D1093623

The Interpretation of
The Acts of the Apostles

By
R. C. H. LENSKI

AUGSBURG PUBLISHING HOUSE
Minneapolis, Minnesota

The Interpretation of
THE ACTS OF THE APOSTLES

Manufactured in the United States of America

TO

AUGUST H. DORNBIRER

NOTE: The translation of the text is an effort in some measure to indicate the Greek wording and the Greek constructions for readers to whom this may be helpful. The following abbreviations are used:

R. = A. T. Robertson, A Grammar of the Greek New Testament in the Light of Historical Research. 4th edition.

B.-D. = Friedrich Blass' Grammatik des neutestamentlichen Griechisch, vierte, voellig neugearbeitete Auflage, besorgt von Albert Debrunner.

B.-P. = Griechisch-Deutsches Woerterbuch zu den Schriften des Neuen Testaments, etc., von D. Walter Bauer, zweite, voellig neugearbeitete Auflage zu Erwin Preuschens Vollstaendigem Griechisch-Deutschen Handwoerterbuch, etc.

M.-M. = The Vocabulary of the Greek Testament Illustrated from the Papyri and other non-Literary Sources, by James Hope Moulton and George Milligan.

R., *W P* = Word Pictures in the New Testament by Archibald Thomas Robertson, Volume III, The Acts of the Apostles.

C. Tr.=*Concordia Triglotta, Libri symbolici Ecclesiae Lutheranae*. German-Latin-English. St. Louis, Mo. Concordia Publishing House.

INTRODUCTION

Luther regarded Acts as a beautiful mirror in which one beholds the truth: *Sola fides justificat.* The fathers likewise admired the contents of the book, noting the great variety of subjects and the immense value of each: the great testimony in regard to the apostolic doctrine and the church; the fundamental outline of church government, church discipline, and church organization; an arsenal full of artillery against the antichrist; a laboratory full of remedies against all soul-destroying errors of faith and offenses in conduct; a larder stocked with all kinds of food for faith, patience, and hope; an inspiration for love and all its works; a very treasury of learning and right doctrine. By adding what students at present see in this great record we should become superficial if we lost or ignored this fundamental viewpoint of an earlier age.

One may say that the skies are now clearing after the critical storms that have raged around Luke and especially around Acts. These storms had very little to do with the things that made Acts so valuable to Luther and to the older students. They hurled their thunderbolts into the isagogical questions, those that concern themselves with authorship, sources, aims and tendencies, historical accuracy, method of composition, agreement with the data in Paul's epistles, and similar matters. A calmer, brighter day has come for Acts. When we consider that in this book Luke mentions one hundred and ten names of persons and many groups of persons besides; gives a long list of places and of provinces in the empire; furnishes all manner of geographical and of historical data that transfer us into an ancient age in which he moved with the greatest freedom and assurance, we see how readily the author made possible many questions for all critics who cared to challenge him on any of these points on the basis of their secular knowledge of the era in which Acts must be placed. No other New Testament book presented so wide and so inviting a field for investigation and for criticism.

But when we now survey the scene, although attacks have not entirely ceased, we must register the fact that the vindication of Luke is complete. Those have gone down in defeat who thought they had made breaches in Luke's citadel. Not even one pinnacle of his fortress did their critical artillery dislodge. The result of all this criticism has been tremendously valuable especially for our age. The sounder the learning, the more extensive the research, the truer the critical tests, the more complete is the assurance that Acts is trustworthy on every point, and that any further investigations will end as the many intensive ones in the past have ended. Acts is today better known as to its external side than it has been at any time since the book was written.

The additions thus made to our appreciation of Acts by the later scholars is of a more secondary nature. Luke himself has been placed into a clearer light. In fact, when we read the words of praise that are now being bestowed upon him we fear that the man, if he heard, would blush. Ramsay, for instance, after a lifetime of research ranks Luke as the greatest of all historians, ancient or modern. His book is called the most beautiful in the world. And so the praise goes on. Acts 27 is regarded as the most perfect account of an ancient sea-voyage ever penned. Luke's character sketches are found to be masterpieces.

We see from this praise that our scholars are captivated by the lesser things: by the writer, his accurate knowledge of externals, his insight into persons and events, his educated mind, his diction, his skill in composition, his personal characteristics, character, etc. Bring all these new treasures — we are grateful, indeed! This, too, is work that must be done. But when all this is said and done, we can only add this new knowledge to the essential contents of the book that was so supremely prized by the fathers. In so much of this scholarship, however, we miss the grand ancient acknowledgment without which all praise of Luke is after all hollow: the acknowledgment that Acts, like Luke's Gospel, was verbally inspired of God.

When we see how Acts emerges from all the critical tests to which the book has been subjected even by hostile eyes with not a single error in the entire complex record, we on our part do not marvel at "the infallible Luke" but recognize the hand of the infallible Spirit who guided Luke's faculties and who thought of us when, through this willing, human instrument, he gave us this piece of inerrant Scripture. Unwittingly these critics have proved a thesis that is more valuable to the believer than the historical accuracy of this beloved companion of Paul's. They merely verify what the church knew and believed from the time when it placed Acts into its sacred canon, namely, that Acts is inspired even as to its words, so that we can trust them also in all minor things as being errorless. What critical work remains to be done, when its final and true results are booked, will be only the adding of the last items in this elaborate proof. And this assurance makes it a joy to offer an interpretation of Acts. Such an interpretation cannot, of course, lose itself in exhaustive discussions of the critical work that has been done on Acts. A large volume would be required for that task, and, when written, would not be an interpretation of Acts and would not be what Luke himself intended Acts to be. His book is all that friendly critics now say it is, and yet it is more.

As a companion of Paul's, Luke, like the other assistants of the apostle, was a preacher. The supreme interest of his life was not medicine, nor the writing of history, nor his friendship for Paul, but the promulgation of the gospel. He wrote his Gospel in order to convert Theophilus and his Acts in order to enlighten this convert in regard to the course of the gospel from Jerusalem to Rome, from Judaism to the Gentiles. The purpose of his two writings is spiritual. To overlook that fact is serious and an injustice to Luke and to his books. So we propose to look well at the beautiful binding, the lovely printing, and the skilful workmanship of this volume from Luke's hands, but only in order to absorb the more delightfully the real things this volume offers.

It is rather interesting to observe how a critic like Harnack of Berlin has shifted from an advocacy (in 1897) of A. D. 78 as the earliest possible date for the writing of Acts to an advocacy of a much earlier date, probably the sixties of the first century. Robertson, in his *Luke, the Historian, in the Light of Research,* 34, writes, "So astonishing a surrender on the part of Harnack created consternation among many critics." For much more is involved than a mere date. The late date, 90-100 A. D., was required in order to make Luke dependent on Josephus in the matter of Acts 5:36, etc. A date after the destruction of Jerusalem in 70 A. D. was required in order to date also Luke's Gospel after that year; for the critics contended that Luke 21:20 with its plain statement about army camps closing in Jerusalem could be only a *vaticinium post eventum,* if not in substance then at least in the form in which this Gospel passage records that prophecy. And now Harnack himself advocates an earlier date.

Ramsay is another scholar who has gone even farther than Harnack. He started with the view that the Acts were of little value historically because, like

John's Gospel, they had been written with an ulterior purpose. But in his *Bearing of Recent Discovery*, p. 89, he confesses: "The more I have studied the narrative of Acts, and the more I have learned year after year about Græco-Roman society and thoughts and fashions and organizations in those provinces, the more I admire and the better I understand. I set out to look for truth on the borderland where Greece and Asia meet and found it here."

This commendable return to a proper estimate of Luke and the Acts has, however, produced some critical romancing which, although largely harmless, calls for a word of caution. Who was Theophilus to whom Acts, too, was sent by Luke? Where did Luke meet him, and what was their relation to each other? The data are extremely meager, and many go too far even when they themselves acknowledge that they are presenting only probabilities or possibilities. It is claiming too much to make Luke a slave of Theophilus in Antioch, to have his master set the young man free and even send him to the great university in Tarsus for a medical education, where he met Saul of Tarsus and formed a friendship that lasted for life. A beautiful romance which a novelist might work into a story or even a film but one that is without substance. Such by-products of criticism, however well intended, must be laid aside.

The fact that Luke is the author of Acts as well as of the third Gospel is so well established that we need not review the evidence. The date of Acts cannot be much later than the date of Luke's Gospel. It is more difficult to assume a long interval between the two compositions than a short one. This dating goes back to Luke's first contact with Theophilus. If this contact reaches gack to Antioch and the early years of Luke, it becomes difficult to explain how Theophilus could for so many years have remained without the certainty which Luke sought to convey to him by means of his Gospel, and why Luke should have waited so many years before finally making the attempt to produce that certainty in his prominent friend. We may say with some assurance that Theophilus came into contact with Luke only a short time before Luke sent him the third Gospel. The prefatory statement of the Gospel shows that its mission was missionary, namely to win Luke's friend for the faith of which he had obtained some knowledge, perhaps through Luke himself. Luke's object was attained. For in the Gospel he addresses Theophilus as κράτιστος, "Your Excellency," a title that was never known to have been bestowed upon one Christian brother by another. Luke follows his first book with a second but now omits this title. How could he do this unless something had intervened? That something must have been the advance of Theophilus from interest to actual faith.

This explains why Luke wrote a second time and continued his Gospel by means of the Acts. It is only natural to suppose that he did not wait long. Thus the date of the Acts and that of the Gospel are not far apart. Both dates come before A. D. 70; the only question is, how far before 70 can we safely go? Tradition says, not far. It tells us that Luke's Gospel was the third in point of time, and that Mark wrote the second after Peter's death in A. D. 64. This is the safest dating apart from the numerous hypotheses regarding this problem.

The dating has something to do with the place of writing. Of the three places suggested for Luke's contact with Theophilus — Antioch years before; Philippi where Luke was for a time left by Paul; Rome, where Luke was at Paul's side — Rome seems most probable. Paul was beheaded in Rome in A. D. 66. We take it that Luke left Rome following this sad event and shortly after that wrote the Gospel to Theophilus and on hearing of his conversion followed this by the Acts. To what place did Luke go? We cannot be certain, and tradition itself has nothing credible to offer.

Another way of dating begins with a consideration of the conclusion of Acts which ends with Paul's being in Rome, a prisoner for two years. It is assumed that Acts was written at that very time in Rome before Paul's trial came to an issue, and that this explains why Luke did not carry the story of the Acts farther and recount the death of Peter in Rome A. D. 64, and that of Paul in A. D. 66. So the Acts would be written before A. D. 62 and the Gospel before that date, perhaps already in Cæsarea. As for Theophilus, he would be located in Antioch or possibly in Philippi. The strength as well as the weakness of this combination rests on the explanation that is given of the way in which the Acts close. Since, however, the dates of the martyrdom of Peter and of Paul are certain, and tradition has Mark write after their death and Luke after Mark (which is certain), an insuperable conflict results between the dating of Mark's Gospel and that of Luke. So we again look at the closing verses of Acts and hesitate to make an explanation of this ending the determining factor in deciding about these interlocking dates. But whatever we decide, let us acknowledge that full certainty cannot be obtained.

This brings us to the interesting problem regarding Luke's original plan of writing. When he began to write the Gospel, did he already then plan to write a second book, namely, the Acts? And did he either at that time or when he began Acts plan to add a third book that would carry the story still farther and include the death of Peter and of Paul, his two heroes in the Acts, and sketches of the work of the other apostles?

A solution of this problem has been based on the word πρῶτος in Acts 1:1. We are told that this means "first" (R. V. margin) and not "former" (A. V.), and that "first" implies both a "second" and a "third" treatise, so that Luke intended to write three books when he began to write the first one. To this is added the further deduction that by ending the second treatise as he does Luke leaves us expecting a third treatise, one that would carry his series of books to a decisive end. The prolog of the Gospel is thus regarded as the prolog for all three books which reveals to us the method Luke pursued in gathering and testing all the material used in them. We are told that for this reason Acts has no prolog that is comparable to the one found in the Gospel but simply a statement that connects this new book with the one that was already in Theophilus' hands.

This view breaks down at what is regarded as its strongest point, the meaning of πρῶτος in Acts 1:1. In the Koine this superlative is freely used for the comparative πρότερον; in fact, Luke never uses the latter but only the former. He uses "first" when only two are involved, and his "first" crowds out "former" which he never uses. See M.-M. 554; R. 280; 663. The contention that at the very beginning Luke intended to write a second treatise cannot be established from the way in which he begins his two books. Other matters ought to be taken into consideration besides the wording of the opening sentences. Luke set out to give Theophilus the certainty concerning the gospel facts, what Jesus began to do and to teach until he ascended to heaven (Acts 1:1, 2), in order to bring his illustrious friend to faith. In his Gospel Luke certainly finished that task and also attained his object in the case of Theophilus. A second, or even a third, book was not needed to give Theophilus the certainty that constitutes faith in Jesus as the Christ. In other words, Luke's prolog to the Gospel is *not* at the same time the prolog for a second and even for a third book. Luke could not have known that he would write even a second book; for he could not tell in advance whether his Gospel would have the desired effect upon Theophilus or not. Even if it should have, the object of a second book would differ from the object of his first book, which had been attained. The moment one considers the books which Luke wrote and thinks of the need of the man to whom they were addressed, the view of a comprehensive preliminary plan of writing on Luke's part becomes unacceptable.

When Luke found that Theophilus had become a believer he wrote him a second treatise with the purpose of giving him further information and of confirming him in the faith. That is the primary and personal object of Luke. Luke performs this second task in just as masterly a way as he had performed the first. He sends Theophilus no mere chronicle of the events that followed Christ's ascension. First, he connects his second book with the first in a simple and natural way. Then he tells the story of the ascension of Jesus, with a brief form of which he had closed his first book, with greater fulness and records how the place of Judas was filled. Then comes the account of Pentecost as introducing the victorious progress of the gospel in its course from Jerusalem to Rome, from Judaism into the great Gentile world to which Luke as well as Theophilus belonged. When tracing this mighty progress for his friend Luke centers especially on two outstanding apostles, the ones that loom up largest in this brief period, Peter and Paul. Here is history, indeed, and a wealth of detail, but entrancing history and more than history, namely, the men who stood at the head of the entire historical progress. The story reaches its climax in Rome just a short time before judgment wiped out the Jewish nation. Here was a record on which the soul of Theophilus could feast, which could deepen his faith with every chapter and rejoice him with the knowledge that he, a former

Gentile, was in this mighty current of Christ which was sweeping out into and through the world.

The idea of publication is stressed by some interpreters. We are told in detail how the ancients went about publishing their books. Our beloved Luke becomes a writer of books for publication, and his rich friend Theophilus the patron through whom he hopes to have publication made. The fact that this idea contravenes the purpose of Luke's writing as expressed by himself seems to be overlooked by these learned students whose ambition it is to have their own books published far and wide. Writers of books themselves, they regard Luke as another. Theophilus becomes incidental. Luke's aim is a far wider circle of readers. But this view needs to be revised. Praise Luke's writing as much as we may, raise its value to the utmost, the fact remains that one man, Theophilus, gave occasion for the composition of Luke's books. Gospel and Acts are intended for him. Both might have gone no farther and have been passed on only to his friends. Let it be noted that Luke nowhere hints at publication. Did he think of publication? The matter took care of itself. Even if Theophilus, after he became a Christian, did not think of giving Luke's writings to the church, those whom Theophilus allowed to read these writings at once clamored for copies, and reproduction of the writings began. But this matter of publication should not unduly influence our view of these books as being originally composed for Theophilus. One man's need of certainty called forth the Gospel of Luke; the success in meeting that need called forth the Acts of Luke. The second builds up the faith wrought by the first. The original purpose of both writings still continues and ought to be recognized.

Where did Luke get his material for Acts? The "we" sections (16:10-17, etc.) speak for themselves — Luke was an eyewitness of the matter recorded in these. The prolog to the Gospel accounts for the rest of the book. Luke obtained his material for the Acts in the same way in which he obtained the material for the Gospel. Inventories have been made of all the contacts Luke had with original witnesses. These witnesses were certainly numerous. Did he have documents? Why not? He surely had a copy of the apostolic letter recorded in Acts 15:23-29; a copy of the letter of Lysias reproduced in 23:25-30; very likely also a transcript of Stephen's defense introduced in chapter seven, which many heard, among them being Paul. Why this question about Luke's sources, especially for the first chapters of Acts, should be as acute as it has been made is hard to understand when we know that Luke secured so much for the earlier period covered by his Gospel. Luke had a wealth of material, much more than he used.

The same is true with regard to the addresses which he recorded. They are exactly like those introduced into the four Gospels. They are for the most part greatly condensed but genuinely true in their condensed form. The critical students make comparisons with the speeches introduced into their books by secular writers. But the addresses recorded in the four Gospels are far superior to any found in secular authors.

Luke's division of Acts has probably always been recognized. Chapter one is introductory. Chapters two to twelve describe the progress of the gospel among the Jews with Peter being the dominant personage. This first half of Acts can be divided into two sections: 1) the progress in Jerusalem (chapters 2-7); 2) the progress in Palestine in general (chapters 8-12). The second half of Acts depicts the progress of the gospel among the Gentiles with Paul as the dominant personage. And again we have two subsections: 1) the progress while Paul was at liberty (13:1-21:16); 2) the progress while Paul was in captivity

(21:17-28:31). The whole depicts the progress of the gospel from Judaism into the great Gentile world or, more tersely stated, from Jerusalem to Rome.

Luke concludes his account with Paul's experiences in Rome. This apostle arrives, remains two years and, though under guard, preaches and teaches in his own house without restraint. This conclusion has puzzled many and has led to many precipitated discussions and hypotheses. The simple fact seems to be that Luke considered his goal attained when his account reached Rome: Paul being the first apostle to work in Rome, the capital of the world. Luke does not seem to share the view of so many that an account of the martyrdom of Peter and of Paul would have made a better ending. Perhaps we ought to revise our opinion in regard to Luke's account of these two apostles. However much he records about them, at the end he lets us see that his interest lies in their work or, more exactly, in the gospel and its success. Yes, we see Paul in the last verses, but the final note is: "Preaching the kingdom of God, and teaching those things which concern the Lord Jesus Christ." This was Luke's supreme interest when writing the Acts; it was to be that of Theophilus. Let it also be ours.

Did Luke issue the Acts in two editions, the first being briefer than the second which is now in our hands? Blass advocated this idea and extended it to the Gospel, supposing that, too, to have been issued in two editions. Zahn took up this idea but confined it to Acts. He has tried to reconstruct the shorter edition from Latin translations and from two Greek texts, notably from D. *Forschungen, etc., IX Teil.* But he is uncertain save for the hypothesis itself that Luke issued two editions of this book.

CHAPTER I

THE OPENING EVENTS, CHAPTER 1

Πράξεις τῶν Ἀποστόλων, "Acts of the Apostles," is the title of Luke's second composition, and this superscription is found as far back as scholars are able to carry their research. This title has remained constant even in the versions. The four Gospels have no titles, for the phrases "According to Matthew," "According to Mark," etc., were added at a later time, chiefly in order to distinguish these writings from each other. Their subject was the same, the εὐαγγέλιον, "the good news" ("gospel" in Old English) concerning Jesus Christ. The question whether Luke himself gave his second account the title it has always borne is affirmed by some although all admit that he left his first account without a title, and those who think that he intended to write a third account are naturally unable to say whether he had a title in mind and what that title might be. Since, however, Luke gave no title to his first account, it is hazardous to assume that he gave a title to the second.

We purposely avoid using the term "books." Luke did not call his first writing a "book" but a λόγος, an account. Both of his writings are of a personal nature and are addressed to one man for reasons that are personal to that man. We are not to think of Theophilus as a patron to whom Luke dedicated books in order that this patron might have them published. That idea has been advanced by men who themselves write books and seek to have them published. So they think that Luke wrote a title for what they call his second book but overlook the fact that he left what they call his first book without a title. When Luke thought of his writings as λόγοι or accounts he needed no titles and used none. The idea of a book is of later origin, hence also we have the captions, including the one that was affixed to his second account and that is still used everywhere.

1) **The first account I made concerning all things, O Theophilus, which Jesus began both doing and teaching until what day he was received up after having given behests through the Holy Spirit to the apostles whom he chose for himself; to whom he also, after he suffered, presented himself alive in connection with many proofs, letting himself be seen by them during forty days and declaring the things concerning the kingdom of God; and while partaking together of salt he ordered them not to be withdrawing from Jerusalem, on the contrary, to be awaiting the promise of the Father, which you heard from me; seeing that John baptized with water, that you, however, shall be baptized in connection with the Holy Spirit not many days after these.**

The periodic sentence with which Luke begins his Gospel is greatly admired as a wonderful example of the literary Koine, and in this admiration one feels a note of disappointment because of Luke's failure to score as highly a second time in the opening sentence of his Acts. But Luke did score just as highly; this time, however, he wrote a complex sentence which in a most concise and certainly masterful way connects Acts not merely with the Gospel in general but with all the salient points of the Gospel, so that these combine into one focus for the great new narrative that now begins. Instead of registering the fact that this is not another *Periode* (B.-D. 464) or remarking that here, too, Luke attains the literary Koine (R. 121), more attention might be paid to the aim and the contents of this complex sentence in summarizing the vital features of the entire Gospel so as to take up the thread of the new narrative.

Luke reaches back to John and his baptism and to the promise of the Father, the baptism with the Holy Spirit, which is now so close at hand; he brings to mind all that he had written about the deeds and the teachings of Jesus up to the time of the ascension; he lets his reader again meet the apostles whom Jesus elected for himself; he recalls the forty days in which Jesus gave all those proofs of his resurrection and spoke of the things of the kingdom in the light of his resurrection; and he repeats the command that the apostles must not leave Jerusalem, for in a few days the promise will be fulfilled. All this is arranged in one grand sentence. With it Luke places his reader just where he ought to be placed in order to go on with the new account. A study of the details of these five verses should not cause us to lose sight of their great sweep through the Gospel which brings us to the front portal of Acts.

We are unable to translate solitary μέν which merely lends a delicate stress to the clause in which it appears; "indeed" is too strong although it tends in the right direction. The older view that δέ should follow, that a contrast is implied, that this must appear at least in the thought, or that, with δέ absent, the construction is broken and results in a kind of anacoluthon, is untenable. See R. 1150. Solitary μέν does not require even a contrasting thought, to say nothing of a δέ. The fact that Luke had already written his second account the reader would see by having that account in his hands as he began to read. "The first account" is all that Luke needs to say in order to place the two side by side. The word λόγος does not mean "book"; the term never means "book," and even when there is a reference to a book, not the book as a book is referred to but only its contents. When Luke refers to a "book," the ancient manuscript roll, he writes βίβλος (Luke 3:4; 20:42; Acts 1:20; 7:42; 19:19) or βιβλίον (Luke 4:17, 20). "Treatise" in our versions is better. Luke wrote an "account" of certain things to Theophilus, a full account, indeed, but only an account, and is now penning another. He is not thinking of publication nor suggesting such a thing to Theophilus.

We have discussed πρῶτος in the Introduction. Luke uses it in the sense of "first" as well as in the sense of "former"; in fact, he never employs πρότερος, even as it is fast disappearing in the Koine, M.-M. 557; R. 280. Zahn supports his view by an appeal to Luke's education as a *grammatikos*; but the appeal must be made to the grammars and the lexicons which register the facts of language. But this implies that the word cannot be referred to as a support for the theory that Luke intended to write also a third book. When Luke writes that he prepared the first account "concerning all things which Jesus began doing," etc., we understand that "all things" is a popular hyperbole; for this statement has the preposition περί, "concerning." One can write "concerning" all things without actually recounting all of them. It is a correct summary of the Gospel when Luke calls it the account "concerning all things which Jesus began both doing and teaching until what day he was received up." The relative ὧν is attracted from ἅ to the case of its antecedent, and the antecedent of ἧς is itself drawn into the relative clause: "what day" for "the day in which."

As far as the use of "began" is concerned, the discussion about the force of this word overlooks two things, that the tense of the two infinitives is present and thus durative, and that the terminus of this doing and this teaching is named to the very day, the day when Jesus ascended to heaven. Jesus "began" (aorist, the start); he engaged in working as well as in teaching (present, the whole course of his work, both activities continuing together); "until what day he was received up" (aorist) records the end. So we dismiss the emphasis on "began" as though this beginning might be of special importance; and also the deduction that Luke implies that what Jesus began the apostles were to continue and to conclude. No; what Jesus began and also continued reached its end the day he ascended.

Nor should one overlook the fact that Luke gives a decided emphasis to the phrase "concerning all things" plus its relative clause by inserting the vocative between them, "O Theophilus." The name Theophilus and all these things regarding Jesus about which Luke wrote to him are thus brought together in what appears to be a significant way.

Does his omission of the title κράτιστε, "Your Excellency," which appears in the Gospel, mean anything? It will not do to say "no," for such high titles (Acts 23:26; 24:3; 26:25) cannot be bestowed upon a person at the beginning of one document and then withheld from that same person at the beginning of another document that is altogether similar. In early Christian literature we are told that no Christian addressed a fellow Christian with such a title. We, therefore, conclude that in the Gospel the title was in place because Theophilus was then not as yet a Christian, but that it is no longer in place in Acts because Theophilus had now become a Christian, for which reason Luke sends him this second account. The gracious and mighty miracles of Jesus (ποιεῖν) and the gracious and true teaching of Jesus (διδάσκειν) had won this man, who was either a Roman knight or a Roman official or a man of very great prominence, to faith. Luke's Gospel had scored a great missionary success.

2) The terminus of the Gospel is the ascension. In Luke 24:51 one verb is used, here, in v. 11 and 22, and

in I Tim. 3:16, another verb occurs, but all five verbs are passive: "he was received up," the agent in the passive being God. Yet in John 3:13; 6:62; Eph. 4:10; Heb. 4:14 we have the active: Jesus himself ascended. Both statements are true, for the *opera ad extra sunt indivisa aut communa*; they are ascribed equally to the different Persons. But before Jesus ascended, as the aorist participle ἐντειλάμενος shows, he gave behests to the apostles, ἐντολαί, as the participle suggests, *Auftraege*. Ἐντέλλω is not the common verb "to command" or "to order" which applies to slaves, servants, soldiers, and the like, but the verb that indicates a more personal relation. Beza has the idea: *Ut facere solent qui ab amicis, vel etiam ex hoc mundo, discedunt* — injunctions such as those leave who part from friends or who leave this world. We need not be told what these behests were. They were given during the forty days and are recorded in Luke 24:47; Matt. 28:19, 20; Mark 16:15-18; John 20:21-23. If anything were yet to be said, this last passage shows that the behests were given "through the Holy Spirit," and that this phrase should not be construed with the relative clause: "whom he did elect through the Holy Spirit." All the acts of Jesus were done in connection with the Spirit who had been bestowed upon the human nature of Jesus. We do not read that the election of the apostles was connected with the Spirit, but John 20:22 specifically informs us that, when Jesus sent forth the eleven, he breathed on them and bade them receive the Holy Spirit.

The relative clause "whom he did elect for himself" is added to "the apostles" in order once more to bring to mind the elective act which constituted these men "the apostles," the specially commissioned messengers (ἀποστέλλω, to send with a commission) of Jesus, we may say, his ambassadors. The middle voice is important: "he did elect for himself"; we may place a good deal into this middle; to represent him, to continue his work, etc. All this, too, lies in the title, "the apostles." Although it is sometimes used in a wider sense to include also the immediate assistants of the apostles (Luke was one), here it refers to the eleven only who received the final behests of Jesus.

Note the position of the phrase "through the Holy Spirit" before the relative clause "whom he elected." In the Greek the phrase might belong within the relative clause, but if that were the case, it would receive the strongest kind of emphasis, an emphasis for which no one could account in the present connection. Since it modifies the participle, "having given behests," no emphasis rests on the phrase. The Greek is content to mark only the past fact that lies in the aorist, "he did elect," whereas the English marks also the relation to other past facts: "he had elected."

3) In another relative clause (οἷς καί) Luke adds that these behests were given after the resurrection of Jesus, during the forty days. Jesus "presented himself alive or as living after he suffered." The aorist παθεῖν is constative and speaks of the suffering as something complete, thus including also the death. To present himself as alive or living (durative present participle) after this fatal suffering implies his resurrection from the dead. This presentation of himself was not a bare presentation but was "in connection with many proofs," sure tokens which made the apostles certain of the fact that their dead Lord was, indeed, alive.

Ἐν does not mean "by," for the proofs were not the means of the presentation but were "in connection with" it. In Luke 24:36 we see just what is meant: Jesus appeared in the midst of the disciples, then, however, he made them feel his flesh and his bones and also ate a piece of fish before them. These proofs were multiplied until they actually became many. This prodigality was intended to remove all doubt so completely as never to permit it to arise again. Luke makes the matter still clearer and adds more data: "letting himself be seen by them during forty days," etc. In this way Jesus presented himself alive. The temporal phrase is placed before the participle for the sake of emphasis. No less than forty days were used for these appearances. Again and again Jesus let himself be seen. The apostles (and others) had time to think, to consider, to talk the matter over, to make any new test they might desire. The present participle fits the repetition of the appearances to their proofs; the agent for the passive, as so often, is expressed by the dative "by them." Thayer calls ὀπτάνομαι a Biblical word, but it has been found elsewhere (Deissmann, *Light, etc.*, 79 and 252: "I am seen," "I let myself be seen"). It expresses exactly what Jesus did when he would suddenly stand in the midst of the apostles.

Valuable is the addition: "and declaring the things concerning the kingdom of God," as recorded in Matt. 28:18, etc.; Mark 16:14, etc.; Luke 24:25, etc., and 44, etc., John 20:21, etc. These were the same things Jesus had been teaching throughout his ministry, but now they appeared in a new light. Romanists insert the thought that Jesus instructed the apostles about the hierarchy, the seven sacraments, etc.

One of the greatest concepts of the New Testament is "the kingdom of God" (Matthew, "of the heavens"). It is misunderstood when earthly kingdoms are used as a pattern for this spiritual concept. An earthly kingdom is a land and a nation on which the king depends. Take his people away, and the king ceases to be king; they, too, are what they are without him as a king. But God (Christ) makes his kingdom, it depends wholly on him and could not exist without him. God's kingdom is found wherever God is and rules by his power, grace, and glory. He makes his own domain and his own people, and never they him. It is the kingdom of the heavens because heavenly powers make it and also give it heavenly character; the kingdom of God (Christ) because he is over and in it everywhere, at once its source and its control. This rule or kingdom goes back to the beginning and extends to eternity. When we look at the power and the omnipotence, it rules the whole universe; when we look at grace, it embraces the whole church; when we contemplate the glory we see heaven and all its inhabitants. The kingdom and rule of grace fills the whole Testament from Adam onward; it is the rule of grace through the Messianic promise. A new era began when the promise was fulfilled in Christ, the era of the New Testament which extends to the end of time.

It is of the kingdom in this sense that Jesus spoke during the forty days. About to ascend on high, he would rule with grace and through the apostles reach out to the ends of the earth. So he rules through their written Word to this day. But since this is a rule of grace, it makes all who are won by grace partakers of the kingdom. It makes them kings unto God (Rev. 1:6) so that they, too, rule with him by means of his Word and have kingly crowns awaiting them (II Tim. 4:8, and all the passages that speak of a crown). See the author's *Kings and Priests* where the entire subject is treated.

4) This verse does not begin a new sentence, for καί only carries the great introductory statement to its conclusion by adding the command to stay in Jerusalem for the coming of the Holy Spirit who had been promised already by the Baptist. Thus in one grand sweep everything from the time of the Baptist until Pentecost is combined with reference to the kingdom.

In συναλιζόμενος we have a *crux interpretum.* If the root is ἁλής, the adjective meaning "crowded," "in a mass," we have the translation of our versions: "being assembled together"; but if the root is ἅλς, "salt," we have the marginal translation of our versions: "eating together," or more precisely: "while partaking together of salt." Rather decisive against the former meaning is the fact that the singular fits only a collective noun, like a multitude, and never only a single person. Then, too, the tense should be the aorist, for the assembling must precede the commanding. Sense and tense are correct if we accept the other derivation, "eating with them," and we have in our favor all the ancient versions and the fathers plus also Luke 24:41-43, where Jesus did eat. Still we lack classical examples for this meaning. See B.-P. 1257.

One is surprised at M.-M. 601 who advocate a difference in spelling so that we have a verb that means "to spend the night with." We may take it that Luke refers to his own Gospel, 24:41-43, 49, where he reports both that Jesus ate broiled (and thus salted) fish and ordered the disciples to remain in the city until they received the promise of the Father. Luke recalls this order because he is now about to report the descent of the Spirit. He even uses the same expression: "the promise of the Father" (Luke 24:49), and adds that they had heard this from him before (the aorist where we prefer the perfect).

5) Ὅτι does not state the reason for awaiting the promise of the Father although it is quite generally so translated: "for" (meaning "because"), German *denn*. How could John's baptizing with water be a part of such a reason? This is the so-called consecutive ὅτι (R. 1001), "seeing that." In view of the fact that John began with water in order to have a greater than he finish by pouring out the Holy Spirit the eleven must stay in Jerusalem. Read Luke 3:16, also John 1:33. We repeat only in brief the exegesis of these passages. John's baptism was the baptism

of repentance unto remission of sins, hence had the Holy Spirit even as this Spirit alone wrought faith throughout the Old Testament era. To reduce John's baptism to a mere water ceremony that was devoid of the Spirit is to contradict Luke 3:3. John began the work with his baptism, Jesus was to finish at Pentecost. We know of none of the apostles who received any other baptism than John's; by receiving it they confessed themselves as repentant and believing.

This ἐν does not imply that the Spirit became the counterpart of "water," a sort of fluid that sprinkled, washed, or even immersed a person. We note fire at Pentecost and not a fluid. Ἐν is here used exactly as it was in v. 3: "in connection with the Holy Spirit"; βαπτισθήσεσθε, like our expression that the Spirit "was poured out," cannot be stressed to get the idea of a fluid. When Jesus was baptized with the Spirit, when the Spirit was poured out upon him, Luke 3:22 describes this as the coming down of the Spirit in a bodily form like a dove. There were different phenomena at Pentecost (sound of wind, tongues of fire), but the act was the same: the Spirit filled the disciples in a miraculous way and gave them great power. This is called "being baptized." And the verb is evidently used in a figurative and unusual way. The apostles had heard this before, but now they are told that the event will occur "not many days after these," a litotes for "after only a few days" (R. 1205). We must note that οὐ is always placed before the preposition (B.-D. 433, 3), that ταύτας is predicative (R. 656): *nicht viele Tage nach den jetzigen* (B.-D. 226), an idiom we cannot duplicate.

Luke has made his masterly connection with his great Gospel account; he is now ready to proceed with the new narration.

6) **Now they, having come together, began to inquire of him, saying, Lord, art thou at this time**

restoring the kingdom to Israel? He, however, said to them: It is not yours to know times or seasons which the Father did place in his own authority. On the contrary, you shall receive power, the Holy Spirit having come upon you; and you shall be my witnesses both in Jerusalem and in all Judea and in Samaria and to the last part of the earth.

Luke uses μὲν οὖν once in the Gospel but twenty-seven times in Acts; there are only a few other instances elsewhere in the New Testament; the favorite combination in Acts is οἱ μὲν οὖν as here, often with a participle. A δέ need not follow although one does follow (v. 7). The particles do little more than to express an accord of the new statement with the one that precedes and may be rendered "accordingly"; no deduction is intended; "therefore" in our versions is too weigthy. There is an ambiguity with regard to the participles as to whether these are to be substantivized: "those come together," or regarded as modifiers: "they having come together." We prefer the latter because it can be carried through while the other at times causes difficulty.

Luke is speaking of the apostles (v. 2); they came together on the Mount of Olives (v. 12) whither Jesus himself led them (Luke 24:50). Some think that the apostles were still in the house where v. 4 and the participle, "partaking together of salt," placed them, so that now the scene of v. 4, 5 merely continues through v. 6-8. Much labor is then expended on v. 9 to show that, without saying so, Luke transfers us to the Mount of Olives. But if Jesus is eating with the apostles in v. 4, why must Luke in v. 6 remind us that they had come together? There is no reason why the apostles should not have asked as they did when Jesus had led them out to the Mount of Olives. Luke is retelling with important additions what he told in the Gospel, 24:50-53. The descriptive imperfect reads as though more was said than Luke records, as though there was some hesitation, and the impression seems to be made that the apostles had talked the matter over and took courage now at last to ask.

In the Gospels κύριος is often only a form of address that indicates respect, but beginning with Luke 7:13 we find the title used as it has ever since been employed in the church in the sense of divine Lord which includes the deity of Jesus and the grace and the redemption which made him our Lord. We shall thus continue to meet "the Lord," "the Lord Jesus," "our Lord Jesus Christ," etc. Direct questions, like indirect ones beginning with εἰ, are called Hebraistic or elliptical: we should like to know "whether." Consider whether this ει is not merely an interrogative particle (B.-D. 440, 3) that adds a note of hesitancy to the question.

The point of the question is the time, whether "at this time" Jesus is restoring the kingdom to Israel. In his answer Jesus distinguishes "times" (longer stretches) from "seasons" (shorter ones, each marked in a certain way). So the apostles do not mean "right away" but "before so very long." The fact that the kingdom is, indeed, to be restored to Israel is taken for granted. The scepter had, indeed, sadly departed from Judah — would it now be restored in Shiloh, in Jesus? Luke 24:21: "But we trusted that it had been he which should have redeemed Israel."

There is a difficulty to determine exactly what the apostles had in mind when they asked this question. We venture to say that they thought of a glorious earthly rule for Israel, the Jewish people, through Jesus, the Messiah, who would soon return in his Parousia. Jesus answers only regarding the times and the seasons and does not explain about the kingdom (see v. 3) and how Israel (the remnant, Rom.

9:27; 11:5) shall have the kingdom restored. The fact that the apostles still expressed strong earthly conceptions by their question can scarcely be denied.

7) The relative clause contains the reason why it is not for the apostles to know even the times to say nothing of the seasons. The word χρόνος denotes a stretch of time but καιρός a definite period that is marked by what transpires in it. The genitive with εἶναι = it does not belong to you, is not your business or concern. The aorist infinitive means "actually to know" and does not exclude the idea that the apostles may know something about times and seasons. Jesus uses the plural to convey the thought that everything regarding time and season is in the Father's province. He placed times and seasons where alone they belong, "in his own authority," for him alone to determine their course and their length. This certainly ought to dissuade all timesetters (Mark 13:32). The fine old exegete Bengel made this very mistake of trying to determine the time of the return of Christ in a calculation that was most miserably wrong. Once for all, as the aorist ἔθετο shows, the Father has put these things beyond our reach.

By saying that they are placed in the Father's authority Jesus does not imply that the Father has not yet determined times and seasons and thus also the date of the end. In Matt. 24:22, and in Mark 13:20 Jesus informs us that the days of the final tribulation shall be shortened for the sake of the elect, and that the Father alone knows that day and the hour. The conclusion is, therefore, that God had, indeed, determined all times and seasons, but had done so by taking all things into account, especially those pertaining to his elect, and that he thus knows these times and seasons even as his omniscience is without bounds. As far as the Son is concerned, only during the days of his humiliation did he restrict himself in the use of this as of the other divine attributes to what was needed in his mediatorial work.

8) After a negative, ἀλλά brings the positive; so decidedly are the apostles not to know that, "on the contrary," their only concern is to be the promise of receiving power for their world-wide testimony. This is spiritual power which is communicated directly by the Holy Spirit in the Pentecostal miracle, a complete and an adequate equipment of mind and of spirit for the great future task. A genitive absolute explains how the apostles are to receive this power: "the Holy Spirit having come upon you." This describes the Pentecost miracle in advance and defines in Jesus' own way what "being baptized in connection with the Holy Spirit" actually means. "To come upon" is certainly far removed from anything like immersion. In a moment Jesus will leave these men, but he leaves them with this great promise; in fact, his leaving is to make good that promise, for the ascension of Jesus was necessary in order to send us the Holy Spirit.

Although the connective is only "and," the thought presented is the result of thus receiving power, and the future tense reads as though being witnesses is a continuation of the promise. This is not an admonition, but only a glorious future fact: "you shall be my witnesses" even as Jesus designated them already in Luke 24:48. They are to be more than heralds (preachers) who proclaim only what they are ordered to proclaim; they are to be herald "witnesses" in the sense of I John 1:1, men who have themselves seen, heard, touched, experienced, and are qualified, even called, to testify accordingly.

We must not pass too lightly over this word "witnesses." In the sense in which the apostles were Christ's witnesses no others were or could be. All the great things they saw could never be repeated; yet all these things had to be made known and made known properly, not only to the men of that age, but to the men of all ages. For this reason the descent of the Spirit bestowed a special equipment upon the apostles. They received the gift of inspiration in the sense of John 14:26, and 15:26, 27. Thus, besides filling the world of their own day with the gospel, by their inspired writings they are witnessing to the end of time. Individual names are, indeed, attached to the four Gospels and also to the other New Testament writings, but what these Gospels report is the testimony of all the apostles. In Acts Luke is only the scribe, the apostles here continue their testimony by deed and word. The same is true with regard to the Epistles. In the whole New Testament we have "my witnesses" speaking to the end of time in a great apostolic chorus. In their testimony speaks "the Faithful Witness'" himself (Rev. 1:5). "My" witnesses = called to witness by me, for me, about me, yea, all about me.

The course of the work of the apostles is outlined in one grand sweep: "both in Jerusalem," etc. The *τε . . . καί*, "both . . . and," is extended by the addition of a second "and." Note that Judea and Samaria are regarded as a unit since only one article is used (R. 787); also that to reach the utmost or last part of the earth involves passing through all the parts that intervene. The city is named first and made prominent because the apostles were to do much work right in Jerusalem, founding and extending there the mother congregation of all Christendom, radiating from which all the sister congregations were to be established elsewhere. Jesus here announces the program which we see carried out in Acts. We know, too, that Paul reached Spain and Thomas reached India.

9) **And having said these things, while they were looking, he was taken up, and a cloud took him from their eyes. And as they were earnestly gazing**

into heaven, while he was going, lo, two men were standing beside them in white apparel, who also said, Galilean men, why are you standing looking into heaven? This Jesus, received up from you into heaven, shall so come in what manner you viewed him going into heaven.

Except for the brief statement in Mark 16:19, we have only Luke's descriptions of the ascension, which are thus invaluable, especially this one in Acts which so graphically describes just what the witnesses saw and thus just what we are so glad to know. The Lord had concluded his address (hence the aorist participle). The eyes of the apostles were resting upon him (note the present tense of the genitive absolute and its emphatic forward position). The verb means to see, to look, to direct the eyes and the attention upon an object. Jesus was not suddenly snatched away out of their sight; this time he did not vanish as he had done when leaving them during the forty days. Now his leaving had a different meaning. Before this, when he would vanish, they knew that he would appear again; now his presence was slowly and visibly taken away, upward, in a heavenly way. They see it all with their very eyes as the witnesses they were to be.

An awed silence comes over them. Jesus spreads his hands over them in blessing (Luke 24:50) and slowly, majestically, mightily rises heavenward from the earth, higher and higher. Their eyes are wide with astonishment and follow him and strain in looking (ἀτενίζοντες, v. 10). Far aloft they see the holy body of Jesus until at last a flimsy cloud folds him in. They still gaze after him — but he is gone. They know whither — he has ascended into heaven.

The verb used is ἐπαίρω, "to lift up." It is passive like the two other verbs that were used with reference to the ascension in the Gospel and in Acts; see v. 2

regarding both the passive and the active. The ascension was visible solely for the sake of the apostles. The moment the cloud hid Jesus from their sight, he was transferred timelessly into the heavenly glory, the abode of God and of the saints and of angels. This is the great article of our faith: "he ascended into heaven." Chrysostom says: "Of Christ's resurrection the disciples saw the final part, not the first part, but of his ascension they saw the first part, not the final part." In ὑπέλαβεν the preposition conveys the idea that the cloud received Jesus by appearing under him. When it is said that the cloud carried Jesus up into heaven, motion is put into the cloud; it served only to hide Jesus. The ascension, like the resurrection, pertains only to the body of Jesus and thus to his human nature in union with the divine. The greatest part of the miracle was that which occurred after the cloud hid Jesus when he was instantly in the glory of heaven, seated at the right hand of majesty and of power in order to exercise these forever also according to his human nature.

Yes, he is visible in heaven as is Elijah. He has the same body that died on the cross and lay in the grave. But he is not confined in heaven like Elijah. He is at the same time wherever he has promised to be, and that according to both natures. It is incomprehensible to finite minds, and all who philosophize about it may know in advance that they are childishly wrong. The recorded facts are true, beyond them no man can go.

The cloud was only the divinely chosen earthly means in a final and appropriate way to remove the visible body of Jesus from the eyes of the apostles. They were to cease looking. Jesus was not rising on and on in the regions of distant space — he was gone — gone where there is no space, no time, or ony other mundane restriction. It is allegory to say that the

cloud served "to make visible the gracious, saving presence of God," or to think of the cloud as "the visible revelation of the presence of God who receives the Son unto himself into the glory of heaven." Let no such allegory becloud the stupendous fact that all in an instant the body of Jesus was in the glory of heaven.

10) Ἀτενίζω refers to strained and earnest looking; the periphrastic imperfect, more than the simple form would do, pictures the continuousness of the act. The added genitive absolute with its present tense, "he going" ("while he was going") pictures once more what the earnest gaze of the apostles saw. In new words Luke describes what the witnesses beheld but now in order to add a second astonishing fact with the interjection "lo" Sometimes καί is added to introduce the main clause. This may be due to Hebrew influence although it is found also in Homer and strongly resembles ἐγένετο καί plus a finite verb (B.-D. 442, 7). This explains the untranslatable καί before the interjection.

Not after the ascension but while it was in progress the two angels appeared. When the apostles looked, there "they were standing beside them in white apparel"; the past perfect of this verb is always used in the sense of the imperfect and is here used descriptively. The presence of these angels marks the ascension as one of Christ's great saving acts. Luke calls the angels in the tomb ἄνδρες, "men" (24:4) and here he again writes "men"; Mark 16:5 has νεανίσκος, "young man." They appear in this form in order to draw as near to those to whom they appear as heavenly spirits can. They are, of course, without sex (Luke 20:35, etc.) but they come visibly as men, young men, images of strength and of beauty combined, never as women or maidens — a point which only the best artists have noted. On the rare word ἐσθῆσις see R. 267. The whiteness of their apparel is noted, which we may take as signifying purity, holiness, heavenliness.

11) No second look was needed to tell the apostles who stood before them in greatness, power, and glory. These angels had come to complete what was necessary in regard to this act of Jesus. They are his spokesmen who at once confirm the ascension and then also connect it with the future return of the Lord. We may say that here we have another part of the answer of Jesus to the apostles concerning the restoration of the kingdom to Israel (v. 6). These apostles are to fill the world with their witness; then at last Jesus will return for the consummation of his kingdom. We cannot entertain the idea that these two men were Moses and Elijah; but were they the same two mentioned in Luke 24:4? If we are asked in what garments Jesus appeared during the forty days and here at his ascension, the answer must be that no man knows, for the witnesses have left no word in regard to this.

The address, "Galilean men," is used less because these apostles were native Galileans (Judas alone was from Judea) than because it would bring back to them in a flash their long and blessed association with Jesus, especially in Galilee. "Why are you standing looking into heaven?" is not a rebuke. It was only natural to gaze after Jesus in this manner. The question intends to turn their minds from mere astonishment to more important thought. The ascension of Christ and his return at the Parousia go together. And these heavenly messengers bring a glorious promise to the apostles at this great moment. For now when Jesus is received up they are once more to hear that he will come again in the same visible way.

For a third time the ascension is described but now by the angel spokesman: "this Jesus, received up from you into heaven," this very one who is known by this his personal name and described by the act just witnessed, he shall return. On the passive participle of the verb see v. 2; compare the verbs in v. 9 and in Luke 24:51. A moment ago the apostles spoke with this Jesus, now his glorious reception into the heavenly world is already accomplished. What this implied Jesus had himself told them: not mere rest while they struggled here below, but a mighty, all-transcending exercise of power and authority. The angels have nothing to add to all that Jesus had told them on this subject; they restate another assurance which the Lord had left his apostles, restate it in the most emphatic and direct form: this Jesus "shall so come in what manner you viewed him going into heaven."

Note the emphatic words: οὗτος — οὕτως — ὃν τρόπον (a set phrase in which the antecedent is drawn to the relative, R. 718), *"this"* Jesus — *"thus"* — *"in the* (same) *way in which"* you viewed, etc. He departed visibly, he shall return visibly; he went to heaven, he shall come from heaven; he went away bodily, he shall come back bodily. It is not added that he will return in all his glory with all the angels of God about him for the final judgment, although Jesus had given these additions. It is not added that every eye shall see him when he returns, also those who pierced him, Rev. 1:7. But one may ask how this can be possible when the earth is a globe, and when he who appears on one side of the globe cannot be seen on the opposite side. All such questions assume that space, time, and earthly conditions as we know them shall continue and govern at the last day. But time shall be no more, space shall no longer exist, heaven shall come down to earth (Rev. 21:1, 2), and a few other tremendous changes that our science never dreamed of will so arrange it that even the most skeptical doubter shall not have the least trouble in getting the fullest view of "this Jesus coming out of heaven" for the judgment also of all skeptics and unbelievers.

12) **Then they returned to Jerusalem from the mount called Olive grove, which is near Jerusalem, a**

Sabbath journey away. They returned "with great joy," Luke 24:52. It is important to know that the apostles returned to Jerusalem even as Jesus commanded (v. 4), and that the following events took place there. It is likewise of interest to know that the ascension occurred on the mount called "Olive grove." Sometimes a name is retained in the nominative, here it appears in the genitive in agreement with the genitive participle, and the nominative must be Ἐλαιών (not circumflexed). On the forms used in the passages in the Gospel see R. 267. The distance from Jerusalem to Olivet was as far as Jews were allowed to walk on the Sabbath, namely 2,000 paces. Luke might have given the distance in terms of stadia; the expression which he uses shows that he is following a Jewish source. "Having a Sabbath's journey" is the Greek idiom. Yet this does not state the entire distance to the place on Olivet from which Jesus ascended, but only the distance to the base of Olivet. Luke 24:50 indicates how far up the mount Jesus took the apostles, namely, to the place where the road branches, one branch going toward Bethany, which lies about 4,000 paces from the city beyond the ridge.

The spot now pointed out to travellers as the one from which Jesus ascended cannot be taken seriously. Because the ascension is so important Luke records the place of it for Theophilus in both the Gospel and the Acts. The view that the ascension occurred on Sunday is refuted by both the forty days mentioned in v. 3, which fix the day as a Thursday, and the distance indicated, for a Sabbath's journey would extend only to the base of Olivet and not to the place on Olivet from which the ascent was made.

13) **And when they came in they went to the upper room where they were abiding, both Peter and John and James and Andrew, Philip and Thomas, Bartholomew and Matthew, James of Alpheus and**

Simon the Zealot and Judas of James. These all were continuing steadfastly with one accord in prayer together with women, also Mary, the mother of Jesus, and together with his brothers.

"They came in" means from Olivet into the city. They did not scatter but at once went up "to the upper room where they were abiding." The relative clause cannot be separated from its antecedent so that it does not define which upper room is referred to, namely *the* one *where* they were abiding. But some make this separation in order to make room for the conjecture that this upper room is the same as the one mentioned in Luke 22:12, where Jesus celebrated the Passover, and for the added supposition that it belonged to Mark's father. But the article in the phrase "to *the* upper room" cannot refer to a passage in the Gospel. "They were abiding" means that the apostles and other disciples were making this room their headquarters while they were in Jerusalem. Nor can it be assumed that all of them, so many men and women, lived in this room. The best guess as to its identity is that it was the room where the apostles gathered after they heard the news of the resurrection, John 20:19, 26.

Such upper rooms were quite common. Sometimes they were merely booths that were erected on the flat roof of the stone building. The author saw many of them in the Holy Land. We shall note them in the Acts; the body of Dorcas was laid out in one of them. Sometimes they were roomy and even ornate like the one with its tiled floor that is mentioned in Luke 22:12. They were used as places for retirement and quiet and, for the company here described, as a place that was free from interruption and disturbance. The fact that the house belonged to a friend of Jesus need scarcely be added. The effort to locate this upper room in the Temple is futile. Nor does abiding in this room contradict Luke 24:53, the constant stay in the Temple; the disciples divided their time between the two places.

Luke introduces the apostles in verse 2. He intends to write about them in this account, presently also to tell how the vacant place of Judas Iscariot was filled. Very properly he lists their names at this point so that Theophilus may also know just who had witnessed the ascension of Jesus. The chief feature of this list is the order of the first four names which constitute the first group. Here Peter and John are grouped together, and James is third, for these three were distinguished by Jesus in Jairus' house, at the transfiguration, and in Gethsemane. Peter is always first but only as *primus inter pares*, for Matt. 18:18 gives to all the apostles the powers bestowed on Peter in Matt. 16:19. The only reason commonly assigned for pairing John with Peter is Luke's further narrative in which the two appear as companions; but the conclusion of John's Gospel shows that the two were also close friends and constant companions. Luke 6:14, etc., just lists the names, but if we make three groups we shall in all four lists find the identical names in each group although in varied order. The present list has four groups that are marked by asyndeton; but if we count three groups we shall find the same name heading each group as in the other lists, Peter, Philip, and James of Alpheus. Andrew and Philip have Greek names.

Philip is from the home of the two pairs of brothers and must be distinguished from the deacon and evangelist Philip. The other name of Thomas is Didymus, "Double" or "Twin." Bartholomew is a patronymic for Son of Tolmai; his personal name was Nathanael, John 1:46; 21:2. Matthew is the former publican, the writer of the first Gospel. The second James is distinguished by the genitive of his father's name: son of Alpheus. The second Simon is distinguished by the apposition "the Zealot," for he had at one time belonged to the militant Jewish party which contended for the honor of the law and the theocracy of Israel. Judas is distinguished from the traitor by the genitive of his father's name. We do not take "of James" in the sense of "brother of James," for we have just had a genitive of the father ("of Alpheus") and also a patronymic. If the last genitive is to be different and to indicate "brother," ἀδελφός would have to be added. If Jesus conquered the world through the testimony of these men, the victory was certainly not due to the men but to their Lord as whose witnesses they appeared.

14) These eleven, Luke states, not only had their headquarters in this upper room, but "were continuing steadfastly in prayer," τῇ προσευχῇ, a *res sacra* that was always directed to God. And they did this "with one accord," ὁμοθυμαδόν. This word occurs ten times in Acts and is a significant adverb to express oneness of heart and mind. Abstract nouns such as "prayer" may or may not have the article in the Greek. The next verses show that Luke does not have in mind a continuous ten-day prayer meeting with audible praying going on constantly. The word προσευχή is at times used in the wider sense of worship. Prayer marked these ten-day gatherings. This word has thus far been found only once in paganism in the sense of "prayer or supplication," in a lone letter, M.-M. 547, and is thus distinctively Jewish and Christian, that is, Biblical.

And now with two σύν Luke expands the group that was thus together in Jerusalem by adding women as one class and the brothers of Jesus as another. He does not say "together with the women" but only "women," an indefinite number and not a fixed group. Who they were we gather in part from the Gospel: those mentioned in Luke 8:2, 3, at the crucifixion, and at the tomb; but in these places a number of them is left unnamed. From Luke 24:49 we conclude that they were from Galilee. Luke names only the mother of Jesus (καί = "also") who was in John's care. With two exceptions in Luke's Gospel he calls her "Mariam," and a few texts have this form here. One cannot say apodictically that some of these prayers were directed to Jesus; if they were, Mary would have prayed to her son as did all the rest that were in the upper room.

A separate preposition adds "his brothers" and does this after mentioning the women. This makes it certain that none of these brothers of Jesus were apostles. In John 7:3-5 they are not even believers. It is generally thought that the resurrection of Jesus brought them to faith so that we now find them here. Who were they? As far as the writer is able to see, the problem is not solved. The answers given are: sons of Joseph by a former marriage; cousins of Jesus, sons of a half-sister of Mary; and the modern answer, sons born to Joseph and Mary after Jesus. Strong objections may be lodged against each one of these views. When the latter is stressed on the strength of the word ἀδελφοί, "brothers," the passage before us raises gravest doubts. Right after "Mary, the mother of Jesus," we read not "*her* other sons" but "*his* brothers." Why is their relation to Jesus instead of their relation to their own mother mentioned if she was their natural mother? Nobody has as yet been able to answer. Mary is under John's care; yet here are her own natural sons, even more than one, and why is she not in their care? We are still waiting for a satisfactory answer. We, therefore, leave the problem where it is and note only that the objections to making them sons of Joseph and Mary are very strong.

15) **And in these days Peter, having arisen in the midst of the brethren, said (now there was together a multitude of persons, about a hundred and twenty): Men and brethren, it was necessary that the Scripture be fulfilled which the Holy Spirit spoke**

in advance through David's mouth concerning Judas who became guide to those who seized Jesus, seeing that he had been numbered among us and obtained the lot of this ministry.

"These days" are those between Ascension and Pentecost. Here for the first time in Acts "brethren" is used as a designation for the disciples of Jesus; hereafter it is the standard term. The present meeting could not have been held in an upper room of a house; a place in the Temple courts also seems unlikely. So we are left without this information. The matter of filling the place of Judas must have been discussed, at least by the eleven, prior to the action that was finally taken. Jesus had appointed no substitute for Judas during the forty days. The fact that the number of apostles must be twelve according to the choice Jesus had originally made which matched the twelve patriarchs and the twelve tribes of Israel and the twelve thrones awaiting them to judge these twelve tribes, was taken for granted. But the eleven do not act by themselves; they wait until as large a number as possible could be brought together and then the eleven act only as brethren who are on a par with all these others. It is the first vivid illustration of what we shall see throughout the Acts and the early church. There is nothing hierarchical in their procedure. The apostles do not constitute a superior order. All are brethren, each having his place and his task; by Jesus' own appointment the apostles have the most important task.

Luke is not certain that exactly 120 were present; in general, he is not so precise in regard to numbers. Therefore his 120 is not symbolical, 12 times 10. In v. 14 he mentions no number. It seems that number was recorded for two reasons: first, because it was the church that acted, and secondly to show the ratio in which the disciples increased, adding 3,000, then growing to 5,000 men, finally increasing to so many that count is lost and many priests are won until the first persecution causes a great scattering. Ὀνόματα "names," is used in the sense of "persons," all of them being true believers. This, however, does not include the women. The phrase ἐπὶ τὸ αὐτό, "at the same place," is used in the sense of "together." It was natural that Peter should take the lead in the matter at hand just as he had done among the Twelve in past days. Nowhere do we note the least indication that he acted with any special right or authority. Today we should say that he served as chairman of the meeting by general consent.

Ἄνδρες ἀδελφοί is the formal address to a body of men and is quite commonly used thus; it is less familiar than ἀδελφοί, so that the translation of the A. V. is preferable to that of the R. V. The assembly consisted of men, otherwise ἄνδρες could not have been used; ἀδελφοί might include ἀδελφαί, just as today "brethren" may include "sisters," but ἄνδρες could not include γυναικές, just as to this day the address "men" omits "women." Throughout the Acts, in all the highly important transactions of the apostolic church, the men and the women abide in their divinely designed places.

Δεῖ may express any type of necessity; the imperfect refers to the necessity of a certain fulfillment of Scripture which was necessary all along and was now recently fulfilled. Some things God foreordains; when these are recorded in Scripture prophecy, the fulfillment is certain because of God's will and foreordination. But in all contingent matters such as the betrayal of Judas prophecy is fulfilled because of the infallibility of the divine foreknowledge. God did not decree the betrayal; Judas determined that himself; God foreknew that ungodly determination, foretold it, however only in a general way, and so Judas fulfilled the prophecy.

Here is Peter's clear definition of Inspiration: in the Scriptures the Holy Spirit is the speaker, and (in this case) the mouth of David is the medium for his speaking. This definition is oft repeated. The Spirit = the *causa efficiens;* the human mouth (pen) = *causa instrumentalis.* The significant preposition is διά "through" a medium or an instrument. And this was done not merely "through David" but through his "mouth," his very utterance. This is Verbal Inspiratian, than which none other ever occurred according to the Scriptures themselves. The prophecies involved are quoted by Peter in v. 20, 21, now, however, saying that they refer to "Judas who became guide to those who seized Jesus," which graphically describes the act of betrayal.

17) Ὅτι cannot be causal "for" or "because"; it is what R. 1001 calls the consecutive ὅτι, here naming the point on which the prophecy rested: Judas was an apostle. If he had not been that, the Scripture could not have dealt thus with him. Peter puts this vital point, consecutive to which was the necessity of the Scripture fulfillment, into a double statement. First "he had been numbered among us," the periphrastic past perfect expressing his ordination as one of the Twelve prior to his act of betrayal. He had received from Jesus this highest station which was graciously bestowed upon so few. Such high honor, such glorious prospects were granted to Judas by the Lord's grace. Secondly, and helping to define the first statement: "he obtained the lot of this ministry." The highest of all offices came to him. Λαγχάνω, "to obtain by lot," is used in the general sense of "to obtain," hence κλῆρος, "lot," can be used with it and is here also used in the broad sense of "portion," the entire expression being a choice one for appointment to an office. "The lot of this ministry" is a portion or share in the voluntary service to which the apostles were called. Διακονία is also

choice, denoting a service freely rendered for service sake in order to help others. At the wedding in Cana not *douloi,* but *diakonoi* assist; in Matt. 22, *douloi,* slaves, invite, but *diakonoi* cast out the guest, and these latter are angels. "The lot of this ministry" is the one the eleven still have; the genitive is partitive and thus shows the great apostolic ministry to be a unit in which each apostle had his share. Back of the Scripture statements is this high position of Judas; this brought him into those prophecies.

18) **This man, accordingly, acquired a field out of the iniquity wage and, on going headlong, burst in the middle, and all his bowels gushed out. And it became a thing known to all that inhabit Jerusalem, so that field is called in their language Akeldama, that is, Field of Blood.**

The R. V. makes these verses a parenthesis, an insertion into Peter's speech. Yet when those who regard these words as a parenthesis admit that Luke wove them into Peter's address, we dismiss this idea and read them as the A. V. does. No parenthesis is indicated save the small insertion for the sake of the Greek readers: "in their language," and "that is, Field of Blood," which every reader at once notes as having been written by Luke and not spoken by Peter who spoke Aramaic. How Judas acquired a field "out of the iniquity wage," the silver paid him by the high priest for his iniquitous betrayal, might be doubtful if we did not have Matt. 27:3-8. Judas did not acquire that piece of ground by himself going and buying it but by throwing that money into the Temple, hanging himself, and confronting the high priests with the problem of what to do with this "blood money." They solved the difficulty by buying the piece of ground to make a potter's field of it. Peter is brief because all his hearers know the facts.

Matthew reports only that Judas hanged himself, but Peter adds the detail that, on falling headlong, his body burst open, and all his bowels gushed out. The two statements are not contradictory. We need only supply the thought that Judas must have hanged himself in a place where his body could fall down far enough to burst open the abdomen with such horrible results. Ahitophel, the Old Testament type of Judas, also hanged himself. The end of the traitor is most terrible.

19) It is not this end alone that Peter recalls to the brethren but also the fact that the whole city came to know of it with the result that that piece of ground was named by the people: Akeldama (*Akeldamach*), which Luke, like Matthew, translates, "Field of Blood." Here again something must be supplied from Matthew's account, namely, the fact that the high priests refused to put the money into the Temple treasury because it was "blood money" just as Judas said he had betrayed the innocent blood. All this became known together with the horrible death of Judas, and this name, "Field of Blood," was the result. The name primarily refers to the blood of Jesus and secondarily to the death of Judas who betrayed Jesus' blood. There is no evidence that Judas hanged himself on this very piece of ground. The later stories of Papias and others are fiction and are in part due to a misunderstanding of Peter's words.

20) **For it has been written in the Book of Psalms:**

Let his habitation become desolate,
And let not one be dwelling in it!

and,

His overseership let another take!

Peter uses the common formula for introducing Old Testament quotations: γέγραπται, the perfect, "it has been written" and thus now stands as so written.

We see that David's "mouth" mentioned in v. 16 and his writing are regarded as being identical, something that is constantly done in the New Testament with reference to Old Testament writers. The γάρ is explanatory. When v. 18, 19 are made parenthetical, this "for" is connected with v. 17, but we see that it connects even better with v. 19. For all that is said of the terrible end of Judas accords with the two passages of the Psalms (69:25; 109:8) which are now introduced; in fact, γάρ may be translated, "for instance." Peter certainly knew the Scriptures well to be able to adduce these two striking statements. He does not cite them as by any means being the only ones that refer to the case of Judas. A glance at Ps. 69, for instance, shows its typical character. The Jews themselves refer many of its statements to the sufferings of the Messiah and thus to the enemies who inflict these sufferings upon him. When he exposed the traitor, Jesus, too, used Ps. 41:9, David's word regarding the traitor Ahitophel (II Sam. 15:31; 17:1, 23), Luke 22:21; John 13:21-27.

Peter cites two passages, one regarding the removal of Judas from his place and position, the other regarding the filling of his vacant place by another. Both passages deal with the enemies of the theocracy during David's time; it is thus that they apply to Judas who by his traitorous act stands forth among these enemies as their chief representative. All those enemies of David's time are the type of whom Judas became the great antitype. It is thus that the Holy Spirit spoke about Judas in advance. When he spoke through David, Judas was fully foreknown. When he quotes Ps. 69:25, Peter renders the LXX quite exactly and makes only verbal changes that retain the full meaning. David's plural is, however, made a singular because the passage is used specifically with reference to Judas.

The two lines are synonymous Hebrew poetry. The second line repeats and thus emphasizes the first with different words. "Let his habitation become desolate," his ἔπαυλις or dwelling, with Judas being forever removed from it; "and let not one be dwelling in it" in the sense of continuing what he was. So the damnable career of Judas ended, and no one was there to continue it.

Palm 109:8 already had the singular and called for no verbal change: "His overseership, his ἐπισκοπή, let another take." This means his high, responsible office, which is not the same as his habitation and dwelling. The abused office must continue. Since the unworthy incumbent is gone, the Lord will provide one that is worthy. This is true even with regard to the lesser positions of ordinary believers. When the Jews scorned to take their places, the apostles turned to the Gentiles, Acts 13:46. It is this second passage which both warrants and leads to the action now proposed, namely the filling of the office of Judas.

21) **It is necessary, therefore, that of the men who went together with us at every time the Lord Jesus went in and went out on us, beginning from the baptism of John until the day he was received up from us, one of these become a witness of his resurrection together with us.**

Οὖν draws the conclusion which forms a necessity (δεῖ) that was brought on by the act of Judas which entailed that another be put into his office. The entire sentence, packed full of a variety of statements, is neatly and compactly constructed. Peter names the qualifications which the man who is to replace Judas must have. He must be one of those who went together with the eleven every time Jesus came to them, walked with them, and then parted from them for awhile during the whole period that extended from the days of the Baptist until the ascension. Only one who had these requirements would be qualified to be the twelfth in the chosen band who were to act as witnesses of Jesus' resurrection.

We at once see from the modifiers that τῶν συνελθόντων refers to going together with the eleven during the whole ministry of Jesus and not as the same participle in v. 6 to only one, namely, this present meeting with the eleven. Peter also says ἐν παντὶ χρόνῳ, "at every time," and not, "in all the time," (ἐν παντὶ τῷ χρόνῳ), and describes these as the times when Jesus "went in and went out on us." The Gospels, too, show that especially during the first part of his ministry Jesus at times left the apostles and then returned to them. Note the designation "Lord Jesus" and compare 1:6 on "Lord." The grammars regard ἐφ' ἡμᾶς as applying only to the first verb: "went in on us," and let us supply for the second: went out "from us" (B.-D. 479, 2); but "on us" would have to fit the second verb if this were a case of zeugma and not the first. "On us" fits both verbs quite well.

22) The period thus covered begins with "the baptism of John," which simply denotes the time when John was baptizing and not merely when John had finished his baptizing. A point to be noted is that Peter connects the Baptist with the ministry of Jesus as the activity of these two is always linked together. This period ends with the ascension, for which Peter uses the same verb he used in v. 2 (which see) and in v. 11. The genitive ἧς need not be an attraction from the dative as R. 717 and B.-D. 294, 2, assert by pointing to one other example found in one other text (D in Luke 1:20); it is the genitive of time within which something occurs. "Until he was received up from us" (the eleven) does not imply that the qualification includes presence at the ascension; for we know of none but the eleven who were present at that time. It seems to be a hasty conclusion that quite a number

possessed the qualifications here laid down by Peter; we venture to conclude the contrary. When investigation was made, only two were found.

The construction is δεῖ γενέσθαι ἕνα, "it is necessary that one become," and "these" at the end takes up and emphasizes the fact that only such men are to be considered. While the predicate (become a "witness of his resurrection together with us") is unemphatic in the Greek it describes the apostolic office according to its chief task, that of testifying to the resurrection of Jesus. This implies that every apostle must himself have seen the risen Lord and be able to testify accordingly. All else that he saw and heard about Jesus must reach a climax in this final sight. For it is the resurrection of Jesus that is the supreme and ultimate proof of his Messiahship, at once the seal and the crown of all his words and his deeds, especially of his Redeemership. Take away the resurrection, and all else crumbles; but when the resurrection is a fact, all else is established (I Cor. 15:13-22). The fact that those who had followed Jesus from the time of John's baptism would also have seen the risen Lord, Peter does not need to state. What he had to say was that one who had followed thus could join the eleven in their official witness-bearing regarding the resurrection.

23) **And they stood up two, Joseph called Barsabbas, who was called besides Justus, and Matthias.** Why only these two? Because only these two met the requirement laid down by Peter. This is so obvious that one is surprised to find the claim that quite a number of men met the requirement, and that only two of these were selected. And on the strength of two texts Zahn claims that Peter did this selecting. By what right were these two singled out and the rest discarded if the Lord was to make the choice. If the assembly eliminated many, and the Lord only one, he

did very little of the choosing. One out of many could just as well be selected by lot as one out of two. It cannot be said that the assembly or that Peter had reasons for eliminating all but two, for that would only be saying that Peter had not stated all the requirements. Only two met the requirements stated by Peter. The entire choice was left to the Lord.

We really know nothing beyond the names of the two here recorded. All that is worth noting is the statement of Eusebius that both belonged to the Seventy. The name Joseph was so common that it became necessary to state also his other names. The first, Barsabbas (Barsabas), is a patronymic, "son of Saba" or "son of the aged." On the significance of the spelling see Zahn, *Forschungen,* IX, 334, etc. Nor is it surprising that a Latin name was added, "Justus," even as Saul became Paul. In the case of Matthias nothing further than the name was needed because no other man with this name was connected with Jesus. From later sources it is concluded that he was also called Thulmai (Ptolomy).

24) **And praying they said: Thou, Lord, heartknower of all, show forth whom thou didst elect out of these two as the one to take the place of this ministry and apostleship from which Judas passed away to go to his own place. And they gave lots for them, and the lot fell upon Matthias, and he was counted as voted in together with the eleven apostles.**

The choice between the two was entrusted to Jesus by means of prayer. When the aorist participle expresses the same act as the aorist finite verb it indicates simultaneous action: when they prayed they spoke. Peter no doubt spoke the prayer in which all joined silently. The emphatic σύ is more than an address; Jesus is asked in contrast to any selection the assembly might make. And the reason for the appeal to him is that he is the "heart-knower" and thus able to choose with unerring insight. If anything is needed to show that Κύριε is here the Lord Jesus (v. 21) and that these believers are directing a prayer to him, the petition itself shows this, the very verb ἐξελέξω being repeated from v. 2 and from Luke 6:13. As their very name shows, the apostles are elected as his own ambassadors by Jesus in person. So Jesus is here asked to show "whom he did elect of these two as the one," etc.; ἕνα is predicative to the relative ὄν. The aorist "did choose" places the act into the past; all that is needed is that Jesus make this known.

25) The office is fully designated; διακονία recalls v. 17. The second genitive, "of this apostleship," helps to lend weight to the entire designation; at the same time it brings out the thought that the chosen one is to be an apostle. The relative clause adds the idea that this place is now vacant. Judas passed out of it to go to what is significantly called "his own place." The two words "place" are in contrast; but this means that, since the first does not denote a locality but, as the genitives show, an office, no stress should be laid on the second as being a locality although in Luke 16:28 we have "place of torment." The fact that Gehenna or hell is referred to is beyond question. Somehow even those who otherwise speak about an intermediate place, a *Totenreich,* "a realm of the dead," unanimously state that Judas went to hell. "His own" place means, of course, the one and only one befitting him. The view that this refers to the burial place his money bought is scarcely worth noticing. "To go" to his own place, an aorist, means that he arrived there, and this verb conveys the idea that he went of his own volition. He, too, made a choice: the high and holy place of his office he passed up and elected to go to this other place in spite of all the efforts on the part of Jesus to stop him.

26) The lots were not given "to them" but "for them." Somebody attended to this. Probably two markers, each with one name upon it, were placed into a vessel which was shaken so hard that one flew out. This one indicated the choice. The custom of casting lots in this way was very ancient; it dates back to Homer; compare Lev. 16:8. The lot fell upon Matthias; the marker that had his name upon it flew out. The verb συγκαταψηφίζομαι, from ψῆφος, the pebble, black or white, which was used in voting, is found only in one other place in Greek literature and is here used, not with reference to voting, but with reference to counting one as having been voted in, as belonging "together with the eleven apostles." The idea that he was in any way discounted as an apostle because he was elected so late is wholly foreign to Acts.

No further example of this Old Tesament method of turning a decision over to God appears in the New Testament. In the Old Testament it was justified since God often intervened in the affairs of Israel in an outward and a direct way; He himself appointed the casting of lots in Lev. 16:8 and in apportioning Canaan. Prov. 16:13. The Moravians wanted to continue this practice in the Christian Church in cases where the Word of God does not decide: in the reception of members, in allotting offices, in sending out missionaries (see, however, Acts 6:2, etc.; 14:23; I Tim. 3:1, etc.; Tit. 1: 5), in entering marriage (where, however, obedience was not compulsory). Even Zinzendorf finally warned, "Those having no call may burn themselves with the lot." Recourse to drawing or casting lots was abandoned already by the apostolic church; we must follow the enlightenment the Spirit affords and the indications of Providence in both church matters and our personal affairs.

CHAPTER II

THE FIRST HALF

The Gospel Among the Jews in Palestine.
Chapters 2 to 12

The time: 31-44 A. D.; Pentecost to the persecution of Herod Agrippa.

The center of activity: Jerusalem.

This missionary range: Palestine, Jerusalem, Judea, and Samaria.

The chief personage: Peter, besides whom appear in a secondary capacity: John, James, Stephen, Philip. Barnabas and Paul begin their activity.

Peter is prominent in six marked instances: 1) At Pentecost in his sermon, chapter 2. 2) In the miracles, that follow, chapters 3 to 5, and 9:31-40. 3) In discipline and in the appointment of deacons, 5:1-11; 6:1, etc. 4) In superintending the work in Samaria together with John, 8:4-25. 5) In bringing the gospel to the first Gentiles, chapters 10 and 11; 6) As a steadfast confessor during the first great persecution, chapter 12.

The First Quarter

The Gospel in Jerusalem, Chapters 2 to 7

THE COMING OF THE HOLY SPIRIT

1) **And when the day of Pentecost was being fulfilled, they were all together at one place.** Luke alone, here and in Luke 9:51, uses this verb, both times

it is the present infinitive passive with ἐν τῷ to designate the arriving of a period or of a point of time. In Luke 9:51 it is not the day of the ascension that is referred to but the final period of Christ's life that culminated in the ascension. Here in Acts the Jewish day of Pentecost is referred to. The difficulty does not lie in the neat Greek phrase but in its translation as far as both sense and tense are concerned. The idea is that, by coming, this day is filling up completely a measure of time that was hitherto beginning to be filled more and more. Yet no mere dating is intended, namely the arrival of the fiftieth day after the Jewish Passover. The phrase is too weighty for that. Luke is thinking of the Lord's promise and of how it is now coming to fulfillment, the arrival of this day making full the measure of time the Lord contemplated when he made the promise. Hence also the present tense is employed. As the hours of this day began, the measure of this time was being filled up, and the thing promised was now due to occur, and Luke states that it did occur. Compare C.-K. 929 for the main thought.

The feminine ἡ Πεντηκοστή without ἡμέρα came to be the name of the festival; hence Luke writes: "the day of the Fiftieth," i. e., of Pentecost. It came on the fiftieth day after the Passover. Coming seven weeks after the Passover, it was also called "the Festival of Weeks." In this year the fifteenth of Nisan, the day of the Passover, occurred on a Friday (which, of course, began at sundown on Thursday). The count of fifty starts with the next day which was a Sabbath and thus brings us to another Sabbath as the day of the Pentecost of this year.

The Christian celebration of the descent of the Spirit did not begin until years later. The name Pentecost was retained, but the count was made from the Christian Easter, which was always celebrated on a

Sunday and disregarded the fact that the Jewish Passover always came on the fifteenth of Nisan, no matter what the day of the week. Thus our Pentecost is also always observed on a Sunday. Passover, Pentecost, and Tabernacles were the great Jewish festivals that were attended by Jews from everywhere. Pentecost, however, lasted only one day. It was the Jewish harvest festival that celebrated the completion of the harvest, Exod. 23:14, etc., and the description in Lev. 23:17, etc. Long after the time of the apostles a second day was added, and the entire festival became what it is for the Jews today, a celebration of the giving of the law on Sinai.

"All" refers to the persons mentioned in 1:12-15 and certainly includes the women; but the estimate that there were 200 seems high. Here ἐπὶ τὸ αὐτό, following ὁμοῦ, must mean more than "together" (1:16), namely "in the same or in one place." What Luke says is that this day found all the disciples in one place, and that none of the entire number was absent. They were ready when the Spirit came.

2) **And there came suddenly out of heaven a noise as of a violent wind borne along, and it filled the whole house where they where sitting. And there appeared to them, as distributing themselves, tongues of fire, and it sat on each single one of them. And they were all filled with the Holy Spirit and began to make utterance with different tongues even as the Spirit kept giving to them to utter exaltedly.**

The Jews stood when praying; sitting implies that the assembly of disciples was listening to some discourse that was being uttered, let us say, by one of the apostles. About nine o'clock (v. 15) a violent noise sounded out of heaven, descended, and filled the entire building where the assembly was sitting on the floor in Oriental, cross-legged fashion. Luke compares the sound to that of a violent wind borne along, i. e., moving forward. It was sound alone and not a wind. The roar started in the sky but soon filled only the house. This mighty sound was surely the symbol of power, and we may recall that both the Hebrew and the Greek words for the Spirit, *Ruach* and Πνεῦμα, denote wind or breath, and that Jesus himself compared the coming of the Spirit to the blowing of the wind, John 3:8. The volume of the sound denotes vast, supernatural power. The Spirit of God thus indicated his coming upon the disciples in an audible manner. But this roar also had the purpose of attracting the mass of people to the spot where all the disciples were gathered. And while the aorist "there came" registers only the fact of the coming, we take it that the roar lasted long enough to effect this necessary purpose.

Much effort is often spent in trying to prove that this οἶκος or "house" could be only one of the thirty halls in the Temple that were called οἶκοι. It is stated that this is the festival, the ninth hour, when all would be in the Temple, the great mass of people that quickly gathered and gathered so that Peter could preach to them. But why would all these disciples be sitting in one of these halls of the Temple at this hour of prayer? And would this roar not cause everybody on the entire Temple grounds to rush to this hall, all the Temple police, all the Sanhedrists likewise? Proving the house to be one of the halls of the Temple proves too much. Note the article: "*the* whole house," evidently the one already referred to in 1:13, 15, where 120 persons had plenty of room. But this was not a "house" in the modern sense of the term, a building with ordinary rooms. We, of course, lack details, but if Luke had a hall in the Temple in mind he surely would have written ἱερόν.

3) The second phenomenon was that of tongues resembling fire and distributing themselves to each

person present. There was no actual fire but only a resemblance to fire. This aorist again registers only the fact and not the duration of the appearance. The crowd speaks only of what it hears and not of what it sees. We may conclude that the flamelike tongues had disappeared by the time the crowd had gathered. Luke writes, "distributing themselves," and then adds, "it sat upon each single one of them." Luke does not intend to write a subject just as we have none when we say, "it rains," "it is lightning," etc. Perhaps we may say that the flamelike tongues appeared in a great cluster and then divided until a tongue settled on the head of each one of the disciples. Compare the phrase ἐφ' ἕνα ἕκαστον, with εἷς ἕκαστος in v. 6, and with the simple ἕκαστος in v. 8. Luke means "on each *single* one," not a single one being excepted, men, women, old, young. These firelike tongues are plainly the fulfillment of Luke 3:16: "He shall baptize you with the Holy Spirit and with fire." Pentecost corrects all other interpretations of Luke 3:16, and of Matt. 3:11. The sound roared indiscriminately in the house, but these tongues sat individually upon each person. The Spirit fills every single believer in the church, uses every one in his mighty and blessed work. Pentecost raises all to the same level.

Why tongues, and why like fire? May we say that these tongues point to the speaking with tongues? When the heart overflows with grace and power, the tongue is kindled into utterance. So all are to have the Spirit, to confess, to pray, and to praise. Firelike tongues may well recall the altar with its holy fire which send the offering up to God. Fire is also a symbol of purity and purification. Each disciple is to make his confession, prayer, praise, testimony a pure offering coming from a holy altar that is burning with sacred fire. Like the noise, the tongues were a supernatural, heavenly manifestation.

4) Once more Luke writes "all," namely "all were filled with the Holy Spirit." This is the miracle itself, the signs are only accompaniments. The emphasis is on the passive verb "they were filled," for it was Jesus who filled the disciples with the Spirit; the aorist simply states the great fact. This is the realization of the promise, "he shall baptize you with the Holy Spirit." At one time the Spirit descended upon Jesus in a wondrous manner; in an analogous way the Spirit came upon and filled all these disciples of Jesus. Through the Spirit he became the Christ (the Anointed), through the same Spirit his disciples become Christians (people anointed).

Yet we must remember that they all had the Spirit even before Pentecost just as did all the saints of the Old Testament. No saving faith was ever possible without the Spirit. In the case of the eleven we must also recall John 20:22. Here, at Pentecost, Jesus sent the Spirit in a new fulfillment of the promises stated in 1:5; John 14:16, 17; 15:26; 16:7. At Pentecost the Spirit himself came to dwell permanently, throughout all the ages, in the hearts of those who constitute the *Una Sancta*, the Christian Church. Hitherto he had, indeed, wrought upon men with his saving power and bestowed also this or that gift; since Pentecost he actually fills the church with his powers and his gifts, and that by way of his own blessed presence. Hence these miraculous manifestations on this day of Pentecost; hence the new influx of power into the disciples, especially into the apostles for this witness-bearing in all the world (1:8); hence also the array of spiritual and charismatic gifts which Paul lists in I Cor. 12:4-11. The effect was the spread of the church throughout the world and the radiation of power from the church in all the world. Once redemption was accomplished, all this could follow and did follow because of the presence of the Spirit. The great channels through which the Spirit dwelling in the church operates are the Word and the sacraments.

Luke properly records that all were filled with the Spirit before he adds that they all began to speak in new languages. The sound and the visible tongues were external, but this miraculous speaking was a personal act due to the inward presence of the Spirit. In Mark 16:17, Jesus promised this gift: "they shall speak with new tongues." These καιναί tongues are the ones Luke here calls ἕτεραι, "other or different" tongues. "Began to make utterance" is scarcely an Aramaic pleonasm but a circumstantial way of stating so important an action. Hence also the following imperfect as the Spirit "kept giving" to them. Every word of these strange languages was an immediate gift of the Spirit. The rare verb ἀποφθέγγεσθαι describes the utterance as being made in an exalted manner.

What this speaking "with different tongues" means is stated in v. 6: "everyone heard them speaking in his own language"; and in v. 11: "we are hearing them telling with our own tongue the great things of God." The disciples spoke in foreign languages that were hitherto unknown to them, in the very languages of the natives of the foreign lands who were presently assembled before them. This is what Luke writes, and the church has never doubted the fact and Luke's veracity and accuracy in reporting that fact.

But serious objection is raised by some commentators who say that Luke's words mean something else, or that he has reported the facts in a wrong way. The miraculous speaking mentioned in 10:46, in 19:6, in I Cor. 12:10, and in 14:2, etc., is referred to. Nearly every objector has his own peculiar view. Some even say that "tongues" means "the language of heaven"! When Luke writes "with different tongues" and later omits "different," the omission is pointed to as proof positive for the fact that there were two entirely different kinds of speaking with tongues. The author has treated the entire subject at length in connection with I Cor. 12:10, and 14:2, etc. Sometimes Luke's sources are questioned. Yet he wrote with full knowledge of the gift of tongues. He had been in Corinth and may well have witnessed this gift in operation. He had Paul at his side who knew all about this gift. We have every reason to think that Luke also met other apostles, certainly Peter, to say nothing of some of the very disciples who here at Pentecost spoke with tongues and still others of the 3,000 who were there to hear that speaking. Still more, the Spirit who bestowed this gift of tongues guided Luke in producing his account.

The gift of tongues is one of the proofs for divine Inspiration. The Spirit who put the words of strange languages into the mouths of the disciples wherewith to speak the great things of God had no trouble in attending to the words of the holy writers so that they recorded what he desired and in the way he desired it.

Many have thought that the confusion of tongues at Babel was counterbalanced here at Pentecost, and that is the chief import of this part of the miracle. Rocholl, *Philosophie der Geschichte,* 275, beautifully states this view: "The speaking with tongues by the witnesses of the Mediator celebrates the resurrection of the unity buried at Babel. . . . It was the first full chord, struck by a higher hand on the discordant giant harp, the strings of which are the nations of the earth," etc. An attractive thought; and yet the diversity of languages has continued unchanged. Even Greek, a world language, did not endure. We must go deeper than Rocholl. The miracle of tongues maintains the diversity but points out into all lands, nations, and tongues exactly as Jesus does in 1:8. The miracle is prophetic, the first full chord of that symphony of confession, testimony, prayer, and praise that was soon to rise to the throne of the Redeemer from the tongues of all the nations of the world.

The gift of tongues was one of the miraculous gifts of the apostolic church and as such, together with other miraculous gifts, served its purpose in attesting the presence of the Spirit at a time when such attestation was needed. Hence it was transient and disappeared when the church grew to such proportions that its very presence and power attested the Spirit's presence within it. The gift was not intended for preaching, and none of the believers in the apostolic church used it for that purpose. The one apostle who preached to so many nationalities did this without the gift of tongues. God had providentially prepared the vehicle of Greek, the world language of that time, for this purpose. Wherefore the New Testament also appeared in Greek.

As they have done in the case of the gift of healing, men have tried to regain the gift of tongues. The last abortive effort started in California, leaped to Scandinavia, ran its course there and in Germany as a Pentecostal movement, and died suddenly when its chief exponents openly confessed that they had been hoaxed by devilish spirits. Those "tongues" had been gibberish, their translation pure imagination. The devilishness consisted in no small measure in attributing this folly to the Holy Spirit.

5) **Now there were dwelling in Jerusalem Jews, men devout, from every nation of those under heaven. And when this sound occurred, the crowd came together and were confounded because they kept hearing them speaking, every single one, in his own language. And all were in amazement and kept wondering, saying: Lo, are not all these speak-**

ing Galileans? And how do we on our part hear, every one in our very language in which we were born?

Luke is concerned only with this class of Jews who were born or reared in foreign parts but had now permanently settled in the Holy City in order to end their days there. They, of course, knew and spoke Aramaic, but they knew, in some cases even still better, the native language of the land where they had dwelt so long. How dearly these Jews loved Jerusalem is evidenced by expressions such as this: "Everyone who is buried in the land of Israel is in as good case as if he were buried under the altar." "Men devout" brings out this idea, earnest and sincerely religious Jews who wanted to spend their last years near the Temple and join in the worship at this great sanctuary. Εὐλαβής, "one who takes hold well," is regularly used in this religious sense. "From every nation," etc., is not as hyperbolic as might be supposed. Few cities and towns, to say nothing of countries in the great Roman empire, were without a contingent of Jews. In his great oration in Josephus, *Wars*, 2, 16, 4, Herod Agrippa states only facts about the Jewish diaspora: "There is no people upon the habitable earth which have not some portion of you (Jews) among them."

6) It was the mighty sound that brought the crowd together at the place where the disciples were gathered. The sound identified the place. We know how quickly crowds gather. Natives of Jerusalem and pilgrims from afar may have been in the crowd, but Luke has already drawn our attention to the great number of foreign-born Jews who are of special importance in this connection. They were utterly confounded "because they kept hearing them speaking, every single one, in his own language." The imperfect brings out the continuousness of the action. Each

foreign-born Jew heard his own foreign language uttered, not once or twice, but for a considerable time. After the plural verb the singular "every single one" individualizes as this is frequently done. Luke means "in his own language" and not "dialect" just as the word used in 1:19 means "language." The list of nations following also excludes the idea that the disciples, whose own Aramaic was the Galilean dialect, were now speaking a number of other Aramaic dialects. Compare v. 11.

7) Luke heaps up the verbs describing the effect upon the hearers. The aorist συνεχύθη states the first impression: the crowd "was confounded." Then two imperfects describe the condition that followed: "they were amazed," dazed by the astounding thing they were witnessing, "and kept wondering" what it could mean and how it could be explained. So the questioning began, first as to the identity of these disciples, secondly as to how they could speak as they did, the two questions belonging together. Luke states only briefly the questioning that went through the crowd.

We need not ask how the disciples were known to be Galileans. The first inquiry, no doubt, was: "Who are these people?" And someone who knew them quickly supplied the information. The question is one of astonishment as the interjection shows. So all these speaking in all these languages were Galileans! That, of course, meant neither "Christians" nor "unlearned," connotations which "Galileans" never had; but it did mean that the disciples were not residents of Jerusalem, and it identified them as what they were. We also have no reason to think that some were not from Galilee.

8) But the fact of their being Galileans shed no light whatever on the miracle. Note that ἡμεῖς is in contrast with ἅπαντες οὗτοι. These foreign-born Jews could certainly understand Galilean Aramaic, but how

could Galileans speak all these different languages, they say, "in which we were born"? To be born "in a language" means to claim that language as one's mother tongue.

9) The list of nationalities is in apposition to the emphatic ἡμεῖς in v. 8, and should be read: "we Parthians," "we Medes," and so on down the list, each group exclaiming about itself. **Parthians and Medes and Elamites; and the Jews inhabiting Mesopotamia and Cappadocia, Pontus and Asia, both Phrygia and Pamphilia, Egypt and the parts of Libya, those along Cyrene; and temporary residents, Romans, both Jews and proselytes, Cretes and Arabians, we hear them telling with our own tongues the great things of God.**

This list is neatly arranged in three groups: $3 + 8 + 3$; the group of 8 in 4 pairs. The countries mentioned describe a great circle about the Holy Land, starting on the east and swinging around westward to the north and ending in the south. A map is instructive also for some of the distances. The two articulated participles head the second and the third group.

The reading Ἰουδαίαν τε has always been a conundrum. How could "both Judea and Cappadocia" be so closely linked together? How could "Judea" occur in this list at all, which is to name only foreign-born Jews? Rather unsatisfactory explanations have been offered. Emendations have also been suggested; Syria, Armenia, Idumea. To Zahn belongs the credit for having cleared up this *crux*. Following an old Latin version, he drops τε and changes Ἰουδαίαν into Ἰουδαῖοι "Judea" into "Jews." Thus those in the second group (Mesopotamia to Cyrene) were Jews; but the third group consisted of "both Jews and proselytes." This emendation makes the grouping symmetrical and at the same time reveals how easily the corruption of the text could have crept in. "Asia" is the great province of which Ephesus was the capital. The first group names nations, the second group countries, the third again nations.

10) Egypt is paired with "the parts of Libya, those down along Cyrene." Simon, who bore the cross of Jesus, was a Cyrenian. Josephus, *Ant.* 14, 7, 2 cites an interesting passage from Strabo that shows how numerous the Jews were not only in Egypt but also in Cyrene.

The third group, like the second, is introduced with an articulated participle and presents temporary residents in Jerusalem (οἱ ἐπιδημοῦντες) : Romans, Cretes, and Arabians. The participle must refer to all three. We do not think, however, that these were only pilgrims who had come for the festival, for this lasted but one day, and that they would come from a place so remote as Rome for so short a time seems improbable. These, too, "were dwelling in Jerusalem" (v. 5) but, as Luke carefully indicates, only for a time. After the 3,000 had been converted, it was an easy matter to gather the exact data that Luke records.

It seems that the apposition "both Jews and proselytes" belongs only to "Romans" and not also to "Cretes and Arabians," most certainly not to the entire two preceding groups as some have supposed. The Jews had two kinds of proselytes: "proselytes of the gate" who were not bound to submit to circumcision, who observed only the seven Noachian commandments against idolatry, blasphemy, disobedience to magistrates, murder, fornication or incest, robbery or theft, eating of blood (Gen. 9:4), and were restricted in taking part in the worship; and "proselytes of righteousness," Gentiles who became complete Jews. The latter seem to be referred to here.

11) When Luke records in regard to all these different nationalities: "we hear them telling with our

own tongues," he intends to repeat and thus to emphasize the statement made in v. 8. The emphasis is on the dative of means "with our own tongues," our own because we were born in them. In v. 8 the question was raised as to how this could be, here the fact is asserted that it, indeed, is. The persons heard are put into the genitive, the things heard into the accusative. The latter are added, namely "the great things of God." While this is a summary, we are safe in saying that the great deeds of God in Christ are referred to, plus the attributes displayed in these deeds.

In this description, which presents merely the essentials, we must retain the idea of order. All these disciples did not shout together in a Babel of foreign languages, but one spoke here, another there, and each was understood by the nationality whose language he spoke. The foreign-born Jews heard what was spoken, understood what was said. From the account it cannot be ascertained whether one disciple spoke more than one foreign language. Nor can we determine whether the disciple himself understood what he uttered and could have translated it into Aramaic. This speaking was also not preaching the gospel to this crowd. Peter did the preaching. The tongues were just what Paul states in I Cor. 14:22, a sign to those who did not believe and, as he further states, one that should be followed by prophesying (preaching), even as Peter also presently began to preach and to explain this sign to all these Jews.

12) **And all were in amazement and were in perplexity, saying one to another, What does this intend to be? Others, however, scoffing, were saying, They have been filled with sweet wine!**

"They were all in amazement" is repeated from v. 7, and emphasizes this condition. Again an imperfect is added which describes the condition of perplexity which could not get beyond the question as to what this thing could intend to be. Some texts have the optative with ἄν, potential: "What this might intend to be?" The indicative is assured and far better, for it implies that it intended to be something although the hearers could not as yet understand what. Ἄλλος πρὸς ἄλλον is not quite reciprocal (R. 747), a Latinism (R. 692). The great bulk of the hearers were sensible; they stopped with their question, gave no hasty answer, were willing to wait for the true and satisfactory answer. They were in the presence of a great miracle that transcended all reason and all experience and deeply felt the effect of it.

13) But among these foreign-born Jews were others who were of a different character (ἕτεροι, R. 749). They, too, heard the great things of God. But they passed the whole thing off with scoffing; they called the disciples tipsy with γλεῦκος, "sweet wine," not "new wine," since the last vintage was four months in the past. Ἔλεγον is descriptive; they passed this scoffing remark on. The perfect "have been filled" is intensive (R. 903) and means that they have reached the point where they are full. Wise men, sensible men! When God works, and the thing is too plain, these fellows appear with their slur. But what they say reveals only themselves and the baseness of their hearts.

PETER'S PENTECOSTAL SERMON

14) We may say that the speaking with tongues continued until the maximum effect had been attained. Then the Spirit ceased to speak through the mouths of the disciples. **But Peter, after stepping forth with the eleven, lifted up his voice and spoke exaltedly to them: Jewish men and all inhabiting Jerusalem, let this be known to you, and give ear to my utterances! For not are these drunk, as you suppose, for this is the third hour of the day. On the contrary,**

this is what has been declared through the mouth of the prophet Joel:

> **And it shall be in the last days, saith God,**
> **I will pour out of my Spirit upon all flesh;**
> **And your sons and your daughters shall prophesy,**
> **And your young men shall see visions,**
> **And your old men shall dream dreams;**
> **Yea, and on my men slaves and on my women slaves in those days**
> **Will I pour out from my Spirit, and they shall prophesy.**

Σταθείς is not ἀναστάς, "having arisen," as though all this occurred while the apostles and the disciples had been sitting. Peter "stepped forth," "took his stand," and the eleven with him, out in front of all the disciples, at some place where he could preach to this crowd and be heard by it. "With the eleven" means that Peter was only the spokesman for them. Matthias was with them. That the apostles should assume this leadership was the intention of Jesus when he appointed them to their office; moreover, the Spirit was now directing and empowering them. Peter had been but an ordinary fisherman, but here Luke's sketch of his sermon shows that it was a masterly, masterful, most effective discourse that was delivered without preparation or premeditation at the decisive moment on this day before an audience of thousands. This was possible only by the aid of the Spirit. Luke indicates the dignity, the solemnity, and the exalted tone when he says that Peter stepped forth with the eleven, lifted up his voice, and spoke exaltedly (the same verb that was used in v. 4) to the great assembly.

Peter uses the form of a complete address. Ἄνδρες is just as difficult to render here as it was in 1:16, and is just as respectful and dignified with Ἰουδαῖοι as with ἀδελφοί; but note the gradation and see how Peter draws nearer and nearer to his hearers as he continues to speak, advancing to "men and Israelites" in v. 22, and finally to "men and brethren" in v. 29 (see 1:16). "Ye men of Judea" in our versions is incorrect, for Ἰουδαῖοι = Jews, those identified with the entire Jewish nation. The Twelve were such Jews although not all were "of Judea." Nor is it correct to say that Peter took no cognizance of the proselytes in the audience when he said "Jews," for every proselyte of righteousness was no longer a Gentile but an out-and-out Jew.

The addition "and all inhabiting Jerusalem" should not be understood so as to exclude those who were living only temporarily in the city (οἱ ἐπιδημοῦντες in v. 10) but so as to include them. Nor is the idea of this expression such that those living in Jerusalem form a class that was distinct from other Jews who resided elsewhere, transient visitors in the city. What would be the object of such a distinction; and does not what Peter here says apply to all Jews, irrespective of residence, as explaining the Pentecostal miracle? "Jewish men" and "all inhabiting Jerusalem" are the same; the latter is only an apposition. It is added in the sense of the "men devout" used in v. 5. The exclamations uttered by these men showed that they were foreign-born Jews, yet their devoutness had impelled them to transfer their homes to the Holy City. Even those residing here temporarily were here because of the same motive. Peter's address makes that plain and honors them by the statement: "All you who love Jerusalem so much as to have come here to live." A participle in apposition has the article even when it does not occur in an address (R. 1107).

Peter, however, speaks to these devout Jews with all authority: "Let this be known to you and give ear to my utterances!" Note the same authority in 4:10

when he is facing the Sanhedrin. Here is no timidity, no uncertainty but only solid certainty and full warrant. Peter is stating divine realities and makes no apologies for them. "This" = "my utterances" = all that follows in the sermon. Peter uses excellent psychology, he meets the questioning of his auditors squarely, without circumlocution. His authoritative tone is enforced by the full impact of what he says.

He even uses excellent homiletics. He states his theme clearly: "This is what has been declared by the mouth of the prophet Joel." Stating it in advance of his text is proper; you may do the same. Then comes Peter's tremendous text. He marks the two parts of his sermon most distinctly, at v. 22 and at v. 29. They clearly expound the vital point of this text for these particular hearers — no homiletics was ever better. The conclusion is brief, direct, and powerful, v. 36. In order to get the full effect of this sermon put yourself into Peter's place and think how you would have met the situation that morning before that audience.

15) With one stroke Peter quashes the scoffers. Only a few readers get the full force of Peter's reference to "the third hour of the day," our nine o'clock in the morning. Following Exod. 16:8, the Jews ate only bread in the morning; the Targum says, not until after the morning sacrifice, hence at about ten; and meat only in the evening at the δεῖπνον or main meal of the day. They drank wine only when they ate meat, which means at this evening meal. This is the sense of Eccles. 10:16, 17. The godlessness of the princes "who eat in the morning" consists in this that they eat all sorts of food, especially also meat, and with it drink wine already in the morning, hence "for drunkenness"; but godly princes "eat in due season," meat, wine, etc., in the evening. "It is the third hour of the day." Yet these scoffers claim that all these

disciples had already partaken of a great meal, not only with wine, but with far too much of it! The very keenness of this one word of reply shows the full clarity of Peter's mind. Peter speaks for "these," pointing to them; he does not need to speak for himself. Note how οὐ is placed far forward in the sentence, putting it in the strongest possible opposition to ἀλλά.

16) The idea of a drunken jargon becomes even blasphemous when Peter states the reality back of this speaking with foreign tongues: "on the contrary, this is what has been declared through the mouth of the prophet Joel," i. e., this that Peter's hearers have seen is the fulfillment of Joel's great prophecy. Many times we read "it has been written," and now in the same sense "it has been declared or spoken," the perfect tense always has its strong present connotation: once spoken (written) the thing stands so now and forever. The speaker implied in the passive is God (v. 17: "saith God"), and διά here, as in every other case of quotation, states the medium or instrument used by God, the prophet or the mouth of the prophet. This passive plus διά, wherever they occur in Scripture, state in brief the entire doctrine of Verbal Inspiration, to wit, that in all Scripture the real speaker is God, and that the holy writers are only his media, instruments, mouthpieces.

17) Joel prophesied about 870 B. C. Peter quotes Joel 2:28-32, compare the A. V. for the Hebrew; the LXX and Peter have a few longer statements. Thus "in the last days" = "afterward," Hebrew; "after these things," LXX. Peter's wording, however, is interpretative, explaining what the Hebrew "afterword" really means, namely the last period of the world which is ushered in by the first coming of Christ and continues until his second coming for judgment. It is with this time in view that God made his promise

regarding the pouring out of the Spirit. So also Peter inserts "saith God" in order to make plain that it is he who promised, "I will pour out of my Spirit upon all flesh." It is this pouring out that had just occurred (v. 33). "Upon all flesh" is universal but not absolute; v. 38 shows both, "everyone" may receive the Holy Spirit but only by repentance and faith. "Flesh" = men as distinguished from angels by having flesh or a body (Rom. 1:3; John 1:14); but men in their sinfulness and their frailty. Here σάρξ is not in contrast with πνεῦμα in the ethical sense. With abstract words "every" and "all" flow together, hence ἐπὶ πᾶσαν σάρκα needs no article in order to mean "upon all flesh." "I will pour out" implies the full gift of the Spirit and thus extends as far as "all flesh." The Spirit who came upon a few disciples at Pentecost has filled others of all languages in all lands the world over and is still extending his activity to more of them. Once confined to the narrow limits of Judaism for such operations as were preparatory to Christ's redemption, the Spirit, now that redemption was accomplished, went out to men generally and extended the church to the ends of the earth (1:8) and symbolized this at Pentecost by letting the disciples speak in many languages.

The chief effect of the Spirit's activity is always prophesying, not in the narrow sense of foretelling future events, but in the broad and far more important sense of voicing the saving and blessed will of God to men everywhere. In I Cor. 14 Paul speaks of this as the best and highest gift of the Spirit; and Luther writes: "What are all other gifts together compared to this gift, that the Spirit of God himself, the eternal God, comes down into our hearts, yea, into our bodies and dwells in us, rules, guides, leads us! Thus now, as concerning this passage of the prophet, prophesying, visions, dreams are *all one thing,* namely the knowledge of God through Christ, which the Holy Spirit kindles and makes to burn through the Word of the gospel." The fact that Luther is correct is shown by Peter when in v. 18 he adds to both the Hebrew and the LXX texts: "and they shall prophesy." This is interpretative and repeats "they shall prophesy" from v. 17.

"Your sons and your daughters" is amplified by "your young men" and "your old men," the possessives referring to the Jews to whom the Spirit first came through the apostles. The three lines of Hebrew poetry are parallel and synonymous statements, which means that all the predicates belong to all the subjects, sons, daughters, young men, old men. So the three predicates form a unit, each predicate saying the same thing with variation, as each subject is only a variation. All shall prophesy, confess, and tell the gospel, and thus the young men shall see glorious visions of its progress and its victories, and the old men shall dream dreams of its blessedness and its power, literally: "dream with dreams," a Hebraism in the translation and not a case of a Greek cognate object.

18) In *καί γε* the particle is climacteric or ascensive, which we try to render by "yea and," meaning, "on top of all that has been said." This emphasis applies to the two phrases: "on my men slaves and on my women slaves." In v. 17 the four *ὑμῶν* refer to the Jewish nation. What a blessed thing it is to have *their* sons and *their* daughters prophesy, etc. But they also have a relation to the God who made this promise and fulfills it with reference to them: they are *his* slaves, etc. And "slaves," *δοῦλοι*, brings out the idea that they belong wholly to God, are wholly subject and obedient to his will. Jesus himself was the *'Ebed Yahweh,* "Servant of Jehovah," and all believers are in a similar position.

Are these still only Jewish believers? Some think so. Yet "all flesh" precedes, the Spirit was to reach out into all the world. Hence we are inclined to think that this "yea and" introduces all who belong to God by faith in Christ, Gentiles plus Jews combined into one. All of them shall have the Spirit and shall prophesy. The Hebrew has: I will pour out "my Spirit" (the accusative); the LXX and Peter the partitive: "of or from my Spirit." We take the sense to be the same, for to have the Spirit is to have some of his power and his gifts, no man can assimilate all of them.

A peculiar question arises as to the difference between the Hebrew and Peter's quotation. The Hebrew has this gradation: your sons — your daughters — your old men — your young men (these two in this order) — the (men) servants — the handmaids. The last two seem to refer only to the Jewish servants. Delitzsch calls them slaves and says that in the Old Testament no slave had the gift of prophecy. He states that the translators of the LXX could not understand how slaves should have this gift and therefore added "my," making them God's *douloi* and *doulai*. But this does not remove the difficulty. For most of these slaves of the Jews were Gentiles, and for even these to receive the Spirit implied that the Gentile world would be blessed. And Peter is right: these persons would no longer be just slaves but *my* (God's own) slaves, even as all believers, whether they are Jews or Gentiles, are purchased and won by Christ in order to be his own and to live under him.

19) Peter must quote Joel's prophecy in full because the second part of it states how long the Spirit, poured out at Pentecost, will continue his work in the world, and because the last line opens the door of salvation to everyone who, in repentance and faith, calls on the Lord (v. 38).

And I will give wonders in heaven above
And signs on the earth below,
Blood and fire and vapor of smoke;
The sun shall be turned into darkness,
And the moon into blood
Before the Lord's day comes,
The one great and manifest,
And it shall be, everyone who shall call on the name of the Lord shall be saved.

It must be well understood that the prophets always viewed the two comings of Christ together without having the interval between the two revealed to them. We have a clear example in the Baptist who in Luke 3:16 speaks of Pentecost and in 3:17 of the final judgment. This also caused a difficulty for him. When he saw Jesus doing works of grace only and none of judgment he wondered whether another was yet to come to perform the work of judgment. Joel's description recalls that of Jesus given in Luke 21:9-11, 25, 26. Joel combines the two, "wonders in heaven above and signs on the earth below," and Peter adds the words "signs," "above," and "below" in an interpretative way.

Τέρας = "wonder," a startling, amazing portent or prodigy. The pagan world also had such portents. It seems that for this reason the New Testament never uses "wonders" alone but always conjoins the word with "signs" or with "miracles." Many of God's signs are, indeed, also portentous wonders, but they are never wonders alone, they are divine indications and thus lie on a far higher plane than pagan portents. "Sign," σημεῖον (σημαίνω, to make known by a σῆμα), is always used with a strong ethical connotation by pointing to the significance of the occurrence and not merely to its strangeness. Hence the word is also used alone. In the parallelism of Hebrew poetry the wonders are not restricted to the heavens, nor the signs to the earth, but in both spheres both shall occur and shall at the same time be astonishing and very significant. The sign language of God cannot be misunderstood, every startling and disquieting phenomenon proclaims that heaven and earth must pass away and all their affairs be wound up.

"Blood," etc., are only specifications, a few of the arresting signs that occur on earth. "Blood and fire and vapor of smoke" appear together at the time of wars and in great calamities in nature. As far as bloody wars are concerned, we have seen this sign often enough, and the Scriptures hold out no hope that it will not be repeated until the very end.

20) The turning of the sun into utter darkness and of the moon into a blood-red glow until its light, too, is extinguished, is the ushering in of the end of the world itself as Jesus described it more fully in Matt. 24:29. In Joel's prophecy this is indicated by the final phrase; πρίν is best regarded as an adverb-preposition, and the infinitive as a noun (R. 1091; B.-D. 395 has the older explanation). "The Lord's day" is the final day of the world, it is peculiarly his because it is the day on which he shall judge the world. But it is no longer a mundane day of so many hours by the clock. The whole universe shall be utterly changed, and time shall have ceased. It is called "day" (the genitive "Lord's" making it definite) because human language supplies no better word. The two adjectives are added by the article and are like an appositional climax (R. 776): "the one that is great and manifest." "Great" in the absolute sense, the positive being stronger than a superlative would be; "manifest" as revealing what this day is to be to the whole universe. The Hebrew adjective is "terrible," and this was translated "manifest" by the LXX. The Spirit allowed Peter to retain the latter because it was satisfactory and appropriate. In fact, the ἐπιφάνεια of the Parousia is emphasized repeatedly, II Thess. 2:8. Κύριος = *Yahweh*; it is his

day in which he will judge the world through Christ, Acts 17:31.

21) The really important statement in Joel's prophecy is the final one which declares that during all this time, from Pentecost to the Lord's day at the end, everyone who calls on the Lord shall be saved. It is this promise that Peter applies in v. 38. Καὶ ἔσται, as in v. 17, is the Hebrew *vehayah* and needs no connective to link it with what follows (R. 1042). "It shall be" is a promise that cannot be broken. What it includes has already existed for nearly two thousand years. "To call upon the Lord's name" (the verb is the middle) means to call him to our aid, i. e., in our spiritual need. The ὄνομα or "name" is that by which the Lord alone is known as the One who has the help we need. This name is his gospel which must first be brought to us in order to reveal the Lord in all his grace in Christ and thus to kindle in us the desire for that grace and help and cause us to call upon his gracious name.

Note the universality in Joel's "everyone who," etc., and ὃς ἄν (ἐάν) indicates expectancy, it is assumed that many will call on the Lord's name. Here is the commentary on "all flesh" mentioned in v. 17. Here grace flows out also to all the Gentiles. "Everyone who" and all similar expressions of universality are like blank spaces in mighty bank drafts which are signed by the Lord and into which he invites us to write our own name by faith. If we do, the draft will without fail be honored by him. Here we meet the great verb "shall be saved," the passive implying the Lord as the Savior. In this verb as in all its derivatives (Savior, salvation, those that have been saved) lies the idea of mortal danger, a mighty act rescuing from that danger, and then also the blessed power that continues to keep in safety forever. The verb has its full meaning here. Its future tense is not to be dated at the last day, but this salvation begins the instant the sinner calls upon the saving name of the Lord. Peter's sermon, as here sketched by Luke, brings to his hearers all the actuality of this great prophecy of Joel as on this Pentecostal day and hereafter applying to his auditors for their own personal salvation.

22) **Israelite men, hear these words! Jesus, the Nazarene, a man accredited from God to you by power works and wonders and signs which God worked through him in your midst even as you yourselves know, him, delivered up by the determinate counsel and foreknowledge of God, you, through lawless men's hand fastening up, made away with; whom God raised up by loosing the pangs of death for the reason that it was not possible that he be held by it.**

On the address compare v. 14 and note that the apposition "Israelites" is a name of the highest honor for Jews which recalls Jacob who prevailed and had his name changed to "Israel," contender with God. So "Israel" and "Israelites" involved the covenant and the highest hopes of Judaism. To call his hearers "Israelite men" was an appeal that they now show themselves worthy of that name. "Hear these words" with its decisive aorist imperative for hearing that actually grasps continues the tone of authority from v. 14.

In one masterly sentence Peter presents Jesus who is back of the Pentecostal miracle and back of the whole prophecy of Joel. The directness, completeness, conciseness with which the essentials about Jesus are combined into one sentence deserve fullest appreciation. The name is put first: "Jesus, the Nazarene." It is the ordinary name by which he was commonly known, the personal name "Jesus" with "Nazarene," from the town of his long residence, added in order to distinguish him from others who had the same personal name: for

Yehoshu'a, later *Yeshu'a* (Joshua = Jesus), was a name that was frequently chosen for sons and meant "*Yahweh* is help," i. e., on or through whom *Yahweh* effects salvation. So also Peter says "a man," his object being to recall Jesus to his hearers as they had seen him so often during his earthly life.

"Even as you yourselves know" appeals to the knowledge of the hearers of the tremendous fact that was so prominent in the case of Jesus: his miracles. Peter purposely uses three terms when referring to them, the three applying to each miracle, yet the three accentuating the great number of the miracles. They were δυνάμεις, τέρατα, σημεῖα, works of supernatural power, creating wonder and amazement but full of heavenly, divine significance as works of divine grace. The whole Jewish world rang with the story of these miracles. By them, Peter says, this man "has been accredited from God to you," and he fortifies this by stating that "God wrought them through him in your midst," οἷς being attracted from ἅ. This no honest and sincere Jew would or could deny (John 3:2; 9:31-33), and when the Pharisees attempted it by claiming they were wrought by Beelzebul, Jesus showed the senselessness of their falsehood.

The fact that God wrought the miracles does not place Jesus on the same level with the apostles who also wrought miracles. It is equally true that Jesus wrought them by his own power as no other man ever wrought a true miracle. All the *opera ad extra* are ascribed equally to the divine Persons. The point of here ascribing the miracles of Jesus to God is not to indicate the source of their power but to bring out their purpose in regard to Jesus: they accredited him to the Jews, for which reason also they were wrought in their midst, so all of them might accept them as accreditations. The perfect participle "having been shown forth or accredited" has its usual strong present force, "still standing thus accredited." Note the juxtaposition: "from God to you." As what Jesus thus still stands accredited to all Israelites worthy of the name the statement itself makes declaration, namely as sent to Israel by God to be for Israel all that he claimed to be and was.

23) The emphatic τοῦτον, "him," "this one," sums up all that has been said: this man so mightily and publicly accredited from God — *him* the Jews murdered! That was their answer to God's seals and accreditations. Here Peter preached the law with its crushing power in order to bring about the conviction of sin and genuine contrition. He in no way softens his words since this would only defeat their purpose. He states the cold, damnable fact: "him, through lawless men's hand fastening up (namely to the cross), you made away with," which means murdered. The ἄνομοι are pagans who are without the Torah or νόμος and follow their pagan gods and heathen ideas. "Through the hand" is Hebraistic for "by means of." The aorist participle προσπήξαντες is used in an absolute sense and may be rendered "having crucified"; ἀναιρέω is often used in the ugly sense of to kill, murder, make away with one. The killing of Jesus by the Sanhedrin through Pilate was an act of the Jewish nation (Matt. 27:25) that involved every Jew who, when the act was made known to him, did not completely disavow and disallow it. Until Peter's hearers did this, he had to uphold the charge: "him you made away with."

But Peter has far more to say; he had to insert the claim that this bloody deed did not happen accidentally or only by the damnable will of the Jews. God could have prevented it in a second. This murder of Jesus happened only because Jesus was "delivered up (handed out to the Jews) by the deliberate counsel and foreknowledge of God." God abandoned Jesus to the murderous Jews in order that they might wreak their hatred upon him (John 19:11); this God did for his own mighty purpose: by the death of his Son to redeem the world. Peter wisely takes his hearers step by step and leads them carefully to faith. Any sincere Jew had to agree that no one such as Jesus was could have been killed as Jesus was unless God were in some way back of his death. Nor would any Jew use this fact in order to absolve his nation of blame for the killing. Ἔκδοτον is a verbal adjective from the aorist stem of δίδωμι and is equal to a passive participle.

In what way God delivered Jesus up to die on the cross is indicated by the weighty datives of means. The success of the betrayal by Judas, which placed Jesus into the power of the Sanhedrin, was due to no cunning or power of men (Matt. 26:53, 54; Luke 22:53b). The death of Jesus was due to "the determinate counsel and foreknowledge of God"; the perfect participle ὡρισμένῃ, "having been fixed or determined on," places the counsel of God back into eternity. God formed his plan of salvation, which involved the sacrificial death of his Son, in eternity and therefore alone gave him over to the murderous Jews. The divine counsel comes first, and on it rests the divine, infallible foreknowledge. The relation of the two is not one of time — in God no before and after exists — but of inward connection. When we consider the actions of men, this relation is reversed; what God determines in eternity regarding them rests on his infallible foreknowledge. "Counsel" and "foreknowledge" are not identical; to make them one and the same is to misunderstand both. The "foreknowledge" is misunderstood when it is regarded as an action of the will, a determination to do something and thus knowing it in advance. Such is the idea of C.-K. 256: *im voraus gefasster Beschluss*, "a decree formed in advance"; for according to C.-K. 226 βουλή means *Ratschluss*, and the fact that this resolve or decree was formed in advance need not be said

24) Here we have the first apostolic preaching of the resurrection of Jesus. Although it is couched in only a relative clause, its force is tremendous. You made away with him — God raised him up! You did it by crucifying him — God did the opposite by loosing the pangs of death! These were hammer blows of the law. So directly were these Jews opposed to God, and God to them. The genitive in "pangs of death" is subjective; ὠδῖνας are birth pains. The idea is that, when Christ died, death was taken with birth pains and suffered them until God delivered death of Christ by raising him up, thus "loosing the birth pains," ending their strain. "The birth pains of death" is generally regarded as being cited from Ps. 18:5, and Ps. 116:3, where the LXX translated *cheble maveth,* "snares of death," "birth pains of death" (the English of Ps. 116:3 also has "sorrows of death"). In the plurals occurring in these two passages the word "snares" and "pains" are indistinguishable, *chēbel* = snare; *chĕbel* = birth pain. But Peter is not quoting either psalm; he is using this expression of his own accord, and no one can prove that he borrowed it from a psalm, or that Luke translated Peter's "snares of death" with the LXX's "birth pains of death." We need scarcely add that for Christ these pains ended at the moment of his death. A few texts have the reading "hades" instead of "death."

Luke alone uses καθότι which here has the force of διότι, "because," "for the reason that." Peter states merely the fact that it was not possible that Jesus should be held by death; he then proceeds to prove this from the prophecy of David and thus once more proclaims the resurrection of Jesus and along with it his exaltation, which also is proved from David's prophecy. Thus Peter reveals the contents of the counsel and foreknowledge of God which gave Jesus into death in order to destroy death by atoning for sin in which lies the power of death. The deity of Jesus becomes evident in this exaltation which enabled Jesus to send down the Holy Spirit with those miraculous results which Peter's hearers see and hear (v. 33).

25) First, then, the proof that, according to the Scriptures, Jesus could not be held by death. Peter is speaking to Jews, hence he quotes a word of David's from the Scriptures. The proof lies in the fact that what God foretold regarding Christ must come to pass. Some critics place Ps. 16 later than the time of David. Peter here contradicts them: "David says," etc.; Paul does likewise in Acts 13:35. The testimony of Delitzsch is to the same effect. The external marks as well as the internal ("David" in the title; the language, tone, poetical fervor, etc.) point to the Davidic authorship of this psalm. Just what situation in the life of David this psalm pictures cannot be historically determined. It was most probably recovery from a severe sickness which prevented David from entering the reconstructed castle on Zion (cf. Delitzsch on Ps. 30).

The LXX is quoted quite exactly which agrees with the Hebrew and expands only a phrase here and there for the sake of clearness. On the general subject of quotations we may say the following: Where it seems necessary the New Testament writers translate the original, or correct the LXX according to the original, or translate interpretatively, and often use the LXX without change. The Holy Spirit guided them throughout, and he has full and free power to deal with his Word in the way that best suits his purposes. He may restate in other words, add to, abbreviate, interpret, etc. We do the same, not only with our own words, but also with those of others and even with Scripture. To demand mechanical, literal exactness of the Holy Spirit and the New Testament writers is to set up for them alone a peculiar canon against which all sensible writers must rebel. The quotation from Joel in v. 17, 18 is reproduced with greater freedom than the one now cited from David. This fact alone shows how well the writers knew their Old Testament even when they did not quote it according to the very letter. See *Introduction to the Critical Study and Knowledge of the Holy Scriptures,* Thomas Hartwell Horne, 7th Ed., II, 281, where the Hebrew, LXX, and New Testament passages are printed in parallel columns, in the original and in translation, together with other helpful material.

For David says regarding him,
I saw the Lord before me always
Because he is at my right in order that I shall not be moved.
Because of this glad was my heart, and jubilate did my tongue.
And besides also my flesh shall tent on hope
Because thou wilt not abandon my soul unto hades
Nor wilt give thine Holy One to see corruption.
Thou didst make known to me ways of life;
Thou wilt fill me with gladness in the company of thy countenance.

In *προορώμην*, the middle voice, the imperfect tense, and the preposition *πρό* each contribute their part so that we have no equivalent in English: for himself, all along, every time he let his glance move in front of him, David saw the Lord *ἐνώπιόν μου*, right before his eyes, and that "always." Nor had he the least difficulty, "because he was at my right" as advocates used to sit at the right side of the clients they supported, "in order that I should not be moved," made to toss to and fro in uncertainty and in fear. The same thought is found in Ps. 23:4: "Thou art with me; thy rod and thy staff they comfort me." The phrase ἐκ δεξιῶν is idiomatic, has no article, always has the plural, and extends "out from" his own right side to where he saw the Lord (*Yahweh*) with the eyes of faith. The aorist speaks of actually being moved. All that this vision meant for David he now unfolds.

26) His heart, in the Scriptures always the center of the personality, was filled with gladness, the same verb that is used for making merry at a celebration in Luke 15:32; and his tongue jubilated, exulted in songs and expressions of praise. The Hebrew has "my glory jubilated." But we question whether the Hebrew "heart, glory, flesh" is identical with the triad found in I Thess. 5:23:."spirit, soul, body." From the abundance of the heart the mouth speaketh; heart and tongue go together. Spirit and heart are not the same. It seems that the LXX translated "my glory" "my tonguc" because "my glory" was used with reference to any illustrious bodily member, especially where this glory is said to jubilate.

Both ἔτι and δέ indicate that what is now added about "my flesh" is the counterpart to both previous statements; heart and tongue are combined as one concept, flesh is the other. "Besides" (ἔτι) what he had to say about his heart and tongue David has something great to say about even his flesh (καί), and this is naturally of a different nature (δέ) than what he had to say of his heart and tongue. His flesh, meaning his body, "shall put down its tent on hope." The verb means "to put down a tent," "to camp in order to rest," and thus simply "to rest awhile." This verb implies only a transient sojourn; a tent is not a permanent structure. "Rest" in the A. V. is more correct than "dwell" in the R. V. The temporary tenting comprises both the bodily life of David and the stay of his body in the grave. In both conditions his flesh makes its tent and camp "on hope," on this as the ground (ἐπί). What that hope contains follows in the next line. The point to be noted is that making camp matches hope, both continue only for a time; when hope reaches its fulfillment, it becomes joy and gratitude.

27) This hope of David's has solid reality under it and thus cannot end in disappointment as do the hopes of the ungodly which have no other foundation than the desires of the ungodly themselves. Jehovah, who has ever been at David's right to keep him from being shaken by doubt and by fear, will never forsake him at the time of death. His hope is sure: "Because thou wilt not abandon my soul unto hades." When David comes to die, *Yahweh* will not abandon his soul or permit it to sink into hell, the place of the damned. *Denn nicht preisgeben wirst du meine Seele dem Hades*, Delitzsch, who also correctly defines the Hebrew verb of which ἐγκαταλείψεις is a correct translation: the abandonment here denied is not merely one which leaves a person in a terrible place after he has fallen there, but one which never even permits him to get into such a place. "It is thus the hope not to die or, dying, not to die, which David utters."

Here ψυχή is in contrast with σάρξ, "my flesh," and not with πνεῦμα or "spirit" and thus refers to the soul as the entire immaterial part of man which in life animates the body and also contains the spirit and personality. Thus body and soul constitute the entire human being. When *psyche* and *pneuma* are paired, the former refers to the immaterial part only as animating the body (translated "life"), the latter to the same immaterial part as representing the ἐγώ or personality and as being able to receive impressions from the divine *Pneuma* or Holy Spirit. From this lower sense of ψυχή the Greek derives its adjective ψυχικός for which we have no equivalent derived from "soul," since the English does not use "soul" in this lower sense of the Greek but only as almost the equivalent of "spirit";

thus we are compelled to translate the adjective "carnal," for it means disregarding the higher nature of the *pneuma* and yielding wholly to the promptings of the animated body. David says, Jehovah will not permit his soul, when at death it is separated from his body, to fall "into hades," εἰς ᾅδην (the better reading), or εἰς ᾅδου, supply δόμον, "into the house of hades."

Sheol is here translated "hades." The word *sheol* is used in a wide sense: at death all men go into *sheol*, and around the word in this sense cluster all the dark, painful, dreadful things that we still associate with death, leaving this bright world, and entering the grave. Neither the Greek nor the English has a true equivalent for *sheol* in this sense; the Greek used its "hades," we use our "grave." It was the best that translation could do.

Sheol is, however, used also in a narrow sense. It is applied peculiarly to the wicked, and all connotations and descriptions are according. The second use complicated matters still more as far as translation is concerned. The Greek again used "hades," but the English could not again use "grave," it used "hell," the place of the damned. As translations of *sheol* both "grave" and "hell" are interpretative and as such perfectly proper. But here confusion sets in. Some retain the Hebrew *sheol* in all passages of the English Old Testament where this word occurs, and "hades" in all the New Testament passages. Pagan ideas are introduced. We are told that the Hebrews had no clearer ideas than their pagan neighbors. Their *sheol* was uniformly "the nether world," the *Totenreich*, the realm of the dead. It was thought to consist of two parts, an upper and a lower part, the one being less terrible than the other. Everything in the Old Testament that clashes with this idea is ignored. This procedure is carried into the New Testament, where it begins with Dives and Lazarus in Luke 16:22, etc. "Hades" is retained in the sense of *sheol* and is now an intermediate place between heaven and hell. Hither all the dead are still said to go, the godly into the upper part, for which the term "Paradise" is appropriated from Luke 23:43, the wicked into the lower part which is not specifically named. Again, all that disagrees with this view — and there is very much, indeed, in the New Testament — is ignored or left as a contradiction.

Fancies go still farther. At his death Jesus is thought to have entered the Paradise part of this intermediate place in order to stay there until his resurrection. Some call this his descent into hell (hades). It is also stated that he opened this place and released all the souls in it so they might enter into heaven; as a consequence this place is now vacant, the godly now going directly to heaven. But the ungodly still enter the nether part. It is not hell but only like hell. But some extend the idea still farther: in this lower part of the intermediate place conversion is still possible. A kind of infernal missionary work is said to be in progress. Jesus himself is thought to have started it in I Pet. 3:19; 4:6.

Not only David's hope is thereby darkened, but the entire Christian hope as well. Two places, and only two, exist in the other world, heaven for all believers, hell with its damnation for all unbelievers. The only difference between the two Testaments is this: the New is clearer than the old on this subject as on all others. In Peter's sermon the New is made to bring out the full reality contained in the Old.

The translation of our versions is unfortunate: "*Thou wilt not leave* my soul in hell (hades)." This reads as though David's soul would, indeed, enter hell (hades), but that God would eventually remove his soul from this place. Even a scholar like Zahn attempts to maintain this sense of the verb. He weakens the force of the Hebrew *'azab* by saying that it *might* mean "abandon" but claims the Greek verb *must* mean "to leave." David is thus thought to say of himself and of Christ that at death their souls would enter, not heaven, but the realm where all the dead are and would be released from this place by means of the resurrection. But did Christ, according to this notion, not take all the souls of the Old Testament saints out of the upper part of this realm of the dead? And David would have been released ahead of his resurrection! And does not the Old Testament itself teach with all clearness the resurrection of also the ungodly, Dan. 12:2? And what about the parallelism? If David's soul entered hades (hell), then Jehovah's Holy One saw corruption. Οὐ — οὐδέ are decisive in negating both lines and not merely the main verbs but also their objects. The soul of David did not enter hell as little as Jehovah's Holy One saw corruption. He preserved both from both.

God, indeed, "gave out" (implied in ἔκδοτον in v. 23) Jesus to be made away with through death, but David already said, "He will not give him to see corruption." He will be dead, indeed, and entombed as one dead, but no corruption, decay, putrefaction would touch his holy body while it lay in the tomb. Recall how the women hurried to the tomb on Sunday morning, fearing that even then they might find corruption too far advanced to handle the body. "To see" corruption means to experience it. Delitzsch notes the major sense of sight which is figuratively employed as the sensus communis by which all experiences, active and passive, are perceived. In his *Biblische Psychologie*, 234, he shows how by this verb and by the singulars eye and ear (not plurals) the Scriptures go back to the unit *sensorium* underlying all perception and all experience. We need not puzzle ourselves about *shachath* and its translation διαφθορά, "corruption." The Hebrew means both "pit" and "corruption," the noun being a derivation from two verbs (Ed. Koenig, *Hebraeisches und aramaeisches*

Woerterbuch, 495). Note the contrast: Holy One — corruption.

Note the far more important contrast: *my* soul — *thy* Holy One. Let us admit it that the former refers to David and to Christ, the latter only to Christ as Peter also proceeds to explain. David's body decayed; not even the slightest bit of decay touched the body of Jesus. "Holy One" (*qadosh,* ἅγιος) is often applied to God, especially by Isaiah; also to Christ in Mark 1:24; Luke 4:34; Acts 3:14; I John 2:20; here and in Acts 13:35, ὅσιος (Trench: opposite of "polluted") is used. "Holy One" thus predicates the holiness of deity of Jesus; it was thus that he did not see corruption. The body of the incarnate Holy One could not be touched by the decay which touches even the bodies of the saints because they are still sinners. David thus prophesied in regard to Christ and his stay in the tomb. And now we see the "hope" on which his flesh rested. Death would bring corruption to his body, but at death his soul would escape hell and enter heaven because Jehovah's Holy One would not see corruption when he would be given into death (v. 23). The body of Jesus, untouched by corruption, would arise on the third day, sin and death being conquered forever. David's body, living or dead, thus rested in the hope, in the hope of its resurrection at the last day, and at death his soul would enter glory.

28) It is thus that the Lord made known "life's ways" to David (the Hebrew has the singular), and we may take the genitive in either sense: "the ways that belong to life," are characteristic of it, or "that lead to life," i. e., life eternal. These ways are repentance, faith, obedience, and hope; and "life" (ζωή, so often in John) is the life principle itself, life in God, with God, in and with Christ who is "the Life," i. e., the fount of life for us. "Didst make known" goes far beyond the intellect; no one can have the knowledge of life's ways

except by having that life and in its living power walking in those ways. The thought is not merely reaching that life hereafter, but having it, enjoying it, walking in its ways now.

The Hebrew: "Satiation with joys is with (or at) thy countenance," i. e., is had where the light of Jehovah's countenance or presence is felt, is rendered in the Greek: "Thou wilt fill me with gladness in company with (μετά) thy countenance." The thought is the same as it is in the Hebrew. The future tense "wilt fill me" means already now and, of course, vastly more after death.

29) Peter adds an exegesis of the main point of David's prophecy. **Men and brethren** (1:16; 2:14), **it is permitted to state with openness to you concerning the patriarch David that he both died and was buried, and his tomb is with us to this day. Therefore, as being a prophet and as knowing that God swore to him with an oath to seat one out of the fruit of his loins on his throne, foreseeing it, he made utterance concerning the resurrection of the Christ that he neither was abandoned unto hades nor did his flesh see corruption.**

Peter first of all makes very clear that David's words were not fulfilled in his own person but were prophecy and dealt with the resurrection of the Messiah. He is deferential: "it is permitted," etc. = "permit me to state openly to you" as my brethren who know that I mean nothing derogatory when I say "concerning the patriarch David," whom I revere with you as a patriarch, the progenitor of a royal line in Israel, first "that he both died," ended his life, "and was buried," these two going together, and secondly, as well-known evidence of the fact, "his tomb is with us to this day." Neh. 3:16 mentions David's tomb; Josephus speaks of it several times. It was about a thousand years old at this time, and Dio Cassius 64, 14 reports that it fell into ruins during Hadrian's reign in the year 133, after which it is no longer heard of. It was at Jerusalem — mute but incontrovertible evidence that Ps. 16 was not fulfilled in David. David's body saw corruption. It was dust.

30) The possibility that David could have been mistaken in his psalm is not for one moment entertained. The conclusion (οὖν) to be drawn is far otherwise, one to which all of Peter's hearers at once agree: "as being a prophet . . . he made utterance," and that "concerning the resurrection of the Christ." The verb ὑπάρχω is often used in the sense of "to be." But Peter must add an important point, the one on account of which he already called David a "patriarch." When David wrote that psalm he did it "knowing that God swore to him with an oath to seat one out of the fruit of his loins on his throne." The form of the participle εἰδώς is perfect, but the sense is always present. "Swore with an oath" may be pleonastic but it is stronger than the verb without this dative of means (R. 1205, 531). See II Sam. 7:12; Ps. 132:11. The phrase ἐκ καρποῦ is partitive: "one out of the fruit," etc., and should be regarded as the object of καθίσαι and not as the subject (R. V.); the additions found in the A. V. have far too little support to be considered. Peter needed to say no more for Jews. They knew that "one out of the fruit of his loins" (the Greek for "loins" is always singular) referred to the Messiah. They, indeed, conceived his throne to be one of earthly grandeur only and had to be taught Luke 1:32, 33.

31) "Foreseeing it," Peter says, David made utterance as he did. He foresaw what he recorded in Ps. 16. This psalm is quoted by Peter, and thus Peter says that David made this utterance "concerning the resurrection of the Christ." As a prophet he spoke by revelation and by inspiration; hence ἐλάλησε, "he made utterance," is the fitting verb. How fully David himself compre-

hended his own utterance is quite immaterial. It is Peter himself who tells us how far beyond the comprehension of the prophets some of their utterances were, I Pet. 1:10-12; II Pet. 1:20, 21. We have no interest in reducing this comprehension to a minimum or in searching out and speculating on its degree. The point is that we ourselves see and believe the literal fulfillment. In the case of David the word was half fulfilled, namely only the clause that his soul would not be abandoned unto hades. In the case of the Christ both were to be fulfilled, this statement and the other that his flesh should not see corruption. Note how Peter repeats the double statement, retaining the sense but not the identical words. Most important, he uses aorist tenses where David had futures: "that he neither was abandoned unto hades, nor did his flesh see corruption." These historical aorists are in place, for they declare that the fulfillment has come in the resurrection of the Christ who is Jesus.

32) **This Jesus God raised up, whereof all we are witnesses.** In "this Jesus," who is presented fully in v. 22 as to his accreditation and his death according to God's counsel, the prophecy of David, which was unfulfilled in his own case, was truly and completely fulfilled: "This Jesus God raised up." It is he and he alone whose flesh did not see corruption. He is the Holy One of *Yahweh* in David's prophecy, the One out of David's loins, "the Christ," fully and gloriously proved so by God's raising him up. By this act God sealed him as the Christ. Note that in this its very first presentation the entire apostolic message centers in the resurrection of Jesus. God centered it there already in David's prophecy, then again in fulfilling that prophecy in the case of Jesus, I Cor. 15:13, etc.

All that Peter needs to add is the clause: "whereof all we are witnesses," namely the whole body of the disciples, all of whom had seen the risen Lord, 500 at one time in Galilee; οὗ must be "of which," of the act of raising up Jesus, and not "of whom," of his person. In order to see the force of this clause for all these Jews, dwellers in Jerusalem, we must recall the full publicity of the death of Jesus (v. 23), plus the report on his empty tomb which the Sanhedrists tried to explain away (Matt. 28:11-15), thereby aiding the publication in the city of what had occurred in Joseph's tomb. The lie that disciples had stolen the body from under the eyes of the Roman guard was too shallow. All that Peter needed to do was to flash the truth on those hearers in connection with David's prophecy. To this day that empty tomb establishes the resurrection of Jesus and the fulfillment of the prophecy. "All we" recalls I Cor. 15:4-8, and what the risen Lord himself expounded to them regarding the prophecies of Scripture as recorded in Luke 24:27; 44-48.

33) But Peter cannot stop at this point. His hearers themselves are witnesses this very day. **Therefore, having been exalted by the right hand of God and having received the promise of the Holy Spirit from the Father, he did pour out this which you yourselves see and hear.** Right here and now Peter's hearers were both seeing and hearing the great effects of the resurrection of Jesus, the miracles of Pentecost. They reveal what the resurrection involved, the exaltation of the risen Jesus, his pouring out the spirit, the miraculous evidence of which all were seeing and hearing. Peter thus goes straight to his goal: he lays up stone on stone with perfect, swift mastery until the arch is complete.

The fact that the resurrection of Jesus as the Christ was not intended to bring him back from the dead for a continuation of his former earthly life did not need to be stated. The resurrection miracle was far too great for so small an effect. Another act accompanied that of raising the incorruptible body of Jesus from the dead: he was exalted by the right of God, οὖν presenting this and what follows as resting on the resurrection. The participle presents this act of exalting Jesus as being preliminary to what follows. "Having been exalted" includes both the glorification of the body at the time of its resurrection and the ascension of that body to heaven. Peter does not say regarding this exaltation that the disciples constitute the witness of it. They saw some of it in the appearances, and the eleven saw the first part of the ascension, but none saw the exaltation in heaven. Peter will offer the other, the Scripture, proof.

The dative is called ambiguous by R. 543: to — at — by the right hand, and some puzzle about the choice to be made when interpreting. But the ambiguity is only abstractly grammatical and not exegetical. This is the dative of means: "by the right" (supply "hand"); and it has been well said that, when the right hand exalts, it does not place on the left side. In all the passages which speak of God's right hand his omnipotence and his majesty are referred to; by these the human nature of Jesus was exalted; Eph. 1:20-23 offers the fullest description.

A second participle is added with the close connective τε which is stronger than καί and indicates that the exaltation and the reception of the Spirit are a double act. The exalted Jesus "received the promise of the Holy Spirit from the Father." Here we have the Holy Trinity, for "Father" implies Jesus as the Son. The fact that the exalted Jesus receives the Spirit from the Father in order to send him forth to the disciples appears in John 15:26; 16:7; compare Acts 1:4. It is thus that the three Persons unite in working out our salvation; we may also compare Luke 3:22. On this centering of all these acts in the Father nothing beyond the fact itself can be offered. "The promise of the Holy Spirit" = the promise which is the Spirit; the genitive is appositional (R. 498). In 1:4 we, therefore, have simply "the promise of the Father." The Spirit is the Promised One, promised as the result of Christ's redemption, to convey that redemption to men and to appropriate it unto them.

And now Peter is back where he began in v. 16: "he did pour out this which you yourselves see and hear," ἐξέχεεν the aorist to express the fact. While τοῦτο might refer to Πνεῦμα, the relative speaks of what Peter's hearers are seeing and hearing, which is not the Spirit himself but the effect of his presence, the miraculous manifestations. They are poured out by the pouring out of the Spirit. Since the Spirit is a person, it is a striking expression to say that he is poured out. In v. 17, 18 we have the partitive "from or of my Spirit," which helps to explain the figure of pouring out. The Spirit is the source and fountain of all spiritual gifts and blessings; where the Spirit is these are richly distributed and bestowed like heavenly streams of grace. Thus both the Spirit himself is said to be poured out and all the gifts which we still see and hear. Compare the literal presentation in I Cor. 12:7-11.

34) Peter offers far more than his own assertions, true as they are. He at the same time offers the proof that is decisive for his Jewish hearers by again quoting the prophet David, this time Ps. 110. **For David did not go up into the heavens, yet he himself declares,**

> **Said the Lord to my Lord, Sit thou at my right**
> **Until I place thine enemies as a footstool of thy feet.**

With assurance, therefore, let all Israel's house be realizing that God made him both Lord and Christ, this Jesus whom you on your part crucified.

The one thing it was necessary to prove was the exaltation of Jesus. The other needed no proof, for the miracles of the outpouring of the Spirit Peter's hearers themselves saw and heard. They also beheld the fact that these effects of the Spirit were observable only in the disciples of Jesus who were assembled before them. The connection with Jesus was thus plain. David is merely called on to reveal just what this connection was. But this is set aside by the critics who deny that David wrote Ps. 110 by attributing it to an unknown and much later writer. Here again we have the parting of the ways, on the one side these critics with their hypotheses, on the other hand Christ and his testimony. Matt. 22:41-46; Mark 12:35-37; Luke 20:41-44 report an untruth if the declaration of Jesus that David wrote this psalm is not reliable. The very words Peter here uses are elsewhere used in the same sense: I Cor. 15:25; Heb. 1:13; 10:13. Other passages of the psalm are likewise used with reference to the Messiah: Heb. 5:6; 7:17, 21. If anything is Scripturally certain, it is that David penned this psalm.

He did not speak of himself in what he said in this psalm but again, as in v. 27, of another who was vastly greater than himself. Peter at once points that out. With γάρ he introduces the proof for the exaltation of Jesus. "David did not go up (ascend) into the heavens." He died and was buried, and the tomb that contained his body was nearby when Peter spoke, had been there for a thousand years. Peter renders the Hebrew dual *shamayim* with the word "heavens." "Did not go into the heavens" refers to the body of David. David ended as every other human being ends. Death separated his soul and his body, the latter rotted in the tomb, and since David was a believer, the former went to heaven to await the last day and the resurrection. In connection with v. 27 we have treated the claim that David's soul went to hades.

And yet this very David says this wonderful thing which cannot refer to himself, which must refer to the Messiah, and which is now seen to be fulfilled in Jesus. "The Lord said unto my Lord," *Yahweh* unto David's *'Adon.* David was king and had no earthly lord above him. Who, then, was this "Lord" of David, this *'Adon,* this mighty dignitary, whom Jehovah seats at his right in eternal triumph over his enemies? All Jews knew that David was here speaking of the Messiah and by calling him "my Lord" was confessing and worshipping him. But the great point of the revelation which David makes lies in what *Yahweh* says to this Messiah Lord: "Be sitting (present imperative, durative) at my right," etc. This is divine exaltation (Heb. 1:13). To only One did *Yahweh* ever say this.

On the idiom ἐκ δεξιῶν see v. 25. God's right and right hand (v. 33) are anthropomorphitic expressions which signify his might and his majesty; and sitting at God's right is to exercise all this might and this majesty. Need we say that this is impossible for one who is only a human being? Need we add that it could not be said of the Son as the Second Person of the Trinity, he who in his very being is already of equal might and majesty with the Father? This was said to the Son as man. In his human nature he was exalted to rule forever with divine might and majesty.

It is as the incarnate Son that he has "enemies" (Luke 19:14). Had they not carried him to the cross? But *Yahweh* says he will place them all as a footstool of the feet of this Lord of David's. The figure matches this *'Adon's* sitting at Yahweh's right. In this way conquering kings showed their triumph by placing a foot upon the neck of some conquered king. But here the figure is magnified — *all* the enemies as a unit, as a permanent footstool of the exalted Messiah. This does not imply that the Messiah rests on the heavenly throne while the Father crushes his enemies for him. Ps. 2:9

makes that plain. The Persons join in all works. Nor is this crushing a strain. God laughs at these enemies and their silly rage against his Anointed. Delitzsch writes: "Temporal history shall end with the triumph of good over evil but not with the annihilation of evil but with its subjugation. To this it will come when absolute omnipotence for and through the exalted Christ shows its effectiveness."

By citing this prophecy Peter accomplished two things: he explained from David's writings how the miracle of Pentecost occurred after having shown from Joel's prophecy *that* it must occur; and he placed David before his hearers as calling the Messiah "his Lord" together with the enemies who would be made the Messiah's footstool. These were *Jesus'* disciples upon whom the Spirit promised by Joel had come with such miraculous manifestations; from whom could this Spirit have come upon them except from Jesus and except from him as exalted at God's right even as David had said? But what about these hearers of Peter's? Were they among the enemies of whom David, too, had prophesied? Peter struck home in the hearts of these hearers with his quotation.

36) The summing up is so masterly that it could have been made only by inspiration from the Spirit even as the entire sermon bears the plainest marks of the Spirit. It has been well said regarding this last sentence: *Tot verba, tot pondera.* Note the same tone of authority in the imperative that was evident at the beginning (v. 14) and in the progress (v. 22) of the sermon. This final οὖν draws the deduction from the entire presentation. Take Jesus (v. 22-24), the Pentecostal miracle, the prophecy of Joel and the two prophecies of David — what do they put beyond question? "That God made Jesus both Lord and Christ," and "let all Israel's house be realizing it with assurance." Any other deduction is false to both the facts and the

prophecies. Note the durative present "be realizing," γινωσκέτω. This is more than mere knowing, it is a knowing that is realization and complete conviction that grows deeper the longer it continues. "Assuredly" or "with assurance" fits this realization; note the noun in Luke 1:4, "the certainty" for Theophilus.

Peter looks far beyond his immediate hearers when appealing to "all Israel's house." No article is needed after πᾶς to have it mean "all" and not "every"; better than the explanation of R. 772 is that of the older grammarian Winer: οἶκος Ἰσραήλ is a proper name. "House of Israel" makes all Jews one great family of the patriarch Israel, all of whose members ought to share his faith. Israel is the third great patriarch, the one from whom the whole people of Israel branched out. The reference is to the human nature of our Lord when Peter says that "God made Jesus both Lord and Christ," this nature, of course, in conjunction with the divine. And "made" includes everything from the incarnation to the final exaltation. "Lord" is divine Lord, David's *'Adon,* the Κύριος (1:6) and ὁ Κύριος Ἰησοῦς (1:21) of the apostles. The word contains power and majesty but always coupled with grace and the highest magnanimity, for this Lord is our Savior. Here the title is joined with "Christ," Χριστός, the verbal adjective from the superior verb χρίω, "to anoint," hence "the Anointed," the Hebrew *Mashiach.* The word refers to an office. As the Anointed, Jesus is our Prophet, High Priest, and King, and in all these offices brings us salvation.

This Lord and Christ had been the great hope of the Jews, but they had converted their expectation into one of a grand, earthly Deliverer and Ruler who would lift the Jews above all nations in supreme power and glory. Therefore they rejected "this Jesus," Peter adding: "whom you on your part (emphatic ὑμεῖς) crucified." *God* made him Lord and Christ, *you* crucified him. On their guilt compare v. 23. The contrast between "God" and "you" is the same as in v. 23, 24, but terser and thus stronger. Peter minced no words. He preached plenty of gospel but drove straight home with the law. And he was content with that. There was no sentimental pleading, belaboring, begging, which so often defeats itself. No sinner does God a favor by accepting Christ. Peter preached the divine truth in all its power; the effect took care of itself.

The Effect of Peter's Sermon

37) **Now on hearing it they were pierced through as to the heart and said to Peter and the rest of the apostles, What shall we do, men and brethren?** Δέ is metabatic or transitional, carrying the account farther. The effect of Peter's preaching was the one intended. His sermon consisted of law and of gospel, and in normal cases it is always the law that first takes effect; yet the gospel must accompany the law, otherwise the law will effect only despair instead of contrition. It is not merely the repeated statement that these hearers of Peter's were involved in making away with Jesus that pierced their hearts but their whole previous attitude toward this Jesus whom God had sent them as "Lord and Christ." They had not accepted him thus, they had treated him as a mere man, many perhaps with indifference, others joined in the hostility of their Sanhedrin. Their eyes were now opened to the wickedness of their previous attitude toward Jesus. All the guilt of their unbelief was revealed through Peter's sermon. This shows us how we must today preach the law in connection with Jesus, the Lord and Christ of God. We must reveal the guilt of unbelief. Unless the sinner is pierced in heart with this guilt, conversion will not be wrought.

The second passive is followed by the adverbial accusative: "they were pierced through as to their hearts." Like a sharp spear the law penetrated their hitherto hard and impervious hearts. The Greek καρδία is always the center of the personality, psychologically the mind plus the will. Far more than the feelings of the hearers were stirred or hurt. "Pierced through" means in a deadly way. By the exposure of it which Peter had made their entire previous attitude of unbelief was struck a deadly blow. These men felt utterly crushed. They were not only hurt but hurt so that they could not rally against the hurt. Their conscience was smitten so that they could not fend off the blow. They had been in opposition to God in their treatment of his grace in Jesus. Denial on their part was impossible. The question they asked is a full admission of their guilt.

They use the plural "men and brethren," for they realized that Peter spoke for all the apostles. On "men and brethren" see 1:16, and 2:29, and note the appeal in "brethren," which asks the apostles to help them as brethren. They use the deliberative subjunctive in their question, thereby indicating that they are utterly at a loss as to what to do in their terrible situation. The question was not intended in a synergistic sense nor was it less than the one asked in 16:30 because "to be saved" was not added. These men were not thinking of doing something *of themselves* to remove their guilt. Their question implies the contrary: 1) a complete confession of their guilt; 2) a complete confession of their helplessness in regard to this guilt; 3) complete submission to the apostles in order that they who have produced the consciousness of their guilt may lead them also to deliverance from this guilt. Peter does not correct their question, nor did Paul do so in 16:30. He would have been in the wrong to answer, "*You* cannot do anything!"

38) **And Peter to them** (the verb is to be supplied from v. 37): **Repent and be baptized, everyone of you, in the name of Jesus Christ for re-**

mission of your sins, and you shall receive the gift of the Holy Spirit. For to you is the promise and to your children and to all afar off, as many as the Lord, your God, shall call to himself.

Peter gives direct answer and tells these men exactly what to do. But this doing is nothing more than the divinely intended reaction of the gospel in the hearts of these men. *They* must repent, *they* must come to baptism, but only as drawn by the gospel and its power of grace. It is our will that moves and acts and yet only because God's grace makes it move.

In μετανοεῖν and μετάνοια we have one of the great concepts of the Bible. The word originally signified to perceive or understand afterward (μετά), i. e., too late; then it advanced to the idea of a later change of mind and thus came to mean "repent." But throughout the New Testament the word has been deepened to mean an inner change of heart that is decisive for the whole personality, one away from sin and unbelief with their guilt unto Christ, faith, and cleansing through Christ. When it is used without modifiers as here, "to repent" includes the entire inner change or contrition and faith (like ἐπιστρέφειν, "to turn," "to be converted"); but when "to believe" is added, contrition alone is referred to but as accompanying faith. So "repent" here = turn wholly to Jesus as your Savior ("Lord and Christ," v. 36) and accept him as such. In order to effect this change of heart Peter had placed so fully before them just who and what Jesus is. It is this Jesus who is thus to draw them to repentance.

The aorist imperative is one of authority and demands a decisive act that is to stand once for all. A present imperative would imply that the repentance is to be renewed daily even as Luther calls the Christian's entire life a repentance.

"Repent" is plural, but "be baptized" has the distributive singular subject "everyone of you." The two acts, however, always go together in the case of adults, and all difficulty disappears when we properly conceive them as a unit. Let us not separate them. The pathological cases of possible repentance without baptism need not concern us. Peter's hearers knew about baptism through the work of the Baptist. Jesus continued John's baptism (John 4:1, 2). This baptism was not only symbolical. As practiced by both John and Jesus and then as being appointed for all nations it bestowed the remission of sins and was thus a true sacrament. The Twelve, as far as we know, had been baptized only with John's baptism.

"In the name of Jesus Christ" for the first time uses "Jesus Christ" as a personal designation, combining the personal "Jesus" with the official "Christ." This later became the regular usage. As in v. 21 and in all these expressions, ὄνομα, "name," designates the revelation by which Jesus Christ is known so that we rely on him. To be baptized "in his name" means to be baptized "in connection with the revelation he has made of himself," the application of water (as instituted by him) placing us into union with him by means of his name or revelation. Baptism seals us with this name and revelation and gives us all this name and this revelation contain, and by receiving baptism we accept it all. A refusal of baptism would be a repudiation of Christ and of all the gifts contained in his name. He who wants a piece of property wants and accepts the deed to it: if he will not have the deed he may be quite certain he does not really care for the property, especially since both property and deed are a gift.

The church has never considered "in the name of Jesus Christ" the formula to be used when baptizing; it employs only the words occurring in Jesus' own command: "in the name of the Father and of the Son and of the Holy Spirit." The εἰς is static and does not mean "into" but, as so frequently in the Koine, "in." What words are we to use: some selected by ourselves, one person using this, another that formula? Would our words be better than Christ's own? The holy name is like a signature and deeds to us all that the revelation centering in this name intends to convey. Are signatures to deeds something immaterial, to be changed *ad libitum?* Banks certainly do not think so. When we baptize, all doubt as to the genuineness of the act is always to be excluded. That is done by the use of the name Jesus gave; it is not done by substituting words of our own even though these be other words taken from Scripture.

"Everyone of you" makes repentance and baptism personal in the highest degree. Salvation deals with each individual. Note the universality: "everyone," no matter what his condition or position may be. One door is open to all, one only. Baptism is pure gospel that conveys grace and salvation from God through Christ; it dare not be changed into a legal or legalistic requirement that is akin to the ceremonial requirement of Moses such as circumcision. God does something for us in baptism, we do nothing for him. Our acceptance of baptism is only acceptance of God's gift.

This is emphasized strongly in the addition: "for or unto remission of your sins." It amounts to nothing more than a formal grammatical difference whether εἰς is again regarded as denoting sphere (equal to ἐν), R. 592, or, as is commonly supposed, as indicating aim and purpose, R. 592, or better still as denoting effect. Sphere would mean that baptism is inside the same circle as remission; he who steps into this circle has both. Aim and purpose would mean that baptism intends to give remission; in him, then, who receives baptism aright this intention, aim, and purpose would be attained. The same is true regarding the idea of effect in εἰς. This preposition connects remission so closely with baptism that nobody has as yet been able to separate the two. It is this gift of remission that makes baptism a true sacrament; otherwise it would be only a sign or a symbol that conveys nothing real. In order to make baptism such a symbol, we are told that Peter's phrase means only that baptism pictures remission, a remission we may obtain by some other means at some later day. But this alters the force of Peter's words. Can one persuade himself that Peter told these sinners who were stricken with their terrible guilt to accept a baptism that pointed to some future remission? Had he no remission to offer them now? And when and how could they get that remission, absolutely the one thing they must have? And how can Ananias in 22:16 say, "Be baptized and *wash away* thy sins!" as though the *water* of baptism *washed* them away by its connection with the Name?

Ἄφεσις, from ἀφίημι, "to send away," is another great Biblical concept: "the sending away" of your sins. How far away they are sent Ps. 103:12 tells us: "as far as the east is from the west, so far has he removed our transgressions from us." Measure the distance from the point where the east begins to the point where the west ends. Nor does David say, "as far as the north is from the south," lest you think of the poles and succeed in measuring the distance. Again Micah 7:19: "Thou wilt cast all their sins into the depths of the sea." Even today the sea has depths that have never been sounded. The idea to be conveyed is that the sins are removed from the sinner so as never to be found again, never again to be brought to confront him. God sends them away, and he would thus be the last to bring them back. When the sinner appears before his judgment seat, his sins are gone forever. This is what our far less expressive "forgiveness" really means. Nor does the guilt remain, for sin and guilt are one: sin gone, guilt gone!

"And you shall receive the gift of the Holy Spirit" means in and by repenting and being baptized. The genitive is appositional; as in v. 33 the promise is the Holy Spirit, so here the gift is the Holy Spirit. In Peter's sermon the Spirit came to work upon the hearers from without, but by bringing them to repentance and to baptism he would actually enter their hearts, be their heavenly gift, and thus put them into actual communion with God. This gift is bestowed upon each and every repentant and baptized soul and cannot, therefore, refer only to charismatic gifts of the Spirit, speaking with tongues, healing, etc., but denotes the gift of grace and salvation which is always present in the heart which the Spirit enters. We do not read that any of the 3,000 spoke with tongues, yet they all received the Holy Spirit.

Here again we must not separate repentance, baptism, the Spirit. Not at some later time were these people to receive the Spirit; not in some later sudden, mysterious seizure; not as a later "second blessing" that would produce a total sanctification or sinlessness by a sudden transformation. Luther wrote against the Anabaptists: "This doctrine is to remain sure and firm, that the Holy Spirit is given through the office of the church, that is through the preaching of the gospel and baptism. There must seek him all who desire him, must not despise the little band in which the preaching of the gospel resounds, but must hold to that band, gathered and staying together in Christ's name."

39) In order to draw all his hearers unto repentance and baptism Peter assures them: "For to you is the promise and to your children," to them first as Jews. "The promise" is the Holy Spirit, "promise" occurs in this sense in 1:4, and in 2:33. It was the intention of God to bestow his Spirit upon the Jews

first. "To you" is emphatic and thus stresses the thought that, if God so graciously purposed to bless them with his Spirit, they should surely not despise his intention. "And to your children" is a most significant addition when we bear in mind that the Old Covenant included children. Certainly, the New Covenant would include them likewise. But how are children to receive the Holy Spirit except by baptism? "Your children" allows no restriction as to age. How the Holy Spirit enters their hearts by baptism is his concern only, ours is to administer that baptism, in no wise doubting, otherwise we could not answer to God.

"And to all afar off" includes all other nations and, of course, also their children, εἰς μακράν (ὁδόν), a phrase that is made a substantive by the article with εἰς being static (R. 593). These "afar off" cannot be restricted to the Jewish diaspora, especially not in view of "all flesh" in v. 17; compare Isa. 49:1, 12; 57:19. "As many as the Lord, our God, shall call unto himself" in no way limits the universality. These are not persons who are chosen by a mysterious decree of election but those who are called by the gospel. Others, too, are called but reject the call in permanent obduracy; these are won by the call and its grace. The aorist subjunctive is futuristic and views the entire calling as a unit that includes all those won by the call as one body. Κύριος ὁ Θεός = *Yahweh Haelohim,* and ἡμῶν means that this covenant Lord and omnipotent God exercises his power in favor of Israel. By means of this possessive Peter unites himself with his Jewish hearers; the God of the Old Covenant is also the God of the New. It is worth noting, both here in Peter's words and beginning with the Baptist, that the Three Persons are mentioned with utmost freedom, and all Jews accepted this Trinity of God without a question.

40) **And with many other words he adjured and kept urging them, saying, Be saved from this**

crooked generation! Luke himself tells us that he is reporting only the essentials. Perhaps Peter had to answer questions and make further explanations literally "with other more words (statements)," more than the ones recorded. The verb is strong: "to protest earnestly," "to adjure," the aorist to express the fact. But the imperfect "he kept urging them" (thus M.-M. 484) describes the chief point of this adjuration, the urging: "Be saved from this crooked generation!" The aorist imperative is passive, and there is no reason for not regarding it so. Some passive forms are to be taken in a middle sense, but scarcely this passive. One might make it permissive, "let yourselves be saved," but scarcely the reflexive middle, "save yourselves."

Here "generation" is to be taken in an ethical sense as the adjective "crooked" plainly shows. The Hebrew *dor* and the Greek γενεά are often so used although this has often been denied in connection with Luke 21:32. The generation here referred to is the entire succession of unbelievers with the Sanhedrin at its head. From it Peter's hearers are to be saved by repenting and by being baptized. "Crooked" is made emphatic by means of a second article (R. 776); σκολιός (Deut. 32:5; Ps. 78:8 = LXX 77:8; Phil. 2:15) is used figuratively. It refers to a warped piece of timber which the carpenters must throw out as being useless. "Be saved" implies that the crooked generation is bound for destruction.

41) **They, accordingly, who received his word were baptized; and there were added on that day about three thousand souls.** Οἱ μὲν οὖν is clearer here than in 1:6; for the article is to be construed with the participle: "those receiving his word" and not all those present on this occasion. Receiving, "consenting to the word, giving it entrance" (C.-K. 281), was one act, hence the aorist participle; "his word" (λόγος)

is the substance of what Peter said. All these "were baptized."

This leads us to a consideration of the question of baptism by immersion. When Luke writes, "They were baptized, and about three thousand were added on that day," he certainly intends to say that they were added by baptism on that very day and not that they were added that day but were baptized later on. Those who accept the plain sense of Luke's statement must show where 3,000 could be immersed in Jerusalem in about half a day. Some speak of the brook Kidron or of one or the other of the pools, but Kidron is bone-dry the greater part of the year, and the pools are not ponds. For several reasons none of the pools that have been mentioned in this connection can be considered. Those who are informed regarding the water facilities of Jerusalem, therefore, regard Luke as saying that the reception took place "on that day," but that the baptizing took place later, namely at the Jordan. But we may wonder why Luke did not then write: "Those who received his word were added on that day, and there were baptized about three thousand." Even this might well mean that they were also baptized on that day. Luke, however, wrote as he did: baptized — added that day. Even the long journey to the Jordan is taken for granted although Luke should then have written, "were baptized in the Jordan," which he, however, did not add.

The question at issue is, however, much more extensive. It involves all other baptisms mentioned in the New Testament beginning with that of John. We have treated the latter in the Gospels (which see). Neither John's nor any other baptism mentioned in the New Testament was administered by immersion. All the evidence is to the contrary, often overwhelmingly so. The issue in regard to the 3,000 who were baptized at Pentecost is vital. This grand baptism, the first in the Christian Church, undoubtedly established the mode also for all future baptisms. Soon the membership in Jerusalem rose to 5,000 men (not counting women and children, 4:4); then Luke loses all count and says only that further "multitudes" were added (5:14), and after that "the number of the disciples were multiplied" (6:1), and again "multiplied," even "a great company of priests" believing (6:7). Were all these thousands also taken to the Jordan for baptism? The claim is often made that all the men among the 120 or more disciples helped the Twelve to baptize the 3,000. This is done in support of immersion, especially when the baptism is placed in Jerusalem and when Luke is thought to say that it occurred "on that day." Immersion requires so much strength that many men would be needed for immersing 3,000. But who alone stepped forth to deal with this multitude? In v. 14 it is "Peter with the eleven," and in v. 37 the multitude speaks to "Peter and the rest of the apostles." This is Luke's answer. Here the apostles functioned in their high office for the first time.

How, then, were the 3,000 baptized? We do not know. The Spirit has withheld the answer. Why? Because the mode is not essential. In order to make it essential the Spirit would have had to state it in plain terms. One mode, however, was not used: immersion. Why, then, should we use it? The church has selected the simplest mode, one that is probably much like the one that was employed in Jerusalem. To insist on one mode and to condemn all others is rather presumptuous. We may add that all the pictorial and the archaeological evidence regarding the mode of baptism in the early church has been gathered by Clement F. Rogers, M. A., *Baptism and Christian Archaeology*, Oxford, Clarendon Press. This man approached his investigation with the conviction that immersion was the primitive and original mode. He found the exact contrary to be true. The most ancient tracings and carvings portray the act of baptism as being carried out by pouring. In this way John baptized Jesus, and in this way other baptisms were administered. All the fonts found in ruins and in excavations are shallow, a few steps down. In some of these immersion could have been possible, but only by laying the person down flat in the font, and then he dared not have been very corpulent. This mass of evidence invalidates the assumption, so often met with, that immersion was the mode of baptism in the early church.

To this day it is by means of baptism that people are added to the church. In the Greek "were added" is enough and needs no phrase which states to whom they were added; the same is true in regard to v. 47. Luke's ψυχαί are "souls" in the sense of "persons." The statement that all of these were men must be denied in view of 4:4, where Luke counts only "men," ἄνδρες, and omits women and children. "Souls" does not exclude children, especially in view of "your children" in v. 39 and of the entire Old Covenant which included children. In 7:14, where the family of Jacob is mentioned, "souls" positively includes every child. The effort to take "your children," τέκνα, in the sense of adult descendants only is ineffectual. All these details, however, must not dim the tremendous fact which Luke here records. Think of 3,000 coming to faith and to baptism on one day, the very first day of what may be called the Christian Church! Thus on one day the great mother church of all Christendom was founded. The first Christian congregation starts off with 3,000 members.

The First Picture of the Mother Congregation at Jerusalem

42) Luke gives us several of these pictures in due succession, and each is intensely interesting. The

Spirit begins his saving work, we are subject to it today. Jesus labored for three years and at last had only some 500 disciples (I Cor. 15:6) ; here 3,000 were added at one stroke, fulfilling John 4:37, 38. **And they continued steadfast in the teaching of the apostles and in the fellowship, in breaking the bread, and in the prayers.**

The entire sketch is presented by means of descriptive imperfects, thus painting the picture. Προσκαρτερέω means "to adhere with strength" to something, the periphrastic imperfect stressing the continuance. We have four datives in two pairs and do not regard the last two as a unit apposition to "fellowship."

The fundamental activity of the first congregation is this firm, continued adherence "to the teaching of the apostles." They were the called teachers and preachers and they began their work at once, there being about 300 hearers to each apostle. This work went on continuously, and all these people not only attended the meetings faithfully but also earnestly adhered to what was taught. Διδαχή is both the work of teaching and the doctrine taught. In this case both meanings flow together.

The deduction should not be made from this passage that people may be received into the church only on their willingness to enter it and that teaching may be postponed until later. These converts were Jews who were fully conversant with the Scriptures as Peter's quotations from Joel and from David show. The one thing they needed was the conviction that Jesus was the Christ. That Peter wrought in them on Pentecost. Thus they were fully prepared for baptism and for membership; they had what we must now first give to those who have never been properly instructed. This teaching after Pentecost was that which we now perform Sunday after Sunday, the teaching and the preaching in public worship.

They adhered "to fellowship," and Luke adds no genitive, nor is "of the apostles" to be understood; this is the fellowship of all the members with each other as well as with the apostles. They were one spiritual body, inwardly one by faith in Christ, inwardly and outwardly one by confessing Christ and by adhering to the one doctrine of Christ that was taught by the apostles. And so they kept together as one body and treated each other accordingly. One faith and one teaching, and thus one body in one fellowship. No parties, schisms, inwardly. Κοινωνία is here *communio* and not *communicatio* or impartation of alms. That point Luke also notes later; it would be out of place so far forward in this account. Already that fact settles the question as to the next two datives; they are not appositions to *koinonia.*

They adhered "to breaking the bread." There is no necessity for stressing the article in the sense of "their bread," that eaten at a joint meal. Even then the Sacrament of the Lord's Supper would be involved, since at this early time it was always celebrated at the end of a meal (I Cor. 11:33, 34 in connection with what precedes). Luke is speaking of the greatest things done in this first congregation and characterizes the celebration of the Lord's Supper by use of the expression that was common at that time: "breaking the bread." To stress this phrase so as to exclude the cup from the Sacrament is just as unwarranted as to have the phrase mean only partaking of a joint meal. The apostles cannot be charged with mutilation of the Sacrament. I Cor. 11:23-29. "Breaking" has been made an essential feature of the Sacrament, yet there is no counterpart for the wine. Breaking was practiced only for the purpose of distribution, the bread of that time never being cut in our fashion. Krauth, *Conservative Reformation,* 723, shows the impossibility of letting the breaking of bread symbolize the killing of a man; see the words of institution in the Gospels and in I Cor. 11.

They adhered "to the prayers," i. e., to the worship in their own gatherings, 4:24, etc., and to the stated devotions in the Temple, 3:1, etc. It seems that this word is used to designate the entire service or worship and not merely the praying. We thus see how Luke first pairs teaching and the fellowship it involves and secondly the Sacrament and the worship which parallels it.

Here we have a brief description of the religious life of the first Christian congregation. All the essentials are present and are in proper order and harmony. The church has always felt that this is a model. One wishes that Luke had said more. Where did this large congregation assemble, for it grew tremendously (4:4; 5:14; 6:1, 7)? Many think of the halls of the Temple. But this was scarcely the case. The one thing certain is that no difficulty was encountered regarding a meeting place. Were these "prayer meetings" in the modern sense of that term? We shall see that only on special occasions were gatherings for the purpose of praying held. The dominating feature is the teaching (Word) and the Sacrament.

43) **Moreover, on every soul fear kept coming; and many wonders and signs through the apostles kept occurring.** Here and again in v. 44 δέ adds something different. The reason for referring "every soul" to non-disciples who came into contact with the congregation is the contrasting subject in v. 44, "all those believing." These outsiders kept experiencing "fear" in the sense of awe. They felt that higher powers were at work among the disciples. It is one thing to have such impressions, quite another to act properly upon them. With the close connective τε Luke adds the "wonders and signs" that were connected with this **fear**; see v. 19 regarding the two terms. The miracles

were intended to impress those that were on the outside. The statement is summary and is placed at the head of the activity of the apostles because Luke does not intend to recount these miracles but to confine himself only to notable instances. Let us not overlook the fact that these were "many," astonishing as τέρατα and significant as σημεῖα. But the apostles were only the instruments (διά) through whom One who was far higher wrought. This differentiates all the apostolic miracles from those of Jesus. God, indeed, wrought those of Jesus (v. 22) but only as the divine Persons work together.

44) **And all those believing kept together; and they were having all things as common and were selling their possessions and goods and distributing them to all according as anyone had need.** This translation reproduces the correct reading. "All those believing" (present participle) "were," in the sense of "kept," together (the phrase is to be understood as it was in 1:16). The imperfect ἦσαν is iterative; the believers made a practice of meeting together. Remember in what different countries they had been born. The Temple had drawn them to live in Jerusalem, and now their believing drew them together in a different, deeper, and far truer way. Faith in Christ was the bond which made one body of these believers even outwardly. This must be added to "the fellowship" mentioned in v. 42. Some think that these thousands lived together, others reduce the number. Both views are unacceptable. The fact that they all found room for their frequent meetings Luke considers it unnecessary to explain.

45) As they were thus drawn together, so they treated each other. "They were having or holding all things as common," κοινά is predicative. This states the main idea, namely how they considered and treated their possessions, not as belonging to the owner only,

but as something in which the rest were to share as need arose. This was not communism but the product of something that communism does not understand. The following imperfects are iterative (R. 884): this selling and this distributing took place from time to time and was individual and wholly voluntary as 5:4 plainly states. It occurred "according as anyone had need." The use of a conjunction with ἄν (or ἐάν) with the iterative imperfect is the classic construction, which is, however, retained in the Koine only in subordinate clauses (C.-K. 367; R. 922). As needy cases arose they were taken care of in this manner. It is a fair conclusion that most of these Jews who had moved to Jerusalem from distant lands and were now believers were well off and were living on their wealth. Yet they had changed their entire attitude toward their wealth and were now using it in fine Christian charity. Volunteers came forward, such as Barnabas mentioned in 4:37, sold some possession or goods, and placed the proceeds at the disposal of the apostles. The fact that among so many believers instances of need occurred is only natural.

The old Mosaic law provided ways and means for taking care of all cases of poverty among the Jews; but the number of beggars referred to in the New Testament shows that these laws were no longer enforced. This old spirit was revived in the first congregation in Jerusalem and chose this means for letting no fellow believer suffer need. It is unfair to say that the Christians thought that their property was insecure because of the hostility of the authorities and therefore gave it away, or that they expected Christ's return in the immediate future and therefore dealt so lavishly. So also the poverty of the mother congregation which was found there at a later date is often attributed to what Luke here records, but this was due to the fact that the Herodian persecution scattered this first congregation to the four winds while famine and hard times set in and caused distress. What Luke describes is a fine display of Christian charity. The same motive is still active in the church today. Many rich still offer large sums, and the rest still bring their portion, and Christian need never waits long for relief.

46) **Day by day both continuing steadfast with one accord in the Temple and breaking bread house by house, they were partaking of their food in exultation and simplicity of heart, praising God and having favor with the whole people. Moreover, the Lord kept adding together day by day the saved.**

The descriptive imperfects continue. Luke sketches the daily life of the first congregation. The three κατά phrases are distributive: "day by day," "house by house"; τε . . . τε correlate the first two participles (R. 1179), "both . . . and." The believers both visited the Temple and broke bread house by house at home. The daily visits to the Temple were made for the purpose of participation in the Temple worship; we see Peter and John thus engaged in 3:1. The separation from the Temple and the Jews generally developed gradually and naturally. Until it was effected, the Christians used the Temple which Jesus had honored and which typified him (John 2:19-21) as they had used it before. Its spacious colonnades and halls afforded them room for their own assemblies.

Many think that "breaking bread" again refers to the Sacrament, but in a brief sketch such as this Luke would scarcely repeat in this fashion. The addition "house by house" would add nothing new since it is self-evident that the Temple was not the place for the Sacrament. "Breaking bread" also refers to all the meals and not merely to such as might precede the

Sacrament as an agape. "House by house" is like "day by day." It does not mean merely "at home" but in each home. Wherever there was a Christian home its residents partook of their food "in exultation of heart," with high delight in the grace vouchsafed them, and "in simplicity or singleness of heart," rejoicing in the one thing that filled their hearts with such joy. This noun is derived from an adjective which means "without a stone," hence perfectly smooth and even, metaphorically, a condition that is undisturbed by anything contrary.

47) "Praising God" was the natural expression of their hearts for the supreme blessing they had found in Christ. So also they enjoyed "favor with the whole people." Taken as a whole, the people of the city thought well of all these disciples. Their fervor in the Temple worship commended them, and their happy conduct with praise to God on their lips made the Jews like them. What a beautiful picture of this morning hour of the church! The goodness of the Lord gave his disciples this period of undisturbed peace in which to grow and increace. The favorable disposition of the populace helped to bring many to faith. So the Lord often gives his church days of peace — do we always use them as did the first church in Jerusalem? Soon the skies would become clouded and the storm of persecution descend to scatter the flock.

In v. 41 we have the passive "they were added," here we see the agent in that passive: "the Lord kept adding together," ἐπὶ τὸ αὐτό occurs in this sense (1:16). The Lord alone can add new members. Those who lay stress on numbers bring in many in ways which they devise. We want numbers, but such as the Lord adds and records in his book, and none, if we can help it, whose names would be only on our books. He adds only by filling the heart with the gospel. "Day by day" in a brief space of time the congregation grew from

3,000 souls to 5,000 men, or some 10,000 souls (4:4). Those added are significantly called "the saved," *οἱ σωζόμενοι.* The substantivized present participle is timeless and expresses quality or condition and nothing more. "The saved" are those who are in a saved condition. "Such as should be saved" (A. V.) is incorrect and introduces a wrong idea; "those that were being saved" (R. V.) is also incorrect, for it suggests the thought that salvation was still in the future; "those that were saved" (R. V., American Committee) is still faulty in so far as it introduces the past tense. An aorist participle would point to the saving act, and a perfect participle (and this is at times used) to that act and the saved condition resulting. The present participle stops with a statement of the quality or condition: "the saved." On the readings found in the A. V. see 3:1.

CHAPTER III

PETER AND JOHN HEAL THE CRIPPLE IN THE TEMPLE

The miracle is notable in itself but is recorded chiefly because of its effect. It aroused the Sanhedrin to its first opposition against the apostles. Luke has no indication as to the time that intervened between Pentecost and this miracle. For doing good Peter and John receive evil.

1) **Now Peter and John were going up into the Temple at the hour of prayer, the ninth. And a man, being lame from his mother's womb, was being carried, whom they were placing day by day at the door of the Temple, the one called Beautiful, to ask alms from those going into the Temple, who, on seeing Peter and John about to go into the Temple, began requesting to receive alms.**

We follow the preferred reading which has *ἐπὶ τὸ αὐτό* concluding 2:47, and not opening 3:1. The A. V. does the reverse and therefore concludes 2:47 with *τῇ ἐκκλησίᾳ*, a dative that is found in several texts. The textual evidence is in favor of the reading translated in the R. V. To put the phrase at the head of 3:1 makes it too emphatic, since the very mention of "Peter and John" shows that they were "together." We are prepared to find them so. In his list in 1:13 Luke has grouped them together (correct the A. V.); they act together in Luke 22:8; John 13:24, 25; 18:16, 17; 20:2, etc.; 21:21, 22. So we repeatedly find these two together in the story of Acts. A close friendship unites them. By nature they were entirely different. Peter was impetuous, John serene. Thus they supplement each other.

Diamond polishes diamond, writes Rieger, and it may well happen that each enhances the luster of the other. God often uses the friendship of believers for the good of the church, especially the friendship of highly gifted men; witness the working together of Luther and Melanchthon.

These two were in the act of going up into the Temple at the hour of prayer. In 2:15 we find mention made of the service held at 9 A. M., here the one held at 3 P. M. is referred to. The Jews counted twelve hours for the day, starting with 6 A. M.; so their ninth hour was 3 P. M. which was called the evening sacrifice. Already in 2:46 we see how the disciples adhered to the Temple and its services. They continued this practice until the Lord himself eventually made it impossible. The Jews always spoke of going "up" to or into the Temple, no matter what the elevation was from which they started. This was said in an ethical sense. The Temple did not occupy the highest elevation in the city.

2) Simultaneous with their going into the Temple, as a second imperfect informs us, a lame beggar "was being carried" into it on some sort of a litter; τις is only our indefinite article "a" man. "Lame from his mother's womb" states that he was born lame, had never walked during the forty (4:22) years of his life. He seems to have been injured at birth so that his ankle bones (v. 7) had not developed or were misshapen. His congenital lameness, especially at the age he had now reached, rendered him incurable. The first two imperfects are descriptive of actions in progress. Peter and John overtook the men who were carrying the beggar in. This very likely occurred somewhere in the large court of the Gentiles. The imperfect in the relative clause expresses customary action as the added phrase shows: "whom they were placing day by day," etc. Relatives or friends did this, and it was

quite a task to carry the beggar such a distance and back home again. Israel was to have no beggars (Deut. 15:4), but the Jews were omitting the weightier matters of the law such as judgment, *mercy,* and faith, Matt. 23:23. We meet beggar after beggar.

This one had his regular station at the gate called "Beautiful," Ὡραία (θύρα or πύλη), from ὥρα, "timely" and thus "blooming," "beautiful." Josephus, *Wars,* 5, 5, 3, describes it as being much higher than the other gates and as being adorned with magnificent silver and gold plates. The Talmud calls it Nicanor's gate after its donor. This great gate was the only one that led from the court of the Gentiles surrounding the Sanctuary and the Temple buildings proper into the court of the women and through this to the court of the men. Opposite this gate was Solomon's Porch, a colonnade. Fourteen steps led up to a gallery, that ran around the three sides of the women's court, and five more steps from this gallery to the gate "Beautiful"; on two sides of the women's court other less imposing gates afforded entrance. We at once see that, while it was work to carry the beggar so far and also up those steps, he certainly had the most promising place for begging. The infinitive with τοῦ denotes purpose.

3) Not waiting until he was deposited in his usual place but already when Peter and John were about to go into the Temple, perhaps before they ascended the steps, this beggar "began requesting to receive alms." This imperfect is not iterative (R. 884) but inchoative: the beggar "began to request," and the tense also holds us in suspense as to the outcome of what he began which was anything but what he expected. The verb itself expresses respectful asking. There is no reason for connecting this request with the liberality manifested toward fellow believers by the Christians described in 2:44, 45, as though the beggar knew all about that and expected some of that liberality

to be shown him. This man was begging in his usual way and was accosting people even before he got to his regular station. "Began requesting alms" would be enough; "to receive" is circumstantial and indicates the outstretched hand that is anxious to take whatever might be offered. Luke draws the picture well.

4) **Now Peter, earnestly looking on him, with John, said, Look on us! And he began to give heed to them, expecting to receive something from them.** Δέ continues the story but introduces a new action which was so different from that which the beggar usually experienced. Peter is the spokesman and later performs the miracle, but John is with him in both. This earnest look of the apostles does not mean, "looking through to the innermost bottom of the heart in order to discover the proper receptivity." Interpretations such as that are due to the view that miracles require faith in advance. This view is here carried to the point of making Peter and John look into the beggar's very heart, which would itself be a miracle. The simple fact is that Peter and John saw only a poor, pitiable cripple and his outstretched, begging hand before them. But why this earnest and intent look? We know of but one answer. The apostles had often seen this cripple begging at the gate "Beautiful," they may even have dropped him a coin now and then. To heal him had not entered their minds. Why not? Because the Lord had not put it into their minds to do such a thing. The apostles did not perform miracles just when and where they thought advisable. In every case they were moved to do so by the Lord and by his Spirit. It is because the Lord so moved them that they now fixed their full attention on the cripple whom they had seen so often on previous days.

Hence also their order to the beggar to look on them which was uttered with the peremptory and authoritative aorist imperative. This beggar must pay close attention to the apostles.

5) And he does. "He began to give heed to them," ἐπεῖχεν (supply τὸ νοῦν), but only in the same way as any man might do when his attention is thus aroused. So little was the thought of faith of any kind in his mind that he supposed only that something would now be given to him, something more than the ordinary small coins he usually received. This is one of a number of plain cases in which faith does not and is not intended to precede but rather follows the miracle.

6) **But Peter said: Silver and gold is not mine; but what I have I give to thee. In the name of Jesus Christ, the Nazarene, be walking! And having grasped him by the right hand, he raised him up, and at once his feet and ankles were made firm. And leaping up, he stood and began to walk. And he went with them into the Temple, walking and leaping and praising God.**

Peter speaks of "silver and gold," the more valuable coins, because the beggar evidently expected an unusually valuable gift from them and because he thought them wealthy. It is a rather hasty conclusion on the basis of this word to suppose that the apostles were themselves dependent on alms; for John had a home and was able to support Jesus' mother (John 19:27). Peter means, "I have no wealth." But the cripple has no time to be disappointed, for Peter immediately adds, "But what I have I give to thee," leading the cripple to wonder what that might be. He had his gift from the Lord — miraculous healing as the seal of the gospel message, that definite form of healing for this particular person as it was indicated to both these apostles by the Lord.

Without adding a single word of explanation, without doing anything to awaken or to increase faith,

Peter utters the command that conveys its own power of compliance: "In the name," etc. Here again is this pithy and significant phrase ἐν τῷ ὀνόματι κτλ., which is so often interpreted in inadequate ways. It does not mean "by the authority of," etc. (R. 649); nor does it mean this in some places and something else in others. See ὄνομα in 2:21 and this phrase in 2:38. Here, as always, the sense is: "in connection with the revelation of Jesus," etc. In addition to what has been said when considering 2:21 and 38 we may state that "name" in the sense of "revelation" not only comprehends Jesus and all his power and grace but also conveys him to us for our apprehension. Paul is acquainted with the phrase "in Christ" or "in the Lord," and uses it often; in the expression "in the name of Jesus Christ" "name" stresses the vital connection with the person Jesus Christ. The power and the grace that make him "Jesus Christ" ("both Lord and Christ," 2:36) are revealed in all that truly makes us know him, that shines out from him, and that is his NAME, the source from which all blessings, also this miracle of healing, flow. On "Jesus" see 2:22; on "Christ," 2:36; the two combined in 2:38; on "the Nazarene," 2:22. "In the name of Jesus Christ, the Nazarene," suddenly brought to the cripple's mind all that he had ever heard about this wonderful person.

"Be walking!" is the present imperative to express enduring action; he is to have the power of walking now and always. Here is no "if" or "but"; here is no process or slow mending. We all know that even when limbs are sound, no human being can at once walk, leap, caper, jump, who has never done so before. The thing must first be learned. But the cripple is not to learn, he is to walk perfectly from the very first instant. Let that feature of the miracle have its just due. In no way did the miracle depend upon the man's faith or will or understanding. Of course, he was to know, to believe, and to act, but all these came about as a result of the healing, they were not conditions or requisites to the healing.

7) Peter grasped him by the right hand, the very hand he was holding out for alms, only in order to raise him up, to make him stand and to walk at once. If Peter and John had walked away, the cripple would have discovered that his feet and his ankles were normal and that he could walk. But no interval was to occur. Peter's effort raised the man from the ground; instantly his limbs were firm, sound, strong, ready to serve their natural purpose. The member grasped is properly in the genitive: took hold "of the right hand."

8) Peter did not need to exert much effort, of himself the restored cripple, "leaping up, stood and began to walk" (inchoative imperfect). Luke's description is vivid. R. 1116 writes: "It is not clear why the present participle occurs, ἐξαλλόμενος, unless it is to note that he kept on leaping and walking alternately." One would expect the aorist, "having leaped up, he stood." The aorist "stood" is constative: without falling he stood upright. Then the imperfect notes that he began to walk, to do just what Peter had told him to do.

He accompanied the apostles as they proceeded up the steps and on through the gate Beautiful, walking, of course, but also leaping and jumping every now and then, overjoyed at the blessing given him even without his asking, praising God who had made him so rich in Jesus' name. But what about us who have enjoyed sound limbs all our lives? So many blessings, so little realization and gratitude! The cripple's first walk took him into the Temple, the very purpose for which we should use our feet, keeping them always in the paths of righteousness for his name's sake.

9) **And all the people saw him walking and praising God; moreover, they kept recognizing him that this was the one sitting for the alms at the Gate Beautiful of the Temple, and they were filled with amazement and excitement at what had come to him. But he holding to Peter and John, all the people ran together to them at the porch called Solomon's, dumbfounded.**

It seems that v. 9, 10 describe what occurred before the Temple service, and v. 11 what occurred after it was over and the people had dispersed. When Luke says that all the people saw him "walking and praising God" he tells us that the man drew general attention to himself. Even after the restored cripple had come to the men's court he continued walking around instead of standing still like the other men and kept calling out words of praise to God. Thus everybody saw him.

10) For a man to act thus was unusual, yet in itself such conduct would not have attracted so much attention. People would only have wondered as to what made him act in this way. By means of the iterative imperfect Luke tells us that, as he thus moved about, group after group recognized him as the very man they had so often seen "sitting for the alms," the article to indicate the alms they had given him from time to time at the Gate Beautiful. They had not seen him sitting thus with his deformed feet and ankles this afternoon — here he was among them, walking around and praising God. Luke uses two nouns to convey the effect; both are strong: θάμβος, "amazement" that came with a shock, and ἔκστασις, "excitement" that throws the mind off its balance. They stared uncomprehendingly at the change that had come over the man.

11) What happened when the service and the worship were conducted is not stated. But these are evidently now over, and all the men pass out of the Temple through the court of the women. Instead of making

their exit by one of the side portals, all those present stream through the main eastern portal called "Beautiful," down the steps to the court below, "at the porch called Solomon's," ἐπί with the dative, not into this porch, but in front of it. This *stoa* consisted of a span of roof which rested on magnificent pillars extended along the entire eastern outer wall of the Temple area. It was named after Solomon, because this side of the Temple area perhaps rested on the old massive foundation walls which rose several hundred feet from the valley beneath and had been left undemolished since Solomon's time. As they went out, the healed cripple clung tightly to Peter and to John. The three got no farther than this court facing Solomon's porch. Everybody ran out to this and surrounded them in a packed crowd. And ἔκθαμβοι, "dumfounded" with amazement, describes the state of their minds; the "greatly wondering" of our versions is far too weak.

12) The beggar clings to Peter and to John. Attention is centered on all three. Amazement with its silent questioning looks to them for an answer and an explanation. The Lord had timed this miracle so as to bring this whole audience before Peter, literally compelling him to preach to these people. His words are straight to the point: Not we have done this but the risen Jesus. While the question seems to be one that is wholly about the beggar, Peter turns it into a matter that is entirely personal to everyone of his hearers. God is attesting this Jesus whom they crucified as the Savior promised by prophecy. Let them repent and share in his blessings! And again we see the authority, the mastery, the effectiveness of this sermon, which strikes straight home into the consciences and the hearts of Peter's hearers.

Now on seeing it, Peter made response to the people: Israelite men, why are you marvelling at this man, or why are you gazing on us as though

by our own power or godliness we have made him to walk? The verb "made response" is used with reference to any situation that requires an explanation, and here certainly was such a case.

Ἄνδρες is used as it was in 1:16, and 2:14, and "Israelites" as in 2:22 which employs the religious name of honor for the Jews with its appeal to their highest hopes and motives. They are to view this miracle as true Israelites should. Thus they are not to marvel at this man and to stop with their amazement — they are to let their thoughts go much farther. The neuter "at this thing" is out of place because τούτῳ is in contrast with ἡμῖν, persons. So also they are not to gaze on the apostles "as though" (concessive ὡς, R. 1140) they had made this man walk (object infinitive with τοῦ, R. 1168) by their own power (effective cause) or with their godliness (meritorious cause, John 9:31, 33) The power did not emanate from the apostles, nor was power given them as a reward of their godliness. To understand that power these people will have to look elsewhere.

13) **The God of Abraham and of Isaac and of Jacob, the God of our fathers, glorified his Servant Jesus whom you delivered up and denied before the face of Pilate, he having judged to release him. But you denied the Holy and Righteous One and asked for yourselves that a man, a murderer, be granted unto you, but the Author of life you killed, whom God raised up from the dead, of which we on our part are witnesses. And on the basis of the faith of his name this man, whom you behold and know, his name made firm; yea, the faith, that through him, did give to him this entire soundness in the presence of you all.** This true explanation of "what has come to this man" (v. 10) all Israelites should know, for it means everything to them personally.

Peter is speaking to Israelites, hence he employs the great covenant name which God gave himself in Exod. 3:6, "the God of Abraham," etc. It is no mere heaping up of words when Peter adds the apposition, "the God of our fathers," for he intends to designate God as the God also of all the descendants of the patriarchs who in times past shared the covenant and the faith with them. "Our" links also Peter and John with all these "fathers." It is to sink into the minds of Peter's hearers that he whom their nation worshipped in all past ages in their covenant relation with him, he it is who as this God and in this covenant of his "glorified his Servant Jesus." It is the same glorification which Peter preached on Pentecost in 2:30-36, namely the resurrection and the exaltation at God's right hand. Not only the miracle is referred to and the fact that God gorified Jesus in and by that. For in v. 15 Peter himself specifically mentions the resurrection, and in v. 16 the miracle is ascribed to the name of Jesus, i. e., to the name of this glorified Jesus. Παῖς is never used in the sense of "Son of God"; this thought is always expressed by the words υἱὸς Θεοῦ. The marginal note of the R. V., "Child," should be cancelled here and in all other passages where it occurs. This παῖς is the great *Ebed Yahweh* of Isaiah, chapters 40-66, the mighty "Servant" of Jehovah, who is his Son, indeed, but the Son who by his incarnation became "his Servant" to work out our salvation.

Now comes the personal turn of Peter's words which is sudden and startling, direct and crushing. On the one side, God and what he did, namely glorified Jesus; on the other side, these Jews and what *they* did, namely denied, rejected, disgraced Jesus. Note the emphatic ὑμεῖς: "whom *you on your part* delivered up and denied before the face of Pilate, he having judged to release him." Note the balance in μέν and δέ (v. 14).

Peter is a master in making these terrible contrasts between God and the Jews; compare 2:23, 24, 36; 4:10, 30, 31. When stating the terrible action of his hearers Peter names only the chief points and these in the order in which they occurred: "they delivered Jesus up" to the pagan governor with the demand that he be crucified, they wanted him made away with forever; then "they denied him before the face of Pilate," boldly, shamelessly, to his very face, declaring that he was not their King (Luke 23:2; John 19:14, 15), disowning him utterly. And this they did after Pilate "judged" or declared his verdict that he would release him, ἐκείνου is far stronger than αὐτοῦ and places pagan Pilate into contrast with the Jews. God glorified Jesus, Pilate wanted at least to release him, but the Jews demanded his death. Even pagan Pilate was better than the Jews. See 2:23 as to how it was possible for Peter to blame all the Jews.

14) Now follows another and a different contrast which is suggested by the word "deny." Jesus they denied, Barabbas they chose in his place. "The Holy and Righteous One" they rejected "and asked for themselves that a man, a murderer, be granted unto them." Being murderers themselves, that was the man they wanted. Note the chiasm which brings the two verbs that have a similar sound but an opposite sense strikingly together: ἠρνήσασθε — ᾐτήσασθε. Compare what is said in 2:27 on "thine Holy One." Holy and righteous are often found together in the sense of separate from sin and pronounced guiltless by the divine Judge. Him who in all his life and his work was spotless and approved of God the Jews denied and thereby declared that they would have nothing to do with him; but they considered it a favor that a vicious murderer be released for them. The middle of αἰτέω is used in business transactions. Here and in Matt. 27:20, and Luke 23:25, the middle brings out the idea

that the custom gave the Jews a right to ask for Barabbas, while in Matt. 14:7 this form emphasizes the right of request because of Herod's oath.

15) The word "murderer" leads to another still mightier contrast (δέ). Over against this murderer Peter places "the Author of life," τὸν ἀρχηγὸν τῆς ζωῆς, life's cause and originator (Heb. 12:2; also C.-K. 179). A murderer takes life although it be only the earthly life; this Author of life has divine life in himself and has thereby become the fountain of spiritual and everlasting life for us. The contrast rises to a tremendous climax: the one destroys the lower life, the other bestows the highest life. To this climax there is added the paradox, "you killed the Author of life." How can life's own Author be killed? One might ask further, "How can Jesus become the Author of life by being killed?" This is one of those great Scriptural statements that cannot be brushed aside by calling it a *praedicatio verbalis*, mere verbal play. "The Author of life" is a divine name for the person of Jesus, yet something human is predicated of him. The Scriptures also have the reverse. And this means that everything human as well as everything divine may be predicated of Jesus, no matter how his person is designated, whether by a human or by a divine name. This can be done because in Jesus a communication of natures and also of their attributes exists — he is the Godman.

Luther points out the practical value of Peter's word for us: "We Christians must know that if God is not also in the balance and gives the weight, we sink to the bottom with our scale. By this I mean: If it were not to be said, God has died for us but only a man, we should be lost. But if 'God's death' and 'God died' lie in the scale of the balance, then he sinks down, and we rise up as a light, empty scale. But, indeed, he can also rise again or leap out of the scale; yet he could not sit in the scale unless he became a man like us so that it could be said: 'God died,' 'God's passion,' 'God's blood,' 'God's death.' For in his nature God cannot die; but now that God and man are united in one person, it is correctly called God's death when the man dies who is one thing or one person with God." *Concordia Triglotta,* 1029, etc. In brief, the entire value of Christ's being killed for us lies in his being the Author of life, God.

Peter now returns to his original contrast: the clash between the deed of the Jews and the act of God. *They* killed the Author of life "whom *God* raised up from the dead." And this divine act is more than a contrast to the deed of the Jews; at one stroke God nullified all that the Jews had done. He contradicted and condemned all that they had done; he approved and sealed his great Servant as being in fact the Author of life, the destroyer of death. God accepted all of Christ's work and sacrifice as being full, complete, sufficient and crowned Jesus with infinite glory.

The phrase ἐκ νεκρῶν, like so many other fixed Greek phrases, needs no article. The absence of the article also stresses the noun. The expression never means "out from among the dead" so that all the other dead are regarded as still lying in their graves. The idea expressed by this combination is one of separation alone, R. 598. The phrase occurs thirty-five times with reference to Christ, a few times with reference to other individuals, and also in a figurative sense. Two of these passages refer to the resurrection of a number of the dead, and in them this standard phrase can have no other meaning than the one indicated. No wonder that the phrase is never used with reference to the ungodly; such usage, to say the least, would be gravely misleading. When they are called from their graves, this return to life is not an escape of their bodies from death but an entrance of their bodies into a state that is far worse than decay in the grave. The idea of this expression is not that, when Christ arose, he left all the other dead behind. God took Christ out of death and returned him to life. That is what the phrase means literally and actually.

"Of which we on our part are witnesses" is the same statement found in 2:32 with the pronoun being neuter (not masculine); compare 1:8. The mighty evidence that the power of the crucified Jesus was still operative was before Peter's hearers in the person of the miraculously healed beggar. No personal power of Peter's and of John's had wrought this miracle. It was like so many that were wrought by Jesus prior to his crucifixion. How was it wrought? Here are the witnesses to testify as to the how. By the power of the risen and the glorified Jesus.

16) Peter is even more explicit. Besides clearly stating the ultimate cause of the miracle, he states also the intermediate, or we may say, mediate cause: "his name made this man firm," made his feet and his ankles strong and firm to bear his body, the verb being used as in v. 7. And united with this "name" is "faith" in the name. Hence both name and faith are mentioned twice and are thus made emphatic. This takes us back to v. 6, "in the name of Jesus Christ," and we must recall what was said regarding "name" as designating the revelation which brings Jesus to us. Name and faith are correlatives, the name (revelation) is intended for faith, intended to awaken trust, to be received and held by confidence of heart. And faith needs the name or revelation as the sure ground on which to rest. All other ground is sinking sand.

We thus get Peter's thought. He gives all the credit to "his name" for making firm "this man whom you behold and know." The power that wrought the miracle lies in the name, for it reveals him who himself is in and with his name. Yet the name is not suspended in the air, the revelation must reveal to some heart, somebody must hold to the name and revelation by faith. So Peter adds the thought that the beggar was healed "on the basis (ἐπί) of the faith of his name" (the objective genitive); and again, "the faith, that (faith) through him" gave the man "this entire soundness in the presence of you all." So the object of this faith is the name and revelation; but this faith is "through him," mediated and brought about by Jesus who is revealed by his name. Peter says that only in this way are he and John connected with the miracle. It certainly ought to be clear that the faith which Peter is here speaking of is that which he and John have and not a faith which the beggar had. We have discussed this point when considering v. 4. Yet the view is held that this beggar had to have faith before he could be healed; that his believing was essential; that his faith cooperated with that of the apostles, etc. But the whole account, v. 1-7, places this healing into that class of miracles where faith is intended to follow, and not to precede the miracle. The view that faith must always precede a miracle is a deduction from only a fraction of the facts.

Note the emphasis on "this man whom you behold and know." The man is physical, visible, tangible evidence of the power of the glorified Jesus as mediated by his name and by faith in him and his name. And this man is but a sample of what that power of the risen Christ does in the hearts of men to this very day. It is a continuation of the miracle by which he attested his power and his grace throughout his own ministry. These attestations, once made, stand for all time. To demand their constant repetition is to declare that the recorded attestations do not fully attest, that the seals which the Lord deemed sufficient are not sufficient. We note, too, that the miracle justified the faith of Peter and of John, justified the faith of all who through it came to believe (4:4), justifies our faith today. It is unwarranted to regard Luke's account as a myth, to assert that the early church added its own ideas and conceptions to some perfectly natural occurrence. If Luke's account portrays only the fancies of Peter and of John or those of the early church, then our faith is as vain as theirs was, and the sensible thing to do is to drop the whole matter and to be satisfied with our ethics.

17) Peter plainly marks the transition to the second part of his address. The first part is objective and states the great facts and, of course, includes also those of the rejection of Jesus; the second is subjective and reaches into the hearts of the hearers in order to win them to repentance. Yet the second rests on the first and could not exist independently. **And now, brethren, I know that you committed it in accord with ignorance as also your rulers.** "Now" is not temporal but logical: taking the situation as it is. The word of address, "brethren," marks the turning point in the sermon and voices the love that now accompanies its appeal. "Brethren" is to be taken in the sense of "*our* fathers" in v. 13, "fellow Israelites," and not as "Christian brethren."

Peter says that he well knows that what these hearers of his as also their rulers had committed (πράσσω is often used with reference to evil acts) was done "in accordance with ignorance." But he does not thereby retract his previous statement regarding the ungodliness of their action (v. 13-15). It was directly against God, and not one particle of the damnableness of it all can be subtracted. Κατὰ ἄγνοιαν refers to the Old Testament distinction between sins for which sacrifices can be made (Num. 15:27-29) and sins for which the sinner's soul is cut off (Num. 15:30, 31); sins done "ignorantly," sins done "presumptuously" ("with a high hand"). On the former note Lev. 4:2, 27; 5:18; 22:14; and notably Heb. 9:7 compared with

10:26. Jesus made this distinction when he hung on the cross, Luke 23:34; Paul repeats it in I Cor. 2:8; Peter speaks of the sins committed prior to conversion as being done in ignorance, I Pet. 1:14. The point to be noted is that pardon is possible for such sins; and of that Peter intends to assure his hearers. The popular notion that ignorance excuses sin so that it is without guilt is wholly un-Biblical.

18) **Moreover, what things he announced in advance through all the prophets' mouth that his Christ suffer, God did thus fulfill.** This presents another consideration for Peter's hearers, hence δέ, "moreover." He restates in other words what he has said in 2:23. Not by accident did God's Christ suffer. If the Jews did not know what they were doing by making Jesus suffer, God knew what he was doing when he gave "his Christ" as a lamb for the slaughter, as the sacrifice for the sins of the world. In fact, God had announced in advance "through all the prophets' mouth," making them all speak with one mouth and voice, that the Messiah was to suffer. Only thus could his Messianic work and purpose be accomplished. And what God had thus announced this he, indeed, did fulfill in just that way. The Jews acted in ignorance, God with full intelligence. Peter states the facts as they are. God did not cause the ignorance. But God's grace and wisdom work in spite of human ignorance, yea, in and through that wicked ignorance they bring about its cure and deliverance from its guilt. On "Christ" see 2:36; "his Christ," sent by God and wholly his, is used in 4:26; Luke 9:20; Rev. 11:15; 12:10. The Greek prefers to place οὕτως in the emphatic position at the end. God gave Jesus to suffer as his Christ and thus also glorified him (v. 13).

19) This rich gospel and effective law lead straight to the gospel call: **Repent, therefore, and turn again for the blotting out of your sins, in order that**

there may come seasons of refreshing from the presence of the Lord, and that he may send the Christ who has been appointed for you, Jesus; whom heaven must receive until the time of the restoration of all things, of which God made utterance through the mouth of his holy prophets from of old.

The double command, to repent and to turn again, points to the necessary result (οὖν) of Peter's address. He had dispelled the ignorance of his hearers, they saw the wickedness of their killing Jesus and the blessedness of God's making him their Messiah. This should surely draw them to repentance unless they intended to continue their opposition to God in full consciousness and thus place themselves beyond pardon. "Repent!" is explained in 2:38. "Turn again" merely re-enforces "repent"; it is our "convert" which is used to indicate the change from sin to pardon in conversion.

The clause with εἰς τό states what the immediate purpose of repentance is: "for the being blotted out of your sins," the passive denoting God as the one that blots out the sins. See the same figure in Col. 2:14; Ps. 51:9; Isa. 43:25. The aorist indicates one erasure. The figure conceives the sins as being written into a record, which charges them against the sinner. The reality back of the figure is God's recalling to mind the sins and bringing them to judgment; blotting them out means that he forgets them so that all trace of them is removed. On "remission" see 2:38.

The clause with ὅπως ἄν states the purpose of repentance that follows upon the blotting out of the sins; ἄν is seldom used with this conjunction (B.-D. 369, 5), and its presence here in no way modifies the sense as the older grammars suppose. "Seasons of refreshing or cooling from the presence of the Lord (*Yahweh*)" are longer or shorter periods of spiritual enjoyment when men who repent and are justified are given times in which to feel the sweetness of God's grace in Christ Jesus without disturbance. They come from God's presence or countenance like sunshine and pleasant breezes. The old legalism of Pharisaism knew nothing about such seasons, for all work-righteousness is like the drive, heat, and sweat of slavery. Difficult times, even fiery trials, alternate with such pleasant seasons. Chiliasts think that these seasons are the millennium, and the absence of the article with both nouns is overlooked by them: *Erfrischungszeiten,* "refreshment seasons." Nor do they notice that Peter makes these seasons the proximate purpose of repentance and not one that is remote.

20) The ultimate purpose is that the Lord (*Yahweh*) "may send the Christ who has been appointed for you, (namely) Jesus." The participle means, "to take to hand" and thus "to appoint" (M.-M. 556); the perfect passive states that, once having been appointed as the Messiah, he remains so. "Jesus" is an apposition which states who this appointed Christ or Messiah is. Compare 2:36. The Lord will send Jesus at the end of the world, and what that means is next stated. Peter also shows how the purpose of our repentance centers in the great Parousia of Jesus. Chiliasts overlook the fact that Peter places the refreshing seasons ahead of the sending of Jesus for his great return (1:11).

21) Peter makes the matter plain by means of the relative clause. The Greek ὃν οὐρανὸν δέξασθαι may, however, be understood in two ways, the accusative being either the subject or the object: "who must receive heaven," or, "whom heaven must receive." Luther chooses the former, our versions the latter. Some think that the latter translation conveys the idea that heaven received Christ's human body and nature in such a manner as to confine them to that place and thus to make it impossible for him to be present any-

where else. It is said that he was like Elijah who, when he is in heaven, is nowhere else and who, when he came to Jesus on the mount, was there only and not in heaven. But the thought is that heaven had to receive Jesus until the day of his return and not that he received heaven for that period of time. Δεῖ stresses the necessity of God's plan which glorified Jesus, permitted him to work with divine power on earth until the consummation is reached, and then sent him as appointed for us (ὑμῖν, as believers).

Thus Christ rules from heaven in glory "until the times of the restoration of all things," those times (ὧν = χρόνων) of which all the prophets of old have spoken. Ἀποκατάστασις means placing things back into their former condition: "in the regeneration, when the Son of man shall sit on the throne of his glory," Matt. 19:28. Compare Rom. 8:18, etc. II Pet. 3:13. "We look for new heavens and a new earth, wherein dwelleth righteousness." Rev. 21:1, 5: "I saw a new heaven and a new earth." "Behold, I make all things new." Paradise will be restored. Here again ἄχρι χρόνων has no article, but the plural does not speak of separate times with intervals between them but refers to eternity but speaks of it in a human way as "times"; for after the restoration has been effected, it will remain forever.

Peter's expression has been misunderstood. Although the Greek terms "seasons" (periods) and "times" always have distinct meanings, these two words have been identified in this passage and referred to the millennial era. At least the term "times" has been referred to this era. So also not only are the seasons placed after the sending of the Christ, but this sending is placed after the times. The old fancy of Origen has also been revived that "all things" must include even Satan and all the damned.

If ὧν refers to πάντων, it becomes restrictive: "only all those things which." It must refer to χρόνων: "those times which the prophets have made utterance about"; the genitive is due to the antecedent and is attracted from ἅ. God mentioned (ἐλάλησεν) these times of the consummation through the mouth of the old prophets, compare Isa. 11:6-9; 35:1-10, etc. Here, as in v. 18, we have διά which is so significant for the Biblical conception of Verbal Inspiration. God is always the speaker, the prophets are always the media or instruments "through" whom he speaks. It is the "mouth" of the prophets which God uses, for the very words they speak are those desired by God, and the "mouth" is mentioned although the written word is referred to. The prophets are called "holy" as being set apart and belonging to God who makes them his mouthpiece.

The neat Greek phrase ἀπ' αἰῶνος, literally, "from the eon," means all along during the past era of the world. The noun denotes an age or eon and includes both the time and what transpires in and distinguishes that time. The R. V. gives a long circumscriptive translation: "which have been since the world began"; far better is that of the American Committee, "from of old."

Peter opens a grand prospect to his hearers which is far beyond his own former conception and that of all other Jews and their earthly Messianic kingdom. Repent, etc., and there shall follow cancellation of all sins, then seasons of spiritual refreshing, finally Christ's glorious return, and the fulfillment of all prophecies concerning the final restoration. The apostles were never afraid to place their admonitions on the mightiest possible base or to appeal to the most powerful motives.

22) Peter instances Moses, Deut. 18:15, 18, 19. **Moses said: A Prophet will the Lord God raise up for you out of your brethren like me. Him shall you**

hear according to all things whatsoever he shall utter to you. Moreover, it shall be, every soul which shall not hear that prophet shall be utterly destroyed from the people.

This is not μέν *solitarium* (R. 1151), for δέ follows in v. 24, which balances Moses and all the prophets since Samuel. In v. 23 δέ is a part of the quotation. The quotation is freely reproduced from the LXX by slightly changing the order of the words in the first part and following the Hebrew in the second part. On quoting see 2:25. Moses had special importance for Peter's hearers. This passage of Deuteronomy was well known and was also by the Jews referred to the Messiah. Peter quotes it for two purposes: as presenting Jesus the Prophet-Messiah foretold by Moses, and as emphasizing the admonition to repent, this being what the Prophet-Messiah has to say to all Israelites. Moses "said" means in his writings.

"The Lord God" is used for the Hebrew as in 2:39 and implies his covenant relation and his power. What God told Moses about the Prophet, Peter repeats as being told to the Israelites by Moses. "Out of your brethren" has peculiar force. When did God ever raise up a prophet for the Israelites from any people except their own brethren? Why, then, add the words that this future prophet would come "out of their brethren"? This is a reference to the human nature of Jesus, but by mentioning it in such a peculiar manner God implies that there will be something about him that is far higher than his Jewish birth. The phrase points to this Prophet's deity. Therefore also he will be only like Moses and not like all the other prophets. Moses was a mediator-prophet, the mediator of the covenant made on Sinai, for which task a man was sufficient. The promised Prophet would also be a mediator but of a still higher covenant, the one that superseded the first and centered in Golgotha. The Jews kept looking for this prophet although in their own way, John 6:14; Luke 17:16. Jesus himself referred to this prophecy of Moses' in John 5:46, 47.

Hence also the gravity of the command and the threat. "Him shall you hear!" the genitive of the person after a verb of hearing, the future tense with the imperative sense of laws: thou shalt; thou shalt not. The sense is "hear and obey" by doing exactly what he says. Peter adds the next phrase and clause as interpreting what this command includes: hear "according to all things whatsoever he shall utter to you." The aorist is constative and sums up all his utterances into a unit, while "all things as many as" distributes them as to their number. The indefinite ὅσα ἄν conveys the thought that, no matter what this Prophet may say, unquestioning obedience is demanded. Certainly, all of God's prophets must be obeyed; yet of none is this said with such peculiar emphasis as of this supreme Prophet.

23) Hence also the threat is made prominent in the same strong manner. Ἔσται, like ἐγένετο, is used without a connective; and "every soul" is to be taken in the sense of "every person." In ἥτις ἄν with the subjunctive there lies the idea that someone may, indeed, not hear that Prophet, may dare to reject the message that he brings by the disobedience of unbelief. Such conduct shall be fatal for him. His doom is sealed in advance. The Hebrew reads, "I will require it of him"; the LXX, "I will execute vengeance upon him." Instead of either of these expressions Peter uses the strong formula which occurs frequently in the Pentateuch beginning with Gen. 17:14: "shall be utterly destroyed from the people." He shall be sundered from the λαός, from God's people, by the death penalty without forgiveness, to be cast out and rejected forever in the final judgment. The threat could not be made stronger The moment we realize wherein all

the things Jesus came to proclaim centered, namely in faith and forgiveness, we see how absolutely fatal the rejection of unbelief necessarily is.

24) **And, on the other hand, all the prophets from Samuel and those in succession on, as many as made utterance, also announced these days.** After μέν in v. 22 we now have δέ, for which "on the other hand" is cumbersome yet reproduces the idea. Moses on the one hand, and not merely one but all the others on the other hand. In one grand chorus they proclaimed "these days," those of the great Mediator-Prophet foretold by Moses, who would grant the seasons of refreshing until the times of the restoration of all things, the days of the entire Messianic era. Peter attributes to all the prophets a vision of the New Testament era up to and including the Parousia. All their prophecies related to these days in one way or in another; for none of them would have prophesied if these days had not been promised.

The prophets after Moses are reckoned from the time of Samuel and his school of prophets. Samuel was not only himself great, he also founded a school of prophets, for which reason the Talmud calls him *magister prophetarum*. The adverb καθεξῆς, "successively," "in succession or due order," is made a substantive by the article. If "those in succession" are Samuel's pupils, the construction is quite regular. Samuel and his pupils in order after him would justify Peter's making the count begin with them and their great teacher, "as many as made utterance" would include the rest. The alternative is to find a mixed construction here: 1) "all the prophets from Samuel on, as many as have spoken"; and 2) "all the prophets, Samuel and those in order, as many," etc. The two statements would be combined into one, which is not satisfactory. I Sam. 2:10 contains a notable prophecy which names "his Anointed." When we are thinking of Samuel we should not forget his anointing of David, the type of Christ, and his relation to the kingdom that began with Saul.

25) All that has been said about Moses and the prophets Peter now drives home. **You yourselves are the sons of the prophets and of the covenant which God covenanted with your fathers, saying to Abraham, And in thy seed shall all the families of the earth be blessed.** This appeal to the highest motives is powerful. Nothing could be more effective psychologically. The pronoun "you" is emphatic, and the predicate with the article makes it identical and interchangeable with the subject (R. 768); in other words, there are none others who are sons of the prophets. The connotation in "sons" as compared with "children" is that of legal standing, of heirship, and thus of succession in carrying on that for which the fathers stood. Peter says, "you are the sons," meaning that this honor and this high position now rest on these his hearers. All that the prophets gave them as sons is theirs to have, hold, and pass on. In all the world none others are found who have a right to this position. The prophets are the spiritual fathers of the Israelites and even the physical fathers of their blood.

"And of the covenant" is added in order to bring out the idea of the full blessedness, greatness, and nobility of this sonship. The position which was once occupied by the prophets as their fathers they now hold as their successors. More than this, the fathers had only the promises of the covenant, these sons are to have the great fulfillment of those promises. Being sons and heirs, the inheritance is now to be paid out to them. Διαθήκη is the Hebrew *b^e^rith,* noun and verb being the same: "the covenant which God covenanted." The middle voice also corresponds with the noun: God disposed of what was his, disposed of it as he saw fit (ἧς is attracted from ἥν).

Always it is God who covenanted and never Abraham. It is always God's covenant and not Abraham's; nor are the two ever coordinated. God did the bestowing, Abraham only received. This covenant was "with your fathers," πρός being used to indicate living relationship and intimate intercourse (R. 625.) Since it was made with Abraham, the covenant included all the fathers, for they were Abraham's sons and heirs even as Peter's hearers now are.

Peter quotes the words of the covenant from Gen. 22:18, but deviates from the LXX by placing "in thy seed" first and by substituting "all the families" (πατριαί) for "all the nations" (ἔθνη), which is evidence that Peter translates the Hebrew independently. Gal. 3:16 establishes the vital point that τὸ σπέρμα of this covenant promise is Christ; in that passage Paul stresses the use of the singular rather than the plural σπέρματα. God said "seed," not "seeds." The great covenant blessing of redemption and salvation was in connection with (ἐν) Christ and not in connection with all the descendants of Abraham. That Seed, that great son of Abraham, had now appeared, and all the blessing promised in him was now actually present. Abraham and the fathers had died in the faith and the hope of it, seeing it from afar and thus appropriating it; Peter's hearers have it right before them. The healed beggar is a sample of that blessing; Peter's sermon is the offer of all the spiritual riches of that blessing. With πατριαί Peter echoes πρὸς τοὺς πατέρας in its connection with οἱ υἱοί. The word refers to families in the widest sense as being derived from one father as the head. We might translate "tribes or clans." But "of the earth" extends the covenant promise and blessing beyond Judaism (1:8), and this universality is intensified: "all the families of the earth."

We challenge the claim that Gal. 3:16 does not apply, and that "seed" is a collective term for the descendants of Abraham, so that they bring the blessing to all the families of the earth. That is the contention of the Jews today: they, the Jews collectively, are the Messiah for all nations, Judaism is the salvation of the world. Isaiah's *Ebed Yahweh,* Servant of Jehovah, is Jewry. The commentators do not, of course, have this in mind; they refer to Christ but associate him with the Jews as a nation. Not only is salvation of the Jews (John 4:22), it is still bound up with the Jews. Zahn writes "that the redemption of humanity depends on whether Israel after its errings will yet finally reach the goal of its destiny," i. e., in a final, national conversion. We, of course, cannot agree with such views.

26) **To you first God, having raised up his Servant, sent him blessing you in turning each one from your wickednesses.** After the strong ἡμεῖς at the head of v. 25 we now have the equally strong ὑμῖν at the head of this verse: "*you,*" what you are by reason of God's past grace — "*to you,*" what comes to you by means of God's present grace. Note the three great words placed together: "to you — first — God." "First" places Peter's hearers at the head of the vast host and the procession of "the families of the earth." They alone had the "Seed," the great "Servant" of Jehovah in their midst, παῖς as in v. 13. "Having raised him up" refers to the entire ministry and mission of Jesus as God's Servant and is thus construed with "sent him to you."

The present tense εὐλογοῦντα causes the grammarians some difficulty. R. 1116 and 1128 regards it as expressing purpose and assumes that the context makes this clear. Such a significance would seem to call for the future participle or the present infinitive. The present participle is descriptive of αὐτόν, "him," and is durative because he blesses continuously. Its present tense is without relation to the aorist of the main verb. Ἐν τῷ with the infinitive is a favorite usage of Luke's although it is Semitic (R. 1072). It is usually temporal, "while," but also has other meanings: *indem, dadurch dass* (B.-D. 404, 3). Here we translate, "By turning each one," etc. This is the turning of repentance as in v. 19. The supreme blessing for any sinner is that Christ turn him "from his wickednesses."

Ἀποστρέφειν is regarded as intransitive by B.-D. 308: "in that each one turn from your wickedness." But this gives the sentence the unsatisfactory sense: Christ blesses when each one turns. The infinitive is transitive: Christ blesses by turning each one. Peter individualizes, for conversion is a personal matter; Christ turns us, but so that we ourselves turn, Jer. 31:18. Peter is using Old Testament phraseology when he speaks of turning from wickedness; note Ezek. 3:19; 18:27; 33:14; Jonah 3:10. With πονερά Peter uses no soft words; it is "wickednesses" in the sense of *Bosheiten, Schurkerei,* active and vicious evil. The plural leads us to think of all the fruits of unbelief. To turn from them means to turn to Christ in a new life. At this point Peter is interrupted by some of the very wickedness against which he was warning. Yet he had said enough to bring a host of his hearers to faith.

CHAPTER IV

Peter and John Before the Sanhedrin

1) News of what had occurred (the healing) and of what was now occurring (the preaching) reached the Sadducees, and they at once interfere with strong measures. **Now while they were speaking to the people, there suddenly stood by them the priests and the commander of the Temple and the Sadducees, thoroughly vexed because they were teaching the people and proclaiming in connection with Jesus the resurrection from the dead. And they laid hands on them and put them in ward for the morrow; for it was already evening.**

Peter did the speaking. "They speaking" means that he acted also for John. The address was just about completed. Before anything further could happen such as happened in 2:37, the authorities swoop down on the scene and arrest Peter, John, and the beggar. The verb denotes sudden, unexpected appearance and is used with reference to the sudden standing of angels beside someone. So absorbed was everyone that the approach of the authorities was not noticed.

Luke names in order: "the priests, the commander of the Temple, and the Sadducees." But this mention of "the priests" in the first place, and the fact that they were few, in no way debars us from thinking that they were the ones who had charge of the service on this afternoon. Their authority was less than that of the commander and of the Sadducees: To think of these "priests" as priest police, and to assume that there were two kinds of police: one that was composed of priests and another of Levites, on no stronger evidence than the appearance of ἱερεῖς in first place in this passage of Acts, is venturesome thinking. These were the regular priests, one of the twenty-four groups that had been selected by lot, whose time of service had been appointed for this day. Somebody had reported to them, and they, in turn, had informed the higher authorities, and so it came about that they were present with these authorities.

"The commander of the Temple" called the *sagan*, was at the head of the entire police force of the Temple which was composed of Levites. In the story of the arrest of Jesus these Levite police are called ὑπηρέται, "underlings"; they went about armed with clubs. Luke uses the plural στρατηγοί (Luke 22:4), from which we conclude that the commander had several lieutenants under him. The chief commander, Zahn claims, ranked next to the high priest, but that he, too, was a priest we decline to believe unless convincing evidence is furnished. Josephus mentions the commander in *Ant.* 20, 6, 2; *Wars*, 6, 5, 3. On an errand such as this present one this commander would not appear without a detachment of Levitical police. That is so self-evident that Luke does not need to mention these "underlings" when he names the authorities that appeared.

"The Sadducees" were members of the Sanhedrin, such as happened to be at hand when Peter addressed the people. They are the persons that instigated the arrest. This Jewish sect rejected the mass of oral tradition taught by the popular schools, claimed that this life was the whole of existence, that there are neither angels nor spirits, and that there is no resurrection of the dead. Although they were few in number, the Sadducees wielded a tremendous influence because they commanded wealth and social position and because the family of the high priest and a number of other priests belonged to their group. "The doctrine of the

Sadducees is this, that souls die with the bodies; nor do they regard the observation of anything besides what the law enjoins them; for they think it is an instance of virtue to dispute with these teachers of philosophy whom they frequent. But this doctrine is received but by a few, yet by those still of the greatest dignity," Josephus, *Ant.* 18, 1, 4. They were the aristocrats, the freethinkers and skeptics among the Jews. They were coarse in manners and lived in Epicurean luxuriousness.

2) What brought them to the scene was the fact that they were "thoroughly vexed" because Peter and John were teaching the people and proclaiming the very doctrine they were opposing, and were doing this ἐν τῷ Ἰησοῦ, "in connection with Jesus," namely by proclaiming that Jesus was risen and by furnishing as evidence of his living power the miracle wrought on the lame beggar. Peter had not yet preached the general resurrection, but these Sadducees drew the correct conclusion that, if Jesus was risen, their whole contention about the impossibility of the resurrection was null and void. Jesus had already answered them, Matt. 22:23-33, but his answer had left them obdurate. Now, when right here in the Temple, under their very eyes, the resurrection was being taught "in connection with Jesus" whom they had brought to the cross, they rise up in their might to decree a summary stop. Note that Luke adds ἐκ νεκρῶν with a second article so that this phrase receives the emphasis (R. 776): "the resurrection, that (namely) from the dead." The dead, no, they cannot arise! On the phrase itself see 3:16.

3) Luke's account is summary. Whether any charges were preferred, whether an altercation ensued, whether the people took the matter quietly, is not said. He states only that these authorities made short work of it, arrested and locked up Peter and John and the beggar. The Greek has the expressive phrase, "they

threw their hands on them," meaning, of course, that not the authorities themselves did this but their "underlings" at their command; so in 3:15 Peter said to all the people, "You killed the Author of life." Strong men took them by the arms and hurried them away.

Τήρησις is "custody," "ward," "imprisonment." Zahn has located the place of confinement on the basis of statements found in the Mishna and places it in one of the vaulted halls above a certain portal; but all we can say is that the place was not the same as that mentioned in 5:18. Evening had come, not, indeed, sunset but late afternoon. Thus it was too late to summon a session of the Sanhedrin in the hope of having it take care of the business on hand. The Jewish law forbade trials at night, a law that was most flagrantly violated in the case of Jesus but was here observed.

4) **But many of those that heard the Word believed; and there came to be a number of men about five thousand.** The aorists are historical and register only the facts. Peter's success was phenomenal. This is a fine example of apostolic evangelization. But remember that these were Jews who knew their Scriptures and not Gentiles or people to whom the true religion is still unknown. Even these Jews needed further instruction, 2:40. The apostles always laid a thorough foundation. Note that "they heard the Word," Rom. 10:17. Thus early "the Word" signified the sum of the apostolic doctrine; in 2:42 it is called "the teaching" or "the doctrine."

Luke says that the entire number of believers in Jerusalem increased from over 3,000 souls (2:41) to 5,000 men, not counting women and children of whom there was, of course, a due proportion. A count must have been made so that Luke could obtain this figure. It was too difficult to count all the souls, at least Luke could obtain only the figure he here recorded. He might have made an estimate of the souls. But his aim is accuracy with no intention of making the figure as large as possible.

5) **Now it came to pass on the morrow that there were brought together their rulers, and the elders and the scribes in Jerusalem and Annas, the high priest, and Caiaphas and John and Alexander and as many as were of high-priestly kindred.**

Luke's Hebraistic ἐγένετο may be followed by καί and a finite verb, by a simple finite verb, or, as here, by the accusative with the infinitive as the subject. The Sanhedrin was brought together by a summoning of its members. Only those "in Jerusalem" were summoned and not those living in country places outside of the city. The phrase modifies the nouns. The Sanhedrin is often designated by naming only two of its constituent groups; a little more impressive is the naming of all three: "the high priests, the elders, and the scribes." Here Luke refers to the high priests in a special way (v. 6) and thus varies the designation by calling the first group οἱ ἄρχοντες, "the rulers." He surely has in mind the group that is otherwise called by the general term "the high priests." "Rulers" befits them in a special way since they had the leadership in the Sanhedrin, Caiaphas being the presiding officer who had the executive power in his hands. There is no reason for including lay rulers who were not priests in this first group. These were classed as "the elders." They were important laymen who had been elevated to a position in the Sanhedrin because of their standing and their experience in judicial matters. The scribes were the rabbis, graduates of the schools, who were chosen because of special ability in interpreting the Tora, i. e., the Law, the Old Testament. All or nearly all of them were Pharisees as were also the elders. The entire number that made up the Sanhedrin was 70 or

72 although not all members were needed for transacting business.

6) Καί particularizes by naming four of them individually and by summarizing the rest of this special high-priestly group. This is an exceptional construction in Luke's writings but becomes almost necessary after the statement in v. 1 that "the Sadducees" had brought about the arrest; v. 6 tells us who the chief Sadducees were, namely all those of high-priestly connection.

Here, as elsewhere, Annas is mentioned as being especially important. He is named first because of his age; Caiaphas was his son-in-law. Annas had been high priest from the year 6 to the year 15. Then several other high priests followed in quick succession. After these Caiaphas held the office from 18-36. Having been high priest, this title was still accorded to Annas, no doubt also because he continued to wield great influence personally and through his family. His son Eleazar had been high priest after him, his son-in-law now held this office, four other sons attained the high priesthood at a later time (Josephus, *Ant.* 20, 9, 1), so that a regular dynasty of the house of Annas was established. The name Annas was common, hence an addition was needed to mark the Annas here referred to. He also had a son by the name of Annas. Caiaphas was a rare name; we know of only this one individual who bore it; hence no further distinctive mark was needed. The Talmud also laid down the principle, that one might promote an individual to a sacred office but not demote him. This idea may well have been operative already at this time when the Romans interfered with the high priesthood so that the office was no longer held for life.

We really know nothing definite about John and Alexander. Zahn identifies John with Jonathan, the son of Annas, high priest after Caiaphas in 36, who was soon replaced by his brother Theophilus, was offered the same office again but declined in favor of his brother Matthias, and was finally murdered in the Temple by bandits. When Luke wrote, all this was history (recorded by Josephus), and this circumstance would explain why "John" is placed third by Luke, if he is, indeed, this Jonathan and son of Annas. All that can be said about Alexander is this, the fact that a Sadducee bearing such a name reveals the foreign influences at work among the sect.

Luke mentions still others who belonged to the high-priestly γένος, "kindred," which some take in a wide sense as referring to relatives of former high priests, but which seems to refer to relatives of the present high-priestly family. These, Luke suggests, were the real leaders of the Sanhedrin, all of them Sadducees, all of them foes of the resurrection and of any preaching about Jesus as having risen from the dead. These most powerful judges, whose verdict was absolutely determined in advance, the two former fishermen from Galilee had now to face.

7) **And having stood them in the midst, they began to question, In connection with what power, or in connection with what name did you do this thing?** The judges sat cross-legged in a half-circle on a raised platform. Temple police brought in Peter, John, and the beggar. They were compelled to stand on the lower floor "in the midst," the judges facing them from all sides. This was the exact manner in which and the exact place where Jesus had stood when facing this court. What memories, what anticipations must have crowded into the apostles' minds! Caiaphas must have presided as he had done when Jesus was tried. But no crime is charged against them, no row of witnesses confronts the disciples. This is only a judicial investigation; the apostles are asked to make a statement regarding themselves. All present know

what that statement will be, one that gravely incriminates themselves together with this court, most especially with its dominating members, the high-priestly Sadducean connection. The imperfect "they began to question" is descriptive and at the same time holds us in suspense as to what the answer will be.

The English cannot reproduce the pointed τοῦτο ὑμεῖς at the end of the question: "this thing — *you*," fellows like you. The pronoun has an emphasis of scorn. "This thing" declines to describe it in any way, for that would bring into prominence the greatness and the beneficence of the deed of the apostles. Not *what* they had done is asked about, for who could condemn the restoration of a congenital cripple; the *way* they had done what they had done, the *means* by which they had done it, are assailed. Sometimes ποῖος is qualitative, sometimes it is not (R. 740). We may here render: "In connection with what kind of power, or in connection with what kind of name?" The Sanhedrists know that the apostles will be compelled to say that the power and the name have reference to Jesus. Now also the Jewish exorcists claimed to do wonderful things by using the formulas of their day, the names of the patriarchs or the name of Solomon, and this procedure was considered proper and orthodox. The question thus implies that, if some other power and especially some other name was used by the apostles, they lay themselves open to the most serious charge. Jesus of Nazareth was regarded as a rank blasphemer in the eyes of the Sanhedrin because he had called himself the Son of God. To use his power and his name for healing, no matter what the blessed result, was using the power and the name that were as blasphemous as this blasphemer himself.

The question with its repeated and thus emphatic "what kind of" is shrewd; it is like a noose thrown around the necks of the apostles. The end certainly does *not* justify the means. Damnable means dare not be used even if, through them, good or apparent good is done. That is the point of the double question. The Sadducees could not, of course, unlike the Pharisees in the Sanhedrin, claim that Beelzebul was the source of Jesus' power and name, for they denied the existence of angels and of spirits. Yet Josephus, *Ant.* 18, 1, 4, informs us that they were base enough, when it served their purpose, to "addict themselves to the notions of the Pharisees because the multitude would otherwise not hear them." The question is here put in a shrewd way so as to gain the support also of all the Pharisees who had their own view of the wickedness of Jesus' power and name. Note that here and in 2:38 and in Peter's answer ἐν ποίῳ ὀνόματι means "in connection with" what name?

8) **Then Peter, filled with the Holy Spirit, said to them: Rulers of the people and elders, if we on our part this day are judicially examined on a good deed to an impotent man, in connection with what this man has been saved, let it be known to you all and to all the people of Israel that in connection with the name of Jesus Christ, the Nazarene, whom you crucified, whom God raised up from the dead, in connection with this One does this man stand here before you whole.**

Peter again speaks for himself and also for John. It was not necessary to state explicitly that on Pentecost Peter was filled with the Holy Spirit when he preached as he did; nor was there need to state that he spoke by the Spirit to the multitude before Solomon's Porch. But here this fact must be noted because it is the first fulfillment of the Lord's promise given in Matt. 10:19, 20. Peter's wonderful defense is not to be credited to his keen powers and his great courage. He and John had not lain awake all night planning what to say. They had not even known what turn things would take. It is the Holy Spirit who puts this telling defense into Peter's mouth. Peter merely uses a shorter formula when he names only the rulers and the elders when addressing the Sanhedrin. Both are most honorable terms; in fact, either could be used alone as a designation of the entire court. Like Jesus, the apostles acknowledge and submit to the authority of the Sanhedrin. Peter used even the most respectful form of address.

9) In the conditional form of the answer: "if we this day," etc., there lies a fine intimation that no just grounds exist for instituting the examination now being made. The emphatic ἡμεῖς, "we on our part," takes up in a dignified way the emphatic and scornful ὑμεῖς of the question. The verb ἀνακρίνω is used in a forensic sense to indicate a preliminary judicial examination on the result of which further legal action may depend. Peter thus tells the Sanhedrin what it is doing; its president had failed to do so. The latter had used only τοῦτο, "this thing," in his question of examination; Peter is proud to state what "this thing" really is because of which he and John are being subjected to judicial probing: "a good deed to an impotent man" (the objective genitive, R. 500). The articles are purposely omitted in order to emphasize the quality of the terms and to generalize the phrase. Any good deed done to any helpless man, a restoration of such a man, speaks for itself. Not only this good deed but any and all like it ought to be beyond criminal suspicion and inquiry by any court. The Sanhedrin should investigate crimes and not good deeds. Yet if this high court must know "in connection with what this man (pointing to the beggar) has been saved (and thus now stands before them as saved," Peter is certainly ready to furnish the fullest information, and this high court may then decree whether any criminality attaches to the means used for the man's wonder-

ful restoration. Ἐν τίνι is neuter because it includes both "power" and "name" in the question; the R. V.'s marginal translation "in whom" is inexact. All five ἐν, beginning with those in the question, are identical in force and mean neither "through," "by," nor "in," but, "in connection with," which is the original sense of this preposition. This sense also gives it so wide a range. Sphere illustrates its idea, for ἐν draws a circle around two concepts.

10) We have noted Peter's tone of authority in 2:14, 36; here it appears again and is expressed with the same imperative: "let it be known to you and to all the people of Israel." So little is there to hide that Peter courts the utmost publicity and would have the world of Judaism know the exact facts regarding this beggar's restoration. The Sanhedrin wants the name stated that is involved in this miracle; triumphantly Peter complies: it is "in connection with the name of Jesus Christ, the Nazarene," that this man stands here before their very eyes ὑγιής, sound, whole, no longer crippled. By naming this name Peter does not need to specify the power in regard to which he also had been asked. All Palestine knew about that power because of the miracles which Jesus himself had wrought.

The old view is still held that in these "name" phrases ὄνομα means "authority," R. 649, or that the phrase is a mere circumlocution. It is, of course, the Hebrew *b^e^schem*, B.-D. 206, 3; but in these phrases and in other connections NAME always denotes revelation; see the discussion in 2:21, 38; 3:6. We believe "in or on the name." The name is inserted before the person as making him known to us, as the means for apprehending him, of connecting ourselves with him. Note the resumptive ἐν τούτῳ in this verse: "in connection with this One" as named and revealed. "Nazarene" is repeatedly used to identify Jesus in the popular way (2:22); and, as in 2:38, "Jesus Christ" designates him as the Messiah (2:36, "Lord and Christ").

The two relative clauses name Jesus as Christ more fully, and the asyndeton makes them the more striking by presenting clashing opposites: "whom *you* crucified, whom *God* raised up from the dead." Here we have the same bold contrast we noticed in 2:23, 24; 3:14, 15, which appeals to the conscience when the divine law reveals the sin. Here again God is shown as nullifying what the Sanhedrin had done. It had intended to abolish Jesus forever, God raised him up and established him forever. Here Peter does not add as he did in 2:32; 3:15: "of which we are witnesses." Their testimony regarding the resurrection of Jesus would be scorned by the Sanhedrists. Peter points to the testimony that even these vicious haters of Jesus cannot deny, namely the healed beggar standing there before their eyes: "in connection with this One," whose name and revelation he has just presented, "this man stands here before you whole." The perfect παρέστηκεν is always used as a present, and παρά, "stands beside," means, "stands here."

Peter says this to men like Annas and Caiaphas here in the midst of their Sadducean following. The whole Sanhedrin had tried to hush up the resurrection of Jesus, Matt. 28:11-15. Here it faced them with even stronger evidence than that which the Roman guard brought from the tomb. No dead Jesus could work a miracle such as this; the risen and glorified Jesus alone could do that. So Jesus had healed when he was alive; lo, so he had healed now after this Sanhedrin had crucified him!

11) Why did Caiaphas and those Sadducees not leap up and denounce Peter in blazing wrath? Did the truth thrown into their faces, hurled at their consciences with such unexpected power dumbfound them

for the moment? Peter continues: **This One is the stone, the one considered as nothing by you, the ones building, the one become corner head. And the salvation is in connection with not a single other; for there is not another name under heaven as having been given among men in connection with which we must be saved.**

Peter was not defending himself and John. There was nothing against which to make a defense. He is doing his part of witnessing (1:8), preaching Jesus Christ to these Sanhedrists as to any other sinners through law and gospel. What this court would do with him and with John mattered not at all; his one concern was to glorify Jesus as the Savior, and in this the Holy Spirit directed his words In his witness he uses Ps. 118:22, yet not as a quotation but in order to recall to the Sanhedrists what Jesus himself had told them on the basis of this psalm in Matt. 21:42-44. Jesus had warned them that this prophecy would be fulfilled; Peter points out that it has now been fulfilled, both parts of it, viz., what they had done, and what God had done. But he centers attention on Jesus, on the unbelief of the Sanhedrists in rejecting him, and on the deed of God in making him the Savior.

"This One" is resumptive and repeats all that Peter has said about Jesus. The article with the predicate "the stone" makes it identical and interchangeable with the subject, R. 769. The figure refers to the spiritual temple of God. In their office as spiritual leaders of the Jewish nation God had appointed these Sanhedrists builders of this temple. How they would function as builders the psalmist had foretold, and Peter now repeats the thought of the psalmist in connection with this stone, Jesus Christ, "the one considered as nothing" by them, unfit to be used anywhere in a building such as they proposed. They rejected Jesus and crucified him. But this very stone is "the one become corner head," the one supreme stone which, laid at the head corner, governs every other corner and every angle in the entire spiritual temple and thus determines the angle at which every other stone is to be laid. How Jesus became this wonderful stone Peter has already stated, namely by God's raising Jesus from the dead. Note that εἰς is predicative: *geworden zum Eckstein*, Hebrew, *le*, R. 481. "Corner head" is without articles and thus stresses the concepts themselves; it is almost a compound.

Sometimes Christ is viewed as the entire foundation (I Cor. 3:11), then again as the cornerstone, as distinct from the foundation (Eph. 2:20). The latter is not the former. Peter loved this passage about the cornerstone (I Pet. 2:4, etc.), for his own name Peter (rock) always reminded him of this Stone. Will these blind Sanhedrists at last see their terrible sin and repent?

12) In plain, literal language Peter presents the fulness of the gospel with its mighty call to salvation. The Greek may or may not use the article with an abstract noun, so that here ἡ σωτηρία is usually translated "salvation," *Heil* (Luther); yet here the article specifies. Peter means "the salvation," that promised in the Messiah. It is this salvation that exists "in connection with not a single other"; ἐν is used like the five ἐν in v. 7 and 10. No second, no substitute, no alternate to Jesus exists so that by connecting with (ἐν) this other we could secure salvation. The noun "salvation," to which the verb "be saved" is added, denotes the act of deliverance plus the resultant state of safety; both are wrought by the Σωτήρ, Savior; see the participle in 2:47. Peter uses the same verb when speaking of the deliverance of the beggar in v. 9, just as Jesus, too, had used it in the case of persons healed in Luke 8:48; 18:42; and with reference to the deliverance from sin in Luke 7:50. The word can be used in

either sense, but here, where Peter speaks of the supreme work of the Messiah Jesus, salvation and saving are to be taken in the spiritual sense.

With γάρ Peter explains by restating more fully and explicitly what he had said. Because of γάρ, οὐδέ cannot mean "neither," this is true also because no other οὐδέ follows. The entire previous sentence is expanded. Elucidating and fuller restatements are generally introduced with explanatory γάρ. Instead of "not a single other" (person) Peter says, "not another name under heaven as having been given among men." Here he again uses "name" as he did in v. 10 and as he used it with such emphasis in 3:16, there adding the correlative "faith" with equal emphasis; see the remarks on that passage.

Name" is again the revelation by which the saving person becomes the possession of the person to be saved. It is the objective means of saving and implies faith in that name or revelation as the subjective means. Jesus comes to us by means of his name; that name awakens faith; and by faith in his name he saves us. Ἄλλος and ἕτερος are often used without a special difference in meaning; and R. 749 thinks that here the latter means only no "other at all." This absoluteness, however, lies in the added phrase "under heaven" and not in ἕτερον itself. We are certainly entitled to retain the difference here; "not a single other" who is in any way *like* and comparable to Jesus brings us salvation; and, excluding the other possibility, "not another name under heaven" that is *different* from his and works on us in a different way.

Instead of a relative clause we have the articulated perfect participle, articulated because otherwise the participle would be combined with ἐστίν and form a periphrastic perfect verb form. This participle adds the very important thought that, to do us any good, the "name" must be given to us, namely by God or by

Christ. Only of a name thus given among men is Peter speaking, any other name would reveal and convey nothing to us. Names are intended as distinctions by which others know us, and the better they know us, the better they can trust us. The perfect participle "having been given among men" implies that, once given, the name remains as our means of salvation.

And here again is universality: "among men," paralleling "on all flesh" in 2:17, and "to those afar off" in 2:39. The name has been given "among men" in order to attract and to draw them with its saving power: "in connection with which we must be saved," ἐν is for the sixth time used in the same sense. This "we" is not a retraction of "among men," not a limitation of the universality. It appeals to Peter's hearers and joins him with them; for he is not offering an academic or abstract proposition which one might debate and regarding which one might hold different opinions but an absolute fact of necessity on which hangs eternal salvation or eternal destruction. Since "to be saved" includes the act plus the condition, Peter can freely include the apostles with the Sanhedrin; the infinitive is constative. The necessity implied in δεῖ is that of the fact: Since salvation is possible only in connection with Jesus, all who desire to be saved *must* embrace his name.

13) **Now, beholding the boldness of Peter and John and having perceived that they were people uneducated and ordinary, they were marvelling, also they were recognizing them, that they had been with Jesus. Seeing also the man standing with them, the one having been healed, they had nothing to say to the contrary.**

The imperfect tenses are descriptive of the situation of the Sanhedrists. Two things made them marvel: the παρρησία of the apostles, the free, assured way in which they bore themselves and spoke, and yet the fact that they were "uneducated," never having attended a rabbinical school, and besides that they were ἰδιῶται, ordinary, common people who had nothing but their own little personal affairs to which to attend. They held no public office of any kind that might give them some training. They understood that the apostles had neither the advantage of rabbinical schooling nor that offered by any other kind of prominence. Associated with this was their recognition of the fact that they had been with Jesus, and that this experience in some way accounted for the effective way in which they spoke and acted. Many, no doubt, had seen these two apostles with Jesus during the Passover week, then, however, paying little attention to them. The Greek retains the tenses of the direct discourse when it expresses what one perceives and recognizes, hence εἰσί and also ἦσαν; the thought of the Sanhedrists was: "they are uneducated" — "they *were* with Jesus."

14) Associated with all this they saw standing beside the apostles the man that had been healed, whom, of course, they had for a long time known as the most hopeless cripple but who was now standing on his feet completely healed — eloquent attestation of every word Peter had spoken. All of this was too much. They were checkmated, "they had nothing to say to the contrary," there just was nothing that they could say. Note how the two τε used in these verses bind the three statements into one compact whole.

Here we have a shining exemplification of the manner in which the Holy Spirit conducts the cases of persecuted disciples. Even the Sanhedrists perceived that a power was sustaining Peter and John. The point to be noted, however, is not the fact that the apostles escaped but that, irrespective of this, they so perfectly maintained the cause of Christ and the gospel. The very judges who compelled them to appear were converted into an audience for the apostles' preaching, and they preached to this audience without the least timidity or restraint and with all power and effectiveness. Such scenes occur throughout the Acts; in this way the gospel reached out to the highest authorities to win rulers, governors, kings for Christ.

15) **But having ordered them to go outside of the council chamber, they conferred with each other, saying: What shall we do to these men? for that a known sign has occurred through them is manifest to all those inhabiting Jerusalem, and we are not able to make denial. But in order that it may not spread farther to the people, let us threaten them no longer to speak on the basis of this name to any man.**

This was a painful situation. The Sadducees, who had caused the arrest, had not expected to find themselves at such a disadvantage. Nothing is left to them but to order the prisoners to step outside and to confer in private. Here συνέδριον designates the hall where the session was held, where the judges "sat together"; the word is also used to designate the Sanhedrin itself. The Greek is picturesque: "they threw together" (words, λόγοι), R. 1202, and thus conferred in private, each giving his opinion. We need not ask how Luke obtained the results of this conference, for since so many were conferring, it was impossible to keep things secret.

16) Luke reports only the gist of what was said and decided. "What shall we do to these men?" is a question of deliberation and doubt, hence the subjunctive is employed. Having arrested these men, they felt that they must do something to them; but what could they do? The honest thing to do was to acknowledge their wrong in having made the arrest; yea, to admit their crime in crucifying Jesus, to repent, and to accept him as the Christ. But their very question implies that these things they will *not do*. They must in some

way maintain their opposition, the only question being in what way.

They admit that they cannot deny the reality of the "sign" wrought through the apostles. It is a "known sign" and by this time "manifest to all those inhabiting Jerusalem." The crowds that saw the healed beggar and heard Peter's address in the Temple court spread the news over all the city; the Sanhedrists admit this to each other. With φανερόν supply the copula ἐστί.

This is the blindness of unbelief. The fact that a known and notable sign has occurred, a sign that signified something, one that had been wrought "through the apostles," they being only the medium (διά) of a higher power, means absolutely nothing to these Sanhedrists personally. They would deny the miracle if they could; the only thing that prevents such a denial is the fact that it is already known throughout the city. This to their great regret. We see how old the motives and the policies of unbelief are. The circumstance that facts are facts and signs are signs means nothing; deny them, get rid of them in some way; it is deplorable that they should be known at all, and they must be kept from becoming better known lest still more people believe them.

17) Ἀλλά corresponds to μέν in v. 16. The only thing left to be done under the painful circumstances is to take effective measures to prevent the further spread of the knowledge of this sign "to the people" (εἰς, not. "among"). The Sanhedrists agree that proper threatening will accomplish this; yet we must remember that they were sorely perplexed to find anything they might do. The subjunctive is hortative: "let us threaten them," aorist to express the one act. They have in mind a threatening command "no longer to speak on the basis of this name to any man." Note λαλεῖν; not "to make utterance" is to keep still. The

apostles are not to mention "this name" nor anything depending "on this name," no matter what it may be. The Sanhedrin intends to muzzle the apostles completely. The phrase "on the name" has the same force as "in the name," the preposition varying only the relation by using the idea of basis instead of that of connection. "Name," however, has the same meaning it had in v. 7, 10, 12; compare 3:16; and the previous passages 2:21, 38; 3:6. They purposely say "this name" without mentioning "Jesus." It has been well said: *sie wollten ihn totschweigen.* (They would kill him by silence.) This significant aversion to pronouncing even the name still exists to this day.

18) **And having called them, they passed the order all through not to make a sound and not to teach on the basis of the name of Jesus.** The threat was implied. To disobey a strict order of the supreme Jewish court was at that time a more serious thing than contempt of court is now. The order is summary and permits no exception of any kind. "All through" is to be construed with both infinitives, but τό modifies only the compound adverb καθόλου by regarding this as an adverbial accusative. The present infinitives are linear and refer to all time to come. They are not even "to make a sound," *etwas verlauten lassen,* on the basis of the name of Jesus. This includes the teaching, but that is also specified because the apostles had been teaching.

"Jesus" is here added, and the usual explanation given is that the Sanhedrin was compelled to mention this name when issuing its order; yet these are Luke's own words, and there is no evidence that "Jesus" was even here uttered by the Sanhedrists. One cannot be sure that they did so. Thus the apostles were no longer to be apostles, the witnesses (1:8; 2:32; 3:15) were no longer to testify. The Sanhedrin nullifies the order and the appointment of Jesus. The whole work of the gospel is to be nipped in the bud.

19, 20) **But Peter and John, making answer to them, said: Whether it is right in the sight of God to hearken to you rather than to God, judge ye; for not able are we on our part not to utter what things we saw and heard.**

The circumstantial participle (aorist of simultaneous action), "making answer to them," intends to mark the importance of the answer to this court order. The answer is very brief but perfect. No man could have given a better one. Peter and John act as a unit. The perfection of the answer lies in the turning of the question at issue back upon the judgment of the Sanhedrin itself; in the formulating of that question in the simple way in which it ought alone to be formulated; and then in the giving of the only answer the apostles on their part are able to make. The whole answer is designed so as to focus on the real issue and to cut off any opportunity to quibble about irrelevant points. The Holy Spirit prompted this answer even as to its wording.

From the Jewish supreme court the apostles appeal to God's own court, to which even the Sanhedrin was amenable: "whether it is right in the sight of God." As the highest religious court of the nation the Sanhedrin itself was always assembled as being in the very sight of God, and its every act was to have the full sanction and approval of God. Peter struck home when he said "in the sight of God." The forensic point in the words employed by the apostles should not be overlooked, for both δίκαιον and ἐνώπιον τοῦ Θεοῦ refer to God as the Judge who pronounces what is δίκαιον, "just," "righteous," in harmony with the divine δίκη or norm of right. The one thing the Sanhedrists need to dread is that the divine Judge should pronounce an action of theirs unjust, contrary to his norm of right.

So the alternative before the apostles is, "whether to hearken *unto you* rather than *unto God,*" or negatively, "whether to disobey men rather than God." "Judge ye" means that, as far as the apostles are concerned, the alternative is decided, and they are ready to abide by the consequences. Elucidative γάρ explains that their position has been taken: "not able are we not to utter what things we saw and heard." This is a litotes which puts negatively what is intended very positively, namely that they are bound to utter these things. The οὐ and the μή cancel each other, B.-D. 431, 1. The inability of the apostles to remain silent about all that they have seen and heard (the Greek uses aorists to express the facts, the English prefers perfects to express the relative time of the facts) of Jesus is moral, spiritual, due to the compulsion of conscience. In the four Gospels we have a survey of what the apostles saw and heard. The emphasis is strongly on ἡμεῖς, both because it is written out and because of its position, verb and subject are reversed: "unable are we," stressing both. The Sanhedrin may judge for itself, what the apostles judge they here declare. Where God is involved, every man must judge for himself, and he is entitled to do so.

There was not a moment's hesitation, not the least trace of fear, but complete outspokenness. The apostles do not leave the impression that they may possibly obey while in their hearts they resolve not to obey; nor do they evade the issue by saying that they will think the matter over. They face the issue like men, squarely, openly.

Compare 5:29. No wonder Luke devotes so much space (chapters three to five) to the events which evoked these declarations that are of the highest moral import regarding human and divine authority. In John 7:48, 49 this very Sanhedrin operated with the directly opposite principle, a principle which now receives its supreme challenge. All human authority must yield to divine authority. It is, indeed, a divine command that we obey the government (Rom. 13:1), but this obedience is never absolute. When the government or any human authority commands what is contrary to God, we are bound to obey God alone. The first members of the church who suffered for this principle were the Twelve, cf., 5:40; the history of all the martyrdoms that followed extends from that time until the present. Tears and blood have ever anew sealed this great principle in this wicked world.

Some individuals have gone too far by having this principle justify rebellion and revolution. The apostles offered only passive resistance and not the sword. Like them, we may use all legitimate means to change the wrong demands made on us, but beyond that we suffer in patience any infliction that may result. It is this great principle that makes for the separation of church and state, that keeps each out of the domain of the other. This is the principle underlying true civil and religious liberty and the liberty of conscience. Endless are the means by which this principle is assailed, endless the efforts of human authority to supersede the divine. The author has treated the entire subject in *Kings and Priests,* see especially pp. 101, 104, 116.

21) **But they, having made further threats, released them, finding nothing as to how they should punish them on account of the people, because all were glorifying God for what had occurred. For the man was of more than forty years on whom this sign of the healing had occurred.**

So the whole proceeding ended in failure. Luke adds the reason that the Sanhedrists found nothing chargeable: "on account, or in consideration, of the people." They dreaded the effect which harsher methods might have on the people, for these glorified

God because of what had occurred. The insincerity and the inner dishonesty of the Sanhedrin is in glaring contrast with the openness of the apostles. Chrysostom has a fine passage in which he compares the two: the Sanhedrists at a loss, the apostles joyful; they afraid to say what they think, these speaking out openly; they dreading to have the report spread, these unable not to say what they saw and heard; they not doing what they wanted, these declaring what they wanted. He ends by asking, "Who, then, were in bonds and in dangers?" The article before the indirect question of deliberation with πῶς merely substantivizes it as being the object of the participle, R. 766.

22) It may well be possible that as a medical man Luke adds the notable detail of the man's age although one need not be a doctor in order to be impressed by this feature of the miracle. The people, no doubt, remarked about the beggar's age when they told the story of his instantaneous healing. With πλείων (and ἐλάσσων) ἤ, "than," is omitted when these occur before numbers, B.-D., 185, 4. The perfect participle is proper in the phrase in v. 21; "what has occurred," which states the viewpoint of those praising God; here, in the relative clause, the past perfect states the standpoint of the reader. The genitive "of the healing" is appositional to "this sign," R. 498.

The Prayer of the Apostles

23) Luke adds the sequel, which incidentally gives us an insight into the prayer life of the apostles. **Now, having been released, they came to their own and reported what all the high priests and the elders said to them.**

There is a question as to who are referred to by "their own?" Many interpreters answer, "The believers." But in v. 31 we learn that *all* were filled with the Holy Spirit and continued to utter the Word of God;

and in v. 32, we read of the multitude of those that believed. And this multitude, no doubt, includes more than the "all" of v. 31. Nor did "all" mentioned in this verse preach the Word. Peter and John came to their fellow apostles; if a few other persons were present, they are not considered in Luke's narrative. The Sanhedrin is usually designated by naming only two of its classes as is done here where "the high priests and the elders" are named. And these are "their rulers and the elders" which were mentioned in v. 5. Stress is laid only on what these foes of Christ and the gospel "said" and not on what Peter and John replied, because the prayer that now follows deals with what these foes ordered, namely, the cessation of all preaching. The apostles pray that God may grant them the ability to go on preaching with boldness (v. 29).

24) **And they, on hearing it, with one accord lifted voice to God and said: Lord Almighty, thou art he that madest the heaven and the earth and the sea and all the things in them, the One that through thy servant David's mouth didst say:**

> **For what purpose did Gentiles snort,**
> **And people put care on empty things?**
> **The kings of the earth stood in array,**
> **And the rulers were gathered together**
> **Against the Lord and against his Anointed.**

For there were gathered of a truth in this city against thy holy Servant Jesus, whom thou didst anoint, both Herod and Pontius Pilate with Gentiles and peoples of Israel to do what all thy hand and thy counsel foreordained to occur.

Instead of launching words of indignation against the Sanhedrin and its unjust demands, the apostles automatically turn to God, the Omnipotent, lay the case before him, and ask him to enable them to resist those demands. A great critical moment has come: all their preaching and teaching must henceforth be done in open violation of the highest legal power and authority of their nation. They must, therefore, depend wholly upon the still higher power and authority of God. "They lifted up voice and said" certainly does not intend to exclude Peter and John. Here we again meet the significant adverb "with one accord." There was no coward among the apostles, no one wavered, all as one man resolved to disobey the Sanhedrin and to rely and to call upon God.

The view that the plural conveys the idea that all those present actually spoke the prayer aloud in unison is as untenable as to think that in v. 19 Peter and John spoke in unison. Some even state that this prayer had been composed and committed to memory some days before, and that it was a general prayer without special reference to what had just occurred. But this view is plainly contradicted by v. 29: "look upon their threats," which clearly refers to v. 17 and 21; and by v. 30: "while thou stretchest forth thy hand for healings," which certainly refers to the healing of the lame man on the previous afternoon. No; we discard such literalism. Luke evidently means that one of the apostles uttered the prayer, and that all the apostles lifted up their voice and spoke through his voice and his words. We pray in the same manner. The pastor's voice is the voice of the entire congregation speaking to God.

Δεσπότης is our "despot," one who rules with absolute and unrestricted power by his will alone, but the Greek word does not have the connotation of arbitrariness and tyranny which we associate with the word despot. In spite of Prov. 11:26 where the LXX used the term as a translation for *'Adon,* it is a question whether *'Adon* was the Aramaic word here employed. The word evidently refers to God's omnipotence, and we might translate it "Lord Almighty." When deciding between the A. V. which inserts the copula: "thou art (God is not in the text) he that made," etc., and the R. V. which omits the copula, we prefer the former. To make all that follows in v. 25, 26 an apposition results in an unwieldy anacoluthon. We then have an extended subject without the sign of a predicate, and the construction continues with a γάρ clause in v. 27. By inserting the copula a construction such as this is avoided. The omnipotent power of God is sketched by describing him as the Creator of heaven, earth, sea, and all things in them, and the mind dwells on each of these tremendously great created objects somewhat as in Neh. 9:6; Jer. 32:17; Rev. 14:7.

25) Although it is supported by four great uncials, the reading ὁ τοῦ πατρὸς ἡμῶν διὰ Πνεύματος Ἁγίου στόματος Δαυεὶδ παιδός σου εἰπών is unacceptable both as to form and to substance. It seems to be an old Jewish-Christian gloss that found its way into the text. Linguistically it is impossible to construe both the Holy Spirit and David after the one διά, to say nothing of the genitive "our father" which precedes this preposition; nor has anyone discovered why David should here be called not only God's servant but in addition "our father," the latter being placed forward for the sake of great emphasis. The A. V. renders in a sensible way, "Who by the mouth of thy servant David hast said," or more literally, "the One that through the mouth . . . didst say." Παῖς = "servant." It is so used with regard to Jesus in 3:13, 26; 4:27, 30. Διά, especially when it is used in connection with "mouth," describes Verbal Inspiration. R., *W. P.*, supposes that a second διά dropped out in the longer reading given above, but this still leaves that reading unacceptable.

The critics reject this apostolic testimony to the Davidic authorship of Ps. 2, and seek to find some other far later author. The testimony of the apostles is rejected although it is inspired (v. 31). Like the Sanhedrists, the critics still regard them as ἀγράμματοι καὶ ἰδιῶται, v. 13. The Old Testament has no superscription for this psalm, and the critics draw the conclusion that therefore David could not be the author of it and thereby ignore the old warning that it is dangerous to conclude anything *e silentio*. The fact that the psalm is nevertheless, ascribed to David is explained by some on the supposition that the term "psalm" was regarded as equivalent to "song of David" although this is contradicted by the fact that many psalms are ascribed to other writers.

We may well regard David himself as a type of Christ, so that the psalm refers to David's ascending the throne of Israel and maintaining that throne by the help of Jehovah in spite of all his enemies. But this is described in a way that is so grand and comprehensive that it plainly reaches out beyond David's person and extends to the Messiah whom David typified also in this respect. Meyer paraphrases the words of the psalm here quoted as follows: "Why do the Gentiles rage" against Jesus, namely the Romans, "and the peoples," Israel's tribes, "imagine vain things," such as they cannot successfully carry into effect, namely the destruction of Jesus? "The kings of the earth," represented by Herod, "set themselves in array" against Jesus, "and the rulers," with Pilate, "were gathered together" with the ἔθνη and λαοί "against the Lord," Jehovah who had sent Jesus, "and against his Anointed." This psalm, of course, goes beyond the opposition that was evident at the time of Jesus and the apostles and includes all opposition down to the end of time. The greatness of the psalm is evident from the fact that it is repeatedly quoted in the New Testament.

26) The ἔθνη, heathen and Gentiles, are paired with λαοί, the plural to denote the tribes of Israel (the

singular is regularly used as a designation of the people of Israel). The question introduced by ἱνατί is one in regard to purpose ("in order that what may occur?") and here inquires as to what possible sensible purpose the heathen could have in snorting against Jehovah and his Anointed. What end had they in view? This verb is used with reference to the snorting of horses and thus denotes the pride and the scorn of strength. These pagans rear, paw, and snort like wild stallions who show their power as though nothing could control them. What for? For nothing.

What is the end to be accomplished by these λαοί by bestowing care, thought, and diligence on things that are κενά, empty, without inner reality or substance? The senselessness manifested by devoting effort to things that are void and hollow ought to be apparent. The whole scheme of abolishing Christ is an empty dream, an insane delusion, and yet ceaseless effort is put forth to realize that dream. These two lines are full of divine scorn and irony.

The psalm advances to the kings and the rulers who stand at the head of their people, and in whom this opposition centers. Παρέστησαν, "stood by," is well rendered, "stood in array." They ranged themselves in line for battle. In the same way the rulers "were gathered together" (ἐπὶ τὸ αὐτό as in 1:16 and repeatedly) for the same opposition. Two great κατά phrases ("down against") state the focus of all this tremendous though vacuous hostility: "the Lord (*Yahweh*) and his Anointed (Χριστός, Luke 3:22)." They will not have this man to reign over them, Luke 19:14. And yet he will reign even over them, over all of them, if not in grace (which they scorn) then in judgment (which none can scorn), Ps. 2:9. It is one of those odd fancies that still find occasional favor (as in R., *W. P.*) that all present sang the lines of the psalm, and that Peter then applied them. Luke, however, records a prayer.

27) What the psalm depicted found one of its most notable fulfilments as to both Gentile and Jewish opposition in the death of Jesus. The conjunction γάρ frequently specifies by introducing an example; it is like our "for instance." Note that the verb "there were gathered" is repeated and put into the emphatic forward position. For the striking feature of the killing of Jesus was this very coalition of his foes, notably Herod and Pilate, who actually again became friends in this strange way. Who would have thought it possible? But it occurred "of a truth" — it actually did. And "in this city," the last place in the world where one would have thought it possible for Jews and pagans, a Jewish king and a pagan ruler, to combine against Jehovah and his Messiah.

Ἐπί, "on thy holy Servant Jesus," fits the idea of the trial to which Jesus was subjected. This monstrous and unholy alliance was directed as the psalm states, "against Jehovah's Anointed" who is fully designated in the prayer. "Servant," the great *'Ebed Yahweh,* is explained in 3:13. He is here significantly called "holy" in order to manifest how monstrous and damnable this combination against him was. "*Thy* holy Servant" shows how Jehovah was involved as the line of the psalm last quoted states. Instead of saying "Jesus Christ," the prayer expands, "Jesus whom thou didst anoint" and lays fuller stress on this point in the psalm and again shows that Jehovah is involved. It is enough to mention the king and the governor, for all the rest that were implicated in the murder of Jesus are included in the phrase "with Gentiles and peoples of Israel." Yes, "of Israel," a poignant genitive!

28) The purpose of this coalition is expressed, not from the viewpoint of Herod and of Pilate, but

from that of God. The enemies of Jesus did not assemble to do what God had foreordained but to carry out what their own wicked will intended; and yet they thereby carried out exactly what God had determined from eternity. Behind their violence in attempting to destroy Jesus there stood "thy hand," the power of God designated concretly and anthropomorphitically, and "thy counsel," the will and plan of God regarding Jesus, his Anointed, which through his very passion and death made him the Savior of the world.

The things these enemies did were κενά, "empty," as far as *their* purpose and intent were concerned; but in God's hand and counsel these vicious things were made to serve *his* purpose and intent. Neither God's hand nor his counsel compelled these enemies to make Jesus suffer and die; their own wickedness did that. But God's hand and counsel foreordained in all eternity that what they did should serve the divine purpose and end, defeat their purpose and accomplish his. It is thus that God rules in the midst of his enemies, and when they do their own wicked will most perfectly, they become mere tools for his high and blessed will. The depth of thought here so tersely expressed is the product only of divine revelation.

29) **And as to things now, Lord, look upon their threats and give to thy slaves with all boldness to go on uttering thy Word while thou stretchest out thy hand for healing and in order that signs and wonders may occur through the name of thy Servant Jesus.**

Acts alone has the form ταvῦν, "as to things now" or simply "now," here referring to the situation that has just developed. In regard to the threats of the Sanhedrin the apostles ask only that God "look upon" them, i.e., take them into account in what he does for the apostles. They do not ask for punishment of the Sanhedrin, nor that God should make its threats null and void; they do not ask for protection against the execution of these threats, nor for anything regarding their own person. All they plead for is the gift of boldly uttering the Word, irrespective of what the Sanhedrin may do. Peter and John had shown this boldness (v. 13), but the apostles realized that this consisted in more than just manly courage, that it was a spiritual virtue and thus a gift bestowed by God. The emphasis is on the phrase "with all boldness."

By calling themselves δοῦλοί σου they bow in humility before God but also state that they have no will but his, that they are wholly dependent on him and wholly bound to his service. The aorist is used in prayers because of the urgency and the intensity it expresses. As true apostles, men sent and commissioned, they merely "utter" the Word, λαλεῖν; it is laid upon their lips and is not the product of their own minds. And here again, as in v. 4, "the Word" is used in its comprehensive and specific sense as designating the gospel of Christ. If God will help them to keep sounding forth (durative infinitive) the Word, all will be well.

30) When they ask for signs, no second request is made, for these naturally accompany the apostolic Word as its seal even as Jesus had also promised; hence also there is no καί or coordination but only ἐν τῷ, Luke's favorite idiom, which certainly does not here indicate means (R. 1073) but has its usual force, "while." Here we have a plain statement by the apostles themselves that a miracle is wrought only when God wills "to stretch out his hand" in omnipotent power. In every case (as noted when explaining 3:4) the apostles waited until God bade them act; they never depended merely on their own judgment. "For healing" is a special reference to the miracle performed upon the lame beggar.

"Signs and wonders" include all miracles of every kind such as the Lord's hand may choose to work. His hand (power) works them but does so through the medium of (διά) "the name" of Jesus; on ὄνομα see 2:21, and the phrases found in 2:38; 3:6; 3:16; 4:8, 10. "Thy holy Servant" is added as it was in v. 27. Some interpreters construe the infinitive γίνεσθαι with ἐν τῷ and coordinate it with ἐκτείνειν, but the subject of the latter is personal, that of the former neuter. Others construe it with εἰς, but this makes the infinitive clause coordinate with a mere man. We construe it as a purpose clause that is dependent on "in that thou stretchest out thy hand"; thus it is parallel with the phrase εἰς ἴασιν, which expresses purpose.

31) **And when they had petitioned, the place was shaken in which they had been gathered, and they were all filled with the Holy Spirit and continued to utter the Word with boldness.**

The answer to the petition was immediate and miraculous. We are helped in understanding this when we remember the great issue (v. 19, 20) with which the petition dealt. God put his sanction and his seal upon the principle uttered in this prayer, did it for all time to come. Δέομαι is the common verb to express begging for something either from men or from God. The shaking of the place is sometimes assumed to have been due to an earthquake; but when an earthquake occurred, as at the death and at the resurrection of Jesus, this is stated, see also 16:26. This shaking had no natural cause but, like the manifestations at Pentecost, was due only to the Holy Ghost. The sign was one of omnipotent power in the divine presence. The verb "they had been gathered together" may be considered the periphrastic past perfect (R., *W. P.*) or the imperfect plus a perfect participle: "they were," namely "as having been gathered" and thus still being together.

A new measure of the Holy Spirit was bestowed on them. The wider we open our hearts, or the wider God is able to open them, the more of the Spirit we receive; verbs of filling are followed by the genitive. Although it is added only as a coordinate fact by means of *καί*, it is the result of this being filled with the Spirit that they all "continued to utter the Word with boldness," the very thing asked for in v. 29. The imperfect tense is not inchoative (R., *W. P.*), for they had been speaking with boldness all along, and the test was now whether they would allow the threats of the Sanhedrin to intimidate them or not. By the Spirit's help they continued their public preaching openly and freely as though the Sanhedrin had never made a threat. They obeyed God rather than men and committed the consequences to God. This was spiritual heroism.

THE SECOND PICTURE OF THE MOTHER CONGREGATION AT JERUSALEM

32) Compare 2:44-47. After the first great influx of members Luke describes the excellent condition of the congregational life; now after a second great influx and after a notable victory over their opponents he again shows us the condition of the church. **Now of the multitude of those that believed there was one heart and soul; and not one was saying that anything of his possessions was his own, on the contrary, for them all things were common.**

Viewed outwardly, the congregation consisted of a great πλῆθος or "crowd" that was made up of a vast variety of people, old and young, rich and poor, with many differences in occupations, gifts, temperament, inclinations, etc. The 3,000 won at Pentecost came from many lands and had different native languages. Luke's last count was about 5,000 men (4:4). Make your own estimate of the total membership when the women and the children are included. What held all these people together was their one faith; they were "those that believed," the aorist participle stating only the fact of their believing.

Faith is the inner and essential bond of union in the church. The Communion of Saints is such by faith alone. Mere outward connection with a church body does not constitute true membership although it may lead to that. This is a spiritual state in the soul and not a matter of outward arrangement. Faith, of course, produces many visible results, for those who believe show their faith in many ways, and all these manifestations are valuable, but valuable only as evidences and fruits of the inner state, the precious saving faith itself.

The outstanding feature which Luke can report is that of this host of believers "there was one heart and soul." As in a living body only one heart beats, and as it is animated by only one ψυχή, so it was true of this great body of believers. Καρδία and ψυχή naturally go together as the pulsing heart and the breath of life. The Greek word for the heart designates the center of the personality, the seat of thought, feeling, and volition; in English the word heart connotes chiefly the feeling. The Greek ψυχή characterizes the soul in so far as it animates the body, it is the "life" of the body. Luke presents the fact that this great outward body of the congregation had one living personality in it. Its whole active life was one in thought, feeling, and will. "They all wanted one thing: to be saved eternally; they all thought one thing: only to be faithful to the Lord Jesus; they all experienced one thing: the comfort of the Holy Spirit." Besser. This means that, despite the great number, no divisions, no factions, no contentions existed.

In this regard the mother congregation of Christendom serves as a model for all time, a rebuke to all her daughters who followed heresies and errors and caused rents in the church, and a rebuke likewise to all members in any congregation that cause strife and disturbance; but a shining example for all congregations that hold in unity to the one faith and doctrine (2:42) and in one mind to the things that make for peace. The condition of the first congregation was one that made for healthy inner and outer growth.

We have already discussed how "for them all things were common," see 2:44, 45. Here the additional feature is added that even in this matter "not one was saying or claiming that anything of his possessions (literally, of the things belonging to him) was his own." Everyone regarded his possessions as not being intended for him alone but to be employed for all as need required. Even in the matter of personal possessions all were one heart and soul. This is truly remarkable, especially in so large a body. "Not one" — usually one or at least a few are opposed to such an arrangement. This is especially true where money is concerned. Selfishness shows itself, often in shameful ways, and will not let true generosity and Christian love flourish. We have already shown that even here in Jerusalem no communism was practiced and have answered the attempts to misconstrue the motives that animated these first Christians; see 2:44, 45.

33) **And with great power the apostles continued duly to give the testimony of the resurrection of the Lord Jesus, also great grace was upon them all.**

In v. 31 the uttering of the Word with boldness refers to the preaching before the general public in the city in order to win new believers. We have, pointed out that Luke says this regarding the apostles and not regarding any and all of the believers. The fact that these latter also testified in their private capacity is taken for granted. When Luke now adds that "the apostles continued duly to give the testimony of the resurrection" we again see that this was their official task; ἀπό in the verb always denotes a giving that is due to an obligation that is to be met. The obligation is indicated by the word "testimony" or witness, which recalls the fact that the apostles were the divinely appointed "witnesses" (1:8). We know that many others had seen the risen Lord; yet here the apostles alone act as the public witnesses. The fact that the others testified in private is self-evident. Yet we are not friendly toward the restriction which some introduce at this place by claiming that the testimony here mentioned was given only to the congregation — why not also to others? The answer usually given, that Luke here writes only regarding the believers, overlooks the fact that the apostles had the appointment "duly to give the testimony" in all Jerusalem, etc. To be sure, as in 2:42, they diligently testified and taught in the congregation; but they also reached out beyond it.

About this testimony the believers had gathered, about it new believers would gather. From it sprang their faith and their love. They needed to have it preached to them ever anew. The resurrection is the crowning work of God in accomplishing our redemption. It was the final proof of the deity and of the Messiahship of Jesus. It attested the full efficacy of his life, his suffering, and his death in removing the barrier that separated us from God (sin) by satisfying every claim of his holiness and righteousness. It showed also that the glorified Savior lived and ruled as the Head of the church to keep and to bless it to eternity. To this day it is Sunday, the day of Christ's resurrection, which assembles the hosts of his believers to the worship of his name. With the close connective τέ Luke unites this preaching with its result, namely "great grace upon them all," namely divine grace through the channel of this testimony, God's unmerited favor which built up the faith and the love of all. In 2:47 we have a different context, and there χάρις means the favor and the good will of the general public.

34) In 2:44, 45 Luke wrote only briefly regarding the manner in which love manifested itself in the congregation; here he returns to the subject and adds an instance of how things were done. **For there was not anyone needy among them; for as many as were owners of lands or of houses, making sales, kept bringing the proceeds of the things disposed of and laying them at the feet of the apostles; and it was distributed to each according as anyone was having need.**

Here γάρ brings evidence of the grace that rested on them: not one in need of the necessities of life. There were many beggars among the Jews. We meet them constantly (3:2 is a sample). The believers had none. The model here given has been followed by the church since that time. Every congregation takes care of its poor and unfortunate, and we need not add how extensive the arrangements are for doing this work through entire church bodies and in regular institutions. Even the world has learned something from the church in this line.

The rich came forward, "owners of lands and of houses." The present participle and the two imperfect verbs are iterative (R. 884) and express what occurred from time to time (R. 1116). The prices or proceeds of the sales were brought into the assembly and deposited beside the feet of the apostles. They seem to be represented as sitting on a platform and at this time managed the distribution of the funds thus voluntarily brought in. The idea to be expressed is certainly not that the rich sold all of their property and thus made also themselves poor. What Luke conveys is that the amounts brought in were large, each seller going to great lengths in disposing of some of his property, and that sales were made only at intervals, when new funds were required.

35) Another iterative imperfect reports the distribution; it is a form of διαδίδωμι, and the passive singular has an indefinite subject: "it was distributed," i. e., by the apostles who still managed everything without assistants. In this simple, though effective, fashion every case of need received proper relief.

36) Luke adds an illustration of this way of giving but singles out Barnabas for the special reason that we may thus early take note of this man, since he came to occupy an important place in the advance of the church. An illustration is in place at this point so that we may properly understand the following narrative which records a flagrant case of deception in this very matter of charity. **And Joseph, the one called besides Barnabas on the part of the apostles, which is, when interpreted, "son of consolation," a Levite, a Cyprian by race, he, having a field, on selling it, brought the money and placed it at the feet of the apostles.**

The elaborate manner in which Luke introduces this man is due to his future importance. His introduction is fittingly connected with a noble act of his that was performed in the early part of his Christian career. He had the common Jewish name "Joseph" which had been given him at the time of circumcision. Since many others had the same name, it is not surprising that he bore also another name. This second name was "Barnabas" and, as we shall find, completely superseded his original name.

We restrict ourselves to the main points regarding this second name; those interested may examine Zahn on our passage who has an elaborate investigation. Luke writes ὁ ἐπικληθείς, the aorist participle, and not ἐπικαλούμενος, the present. The latter would mean that Joseph was always called Barnabas, the former means that he got this name from the apostles, and ἀπό is the correct preposition, "from," not ὑπό, "by." One of the apostles must have called Joseph by this name; originating thus, everybody (not only the apostles) called him by this name. Luke translates the name for Theophilus. Why? Because Theophilus is not merely to know its meaning but is at the same time to see how a name that had such a meaning was given this man by the apostles. Luke is the last man to dispense mere etymological information. The interpretation or rather translation of Barnabas is "son of consolation." Luke mentions all this regarding the name in advance of the statement that Joseph was a Levite in order to bring together everything regarding the name. The fact that Joseph was "a Levite" is again no mere biographical item without further relevancy. Joseph was the first Levite to be won for the gospel by the apostles, won immediately after the Sanhedrin had uttered its dire threats to Peter and to John. His conversion was the first breach in the hierarchical walls and, coming at just this critical time, brought great consolation and encouragement to the apostles. That is why they gave him the new name, one which caused his original name to be discarded.

The onomastic debate with regard to "Barnabas" is rather severe and has taken on renewed energy. The charge that Luke mistranslated is rather beside the point since he was for so long a time and so well acquainted with Barnabas himself. And at least some of the Twelve most certainly knew Barnabas intimately. Meanings such as "son of prophecy," "son of a prophet," "son of consolation" in the sense of preaching in a comforting way, or Deissmann's "son of Nebo," an idol whose downfall Isa. 46:1, 2 prophesied, find no support in Luke. If Joseph's preaching gave him his name, why did he preach so early, and why was he called "son" and not, as one should expect, "father of consolation"?

The fact that he was a Cyprian by race is added because he and Paul made their first missionary journey to Joseph's homeland, the island of Cyprus. He was thus a foreign-born Jew. His father seems to have given up his station as a Levite and to have moved to Cyprus; see the list of foreign-born Jews in 2:9, etc. Joseph, however, remained a Hebrew Jew and, like Paul, did not become a Hellenist. The fact that he was at this time in Jerusalem, aside from other reasons, may be explained by the circumstance that his relatives, his sister Mary and his cousin Mark, lived here. It is only a conjecture that Joseph was one of the Seventy, a conjecture that disagrees with all that may otherwise be safely assumed.

37) The genitive absolute, "a field being for him," i. e., "he having a field," shows that he possessed wealth; he was like those mentioned in v. 34. The statement regarding what he did with this field is worded exactly like that in v. 34, 35, and only uses the aorists instead of the iterative tenses. The singular τὸ χρῆμα, instead of the usual plural, seems to signify the sum of money as a whole.

CHAPTER V

Ananias and Sapphira

The deceit of Achan, Josh. 7:1, etc., and his severe penalty, which occurred when Israel first entered Canaan, are recorded as a warning for the entire Old Testament Church. The deceit of Ananias and of Sapphira, which happened when the Christian Church began in Jerusalem, and their severe penalty are recorded as a warning for the entire New Testament Church. The first danger to the young church came from the outside when the Sanhedrin struck at Peter and at John. This had been safely met, and the church continued on in its successful course. Now follows the second attack of Satan from within the sacred circle of the congregation itself: the hearts of two disciples had become false, two hypocrites are unmasked. Rich members, also Barnabas, sold land or property and laid the proceeds at the feet of the apostles to be used for the needy. Ananias and Sapphira do the same, but their act is in reality the absolute opposite, and judgment overtakes them. Here God's attitude toward all hypocrites in the church is recorded whether his judgment strikes them at once or is delayed for a time.

1) **Now a man by name Ananias with Sapphira, his wife, sold a property and held out for himself something from the price, his wife also knowing it together with him; and having brought some part, he placed it at the feet of the apostles.**

Because of the gravity of the offense the names of the offenders are not withheld; τίς is used like our indefinite pronoun. Throughout the account Ananias is linked with his wife who was not the jewel (sapphire) after which she was named. They both sold the property. It is usually assumed that this parcel of ground (v. 3) was all they owned, but the indefinite *κτῆμα*, without the article, makes the impression that this property was only one of their possessions. Nor did Barnabas or any of the owners mentioned in 4:34 sell all their real estate for the benefit of the needy.

2) Selling the property and retaining a part of the price were but two elements of one transaction. The whole procedure was planned in advance. In order to place the matter beyond question the genitive absolute, "his wife also knowing with him," is added. We cannot agree with those who think that the idea of retaining part of the price came to these two people only after the parcel had been sold, that perhaps the sight of so much money stirred the cupidity of the couple, that thus an originally right motive went wrong. No sinner should ever be painted blacker than he is, but on the other hand, no sinner should be whitewashed to hide some of his blackness. Here there was no change of mind, no yielding to a sudden impulse. The heart of husband and wife had grown cold and dead in regard to faith. Their sin was not merely cupidity but the worst and the boldest type of hypocrisy. Satan had entered where Christ could not remain.

Husband and wife were "one heart and soul" (3:32) in evil. Whereas the one should have restrained the other, neither did so, but each aided and abetted the other, both were equally guilty. This premeditation, this conspiracy made the sin so terrible. They had to talk the matter over, had to say to each other what was in their hearts, had to tell each other what to do and how to act so that nobody should know. For such conduct calousness is required; theirs were two seared consciences. Neither had scruples or compunctions of conscience. And thus Ananias carried out the deed.

We must imagine that the congregation or a part of it was assembled for worship. The apostles are present to lead and to teach. Ananias has the bag of money with him; and when the time came to make the offerings, he went forward and in the sight of all deposited the bag. "At or beside the apostles' feet" (the same expression used in 4:34, 37) represents the apostles as seated on a platform. To those who looked on, Ananias appeared as a second Barnabas. Words of praise, at least thoughts of commendation, accompanied the act of Ananias. He acted with perfect assurance, certain that no one could possibly detect his deception. He never thought of God or of Christ who were present in that assembly according to their promise. And so the deed was done.

The supposition that Ananias aimed at attaining more than praise, that he aspired to a leadership such as Barnabas had gained, cannot be substantiated from Luke's account. Why Barnabas received his second name is explained in 4:36; that he sold all his possessions is not stated nor is it to be assumed; he became prominent at a later time and only for this reason is he here cited as an example. The mere juxtaposition of Barnabas and Ananias with its contrast of sincerity and base hypocrisy involves no more than is thus indicated, which also is certainly enough.

3) **But Peter said: Ananias, for what reason did Satan fill thy heart for thee to belie the Holy Spirit and to hold back for thyself something from the price of the land? Was it not, remaining** (unsold), **remaining for thee? and sold, was it not still in thy power? Why didst thou put this affair in thy heart? Thou didst not lie to men, but to God!**

Ananias had just laid down the money and had most likely added a few words that expressed his intention. He, no doubt, expected Peter or one of the other apostles to answer with words of acceptance and personal commendation. Instead of this there came the exposure of his fearful sin like a bolt out of the clear sky. How did Peter gain such complete knowledge about the sin of Ananias? One answer to this question is found in 1 Cor. 12:10, "and to another discerning of spirits." In the case before us Peter had even more, namely the direct revelation of the Holy Spirit concerning Ananias and his wife. Did this revelation include the judgment to be visited upon Ananias? Peter announces the judgment upon Sapphira but not that upon Ananias. We can get the answer by inference only since we do not have a direct statement by Luke himself. It seems that the revelation given to Peter included the judgment awaiting both Ananias and his wife. Why should God have revealed less than this to him? Sin and judgment belong together. Was Peter to be dumbfounded by the sudden, terrible death of Ananias, frightened, perhaps, that he had helped to kill him?

But why did Peter not announce the judgment upon Ananias as he did that upon Sapphira? The explanation is not acceptable that he did not know that Ananias was to die but from his death concluded that Sapphira was likewise to die. So Peter would speak partly as a result of revelation and partly on the basis of deductions of his own. In a matter of life and death that cannot be considered likely. It seems rather that Peter spoke only such words to Ananias that the Spirit inspired him to speak, and that the Spirit withheld the announcement of the death of Ananias in order to make it absolutely clear to all those present that this judgment was wholly a divine act and not one that was in any way due to Peter, or one in which he served even as an instrument. After this was clear from the first instance, Peter could announce the Spirit's judgment in the second case without leaving the slightest impression that he was inflicting the penalty or was the agent in the infliction.

The questions asked by Peter assume complete knowledge against which denial is impossible. Peter's questions are unanswerable. Ananias has no excuse to offer and can state nothing in extenuation of his guilt. So the sinner is always dumb before God: "and he was speechless," Matt. 22:12; or if he should venture a defense he would be condemned out of his own mouth. "Why did Satan fill thy heart?" refers the guilt back to its real source and implies that Ananias could and should have resisted Satan. With διατί Peter asks for the reason — Satan's reason was the damnation of Ananias — what reason could Ananias have had? "Filled" means that Satan took complete control of the man, and that his was done with the full consent of Ananias.

Here again (4:32) "heart" is the center of the personality, including especially the mind and the will. When Ananias became a believer, the Holy Spirit filled his heart and cast out and kept out Satan and his power. But Ananias had turned away from God's Spirit and had once more opened his heart to Satan and to all his devilish suggestions. How a man, once won for God, can again turn to the devil is a mystery no one can solve. We know the fact only too well but we cannot understand how any sane man's will can so turn to his own destruction.

The two infinitives do not denote purpose, do not state the intentions of Ananias; they express result (R. 1089): "so that thou didst belie and didst hold back for thyself." The deed has gone far beyond its original intent, it is fully accomplished (two aorists). "Belie" is followed by the accusative as in the classics: in v. 4

it governs the dative. The sin of Ananias is here truly described. All sins are, indeed, committed against God, and those of believers especially against the Holy Spirit. Ananias permitted Satan to influence him to the extreme and to beguile him to carry out a deed that emanated wholly from Satan and to offer it as a deed that was prompted wholly by the Holy Spirit; yea, to present this deed to the Spirit himself, in the very church where the Spirit wrought, before the special agents, the apostles, through whom the Spirit wrought, a deed which the Spirit was to accept as being wrought by him when it was wrought wholly by the power of Satan. Thus, deliberately, mockingly, Ananias belied the Spirit and attempted to palm off a devil's work on the Spirit and hoped that the Spirit would not detect the deception; yea, he would leave the impression that the Spirit had produced this devil's work!

The second infinitive defines the lying act more clearly: "to hold back," etc. It is dreadful enough to sin and to admit that we followed the evil one; but what shall we say of him who sins and then not only pretends that the Holy Spirit prompted his sin but also that it is a divine work and then proceeds to bring it to God as a holy offering?

4) The sin of Ananias was altogether gratuitous. It was without rime or reason. The double question is so compact in the Greek that we cannot translate it into English with a like compactness. Ananias was entirely free to keep his land for himself or to sell it. The present participle μένον, "remaining," means: "remaining as it was, unsold and in thy possession"; and the imperfect ἔμενε: "was it not remaining for thee," no one asking thee to make a change? The interrogative particle οὐ, here found in its strong form οὐχί, brings out the fact. Ananias was compelled to answer "yes"; he knew that he could have kept his

land. he sinned with full knowledge. The enclitic σοί is accented and placed before the verb because it has a strong emphasis: "was it not remaining *for thee,*" wholly and entirely for thee alone.

The question is extended. But now the aorist neuter passive participle πραθέν (from πιπράσκω) speaks of the land as "sold." Although it had been sold, nothing was changed: "Was it not still in thy power?" The imperfect ὑπῆρχε expresses continuance, "still it was in thy control" (ἐξουσία) for thee to do with it in all honesty and uprightness as thou mightest wish. He could have retained the whole sum he had received for the land, and no one could in the least have blamed him; or he could have brought as an offering for the needy any portion of the money, small or large, as he might have desired; the only requirement set was that he make no false pretense about it. Did Ananias know this? Most certainly. Again the deliberateness of his lie is revealed.

"Why didst thou put this affair in thy heart?" the middle ἔθου, "put it there for thyself." Τὸ πρᾶγμα τοῦτο is not merely this idea or plan but the whole transaction as now carried out. "Why," τί ὅτι, *quid est quod,* "what has occurred that" (R. 965), asks about the terrible change that has occurred in the heart which made it possible for Ananias to lend his heart to this deed. To place in the heart means more than "to conceive" (our versions); "heart" includes the will as the center of the personality, and Peter does not refer only to the conception but also to the entire execution of the plan. Something had occurred in this man's heart: Satan had usurped its control. And thus he lied not merely to men but to God himself.

The deed is considered only with reference to God. Ananias is sadly mistaken when he thinks that he is dealing with men; he is dealing directly with God himself. He could and should have known that.

This is in a way true of every sin, especially of every conscious sin; but it is most directly true of every act of hypocrisy, in all matters of worship, wherever God is directly concerned as here in this lying offer to God. Peter's word to Ananias undoubtedly identifies God and the Holy Ghost. This is often denied, and the claim advanced that the lie was made to God indirectly through the Holy Ghost, the latter serving only as the medium. But this virtually declares that the Holy Ghost was as ignorant of the fraud as men were. God is not behind the Holy Ghost as he is behind the apostles and the church so that whatever is done against them is done mediately also against God. The Holy Ghost is God; the sin was committed against him as God. The old dogmaticians and the church are right when they here find a clear expression of the deity and the personality of the Holy Spirit, the Third Person of the Godhead.

5) **And Ananias, hearing these words, having fallen down, expired; and there came great fear on all those hearing it. And having arisen, the younger men wrapped him up and, having carried him out, buried him.**

With the words ringing in his ears, the λόγοι, the things Peter was saying, Ananias suddenly collapsed and expired (this verb is used only in Acts but is found also in LXX and in Hippocrates). Neither Peter nor the words he uttered killed Ananias. All natural explanations such as a stroke of paralysis, heart failure, etc., that was superinduced by the sudden shock at finding himself exposed, prove insufficient when they are applied to two persons as must be done here, the death of the second being announced the moment before it occurred.

Why was Ananias granted no time for repentance? We have no warrant to inquire into the secret counsel of God in either this or any other case. That question belongs in the domain of divine providence where hundreds of things are beyond our comprehension. God alone knows when and how to interfere with his judgment. He is not accountable to us, and no questioner should forget this truth. His mercy, like his judgment, is beyond question. Even if he were to uncover these to us, our poor minds would not be able to grasp them. Was Ananias lost? "Not to desire to know where the best of all teachers wants us not to know, is a wholesome and faultless ignorance." Gerhard. As far as we are concerned, the object of this judgment upon Ananias is to inspire us with fear that we may guard ourselves against the machinations of the devil. This was the effect produced upon the first church.

The present participle "those hearing" = "the hearers," i. e., those present who heard what Peter said. In v. 11 more is said. This fear was the effect of the power and the judgment of God that were manifested in so sudden a manner. It was awe for faith, fright for the flesh. On the latter, the third use of the law, compare *C. Tr.*, 965, etc., 9 and 19.

6) The dead body must be removed and buried. Why was Sapphira not called to her dead husband's side; why was he buried immediately without her knowledge? The answer appears in the sequel: the same judgment awaited her. But we must remember that all this is an act of God's Spirit and not of Peter nor of the apostles. It was proper that "the younger men" should attend to this sad task. In v. 10 they are called "the young men," and the change of words indicates that no officers of the church are referred to as some have supposed. The next chapter will tell us about the first officers. The two words used do not signify youths or boys but men between twenty and forty years

of age. The implication is that older men were also present as well as the apostles (v. 2) and not merely Peter. The entire account reveals a full assembly.

When bodies are not embalmed in Oriental countries burial is greatly hastened; in the case of the Jews this hasty burial made possible also the early cleansing from the defilement contracted by touching the dead. Burial took place on the day of death or, if the hour of death was late, the next morning. The wrapped body was carried to the cemetery and buried without a coffin. The writer witnessed such a Jewish funeral procession at Jerusalem: men marched in ranks, the body was wrapped in its garments and carried on a bier of two long poles with bands stretched across them. No covering hid the body, several men carried the poles on each side. In a manner similar to this Ananias was carried out.

7) **Now there occurred an interval of about three hours, and his wife, not knowing what had occurred, came in. And Peter answered to her, Tell me whether you disposed of the land for this much? And she said, Yes, for this much.**

Luke regularly records only the facts and leaves their combination and relation to the reader. It has been well said that this manner of writing expects a good deal on the part of the reader. Our historians are prone to relate everything and to leave very little to the reader. So here we should like to know why both had not come together, why the interval was three hours, why Sapphira came at all, etc. Was she worried because of her husband's long absence? The text supplies nothing. Was it all planned with a view that Ananias should precede her and receive the plaudits of the congregation, and that Sapphira was later to furnish the occasion for a second congratulation? It almost seems so.

The three hours have been regarded as being the interval between the regular Jewish hours of prayer, but this was longer, the morning devotion being held at nine, the evening devotion at three. All that Luke states is that Sapphira was ignorant of what had happened three hours before and came into the assembly in the usual way. She must have known that the meeting was to continue for so long a time or longer. Were there matters other than worship that required so long a time, or did teaching take up so much time? We see no reason for making διάστημα a nominative absolute that is merely inserted to mark the time (B.-D. 144; R. 460), so that ἐγένετο καί plus the finite verb is the idiom Luke often uses; why not let this nominative be the subject: "there occurred an interval," etc.?

8) Sapphira probably looked about the room for her husband. "Answered to her" does not imply that she asked a question to which Peter replied. The verb is frequently used with reference to a statement called forth by a situation. So here it means simply that Peter had waited for Sapphira to enter in order that he might address her as he did. Before she sat down, Peter called to her. "For this much," genitive of price, gives the impression that the sack of coins had been left untouched where Ananias had deposited it on the platform, and that Peter now pointed to it and Sapphira recognized it. One should think that the question, asked in this manner, should have made the woman hesitate. Why did Peter ask so significantly in regard to the actual amount: "for so much"? That question must have struck her conscience since she knew that it was not for so much but for more. But no, Sapphira is not startled. She clings to the agreement made with her husband to say "for so much," and Satan is supporting her as he did Judas when Jesus gave him a final warning. With all positiveness she

affirms, "Yes, for so much!" This was loyalty but of the wrong kind. With this word Sapphira forfeited her opportunity for repentance. This final "yes" to the sin was yes also to her judgment.

9) **But Peter said to her: Why was it agreed for you to tempt the Lord's Spirit? Lo, the feet of those that buried thy husband at the door, and they shall carry thee out! And she fell at once at his feet and expired; and, on coming in, the young men found her dead and, having carried her out, buried her beside her husband. And there came great fear on the whole church and on all that heard these things.**

Peter's question is an exclamation of grief, τί ὅτι as in v. 4. He reveals some new features of the sin. They had deliberately agreed, had formed this conspiracy with resolute purpose. The impersonal passive may have the dative as it is found with a passive or after σύν. By carrying out their agreement they have deliberately tempted the Lord's Spirit. The aorist infinitive states a result; it is like the two infinitives occurring in v. 3: "so that you tempted." This Israel had done in order to see whether the Spirit would permit its wickedness to pass unpunished, Num. 14:25; Ps. 95:8, 9. We need not say that Ananias and Sapphira intended their act to be such a temptation of the Spirit whom the Lord (Jesus) had sent; it was this, nevertheless.

Sinners often call their sins by mild but untrue names. When the light of God falls upon them, all shams disappear. Every imitation of faith and of love tempts the Spirit, challenges him. Will he know, will our cunning not deceive him? "Be not deceived, God is not mocked."

"Behold the feet," etc., needs no verb to complete its sense for it is an exclamation. The footsteps of the returning young men were heard. Now, only a moment before her own death, Sapphira learns that her husband is already buried. "They shall carry thee out" states only the fact. Why this was said to her and not to Ananias also is discussed above.

10) Her death ensued on the instant. When the young men came in they found another such sad task awaiting them. The first two and the most awful hypocrites in the Christian Church were buried side by side. It is often asked whether they committed the sin against the Holy Ghost. This may be safely denied because an outstanding mark of this sin is blasphemy, a feature that was absent in the case of Ananias and Sapphira.

11) The effect produced by these two deaths that had occurred in the very assembly of the congregation must have been tremendous. Luke again notes the fear and its greatness; not, however, fear of the apostles but of the Spirit before whom the lies found in every heart are open to view, and who is able to smite the sinner in the very midst of his sin. This fear came "upon the whole church."

Here Luke for the first time uses ἐκκλησία with reference to the body of the believers in Jerusalem, whether they were gathered in an assembly or not. It is so used in Matt. 16:18, but in a still wider sense, for it refers to the body of believers of all future time. In Matt. 18:17 the word denotes the local congregation. This double use continues to this day. The term is derived from ἐκκαλεῖν, "to call out," as when a herald calls out the citizens to meet in assembly. The assembly of Israel was called its *ecclesia*, 7:38. "All those that heard these things" were the people who were not connected with the congregation. In v. 5 the present participle denotes the immediate hearers who were present in the meeting; here the aorist participle refers to those who later learned of the matter, and the preceding *ecclesia* restricts these to outsiders.

THE THIRD PICTURE OF THE MOTHER CONGREGATION IN JERUSALEM

As he did in 2:43-47; 4:32-35, Luke pauses also at this point to present a survey of the congregation and briefly notes the main features of the great and continuous progress.

12) **Now through the hands of the apostles there continued to occur many signs and wonders among the people. And they were all with one accord in the porch of Solomon. Yet of the rest no one dared to join himself to them, but the people kept magnifying them.**

What has been recorded in the previous brief descriptions holds good for the present account and need not be repeated. Some new, notable features are added, especially the signs and wonders (see 2:19 on the terms) of which Luke records that they were many, πολλά being placed emphatically at the end. These were miracles of grace and of healing, and we note that Luke places them in strong contrast with the one miracle of judgment he has just recorded. The singular "through (the) hand," the phrase being little more than a preposition, denotes only agency in general, but the plural "through the hands" points to the actual placing of the hand or the hands upon the sufferers. In Luke's first description of the congregation signs and wonders were noted (2:43); these have now greatly increased.

The usual meeting place of the entire congregation was "the porch of Solomon" (see 3:11) before which Peter and John had been arrested. Here "all" (ἅπαντες, stronger than πάντες) kept meeting "with one accord." Although they had been threatened never again to use the name of Jesus, the apostles used it right here in the Temple court. Thus far those threats had remained empty. The long, roomy colonnade afforded ample space for the assembly of the thousands of Christians. Although all of them were Jews, they now constituted a separate body and thus met "with one accord." This spacious porch was also ideal for the work of the apostles in ever making new converts. Here the Jews gathered daily in multitudes, and the Christians, too, joined in the regular services so that no outward division as yet appeared.

13) Yet the Christians were a distinct body and were recognized as such with the result that no outsider ventured to join himself to them. This concurs with the fact that the people kept magnifying them (compare 4:21 and 2:47) and speaking highly of them. Had it not been for this general favor and praise, undesirables would have crowded in and disturbed the gatherings of the believers in all sorts of ways. To whatever degree the miracles prompted this high regard, the effect here described is not that "the rest," the Jews generally, stayed away from the gatherings of the Christians; they were evidently drawn by the preaching and the teaching that went on diligently here in Solomon's porch.

14) **Moreover, the more were believing ones added to the Lord, crowds both of men and women.** Μᾶλλον refers to this magnifying on the part of the people, and δέ adds the statement as something that went beyond what has just been said. The attitude of the people helped in producing new believers. Many would at any rate have been won, but now this occurred the more. In 2:47 the Lord kept adding; the parallel is now passive, "believing ones kept being added to the Lord." In 4:4 Luke could still state figures, but only with reference to the men, 5,000 of them; but now all count has been lost, no figures could be secured, and all that Luke can write is that "crowds both of men and of women" were added to the thousands already in the faith. Why this manner of expression should be

called popular exaggeration is hard to see; "crowds" does not mean "little groups." A general movement set in which was due to the favorable attitude of the people as such. Luke considers πιστεύοντες and "were being added to the Lord" quite sufficient for the intelligent reader who will understand that these people believed in the Lord (Jesus) and were brought to such faith by the preaching of the apostles. Since 2:41 baptism has not been mentioned, but it certainly is understood that all new believers were, like those 3,000, received by baptism.

A few oddities must be noted. The section from 12b to 14 has been considered an insertion by a strange hand, or a marginal note that was introduced into the text, or a section transposed from 4:31. Why? Not on the basis of textual evidence but because v. 15 is supposed to be a continuation of 12a. Yet v. 15 properly joins v. 14 and could not fittingly be connected with 12a. B.-D. 365, 1 considers v. 14 a parenthesis and calls it harsh because v. 15 is said to match illy with v. 13. There is no parenthesis. At this point, too, we can see how unwarranted is the opinion that in v. 13 κολλᾶσθαι signifies "to join" in the sense of believing, and that "dared not join" refers to a certain party that kept entirely aloof. Here in v. 14 we see how Luke expresses this kind of joining: "were added unto," the same verb he used in 2:41, 47. Verse 13 speaks of intrusions, men fastening themselves on the assemblies of believers in order to harass them.

15) **So that they kept carrying the sick even into the street and kept placing them on little beds and pallets in order that, as Peter came, at least the shadow might overshadow some one of them. Moreover, there kept coming together also the crowd from the cities around Jerusalem, bringing sick and any oppressed by unclean spirits, who continued to be healed all.**

Ὥστε with the infinitive expresses actual result. The claim that we must connect this verse with 12a overlooks the fact that, the more signs and wonders occurred, the less reason was there to carry the sick into the streets. Luke intends to show that the people magnified the Christians, and that numbers of men and women came to faith, and that the result of this circumstance was that they kept carrying the sick out even into the streets, etc. This, as Lukes states it, was a result of the attitude of the people, of their tremendous confidence; not, as some regard Luke as saying, a result only of the occurrence of many miracles. The present infinitives denote iterative action. With the feminine πλατείας supply ὁδούς. The diminutive κλινάριον denotes a little bed, and κράβαττος (κράββατος) a pallet or camp roll. The sick were carried out into the street and then deposited on some sort of a bed to await Peter's coming. No distinction is here made between rich, soft beds and hard, poor couches.

The sick were arranged in this manner in order that they might be directly in the path of Peter so that he could not avoid seeing them and could heal them without losing time by going to their homes. The idea to be expressed is that he did so heal them. For κἄν (note the crasis for καὶ ἐάν), which has come to be a mere particle (B.-D. 374), states that "at least," i. e., if no more were done by Peter, his shadow might overshadow some one of them here and there and evidently thus transmit the healing. Some texts have the future indicative after ἵνα, a construction which is found in the Koine.

This trust that even Peter's shadow would heal them has been called superstition or faith coupled with superstition. The question has also been raised as to whether healing was actually thus transmitted. If Peter's shadow had not healed, the fancy that it might heal would have at once been dissipated. Many unfortunates asked Jesus to touch them and to heal them in this manner; to ask for the touch is not more superstitious than to look to the shadow. In Mark 6:56 the touching of even the garment of Jesus healed; in Acts 19:12 the handkerchiefs of Paul accomplished a like miracle. The physician Luke describes these effects and in no way suggests that the apostles or Jesus found anything superstitious or wrong in this faith. The important feature in all these healings is the fact that contact was in some way sought with the person transmitting the healing. The διά in v. 12 states that the Lord used the apostles as the personal media for the signs and wonders. It was throughout his power that wrought the healing.

More must be added. All healings emanate from the Lord and his will; the apostles are no more than his instruments. Once this is understood, we shall not lay stress on the will or the consciousness of the apostles. In Matt. 9:20 it was the will of Jesus that healed the woman who touched the tassel of his robe from behind. It is his will that operated through the apostles, through their hands (v. 12) and through Peter's shadow. As far as the will of the apostles was concerned, this was wholly in accord with the will of Jesus. The rich outflow of healing power from Jesus at this time meets the abundant faith that sought this healing power and manifested itself in such striking ways. Here faith in Jesus' power preceded the healing; this was not the case in 3:4 and in other instances — see the discussion on this passage. No man who came to Jesus or to the apostles in faith remained unhealed, and not a few were healed without previously having had faith in order to be brought to that faith. All this, too, was at first faith only in the power of Jesus to heal. That was enough to begin with; but this incipient faith was to advance to the higher faith which would rely on him for healing and for saving also the soul. This subject must be studied in its entirety; those who busy themselves with it merely as they happen upon it here and there will naturally draw inadequate and wrong conclusions.

16) For the first time the history of the church reaches out beyond Jerusalem proper, namely to the towns around the capital (πέριξ is an adverb with the genitive and is like the preposition περί). Even from these places the sick were brought in. As he does in his Gospel, so here in Acts Luke differentiates and describes the demoniacs and never for a moment confuses them with people who were suffering from ordinary ailments. Here he mentions them for the first time in Acts and calls them "oppressed by unclean spirits," agitated, vexed. Note that ὑπό points to these spirits as being the personal agents; and "unclean," filthy, vile, points to their unholy character. On the entire subject of demoniacal possession see the comment of the author on Matt. 4:24; 8:28; Mark 1:23; Luke 4:33.

The idea expressed in οἵτινες is "any such," no matter who they were or how severe their case. They continued to be healed *all*, ἅπαντες, as in v. 12, is stronger than the simple πάντες, "all altogether," without a single exception, the word being placed emphatically at the end. Note the imperfect tenses throughout the entire paragraph, all of them are descriptive and picture what was going on at this time; they are also continuative and iterative. These open tenses at the same time imply that something is to follow that interfered with this grand work and progress. In fact, that is why Luke places this sketch at this point of his narrative.

Peter continues to stand out pre-eminently. This may be due to the fact that the apostles had not as yet scattered but remained together and moved about and acted as one body. Thus Peter spoke for all and in the case of the healings acted for all; note v. 29. The people thus looked to Peter and trusted that even his shadow would cure the unfortunate. Neither the other apostles nor Luke see an undue assumption of authority on Peter's part in this fact, on the contrary, all feel that through Peter they are acting as a unified body, and that is the way in which they intended to act.

Here the promise of Jesus regarding healings and signs was fulfilled in a notable manner; the miracles of the apostles appeared as a direct continuation of the extensive healings wrought by Jesus himself. His power in and through the apostles thus in the most manifest way connects their work with the work he did during the days of his earthly ministry. The success was phenomenal. It now seemed as though the entire population of Jerusalem and that of even the surrounding towns would soon be won for Christ; and once the capital became Christian, what might not be expected from the nation as a whole?

The Twelve Arrested and Miraculously Released

For some time the Sanhedrin tolerated the bold disobedience of its peremptory orders not to speak or to teach in Jesus' name and with growing concern watched the growth of the Christian movement. The members of this body were, however, convinced that this could not be permitted to continue much longer unless they were ready to abdicate their position in favor of the apostles. The tension increased until finally, without an especial cause or occasion, the cord snapped.

17) **Now, having arisen, the high priest and all those with him, the local sect of the Sadducees, were filled with passion and laid hands on the apostles and put them in a public ward.**

These same Sadducees caused the arrest of Peter and of John in 4:1, 2. This time the high priest takes the lead, and he and his following take summary action. "Having arisen" means, "having proceeded from inaction to action"; he and his followers refused to remain inactive. Because in 4:6 "high priest" is appended to the name Annas, it is supposed that this same individual is referred to also in this place and Luke is accordingly charged with inaccuracy. But in 4:6 the names are arranged according to seniority, and "high priest" indicates only the general status of Annas. Neither there nor here does Luke make Annas the ruling high priest, for Caiaphas held this position.

These Sadducees have the leading position in the Sanhedrin and maintain it also in this case by ordering the arrest on their own authority and afterward call a session of the Sanhedrin. Our versions translate, "which is the sect of the Sadducees"; R., *W. P.*, "the sect of the Sadducees" or "the sect which is of the Sadducees." But the high priest and those with him were only a small part of this sect, nor were they a little sect within the sect of the Sadducees. Hence these translations are unacceptable. Moulton (in R. 1107) puts us on the right track when in 13:1 he translates the same attributive participle, "the *local* church"; a papyrus has this participle in the sense, "the *current* month." So Luke means "the *local* sect of the Sadducees." Αἵρεσις means "choice," a chosen opinion or tenet, and thus the party holding that tenet, "a sect"; it often has a connotation of reproach.

First the motive, then the act. They were filled with passion, filled to overflowing, could not longer contain themselves. The noun means "hot steam"; it is derived from ζέω, "to boil." That this was "envy" (A. V. margin) or "jealousy" (R. V.) is a deduction made from what is regarded as the general situation, but this is too narrow. These Sadducees were wrought up because the apostles were boldly continuing their preaching of Jesus. We have their own statement for this in v. 28.

18) On this occasion all the apostles are summarily arrested; of course, by the Temple police on an order of these Sadducees. Where and how this was done we are left to surmise. We have only one clue in v. 26, where the Temple commander and his men proceed alertly because they were afraid of the people present. We thus conclude that the arrest mentioned in this verse was made at a moment when the people were absent. The culprits were placed "in a public ward." Since Luke always writes with great care and exactness, it is fair to conclude that this was not the same place of confinement as the one referred to in 4:3, but was one of the common jails, in regard to the location of which we are left uninformed. Thus at one sudden stroke and without the least warning the leaders of the entire church in Jerusalem were snatched away. Lodgment in jail was no more pleasant or honorable in those days than it is in ours; the procedure seems to be a deliberate attempt to subject the entire leadership of the believers to public disgrace. Criminals are summarily arrested but not decent men. Peter and John seem to have been placed only under guard for the night; the Twelve are now thrown into jail under lock and key.

19) **But an angel of the Lord, during the night, opened the doors of the prison and, after leading them out, said, Be going and, having taken a stand, go on speaking in the Temple to the people the words of this life! And having heard it, they went at dawn into the Temple and began to teach.**

To say that Luke is less vivid here than he is in the similar account in 12:6-10 is to overlook the great differences in the situations. Peter was to be executed, was fastened in chains and most heavily guarded in a far stronger prison; the Twelve were confined in the common jail. So Luke has less to say here, but what he says is surely vivid enough. We make no apology as far as the veracity of Luke's account is concerned. We find no legendary element in the narrative, no clothing of any fact in symbolical form, no friendly jailor or courageous Christian who released the apostles. Meyer is correct: *Das ist einlegende Schwindelei.*

Some time during the night (the phrase needs no article) an angel appeared in the prison where the apostles were confined, miraculously opened the locked doors from the inside, and himself led the apostles out (note the close connective τε which makes the whole action but one procedure). The guards saw nothing. Twelve men witnessed this act, saw and heard the angel, and were not deceived as to his identity. Some say that this release amounted to nothing since the apostles were promptly rearrested. But the rearrested apostles were in a position that was far different from the one that obtained at the time of their first arrest. The outcome of this affair was turned in favor of the apostles by this miracle; the time of peaceful development for the church was yet to continue.

20) The angel leaves the apostles with specific directions which in point of boldness, were like an open challenge to the Sanhedrists who had caused their arrest. They are to go and to take their stand or position in the very court of the Temple where they had been preaching constantly, and are to "continue to utter all the utterances of this life" to the people. Both λαλεῖτε and ῥήματα say nothing about the subject matter to be uttered, they make plain only that the apostles are to speak as they did before. The subject matter is contained in the emphatic qualitative genitive "of

this life," the divine ζωή. In John 6:68, Peter had confessed regarding Jesus, "Thou hast utterances of life everlasting." The demonstrative does not refer "in sense" to ῥήματα (R. 497, 706) but is placed correctly: "this life," the one you are preaching in connection with the resurrection of Jesus, the one that is so objectionable to the Sadducees, the one that is salvation indeed. We do not need the capital letter of the R. V. even as it is not needed in John 6:68, nor the appeal to the Aramaic as though the angel had said, "these life utterances," and Luke had misconceived the sense. "Utter the utterances" implies that they were given to the apostles by the Lord, and "of life" that they conveyed this life to men.

21) One text adds: "and each one went home," which is certainly true. It was still night, the Temple gates were still locked, the time still too early to carry out the angel's order. But *sub lucem,* "under the dawn," when the gates were first opened for the early service at dawn, the apostles entered the Temple courts and began their teaching (inchoative imperfect). This was God's answer to the Sadducees. Rejecting "this life" themselves, they were resolved to prevent all others from accepting it even as Jesus had said in regard to the Pharisees, Matt. 23:13.

Now the high priest having arrived and those with him, they called together the Sanhedrin and all the eldership of the sons of Israel and sent to the jail in order that they be brought. But the underlings, on coming, did not find them in the prison; and having returned, they reported, saying, The jail we found as having been locked in all safety, and the guards standing at the doors; but on having opened, inside we found no one.

Granted that the addition of the words "having arisen early" in a very few texts reports a fact, the reason for this very early appearance of the high priest and his coterie would not be due to the fact that the high priest officiated in person at the early morning service; we should rather suppose that this early beginning was made in order to hasten on their way the messengers that were to summon the members of the Sanhedrin. Luke never reports irrelevant matters, and this functioning of the high priest at the early service would be one of these. Παρά in the participial form refers to the Temple which has just been mentioned.

The twofold designation, "Sanhedrin and all the eldership of the sons of Israel," has led to the conjecture that two bodies were summoned, or that the eldership was called in as advisory, in the capacity of assessors. But no historical evidence for such a second body has been found. The Sanhedrin was certainly large enough in itself. We have a similar twofold designation in Mark 15:1. In each instance a plenary session in indicated. Συνέδριον refers to the function of the body sitting together and taking counsel; while γερουσία indicates its dignity as being composed of γέροντες, old and honored men; hence it was also called the presbytery. "Sons of Israel" is only a more dignified term than "of the people." The Sadducees were presenting a case of major importance and they, indeed, had no less than twelve men to present as criminals.

The Sadducees summoned the members of the high court and then also sent a detachment of Temple police to bring the prisoners from the δεσμωτήριον or jail. These Temple police were Levites, were a large body that was generally armed with clubs, were under the orders of a chief commander who, in turn, had lieutenants under him. They are usually termed ὑπηρέται, "underlings." The high priests and the Sadducees imagine that they have everything in their own hands and are fully determined to crush the entire movement. They were due for a rather rude awakening.

22) The detachment of "underlings" proceeds on its errand. Luke states only the facts that they did not find the apostles in the jail and that they returned and made due report to their superiors.

23) Here we learn more although the report, too, states only the facts in the succinct way of military reports. First of all, they report that they found the jail still duly locked in all safety, the perfect participle bringing out the thought that, once locked, it had remained so until these underlings themselves unlocked it. Secondly, they also found the guards standing at the doors. In other words, on arriving, they found nothing whatever amiss — locks and guards were in order. But now comes the shock: "on having opened up, inside no one did we find." The twelve prisoners had vanished into thin air. One can imagine the expression on the faces of the Sadducees when they heard this report.

24) **Now when they heard these words, both the commander of the Temple and the high priests, they were much perplexed concerning them as to what might have occurred. But someone, having come, reported to them, Lo, the men whom you placed in the prison are in the Temple standing and teaching.**

Only the commander of the Temple police and the high priests are named because they had made the arrest; the rest of the Sanhedrists now learned of the matter for the first time. The commander is named first because he was responsible for all his men through whose fingers these prisoners had slipped. The preposition διά in the verb intensifies it: "thoroughly perplexed concerning them," i. e., the words or statements just made. In the indirect question: τί ἂν γένοιτο τοῦτο, we have an instance where a misconception of the meaning may mislead not only some translators but a few grammarians. Neither the sense nor the grammar yield the translation, "whereunto this would grow" (our versions, Luther, R., *W. P.*). This translation would require the present optative. The aorist optative compels us to translate, "what might have occurred" (B.-D. 299, 2: *was da wohl geschehen sei; wie das zugegangen sei*). The perplexity was caused by what had just been reported and the astonishment as to how in the world such a thing could have happened. It was not as yet caused by a regard for the future and what might happen.

In the New Testament the direct discourse is preferred to the indirect, hence so few examples of indirect discourse with the optative occur, and these occur only in Luke's writings. They represent the potential optative with ἄν which is taken over from the direct question without change, B.-D. 385 and 386. Only the apodosis is used in these indirect questions, the protasis, εἰ with the optative, does not appear.

25) In the midst of this perplexity there comes a messenger with the news that the men whom the Sanhedrists had locked up were in the Temple this very instant, back in their accustomed places, standing there as usual and proceeding with their teaching of the people. This messenger was, no doubt, a Levite, at least someone who knew all about the arrest of the previous day. But note that the news reaches the perplexed Sanhedrists just at this psychological moment as though the Lord had timed it so. If the Sadducees had heard this news sooner they might have kept it to themselves; now it came to the ears of the entire Sanhedrin and certainly had its effect.

THE TWELVE BEFORE THE SANHEDRIN

26) The situation had taken on an unexpected complexion. **Then the commander, having gone with the underlings, brought them, not with force, for they were fearing the people lest they be stoned.**

The chief commander had not thought it necessary to go to the prison in person, now he finds it decidedly necessary to go to the Temple court, for the situation has become delicate. He takes with him the Levite police who have just made their astonishing report. The texts with the reading ἦγεν describe, those with ἤγαγεν merely state the fact. From the prison the apostles were to have been brought "with force" like prisoners who are being haled before their judges; nothing of the sort is now attempted, "not with force," but the apostles are brought as men who have been requested to appear. They accompany the commander of their own accord; not a hand is laid upon them. And Luke states the reason (γάρ) : the commander and his men feared the people, crowds of whom were again listening to the teaching. That was real fear "lest they be stoned."

We see no reason for being in doubt in regard to the construction of this clause; it is not a purpose clause that is dependent on the phrase "not with force" (R., *W. P.*) ; but it is dependent on "they were fearing" and states what was feared. See R. 995; B.-D. 370. Sections of the Temple were still being rebuilt; in fact, this rebuilding was not completed until shortly before the war and the final destruction of the entire Temple. So stones were at hand as in John 8:59; 10:31. The Jews were also extremely excitable, and when they were suddenly aroused knew no limits in their mob violence. Here we see the high esteem which the apostles enjoyed among the common people; it was highly dangerous to make a false move against them in the presence of the people. And all this occurred while the great Sanhedrin was kept waiting.

27) **Now, having brought them, they made them stand in the Sanhedrin. And the high priest inquired of them, saying: With an order we gave orders to you not to be teaching on the basis of this name; and lo, you have filled Jerusalem with your teaching and intend to bring on us the blood of this man!**

While the Sanhedrists were seated on a semicircular platform, the apostles were literally made to stand (the verb is transitive) "in the Sanhedrin." So John and Peter, and so Jesus, too, had stood. Caiaphas presides, and it is he that "inquired." But the form of his address is not a question, it is an assertion in an accusing tone that demands a reply in defense.

28) Not a word does Caiaphas breathe about the manner in which the apostles escaped from the prison — he surely had his suspicions regarding that. It would have been a fine thing for him and for the other Sadducees, who did not believe in angels, to hear it attested by twelve witnesses before the whole Sanhedrin and all the Pharisees who were in it, who did believe in angels, that an angel had opened the prison and had led them out. So not a word regarding that subject. But a strong word regarding the awful crime of the apostles who had flagrantly disobeyed the strictest orders of the august Sanhedrin in no way ever to be teaching ἐπὶ τῷ ὀνόματι τούτῳ, with "this name" and what it stands for and reveals as the basis (see 2:21).

"With an order we gave orders" is the Greek reproduction of the Hebrew infinitive absolute and yet follows similar Greek constructions which, by adding the cognate noun, emphasize the force of the verb: "we issued strictest orders to you," R. 531. The infinitive is properly durative: "not to be teaching." Here we again see the unwillingness of these foes of Jesus even to utter his name "Jesus"; "this name," "this man" is all that they can bring themselves to say. *Sie moechten ihn totschweigen. Fugit appellare Jesum; Petrus appellat et celebrat.* Bengel. The high priest's feeling on that point is correct, for this name will prove his destruction.

But what have the apostles done? "You have filled Jerusalem with your teaching!" No less. And this is true in fact and not an exaggeration. The perfect is extensive (R. 895) ; it reaches from the past to a point in the present; the accusative indicates what is filled, and the genitive that with which the filling has been accomplished. "Jerusalem" has the article, *das Jerusalem* (German), it is feminine because it is the name of a place. This very teaching, this reprehensible doctrine (2:42) the apostles have spread over the entire city in bold violation of the Sanhedrin's stringent command.

Thus far Caiaphas kept the judicial tone, his words sounded like a stern indictment. Now the judge turns defendant and speaks in behalf of his own personal cause and even in an injured tone. He is recalling the bold words of the people that were, no doubt, first uttered by him personally and then caught up by all of them when Pilate refused to assume the guilt of Jesus' blood as recorded in Matt. 27:25. But he is now thinking only of himself and of the Sanhedrin. When they stood before Pilate they were morally certain that there would be no such guilt and boldly offered to take it upon themselves if such guilt there should be.

Why should that offer and especially the word "blood" have remained in this high priest's mind now to be recalled in the presence of apostles? Why should he say, "you intend (the verb expressing purpose,

R. 878) to bring on us the blood of this man" if no guilt attached to the shedding of his blood and to the part the Sanhedrin had played in that shedding? This is the secret working of conscience which makes a coward of this hardened criminal. He sees frightful intentions in the hearts of the apostles and in the growing success of their work. They were resolved to dethrone the high priest, to overthrow the Sanhedrin, and thus to wreak vengeance on them for "the blood of this man." His blood is haunting this Jew, has gone on haunting Jews ever since; but all they do is what Caiaphas here does: betray the thought and charge men with trying to execute it instead of repenting before God.

29) **Answering, however, Peter and the apostles said: It is necessary to obey God rather than men. The God of our fathers raised up Jesus whom you on your part laid hands on, hanging him on wood. Him as Leader and Savior God exalted with his right hand to give repentance to Israel and remission of sins. And we are witnesses of these things, also the Holy Spirit whom God gave to those obeying him.**

The indictment is met by a perfect defense. The singular "answering" presents Peter as the speaker, and the plural "they said" makes the words of Peter the words of all the apostles. First of all, Peter summarily restates what he had said already in 4:19, 20, with the difference that now the great principle is stated abstractly in the briefest form: "It is necessary to obey God rather than men." The "we" of our versions is due to the awkwardness of the English; the Greek expresses the general idea that "one must obey," the German, *man muss gehorchen.*

This dictum is axiomatic for all except atheists and agnostics. Its tremendous significations have been fully discussed in connection with 4:19, 20. But in any given case of supposed conflict between these two authorities "God" and "men," how are we to determine that God really says and orders what men object to, deny, and forbid? Peter answers this question in a full and direct way for the apostles. The Sanhedrin would readily admit the general principle, but it would deny that, by filling Jerusalem with the name of Jesus, the apostles were obeying God and thus rightly placing his authority above that of the Sanhedrin. This, then, is the real point. Men who have erring consciences convince themselves in some way of their own that they are obeying God, whereas, like the Sanhedrin here, they are not but are, perhaps, doing the very opposite. This is not the case with Peter's defense. We may test it today. The apostles were, indeed, obeying God when they disobeyed the men of the Sanhedrin.

30) For God did these things with regard to Jesus and made them and the Holy Spirit the witnesses. They must, therefore, testify and, if men forbid, must obey God rather than men. "The God of our fathers" is a designation that has strong connotations. First, all the hopes and the expectations of our godly fathers rested on God's Messianic promises. Secondly, they were our fathers, and we ought to be their true children by sharing those promises and those hopes now that they have been fulfilled. Thirdly, "our" refers to the Sanhedrin as well as to the apostles; the very pronoun is a call to faith.

The emphasis is on what *God* did, for the apostles are obeying *God* rather than men. And now Peter once more uses two fearful contrasts that were employed so crushingly in 3:13-15, and 4:10: *God* raised up the Jesus *you* killed. *Your* action was directly against *God*; *he* nullified what *you* did, yea, elevated Jesus into his eternal office. Thus, in the most effective way Peter at this very moment does his part by testifying as God's witness and by filling even this hall of the Sanhedrin and the ears of all the Sanhedrists with the name of Jesus.

It is contended that the statement, "God raised up Jesus," does not refer to the resurrection but to the entire act of sending Jesus for his work. Peter cannot mention the resurrection before the crucifixion. Moreover, we are told that we here have the proper chronological order: God raised up Jesus by sending him; the Jews crucified him; God exalted him (by raising him from the dead and by enthroning him in heaven). But this is specious. Peter is not following chronology but is hurling contrasts at the Sanhedrists. The strong asyndeton in v. 31 is not a parallel to the relative ὅν in v. 30; a relative and then an asyndeton do not denote a chronological succession. No; Peter at once announces the mighty deed of God: raising up Jesus from the dead. Everything turns about this central act of God's. As he had done in 4:10, he compels especially the Sadducees in the Sanhedrin who deny the resurrection to face this fact of the resurrection of Jesus. And whereas the Sanhedrists avoided the very name as though even to pronounce it brought defilement upon them, Peter joyfully utters this blessed name and sounds it forth into the ears of these Sanhedrists.

There stands the great fact: *God* raised up Jesus. And here stands its opposite: "whom *you* laid hands on by hanging him on wood," the modal participle which expresses action that is coincident with that of the verb. The verb is expressive of exactly what the Sanhedrists did although they used the hands of others. Moreover, it agrees with the participle: "by hanging him on wood," ἐπὶ ξύλου, which is usually translated, "on a tree." The expression is Jewish for the Jewish thought that is expressed in Deut. 21:23; Gal. 3:13, that one who was executed by being hanged on a beam of wood was by that act declared to be accursed. The Jews suspended the dead body of a criminal after execution; so Christ's dead body hung on the cross. Not only did the Sanhedrin bring about the death of Jesus, a death that was shameful in the eyes of Romans (crucifixion), but they inflicted upon him the death of those who are accursed by God (suspension on wood).

31) The succession of thought is by no means chronological, for with the emphatic τοῦτον Peter in typical Greek fashion resumes all that he has just said about Jesus in v. 30. He is not adding a third act in a series of three but is stating what God's act in raising up the Jesus whom the Jews hanged as one accursed really signifies, namely that "by his right hand God exalted him as Leader and Savior." God's right hand always signifies his power and his majesty; on this dative with the same verb compare 2:33.

Because ἀρχηγόν and σωτῆρα are without articles they are predicative: God exalted him "as Leader and Savior"; the idea is not that of purpose "in order to be a Leader," etc. The two terms, taken together, state what Jesus is. In 3:15 we have ἀρχηγός with a genitive while here this definitive title is absolute. In an effort to find one English term that will fit both passages many translators use "Prince," German *Fuerst,* although the connotation in these translations is not that associated with the Greek word. *Archegos,* like "Savior," refers to what Jesus does for us; he is a fountain, source, author, beginner for us and, as we see from "Savior," the beginner and author of salvation for us. In 3:15 we say "Author of life," here, if we had a similar genitive, we could say "Author of salvation," and this is indeed the sense. "Prince" would indicate that we honor his royal position, that *we* do something for *him*; it may also imply that he is not yet King. On the idea contained in "Savior" compare 4:12 (3:47).

Christ's exaltation always refers to his human nature which is in the *unio* with the divine. The term includes the resurrection which was already a glorification and also the *sessio* in heaven. But only through the medium of the human nature by which Jesus lived under the law, suffered, and died for our sins is he now our Leader and Savior, bringing us to the salvation he has prepared for us.

God exalted him as such an Author of salvation for our sakes, "in order to give (infinitive of purpose, effective aorist) repentance to Israel and remission of sins." This shows how the salvation is made ours. It is wholly by a gift of grace, τοῦ δοῦναι; both repentance and remission are given. The former is wrought in the heart through the Word, the very Word Peter is here preaching so effectively; the latter is given through the divine declaration of justification which absolves the repentant sinner from his sins. The two are simultaneous but always occur in this order and never in the reverse order. The moment repentance is wrought in the heart the act of remission follows in heaven. On μετάνοια and on ἄφεσις see 2:38. "Israel" is mentioned as the recipient of the gift in the sense of 1:8. The gift was intended for Israel in the first place, and Peter had only Israelites before him.

32) These are the profound things that *God* has done for this most vital purpose. "And we are witnesses of these things" or "of these said things." The idea contained in "witnesses" is not only that the apostles themselves saw these said things and could thus testify regarding them. Seeing the nature of these things and their divine purpose, it would be absolutely criminal if they, the witnesses, did not testify and proclaim them to all Israel. Such negligence would certainly be disobeying God in the most wicked way.

When the Sanhedrists attempt to silence them these Sanhedrists disobey God. The apostles cannot permit themselves to be thus silenced, for that keeping silent would imply putting the authority of men in the place of that of God. The logic and the moral rectitude are as clear as crystal.

When Peter adduces the Holy Spirit as another witness in the relative clause, "whom God gave to those obeying him," he intends to state that the testimony of the Spirit is mediate, he using the believers as his media. The idea is not that they are all to preach and to teach as the apostles did, but it is much broader. The apostolic office is kept distinct (1:22). The Holy Spirit is in the hearts as a gift of God to all who by faith in Jesus obey God. All that the Spirit has wrought in these obedient ones is the Spirit's living testimony to Jesus and to what God has made Jesus to be. The fact that Jesus is the exalted Savior is apparent in every believer who has Jesus and his salvation in his heart and confesses these by lip and life. The apostles are not only God's witnesses, their testimony is accompanied by the great fact that is before the eyes of all men, namely that all those who are with the apostles have God's Spirit in their hearts, and that he speaks in and through them. "Those obeying God" include the apostles, although their service as special apostolic witnesses is not excluded. "Obeying" recalls the same verb used in v. 19. What about these Sanhedrists? They are evidently not among those who obey God with the blessed obedience of faith; they have closed their hearts against the gift of the Holy Spirit, against the gift of repentance and remission, against Jesus, God's Savior.

This apostolic address is far more than a defense against an indictment. Peter preaches law and gospel to the hearts of the Sanhedrists, if possible, by God's grace in Christ, to convert and to save them. Note that he speaks to these Sanhedrists about the Holy Spirit as though the Holy Trinity were known to them. This knowledge of the Trinity is assumed already in the preaching of the Baptist and thereafter with never a Jewish objection based on unitarian conceptions of God being uttered. The claim that the Old Testament did not reveal the Trinity to the Jews is without basis in fact.

33) Peter's words reached the heart. **But they, having heard, were sawn in two and were intending to make away with them.** We have the same strong figure in 7:54. We prefer to retain it instead of modifying it: "were cut to the heart" (our versions). The verb is passive and states what Peter's words inflicted. Here the infliction was not salutary, but note a similar passive in 2:37 where it had a salutary effect. The verb states only how pained the Sanhedrists were by the truth concerning their murder of Jesus and their hostility to God; it does not say anything about the rage of these men. The next verb, "they were intending" (to be understood in the same sense as in v. 28 and not "took counsel," A. V.), states that the Sanhedrists were forming the purpose in their hearts to "make away with" the apostles, to murder them. From the treatment accorded Jesus as well as that accorded his apostles we note the type of men that constituted the supreme court and the highest leadership of the Jews: men who had committed murder and were ready again to commit murder.

Would it not have been wiser for Peter to have toned down his words? Many have adopted that sort of wisdom and by doing so have persuaded themselves that they were better witnesses than Peter, more obedient to God than were the apostles. They have never sawn a sinner in two by a preaching of the law. They convert painlessly. Alas, their conversions are only counterfeit. Both verbs are imperfects, both describe conditions, both imply that something definite followed. If the reading ἐβουλεύοντο be preferred to ἐβούλοντο, the former would indicate a little more than intention, namely an openly voiced resolution on the part of some of the Sanhedrists to make away with the apostles. "Were intending," in fact, implies as much, for the intention could not be known unless it was expressed in words.

34) **Now one in the Sanhedrin, a Pharisee, by name Gamaliel, a lawteacher, in honor with all the people, having arisen, ordered to put the men outside for a little while.**

"One in the Sanhedrin" means a member of that body. "A Pharisee" describes him as being a member of the party that was opposed to that mentioned in v. 17 and even more fully in 4:5, 6. This point is of great importance for the sequel. The Sadducees were thwarted by this Pharisee and his followers in the Sanhedrin; a compromise was effected, the apostles were only scourged. "By name Gamaliel," the common dative for introducing names, at once shows to all who know anything about this famous teacher what weight a word of his would have. He was not only "a lawteacher" but one "in honor with all the people" (ethical dative), famous among the Jews. This important personage, as was the right of any member of the Sanhedrin when an executive and **private session** was desired by him, ordered the prisoners to be taken out βραχύ, "for a little," the neuter adjective used as an adverb.

Φαρισαῖος, from the Hebrew *pharash,* means "a separatist." This designation came to be the name of a member of the Jewish party that is prominent everywhere in the New Testament. Organized after the exile, this party insisted on the strictest outward observance of all legal regulations and also of the tradition that added a mass of rabbinical regulations to the

Mosaic laws. They were extreme formalists who ignored everything spiritual in the Scriptures, under their formalism hid much that was morally vicious, and yet were proud of their holiness. They were honored as being holy by the people generally, were absolutely self-righteous and thus violently opposed to the doctrine of grace and liberty that was proclaimed by Jesus. They are accurately described by Jesus himself in Matt. 23:13-39.

This Gamaliel was the grandson of Hillel who was famous in Jewish tradition. Hillel flourished about 37-4 B. C. We know nothing about his son Simon; but Simon's son Gamaliel, whom Luke introduces here, was one of the seven men who were accorded the title "Rabban." He developed his grandfather's teaching and founded a dynasty of famous men which continued for about four centuries. This Gamaliel, called "the old," to distinguish him from his grandson of the same name, must have been famous for many years before the incident recorded in this passage. Saul was a pupil of his (22:3), and it is just possible that Saul himself was present (but not as a member) at this session of the Sanhedrin and heard Gamaliel's address. Much has been made of this Pharisee in Christian tradition and legend. Zahn loves to trace such things, see his *Apostelgeschichte*, 219, etc.

35) **And he said to them: Israelite men, take heed to yourselves about these men, what you are about to do. For before these days, there arose Theudas, claiming himself to be somebody, to whom there was inclined a number of men about four hundred, who was made away with, and all as many as kept on obeying him were dispersed and came to nothing.**

Gamaliel addresses his colleagues in the same honorable fashion as did Peter the Jews in 2:22, and in 3:12. He counsels caution and advises that his colleagues forget not to consider their own interests in case of any precipitate action into which their passion may otherwise lead them. Many, no doubt, thought that he was referring to the danger from the people (v. 26) who held the apostles and believers generally in high esteem (v. 13), but Gamaliel has a different self-interest. He bids his colleagues look farther. Yet his own view and his conclusions proved to be entirely wrong. The Lord, however, used his spurious wisdom to extend the great work that was going on in Jerusalem with full vigor.

36) He sketches briefly the career of a certain Theudas, who was known to his colleagues, who claimed himself to be somebody, secured a following of 400 men for his rebellion, and was soon killed with the result that those who still adhered to his ideas were dispersed and faded into nothing, *ad nihilum.* His entire movement ran its full course without aid from the Sanhedrin. We see the drift of Gamaliel's argument: this Jesus-movement will most likely fade out of itself. Why should the Sanhedrin dip its hands into the blood of these twelve men who still "keep on obeying" Jesus as the followers of Theudas did even after he was slain?

But this little bit of history recounted by Gamaliel, which Luke records without comment as to its correctness, has become the occasion for considerable debate because of statements made by Josephus. In his *Ant.* 20, 5, 1 he, too, reports about a certain Theudas who incited a rebellion and came to a miserable end; but this man appeared about thirteen years after the time of Gamaliel's address. Gamaliel mentions 400 men as constituting the following of the man whom he has in mind, Josephus writes of this man that "he persuaded a great part of the people." Not a few conclude that Josephus is right, and that something is wrong with Luke's account. To make this conclusion more plausible they date Luke and Acts late enough so that Luke could have read Josephus. And Luke is then thought to have invented this part of Gamaliel's address. Men like Ramsey, Robertson (*Luke the Historian*, 160; *W. P.*), and others still think that at least a problem exists and themselves propose to wait until it has been solved. There is no problem whatever in regard to Luke who never read a line of Josephus. Any problem there may be pertains only to Josephus whose mistakes and inaccuracies Zahn, among others, has sufficiently pointed out. Whether Josephus speaks about this Theudas mentioned by Gamaliel, confused the dates, or reports about another Theudas who was active thirteen years later, leaves Gamaliel's statements unaffected.

37) **After him there arose Judas, the Galilean, in the days of the enrolment and drew away people after him; he also perished, and all as many as kept obeying him were scattered abroad.**

This refers to the enrolment for taxation mentioned in Luke 2:1, 2. Gamaliel's expression "in the days of the enrolment" speaks of this as a well-known period. Judas, born in Gamala in Gaulonitis, is called "the Galilean" because of the scene of his revolt which was of far greater proportions than that of Theudas. But he, too, perished, and his following, too, was dispersed so that his efforts likewise ended in nothing.

Usually little is said in regard to Josephus and his account of this Judas, but in this case Josephus' account is worse than that in regard to Theudas. Zahn charges Josephus with *heillose Verwirrung* regarding Judas and other men of like aims as well as in regard to the taxation under Cyrenius in Palestine. Josephus produces a tangle by duplicating Judas, so that he mentions one who was active during the taxation at the end of the life of Herod the Great and another who was active toward the close of the first century. We need not enter into the details which pertain only to Josephus and not in the least to Luke. We add only that the rebellion was of grave proportions, that Judas sought royal honors, and that Josephus, both in the case of Theudas and of Judas, suppresses the Messianic claims that helped to attract the following of these men.

38) In view of these two plain historical instances Gamaliel offers what has become his famous *counsel of indecision*: Be careful — do not decide — wait, wait and see! **And as to now I say to you, stand away from these men and let them be! For if this counsel or this work is of men, it will be overthrown; but if it is of God, you will not be able to overthrow them — lest perchance you be found even fighting God.**

Ταννῦν, "as to the things now," as to the present situation, this, namely, in view of the two historical instances that were well known to all present, Gamaliel advises his colleagues "to stand away from these men" and not to think of killing them and "to let them be," which we may also translate, "to dismiss them." Gamaliel then makes plain his method of reasoning. There can be only two possibilities. He takes up each and draws the conclusion. First, if this counsel or this work — call it what you please — is "of men," has its origin and its source of strength only in weak, erring, deluded men, "it will be overthrown." That is undoubtedly true. Every religion that is built and founded on men will go down in failure. The only oversight in Gamaliel's statement is that he did not say *when* it will be overthrown. He and his colleagues may be dead and gone by the time this human thing, if it be human, is finally overthrown. The question for Gamaliel was as to how long he could wait. How long have some pagan religions endured? How old is Mohammedanism? God will overthrow every false religion and every false religious movement in the end, but can we sit down in indecision until this final proof is produced?

39) The other alternative is equally faulty. If it is "of God," has its source and strength in him, "you cannot overthrow it." "Lest perchance" requires that we supply in thought: "Take heed, lest," etc.; and καί is elliptic: "not merely fighting men but *even* fighting God." Shall they, then, do nothing? Shall they sit on the fence and wait and wait, afraid to strike for God lest they strike against God? This counsel has been called wise but it offers only the folly of indecision where decision is imperative. And with its indecision there goes hand in hand the implication that God has not supplied us with means to make the true and safe decision, so that only the final fate of any religion can decide whether it is of God or of men.

Gamaliel belongs to that class of men whom the most convincing evidence does not convince. They still demand other evidence, more and more signs, Matt. 12:39, etc. Their answer to all the evidence furnished by Christ is: "Yes — but!" Gamaliel lacked one thing: the consciousness of sin. The veil of his Pharisaic work-righteousness blinded him to his guilt. Peter's call to repentance did not move him to contrition. So this wise Jew continued in his folly.

R. 1018 compares the two conditional sentences employed by Gamaliel, first, ἐάν with the subjunctive followed by the future indicative (expectance); secondly, εἰ with the indicative followed by the future indicative (reality), and finds that Gamaliel is giving the benefit of the doubt to Christianity. This, however, is not the case. The conditional forms used keep the balance and incline neither way. The reason for using these forms lies elsewhere. In the one case Gamaliel rightly thinks of the future: "if it shall (turn out to) be of men"; in the other case he just as rightly thinks of the present: "if it is of God." Both are suppositions on his part just as all conditions are suppositions and nothing more. In the one case Gamaliel supposes something future with a future result; in the other something present with a future result. He has not a mite more certainty for the one case than for the other — yes, masterly indecision.

40) **Now they obeyed him; and having called the apostles, after administering a hiding, they gave orders not to be speaking on the basis of the name of Jesus and released them.**

Literally, "they were persuaded to him," the Greek for, "they obeyed." No one of the Sanhedrin arose to point out the fallacy in Gamaliel's argument, and no one called attention to the fact that by rejecting and crucifying Jesus they had already decided that this entire movement was *not* of God. The Sadducees lost, the Pharisees won. This friction between the two parties explains much, particularly also the scourging administered before the apostles were released, δείραντες, literally, "after flaying them." They were stripped and given thirty-nine blows with rods across the back (Deut. 35:3; II Cor. 11:24; compare, Matt. 10:17, and Acts 22:19). This severe treatment was not so much to be a punishment for what the apostles had done but rather an emphasis on the renewed order not to be saying a word "on (the basis of) the name of Jesus" (see 4:17, 18). To be beaten thus was no small disgrace; before Roman judges Roman citizens dared not be treated thus. The Jews had no such restrictions.

41) **They, therefore, were going from the presence of the Sanhedrin rejoicing that they were deemed worthy to be dishonored on behalf of the Name. And every day in the Temple and from house to house they were not ceasing to teach and to proclaim as good news Jesus the Christ.**

Οἱ μὲν οὖν is Luke's favorite turn of expression, see 1:6; a δέ need not follow. The imperfect with its present participle is beautifully descriptive and pictures the apostles going from the presence of the Sanhedrin and rejoicing as they went. The scourging took place in the presence of the Sanhedrin; Jesus, too, was scourged in the presence of Pilate. Gamaliel also went away, but certainly not rejoicing. If this work was "of God," would not forbidding it and scourging its agents be fighting God? But there was no doubt in the hearts of the apostles.

Note the sharp oxymoron (bringing together contradictory terms) in "deemed worthy to be dishonored." These disgraceful stripes the apostles considered badges of honor. In the great and blessed fight *for* God they had not been undecided and inactive like Gamaliel but had done their part valiantly and as true soldiers of the cross bore honorable wounds to attest their noble loyalty. This was the first instance of what Paul writes in I Cor. 4:9: "I think God hath set forth us the apostles last of all, as men doomed to death; for we are made a spectacle unto the world, and to the angels, and to men." "On behalf of the Name" makes ὄνομα emphatic, for from the beginning (4:7) everything had turned on this "Name," the term being used as explained in 4:2; 2:21. Here it is used in an eminent sense.

42) Never for a moment did the apostles cease their blessed work. "Every day" they continued, and this openly "in the Temple" where the Sanhedrin and the Temple police could see and hear them, and, of course, also κατ' οἶκον, which is distributive, "from house to house," and not merely adverbial, "at home." They continued to fill Jerusalem from center to circumference with the Name. They scorned to work only in secret. They knew no fear. The imperfect, "they were not ceasing," with its complementary present par-

ticiples is still descriptive, and "were not ceasing" (negative) is a litotes for "were ever continuing." The first participle, "teaching," is made more specific by the second, "proclaiming as good news Jesus the Christ"; τὸν Χριστόν is predicative: "as the Christ." Here we have the first instance of εὐαγγελίζεσθαι in the Acts in the full sense of preaching the gospel, and with it the mighty name "Jesus" and its full significance in "the Christ," the Messiah of God (2:36). This "name" fittingly closes the present narrative.

This was the opposite of indecision. This was the divinely wrought certainty that had long ago made the final decision. This was the joy that came from that certainty. The apostles never for a moment complained of the injustice they had suffered at the hands of the authorities; they did not boast of their own courage and fortitude or concern themselves about defending their personal honor against the shame inflicted on them. If they thought of themselves at all, it was only that they might prove faithful to the Lord by working for the honor of his great blessed Name. All else they committed into his hands.

CHAPTER VI

The Election of the Seven

In chapters six and seven we have the story of Stephen. There is no reason for thinking that a special document was intercalated at this point by Luke or by some redactor. There is a perfect connection with the preceding. After being told about the great growth of the congregation and of its manner of taking care of the needy, we now learn that this work grew beyond the capacity of the apostles, and thus we come to Stephen, one of the seven deacons who is forever distinguished as the first martyr of the Christian Church. This fact justifies Luke for allotting so much space to Stephen and to his address in this account. At the end of the narrative about Stephen we catch our first glimpse of Saul.

1) **Now in these days, the disciples multiplying, there occurred a murmuring of the Hellenists against the Hebrews because their widows were being overlooked in the daily ministration.**

Nothing of note occurred after the agitation reported in the previous chapters. The apostles continued their great work strenuously and without interference. The genitive absolute reports their continued great success: "the disciples multiplying." It has been conservatively estimated that at this time the total number of the disciples was between twenty and twenty-five thousand. This vast increase, Luke intimates, occasioned the murmuring, subdued complaint, of the Hellenists against the Hebrews, that the widows of the former were being overlooked in the daily dispensation of support, which is beautifully called the διακονία or "ministration" which freely renders service and help for the benefit of those concerned. Here Luke calls the believers μαθηταί, "disciples," from μανθάνω, "to learn," but not in the sense merely of "pupils" who are still under instruction but rather in the sense of those who have already learned. And even this is not enough, for this learning was not merely intellectual, it involved the acquirement of the very spirit of the teacher. These disciples had become like their Master, they were following in his footsteps.

The Ἑλληνισταί (a word not found until it was used by Luke) were not Ἕλληνες, "Greeks," either by extraction, by religion, or in the broader cultural sense. They were Jews fully as much as the other class that is called "Hebrews." We read of all sorts of Hellenists in 2:9-11 and find their synagogues mentioned in 6:9. They had been reared in foreign lands, had replaced the Aramaic with the Greek language, and thus read their Scriptures only in the LXX translation. In the diaspora the second and the third generations lost their Aramaic to a great degree as the inscriptions on their tombs show. Yet they in every way remained loyal Jews. Among them there were proselytes (2:10), but these had completely adopted Judaism and thus are also designated as Jews. These Hellenists were scattered over the entire Roman world.

The Ἑβραῖοι were the Jews of Palestine and of the great eastern diaspora, Babylon, etc. Their native tongue remained Aramaic, they used the Hebrew Scriptures in their synagogues, their Greek was for the greater part imperfect, and they took a certain pride in being "Hebrews" (II Cor. 11:22; Phil. 3:5). There was, however, no clear dividing line between these two great classes of Jews. Jesus, who lived only in Palestine, needed no interpreter but himself spoke Greek to Pilate. On the other hand, Paul, who who was reared in Tarsus, perfectly preserved his

Aramaic and knew his Hebrew. So also the attitude of the two classes is devoutly Jewish. "To Hellenize" meant to adopt Greek or pagan modes of life, and this corruption had contaminated the Jews, even some of their aristocratic priests, but the Hellenists we read about in the New Testament had not Hellenized themselves in this manner.

The complaint was not directed against the apostles although they must be classed as "Hebrews." It seems as though the majority of the congregation consisted of Hebrews, and that the apostles had used assistants from this class for dispensing the needed charity. How this had been done, and how widows of the Hellenists had thus come to be overlooked, we are unable to say. We see only that the complaint was justified. How much party feeling between Hellenists and Hebrews was involved is difficult to say.

2) **And the Twelve, having called to them the multitude of the disciples, said: It does not please us that we, having forsaken the Work of God, keep ministering to tables. Look out for yourselves, therefore, brethren, seven attested men from yourselves, full of the Holy Spirit and of wisdom, whom we shall appoint for this need. But for our part, we will continue steadfast in the worship and in the ministration of the Word.**

The apostles function as the leaders of the congregation. They act promptly and do not let the case become acute. Although they are apostles, they make no decision of their own a law for the congregation. There is not the least trace of popery; they deal with the members as brethren. The Twelve called the meeting and not Peter. In order to do so they must have discussed the matter among themselves and naturally would offer some proper plan for the congregation to adopt. But this amounted only to making a motion in the meeting and seconding it, after which all voted.

Luke does not need to say that only those who had attained the proper age took part in this meeting in accord with the spirit of the Fourth Commandment, Eph. 6:1; Col. 3:20; likewise, he need not mention the fact that only the men voted in accord with the Jewish practice which was based on Gen. 2:18-23; 3:16, and was for this very reason the apostolic practice, I Tim. 2:12-14. This point has now become controversial, but exegetically neither the apostolic practice itself nor the grounds on which it rests, God's creation and thus nature and the condition produced by the fall, can be controverted.

Perhaps Peter spoke; if this was the case, he did so merely for all the Twelve. The personal pronoun ἡμᾶς lends force to the impersonal οὐκ ἀρεστόν ἐστι, so that this means: "It does not please us." The matter is well stated: "that we, having forsaken the Word of God," i. e., the preaching and the teaching of this Word, the essential task to which the apostles were called by the Lord, "keep ministering to tables," to dispensing food for the needy. We now have διακονεῖν to correspond with the διακονία used in v. 1. The apostles were, indeed, "to minister," but in distributing the Bread of life and not in attending to the distribution of ordinary food supplies. The words are general. Therefore it is impossible for us to learn just how the apostles had been ministering to tables. Yet we may safely say that "tables" does not refer to the love feasts that were taking place at different houses and preceded the Eucharist. The food for these feasts was brought by the participants who readily shared with the needy. Luke has already informed us that this ministry refers to administering and distributing the large sums of money that were derived from the sale of property. From this fund the daily ministration was made.

At first the apostles shouldered this extra task without much difficulty. But now it had grown to undue proportions and interfered with their essential work. The fact that some widows were thus overlooked was only one evil result; the apostles point to one that is still worse; their being forced into a task that really does not belong to their office. This point is worth noting. The theory that all offices in the church are derived from one central office and really constitute parts of it finds no support here. This theory has led to such ideas as that when the janitor rings the bell, sweeps the church, lights the lamps, he is only substituting for the pastor. The apostles have a different view and clearly state what the obligation of the Christian ministry is. Other tasks may arise, but these are extraneous, to be turned over to other hands. The apostles were not delegating a part of their divine office to others — they could not. They were relinquishing tasks that were not a part of this office, that were interfering with that office. To be sure, these tasks, too, need to be performed, but this necessity does not make them a part of the divinely instituted office of apostles and pastors.

3) The selection of the men for this task is left to the congregation. If these men were to serve as assistants to the apostles in their apostolic work, the selection would have been made by the apostles. So Paul selected his assistants, and we know that he declined Mark's services. But these men were to be the aids of the congregation in the ministration at tables, and so the congregation was properly told itself to choose them. The apostles merely make the proposal, suggest the necessary number, and name the qualifications the men should have. And we must note that the congregation freely adopted these restrictions. Just why seven were proposed no one knows. It is, of

course, a sacred number, but here practical considerations evidently governed. If these men were to have been assistants of the apostles, we should expect the number to be twelve and not seven. It is only a conjecture to say that at this time seven special meeting places were used by the congregation. The reason for selecting seven seems to have been obvious to the congregation, but what this reason was we cannot say.

The present participle "attested," "witnessed to," is qualitative and the present tense for this reason. Men who were known for their character and their ability are referred to; this was naturally consented to. Likewise, the requirement that they should be "full of the Holy Spirit and of wisdom." It is well that "wisdom" is added, for this helps us to understand just what is meant by being full of the Holy Spirit. All the disciples had the Holy Spirit, all had received one gift or another from him. The men needed for the task here considered ought to have one notable gift in an especial measure, namely to such a degree as to be recognized by the members generally. This was "wisdom," the ability and the readiness to apply Christian knowledge to the practical affairs of life. We at once see how necessary this gift of the Spirit would be, and how the congregation readily agreed to look for men only of this marked type. Moreover, where the Spirit gives wisdom, other gifts will also be present.

"Whom we shall appoint for this need" has no emphatic "we" and in no way implies anything hierarchical. After the election of the men by the congregation the apostles, who had had this work in their hands thus far, would turn it over to them. The idea that a fitting ceremony would be included was only natural (v. 6).

4) After this arrangement has been made, the apostles expect to devote all their time to what proper-

ly constitutes their divine office which they summarize briefly as "the worship and the ministration of the Word." The term προσευχή is frequently used in this wider sense of worship of which prayer constitutes the prominent part. That the newly created office, like everything else belonging to the life and the activity of the congregation, would be under the guidance and the leadership of the apostles and their divine office, goes without saying.

5) **And the word pleased before the entire multitude; and they elected for themselves Stephen, a man full of faith and of the Holy Spirit, and Philip, and Prochorus, and Nicanor, and Timon, and Parmenas, and Nicolaus, a proselyte, an Antiochian, whom they set before the apostles. And praying, they placed on them the hands.**

We may say, "the proposition" was accepted by vote. The construction with ἐνώπιον is the language of the LXX, and ἤρεσεν is like the Latin *placuit* when a vote is taken. The entire assembly unanimously voiced its agreement. The election was held, but we do not know in what manner except that the apostles do not seem to have made the nominations. The two most prominent men, as the following record describes them, are placed at the head of the list; we know nothing further concerning the rest. Stephen is especially distinguished as "a man full of faith and of the Holy Spirit." If πλήρης is the reading adopted, this word is regarded as indeclinable (B.-D. 137, 1). In v. 3 the order is: "full of the Holy Spirit and of wisdom"; here: "full of faith and of the Holy Spirit." First the source, and then the fruit; again the fruit, and then its source. What Luke means by "faith" we see in the following: the power of personal conviction expressed in most convincing wisdom (v. 10). Stephen's address before the Sanhedrin is the sublime expression of that faith. Philip became the evangelist and is not to be confused with Philip the apostle.

All the men chosen bear Greek names, but it would be a hasty conclusion to state that all were Hellenists when we remember that two of the apostles, who were certainly Hebrews, had Greek names, namely Andrew and Philip. We, therefore, decline to draw the conclusion that, since the complaint came from the Hellenists, the Hebrews generously turned the whole work of ministration over to the Hellenists. Some of both classes of Jews were elected, the only fair and proper course. The one named last was even a proselyte. To select one of this class was also wise. When Luke adds that he was an Antiochian, some think that this manifests Luke's personal interest in Antioch as being the home city of himself and of Theophilus (Robertson, *Luke the Historian, etc.,* 22). The truth lies rather in this that, as he does in the case of Stephen, Luke writes with a view to what follows. Antioch was to become the great missionary center. More serious is the idea expressed by a few of the fathers and by some recent scholars that Nicolas became apostate and founded the Gnostic sect of the Nicolaitans mentioned in Rev. 2:6, 14. He would thus be mentioned last by Luke as a kind of traitor, like Judas. But the sole evidence furnished for this view by Irenaeus, Tertullian, etc., seems to be the name. It ought to be understood that decidedly more evidence is required in a matter of so serious a charge.

6) "Whom they set before the apostles" makes the impression, that it took some time to effect the election, and that the apostles entrusted the election entirely to the congregation. They, too, were the ones to be satisfied. After the election had been held, these seven were certified as the congregation's choice.

Luke continues with a plural participle and a verb, but evidently not the congregation but the apostles laid their hands on the seven and installed them in their office. The word "apostles" is not written because Luke has just mentioned them. The Lord's blessing was invoked upon the elected men, and the hands were laid on them in this Old Testament symbolical act, which transferred the office with its duties and privileges and pictured the bestowal of the divine blessings that were necessary for this important work. Compare Num. 27:18; Deut. 34:9. This rite was freely adopted by the early church; we read of it in 13:3 in connection with missionaries, and in I Tim. 4:4; 5:22; II Tim. 1:6 in connection with elders. We still use it in connection with confirmation and ordination. It was always symbolic and never charismatic.

The entire account shows that these seven men received only the office of deacons, their duty being to care for the poor and the needy as almoners. The preaching and the work of the Word remained wholly in the hands of the apostles (v. 4). The idea, often voiced, that after Pentecost the believers as such preached is without support in Luke's account. So also the idea that, because Stephen argued with the Jews in their synagogues, and Philip became an evangelist, their diaconate included public preaching and teaching, and their installation was an ordination, goes beyond the facts as Luke reports them. These seven were in no sense presbyters of the Jerusalem congregation; they were not elected for that purpose. What is later reported about Stephen and about Philip has nothing to do with their official duties in the congregation. These activities were the result of gifts and of opportunities that extend beyond their special office. The offices that came into being in the apostolic church were not fluid but well defined.

7) **And the Word of God continued to grow; and the number of the disciples went on multiplying**

exceedingly; also a great multitude of the priests were becoming obedient to the faith.

Luke inserts this little account of the progress made in Jerusalem in order to show that neither the attack of the Sanhedrin nor the defect that had developed in the congregation in any way checked its growth. Compare 2:41; 4:4; 5:14, and now 6:7. The imperfect tenses describe and at the same time show steady continuation. "Continued to grow" speaks of the Word of God as a living thing; and it, indeed, grows as it enters and fills more and more hearts. "Went on multiplying exceedingly" is not an exaggeration as the clause with τε proves which adds that "a great multitude of the priests" were won. These had held off the longest but were now coming in numbers. To speak about plebeian priests contradicts the fact that all the priests were on the same level who were divided into twenty-four courses, each taking its turn in the Temple and portioning out the different tasks. There were no ranks or grades among them. "Were becoming obedient to the faith" is an expression similar to the one found in 13:8; Rom. 1:5; 16:26. We see no reason for not understanding πίστις in the objective sense, namely as that which faith holds, Christ, the gospel, salvation in Christ. To understand the word in the subjective sense, faith in the sense of the action of believing, raises unnecessary difficulties.

Stephen Brought to Trial

The Lord's hand had restrained the enemy for a long time. Finally the awful blow fell that was to scatter the congregation far and wide. It fell suddenly and in a way that was altogether unexpected: one of the deacons was brought to trial.

8) **Now Stephen, full of grace and power, was doing great wonders and signs among the people. But there arose some of those out of the synagogue**

called that of the Libertines and of the Cyrenians and of the Alexandrians, and of those from Cilicia and Asia, disputing with Stephen. And they were not strong enough to withstand the wisdom and the Spirit by whom he was speaking.

Once again Luke draws attention to the spiritual qualifications of Stephen, he was "full of grace and power," for Stephen is the first man in addition to the apostles to perform miracles, "great wonders and signs," the two terms being combined as usual (see 2:19). "Many" could not be added, for Stephen's career was cut short; but "great" is added in order to indicate that Stephen's miracles were of the same quality as those of the apostles.

In v. 3 and v. 5 note "wisdom, faith, and the Holy Spirit," two personal effects and their divine source. Now "grace and power" are added. Both are direct gifts of a different kind that are plainly charismatic in their nature and enable their possessor to work miracles. This is not χάρις in the sense of pardoning grace, for that Stephen had when he first came to faith, but the special *favor Dei* that was connected with the δύναμις or power bestowed on him at this time as something exceptional and not granted to the other deacons: the ability to perform miracles. In other words, the Lord singled out Stephen (grace) as his instrument through whom he wrought miracles (power) when and where the Lord desired (compare 3:4). The congregation had made him a deacon, the Lord made something far greater out of him. As stated in connection with v. 6, the latter had nothing to do with his work as a deacon. We add that Luke does not say a word about Stephen's being a preacher or a teacher. He had neither a mediate nor an immediate call to that work.

9) From Luke's account we gather that Stephen was assailed by a number of Hellenistic Jews because

his wonders and signs drew especial attention to him. Why they did not attack one or the other of the apostles but selected Stephen is not indicated. Luke states only the fact. The usual view is that Stephen made bold to invade the synagogues of these Jews and thus forced disputes regarding Jesus as the Messiah. The opposite is true. These Jews arose against Stephen and forced a dispute upon him, not in a synagogue of theirs, but in such a place where they were able to meet Stephen, probably in the court of the Temple or somewhere on the street. Stephen was a Hellenist as were his attackers, and this may have caused them to single him out although Luke does not say this.

We must note that τινες τῶν ἐκ . . . καὶ τῶν ἀπό indicates two general groups, and that "synagogue," although it is often used as a designation for a building, must here have its original meaning: "gathering, congregation, mob." The word is applied only to the first group; the Libertines, Cyrenians, and Alexandrians formed a congregation, not so "those from Cilicia and Asia" — at least Luke does not say so. The fact that Luke does not refer to a building appears also from the circumstance that no synagogue would be called by a name that included three nationalities; on the other hand, no grammarian has supplied "synagogue" with either the first three nationalities alone or with all five. How R., *W. P.*, can say that Luke may have referred to five synagogue buildings, is rather difficult to understand. By using ἀπό Luke excludes a reference to even two synagogues. The Talmud speaks of 480 synagogues in Jerusalem, but if there had been that many or even a thousand, this would not affect what Luke here states.

Luke uses the aorist: "there rose up some" in dispute. This aorist cannot be constative as speaking of a series of acts. It follows an imperfect and is in turn followed by an imperfect, and, therefore, if a series of disputes were implied, we should have an imperfect and not an aorist between imperfects. Moreover, the subject of this aorist is "some," a group made up of five nationalities. These arose in dispute. This does not mean that now the Libertines arose, now the Cyrenians, and so forth, today in this synagogue, tomorrow in that?

Some commentators draw on their imagination and ask: "Was not Saul from Cilicia, would he not be in the synagogue of the Cilicians, and would not this brilliant pupil of Gamaliel's be the first one to oppose Stephen when he invaded this synagogue?" R., *W. P.*, regards this story as "practically certain." As to Luke, he reports that "some" who were possibly chosen for this purpose from two groups (the one composed of three, the other of two nationalities), all of them Hellenists, on one occasion engaged Stephen in a decisive dispute.

The Libertines were freedmen and their descendants, the Latin *libertini.* This term ignores the earlier distinction between *liberti* as a designation for freedmen and *libertini* as a designation for their descendants. This term is geographical like the rest, and to hear it mentioned was to think of Rome, whither two generations before, in 61 B. C., Pompey had taken many hundreds of captive Jews who were then sold as slaves. Numbers of them and of their descendants gained their liberty and were considered Romans. They were rapidly Hellenized. Zahn draws attention to the inscriptions on tombs and to the fact that only one of the seven synagogues found in Rome is called that of the Hebrews. The circumstance that numbers of these freedmen migrated to Jerusalem is most natural, for, like other Jews of the diaspora, those listed here and in 2:9-11, they felt drawn to their great sanctuary in the Holy City. It is entirely probable that some of the *libertini* were among the "Romans" mentioned in 2:10, even some who refused to believe at that time and now withstood Stephen. On the Cyrenians see 2:10. The Alexandrians were from Alexandria in Northern Egypt, two of whose five divisions were inhabited by Jews. Alexandria was the main seat of Hellenistic Jewish learning. Cilicia is a province in the southeastern corner of Asia Minor, while Asia (here without the article) is the province by this name, whose capital was Ephesus. All these Hellenistic Jews, like Stephen himself, had their present permanent homes in Jerusalem.

10) Luke follows with imperfects that are descriptive but not ingressive (R., *W. P.*). They are open tenses and imply the definite action expressed by the following aorists. These Hellenists were many against one, but despite their number they had not the strength (imperfect) to resist successfully (aorist infinitive) "the wisdom" (see v. 3) and the Holy Spirit granting that wisdom, by whom Stephen kept speaking in this debate. "By whom" = by whose assistance. Luke pictures the situation.

11) Now the result that followed. **Then they suborned men,** (these) **stating, We have heard him uttering blasphemous utterances against Moses and God. And they stirred up both the people and the elders and the scribes; and having come upon him, they snatched him and brought him to the Sanhedrin, besides they set up false witnesses,** (these) **saying: This man does not cease uttering utterances against this holy place and the law. For we have heard him saying, This Jesus, the Nazarene, will destroy this place and will change the customs which Moses gave to us.**

When fair means fail, unbelief is prone to resort to foul means, thereby condemning itself. The narrative proceeds by using aorists, all of which report the outcome of the action described in v. 10. "They suborned men," etc., literally, "threw under," is the regular term for securing perjured witnesses. There is no reason why these "men" could not have been selected from the disputants named in v. 10. It is also plain that these men were to serve as witnesses at the trial to which these opponents of Stephen hoped to bring him — a plan which succeeded. These very men were the ones put forward as the "false witnesses" referred to in v. 13; the idea that they were not the same men lacks support.

Λέγοντας introduces what these men are to say, namely to charge Stephen with "blaphemous utterances against Moses and God." This greatest Old Testament prophet and mediator of the covenant is combined with God as the object of one preposition which practically makes "Moses and God" one concept; for whatever would be uttered against Moses would *eo ipso* be spoken also against God. What these utterances were to be we hear presently; only their general character is stated in advance.

12) With this devilish plan in mind, the Hellenists begin operations. They inaugurate a violent agitation throughout the city and soon succeed in stirring up "both the people and the elders and the scribes," τε — καί, "elders and scribes," being a unit and meaning as much as Sanhedrists. Since so many Hellenists started on a definite campaign simultaneously, it is little wonder that a great agitation resulted. It certainly lasted more than a day or two. The idea of blasphemy against Moses and God stirred up the most violent passions in almost any Jew. The fact that such a charge was prefered from many quarters certainly made it appear to be true. The Sanhedrists, no doubt, responded most readily although it was not an apostle

that was being accused; they must have become more alarmed than ever because so many priests accepted Jesus (v. 7).

Luke simply relates the facts in the briefest fashion. With τε he closely connects the arrest with the successful agitation. This means that, as soon as preparation was well under way, Stephen was to be apprehended and put to trial. This, too, succeeded. How and where his foes captured him is immaterial to Luke. Perhaps it was in his own home or when, upon some occasion, he ventured into the street that they accosted him, caught him, and led him away to the Sanhedrin. The verbs make one think of a wild animal leaping on its innocent prey, burying its fangs in the flesh, and carrying it off.

One of the remarkable features of this story is the circumstance that these vicious and bloodthirsty Jews do not plan simply to capture and to kill Stephen without further ceremony. No; they plan on a trial, prepare witnesses, then secure Stephen and place him before the high court. They just *will* have the legal machinery! It was so in the case of Jesus. Although their motives were insincere and all the means criminal, this show of legal right seems in some way to hush their consciences.

13) We have no reason to think that the Sanhedrin was assembled and waiting when Stephen was brought in. All that Luke wishes to convey to us is the fact that Stephen was placed before this high court to be tried for the worst crime known in its criminal code. How long a time was required to assemble the Sanhedrin is an immaterial detail. So also the proceedings previous to the calling of the witnesses. We have heard the indictment in v. 11; Luke needs to report only its substantiation by means of testimony. The accusers (v. 9) have their witnesses ready. Luke at once calls them "lying" or "false"

witnesses and by the use of that expression intends to indicate that they consciously testified falsely and thus perjured themselves. The proof is furnished *in extenso* in Stephen's own address which shows what he did say in his dispute (v. 9) and at any and all other times.

First the preamble: "This man does not cease uttering utterances against this holy place and the law." Not once or twice but without changing his utterances he assails "this holy place and the law." The view that by "this holy place" the witnesses referred, not to the Temple, but to the city of Jerusalem with its Temple, is unsatisfactory since it cannot be shown that this designation was ever so used. If a holiness of the city might be spoken of, this emanated only from the Temple; and any utterance against the city would be blasphemous only because it was really spoken against the Temple. As far as destruction is concerned, the Temple would be the last structure to be destroyed; its destruction would thus involve that of the city. Far more important is the combination of "this holy place" with "the law" which refers to Mosaic regulations that centered in the Temple (not in the city save as the Temple in that city is referred to). Of necessity the two belong together, for any derogatory utterances against either would involve the other. God (v. 11) was behind both.

14) The actual testimony is introduced with γάρ: "We have heard him declaring, 'This Jesus, the Nazarene, will destroy this place and will change the customs which Moses gave us.'" This sentence purports to be a direct and verbatim quotation from Stephen's own lips; but in reality it is only a restatement of what these witnesses claimed Stephen had said. The case is quite analogous to that of Jesus who was alleged to have said about the same thing (John 2:19-22; Matt. 26:61; 27:40). In both cases no effort

is made to understand what the person charged actually said, and what his words really mean, but only to use his words against him by making him say or imply what he never actually said or really implied. Luther makes the application: "We ought on this account raise no high complaint against such unfair accusations. The devil knows no other way than to lie and pervert and interpret in the worst fashion what has been said well and properly. This we must look for and must wait until God comes and proves whether they have spoken truth or whether they have lied. In the meanwhile we must content ourselves that, together with beloved Stephen, we have the testimony of our conscience that we are not trying to blaspheme or teach people wrongly and mislead them."

After one fashion or another commentators endeavor to determine exactly wherein the lie of these false witnesses consisted, and some of them pare down the lie to very moderate proportions. Fortunately, we have Stephen's own reply. He takes up these charges in detail and first refutes the charge that he blasphemed God; secondly, that he blasphemed Moses and the law; thirdly, that he blasphemed the Temple. In fact, he proves that he does the very opposite, and that in the true sense of God's own Word, that Word which these Jews constantly resisted and whose prophets they killed. Nor was Stephen, as little as Jesus, condemned on the basis of this false testimony but because he spoke the truth, especially the truth about his own accusers and judges.

15) After the depositions of the perjured witnesses had been received, all eyes turned upon Stephen. **And all those sitting in the Sanhedrin gazing earnestly on him, saw his countenance as an angel's countenance.**

What made the entire Sanhedrin gaze thus at Stephen? Was this only a look of interest which is apt to be manifested when a defendant reaches the dramatic moment for his own defense? No; it was what these Sanhedrists saw: Stephen's face like an angel's face. Aorist participle and aorist verb express simultaneous action. Did Luke mean only that "with beaming countenance" and "unafraid" Stephen "enthusiastically" entered on his defense? Then Luke, the great historian, used extravagant, not to say false, language. Even great joy and exalted expressions on a man's face would not make a body of men think they were seeing something "like an angel's face."

We must recall the promise of Jesus given to the disciples that at their trials before tribunals the Holy Spirit would inspire them (Matt. 10:19, 20; Mark 13:11-13; Luke 12:11; 21:14, 15). This was Stephen's supreme hour. That Spirit now filled him to such an extent that his countenance shone with supernatural radiance, light, and power, which were comparable only to those that appear on an angel's countenance. The Sanhedrists gazed in astonishment. They were struck by this phenomenon — struck but not moved. They who were proof against the angelic truth Stephen uttered would certainly not be moved by his angelic face. They had seen other phenomena, for instance, the restored cripple (4:14) and the miracles of Jesus, and had become more obdurate than ever. The appearance of Stephen's face had a purpose with reference to the Sanhedrin and all who witnessed the trial. A hush fell upon them; they were gripped by that light on Stephen's face until his address reached its climax. How did Luke know all this about Stephen? There were witnesses enough, and one especially, Luke's dearest friend Paul.

CHAPTER VII

STEPHEN'S DEFENSE

1) **And the high priest said, Are these things so?** On εἰ introducing a direct question see 1:6; ἔχω with an adverb is practically our "to be." German: *Verhalten sich diese Dinge also?* But this question is by no means equivalent to the procedure followed in our courts when the judge asks the prisoner whether he pleads guilty or not guilty. Here the prosecution had closed its case, and the high priest Caiaphas who is presiding over the court turns the case over to the defense. We should also say that the question of the high priest was *not* abrupt but the expected and necessary question, and that neither this nor anything else "broke the evident spell of the angelic look on Stephen's face." The radiance continued; and its hushing effect continued until v. 54, when it was dissipated by rage.

2) **And he said, Men, brethren and fathers, hear!** Stephen intends to speak at length, hence the command to hear. Ἀδελφοί are all those present, πατέρες the members of the Sanhedrin in particular. The address is dignified, respectful, from the standpoint of one who belonged to the Jewish nation ("brethren") and was under Jewish authority ("fathers").

Stephen's defense has often been underestimated and even criticized. It has been stated that, if it had not been for the impression made by Stephen's bearing and his eloquence, he would have been called to order after the first few sentences for digressing from the point at issue. Such statements are unwarranted. Why should an address that was not pertinent, or that was faulty in other ways, have so much space allotted to it in Acts? Stephen spoke by direction of the Spirit, in later years Luke recorded his words by the prompting of the Spirit. Such an address must show the marks of the Spirit. It certainly does.

Things were at passion heat, the charge lodged against Stephen was the most heinous crime known to Judaism. If you had been in Stephen's place, what would you have offered in defense? Stephen begins in a quiet tone and proceeds with studied deliberation. Accused of speaking against Moses, God, the Temple, and the law and customs, he speaks of them in due order and at some length and reveals just how he does speak of these subjects, namely in the closest connection with God's own Word. Apparently not making a special defense at all or with one syllable referring to his accusers and their false witnesses, he is yet utterly refuting them and making the most effective defense. What could be blasphemous about a man who spoke as reverently and as Biblically as this man did? Yet into his address Stephen weaves the old disobedience and unbelief of Israel. Joseph is sold by his wicked brothers (v. 9), Moses is scorned (v. 25-28), the very Moses whom God made a deliverer (v. 35), the very Moses who spoke the great Messianic promise about the Prophet like himself (v. 37), and whom the whole nation refused to obey (v. 39, 43). It is thus that the final invective is prepared for a ringing denunciation of Israel's vicious unbelief as a call to repentance; it is uttered in the very tone and manner of the old prophets. Beginning so calmly, the defense ends so powerfully and turns the tables completely by putting accusers, witnesses, and court itself on the hopeless defense. To date no one has offered to outline a better defense for Stephen.

How did Luke secure this address? It was delivered in public, followed the Scripture story in simple fashion, may have been recorded by the secretaries of the Sanhedrin, was certainly heard by Paul. The one thing to be noted is that the address differs markedly from Luke's own manner of writing and contains points that were entirely beyond Luke's knowledge. In other words, Luke could not have invented this defense, or made up this address for Stephen, or developed it from a general report of its contents. Luke had a rather exact report of this address; and this helps to establish the exactness and the reliability of all the briefer addresses he records. The theme of the address is not formulated by Stephen himself but is apparent:

GOD'S GRACE IS MET BY ISRAEL'S DISOBEDIENCE

I. *God's grace manifested in Abraham and the disobedience of the patriarchs.* The emphasis is on *God.*

II. *God's grace manifested in Moses and the disobedience of Israel.* The emphasis is strongly on *Moses.*

III. *God's grace manifested in David and in Solomon.* The emphasis is on *the Temple.*

Conclusion: The present disobedience.

The God of the glory appeared to our father Abraham, being in Mesopotamia, before he dwelt in Haran, and said to him, Go out from thy land and from thy kindred and hither! into the land which I will show thee. Then, having gone out of the land of the Chaldeans, he dwelt in Haran.

The first words strike the keynote: *"the God of the glory,"* (LXX Ps. 29:3). That does not sound like blaspheming God. The genitive is qualitative: the God who is distinguished by the glory, not by glory in general, but by his own specific glory (note the article), the radiant revelation of his divine attributes, of any or of all of them as God permits them to manifest themselves.

It is charged that Stephen misarranged his data when he placed this appearance of God *before* Abraham's residence in Haran and when he locates the previous residence of Abraham (which was Ur) in Mesopotamia. But this charge is unwarranted. It rests solely on the claim that Stephen quotes the words of Gen. 12:1. These were, indeed, spoken in Haran, but their utterance there may have been only a repetition of the original command given in Ur. That this supposition is true may be judged from the omission of the phrase "and from thy father's home," which omission shows that Stephen is not merely quoting Gen. 12:1, but knows exactly what he is saying. In Gen. 11:31, Terah and his family do not leave Ur of the Chaldees of their own will, for already at that time their final destination is said to be "the land of Canaan." Why? Because of the divine revelation. We have the same thought in Gen. 15:7 (see Neh. 9:7): God brought Abraham out of Ur of the Chaldees. To make the measure more than full: Philo and Josephus (*Ant.* 1, 7, 1) corroborate Stephen. In regard to the location of Ur, Stephen located it where it was.

Stephen spoke before an audience that was thoroughly versed in Scripture and he would have made a frightful impression if his first sentences had contained two palpable errors. His critics in the Sanhedrin would have halted him right then and there if his statements had, indeed, been erroneous.

3) We have no reason to think that God spoke only to Terah in Gen. 11:31, and not also to Abraham, or that he did speak words that were similar to those

he repeated in Gen. 12:1 to Abraham alone. The original word was one that combined a command and a great promise. By obeying the command Abraham displayed his full faith in the promise. Stephen points out the fact that Abraham's faith began already in Ur. He speaks of Abraham only because he is the father of believers who rose to tremendous prominence in contrast with all his disobedient and unbelieving descendants. Already in Ur, God began to establish with him the covenant that culminated in Christ, the very covenant the accusers and judges of Stephen were rejecting by repudiating Christ and by now bringing Stephen to trial for his abiding in that covenant by obeying and believing in Christ. John 8:56-59. The address shows its perfect approach by thus beginning with God and Abraham and the promise of the covenant. Were Stephen's hearers still the sons of Abraham?

4) Abraham obeyed, left the land of the Chaldees, and went to Haran. He thus set out for the land that God would show him. The reason for his stopping in Haran is now indicated. **And thence, after his father died, he caused him to migrate into this land in which you are now dwelling, and he did not give him an inheritance, not a foot's space. And he promised to give it to him for a permanent possession and to his seed after him, he not having a child.**

The residence in Haran was temporary; it continued only until Abraham's father Terah had died. But here again, Stephen, like Philo, the celebrated Jewish contemporary of Christ, seems to be in conflict with Genesis. Terah is said to have been 70 years old when Abraham was born (Gen. 11:26), and he died in Haran at the age of 205 years (Gen. 11:32). Abraham was 75 years old when he left Haran (Gen. 12:4). Thus $70 + 75 = 145$; and 60 years must be added to make the total 205. Then Stephen would be wrong: Abraham did not leave *after* his father's death but 60 years before he died. Philo, the Jewish tradition, and thus Stephen are said to have followed an older report which attempted to save Abraham's filial piety toward his father. Over against the Samaritan Pentateuch, which makes Terah's age only 145, the Jewish text must stand that his age was 205. The view that in Stephen's address "died" refers to a spiritual death is without foundation. The solution lies elsewhere. In Gen. 11:26 Terah is said to be seventy years old "and begat Abraham, Nahor, and Haran." Abraham is mentioned first because of his greater importance and not necessarily because he was born first. He was the founder of the chosen nation, Nahor was the grandfather of Rebecca, and Haran was the father of Lot. Now Abraham's son Isaac married the granddaughter of Abraham's brother Nahor. It is fair to conclude that Nahor was much older than Abraham, i. e., that in Gen. 11:26 the names are not arranged according to ages but according to importance. Aside from the inspiration by which Stephen spoke and Luke wrote, it does seem that in the simple matter of adding a few figures Stephen (Philo, too) would not have made such palpable errors.

From Haran God transferred Abraham (μετοικίζω) to "this land in which you are now dwelling" (static εἰς, and this εἰς is not repeated after the verb as R. 566 thinks), namely Palestine. The emphatic ὑμεῖς intends to connect Stephen's hearers with God and Abraham and the covenant.

5) But the remarkable fact was that God gave Abraham no "inheritance" in this land, not as much as "a foot's space," on which to plant a foot. The field purchased by Abraham in Gen. 23:9-17 was not a gift of God to him, in fact, was only a burial place. All

that Abraham had received from God was the promise that God would give him the land as a permanent holding (εἰς κατάσχεσιν) and to his seed after him — but Abraham had no child. It was all grand and good, but it all required faith, an immense faith on Abraham's part. Not seeing, he yet believed. In the genitive absolute, "a child not being for him," the negative οὐ instead of μή is more decisive (R. 1138) as marking the actual fact at that time.

6) **Moreover, God spoke in this way, that his seed will be a foreigner in an alien land, and that they should enslave it and ill-treat it for four hundred years. And the nation to which they shall be slaves I myself will judge, said God; and after these things they shall go forth and shall serve me in this place.**

Transitional δέ adds another feature, a statement concerning a matter that taxed Abraham's faith still more: 400 years would elapse before his descendants would come into possession of the promised land. "In this way," in this strange manner, did God speak. This is a reference to Gen. 15:13-16. Abraham's seed was to be a πάροικος, one dwelling beside another without right of citizenship "in an alien land," one belonging to others. "They shall enslave" Abraham's seed "and shall ill-treat it," the plural subject needing no further definition.

Stephen quotes the 400 years mentioned in Genesis while Exodus 12:40 has 430 (Gal. 3:17); Josephus gives both figures. It is best to regard 400 as a round number instead of trying to devise two ways of counting the years. To be enslaved and ill-treated was not a pleasant prospect but an added burden to Abraham's faith. Yet Canaan afforded no room for a second nation to develop beside the Canaanites; in Egypt there was abundant room and thus also much less danger of contamination by idolatry. God knew what he was doing; we now see it after the event; Abraham could not foresee it and had to rely on faith.

7) Indirect discourse is never long sustained in the New Testament; so here Stephen turns to the direct and continues his reference to Gen. 15. Not with indifference will God view this treatment of Abraham's seed in Egypt. He lets his people suffer, but in his justice he always reckons with the oppressors and the persecutors. He did so in the case of these Jews who were spending their time of grace by persecuting the apostles, now Stephen, and presently the entire congregation of believers. Note the emphasis on ἐγώ, both because it is written out and because it is placed after its verb which stresses both. This judgment came upon Egypt in the form of the ten terrible plagues. Δουλεύω is used transitively in v. 6: "to enslave"; intransitively in v. 7: "to be a slave." The former use is found in the dictionaries.

The indefinite relative ᾧ ἄν (or ἐάν) leaves the guilty nation unnamed. At the time appointed, however, Abraham's seed (now the plural) shall go forth out of this bondage, out of that foreign land, "and shall serve me in this place." The last phrase is possibly an allusion to Exod. 3:12, "in this mountain," but is not a quotation (R., *W. P.*). Λατρεύω is used with reference to the divine service of worship which all should render while λειτουργέω designates official service. This promise was spoken in Canaan, and "this place" is thus definite.

8) **And he gave him the covenant of circumcision; and thus he begot Isaac and circumcised him on the eighth day; and Isaac, Jacob, and Jacob, the twelve patriarchs.**

In addition to the aforementioned promises God gave to Abraham "the covenant of circumcision." This is almost an appositional genitive but is probably qualitative since circumcision was considered the sign and seal of the covenant, the latter consisting of the promise that Abraham should be the father of many nations (Gen. 17:5). The ordinary word for covenant was συνθήκη, but the LXX translated *b^e^rith* διαθήκη, apparently because it has less of the idea of mutuality even as it is also used in the sense of "testament." For the covenant was wholly one-sided: God "gave" it to Abraham, and it is always called God's covenant and never Abraham's. Here there were not two equals making an agreement; here there was no exchange of this for that. Here there was only a giver and a recipient, only a great blessing and the obligation properly to receive and to use it.

The seal of this covenant was circumcision, περιτομή (from περί and τέμνω, "to cut around"), the cutting off of the foreskin. It was performed by the father on the eighth day (even if this occurred on a Sabbath); today it is performed by the rabbi or by a special officer (*mohel*). Associated with it was the giving of a name. The religious idea embodied in this act was the placing of the child into and under the covenant with all the blessings, promises, and obligations resulting therefrom. Involved in this is the idea that the child be spiritually renewed as now being in the covenant in that the removal of the foreskin sanctified procreation among the covenant people.

In order to understand why this act was limited to males we must disregard our modern ideas of individualism and of the equality of the sexes and go back to the creation of man and note that Eve was made for Adam. All girls were in the covenant through their fathers, for the covenant line was transmitted only through the men. We may call circumcision an Old Testament "sacrament," but it was such in a modified sense even as the covenant was altogether promise with the ultimate fulfillment coming in Christ. The circumcision found among other ancients has another significance, that of Mohammedanism being only an imitation of the Jewish rite.

"Thus," in this covenant, Abraham begot Isaac and circumcised him on the eighth day, and the line of covenant bearers was continued from Isaac through Jacob (not Esau) and then branched out through all of Jacob's sons who were called the twelve patriarchs as being founders of long lines of descent.

We thus see how Stephen thought of God, how Scripturally he connected him with Abraham and the chosen nation to which all the Jews belonged by virtue of the old covenant and its seal. What a hopeless undertaking to prove that Stephen was a blasphemer of God (6:11)! Where in the Sanhedrin itself was there a man who could honor the God of Abraham, Isaac, and Jacob more?

9) When Stephen sketches the story of Joseph he does it as one who is still speaking of God, and he adds how God fulfilled the promise to Abraham (v. 6, 7) by raising up a nation from Abraham's seed and finally establishing it in Canaan. Another feature is interwoven with this: it was God who made Joseph the savior of the patriarchs and did this despite their hatred of their brother. Joseph thus appears as a type of the eternal Savior Jesus. Such a reading of Israel's patriarchal history glorifies God by a true spiritual insight and makes this section a genuine link in the historical apology of Stephen. **And the patriarchs, having envied Joseph, sold him into Egypt. And God was with him and took him out of all his tribulations and gave him grace and wisdom before Pharaoh, king of Egypt, and established him as governor over Egypt and his whole house.**

Here there is the first defection from the covenant: the patriarchs were filled with envy toward one of their number, the aorist participle stating only the historical fact. But God used this evil unto good, yea, unto good for the very ones who perpetrated it. In this way Stephen thought of God. In ἀπέδοντο the preposition implies the sale; compare 5:8. The patriarchs duly gave from themselves (middle) their brother in the bargain in which they were duly paid. They got rid of Joseph; so the envious Jews (Matt. 27:18; Mark 15:10) got rid of Jesus. Joseph was sold into Egyptian slavery.

10) "And God was with him." In this significant flash Stephen emphasizes the contrast between God and the wicked patriarchs. What God did with Jesus was also the very opposite of what the Jews did; Peter drove this home in 4:10-12; 5:30, 31. God was with Joseph in a most effective manner: he took him out of all his afflictions (θλῖψις, from the verb that means to press or compress); he gave him χάρις, undeserved divine favor, and wisdom before Pharaoh for interpreting the king's dreams, etc.; and thus he established him (set him down) as governor over Egypt and the whole house of the king: "governor" in the sense of grand vizier, prime minister, second only to the king himself; over his whole house like the Frankish *Major Domus*. He raised him from a slave to a vice-king. Pharaoh is the title of all Egyptians kings, *per-'o* = "great house." God is still the subject of "established" and not Pharaoh (our versions), which translation is not necessitated by "his" (Pharaoh's) house, at least not in the Greek. Stephen is reciting all that *God* did by nullifying what the patriarchs had done and by working out *his* plans for Abraham's seed.

11) **Moreover, there came a famine over the whole Egypt and Canaan and great tribulation; and the fathers were not finding provisions. But Jacob, on hearing that there was grain in Egypt, sent out our fathers the first time. And at the second time Joseph was made known to his brothers, and Joseph's family became manifest to Pharaoh.**

And Joseph, sending, called to him Jacob, his father, and all his kindred, in all seventy-five souls. And Jacob came down into Egypt, and he himself came to an end and our fathers; and they were transferred to Shechem and deposited in the tomb which Abraham bought for a price of silver from the sons of Emmor in Shechem.

The story is continued with δέ which adds the great chapter on Joseph, the deliverer, and on the faith of the patriarchs in Egypt. "There came a famine" reports the fact; "they were not finding" describes the situation. Being herdsmen who had numerous flocks, this famine made their situation trying, indeed.

12) Egypt was the great wheat country of the world, in later times the granary of Rome (Acts 27:38). Why Egypt had wheat throughout the seven years of famine is not stated, but it was due to Joseph. Verbs of perception have the complementary participle in the accusative when this refers to what is perceived, hence ὄντα after ἀκούσας (B.-D. 416, 1); another explanation is that of indirect discourse, the participle retaining the tense of the direct (R., *W. P.*). The diminutive σιτίον is rare. Grain was all that the fathers secured on the first journey to Egypt.

13) But on the second journey Joseph was made known to his brothers, or, taking the passive in the middle sense, made himself known to them (B.-D. 191, 2). Καί adds the effect with which Stephen is here concerned, namely that Joseph's γένος or family became manifest to Pharaoh, i. e., he now knew all about it. In Gen. 41:12, Joseph was introduced as a Hebrew, but now Pharaoh learns much more. Note that "Joseph" is repeated because of the importance and the dignity in his name.

14) It was this knowledge, brought to Pharaoh, that enabled Joseph to transfer his father and his entire relationship from Canaan to Egypt and to take

them out of the famine-stricken land to one that was well supplied with food, with one of the family serving as vice-ruler. But this move was a fulfillment of the word spoken to Abraham in v. 6. Here in Egypt God intended to let Jacob's family grow into a nation. On ἐν used with figures see R. 589: "amounting to," or "in all." Winer called this construction Hebraistic, but the papyri have this construction in all its varieties. In Gen. 46:27; Exod. 1:5; Deut. 10:22, the number of "souls" (persons, as in 2:41, which certainly included every child) is only seventy, while in the first two of these passages the LXX has seventy-five. This is a mere matter of counting. The descendants of Jacob that went to Egypt were sixty-six in number (Gen. 46:26), but counting Joseph and his two sons and Jacob himself (Gen. 46:27), the number is seventy. In the LXX all the sons of Joseph whom he got in Egypt were counted, "nine souls," which, with the sixty-six, made seventy-five. Various other ways of counting are suggested in order to explain this number; the one indicated is correct.

15) Thus Jacob completed his life (τελευτάω) in Egypt, both he and the fathers, including Joseph — far from the land of promise.

16) Yet we see their faith in the promise. They only sojourned in Egypt, their real home was Canaan, and so they were all eventually buried there. Jacob was at once buried in Abraham's tomb Machpelah in Hebron. Read about his grand funeral in Gen. 50:1-13. Stephen is brief and speaks only of the fathers and states that their bodies were eventually transferred to Shechem. We know this only in regard to Joseph, for we learn that his body was embalmed (Gen. 50:26) and, according to the oath he had exacted from the children of Israel, was buried in Shechem after the Exodus (Josh. 24:32). The Old Testament reports nothing in regard to the brothers of Joseph.

It is Stephen who here tells us that they, too, were buried in Shechem together with Joseph. Jewish tradition, no doubt, preserved this information, and there is no reason for doubting it.

There is a difficulty in the statement that *Abraham* bought the tomb in Shechem from the sons of Emmor in Shechem. In 33:19, etc., it is *Jacob* who buys a piece of ground from these owners in order to erect an altar in that locality. Two solutions are offered. Perhaps some scribe wrote "Abraham" instead of "Jacob" in this passage; many are satisfied with this solution. Yet in Gen. 12:6 Abraham is in Shechem long before Jacob was there; and it is not at all improbable that Abraham made the original purchase, but after his departure from this place the land was again occupied by its original owners until Jacob repurchased it as Gen. 33:19 reports. "Sons of Emmor" are the tribe; the term is like "sons of Israel."

---

17) We come to *the second part* of Stephen's defense. The emphasis on God continues; but now Stephen refutes the charge that he is blaspheming *the law and Moses, the lawgiver.* Most emphatically he acknowledges that both were sent by God. Yet Stephen tells this part of the history so as to bring out all of the old opposition to Moses and to the law and thus to God himself, an opposition that finally culminated in the rejection of God's Anointed. Thus the faith of Abraham waned; yea, the faith of the fathers suffered an ominous decline.

Now as there was drawing nigh the time of the promise which God communicated to Abraham, the people grew and multiplied in Egypt until there arose a different king over Egypt who did not know Joseph. This one, by using fraud on our race, ill-treated our fathers so that he was causing

their babes to be exposed that they might not go on living.

The time set for the fulfillment of the promise as it had been told to Abraham (v. 7) was now drawing near; ἧς is attracted from ἥν. The aorists report the fact of the great increase of the Israelites in Egypt. It was this increase that worried the new king.

18) The statement that this king "arose" and that he knew nothing about Joseph points to a dynastic change in Egypt. "The previous dynasty had been that of the Hyksos; the new king was Ahmes who drove out the Hyksos." Knobel. The statement implies that until the time of the rule of this king the Israelites had flourished unmolested; but now their troubles began. Until this time the memory of Joseph and of all that he had done for Egypt brought favor to the Israelites; but this king neither knew nor cared for Joseph, he looked at the Israelites with cold, political eyes and saw that, if they continued to increase, their power would endanger the kingdom.

19) Thus the affliction began. The fraud used on the Israelites was the ill-treatment that the king ordered their babes to be exposed in order to cause them to die. This fraud broke the old agreements and promises originally made to the Israelites. Stephen contents himself with mentioning only the worst part of the ill-treatment visited upon the Israelites, the destruction of their male children. As long as "the fathers" is regarded as the subject of τοῦ ποιεῖν, there will be wavering between the consecutive (A. V.) and the final (R. V.) idea of this infinitive. But when no new subject is expressed with an infinitive, its subject is the subject of the main verb, here οὗτος, the new king. Through his decrees this Pharaoh made those babes ἔκθετα (verbal adjective from ἐκτίθημι), "exposed ones," exposed to die; he did this regularly, present infinitive, by enforcing his decrees.

The infinitive is consecutive. But εἰς τό with its present infinitive expresses purpose: "for them not to go on living," litotes, "for them to die."

20) This was the terrible situation obtaining when Moses was born. **At which season there was born Moses, and he was fair unto God; who was nourished for three months in his father's house. But having been exposed, the daughter of Pharaoh took him up for herself and raised him up for her own son.**

Stephen intimates that God is with Moses from the very beginning. His birth occurred at this terrible season, καιρός, a period that is marked by what distinguishes it. "Fair or beautiful to God" is not a Hebraistic superlative (R. 671); the dative is ethical and has a distinct personal flavor (R. 537). Here and in Heb. 11:23 ἀστεῖος is taken from the LXX translation of Exod. 2:2; it really means "citified" but is used widely in the sense of refined beauty. Note how Stephen connects Moses with God even when Moses was still a babe. The Greek loves to construct his sentences in an unbroken chain; hence these relatives: "at which season" — "who was nourished." For three months only could the babe be kept at home.

21) Finally he had to be exposed to death; but he was saved in a most remarkable way and was reared as the son of Pharaoh's own daughter who, as Josephus, *Ant.* 2, 9, 7 reports, called him παῖς μορφῇ θεῖος, "a lad divine in form." Both verbs are middle: "she took him up for herself," i. e., appropriated him, and "nourished him up for herself for her own son," i. e., adopted him. R., *W. P.*, following Vincent, thinks that the idea of adoption is expressed by the first verb, but that is evidently not the case, for then the second verb and its phrase would be superfluous. Pharaoh's daughter first appropriated the baby and eventually adopted him as her own son. Moses became a member of Pharaoh's own family.

This is one of the many instances in which God seems to play with his enemies: Pharaoh's own daughter saves, adopts, rears, educates God's great deliverer of his own enslaved people. Ah, if she could have known what God was having her do! And here we have another type of Jesus who also nearly perished as a babe, who also was saved even in Egypt, and who also became a deliverer, yet one who was far greater than his type Moses. This typical feature in the child Moses could scarcely, however, have been known to Stephen.

Sometimes it is thought that the act of taking up the child as here described was equivalent to that of the Oriental father who, on the birth of a child, took it up in his arms in order to signify that he acknowledged and intended to rear it, whereas, if he had refused to do this, the child would have been rejected by him and left to perish. It is certainly stretching the point to present Pharaoh's daughter as thinking of herself as performing such a paternal act.

22) **And Moses was educated with all the wisdom of the Egyptians; and he was mighty in his words and deeds. And when a time of forty years was being filled for him, it came into his heart to visit his brethren, the sons of Israel. And on seeing one being wronged, he defended and exacted vengeance for the one being abused by smiting the Egyptian. Now he was supposing that his brethren were understanding that God through his hand was giving salvation to them; but they did not understand. And on the following day he appeared to them while fighting and tried to reconcile them for peace by saying, Men, you are brethren! Why are you wronging each other? But the one wronging his neighbor thrust him away from himself, saying: Who established thee as a ruler and judge over us? Thou, dost thou want to make away with**

me the way thou didst make away yesterday with the Egyptian? And Moses fled at this word and became a foreigner in the land of Midian where he begot two sons.

Even the mighty man Moses, having arrived at full manhood and being a man of power in every way, was an utter failure without God. No divine work can be done without God. Stephen tells the story at length in order to follow it with the glorious story of what Moses accomplished for Israel when God was with him. Was there any man present who could speak more Scripturally about Moses and show more clearly how God brought the Old Testament mediator to his great office?

The priestly cast of the Egyptians was famed for its knowledge of science, mathematics, astronomy, and medicine, and constituted the nobility about Pharaoh. Compare I Kings 4:30. In all their wisdom was Moses educated; with abstract nouns "every" and "all" flow together, hence πάσῃ σοφίᾳ "all (every) wisdom." And this magnificent education and training were not wasted; they produced a man who was powerful in word and deed, mightily equipped for leadership. Note the similar expression in regard to Jesus in Luke 24:19. Power is referred to and not mere readiness of tongue which explains Exod. 4:10, 15.

23) Moses, too, felt this urge of leadership. He was now reaching the age of forty or full maturity. Men lived longer in those days, and we must reckon accordingly. So although he was without a call from God, with the thought just arising in his own heart, as Stephen carefully states, he proceeded to see for himself, with his own eyes, "his brethren, the sons of Israel," as to what he might do for them.

It is difficult to render the Greek idioms into acceptable English. Thus the clause: "when there was being filled up for him a forty years' time" = when he was about forty years of age. A thought or idea that arises in the heart is in Hebrew said "to go up upon the heart." To think about its going up "out of the lower deeps of one's nature" is a misunderstanding; for in Isa. 65:17, and Jer. 3:16 the expression is used in a good sense with regard to the memory of former glories; and in I Cor. 2:9 it is used negatively with regard to great glories. With reference to Moses the expression is not used in a bad sense but indictes only that the idea was his own conception. "To look for one's self upon" = to visit with the connotation of help. It is thus used with reference to God in Luke 1:68, 78; 7:16: Heb. 2:6; also with reference to judicial visitation (C.-K. 999).

Here the act of Moses is entirely beneficent. For he intends to look upon "his brethren," his own blood and kin, "the sons of Israel," the heirs of God's covenant. Both terms are highly significant. Although he was reared and had grown to manhood in the pagan court, Moses had not become an Egyptian in heart and soul. These enslaved Israelites were his real brethren, he was one of them. Yes, one of them as "the sons of Israel," not merely nationally but spiritually. Moses had not lost his faith, he shared Israel's hopes and Israel's spirit. The fact that they were nothing but slaves did not alienate him. One wonders at the man. How had he escaped all the idolatry in the midst of which he had been reared? How had the faith of Israel been put into his heart and been preserved there?

24) Living at the capital and at the king's court, Moses must have gone some distance in order to see the Israelites in their oppression as slaves. Only two striking instances of what he found are preserved. He saw an Israelite being wronged by an Egyptian in some shameful way, a taskmaster lashing the defense-

less slave. Not only did Moses come to the Israelite's defense, but he also exacted vengeance for the oppressed by smiting the Egyptian, and that fatally. In Luke 18:7 we find ποιεῖν ἐκδίκησιν used in the sense of to do what the law of right exacts, hence to avenge; see the verb alone in Luke 18:3. We at once see the love and the loyalty of Moses to his brethren, but also note that his tremendous power and energy are badly misdirected. He is by no means as yet ready for the great task of which he is dreaming. He acts without a call or direction from God.

25) A parenthetical δέ indicates his thought and his motive: "Now he was supposing that his brethren were understanding that God through his hand was giving salvation to them." Note the durative tenses. Νομίζω has the accusative with the infinitive, and the indirect discourse retains the present tense of the direct: "God through my hand is giving," etc. Note that "God" and "through his hand" are placed close together. The astonishing thing is that Moses already feels himself to be the deliverer of his people, an instrument of God. "Through his hand" = through his agency. We are unable to see how Moses arrived at this idea concerning himself. He even supposed that his brethren were understanding this, and that, when the one he had rescued would tell about the mighty Moses who delivered him, they would all look up to him. Much is veiled here. It seems as though Moses had left the Egyptian court for good in order to become the great deliverer (σωτήρ) of his own people. But he was sadly mistaken: his people understood nothing of the sort.

26) This truth was brought home to Moses on the very next day. "He appeared," suddenly stood beside two of them who were engaged in fighting (present participle) and tried to compose them (conative imperfect) for peace by appealing to them that

as brethren they ought not to wrong each other. In the question ἱνατί asks "to what purpose" they were doing each other wrong. The rebuke was perfectly proper and mild, Moses did not even take sides. What, indeed, could either gain by hurting the other?

27, 28) Then Moses had his eyes opened. The one who was wronging the other, that very one, thrust Moses away with a sharp question: "Who established thee as ruler and judge over us?" And with the accusing question: "Certainly *thou* dost not want to make away with me what way thou didst make away yesterday with the Egyptian?" This is the force of the question with μή which strongly demands a negative answer. In v. 21 the aorist ἀναιρέω is used in its neutral sense, simply, "to take up"; here, as in 2:23 and so often, it is used in its evil sense, "to make away with," "to murder." Note how με σύ are abutted, and the emphasis is on "thou"; ὃν τρόπον, the adverbial accusative, has the antecedent drawn to the relative. These questions must have come as a shock to Moses. The castle Moses had erected out of his own suppositions came down about his head. He was usurping the place of "ruler and judge over his brethren." God had not appointed him. His whole proceeding was wrong. His own brethren considered his deed of yesterday plain murder — and it was that. They thrust him away.

Pharaoh also heard of it and sought to bring Moses to account. When, in Heb. 11:27, Moses is said to have left Egypt "by faith, not fearing the wrath of the king," this means that the did not seek to remain in Egypt, to placate the king's wrath, who, of course, was more wrathful than ever because Moses left; but now he places both his people and their deliverance as well as himself entirely into God's hands. This was a mighty act of faith.

But Stephen has a purpose in bringing out so pointedly the fact that Moses' own people did not understand, and that the very Israelite who was in the wrong thrust Moses away. Stephen returns to this in v. 35. So far is he from blaspheming Moses that he views Moses as a type of Christ. Both were denied, both were thrust away by Israel, and God made both the deliverers of Israel but he made Christ such in a far higher sense.

29) Ἐν τῷ λόγῳ, "in connection with that word" (which B.-D. 219, 2, however, makes *wegen,* and R. 589 the occasion, the preposition being used in its original sense) "Moses fled." He became "a foreigner" (πάροικος as in v. 6) in Midian; but despite his long stay in Midian he did not become a Midianite. During those forty long years he remained a true Israelite and waited for his people's promised liberation (v. 6). The fact that he married and "begat two sons" in Midian makes his remaining a foreigner in the land only the more significant.

The plans of Moses had failed swiftly, utterly; God's plans were moving with perfect success. Moses needed not only the forty years of Egyptian schooling but forty more of desert schooling in order to make him the man God wanted.

30) **And forty years having been fulfilled, there appeared to him in the wilderness of Mount Sinai an angel in a flame of fire of a thornbush. And Moses, on seeing it, wondered at the sight; but as he came near to observe it, there came the Lord's voice: I, the God of thy fathers, the God of Abraham and of Isaac and of Jacob! And become trembling, Moses dared not observe. And the Lord said to him: Loose the sandal of thy feet, for the place where thou standest is holy ground. Seeing, I saw the ill-treatment of my people in Egypt, and**

their groaning I heard; and I came down to take them out for myself. And now hither! I will send thee to Egypt.

The life of Moses may be divided into three periods of forty years each. While he was pasturing his flock in the wilderness of Mount Sinai he suddenly saw a thornbush on fire which was burning intensely but not burning to ashes. On "Mount Sinai" see R. 760. Ἐν φλογὶ πυρὸς βάτου is exceedingly compact, the nouns without articles being stressed in their own meaning: "in a thornbush's fire flame," the two genitives being descriptive (R., *W. P.*). Since βάτος is any thornbush, it is impossible to determine its variety botanically, and quite unnecessary.

The bush is symbolical of Israel, which, too, was a lowly bush and not a towering tree like the Egyptians. The flame of fire in the bush symbolizes Israel's fiery affliction which, although it was due to the Egyptians, had Jehovah back of it. The fire burned with hot flame but did not consume the bush; so Israel's affliction burned but did not destroy.

The ἄγγελος here mentioned is called both *Yahweh* and *Elohim* and is thus God himself. This is the *Maleach Yahweh* who is mentioned again and again in the Old Testament but never in the New; compare Gen. 22:11, etc., and 48:15, etc. In order to determine with exactness who is referred to all the passages that treat of him must be combined and compared. Thus he will appear as the *angelus increatus* and never as a created angel although some contend for the latter. Other angels are always representatives of a class, this angel is always the specific revelation and personification of God himself.

Regarding the identity of this *Maleach* with *Yahweh-Elohim* there is not the slightest doubt. The question whether we may say more, namely that this *Maleach* is the Old Testament appearance of the Son, the Logos, and thus an anticipation of the Incarnation, is answered by two observations: 1) In some passages this *Maleach* speaks and acts like God and is yet distinguished as a separate person; 2) All his activity is the mediation of salvation so that Malachi 3:1 calls him "the Angel of the Covenant." When this is compared with the New Testament revelation of the Logos and of his Incarnation, the deduction is sound that the great Maleach of the Old Testament was, indeed, this same Logos. When C.-K. will not make this deduction because he thinks that the New Testament revelation in Christ was wholly new (Gal. 3:19; Heb. 2:2), he is answered by John's Prolog, by John 8:56-58, by Heb. 3:1, "the Apostle" Christ Jesus, and by every similar passage. In this as in many other respects the Arian inclinations of von Hofmann have influenced some exegetes and theologians. When C.-K. finally introduces the apocalyptic Jewish literature, we see the source of much of the confusion regarding the Old Testament manifestations of God and must reply that these revelations will never be seen in their clear reality when they are viewed through the medium of such Jewish literature and will be lost altogether when it is thought that even these Jewish apocalyptic ideas originated in Persian and other pagan sources.

31) Attracted by this astounding phenomenon, Moses was in the act of approaching it in order to inspect it more closely when "the Lord's voice" rang out from the burning thornbush. The ὅραμα or "sight" was the strange fact that a bush should be on fire here, where there was no one to set it on fire. Vastly stranger it was that it should burn and burn without consuming itself. This was not an ordinary fire but a miracle of God. Moses saw only this flaming fire from which the voice spoke and no form of any kind in the fire. The voice alone indicated that the Lord was revealing himself by means of this fire.

32) The Lord at once makes himself known by proclaiming his full covenant name: "I, the God," etc. From "the fathers" God goes back to Abraham, Isaac, and Jacob and thus strongly expresses the truth that this appearance has a connection with his great covenant. He appears here on Sinai because here he will renew and advance his covenant with the children of Israel when Moses, through God's mighty hand, has freed them from Pharaoh and brought them to this place. No wonder that Moses was trembling and dared not raise his eyes to look at those flames. Behold, this is how Stephen thinks of God and of Moses!

33) The order to remove "the sandal of thy feet," a distributive singular, is to induce Moses to realize fully that he is standing in the presence of God himself, which makes the entire place "holy ground." The perfect ἕστηκας is always used in the sense of the present: "thou standest."

This is an Oriental idea: to remove the sandals in the presence of a superior, to walk in bare feet in any sanctuary. Thus the priests did in the Temple, thus must all who enter Mohammedan mosques do today, thus the Samaritans do on Mt. Gerizim. See how Aaron and his sons were sanctified, Exod. 29:10; Lev. 8:23. Entrance into the mosques, even that on the site of the Temple in Jerusalem, is now compromised. All the author had to do was to put on huge slippers over his shoes. These were furnished at the doors by an attendant, but these slippers were imperative unless one entered in his stocking feet. The keepers of the synagogue of the Samaritans at Nablous did not require this, but their great sacrifice on Mt. Gerizim is another matter.

34) And now at last Moses receives his divine commission to deliver Israel. God condescends to speak in a human way about his looking down on the

ill-treatment of his people in Egypt and hearing their pitiful groaning. The ἰδὼν εἶδον is a reproduction of the Hebrew infinitive absolute after the fashion of the LXX, which emphasizes the verb by means of its participle: "I surely saw"; it is found in the New Testament only in quotations. The Greek is content with the mere past fact, "I saw — heard," whereas the English requires the time relation of the perfect, "I have seen — have heard." Thus also we have "I came down" and the infinitive of purpose, the middle from ἐξαιρέω, "to take them out for myself," i. e., to effect their deliverance (effective aorist). Thus Moses receives his commission: "And now thither!" We must connect the adverb δεῦρο with ἀποστείλω (R. 932): "come, I will send thee," and the verb means, "send with a commission to execute," and thus means more than πέμπω although both are generally translated "to send." Stephen thus exalts Moses.

35) But he is not merely reciting the Old Testament story of Moses. He has a purpose in his selection. From the divine commission of Moses, Stephen proceeds to what this commission really implied regarding Israel. He reads the Old Testament with the clear, deep insight of Paul. **This Moses, whom they denied when they said, Who established thee as a ruler and judge? this one God has commissioned both as ruler and ransomer with the hand of the angel that appeared to him in the thornbush. This one led them out by doing wonders and signs in Egypt and in the Red Sea and in the desert for forty years. This one is the Moses who said to the sons of Israel, A prophet will God raise up from you out of your brethren, like me. This one is he who came to be in connection with the assembly in the wilderness, in company with the angel who was speaking to him in the mount of Sinai, and (in company with) our fathers; he who received living say-**

ings to give to us; he to whom our fathers did not will to become obedient but thrust him away and were turned in their hearts unto Egypt when they said to Aaron, Make us gods who shall go before us! For this Moses who brought us out of Egyptland, we do not know what happened to him.

The entire passage is one chain: five emphatic "this" terminating in two "he who (to whom)." It is like a grand pyramid, and the capstone is Israel's idolatrous unbelief.

The trouble lay not with Stephen and his treatment of Moses, it lay with the treatment Moses received from Israel at the beginning and continued to receive, yea, was receiving right now from Stephen's accusers and judges. Stephen's defensive is turning into an offensive. Not he is on trial, but his judges are. Stephen, however, is not judging them, he is letting God's Word, Moses himself, do that just as Jesus did in John 5:45-47. So in the very first place it was "this Moses" whom they denied and repudiated at the beginning as not being a ruler and judge for them, whom in spite of them God made both ruler and vastly more than judge. We have the same verb "denied" that was used with regard to the rejection of Jesus in 3:13. The aorist participle εἰπόντες refers to the one statement that is requoted from v. 27. Only one man uttered it, but it is rightly attributed to all the Israelites, for their whole history shows that very attitude. This repudiated Moses who was made the old covenant mediator is the very type of Jesus who was also repudiated by the Jews and yet was made the everlasting Mediator.

Although he was repudiated as "ruler and judge" (the two functions always going together in ancient times), God commissioned Moses as "ruler and ransomer" to operate in this vastly higher function with the help and agency (σὺν χειρί, compare the phrase in

v. 25) of the angel that appeared (aorist to indicate the one appearance) to him in the thornbush, whose name and identity that angel himself declared (v. 32). Ἄρχων is rather general: "ruler," prince, author, and the like; here it means the head and leader of the young nation. But λυτρωτής is far superior to "judge." This title is purposely chosen in order to bring out fully the parallel with Christ who was a "ransomer" in the supreme sense. Although it is rare, the term is made plain by its cognates in the Greek. All of these involve a λύτρον or ransom price of some kind; in Christ's case the price of his own blood and death. Our word "redeemer" tends to lose this definite sense, "ransomer" retains it. The tendency to reduce this term to "liberator" (the cognate terms similarly) must be resisted. Moses, too, paid a great price in leading Israel out of its bondage. The burden which often crushed his soul, the fearful sins of this people are indicated in part in the following. The perfect ἀπέσταλκε is not a mistake for the aorist (B.-D. 343, 2), nor is it a perfect in a chain of aorists; it is the vivid perfect in narrative (R. 897), and we may add that it conveys the idea of the permanence of the appointment.

36) Another "this one," which emphasizes the previous ones, tells Stephen's hearers that this repudiated leader accomplished the liberation of Israel. And how did he accomplish this? By all the "wonders and signs" (see 2:19) in Egypt, the Red Sea, and the wilderness "for forty years" (accusative of extent of time). In these many signs connected with Israel's release Moses again typified Christ.

37) "This one is the Moses" intensifies all these demonstrations by adding the name "Moses" because of the greatness of what is now predicated of him. He, yes, he it is who prophesied so distinctly about the Christ "to the sons of Israel," sons and thus heirs

of the covenant and the faith of Israel, all of whom ought to be true sons in that covenant and that faith. On the prophecy itself see 3:22, and note that "like me" again and more decidedly than ever makes Moses the type of Jesus, each being a mediator, Jesus being the supreme one.

38) The fifth "this one" brings out this mediatorship of Moses which made him the type of the eternal mediator. For in connection with, ἐν, the assembly (ἐκκλησία, see 5:11) of the children of Israel in the wilderness, namely on Mount Sinai, he was in company (μετά) with both the Angel Jehovah who spoke to him on Sinai (v. 30-34) and with our fathers. Note that μετά has two objects: "in company with the angel and our fathers"; to be with both made him the mediator of the old covenant (in this respect surpassing all other prophets) and the great type of Jesus. It conflicts with the line of thought followed by Stephen when Gal. 3:19; Heb. 2:2; Josephus, and "a well-defined Jewish interpretation" concerning angels (plural) in connection with the giving of the law, are introduced; for Stephen carefully refers back to v. 30, etc., to the one ἄγγελος or messenger who was God himself. He is not to be confused with created angels.

A signal feature of this mediatorship is briefly mentioned in the first relative clause: "he who received living sayings to give to us," received them from God in order to bestow them on us, Stephen regarding himself as one of them. The reference is to the divine law. Since Moses was the medium of its transmission, this law in a signal manner made him the mediator of the old covenant (given to Abraham, v. 8). Λόγια are simply "brief sayings," here those of the Decalog. Any other use of the word, pagan, Biblical, or ecclesiastical, means no more even when the "oracles of Delphi," the "Logia" that Papias said Matthew wrote, or the "Logia of Jesus," extracanonical sayings of Jesus from the Oxyrhynchus papyri, are referred to.

More important is the question as to how Stephen could call the Ten Commandments "living." That view is too narrow which fails to connect them with the entire old covenant and forgets that this covenant was entirely gospel, God's grace in the promise of the Messiah and salvation. We have those "living logia" in connection with the new covenant and its fulfilled promises in Christ. The living power of God is in them. They are even "unto life," Rom. 7:10, 12, 14; Gal. 3:12; but not to the sinner (Gal. 3:21). For him they are only an aid to the gospel in restoring him to life.

39) Once more, and with another relative, Stephen points his hearers to Moses but now he points to him as once more being rejected by these false "sons of Israel": "he to whom our fathers did not will to become obedient but thrust him away (significantly repeating the verb from v. 27) and turned in their hearts (in the very center of their being) unto Egypt." "Did not will" is the very verb Jesus used in Matt. 23:37. There is where the seat of unbelief is always found; and this will is in the heart. Not the bondage in Egypt attracted the Israelites but, as the following shows, the feasts of Egyptian idolatry.

40) Stephen does not speak only in general terms when he thus charges the fathers with the rejection of Moses at Sinai. With εἰπόντες (aorist as in v. 35) he specifies; the Israelites demanded that Aaron make them an Egyptian idol: "Make us gods!" The enormous guilt of this demand needs no emphasis. The relative clause with the future tense denotes purpose (R. 960): "who shall go before us" on our way back to Egypt. The living God led them out with omnipotent miracles; the dead idols of Egypt, manufactured in the desert by their own hands, are to

nullify all this and to lead them back. In the plural "gods" the one true God is denied. The plural is one of category, hence the manufacture of one idol was sufficient.

The excuse for turning from God is the fact that they do not know what has become of "this Moses," the contemptuous use of οὗτος (R. 697). The relative clause may be concessive: "who (although he) brought us out of Egypt-land"; again it may be derogatory: "this Moses, who (we are sorry to say) brought us," etc. The subject is a pendent nominative (R. 459) which is often used in popular language. Moses remained on the mountain peak with God for forty days; hence the light and slighting statement: "We do not know what occurred for him," i. e., what has become of him. He was no longer a concern of theirs. Thus again Moses was repudiated, the covenant cast aside, the faith of Abraham spurned, the omnipotence and the miracles of God regarded as nothing. Why is Stephen bringing these histories forward so prominently? Because he is preparing for his climax: in their rejection of the mediator Moses these disobedient, unbelieving fathers were the type of Stephen's present hearers in their still more vicious rejection of the Mediator Jesus.

41) **And they made a calf in those days, and they led up a sacrifice for the idol and went on making merry in connection with the works of their hands.**

Right here at Sinai the Israelites staged a regular idol festival. The verb "made a calf" is found only here but is a clear compound. This μόσχος is a ταῦρος, a calf that has grown, but not to full maturity, the bull god Apis of the Egyptians. The writer visited the Tomb of the Bulls which is underground and in the desert. It has a long passageway with chambers on each side, and each chamber contains a granite sarcophagus weighing tons and a lid to correspond. The embalmed, mummified bulls were not there, but the monstrosity of such worship of brutes still stared one in the face. Stephen mentions the two chief acts: bringing up the burnt sacrifice (*θυσία*) for the idol as he properly names the bull, and then the continued making merry (imperfect, descriptive), the same verb that occurs in Luke 15:23, in the parable of the Prodigal. They did not only "rejoice in the works of their (own) hands" (our versions), in the idol they had made, but also "made merry," celebrated a grand feast with dancing, singing, etc., "in connection with the works of their hands," the idol with all its paraphernalia.

42) Stephen passes over the rest of the story and mentions only the punitive act of God, his turning from Israel and giving them up to their idolatries, as Amos 5:25, etc., describes it. **But God turned and gave them over to serving the host of heaven even as it has been written in the prophets' book:**

> **Certainly, you did not offer to me slaughter victims and burnt sacrifices**
> **For forty years in the wilderness, House of Israel?**
> **Yea, you took up the tabernacle of Moloch**
> **And the star of the god Rephan,**
> **The figures which you made in order to worship them.**
> **Yea, I will transfer you beyond Babylon.**

"God turned" (the verb is here intransitive). When the sinner determines to follow his wicked course, God punishes him by giving him over to his sin and thus uses sin to punish sin. A downward progression results until the effects of sin destroy the sinner, and he is blotted out. Nothing can be worse than to have God turn and let the sinner who has turned from him go on into judgment. "God gave them over to serving the host (army) of heaven," which is Sabaism, worship of the sun and other heavenly bodies instead of the Lord of hosts. "Gave them over" occurs in the same sense three times in Rom. 1:24, 26, 28, where God speaks of abandoning the heathen to their lusts, three times "like clods on a coffin in a grave" (R. *W P.*). Λατρεύειν refers to religious service as in v. 7.

Instead of quoting more from the Pentateuch or alluding to its expressions, Stephen lets the prophet Amos speak for him and uses the regular formula of quotation γέγραπται, "it has been (and thus remains forever) written." The twelve minor prophets were regarded as one book. The μή in the question in the first two lines of Amos' words demands a negative answer: Israel did *not* bring its sacrifices to God during the forty years in the wilderness. What sacrifices were still brought God could not accept. The following lines show that idolatry filled the hearts of the nation. Even circumcision, the sign of the covenant, fell into disuse. The two Hebrew words denote burnt offerings and meat offerings, but the LXX translated them with two words, both of which mean sacrifices slaughtered and burnt. Stephen follows the LXX throughout with but slight change, and since in the next three lines this deviates so far from the Hebrew, it would seem that he spoke Greek and not Aramaic when making his defense.

Amos prophesied between 810 and 783 B. C. against the Northern Kingdom in the time of Jeroboam II, when Uzziah reigned over the Southern Kingdom. When he points out the sin, godlessness, and idolatry of the Israelites of his time, he refers to the Israelites in the desert during the forty years under Moses. Those old idolatries are still going on and are, therefore, the more worthy of punishment. The forty years may be regarded as a round number. They were in reality thirty-eight, yet forty appears in Num. 14:33, and Josh. 5:6. Moreover, the germs of this defection were found already at the start of this period. In "House of Israel" Amos sums up all the generations of Israel since Moses' time, for this wickedness manifested itself ever anew.

43) The Hebrew reads as follows:

"Yea, you have borne the tabernacles of your king
And the shrine of your images,
The star of your god which you made to yourselves.
Therefore will I cause you to go into captivity beyond Damascus.

See Delitzsch on the passage in Amos. The thought of Amos is: the king, whose tabernacle, and the images, whose shrine they bore, was a star which they had made their god, an astral divinity. They made images of their star divinity and carried them in a little casket-like temple which was placed on a portable rack (*Gestell*) of some kind. This method of worship the Israelites copied from the Egyptians among whom sun worship and star worship existed from the earliest times. We need recall only that *Ra* was originally their supreme god, namely the sun, the prototype of all their kings, who was worshipped also as Osiris and in Apis, the bull. *Mentu* and *Atmu* are only the rising and the setting sun, i. e., *Ra* divided; *Phtha* and *Amon* (*Amon-Ra*) were later advanced to first place as gods. The oldest translations show how wrong the transpositions of the LXX are. But worst of all, the LXX read the Hebrew word for "your king": *m l k k m* (omitting the vowel points) as "Moloch"; and made "Rephan" a god out of the Hebrew *kiyun*, "shrine," by misreading two of the unvocalized letters: turning *k* into *r*, and *y* into *ph*. And a great deal of difficulty has resulted from this infelicitous misreading.

There is no god "Rephan." The Israelites knew nothing about Moloch during those forty years, and the effort to identify Moloch with Saturn, the one being worshipped by allowing children to burn up in his heated arms, the other said to devour his children, thus making Moloch a star divinity, is misdirected. When Rephan is identified with Satan, this is only another fancy. We may also note that Deut. 4:19 forbids the very type of idolatry to which Amos refers, the worship of sun, moon, stars, and the host of heaven; and Ezek. 20:7, etc., states positively that the Israelites would not relinquish "the idols of Egypt." All the evidence is in favor of the view that in the wilderness Israel practiced Egyptian and no other idolatry.

The last line is simpler. Amos wrote: "beyond Damascus," so also the LXX; Stephen substitutes "beyond Babylon" because the prophecy had been fulfilled long ago, the people having been carried so far beyond Damascus as to have been scattered even beyond Babylon. Amos speaks of the Northern Kingdom.

The question that is of moment here is how Stephen, speaking by the Spirit, could retain the faulty and baseless rendering of the LXX, especially the terms "Moloch" and "Rephan"? The answer is: "Because these names are negligible for the purpose Stephen and the Spirit had in hand, the bringing home to Stephen's hearers their like opposition to God." Even the LXX left "the star" as a god and an idol. Besides, we have the original Hebrew so that actual error even in so insignificant a matter is obviated.

---

44) The *third part* of the address refutes the charge of blasphemy against the Temple. Stephen briefly reviews the story of the Tabernacle and of the Temple and ends with a quotation from Isaiah that is directed against an overestimation of the Temple. The reply scorns to enter into details, it throws on the screen the Scripture story and view of the Temple as

being also Stephen's view and lets that suffice. The entire bearing of Stephen, as it is reflected in his address, is that of power backed by divine certainty, so that he is in reality not defending himself but rather trying to bring his judges to repentance.

The Tabernacle of the Testimony was for our fathers in the wilderness even as he appointed who spoke to Moses to make it according to the model which he had seen.

Note the contrast between "the tabernacle of your king" (god) in the quotation from Amos and this "Tabernacle of the Testimony," by which, in connection with which, and in which God testifies to Israel regarding himself and regarding all his covenant grace. The LXX thus translates the Hebrew "tabernacle of coming together," i. e., where God meets his people and reveals himself. This is not literal but substantial correctness so that Stephen adopts the expression. This was the true tabernacle for the fathers, but all that Stephen can say about it is that Moses made it after the heavenly pattern and that thus the fathers had it. What more could he say when they carried that idol tabernacle with them? "It was for the fathers" is the idiom for "the fathers had it."

Stephen points to its divine origin when he says that he who spoke to Moses (God) ordered him to make it according to the model which he had seen while he was with God on the mountain. The very design was God's so as to connect this Tabernacle entirely with God. Τύπος is "blow," then the mark made by a blow, the imprint, and thus the design, pattern, or model. Stephen tacitly points out the fact that Israel did not always have the Temple which the Jews so fanatically adored at the present; a long time elapsed before they ever thought of a temple — surely a sobering thought.

45) **Which our fathers, having received in turn, brought in in company with Joshua, in connection**

with the permanent possession of the nations which God pushed out before the face of our fathers until the days of David who found favor before God and asked for himself to find a habitation for the God of Jacob.

In the flexible Greek fashion all that Stephen says about the Tabernacle and the Temple, v. 44-50, is one grand sentence. The participle "having received in turn" is to be construed with "brought in in company with (μετά) Joshua." The Tabernacle was delivered to them by Moses when Joshua brought the fathers into Canaan. This was "in connection with the permanent possession (κατάσχεσις as in v. 5) of the nations," the Canaanite tribes, "whom God pushed out," etc. The genitive "of the nations" is not subjective so that the phrase would mean: "at the time when the nations held permanent possession"; the genitive is objective: Israel came into permanent possession of these nations, i. e., of their land, they having been driven out by God (ὧν is attracted from ἅ). "Which they brought in . . . until the days of David" indicates briefly that for a period that covered hundreds of years this Tabernacle was all that Israel had.

46) Another relative clause brings us to the last chapter of the Tabernacle. It was David who found such favor (χάρις) with God that encouraged him to ask for himself (middle), as a special manifestation of that divine favor, "to find (object infinitive) a habitation for the God of Jacob." This infinitive clause is an appropriation of the beautiful language of Ps. 132:5. Besides this psalm read II Sam. 7:1, etc., regarding David's plans. Σκήνωμα is poetical language, as is also εὑρεῖν. David has in mind a permanent place of worship, a beautiful temple, yet he calls it no more than a "tent" and speaks of finding it when he thinks of building a fitting temple. Instead of using a mere pronoun Stephen keeps David's impressive dative "for the God of Jacob."

47) An adversative δέ takes us to Solomon. **Solomon, however, built him a house.** Not before this time did Israel have a temple. Even David had to content himself with the old Tabernacle. Somehow God did not seem to be so anxious about a temple. He even let David ask in vain for the privilege of building one (I Kings 5:3; I Chron. 22:7, etc.; 28:2, etc.) and put this event off until Solomon's time. David was a man of war and blood, Solomon (*Sh^elomah, Friedrich*) a man or prince of peace; the one was a type of Christ conquering foes, the other a type of Christ reigning in peace. Stephen is satisfied to mention only the fact that Solomon finally built "a house for him," nor does Stephen call it any more than that.

48) In fact, over against the Jews who valued their Temple extravagantly, far more than they valued the true worship of God by faith and obedience to him, and desecrated even this "house" with their godless obduracy, Stephen shares Solomon's own conception of the Temple (I Kings 8:27): **nevertheless, not the Highest in things made with hands doth dwell,** nay, not he, whatever creatures may do. The negative is purposely placed with the subject: "not the Highest," and our versions ought to be amended accordingly; for to construe the negative with the verb even alters the sense. See R., *W. P.* For, indeed, all that others can do is "to dwell in things made with hands." That is one difference between them and the Highest, one of the great titles for God. It is because of his infinite exaltation that he is beyond all man-made things. We have only the neuter plural and not "temples" (A. V.) or "houses" (R. V.). So also the contrast between the two is heightened by placing them side by side in the Greek: "the Highest — in things made with hands." When Stephen speaks thus about the Temple, the very one built by Solomon, he has God's own Word to sup-

port him: **even as the prophet states,** namely Isa. 66:1, 2, with only slight verbal difference between the LXX and the Hebrew.

49, 50) The quotation is exactly to the point.

> **The heaven a throne for me,**
> **And the earth a footstool of my feet!**
> **What kind of house will you build me? saith the Lord;**
> **And what a place of my rest?**
> **Did not my hand make all these things?**

Here God himself speaks and declares what he thinks of any and every temple built for him by men. The superstitious reverence of the Jews for their Temple here finds its divine answer. These Jews treat the Highest as though he were some pagan god or pagan idol that had to have some sort of temple for its home. Because Stephen has spoken of God as being exalted above all man-made temples, they are now putting him to trial. Because he will not make God an idol that needs must have a temple, they are ready to condemn him for blasphemy of their Temple. We must note the full force of what Stephen says, in particular how his words regarding the Temple naturally merge into the denunciation of v. 51, etc., without either break or pause.

Even the heaven is only God's throne, a royal seat for him. Heaven itself is not a house or a temple for him; it is only one of the things he has made. As for the whole earth, it is vastly less, nothing more than a footstool for his feet, so far beneath him, one of the insignificant things he has made. Why does Isaiah say these tremendous things to the Israel of his time and to the future Israel that would return from its seventy years of captivity in Babylon to build him another temple? Because of their wicked and obdurate hearts.

That is exactly why Stephen, too, hurls these same words at his present hearers, whose hearts are of the same kind. What kind of a house is it that people such as this will build for *Yahweh* who is here confronting them? The Herodian Temple was even now in the process of being rebuilt. And what a place of his rest are they trying to provide, where he may enter and abide among them? They have forgotten his infinite greatness which Solomon remembered, II Chron. 6:18. They do not draw the proper conclusions from the fact that it is he who made all these things, even heaven and earth and all that is therein. They no longer know that God looks only to him who is of a contrite spirit and who trembles at his Word lest perhaps he fail to observe it (the continuation of Isa. 66:2, then also v. 3). When they build with hearts like that, every offering in their Temple so builded is an abomination to *Yahweh*, the blood of every ox like that of a murdered man, every lamb like a dog with his head cut off, every oblation like swine's blood, and their burning incense as though it were intended to bless an idol. Stephen does not add these statements of Isaiah, but these words help us to understand the lines which he quotes.

Neither the Lord speaking through Isaiah, nor Jesus (John 2:19; 4:23, 24), nor Stephen say that no temple and no places of worship shall be built. God vouchsafed his presence in the ancient Tabernacle and in Solomon's Temple (II Chron. 7:1-3). How, by whom, and in what spirit temples are to be built Solomon and Isa. 66:2b show us. But to build temples and churches, to make them grand and imposing, to fill them with crowds for great services while hearts are without contrition, obdurate before God's Word, is to treat God as an idol to whom we may dictate as we please, to invent what his will and word is to be to suit our own perverted hearts. That is the kind of house many still build, a place where they offer rest to the Highest. The view of critics that Isaiah's words refer to a temple which the Jewish exiles proposed to erect in Babylon, or refer only to the Samaritan Temple on Mt. Gerizim, need not be refuted at this place. Compare Aug. Pieper, *Jesaias II*, 653, etc.

---

51) What follows must be called *the conclusion*, for while it continues the account without a break, it pertains to all that precedes. Like one of the prophets of old, in the very spirit of Isaiah from whom Stephen has just quoted, he hurls the countercharge of wilful obduracy against his judges. He wields the law on the conscience of his hearers with the boldness and the fearlessness of a Peter (2:36; 4:10-12; 5:29-32) in order to crush these wicked Jews in repentance.

Stiffnecked and uncircumcised as to heart and ears, you on your part always fall against the Holy Spirit; as your fathers, also you! Which of the prophets did your fathers not persecute? And they killed those who made advance announcement about the coming of the Righteous One, whose betrayers and murderers you on your part have now become: people such as received the law on dispositions of angels and did not observe it!

The invective is deliberate, measured, with not a word too much, like a surgeon who cuts deep in order to let the fearful corruption out. "Stiffnecked" = with a neck or a back (τράχηλος) that will not bend; obstinate. "Uncircumcised as to hearts and ears" = bearing the covenant sign only outwardly and not inwardly in its intended force, which involves the cutting off of all opposition to God and to his Word. The dative is neither locative nor instrumental but a dative of relation (B-D. 197): "in regard to hearts and ears." As to their hearts and their ears these Jews were no better than the uncircumcised heathen. John 8:44. The ears are the organs for hearing God's Word and his will, the heart the organ for receiving, believing, obeying that Word and that will. The hearts are mentioned first because they control the ears and in the obdurate make them deaf to God.

Although it is added only coordinately (*καί*), we now have the proof for these designations: "you on your part (emphatic ὑμεῖς) always fall against the Holy Spirit," which uses the idiomatic Greek verb for opposition and resistance. "Holy Spirit" is in place because it is this Person who comes to us in the Word in order to work contrition and faith. To resist him is to cut ourselves off from the very means by which alone we can be saved. This resistance begins with individual acts and eventually becomes a fixed *habitus* which permanently closes the heart so that the Spirit can no longer have his work in us. This is hardness of heart or obduracy.

Why the Word melts some hearts while others deliberately and permanently harden themselves against it, no man knows. The former is due wholly to God's grace, the latter is due wholly to man's guilt. No one cause for both exists. When synergism or determinism are taken to be such a cause, the fact is overlooked that both are non-existant. Man cannot aid the Spirit with his unregenerate or natural ability, nor is the *gratia* of the Spirit *irresistibilis*. The conversion of the sinner is easy to explain, for the *gratia* is *sufficiens* to work conversion in him; the obduracy remains a mystery because of this very sufficiency of grace, which, as was the case in these hearers of Stephen, secures only the opposite effect. In this respect Stephen's hearers proved to be true sons of their fathers: "as *your* fathers (Stephen takes care not to say *our* in the present connection), also you." Israel's history reveals a damnable ancestry, and the descendants are still multiplying rapidly.

52) Stephen fully establishes this connection of evil spiritual descent; Jesus did the same in Matt. 23:29-32. What did "your fathers" do? They persecuted every one of the prophets through whom the Holy Spirit spoke to them. Stephen's question which asks them to name one who was not so persecuted is not a rhetorical exaggeration. "Who even today, according to the statements of the Old Testament, is able to name a prophet who was received with approval and enthusiasm as other nations received their great spirits and prophets? From Moses and Samuel until Malachi and John the Baptist the true prophets who arose in Israel came to experience ungrateful disregard, haughty contradiction, open rebellion, and, as Jesus also says regarding all the prophets, persecution from the people of their nation, from the princes and the priests, from their own nearest relatives." Zahn. As far as murder is concerned, Stephen does no more than to repeat the charge which Jesus made in Matt. 23:31, 35, 37; Luke 11:47, etc.; 13:34. The fact that the murderous intent did not always succeed, as was the case with reference to Elijah, Jeremiah, etc., made those who had this intent nonetheless murderers. Such, Stephen tells his hearers, were "your fathers."

The words are perfectly chosen when he describes the prophets as "those who made advance announcement about the coming of the Righteous One." That announcing was their chief, their blessed work; they were God's own heralds. What did it, then, mean to persecute and to kill them? "Coming" is the great Messianic term; it is a comprehensive designation of the Messiah's entire life and work. Jesus is repeatedly called "the Righteous One" in the supreme sense; see 3:14, and compare 22:14; I Pet. 3:18. Here this designation is in glaring contrast with "betrayers and murderers." What their fathers did to such an eminent degree these judges whom Stephen faces have exceeded "now," in the recent past. The Greek is content to use the aorist with reference to a recent occurrence: "became," whereas we prefer "have become." By hiring the traitor Judas the whole Sanhedrin made itself "betrayers" of the Righteous One; and by forcing Pilate to crucify him *they* became his "murderers." Note the emphasis on ὑμεῖς and how fully and terribly their connection is established with "your fathers," the persecutors and the murderers of the prophets.

53) R. 728 makes οἵτινες causal (which it often is): "since you are such as"; but B.-D. 293, 2 sees correctly that here (and elsewhere) this relative is used when the general characteristic of definite persons is stated: *you* — "people who," "people such as." Yes, they were this very kind. They received the law in a most heavenly way but did not guard or observe it. All this frightful crime would be bad enough if they had never had or heard of this law of God; but God had made them his chosen people and had given them his glorious law, and they treated it in this manner. The tables are thus completely turned. Stephen stood accused of speaking against the law, but the Sanhedrin itself is convicted of utterly breaking and abandoning the law.

The phrase εἰς διαταγάς is a crux as far as translating and explaining εἰς is concerned. See our versions and the R. V. margin and what they think the Greek means. Many explanations are offered, Zahn is undecided. Fortunately, the sense is clear as Deut. 33:2; Gal. 3:19; Heb. 2:2 show. The angels were active in the giving of the law on Mount Sinai. The genitive "of angels" is subjective: they made "dispositions," shall we say "arrangements," the Germans say *Anordnungen.* Deissmann has found the word used in the sense of an order, a disposition one has made, a testamentary disposition, an imperial or a divine ordinance (*Light from the Ancient East,* 86, etc.). In this case εἰς does not equal ἐν; nor is it "unto," "in accord with," or the predicative εἰς (R. 596), "as" (R. V. margin). It is best to take εἰς in the sense of "upon" or "on," German *auf*. But when "angels" are supposed to include the angel mentioned in v. 30 and 38, or when the plural is identified with this one angel, who is God himself, we cannot agree. Stephen exalts the law: heavenly angels helped in its giving, yet the Sanhedrists disregarded it; Paul's emphasis in Gal. 3:19 is the reverse; *only* angels were used.

STEPHEN STONED

54) It is usually assumed that Stephen's address ends at this point, that it was broken off here, and that he intended to close with some word of gospel. He did close with a wonderful gospel utterance (v. 56); the interruption did not come until after he had spoken it. Luke pauses to tell us about the preliminary effect that was produced by the law Stephen was uttering, which already shows what effect the gospel would have.

Now, while hearing these things, they were being sawn in two as regards their heart and began gnashing their teeth against him. But being full of the Holy Spirit, on earnestly looking to heaven, he saw God's glory and Jesus standing at the right of God and he said, Lo, I behold the heavens having been opened, and the Son of man standing at the right of God!

The imperfects used in v. 54, as the present participle shows, go back to the preceding verses and describe what was happening while Stephen was uttering the severe indictments of the law. No pause occurred at this point. Yes, Stephen's words went home and produced an inner and an outer effect. There are always *motus inevitabiles* when the Word is rightly preached; no man escapes some effect, no man is the same man that he was before that Word reached him.

Here the effect was utterly hostile. Luke again uses the strong verb employed in 5:33, "they were being sawn in two," but here with the dative of relation "as to their hearts," the same dative that occurred in v. 51 (B.-D. 197, who adds that this dative predominates over the accusative of relation). These hearts (the heart is always the center of the personality) did not bend or bow to the law in a manner that indicated contrition; they were stiff and hard like dried wood, and the law could only saw them in two with its sharp teeth. The outward evidence was the fact that, as they sat and listened and heard more and more what Stephen was saying to and about them, they began grinding their teeth at him in suppressed rage. Yet they kept their seats; Stephen could still be heard.

55) And so Stephen spoke his final word. It became an involutary exclamation, for at this moment a wonderful thing happened. Although he had spoken under the Spirit's influence during his entire address, at this moment he became filled with the Spirit and, on earnestly looking up toward heaven (he was in the hall of the court), "he saw God's glory and Jesus standing at God's right." By the help of the Spirit his mortal eyes were enabled to look right into heaven. The words ἀτενίσας, εἶδε, and the following θεωρῶ are an answer to the idea that Stephen saw only mentally, in his own mind or imagination, or, as is usually said, "in spirit." No; this was an outward reality, even as the Holy Spirit is mentioned who gave this ability of sight to Stephen's eyes.

The first martyr of the Christian faith is going to his death; and he becomes the leader of the long, long line of future martyrs. Therefore this sight is granted to him, not as though it were intended for him and his strengthening alone, but through him for all of them. So the glory of God shines for all of them as they near death, so the Savior stands ready to receive them. Through Stephen's eyes they are all to see. "God's glory" is one concept, the Hebrew *k*ᵉ*bod Yahweh,* all the majesty of God shining in heavenly light. The Spirit enabled Stephen to look at his glory without its blinding his eyes. That glory was over him in the midst of all his enemies.

"And Jesus standing at the right hand of God" (on this phrase see 2:25; this perfect participle is always present in sense) signifies that he had arisen to come to the aid of his confessor, to receive him unto himself. God's "right" or "right hand" is invariably his power and his majesty; and to stand at God's right, like sitting at his right, is to exercise this infinite power and majesty in an unlimited way. This surely refers to the human nature of Jesus as it participated in the divine majesty or attributes (δόξα). To understand this aright one must consider all the passages that speak of God's right plus their contexts. It goes without saying that what Stephen beheld was adapted to his eyes, and at the same time the Spirit gave to his eyes the ability to see this heavenly glory and Jesus.

Strange interpretations have been given to Luke's words. Thus it is said that Jesus is standing and not sitting with God on his throne; that he is not revealing himself as coregent with God but as the servant of the King of heaven, the one who is next to the throne, who is ready to obey the nod of the King and his will in the whole domain of his rule. An older view claims that Jesus' standing thus in heaven means that, when in his human nature Jesus is sitting or standing in heaven, he is closed there so that he cannot at the same time and in the human nature be present on earth (Calvin, *Institutiones* IV, 17, 16), and that we must interpret Matt. 28:20; 18:20; the words of the Lord's Supper, and all similar passages according to the limitation this reasoning places upon the body, the bodily presence, and the human nature of Jesus in his glory. The basic deficiency of these reasonings has often been pointed out. They play one passage of Scripture against another instead of letting one class of passages illumine and interpret the other class. *Scriptura ex Scriptura explicanda est,* always and always, and not by rationalizings of human minds regarding some passage or passages so as to make them conflict with other passages.

56) Thus the Holy Spirit himself completed Stephen's address for him, completed it in a most miraculous way and with the most effective gospel word. Unlike Peter, Stephen did not need to preach to the Sanhedrin the resurrection and the exaltation of Jesus (3:10, 15), here Jesus himself preached it by revealing himself to Stephen in his heavenly glory and causing him to reveal to the Sanhedrin what his eyes were seeing. This was the fulfillment of the very word Jesus himself had uttered before this very Sanhedrin when he was on trial, Matt. 26:64. They now hear that this Jesus whom they crucified is standing in the heavens as the eternal Messiah at God's own right of majesty and power. Stephen is not relating what he saw on some former occasion, but what it is granted him to see at the very moment of his speaking. Far removed and yet not removed is this Jesus; for the heavens stand open (the perfect participle with its present connotation), and he is standing as one who has risen for action. Yes, it was all for Stephen, for his comfort and his assurance. There stood the almighty Son of man whose power maintained his great confessor. But it was intended also for the Sanhedrists. Whom were they opposing? The glorified Son of man, the heavenly, eternal, almighty Messiah of God.

The title "the Son of man" is discussed at length in connection with the writer's interpretation of Matt. 8:20; Mark 2:10; Luke 5:24; John 1:51, to which the reader is referred.

57) While the crushing rebukes of the law were being administered, the Sanhedrists had remained in

their seats although gnashing their teeth; the great gospel testimony of Stephen, although it was produced by a miracle of God, causes the Sanhedrists to rage like wild beasts that are demanding blood. Is it possible that the gospel can affect men's hearts in such a way? It did in this case. **But uttering yells with a great voice, they held their ears and rushed with one accord upon him; and having thrown him out of the city, they began stoning him.**

Pandemonium broke loose. All legal formalities were cast aside as mob rage and violence suddenly came into control. We do not understand how some interpreters can insert into Luke's description the formal passing of a death sentence. According to Jewish law it would have been ineffective because a second session of the Sanhedrin which was held at least a day later was necessary for legal confirmation, and in addition to that the governor's consent to the execution was mandatory. No; a mob storm breaks loose and hurries Stephen to his death forthwith.

The shouting and the holding shut of the ears implies that Stephen's words were considered the most awful blasphemy. Lest they hear another word like that they shout with might and main to drown out Stephen's voice and stop their ears so that no word of his may enter them. Then, as though actuated by one impulse, they dash upon this blasphemer and thrust him outside of the city and there begin to stone him. All this happened without delay. But note that Luke first has a chain of aorists that fall like blow upon blow; the shouting — the holding the ears shut — the rushing upon Stephen — the expulsion from the city; and then uses an imperfect which arrests our attention to view what is going on, the process of stoning, for, before it is finished, something else must be told. This imperfect is repeated in v. 59 and holds us in suspense still longer in anticipation of what is yet to be added. This use of the imperfect is an excellent example of how the tense is employed to hold the reader in suspense.

58) We know that attempts were made to stone Jesus for blasphemy in the very Temple courts (John 8:59; 10:31, etc.). Why Stephen was thrust out of the city in agreement with Lev. 24:14 (Heb. 13:11), we cannot say, unless it was done because of the strange twists of the mob mind which, in the midst of its lawlessness, sometimes clings to legal formality. Points to be considered in reconstructing the story are these: building was going on in the Temple area, and stones were ready at hand there — the paved streets afforded no suitable stones — just where the Sanhedrin met is a question — outside of the city plenty of stones were available.

We are not impressed by the argument that these supreme judges and dignitaries of the Sanhedrin were incapable of the coarseness here described, and that Luke intends to change the subject of all the verbs to other unnamed persons. We know what these men perpetrated upon the helpless Jesus in Matt. 26:67, 68, and in Mark 14:65. They really do less here. But, of course, to the Sanhedrists we must add their Levite police force, into whose hands Stephen must have been given for the trial; we must also add the crowd of Hellenist Jews who had arrested Stephen and brought him in and acted as his accusers, together with their suborned witnesses. Many persons may have been thronging outside of the doors, these were augmented by people who had been attracted to the scene. A force of police rushed Stephen to the scene of execution. Sanhedrists went along, and a crowd that grew as they went followed.

But what about the loss of the Jewish right to execute criminals? Note that the Sanhedrin had not passed a verdict and thus was not legally liable. The whole action was one of mob violence and could be classed as a popular outburst of rage against a fearful blasphemer. Pilate was not eager to do justice in a case such as this, the less so since he himself had grave reasons to fear the Sanhedrin because of outrages he had perpetrated. We need not date this event later than the rule of Pilate, place it into an interim when Pilate had been withdrawn and his successor had not yet arrived. Pilate was at Caesarea at this time.

And the witnesses placed their robes at the feet of a young man called Saul. The witnesses had to cast the first stones in order to attest that they had sworn and witnessed truly (Deut. 17:6); otherwise they would be adding the crime of murder to that of perjured testimony. The long, loose outer robe had to be laid aside in order to permit free use of the limbs in the violent action of throwing stones. The thought is not that some individual, here by chance Saul, was selected to guard these robes lest someone make off with them during the excitement. We must assume that Saul was acting in an official capacity, either alone or in conjunction with others who were superintending the stoning. This is made probable by what is related in the sequel about his prominent activity under the authority of the Sanhedrin. We see what a position he had attained as a disciple of the great Gamaliel who was a member of the Sanhedrin (5:34). "Young man," νεανίας, is not a youth in our sense of the word but a man come to maturity; Saul must have been about thirty years old at this time. This is only an estimate, yet it is based on all the available data.

59) **And they were stoning Stephen, calling out and saying, Lord Jesus, receive my spirit! And having kneeled, he shouted with a great voice, Lord, place not this sin against them! And having said this, he fell asleep.**

The repetition is tragic and is made more so by the imperfect tense. The terrible process of stoning a man to death was going slowly onward. An aorist would mean that the final, fatal stone had been thrown. Note that Luke now adds the name: "And they were stoning Stephen" — yes, this proto-martyr, this first confessor of Christendom to seal his faith with his life. As stone after stone crashed against his body, he raised his face to God and after the pattern of Jesus' own dying prayer (Luke 24:46) asked the Lord Jesus (see 1:21) to receive his spirit. That prayer was heard. Stephen's spirit, the immaterial part of his being, left his body and was received by Jesus into the glory and the bliss of heaven, there to await the last day when his body would be raised up to be again united with his soul and to participate in its heavenly joys. So Paul longed "to depart and be with Christ" (Phil 1:23).

Here there is no "oblivion" for the soul at death. The idea of a *sheol* or hades as a *Totenreich* or intermediate place for souls, lying somewhere between heaven and hell, seems to be foreign to Stephen's mind, who sees only the heavenly glory of God and Jesus at God's right standing to receive his martyr's spirit. *Fecisti me victorem, recipe me in triumphum.* Augustine.

60) Stone after stone struck Stephen. He sank to his knees, literally, "having placed the knees," yet he did not do so in the humbleness of prayer before the Lord but simply because he had been severely struck by well-aimed stones. At the very moment of death, like Jesus, he rallies all his fast-ebbing strength and at the top of his voice so that all in the crowd may hear he shouts his final prayer which asks God not to place this sin against his murderers, the dative of disadvantage. In the aorist negative commands are in the subjunctive and not in the imperative. In prayers, for instance in the Lord's Prayer, the aorist denotes urgency and fervency; so it does here. This prayer for his enemies Stephen had also learned from Jesus. R.,

W. P., regards this aorist as ingressive, it is effective. The verb accords with its opposite, ἀφιέναι, "to dismiss" or send the sin away (ἄφεσις). Stephen's prayer had one most notable fulfillment, namely Saul. Being a young man like Stephen, Saul soon stepped into Stephen's vacant place, took up the martyr's work, and carried it forward with great power.

And so Stephen "fell asleep." This time Luke uses an effective aorist which marks the ending of an action. The two aorists used in this verse thus bring the final outcome of the previous imperfects. Although he experienced a violent and terrible form of death, Stephen "went to sleep." This is not a euphemism which would hide the fearful reality but literal truth. This expression is regularly used in the New Testament with reference to the dying of believers. By the use of this very word for death the resurrection is implied. But only the body falls asleep; the soul does not sleep but is with the Lord, awaiting the awakening of the body.

CHAPTER VIII

The Second Quarter

The Gospel in Palestine, Chapters 8 to 12

THE GOSPEL IN SAMARIA

The stoning of Stephen ushered in the first general persecution. The church had grown extensively; it was to grow more than ever, but now by being spread abroad. Luke's figures and further notes about the growth make the estimate of 25,000 believers in and near Jerusalem at the time of Stephen's martyrdom seem conservative. The persecution aimed to destroy the infant church; in the providence of God it did the very opposite. It started a great number of new congregations especially in all of Palestine, each becoming a living center from which the gospel radiated into new territory even as Jesus had traced its course by adding after Jerusalem "all Judea and Samaria" (1:8).

1) **Now Saul continued to agree with his taking away. Moreover, there arose on that day a great persecution against the church in Jerusalem; and all were scattered abroad through the regions of Judea and Samaria except the apostles.**

It is the strong durative sense of the periphrastic verb form that makes the statement about Saul so important in the present connection. To be sure, he agreed with full approval to Stephen's "taking away," the word that has the sinister meaning of murder; but he continued in this agreement, and it is thus that, starting on the very day of Stephen's martyrdom, a persecution began that Luke rightly calls "great." For so thoroughly did Saul agree to what was done with Stephen that he moved to do the same thing with the entire church in Jerusalem. In other words, Saul became the prime mover in this persecution. That is why the statement regarding him is put here in connection with the word about the persecution.

The A. V. is right in beginning the new chapter as it does. The casual mention of Saul in 7:58 is only preliminary to this more serious statement which connects Saul with the persecution. He was a man of tremendous energy and sound logic. Stephen's death should be followed up, the entire Christian movement should be crushed. Saul placed himself forward in making the effort.

Beyond saying that the persecution began that very day and that Stephen was its first victim Luke reports no details. With the historical aorist he states only the effect that the Christians were scattered abroad all over Judea and Samaria. Τὰς χώρας, "the regions," does not mean that they went only into the country districts and avoided the cities. Samaria became especially attractive to the Christians, for they were losing their antipathy toward the Samaritans, and in this country, so close at hand, the Sanhedrin and its minions could exercise no authority. "All" is to be taken in the popular and not the absolute sense. The apostles, however, remained in Jerusalem. In explanation we may note that Jerusalem was still the headquarters for the work among the Jews, and the apostles were to remain here until the Lord should direct them elsewhere. As far as fear was concerned, they had none as they had already demonstrated (4:8, etc.; 5:30, etc.)

2) **Yet devout men buried Stephen and made great lamentation over him.** This is added lest a wrong deduction be made from the foregoing. In the

first place, the Jews always buried on the day of death, if possible; and in Stephen's case no delay of any kind was necessary. As soon as the crowd about the dead martyr dispersed, men of the type of Joseph of Arimathaea and Nicodemus took a hand and gave the poor, battered, and bloody body decent burial. Their very act shows them to be "devout" (see 2:5), sincere, and of honest hearts, men who deeply deplored what had been done. Luke's designation can scarcely refer to Christians against whom adverse measures must have been taken that same day.

So also these men made great mourning over him, κοπετός, the beating of the head and the breast while wailing in Oriental fashion. Luke loves contrasts, so he tells us that, while such men were still to be found in Jerusalem, this other man, Saul, began his bloodthirsty work.

3) **Saul, however, began to lay waste the church, entering in house by house and, haling men and women, was committing them to prison. They, therefore, on being scattered abroad, went on through, proclaiming as good news the Word.**

This is the way in which Saul continued to agree to Stephen's death. The verb indicates the devastation caused by a wild beast, and the imperfect is best regarded as conative. On ἐκκλησία see 5:11. The κατά phrase should be construed with the participle; though the noun is plural and has the article the phrase is distributive as in 22:19 and 26:11 (B.-P. 634). These latter passages refer to different synagogues in which beatings were administered in the different cities and thus cast no light on the proceeding of Saul in Jerusalem where the victims were committed to prison. We are thus not warranted in thinking only of houses in which assemblies were held; these were private homes, the article indicating those in which Christians might be living — these Saul invaded.

Many had to suffer, Luke noting that even women were not spared. The participle "haling them," dragging them with violence, as well as the main statement, "he kept duly giving them over into prison" (thus literally), show that Saul had been given a force of Levitical police by the Sanhedrin in order to execute his orders of arrest in Jerusalem, and that, therefore, Saul was the chief agent of the Sanhedrin in this persecution. In fact, it seems that but for him such strong measures would not have been taken. This ferreting out where Christians lived and then falling upon them with a force of police made all Christians unsafe in the city and necessarily caused the great exodus in harmony with Jesus' own orders, Matt. 10:23 (Acts 14:6).

4) Now a further contrast: Saul ravaging the church, but the dispersed Christians spreading the gospel. Incidentally, we here see how God was turning this persecution to his own great ends. Saul thought he was crushing the Christian movement; in reality, the harder he worked to do so, the more he himself helped to spread that movement. We have οἱ μὲν οὖν as in 1:6, and this subject is modified by the participle: "they, therefore, on being scattered." In whatever territory they passed through "they told as good news the Word," here this verb has an object as in 5:42. Luke uses εὐαγγελίζομαι in its ordinary sense as in Luke 1:19; 2:10; 3:18; and not in the official sense of "to preach." These were ordinary Christians; they did not set themselves up as preachers but told people why they had to leave Jerusalem and thus testified to their faith in Christ Jesus. They fulfilled the duty that is to this day incumbent on every Christian. In 11:19 Luke indicates how far this dispersion reached: to Phoenicia, Cyprus, and Antioch. This does not indicate the use of a separate document; Luke is evidently proceeding in due order by telling us first of what happened in

Samaria and then reporting what happened in more distant places.

5) So we see how Philip came to work in Samaria. **Now Philip, having gone down to a city of Samaria, was proclaiming the Christ to them. And the multitudes with one accord were giving heed to the things being declared by Philip while they were hearing and seeing the signs which he was doing. For many of those having unclean spirits — shouting with a great voice, they kept going out; moreover, many having become paralyzed and lame were healed. And there was great joy in that city.**

After having stated that all the apostles remained in Jerusalem (v. 1), we understand that Luke refers to the deacon Philip (6:5) and not to the apostle Philip (1:13). The congregation at Jerusalem was sadly disrupted; the deacons were no longer needed, and Philip was thus free to leave. We have already indicated why Samaria, so close at hand, offered an attractive refuge to the Christians. We must combine Philip's preaching with his power to work miracles. These gifts of God made him what has been called an evangelist, a missionary preacher. He was thus more than the ordinary Christians who spread the gospel only as a part of their general Christian calling; yet he and his work remained under the authority of the apostles and of the mother congregation in Jerusalem (v. 14) so that he acted with their approval and as their agent. "The Christ" = the Messiah whom the Samaritans, too, expected (John 4:25) although they accepted only the Pentateuch. "The Christ" is the same as "the Word" (v. 4).

On the basis of both textual and other evidence we ought to read: "to a (not the) city of Samaria" (compare the same expression in Matt. 10:5). Even the texts that have "the" seem uncertain, for Aleph has the reading "Caesarea" in place of "Samaria," and B has "Paul" instead of "Philip" in v. 6. Luke never uses the appositional genitive when naming a city so that "the city of Samaria" would be "the city," the one called "Samaria." "Samaria" always refers to the country bearing that name. At this time the city which was at one time called "Samaria" had the name "Sebaste." The usual explanation that we here have an appositional genitive must therefore be dropped. Luke does not name the city. Yet in all probability he has in mind the old city of Shechem, which was later called Neapolis, and at present has the name Nablous, which is located at the foot of Mount Gerizim, the center of the Samaritan worship ("this mountain," John 4:20, 21), and is to this day maintained by the dwindling remnant of Samaritans. In 1925 the writer met their high priest, visited their synagogue in Nablous, and inspected their sacred scrolls. To the Samaritans this city was what Jerusalem was to the Jews. Here the magician Simon would most naturally establish himself. Near this city, at Sychar, Jesus had taught with success for two days (John 4:39-42). When coming from Jerusalem, Philip would reach this city first and have every reason to stop and to work here. Compare the data in Zahn, *Apostelgeschichte*. The temporary order not to preach in Samaria (Matt. 10:5) had been rescinded by Jesus in Acts 1:8.

We thus see why Luke devotes some space to Philip's success in Samaria. It is not just a city such as Sebaste that was won for the gospel but the religious center of the entire Samaritan people. After being driven from one religious center, another such center was promptly being won. Saul was not succeeding in stopping the preaching and the spread of the gospel.

6) The imperfect tenses, starting with v. 5, continue descriptively and picture the remarkable progress until they end in two aorists (v. 7, 8). Supply **νοῦν**

with προσεῖχον. "Multitudes" were giving heed to the things being declared by Philip, which means that they came to faith. The success of the apostles in Jerusalem was being repeated in the Samaritan religious center. Luke's favorite ἐν τῷ with the infinitive in the sense of "while" reports that seeing and hearing the signs (see 2:19) accompanied the preaching the Samaritans heard from Philip. These signs, like all those wrought by Jesus and the apostles, attested and helped to seal the preaching as being truly a message from God. We may compare Philip with Stephen in this respect (6:8) and remember that every miracle was wrought only by a direct communication from God (Christ), see 5:15.

7) Even many demoniacs were healed. The subject of demon possession is treated in connection with Matt. 4:24; 8:28; Mark 1:23; Luke 4:33. The construction is anacoluthic. It begins with the persons of the afflicted and ends with the demons of these persons as the subject of the verb; and while τὰ πνεῦματα which is implied in βοῶντα is a neuter plural, the verb is not made a singular and thus regards the *pneumata* as persons. Luke implies that demoniacs came to Philip, and that all who came found deliverance. These unclean, vile spirits acted just as did those that were driven out by Jesus: they always shouted with hideous cries when they were compelled to leave their poor victims. The witnessing of these miracles which so clearly testified to the complete victory of Jesus over all the power of hell, rightly impressed the Samaritans.

Luke adds the sad cases of the paralytics who had been lamed on one side of the body by a stroke. These, too, appear frequently in the story of Jesus, every one being a hopeless case to this day as far as medical help is concerned. These, too, were healed, and Luke now reaches his aorists which close the story.

8) No wonder the joy in that city became "abundant," πολλή. Jesus had entered it with his gospel to free the souls and with his signs to heal even the bodies.

9) Philip, however, had more to contend with than the perverted Samaritan religion. Here in the old religious center of the Samaritans Simon was holding sway over the minds and the hearts of the people by means of his occult Oriental black arts. His story is introduced by Luke as an indication of the success of Philip in freeing the people from the hold this charlatan had upon them. This is the main object of Luke's account. As far as the man himself is concerned, he is of minor importance, for which reason also Luke closes his account regarding him at v. 24.

Now a man, by name Simon, was already in the city practicing magic and astonishing the nation of Samaria, declaring himself to be someone great; to whom all from small to great were giving heed, declaring, This one is the Power of God, the one called Great! Moreover, they were giving heed to him because he had astonished them with his magical arts a long time.

Δέ turns to the new subject, and τίς is only our indefinite article. When Philip came to the city he found that this Simon had been fully established there for some time and was practicing magic (μαγεύων) and filling the people with astonishment.

He is called Simon Magus and plays a great role in the traditions of the second and the third centuries. None of these reports are worthy of much attention although some commentaries give them space. Zahn discusses them at length. The participle μαγεύων has no connection with the Magi who appear in Matt. 2:1. This Simon belonged to a class of charlatans that were rather common at this period, who practiced occult arts in order to impress the people and to gain a following. Much was plain sorcery which was at times combined with a shrewd use of natural laws that were otherwise unknown. The range of their arts extended from the conjuring of demons, dealing with the dead, influencing the gods, to charms for healing, divination, stargazing, and the like. The more pretentious employed formulae and ideas that were derived from Oriental theosophy and mystic cults, or combined these with Greek ideas. The type of magic employed must be deduced from what Luke himself states. He was certainly successful, for he astonished not only the city but, as Luke says, "the nation of Samaria." It is this power of the man among the people as a whole that shows us what the gospel really accomplished through Philip's activity.

Simon must have performed prodigious feats of conjuring, for in v. 11 Luke uses the noun ταῖς μαγείαις. What these feats were is of less importance than the man's claims and the credence these claims found. He declared "himself to be someone great." This is more than *etwas Besonderes* (neuter), B.-D. 301, 1. He purposely kept the designation of himself indefinite and veiled and thus made a deep impression on the imagination of men who love the mysterious. But there is no evidence that he claimed "to impersonate God." Jerome's report that Simon said: *Ego sum sermo Dei* (the Logos), . . . *ego omnipotens, ego omnia Dei,* is a late fancy that is contradicted by Luke's plain words. Simon kept the people guessing. Even Samaritans who had the Decalog in their Pentateuch, would not have suffered the use of these titles if Simon had, indeed, used them.

10) Simon achieved what he wanted: "All from small to great gave heed to him"; we should say, "both young and old," or, "both high and low." What *he* conveyed by hinting *they* supplied by their own superstitious imagination and declared him to be no less than "the Power of God, the one called Great." This

is not deification. It would be among pagans who had many gods but not among Samaritans. These thought of a manifestation of God's power in the person of the man Simon, of that power which is supreme. The positive "great" is used in the absolute sense and replaces the superlative. Note that, when the predicate has the article, subject and predicate are identical and interchangeable, R. 768. Luke does not report that Simon was identified with God himself, and we have no right to put into his words more than he himself implied. Zahn follows Klostermann in making ἡ μεγάλη the transliteration of the Hebrew participle piel of *galah*: *m*ᵉ*galleh*, and in noting that this Hebrew verb is always translated ἀποκαλύπτειν by the LXX. The people thus esteemed Simon as God's great instrument for revealing everything, also God himself. Thus they followed the hint stated in John 4:25, where the Samaritan woman told Jesus that the Messiah would tell them all things. But Zahn is the only commentator of note who adopts this ingenious explanation of Klostermann's. Both men fail to make clear how Luke's simple Greek adjective could convey the idea to the reader that a Hebrew piel participle is being referred to. Why did Luke not write the corresponding Greek participle ἀποκαλύπτων?

We should not identify this Simon with the one mentioned by Josephus in *Ant.* 20, 7, 2, whom Felix used to seduce Drusilla away from her husband Azizus, king of Emesa. Luke does not make him a spurious Messiah, a rival of Jesus. He is only a notable representative of the superstitious religious imposters, of whom the world was full at this time. He is to be put into the same class with Elymas (Acts 13) and the famous charlatan Apollonius of Tyana, who flourished in the same century. The Satanic influence of these imposters is evident.

11) What made the case so difficult for Philip's work was the fact that by means of his arts Simon had held the people "a long time" (dative of time *when* an action takes place; this construction is restricted to words like day, night, year, etc.). The perfect infinitive agrees with this dative. Philip found the man's hold on the people deep and strong. But we already know that Philip broke this hold; even Simon gave way to Philip.

12) **Now, when they came to believe Philip proclaiming the good news concerning the kingdom of God and the name of Jesus Christ, they were being baptized, both men and women.**

We see to what the "giving heed" mentioned in v. 6 led: men and women "came to believe," an ingressive aorist (not a constative, as R., *W. P.* states), hence it is followed by the imperfect. Πιστεύω with the dative means to believe the person and what he says. So here these Samaritans accepted all that Philip was proclaiming as good news "concerning the kingdom of God (see 1:3) and the name (see 2:21, 38; 3:6) of Jesus Christ (see 2:38)." They came to believe the good news concerning God's rule and reign of grace, pardon, and salvation as this was revealed (ὄνομα) in the person named Jesus and in his office as Christ. Luke gives us a brief summary of Philip's gospel preaching; it centered in the kingdom and in the Name. It does so to this day. The Name is the great door that admits into the kingdom.

And thus Luke states that "they were being baptized, both men and women," the imperfect stating that this occurred continually as they came to faith. We see that Luke makes the account of what happened here in Samaria somewhat of a parallel to what had happened in Jerusalem. At the time of the first ingress of believers, cf. 2:40, their being baptized is recorded; the same is done here at the time of the first influx of

Samaritans. Here, too, no hint regarding the mode of baptism employed is offered. Immersion, however, is out of the question, no place that would be suitable for using this mode is found at Nablous. Yet "they were being baptized" without the least difficulty. Jesus had sown the seed at Sychar in Samaria, Philip was reaping the great harvest (John 4:37, 38). Simon's hold on the people was entirely broken.

13) **Moreover, Simon himself also came to believe and, on having been baptized, continued to hold to Philip; and beholding that signs and works of power kept occurring, he was amazed.**

He who had amazed others by his magical arts and claims was now himself kept in a state of amazement (imperfect tense) by what he kept seeing (present participle), the miracles that kept occurring (again a present participle, here in the construction after a verb of seeing). Luke does not use the usual expression "signs and wonders" but writes "signs and power works" as emphasizing what Simon saw in the miracles: their significance and their power. On the basis of what is related later it is usually assumed that Simon's faith was only a sham, but Luke uses the same verb and the same tense with reference to him as he does with reference to the people; he even adds that Simon remained in close attachment to Philip. The man did believe. The fact that he later went wrong, and that his young faith was perverted and lost, is something that followed. All that Luke intimates regarding this outcome is the fact that Simon was too much captivated by the miracles he saw. The probability is that he came to regard them as being in the same class with his own magical arts but far superior to what he had been able to produce.

It is unwarranted to claim that in the case of Simon's baptism we have "clear proof that baptism does not convey salvation." The Baptist taught and practiced the baptism of repentance and remission of sins. The 3,000 were told to be baptized "for the remission of sins." Paul's sins were washed away by his being baptized (22:16). Baptism is "the washing of regeneration and renewing of the Holy Spirit" (Tit. 3:5). Baptism is what it is irrespective of its recipient. A gold piece that is treated as being worthless is no less a gold piece. The only deduction that can be legitimately made on the assumption that Simon had only a sham faith at the time of his baptism is that baptism does not work mechanically, as an *opus operatum,* which means that the saving grace it conveys must be apprehended by the heart. The fact that a man does not appropriate something is not a proof that there was nothing to appropriate.

14) It must have been some time after Philip had begun his work and not until his success attained the proportions recorded by Luke that the apostles came to Samaria. **Now, when the apostles in Jerusalem heard that Samaria had received the Word of God, they commissioned to them Peter and John who, having come down, prayed regarding them that they might receive the Holy Spirit; for as yet he had not fallen on anyone of them, and they had been baptized only in the name of the Lord Jesus. Then they began to lay their hands on them, and they began to receive the Holy Spirit.**

Since the congregation at Jerusalem had been scattered far and wide, the good news that came from Samaria must have brought joy to the apostles who had remained in the city (v. 1). We see nothing hierarchical in their action of sending two of their number to Nablous to Philip to review this new increase of believers.

It is not hyperbole when Luke writes "that Samaria has received the Word" (the tense of the direct discourse being retained), for this does not mean "all

Samaria" but Samaritans as distinct from Jews; note 1:8. The Word was advancing from Jewish into Samaritan territory — a most significant progress. Since the return from Babylonia a gulf had existed between these two peoples and, lo, it was now being bridged by the Word of Christ. And this was being done, not by an apostle, but by one of the former deacons. That certainly concerned the apostles, and they sent the two most important individuals of their number to Philip. The idea to be conveyed is that all the believers constitute one body whether they were formerly Jews or formerly Samaritans. This oneness is expressed by the mission of Peter and of John.

15) Their mere visit to Nablous would, however, have meant too little; that would have made manifest no more than outward oneness between the old and the new wing of the church. On their arrival Peter and John, therefore, prayed for the Samaritan believers in order (ὅπως, purpose) that they might receive the Holy Spirit. For it is this Spirit who makes the church one. When he dwells in all believers through the Word and faith, they are all made one spiritual body with Christ as the head and with his apostles as his chief ministrants of the Word.

16) The reason for their prayer is explained by the γάρ clause: the Spirit had not yet fallen upon any of the Samaritan believers (periphrastic pluperfect). The very expression indicates that the charismatic gift of the Spirit is being referred to, which comes in a miraculous way and is apparent to all who might be present. "Had fallen" recalls what had happened at the time of Pentecost. The Samaritan believers had not yet been distinguished by this sign of the Spirit's presence; it had been delayed until this time.

"They had been baptized only," etc. The periphrastic pluperfect with **ὑπῆρχον** instead of **ἦσαν, R. 1121,** is used, but this by no means intends to say that at this time these Samaritans had received no more than baptism from the Holy Spirit or, as some would say, baptism as a mere symbol so that through the apostles they were now to receive the Spirit himself. They had been baptized as believers, they had received Word and sacrament and all that Word and sacrament bestow, the Holy Spirit in their hearts, and thus regeneration, conversion, justification, the power of a new life, in a word, salvation. They had received the supreme gifts of the Spirit "only," but these are invisible. Baptism was the one gift that was also an outward mark of their having the Spirit.

Still other marks were to be granted them, seals and signs that they were true members of the spiritual body that is created by the Spirit. These were the charismata of the Spirit, those gifts which the Spirit distributes freely in the church (I Cor. 12:7-13). In these earliest days of the church's history he distributed them miraculously, most wonderfully at Pentecost in the speaking with tongues, after that in a less wonderful way here at Nablous; then in 10:44-48 (11:15), in 19:6, and in the congregation at Corinth.

17) So this manifestation of the Spirit was now bestowed upon the Samaritan believers. As was the case in 19:7, this was done through the laying on of hands; see 6:6 for this symbolic rite. On Pentecost, in the case of Cornelius, and in Corinth, the Spirit did not make use of such a rite. Here and in 19:7 its purpose is apparent: the Spirit uses the chosen apostles of Jesus in order to unite all his believers into one spiritual body and to make this apparent. Not two or more churches were to be established: one that was Jewish, another that was Samaritan, others that were Gentile; no, only one, in which all believers were to be on the same level. In order to get the full import

of this fact we must project ourselves backward into those days when Jew, Samaritan, Greek Gentile, barbarian Gentile were as widely separated from each other as the poles. The Spirit had his mighty reason for waiting until the arrival of the apostles before bestowing his charisma in Samaria.

In order to avoid wrong deductions, let us note that none of the 3,000 new believers at the time of Pentecost received the gift of tongues but only the 120 whom Jesus himself had long ago brought to faith; in 10:44-48 the new believers received this gift. After Pentecost, as the church grew by leaps and bounds, speaking with tongues did not occur, but at a far later time this gift reappeared in the congregation in Corinth. It was exactly as Paul states in I Cor. 12:11.

No charismatic gift was bestowed in connection with the baptism administered by the apostles — remember Pentecost; the baptism of Philip lacked nothing which the apostles had to add. The Spirit's manifestations at the time of Pentecost, here in Samaria, and then in Caesarea had their own special purpose, and this by no means concerned just those who received gifts miraculously but extended far beyond them. As to far more necessary and valuable charismata that were bestowed unobtrusively, note Stephen (6:10) and note Paul's estimate and advice (I Cor. 14:1). Only by strange processes of reasoning could the older view arise that in the coming of Peter and of John to the Samaritans lies support for the rite of confirmation as a sacrament of the church (Cyprian, *Epistle* 73).

18) **Now, when Simon saw that through the laying on of the hands of the apostles the Holy Spirit was being given, he offered them money, saying, Give also to me this power, that on whom I lay the hands he may receive the Holy Spirit.**

When Peter and John came to Nablous, a gathering of all the believers was probably held, and the apostles laid hands on some of them, and these began to speak with tongues. It was this that Simon saw and that made him desire to possess the same ability he thought the apostles had. When it is said that those speaking with tongues were transported into "ecstasy," this is without the support of any passage dealing with this gift. It is likewise exaggeration to suppose that every believer had hands laid on him, and that all spoke with tongues. This view misunderstands the purpose of this manifestation. What was done in the case of some counted for all; this was not a matter that pertained to individuals but to this entire body of Samaritan believers and to all others who might yet come to faith. This manifestation happened once, and that was all. Its significance as a sign for all believing Samaritans was thus established and needed no repetition.

19) Simon was still bound by his ideas about magical acts and thus rated what he saw the apostles doing as something of the same order but grander than anything he himself had been able to do. He had paid out money to learn his feats of conjury and so made bold to offer money to Peter and to John in order that they might teach him how to perform this new and astonishing feat. When estimating the import of this offer the fact is often overlooked that Philip had already been working many signs even on demoniacs and paralytics, and that Simon, nevertheless, had made no attempt to acquire this power. This makes his present offer appear like a relapse into his old life and ways. He believed and was baptized (v. 13) but now fell back into his love for occult arts. The worst feature about this relapse was the fact that he regarded the Holy Spirit as being merely some sort of mysterious effect that could be brought about by

one who understood the secret art. Any derogation of the Holy Spirit is dangerous in the extreme as we see in the case of Ananias and Sapphira (5:3, 9). Simon's offer of money eventually coined the term "simony" as a designation for the purchase of church offices and the revenues connected with them.

20) Was Simon planning to return to his old life by adding this new art to his old ones? He was certainly severely reprimanded by Peter. **But Peter said to him: Thy silver be with thee in perdition because thou didst suppose to acquire the gift of God through money! There is not for thee part or lot in this matter; for thy heart is not straight before God. Repent, therefore, of this thy baseness and beg the Lord if, perhaps, the project of thy heart will be remitted for thee. For I see that thou art in gall of bitterness and bond of iniquity.**

The optative of wish εἴη is construed with static εἰς and = "May thou and thy silver be in perdition!" This is an imprecatory wish. This wish is really a judgment and one that is fully justified, since any man who has the idea that money may purchase the powers of the Spirit is on the verge of committing blasphemy against the Spirit and should, therefore, be damned. Ἀπώλεια, "destruction," is regarded as annihilation by those who wish to abolish hell from the Scriptures, whereas its Biblical meaning is the complete ruin of the sinner in the loss of salvation and life and in the doom of eternal death. "Thy silver with thee," the means of the sin together with the sinner. The use to which we put our money stamps our character upon it.

This judgment of imprecation is at once substantiated, ὅτι, "because." This former conjurer imagined that he could acquire the gift of God through money. Peter says nothing about the insult Simon offered him by the proffer of money in such a deal; he at once points out the worst feature the insult offered to God by imagining that *his gift* was like a conjurer's trick that could be *bought with money.* "The gift" is really generic, for anything that constitutes such a gift is referred to. Here the Holy Spirit is himself the gift; for only one filled with the Spirit would be used by him to convey such spiritual gifts by the laying on of the apostles' hands. Peter is opening the eyes of Simon to the damnableness of his proposition.

We should note that Simon's story is told so fully because it is a parallel to that of Ananias and Sapphira. Both stand out in the first church as glaring examples of the frightful attempt by means of money to obtain what can be obtained only by God's grace. So men still think they can buy honor in God's kingdom, yea, salvation itself, by means of money contributions to some church cause, whether they acknowledge their secret intent or not.

21) "There is not part or lot for thee" = thou hast neither part not lot, the two terms emphasizing the same idea, namely that Simon has completely excluded himself from any participation "in this matter." This meaning of λόγος, the matter under discussion, is well established. But we must not narrow its sense in this statement to the transmission of the Spirit by the bestowal of a spiritual gift. "This matter" includes everything connected with the Spirit and his gifts. Simon was unfit to receive even the gift that so many Samaritans were freely receiving. We must note that he had not knelt down with them to have hands laid on his head so that he, like others, might speak with tongues. He had only stood by and conceived his vicious project of purchase. It was thus that he completely excluded himself from all contact with the Spirit.

This answers the objection that is based on too narrow a view and makes "this matter" refer only to the laying on of hands for bestowing the gift of tongues. Those who see that this view is too narrow and that it does not fit the context offer an unsatisfactory remedy by letting λόγος mean "this Word and gospel of Christ" by appealing to the use of "Word" in v. 14 and 25, and also to the context, that Simon's heart is not straight before God. Yet the context does not deal with the gospel Word, its preaching (v. 25) and its reception when preached (v. 14). All is clear and the context fully satisfied when "this *logos*" is taken to refer to this entire matter of receiving anything from, or transmitting anything as an agent of, the Holy Spirit.

From that Simon completely excluded himself in that his heart was no longer "straight," sincere, honest, true, in God's sight. "Heart" is always the center of the personality with all that characterizes it in mind and in will. It is thus that God always looks at our hearts and sees our inmost character. We are unable to judge the heart, and there is no worse vice in the church than what the Germans call *Herzens-richterei,* presuming to judge other men's hearts. Peter was not doing that, for Simon himself had fully revealed the crookedness of his heart, and Peter was judging him on the basis of that revelation.

So we may judge men on the basis of their clear and undeniable actions. Often a pretense of doing no more than that is made when evil motives are attributed to fellow men in attempts to injure them. Then our own hearts are no longer "straight before God." Then we pretend to see a splinter ("mote" is incorrect) in our fellow man's eye the while we carry a beam or plank in our own eye. In the case of Ananias and Sapphira, Peter acted under special revelation from the Spirit, which makes that case entirely exceptional.

22) Simon is shown how he appears in God's eyes. At the same time he is told what to do in order to be restored. He is to repent from this baseness; see this verb in 2:38, and not that it is here used in its narrower sense: true contrition and sorrow of the heart for sin. It is thus construed with the sin from which Simon is to repent and turn, and he is told to seek remission for that sin. Peter rightly calls it "this baseness," κακία, which is not the same as "wickedness" (our versions), the word for that is πονηρία. While the two terms are synonymous, the former is milder, it is the German *Schlechtigkeit*, the opposite of ἀρετή or excellence (C.-K. 558), while the latter is active, vicious wickedness. The idea expressed is that of loss as in good-for-nothingness, here with reference to a spiritual condition that has become spoiled, bad, depraved.

This contriteness is to be combined with the humble, begging prayer for the divine remission of the sin and guilt involved in his ἐπίνοια, the thing that has come upon his mind, his frightful "project." Peter's two aorist imperatives are intended to make Simon see the urgency of Peter's commands. By using δέομαι Peter bids Simon throw himself at the Lord's feet as a beggar; and the εἰ with the indicative expresses expectation (B.-D. 375) which is in this case lessened by the addition of ἄρα: "if, perchance, he will," etc. The implication of this conditional form is not regarding the Lord's willingness to remit but in regard to Simon's contrition and begging as being necessary for enabling the Lord to extend remission. Unless Simon's heart changes, he himself will prevent the Lord's remission. Therefore, too, Peter says, "the project of thy heart," for the seat of this sin is in Simon's heart, and the Lord will see his very heart, and no outward contrite begging will deceive him. In "shall be remitted," literally, "shall be sent away," we have the Biblical term for freeing the sinner from his sin and his guilt; see the explanation of the noun ἄφεσις in 2:38.

23) The γάρ explains to Simon how serious is his condition. His "project" betrays the terrible condition existing in his heart. Peter sees Simon "in gall of bitterness and bond of iniquity," for that is what his project reveals concerning himself. His entire person is concerned; the construction ὁρῶ σε ὄντα is classical, and εἰς is static, "in," not "into," R. 593. Both genitives are appositional: gall that is bitterness, and bondage that is iniquity, the absence of the articles stressing the force of the nouns themselves. On "bitterness" compare Heb. 12:15. The entire expression describes Simon's spiritual state. Bitterness, however, does not refer to "bitter enmity" on Simon's part, not to embitterment and "bitter anger" against the apostles or the Lord. The latter idea has influenced the interpretation of the next verse. As in Heb. 12:15 the "root of bitterness" means a root out of which bitter fruit grows, fruit which the Lord abominates, so here "gall of bitterness" is that fruit. The Lord will not taste it and must cast it away. The next expression is more literal and helps to explain the former: Simon's iniquity is a bond that firmly holds him, wrapped, as it is, all about him.

24) **But, answering, Simon said, Do you yourselves beg in my behalf of the Lord that nothing may come upon me of the things you have mentioned!**

A few texts add the statement that he continued weeping greatly: ὃς πολλὰ κλαίων οὐ διελίμπανεν. Is there anything wrong about this answer? Yet, just about everything about it has been found wrong. Why? Because of the later tradition which presents Simon as the father of heresies, the founder of the first heretical sect, a man who deified himself. Instead of interpreting Luke's words as they stand, they are interpreted in conformity with this tradition, and the matter settled in advance: Simon could not have repented, he did not repent, and all that Luke states is made to conform to this view. What is wrong in his asking for apostolic intercession? If some other sinner had done the same, the commentators would praise him; but Simon is accused of merely referring Peter's command back to him: You apostles go and beg of the Lord if there is begging to do! This is not fair to Simon. Simon asks for the apostlic intercession in his behalf as one who first of all earnestly prays for himself.

Then his desire to escape the things about which the apostles have warned him is regarded proof positive that Simon did not repent and desired only to escape the apostles' threats. No account is taken of the fact that Simon had just recently been brought to faith, in fact, although in v. 13 Luke writes, "he himself came to believe," this plain assertion is interpreted to mean that he only pretended to believe. It is not to the credit of some exegetes that they allow later tradition not only to modify but to reverse the words of the inspired text.

As to fear, shall we forget the warning Jesus himself gave about being cast into hell, Matt. 5:22, 29, 30; 10:28; 18:9? If it was wrong for Simon to fear as he did, was it right for Peter to threaten him as he did? Luke, moreover, leaves Simon at this point as he is pleading for the apostolic intercession. Could he do that if he intended his readers to understand that Simon failed to repent? He could not! Luke's words permit only one interpretation, namely that Simon did repent, that Peter's strong words were not in vain.

Yet Luke's leaving Simon with this petition on his lips has been thought to imply that Simon continued in his evil ways, and that the only reason Luke does not say as much is that he intended to write a third book in which he intended to tell us more about Simon and his wicked heresies. It is certain that Luke intends to say that Simon repented. The next verse corroborates this fact. *If* this is the same Simon who afterward introduced the first heresies, Luke intimates it in no way. All that Zahn, for instance, reports of the later tradition, as he himself admits, is invention, much of it based on Simon's magical arts. It seems as though his former practice of magic is the basis for the traditional connection of *his* name with those old heresies and fictions. And Luke is not responsible for these views.

25) **They, therefore, after testifying and uttering the Word of the Lord, began to return to Jerusalem and were proclaiming the good news to many villages of the Samaritans.**

In regard to Luke's favorite "they, therefore," see 1:6. We should note that both aorist participles fit the idea that the Word was altogether that of the Lord, and that the apostles merely uttered it as being his. With this they supported all that Philip had done and did all they could to strengthen the faith of the Samaritan believers. Then, as the imperfect states, they began their return to Jerusalem, left the whole work in Philip's hands, and thus acknowledged his competence. It was still their place to be in Jerusalem. But they proceeded slowly and evidently traveled about here and there and thus "evangelized many villages of the Samaritans" (the verb is here used with the accusative of the persons). Peter and John thus helped materially in winning Samaria for the gospel.

THE ETHIOPIAN EUNUCH

26) Only one man is concerned in this account, but his conversion is of the utmost importance for the

early history of the church, hence the space devoted to him by Luke and the place assigned to this account, being introduced between the conversions in Samaria and the conversion of the apostle to the Gentiles. The unnamed Ethiopian eunuch is *the first Gentile* converted to the Christian faith. He was, indeed, not a pagan but a proselyte of the gate and thus, however, still regarded as a Gentile by all Jews. It is by the Lord's own direction that the gospel is thus beginning to reach out into the great Gentile world; and it is the evangelist Philip who is distinguished as the man who, besides opening up Samaria to the gospel, brought in also the first Gentile convert. Through him the gospel first entered Africa, and that not in lower Egypt among the many Jews in Alexandria, etc., but in the more distant interior land of the Ethiopians who were a type of Negroes.

Now an angel of the Lord spoke to Philip, saying, Arise and be going toward the south on the road that goes down from Jerusalem to Gaza; this is desert. And having arisen, he went.

It is decidedly noteworthy that the Lord employed the service of angels for bringing the first Gentiles into his kingdom, here the Ethiopian eunuch, and in chapter 10 Cornelius, the centurion of the Italian cohort. We have no details about the appearance of the angel to Philip; only the great fact that this heavenly messenger gave directions to Philip, who promptly obeyed them, is recorded. "Arise" simply means that Philip is to make ready for his long journey; compare 5:17. "Be going" is the durative present imperative to indicate an act that will take some time. When the persecution broke out in Jerusalem, Philip had gone north to the Samaritans; he is not to continue in that direction but is to return to Jerusalem and from there to go "toward noon," i. e., southward, in an altogether unexpected direction. The Lord does not call one of his apostles in Jerusalem. He chooses his own instrument for the task he himself maps out. Philip is to take the road that goes down from Jerusalem to Gaza, the old Philistine city on the coast. The data regarding this city need not occupy us as it is mentioned only to designate the road that Philip is to take.

The remark, "this is desert," refers to the road. While the feminine demonstrative might refer to Gaza, a remark about its condition would be irrelevant since Philip was not to go to Gaza, nor was the city ἔρημος at this time. The angel designates which one of the roads Philip is to take: not the one that leads through the more populous sections of the country but the one that leads through the rather uninhabited parts. We are unable to determine which road this was. Any road would pass through uninhabited territory after leaving the hills; and we do not know how far toward Gaza Philip had to go. The claim that this clause is not a part of the angel's directions but only a remark made by Luke, leaves Philip to conjecture which road to take and has Luke write as though there was only one road and that one desert.

The fact that Philip is thus shown just where to go is plain, but we cannot see the force of the objection which denies that the eunuch chose this road, chose it because it permitted him to be more undisturbed in his study of the Scripture roll he had recently acquired. On this road Philip, too, encountered no interruption in dealing with the eunuch.

But why did the Lord not send the angel to instruct and to baptize the eunuch and leave Philip in his successful work in Samaria? We have an answer to this question. The Lord bestowed the office of the ministry upon men and not upon angels, and we find that the Lord in every case makes use of the men he has called and honors their office and their work accordingly. So Philip is off on his long journey afoot; the time and the effort spent in winning the eunuch are not too great.

27) **And lo, a man, an Ethiopian, a eunuch, a lord under Candace, queen of the Ethiopians, who was over all her treasure, who had come to Jerusalem in order to worship; and he was returning and sitting on his chariot and was engaged in reading the prophet Isaiah.**

Luke may well utter an exclamation at the thought of the man Philip found travelling on this lonesome road. He merely reproduces the astonishment that Philip himself must have felt. Luke immediately records all the details although some of them Philip did not learn until a little later when he conversed with the man. He was an Ethiopian, a black man! Αἰθίοψ, from αἴθω, "to burn," and ὤψ, "countenance," points to race and nationality and not merely to residence. Thus the idea of his being a Jew who had risen to great power in Ethiopia is at once excluded. In fact, the entire narrative points to the fact that this man was a Gentile. Philip's first glance at the man put him face to face with the question of receiving Gentiles into the church. The apostles had not as yet encountered the question: "On what terms and in what manner are Gentiles to be received?" Yet in this case Philip was relieved of hesitation or difficulty. The Lord had sent him through the word of an angel and was even now directing him.

This man was a eunuch, which must be taken in the literal and not in the official sense, since his official position is described in the following. We learn only the fact and not how he became a eunuch. Yet he was a δυνάστης, a man of authority and power, "a lord." We translate the Greek genitive "of Candace" with the idea "under" this queen of the Ethiopians. This intermediate title is explained by the relative clause which states that this man was the royal treasurer, γάζα being a Persian word for "treasure" which is used in both the Greek and the Latin (γαζοφυλάκιον, "treasury," a place where the treasure is kept, Mark 12:41 and elsewhere).

In Ethiopia the royal descent was by way of the mother. The queen mother transmitted the inheritance to her son but herself exercised the rule, and though the son was regarded as king and given divine honors, he was confined to the palace while his mother reigned. In the year 25-21 B. C. a one-eyed Candace fought the Romans and saved her kingdom by a favorable peace.

"Candace" is only a title like Pharaoh, Sultan, Czar, etc. The history of missions has made this title famous. In 1853 Pastor Louis Harms, of Hermannsburg in Hannover, Germany, a small inland town, had a vessel built with funds he collected, and sent the first missionaries he had prepared to their destination in Africa. He called the vessel *The Candace.* This missionary enterprise was highly successful and stands out as one of the great monuments of faith in the history of modern mission endeavor.

The kingdom of the Ethiopians was not Abyssinia, the old kingdom of Aksum (Axum), but a domain whose boundaries shifted at times. It began at Assuan on the Nile and extended beyond Chartum and since the eighth century B. C. was known as "Ethiopia" to the ancients. It was inhabited, not by semitic, but by hamitic, Negro-like tribes. This powerful kingdom had two great royal cities: Meroë on the island in the Nile by the same name, and one farther down on the river Napata.

When Luke adds that the eunuch had come to Jerusalem to worship (future participle, denoting purpose, R. 1128) he informs us that this Gentile was a proselyte of the gate. In 2:10 we read about proselytes of righteousness; these had become completely Jewish and had really been absorbed into Judaism and had lost their character as Gentiles. No eunuch could be- more than a proselyte of the gate, since because of his mutilation he was debarred from entering the inner Temple courts (Deut. 23:1). Yet read the great and special promises of the Lord to godly eunuchs as recorded in Isa. 56:4, 5. These second-class proselytes, who were exceedingly numerous in the Jewish diaspora, did not submit to circumcision and were bound only to the so-called Noachian commandments (Gen. 9:4-6) against idolatry, blasphemy, disobedience to magistrates, murder, fornication or incest, robbery or theft, and eating of blood. They were quite generally open to the gospel and received it with great readiness; in the New Testament they are designated as *σεβόμενοι* or *φοβούμενοι τὸν Θεόν*.

Recently discovered papyri, dating from the fourth and the fifth centuries B. C., mention a Jewish military colony that was at first under Pharaonic, then under Persian, later under Ptolomaic, and finally under Roman jurisdiction. It was located at Syene and the island Elephantine which were close to the boundary of Ethiopia. By way of business and financial contacts the treasurer of the queen could easily come into contact with these and perhaps also with other Jews.

The sincerity and the devotion of this proselyte are evident when we note that he undertook a journey of some 200 miles that was difficult at best and not without danger in order to visit Jerusalem and the Temple although he was debarred from entering beyond the court of the Gentiles. He is after a fashion the counterpart to the Queen of Sheba who came from southern Arabia on a similar long journey. Tradition reports his name as Indich or Judich.

28) Verse 27 is minus a verb and is to be regarded as an exclamation — such a man is awaiting Philip! On his return homeward after his visit in the holy city he is riding in his chariot with his driver, absorbed in reading a newly acquired parchment roll of the prophet Isaiah. The imperfect tenses picture him as Philip saw him. He might have chosen a more interesting road homeward. It is fair to conclude that he chose this lonely road in order to read the roll which he had recently acquired and was now eager to study and to absorb. It was surely the Lord's providence that had placed Isaiah, the evangelist of the Old Testament, into this devoted proselyte's hand and had led him to turn to the very choicest part of the book of this prophet at the time of Philip's approach. God had prepared this pupil for his new teacher. He was reading aloud, perhaps with some difficulty, for the ancient manuscripts did not write the words separately, had no punctuation, no breathings, and no accents. His copy must have been made from the Greek LXX, and Philip conversed with him in Greek, the language everywhere current.

29) **Now the Spirit said to Philip, Go to him and attach thyself to this chariot. And having run to him, Philip heard him reading Isaiah, the prophet, and said, Dost thou understand what thou art reading? And he said, How, then, could I unless one shall guide me? And he besought Philip to come up and sit with him.**

The Spirit never has difficulty in communicating with a person so that the latter knows from whom the communication comes. All *ifs* and *buts* are removed for Philip in regard to the important personage who is evidently a Negro, riding in his stately chariot. To Philip the Spirit speaks and not to the eunuch when the way of salvation was to be expounded to the latter. "Therefore we ought and must constantly maintain this point, that God does not wish to deal with us otherwise than through the spoken Word and the Sacraments." *C. Tr.* 497, 10. In the preaching of the gospel God adheres to the means and to the office he himself has given us; dreams, visions, voices, and the like he may use for other purposes but not for this one. We may translate the aorist passive imperative, "be joined," or as a middle, "join thyself."

30) The chariot seems to have been moving slowly ahead of Philip so that by hastening his steps he soon came to walk beside it. It is rather farfetched when R., *W. P.*, says that "probably Philip jumped on the running board on the chariot." Walking thus, without intruding, Philip heard the man reading from Isaiah and, perhaps as the man paused and looked up, Philip asked the question whether he understood what he was reading. The ἆρα is a word of interrogation, γε is strengthening and lends a touch of doubt.

31) The eunuch not only acknowledges his inability but states that he needs a guide. The sentence is a mixed condition: in the apodosis it has the optative with ἄν (potentiality): "How then could I"; in the protasis ἐάν (= εἰ) with the future indicative (reality): "unless one shall guide me," and γάρ is added like the German *denn* (B. D. 452, 1) so that the force is: "No, for how could I," etc. And promptly the eunuch beseeches Philip (the verb is strong) that "having come up (into the chariot), he sit with him," to guide and to instruct him. All three aorists, verb, participle, infinitive, imply that the request was granted (B.-D. 328); a verb in the imperfect would imply that something else followed.

32) **Now the section of the Scripture he was reading was this:**

As a sheep to the slaughter he was led;
And as a lamb before the one shearing him is dumb

So he opens not his mouth.
In the humiliation his judgment was taken away.
His generation who shall recount?
Because taken from the earth is his life.

The passage that caused the eunuch difficulty was Isa. 53:7, 8, which Luke records for his reader from the LXX. The chief variation from the Hebrew is in the fourth and in the last lines:

"He was taken from prison and from judgment;
. . .

For he was cut off out of the land of the living."
A glance at the text shows that even these are but variations in form and not in thought. Both Delitzsch and Aug. Pieper (*Jesaias II*), each in his own way, vary from the translations found in our Old Testament according as they read the Hebrew and construe the last line. These intricacies need not detain us; for the eunuch had no difficulty in reading the words and the sentences in his LXX copy of Isaiah, his difficulty was vastly greater, namely what the prophet really meant by this entire section.

For ourselves we note cursorily that Isaiah is depicting the great *'Ebed Yahweh*, τὸν παῖδα τοῦ Θεοῦ Ἰησοῦν, "the Servant of God, Jesus," (Acts 3:13, 26; 4:27, 30) in his suffering and his death. Patiently, silently, without resisting, the great Servant of Jehovah, "was led as a sheep to the slaughter." Pieper: "Maltreated was he; but he — he bowed himself." His silent submission is emphasized: "And as a lamb," etc. Delitzsch and Pieper translate the Hebrew in the same way.

33) "In his humiliation his judgment was taken away," the judgment executed upon him as our substitute. He rendered full satisfaction and atonement; all claims were satisfied. Delitzsch translates the line

as it is found in our Old Testament (see above); but Pieper lets the Hebrew preposition *min* mean, not what it usually does, "from" but "by means of." He does this for internal reasons, but his reason is by no means satisfactory. The rendering of the LXX which the eunuch had is thus substantially correct.

There is disagreement in regard to the next line: "His generation who shall recount?" In both Isaiah and here in Acts the sense is that the suffering and dying Servant of Jehovah shall have a vast progeny, a generation (the word is used in an ethical sense, as a designation of those who become his own by faith), *dor*, γενεά, that no one can number. Delitzsch: "And among his cotemporaries who considered: Torn away was he out of the land of the living"; Pieper: "And as to his generation — who mourned, that he was torn," etc. Those internal reasons again obtrude themselves: the idea that Isaiah could not speak of Christ's deliverance and the fruit of his death so early, namely ahead of a narration of his death. Why could he not? Especially since he is writing poetry? The moment we remember this, the matter is cleared up.

The Hebrew verb is *siach*, German *sinnen* (Delitzsch, *bedenken*; not Pieper's *beklagen*), LXX διηγέομαι. And in the Hebrew as well as in the Greek the accusative "his generation" is the object of this verb. Why must we read it adverbially, "as to his generation" (Pieper), or "among his cotemporaries" (Delitzsch)? The same is true in regard to the next line. Why must *ki* be "that," recitative or otherwise? Why not leave it "because"? And so we are in the clear. This *dor* or generation is not the contemporary Jewish nation. Why let it deal so prominently with what it failed to consider or lament? The prophet says: "His generation who considered?" and then states why the question is asked: "Because taken from the earth was his life." Taken from the earth, how could he have a generation? Yet behold, what a vast generation is his, all these believers in all the ages! And the LXX is about correct: "Who shall declare, recount, set out in detail his generation?"

34) Wonderful these words of the prophet! So and yet a mystery! **And answering, the eunuch said to Philip, I beg thee, concerning whom does the prophet say this? concerning himself or concerning someone else?**

The Greek "answering" is often used in a wider sense with regard to any statement that meets a situation. The eunuch had, indeed, struck the heart of the matter. Who was this wonderful person of whom the prophet was speaking? Could it be the prophet Isaiah himself? Was he not an *'ebed* of Jehovah, might he be *this* "Servant"? The difficulty the eunuch had was this, that the prophet did not seem to meet the requirements of this passage and yet he could think of no other person to whom they might be properly applied. To be sure, the eunuch had not heard the modern Jewish answer that the Jews themselves are this wonderful "Servant of Jehovah," their nation that has suffered so much is the Messiah!

We are unable to say how much the eunuch had heard about Jesus while he was in Jerusalem; yet his prompt acceptance of Philip's interpretation would indicate that he had learned much of the story of Jesus and needed only to have the prophecies of the Old Testament properly connected with what he had heard in order to bring him to the Christian faith. This, too, explains the readiness with which Philip proceeded to baptize him.

35) **And Philip, having opened his mouth and having begun at this Scripture, proclaimed as good news to him Jesus.**

The circumstantial phrase about opening his mouth intends to mark the importance of Philip's words. He began with this prophecy of Isaiah, referred to other prophecies much as Jesus once did (Luke 24:27, 45), and so preached the whole blessed gospel of salvation in Jesus' name. "What flowed from the preacher's lips concerning the Word of life, how he preached of the Crucified One in words ever more fiery and enthusiastic, and what transpired in the soul of the hearer, how his heart burned within him, how the scales fell from his eyes, how light upon light illumined him, how, perhaps, tear upon tear rolled down his cheek, all this the record does not describe, words cannot reproduce it properly. Enough, there must have been another upon the chariot, the Holy Spirit, who opened the mouth of Philip and the heart of the treasurer; and the result was that this apt pupil of the gospel could exclaim:

> 'Now I have found the firm foundation,
> Where evermore my anchor grounds!'

Oh, that this might be the result of all our preaching and hearing, Bible reading and explanation, meditation and praying, the knowledge and ever-firmer conviction: Jesus is the Messiah as the prophet promised, as this sinful world needs him!" Gerok.

36) **Now as they were going along the road they came to some water. And the eunuch says: Lo, water! What hinders me to be baptized? And he ordered the chariot to stop; and they both went down to the water, both Philip and the eunuch; and he baptized him.**

No trace of a stream or a lake is found in this region, nor of a record of such water. The problem is not where to find enough water for immersion but where to find water at all. Robinson suggests the *Wady-el-Hasy* between Eleutheropolis and Gaza, not far from the old sites of Lachish and Eglom. The difficulty in regard to the water is not removed by supposing that Philip did not go from Samaria to Jerusalem and from there take a road toward Gaza but took some road directly from Samaria. This contradicts v. 26, which binds Philip to some road that led from Jerusalem to Gaza. Philip must have expounded baptism to the eunuch. It is thus that he exclaims, "Lo, water!" with a happy ring in his voice. When asks about a hindrance to his being baptized he intends to indicate that he knows of none but leaves it to the fuller knowledge of his teacher as to whether his supposition is correct.

37) The textual evidence for this verse (see A. V.) is too slight to admit it into the text. It states what may well have transpired. The objection is textual only, and remarks such as that the words sound like some pedantic preacher asking his convert for a final, formal confession are unwarranted. A confession of Jesus as the Christ was always a prerequisite for baptism.

38) Philip consents. The eunuch orders his driver to halt the chariot, and Philip and the eunuch go down to the water, and the baptism takes place. The subject is made certain: "both Philip and the eunuch," because the eunuch had ordered his driver to halt the chariot, and this man was not concerned in the matter of the baptism. Καὶ ἐβάπτισεν αὐτόν includes the entire baptismal act: "and he did baptize him," all that preceded and that followed was not a part of this sacramental act. The reader is referred to the discussion on baptism in 2:38, 41.

Eusebius reports about a small pool that was formed by a spring near the road, Robinson speaks of a small temporary stream. Neither here nor elsewhere do we read that a robe or garment was laid aside before baptism. We are left to suppose that the two men went to this water, and that the baptismal act was an application of water by pouring or by sprinkling. Those who make the words "they both went down εἰς, into, the water" a part of the baptismal act in order to obtain immersion by means of εἰς τὸ ὕδωρ, "*into* the water," prove too much: Philip went down under the water as well as the eunuch. This is true also in regard to the following words.

39) **But when they came up from the water, the Lord's Spirit snatched Philip away, and the eunuch saw him no more, for he proceeded to go his way rejoicing. Philip, however, was found at Azotus; and, passing through, he proclaimed the good news to all the cities until he came to Caesarea.**

We may translate, "they went *down into the water*" (v. 38), and now, "they came *up out of the water*," and may with R., *W. P.* even emphasize: "Not from the edge of the water, but up out of the water"! The difficulty lies in ἀμφότεροι, "both," Luke even adding: "both Philip and the eunuch." To be sure, εἰς and ἐκ are correlatives: as far as the one takes "into," so far the other takes "out of." But these prepositions apply to "both Philip and the eunuch." Take your choice: *to* the water, *from* the water; or stepping *into* and again stepping *out of* the water; or *down under* the water and again *up from under* the water. Total immersion if you prefer, but for *both*. Not we but Luke combined them.

If Philip was merely induced to say good-by and to tear himself away, Luke chose a strange way in which to tell us this. Πνεῦμα Κυρίου is an unusual expression, yet it conveys the idea that both the Spirit and the Lord (Jesus) removed Philip and did it suddenly and miraculously. All at once he was gone, "and the eunuch saw him no more." I Kings 18:12; II Kings 2:16. Nor is γάρ strange. It explains that the eunuch simply went on his way "rejoicing" and did not try to find Philip by changing his journey and seeking until he located him.

Here this eunuch passes from our view. He had much, he would desire more. In his position and with his means he could secure all else. We have all almost without effort, yet do we always appreciate it and rejoice? Tradition makes the eunuch an evangelist in Ethiopia who soon baptized the queen, etc. We know only that Christian missionaries reached the Ethiopians 300 years later.

40) In one instant Philip was walking beside the eunuch, in the next he was found in Azotus (Asdod), many miles away. To be sure, "he was found" means that people found him there; but this also means that the place where he was found just before this was on the road with the eunuch. "He was found" does not mean that Philip walked away from the eunuch and wandered about until he turned up at Azotus. Luke does not intend to carry on the story of Philip which he evidently knows in all its interesting details. So he states summarily that Philip evangelized the coast towns beginning with Azotus and terminating at Caesarea where he then made his home. We take it that he worked in Ekron, Rama, Joppa, and elsewhere in the plain of Sharon. We have ἕως used as a preposition, the genitive of the infinitive as its object.

CHAPTER IX

SAUL'S CONVERSION

Luke takes up the thread of his narrative which he broke off at 8:3. The importance of Saul's conversion is made prominent in Acts. It was very dramatic, and its effects were most far-reaching. As a conversion it clearly brings out the essentials of every Christian conversion: Saul's contrition and his faith. As a particular conversion it has its individual and exceptional features as has every other conversion, features that cannot be duplicated. These points must be borne in mind, both in order to understand Saul's conversion and in order to avoid false deductions concerning other conversions.

In this chapter Luke furnishes us his own historical account of Saul's conversion; in two subsequent chapters Paul himself tells of his conversion in two addresses. In each instance he has a specific purpose in view and tells the story so as to further that purpose. Therefore, in dealing with the accounts of this conversion it is proper to take up first of all and by itself Luke's objective, historical narrative which aims to present merely the facts as they occurred. Then in due order we may examine Paul's own accounts from the angle of the purposes which induced him to tell his audiences what he had experienced. This is Luke's own method, which first gives us chapter 9, and then chapters 22 and 26.

The time between Christ's ascension and Stephen's martyrdom was probably three or four years. Soul was converted about the year 35 and returns to Jerusalem in 38.

1) Now Saul, still breathing threat and murder against the disciples of the Lord, having gone to the high priest, asked in due order from him letters to Damascus to the synagogues in order that, if he found any being of that Way, whether men or women, he might bring them bound to Jerusalem.

Saul's ardor for persecution had not abated; he still continued to blow his breath, reeking with threat and murder, against the disciples of the Lord —this is the force of Luke's picturesque words. The participle with εἰς means *einschnauben auf jemand.* It is unsatisfactory to say that the genitives are partitive (R., *W. P.*), or that they are analogous to the genitive after verbs of smelling (R. 507) and to illustrate by a horse sniffing the smell of battle (R., *W. P.*). Any analogy with verbs of smelling lies not in what one smells but in what one smells of, in the odor he gives off (B.-D. 174); and still better is the idea of cause: threat and murder caused Saul to breathe out against the disciples (Stellhorn, *Woerterbuch,* on the verb).

The word "murder" is significant. The supposition that it refers only to Stephen's death is questionable. Stephen was already dead; Saul was raging against other disciples. The fact that he had succeeded in having others put to death is certain, and the objection does not hold that Luke should have recorded these martyrdoms, for he recorded that of Stephen only because it marked the great turning point in the course of the history of the church, which sent the gospel out into the wide world.

2) Caiaphas was still the high priest, for not until the year 36 did Jonathan, a son of Annas, and in 37 Theophilus, another son of Annas, succeed Caiaphas; the latter were not sons of Caiaphas (R., *W. P.*). The authorization Saul desired was not requested from the high priest alone but from him as being head of the

Sanhedrin who issued "the letters" on vote of the entire body as we see from 22:5; 26:10.

The middle ᾐτήσατο is not to be understood in the sense that Saul asked these letters "as a favor to himself" (R., *W. P.*); the middle of this verb is used with reference to business transactions, when business claims are made. So here the great business of persecuting the Christians had been officially delegated to Saul, and in prosecuting this business of his "he asked in due order" for documents that would enable him to execute this business of his also in Damascus. While Saul had his heart and soul in this persecution, it was not a private enterprise of his, could not be in the nature of the case, but an official enterprise of the supreme Jewish court itself with Saul as its head agent. For the persecutions in Jerusalem he had as his assistants a body of Levite police that had been granted him by the Sanhedrin in order to hale men and women to prison (8:3) and he was similarly equipped with police when he was authorized to operate in Damascus.

Damascus, the oldest city in the world (apparently a city already in Abraham's time, B. C. 1912, Gen. 14:15; 15:2) that still exists as a famous city, had a large number of resident Jews and, as Luke's plural shows, a number of synagogues. Nero butchered 10,000 Jews in Damascus. It was under the rule of King Aretas three years after the event narrated in this section and must have been strongly Jewish when Saul went there on his errand. The Roman emperors granted the Sanhedrin authority over Jews outside of Palestine, and Aretas was a Roman vassal. What this authority included and in what territory the Sanhedrin might exercise it, is uncertain; but Saul's expedition to Damascus evidently assumes that arrests could be made there and the prisoners brought to the Sanhedrin in Jerusalem for trial. We have "both men and women" as in 8:3.

The word ὁδός, like the Hebrew *derek,* is extensively used in the metaphoric and ethical sense as a "way" or course of life, both as being marked out to be followed and as being followed. For the objective idea of *Sittenlehre* is not enough; in Matt. 3:3 the Baptist proclaims "the way of the Lord," which certainly includes doctrine as well as moral regulations; in Acts 2:28 the plural is used. Especially noteworthy is John 14:6 where Jesus calls himself "the Way." A genitive or other modifiers are often added in order to describe "the way." The wicked also have their way. Here the word is used without an addition save the article: "the Way" κατ' ἐξοχήν, the Christian faith, conviction, confession, and life as taught by and centering in Jesus. The genitive is qualitative: "any being of the Way," who thus differed from all other Jews. These were to be arrested and brought bound (having been and thus continuing to be bound) to Jerusalem.

3) **Now, as he was journeying, it came to pass that he was approaching Damascus. And suddenly there flashed around him a light out of heaven; and, having fallen on the ground, he heard a voice saying to him, Saul, Saul, why art thou persecuting me? And he said, Who art thou, lord? And he: I am Jesus whom thou art persecuting. But arise and go into the city, and it shall be told thee what it is necessary that thou do.**

Luke's favorite ἐν τῷ with the present infinitive means "while," and the accusative with the infinitive is the subject of ἐγένετο. Saul had almost reached his goal and was elated by the prospect of what he would accomplish in destroying the church. He is in the full ascendency of his power. Then "suddenly" Jesus stops him. A miraculous light flashed out of heaven and enveloped him. It was noonday (22:6), and the light was brighter than the sun (26:13) ; it was not a momentary flash but, coming with a flash, shone around Saul for a time (26:13).

4) Instantly Saul dropped from the animal he was riding and fell prostrate to the ground and then heard the voice that said to him, "Saul, Saul, why art thou persecuting me?" In regard to the difference between ἀκούω with the accusative φωνήν and in v. 7 with the genitive τῆς φωνῆς, compare 22:9. The accusative refers to the voice as saying something, the genitive to the voice as coming from someone. There is not a contradiction between 9:7 and 22:9.

One should go through the Scriptures and note these duplications: Saul, Saul — Martha, Martha — Jerusalem, Jerusalem — David's lament over Absolom, and others. In varying ways they express an emotion of deepest concern but never anger. Why, yes why, was Saul persecuting Jesus? This question called upon Saul to probe his soul in regard to the terrible work in which he was engaged. To persecute the disciples is to persecute the Master. *Caput pro membris clamabat.* Augustine. Jesus spoke in Hebrew (26:14), and we take it that the dialog was carried on in this language. Jesus does not at once identify himself. Saul hears only this question coming from one in heaven, the light of whose blinding, heavenly presence and glory was shining about him.

5) Thus, when the voice from heaven paused, the question came from Saul's lips: "Who art thou, lord?" It should be evident that "lord" is here not to be taken in the sense of God, for then Saul would not ask. This is "lord" in the sense of any superior person or being. From I Cor. 9:1 and 15:8 we learn that Saul *saw* the glorified Jesus. These passages have nothing to do with the question as to whether Saul ever saw Jesus while he lived on earth. We have no evidence whatever that Saul saw Jesus in the days of Jesus' earthly life. In any

case, the glorified, heavenly presence of Jesus differed vastly from his presence in humiliation.

Now those standing by saw no one but heard only the voice but not what it uttered. The sight as well as the words of Jesus were intended for Saul only. So he saw and so he heard and understood. Jesus knew how to appeal to Saul's eyes, ears, and consciousness so that they apprehended.

Jesus then names himself and states only his personal name "Jesus," the one that had been given him on the day of his circumcision (Luke 2:21); for it is his identity that is to be established. Yet Saul received far more than this mere name. This was Jesus in glory, he whom the Jews had rejected and crucified, he whom God had exalted to the glory that now enveloped Saul. The tremendous reality and truth of this fact swept over Saul's soul like a flood. And this makes us feel the impact of the contrasted pronouns: "*I*, I am Jesus, whom *thou*, yea, thou art persecuting!" That charge, that accusation of persecuting is thus driven into the soul of Saul to the hilt. Here was the revelation, not only of Jesus, who with one stroke swept away all the lies Saul had believed about him as a mere man, etc., but also the revelation of what Saul was engaged in: persecuting this glorified Jesus in his disciples: "I — thou!"

At this point note the insertions made in the A. V., partly from 26:14, partly as a reminiscence of 22:10. Written, perhaps, on the margin at first, the additions were eventually interpolated into the text.

6) Ἀλλά breaks off. Its force is: I will not speak further of what thou art doing *but* of what thou shalt now do; the adversative idea of ἀλλά is conserved. Jesus orders Saul into the city where he will be told what he must do.

Some important points ought to be noted at this place. Jesus preaches the law to Saul; he confronts him with his sin and his crime; he smites and crushes Saul's heart with a consciousness of its awful guilt. But Jesus does not preach the gospel to Saul, he orders him to go to a place where the appointed minister of the gospel will proclaim this to him; for "what is necessary that thou do" does not refer to works of law but to believing and receiving the grace and the pardon for his sins.

Here we again see how Jesus honors his ministry. Philip is sent to the eunuch by an angel, it is not the angel who is sent to teach the eunuch. And this is the case wherever the gospel is to be offered. The essentials for Saul as a sinner were contrition and faith; the moment these were wrought in him he was converted. Just at what moment this inner turn was wrought in Saul, in other words, at what instant faith was kindled in him, no man can say, nor need we know. One thing alone is certain: when Jesus smote Saul with the law, this crushed him but did not kindle faith in him. It is often said that Saul was converted on the road to Damascus. Strictly speaking, this is not the fact. His conversion began in his encounter with the law but it was not accomplished until the gospel entered his heart by faith, and that did not occur on the road but in Damascus.

Jesus converted Saul, and he did it through his regular means, the law and the gospel; and no conversion was ever wrought without these means. In this instance Jesus applied the law immediately as he had done when he preached to sinners on earth; he applied the gospel mediately through his servant in Damascus. The law was not stronger because it was applied immediately, nor the gospel weaker because it was applied mediately. Saul was not converted irresistibly. In 26:19 Paul says pointedly that he "was not disobedient to the heavenly vision," which implies that he might have answered it by disobedience. If conversion were irresistible, then all who remain unconverted could charge God with their damnation. When Jesus confronts the sinner with his law and his gospel, and the sinner, nevertheless, remains unconverted, the fault is wholly the sinner's own, Matt. 23:27; Acts 7:51; 13:46; 28:25-28.

As far as the outward circumstances of Saul's call and conversion are concerned, these were fashioned by the Lord with a view to Saul's apostleship. This applies especially to his vision of the glorified Jesus, I Cor. 9:1. The Lord was qualifying him for his future work in order that, although he was called so late, he might, nevertheless, be on a par with the other apostles. In this respect Saul's case was entirely exceptional even as the Lord needed only one apostle of this kind. All else, time, place, etc., was in God's gracious providence, who chooses these for all sinners with a view to one result only, namely that they may be as favorable as possible to the success of his grace.

7) **Now the men, those traveling with him, were standing speechless, hearing the voice, yet beholding no one.**

These men constitute the police force that Saul had with him. At the first flash of the superearthly light they, too, fell prostrate (26:14); upon recovering, they now stand speechless, in utter astonishment because of what is happening especially to Saul who is lying on the ground and talking with someone who is unseen by them.

Here there is an opportunity to establish a contradiction. Luke says they "heard the voice"; but in 22:9 it is stated that they "heard not the voice of him that spoke to me (Paul)." Aside from the different cases of φωνή used in these two instances as explained above the sense is plain: they heard the sound (9:7) but heard not the words and understood not the sense of the sound (22:9). This is an exact parallel to the light: they saw the light of Jesus' presence but saw nothing of Jesus himself standing before Saul in his glory. We have an analogous instance in John 12:28, etc. To see and to hear what they did see and hear was sufficient for these Levite ὑπηρέται or underlings; all that they were to know was that a vision from heaven had come to Saul and that a heavenly being had spoken to him.

The three accounts of Saul's conversion have received a great variety of treatment. The whole story is converted into a drama of the imagination: its background are the twinges of Saul's conscience, its actual occasion is a sudden thunderstorm with a stunning flash of lightning, a bolt laying everyone prostrate. Psychology offers its own solution by speaking especially of scruples of conscience and inner battles that were brought on by Stephen's speech and also by his death and the manner in which he died. But Saul had no scruples or misgivings of any kind. He was in the full flush of his persecuting enthusiasm; he was ready for many more killings (v. 1). He was burning with zeal for the right and was seriously fighting the wrong. Then Jesus suddenly appeared to him, and Saul was overwhelmed with the realization that he was fighting for the wrong and against the right, yea, against God's Messiah himself. In an honest character such as Saul had this caused conversion by a terrible struggle that was superinduced by the vision of Jesus.

The psychological aspect is easy to understand. This vision of Jesus was not something that transpired only in Saul's own soul either as imagined by himself or as wrought in Saul's soul by the Lord. In addition to the accounts in Acts, I Cor. 9:1, and 15: 8 disagree with such a view. Jesus actually appeared to Saul. The issues involved in a proper conception of Saul's conversion extend beyond the man himself. When Jesus brought him to conversion he changed not only his life but made him the foremost apostle. Was this man mistaken in regard to what happened on the road to Damascus? Did he labor under psychological delusions and the like? The cause must measure up to the effect. The apostleship of Paul, as it is recorded in the New Testament, cannot be traced to anything that was merely subjective, mistaken, unreal. Luke recorded the realities, and they will ever stand as what they are.

8) **And Saul was raised up from the earth; moreover, with his eyes standing open, he continued to see nothing; and leading him by the hand, they brought him into Damascus. And he was for three days not seeing and did not eat or drink.**

We regard the form ἠγέρθη as a true passive: "he was raised up," instead of taking it in the sense of the middle: "he raised himself up," "he arose." Why should his attendants not assist their commander? But it was discovered that he had been blinded. The genitive absolute has the perfect passive participle: "his eyes having been opened and remaining so." It was found that he was not blinded by the great glare of light only for a time but that "he continued to see nothing," the durative imperfect. His men had to lead him by the hand, and it was thus that the great persecutor and destroyer of the Christian Church entered into the city that he had selected for his new triumphs.

9) Saul continued to be blind for three days. We do not regard the expression as a periphrastic tense because then the negative should be οὐ; μή is the regular negative used with the participle and shows that it is only the predicate. Saul's sight was miraculously restored. He also fasted. He is in a depressed and wretched condition. Luke states only the outward facts. His fearful sin lay heavily upon him, and the Lord permitted it to crush him for three days. A good deal was required to grind down this mighty Pharisee and implacable foe of the gospel. Shut off from the world,

blind, abstaining from food, with no one to help his soul's distress, his proud self-righteousness was conquered, and there remained only a sinner in the dust who ever after felt himself chief of all sinners. I Tim. 1:15. The supposition that this experience left Paul with weak eyes is one of the many hypotheses in regard to Saul; but this one militates against v. 18. When the Lord restored Saul's sight he restored it completely and not halfway.

10) **Now there was a disciple in Damascus by name Ananias. And the Lord said to him in a vision, Ananias! And he said, Lo, I** (hear), **Lord! And the Lord to him: Ananias, go into the narrow street that is called Straight and seek in Judas' house a Tarsian by name Saul; for lo, he is praying, and he saw a man by name Ananias come in and place the hands on him in order that he might recover sight.**

On μαθητής see 6:1; τις is our indefinite article. In 22:12 a little more is said about Ananias, especially that he was esteemed by all the Jews — and Saul was in a Jew's house. The Lord prepared Ananias for Saul, and Saul for Ananias; but we must note that the Lord is also preparing the way for Saul among the disciples at Damascus, who had heard of his frightful deeds and of his coming to Damascus to add to them.

The Lord called as he once did to little Samuel, and Ananias answered: "Lo, I, Lord!" meaning that he is giving ear and heart to hear what the Lord may say.

11) He receives orders as to just what to do in order to find Saul and is told that Saul is praying and that he is expecting Ananias and what Ananias will do for him. Ananias, we see, knows where Judas lived, namely in the ῥύμη or "narrow street" that bears the name "Straight." Damascus, Jerusalem, and other cities had and still have such narrow streets, and but

few of them are straight for any distance; wider streets are called πλατεῖα (feminine adjective, supply ὁδός). We passed through this street in Damascus in 1925. Yes, we visited Judas' house, etc. But when we were to see the window in the wall from which Paul was let down in a basket, lo, they were building a new wall — only the place up in the air was left where they said the old window had been. We certainly had our doubts regarding even the street "Straight."

A Ταρσεύς is a native of Ταρσός, the capital of Cilicia in southwestern Asia Minor. It was at one time a large, free city that was not under a Roman governor; it was also renowned for learning and schools of philosophy. "A Tarsian," of course, differentiates this Saul from any others bearing this name, but 21:39 shows that this term conveys more: Saul was "a citizen" of Tarsus and not merely in the sense in which we ordinarily understand citizenship, as having been born in Tarsus, which would have made him only "a resident," but as being the son of a family that had originally been located in Tarsus by one of the Seleucid kings, or as the son of an ancestor who had been granted the rights of citizenship for distinguished services to the state. Ramsay, *St. Paul the Traveller and the Roman Citizen*, 31, etc. Saul had this standing in Tarsus for life; it was no mean distinction even apart from his Roman citizenship.

"For lo, he is praying" is added as having a special meaning for the mission of Ananias. This is not the common daily praying of a strict Pharisaic Jew, which would not warrant such an exclamation as "lo"; this praying marks Saul as a changed man — praying, no longer breathing threat and murder (v. 1). The raging lion has been changed into a bleating lamb. "Praying" means that Saul is in deep distress, and that the Lord is now engaged in answering that prayer, and that this mission of Ananias is a part of that answer.

12) In fact, the Lord has already shown Saul how his prayers were to be heard. For what the Lord tells Ananias to do he has already revealed to Saul in advance, namely in a vision, showing him that a man by the name of Ananias would enter, lay his hands on him, and restore his sight. In other words, Saul has been duly prepared for and in a wonderful way already introduced to Ananias. He is expecting the Lord's messenger and is now praying for that very reason. Indirectly, in the purpose clause: "in order that he might recover sight," Ananias learns what he is to do for Saul.

13) **But Ananias answered: Lord, I heard from many concerning this man, how many base things he did to thy saints in Jerusalem; and here he has authority from the high priests to bind all those calling upon thy name.**

It is unwarranted to call these honest words of Ananias' his "protest to Jesus against any dealing with Saul," and "an illustration of our own narrow ignorance in our rebellious moods against the will of God." This is not even a case like that of Zacharias who doubted Gabriel's word and was struck dumb because of that doubt. With simple openness Ananias tells the Lord what he has heard from many about this man Saul (the aorist ἤκουσα whereas we use the perfect to refer to recent events, R. 842). Saul's record was certainly bad. The many from whom Ananias had heard it were very likely fugitive Christians who had fled from Jerusalem to Damascus. Besides, reports travelled swiftly in those days.

The dative of disadvantage "to thy saints" is quite noteworthy because it appears so early in naming and describing the disciples. The word ἅγιοι is strictly Biblical in sense and describes the disciples as having been removed from the sinful fellowship of the world and by the sanctifying power of God placed into fellowship with the God of redemption and salvation. They have experienced the ἁγιάζειν of God and his Spirit, they are in possession of Christ's salvation. See the elaborate article in C.-K. 34, etc. and note 53. The change which makes them *hagioi* is that which removed their sin and guilt by justification and continues to build them up in a new life by sanctification. "Saints" came to be a standard term for the believers; they are the ἡγιασμένοι of 20:32; 26:18, those who have experienced and thus still experience the sanctifying grace that makes them God's own. "Thy saints" = those who are in blessed fellowship with the Lord.

14) Ananias also knows all about Saul's plans regarding the Christians in Damascus, his authority to bind "all those calling on thy name" (7:59). This expression makes prominent the full confessional characteristic of the saints, I Cor. 1:2; Rom. 10:13. "Thy name," so hated by the Jews, is not merely **"Jesus,"** or "Jesus Christ," but he with all that he has revealed about himself; note carefully ὄνομα in 4:12, and follow the term from 2:21, 38; 3:6 onward. To call on this name is to confess it as being the bearer of salvation, to pray and to worship in this name, and to expect all help in time and in eternity from him who is revealed by this name.

15) Ananias really puts a question to the Lord. He lays all this in regard to Saul before the Lord in order that the Lord may enlighten him regarding Saul. **And the Lord said to him: Be going; because this one is a chosen instrument for me to bear my name before both the Gentiles and kings and Israel's sons. For I will show him how many things it is necessary that he suffer in behalf of my name.**

The Lord complies with the implied request of Ananias and gives him a glimpse of what Saul is to accomplish in the future. Ananias is merely to aid in the first step. The present imperative is quite mild: "Just be going — everything is all right!" With ἐστί μοι, "I have in him," the Lord tells Ananias what he sees in Saul: from now on he is to be "a chosen instrument" for a most mighty task and for a most wonderful distinction (v. 16). Σκεῦος is any kind of utensil and has the meaning "vessel" (a container) only where this is especially indicated. Since τοῦ βαστάσαι (infinitive of purpose) means to lift, to carry with the hands or on the shoulders, the idea of a vessel is excluded. As the Lord's instrument Saul will take up and carry the Lord's name or revelation (ὄνομα as before) before the Gentiles, etc., holding it up for them to see and to adore. The genitive ἐκλογῆς is qualitative, R. 496, "attributive," and is used instead of an adjective but in a stronger sense: "an instrument of choice," i. e., "chosen." It is the Lord himself who chooses his tools for his tasks. They are his tasks — who shall dictate to him the tools to be used?

The great task of Saul was to take the gospel to the Gentiles (Rom. 1:16). It must have come as a surprise to both Ananias and Saul himself when Ananias told him what the Lord had said. He did become the apostle to the heathen world in an especial sense. "The Gentiles" and "kings" are combined by τε καί, "both and," since the rulers before whom Saul testified were with few exceptions pagan. Yet "Israel's sons" (see 7:37) are added as the secondary field of operation for Saul. The Lord had all of Saul's work mapped out in advance.

16) A great work, and now a great honor: the many things Saul would suffer "in behalf of my name," this significant ὄνομα again. "I will show him" with its preposition ὑπό means: "I will place *under* his eyes and thus show him," but this is not a showing in advance, by prophecy, but a showing from time to time as occasions for suffering arise. To be sure, this word which Ananias would repeat to Saul foretold that he would have much suffering awaiting him; "I will show

him" goes beyond that and includes also the idea that the Lord would be present with Saul and each time point out what he must suffer and help him to endure it. In βαστάσαι the idea of bearing a great burden is expressed; now with παθεῖν a mighty load is added in the shape of suffering. Both aorists are constative and at the same time imply successful bearing and suffering. Δεῖ may be used for any type of necessity; here it is the necessity arising from bearing the Name before the Gentiles, etc., which is indicated by the ὑπέρ phrase, "in behalf of my Name."

Heavy work in distant lands — much suffering arising from that work! What a prospect! And the Lord reveals this in advance. Will Saul not flee from it all? No danger. Remember Matt. 5:10-12, and also how Jesus constantly told the Twelve what awaited them. It is the Name that makes this great work so attractive, the Name which lends glory to the suffering. Recall 6:41. To this day it is true that, if we would join the illustrious company of the great prophets of God, we must suffer for the Name's sake.

17) **Now Ananias went away and went into the house; and, having placed upon him the hands, said: Brother Saul, the Lord commissioned me, Jesus who appeared to thee on the road on which thou wert coming, in order that thou mayest recover sight and be filled with the Holy Spirit. And immediately there fell off from his eyes as if scales, and he recovered sight. And having arisen, he was baptized; and having received food, he got strength. Moreover, he was for some days in company with the disciples in Damascus.**

It is supposition that the vision of the Lord was granted to Ananias at night and that he executed his commission the next morning. If such had been the fact, a word or two would have indicated it. Ananias reaches the house without difficulty and is brought to

Saul who sits there in his blindness waiting for what the Lord had communicated to him (v. 12). Luke records only the pertinent facts. This does not prevent us from supplying what took place. Did someone not admit Ananias to the house and lead him to Saul? Why, then, say that nobody was present except Ananias and Saul? There is no reason why Judas himself and several others were not present. Who gave Saul nourishment (v. 19)? There must have been a great deal of excitement for all the residents of that house! Luke has left ever so much untold in order that we may the more regard what he has told.

So the hands were duly laid upon Saul's head, this symbolical act (see 6:6) being the more important for the blind man. In connection with this act Ananias speaks the great word of absolution to this frightful sinner Saul who is now certainly contrite enough. Jesus himself pronounced absolution in many different ways; note Luke 23:43. Absolution is what this chief of sinners needed most and first, and then all that follows absolution. Already the address, "Brother Saul," absolves. It cannot mean "brother" in the superficial sense in which many use it, nor in the sense of brother Jew. "Brother" was sweet music to Saul's ears. That word admitted him into the communion of "saints" (v. 13), all his past guilt was erased.

"Brother" has material significance, for the next word is ὁ Κύριος and states what the "Lord" has commissioned Ananias to do, that Lord who appeared to Saul on the road which he was traveling three days ago (ῇ, R. 716), Jesus, who there had crushed Saul with the revelation of his guilt. The sight of that Lord had blinded Saul's eyes. So spiritually blind had he been up to that moment. And now, in token of his pardon of Saul's guilt, that same Lord is removing that blindness from Saul's eyes, is restoring sight to him. For the eyes of his soul have been opened to the sight of faith.

Do not ask just when the first spark of saving faith entered Saul's dark soul. It is enough to know that he now believes. And he is to be filled with the Holy Spirit, this supreme gift is to be bestowed upon him by means of the baptism that followed immediately. There is no indication in any of the three records or in other references to Saul's conversion that he received charismatic gifts; we have no right to assume that he did. The spiritual power of the Spirit filled Saul, and at this moment that means more than any charismatic gifts.

18) Saul's sight returned instantly. Saul describes the sensation he felt when he speaks of scales or flakes that fell from his eyes. Those present saw only that his sight had been fully restored, the blinded eyeballs again saw. To Saul it seemed as though scales were dropping away and thus again permitting vision. As his blindness had something symbolical about it, so also has this new granting of sight.

Very briefly, with but two words, Luke records the baptism. Some put a good deal into ἀναστάς, "having arisen"; they think that this word indicates that Saul was taken to the river Abana — some mention Pharpar — and was there immersed. But this journey to the river does not seem to fit into the context, for in rapid succession Luke relates that Saul is sitting in a room as a blind man, that he has his eyes opened, arises, and is baptized, and then takes food and is strengthened — all apparently occurring in that house. Yet in spite of this some claim that he was immersed. R., *W. P.* writes: "possibly in the pool in the house of Judas, as today water is plentiful in Damascus"; Zahn thinks that Saul was baptized in the *Badezimmer* (bathroom) in Judas' house.

But very few houses are furnished with pools. When we visited Damascus in 1925 we noticed that even the vast courtyard of the Great Mosque, the greatest in the world, contained only a fountain, and we observed a moslem making most thorough ablution — he could *not* have immersed himself. The grandest house in Damascus had 365 rooms, and there were fountains in some of the rooms and a pool in the courtyard, but not for the purpose of swimming in them but only for ornament. Our hotel, the Grand Victoria, where Balfour and Allenby stopped, the best in the city, was third-rate in its accommodations. Immersion would be possible, but only in one of the seven channels into which the Abana (now Barada) River is divided in order to furnish irrigation and a general water supply for the city. The city is made by this river, the waters of which are conducted in small channels. Beyond the city these waters disappear in the desert sands. One channel flowed past the hotel, but it was quite shallow, yet in a deep place we saw a bather; there a person could have been immersed. The Pharpar flows at a distance from the city; when we crossed it we saw only a brook.

The claim that Saul was baptized by immersion involves the assumption that ἀναστάς, "having arisen," implies the fact that he was conducted to one of the channels of the Abana. But this circumstantial participle is inserted merely to mark the importance of an act: a person gets up to do this or that. A fitting sample is found in 5:17. Saul had been sitting; he would naturally arise for the baptismal act.

More important than these speculations is the fact that Saul was promptly baptized. He accepted, yea, desired this sacrament with the pardoning and regenerating grace it conveyed to him; it was at the same time the divine seal of grace and of the Spirit and made him Christ's own. After the administration of this sacrament he ceased to be a Jew and was, indeed, made a Christian.

We are left to conclude that Ananias administered the sacrament just as Philip had done in 8:38 in the case of the eunuch. As far as Luke's record shows, the disciples who were living in Damascus, although they were numerous, had not yet withdrawn from the synagogues and had no organization of their own with elders or pastors. So Ananias administered baptism to Saul by the right of his royal priesthood as a believer. Since the Christians in Damascus were as yet without pastors, Ananias, of necessity, assumed this function. In the present instance, however, all doubt was removed by the commission he had received directly from the Lord, which certainly contained the order not merely to restore the sight of his eyes to Saul but also to receive him as a "brother" in the fellowship of the "saints." A vessel filled with water was brought in, some of the water was applied to Saul as Jesus had directed in Matt. 28:19, in the name of the Father, etc., and the blessed act was completed.

19) Saul was a changed man. Since he had been weakened by his fast of three days' duration, he now took food and restored his physical strength. When Luke writes that Saul was in the company of the disciples "for some days," we feel that he intends to state just that. We have no particulars in regard to Judas, to whose house Saul was first conducted; it is fair, however, to conclude that this man was a Jew and not a Christian. Saul now changed his abode; he went where he now belonged, among the disciples. It took some time for them to circulate his story, for him to get acquainted with them and thus gradually to get his bearings in this new city.

Those who introduce what v. 20 states at this point anticipate matters. On the other hand, it is supposed that during these days Saul underwent a course of instruction in the doctrines of the gospel. The μετά phrase does not imply such a thought, and Gal. 1:1-12, and the entire argument in Galatians, chapters one and two, is to the contrary. Saul received his entire gospel directly from the Lord as he declares, "by the revelation of Jesus Christ." He was not to be a preacher or an evangelist like Philip, who could operate with the gospel that was received at secondhand; as an apostle and as one who was on an equality with the other apostles Saul needed to receive the gospel at firsthand. And he received it so, by direct revelation. This may explain his being filled with the Holy Spirit, v. 17.

20) **And immediately in the synagogues he began to preach Jesus, that this one is the Son of God. And all those hearing it continued to be amazed and to say: Is not this the one who ravaged in Jerusalem those calling on this name? and here he had come for his that he might bring them bound to the high priests! Saul, however, was being filled the more with power and was confounding the Jews dwelling in Damascus, proving that this one is the Christ.**

We see the energy of the man. A few days pass, only enough to get his proper bearings, and then he begins his work as a herald (ingressive aorist) in the very city in which he had planned to do far different work. Some think that he began on the very day of his baptism; but that is not what Luke says. Saul preached "Jesus." What about him? "That (epexegetical ὅτι) this one is the Son of God." Add v. 22: "that this one is the Christ." Compare Luke 22:70. The strong demonstratives are exclusive: "this one and this one alone." Saul had seen this Son of God in his heavenly glory; he preached as an eyewitness. "I am Jesus" he had heard him say with glorified lips, the very Jesus who had walked, wrought on earth, had been killed by the Jews, and raised to glory by God — him Saul preached as the Messiah.

We meet the assertion that Paul never called Jesus "the Son of God"; and yet here is the fact — Luke has it from Paul himself. The very first thing which he did when he began his work was to preach Jesus as the Son of God. Luke, the great associate of Paul, here records what "the chosen instrument" (v. 15) of the Lord preached from the beginning. Robertson adds: "With this faith he can shake the world. There is no power in any other preaching."

21) Now the imperfect tenses begin; all of them are descriptive and at the same time lead us to look forward to what followed. First to be mentioned is the amazement of all who heard him in the synagogues of Damascus, and we may include Christians as well as Jews, for the withdrawal of the Christians from the Jews does not seem to have been effected as yet. They continue exclaiming, "Is not this the one," etc! The thing seemed incredible especially to the Jews. Note the recurrence of the expression, "those calling on this name" (v. 14) with the significant ὄνομα; also, "to bring them bound" (v. 2), the same perfect participle. All knew about the authorization and the instructions from the high priests with which Saul had arrived, his Levite police guard (the "men" in v. 7) had told for what purpose they had come under Saul's leadership. How was it possible that the persecutor-in-chief had turned preacher? The question ends in a declaration: "and here he had come for this," the purpose being stated with ἵνα.

22) As Saul preached he grew in power "the more" and caused consternation in the ranks of the Jews. The passive is usually taken in the middle sense, "he grew in power" ("increased in strength," our versions), but it really means that power was bestowed upon him, and this in increasing measure as his work went on. The result is added coordinately: "he continued to confound the Jews resident in Damascus"; as in 6:10 Stephen proved invincible, so also Stephen's greater successor. "Proving that this one is the Christ," the Messiah promised by the Scriptures, indi-

cates how the Jews were confounded. Those proofs were conclusive, overwhelming, and silenced the opponents. Then the same thing happened that had occurred in the case of Stephen; unable to refute the argument, these opponents resolved to kill the man who presented it.

Here we have Saul's first activity in the synagogues. An efficient pupil of the great Gamaliel, competent, therefore, to expound the Scriptures, he secured opportunity to speak in the synagogues. The service was such that any competent and qualified person was allowed to speak, and sometimes replies were made. In all his work in every city the apostle first visited the Jewish synagogues. They provided him with openings, and with the advantage there gained he proceeded. Not for a number of years was Saul as yet to extend his work to the Gentiles. The Lord was still training him, restraining him as he did Moses in Midian (7:29, 30) until in due time the door into his great life's work would open before him.

23) **Now, when many days were being fulfilled, the Jews resolved to make away with him; but their plot became known to Saul. Moreover, they were watching even the gates both by day and by night in order that they might make away with him. However, his disciples, having taken him at night, let him down through the wall by lowering him in a basket.**

These "many days" comprise three years (Gal. 1:18). Saul's visit to Arabia (Gal. 1:17) must be placed within this period. We know the fact of this visit but neither the occasion and the purpose nor the exact place or the duration. It is often supposed that Luke should have written about this journey to Arabia; but he does not record all that might be of interest to Theophilus and now to us. He follows a definite plan and records only the vital and the really significant matters of the apostolic story. This visit of Saul to Arabia was negligible for Luke's plan of Acts. Unless we find the clue to his plan of writing we shall fail to understand at many points.

It was thus after Saul's visit to Arabia, when he renewed his activity in Damascus, that his Jewish opponents took decisive action. The aorist *συνεβουλεύσαντο*, exactly as in Matt. 26:4, means that at a called meeting the formal resolution was passed, its contents being stated. In the case of Jesus it was to get hold of him with cunning and to kill him; in the case of Saul it was "to make away with him," *ἀναιρέω*, the verb which in 2:23; 5:33, 36; 7:28 means murder. Moral considerations never seemed to weigh in the balance when Jesus was concerned. "Took counsel" in our versions is too weak. Saul's fate was decided.

24) All we know is that Saul learned about the plot in some way. The imperfect describes what measures were taken to prevent his escape. His enemies "were even guarding the gates (of the city) both by day and by night," the genitives of time. Saul must have been in hiding because he knew about the fate that was intended for him. In II Cor. 11:32 we see that the ethnarch of King Aretas, who governed the city for him, agreed to the plot to apprehend Saul. The Jews had most likely denounced Saul as being a most dangerous man so that he had issued orders to his guards at the gate to capture him in case he tried to pass through it. He did not need to appoint the Jews as such guards. These volunteered to watch lest Saul in some disguise, reckoning with the inability of the governor's men to recognize him, should manage to evade them. Since the gates of the walled city were sealed, it would be only a matter of time until Saul was located and done away with. An efficient plot — that did not materialize. They watched and watched while Saul was already on his way to Jerusalem.

25) Saul's escape was effected in the simplest manner. Some of the houses that adjoined the wall around the city had windows that were high above the wall itself. From such a window Saul was lowered in a basket, σπυρίς, referring to its roundness; it is called σαργάνη in II Cor. 11:33, referring to its being plaited. We must note the expression "his disciples" which points to the success of Saul's work in Damascus; these men were converts of his. The fate of Stephen was not to be the fate of Saul. The Lord needs martyrs and secures them, and each is given his crown; but he also needs workers and provides them, and each receives his great reward.

26) **Now, having come to Jerusalem, he was attempting to join himself to the disciples; and all were fearing him, not believing that he was a disciple. Barnabas, however, after he got hold of him, brought him to the apostles and recounted to them how on the road he saw the Lord, and that he spoke to him, and how in Damascus he spoke boldly in the name of Jesus.**

The imperfect tenses picture Saul's difficulties on arriving in Jerusalem and at the same time point to what follows, namely their removal. When we remember the Jews' method of reckoning time, the three years of Saul's absence from Jerusalem (Gal. 1:18) most likely imply one full year and parts of two other years. So Jesus lay in the tomb all day Saturday and only a part of Friday and of Sunday, and yet the time spent in the tomb was counted as three days. Another point is Saul's absence in Arabia, likewise the war between Herod and King Aretas, which interrupted intercourse between Damascus and Jerusalem. Thus when Saul suddenly reappeared to join himself to the disciples in their meetings for worship and in social intercourse, he encountered doubt and suspicion, nobody really believing that he actually was a disciple as he claimed to be;

the tense of the direct discourse is retained after ὅτι. It did seem quite incredible that the most violent persecutor of the Christians, who had caused so many to flee from him and had wrought so much havoc, should himself have turned Christian. Was he, perhaps, pretending in order presently to do still greater damage?

27) It was Barnabas, who has already been introduced to us in 4:36, 37, who brought this situation to an end. Luke again states only the fact. We ask, however, how Barnabas came to act as intermediary. Had the two men met earlier in life? The conjecture is offered that both had attended the university in Tarsus years before. There is greater probability that Barnabas, who afterward was in such close and long association with Saul, was drawn to him from the beginning. Natural affinities appear even among leaders of the church. We need no further information at this point.

Barnabas "got hold of" Saul. This verb always governs the genitive, here αὐτοῦ is understood (B.-D. 170, 2), and αὐτόν is construed with ἤγαγε. He took Saul and made a complete investigation, and after he had obtained the remarkable story he took Saul to the apostles themselves and recounted it to them, laying stress on the three vital points: first, that Saul had seen the Lord; secondly, that the Lord had spoken to him; thirdly, that in Damascus Saul had spoken boldly in the name of Jesus (ὄνομα as in all previous passages beginning with 2:21).

The point of these two indirect questions that have a declaration between them (R. 1047) is evidently not merely that Saul is a fellow believer, but that the Lord qualified and made him a fellow apostle. That, too, is the reason that Barnabas takes Saul not merely to the congregation but to the apostles themselves. To have seen the risen and glorified Lord was a requisite for the apostolate. While Luke says only that the Lord spoke with Saul without intimating what this was about, the next statement, that Saul spoke in Damascus as he did, makes plain that the Lord authorized Saul's preaching. Verse 15 was also, no doubt, reported by Barnabas.

Luke writes that Barnabas took Saul to the apostles. This is made more specific in Gal. 1:18, 19, where Saul himself speaks of this visit to Jerusalem. It was brief, lasting only fifteen days. Saul's purpose was to become acquainted with Peter (ἱστορῆσαι, the aorist indicating that this was accomplished). He met only two of the apostles, Peter and James. The latter was not John's brother but the one called "the brother of the Lord." There is much debate in regard to the identity of this James (see 1:14, the brothers of Jesus; 12:27, James being one of them). As far as Luke's plural "to the apostles" is concerned, this is in order if James is regarded as an apostle in the wider sense as was Barnabas as well as others; the eleven were busy elsewhere. In v. 29 "the Hellenists" are only two or three and not all the thousands that were living in Jerusalem; in 8:18 "the apostles" signifies only "Peter and John." The same is true with regard to many other plurals, and there is no need to posit a contradiction between Luke and Galatians.

28) So the ice was broken. **And he was in company with them, going in and going out in Jerusalem, boldly speaking in the name of the Lord. He was engaged both in speaking and in disputing with the Hellenists; but they were undertaking to make away with him. Now, on learning it, the brethren led him down to Caesarea and sent him forth to Tarsus.**

"In company with them" means with the apostles. Saul was not only accepted as a genuine disciple; the apostles treated him as a fellow apostle. It was thus that he went in and out in their company "in Jerusalem," εἰς = ἐν, as so often in the Koine, which sets aside the older forced explanations which even take us out of Jerusalem and then "into" it again.

29) Luke says only that, while he was in company with the apostles, Saul "was speaking openly or boldly in the name of the Lord," i. e., in connection with that name or revelation. We take it that this was not preaching but private utterance. While the participle is a form of the verb used in v. 27, which includes synagogue preaching (v. 20) in Damascus, the situation obtaining in Jerusalem was entirely different. Here the Christians had their established preaching, and Paul would not have intruded. As to the synagogues in Jerusalem, these were at this time not open to the apostles and certainly were not used by them. They had found the courts of the Temple far better suited to their purpose. Note carefully that this participial clause still speaks of Saul as being in company with the apostles, referring to Peter and James.

What Saul did is stated separately, the imperfect tenses showing that he began to speak as well as to dispute with the Hellenists but did not get very far with them. The ἐλάλει implies that Saul accosted a Hellenist here and there, and the συνεζήτει that he occasionally managed to engage in a dispute; but that was all. Some think that Saul entered the synagogue of the Cilicians since he was from Tarsus of Cilicia, but Luke does not say this. We found that this was not probable in regard to Stephen in 6:9. All comparisons with Stephen are, therefore, problematical: that Saul stood in the very synagogue where Stephen had once stood, that in the very place where Saul had contradicted Stephen and had been thoroughly defeated he now used the same arguments against the Hellenists that Stephen had used.

As far as Stephen is concerned, we do not know whether he ever engaged in debate with Saul even outside of the synagogue. Only this is true, and we may make the most of it, that, like Stephen, Saul argued with a few Hellenists where he happened to encounter them, and that very quickly, as in Stephen's case, when counterargument failed, these Hellenists planned to use the more effective answer of murder, ἀνελεῖν. These Hellenists had silenced Stephen's voice with his own blood and undertook to do the same with Saul's voice. On the Hellenists see 6:1. Saul seems to have selected them, not because he himself was a Hellenist, but because he, too, was born in Hellenistic territory and thought he could accomplish something with regard to them. But the undertaking of these vicious opponents came to nothing as the imperfect indicates. Note the difference: in v. 23 συνεβουλεύσαντο, a formal resolution passed at a meeting, here ἐπεχείρουν, an undertaking by individuals.

30) According to 22:17-21 the Lord himself directed Saul to leave Jerusalem. This is what really induced him to do so. All that Luke adds is that the brethren got to know about the undertaking of the Hellenists. Saul, we assume, told them also about the Lord's communication to him. The brethren, of course, only a delegation, "brought him down to Cæsarea" and carefully guarded his person on this journey lest his bloodthirsty enemies should fall upon him on the road and thus after all succeed in making away with him. From Cæsarea Saul could travel to Tarsus by either sea or land.

Here we come to the greatest gap in the record of Saul's life since we saw him at Stephen's death. Saul is lost to view for about eight years; see 11:25 where Barnabas brings him forth from Tarsus. For more than ten years after his conversion and call the Lord's chosen instrument for bringing the gospel to the Gentiles (v. 15) is not active in his great special mission. All we can say is that this was the Lord's will. We should think that Saul was ready for his task, and his task was ready for him immediately after he had been called; the Lord evidently knew better.

What did Saul do during those years he spent in Tarsus? The sacred record is silent on this matter as it is in regard to Paul's sojourn in Arabia. "He preached and missionated," some tell us. But we do not learn about the gathering of a congregation in Tarsus, nor about converts even in Cilicia, and the time spent there is eight years. It is, indeed, precarious to say that at any place in his account Luke should have told us this or that. Here, however, it is plain: if the great work among the Gentiles had begun in Tarsus, and if so many years of Saul's life were devoted to it, Luke simply could not have passed this by in silence. Ramsay's hypothesis is that Saul was not yet fully conscious of his mission to the Gentile world and still thought that the door to Christ was through the synagogue. He forgets the Jews in Tarsus; he himself assumes that a colony of Jews lived in Tarsus (see v. 11). Why did Saul, then, do nothing among these Jews? Ramsay touches only half of the problem. Saul did no work in Tarsus.

Some fill in the account at this point and speak of "the scene at home when this brilliant young rabbi, the pride of Gamaliel, returns home a preacher of the despised Jesus of Nazareth, whose disciples he had so relentlessly persecuted. What will father, mother, sister think of him now?" This scene is expanded. Saul's subsequent poverty is explained by surmising that his father disinherits him as the Jews to this day regard as dead any child that becomes a Christian. Yet all that we know is that years later Saul's nephew warned him in Jerusalem (23:16). We do not even know why Saul returned to Tarsus, and we ask, "Would he remain there for years with parents that regarded him as dead?"

31) **Accordingly, the church throughout the whole of Judea and Galilee and Samaria continued to have peace, being built up and, walking in the fear of the Lord and in the encouragement of the Holy Spirit, was being multiplied.**

This little summary is similar to 2:44-47; 4:32-35; and as far as multiplication is concerned, compare 2:41; 4:4; 5:14; 6:7; 8:25. On μὲν οὖν see 1:6. After Saul had been converted, the persecution of which he had been the driving spirit ceased. And Saul was now some distance removed, a renewal of persecution that might be prompted by the hatred the Jews might manifest toward the Christian Paul was obviated. It was thus that the church had peace, meaning quiet and rest.

On ἐκκλησία see 5:11, and note 8:1, 3. This word is here used in the same sense as denoting the body of believers. The fact that this body is now spread out over three provinces does not change the sense of *ecclesia.* The bond that makes all these believers one is that of faith. Even when it is extended to the ends of the earth it will be just ἡ ἐκκλησία. This concept has a spiritual content even when it is applied to a local congregation only, for the genuine believers always constitute the church, irrespective of mere adherents.

On κατά in the sense of "throughout" see R. 607. It seems that the countries are mentioned in the order of their importance, thus Galilee before Samaria, although Luke records nothing of special historical importance about Galilee. He mentions these three because the church was well distributed throughout these three, which was not the case as yet in other provinces, only scattered congregations having been founded in them.

The imperfect tenses and the present participles are descriptive of the condition and the progress. The οἰκοδομουμένη is undoubtedly the New Testament spiritual edification. This word cannot here refer to outward growth since this is mentioned separately. This conception is not to be externalized as meaning only that the church ordered and developed her internal affairs; nor be reduced to only the devoutness of religious feeling which is furthered by the peculiar type of preaching that aims at this effect. The latter was made the aim of cultus preaching by Schleiermacher who had many followers in Germany. Edification is the strengthening of the entire religious life and activity by means of the Word and the Sacrament. Church organization and the like is a different matter. To this the apostles as yet devoted little effort.

The verbs and the participles are arranged chiastically, the verbs being placed outside, the participles inside, so that one participle refers to each verb. "Walking in the fear of the Lord," etc., the church continued to multiply "in numbers." Combined with the inner upbuilding was the strong outward growth, for "multiplied" means great increase. Palestine was being rapidly Christianized. Luke states how, namely by the church walking in the fear of the Lord and in the comfort of the Holy Spirit. The spiritual power of the church evident in its membership attracted and won men.

"The fear of the Lord" (Jesus) with its objective genitive means that the church dreaded to do anything that might displease and offend the Lord. In their daily life and walk the members had Jesus present with them. This is high praise indeed, for this strong motive is largely absent today; church members too often persuade themselves that the Lord does not mind their worldliness and love of praise from men.

Combined with this fear was "the encouragement of the Holy Spirit" which with its subjective genitive refers to the Spirit's *Zusprache,* his aid in encouragement, direction, and comfort. As the other Paraclete promised by Jesus, he acted as one called to the side of the believers in order to help them in every way. This presence of the Spirit is always mediated through the Word by means of which he speaks to us and keeps us encouraged and strong in the faith. The early Christians did not listen to the spirit of the world and of the flesh. Very unobtrusively Luke here points to the sources of power in the church. When the members walk with the fear of the Lord before their eyes and with the Spirit's encouraging voice in their hearts, the church will be strong and will also surely multiply.

Peter at Lydda and at Joppa

Having practically concluded the preliminary account in regard to Saul, Luke returns to the activity of Peter. We see him at Lydda, at Joppa, and then at Caesarea. He serves as an example of the type of work the apostles generally were doing; yet he is selected by Luke because it was his lot to bring the first Gentiles into the church in such a way as to open the whole question regarding the admission of Gentiles into the church. Philip's baptism of the eunuch was the modest preliminary.

32) **Now it came to pass that Peter, in going through to all, came down also to the saints inhabiting Lydda,** the Old Testament Lod, the Roman Diospolis, the present Ludd, on the road from Jerusalem to Joppa. The accusative with the infinitive is the subject. The participle is only incidental and yet casts a light upon the present work of the apostles. Peter visits Joppa "in going through to all," διὰ πάντων. This must be masculine on account of the following καί which brings out the fact that he "also" came to the saints at Lydda; our versions should be corrected. Peter is alone. There is too much to be done to permit the apostles to go out two by two.

And Peter's program is extensive: he intends to visit "all," to cover the entire church. It would seem as though other apostles had the same program. Since the churches as yet had little or no organization they could not be left to themselves, and therefore the apostles felt obliged to visit them from time to time. That would take them away from Jerusalem for longer periods of time. It was such a visit that Peter was paying "the saints" at Lydda, the same significant term as in v. 13.

33) **And there he found a man by name Æneas, since eight years lying on a pallet, who had been paralyzed. And Peter said to him, Æneas, Jesus Christ heals thee! Arise, and spread** (the bed) **for thyself! And immediately he arose.**

Luke records this event with such brevity because he is concerned, not so much about this sick man, but rather with the effect produced by the miracle wrought upon him. This man is a parallel to the cripple at the Gate Beautiful in the Temple, 3:2, etc., parallel especially in helping to bring many to faith. Some think that this paralytic was a disciple but he was not, for how could Luke write ἄνθρωπόν τινα, "a man," *ein Mensch*, instead of "a believer," "a disciple"? Compare his account about Tabitha in v. 36. Yet healing fell into this man's lap just as it fell into the lap of that beggar in the Temple.

This, too, was a very serious case: paralysis for the past eight years so severe that the sufferer had to spend the day on a κράββατος or pallet (8:7). The ἐξ is the Greek idiom, it counts from the far point and is our "since."

34) Since Peter calls him by name, others must have spoken to him about this man. The reversal of subject and predicate puts emphasis on both: "*heal* thee doth *Jesus Christ*." R. 866 calls this an effective aoristic present because of its punctiliar force; the main point is that it states a tremendous fact. Instantaneously the man *is* healed. "Jesus Christ" (see 2:38) does the deed and not Peter. In 3:6, Peter said, "In the

name of Jesus Christ." The sense is the same. Since Jesus here and now heals him, the man is told to get up and to spread his pallet for himself, a task others have had to perform for him during all these years. This verb στρωννύω occurs in Matt. 21:8, where the people spread branches on the road for Jesus, and in Luke 22:12 where the upper room was spread with floor tiling. The sense is proably that Æneas is to take up his pallet and lay it away somewhere, doing this for himself as it had been done for him every evening when he was undressed and transferred from his pallet to his bed for the night.

35) **And all those inhabiting Lydda and Sharon saw him, they who turned to the Lord,** οἵτινες, *quippe qui*. The effect spread from the town through the beautiful coast plain which extends about thirty miles toward Cæsarea. So many saw the man, recognized the miracle in its true significance, and in faith turned to the Lord, that Luke could write "all." This added to the labors of Peter. How long he labored here we do not know; he later moved on to Joppa.

36) **Now in Joppa there was a woman disciple by name Tabitha, which, when translated, means Dorcas. This one was full of good works and almsdeeds which she was doing. But it came to pass in those days that, having become sick, she died; and having washed her, they placed her in an upper room.**

Transitional δέ takes us into the new account, to Joppa, the present Jaffa, the old port of Jerusalem, one of the most ancient of towns. Philip had, no doubt, worked here, and the first local Christians may have been fugitives from Jerusalem (8:1). Without further explanation we learn that there was a Christian congregation in Joppa. We are introduced to one of the woman disciples by the name of Tabitha, from the Aramaic *tzebiah,* which Luke translates by the Greek

Dorcas, both names meaning a gazelle doe, the emblem of grace and beauty. This name was frequently given to girls. The relative is feminine, ἥ, the gender being attracted from the antecedent. R. 714 makes the relative personal. The account contains no reference to relatives and leaves the impression that Tabitha lived by herself. Her special interest in widows leads us to surmise that she herself was a widow who had no children. Although she lived alone and seemingly had no special object in life, this disciple fashioned a most important place for herself in the life of the young congregation.

She was "full of good works," which includes a variety. Luke specifies by naming one class of these works especially: "and almsdeeds which she kept doing," aiding the poor to the extent of her ability. In this activity she invested her money, time, and strength. She is not represented as a deaconess in the church; in fact, we may safely assume that such an office had not yet been established. Tabitha's work was entirely voluntary; but with a true instinct she chose no work of doubtful propriety with which to serve the Lord in the church, no work that had a worldly taint but one that was fully in harmony with the gospel. Hers were in every respect *good* works, ἀγαθός, good in the sense of truly beneficial, and *mercy*-deeds, the Greek word being derived from ἔλεος, "mercy." "Good works grow from faith and are but the very Word of God in its deed and fulfillment, which has been implanted in us by faith." H. Mueller.

Luke emphasizes the abundance: "full" of good works and almsdeeds "which she kept doing" (durative imperfect). She reaped a rich harvest. She did not tire, discouragements were overcome, she continued faithful in her service to the end. "The sweet odor of the ointment filled the house when the vessel which had stood in a place aside broke." Besser.

37) It was "in those days" that Tabitha became sick and died. We are left to read between the lines that there was a divine providence in the fact that this death occurred at just this time. Peter was within reach. The Lord intended to distinguish this humble woman in a signal way, namely by raising her from the dead. He had given much to the church in Joppa when he gave her to it; now he intended to give the church still more in her.

With sadness they took her body to the upper room and washed and prepared it for burial. The participle λούσαντες is masculine although this washing and this preparing of the body were done by women; the gender is indifferent because no subject is named. Since no house has been mentioned, there is no article with "upper room." An ordinary house would have only one "upper room" which was built on the flat roof and used as a place of retirement. We have no information to the effect that the bodies of the dead were usually placed in upper rooms before burial. Luke relates this in regard to Tabitha because an exception was made in her case. According to the regular custom she should have been buried soon after death; instead of that her body was kept until Peter could arrive. For this reason it was placed in the upper room.

38) **Now Lydda being near to Joppa, the disciples, having heard that Peter was there, commissioned two men to him, beseeching him, Do not delay to come through to us!**

At this point nearly every commentator asks questions that are not answered by the text. Were the two messengers sent after Tabitha had died or before her death? If she was already dead, why was Peter called in such haste? Did they entertain the thought or the hope that Peter might bring her back to life?

Luke makes note of the comparatively short distance between Joppa and Lydda (ἐγγύς is here construed with the dative, and not with the customary genitive), it was only about nine miles. The aorist participle adds the detail that the disciples at Joppa had heard the news that Peter was in Lydda. We can follow only the natural impression made by the brief narrative that the Christians in Joppa had for some time had news of Peter's presence in Lydda but that the thought of sending for him had occurred to no one until after Tabitha had died. Then, as far as hopes and expectations are concerned, all that we can safely say is that the disciples at Joppa requested only that Peter might come and, like true disciples of Christ, committed everything else into the Lord's hands.

"Do not delay," etc., implies that the disciples knew that Peter intended to visit them also, but they beg that he may come at once. In negative commands or entreaties μή with the aorist subjunctive is the regular form but is just as urgent as the positive command with the aorist imperative. "Do not delay" is a litotes for, "Hurry." In that climate the dead are commonly buried on the day of death or, if death occurs too late in the day, the next morning. Peter could be brought from Lydda to Joppa in five or six hours, thus on the same day, if Tabitha had died in the morning, or the next morning if she had died at evening. A delay on Peter's part would have necessitated burial before he could arrive.

Now this petition that Peter hurry does carry with it the silent, humble hope that the Lord's grace might use Peter to return Tabitha to the church at Joppa. Yet, when finding this hope in the petition, we must remember, what also these disciples seem to know, that none of the apostles worked miracles at will. Hence no request is made to Peter to work a miracle upon Tabitha. In every case the Lord and his Spirit directed those to whom the gift of performing miracles had been granted, and they proceeded only when and where they were so directed. What the Lord's will was in the case of Tabitha none presumed to say, and we shall see that Peter himself did not at first know So in all that prompted this message to Peter their thought was only to bow to the Lord's will while trusting in his boundless grace.

39) **And, having arisen, Peter went with them, whom, on having come, they led up into the upper room. And there stood by him all the widows sobbing and showing on themselves tunics and robes, as many as Dorcas made from time to time while yet with them.**

Peter responded promptly. The Greek reads literally: "whom, having gotten to their side (παρά in the participle), they brought," etc. This makes the impression that Peter had been summoned on Tabitha's account and not on account of the disciples in order to administer comfort to them, to preach a funeral sermon, as we should say. Yet even now no request of any kind is made. Peter is taken up to the dead woman's side where he finds that she is wrapped and swathed for burial. But here, beside that loving heart and those busy hands that are now still in death, Peter is shown what this woman meant to the church and what the church had lost in her. It was done in a simple and a most natural way. All the widows for whom Tabitha had made garments are present. How could any of them be absent at this time? "All" is not too strong, for in that congregation there were not overly many.

Their feelings soon gave way in that upper room as Peter questioned and they answered so that he might know fully. They sobbed aloud. This was mourning which was far different from that manifested in the house of Jairus with its noisy, hired mourning women and fluteblowers. This was not such artificial mourning as that. The widows showed Peter garments that had been made by their dead benefactress. Note the middle voice ἐπιδεικνύμεναι, for it conveys the idea that they were showing what belonged to themselves, they wore the very garments Tabitha had made for them, ἐποίει, iterative imperfect, from time to time, now a garment for this penniless widow, now one for that.

The χιτών is the tunic that is worn next to the body, the ἱμάτιον, the robe or cloak that is worn over the tunic, the Latin *pallium*. The one was as much a necessity as the other. The *himation* was really a large, oblong piece of cloth, one corner of which was draped over the left shoulder and fastened under the right shoulder. This garment was ample enough to reach to the ground. It generally served as a covering for the sleeper at night. We must not miss the pathos indicated in the addition μετ' αὐτῶν οὖσα and in the placing of her name at the end: "she — being with them — Dorcas." Now her body was there, but not — Dorcas! *die Dorkas* (German). Catch the lingering tone of affection.

Luke now uses the name "Dorcas," partly for the sake of his own Greek reader who would know the meaning of this Greek name, "*Gazelle*"; and partly, it seems, because even in Joppa the orginal Tabitha had been replaced by its Greek equivalent. "And their works do follow them" is here illustrated in a peculiarly touching manner. What will be the nature of the works that follow you and me?

So Dorcas was a dressmaker, but instead of enriching herself by sewing only for money she enriched her soul by sewing for love. The garments she made for the poor she really made for the Lord, and she has had many successors, both with the needle itself and in other ways. She had only one talent, but see how much she made of that! Many who found themselves in her circumstances would have felt that they could do nothing; she saw the one opportunity and avenue open for her and made the most of that. We think that she sewed also for the children of these widows who were half-orphans; these would not be present at such a solemn time as this.

40) The whole scene must have had a deep effect on Peter. The garments which had passed through the loving hands now resting from their labors spoke more eloquently to him than the subdued and broken sobs of the widows who wore them. **But Peter, having thrust them all outside and having kneeled down, prayed; and having turned to the body, he said, Tabitha, arise! And she opened her eyes, and, on seeing Peter, she sat up. And having given her a hand, he raised her up; and having called the saints and the widows, he presented her living.**

What is here recorded bears some resemblance to the procedure followed by Jesus when he raised to life the daughter of Jairus, yet the differences predominate. Peter kneels and prays, he permits no witnesses to remain in the room, and he finally summons all the disciples. Peter's miracle is thus not a duplicate of that performed by Jesus; the resemblances are due only to the nature of the two cases.

Why did Peter thrust them out? Ἐκβαλών is a strong word, they were reluctant to leave. We have the answer in Peter's subsequent deed: he kneeled and prayed. The Greek idiom is, "having placed the knees." Peter wanted to be alone with the Lord. Peter did not disregard the unspoken longing of the disciples that the Lord show his grace by restoring Dorcas to life. But up to this moment he had no intimation from the Lord as to his will. In deepest humility, on his knees, he now asks the Lord to reveal his will.

We need not hesitate to add that he prayed the Lord to grant the unspoken desire of the saints, a desire that had been kept within godly bounds and did not even venture to utter itself in words, to say nothing of clamoring for satisfaction. It seemed to be one of those pure and holy desires which the Lord loves to satisfy. So Peter lays the case before the Lord and in connection with it the great cause to which this case belonged.

Peter's action after his prayer shows that the Lord gave him an answer, the answer on which Peter's act rests. It was not Peter's "sublime faith" that performed this miracle. The Lord's sublime power wrought it; Peter had the Lord's word which had been communicated to him then and there. The fact that he believed that word is a matter of course.

When Peter turned to the body and said, "Tabitha, arise!" there was no question as to what would happen. Peter was not making a trial of his own faith. Peter was acting on the Lord's word. No apostle ever failed when he had that word; in no case was there a half-effect; but, of course, in no case did an apostle act without the Lord's word. Peter did not say, "In the name of Jesus arise!" but his words implied that and nothing else.

It is incorrect to say that as a result of his prayer Peter treated the body as though it were no longer dead. Luke says he turned to "the body," yet he did not address the body, which would have been folly, but the person. But this does not offer support to the spiritualistic notion that the spirit of Tabitha hovered near the body and thus heard Peter's command. Why introduce our rationalizing ideas of space when it is not the voice and the power of Peter that are at work but the promise and the power of the almighty Lord which work in a way that is absolutely incomprehensible to us? The Lord made Tabitha hear; the Lord returned her soul to her body; the Lord did this in connection with the word he had bidden Peter to speak.

Luke describes only the outward side of what occurred. "And she opened her eyes," the eyes that but a moment ago were broken and sealed in death. We ought not to think that there was a gradual return to life because Luke records several actions. Dorcas was instantaneously and completely restored when Peter spoke. No steps, no gradations followed. Life in full energy was back in her body; the former disease which had been active in her vital organs had disappeared; the incipient decay that had been superinduced by death was removed at a stroke. Dorcas was as one waking out of deep sleep. This is what Luke has in mind, for the first thing an awakened sleeper does is to open his eyes. Naturally, too, on seeing Peter standing beside her, she sat up. For this she needed no help. Her body was swathed in linen strips for burial, yet this did not prevent her from assuming a sitting posture. We have the analogy of Lazarus coming out of the tomb.

41) At this point Peter might have opened the door and called in the waiting disciples. He first gave Dorcas his hand and raised her to her feet. It seems that her arms had not been wrapped against her body. Lazarus, too, was able to stand in his grave wrappings and to appear at the door of the tomb. When Dorcas thus stood beside her bier, Peter called in "the saints and the widows," "saints" as in v. 13, and *καί* does not add a new class but only specifies "the widows" as the ones mostly concerned. What a scene that must have been when Peter presented Dorcas — "living"! That is a way the inspired writers have! They record the most dramatic and stupendous events in a few calm words. They always let the immense facts speak for themselves.

42) **And it became known throughout entire Joppa, and many believed on the Lord. And it came to pass that for many days he remained in Joppa with Simon, a tanner.**

Luke returns to the matter of chief interest, that of the church and its development. A miracle that was as stupendous as this one had been could not but become known throughout the entire city (κατά as in v. 31). That, too, was the Lord's intention. We see that the same effect was produced in Lydda (v. 35). Many "believed on the Lord," ἐπί, rested their confidence and trust on Jesus, on his grace and his power for salvation. The idea is not that miracles as such work faith, but miracles are seals of the Word and attestations of its power and thus aid in producing faith. They are such seals to this day, for, once affixed to the Word, they remain there and need no repetition, and there is no need of new seals as though those affixed by the Lord had lost their validity.

43) Luke likes ἐγένετο, "it came to pass," a sacred way of stating notable facts that he had learned from the LXX. And here again the accusative and the infinitive are the subject. The way had been opened to gather a great harvest in Joppa, and Peter remained "many days" (v. 23) in order to help bring it in.

The noteworthy thing is that Peter accepted the hospitality of "a Simon, a tanner." The handling of hides made this man ceremonially unclean from the Jewish standpoint Christian though he was. Peter disregarded these Jewish scruples and lived in this man's house during the entire time of his stay in Joppa. Recall that Peter and John had been with Philip in Samaria. The old Jewish legalism is dropping away; the next chapter shows the decisive and the complete break. At this point Rieger remarks that a tanner's house was provided for St. Peter, but now a castle scarcely suffices for St. Peter's successors.

CHAPTER X

CORNELIUS:

THE RECEPTION OF GENTILE CHRISTIANS

Luke devotes so much space to the story of Cornelius because it marks a new departure in the work of the apostles. What had been indicated by the baptism of the Ethiopian eunuch is fully established by the baptism of Cornelius and of his household. The eunuch went his way, but these Gentiles in Caesarea remained and thus formed the vanguard of the great army of Gentiles that soon entered the church. What Peter did in the case of Cornelius was a preparation for the entire work of Paul, who was waiting in Tarsus during these years.

1) **Now a man in Caesarea, by name Cornelius, a centurion from the cohort called the Italian, pious and fearing God with all his house, doing many almsdeeds for the people, begging of God always, saw in a vision plainly about at the ninth hour an angel of God come in to him and say to him, Cornelius!**

Joppa was a very ancient city, but Cæsarea was most recent, having been built by Herod the Great in ten years and named in honor of the Roman Cæsar. After Herod's time it became the resident city of the Roman governors.

Cornelius is described at length. He was a centurion in the Roman army, an officer who commanded a century or 100 men. He belonged to the Italian cohort which was stationed in Cæsarea at this time; thirty-two such Italian cohorts were stationed in the different provinces of the empire. They were made up of Italian volunteers and were considered the most loyal Roman troops. A legion consisted of ten cohorts plus auxiliary troops. Each cohort had six centuries and the same number of centurions. No longer is Luke's statement challenged, that there was a cohort in Cæsarea and this province of the empire at the time of which Luke speaks.

It must have been late in the year 37 or early in 38 when Saul left Jerusalem and went to Tarsus via Cæsarea. Peter must have gone to Lydda, Joppa, and then Cæsarea not long after Saul had departed, namely in the summer of 38. Herod Agrippa I, a prisoner in Rome under Tiberius until the latter's death on March 16, 37, was appointed king over his uncle Philip's tetrarchy (Luke 3:1) by the new emperor Caligula but did not arrive in Palestine until late in the summer of 38. Perhaps already in April, 37, Marullus was appointed procurator of Judea, and he must have had this Italian cohort in Cæsarea. Not until early in 41 did Emperor Claudius make Agrippa I king over all Palestine, which explains how he could execute James and imprison Peter in Jerusalem. Marullus ruled as procurator. Agrippa I suffered a miserable death after the Passover of 44, after ruling all Palestine for only a little over three years.

2) When Luke writes: "pious and fearing God with all his house," the adjective marks the godly character of the man, the participle, however, brings out the fact that he and his whole family were proselytes of the gate. On the two kinds of proselytes see 2:10 and 8:27. The important point that is vital for all that follows even as far as 15:7-11, is that Cornelius and his household were still Gentiles and were regarded as such by all Jews, were considered as standing only at the gate of the pale of the Jewish Church and were debarred from passing beyond the court of the Gentiles in the

Temple. None such had as yet come into the Christian Church save the eunuch; those called "proselytes" in 2:10 were such in the full sense of the word and hence were regarded as Jews.

The great question which the Lord compelled Peter and the church to face in the person of Cornelius was whether the way into the Christian Church was to be only through Judaism and the synagogue or also direct from Gentilism and paganism by faith and baptism alone. It was exceedingly difficult for many Christians who had come into the church from Judaism to find and to accept the true and the God-pleasing answer to this question. The Lord made that answer exceedingly plain and forceful through Cornelius. That answer had to be clear in the minds of all before the gospel could reach out into the vast Gentile world.

From the beginning Cornelius appears "with his whole house" around him, his family and his slaves, and soon we note even his friends (v. 24). This was more than just family religion; this man's faith reached out all around him. While he was a proselyte of the gate, we are not at all sure that as much can be said regarding all the rest whom Peter met in his house. Cornelius cultivated the two outstanding virtues of the Jewish religion: he gave abundant alms and he was diligent in prayer. The beneficiaries of his charity were "the people," λαός so often signifying the Jewish people. He had found so much through them that he made generous and grateful return. Luke uses δεόμενος, which takes the genitive as a designation for praying, the verb which means "to beg of God"; in v. 4 we have the regular word for "prayers."

3) He was thus engaged when there came an answer to his prayers that he had not expected. "At about the ninth hour" refers to the hour of the evening sacrifice in the Temple at Jerusalem, three o'clock in the afternoon, the hour that was used for prayer also

by devout Jews who lived far from the Temple. Luke's ὡσεὶ περί is due to the non-existence of clocks and thus to the inability to be entirely exact; moreover, according to the season and the amount of daylight, the hours were longer or shorter. Suddenly Cornelius saw an angel of God; the two aorist participles are punctiliar, not "coming in" and "saying," but that he "came" and "said." We meet these visions frequently; note that of Peter in v. 10, etc. Instead of being confined to ordinary perceptions, the mind and the senses are able to see the supernatural that the Lord intends to reveal. Cornelius was wide awake, entirely master of his mind and his senses, but now he saw the coming of the angel with his eyes and heard the words of the angel with his ears and recognized the angel as the person that he was. The direct address, "Cornelius," implied that this heavenly messenger had a communication for him.

These visions are never mere subjective autosuggestions or the mind's own productions. The angel was actually present, was as real as though a man stood before Cornelius. He spoke audibly so that Cornelius heard his voice and his words. The veil which confines us to this natural world was withdrawn; Cornelius was enabled to see and to hear this angel from the heavenly world. Each vision is confined to definite limits and does not extend beyond these; for it is a revelation of the facts and truths desired by the Lord and hence does not go beyond these. Rationalism will always either deny them outright or will seek natural or pathological explanations for them. Sudduceeism still continues.

4) **And he, gazing earnestly on him and become trembling, said, What is it, Lord? And he said to him: Thy prayers and thy alms went up for a memorial before God. And now send men to Joppa and summon for thyself a Simon who is surnamed Peter; he is lodging with a Simon, a tanner, who has a house beside the sea.**

Cornelius could not do otherwise than to rivet his eyes upon this heavenly being and could not do otherwise than to tremble at his sight. This is quite regularly the effect produced when sinful men come into visible contact with the other world. As in v. 3, so here, too, the participles are historical aorists which intend not to describe but only to register the facts: he gazed, he became trembling. Cornelius properly addresses the angel as "lord." In the Gospels we constantly have κύριος in this sense when a person is addressed as a superior. Eventually the word came to be used as a designation for Jesus as the divine Lord, the Second Person of the deity. We have the two uses in English today: "lord" (some man) and "Lord" (Jesus as God).

When the angel tells Cornelius that his prayers and his alms have come up "for a memorial" before God, the phrase conveys the truth that God intends to remember these prayers and these alms, to take account of them in his grace towards Cornelius. It should not be necessary to say that no work-righteousness is implied but something vastly greater than any claims of human merit. The prayers and the alms revealed the condition of the heart of Cornelius. They were, indeed, good works but are here regarded like the good works of the righteous at the time of the final judgment when Jesus will use them as the evidence of faith and the absence of such good works as the evidence for the absence of saving faith (Matt. 25:34-46). God was thus judging Cornelius by these works of his.

The expression that these works have come up as a memorial before God is anthropomorphitic and speaks of God as a great king who made a permanent record and now proceeds to reward Cornelius. We now see why Luke used the participle "begging" as a designation for the praying of Cornelius (v. 2). Cornelius did more than merely to use the office of Jewish prayer; he begged God to enlighten his heart, to fulfill the great Messianic promises, to grant him a share in those promises. These were the petitions that were now to receive a notable answer. That, of course, was wonderful grace for Cornelius personally. But our view must not be too narrow. Others, as devout as Cornelius, received no angelic message, no miraculous answer. God was using Cornelius for a far higher purpose, namely to open the door of the church to all the Gentiles. For this he chose Cornelius; he might have chosen another. God manages his own affairs in his own superior and most perfect way. It is not necessary to make ἀνέβησαν a timeless aorist (R., *W. P.*) when it is plainly the English perfect "have come up," an ordinary recent past act.

5) Although God sends an angel to Cornelius, that angel is not to preach the gospel to him. Again, as in the case of Philip, God honors the ministry he has established. Angels may help to connect men with God's appointed preachers, they are never allowed to do more. So Cornelius is told just what to do to get Simon Peter. Note the middle imperative, "summon for thyself," which indicates that Peter would have a message for Cornelius.

6) The two Simons are carefully distinguished, each with the indefinite pronoun that is equal to our indefinite article: "a Simon." The passive ξενίζεται = he is received as a ξένος or guest, i. e., "he lodges." The fact that Peter's host is a tanner is again mentioned but apparently only in order to identify him, and for the same reason the detail is added that he has a house ("for him is," idiom) along by the sea (no article is needed in the Greek). Tanneries required much water, and Simon seems to have done his tanning where he lived. There is here no idea of ceremonial uncleanness as a motive why Cornelius should not be afraid of sending for Peter.

7) **And when the angel who was speaking to him went away, having called two of the house-servants and a pious soldier of those holding to him and having recounted to them everything, he commissioned them to Joppa.**

We here learn more about Cornelius. He, of course, at once acted on the word of the angel. The fact that he had a number of οἰκέται (a mild term for slaves who were used as house servants) is not surprising considering his station. The soldiers, of course, were under his command; but we see that he selects one "of those holding to him" who is called "pious," the very adjective that was applied to Cornelius himself in v. 2. See the participle προσκαρτεροῦντες in 1:14; 2:42; 6:4 (these with neuter objects), and in 8:13 (with Philip as the object). A number of soldiers held to their commander because of his religious convictions which they shared.

The idea that these soldiers were merely attendants of their commander does not satisfy the expression, another word would be used to express that thought. It is only a guess to say that the soldier was sent along to protect the two slaves — they needed no protection, for no danger threatened them on the road. These three men were selected because they were spiritually closest to Cornelius. Their respective stations did not matter; as for that, all three messengers might have been slaves or soldiers. The point is that we here have a Roman officer who shared his religion with those who were far beneath him. Military officers usually act very superior to those beneath them; their official pride makes them aloof. The more noteworthy is what we note in this centurion of the elite Italian cohort.

8) We see why these particular men were selected. Cornelius "recounted everything to them," took them completely into his confidence. They were not given a mere formal order to summon Peter but were told all about the angelic vision. This most sacred and intimate

matter Cornelius shared with these men; they had to be men of a type in whose case such a thing was possible. All these points are of great value and help us to understand why Luke goes into such detail.

9) **Now on the next day, while they were travelling and drawing near to the city, Peter went up on the housetop to pray at about the sixth hour; and he became quite hungry and was desiring to taste something. But while they were making ready, there came over him an ecstasy, and he beholds the heaven having been opened and coming down a kind of receptacle like a great linen sheet being let down by four corners to the earth, in which there were all the four-footed and creeping things of the earth and flying things of the heaven. And there came a voice to him, Having arisen, Peter, slay and eat! But Peter said, By no means, Lord, because never did I eat anything common and unclean. And again a voice a second time to him, What God made clean, do thou stop making common! Moreover, this occurred three times; and immediately the receptacle was received up into heaven.**

The two genitive absolutes picture the three messengers on the way and drawing near to the city. About this time, at noon, one of the regular Jewish hours for prayer, Peter retires to the housetop where all is quiet in order to pray. The aorist indicates that he was offering definite prayers and not merely praying in general, which would require the present infinitive. As the Lord prepared Ananias for Saul and Saul for Ananias (9:10-12), so, after preparing Cornelius, he now prepares Peter. The δῶμα is simply the flat housetop and not the upper room built on the housetop, to designate which Luke would have used the regular word as he does elsewhere. It appears as though this tanner was too poor to have such an upper room in his house. Yet we must not imagine that Peter was out on the open roof under the noonday sun. When travelling through Syria and Palestine we saw many smaller houses with booths on their roofs. Some shelter similar to this may have been used by Peter.

The messengers had made good time. Starting after three in the afternoon, they were now, at noon of the next day, entering Joppa. They had covered the distance of 250 stadia or 24 miles by traveling even at night. They traveled on foot as a matter of course.

10) It may have been due to fasting. At any rate, Peter became "quite hungry," πρός in the adjective denoting addition: "very hungry." This adjective, as M.-M. 550 remark, is one of the diminishing number of New Testament words of which it must be said, "Not found elsewhere." The imperfect ἤθελε describes Peter's desire to eat; Luke uses γεύσασθαι, the active of which means, "to make taste," and the middle thus, "to taste for oneself." Peter longed for the taste of food. R., *W. P.*, ingeniously suggests that Peter perhaps smelled the food being prepared below in the house. At least Luke informs us that the folks were getting a meal ready. This seems to have been a delayed ἄριστον which was usually eaten at ten o'clock and was not the δεῖπνον, the main meal which was eaten toward evening.

Then came the ἔκστασις which Luke describes in detail. The word describes a condition when the mind and the senses are lifted out of their natural surroundings and functions and are enabled to receive supernatural impressions and revelations by means of visions or other divine modes of communication. Compare Delitzsch, *Biblische Psychologie*, 285. A case in point is that of Stephen, 7:55, 56. The ὅραμα of Cornelius refers to the same thing although it is named according to what he actually saw, while ἔκστασις names the condition in which the person is when he sees, hears, etc. Such a vision and ecstasy is divinely wrought and has nothing to do with morbid states which are self-induced such as spiritualistic trances.

11) In describing the vision Luke employs the vivid present, "he beholds." Peter's eyes saw the heaven standing open (the perfect participle with present connotation), and out of its superearthly radiance "coming down" σκεῦός τι, "a kind of receptacle," which is described as a great ὀθόνη or linen sheet that was being gradually let down to the earth by four corners.

12) Luke continues: "in which there were," etc. We take it that the great sheet came to rest in front of Peter so that its contents were clearly visible to him and were within his reach: "all the four-footed and creeping things of the earth," first the neuter adjective and next the neuter noun, "and flying things of the heaven," another neuter adjective. The reason "the things swimming in the waters" are not included is because all the creatures were alive, and fish would not be alive in a sheet and out of the water. We need not translate, "all manner of," for the sense is plain without an interpretative rendering. The point of emphasis lies in this πάντα which includes creatures that were regarded as "unclean" as well as those that were regarded as "clean" by the Mosaic law. Here all of them were together in the same pure, clean, white linen sheet, all alike let down by invisible hands from the open heaven and thus from God himself.

13) Then came a voice, evidently out of heaven, we assume an angel's voice, which bade Peter slay and eat. The circumstantial ἀναστάς illustrates what we said on the use of this participle in 9:18. Note that θύω means, "to make go up in smoke" and thus, "to kill as a sacrifice to God," finally merely, "to slaughter or slay." It is God himself, then, who here abrogates the old Mosaic commands regarding clean and unclean animals and foods, and this is an illustration of the abrogation of all the Mosaic regulations regarding clean-

ness and uncleanness — a far-reaching command, indeed.

14) But here Peter reveals himself as the same character that is presented to us in John 13:8, where he refused to let Jesus wash his feet. So here he, too, refuses: "By no means, Lord! Because never yet did I eat anything common and unclean." To get the force of this answer note that μηδαμῶς, because of its μή, expresses Peters thought: "In no way let it be" with the optative of wish εἴη, or with the imperative to the same effect ἔστω; while οὐδέποτε with its οὐ states the negative fact: "never did I eat." If Peter had said οὐδαμῶς, the refusal would have been far more blunt: "In no way will I do it." Peter's is not a mild protest, nor is it a downright refusal; it is a shocked declining of the very idea. Why he is shocked he states with ὅτι, because during all his life he never ate a thing κοινόν, this to be understood as ἀκάθαρτον, "common" in the sense of "unclean," prohibited in the Mosaic regulations regarding food. The force of the reply is: "Goodness, Lord, do not ask me to do that!" Compare Lev. 11; Deut. 14. The Greek construes the negative particle οὐ in οὐδέποτε with the verb: "did *not* ever eat"; we combine it with the object: "I ate *nothing* ever." While it is like the Hebrew *lo — kol,* it is common in the Koine. R. 752.

This reaction of Peter's is most noteworthy as revealing to us the deep hold the old Jewish regulations about ceremonial cleanness had even upon the apostles, and how much was necessary to break this hold and to open the door of the church to the ceremonially unclean Gentiles. The Lord himself had to intervene as he here did in order to bring about the break that simply had to be made. It was revolutionary in the highest degree even for the apostles. Even they needed much time to recognize that all the ceremonial laws were only temporary, intended only for the old covenant, in force only until the Messiah should come, and not the divine will for all time. Peter answers the Lord because he knew that this was his command although an angel had uttered it.

15) The answer Peter receives is stunning and given in a tone of mighty warning. It is the same voice that replies although Luke again writes only "a voice"; "again a second time" is pleonastic, and the phrase with ἐκ is idiomatic. In negative commands with the present imperative an action already begun is ordered to stop, i. e., not to continue, R. 851, etc. So here: "Stop making common!" "What God made clean," God himself, actually made clean (aorist), refers, not to some present act, but to his act in abrogating all the Mosaic regulations through Christ who by his death and his resurrection fulfilled the promises of the old covenant and thus established the new; hence also the aorist, "did make clean."

All the old Mosaic regulations were to make Israel a separate people and prevent their intermingling with the pagans who surrounded them. They all served to preserve Israel and its treasured promises lest these latter be dissipated and lost. This was done, of course, in the interest of Israel but equally in the interest of the Gentile world, for the preservation was made for the sake of the human race. After the fulfillment had been wrought through Christ, its blessings were to go out to all nations. Israel's separation had served its purpose. The veil in the Temple was rent. "The middle wall of partition" had been broken down, Eph. 2:14; now there was "neither Jew nor Greek," Gal. 3:28; the old had decayed and vanished, the new had come in Christ, Heb. 8:13. A test was made in the matter of meats in the case of hungry Peter. He was warned to stop contradicting God by making unclean and unholy what God had relieved of this stigma and had thus cleansed. It sounds like an angel's word, for he is speaking of what God has done.

16) This occurred three times, and then the great sheet was suddenly received up into heaven. Did Peter refuse a second and even a third time after that first forceful warning? It seems so. Here there is shown the patience of the Lord in giving us time to adjust ourselves to the truth. Three questions were put to Peter in John 21:15, etc.; three prayers were uttered in Gethsemane; three times Paul besought the Lord to remove the thorn in his flesh, II Cor. 12:8. We often note threefold repetitions. Ordinary emphasis is attained by one repetition; the double repetition intensifies still more.

17) **Now, while Peter was greatly perplexed in himself as to what the vision he saw might mean, the men that had been sent by Cornelius, having inquired through for the house of Simon, stood at the portal and, having called out, were trying to learn whether Simon, called Peter, was lodging there. Now, Peter continuing to reflect concerning the vision, the Spirit said to him; Lo, three men are seeking thee. Now, then, having arisen, go down and be going with them in no respect doubting, because I myself have sent them.**

After the vision had ended, the imperfect compound with διά describes Peter as sitting there on the housetop "thoroughly perplexed." The idea is not that he did not understand the vision itself, namely as far as unclean animals were concerned; that was too obvious. Peter realized that the vision meant much more; "what it might be," i. e., it had him thoroughly unsettled. The indirect question with the optative and ἄν is the apodosis of a condition of potentiality and is retained unchanged from the direct question, the protasis, of course, being understood: "What might this be if it were explained?" What bearing did it have? What application should Peter make of this warning not to make common what God had cleansed?

The answer was to be found at the portal that led into the courtyard of the house. There were the men that had been commissioned (perfect participle: now acting on their commission) by Cornelius. The aorist participle states that they had succeeded in inquiring their way through (διά) to Simon's house which was along the seashore. Again we note that Simon could not have lived in a pretentious house. The portal was probably a passageway that led through the building itself into the inner yard.

18) Here they had called aloud until someone came and opened the doors, and at the moment they were trying to learn (the imperfect, although some texts have the aorist) whether the Simon who had the additional name Peter was lodging there.

19) Leaving them in that act, Luke takes us back to Peter who, in the genitive absolute, is pictured as still being engaged in reflection concerning the vision, i. e., concerning its import, the double compound (a hapaxlegomenon) signifying that his mind was going through and through (διά) and stopping in (ἐν) what he had seen in order to discover its full meaning. In the midst of this effort "the Spirit spoke to him" in the same way that Peter had often experienced, especially when he was directed to perform this or that miracle.

The words of the Spirit are actually stated in this case. Peter is not left to draw timid conclusions from the vision; the matter is so important in every way that the Spirit himself proceeds to show Peter the full bearing of the vision. "Lo, three men are seeking thee!" excludes the implication that Peter heard the men calling in the street below and overheard even his own name in the inquiry they made. No, this is the first information granted him. But so much is plain: the coming of these men is not accidental, their coming at just this moment is somehow connected with the vision and its real import. Some texts read "two," a few omit the numeral. These are variations that may be disregarded.

20) The claim that ἀλλά has an adversative force in all connections is naturally also made in the present instance, but this claim can be upheld only by inserting an adversative idea that Luke fails to indicate: "Three men are seeking thee; *but* (do not let yourself be sought and do not hesitate any longer, *on the contrary*), having arisen, go down!" But Peter had not been hesitating, had not been letting himself be sought; there is no "but" and "on the contrary," R's doubt in *W. P.* is groundless. This is the copulative ἀλλά which is described in R. 1185, etc.; it is continuative and adds an accessory idea and is to be translated "yea" or "now then." Peter's arising and going down now that he knows that these men are seeking him is to follow as a matter of course. Note another ἀναστάς (v. 13; 9:18), here it means as much as "hurry" and go down.

But he is to do more: he is not merely to go and to find out what they want, he is to accede to their request, to be going with them, and to do this by dismissing any misgivings on his part. The διακρινόμενος is in Peter's mind and not in his conduct (R., *W. P.*), and μηδέν is adverbial, "as to not a thing." It is very well to tell one not to waver in his own mind, to let nothing make him judge for himself now this way and now that way (διά, note also the middle voice); it is quite another thing to get a man's mind to the point where he will actually not do that. This other thing the Spirit accomplished with one simple stroke: "because I myself (emphatic ἐγώ) have sent them" (so that they are now here).

Here is the counterpart to "God" in v. 15: if God cleansed, Peter ought to be satisfied; if the Spirit said to go with these men, Peter ought to drop any misgivings about going. When we have God's authority, any scruples on our part insult God. On God's authority we must act even if we do not fully understand all that he commands or promises. Too often our trouble is that we invent his authority for what he does *not* want us to do; and when we do what he disapproves we refer it to him as having demanded it.

21) **And having gone down, Peter said to the men: Lo, I am the one whom you are seeking! What is the reason on account of which you are here? And they said: Cornelius, a centurion, a man righteous and fearing God, also attested by the whole nation of the Jews was directed by a holy angel to summon thee for himself to his house and to hear utterances from thee. Accordingly, having called them in, he lodged them.**

Peter now acts with perfect assurance. He introduces himself as the man they are seeking and, of course, is anxious to know the αἰτία, here "the reason" for which they are here. The Spirit had intimated nothing in regard to that point; all that was accomplished was to make the connection between Cornelius and Peter on the basis of Peter's vision. All else would follow in natural order step by step.

22) The men related their errand briefly. They introduce Cornelius fully so that Peter may exactly understand with whom he is dealing. What we know from v. 1, 2 is amplified. Now we have δίκαιος, "righteous," which is often disposed of with the remark that Cornelius observed the Jewish regulations. But he was not circumcised, he did not live kosher — a point of special importance in regard to Peter's visit at his house —he was not a full-fledged proselyte. This explanation of "righteous" will not do. The term is always forensic, it is exactly like the Hebrew *tzaddiq* and is well defined by C.-K. 309: he who is able to stand before God, whom God justifies, the God-fearing man. In this case the judge is God and not men, for they are spoken of separately. After adding the connection

with the synagogue the messengers state that Cornelius is "attested by the whole nation of the Jews," meaning, of course, the entire body of Jews in Cæsarea; "of good report" (A. V.), "well reported of" (R. V.) gives only the general sense of the participle.

This is the man who "was directed by a holy angel" to summon Peter. The verb means that he received a communication, and "by an angel" implies that God sent this word; there is no idea of "warning" as in our versions. The implication is only that Cornelius received directions in answer to petitions he had made. He was to summon Peter "to his house" — an important point; Peter is to enter this Gentile's house. Now, no strict Jew would think of doing such a thing because of the defilement involved. Here Peter began to see the real import of his vision. Peter is to lodge with this Gentile, to eat of his non-kosher food, etc. So all of this was contained in the vision of those many unclean animals and birds. And the Spirit had told him not to waver in regard to anything. This summons is to the effect that Cornelius may hear utterances from Peter, i. e., whatever the Spirit may give him to utter to a man such as this. In other words, here God was not only opening the door to the Gentiles for Peter but literally thrusting Peter in; he, too, was receiving directions from God and could not but comply.

23) The men had a long, hard trip behind them and, Gentiles though they were, Peter invited them into the house and lodged them for that day and the night, his own host also welcoming these guests. Yes, Peter had a great deal more than food to digest when, hungry as he was (v. 10), the meal that was in preparation (v. 10) was now served to him and to these three unexpected Gentile guests.

Now on the morrow, having arisen (circumstantial as in 9:18; 10:13, 20), **he went out with them, and some of the brethren from Joppa went along**

with him. And on the morrow they went into Caesarea.

The journey was begun the next morning, and six brethren from Joppa went along (11:12), which made a party of ten. We cannot say that Peter was fortifying himself with witnesses, for these men saw only what happened in Cæsarea after Peter had gotten there, and the important matters, the vision of Cornelius and that of Peter, were beyond their direct ken. The brethren went along because of their interest in what was transpiring.

24) They traveled all day, put up for the night, and arrived in Cæsarea the following day (see v. 30). We take it that everything had been planned in advance by Cornelius so that he knew just when his messengers and Peter would arrive.

And Cornelius was expecting them, having called together his relatives and close friends. If Peter had not been found or had not accompanied them, the messengers would probably have traveled all night and would thus have arrived that night. After the night had passed and they had not arrived, Cornelius was in high expectation and knew approximately when his men would return and bring Peter with them. So he summoned all his relatives and also his close friends. All these were alike in their faith, all had been informed in regard to what Cornelius had done, all were anxious to hear what message Peter would bring them. The congregation is assembled and is waiting eagerly for the preacher. One cannot but admire this Roman officer. He is the leader of this flock; many of them owed their faith to him and to his influence. Only one man is needed to start a congregation if he is at all the man he ought to be. We should like to have some details about these relatives and these friends. But that is the way with us, we always want to know more than is related.

25) At this point Codex Bezae and a few other codices read: "Now Peter coming near to Cæsarea, one of the slaves, having run forward, made clear that he had come; but Cornelius, having jumped forth and" — then continuing as in our text: "having met him, on having fallen down," etc. In spite of the fact that, according to v. 24, the travelers are already in the city while this reading still has them drawing near to it, Zahn regards this reading seriously. What follows also contradicts such a view. But Zahn maintains his hypothesis that Luke issued Acts in two editions, the first being represented in Codex Bezae. The many changes, additions, etc., in this first edition (see our introduction to Acts) receive considerable attention in Zahn's commentary but deserve little notice and most likely represent some ambitious scribe's effort to improve Luke's original.

Now, when it came to pass that Peter came in, having met him, Cornelius, on having fallen at his feet, did obeisance. But Peter raised him up, saying, Rise up; I myself also am a man!

Not on the street of the city or on the road to the city did this meeting occur (Zahn supposes the latter) but, as Luke here states, when Peter went in, namely into the house of Cornelius. Then, as was proper for the head of the house, Cornelius met Peter in what we may call his reception room. Note that we have three εἰσελθεῖν: in v. 24 they go into Cæsarea; in v. 25 Peter goes into the house of Cornelius; in v. 27 Peter and his host go into the room where the assembly is waiting for them. All this follows in proper sequence, but Codex Bezae alters it in order to introduce its addition in regard to the slave's running in and Cornelius' leaping up and running out of the city, etc.

The construction ἐγένετο with the subject τοῦ εἰσελθεῖν τὸν Πέτρον was rather difficult for the older grammarians. Winer calls it a construction that drives the infinitive with τοῦ beyond all bounds and shakes his head at a man like Luke for using it. Meyer speaks of the impossibility of explaining this use of the infinitive in a rational manner and calls it a lone instance of a linguistic *Fehlgriff*. But such views are a thing of the past. B.-D. finds that τοῦ may be added pleonastically to nearly any infinitive but that a ὅτι sentence cannot be converted into such an infinitive, this being possible only with regard to ἵνα and ὥστε clauses. So one breathes easier. R. 1067, etc., regards this infinitive with τοῦ which is used as a subject as a Hebraism and finds examples in the LXX and elsewhere. Other explanations may be disregarded. Compare Luke 17:1, and I Cor. 16:4. The genitive force of τοῦ has been lost.

Cornelius falls at the feet of Peter and thus makes obeisance to him as to a supernatural messenger sent to him from God. This is the first time Peter had such an experience. The translation of our versions, "worshipped him," is misleading unless we remember the inferior sense of this verb in many connections, even as "your worship" is only a title of honor for magistrates, etc. Cornelius was not paying divine honor to Peter but was going beyond the limit that a minister of God or even an angel can accept, Rev. 19:10, etc.; 22:8, etc. This act of Cornelius' does all credit to his humble and willing spirit; but Peter's refusal to accept such an honor does equal credit to him. In great St. Peter's in Rome they still kiss the big toe of the bronze statue of St. Peter; the writer saw a woman and her baby in the act, and if the guide, a learned Italian professor, may be believed, that bronze toe is kissed away and has to be renewed about every so often. Peter ought to visit St. Peter's.

26) Peter promptly raised Cornelius with the peremptory aorist imperative, "Rise up!" and added that he himself was only a man, ἄνθρωπος, a human being. Let all dignitaries in church and in state remember

that. Orientals are far more demonstrative by bowing down their faces to the earth than we Occidentals are. This discounts the obeisance on the part of Cornelius but yet leaves it too strong for Peter.

27) **And conversing with him, he went in and finds many having come together and said to them: You on your part understand how unlawful it is for a man, a Jew, to be in close contact with or to be visiting with one of another nation. And yet to me God showed to declare no man common or unclean; wherefore also without gainsaying I came on being summoned. Accordingly, I ask for what reason you summoned me.**

A beautiful picture: Peter and Cornelius in conversation as they enter the larger room where the whole company sat as an audience. Luke uses the historical (aoristic) present: Peter "finds many having come together." So many that it surprised him. The messengers had not told him that, and Cornelius had probably just mentioned the fact that others were in the room into which he led Peter.

28, 29) In a simple but very direct fashion Peter explains his presence in the house of a Gentile, in contact with this Gentile audience. Note the pivotal points: *you* know — yet to *me* God showed — wherefore I came —— accordingly I ask. Since all Peter's hearers know that it is ἀθέμιτον for any man who is a Jew (the second noun is predicative to the first) to maintain close association with one of another nation, i. e., a non-Jew, or even to be going to him, i. e., keep visiting him, they will naturally want to know how Peter, a Jew, can enter among them for an association that because of its nature must be close, in fact, very close. From the Jewish standpoint such conduct would, indeed, be entirely contrary to law and custom. The κολλᾶσθαι, "to glue oneself to," refers to close association, and προσέρχεσθαι, going to someone, both being durative, to making a practice of such actions, the second being less serious than the first. The Mosaic law had no specific prohibition to this effect, but the entire law with all its regulations had such a prohibition as a result. The man who acted otherwise was going contrary, not to one item of the law, but to the law in its entirety. This was thoroughly understood in Judaism, and Peter takes it for granted that these Gentiles, too, know all about it.

Exceptions are sometimes cited, but King Izates, mentioned in Josephus, *Ant.* 20, 2, 4, etc., is not a true exception, nor are the other cases of making Jewish proselytes. The assumption that the rule of strict separation did not apply to proselytes of the gate, hence not to Cornelius, is mistaken. Why does Peter then speak as he does? Only proselytes of righteousness (of the Sanctuary) were considered the equals of Jews, and the rabbis often spoke very slightingly even of these, as when they were called *sicut scabies Israeli.* The rule of exclusiveness here stated by Peter was not merely a piece of Pharisaic rigorousness, it was the general rule of Judaism. And the rule itself was general and not to be reduced to the regulation that no Jew was to go to Gentiles of his own accord, which would excuse Peter who had been summoned. Peter says to this assembly: "You know what the law is for Jews in this matter, and you see me here in this house and in your company in direct contravention of this law."

Peter confesses that he would never voluntarily have gone contrary to that fixed principle of Judaism, Christian though he now was. It was God who showed him (in the vision) to declare no man common or unclean in the Jewish sense. On the two adjectives see v. 14, 15, and note that Peter is practically quoting and therefore used μηδένα and not οὐδένα. Καί is copulative and yet connects adversative clauses; we do not use "and" in that way and hence translate "and yet." The Greek mind was nimble enough not to need more than καί, which explains what we may call its idiomatic use. "To me," Peter says, God showed; hence without demurring, I came on being summoned. Peter is acting on divine orders; he himself has them apart from what God had communicated to Cornelius. Since these things are now clear, Peter asks for what reason he was summoned, λόγος being used in the sense of "reason" and not of "intent."

30) **And Cornelius said: Four days ago, until this hour I was praying, the ninth hour, in my house; and lo, a man stood before me in brilliant apparel and says: Cornelius, thy prayer was heard and thy alms were remembered before God. Send, therefore, to Joppa and call unto thee Simon who is also called Peter; he is lodging in Simon's, the tanner's, house by the sea. Forthwith, therefore, I sent for thee; and thou on thy part didst well in having come. Now, therefore, we all on our part are here present before God to hear all things, that have been commanded to thee by the Lord.**

The sum of what Peter and Cornelius state before the assembled company is that God himself has arranged this meeting for them. God himself was here opening the door of his church to the entire Gentile world wholly apart from Judaism and the synagogue. That is the feature of the history that Luke here sees and leads his reader to see. This is something that by far transcends Cornelius and Peter, something that must be understood in that light. The phrase with ἀπό is idiomatic and is similar to the use of ἐκ; the Greek always counts forward from the remoter end to himself, we do the reverse. "From the fourth day" = starting at that point. On that day Cornelius was praying "up to this hour" of the day, the time of day that it was now when he was speaking; and by "this hour" he means "the ninth" (v. 3), three o'clock in the afternoon. R. 471 notes that in μέχρι ταύτης τῆς ὥρας we have point of time which is then explained as denoting the entire "ninth hour" by the accusative τὴν ἐννάτην (ὥραν); this, however, is not the object of the participle ("keeping the ninth hour of prayer," R. V.) but merely denotes extent of time: praying that long. Fasting (A. V.) is not in the accepted text. "In my house" means in private devotion, all alone, and not in the local synagogue.

31) Cornelius describes the angel who suddenly stood before him as "a man," which agrees with all the other passages that mention angels, Mark 16:5, "a young man," Luke 24:4, "two men," etc. Although the angels are sexless, they never appear in the form of a woman or of a child (cherubs) but in a form that symbolizes power and authority, a point that ought to be noted when angels are portrayed in church decorations. So also the "brilliant apparel," pure white as is sometimes noted, shining with superearthly radiance, symbolizes holiness. Cornelius retells what the angel had said about his prayer and his alms in v. 4.

32) Then he repeats the order he had received to call Peter from the tanner's house in Joppa. Here the point must not be overlooked that Peter is to come to this Gentile's house. He was already at a tanner's house, at the home of a man who was considered unclean from the Jewish standpoint because he handled hides; he is to go much farther: the one step was to lead to the next, to the one that was really important for the spread of the gospel.

33) Cornelius complied with the angel's orders very promptly and expresses his happiness that Peter, too, came so readily. R., *W. P.*, calls καλῶς ποιεῖν a regular formula for expressing thanks (Phil. 4:14; II Pet. 1:19; III John 6), the participle neatly bringing out the act for which thanks are extended. The sense is: "We certainly thank thee for having come." And now,

in a fine conclusion Cornelius adds: "Here we all are to hear what thou hast to tell us!" Every word and every turn of expression is important.

"Now" the great moment has come to which all these supernatural communications have led. "We all on our part are present here" (note παρά), eager and anxious, ἀκοῦσαι, aorist, to hear effectively and thus hearing to obey. "In the presence of God" with his eyes resting upon us voices the faith that all these Gentiles had received in their hearts because of their connection with the synagogue. Cornelius indicates his military training when he says, "All things that have been commanded thee by the Lord," the perfect participle implying that they stand as the Lord's permanent orders. As military orders, especialy those of the commander-in-chief, are obeyed without question, so Cornelius and all those present intend to obey what the Lord (here referring to God) will communicate to them through Peter.

This is, indeed, a model congregation, model in its attitude toward God, toward his Word, and toward his minister. Here there is true willingness to receive, believe, and obey. Here there is no "if" or "but"; they will accept "all things." Why? They come from the Lord God. Here there is implicit faith, which, however, rests, as it must, on the explicit. They do not as yet know what Peter will say but they do know that what he will say comes from God, and so they are willing to believe.

When this example is held up to our congregations, let it not be overlooked that our congregations must have the same assurance regarding their preachers, that what they say is, indeed, "all that has been commanded to them by the Lord." For with this expression Cornelius paints the model preacher.

34) **And having opened his mouth** (the sonorous formula for proceeding to an important address),

Peter said: Of a truth I am comprehending that God is not a respecter of persons, but in every nation the one fearing him and working righteousness is acceptable to him. The Word which he sent to the sons of Israel, proclaiming as good news peace through Jesus Christ, this is Lord of all.

Luke first mentions two preliminary statements that are parallel to each other and decisive for all that follows, one about God and one about his gospel Word. Peter confesses that "of a truth," literally, "on the basis of reality," he is comprehending (simple progressive present), grasping more and more that God is not a respecter of persons, partial to the Jew merely because he is a Jew, unfair to the Gentile just because he is a Gentile. Προσωπολήμπτης occurs only here and in Chrysostom, but its cognates are used; it refers to a judge who looks at a man's face and renders a verdict, not in accord with the merits of the case, but according as he likes or dislikes the man. The notion of bribery does not lie in the word.

35) In reality God does the contrary (ἀλλά): "in every nation" he accepts only those who fear him and work righteousness. Jew and Gentile who fail to do so he rejects. God is a just Judge. This is the fear of which both Testaments speak constantly, the mark of godly men, the fear of reverence, faith, obedience. And ὁ Θεός is the true God who reveals himself in the Scriptures and not God as some imagine him according to the formula:

> *Jud', Heid' und Hottentott,*
> *Wir glauben all' an einen Gott.*

Both "God" and this "fearing" are definitely revealed in the Word, and neither term is to be determined by men. A wrong conception of God involves a wrong conception of what fearing God means; and vice versa. No greater insult can be offered to God than to disregard his Word concerning himself and our relation to him. In no way does Peter say or imply that a pagan who is serious about what he is pleased to call god is accepted by God.

The first participial designation would suffice, but a second is added in order to make the matter still clearer. Both participles are present, durative, qualitative, substantivized by the article. We have both ὁ ποιῶν and ὁ ἐργαζόμενος δικαιοσύνην with no difference in sense; they are allied to similar expressions such as "pursuing righteousness, faith, love." Thus an attitude of life is referred to, one that is bent on securing "righteousness," a quality of soul and of life that God's verdict approves.

This is far more than doing single deeds and something totally different from doing deeds that men in their verdict are pleased to judge as righteous. See C.-K. 315. The sinner does righteousness when he repents, and a mark of this condition of righteousness is daily contrition and repentance. The contrite sinner does righteousness when he believes and accepts God's pardon in Christ Jesus, and the mark of this condition of righteousness is faith daily renewed. The believer does righteousness when by faith he runs the way of God's commandments, follows in the footsteps of Jesus, bows to the first table of the law and then also to the second.

Doing righteousness is not the simple matter that some make it. Let them look at Cornelius! If his honest pagan convictions had been sufficient, why did he seek the synagogue? If the synagogue had been enough, why was Peter here? A few moral rules of life apart from the Triune God, without Jesus, the Redeemer, are a travesty on Peter's words and will bring tragedy to their advocates. The verbal adjective δεκτός, "one received," refers to God's judgment.

36) As Peter's view is broadening in its true comprehension of God, so also is it in its true comprehension of God's gospel Word. No man can fear God and work righteousness and be accepted by God without the gospel, that gospel as a promise of the Messiah in the old covenant and as fulfillment in Jesus in the new. Peter says that God commissioned this Word, sent it with a message (ἀπέστειλε) to the sons of Israel, "sons" (not "children," our versions). The connotation in "sons" is valuable: these were the legal heirs of Israel who inherited his position and prerogatives in the covenant (see the term in 5:21; 7:23, 37; 9:15; it always has the same high connotation). Not because they were "children" and dear to Israel (τέκνα) but because they were the "sons" and heirs of Israel (υἱοί) did God send his great gospel of Christ to the Jews, and being "sons," they had the high and holy obligation to be like their father Israel in faith.

When he describes this Word and its contents, Peter says of it: "proclaiming as good news peace through Jesus Christ." This is the εἰρήνη, Hebrew *shalom*, of which Jesus Christ, in his person and his office combined (see 2:38), is the Mediator (διά). He purchased and won this "peace," the fruit of his salvation, and bestows it by proclaiming the good news of it, which εὐαγγελίζεσθαι of the Word awakens and is intended for faith. Since it is here used in connection with "the Word" and the verb "gospelizing," "peace" must refer to the saving peace of salvation for sinners when God accepts the sinner for Christ's sake and remits all his sins. This mighty statement should not be toned down by introducing peace between Jew and Gentile, between nation and nation, man and man.

With the resumptive οὗτος Peter declares, "This (i. e., Word) is Lord of all" (i. e., of all men), namely of Jew and Gentile alike. It and it alone is the divine Ruler of men; it alone directs, guides, blesses them.

The emphasis is strongly on this last predicate "Lord of all" which includes also the Gentile world. As Christ is our saving, beneficent Lord, so is his gospel which brings him to us. It is "the gospel of peace" (Eph. 6:15), of peace with God, and rules our hearts in such a way that we enjoy the fulness of this peace. What a glorious thought: all men under this one Lord, the Word which proclaims peace! A few of the fathers thought that "Word" signified the Logos as sent to the sons of Israel, but that would illy fit the context.

Our versions with their parenthesis and their labored construction of this and the following verse, and still more the grammars with their efforts at construing these verses which lead them even to amend the assured reading of the text, exhibit the confusion that has resulted from failure to understand what Peter says. B.-D. 162, 7 and 295 reject Κύριος when not a single text exists without it; some texts omit ὅν. The parenthesis is peculiarly unfortunate and makes the statement a side-issue, namely that Jesus Christ is Lord of all. What perplexed so many is the accusative τὸν λόγον at the beginning of the verse; they thought that this was intended as the object of οἴδατε in v. 37 and did not hesitate to make ῥῆμα its synonym (our versions, for instance). Τὸν λόγον is accusative by inverse attraction to its relative, of which construction there are many other examples, I Cor. 10:16; Matt. 21:42. This usage is so common that it should have been readily recognized, likewise that οὗτος is resumptive as it is in a number of cases and so plainly resumes all that has been said about this λόγος that was sent to Israel.

37) After the two great opening statements in regard to God and the gospel, which voice the heart of what Peter has to say to his Gentile hearers, he launches into the body of his address. That is why he uses no connective and thus indicates that his main discourse now begins. **You yourselves know the**

utterance that came down through the whole of Judea, having begun from Galilee after the baptism which John heralded, Jesus from Nazareth, how God anointed him with the Holy Spirit and power, who went from place to place doing good and healing all those tyrannized by the devil because God was with him. And we, we are witnesses of all things which he did both in the country of the Jews and in Jerusalem.

Peter reviews briefly what his hearers already know and contrasts ὑμεῖς with the ἡμεῖς occurring in v. 39: "*You,* you know all this; *we,* we were the actual witnesses of all this and can thus testify and assure you that you heard the truth." They heard the ῥῆμα, "the utterance" that men made when they told what follows; this talk went through the whole of Judea after starting with great volume from Galilee after John the Baptist preached his baptism and had thereby prepared the way. The news was spread abroad in exactly such a manner. It began after John had come, started with great volume from Galilee, then filled all Judea. The τὸ ῥῆμα does not resume and continue the τὸν λόγον of v. 36. The latter refers to the gospel itself with all its contents while the former means that men spoke and were not silent but told about Jesus.

But ἀρξάμενος causes the grammarians and the exegetes some difficulty. Zahn thinks that it is a solecism; others decide for the neuter and have a few texts to support them (B.-D. 137, 3) but fail to explain why the masculine appears in all the other texts. Although the participle is masculine it modifies the neuter τὸ ῥῆμα. We have the same phenomenon in Luke 24:47, where the same participle is in the nominative when the construction demands the accusative. The masculine nominative is retained unaltered in the Greek and is neither solecism nor anacoluthon (R., *W. P.*, and 413); πλήρης is similarly retained without being declined.

38) "Jesus from Nazareth" does not depend on οἴδατε in v. 37, for it is the object of ἔχρισεν and is proleptic for the sake of emphasis, and αὐτόν is pleonastically inserted where the name would otherwise be placed. The clause with ὡς is in apposition with τὸ ῥῆμα. The news that passed from mouth to mouth and filled the land was: "How God anointed him — Jesus from Nazareth — with the Holy Spirit and power." That anointing took place immediately after the baptism of Jesus. The verb is the historical aorist and reports the one act of anointing and uses the sacred, ceremonial verb χρίω (not ἀλείφω). This verb does not refer to the Incarnation or to Nazareth (Luke 4:14) because Jesus is here said to be from Nazareth, or in a general way to the entire life of Jesus.

Peter is speaking to Gentiles who have come into contact with the synagogue; they seem to need no explanation in regard to the Holy Spirit and how that Spirit could anoint Jesus. The Old Testament must be far clearer in regard to the three Persons of the Godhead than the critics are willing to admit. With the Holy Spirit "and power" makes emphatic the feature of the anointing that was so prominent in all the work of Jesus: he was full of power. The Spirit and the power had come upon him. This refers to his human nature. Peter says still more, namely, that God was with him. Thus all three Persons cooperated in our redemption. We see no reason why the miraculous anointing of Jesus could not have been generally known and reported as Peter here states. Those who witnessed it certainly told others.

The Greek often uses the relative pronoun in an emphatic manner where we should begin a new sentence. So here and again in v. 39 we have: "who" = "he who," he was the one who went from place to place (διά in the verb) "doing good and (to be specific) healing (even the worst imaginable ailment) all those tyrannized by the devil." In this graphic way the demoniacs are described. It is the physician Luke who records these words; compare 5:16; 8:7; and the entire subject as discussed in connection with Matt. 4:24; 8:28; Mark 1:23; Luke 4:33. Peter ascribes demoniacal possession to the devil, διάβολος ("slanderer"), the head of the hellish kingdom who acts through his spirit subjects. All that Jesus did showed that "God was with him," μετά, in company with him; compare Luke 1:66; John 3:2; and the great statements of Jesus himself, John 8:16, 29; 10:30; and many others. Peter is showing his hearers the man "Jesus from Nazareth" of whom all men spoke at the time he was on earth and reveals his connection with God.

39) Now the emphatic ἡμεῖς. Peter's hearers only knew. Peter and the other apostles — for of these he speaks and not of the six brethren from Joppa — had been actual eyewitnesses inasmuch as they had themselves seen "all things which he did both in the land of the Jews (in general) and in Jerusalem (the capital, in particular)"; ὧν is attracted from ἅ. With this emphatic "we" Peter assures his hearers of the full truth of what they thus know about Jesus.

Whom also they made away with by hanging him on wood. This one God raised up on the third day and gave him to become manifest, not to all the people, but to witnesses designated beforehand by God, to us, such as ate with him and drank with him after that he arose from the dead.

Peter does not say that his hearers know also these things. They knew that Jesus had been crucified. But Peter prefers to consider the death and the resurrection as a unit and, apart from anything his hearers had heard, himself to present this part of the gospel story. The pronoun "whom," like the one used in v. 38, is emphatic and really begins a new sentence: "him, whom," he it was whom they made away with, (ἀνεῖλον), the verb we have met so repeatedly. Καί = even this they did, leaving the subject of this frightful deed unnamed, "they," yes, "they." But he adds the aorist participle of means: "by hanging him on wood" as one who was accursed in the eyes of all Jews; see the explanation in 5:30, and the explanation in Gal. 3:13. We feel the throbbing contrasts that we have seen Peter use against the Sanhedrin and the Jews (2:36; 3:13-15; 4:10; 5:30, 31): *God* anointed him, *God* was with him, but they *even* made away with him, and then *God* raised him up. Here only καί points to the contrast. Peter shows no bitterness toward the Jews who killed Jesus.

40) With a decidedly emphatic resumptive τοῦτον, "this one," which includes all that has thus far been said about Jesus, especially what was said about his being killed as being accursed, Peter states the great fact of the resurrection of Jesus and the evidence for that fact. The fact is simply that "God raised him up on the third day," here ascribing the resurrection to God, in v. 41 to Jesus himself. Both are equally true since all the *opera ad extra sunt indivisa aut communa* according to Scripture testimony. God did more: "he gave him to become manifest," i. e., granted that Jesus appeared. This was not a gift to Jesus but, as the following datives state, a gift to us. The manifestations of the resurrection continued for forty days in the repeated appearances of the risen Savior.

41) Peter tells this very carefully. Someone may ask why everybody did not see the risen Jesus. Peter says that God gave his being manifest "not to all the people." These manifestations were intended for the specific purpose of attesting the resurrection of Jesus to the whole world, attesting it beyond a doubt. God could not use anybody and everybody for that task and high honor. When the people who wanted Jesus hung on wood as being accursed heard from the Roman sol-

diers at the tomb how Jesus had arisen, they bribed these indirect witnesses to lie and to deny the resurrection. People, who in spite of all that they had seen and heard of Jesus had, nevertheless, refused to have faith in him, were unfit to be witnesses of his resurrection, and an appearance of Jesus to them would have increased their unbelief by that much. God thus chose his own witnesses. The participle states that he selected them with his own hand, for they had to be prepared and qualified properly to attest the resurrection.

"To us," Peter says, God gave Jesus to become manifest. The pronoun is emphatic by position, "to us," his believers, 500 at one time, I Cor. 15:6, in particular to the apostles to whom Jesus showed himself repeatedly and before whom he ascended to heaven. How complete and how intimate this manifestation was Peter indicates by means of the relative clause: "such as ate with him and drank with him after that he arose from the dead." Οἵτινες is to be construed with "we" in the inflectional endings of the verbs, and the eating and drinking refer to Luke's own statements made in 1:4; Luke 24:42. In fact, Peter here speaks as though eating and drinking may have gone beyond what these passages state.

Peter is now acting the witness. He is so specific and exact in his testimony that these Gentile hearers of his who may have heard something about the resurrection of Jesus shall now receive solid assurance. Peter's testimony is that of an eyewitness. In I Cor. 15:4-8 Paul lists the essential witnesses on whose testimony our faith rests. Here Peter ascribes the resurrection to Jesus himself; on ἐκ νεκρῶν and its misinterpretation see 3:16.

42) **And he charged us to herald to the people and to attest that this One is he that has been ordained by God as Judge of quick and dead. To**

this One all the prophets bear witness that every one believing in him receives through his name remission of sins.

Peter means that Jesus gave the order to the apostles to herald, etc. In v. 40, God is the subject and he might be the subject also here in v. 42 if it were not for the following phrase "by God." Both infinitives are effective aorists: "to herald and attest" so that the work is thoroughly, effectively done and leaves nothing to be added.

Κηρύσσειν means to proclaim aloud as a herald, to make an announcement, "to preach" in this sense. The herald announces what he is ordered to announce, no more, no less, and without alteration. That remains the preacher's task to this day although many think that they are authorized to herald their own ideas. Only one message has the Lord's authorization. Any alteration of that message, any substitution for it, is not only empty but, when it pretends to be the Lord's true message, makes the herald who proclaims it a liar, a false prophet.

When Peter says τῷ λαῷ and uses the same word that occurs in v. 41, the reference is to Israel, λαός being steadily used in this restricted sense; "the people" is not to be understood in the sense of men in general, the word for this would be ἄνθρωποι. Peter refers to 1:8, the command to begin preaching in Jerusalem and in Judea, i. e., among the Jews. The idea to be expressed is that thus far and by the Lord's own direction the heralding has been limited to "the people," the Jews, as it was, indeed, natural that it should be. This heralding was to be an attesting, the depositions of sworn witnesses as though they were under oath to God.

The climax of their heralding and solemn (διά) attestation was to be "that this One is he that has been ordained by God as Judge of quick and dead." Here the deictic οὗτος is again resumptive and gathers up all that Peter has said about "Jesus from Nazareth." He whom God anointed, etc., whom God raised from the dead and gave to be manifest as risen — he is the One, he alone, who has been ordained and stands as thus ordained (this is the force of the perfect participle) by God as Judge of quick and dead. He who by his death and his resurrection redeemed men shall at the last day judge them as to whether they accepted his redemption or not. A natural, yea, an essential connection demands this ordination or appointment of Jesus as the final Judge.

It should be evident that this ordination pertains to his human nature even as Peter used the human name "Jesus from Nazareth." "For . . . to have all judgment . . . are not created gifts, but divine, infinite properties, and yet these have been given and communicated to the man Christ . . . . what Holy Scripture testifies that Christ received in time he received not according to the divine nature (according to which he has everything from eternity), but the person has received it in time *ratione et respectu humanae naturae,* that is, as referring, and with respect to, according to the assumed human nature." *C. Tr.* 1033 etc., 55, etc. John 5:22 and especially 27; Acts 17:31.

"Quick and dead" need no articles (R. 419), they are like other pairs. The "quick," "living," are those who shall still be alive at the end of the world. "Quick and dead" put it beyond question that Peter is speaking of the final judgment. Yet even here Peter is not stressing the universality of the gospel and of Jesus' work. He is stating only the great acts of God regarding Jesus. How they apply to his present Gentile hearers who are in a class other than the Jews, Peter made plain in his very first sentence (v. 34).

43) The note of universality struck at the start resounds again at the end of the address. **Τούτῳ** is now

more emphatic than ever as embracing all that has thus far been said regarding Jesus, *"to this One,"* yea, to Him, all the prophets of the Old Testament who were known to Cornelius and all these Gentiles through the LXX bear witness that he and he alone is the Savior. The object of μαρτυροῦσιν is the clause with the accusative and infinitive which summarily states what all the prophets testify and is thus in indirect discourse. All the prophets unite in saying that "remission of sins receives through his name everyone believing in him." This is the Greek word order which places a strong emphasis on both object and subject by putting the former first and the latter last — read it aloud in order to get the effect. See the discussion of ἄφεσις in 2:38. This complete riddance of sin and guilt is received by every believer through Jesus' name.

The aorist λαβεῖν is used to indicate the one effective act of receiving. Remission and riddance of sins are bestowed on him by God, and thus he has them. The reception is effected "through his name," διά presenting his Name as the medium that effects the remission. It is, of course, the objective medium, God's great means for ridding the sinner of his guilt. It is essential, however, to see what ὄνομα means. Review the term as it is discussed in 2:31, 38; 3:6, and in the following passages. In all of them it is the revelation which brings Jesus and his person and his saving work to the sinner. In all these phrases and connections the "name" does not mean "authority" or "power." Compare what C.K. has to say on pages 800 and 803: God's name = "what God is as the God of the saving *revelation*", praying in Jesus' name = on the basis of and in connection with what has *unveiled* itself in Jesus. C.-K. also discusses the latest literature on the subject, omitting, however, S. Goebel, *Die Reden unseres Herrn nach Johannes*, II, 120, which is especially fine.

No remission is possible except "through his name." But this *name* as the revelation of what Jesus is and what he did and thus is for us always has as its correlative *faith,* the knowledge of this name and the confidence of the heart which embraces all that this conveys and clings to it and relies upon it in life and in death. Faith is thus the subjective means of remission. Peter says that "everyone believing in him" receives remission, the present participle is subtantivized and describes the person as continuing in faith. The name with all that it embraces and reveals produces this confidence by deserving in the highest degree that all sinners rely upon it and upon it alone for remission. When Peter says "everyone believing" he reverts to v. 34, and gently but most effectively opens the door of the gospel and of the Christian Church to the Gentiles sitting before him in rapt attention. It was, indeed, a great hour in the progress of the gospel!

44) **While Peter was still uttering these utterances, the Holy Spirit fell upon all those hearing the Word. And amazed were the believers of the circumcision, as many as came with Peter, that also upon the Gentiles the gift of the Holy Spirit was being poured out. For they began to hear them speaking with tongues and magnifying God.**

Here we see how God himself finished the work which he had inaugurated and directed from the beginning. In 11:15, Peter says that the Holy Spirit descended "when I began to speak"; he had intended to say much more, but all that he had to reserve until some later time. God spoke in his own mighty way at this point by sending the Holy Spirit upon these Gentiles. The verb "fell" denotes the suddenness and also the descent from above.

45) Before Luke continues the narrative proper he records the amazement of the six Jewish Christians who had come from Joppa with Peter. They are dumb-

founded "because the gift of the Holy Spirit is being poured out also upon the Gentiles." The Greek retains the present tense "is being poured out" of the direct discourse of these Jewish believers; but it includes more than this one instance of outpouring and states that as a general thing, as this striking case shows, the Gentiles were receiving "the gift of the Holy Spirit," i. e., were by God himself being placed on a par with all believers from Judaism. That was the astounding thing. It was God and God alone and most directly who gave "the gift." At this time he preferred to dispense with the laying on of hands (8:17); he did not even wait until these Gentiles had been baptized. That is a minor point. At Pentecost the 3,000 received the Spirit charismatically neither before nor after their baptism. The Pentecostal charisma was never repeated in the congregation at Jerusalem. There were signs and miracles many but no speaking with tongues.

Confusion has resulted by failing to notice that "the gift of the Holy Spirit" referred to at this point is the same gift that was bestowed at the time of Pentecost, a charisma, and only a charisma and not the gift of the Spirit, and certainly not the gift of sudden total sanctification. All those who spoke with tongues at the time of Pentecost were already saved, and none of those who were saved that day received the Spirit miraculously and spoke with tongues. All those who heard Peter in the house of Cornelius had faith and were saved before the Spirit came and gave them the ability to speak with tongues. The same is true with regard to the Samaritans, 8:15-17. This falling of the Spirit upon people, this charismatic gift of the Spirit, is entirely separate from the Spirit's reception by faith for salvation and by baptism for regeneration and renewing (Tit. 3:5).

When this is understood, Luke's account will not be referred to in order to deprive baptism of its saving power as though the Spirit comes apart from and without baptism, and as though baptism is only an empty symbol and sign. Peter did not regard baptism thus in the present instance. Since these Jewish Christians called the charismatic gift of the Spirit a pouring out, some say it was "the baptism of the Spirit," or "that these Gentiles were baptized with the Spirit." That may pass but only as long as this "baptism" is viewed as charismatic and as nothing more.

46) With γάρ Luke explains "the gift of the Holy Spirit": Peter and his companions "began to hear them speaking with tongues," ἤκουον, the inchoative imperfect. Note αὐτῶν λαλούντων γλώσσαις, and in 2:4, λαλεῖν ἑτέραις γλώσσαις; then also μεγαλυνόντων τὸν Θεόν, "magnifying God," and in 2:11, τὰ μεγαλεῖα τοῦ Θεοῦ — the language is strikingly similar. We have these three in a direct line: 2:2-13; 8:15-17; and now 10:44-46. The miracle is the same, a sudden speaking in languages the speakers had never learned, first by Jewish, secondly by Samaritan, and now thirdly by Gentile Christians, the plain intention being to show that God made no difference between them, in particular by placing the Samaritan and the Gentile believers on a par with the Jewish believers. One Spirit — many tongues!

But some do not share this view. In 2:4, Luke writes ἑτέραις: they spoke with *"other"* tongues; and here he leaves out this adjective. So in Jerusalem the speaking was done in "other" human languages, but here in Cæsarea in no human languages. There were *two* kinds of speaking with tongues. And this argument is based on the omission of the word "other." But what, then, were these tongues if they were not "other" human languages? Various suggestions are offered, but none of them are acceptable.

We have discussed this subject in connection with 2:4 and find full confirmation here. Peter and Cornelius must have spoken in Greek, and Peter's speech must have been made in that language. And now first one and then another — certainly not several in a babel — "magnified God" by speaking in some other and strange language, one in this, another in some other. This phenomenon occurred again in 19:6. The identity of the occurrence with that of Pentecost is placed beyond question by 15:8: "giving them the Holy Spirit, even as unto us" at Pentecost; also in 11:15-17. At Cæsarea, however, no strangers were at hand to be impressed by the miracle of tongues. The object of the miracle was different, namely to reveal to all present how God "made no distinction between us (Jewish believers) and them (Gentile believers)," 15:9.

47) **Then answered Peter, Can anyone forbid the water so that these be not baptized, such as received the Holy Spirit as also we ourselves? And he ordered that they be baptized in the name of Jesus Christ. Then they requested him to remain for some days.**

"Answered," as frequently, is used in the wider sense of responding to a situation. "Certainly no one can forbid," etc., μήτι, the interrogative particle, expects a negative answer. Peter asks whether anyone is able to hinder it that the water necessary to baptize these Gentiles be brought and the sacrament be duly administered. Was anyone able to offer valid objection? He was sure that no one was able.

The verb of hindering, κωλύειν, is construed with τοῦ μή and the infinitive, but the sense with μή is: "so that not" (B.-D. 400, 4), it is consecutive; μή is omitted when the infinitive is unmodified (B.-D. 392, 1), and sometimes μή seems redundant according to us (B.-D. 429). This is more exact than R., *W. P.*, that the negative may or may not appear after a verb of hindering.

Οἵτινες is causal: "since they received," etc., R. 728. It is God himself who makes Peter so certain, for he had given these Gentiles the Holy Spirit. "As also we ourselves," and again in 11:15, "as on us at the beginning," also the context of 11:15-17, are decisive as far as the miracle of Pentecost and this one here in Cæsarea are concerned: they are identical.

When Knowling interprets, "The greater had been bestowed; could the lesser be withheld?" he has reversed the two. Paul regards the gift of tongues as being the least of all and shows the Corinthians something far better, I Cor. 12:31. Baptism with its regenerating and renewing grace (Tit. 3:5) vastly excels the transient speaking with tongues. Peter makes no wrong comparison in his question. He implies that the gift of tongues is God's indication that these Gentiles are just as acceptable to him as the Jews (v. 34, 35), therefore baptism and Christianity are intended for them. We should not confuse the gift of the Spirit, which is but a transient charisma, with the gift of the Spirit in and through Word and sacrament, which is permanent and eternal salvation.

When Peter asks about someone hindering the water he is not thinking of the Mediterranean or some body of water but of water to be brought in; somebody might try to prevent its being brought in. We may hinder a person from going to a body of water but never the body of water itself. Peter's question does not suggest immersion. It sounds as though the whole company was promptly baptized with water that had been brought into the room where all were assembled.

48) The aorist verbs and infinitives imply that what they speak of was done. We should note the passive, "that they be baptized," and that Peter does not say "to baptize them," active. We give an order to do something and not that something be done. It is this passive infinitive that prevents us from agreeing with those who say that Peter ordered the disciples from Joppa who had accompanied him to baptize these Gentiles and then cite I Cor. 1:16, and John 4:2, with the

remark that the apostles considered it less their duty to baptize than to preach, and overlook the fact that this does not agree with Matt. 28:19, where Jesus puts baptizing and teaching (two participles) on the same plane. As to I Cor. 1:16, Paul congratulates himself that the Pauline party could not point to him and make his administration of baptism the basis of their party.

The apostles do not share the view which makes baptism only a symbol instead of a channel of grace. We remember that Cornelius had been ordered to call Peter and not also the brethren of Joppa and that Peter had been ordered to go and not also others. The six brethren went along of their own accord. Peter "ordered that they be baptized" (or "them to be baptized," our versions) means that he gave an order for water for the baptism. And none of the six brethren were able to object. Peter first asked whether any one of them was able to offer valid objection, and none could. Then he called for the water and baptized the Gentiles. A strange thing, indeed, if he had not done so with his own hands! Here we have this first body of Gentiles entering the church, entering it through Peter, God making all the arrangements for Peter, and yet Peter telling ordinary brethren to do the baptizing! But the idea behind this view is that these Gentiles were immersed, underwent Zahn's *Vollbad,* and that was too great a task for Peter, he shifted it to the six brethren. Even so if it be considered a task, why did Peter not help?

Baptism was the decisive act. That admitted these Gentiles into the Christian Church, admitted them directly from Gentilism and without first having to pass through Judaism. That is why Luke says no more about Cornelius or the congregation that was thus formed in Cæsarea. His story has been told: in Cæsarea the Gentiles first entered the Christian Church. The aorist tenses imply that Peter gladly remained "for some days." But this means a good deal as 11:3 indicates. Peter had not only entered a Gentile's house and thus defiled himself according to Jewish ideas, he remained and lodged in the home of Cornelius, ate his Gentile host's food which was anything but kosher. All this was decisive for Peter himself. He on his part was sloughing off the old Jewish legalism and ceremonialism. *Aurei dies!* Bengel exclaims; yes, these were golden days for the entire church.

CHAPTER XI

PETER JUSTIFIES THE RECEPTION OF THE GENTILES

1) **Now the apostles and the brethren, those throughout Judea, heard that also the Gentiles received the Word of God.**

The news of all that had occurred in Cæsarea, no doubt, spread rapidly, chiefly, however, the great fact itself that "also the Gentiles" had become Christians. The point to be noted was that as Gentiles, without first becoming full Jewish proselytes like those mentioned in 2:10, "they received (we should say: had received) the Word," meaning that, by having thus received it, they had been admitted into the Christian Church. This, indeed, was important news. Where the apostles were when they heard this Luke does not say. The assumption that they were in Jerusalem is not verifiable; like Peter, they were busy here and there, which explains why Luke does not mention their location. The brethren throughout Judea include those in Jerusalem; κατά may be considered distributive (R., *W. P.*), The news, no doubt, penetrated also to other places, but Luke is concerned especially with Judea which includes Jerusalem.

2) **And when Peter went up to Jerusalem, those of the circumcision began to contend with him, saying, To men having foreskin thou didst go in and didst eat with them.**

We have no way of knowing how long Peter remained in Cæsarea and how soon he returned to Jerusalem. To speak about a year and to include work in other places is an unnecessary insertion. In v. 12 the six brethren from Joppa appear in Jerusalem with

Peter. This makes it unlikely that Peter waited so long a time before going back to Jerusalem, or that he first toured Galilee. It is most probable that the interval did not extend beyond two or three weeks, and that thus these six brethren from Joppa were still in Peter's company.

In Jerusalem, Peter met objection to his course of action in Cæsarea. "Those of the circumcision began to contend with him," inchoative imperfect, leaving the outcome of this contending to be stated in the sequel. In 10:45, "the believers of the circumcision" intends to say only that the six brethren with Peter were circumcised Jewish Christians and to contrast them with "the Gentiles" who were not circumcised. Here, however, "those of the circumcision" has a narrower sense, namely those who contended for circumcision as being necessary for membership in the Christian Church, the circumcision party. In Gal. 2:12 the designation is still narrower: the circumcision party as Judaizers and legalists. The beginnings of this party appear here in this contention with Peter. When the proponents of these views developed into a permanent party in the church and caused Paul so much trouble, they mixed the gospel with the old Jewish ceremonial legalism by contending that this latter alone was the true gospel.

3) The attack on Peter centered in the point that he had gone in to and had eaten with "men having ἀκροβυστία, the prepuce, foreskin," i. e., uncircumcised men. The point at issue is not that Peter should not have gone in to them, and that it would have been different if they had come to him; the latter would have been just as bad. The point is that simply to go in and then — still worse — to eat was wrong, to say nothing of baptizing such men and receiving them into the church. This circumcision party appealed to the Mosaic regulations which were clear in regard to circumcision and kosher foods. Already these regulations,

they claimed, condemned Peter's proceeding as being totally wrong. This contention was perfectly correct — *if*, indeed, the Mosaic regulations were still in force; then the only way into the church was through the synagogue.

To appreciate this point we must remember that until this time all the believers, even those in Samaria, were recruited from the circumcised. To bring in uncircumcised men, to enter into full fraternal relation with them in their own houses and at their own tables was a revolutionary innovation. The whole question as to whether this dared to be done came upon these Jewish Christians with a suddenness in the conduct of Peter who had gone and done this astounding thing. The fact that some should object was certainly natural, especially since they were not as yet fully informed as to how Peter had been impelled by God himself to do what he had done. The wonder is that all of them did not object, and also that not a single apostle objected. It has been well said that here Peter was certainly not treated as a pope, to say nothing of an infallible pope. With refreshing openness he was taken to task for his conduct.

4) **But Peter, beginning, proceeded to set out** (the matter) **in order for them, saying: I for my part was in Joppa city praying and I saw in an ecstasy a vision, a kind of receptacle coming down, like a great linen sheet being let down by four corners out of heaven, and it came to me. Into which having earnestly gazed, I began to consider and saw the four-footed things of the earth and the wild beasts and the creeping things and the flying things of the heaven; moreover, I heard also a voice saying to me, Having arisen, Peter, slay and eat! But I said, By no means, Lord! because a common or unclean thing never yet came into my mouth. Yet there answered a voice a second time out of heaven,**

What God did cleanse, do thou stop making common! Moreover, this occurred three times; and all were drawn up again into heaven.

We are agreed that the contention with Peter and his reply occurred at a meeting of the congregation at Jerusalem. That, too, explains the elaborate way in which Luke introduces this reply of Peter's. Ἀρξάμενος is circumstantial but scarcely pleonastic; it marks the importance of the reply as now begun, parallels the adverb "in order," and means "beginning" and not "from the beginning" (A. V.). Peter began and went on telling the whole story just as it had happened. He did not argue in the least; he let the facts speak for others just as they had spoken for him. The imperfect ἐξετίθετο should receive more attention, "he proceeded to set out." It continues the previous imperfect διεκρίνοντο. Both are descriptive, but both intend to hold the reader in suspense as to the final outcome which is recorded by the aorists in v. 18 after Peter has delivered his address. Here were these people contending with Peter, here was Peter telling his story. What was the result? Verse 18 tells us.

5) Peter tells the story as we already know it from 10:9-16 (the vision of Peter) and the following. Only a few variations need receive attention. Ἐγώ is emphatic, "I on my part," or, "as for me, I was in Joppa city," etc. "Ecstasy" and "vision" have been explained. The point of emphasis in Peter's story is, of course, the fact that God sent the vision of the great sheet to him. He was engaged in his devotions and had no idea of what was coming, least of all that he should have any dealings with Gentiles. He was not even in Cæsarea but miles away. He adds the point that the great sheet "came up to me," which explains how he could see its contents.

6) The aorist participle states how he fastened his eyes on the sheet; the imperfect of the finite verb how

he began to put his mind on it; then the aorist of the verb how in a flash he saw all the creatures in the sheet. Participle and verbs picture the action perfectly. The imperfect especially shows the mind bent on discovering what the sheet held, the aorist suddenly brings the effort to an end. The list of creatures has the one addition "wild animals," even as in "the four-footed things of the earth" and in "the flying things of the heaven" the idea is that the animals and the birds were unconfined, wild, not domesticated, few if any of them being permitted to Jews as kosher food.

7) Yet "a voice" bids Peter to use these creatures as food. Peter does not try to identify this voice.

8) It was certain to him that he was dealing with the "Lord," and he states how he made answer to him in words that his present objectors would certainly have used if they had been in Peter's place. This was the very point at issue: Peter's eating ceremonially common or unclean, non-kosher food. He shrank from the very idea. He had a clean record thus far. Never had a particle of such food come into his mouth. He had felt exactly as those of the circumcision do who are now taking him to task. Peter said "no" to the Lord. That was not a small thing. Could his objectors have done more?

9) Then Peter relates the exact answer he received which ordered him to stop making common what God himself had cleansed. We have explained this cleansing in v. 15. Peter had the Lord's answer to his objection, and it certainly constituted the answer also for *his objectors.* Let them right here and now stop making food common and forbidden which God himself had made clean and even bade Peter eat! A statement of the simple fact of what had occurred was far more effective than any argument or reasoning of a general nature could have been.

10) And what Peter tells occurred no less than three times. Let nobody, then, attempt to say that there must be some mistake. And let all note that Peter held out to the end by stressing his old Jewish prejudice and refusal. No, that was not commendable; it showed no virtue in Peter, it showed only God's patience with his ignorance and his narrowness. Perhaps some of these men may have wondered whether, if they had been put into Peter's place, they would have held out as long as he did. Yet the vision had accomplished its purpose, it was withdrawn into heaven whence it had come, it did not merely vanish. To the last Peter knew, and now his hearers are to know, that he had been dealing with the Lord.

11) **And lo, forthwith three men stood at the house in which we were, having been commissioned from Cornelius to me. Moreover, the Spirit said to me to go with them, in no respect doubting. And there went with me also these six brethren, and we went into the house of the man. Now he reported to us how he saw the angel in the house stand and say: Send a commission to Joppa and summon Simon, surnamed Peter, who will utter utterances to thee by which thou shalt be saved, thou and all thy house.**

Remarkable, indeed, ("lo") was it that at this precise moment those three men who had been commissioned by Cornelius should have appeared. God had sent the vision to Peter, and the Holy Spirit now furnishes the interpretation. No, not by accident did those messengers appear "forthwith."

12) Peter would have hesitated to go with them to a Roman centurion and a Gentile; he was just like the men who had raised objection to what he had done. It was the Spirit himself who told Peter to go with the messengers and to stop doubting, letting his judgment go now this way and now that (διά and κρίνω). Does

any man intend to say that Peter should have done otherwise than to obey the Spirit and to go as he was bidden? Even in Joppa six of the brethren, the ones who are now here with Peter, were so interested that they went along with him. And so, Peter says, "we went into the house of the man." Even these six brethren who also were of the circumcision (10:45) did not hesitate.

When Peter says in v. 11, "in which we were (ἦμεν)," he is already thinking of these brethren; a variant is ἤμην, "I was." Objection had been raised to Peter's even entering the Gentile's house (v. 3). That is why Peter is so specific on that point. If entering was already wrong and defiling, eating at a Gentile's table could be no worse and hence is not discussed.

13) Peter now tells what God had been doing at the other end by preparing Cornelius and having him summon Peter. He properly quotes the centurion himself and not the messengers in whom he had confided. Here was much more that was astonishing, indeed, but revealed that Peter was only God's agent, and that God himself was the author of everything. An angel had entered into this Gentile's house. He evidently did not fear contamination. God had, of course, sent him to that house. This angel directs Cornelius to summon Peter. Both the summons to Peter and his own orders to obey that summons came from God. Why should any Christian man object?

14) The relative clause in regard to what Peter would do is not found in 10:5, 6, and in 10:22. Here we have a fuller narration. This highly pertinent clause is added in order to let Peter's hearers know what God's great purpose was in bringing Peter into this Gentile's house. He was to tell Cornelius what would save both him and his house (family). It was a matter of saving this household; on the verb and on the noun see 2:47; 4:12. Λαλήσει ῥήματα is important, "he

shall utter utterances," he shall be the Lord's mouthpiece and receive what he is to say from the Lord. "In connection with" these utterances the Lord would save this family, for his word and his grace would be in every word uttered.

"Shall be saved" is passive and implies the Savior as the agent. Despite his connection with the synagogue, Cornelius had not yet found salvation as is clear from 4:12. What Peter says brings out the very thing all these Jewish Christians must realize, namely that they were not saved by circumcision or legal ordinances of Moses but solely and also completely by the utterances which contain the gospel and are connected with the Savior. And these utterances were sufficient to save any man, be he Jew or Gentile.

15) **Now, when I began to make utterance, the Holy Spirit fell on them just as also upon us at the beginning. And I remembered the utterance of the Lord, how he was saying, John baptized with water, but you, you shall be baptized in connection with the Holy Spirit. If, therefore, God gave to them the equal gift as to us as having come to believe on the Lord Jesus Christ, I, who was I, as able to hinder God?**

Here we have the tremendous climax of all that God did in this case. Luke frequently uses the idiom ἐν τῷ with the infinitive, usually the present infinitive but occasionally also the aorist as here. Peter had scarcely begun to speak — we know how little it was that he said, 10:34-43 — when God did the decisive thing as far as putting the Gentiles on an equality with Jews in the matter of receiving them into the church was concerned: he gave them the charisma of the Spirit, namely to speak with tongues, exactly as he had done ἐν ἀρχῇ (many phrases need no articles), "in the beginning," for us, namely at Pentecost. We have discussed the identity of this gift in connection with 10:44-46.

16) When Peter witnessed the charisma at Caesarea, there at once flashed into his memory the Lord's own utterance and promise which he had made just before his ascension, that word and promise which had been spoken already by the Baptist in Matt. 3:11, "how he was saying" (added circumstantially), "John baptized with water, but you, you shall be baptized with the Holy Ghost," see the interpretation in 1:5, also in Matthew. The promise of the Baptist and of Jesus was fulfilled at Pentecost and had an extension in Caesarea, and Peter at once saw it.

17) This is clinched by the conclusion which Peter drew and was intended to draw (οὖν). The condition is one of reality which has the apodosis in the form of a question in order the more forcefully to impress Peter's hearers. If God gave the identical gift to them (Gentiles) as also to us (Jews), they as well as we having come to believe on Jesus, who was Peter and what power had he to interfere and to prevent God from doing such a thing? Τὴν ἴσην δωρεάν is "the like gift" (our versions) in the sense of "the same," "the equal gift."

It was God who placed these Gentiles on an equality with the Jews in so far as both believed on the Lord. The unmodified participle πιστεύσασιν is to be construed with both αὐτοῖς and ἡμῖν: "to them as also to us as having come to believe," R., *W. P.* Our versions and many commentators would refer this participle only to ἡμῖν, but such a construction would require the article. It is this having come equally to believe that induced God to bestow the equal gift (gift, also in 10:45) *"on them* as also *on us."* The participle is plainly predicative. Having come to faith is the essential thing. By faith the Spirit takes possession of the heart and saves; then, as God deems fit, he may bestow the Spirit also in a charismatic way whenever the interest of the gospel requires this.

Peter asks his critics whether they thought that he was able to prevent God from dealing with these Gentiles as he did. Two questions are fused into one: "Who was I?" and, "Was I able?" The very idea that Peter might hinder God in this bestowal is preposterous. Did his critics intend to claim that he should have attempted that? The question asked them involves also whether they would so hinder God.

18) **Now, having heard these things, they were quiet and glorified God, saying, Then also to the Gentiles did God give the repentance unto life!**

Here the imperfects "began to contend" and "proceeded to set out in order" which occur in v. 2 and 4 are brought to their completion in the two aorists "were quiet and glorified." Here were critics, indeed, but when the actual facts were placed before them, they sought not to carp, they were convinced, they capitulated, "they were quiet" as to any further objection; nay, more, they glorified God, and that for the real and essential thing which is expressed as a deduction by ἄρα, "then" or "accordingly," namely that "also to the Gentiles did God give the repentance unto life." "Then" refers to all that Peter had said, most especially to the last part of his address, the bestowal of the Spirit by the charisma of tongues. That was the evidence of something far greater, the bestowal of "the repentance" which brought "life," ζωή, spiritual, everlasting life.

On μετάνοια see 2:38; it consists of contrition and faith, the turn of the heart from sin to Christ and his pardon. Where this is found, "life" enters, namely the life of faith which is connected with Christ, the Life. This life is invisible, it is in the soul or heart, in this respect it is like our physical life; but, again like our physical life, wherever it is present it manifests itself in endless ways. Those who are spiritually alive love the Lord, confess him, worship him, pray to him, feed on his Word, serve him, etc.

God has succeeded in opening the door of the church to the Gentiles; he succeeded also in having the Jewish Christians who were already within the portal welcome these incoming Gentiles and praise him for bringing them in.

THE CHURCH AT ANTIOCH

19) Once more, as he had done in 9:31, Luke reverts to Stephen's death; *οἱ μὲν οὖν* is used as it was in 1:6. **They, then, that were scattered due to the tribulation that occurred in the case of Stephen went on through as far as Phoenicia and Cyprus and Antioch, speaking the Word to no one except only to Jews.**

As a result of the first persecution Luke related to us the conversion of Saul and his story as far as the return to Tarsus; then Peter's activity outside of Jerusalem which ended with the acceptance of Gentile converts by the brethren in Jerusalem. Now, again reverting to the persecution, Luke records the story of Antioch.

According to a conservative estimate there were 25,000 Christians in Jerusalem at the time of Stephen's death. The great dispersion that ensued as a result of Saul's activity scattered quite a number of these to rather distant and safe parts. Some of them naturally migrated into Phoenicia, into cities like Tyre, Sidon, and Ptolomais along the Mediterranean; others crossed to the great island of Cyprus where many Jews dwelt; finally — and this is the important point to Luke — a goodly number went as far north as

Antioch and thus bring this future center of Christianity to our notice for the first time.

The data in regard to Antioch are compiled in the Bible dictionaries.. We note that because of its population of half a million Antioch was rated as the third city in the entire Roman empire, being outranked only by Rome and Alexandria. At one time it had been the residence of the Seleucian kings; later it became the residence of the Roman procurators of Syria. Lying a bit inland on the Orontes River, its seaport was Seleucia from which Paul started his sea voyages when he set out on his great missionary tours. Cilicia bordered on Syria, and Tarsus was not far distant from Antioch. Many Jews were residing in this pagan city which exhibited both the splendor and the vices of the Roman and the Oriental paganism. Starting with the present account of Luke, Antioch loomed large in the entire early history of the Christian Church.

When Christian fugitives from Jerusalem, all of whom were native Jews or complete Jewish proselytes, settled in Antioch they naturally spread the gospel among the Antiochian Jews in the synagogues of the city, and Luke notes that this was the extent of their first missionary efforts. These limited missionary efforts were not due to a question of language as between the Aramaic of the Jews in Antioch and the Jewish Christians from Jerusalem, on the one hand, and the Greek of the general population of Antioch, on the other. Greek was known to all. In fact, to this day, as we ourselves found in our eastern travels, men residing in these territories speak several languages with ease. In Caesarea, in the house of Cornelius, Peter spoke Greek although he had been but a fisherman on the Lake of Galilee.

20) **But some of them were Cyprian and Cyrenian men, such as, on coming to Antioch, began to**

speak also to the Greeks, proclaiming as good news the Lord Jesus Christ.

The decisive points are: first, the reading "Greeks" and next, the chronology. We must have the reading Ἕλληνας, the common word for pagan Greeks which is often used in contrast with "barbarians," the term for natives of all kinds who did not speak Greek and had no Greek culture. Greeks and Jews are also frequently paired and contrasted. Both were on a higher level in the old world although they differed from each other, and all barbarians were beneath them.

The texts which have Ἑλληνιστάς, "Hellenists," "Grecians," cannot be correct, for these were Jews, namely Jews who had been born outside of Palestine but were of Jewish blood and religion just as much as those who had been born in Palestine. In 2:9-11 we have quite a list of such foreign-born Jews; the 3,000 converts made at the time of Pentecost were, for the most part, such Hellenists. In 6:1 we have discussed the two types of Jews, "Hebrews" and "Hellenists." When Luke states in v. 19 that the Christians at first spoke the gospel to Jews only, the "Jews" were these foreign-born Jews or Hellenists, at least for the greater part, since the proportion of Jews who had been born in Palestine was not so large in Antioch. To say that the gospel was spread among such would mean nothing, for this had been done on an extensive scale on the day of Pentecost and had been done ever since that time. But to say that some Christians were now preaching Christ to pagan Greeks, that, indeed, was a new thing, one that was revolutionary for the Jewish ideas that were still prevalent in the church, and vastly important for all future history.

That, too, is why Luke specifically mentions the Christians who first made this advance in Antioch, namely, not native Palestinians, but Hellenists, Jewish Christians who had been born in Cyprus and in Cyrenia — they began to speak (inchoative imperfect) to these pagan Greeks. Luke omits any further characterization such as he used in connection with Cornelius in 10:2, to the effect that they were "fearing God," φοβούμενοι τὸν Θεόν, one of the standard expressions for designating proselytes of the gate. No, these were just heathen Greeks without synagogue connections. Here, then, is the continuation of what Peter did at Caesarea; it is even an advance on that.

Now Luke does not date this offer of the gospel to pagan Greeks. He gives us only the general historical connection and places this account *after* the story of Cornelius. Luke's indefinite chronology does not, however, justify the view that the extension of the gospel to pagan Greeks precedes the extension God made to proselytes of the gate in Caesarea. If pagan Greeks were already being brought into the church in a great Jewish center such as Antioch, would God go to all the trouble that Luke reports in order to have also Greek proselytes of the gate brought in? The report of the action in Antioch reached Jerusalem promptly and caused no commotion whatever. How could it have been received without dissent if the action of Peter in Caesarea *afterwards* called forth criticism? No; we must leave the events in the order in which Luke records them. These Cyprians and these Cyrenians heard what Peter had done, knew what had been said in Jerusalem that "also to the Gentiles God gave the repentance of life" (v. 18), and thus preached the gospel to Gentiles, namely Greeks in Antioch. Luke makes everything plain. In spite of the directions given by God in the case of Cornelius most Christians still clung to their old Jewish narrowness and confined their missionary efforts to the Antiochian Jews; only the men of Cyprus and of Cyrenia eventually went farther by acting consistent with God's will as this had been revealed at Caesarea in the case of Cornelius.

21) The gospel achieved a pronounced success among the heathen Greeks. **And the Lord's hand was with them, and a great number that came to believe turned to the Lord.** This was due to "the Lord's hand," the anarthrous Κύριος signifying *Yahweh*, which Luke distinguishes from the articulated Κύριος which precedes and follows. The Lord's hand is his power which worked in a providential way in making everything favorable for these disciples to bring the gospel to these Greeks. He opened many doors to them. This is essential in all missionary work. The work is God's and not ours, and he either opens the doors or leaves them closed. So many have the idea that they themselves may decide where to work; but it is futile to beat against closed doors.

Thus a great number of heathen Greeks were converted to Jesus. The aorist completes what the imperfect used in v. 20 left unfinished: they began to speak, and a great number turned. No issue should be made of the use of the article with πιστεύσας since this only makes the participle attributive whereas it is predicative in v. 17. Luke describes the great number, it was a number "that came to faith"; of course, he could have omitted the article if he intended to say "a great number on coming to believe." The aorist participle is ingressive.

22) **And the report concerning them came to the ears of the church that was in Jerusalem; and they sent forth Barnabas as far as Antioch, who, having come and having seen the grace of God, rejoiced and proceeded to exhort all with the purpose of the heart to remain with the Lord because he was a good man and full of the Holy Spirit and faith. And a considerable multitude was added to the Lord.**

Literally, the word or substance concerning these Cyprians, etc., "was heard in the ears" (static εἰς).

Luke says that the news came to the church, "the one being in Jerusalem," the mother church. He does not say that the word reached the apostles. The only fair conclusion is that the apostles were absent from Jerusalem as we, for example, saw Peter busy at Lydda, Joppa, and Caesarea. It is unwarranted, on the basis of the expression "the church in Jerusalem," to draw the conclusion that the believers in Antioch were not yet a church. When, then, did they become a church? On ἐκκλησία see 5:11; the church is where believers are found.

It was due merely to the absence of the apostles from Jerusalem, which left Barnabas as the best available man, that the mother church sent him to Antioch. Besides, he, too, was a Cyprian and would thus be the most suitable man to see what his countrymen were doing in Antioch. The view that Peter was not acceptable as the commissioner, and that, therefore, his services were "discounted" for the present task is unwarranted. Peter was absent. Why was some other apostle not sent? Plainly because the other apostles, too, were absent. In 8:14 the apostles do the sending and not the church. The church did not direct the apostles; the apostles always directed the church, and the church always looked to them for its leadership.

The church acted in the present case because it was thought that the apostles would be absent for some time. It was too long to wait until some of them returned; thus it came about that the church acted independently. In this the church had the example of the apostles as recorded in 8:14 (Philip's work in Samaria). The idea behind this procedure was the same idea that had been followed in that advance movement, namely that all believers everywhere constituted one spiritual body that still had its headquarters in Jerusalem, from which center the apostles still carried on their work, and to which they returned from time to time. The church in Jerusalem acted in good faith and with due wisdom, and the apostles certainly approved its action when one after another finally returned.

23) So Barnabas went. What he was to do we see from what he did. All doubt as to the reception of Greeks into the church had been removed. That matter was settled completely in v. 18. Barnabas shows that he had no instructions to question the right of these Greeks to come into the church. While it was a new movement and should thus come under the supervision of the central church, the headquarters of the apostles, anything beyond that was not contemplated. For those in Antioch, too, it was worth much to remain in connection with the apostles and to have their approval for all their work. A true spirit of unity was back of this commission of Barnabas and of all that he did in its execution. That spirit is often lacking today, sometimes to the extent that even this mission of Barnabas is not properly understood.

Barnabas rejoiced because of the grace of God which he saw in Antioch. Note the *suavis paronomasia* between τὴν χάριν and ἐχάρη. Luke sees more than the faith and the conversions Barnabas found in Antioch, where so many Greeks now believed and confessed. These were the results, God's grace was the ultimate source. He saw the cause in the effect. To be sure, Barnabas had eyes to see — that is why he was sent on this mission. Every task calls for a competent man. Barnabas found nothing that needed to be corrected in Antioch. How many congregations could today be visited by a man like Barnabas without his finding something, even much, to correct? Take this very thing of receiving members by just letting people come into the church in order to augment the number without the proper instruction and separation from their old heathen life and connections! Some day a greater than Barnabas will come, see, and — not rejoice.

So all that Barnabas found it necessary to do was to exhort all "that with the purpose of the heart they remain with the Lord." The imperfect pictures Barnabas as continuing this exhortation, and the present infinitive speaks of continuous remaining. A good start is excellent, but we must endure to the end. Because a text or two has ἐν, "in the Lord," the R. V. margin offers its translation.

Προσμένειν has the dative τῷ Κυρίῳ; to remain with the Lord was the burden of Barnabas' exhortations, and to do this "with the purpose of the heart," i. e., with the set determination of the center of the personality (καρδία). Thus Barnabas sought to confirm the believers in Antioch, especially also the recent ones, the Greeks. Since he found everything in such excellent order, it was not necessary that he return to Jerusalem to make report; he most likely sent word in some other way.

24) The reason that Barnabas showed such interest in the growing church at Antioch was his personal character. Barnabas has been only slightly introduced thus far (4: 36, 37), hence Luke tells us more about him. In that he was "full of the Holy Spirit and faith" he was a man like Stephen, of whom Luke records the same thing in 6:5. The Holy Spirit had taken possession of his heart through the Word and filled it with strong and virile faith. When Luke calls him "a good man," this other description is the basis of his goodness. "Good" is a rather pale translation of ἀγαθός. Since it is his exhortation that Luke explains by calling Barnabas "a good man," we shall hardly go amiss in making the adjective mean "competent," "capable," "serviceable," i. e., good in what he was able to do for others (C.-K. 4) just as κακός means "good for nothing" in whatever respect one

ought to serve his purpose. Here, then, was not a man who judged the situation in Antioch superficially and merely uttered words of praise to please everybody. Such supervisors of the church do her no good because they are not "good" men. It was a blessing for the church in Antioch to have the approval and the support of a "good" man like Barnabas.

This description of Barnabas has led to the conclusion that Luke himself was one of the Greeks who had been won for Christianity in Antioch. It is thought that he was a member of the congregation at Antioch, and that Theophilus also resided there. Thus Luke would have met Barnabas himself and presently also Saul. Some of the ancient fathers call Luke a Syrian from Antioch, although again, it seems, he is reported to have come only from a former Antiochian family. Attention is drawn to the fact that he seems to take a special interest in Antioch, for instance in 6:5 where he tells us that one of the seven deacons was an Antiochian proselyte. All this is interesting but not conclusive. We fear that even the closest scrutiny will find the available data and hints as to Luke's home, family, etc., too slight to advance us beyond hypotheses.

The presence of Barnabas in Antioch soon resulted in far more than a visit with a consequent return to Jerusalem. He himself entered actively into the work. Stimulating all the others and helping on his own part, "a considerable multitude was added to the Lord." Not merely to the congregation but "to the Lord"; the passive implies an agent which we may take to be the Word. Luke does not say whether these new members were Jews or Greeks; his manner of expression leaves the impression that this difference was no longer of moment. The congregation was growing apace; it had a wonderful future before it in the Acts and in the centuries beyond.

25) **He, however, went out to Tarsus to hunt up Saul and, having found him, he brought him to Antioch.**

Here there is room for the play of the imagination. We note that Saul returned to Tarsus in 9:30, but that was seven or eight years ago. During this period of time Saul simply drops out of sight, and that is the best that can be said. Some "imagine" that he worked in Tarsus and in Cilicia on the basis of Gal. 1:21, but he then accomplished nothing, for there is no evidence that a single congregation was started by him during those years. Ramsey supposes that Saul was not as yet clear in regard to his mission to the Gentiles, still had the idea that the door to the church led through the synagogue; but Saul did not work even in the synagogue in Tarsus. If we feel that an explanation is necessary, let us say that Saul waited for God's call as this was promised to him when God told him to leave Jerusalem, 22:17-21. It was a long wait, but Saul bore it well, and now the call came.

What led Barnabas to think of Saul? All we know is what Barnabas did for Saul in 9:26, etc., and we are entitled to add that Barnabas knew that the Lord's intention concerning Saul was to use him as a chosen instrument especially among the Gentiles (9:15). The Gentiles were now beginning to come into the church in large numbers. May that fact not have turned the thoughts of Barnabas toward Saul? Let us say that the Lord guided the thoughts of Barnabas. Seven years or more are certainly a long time. How did Barnabas know that Saul was still in Tarsus and that his journey to that place would not be in vain? We have no clue in regard to this point. All we know is that he located Saul and that he succeeded in bringing him into the great work that was going forward in Antioch.

26) **And it came to pass for them that even for a whole year they were brought together in the church and taught a considerable multitude, also the disciples bore first in Antioch the name Christians.**

This was the year 43 or 44. The important point is that Barnabas and Saul were in close association in the work at Antioch for an entire year. Energetically and in friendly fellowship they worked, successfully teaching a large multitude and bringing them into the church. All three aorists are subjects of ἐγένετο, to which αὐτοῖς is added as a dative of advantage; Luke states what occurred "for them," Barnabas and Saul. The infinitives are historical aorists which intend simply to report the facts. Luke shows how the two men became intimate in their great work. The "multitude" refers to outsiders who were taught so as to be brought into the church. It is fair to assume that not a few were Greeks and thus needed a thorough teaching.

By being added with τε, the third infinitive is connected with both infinitives that precede and thus states that it was during this year that the disciples bore (or ingressive: came to bear) the name "Christians." This is an interesting fact. It is at once evident that the disciples did not invent this name for themselves. They always and for years to come called themselves as Luke himself here calls them, "disciples" (see 6:1), or as he has repeatedly called them, "saints" (see 9:13) also, "brethren" (1:15) also, "those believing" or "believers" (πιστοί).

"Christian" appears twice more in the New Testament, in 26:28, and in I Pet. 4:16, each time as a name that was given to the disciples by others. Since the name was derived from "Christ," the Greek word for "Messiah," it is certain that the disciples got this name in Antioch and not from the Jews who would never have connected the Messiah with the disciples either in a derogatory or in any other way. The Greeks invented this name. Philologians have much to say in regard to the Latin ending ιανος which is appended to a Greek name by Greeks; then, too, they discuss Χρηστιανός, which appears as a variant of Χριστιανός (Codex Sinaiticus) and was used extensively by others e. g., Tacitus, Χρηστός also being used in place of Χριστός. In the days of the Roman persecutions the very name was certainly enough to condemn a man. The question is debated as to whether already in Antioch "Christians" or "Chrēstians" was intended as a vicious title or was used only to distinguish the disciples of Christ from the Jews. Monographs have been written on this subject.

As far as Luke is concerned, the active aorist infinitive χρηματίσαι, "to bear a name," means only that outsiders bestowed the name. As to the spelling of the word by Luke, it is impossible to show that he wrote the name "Chrēstians" and did it in order to show that it was intended as a vilification. The fact that this designation became opprobrious during the persecutions need not be pointed out. There is evidence that the mispronunciation was due to ordinary vulgarity even as Tacitus writes: *vulgus Chrestianos appellabat.* He himself spells *Christus* correctly in the same sentence. Since it was given them by outsiders, the disciples would for a long time be reluctant to adopt the name. Moreover, their reverence for Christ would restrain them from using a designation for themselves which embodied his holy name. We thus conclude that, when the opprobrium attached to the "Christians" is emphasized, we should be content with the reference to the days of Roman persecution and not go back to Antioch and the first invention of the name. There is no indication that during this early period any hostility toward the disciples was manifested in Antioch.

27) **Now in these days there came down from Jerusalem prophets to Antioch. And one of them, by name Agabus, was signifying through the Spirit that a great famine was about to be on the whole inhabited earth; which occurred under Claudius.**

"These days" refer to the year Luke has just mentioned, probably to the middle of the year, since it took some time to gather the money for the proposed relief. Here we note "prophets" in the church for the first time; in 13:1 we have "prophets and teachers." The prophets are far more prominent in the Old Testament than in the new; some of them are towering figures. In the New Testament only the apostles rank with those prophets. The prophets, properly so called in the New Testament, are men of less importance, we may call them Christian teachers to whom the Spirit at times made special direct communications of but minor import. We learn about Agabus as their representative and about two of the communications that he transmitted, the one regarding the famine and the other regarding Paul (21:10, etc.); then also the daughters of Philip are mentioned (21:9). The apostles themselves were prophets in this sense.

Besides this we read about the gift of prophecy which Paul extols as being far superior to the gift of tongues, cf., First Corinthians. This gift any Christian might acquire, and Paul urges all to seek it (I Cor. 14:1). It consisted in thoroughly understanding the Word and in adequately presenting it. Thus we find "prophets and teachers" combined in 13:1. The apostles, of course, had also this gift in an eminent degree, and next to them are their assistants such as Judas and Silas (15:32).

28) When it is asked why these prophets went from Jerusalem to Antioch, we prefer to think that their purpose was to deliver the very message which one of them, namely Agabus, conveyed. It is not necessary to think that he received this revelation only after coming to Antioch; it may have come to him in Jerusalem with the intimation that it was to be conveyed to the brethren in Antioch. Note the verb "was signifying." The imperfect expresses repeated action, and the verb itself implies that he used some symbolic action in connection with his revelation after the manner indicated in 21:11. Luke states no details but only the message itself, that a great famine was impending, μέλλειν with the future infinitive pointing to a famine that is close at hand.

When Agabus states that this famine was to be "on the whole inhabited earth" he indicates that it was to be "great" in its extent. Drought and crop failures would produce famine conditions which affected now this part, now that with more or less severity, so that conditions of distress would affect the whole inhabited world. We need not restrict τὴν οἰκουμένην (γῆν) to the Roman empire; for if all these lands suffered more or less, the barbarian countries would certainly not escape.

Luke has thus far furnished no dates; that is why, writing years afterward, he adds: "which (ὅστις = "which very one," R. 728) occurred under Claudius," ἐπί, "in the time of," R. 603. Claudius reigned from January 41 to October 54. Much of his reign was marked by famine conditions as Roman writers (Suetonius: *assiduae sterilitates*, Dio Cassius, Tacitus) and Josephus report. The entire empire was not affected equally at the same time and just for one period, but crop failures were wide-spread, and certain regions suffered great distress because they were unable to import much from sections that were less affected.

Zahn's deduction from Luke's remark, that Agabus must have spoken his prophecy *before* Claudius came to the throne, i. e., before January 41, conflicts with his own statement that "in these days" signifies in the year mentioned in v. 26, which must be the year 43-44. Luke's phrase "under Claudius" is written, not with reference to Agabus, but with reference to Luke's own time of writing. On the reading in the Codex Bezae with its "we" as implying Luke's own presence here in Antioch see 16:10.

29) **And of the disciples, as anyone was well off, they determined, each one of them, to send for ministration to the brethren dwelling in Judea. Which also they did, commissioning it to the elders by hand of Barnabas and Saul.**

It seems that a link is missing between the general prophecy of Agabus and this action of the congregation at Antioch. How did the brethren at Antioch know that the church in Judea would soon suffer? Luke evidently intends that his reader supply the link. From what Antioch proceeded to do, namely to gather funds for Judea, it is plain that Agabus must have specified that the impending famine conditions in the world would presently bring distress to the church in Judea. The Lord himself sent Agabus from Jerusalem to Antioch at the proper time, in advance, to prepare the necessary relief.

This, it seems, was set under way promptly after the revelation had been received. Everyone of the disciples in Antioch took part, and this was done by joint action of the church. The sentence has been called awkward, and yet it neatly brings out these two points: "they determined" (plural), jointly as a body; "of the disciples, as anyone was well off, each one" (singular), not one holding back.

No; they did not tithe. Saul and Barnabas, although they were former Jews, did not gather funds in this manner. In this very first instance in the Christian Church, when relief on a large scale had to be provided, the correct principle and method were adopted: "as anyone was well off," the imperfect signifying "continued to be well off or prosper." This implies that funds were gathered gradually and that each kept giving as he could from time to time, perhaps from Sunday to Sunday. We know how Paul proceeded later on when relief was again necessary for Jerusalem and when he gathered funds from all the Gentile congregations. It was here at Antioch that his later method was first applied. Εἰς διακονίαν, "for ministration," recalls "the daily ministration" of food and relief to the widows mentioned in 6:1. The same beautiful word is used which denotes help for the sake of help.

30) Already the aorists (v. 29) imply that this thing was done, but Luke adds, probably because it covered so long a period: "which also they did," etc. When the relief became necessary, Barnabas and Saul were the commissioners who were sent from Antioch to the elders in Judea to administer the needed help. This took place after Herod had killed James (12:2), had attempted to kill Peter, had abused the church in Jerusalem (12:1), and had died a most terrible death (12:23), after the Passover of 44. The worst of the famine occurred during the next year.

The relief was sent, we are told, "to the elders." This term comes as a surprise since Luke has not mentioned elders; but he is writing from his own later standpoint and for a reader who knew what elders were. We might call them pastors. They had charge of the congregations in all their church affairs and attended to the services, the teaching, and the spiritual oversight. Πρεσβύτεροι, "elders," designated them according to their dignity, while ἐπίσκοποι described them from the viewpoint of their work as "overseers," "bishops," both terms denoting the same office. The apostles called themselves "elders," I Pet. 5:1; II John 1; III John 1.

We do not know when this office was inaugurated; it came about naturally as an inheritance from the synagogues with their management by elders. At times the majority of the Jews in a town or a synagogue were converted to Christianity. At first the apostles remained and worked in Jerusalem, but when congregations sprang up everywhere, they were absent from Jerusalem, and elders had to manage even this congregation, to say nothing of the many others. Here Luke speaks of the elders in Judea. Since they were the managers of the congregations, Barnabas and Saul naturally worked through them.

A number of questions arise at this point. Did Saul go to Jerusalem on this relief journey, or did he avoid Jerusalem and dispense relief only in Judea? If he went to Jerusalem, did he meet any of the Twelve there? If he went to Jerusalem, why did he fail to mention this visit in Gal. 2:1? Must we conclude from Gal. 2:1 that he kept away from Jerusalem on this relief journey? Or is this relief journey identical with the journey and the visit described in Gal. 2:1, etc.?

As far as the facts are concerned, Saul and Barnabas went to Jerusalem, for in 12:25 they return from this city after finishing their ministry of relief. Secondly, it is impossible to identify this relief journey with the one described in Gal. 2:1, etc., which was ordered by revelation. The visit referred to in Gal. 2 is undoubtedly identical with the one recorded in Acts 15:1, etc. How could Paul then omit this relief journey from his Galatian letter? Whether we can answer that or not, he did so omit it. To insist that such an omission would destroy his whole argument in Gal. one and two is answered by the simple fact that Paul did not think so. But perhaps Paul omitted mention of this relief visit in Galatians because he failed to meet any of the Twelve on this visit. That is possible. But that explanation only raises more questions.

A glance shows that 11:30 and 12:25 must be considered together: Barnabas and Saul are commissioned to bring relief to the brethren in Judea — on completing the relief Barnabas and Saul return from Jerusalem. But why does Luke interlard all that he records about Herod (12:1-23) between these two statements? The matter is simple. The famine and its relief occurred in the summer or the fall of 44 or in 45, hence *after* Herod's death (12:23). But the prophecy of Agabus and the beginning of the gathering of funds occurred *before* this Herodian persecution. Now instead of telling his reader merely that the gathering of contributions for relief was undertaken in Antioch, then reporting about Herod, and finally adding that Barnabas and Saul were sent to convey the relief, Luke at once says that the relief was duly conveyed (11:30). But in 13:1, etc., Barnabas and Saul are commissioned for their first great missionary journey. They were then back in Antioch; that is why their return is mentioned in the preceding verse, in 12:25.

We are sorry to note that Lightfoot draws such a wretched picture of the Twelve and also of Saul. He confuses the dates. Saul and Barnabas bring the relief in the midst of the Herodian terror, James is dead, Peter has fled, the Twelve have taken to cover, "every Christian of rank" has left the city. Saul and Barnabas steal into the city, hurriedly deposit the relief funds, and depart. Ramsay says correctly: "It was not men like that who carried Christianity over the empire within a few years."

But Ramsay has his own story. Besides confusing 11:30 and 15:1, etc., he has Barnabas and Saul bring loads of provisions instead of money and has them in person attend to distributing these provisions to all the needy — in person in order to produce the greater effect of this charity as coming from Antioch; and all this took weeks, for Judea was included. To give the final touch to all this we are left to conclude that these weeks occurred during the Herodian persecution, and that the apostolic council met at the same time! When over a decade later Paul took up his great collection for famine relief in the Gentile churches he brought the money So Barnabas and Saul brought funds. They most likely went first of all to Jerusalem and from there turned in various directions into Judea and distributed this relief money. Then they returned to Antioch. The apostles were busy in various fields. Herod had been dead for months.

CHAPTER XII

The Persecution Under Herod Agrippa I

1) **Along that period of time Herod, the king, put forth his hands to abuse some of those belonging to the church.**

We have explained the chronology of events in 11:30. Herod's persecution occurred "along about that καιρός or period of time." The prophecy of Agabus preceded Herod's persecution and his death, and this, in turn, preceded the famine and its suffering and the relief brought by Barnabas and Saul. Herod died after the Passover of 44, the famine followed toward the end of 44 and continued into 45. "Herod, the king," refers to the Herod who was at this time the actual king of all Palestine and not merely, like his uncle Herod Antipas, often called king while he was only a tetrarch. This is Herod Agrippa I, a grandson of Herod the Great, a son of Aristobolus and Bernice. We have told his story in connection with 10:1: He was a prisoner in Rome until Tiberius died, was made tetrarch on the occasion of the accession of Caligula, and then king of all Palestine by Claudius in 41, and thus became the first and only Herodian who ruled as king over all Palestine after the death of Herod the Great. He died three years after his appointment as king. He was a treacherous, superficial, extravagant prince, although not as bad a character as his grandfather had been. Jerusalem was his capital. Since his elevation to the kingship he courted the favor of the Jews, especially that of the bigoted Pharisees, and played the role of zealous protector of the Jewish faith and cultus. The hostility which developed some years before, when Stephen was slain, found in him a new protagonist, which explains what follows.

He began suddenly to take active measures against the Christians by putting forth his hands (through his minions) to abuse or ill-treat "some of those from the church," οἱ ἀπό is often used with reference to the members of a corporation. Luke writes only "some" without specifying who are referred to although we may assume that he selected his victims. The idea that he observed them in their attendance at the Temple and gave orders to expel them from the courts and the worship, is too general and mild. The view that Peter's action in Cæsarea when he permitted Gentiles to enter the church stirred up Herod's animosity, is rather superficial. Κακῶσαι implies that he arrested some of the more prominent Christians, had them scourged and abused in other ways, and thus began his further bloody work. These first victims escaped death, otherwise Luke would have used a stronger verb than "abuse."

2) **Moreover, he made away with James, the brother of John, by means of the sword.**

During the persecution that followed upon Stephen's martyrdom some Christians were no doubt killed. James is usually called the second martyr, yet, in reality, others preceded him. Although he was one of the Twelve, Luke makes only brief mention of the martyrdom of James. This has been found strange, and some say we do not know why Luke did not tell the entire story for he certainly knew all the details. Luke, however, follows a definite plan. The story of Stephen was vital for that plan since the death of Stephen led to the extension of the church in all directions, even to distant lands. The martyrdom of James had no comparable effect, hence the brevity of the record. The importance of this bloody deed lies only in the fact that it singled out an apostle and that it showed the temper of Herod and indicated to what lengths he intended to go.

We again have the significant verb ἀνεῖλε (ἀναιρέω), "he made away with," which always denotes murder and criminal killing; in the previous chapters it is constantly used with regard to the death of Jesus. The dative of means, μαχαίρᾳ, shows that James was beheaded by an executioner as the Baptist had been by that other Herod. James was thus arrested. He may also have been brought to trial before Herod or have been summarily executed after his arrest. The fact that James was at first the sole victim is most likely due to the circumstance that he was the only one of the apostles who happened to be in the city at the moment.

Clement of Alexandria tells a story which he claims to have received from his Christian ancestors to the effect that the soldier who led James from the court room, after witnessing the joyful confession James had made, was so deeply affected that he on his part confessed himself a Christian, whereupon he was led out to execution together with James. On the way this soldier asked James to pardon him for having served as the tool of the king. James thought a little while and then turned and said, "Peace be with thee!" and kissed the soldier. An affecting story, but whether it is true or not, no one can say. See Eusebius 2, 9.

3) **And, on seeing that it was pleasing to the Jews, he in addition arrested also Peter — now they were days of the unleavened bread — whom also, on capturing, he placed in prison, delivering him to four quaternions of soldiers to guard him, intending after the Passover to bring him up to the people.**

To see their king take such strong measures against the Christians delighted the hostile Jews to the highest degree. It was the king's very purpose to gain this vigorous approval. In the combination προσέθετο συλλαβεῖν, "he added to seize," a Hebraism, the verb takes the place of an adverb, and the infinitive expresses the main idea: "he in addition arrested" also Peter. Greatly encouraged by the first execution, the king proceeded to the next one.

Again we ask why Peter was the one to be arrested, and also why Herod did not arrest more or even all of the apostles. The only satisfactory answer is that the other apostles were absent at this time. When James returned, Herod made away with him; now when Peter came back to the city he, too, fell into Herod's hands. The interval between these two events seems to have been quite short.

The parenthesis is indicated by δέ, and ἡμέραι is the predicate. "They were days of the unleavened bread" means that it was Passover time when all leaven was scrupulously removed from the house for the duration of the entire festival week which began at sundown on the fourteenth of Nisan, the evening on which the Passover lamb was eaten (Matt. 26:17), Num. 28:16, 17. The entire week was called τὰ ἄζυμα (λάγανα, cakes), *hammatzoth.* It seems that Peter had come to Jerusalem in order to spend the Passover week with the mother congregation.

4) Upon his arrest Peter was lodged in prison, which was very likely located in Herod's palace, and was put under the heaviest kind of guard. The reason for this was the fact that Herod had heard that the Twelve had once been locked up securely, and yet that on the next morning their prison had been found empty. The king intended that such an occurrence should not be repeated. So he had Peter delivered to four quaternions of his soldiers who were "to be guarding him," one set of four soldiers doing guard duty in

the way indicated in v. 6 for one watch of six hours, and so each set in rotation.

It was Herod's intention "to bring Peter up to the people" the day after the Passover proper. That means that he was to be led up out of his dungeon cell to the hall of trial where all who cared to could be present, and from there to be led away to execution where all who cared to could witness the act which demonstrated the king's wonderful zeal for the integrity of the Jewish faith.

"After the Passover" means after the Passover meal on the evening of the fourteenth of Nisan, namely on the fifteenth. The plan was to duplicate the execution of Jesus who also died on the fifteenth of Nisan. Herod intended to impress the thousands of people who attended the festival from far and near. In Matt. 26:5, the Sanhedrin planned to wait until the festival week was past because it feared the people, the pilgrim hosts attending the festival who were captivated by Jesus. Their plan was frustrated when God allowed Jesus to fall into their hands on the night between the fourteenth and the fifteenth. The Jewish rule was: *Non judicant die festo.* It was broken in the case of Jesus; it was again to be broken in the case of Peter.

"After the Passover" is generally taken to mean "after the entire Passover week," which identifies "days of unleavened bread" and "Passover." Πάσχα has this wider meaning, but it also has the narrower which then refers to the ceremonial meal when the Passover lamb was eaten on the evening of the fourteenth of Nisan. Here the narrower meaning is in place because of the context and because "days of unleavened bread" precedes. "After the Passover" specifies on which particular day during the days of unleavened bread the execution was to take place.

The king's plans were made, and due measures had been taken to see that they would be carried out.

5) **Peter, accordingly, was being kept in the prison. Prayer, however, was being made strenuously by the church to God concerning him.**

The two imperfect tenses describe the situation and ask the reader to visualize and to dwell on it. Which will be the stronger, the dungeon and its guards or the prayers of the church? The entire congregation was making prayer to God; ἦν and the present participle are the periphrastic imperfect. Whether we prefer the reading περί or ὑπέρ the sense is that the prayer so strenuously made to God was "concerning" or "for" Peter in the sense that his mortal danger was laid before God who was asked that his will be done. God had allowed Stephen and recently also James to die; it might be that Peter's name was to be added to those of these martyrs, and yet God might deliver Peter even now (21:14). Human impossibilities are not impossibilities to him.

6) **Now, when Herod was about to bring him before them, on that very night Peter was sleeping between two soldiers, having been fettered with two chains, also guards before the doors were keeping the prison.**

The imperfect tenses still describe, but we are carried forward to the critical night, the one that it was Herod's intention was to be Peter's last on earth. Herod was very close to bringing him before them (προάγειν), thus carrying out his murderous plan. Hope seemed to be gone, rescue or deliverance impossible. God often lets a case become desperate and delays to the last in order that we may the more clearly recognize that the deliverance comes from him. It was "in that night," on the evening of which the Passover lambs were eaten.

Luke states how Peter was guarded: he lay sleeping between two soldiers and was chained to one on each side so that he could not stir even in his sleep without arousing these two guards who were stretched out at his sides. In addition (τε) guards manned all the doors of the prison. This is usually referred to the other two soldiers of the quaternion on duty; but while these may have stood inside or outside of the door of Peter's cell, the prison was kept by other guards, some of whom were stationed at each exit. Each quaternion when it was on duty, was responsible with its life for Peter's safekeeping; but the prison itself had many more guards, in fact, as the Codex Bezae reads, the entire cohort of the king's soldiers. Herod would certainly have quite a force of troops in Jerusalem at the time of the Passover when thousands of pilgrims were in the city.

7) Now we have the aorists which report the outcome in detail. **And lo, an angel of the Lord stood by him, and a light shone in the cell; moreover, having slapped the side of Peter, he awoke him, saying, Arise in haste! And his chains fell off from his hands. And the angel said to him, Gird thyself and bind on thy sandals! And he did thus. And he says to him, Throw thy robe around thee and be following me! And, having gone out, he was following. And he was not aware that it was true what was occurring through the angel but was thinking he was seeing a vision.**

The very thing that Herod intended to prevent, a recurrence of what had happened in the case of the Twelve when the Sanhedrin had imprisoned them, God made reality. God accepted Herod's challenge, and Peter was as easily released as the Twelve had been. Out of the fetters, the cell, the prison, out from among the special and all other guards, Peter walked as though they had not been there. The account is as lucid and clear as it can be; yet it has been considered a piece of fancy, and men have undertaken to tell us what happened. There is the lightning story; Peter is released by the head jailor — yet the quaternion paid for it with their lives; the king himself had Peter released — yet he killed the four guards; how Peter got out nobody knows, he just imagined that it was through the agency of an angel.

Comment is almost unnecessary. The guards are as though they were not there; none of them is conscious of what was happening. The angel and the light that filled his cell (οἴκημα, the place in the building) Peter saw when he awoke. Let us not overlook the fact that Peter was peacefully asleep. He did not lie there and worry on this apparently his last day on earth. What he would say at his trial and how he would act was dismissed from his mind; he had his Lord's own promises, which he had already tested twice before when he was a prisoner before the Sanhedrin (Matt. 10:19, 20; Mark 13:11-13; Luke 12:11; 21:14, 15). Thus Peter, having committed his soul to the Lord, slept in peace! At the angel's command to arise, the chains by which he was fastened to the soldiers at his wrists, at once drop off noiselessly. Ἀνάστα is the short form of the second aorist imperative active instead of ἀνάσθητι.

8) Peter acts as though he were in a dream and has to be told everything. He is ordered to fasten the belt about his tunic and to put on his sandals; the two imperatives are the middle voice: "gird thyself," "bind under for thyself." The belt had been unfastened and the sandals laid aside for sleep. When Peter has done this, he is told to throw his long loose outer robe around him and to be following the angel. He probably slept on the robe by drawing it over his body as well as he could. The aorist imperative to express the one act is also middle and reflexive, but the order to follow is properly the durative present.

9) Peter followed the angel as though no doors blocked his way. Did they open and then close noiselessly? No guards saw or heard anything. Peter him-

self could at the moment not tell whether what was occurring through the instrumentality (διά) of the angel was real (ἀληθές), or whether it was a vision that had come to him in his sleep. Luke had heard this from Peter's own lips. Note the three imperfect descriptive tenses; the present participle and the present infinitive are the same: "the thing occurring"; thought "to be seeing."

10) **And, on having gone through a first and second guard, they came to the gate, the iron one, the one leading into the city, which automatically opened for them; and having gone out, they went forward along one narrow street, and immediately the angel was gone from him.**

We need make no difficulties for ourselves. In v. 9 Peter and the angel go out of the cell and leave behind the quaternion that had been especially commanded to guard Peter. Now they pass through two other guarded portals and thus get into the great open court from which a great gate led to the street. The repetition of the article gives the noun as well as its two modifiers individual attention and forms a sort of climax (R. 762, 764): "the gate, the iron one, the one leading to the city." This final barrier was impressive. It was made of iron and thus very heavy and was locked with a massive bolt so that a number of men were required to open it. The other two had been ordinary doors. This massive gate opened of itself and let Peter and the angel out, and then, of course, closed just as automatically. That this happened just as the guards were changing is one of those unacceptable suggestions. There lay the prison undisturbed, all its locks and its bolts in place, all its many strong guards in their places — but the prisoner was gone.

The great gate probably opened upon a wide street (πλατεῖα) from which a narrow one (ῥύμη) turned off. The angel guided Peter forward along this one narrow street and thus some distance from the prison and then suddenly disappeared; ἀπέστη is the opposite of ἐπέστη in v. 7.

11) **And Peter, having come to himself, said: Now I know truly that the Lord sent forth his angel and took me out of Herod's hand and all the expectation of the people of the Jews.**

Peter's impression that it was all a dream continued until he stood alone on that narrow street in the dark night. All his movements had followed the directions and the leading of the angel, now he had to think and to act for himself. His natural consciousness returned. He now knew that he had not seen a mere vision, but that what he had seen was full reality. In v. 9 "he was not knowing" (ᾔδει used as an imperfect); in v. 11 he says, "Now I am knowing, do know." First, that Κύριος (*Yahweh*) had actually commissioned his angel, and that he had actually taken him out of Herod's hand or power, and thus out of all that the Jews were expecting, namely that Peter would be killed on the very anniversary of Jesus' death, killed without hope or help of rescue as James had been a short time before this. Peter is making an inventory of what God has done for him and what this really implies. The aorists state the two facts; ἐξείλετο is a form of ἐξαιρέω. God's intent is plain: Peter is not yet to suffer martyrdom, not yet is John 21:18, 19 to be fulfilled. Having been given his liberty, Peter is to use it to escape from Herod. God used supernatural means to free him but intends that from now on Peter is to use natural means and prudence to remain free.

12) **Also, on considering, he went to the house of Mary, the mother of John, the one surnamed Mark, where were many, having been assembled and praying.**

The participle states that Peter saw everything together, i. e., viewed his present situation in relation to what his next steps should be. On thus considering he went to the house of Mary who is identified by naming her son John, whose other name was Mark, by which name he is best known to us; he became the writer of the second Gospel. We again meet Mark in v. 25, and then in 15:5, 13. In Col. 4:10 he is called the ἀνεψιός or cousin of Barnabas. In I Pet. 5:13, Peter calls Mark "my son"; in analogy with I Tim. 1:2, where Paul calls Timothy his own son in the faith, it is fair to conclude that Mark was converted by Peter.

Luke states that many disciples were gathered together in Mary's house this night of the Passover and were praying for Peter. We have two predicative participles, for since one is perfect and the other present, neither can be combined with ἦσαν as a periphrastic verb form. Having been collected, they were now thus. Whether Peter knew that he would find many here is not indicated by Luke although some interpreters assume this to be a fact and build up their combinations on this assumption.

Let us at once state that Peter's object was first of all to notify his friends about his miraculous deliverance. Whether he would find many or few at Mary's house made little difference as to that object, for the whole church was deeply concerned about him, and he could not communicate with all that night. The fact that Peter found many at Mary's house was providential. Let us not forget how the Christians after the death of Stephen, and how Peter, remembering that, might well have expected another flight now that Herod was maltreating Christians, had beheaded James, and was attempting to do the same with Peter himself. It is not at all certain that Peter expected to find an assembly in Mary's house.

We take it that Peter's release was effected not long after midnight, for a new quaternion would go on duty at that time. This would allow until six A. M. before the escape was discovered, when a new quaternion came on duty. He who miraculously led Peter out of prison would scarcely permit a premature discovery of the escape. Those two soldiers within the cell snored peacefully on until well toward six o'clock.

No objection can be raised to the assumption that Mary's house often served as a place of meeting for a group of the disciples, and that the house was large, that Mary was rich, that she was a widow, a woman of character, and all that. But when we are asked to believe that hers was the house in the upper room of which Jesus celebrated the last Passover and instituted the Sacrament, that Mark was the man bearing the pitcher of water whom Peter and John were to follow, that Mary's husband was still living at that time, that Mark was present at the last Passover of Jesus, that he was the young man clad only in a sheet, which sheet was snatched from him when he ran for his life near Gethsemane — we regard this as one of those syntheses which Zahn's great *Kombinationsgabe* has produced.

But there are serious objections to this combination of facts. From this assembly on the night of Peter's escape we are asked to leap backward across a space of about fifteen years to the night of Jesus' last Passover, make the houses the same, and weave in everything else — that is the basic part of this hypothesis. This demands too much of us. Moreover, when Jesus delegated Peter and John to go and to prepare for the Passover, no man could even guess whose the house would be — it was *not* one where Jesus had been often; for Jesus states that its upper room would be tiled, the implication being that the disciples had never before set foot in it. No one but Jesus and the Twelve were present at the Passover: one proof of this is the fact that Jesus had to wash the feet of his disciples. If Mark was there, how did it come that he followed the procession clothed only in a sheet? Would any man clothed only in a sheet walk out through the city streets and into the country to the neighborhood of Gethsemane? Men slept in their tunics. How long did it take to put on a tunic, throw a robe around the shoulders, and then run out? We cannot accept Zahn's view.

13) **Now he having knocked at the door of the passage, there came to it a maid to answer by name Rhoda; and on recognizing the voice of Peter, due to her joy, she did not open the passage but, after running in, she reported Peter to be standing before the passage. But they said to her, Thou art crazy! Yet she insisted that it was so. They, however, went on to say, It is his angel! But Peter remained there knocking; and having opened, they saw him and were amazed.**

Here we have one of the beautiful detailed paintings of Luke. It is like the human interest stories that are so constantly published in the daily press of today. Four lines in 11:19, 20 dispose of the collection and the sending of the funds for relief; many lines fully describe Peter's experience.

According to Luke's account an outer door led into a passageway through the building that faced the street into an inner court. When Peter knocked at the door, a maid came to answer his knock (ὑπακοῦσαι, aorist), and Luke preserves even her name: Rhoda, our Rose or Rosa. R., *W. P.*, comments on these beautiful names for women such as Dorcas (Gazelle), Euodia (Sweet Aroma), Syntyche (Good Fortune). Luke's mention of the maid's name perhaps indicates that Peter knew the household well. As all her actions show, Rhoda herself was a Christian. Maids were used as portresses (John 18:16, 17); they were often, no doubt, slaves, although it is not likely that Rhoda was a slave.

Peter's knocking was heard in the dead of the night. Many disciples were gathered somewhere in the house.

Herod had maltreated some of the Christians, slain James, and was counting on slaying Peter. That knock at the outer door must have caused great fright among the gathered disciples. Their first thought must have been that Herod had sent soldiers to make more arrests, and that in some way he had found out about the gathering at Mary's house. Who should go to the door and answer that knocking? Surely, they would not send just this girl even though answering the door was her regular duty. Some brave man or two ought to have gone. But no, Rhoda goes. To be sure, her answering the door would not arouse suspicion and might afford the disciples time for flight. Bravely Rhoda goes. Let us remember her for that. With palpitating heart she listened in order to learn who was seeking entrance in the middle of the night.

14) On asking, Rhoda at once recognized Peter's voice — another sign that Peter was well known at that house. Straightforward, with nothing flighty or superstitious about her, she believes the evidence of her ears. Not for a moment does she hesitate and reason that this cannot be Peter, that he is far away in the terrible prison under heaviest guard. Instantly her heart is flooded with joy so that she forgets to unlock the door, runs back pell-mell to the assembled disciples, and shouts the great news. One must not sit in his study and coldly view this action. All the emotion, the sudden plunge from dreadful fears to the very extreme of joy in this maid's heart must be felt by the reader. "Peter is standing before the portal! Peter himself is standing before the portal!" she shouts to the assembly. The perfect ἑστάναι is always used in the sense of the present.

15) The answer she received was that she must be demented, we should say crazy. But Rhoda insisted that it was as she declared; with an adverb ἔχειν always has the sense of "to be," the present tense is that of

the direct discourse: *es verhaelt sich also.* Rhoda was the only one of that entire company who kept her balance. Although it was one against all, she did not waver. In the face of her constancy and under the necessity of explaining that voice which Rhoda had heard the disciples fell to saying (descriptive imperfect, which also holds us in suspense as to what the fact would turn out to be): "His angel it is!' i. e., that is who it must be.

Since ἄγγελος means "messenger," and angels are so called because they are God's messengers, some think that the exclamation meant that Peter had sent some messenger from his prison cell, and that Rhoda had heard this messenger say something about coming from Peter and had thus imagined that it was Peter himself. But this is untenable. These disciples could not shake off their mortal fears for Peter and leaped to the conclusion that he was already dead, and that his guardian angel had come to tell the sad news. It was a wild idea, but fears inspire weird notions. Matt. 18:10, and Heb. 1:14, plus old Jewish ideas may have been commingled in their minds. It is difficult to be entirely sure. We recall the cries of the apostles on the night they saw Jesus walking on the water, Matt. 14:26. The one thing that was the fact the company in Mary's house absolutely refused to believe. After praying for Peter's deliverance the thought that God might deliver him seemed incredible to them.

16) All this was going on while Peter was standing before the locked passage. To show that he was still there he kept on knocking. Finally there was only one thing to do, to stop arguing and to unlock that door. The plural shows that practically everybody went to the door. Imagine their perturbed state and the excitement as to what opening that door would reveal. When it swung back — there stood Peter! Rhoda was right, everybody else was wrong. The unbelievable

was fact — "they saw him." And now the sudden and terrific reaction: "they were amazed," ἐξέστησαν, their minds were completely upset.

17) They, of course, took him in, and a hubbub ensued. **Now, after beckoning to them with the hand to be silent, he recounted to them how the Lord had led him out of the prison. He also said, Report these things to James and the brethren, and having gone out, he traveled to a different place.**

Peter had to gesture with his hand in order to bring the excited company to silence. Then he told the entire story of his miraculous deliverance and asked that it be reported also to James and to the brethren, namely to the entire congregation. Without further delay Peter left them and proceeded to another place.

Why does Luke not name this place? The answer that Peter went into hiding in Jerusalem itself is too improbable to be accepted; besides, nearly all interpreters are agreed that he left the city. But why make so much ado about the place to which Peter went when Luke considered it too unimportant to be mentioned? Did Herod not die shortly after this Passover? Then all danger was past. Herod had no royal successors, Roman procurators once more governed. So Peter was free to come and to go as he might please. That is why Luke says only "to a different place." He does not say to what places the other apostles had gone at this time and for the same reason: the matter was of no special importance.

Zahn finds a hint here that Luke intended to write a third book in which the story of Peter was to be continued in detail. Luke, he tells us, would mention this "different place" in that third book. The supposition of a third book cannot be supported by an omission such as this. The reason Peter sent no word to the other apostles was the fact that they were not in Jerusalem at the time but at work elsewhere. The Apostle

James, it seems, had been seized by Herod and killed because James happened to return to Jerusalem for a visit; Herod had arrested Peter and probably intended to do the same with any of the other apostles who might come back.

Romanists fill out the blank which Luke left regarding the place to which Peter fled from Jerusalem by claiming that he went to Rome and remained there for a ministry of twenty-five years as the first pope of the church. This idea is fantastic. Luke wrote the Acts in order to show how the gospel took its course from Jerusalem to Rome, the first apostle to arrive there being Paul, and he a prisoner, and all the while Peter had been in Rome, had been there as a pope, and Luke never said a word about it in the entire Acts, did not even incidentally mention Rome when Peter left Jerusalem but wrote only "a different place." And when Paul finally proposed to visit Rome and wrote to Rome from Corinth he forgot to send greetings to Peter, and after he was in Rome and wrote to others from Rome he again forgot to send greetings from Peter. Thus there is no basis for Rome's contention.

The way in which James is mentioned here, and the fact that Peter sends word especially to him, prepare for 15:13; Gal. 1:19; 2:9, 12; James 1:1. In Gal. 1:19 Paul calls him "the Lord's brother"; the question as to what that relationship implies has been discussed in connection with 1:14, where Luke mentions "his (Jesus') brothers." He must have been the chief elder of the congregation at Jerusalem and, as 15:13, and Gal. 2:9 would imply, chief because of his personal character and ability. In 11:30, the Judean elders are mentioned but no apostles. The conclusion is evident that at this time the apostles no longer had personal charge of the congregation at Jerusalem.

After the great scattering that followed Stephen's stoning and Saul's cruel persecution the congregation again grew. At what particular time elders were placed in charge of it no one knows. During that first persecution the apostles remained in Jerusalem (8:1), but when Saul was converted and quiet again came, we see Peter working at Lydda, Joppa, and Caesarea; the other apostles must have gone out from Jerusalem in the same manner. So already at that time elders must have been chosen by the Jerusalem church, among them was James who from that time onward had charge of the congregation and of all its affairs.

18) **But when day came, there was no small disturbance among the soldiers as to what, then, had become of Peter. Herod, however, when he had made search for him and not found him, after putting the guards to an examination, ordered them to be led away to execution. And having gone down from Judea to Caesarea, he was spending time there.**

There was great excitement among the soldiers, which includes the entire garrison of the palace of Herod. Ἄρα implies: "since Peter was gone," and τί may be considered an accusative adverb, R. 916. The great question was: "What became of Peter?" as our idiom would state the question. He had vanished into thin air. This happened "when day came," as we take it, about six in the morning when the new quaternion came on duty. Herod, of course, was soon informed.

19) He scarcely made the search in person but made it by means of his chief officers. If Peter had somehow gotten out of his cell, how had he managed to get through the guards and the doors, the first, the second, and then the great iron gate? But thorough search (ἐπί in the participle) revealed not even a trace of the prisoner; he was just not to be found. The first two participles report the preliminary actions, the third what followed them, namely a judicial examination with Herod acting as judge. He grilled the four

guards from whom Peter had escaped. Of course, his questioning brought no results, and Herod then commanded that they "be led away," ἀπαχθῆναι, which is like the active in Luke 23:26, a judicial term which may have a modifier as it does in Matt. 27:31, and again may not. The four guards were forthwith summarily executed. It was the military law that the guards of a prisoner were liable with their lives for the security of the prisoner specially committed to them.

And yet one wonders at Herod. His chagrin was great; what about "all the expectation of the people of the Jews" (v. 11)? If Herod had not had the example of the Twelve recorded in 5:19-24, if he had not posted that extra heavy guard to prevent a recurrence, he might have been justified in giving the limit of the law to the poor guards. But he certainly must have felt that a higher hand was behind this inexplicable disappearance of the apostle whom he had planned to kill that day. Did he execute these guards merely to save his face? We know that he left the city, dropped all further persecutions, and spent some time in Caesarea. This is the force of διέτριβεν, the durative imperfect, which is used with or without a noun such as "time," "day," etc.

20) **Now he was in a hot quarrel with Tyrians and Sidonians. With one accord, however, they were present with him and, having persuaded Blastus, the one over the bedchamber of the king, they were duly asking peace because their country was being nourished from the king's.**

How the hot contention arose is not indicated. Tyre and Sidon lie on the coast of Phoenicia which was only a narrow strip of land extending along the coast. This territory belonged to Syria and not to Herod's domain, yet it was dependent on "the royal land" for the greater part of its foodstuffs, especially grain and cattle, being shut off from Syrian imports by rough mountainous heights. Whatever the cause of the rupture might have been, Herod had discontinued the supplies from his country. Tyre and Sidon were rich due to their maritime trade, yet they suffered under Herod's punitive measures. Thus a delegation of Tyrians and Sidonians was present in Caesarea for the purpose of asking peace.

The imperfect tenses are in place because the outcome of the negotiations was still uncertain. The middle ᾐτοῦντο, "were duly asking," indicates that the matter was a piece of business; the negotiations were official. The delegation had made Blastus, the king's chamberlain, "the one over the king's bedchamber" (the Greek lacking our ready title), their friend. We need not ask how they "persuaded" him; bribes have always been effective. He was using his influence with the king. Διὰ τό with the present infinitive states the reason for both the presence of the delegation and for their petition.

21) **And on an appointed day Herod, having put on royal apparel, after having sat down on the throne, was making an oration unto them; and the people kept calling, Voice of a god and not of a man! And immediately the Lord's angel smote him because he did not give the glory to God. And having come to be eaten of worms, he expired.**

From Josephus (*Ant.* XIX, 8, 2) we learn that the fixed or appointed day was the second in a grand celebration of games after the Roman fashion in honor of a victory and triumph of the emperor Claudius on his return from Britain and not in honor merely of his birthday or of the anniversary of his reign. On this day Herod gave his answer to the Tyrian and Sidonian ambassadors in the great theater where the games were being celebrated. The affair was made a magnificent occasion inasmuch also as the answer was favorable.

Luke says that Herod had arrayed himself in royal apparel. That is putting it mildly; Josephus speaks of a στολή or festal robe wrought in silver so that on this morning the slanting rays of the sun made the king glisten and sparkle with brilliance.

The theater was filled with the δῆμος, "the people" considered as a body politic (λαός would be the people at large, ἔθνος the nation, ὄχλος just an unorganized crowd). In their hearing the king, seated on the βῆμα, the elevated stage with its chair or throne, delivered an oration to the ambassadors, ἐδημηγόρει, the word indicating the desire for the favor and the praise of the δῆμος. The king was mounting to the pinnacle of his glory. The games spoke of the great favor Herod was enjoying at the hands of the emperor; the games reflected the glories of Rome; all the important and dignified personages of Herod's kingdom were present among the *dēmos*; then there were these ambassadors from Tyre and Sidon with their humble suit for peace. In his blazing silver apparel and with his demogogic oration the king was grandly rising to the occasion.

22) And then the shouts began among the *dēmos*: "A god's voice and not a man's!" As far as the people were concerned, most of them were pagan idolaters and used to deifying the Roman emperors, and this shouting was no more than a bit of flattery to tickle the vanity of the king. His theatrical robes, his entire grandiose bearing on this special day for which the affair was staged invited the flattery which ranked Herod among the gods as was the case with regard to the Roman emperors. But Herod was a nominal Jew, the king of the Jewish nation, and, as we have seen in connection with his persecution of the Christians, one who posed as a most zealous exponent of Judaism, its great defender against Christian encroachments. This Jew permitted those shouts that deified him to continue instead of instantly hushing them as being utter

blasphemy; he let these pagan idolaters make a pagan god of him and enjoyed it.

We must note the imperfect tenses in v. 21, 22. They picture what was happening and intimate that something decisive followed as the outcome. The aorists used in the next verse record what that outcome was.

23) Immediately, right there in the theater, Herod was struck by the Lord's angel ἀνθ' ὧν, "in exchange or in return for which things", i. e., because he did not give the glory to God, namely all divine glory, instead of accepting such glory for his own person. Καί adds what this smiting of the angel implied: "he came to be eaten of worms," σκωληκόβρωτος, and thus died, ἐξέψυξεν, the lower word, "breathed out his ψυχή," not the higher, "breathed out his πνεῦμα." The *psyche* is man's immaterial part in so far as it animates his physical body, hence it is often translated "life." So all that Luke says and properly can say is that life went out of him. This was the frightful and sudden end of Agrippa I which came to him after only three short years of royal reign; he died at the age of 54.

The manner of his death is plainly marked as a *Gottesgericht*, a signal and visible judgment of God. A number of similar horrible deaths through masses of maggots eating the victim's putrifying body as though it were already a corpse are reported, all of them coming to human monsters. Read Josephus on the death of Herod the Great, *Ant.* 17, 6, 5; II Maccabees 9:5, 9 on the death of Antiochus Epiphanes who bitterly persecuted the Jews and is prominent as a type of Antichrist. Pheretima, queen of Cyrene, celebrated for her cruelty, was eaten by masses of worms while she was still alive; Herminianus, Roman governor of Cappadocia, who cruelly persecuted the Christians, was another; also the emperor Galerius, the last Roman emperor to persecute the church. The historian Niebuhr adds also Philip II of Spain who was noted for his cruelties and his persecutions.

As far as Josephus and his account of Herod's death are concerned (*Ant.* 19, 8, 2), he states that Herod lived only five days after being stricken in the theater and agrees that it was due to the fact that he accepted the blasphemous praise. Josephus always writes with an eye to the Romans and thus says nothing about the worms eating Herod's vitals but tones this down to pains and trouble in Herod's "belly." In *Ant.* 18, 6, 7 he tells of the time when Herod was a prisoner under Tiberius in Rome, how he saw an owl sitting, and how a German fellow prisoner worked his way toward him and prophesied that this owl meant good luck, and that he would soon be elevated to the highest position; but that if he should again see an owl, it would be the reverse, that he would then live only five days. Josephus claims that while he was in the theater he saw an owl sitting upon a rope and died after five days in fulfillment of the German's prophecy. If any basis in fact exists for this story about the owl, we set it down as an instance of second sight.

Zahn seems to find a connection between this owl as a messenger (ἄγγελος) of evil and Luke's angel (ἄγγελος) who smote Herod and thinks that Josephus, who wrote his *Antiquities* in the year 93 or 94, must have read Luke's statement in Acts. No angel was visible when Herod was stricken; the fact that God employed the agency of an angel in visiting his sudden and swift judgment on Herod was the conviction of the apostles who had the illumination of the Holy Spirit.

24) **The Word of God, however, went on growing and being multiplied.** That is the way in which the histories of the persecutions always end. Herod perished, the Word just grew more than ever. Note the imperfect tenses: grew and grew, etc. Both verbs mean that the Word itself increased by entering more

and more hearts. In the parable of the Sower the seed thus multiplies itself; in the parable of the Pounds the capital multiplies by being used in trade. It is a wonderful view of the vital life of the Word. It actually thrives under persecution. Yet we so often hang our heads when God sends persecution here and there. Ten most bloody persecutions ravaged the church under the pagan Roman emperors, and, when they had spent themselves, Christianity had permeated the empire, and in due time a Christian emperor ascended the throne.

25) **Now Barnabas and Saul returned out of Jerusalem, having fulfilled their ministry, having taken along with them John, the one called Mark.**

We have discussed this passage in connection with 11:30, which see. Herod died in 44, the relief was sent from Antioch *after* Herod's death and not before, for the famine and its distress came later. In 11:30 only Judea is mentioned, here, however, we see that Jerusalem was included, and no deductions can be made from "Judea" that would exclude the presence of Barnabas and Saul in Jerusalem.

A curious textual question arises because of the fact that two great uncials read εἰς, "to Jerusalem," instead of ἐξ or ἀπό, "out of" or "from." But in spite of Westcott and Hort who adopt εἰς this reading must be rejected as contradicting the context and also 11:30. The grammarians raise another question regarding the aorist participle συμπαραλαβόντες by stating that it might denote action that was subsequent to that of the main verb "returned"; it indicates coincident action in the very nature of the case, R. 862. We have met Mark in v. 12; we shall meet him again in 13:5, 9. We see how he got to Antioch and could be taken along on the first great missionary journey by Saul. Since he was a cousin of Barnabas, the latter must have advocated taking him along, to which Saul readily consented.

CHAPTER XIII

THE SECOND HALF

The Gospel Among the Gentiles in the Empire
Chapters 13 to 28

The time covered by this period extends from 45 to 62, from the first missionary journey to Paul's imprisonment in Rome.

The action moves through the Roman Empire in a grand sweep. Mission work reaches its highest development.

The chief personage is Paul; at his side appear his notable assistants. We also again meet Peter in chapter 15, and James in chapters 15 and 21.

We see the progress of the gospel first, with Paul at liberty (13 to 21:16); then, the progress with Paul in captivity (21:17 to 28:31). Three great missionary journeys are prominent while Paul is at liberty. Besides Jerusalem, Antioch, the center from which the journeys were made, attracts our attention; then Corinth and Ephesus and other localities become important centers of Christian activity. When Paul is in captivity, Caesarea draws attention but only as the stepping-stone to the final goal which is Rome. Thus Luke's objective is reached: the great transition of the gospel from its original center in Jerusalem and Judaism to its grand new center, Rome and the vast Gentile world.

The Third Quarter

The Progress of the Gospel with Paul at Liberty

THE FIRST MISSIONARY JOURNEY: THROUGH THE ISLAND OF CYPRUS

1) Barnabas and Saul are back at Antioch after their brief mission of relief (11:30; 12:25). **Now there were in Antioch throughout the present church prophets and teachers, both Barnabas and Symeon called Niger and Lucius, the Cyrenian, also Manaen, Herod the tetrarch's child companion, and Saul.**

Transitional δέ transfers us to a time that is later than that mentioned in 11:26 and in 11:30 and 12:25. Luke advances us from the summer or the fall of 44 to the year 49. Zahn has corrected the 50 which is found in his *Introduction to the New Testament* III, 482, Chronological Table, to 49, in his *Kommentar*, 868, in accord with a recently discovered inscription.

Saul and Barnabas are to be sent away on a missionary tour that will necessitate their absence from Antioch for some time. Luke thus mentions the most prominent "prophets and teachers" in the congregation at this time. Three of these would remain at Antioch. We give κατά distributive force "throughout the church" in Antioch because we think of the church as being distributed over the large city and having a host of members.

The added οὖσαν is taken to mean *in der dortigen Gemeinde* (B.-D. 474, 5), "in the local church" (Moulton in R. 1107); but the participle is not to be construed with "in Antioch": "the church being in Antioch, being there"; we take it to be temporal: "being" at the time of which Luke writes: "the *present* church." It is not said that the church had these five illustrious teachers in 44; it has them now in the year 49.

"Prophets" is explained in 11:27, and here refers to men who are able to expound the Word. The context does not suggest prophets of the type of Agabus, to whom God communicated future events. These men served the congregation in the regular manner. "Prophets and teachers" thus go together: men who thoroughly understand the Word and are at the same time able to teach it to others. Hence, too, we decline to let the two τε divide the five named into three prophets and two teachers. For certainly Saul, the very last in the list, had already received direct communications from the Lord (among others also the one mentioned in 22:17, etc.), while we do not know whether Barnabas had received such communications. B.-D. 444, 5 does not divide into groups, yet Luke evidently intended to indicate two groups although we do not see why he divides the list of names. When Barnabas is placed first and Saul last, this seems to imply that the names are arranged according to the time of the conversion of those named or, possibly, according to the time of their entrance into the church at Antioch.

Barnabas and Saul we know. The fact that Symeon had the Roman name Niger in addition to his Aramaic name and was so designated by the Greeks, is only a common feature and really states nothing definite about the man. If he were the Simon who bore the cross for Jesus, Luke would have so identified him. *That* Simon came to distinction because of his two sons (Mark 15:21) and hence not because of a later prominence of his own. The fact that Symeon was not a Cyrenian like Lucius also proves that he was not Simon, the crossbearer. Lucius is designated as a Cyrenian and may have been one of those who fled after Stephen's death and first preached the gospel to the Greeks in Antioch (11:20). B.-D. 268 calls attention to the article "*the* Cyrenian" and thinks that it was perhaps intended to distinguish him from Luke, whose name appears also as "Lucius." Zahn, who finds Luke indirectly referred to in 11:28 (Codex Bezae), scouts the idea that he could have here listed himself as one of the great teachers in Antioch. Symeon is designated by his second name because there are many other Symeons or Simons; Lucius by his birthplace for a similar reason; but Manaen by his connection with the tetrarch, Herod Antipas, whose child companion he had been, σύντροφος, *Milchbruder*, *collactaneus* (Vulgate), nourished and brought up together with this Herod. That would make Manaen about 69 years old, for Herod Antipas was born in 20 B. C. Some interpreters identify Manaen with the βασιλικός mentioned in John 4:46-53; but this is only a guess. With more assurance we may say that Manaen was of aristocratic if not princely birth and thus stands out among the disciples. His princely education was an asset in his present leadership.

On the basis of a hypothetical first edition of Acts, Zahn thinks that a sixth name was added between Lucius and Manaen, namely that of Ticius, an Antiochian, whom Zahn supposes to be Titus, one of Paul's later assistants, this being the only mention of him in Acts. Aside from the hypothesis itself (*Forschungen IX*) and Zahn's alteration of "Ticius" to Titus, he fails to show how Luke could issue a second edition and from it omit this most certainly important name.

2) **And while they were engaged in a divine service to the Lord and on fasting, the Holy Spirit said, Separate now for me Barnabas and Saul for the work to which I have called them for myself. Then, after having fasted and prayed and laid the hands on them, they released them.**

The great hour had come: the call to the Gentile world, even to stand before kings! Saul had waited all these years, from 35 to 49, and had been working here in Antioch for about six years. Now at last he was to go out into the pagan world, not alone, but together with his close friend Barnabas. The Attic orators used the word λειτουργεῖν to designate any free service rendered to the state, in the LXX it is used with reference to the official service rendered by priests and Levites, and in the New Testament with reference to any sacred official service (Rom. 13:6, and 15:27 are not exceptions.) Here the participle must mean that these five men were not merely generally busy in their official capacities as prophets and teachers but were in the midst of a divine service with the assembled congregation; it may well have been one of the regular Sunday services which included the entire congregation as such.

The early Christians retained the Jewish religious custom of fasting. The law prescribed only one annual fast on the Day of Atonement, hence this is also called The Fast (Acts 27:9). A few additional fast days had been arranged by the nation itself in memory of sad experiences. The Pharisaic fasting was self-imposed and was observed for the sake of acquiring merit. Yet pious Jews also fasted in all sincerity, and it was this custom that was followed by the Christian Church. This fasting was always partial. (The writer's parents never ate before the Communion.) It is correct, the pronoun αὐτῶν refers only to the five men, but the first participle insures the presence of the congregation.

We find no danger in thinking that the church as such was present. Barnabas and Saul belonged to the congregation as prophets and teachers. The members were certainly concerned in the mission of these two. The Holy Spirit alone was their Sender and not the congregation, and certainly not the other three teachers. In 14:26, etc., we see that the church commended Barnabas and Saul to the grace of God for the work which they did and that they returned and made a report to the church. We are not told how the Holy Spirit spoke as he did although it is usually assumed that it was by means of a special revelation to one of the three teachers who was to remain, but this is done largely because we know of no other way unless Saul himself received the revelation. We say the latter only because Saul had previously received such revelations, cf., 9:12, and 22:17, etc.

The order of the Spirit was: "Separate now for me Barnabas and Saul," etc. Here the second person plural cannot refer to the five men who are included in the αὐτῶν, because two of them were to be separated; this command is addressed to the entire church. It was to give up the services of Barnabas and of Saul and let them serve the Holy Spirit elsewhere. Δή is rare and has a note of urgency. It emphasizes the imperative and is like the Latin *jam* or the German *doch*. There is no real equivalent in English, hence it is left untranslated in our versions; it is an emotional particle, and we may render: "Do now separate!" Note the perfect: for the work to which "I have called them for myself" (middle). What this work was we know from 9:15; 22:14, 15, 21; 27:16, in regard to Saul, and this was now to apply also to Barnabas.

3) What the Spirit ordered was promptly done. We do not think that the commissioning service was set for a later day. We take it that the service was now turned into a commissioning service. It was considerably prolonged. Thus with fasting, praying, and laying on of hands, the latter by the presbyters and not by the three other prophet-teachers who were left behind, "they released them," namely the whole church at Antioch. Luke is careful not to say: "they sent or they commissioned them," which would have been untrue.

The substance of the prayers we know from 14:26: "they were recommended to the grace of God for their work." It was a great day for the entire church.

The laying on of hands was used in connection with the seven deacons and is explained in 6:6. It is here again used in the same symbolical way. This, of course, was not ordination for Barnabas and for Saul, who were already "prophets and teachers." Yet it was the ceremony the church deemed proper formally to carry out the will of the Spirit in order to separate these two for their special work. We have no divine command for ordination, and when we now ordain we merely follow in the footsteps of the apostles and the early church by solemnly setting men apart for the holy ministry. So we also adopt the laying on of hands for our ordination and also for our confirmation of catechumens. We are free to do this and equally free not to add the ancient fasting. The virtue of these rites does not lie in the symbol of the hands being laid on but in the prayers of the church for those who are thereby set apart, prayers that are efficacious with God.

4) **They on their part, therefore, having been sent out by the Holy Spirit, went down to Seleucia and from there sailed away to Cyprus.**

Luke writes αὐτοί with a natural emphasis and refers to Barnabas and Saul, and μὲν οὖν is used as in 1:6. Luke purposely repeats that it was the Holy Spirit who had sent them out, and had done that by an immediate call. So the two went the short distance from Antioch to its harbor town Seleucia at the mouth of the Orontes River, found a ship there, and sailed for Cyprus, the island of which Barnabas was a native; see 4:36. The distance was not great. The Spirit evidently let them choose the locality where they wished to labor, and they followed natural lines by returning to the old homeland of Barnabas where he knew the type of people that would be met. It is one of Luke's literary habits always to name the harbors in connection with the voyages; this has been attributed to his love for the sea which was so characteristic of the Greeks. We are not told how this tour was financed. Money was required for the passage on the boat and also otherwise. It does not seem that the congregation at Antioch supplied the funds. All that one may conclude is that Barnabas and Saul went quite on their own.

5) **And being at Salamis, they began to proclaim the Word of God in the synagogues of the Jews. Moreover, they had also Mark as attendant.**

The actual work of proclaiming the Word started at Salamis, and that method was at once used which Saul followed ever after: they began in the synagogues. That was a simple and an easy way. As teachers and speakers who were efficient and able in every way, who were themselves of Jewish birth and training, permission was always freely given them to address the synagogue congregations and to expound to them the Old Testament prophecies concerning the Messiah and their fulfillment in Jesus. This was, of course, mission work only among the Jews, but it was done among the Jews of the diaspora, in pagan cities, and was intended to reach out from the synagogues to the Gentiles of those cities.

It is often thought of as following the rule or, shall we say, the principle: to the Jews first and then to the Gentiles. But this was not a mere rule. The wall of partition (Eph. 2:14) had been removed, *together* they were to become Christians. It was this far deeper principle that Barnabas and Saul followed when they entered the synagogues first. The Jews had the Scriptures and the Scripture knowledge of God. Therefore the beginning was naturally made with them. Salvation was of the Jews (John 4: 22), the Messiah was David's son, redemption was wrought in Israel. The gospel was thus offered first to the Jews throughout the diaspora so that the Jews might lead the Gentiles into the Christian Church. It would have been abnormal to follow any other course; in fact, wrong to ignore the Jews.

At this point Luke remarks that Mark was a third party in the work but only in the capacity of an attendant; he was the ὑπηρέτης, literally, "under-rower in a trireme," and then anyone under the orders of another, "an underling." This word is used with reference to the Levite Temple police who were under the orders of their στρατηγός or commander, for instance at the time of the arrest of Jesus in Gethsemane and at the Jewish trial of Jesus. This shows what Mark's duties were: he was to do what Barnabas and Saul ordered him to do. The view that he was to baptize the converts is untenable. The administration of this sacrament was not a chore but as sacred and important as the preaching of the gospel itself, for it had been commanded by Jesus as much as the preaching had. Mark did whatever Barnabas and Saul asked him to do; they assigned his duties. This is the force of "underling." They may have used him also for teaching, perhaps also even for baptizing or helping to baptize on occasion. All depended on what might be needed. Some of his duties were prabably those of an ordinary servant. It was through the instrumentality of his cousin Barnabas that he was taken along. Luke mentions his presence in Jerusalem in 12:12, and shows how he was brought to Antioch in 12:25.

6) **Having gone through the whole island as far as Paphos, they found a man, a magus, a false prophet, a Jew, whose name was Barjesus, who was with the proconsul Sergius Paulus, a man of understanding. This one, having called to himself Barnabas and Saul, earnestly sought to hear the Word of God. But Elymas, the magus — for thus his name is translated — began to stand against**

them, seeking to turn the proconsul aside from the faith.

All that Luke states in v. 5 is that, upon arrival at Salamis, they adopted the practice of preaching in the synagogues. Now we read that the missionaries crossed the entire island by following its southeastern shore line — the interior is mountainous — to Paphos at the western end. Luke does not intend to furnish an itinerary nor to describe what was done at each place. We have no details about Salamis. There were no places of importance along the route to Paphos. The old Paphos had been destroyed by an earthquake in 15 B. C. With the aid of Augustus the new city was built at some distance from the site of the old ruins, at a spot where a bay faced south. Here the Roman proconsul had his residence.

The reliability of Luke's statement was formerly challenged on the ground that Cyprus was an imperial province and hence was not governed by a proconsul but by a propraetor. That was, indeed, true at a former time, but at this time Cyprus had been made a senatorial province, and its governor thus was a proconsul as Luke states. The island later again became an imperial province. General Cesnola discovered an inscription on the north coast of Cyprus which was dated "in the proconsulship of Paulus," the very Sergius Paulus of Acts. Robertson, *Luke the Historian, etc.*, 182.

We are granted only one glimpse of the work done in Cyprus: Saul's clash with a Jewish charlatan before the proconsul of the island. It is a parallel to the experience Peter had with Simon Magus as recorded in 8:9, etc. As far as the record goes, the work went on in its regular course with nothing especially to be noted. Here in Paphos the clash with the magus is important, not for its own sake, but for the effect it had on the proconsul. After he had been won for the gospel, great success was assured. This μάγος was a man of the type of Simon Magus, of whom μαγεύων and μαγεῖαι are predicated in 8:9, 11, the practice of magical arts, which were usually, however, associated with occultism and strange religious claims. This man was "a pseudo-prophet," who mixed his arts with false religious doctrines which were most likely concocted by himself. He was a "Jew," of course, no longer in religion but only by birth. He was a man of less importance than Simon Magus and spread no mysterious halo of divinity about himself.

7) He had managed to attach himself to the proconsul whom Luke characterizes as συνετός, which is more than φρόνιμος, "sensible," and means rather the quality of understanding, ability to put his mind on an object and to grasp it. This charlatan, unlike Simon Magus, cared nothing for the ordinary people but, like so many of his ilk in this era, sought to impress only some great personage and subject him to his control. The fact that he should have had a hold on a man of understanding such as Sergius Paulus was is not so strange when we recall what Juvenal reports regarding the Emperor Tiberius, "sitting on the rock of Capri with his flock of Chaldeans around him." Shallow men like Pontius Pilate scoffed at truth and anything serious, others who were dissatisfied with ordinary idolatry fell for the impressive and cunning deceivers who offered mysterious and apparently supernatural arts invested with strange Oriental philosophies.

Yet when this proconsul heard of Barnabas and Saul and the stir they were causing in Paphos he summoned them and, as Luke expresses it, ἐπεζήτησεν, "earnestly sought," to hear the Word of God, i. e., this teaching which they had to offer. The aorist of the verb and the infinitive imply that he obtained what he sought and fully heard that Word, namely the gospel. Barnabas and Saul had a public audience with the governor, at which they could speak at length and fully inform their great hearer.

8) And now we come upon a linguistic problem that is connected also with the variant readings of the codices and of the ancient versions. Does Luke intend to say that "Elymas" is a translation of ὁ μάγος, and is "Elymas" then an Arabic or an Aramaic term that is equivalent to a professional title like "professor" which was appropriated by the old mesmerists, the present mediums, and others? This has been the usual view. Attempts were made to clear up the etymology by reference to the Arabic verb *'alima,* "to gain insight," "to grasp," and the noun *'alim,* "magician," "diviner."

The contention of Zahn and others is that "Elymas" is not intended to be a translation of ὁ μάγος which needs no translation but of the man's name "Barjesus," a patronymic with "bar" to be understood in the sense of "son." The process starts by regarding "Elymas" as a Greek term to which the Aramaic "Barjesus" is then fitted. The result is that "Elymas," a corruption of *'Etoemus* (*'Etimas*), is really *paratus* = "the Expert"; and "Barjesus," when this is derived from the Hebrew *shavah* which in the piel means "to smooth," "to finish" (omitting *bar* = "son"), is something of an equivalent of "the Expert."

This "Son of the Expert" or simply "Expert," the "ready man," began to oppose Barnabas and Saul and sought to divert (διαστρέψαι, turn this way and that by raising objections) the proconsul, his patron, from the faith, the article pointing to the objective sense of "faith," i. e., from the Word intended for faith. The imperfect tense and the present participle reveal only the attempt and point forward to the outcome. The devil had his advocate at the proconsul's side who was seeking to defeat the messengers of God. The trickster feared that he would lose control and be ousted. Evil men are always in the road to prevent the gospel from saving others. Spurious science and false religious teachings know they will be ousted if the gospel has full sway.

9) **But Saul, also Paul, filled with the Holy Spirit, earnestly looking on him, said: O full of all guile and all villainy, devil's son, enemy of all righteousness, wilt thou not cease to turn aside the Lord's ways, the straight ones? And now, lo, the Lord's hand on thee! And thou shalt be blind, not seeing the sun until a season! And immediately there fell on him a mist and darkness and, going around, he began seeking hand-leaders.**

In the simplest way, with a mere ὁ καί, which R. 734 thinks might be intended as a relative, Luke introduces the name "Paul" instead of Saul. From this point onward he intends to use only the name Paul except where the apostle may speak of himself. The reason for making the change at this point is plain. Up to this moment it is always "Barnabas and Saul," which implies that Barnabas exercised the leadership; but now the Spirit descends on Saul, and from this point onward the leadership rests with him. Here, then, was a fitting place to indicate that Saul now used his Roman name Paul because he worked among Greeks to whom *Sh'aûl* would sound too foreign.

Saul did not receive or himself take the name Paul at the time of his baptism in Damascus. If that had been the case, Luke would have called him Paul from that time onward. The idea that conversion "made Saul a Paul" is not correct. Saul did not assume the name Paul here in Paphos and did not choose "Paul" because of the proconsul's name "Paulus." These suggestions, as Farrar says, contain "an element of vulgarity impossible to St. Paul." Augustine thought that he chose "Paul" from motives of humility since the word means "little"; but almost the opposite is true. "Paul" had a proud ring in those days as suggesting the glories of the Aemelian family (Page).

On the eighth day, at the time of his circumcision, the father named his little son after the one Jewish king who had been chosen from the tribe of Benjamin, the tribe to which the family belonged; thus he received his Jewish name "Saul." But he was born a Roman citizen of the great city of Tarsus and thus received his Roman name (Latin) "Paul" on the ninth day. Like his Jewish name and like so many names of children, this was chosen because it was borne by illustrious persons of the Roman world. Other Jews had Greek names; the apostle and the evangelist were both named Philip after the tetrarch of that name. Saul's father gave the child a Roman and Latin name because he was a Roman citizen with all the rights in the Roman empire this implied. The child had both names from infancy. When his father called him he shouted, "Saul, Saul!" but when the Greek boys with whom he played called him they shouted, "Paul, Paul!" In his early connections with Jews he was called "Saul" as Luke has named him up to this time; from now on as he henceforth worked chiefly among Gentiles, "Paul" was the name he used, and Luke makes the change by showing that it began at this point. That is why Luke writes only ὁ καὶ Παῦλος and says nothing about his assuming this name; he always had had it.

It was not Barnabas but Paul who at this critical moment was filled with the Holy Spirit and was made the divine instrument for bringing judgment upon Barjishwan — Hetoimos (as Zahn calls him). Up to this point in the narrative Barnabas is always named first. Here in Cyprus, his native land, he properly took the lead. Now that the missionaries are about to leave the island, Paul will be the leader. This was

God's intention regarding this "chosen instrument" for the work among Gentiles; and with it, no doubt, went also Paul's own higher qualifications for the leadership. Moreover, Paul would continue in this work among Gentiles long after Barnabas.

When Paul now denounces the trickster and tells him that he will be blinded he does this, not by his own power, but through the Spirit. It is the same thing that occurred in Peter's case, who exposed Ananias and his hypocrisy by the Spirit's revelation and not by any powers of his own. To say that being filled with the Holy Spirit means being filled only with "a high degree of agitation," *in hochgradiger Erregung*, is unwarranted. A holy indignation did, indeed, move Paul just as it moved Jesus when he denounced the Pharisees and announced their judgment, cf., Matt. 23:13, etc. But Paul could never have brought blindness on this charlatan by even the intensest indignation. A mere volition on the part of an apostle never worked a miracle; the Lord and his Spirit use even the apostles only as instruments to carry out their volitions.

10) Paul is not carried away by his indignation, for his words have cold logic in them, in this respect being like the denunciation of the Pharisees on the part of Jesus. First, the evil in the man's heart, his inner motives are named; next, what these make of him in God's sight; then, what they ever lead him to do. "And now" rests the penalty of the Spirit on this clear basis. First, the full evidence of outrageous guilt; then, the verdict announcing the punishment. The Spirit, speaking through Paul, is absolutely just.

The Greek uses "O" sparingly, which makes it only the stronger when it is used. "Full of all guile and all villainy" exposes exactly what was in this man's heart. These were the motives back of his opposition to the missionaries and his efforts to keep the proconsul from the faith. Δόλος is "bait" and then the cunning that uses it to catch its victim; the word is very much in place here: the proconsul was the victim who was to snatch at the bait this fellow was offering by his arguments against the faith. Ῥαδιουργία, "the ability to do a thing easily," is used in the sense of "unscrupulousness," when one acts without the least compunction or hesitation as to the damage he may do to others in gaining his ends, hence "villainy." The fellow was ready to do or to say anything in order to keep his hold on his victim. Twice Paul adds "all," which marks the extent of this man's viciousness.

What this really made of him Paul states in plain words, "a devil's son," υἱός is to be understood in the ethical sense as described in John 8:44. "Son" and "sons" are used in both an evil and a good way. We have "sons of light," "sons of Israel," or "of the prophets," etc.; in II Thess. 2:3, "son of perdition." Children are dear to men; but in ethical connections the son reflects the father or the quality and thus represents the one or the other. A devil's son is not only his offspring but one in whom the devil's characteristics reappear. "Devil" is Satan without stress on the etymology "slanderer." Those who understand "Barjesus" as meaning "son of Jesus" (Joshuah) find a contrast to this name in "devil's son." Paul specifies the ethical feature when he adds "enemy of all righteousness." An ἐχθρός is a hating personal enemy, and δικαιοσύνη is righteousness or right in the forensic sense as meeting the approval of the righteous divine Judge. Anything of that sort this man hated, for it would utterly condemn and destroy him and his vicious practices.

The motive, the man, and now the deeds: "Wilt thou not cease to turn aside the Lord's ways, the straight ones?" The addition of the adjective by means of a second article makes a kind of apposition and climax, R. 776. These blessed ways of the Lord, these teachings of his that lead to faith, that are straight and true in every part and not crooked, not tricky, with no ulterior design, this fellow intends never to cease turning this way and that (διαστρέφων as in v. 8), to twist and to pervert by his objections, making them appear as what they are not, as something evil according to the evil that fills his own heart. The question is strongly rhetorical, for it has οὐ with the subjunctive (futuristic, R. 942) as though the answer is to be "yes" while the sense is: "No, thou wilt not cease doing this!" The fellow would let no moral consideration of any kind stop him in his nefarious doing.

11) But the Spirit has a way that will stop him: "And now" as the legitimate deduction from this character and conduct, "lo, the Lord's hand upon thee!" Why insert "is" and weaken what is an exclamation and not a cool declaration? Paul, as it were, sees that hand or almighty power of the Lord Jesus striking this devil's son. The fellow is to be blind and not see the sun until the time (καιρός) set by the Lord. This blindness for a time is a judicial penalty; it is by no means all that he deserved, but in his grace God moderated it by not cutting off the opportunity for repentance. It was a preliminary judgment like so many that God inflicts on wilful sinners in order by such severe means possibly to turn them from their evil ways. These judgments, if they are spurned, prefigure and announce the final, fatal judgment. God warned Pharaoh with ever greater severity until the cup of his obduracy overflowed; then came the final stroke. This man's wilful blindness was punished by miraculous physical blindness. The penalty often corresponds to the guilt. If this penalty would fail of its proper effect, a greater

penalty awaited him, the darkness of everlasting death. The devil's son would then end in the devil's eternal night.

The man was struck blind instantly. Those who think that this was effected gradually because "a mist" is mentioned before "darkness" disregard the aorist with its adverb. Sight was blotted out at once. "Mist and darkness" are one idea, and mist is added in order to show that the eyeballs were filmed so that their sight went out like a light that is blown out. The effect was that, "going around, he began to seek handleaders," a compound noun for which we lack a current equivalent. He would mislead the proconsul, he now sought someone to lead him, and that not amiss.

Here the man disappears from view. No one knows how long his blindness lasted. Zahn thinks that he was certainly cast off by Sergius Paulus and that eight years later he appeared as "one of the friends" of the procurator Felix (Acts 24:24), the fellow who was employed to lure away Drusilla, the daughter of Agrippa I, from her husband Azizus, the king of Emesa (Joseph, *Ant.* 20, 7, 2), in order to marry Felix. He is described as a Cyprian Jew and a magician. As to his name, the "Simon" found in the texts of Josephus is due to Christian copyists who placed this name in the margin and then into the text, thinking that the Simon Magus of Acts 8 was referred to; the name was "Atomon" and seems to be the "Hetoimon" ("Elymas," see v. 8) of Luke. All that one can say is, interesting if true.

12) **Then, on seeing what had occurred, the proconsul believed, dumbfounded at the teaching of the Lord.**

This punitive miracle dumbfounded the proconsul The undeniable power manifested in it he rightly connected with "the teaching or doctrine of the Lord

(Jesus)," thereby showing himself συνετός, "one understanding" (v. 7), by putting his mind and what had occurred together properly. He saw the same power in the miracle and in the doctrine which it sealed.

Luke writes the simple, positive, assuring aorist: "he believed." We have no reason whatever to discount the word. The reasons brought forward for doing so are invalid the moment Luke's account of the work in Cyprus is viewed as a whole. We at once see that the proconsul is the only convert that is mentioned as a result of the entire work done in Cyprus. That speaks rather plainly. It was not Luke's intention to report in detail. He mentions only two towns, Salamis where the missionaries landed and Paphos from which they left. It is not even stated that converts and congregations resulted in these towns. Yet many were undoubtedly converted, and a number of congregations was left behind.

Is it any wonder, then, that Luke writes regarding the proconsul only that "he believed"? Why ask for more, that he was baptized, that this included his family, that he was received into the church, etc.? And because all this is not in the record, why question whether it occurred? Luke expects his readers also to be συνετός. Why these suspicions that the proconsul was perhaps not baptized because of his Roman office, because he had to take official part in certain official religious idolatrous rites? Another view is that, if a proconsul had been converted to Christianity, Roman and Greek historians would have recorded that fact. They certainly did not record the fact that this proconsul was a pupil of the Jewish magus. "He believed" — that aorist stands as a tower — the very governor of the island, a Roman, believed! Luke makes this fact most impressive by saying nothing about other believers. He lets his reader himself say this.

This first stage of the first missionary journey of Paul was eminently successful. The one high point of success scored speaks volumes. And we should not think that, because in the next verse it is stated that the missionaries left, they departed the very day after the proconsul believed. They left when it was safe to leave their work in Paphos. In his chronological table Ramsay allows from March to July for the stay in Cyprus.

The First Missionary Journey: Pisidian Antioch

13) After the work is completed in Cyprus, new territory is sought. **Now having set sail from Paphos, those around Paul went to Perga of Pamphilia. John, however, having withdrawn from them, returned to Jerusalem. But they on their part, having gone through from Perga, arrived at Antioch, the Pisidian.**

The passive of ἀνάγω is used in a nautical sense, "to put to sea," "to set sail." The Greek says literally, "go up" on the sea and "come down" to land, speaking as it appears to the eye. The voyage from Paphos to the coast of the mainland was easily accomplished, there being frequent shipping facilities. Instead of stopping at the harbor town Attalia (14:25), they sailed up the Kestros River and landed at Perga. The observation is certainly correct that, when Luke writes "Perga of Pamphilia," he is not locating Perga for his reader, not distinguishing it from some other Perga. Pamphilia was selected as the next missionary field and is mentioned for this reason. It is true that Paul first went up to Antioch and worked there, but equally true that on the return journey work was done in Pamphilia.

In οἱ περὶ Παῦλον we have the classic idiom for "Paul and his company," he being included (B.-D. 228). Significant is the naming of this group after Paul. It is not "the Barnabas party" but "the Paul party." Luke writes thus because after the stay at Paphos the main person and leader is Paul. Let us understand that this gravitation of Paul to the leadership was entirely natural. In personality, in personal force, as in education, Paul outranked even a man like Barnabas. Although it had been held back all these years, the simple greatness of the man now began to be revealed. That fact made it easy for Barnabas to fall into second place.

It is Ramsay who connects Perga, Mark's leaving, and the haste to Pisidian Antioch by starting from the assumption that Luke joins together what inwardly belongs together. The three statements are usually treated separately. The only direct light we have on Mark's defection is the remark made in 15:38, 39 that "he did not go with them to the work" and that Barnabas and Paul fell out with each other in regard to taking him along on a second missionary journey. What really was the trouble still remains veiled. We hastily acquit the mosquitoes at Perga, not because they stung Paul and Barnabas as well as Mark, but because no stay was made at Perga at this time. The charge of homesickness, that Mark went *zu seiner Mutter* (to his mother), is unfair. We find nothing convincing in the surmise that Mark did not relish the transfer of leadership from Barnabas, Mark's cousin, to Paul. Mark was only an attendant (v. 5), and the shift of leadership was entirely natural. Mark could not take umbrage as long as Barnabas did not. Still less likely is Mark's dissatisfaction with Paul's work among the Gentiles, for Barnabas stood for the same work, he as well as Paul having cast away Judaistic ideas.

That leaves Mark's lack of courage, which agrees with chapter 15:38, 39. It may well be possible that something had occurred at Perga which took the heart out of Mark. Ramsay asks the question as to why Paul went straight on from Perga to Pisidian Antioch, a long hard journey that was full of dangers at that. Why was no work done at Perga at this time but only later? Ramsay finds the reason in Gal. 4:13, 14, Paul's "infirmity of the flesh." Paul had to leave the hot lowlands and get into the higher interior without delay. Thus he hurried straight on to Antioch, 3,600 feet above the sea; here he might hope to recover.

What, then, was Paul's ailment? Ramsay diagnoses it as malaria which with its sudden attacks incapacitated Paul for several hours at each recurrence, prostrated him utterly, and was accompanied by frightful headaches. Since Paul was in this condition, Mark lost heart. In 15:38, 39 Paul still mistrusted Mark. Suppose Paul should have another siege of the malady, what would Mark then do? Was this Paul's "stake in the flesh" (II Cor. 12:7)? It could not have been even if we stress the accompanying headaches; the ailment was temporary.

Ramsay's combination would also explain why Barnabas went on with Paul. He and Paul had been commissioned together by the Holy Spirit (v. 2); if Paul went on, Barnabas dared not withdraw and go with his cousin. The view that in Gal. 4:13, 14 Paul refers to some eye trouble that made his face look disagreeable is only a conjecture which does not even fit in with the language used. In v. 9 Paul "sets his eyes" on the magus, and that bars out any affliction of the eyes. The hypothesis of epilepsy is even less likely; a man who was subject to epileptic fits could not possibly have the mentality and do the work of this apostle. Besides, this ailment of which Paul complains does not seem to have been continuous. Only the Galatians saw him when his condition was very bad.

As far as "Galatia" is concerned, namely the debate as to whether Paul worked in southern Galatia or in northern Galatia, the question is settled. It was southern Galatia which included the very cities Paul was now entering before he returned to Perga which is located in Pamphilia.

14) After Mark had left them, Paul and Barnabas pressed on to Pisidian Antioch. According to Luke's record this was not a missionary tour, the travelers went straight through to Antioch. Antioch was not in Pisidia but on its border, hence Luke does not write "Antioch of Pisidia" (like "Perga of Pamphilia") but "Antioch, the Pisidian," the city thus being distinguished from Syrian Antioch and other towns of that name. It was a Roman colony like Philippi, a free city, and among its inhabitants there were many Jews. It was located in the Roman province of Galatia which included the ethnographic *Regiones* Pisidia, Phrygia, and Lycaonia. Until the return to Perga the journey was made entirely in Galatia. Antioch was a most desirable place in which to plant a Christian congregation.

And having gone to the synagogue on the day of the Sabbath, they sat down. But after the reading of the Law and of the Prophets the synagogue rulers sent to them, saying, Men and brethren, if you have some word of exhortation in your minds, say on!

We should begin a new sentence with *καί*. It has been asked how it was possible that in Antioch two Sabbaths were sufficient to produce such a decisive result among the Jews as well as the Gentiles when at other places similar results were more slowly achieved. But Luke is specific. The work began in the synagogue and moved with rapidity. After Paul and Barnabas had found lodging they most likely introduced themselves to the Jewish leaders, and when the Sabbath came, they sat down in the audience. Whether special seats were set aside for visiting rabbis is not known. The Greek often has the plural for "Sabbath"; the word is treated somewhat like names of festivals.

15) Luke has a double purpose in reporting the following sermon preached by Paul. It is a sample sermon which shows just how he presented Christ and the gospel in the synagogues. It is more: in this sermon we see how the Jews became hostile and then proceeded to persecute, which was one of the usual experiences of Paul.

Each synagogue had its managers who were called "elders" or as here "synagogue rulers"; one of these served as chairman or head of the others. All the synagogue's affairs were in the hands of the rulers. Since there were no pastors, the rulers managed the services so that the lessons were read, the prayers and the responses were recited, and necessary business attended to. Whenever possible, however, competent rabbis were asked to address the people. This was done by request or permission of the rulers. Men of the necessary schooling and ability were not numerous and happened along as visitors only occasionally. When Paul, the famous pupil of Gamaliel in Jerusalem, and Barnabas, a Levite and resident of Jerusalem, appeared in Pisidian Antioch, the elders even sent the *chazzan* or synagogue clerk to the rear where they were sitting and invited them to come forward to address a word to the people. This was in regular order, was not possible every Sabbath, and was appreciated the more on that account.

This occurred after the regular part of the service had been concluded, the main features of which Luke mentions, namely the reading of the Law (Torah, Pentateuch) and of the Prophets (a term that included the historical books from Joshua through Kings). The Pentateuch was divided into fifty-four lections called *parashas*, fifty-four so as to suffice also for the Jewish leap year, the Prophets into fifty-four *haphtarahs*; one of each of these lections was read each Sabbath. These two lections were themselves a fair-sized sermon. The Palestinian and the eastern Jews, the so-called Hebrews (see 6:1), used the Hebrew text which was translated into the vernacular Aramaic, for the majority of these Jews were no longer fully conversant with Hebrew. But in the Hellenistic diaspora, thus also here in Antioch, the LXX was used which need not be translated since all understood the Greek. This explains the presence of so many Gentiles, proselytes of the gate and prospective proselytes, in these synagogues. The Jews themselves were the Hellenists mentioned in 6:1; on the two kinds of proselytes see 2:10. The second class of proselytes were always open to the gospel, were readily won for the gospel, and thus formed the avenue for reaching the Gentile Greeks in general.

The idiom ἄνδρες ἀδελφοί is explained in 1:16; it is at once polite and dignified. Perhaps λόγος παρακλήσεως was a standard term for an address such as is here requested, the genitive denoting "exhortation," encouragement to believe the Word and to live according to its precepts. It did not necessarily imply an exposition of the lections read for that Sabbath although the address might take up some word in one the other lection or might start with such a word. What the visiting rabbi might desire to say was left entirely to him. The address would be quite informal, at least in most cases: so here "any word in you," *in animis vestris,* that in your mind and heart might seem profitable for the people to hear. This invitation was just what the missionaries desired.

16) **And having arisen and having motioned with the hand, Paul said, etc.** It is Paul who responds and makes the address; he is now the leader. The Jewish teachers sat when making an address. Both in Constantinople and in the Great Mosque at Damascus the writer saw the Mohammedan speakers sitting cross-legged, the latter speaker being very dramatic and fervent in his Arabic address. But in the Greek Catholic church in Damascus the patriarch, as well as the new bishop whom he installed, together with the other bishops and clergy stood during the entire ceremony and while the patriarch made his address to the new bishop and the latter responded. In the Hellenistic synagogues it was customary for the speakers to stand. Since the ordinary part of the service was at an end, the audience in the large synagogue had begun a conversation, and when Saul went forward and faced them he motioned for silence. Ἀναστάς is so constantly used circumstantially for proceeding with an act that it does not assure us that Paul stood; but in 17:22 he stood, and we assume that he followed this Roman custom here.

It is, of course, problematic what lections had been read on that Sabbath, nor have we the lections as they were arranged in those early days. From two words, both of which are distinctive, in Paul's address one might conclude that the lection from the Torah was Deut. 1, and the lection from the Prophets Isa. 1. These words are ἐτροφοφόρησεν (v. 18), which appears in Deut. 1:31; and ὕψωσεν (v. 17), which appears in Isa. 1:2, in the LXX. The historical part of Paul's address may have been suggested by Deut. 1. The address names: **Israelite men and those fearing God** and bids them **hear,** and uses the authoritative aorist imperative and not the milder present. This implies that quite a number of these proselytes of the gate, who are regularly called οἱ φοβούμενοι τὸν Θεόν, must have been present. Paul names them side by side with the Israelites. The proselytes would sit in a place that was especially set aside for them. The women were seated behind some screen where they would be invisible to the men. Paul had no occasion to name them in his address. When Paul says "Israelites" he appeals to the highest motives in his Jewish hearers; see the term in 2:22.

Inferior homiletics receives no support from Paul's address at Pisidian Antioch. The theme is plainly marked in v. 23, and three of the parts are marked, each with ἄνδρες ἀδελφοί (v. 16, 26, 38). Here is the outline:

UNTO ISRAEL A SAVIOR, JESUS

I. Israel's history leads up to him.

II. God fulfilled his promises to Israel by raising him from the dead.

III. In him alone is forgiveness and justification.

Even a little study shows how well the sermon fit the time, the place, and the audience. Put yourself in Paul's place and say what you would have spoken in Antioch.

17) **The God of this people Israel elected for himself our fathers and exalted the people in the foreign sojourn in Egypt's land and with a high arm led them forth out of it. And for about a time of forty years he bore them as a nursing father in the desert.**

Paul begins his address as Stephen had begun his defense: by a review of Israel's history. The tone and the object, however, are different. Through the history recounted by Stephen runs the note of Israel's disobedience in rejecting Christ; Paul's account of the history shows God's grace blessing Israel. Impressively Paul begins with "the God of this people Israel." He says "of this people Israel" because he is speaking to Gentiles as well as to Jews, and the pagan nations had been idolaters and had not worshipped the true God. The Jews sometimes carried their ancestry back to Abraham (John 8:39), sometimes to Jacob or Israel (as here) and thus to "our fathers," the twelve patriarchs (Rom. 9:5). This great and only God, who in the Old Testament is named from his people Israel, in whom the Gentile proselytes of the gate now also believed, by a signal act of his free grace "elected for himself (middle voice) our fathers" in his great plan of grace for all men to be the bearers of his promises to the world and to be the nation from whom the Savior of the world should be born according to the flesh. A brief and yet mighty statement; a perfect way to begin a sermon, namely with a statement that arrests attention by its importance and promises that the following will remain on this high plane.

Equal in force is the next statement: "and he exalted the people in the foreign sojourn in Egypt's land" by making them strong and numerous and by granting them his covenant promises and the true worship. Λαός is always the covenant people; and the verb does not mean merely that he let the people grow up to be big but that he placed them on a high plane. While they lived as πάροικοι, "foreigners," not natives in παροικία, the state of aliens, in the land of Egypt, God still kept them as his own people. And when the time came, God ended that alien state by leading his people out "with an arm exalted." The μετά does not speak of this exalted arm as the means or instrument by which God led out Israel but as the accompaniment: "in company with an arm exalted."

This arm went along with Israel at the time of the exodus; they saw it in the pillar of cloud by day which became a pillar of fire by night. God's arm is his power and his majesty; where his arm is, there he is: God who exalted his people led them to their own land with an exalted arm. Behold all this grace! Then think of its ultimate purpose!

18) We regard this verse as an independent sentence and not as subordinate to the next verse. Like a nursing father God carried his people through the desert. The reading ἐτροφοφόρησεν, both here and in Deut. 1:31, is decidedly to be preferred to ἐτροποφόρησεν, "he bore their manners." The former is a rare verb and was easily changed to the commoner verb by altering only one letter. But the Hebrew justifies the former verb: "he bare thee as a man doth bear his son." Paul knew the Hebrew as well as the LXX. There would be a note of blame in saying that God bore Israel's manners for forty years; for we know what those manners were (7:39-43); but Paul's tone is the very opposite; it shows God's wonderful grace toward Israel. All those years God tenderly cared for Israel like a father nursing his son. He fed the people with manna and kept them so that they did not perish. The fact that their own unbelief extended the journey to forty years is not the point here; God kept them in spite of their unbelief.

19) **And having destroyed seven nations in Canaan land, he distributed as a heritage their land about four hundred and fifty years; and after that he gave them judges until prophet Samuel; and thereupon they asked for themselves a king, and God gave them Saul, son of Kish, a man of Benjamin's tribe, for forty years.**

Paul proceeds from the entrance into Canaan through the era of the judges to the end of Saul's reign. The chief point of this presentation is the truth that *God* did all that is here recited. His agency in the history is brought to view. It was he who destroyed the seven Canaanite nations (cf., Deut. 7:1, where their names are recorded); he who distributed their land to the people of Israel as an inheritance.

The correct reading continues with ὡς (there is no καί before it) and places the dative of time in v. 19 and not, as the A. V. does, in v. 20 by placing the dative after the μετά phrase: "and after that . . . about the space of 450 years." R. 527 does not give much helpful information on this dative; B.-D. 201 furnishes full evidence for this use of the dative as denoting length of time instead of an accusative with transitive verbs; this is apparently done in order to avoid two consecutive accusatives, one being the direct object of the transitive verb and another indicating the extent of time. Zahn says that placing the dative of time into v. 19 lets Paul say that distributing the inheritance covered that much time. The round number "about 450 years" covers the time from the sojourn in Egypt to the possession of Canaan. According to 7:6 (Gen. 15:13) 400 years were spent in Egypt, forty additional years in the journey through the desert to Canaan, and about ten further years for conquering the land, which is certainly close to 450 years. Paul says that during these many years, almost half a millennium, God dealt so graciously with his λαός.

20) Zahn resorts to an emendation of the text by eliminating μετὰ ταῦτα and making v. 20 read: "for about 450 years he gave judges," etc., and makes the period of the judges 450 years, which is in contradiction with I Kings 6:1, which makes the entire time from the exodus from Egypt to the fourth year of Solomon's reign only 480 years. Nor can the 450 years be reckoned according to the incorrect reading of the A. V. "after these things," after the entrance of Israel into Canaan, for this would advance us into

the reign of David and beyond that of Saul, neither of whom Paul has as yet mentioned.

The claim is unwarranted that Paul had a different method of reckoning from that employed in I Kings 6:1, which arrived at 480 years from the exodus to the time of Solomon, namely that Paul merely added together the years of the judges and disregarded the fact that the terms of the judges frequently overlapped and thus secured 450 years; the Jews are charged with doing the same thing. Paul's 450 years have nothing to do with even the longer era that began with the conquest of Canaan. R., *W. P.*, counted the 450 years from the birth of Isaac to the conquest of Canaan. But it is sixty years from Isaac's birth to Jacob's, seventy more until Jacob goes to Canaan, 400 in Egypt, forty in the wilderness — 570!

It is again God who gave Israel judges until the last one who was even more than a judge, namely "prophet Samuel" who is even regarded as one of God's great prophets.

21) Finally they asked for themselves a king. Paul is not reciting the faults of Israel but God's leadings which culminated in the Messiah. Hence he mentions only the request for a king since in response to it God gave them Saul. It was God who did this. It is a misunderstanding to say that Paul adds Saul's lineage, "son of Kish, a man of Benjamin's tribe," because the apostle himself came from that tribe and himself was named Saul. No motive of pride actuated Paul in making this addition. He mentions Saul's lineage for a most pertinent reason. It was not from the tribe of Benjamin, not from the royal line of Saul, that the Savior came but from David who replaced Saul.

The Old Testament nowhere states the length of Saul's reign. In I Sam. 13:1 the age of Saul when he became king had already been omitted when the

LXX made their translation. Here again Jewish tradition is supposed to have furnished the omitted information by making Saul's reign forty years, equal to that of David and of Solomon. Josephus is usually quoted in support of this view, but in *Ant.* 6, 14, 9, in the statement that Saul reigned eighteen years while Samuel yet lived and twenty-two after Samuel was dead, the word "twenty" is not genuine, and the word "two" seems to be taken from the corrupted passage I Sam. 13:1. Elsewhere Josephus makes Saul's reign only twenty years — a sample of the reliability of this historian. Paul's forty years should be taken as extending back to Samuel just as the 450 years extended back and allowed seventeen to nineteen years for the judgeship of Samuel and twenty to twenty-two for the kingship of Saul. Keil, *Biblischer Commentar, Josua, Richter und Ruth,* 212.

22) **And after having removed him, he raised up David for them for king, to whom also he said, giving testimony, I found David, him of Jesse, a man according to my heart who will do all my will. Of the seed of this one God according to promise brought for Israel a Savior, Jesus, John having heralded in advance before the presence of his entering in a baptism of repentance to all the people Israel. And as John was fulfilling his course he went on to say: What do you suspect me to be? I am not he! But lo, there comes after me he, the sandals of whose feet I am not worthy to loose.**

All that Paul says about Saul, the Benjaminite king, is that God removed him. This, however, does not refer to Saul's death — he killed himself — but to his rejection by God when Samuel was commissioned to anoint another as king in Saul's place. God allowed Saul to continue to reign for a time but only as one who had been rejected. In place of Saul, God "raised up David for them for king" (εἰς introducing the predicate, resembling the Hebrew *l*[e], R. 482). Of Saul, Paul says God "gave," of David, God "raised up," a more significant term which includes all that made David the king he was. Paul makes this prominent by letting God himself testify concerning David; the action of μαρτυρήσας is simultaneous with that of εἶπε due to the nature of the actions. What God said was testimony.

Paul is not quoting, has no formula of quotation, and cares only to state the substance of the divine testimony regarding David. Thus Ps. 89:20, and I Sam. 16:7, 12 are used, and one expression is taken from Isa. 44: 28, where it is used with reference to Cyrus, but it applies to David just as well or even better. David allowed God to make his heart and his life what they were. "Him of Jesse," i. e., Jesse's son, points to David's father as being but a common man; yet under God's gracious leading he eventually found this man's son David "a man according to my heart," an individual as God wished him to be. David's great sins did not alter this testimony of God, for David repented.

The relative clause shows to what this testimony referred, namely to David's willingness to do all the θελήματα of God, the different things that God willed. In this respect David was the opposite of Saul, to whom Samuel had to say, "To obey is better than sacrifice," and then, "Thou hast rejected the word of the Lord, and the Lord hath rejected thee from being king over Israel," I Sam. 15:22, 26.

Paul brings into prominence the high, godly caracter of David because the Messiah was to be David's son. When he thus distinguished David, Paul had the fullest consent of all his hearers, especially of the Jews who knew all about David and who fully believed that the Messiah would come from David's line. When Jesus asked the Pharisees whose son the Christ would be, they promptly answered, David's son (Matt. 22:41, etc.), and many an afflicted person appealed to Jesus as "the son of David."

23) The emphatic demonstrative τούτου, "of this one," placed at the head of the sentence, sums up all that Paul had said about David and now, leaping across the space of a thousand years, connects Jesus with him: "of the seed of this one," etc. This clear statement that Jesus was "from the seed" of David ought to give pause to all those who deny that Mary was a lineal descendant of David and refuse to understand Luke's genealogical table (Luke 3:23, etc.) as being that of Mary. Read Rom. 1:4: "Jesus Christ, which was made (τοῦ γενομένου) of the seed of David according to the flesh." If Joseph alone was of David's blood and not Mary, if, therefore, Jesus was only legally David's son through his foster-father, how could he be "from (ἀπό, Rom. 1:4, ἐκ) David's seed"? That exegesis is wrong which denies Davidic descent to Mary and Davidic blood to Jesus. When we are told that in the present passage Paul is not speaking of the birth of Jesus but only of his office, and that this is made certain by εἴσοδος in the next verse, we challenge this claim. Paul speaks of both the birth or descent of Jesus and of his office. "According to promise" even connects the two, for it was God's promise that one of David's blood should be the Savior, II Sam. 7:16; Isa. 11:1; Jer. 23:5, 6; Zech. 3:8 (Luke 1:32, 33). Without the Davidic birth and blood there is no Messianic office.

In one simple, direct statement Paul declares that God made Jesus the Savior: "God according to promise brought for Israel a Savior, Jesus." "God" did it; Paul made God's agency very prominent throughout all of Israel's history, and here that agency reaches its climax. The choice between the reading ἤγαγε and the slighty supported ἤγειρεν, is easy, because the latter is drawn from v. 22: "raised up" David; and we regard the reading ἀνήγαγε as a conjecture for which there is little support.

This very verb ἄγω, "brought," occurs in the promise Zech. 3:8, and its use with the dative "brought for Israel" is most proper. The expression is only a variation of Peter's declaration: "God made this Jesus both Lord and Christ" (2:36). Paul has been recounting Israel's history under God and thus he says that God brought Jesus "for Israel." The Gentiles present were to hear that the Savior was presented to Israel according to the promise made to Israel; the fact that this Savior was intended also for them they would hear presently (v. 39).

Note that the great name "Jesus" is placed emphatically at the end and that it thus balances the equally emphatic genitive "of this one (David)" at the head of the sentence. No play on words is intended in σωτῆρα Ἰησοῦν although "Jesus" itself signifies "savior" (see 2:38). "Savior" puts the whole office and work of Jesus into one word, and that word signifies not only what Jesus did but what he still does — he is and remains the one who saves. All that the Scriptures say about salvation lies in this one term. "Savior," plus its derivatives, refers to the act of rescuing from mortal spiritual danger and includes the further continuous act of keeping in the condition of spiritual safety. All that God had planned from the very beginning when selecting the fathers (v. 17) God had carried out when he brought Jesus to Israel and presented him as the Savior according to the promise.

What a glorious statement for these Jews to hear! They gloried in that past history with all its illustrious names and with God in and over it all; and now it was crowned by God's bringing to them this promised Savior. We know of no more perfect approach that Paul could have made to the mighty theme of the Saviorhood of Jesus for this audience of his.

24) The added genitive absolute describes how God brought Jesus for Israel as a Savior. We must note the grandness of the language and of the underlying imagery. Note, "before the presence or face of his entering in," Hebraistic, as though this Savior came in divine power and majesty. A great herald came before him who announced his coming for Israel by proclaiming "a baptism of repentance for all the people Israel." It was thus that God brought Jesus to Israel. Paul's hearers knew about Jesus and about the Baptist; all he needed to do was to present the great facts as they had occurred.

In the verb "to herald in advance" (πρό) we have the prophecy that John should be the "voice" crying in the wilderness. What heralding a baptism meant all Jews would know, all of whom were conversant with the Jewish lustrations and cleansing ceremonies. This herald John, they understood, came in advance in order to prepare the people of Israel for the coming of the Savior. Carefully, despite all brevity, Paul adds the qualifying genitive baptism "of repentance." It demanded repentance, was intended for the repentant only, but the entire people of Israel were to accept it by such repentance. On the concept repentance see 2:38, and on John's baptism 1:5. God intended John's work only for the Jews, and in due time, as now, the blessing of it would go out to all the world.

25) Paul shows the greatness of this Savior Jesus by the word of the Baptist which John 1:19, etc., recounts so fully, also Luke 3:15, etc.; Matt. 3:11. This occurred when John was finishing his course, i. e., when Jesus had already begun his ministry. Many of the people quietly thought (ὑπό in the verb) that John him-

self might be the Christ. The imperfect ἔλεγε pictures his answer. One may draw the question and the answer together: "What you suspect *me* to be *I* am not," the emphasis being on the pronouns (B. D. 298, 4; R. 738); or one may divide: "What do you suspect *me* to be? *I* am not (what you thus suspect)!" *what*, not *who*.

The utter folly of thinking that a mere man like John could be the Messiah and Savior is brought out by saying that one as high as John was, so high as to be suspected of himself being the Messiah, was not worthy of stooping before the real Messiah in order to render him the service of the lowest slave, that of untying his sandals to take and to cleanse them and of washing the dust from his feet. It was a concrete and striking way of pointing out the deity of the Messiah. The exclamation "lo" helps to make it strong; ἔρχεται is Messianic, the Messiah was "the One coming."

This first part of Paul's discourse is purely historical — all a series of facts — all straight testimony. All these things God had done — no "if" or "but" about it. Every word must have gone directly home.

26) Paul marks *the second part* of the discourse most plainly by once more addressing his hearers: ἄνδρες ἀδελφοί (see 1:16). We may extend this second part to v. 37, after which Paul addresses his hearers for a third time. Two historical facts are presented: Jesus' death and his resurrection. Both, however, are presented in such a way as to bring out their full significance. The Jews of Jerusalem killed Jesus but by doing this ignorantly fulfilled the divine prophecy. God raised Jesus from the dead and completed the fulfillment. This resurrection attests the Messiahship of Jesus by God's own act. The prophecies are quoted to fortify the fact. Here again are straight facts but facts set into the proper divine light.

Men and brethren, sons of Abraham's stock, and those among you fearing God, to us the word of this salvation was sent out.

The apposition appeals most strongly to the theocratic position and feelings of Paul's Jewish hearers. In v. 17 this appeal was made through Israel, now it reaches back also to Abraham with whom the covenant was originally made. By adding Abraham to Israel Paul produces a cumulative effect. Paul is asking his Jewish hearers to show themselves as true sons of Israel and of Abraham. All that is said about υἱός in v. 10 applies also here. The translation of our versions "children" misses this important point; "children" would be τέκνα, the connotation being "dear children." "Sons" are far more, namely the heirs of Abraham and Abraham's stock, they in whom all that Abraham and his race stand for is to live on undiminished, they who ought to perpetuate the character, the faith, the lofty standing of Abraham and of his descendants. As such "sons" Paul addresses his Jewish hearers. The Gentiles present Paul addressed by the title he had formerly given them (v. 17); as men who have come to the right knowledge and the true fear and the worship of God and have forsaken all idolatry, they, too, are now to show themselves as such.

Paul has mentioned Jesus as "Savior" (v. 23); "the word of this salvation" links up with that Savior. This word sets forth what makes Jesus the Savior and how he is our Savior. Hence it was sent out, commissioned forth for all, Jews and Gentiles alike, to hear, know, believe, and thereby to receive salvation, σωτηρία, deliverance from sin and the safety that results (it is like Σωτήρ in v. 23). The ὑμῖν of a few texts should not be urged against the ἡμῖν of the many and most important. Paul could have used either; both would include all his hearers, and that irrespective of the preceding ἐν ὑμῖν. The difference is only this, by saying "to us" this word was sent Paul includes Barnabas and himself with all his hearers, while "to you" would refer only to his hearers. The great word of this salvation, Paul says, is now here for all of us to accept and thereby to be saved.

27) **For, those dwelling in Jerusalem and their rulers, having failed to understand this and the voices of the prophets that are being read on every Sabbath, they, by passing judgment, fulfilled them. And though having found not a single cause for death, they asked Pilate in due course that he be made away with. Moreover, when they had finished all the things that have been written concerning him, having taken him down from the wood, they placed him in a tomb.**

With γάρ Paul introduces his presentation of the death of Jesus on the cross. This is not a statement of a reason but an explanation of what is contained in "this word of salvation" which Paul says has been sent out to us. "For" means: "in order that I may explain." There is not the least indication that Paul is here contrasting the murderers of Jesus with his present hearers and no reason for such a contrast.

The death of the Savior Jesus was brought about by the people of Jerusalem and their rulers, the Sanhedrists. Peter, too, accuses the former just as Paul does here (2:23). The simple fact is that the Sanhedrin could never have forced Pilate to crucify Jesus if the populace of Jerusalem had not seconded their rulers. If the people had objected and demanded the release of Jesus, Pilate would have been encouraged to deny the ungodly demand for Jesus' death. Paul, too, brings out the truth that both people and rulers acted in ignorance (3:17; I Cor. 2:8; compare Luke 23:34). This was criminal ignorance, and Paul states the guilt of it in the causal participle "having failed to understand," which is not ingressive (R. 858) but effective.

Does τοῦτον refer to Jesus as our versions translate? This antecedent would be too remote. Since v. 26 Paul had advanced to a new part of his discourse, and the masculine λόγος immediately precedes. These people and their rulers failed to understand both "this," the word of salvation regarding Jesus as the Savior, and the voices of the prophets which already contained that word. What increased the guilt of the latter was the fact that these prophets were constantly being read in their synagogues; on every Sabbath they heard them and yet failed utterly to understand the word of salvation in them, the word about Jesus, his atoning death, and his resurrection. Καί cannot be "also" for the reason that the main verb can never be added to a participle by an "also" or some other coordinate conjunction; those who attempt it here change the participle into a second finite verb: "because they failed to understand . . . they also fulfilled," but Paul subordinated. So καί connects τοῦτον and τὰς φωνάς.

The grammatical references of κρίναντες ἐπλήρωσαν are misunderstood in our versions, apparently because τοῦτον is referred to "him" (Jesus). Since neither the participle nor the verb have an object expressed in the Greek, the participle is given the object "him" and the verb the object "them" (voices): "fulfilled *them* by condemning *him*." But the participle has no object in the Greek, and the two objects, "this" (word of salvation) and "the voices of the prophets," etc., belong equally to "having failed to understand" and to "fulfilled," as they failed to understand both, so they (inadvertently and ignorantly) fulfilled both. And κρίναντες states how they did the latter: "by passing judgment," i. e., by that act (aorist).

The verb κρίνειν is neutral and means neither to acquit nor to condemn but only to judge. Because of their failure to understand these men were fit to do neither, acquit or condemn or to judge in any sense.

Yet they went ahead and acted the judge, they passed judgment. Of course, when one does this he must either acquit or condemn. These men did the latter. In this way their blind ignorance led them to fulfill their own prophets, do the horrible acts their prophets had foretold regarding them. Incredible — yet true to the letter!

28) The indefinite participle which speaks of their act of passing judgment is now described. They found not a single "cause of death" yet demanded Jesus' death. This is legal language. This finding is judicial, the legal finding of a judge on the basis of legal evidence. Αἰτία is a legal indictment, and the genitive θανάτου qualifies it as being one the penalty for which is rightly death. In the negative "not a single one" there lies the implication that several indictments were tried, but that not one of them was supported by evidence that a court could allow.

This applies fully also to the charge on which Jesus was condemned by the Sanhedrin, that by calling himself the Son of God he had blasphemed. The Sanhedrin merely grasped at that as a last resort. The moment Jesus had uttered his yea to the question put to him, the verdict guilty was rendered. No opportunity was given Jesus to offer proof that his yea was true in fact and the opposite of blasphemy. He was pronounced guilty without in the least permitting him to produce evidence on which the court might render a finding. That is why the Sanhedrin dared not tell Pilate on what grounds it had condemned Jesus to death but threw up a lying smoke screen of findings it had never even attempted to find: "we found" (i. e., legally), Luke 23:2; but Pilate had to answer: "I find" (legally, as judge), John 19:4.

Although it had no finding, the Sanhedrin and the people "asked Pilate in due course that he be made away with." The wording is again legal; for this verb is middle and in this voice is used to designate all sorts of business transactions. It does not mean that "they asked as a personal favor for themselves" that Jesus be executed. Roman governors did not grant such favors. In due course the great Jewish court came to Pilate's superior court with the legal request that the Roman court accept the Jewish verdict. This was a piece of legal business. The Jews could execute no one; all their death verdicts were subject to the Roman governor's review. Now the outrageousness of the Sanhedrin's procedure is revealed: without a single finding legally laid down by their own court they come in due form and make the formal legal request of Pilate's court to have Jesus executed! The aorist ᾐτήσαντο implies that they actually succeeded. The verb ἀναιρέω is constantly used in Acts with reference to the judicial murder of Jesus; he was to be made away with, executed.

29) Paul is brief; his aim is to show how the guiltless Savior Jesus came to his death through the guilty and ignorant Sanhedrin and the people of Jerusalem. For this reason he does not alter the subject when he now speaks of what was done with the body of Jesus. He simply says that *they* buried him. But first the important clause: "when they had finished (the Greek needs only the aorist) all the things that have been written (and still stand so, perfect participle) concerning him" — yes, they finished all of them! They were plainly written for anyone to read and to know, and yet, without an inkling of what they were thus really doing, they did all these things. This was the vital point for Paul's hearers, that God himself had had all these things regarding Jesus, his sufferings and his death, recorded in the prophets. To see them there in the inspired books and then to see them in actuality in Jesus, this was bound to go home. In this light of prophecy the shame of the cross disappeared; in this

light of prophecy the guilt of the Jewish rulers and of the people in Jerusalem cried to heaven.

We must not miss the added touch in the participial clause: "having taken him down from the wood." We have explained this "wood" which our versions translate "tree" in 5:30, and have shown that in the estimation of Jews hanging on wood involved being accursed. Paul's hearers knew that Jesus had been crucified at Jerusalem; when he speaks of it, Paul brings out the Jewish point of view that the Sanhedrin and the people had not merely succeeded in having him made away with but by having this done so that in the eyes of all Judaism he was accursed. See the exposition of Gal. 3:13. After taking him down they placed him in a tomb. Dead, buried, accursed at that. His foes thought they surely had destroyed him, were absolutely done with him, would never be disturbed by him and all this was done just as it had been written, and they never realized that it had been written about them.

The passive "that he be made away with" (v. 28) shows that the rulers and the people did not do this with their own hands; and this applies to taking down the body and placing it into the tomb. By having Jesus killed these rulers necessitated the disposal of his body, and thus it can be said that they did these acts. The usual explanation is that Joseph of Arimathaea and Nicodemus are referred to since both were Sanhedrists. But this is only a formal explanation and hence is not satisfactory. Peter charged the Sanhedrists to their faces that *they* killed Jesus; in the same way *they* buried him. Both were done by forcing others to perform these acts.

This is the first subpart. It stands out in strong contrast with the preceding. In v. 17-25 the agent is *God* throughout: *he,* he did all all that is said; but in v. 26-29 the agents are the blind *people and the rulers*:

they, they do all that is said. When Paul now proceeds, it is again *God* who is the great agent. The address pivots on the agents. Its convincing force rests on these marked pivots.

30) **But God raised him from the dead, who appeared for many days to those who came up with him from Galilee to Jerusalem, such as now are his witnesses to the people.**

The contrast is tremendous: the people and the rulers made away with Jesus as one who was accursed, God did the absolutely opposite. God reversed and nullified what they did, yea, by raising him from the dead whom they had killed as one who was accursed God set his seal upon him as being the Savior. It is the same stunning contrast and opposition as that used by Peter when he faced the people in Jerusalem and the Sanhedrin, the very murderers of Jesus (2:23, 24, 36; 4:10; 5:30, 31). Note how succinctly the fact is stated as a fact: "But God raised him from the dead!" On ἐκ νεκρῶν see 3:16. This deed was one of omnipotence. There it is recorded in Scripture for all who will to rage against; but it is unchangeable, impregnable as ever. Modernists may hurl themselves against it, they injure it not a whit, they injure only themselves.

31) A second fact and deed is added with ὅς which in the Greek so often = "he who." Paul does not continue with God and say: "God manifested him." Yet he does not detract from the first mention of God and what God did. He also maintains all that he said when stating that God "raised him from the dead." Jesus was made alive. He, he himself was the one who appeared as living and raised from the dead and not once only but "for many days," in the Greek idiom "for more days (than a few)," forty in all. To whom? "To those who came up with him from Galilee to Jerusalem," to those who had known him longest and best, who could not be deceived. Paul is not speaking of himself and of

his vision of the risen Lord. He uses ὤφθη, the aorist passive of ὁράω, "he was seen," or intransitive, "he appeared," which is employed four times in I Cor. 15:5-9.

But his resurrection was not intended for these friends of Jesus alone. It concerned all the λαός or Jewish people, namely in the special sense developed in v. 17-25. So many of them were scattered far and wide over the earth and could not all be direct witnesses of God's saving acts. This was the case in regard to all Israel's past history and God's deeds in that history. The true witnesses testified to all those facts. That is the case with regard to Jesus, his work and suffering and death and now in particular his resurrection. God chose the witnesses by whom he intended to attest this great deed of his and the living presence of the risen Savior. Οἵτινες expresses quality: "such as now are his witnesses to the people." Having seen the risen Jesus again and again, they, as many of them as there are, constitute his eyewitnesses who are qualified in every way to testify to all that they have seen.

Paul first presents the facts that God raised Jesus from the dead and that Jesus appeared to chosen witnesses. Up to this point all has been objective, but now with the marked ἡμεῖς ὑμᾶς there comes the subjective: the good tidings *we* bring to *you* of the fulfilled promises to which are added some of these promises concerning the Messiah's resurrection with brief elucidation. Down to its minor parts the discourse is arranged with exactness in a perfect progression, logically and psychologically.

32) **And we on our part to you on yours are proclaiming as good news the promise come to the fathers, that God has completely fulfilled this to us, their children, by having made Jesus to appear; as also it has been written in the second Psalm: My Son art thou; I today have begotten thee. Moreover, regarding that God made him appear from the dead not still about to return to corruption he**

has declared in this way, I will give to you the holy things of David, the trustworthy things! Because also in another he declares, Thou wilt not give thy Holy One to see corruption. For David, having served his own generation by the counsel of God, fell asleep and was added to his fathers and saw corruption; but he whom God raised up did not see corruption.

Both pronouns occurring in v. 32 are accented and are aided in their emphasis by their juxtaposition. "We on our part" = Paul and Barnabas, and "to you on yours" are Paul's Jewish hearers. To them these messengers are here and now proclaiming as good news "the promise that came to the fathers."

33) Not the promise as such, but the fact "that God has completely (ἐκ in the verb) fulfilled this to the children (of the fathers), namely to us (Paul, Barnabas, and the Jewish hearers), by having made Jesus to appear." The ὅτι clause is appositional to "the promise." Ταύτην is put forward for the sake of emphasis: "this," this very promise, for which the fathers waited so long, God has now finally fulfilled for their children, the perfect tense implying that the fulfilling now stands as such. The reading τοῖς τέκνοις ἡμῶν (R. V.) makes no sense. Paul had no children, and the promise was fulfilled not merely for the children of his Jewish hearers and not the hearers themselves. We must read either "for their children" (αὐτῶν) as in the A. V., or "for the children, namely us" (ἡμῖν). Since the promise was made to the fathers and not to the Gentiles, Paul says properly that it was fulfilled for the children of those fathers, the Jews, leaving out the Gentiles. The whole work of Jesus was done among Jews. The fact that the Gentiles were to participate in it changes nothing of what God did. Throughout the discourse one sees how Paul is laboring to win his Jewish hearers; throughout he depicts what God did for the fathers and finally for

their children. Paul has no fears for his Gentile hearers. So he now freely says, "To the children, to us."

We refer ἀναστήσας Ἰησοῦν to God's act of raising up Jesus as the Savior and not to the act of raising him up from the dead. With δέ, "moreover" (slightly adversative), Paul then adds ἀνέστησεν αὐτὸν ἐκ νεκρῶν, the act of raising Jesus from the dead. This δέ prevents us from referring both the participle and the finite verb to the resurrection. If both referred to the same act, the former and not the latter ought to have the modifier "from the dead." But the participle should not be restricted to the incarnation and the birth of Jesus: "by having made Jesus to appear (or to arise)" the entire career of Jesus from beginning to consummation is referred to, which thus includes also his resurrection. The verb "completely fulfilled" refers to the entire career; it cannot mean that by the resurrection of Jesus the final item of complete fulfillment was added. As far as that final item is concerned, that is specified in v. 34. When in v. 23 Paul says "Savior," in v. 26, "the word of this salvation," and in v. 32 εὐαγγελιζόμεθα, he is not speaking only of the resurrection of Jesus but of all that he was and did, including his glorious resurrection.

It is this act on the part of God, this making Jesus to appear or arise in general, of which Ps. 2:7 speaks. Peter quoted this psalm in 4:25, 26. In Heb. 1:5 our passage is quoted to show that God exalted Jesus above the angels. Peter attributes this psalm to David although it appears without a caption. The contents are plainly Davidic. The reply that in general speech "psalm" meant a song composed by David overlooks the fact that many psalms were attributed to Asaph, to Solomon, and to others. Some think that Paul cites David because in v. 22 he had brought Israel's history up to the time of David; but he also quotes Isaiah. When some texts read "the first" Psalm, we note that the two psalms were read as one lection in the synagogue, which regarded the first Psalm as the introduction to the entire book of Psalms.

The Hebrew and the LXX agree: "My Son art thou; I myself (emphatic ἐγώ) today have begotten thee." The reference is to II Sam. 7, especially to v. 13 and 16, to the Seed of David (Jesus) who should reign in the Davidic kingdom and on the Davidic throne forever. It is this everlasting King himself who quotes Jehovah as declaring to him, "My Son art thou," etc. God made that declaration to Jesus himself when at the time of his baptism he anointed him with the Spirit: "Thou art my beloved Son." Luke 3:22. It was then that Jesus assumed his office as Savior. That declaration was repeated at the time of the Transfiguration of Jesus, cf., Luke 9:35.

Although they are even verbally almost identical with the word occurring in the psalm, these two words of the Father to his Son Jesus are often overlooked. In the psalm David says that this declaration was made long ago. He speaks of II Sam. 7. Then Jehovah said, "Yet have I set my King upon my holy hill of Zion!" and that King declares that Jehovah said to him, "Thou art my Son," etc. Regard it all prophetically with reference to what the Father did with Jesus when he brought him to Israel as the Savior (23); or regard it as prophecy, as what was done already in David's vision as regards the everlasting King on his throne. In either case "I myself today have begotten thee" is figurative regarding Jehovah's placing this everlasting King on his throne. The inauguration of a King who rules forever on an everlasting throne in an eternal kingdom is for Jehovah the begetting of a Son, a King who rules eternally like Jehovah himself. That prophecy was fulfilled, Paul says, when God raised up Jesus as the Savior. The statement about Jesus, like that of the psalm, is general; hence Paul follows it with a further elaboration, and we must read the whole together in order to get its force.

The passage occurring in the psalm does not speak of the *generatio aeterna,* not of the inner Trinitarian relation of the two Persons, not of eternity but of time. Likewise, the psalm does not speak of the Incarnation, the conception, and the birth of Jesus. Many, however, think that it speaks of the resurrection of Jesus, and that the reality back of the figure of generating is the raising from the dead. They, therefore, also let ἀναστήσας mean "having raised from the dead." It sounds attractive to hear that Jesus was made Savior and King forever by his resurrection. But how about his suffering and his death, his whole office and his life? And look at Luke 3:22, and 9:35. No, this raising up, making to appear, the word of the psalm, refer to all that God did in setting him forth as the Savior and most certainly includes also his resurrection, but most certainly also includes all else as well and does not refer to the resurrection alone.

34) With δέ, "moreover," Paul now turns to the resurrection: "regarding that God made him appear from the dead," ὅτι is slightly causal. This resurrection, however, involves more than the fact that Jesus was brought back to life. So were Lazarus and others, and then they again died. Jesus was raised "not still about to return to corruption." Μηκέτι = "not still," not after all to fall a prey to corruption; it does not imply that by dying Jesus had seen corruption but was not again to see it. The translation "no more" in our versions is inadequate. Paul tells his hearers that God "has said" (formula of quotation like "has been written") something in Isaiah 55:3 in regard to the mighty act of raising Jesus from the dead never to see corruption; God promised, "I will give to you the holy things of David, the trustworthy things." Paul follows the

LXX because the point is τὰ πιστά, "the things trustworthy," *hanne'emanim*, that can never be broken or abrogated. They are "the holy things of David," Hebrew, "the David mercies," a standard term for the covenant promises as made to David by God in II Sam. 7 (see above), Ps. 89:36, 37.

"David mercies" introduce an epoch in the history of the covenantal prophecies and promises in that David was promised the Seed who should rule his throne and his kingdom forever. That was more specific than the promises given to Abraham. Now Paul says that God spoke thus about these absolutely reliable David mercies with a view to what he intended to do in regard to Jesus, namely realize these mercies in Jesus, raise him up as the Savior (v. 33), and raise him from the dead incorruptible and never to see corruption, and thus to be the eternal Messianic King. In short, τὰ πιστά are absolutely reliable, sure, trustworthy, because they are realized in him who is beyond being touched by corruption.

We may add that Isa. 55:1-3 is an invitation to the Gentiles; the covenant made with Israel is intended for them also; the trustworthy mercies of David are to be theirs. This makes the quotation the more significant for Paul's audience in which there were many Gentile hearers. Aug. Pieper, *Jesaias II*, 444, etc. The interpreters usually think only of Israel. Paul quotes freely, adding: "I will give to you."

35) And now comes the capstone to this arch of prophecy. In Psalm 2:7 David had the Messiah in mind, Jesus in his whole office; in Isa. 55:3 the prophet had Jesus in mind, his resurrection, his being beyond all corruption. Now God spoke as he did in Isa. 55 "because" (διότι) in another psalm, namely 16:10, he says in so many words through David, his mouthpiece: "Thou wilt not give thy Holy One to see corruption." Jesus dead, entombed, raised from the dead, then and

forever free from corruption or decay of body is, indeed, the Savior forever. Peter used this same passage from this psalm in 2:27, where the details are fully elucidated. Even the explanation added by Paul contains what Peter added at greater length.

36) For David himself certainly saw corruption and hence could not be this "Holy One," hence could not be the Messianic King. After he had served his generation (indirect object) according to God's counsel he fell asleep. The dative cannot be temporal, "in his own generation," for the simple reason that no man ever serves in any but his own generation. The point is not when David served but how far his service extended, namely to his own generation alone. The Messiah had to serve all generations; and this Jesus does because he was raised in incorruption to live and to rule forever. If David served his own generation (indirect object), "the counsel of God" cannot be an indirect object. Yet that leaves two constructions possible: "served by," or, "fell asleep in the counsel of God." But plainly the chief point is that David died (main verb) and not that he served (only participle). Why, then, attach all the modifiers to the participle, the minor action? The point is that God let David fall asleep for good and all, aorist. It was God's counsel to let him die and be gathered to his fathers and his body thus to see (experience) corruption. On "see" (eye, ear, singulars) note Delitzsch on 2:27; "fell asleep," ingressive aorist as in 7:60. David "was added to his fathers" in the grave. The expression must refer to the grave, since the next clause states that he saw corruption, his body turning to dust in the grave.

37) Jesus' case was far otherwise. In him all those promises were fulfilled. God raised him up, and he did not see corruption but lives to serve and to save forever. Here the relative ὅν is again emphatic: "he, the one whom," etc. Through the first part of the dis-

course and through the second there runs the word "God," what God did and said. All are divine facts which need only to be seen aright and in their true bearing.

38) In *the third part* of the discourse Paul presents the saving power and grace in Jesus to everyone who believes and warns against unbelief. **Be it known, therefore, to you, men and brethren, that through this One remission of sins is being announced to you; and in connection with this One everyone believing is justified from all things from which you could not be justified in connection with the law of Moses.**

With οὖν Paul comes to the conclusion that must be drawn from all that precedes. Two things follow: 1) the objective fact that remission is being announced; 2) the personal fact that every believer is justified. Both facts are most closely connected with "this One" whom Paul has fully and clearly presented as the Savior brought to Israel (23) by God. "Be it known to you" ushers in these weighty announcements in an authoritative tone. The address "men and brethren" (see 1:6) is this time without appositions which distinguish Jews and Gentiles (v. 17 and 26). The Savior is intended for all alike.

Διὰ τούτου, "through this One," makes Jesus the Mediator, and the demonstrative, in the idiomatic Greek fashion, sums up all that has been said about Jesus. Through Jesus as the one divine channel remission of sins is conveyed by the public announcement which presents him. Jesus, crucified and risen, brings us remission. On this ἄφεσις see 2:38, and note 10:43. It means that the sins are sent away from the sinner forever. To see the last of your sin and guilt, to see it all vanish like vapor in the hot sun of grace and pardon in "this One" as though you had never sinned, is certainly blessedness and joy to anyone who realizes what sin is. There is a passive sense in the word "remission"; God himself sends the sins away. This helps us to comprehend διά. It is only by way of Jesus that God can possibly come and remove our sins from us. All of them are contained in the plural "sins," everything in us whereby we have missed the mark set for us by God's holy law.

This remission "is being announced," κατά in the verb has the note of solemnity, *wird feierlich verkuendigt.* Paul's present passive means more than that he and Barnabas were now making the great announcement; the real agent is God; this is also true with regard to "is justified" in the next verse. We see that throughout the entire address God is the one agent. This is a supreme way of composing an address, it was certainly effective for both classes of Paul's hearers. The verb is pregnant, "announced to you," for you to believe, accept, receive, possess. The gospel is always "announced" or preached thus. The very announcement reaches into the heart in order to kindle faith. Who can hear this remission announced to him without wanting it? A special, wicked, ugly effort is necessary to keep faith from arising in the heart.

39) With a coordinate statement Paul repeats and sets the matter in a still clearer light before his hearers. Our inflexible English compels us to reverse the clauses. The emphasis is on the modifier: "from all things from which you could not be justified in connection with the law of Moses." The two phrases are in direct contrast: ἐν τῷ νόμῳ Μωϋσέως and ἐν τούτῳ, "in connection with the law" and "in connection with this One." The idea is not that some sins can be removed by the law, and that others remain which the law is unable to remove; no, all sins are referred to. As long as our connection is only with the law of Moses, its demands and requirements, we shall break them often and in this law find no means to remove our sin and our guilt.

Here we meet the verb δικαιοῦν for the first time in Acts. It is always a forensic term with a personal object, and in the New Testament is used only in the religious sense as referring to the verdict and judgment of God which is always favorable: "to justify," that act of God by which as the Judge he declares the sinner just and acquits him from his sin and his guilt. See C.-K. 324, who has a treatment that is so exhaustive that every student should examine it in its entirety. It does not mean "to free" except in the forensic sense just stated (B.-P. 308 is misleading); in the Scriptures it never means "to make just," "to deem worthy" (R., *W. P.*). Justification is no less than the central doctrine of the Word, *the articulus stantis aut cadentis ecclessiae,* the destruction of which destroys the church itself so that it remains Christian no longer. Paul tells his hearers that if they appear before God's judgment bar in connection with the law of Moses as their hope, God cannot acquit them. It is utterly impossible, for the law brings only condemnation to the sinner.

This is Paul's first summary statement regarding works of the law and their utter hopelessness to secure the favorable verdict of God. He has made his letters ring with this doctrine. Jesus most strenuously opposed the Pharisees who trusted in the law. The world is full of followers of these Pharisees who in one or in another way still operate with works as the certain way to heaven.

The sinner's hope is only "in connection with this One." The phrase does not belong to the participle: "everyone believing in this One," but to the verb: "is justified in connection with this One." The connection with him is made by this believing. The participle is used without a modifier: "every believer." And this is another cardinal concept of Scripture: πιστεύειν (πίστις, ὁ πιστός), compare 2:44. "To believe" is to put all trust for remission, justification, and salvation in Christ alone as the Savior (v. 23). By believing, by our confidence in him and in the saving power of his death and his resurrection we are put in vital, spiritual connection with him. Paul tells his hearers that everyone who appears before God's judgment bar in connection with this Savior, he and he alone "is justified," the present tense is durative: "is and remains justified" as long as he is "one believing." In this way Jesus is the Savior. Do you want to be acquitted of all sin and guilt by God, now, in the instant of death, at the last great day? Then let this Savior fill your heart with complete reliance on him.

"Everyone believing" is like the blank line in a signed check or draft, on which you are to write your name over the signature Σωτὴρ Ἰησοῦς (v. 23). This is the universality of grace, remission, and justification. Paul was speaking to Jews and to Gentiles, and "everyone believing" applies to all of them. In the previous sentence ὑμῖν is plural, here πᾶς ὁ is singular. Paul is a master in using these two. Being justified is personal, individual. Every sinner is judged separately. The verdict is always rendered in the singular: "Thy sins are remitted for thee! Go in peace!"

In these two short verses we have Romans and Galatians in a nutshell. Justification by faith alone — *Sola Fide* — is an endless, inexhaustible theme. "The way to salvation, so slowly and with such difficulty prepared for us — slowly through the time of preparation in the old covenant — with difficulty, through the bitter suffering and death of Jesus: and yet so short and so pleasant for us to travel — short, for all that we need is to embrace the cross of Christ by faith — pleasant, for here we find remission of sins, life, and salvation." Gerok.

40) Paul closes his address by prodding the consciences of his hearers and warning them against Israel's greatest sin, unbelief. **See to it, there-**

fore, lest that arrive which has been spoken in the Prophets:

> **Look, you despisers, and wonder and vanish away!**
> **Because I am working a work in your days,**
> **A work which you in no wise shall believe if one detail it for you.**

Note that μὴ ἐπέλθῃ is not followed by a dative; hence it does not mean, "lest there come upon you," but only, "lest there arrive." "The Prophets" are that portion of the Old Testament which is regularly designated by this name which does not, however, include Daniel. Paul quotes from Hab. 1:5, according to the LXX with slight change. The prophet's words are not a prediction concerning Paul's present hearers. Paul uses them only as a warning. He has in mind a possible analogy or resemblance. Unbelief in regard to Jesus would make his hearers like those whom Habakkuk threatened. By unbelief they would put themselves into the same class with those despisers of old and would, of course, invite the same judgment.

41) The LXX translate as though their Hebrew text read *bogdim*, "despisers," instead of *bagoyim*, "among the heathen." The imperatives are aorists and thus peremptory. The God of might and majesty is speaking. He calls to the blind Jews, "Look!" and as a result "wonder!" and as a result "vanish away!" The judgment descending upon them is the terror behind these imperatives. It shall rise, like a tornado, fill them with astonishment, and then strike them and wipe them out completely.

What this calamity is, the prophet describes by bringing out powerfully that it is wholly God's work. "Because a work I work in your days" means a most terrible work, and I, I myself (emphatic ἐγώ), work it. To the prophet's hearers the present tense sounded as though God were already busy with that work. So incredible will that work be that, if one were to tell about it in advance, no one would in any wise (strong οὐ μή with the futuristic subjunctive) believe it, i. e., give it credence. The conditional clause is strong: "if one shall detail, recount it piece by piece (διά), and spread it out (ἐκ) for you." The prophet did so detail it by depicting how the Chaldeans would sweep down upon Israel and utterly destroy it. It was literally true, but not a single Israelite believed the prophet until the horrible destruction came upon the nation. Paul practically asks whether such unbelief is now to repeat itself in the case of his hearers. We know what calamity it was soon to bring on Jerusalem and on Palestine.

42) **And as they were going out they were beseeching them for the next Sabbath to speak to them these utterances. Moreover, the synagogue having broken up, many of the Jews and of the worshipping proselytes followed Paul and Barnabas, who, speaking to them, kept urging them to continue in the grace of God.**

This was the effect of Paul's sermon. It was entirely favorable as the two statements in regard to what the hearers did show. Paul and Barnabas were asked to speak again on the next Sabbath, and many Jews and proselytes followed them to hear more immediately. So we discount the idea that Paul ended his sermon with a warning because he saw some of the Jews scowling. The two imperfects παρεκάλουν and ἔπειθον intimate that more will follow. We need not debate long as to how this going out of the synagogue and its breaking up should be understood. When the service was ended, and as they were going out among the large audience, Paul and Barnabas were asked to return the next Sabbath (construe εἰς with the main verb), of course, by those who had the authority, the synagogue elders; then after the audience had left the building, and Paul and Barnabas finally started for their lodgings, many of the audience followed them.

43) This shows the powerful impression Paul had made. There was no difference between the Jews and the Greek proselytes in this respect, for both classes are found in the group that follows the missionaries. Like φοβούμενος, also σεβόμενος is regularly used as a designation for a proselyte of the gate. Luke reports only the gist of what Paul and Barnabas said to these men who could scarcely separate themselves from them; it was the admonition to remain in the grace of God. The implication is that they were in this grace, that they believed Paul's message about the Savior Jesus. The one thing necessary, then, was to continue in this grace. One feels that Paul and Barnabas are thinking that opposition to this grace will arise and will try these young believers. In this they were right.

44) **Now on the coming Sabbath almost the whole city was gathered together to hear the Word of God.**

We now learn what the imperfect tenses used in v. 42, 43 intimated, namely what eventually happened. The talk about Paul and Barnabas and the sermon the former had preached spread through the city, the proselytes telling all their Greek friends with the result that a vast interest was aroused, and almost the whole city turned out to hear the Word of God. What interested all these Gentiles was the fact that without becoming Jews and adopting the Jewish separative laws they could be received into the full communion of faith. Paul and Barnabas were certainly succeeding in Pisidian Antioch.

45) **But the Jews, on seeing the crowds, were filled with passion and began to speak against the things uttered by Paul, blaspheming. Also speaking boldly, Paul and Barnabas said: To you was it necessary that the Word of God be spoken**

first. Since you are thrusting it away and are judging your own selves not worthy of eternal life, lo, we are turning to the Gentiles! For so has the Lord enjoined upon us:

> **I have set thee as a light of Gentiles**
> **For thee to be for salvation to the uttermost part of the earth.**

Luke says nothing about rabbis and that they stirred up the Jews during the week and were envious on this second Sabbath because so many came out to hear Paul while nobody in particular came out to hear them. The Jews were wrought up, not during the week, but on this Sabbath, not by agitators, but at sight of these crowds of Gentiles. Nor were the Jews afraid of losing the Jewish character of their synagogue services. Their ζῆλος, "zeal," "passion," was inflamed by the Gentiles as Gentiles: all these pagans were coming to share with them. This was not clerical jealousy between rabbis and Christian ministers which points a warning for professional men but the dislike of established church members who were unwilling to let a large number of outsiders suddenly come to share their religious prerogatives and blessings.

From Luke's account we are unable to tell whether the uproar began in the synagogue after the service was in progress and Paul and Barnabas spoke as they had been requested on the Sabbath before or already outside of the synagogue. It does not seem possible that all these people could have found room within the building. The imperfect is inchoative; the Jews began speaking against the things that were uttered by the missionaries. The outcome is held in abeyance for the moment by the imperfect tense. Not reason but heat and passion dictated this contradiction. Luke, therefore, does not intimate what objections were raised. He says only that the objections were vicious and went to the length of blasphemy, reviling this Jesus whom Paul and Barnabas preached as being the Savior promised to Israel by God.

46) The aorist now states the outcome. Argument against this blasphemous passion was useless. The rupture had come. Paul and Barnabas accept it. It is for this reason that Luke gives such prominence to the story of Pisidian Antioch. Here for the first time in Paul's missionary experience the open breach with the synagogue occurred. Paul was to have this experience again and again. It was to become typical of his work. So Luke describes at length how it began. In Cyprus nothing comparable to this had occurred. Here in Antioch Paul's sermon at first won the Jews; v. 42, 43 are plain in regard to that point. We have the whole sermon and can judge that it could not but win the Jews since God, their God, had done all that Paul recounted. What caused the break was the proclamation of the universality of God's grace in Jesus, the opening of the door full and wide to all the Gentiles. This stirred the Jewish exclusiveness and particularism to violent opposition when so many Gentiles now came. So the break came and it was decisive in every way.

How Paul and Barnabas accept it is fully recorded, and it should be noted that both are agreed in the matter. "To you," they say, "to you as the people whom God originally chose for the high mission of bringing salvation to all the world, it was necessary because of this your mission that the Word of God in regard to the fulfillment of his promises in Jesus, the Savior, should be spoken *first*, before that Word was brought to the Gentiles." Paul and Barnabas have done that.

The boldness (παρρησιασάμενοι) of the statement they make is evident from what follows. Since the Jews here in Antioch are thrusting that Word away and by that act are pronouncing on themselves the judgment that they are unworthy of eternal life, because of their unbelief not fit to have the eternal life the Savior bestows, "lo," let it surprise you, indeed, "we are turning to the Gentiles," who, as you see, are so eager for this Word, so ready to hear about the Savior, Jesus, and to accept the eternal life which you will not receive through him. That attests the break, states clearly who is making it, places the guilt where it belongs, and defines exactly what that guilt is.

Paul states what thrusting away the Word really means. By doing so the Jews themselves act as judges in their own case. They do not want the Word, their judgment, therefore, is that they are not worthy of the eternal life which that Word brings. They, indeed, blasphemed that Word as Paul spoke it, they scorned it as though it were nothing; Paul and Barnabas lift it high by pointing to the life it brings. And they tell these scorners what they are really doing. In his grace God regarded them worthy to receive that life through the Savior; they regard themselves unworthy. Whereas God intended to place them in the van, at the head of all the Gentiles, they put themselves entirely out of the procession. They have only themselves to blame.

"We are turning to the Gentiles!" Here at last Paul's mission as originally defined by Jesus comes to full realization: "to bear my name before the Gentiles," 9:15. The gospel will be preached to the Gentiles alone wherever the Jews thrust it away. The gospel will leave the synagogue completely and will gather its own assembly and church. The doom is settling down on the synagogue and the Jews; for nearly 2,000 years that doom has now remained. It will remain to the end.

47) When Paul uttered his strong warning in v. 40, 41 he let one of the prophets of the Jews' own Bible speak for him. Now that Barnabas and he are taking the decisive step of turning to the Gentiles, he does the same. Isaiah is their spokesman cf., 49:6.

This is done in order to close the mouths of the Jews. If they rage against Paul and Barnabas because of their turning to the Gentiles they must first square accounts with the great *'Ebed Yahweh,* Jehovah's Servant, who himself stated what Jehovah declared to him, namely that it is a light thing to raise up the Jews and the Israel of the diaspora, but that the greater and mightier part of the work of this Servant is to be that done upon the Gentiles. Paul and Barnabas say: "So the Lord (Jesus) has enjoined upon us" (perfect: his order stands). The sense is that, when Jehovah told the Messiah, his Servant Jesus, that he was to be a light for Gentiles, and when this Servant so declared, this was an order for all the messengers through whom this Servant works to preach also to the Gentiles in order that light and salvation might be brought even to the farthest end of the earth.

God himself has appointed his Messiah "for a light of Gentiles" (predicative εἰς, R. 482). The genitive is objective, this light is to illumine them. They are in darkness without the Old Testament Word. It was the Messiah's great task to be their light. The infinitive with τοῦ denotes purpose: "in order that thou be for salvation to the uttermost part of the earth." All Gentiles, however far removed from the center Jerusalem they may be, are to have this light. The εἰς is again predicative: Jesus is to be the salvation of the Gentiles ("Savior" in v. 23). God has appointed him to be this, has done it in the distant past, and that act stands. And now the messengers of Jesus are proceeding in accordance with that will of Jehovah.

48) That was a stunning reply which the Jews could answer, not by reason, but only by violence. **Now hearing it, the Gentiles began to rejoice and to glorify the Word of God; and they believed, as many as had been ranged in order for life eternal.**

The two imperfects reach a climax in the aorist "they believed." What angered the Jews delighted the Gentiles, namely to hear that the gospel was intended also for them, for them directly without the necessity of first becoming Jews and submitting to all the Jewish regulations. Happy to hear it, they glorified "the Word of God," meaning the Word in the sense in which Luke has continually been using it, the gospel of Jesus, the Savior. It is always so: whereas some spurn that Word, others receive it joyfully. So these Gentiles "believed," the aorist stating the fact.

Yet not all of those who had come to the synagogue on that Sabbath but only those "who were such as had been ranged in order for life eternal" believed. Τάσσω is a military term that means to draw up in rank and file and is then used generally for placing in an orderly arrangement and then to appoint and even to agree. The English "ordain" (our versions), *verordnen* (Luther) serve well enough, even better than "appoint" (R., *W. P.*) as long as the sense of the original is not rejected. For in τάσσω there lies a τάξις, a certain order, here the *ordo salutis*. Verb and noun go together. The periphrastic past perfect may be either passive or middle: "had been ranged in this *ordo*" by God; or "had ranged themselves in this *ordo*." Since no man is able to put himself into the *ordo salutis* by his own powers, it makes little difference which we choose. It is like *bekehrt werden* and *sich bekehren*. The point is to exclude all synergism. The context helps us. Here we have a contrast: the Jews thrust away the Word; these Gentiles glorify the Word. By their own fault the Jews are out of the τάξις; by God's grace these Gentiles are in it. Again the contrast: the Jews regard themselves unworthy of eternal life; these Gentiles are in line for eternal life. Who put them in line? God did so by sending Paul and Barnabas and his Word and his grace and by making both come in contact with their hearts. He did the same for the Jews and would have preferred to have them in the same blessed *ordo* but for the criminal wickedness with which they removed themselves from this *ordo* by blaspheming instead of glorifying the Word.

Although this passage deals with the doctrine of conversion, it has often been regarded as a pronouncement regarding predestination. This view began with Jerome who revised the old Latin rendering *destinati* or *ordinati* to *praeordinati* in order to make the coming to faith and salvation the product of a predestinatory eternal decree. Calvin is the great exponent of the *decretum absolutum;* those included in this decree are irresistibly brought to faith and held in it, and all others, even if they do believe for a time, are doomed by this same decree. Others conceive the decree as merely including the former and omitting the latter. Calov pointed out that Luke did not write προτεταγμένοι, and that neither τάσσειν nor τάσσεσθαι nor the context refer to eternity.

"Life eternal," so often found in the discourses of Jesus in John's Gospel (see John 3:15, 16), is the spiritual ζωή implanted in regeneration, fed by the Word and the Sacrament, passing unharmed through temporal death, then entering the heavenly state of glory. It dwells in the soul by faith but extends also to the body. Jesus will raise up those who have this life at the last day, John 6:54. "Life eternal" does not refer only to the heavenly life to come.

49) **Moreover, the Word of the Lord was being carried through the whole region.** The imperfect describes this spread in its progress; new believers were being won in the entire region. How long this continued until Paul and Barnabas were driven out can only be estimated; a period of approximately six months is probable. Ramsay regards χώρα here and elsewhere in Acts as a technical term for *Regio,* the

administrative district with Antioch as its center. He calls it "the Phrygian Region of (the province) Galatia." Since Galatia was so large, these "regions" were established; in each regional center the governor had his officials and visited these centers from time to time; thus also those living in the *Regio* would have much occasion to visit the center and thereby come into contact with the gospel. Ramsay's view seems sound until one gets to 16:6 and 18:23, where it cannot apply. We thus understand χώρα in the sense of territory, an indefinite region.

50) **The Jews, however, incited the worshipping women, those prominent, and the chief men of the city and stirred up a persecution against Paul and Barnabas and expelled them from their borders. But they, having shaken off the dust of the feet against them, went to Iconium. Yet the disciples continued to be filled with joy and the Holy Spirit.**

These women were proselytes, and Strabo and Juvenal report that throughout the empire many pagan women were proselytes of the synagogue. On the distinctive participle σεβόμενος see v. 43. The prominent women who were married to influential men were incited and also the chief men of the city, those who had government offices in the city and others who had considerable influence. The Jews had to work through others because they were not sufficiently numerous and powerful to take matters into their own hands.

Luke is reticent in regard to Paul's sufferings; so all that he records is the fact that the machinations of the Jews succeeded in stirring up a persecution against Paul and Barnabas the result of which was that the two were expelled beyond the borders, not merely of the city, but also of its environs. This means that magistrates of the city took action and not officials of the province. Only this city and its neighborhood were forbidden them and not the entire *regio* or all of Galatia. In II Tim. 3:11 Paul speaks of these days: "Persecutions, sufferings, what things befell me at Antioch," etc. In II Cor. 11:25 he states that he was thrice beaten with rods, and that means by the lictors in cities that were Roman colonies such as Antioch. One of those beatings may well have been suffered in Antioch. The entire city at first flocked to hear the gospel, now the current flowed in the opposite direction.

51) The expression "shaking off the dust of the feet" goes back to Jesus, Matt. 10:14; Mark 6:11; Luke 10:11. One commentator regards this as being only a phrase — the two left willingly. Another, "a dramatic gesture that forbids further intercourse." Still another finds in it "a gesture of protest." We also find the view that it is "a symbol that the very soil of the place was defiling." But they shook off only dust. In v. 50 Luke purposely retained "the Jews" as the subject although the expulsion took place through the magistrates who were the tools of the Jews. So now the dust was shaken off against these Jews and not against the whole city, which would have included the Christians. The act is symbolic; how serious it is Matt. 10:15 states; and it means that the dust is left behind as a testimony or witness (Mark 6:11) that the kingdom had been brought near by the feet of these messengers whose dust was thus left behind (Luke 10:11). That dust will testify on the day of judgment that wicked obduracy drove the messengers away.

So with sore backs Paul and Barnabas went on to Iconium. The fact that this was a Phrygian city is plain. Just where it belonged at this time is debated by the authorities. The question is intricate because at various times the city belonged to Pisidia, to Phrygia, and to Lycaonia, these signifying ethnographic districts and not Roman provinces. Ramsay makes it a part of the *Regio* of Antioch; but it naturally belonged with Antioch, both being Phrygian. So also Lystra and Derbe belonged together, both being nationally Lycaonian. Zahn makes Iconium a Roman colony. Later on this city became more renowned than Antioch.

52) The expulsion in no way injured the disciples who were left destitute of these leaders. They had the best Paraclete, the Holy Spirit, who filled their hearts and also gave them joy. The imperfect describes this condition as one that continued indefinitely. Luke does not refer to a charismatic presence of the Spirit but to the gracious spiritual presence that was mediated objectively by the Word and subjectively by faith in "the Savior Jesus" (v. 23).

CHAPTER XIV

THE FIRST MISSIONARY JOURNEY: ICONIUM, LYSTRA, DERBE, AND THE RETURN

1) Luke intends to give us only a brief account of the work in Iconium. Into the present short chapter all the rest of the work that was done on this missionary journey plus the return to Syrian Antioch is compressed. His plan seems to be to picture characteristic experiences encountered in this first effort to extend the gospel from the synagogue into the Gentile world in general. In Iconium great success is paralleled by strong opposition. Yet the work is accomplished, and before the opposition comes to its climax, Paul and Barnabas prudently leave.

Besides the remarks made in connection with 13:51 let us note that some of the former pictures of Iconium must be revised. A colony of Jews was prominent in the city; it had only one synagogue which was not as large as the one at Antioch but had men in it who were influential enough at last to enlist the aid of the magistrates in taking violent measures against the gospel messengers. The rest of the population was divided between Greeks and the older Phrygian stock of natives. There were, however, no Roman officials in it at this time. The greater prominence of the city when it became a Roman colony and outshone Pisidian Antioch was achieved at a later date. Several Roman roads entered the city, and the great highway that extended east and west passed through it. Paul and Barnabas had come about forty-five miles from Antioch and considered Iconium a city that was sufficiently important for the planting of a Christian congregation. It was Paul's constant policy to enter the greater centers from which the gospel might spread into neighboring territory. But on this first journey Antioch is the largest place which he visits. He grew as he worked until he eventually fixed his heart even on Rome.

Now it came to pass in Iconium that together they went into the synagogue of the Jews and spoke so that a great multitude of both Jews and Greeks believed.

It should be well noted at the outset that all the verbs of this paragraph that refer to Iconium are aorists. We have a recitation of facts from the time of the arrival to the time of the summary departure. Another feature is that Paul and Barnabas are indistinguishably combined; from κατὰ τὸ αὐτό onward they speak and act "together." Paul did not always do the speaking, Barnabas undoubtedly did his share of it. Paul would see to it that he did.

R., *W. P.*, thinks that these aorists covered only one Sabbath's speaking and calls it "a tremendous first meeting." But Luke does not say "on the day of the Sabbath" as he did in 13:14, and does not say "God-fearing Greeks" but "Greeks" in general. The claim that these were only proselytes is met by the fact that in the preceding chapter Luke always used the distinctive terms when he referred to proselytes and does not use one of them here. Some of the Ἕλληνες, to be sure, were proselytes of the gate, but by no means all of them. This view is not affected by the use of τὰ ἔθνη in v. 2; it is rather upheld, for these "Gentiles" were the unbelievers, not only unbelieving Greeks but Phrygians as well, who were placed in opposition to the ἀδελφοί, "brethren" or believers.

Nor, on the assumption that all was accomplished by one Sabbath day's preaching, should we stress οὕτως to mean that the missionaries preached "so" exceptionally as to produce a phenomenal result: "*so* plainly, *so* convincingly, with *such* an evidence and demonstration of the Spirit, and with *such* power; *so* warmly, *so* affectionately, and with *such* a manifest concern for the souls of men; *so* from the heart, *so* earnestly and seriously, *so* boldly and courageously." This is overdoing a good thing as though at other times and in other places Paul and Barnabas did not speak *so* and *so* and *so* and hence had no *such* phenomenal results. We cannot thus separate and emphasize οὕτως which has no emphatic position but is to be combined with ὥστε: "so that."

All these "Greeks" were not in the synagogue on that day, and certainly not those who were not proselytes. These aorists are constative. Luke is giving us a summary. He first describes the success without saying how long it took to achieve it. Yet we may regard the aorist πιστεῦσαι as ingressive, "came to faith." As the missionaries spoke Sabbath after Sabbath, more and more Greeks were attracted until a crowd of both Jews and Greeks came to faith. This infinitive shows what was spoken, namely the gospel of Jesus the Savior (13:23). How Paul, for instance, preached it Luke has reported in 13:17, etc. Luke does not need to report that again; and he certainly cannot mean that at Iconium the preaching was better than it had been at Antioch. Look at that sermon delivered at Antioch and ask yourself how it could be improved. While the chief purpose of the account in regard to Antioch is to relate how Paul and Barnabas for the first time turned to the Greeks in general (13:46), the secondary purpose is evidently to exhibit the manner of Paul's preaching on his missionary tour. In order to understand what occurred in Iconium we should not forget Antioch. We must especially note that here "Greeks" is to be considered in the light of 13:46, namely Greeks in general, also such as were not proselytes.

2) **But the Jews who came to be disobedient stirred up and embittered the souls of the Gentiles against the brethren.**

This is the second effect of the preaching, a party of Jews "fixed in disobedience"; the aorist ἀπειθήσαντες conveys the idea that they had come to this fixed state. The participle itself means to be unpersuaded, thus to refuse belief, and thus to refuse to obey. The two latter meanings merge. Faith is at times called obedience; and unbelief disobedience. This is due to the fact that the Word demands faith, consequently responding with faith is to obey, refusing faith is to disobey. The point to be noted in this characterization is the fact that these Jews had heard the gospel in their synagogue and yet rejected it; the participle could not be applied to men who had not yet heard the Word or had not heard it sufficiently. Another noteworthy point is the observation that, as was the case in Antioch, Jews were again the opponents of the gospel and offered violence to its ministers. They have this unenviable distinction; the Gentiles are only drawn into it through the agency of these Jews. We note that in 26:19 Paul says with reference to himself and his own conversion: "I was not disobedient"; note also Heb. 12:25: "See that ye refuse not him that speaketh." This is the sad feature especially in regard to missionary preaching, that some become fixed in disobedience and, though salvation is knocking at their doors, deliberately turn to perdition.

Fixed unbelief is ever morally vicious. It does not always go to the extreme, but when the circumstances are favorable, it ignores every moral consideration in vilification of the gospel and in taking base measures against its adherents. So these Jews did not content themselves with rejecting the gospel, the devil plagued them to such an extent that "they stirred up and embittered the souls of the Gentiles against the brethren." These Jews started an agitation against the converts by stirring up the Gentile population with slanderous reports about the brethren. Here κακόω has the non-classical, later, and rarer sense of "to embitter," to make evil-minded against someone. A uniformly used weapon against the gospel and its true believers is this process of poisoning the minds of those who as yet do not know the gospel.

A discrepancy has been found between what Luke here states that the hostile Jews succeeded in doing (the aorists imply success) and what the next verse states, namely that Paul and Barnabas spent much time in Iconium working openly. In order to remove this supposed difficulty some would eliminate v, 3 or dispose of it as a marginal remark. Reference is also made to the reading of the Codex Bezae which speaks of "a persecution" and of how "the Lord quickly gave peace." Let us say in general about this codex and the many additions it offers to the accredited text that it is a late effort to improve on Luke and is taken too seriously by certain interpreters. Luke knows of no "persecution" that was followed by a sudden providential "peace" which then enabled Paul and Barnabas to continue their work. The romance regarding Thecla is introduced with a trial for Paul and Barnabas in which the magistrates discovered the falsity of the charges and acquitted the prisoners, and thus the Lord provided peace; Thecla is regarded as a convert who was gained in Iconium.

These views are answered when we note that the Jews succeeded in embittering only the souls of the Gentiles. Beyond that they were not successful. Again, this viciousness was directed "against the brethren" and not against Paul and Barnabas in particular. This phrase excludes an arrest and a trial of Paul and of Barnabas. The attack took in all the believers; we may say it "bit off more than it could chew." In regard to tangible results, this general attack furnished none that

Luke could record. The effort put forth dissipated itself largely because it tried to take in too much territory. The feeling that was temporarily aroused subsided.

Luke writes that the Jews worked on "the Gentiles," he does not say on "the magistrates," he does not even say on "the Greeks," those who had Greek culture and education. These Jews wasted their efforts in trying to stir up too many people. They tried to set too many against too many and so accomplished nothing. And that is exactly what Luke implies in v. 3. The work of Paul and Barnabas was not stopped. Where, then, is the discrepancy? There is none in Luke's account.

What Luke tells us is that in Iconium, too, a hostile party of Jews soon formed and vented its hostility by turning the Gentiles generally against the Christians. Under this handicap Paul and Barnabas labored, but it did not hinder them to any notable degree. They worked right on. Read what Luke says. He does not refer to "a first explosion" in v. 2, to be followed by the "second" in v. 5. Luke knows of only one.

3) **A sufficient time, therefore, they spent boldly speaking in the Lord, he bearing witness to the Word of his grace by granting signs and wonders to occur through their hands.**

The close connection of this verse with the two preceding verses is shown by οὖν, which means that, with the situation as indicated, many Jews and Greeks turned into believers. Because other Jews stirred up the Gentiles, Paul and Barnabas spent a considerable amount of time in Iconium, meaning enough time fully to establish a permanent Christian congregation. "Boldly speaking" does not mean "copious and commanding eloquence." Paul always spoke with boldness, the participle implying free and open speaking that holds nothing back. He later asked the Christians to pray that he might speak thus, Eph. 6:19, 20. Luke notes that Paul and Barnabas spoke thus here in Iconium because the Jews had embittered the Gentiles. That did not make the preachers timid and hesitant lest they say too much; they spoke with utmost freedom, held nothing back, cared not who heard them. Warmth and eloquence there may have been also, but Luke says nothing about that. The gospel will cause offense — let it. So many try to preach it with an eye to their personal interest by toning down unpopular doctrines, flattering themselves that they are up-to-date, progressive, even wise. Not so these two great heralds.

We have no smooth translation for ἐπὶ τῷ Κυρίῳ, really, "on the basis of the Lord," and thus render "in the Lord." The Lord was the reason of their courageous freedom of utterance. But not merely in general as inspiring them with confidence that by relying on his commission and promise they had nothing to fear; here in Iconium the Lord "was bearing witness to the Word of his grace" in a signal manner. He was testifying that the Word preached by his messengers was, indeed, his Word, and at the same time, by the manner in which he bore this testimony, he made plain who he really was — not a Jesus dead and buried, his body gone, no one knowing what became of it (this is the gospel of many today) — but a Jesus risen and glorified, the Savior in heaven, exercising the divine power and majesty as the great Head of the church.

There is no καί preceding διδόντι so that it describes the manner of μαρτυροῦντι: "he testifying by granting." A precious name is here used as a designation for the gospel. In Paul's sermon in Antioch he called it "the Word of this salvation" (13:26); and Luke, "the Word of God" and "of the Lord" (13:44-49). It is also "the Word of grace," which the Lord's grace uses as its tool and instrument for reaching the sinful and guilty souls of men in order to bestow itself upon them, free them from sin, guilt, and all condemnation, and unite them to the Lord as his own. The Word is thus the means of grace, the divine channel through which grace flows to the sinner. I Cor. 2:1-5. Χάρις is here, as throughout, the Lord's favor and love which is shown to those who, because of their sin and guilt, do not deserve it. The word always connotes guilt and signifies the love which would remove that guilt.

This Word of grace the Lord attested as what it was, the bearer of divine grace to the sinner, by means of miracles of gracious healing and deliverance from fearful ailments. These "signs and wonders" (see 2:19 on the terms) the Lord appended as seals and credentials to the Word; it was like signing his own name to it. All those credentials stand to this day and are for this very reason not repeated; for genuine seals need no further seals to prove them genuine. If seals must have still other seals, this would prove only that none of them are sufficient, which is the claim of those who deny the reality of miracles.

Luke reports no signs that might have occurred in Antioch, and in the case of Paphos only that of striking the magus blind. Let us note this when Luke writes that here in Iconium Paul and Barnabas wrought miracles, the Lord "granting," "giving" them. No apostle or other Christian ever wrought a sign at will but only when the Lord so willed and by his Spirit prompted and directed the act (see 9:40). Compare Heb. 2:4: "signs and wonders . . . *according to his own will.*" Here the signs and wonders were a tremendous testimony regarding the Word for Paul and Barnabas and for all who saw them and all who heard them. The hostile Jews might agitate all they pleased, the Lord made his Word only the stronger. "Through their hands" does not necessarily imply the laying on of hands although this symbolic gesture may have been used (on its significance see 6:6). Διά is important, for it makes Paul and Barnabas the Lord's media and nothing more. The Lord used their hands when and where he desired.

4) **Now the multitude of the city was split, and some were with the Jews, some with the apostles.**

Note how δέ corresponds to μέν in v. 3 and balances the two statements: the long stay — the whole city split. But v. 4 says more, it goes back to v. 2. Those wicked Jews were the rallying point of the one party (οἱ μέν), and the apostles the center of the other (οἱ δέ). The entire Gentile population was divided into two opposing camps; σύν is used exactly as when we say, "I am *with* you" on any question. A point not to be overlooked is the fact that Paul and Barnabas filled the entire city with the sound of the gospel, filled it so that practically no person remained neutral. In this they had the aid of the hostile Jews. The more these agitated, the more the gospel became known. People simply had to go and hear what these men were teaching and doing.

Paul never went off into a corner, gathered a handful, and then thought his task done. Even in Athens he had the philosophers of the city around him. So he thoroughly evangelized Iconium. Warneck says: "It is not rhetorical hyperbole when Paul says of himself that he filled *the world* with his gospel, Rom. 10:18; 15:19; Acts 17:6." "But thanks be unto God, which always leadeth us in triumph in Christ, and maketh manifest through us *the savor of his knowledge in every place*," II Cor. 2:14. In those days all sorts of exotic religious wares were offered (see the samples in 8:9, etc.; 13:6, etc.), but Paul never failed to lift the gospel above everything human and filled entire cities and districts with his message.

Here Luke uses the word "apostles" with reference to both Paul and Barnabas; the term is used in the wider sense. So James, the Lord's brother, is an apostle

(Gal. 1:19); Epaphroditus (Phil. 2:25); Sylvanus and Timothy (I Tim. 2:6); Andronicus and Junia (Rom. 16:7); and there are false apostles (II Cor. 11:13). The gospel always causes a division, one that is at times sharp and painful. Jesus himself said it would do so, Matt. 10:34, etc., and elsewhere. Sometimes Christians do not like this, and the children of unbelief constantly reproach us for bringing about this disharmony or whatever they are pleased to call it. But this is the very nature of the gospel. The only way to avoid it is to preach and to believe some sham gospel, and even that may cause division. When light comes, darkness resents it; when righteousness appears, the unrighteous assail it; when life comes, the powers of death bestir themselves to destroy it.

Even without becoming polemical the gospel interferes with what the heathen regard as their dearest treasures. Many heathen religions are syncretistic, but in the case of Jesus there is either the acceptance of faith or the rejection of unbelief. Warneck is right: "Over against the Son of God indifference is impossible; no one can erect an altar for him at the side of the idols he may have in his pantheon." Many religious errors are unionistic; they tolerate and fraternize each other. But the gospel and its truths cannot compromise nor fraternize with a single error.

5) Luke has described the situation which at last came to a climax. Paul and Barnabas did not avoid or fear the issue and did, of course, not provoke it although in all probability they expected it in some form or other (13:50). **And when there occurred an onset of both the Gentiles and Jews with their rulers to outrage and to stone them, having become aware of it, they fled for refuge to the cities of Lycaonia, Lystra, and Derbe, and the region round about; and there they continued proclaiming the good news.**

Real persecution at last raised its head. Here there was fulfilled what the Lord had told Paul in advance: "I will show him how many things he must suffer for my name's sake" (9:16). There was an actual "onset" or "assault," (Luther, *Sturm*) and not a mere plot. A mob was formed and got under way in order to locate Paul and Barnabas in order to heap insults upon them and to stone them. It was composed of both Gentiles and Jews plus the rulers of the latter. We cannot understand how B.-D. 393, 6 can translate ἐγένετο ὁρμὴ . . . ὑβρίσαι *sie beschlossen, beabsichtigten;* this was not a meeting that passed a resolution of intentions.

The other view is that the mob actually seized Paul and Barnabas and began to revile and to pelt them with stones, and that συνιδόντες, on considering the matter, Paul and Barnabas took to flight — to be sure, a wise consideration. The participle, however, does not mean "considering" or "having considered," but, as in 5:2 and 12:12, to know something together with somebody else. Somebody rushed in and warned the intended victims; the mob never found them.

We should note that this time the animosity was not directed against the brethren, but that it concentrated upon the two principals alone. Those Jews had no success when they endeavored to embitter the city (v. 3); this time they sought an objective they could quickly reach. These considerations indicate that it is difficult to determine who the "rulers" were, whether these were the Jewish elders or these together with the city magistrates. Some think of the latter. But what about the stoning? We are told that this was to be only a pelting with stones in order to drive the victims out of town. Nor does 13:50 decide the question. There the city magistrates did have a hand but did not join a mob and yet got rid of Paul and Barnabas. It is asking rather much of us to believe that the city magistrates joined the Jewish elders in a mob. This was a large and important city, and the dignity of the magistrates was accordingly. If they had taken a hand, we should have had a repetition of the events which occurred at Antioch and not a mob. Luke uses the inverse order because the Gentiles (again he does not use "Greeks," v. 3) formed the larger crowd, the Jews were a smaller number, their elders were the real leaders, and stoning was to be the method of summary execution in regular Jewish style.

6) Κατέφυγον means "to flee for refuge." Paul and Barnabas are not cowardly but prudent. When it was necessary, Paul risked his life, otherwise he did not. His work had been completed in Iconium, the whole city knew about the gospel. The missionaries did not flee because they were defeated; they merely left one victory behind in order to start winning another. They acted in accord with Matt. 10:23.

Lystra and Derbe belonged to the ethnographic section of Lycaonia. The old native languages were still spoken in these ethnographic sections, and so the old names survived. Lycaonia was, however, Roman territory only in part, namely in that part containing Lystra and Derbe. One might call it "Roman Lycaonia." But the old name was *Galatica Lycaonia* because it was incorporated into that Roman province. The other part was not Roman because it was being ruled by King Antiochus and hence was called *Lycaonia Antiochiana.* Paul confined himself to Roman territory.

"The region round about" is added to show that the gospel penetrated into the entire section as this had been the case in 13:49. The imperial road from Antioch to Iconium passed on to Lystra and Derbe. Zahn makes Lystra a Roman colony, and also Derbe which was located near the passes that crossed the Taurus range. It was a high honor for a provincial city to be made a *colonia,* for this demonstrated the interest of the emperor who regarded the city as worthy of the residence of Roman citizens, the aristocracy of the empire. About 300 Roman citizens were placed into such a city, which did not itself have citizenship. The city thus became a military outpost of Rome, an advance guard of the mother city, a small edition of Rome itself. In times of peace the military feature was not prominent. The most important feature of the transfer of the work to Lystra and Derbe is that neither place had a synagogue of Jews. Paul and Barnabas were now in completely Gentile and pagan cities — a most important step in their work.

7) Now at last we have an imperfect tense (periphrastic) which indicates that the two continued preaching the gospel. In v. 20 Paul and Barnabas reach Derbe. The view that they had taken along disciples from Antioch and Iconium on account of the Lycaonian language is untenable, because such disciples could themselves not have spoken Lycaonian — the natives of Iconium spoke Phrygian. Greek was spoken everywhere. In the Orient it is today a simple matter for men to speak several languages, they seem to grow up that way.

8) **And in Lystra there was sitting a man, impotent as to his feet, lame from his mother's womb, who never yet did walk. This one was listening to Paul speaking; who, on earnestly looking at him and seeing that he had faith to be made whole, said with a great voice, Arise on thy feet upright! And he leaped up and began to walk.**

In v. 6 we have the feminine singular Λύστρα, here the neuter plural Λύστρα: both are names of the city. Luke intends to narrate an experience in an entirely pagan city: first Paul and Barnabas are treated as gods, next as devils. This is only a glimpse into the work done in Lystra, one that is significant in every way. The miracle is almost a duplicate of that wrought by Peter and John. In the former instance there are two companions, Peter and John; here two, Paul and Barnabas — both times there is congenital lameness of the worst type — both times unsolicited healing — both times great results. But withal there are also great differences: the one man is a Jew, the other a pagan — the one is minus faith, the other has faith — in the one case many believers are the result, in the other a great manifestation of pagan idolatrous ideas. The fact that Luke was aware of the parallel should not be disputed, but the claim that Luke invented this miracle in order to make Paul the equal of Peter is unwarranted.

This man was not a beggar as was the one healed by Peter and John. Luke carefully notes the begging of the latter yet says not a word to that effect about this man. So he says nothing about a synagogue because none existed in Lystra. The man is described as sitting (imperfect), for he could not even stand. The description continues in v. 9, the tenses holding us in suspense until the aorist relates what Paul did. Luke's detailed description of the man's condition has been noted. We may say that Luke's interest as a physician is evident in this. First, we learn that the trouble lay in his inability to use his feet, the dative "as to his feet" being a dative of specification which is often used in place of the accusative; R. 523 regards it as the locative with adjectives. Secondly, this condition was congenital, "from his mother's womb," he was probably injured at birth. Finally, the man had never walked, the aorist merely stating the past fact as such whereas we should use the past perfect. Here was a case that was absolutely beyond human help.

9) The cripple was listening to Paul's speaking. In this respect he differed from the beggar in the Temple. It is entirely probable that Paul was recounting some of the miracles of healing wrought by Jesus. The cripple was thinking of himself and of how Jesus might have healed him, too, if he only had been there. But

the idea to be expressed is by no means that by casually looking at him Paul saw that he had this faith τοῦ σωθῆναι, "to be made whole" ("saved" from his condition, the infinitive after a noun with the idea of complement, R. 1076). This ἀτενίσας is the same as that occurring in 3:4, the result of an intimation of the Holy Spirit that a miracle was to be wrought upon the man.

The thesis is sound that no man wrought a miracle without this specific direction on the part of the Spirit. Miracles were never wrought promiscuously at the will of the apostles. Paul saw that the cripple had this faith by observing the eyes and the bearing of the cripple. Or did the man voice this faith? It is often assumed that Peter, too, looked and saw faith in the beggar; but the opposite is true, he saw the beggar expecting and thinking of nothing but a good-sized gift of money, wherefore Peter also told him he had no money to give. Faith sometimes preceded the healing (here), sometimes followed (Peter's beggar).

10) As he had done in Iconium and had not done in Antioch, the Lord intended to attest the gospel by signs and wonders in this city (v. 3). So "with a great voice" that expressed the great divine authority and the great divine power now to be manifested Paul commanded this cripple to arise on his feet. And he leaped up at once (the aorist of ἅλλομαι expressing the one act) and did not only stand upright but "began to walk" (the imperfect to indicate the action that continued indefinitely).

11) Luke's interest does not lie in this cripple's personal story, for not another word is said about him. The miracle is described for the sake of the strange result it produced. **And the multitudes, on seeing what Paul did, lifted up their voice, saying in Lycaonian, The gods, having become like to men, did come down to us! And they began to call Barnabas**

Zeus and Paul Hermes, since he was the one leading the speaking. And the priest of the Zeus that was before the city, after bringing bulls and garlands to the portals, together with the multitudes was intending to sacrifice.

Peter had encountered the superstitions of Simon Magus in Samaria, Paul a lesser magus in Paphos; it is now that Paul and Barnabas encounter the idolatrous Greek mythology that was prevalent in the Roman world. From the narrative one gathers that the cripple was one of a large audience to whom the gospel was preached and that the healing occurred at the conclusion of the preaching. It is not stated where the gathering occurred save that it seems to have taken place outdoors in some square of the city. We note incidentally that the missionaries seem to have had no trouble whatever in reaching multitudes of the general population, entirely pagan though they were. Only incidentally we learn that converts were made and that a congregation was organized and that elders were appointed (v. 22, 23).

The crowds that witnessed the miracle were native Lycaonians; there were perhaps some Greeks among them. They at once called to mind their old mythology and in their excitement in a natural way reverted to their native Lycaonian language and declared that once more the gods had taken on the likeness of men and had come down to them from Olympus. Did not Ovid in his *Metamorphoses* VIII, 626, tell the story that Zeus and Hermes had appeared in the form of men in the neighboring region of Phrygia? And now the story of Baucis and Philemon was being re-enacted in a new way in Lycaonia! Our versions use the Latin names Jupiter and Mercury instead of the Greek Zeus (genitive Διός) and Hermes. But this does not justify the assumption that Luke substituted Greek gods for what were actually Phrygian divinities and the claim that the main god's name was Papas or Pappas and that there was a secondary god Mēn.

12) But Luke himself answers this claim. He states that Paul was called Hermes because he led in the speaking. It was the Greek god Hermes and he alone who was thus indicated. In the Greek mythology Hermes was the messenger of the gods, the spokesman of Zeus, who was eloquent in speech and the legendary inventor of speech. What Phrygian god fits this description? Hermes was beautiful and graceful. The statues show him in the position of a swift runner bearing messages. Paul scarcely fits that description, wherefore also Luke indicates that it was not his form and figure but his ability in speech that suggested the identification.

Nothing is said as to why Barnabas was thought to be Zeus. But we may say that he was older and may venture the suggestion that he was of a more imposing stature. Perhaps because the people feel certain that Paul was Hermes, Barnabas was made Zeus without further question. It is not likely that afterward, in Gal. 4:14, Paul had this episode in mind when he wrote that the Galatians had received him "as an angel of God." A Greek god and a divine angel are rather different; besides Paul adds "even as Christ Jesus." His letter was written to all the churches in Galatia and not to Lystra alone. Analogous to Paul's comparison with an angel are II Sam. 19:27; Zech. 12:8; Mal. 2:7, and not the idea of his being a Greek god.

13) Acting on the extravagant surmise that the two gods are disguised as men, preparations are made to offer sacrifices in the temple of Zeus. "The Zeus that was before the city" was the temple dedicated to this god which contained his statue and was probably situated on some eminence just outside of the city. Most ancient cities were walled so that their boundaries were very definite. The Codex Bezae has the plural

"the priests," but the preferred reading has but one priest. Luke speaks of "the priest" as the chief priest by whose order alone things could go forward; and it is self-evident that this lone man could not have brought several bulls with their garlands and himself slaughtered and cut them up for the sacrifice.

These ταῦροι were "bulls" and not "oxen," and they were decorated with "garlands" of flowers while being led to the sacrifice. This was good Greek custom and indicates that this was the temple of Zeus and not that of some Phrygian god. It is not the plural "gates" that indicates that these belonged to the temple or rather to its surrounding court instead of to the city; but the nature of the case. Yet it is held that the city gates are referred to for the reason that Paul and Barnabas, the supposed gods, were in the city. But where was the altar at the city gates, where all the other things that were necessary for a regular Greek sacrifice and celebration? Why would a sacrifice before a city gate honor Paul and Barnabas more than one at the temple's altar?

This answers also the other question as to how sacrifice at the temple of Zeus could honor Paul as Hermes. A sacrifice to the chief god was intended also for any other god, especially if no temple of that minor god was at hand. And was not Hermes the messenger of Zeus? The pressure for this sacrifice came from the ὄχλοι, the crowds; hence they were present when the sacrifice was now about to be made. The presence of Paul and Barnabas was not required, for did not gods know when sacrifices were being offered to them? The proximity of Paul and Barnabas was enough. Codex Bezae again has the variant ἐπιθύειν which means, "to sacrifice in addition," to bring an extra sacrifice.

14) Paul and Barnabas were blissfully ignorant of what was under way. By calling this temple and its statue "the Zeus before the city," just as many temples

so situated bore names accordingly (as today "St. Paul's outside of the walls," the great Roman Catholic church outside of Rome) Luke implies that Paul and Barnabas were in the city.

But having heard it, the apostles Barnabas and Paul, having rent their garments, sprang forth into the multitude, yelling and saying, Men, why do you do these things? We, too, on our part are human beings of like sensations with you, proclaiming as good news for you on your part to turn from these useless ones to God alive, who made the heaven and the earth and the sea and all the things in them. He who in the generations gone by let all the Gentiles go their own ways and yet he did not leave himself witnessless, working good by giving to you rains from heaven and fruit-bearing seasons, filling your hearts with nourishment and happiness.

How the apostles learned what was in progress is left unsaid. Luke would have used a different participle than the one employed in the text if they had been summoned or invited. Barnabas is named first because of the order followed in v. 12. The act of tearing the garment consisted in grasping the tunic at the neck with both hands and giving a downward pull and tearing a rent of four or five inches in the tunic. It was always the tunic (χιτών) which was worn next to the body that was thus torn and not the long, loose outer robe (ἱμάτιον). In the expression "to rend τὰ ἱμάτια," the noun is used in the wider sense of "garment." The robe was made of heavy material that was too solid to be torn and hung loosely upon the body.

This act symbolized grief and pain at seeing or hearing anything that was actually blasphemous or sacrilegious. The whole idea and the act of these Lystrians were sacrilege. To go about with a torn tunic thus was evidence of what the wearer had experienced.

Already the news caused the apostles (see v. 4) to rend their garments. "They sprang out into the multitude" (ἐκ in the verb and εἰς corresponding) means simply that the apostles rushed out from the place where they were into the crowd at the temple in the most violent agitation and at the top of their voices (κράζοντες, "shouting") stopped the proceedings then and there.

15) Luke records what amounts to a brief address which was probably spoken by Paul. Shouts of, "Stop! stop!" may well have preceded this little address. When the apostle says "men" he is abrupt and not discourteous; we use "men" in the same way. The τί means "why" and is not predicative, could not be with a transitive verb (R. 736). This question bids these people consider why they are doing these things in order that, realizing why, they will at once cease and regret their undertaking.

We must note the strong correspondence between the emphatic pronouns ἡμεῖς and ὑμᾶς: "we on our part," "you on your part." Why treat the apostles as gods when they are only men, yea, men engaged in telling the good news that these their hearers are to turn from these very gods to the one who really is God and has long proved even to them that he is? Καί is scarcely adversative "and yet" but simply "also": "Men, we also are (only) human beings," ἄνθρωποι, *Menschen.*

This fact is intensified by the addition "of like sensations with you," ὁμοιοπαθεῖς ὑμῖν. This word does not mean "of like passions" or "of like nature." The gods were considered ἀπαθεῖς, unlike human beings. In these adjectives the verb πάσχω refers to suffering the vicissitudes connected with human existence. Paul and Barnabas suffer all such vicissitudes just as these men do and are not exempt, lifted to a plane above them as gods were suposed to be. This statement directly denies the notion of these pagan people that the apostles were gods in the likeness of men (v. 11).

But that is not all; the apostles are here in Lystra "engaged in proclaiming as good news that *you*, you Lystrians, given to idols, turn from these useless ones to God alive," etc. It is the greatest good news in the world to learn that all idols are μάταιοι (masculine, supply θεοί), that there is a "God living" who is attested as such even to the pagan world, and that we should turn from the useless to the genuine. We construe ὑμᾶς with the infinitive and not with the participle, for the infinitive calls for a subject, the participle needs no object.

In order to appreciate the full force of what is said we must note that μάταιος is used specifically with reference to heathen gods and idols. The adjective refers to that which does not accomplish its purpose and thus disappoints, while κενός is that which is empty. These heathen gods fail utterly in what their worshippers expect of them as gods. The adjective goes no farther. Of course, they are "useless" as gods because they are in reality οὐδέν, "nothing" (I Cor. 8:4). Recall the famous passage Isa. 44:10-17, which describes how a man cuts down a tree and with part of it cooks his dinner and makes a fire to warm himself and out of some of this wood manufactures a god for himself and worships it. Isa. 37:19; Hab. 2:18, 19. No wonder such gods are absolutely useless! It is pure fiction that actual supernatural beings exist which correspond to such images. All this applies to the fictions which men today call "God," using the capital letter, although no material image is made; such fictional images are also μάταιοι.

Over against them is set Θεὸς ζῶν, "God alive," "God living." No article is necessary because only the one exists. The contrast between "useless ones" and God "living" brings a great advance in the second designation. Instead of saying "useless" and then "useful," the apostle at once states the full reason that makes

God useful: God is alive, living, is and does all that the term "God" implies even far beyond the expectation of his worshippers. The evidence for his living existence is before the eyes of even the pagan world: it is he "who made the heaven and the earth and the sea and all the things in them" including men themselves, the four terms spreading out his mighty creations so the mind may grasp them the better. Ps. 19:1; Rom. 1:20

16) In addition to this evidence in creation the living God attested himself by means of the constant benefactions of his providence. He did this even in the case of the Gentiles whom "in the generations that have passed" (perfect participle) he permitted to go their ways. There is a contrast with the present and God's work of now sending the gospel to the Gentiles. "Their ways" gives ὁδοί an ethical sense just as "the Way" is used with reference to Christianity in 9:2 (see the explanation). The plural signifies that the Gentiles followed many different ways, their very multiplicity revealing that they were wrong ways.

No effort is made to show why God permitted the Gentiles to wander thus, for the point to be made here is that he had nevertheless not cast off the Gentiles When we now ask why this was done in regard to the Gentiles we must, first of all remember that Gentiles and their pagan ways should never have come into existence. God destroyed the godless race of Noah's time. Was that not judgment enough? Noah began a new race, began it with the true God, bequeathed that knowledge to his descendants, even the knowledge of the judgment of God through the Flood. How could paganism then begin? The answer is plain. If God accepted the fearful defection that developed into idolatrous cults and let the Gentiles go on in these cults he at the same time prepared universal salvation in and through Israel until he could now send the gospel to all men. Compare 17:30. The real story is that because of their own fearful guilt men lost the true God and the true religion, and that God prepared to restore it to them and in due time did so.

The contention that τὰ ἔθνη refers to "the nations" in the sense that the Jews and the Samaritans are included because "in their ways" does not mean "in their *own* ways," ἑαυτῶν instead of merely αὐτῶν or ταῖς ἰδίαις ὁδοῖς is not in keeping with the context. In spite of their defections and their idolatries the Jews are never included with the Gentiles as forming one class of men. God gave more than the evidence of creation and providence to the Jews; he used the Jews alone as a means for eventually spreading the gospel to the Gentiles even to the ends of the earth. God shaped the way of the Jews in a manner in which he did not shape "the ways" of the Gentiles.

17) Although v. 16 begins with ὅς, it is really an independent sentence, and v. 17 is its second part. The printing should be according: "He it was who, indeed, permitted . . . and yet did not leave himself unattested," etc. He had not turned forever from the Gentiles although his displeasure rested upon them because they had abandoned him and the true religion, and although in just judgment he let them go on in their ways. During the entire time of their abandonment of him he kept on attesting himself to them in the most effective manner. The second participle depends on the first, and the third on the second: "working good (in the sense of what benefits) by giving and by thus filling," etc. All good things of this earthly life are wrought by God.

Some think that "rains" are mentioned because Lystra often suffered drought; but "rains" are mentioned especially because they came "from heaven" and thus from God. Through them he gives fruit-bearing seasons with all their rich abundance. The miracle of the seasons and of their abundance of fruit, which is repeated year after year, is one of the great attestations of God to himself that is fit for all men to see: "The eyes of all wait upon thee," etc., Ps. 145:15. Thus God "fills your hearts with nourishment and happiness." The expression is concentrated. It is the body that is filled with the nourishment so that the heart is made glad; instead of mentioning both body and heart, the latter is selected because the food is the means for the heart's delight. Here "heart" means the seat of thought, feeling, and will, the center of the being.

Paul is preaching natural theology as he does in 17:24-29; Rom. 1:19-23. We may add the great passages found in the psalms. It was the direct way to the heart of Gentiles. In Antioch, in the case of Jews and proselytes of the gate he referred to God in Israel's history (13:17) as the direct way to their hearts. True natural theology leads to a correct knowledge of God; we need it even in the case of Christians. It contains no gospel yet is a step toward revealed theology with its gospel fulness. In the face of God's revelation and self-attestation in nature it should be impossible to believe in gods and idols (17:27, 28).

18) **And by saying these things hardly did they restrain the multitudes from sacrificing to them.** The sincerity which went to the length of inaugurating this sacrifice was because of its very nature strong and hard to turn from its course, which makes what follows the more striking. After a verb of hindering μή with the infinitive is called pleonastic.

19) **Now there came to them Jews from Antioch and Iconium, and, having persuaded the multitudes and having stoned Paul, they were dragging him out of the city, supposing him to be dead. But the disciples having surrounded him, after arising, he went out with Barnabas to Derbe.**

Luke adds a dramatic touch by placing these two clashing incidents side by side, first making pagan deities of Paul and Barnabas and then stoning Paul and dragging him out as dead. There is no need for the textual additions that the apostles spent some time in Lystra before this attack on Paul occurred. The hatred of the Jews both in Antioch and Iconium was so intense and persistent as to pursue him to Lystra. The impression is not left on the reader that these were Jewish merchants who had come to Lystra on business and accidentally found the apostle at work in this city. This was a combination of Jews from the two cities in which Paul had worked and from which he had been driven out. He had left many converts behind, and that circumstance kept the Jewish hatred alive. In some way Jews from both cities got together and planned to follow the apostles to Lystra. Yet we do not read about any Jews in Lystra with whom they joined hands.

Luke relates only the facts that occurred and does this in the briefest way. So we are unable to say why Paul alone became the victim of stoning and not Barnabas also. These Jews persuaded the multitudes. There is no need to ask by what means when the basest lies were used even against Jesus. As far as the city crowds were concerned, it was not difficult to persuade them, for were not the apostles attacking their gods as being "useless"? How easy, too, to brand the entire story of Jesus as nothing but an invention in spite of the miracle wrought on the lame man, the effect of which had begun to wane. The upshot was a mob that somehow got hold at least of Paul and stoned him. They certainly would have included Barnabas if they could have caught him. To say that they passed him by is a grave injustice to this noble companion of Paul's. In Iconium the plan included the stoning of both Paul and Barnabas.

Since Jews were back of the original plan and now its execution, this stoning was the Jewish idea of doing away with Paul. Pagans would probably have beaten him to death. This is corroborated by the procedure of dragging the victim outside of the city after they thought he was dead (perfect "has died" used for "is dead"). That pagan mob could not be persuaded to perform the execution in proper Jewish style, to wait until Paul was first dragged out and then stone him; they stoned him on the spot and then dragged him out. These pagans would have permitted Paul to lie in the street; but the Jews had to have him thrown outside of the city. The imperfect ἔσυρον conveys the thought that this was not the end of the matter.

20) The aorist that follows brings the outcome. Paul lay somewhere along the road beyond the city gate. The mob had finished its work and had dispersed. Thus the disciples finally reached him and stood around his battered body with torn hearts. Incidentally we learn that there were "disciples" in Lystra. Luke seems to regard it as a matter of course that the apostles had succeeded also in Lystra. To be sure, they had! Nor have we any reason to think that the number of converts made was small. They had been won directly from paganism.

Was Timothy in this circle of disciples who were grouped around Paul? Luke introduces him in 16:1, but at that time he was already a disciple. In I Cor. 4:17 as well as in II Tim. 1:2, Paul calls him "my beloved child" (τέκνον), which makes it rather certain that Paul had converted him, and that would of necessity have occurred on this first visit of Paul's to Lystra. When R., *W. P.*, writes: "Timothy, a lad of about fifteen, would not soon forget that solemn scene," Timothy's age is estimated too low, for in 16:1-3, only a year later, Paul takes him along as one of his assistants; he must have been past twenty.

The disciples had come to give Paul a decent burial as devout Jews had once buried Stephen after his stoning. But, as Luke states with astonishing brevity, "after arising, he went into the city." Was this a miracle? Luke does not even hint that it was a miracle. This would have been the place to invent one in order to glorify Paul as the only apostle who had returned from death to life, but the Scriptures contain no invented miracles. It is not difficult to see what had happened: a stone had rendered Paul unconscious, and he remained so until this time. That was, indeed, providential preservation. But we must not understand Luke's brevity to mean that Paul simply got up and walked off. He regained consciousness, showed signs of life, was finally assisted to his feet, and so went painfully into the city. Was it under cover of night as Zahn thinks on the basis of some readings? Those readings are valueless. In II Cor. 11:25 Paul recalls this experience: "once was I stoned." But the next morning he and Barnabas left for Derbe. Paul did not spare his poor body although it was bruised and sore. He suffered violence, but again as one who moves on to new conquests. He had come to Lystra and left a Christian church behind.

21) **And having evangelized that city and made many disciples, they returned to Lystra and to Iconium and to Antioch, making firm the souls of the disciples by exhorting them to remain in the faith and that through many tribulations we must go into the kingdom of God.**

Two participles dispose of the work done in Derbe (see v. 7), both are constative aorists; they evangelized the city, which means just what it says, filled the city with the gospel news; and again they labored with success, they "discipled" a goodly number; this word is explained by the noun *μαθηταί* which occurs in 6:1. Nothing that was of exceptional import occurred. Derbe was on the Roman frontier so that no new cities were visited in this territory. The two apostles retraced their steps in spite of the hostile Jews and the painful experiences they had had in those three cities.

22) It was wise, indeed, to return to the young congregations they had founded so that they might confirm them in the faith and help them to organize and to elect elders. The present participle does not express future action (R. 892); since it follows a constative aorist, the present participle serves as a complement by spreading out the action (B.-D. 339, 2). Returning does not refer merely to arrival in these cities but to a return that was at the same time an official visit that included the activity of making "the souls of the disciples" firm. The word ψυχαί is here not a contrast to or a distinction from πνεύματα but denotes man's entire immaterial part as the seat of the spiritual life.

The second participle modifies the first and shows how this firmness was achieved. The apostles exhorted the disciples to remain in the faith (present durative infinitive), and "the faith" is objective, *fides quae creditur*, the infinitive denoting subjective faith, *fides qua creditur*. The thought is the same as that expressed in 2:42, "remaining steadfast in the teaching of the apostles." That was the essential point. Beginners who have not been made firm as yet are in danger of falling away. A good beginning is a great achievement, but a good continuation is its normal and essential result. Conversion must pass on to preservation.

When Luke follows the infinitive with a ὅτι clause instead of a second infinitive, this is not an example of zeugma (one verb with two objects, only one of which fits the verb). The participle παρακαλοῦντες fits both (*contra* B.-D. 479, 2), and both are indirect discourse without supplying λέγοντες before ὅτι (*contra* B.-D. 397, 6). The danger these disciples faced was the persecutions they might have to suffer, compelling examples of which they had in the case of the apostles who had suffered in all these cities except Derbe. The one thought that had to be impressed upon them was that persecution belonged to the normal state of Christians. The world always hates them; moreover, tribulations are to help to develop their strength of faith.

Δεῖ expresses any type of necessity, here the one that is due to the nature of discipleship in a wicked world: "it is necessary that we enter the kingdom of God through tribulations," θλῖψις, the pressure that squeezes painfully. On the kingdom in general see 1:3; here, as also the aorist infinitive shows, the kingdom of glory is referred to, God's and Christ's eternal glorious, heavenly rule. The thorns prick us as we climb upward to that kingdom, but the roses await us there. Here the cross, yonder the crown. Rationalism urges us to forget the hereafter, makes this life the whole of religion, accuses us of otherworldliness and of disregarding what we ought to do in this life. But take away the glorious Christian hope, and what have we to live for? Let the full hope of the blessedness to come shine out, and all our earthly days are lighted with heavenly light and filled with highest purpose, courage, and strength.

23) **Moreover, after by vote appointing for them elders from church to church, by praying after fastings, they commended them to the Lord in whom they had believed.**

As in II Cor. 8:19, χειροτονέω means to vote by stretching out the hand. In 10:41 the compound with πρό has God as the agent; but even when it is thus used with reference to an individual and not to an assembly, the idea of a vote is not removed from this verb. We may translate "designate," "elect," "appoint"; but the one designating or appointing voted to do so. Luke would make an important point by using this verb here. For the question at issue is whether Paul and Barnabas chose these elders without congregational participation or whether they conducted a congregational meeting in which a vote was taken by show of hands, the congregation choosing with participation of the apostles and under their guidance. The latter is undoubtedly correct, just as the praying with fastings by no means includes only the two apostles but each congregation as well. The method used is fully explained in 6:2-6. The point to observe is that both participles refer to the subject of παρέθεντο, to Paul and Barnabas, and are thus used in a wide sense. The apostles presented the matter, had the eligible men named, had the vote taken, and thus appointed those chosen and ordained them as the elders. The ceremony of laying on of hands was certainly used, for in I Tim. 5:22 the very act of putting a man into the ministry is called "laying on hands"; compare I Tim. 4:14; II Tim 1:6. On this ceremony see 6:6.

We have discussed "elders" in 11:30. The apostles followed the pattern of the Jewish synagogues with their elders and had them elected in the same way. There is nothing hierarchical whatever throughout the New Testament. Only one advance must be noted in the case of these Christian elders, namely the ability to teach. See the qualifications as these were laid down a few years later by Paul in II Tim. 3:1-7, and in Tit. 1:5-9. The choice was thus narrowed to a very few men. It is fair to conclude that these were Jews even in these Galatian congregations, including Derbe and Lystra where no synagogues existed. Jews alone were sufficiently versed in the Old Testament, the sole Scriptural basis of the Christian teaching. No deacons in addition to elders are mentioned at this ear y time, and we conclude that this office was introduced later.

While these historical points regarding the first organization of the apostolic church are of utmost interest, they constitute no law for the Christian Church which binds us to repeat every feature and method. But the example of the apostles stands for all time as having been given under the direct influence of the Holy Spirit. Some of the various types of organization found in the church today reflect the spirit of the gospel and of its apostles less than others, and we decline to adopt the former, namely those that are hierarchical and monarchial and that curtail the rights of the congregations.

The κατά is distributive: "church by church." Each was an ἐκκλησία by itself that was independent of a Jewish synagogue, a distinctive Christian body. All the members were μαθηταί, "disciples," believers, and in that sense "saints" (see 9:11); on "church" see 5:11. The work of securing "elders" was of the highest importance and was hence accompanied "by praying with fastings" as was done in 13:3. But we see that fasting was secondary to praying, "with fastings" meaning as an aid to praying. On the general practice of fasting see 13:2; it was used as a spiritual aid on special occasions. Cooking and eating and all that these entail were set aside for the day in order to be entirely free for the higher things. The prayers were spoken before the vote and at the time of the ordination of the elders. The plural "fastings" scarcely implies repeated fasts but fasts on the part of the disciples.

After the congregation had been properly organized and spiritually fortified, the apostles said good-by. They had done all that they could do and thus "committed them to the Lord on whom they had believed." The verb means "to place at someone's side." This Jesus did with his spirit when he was dying (Luke 23:46). All these converts belonged to the Lord; he would take care of them in the days to come. Luke seems to be quoting from words that were uttered at the parting services. So we still part and commit each other to the Lord.

The relative clause is relative only grammatically and in reality states the reason for committing these disciples to the Lord: they had put their trust in him the moment they had become disciples. That they should now be placed into the Lord's care in a special way was what their own hearts desired. Having been deposited at the Lord's side by the prayer of the apostles, they did not feel themselves in a strange or in a false position, and when the Lord saw them thus placed at his side he did not regard them as people whom he had never known. Since they had believed and trusted in him, he would reward their confidence in him and in the commitment of the apostles.

24) **And having gone through Pisidia, they came to Pamphilia. And having spoken the Word in Perga, they went down to Attalia; and thence they sailed away to Antioch whence they had been given over to the grace of God for the work which they fulfilled.**

The return is made by the same route by which they had come. The time consumed on this first missionary journey is estimated at about eighteen months; no exact figures can be given. On the geography of Pisidia, etc., see 13:13, 14.

25) The reasons that induced Paul to hasten away from Perga on first landing there have been stated (13:13, 14) Luke's brevity is here like that employed in the case of Derbe (v. 21) and must not deceive us as to the work accomplished by "speaking the Word." We must understand that here, too, a congregation was established. Ships came up the Kestros River to Perga, but when the two missionaries were ready to return they went down to the regular seaport Attalia and found passage there. Luke likes to name the harbors.

26) So they sailed back to Syrian Antioch and landed at the harbor Seleucia. When Luke writes "whence they had been given over," etc. (periphrastic

past perfect tense), he is most exact, for that was exactly what had been done (13:2). The Holy Spirit had required their services, and the church at Antioch had given up these two teachers for this work. They had been given over "to the grace of God for the work," etc. God's grace was to use them as its tools and instruments. This is a true and expressive description of all missionaries: they are the instruments through whom God's grace works. Not they work, in the last analysis, but grace. What a blessed position to be thus used by grace! And now the work was fulfilled; grace had accomplished what was to be done on this first journey into heathendom. What elation must have filled the hearts of the two returning missionaries! Victories, even great victories, could be reported.

27) **Now having come and having brought together the church, they went on reporting what great things God did in their company and that he opened to the Gentiles faith's door. And they continued to spend not a little time with the disciples.**

Imagine this scene: the entire congregation and these two, the first Christian missionaries who went forth into heathendom, and their long report of which the assembly could not hear enough. Significantly they tell not of what *they* did but of what *God* did. Luke 19:16: "*Thy* pound hath gained ten pounds!" The glory belonged wholly to God. So it is still, and let us not make this a mere phrase of the lips. With μετὰ αὐτῶν they say that they only accompanied God when he did all these great things. And that was the literal fact.

Καί is epexegetical and among "what great things" God had done specifies the one that was of such vast importance and of such far-reaching consequences at that time: "and in particular that he opened to the Gentile faith's door," letting them in through the door that bore only the one sign, "Faith," above it. The figure of the door is frequently used and simple. But "faith" was epoch-making in this connection. The genitive is appositional: faith is the door. The fact that it leads into the kingdom of God, and that this is faith in Jesus, is understood. This is salvation by faith alone without any of the Old Testament ceremonialism, neither as connected with the gospel in its Old Testament form of promise, nor with the legalism which the Jews and especially the Pharisees had built up in their own false way. Luke, of course, gives his reader only the briefest summary, but despite its brevity we see that the result of the apostles' labor was immense.

28) Paul and Barnabas had a strenuous time behind them. Paul bore marks of it in his body for life (Gal. 6:17). So they spent some time in Antioch "with the disciples," Luke using the term that was most current among the Christians themselves. It has been estimated that they remained in Antioch from the fall of 51 to the spring of 52. In v. 27, 28 Luke uses imperfect tenses, both of them intimating to the reader that more is to follow.

CHAPTER XV

The Apostolic Convention at Jerusalem

1) Outstanding in the history of the apostolic church is this apostolic convention at Jerusalem and the spirit and the manner in which it settled the great question regarding what was necessary for salvation and thus for membership in the Christian Church. Underlying the entire situation and the way in which it was handled was the conviction that the church was one no matter how many and how widely scattered throughout the world its members were. Despite the gulf which had existed between Jews and Gentiles for so many ages the thought of two churches that were to be diverse in teaching and in practice, one of them Jewish with one way of salvation and one set of requirements for membership, and the other Gentile with another way and with different requirements, never entered the minds of the apostles or the people. The way of salvation was one, and the church was one and could not be two. The conflict that arose must be settled and was forthwith settled on this basis. Jews and Gentiles remained one church; a right and Christian *modus vivendi* was established. It was not the one existing in the synagogue between Jews and proselytes of righteousness as full members and thus constituting the first class on the one hand, and on the other hand proselytes of the gate as nominal members who were regarded only as a decided second class. Jewish and Gentile Christians remained on the same level in every way, their living together in full unity was mediated by Christian love in the domain of liberty in the adia-

phora or nonessentials. Luke's account and the far-reaching effects of this apostolic convention are not understood until all this is clearly apprehended.

And certain ones, having come down from Judea, began teaching the brethren, Unless you shall be circumcised after the custom of Moses you cannot be saved.

Luke introduces this account with a simple *καί* and a comparison with v. 35, 36 shows that what is now recorded occurred at and not after the time which Luke says Paul and Barnabas were spending at Antioch, cf., 14:28. Zahn dates the council in the spring of 52; others place it earlier. All these dates are based on estimates as Luke mentions no exact dates. After Peter had baptized Cornelius and his house in Caesarea he was severely taken to task by "those of the circumcision" on his return to Jerusalem (11:1-3). The matter was settled at that time, yet not in such a way that the question in regard to receiving pagan converts did not again arise. It arose in Antioch when certain unnamed persons came up from Judea — Luke has before this mentioned the country when he had chiefly Jerusalem in mind — and began to spread their Judaizing views and gravely disturbed the simple faith of the Gentile disciples of whom Antioch had so many.

Their teaching is quoted in brief. Circumcision is necessary for salvation; negatively, without circumcision no salvation. But this teaching was not stated merely as doctrine, in a general form, but practically, personally, applying the doctrine: "You cannot be saved unless you shall be circumcised after the custom of Moses." All the uncircumcised Gentile Christians in Antioch were thus pronounced unsaved. Faith in Jesus Christ was not enough to save, circumcision must be added. The issue was centered on circumcision alone with a kind of inconsistency, for if circumcision was essential as required by the usus of Moses, then what about all else that Moses had required? Consistency would soon have introduced the entire legal system.

In 11:3 the issue was centered on eating unclean food in Cornelius' house; also in Gal. 2:11, etc. Now circumcision was necessary in the old covenant; it was a part of the covenant itself (Gen. 17:10, 11), so that by rejecting circumcision one was rejecting the saving covenant. Thus it came about that, when the new covenant which rested wholly on Jesus' blood was established, circumcision together with the entire old covenant was at an end. Circumcision, the whole old Mosaic system, had lost its import and efficacy. It was hard for Jews who had grown up in this system to realize this truth; but it was a fact, even a most blessed fact, for the sole function of the old covenant was to lead to the new.

When the end of the old covenant came, circumcision ceased to be what it had been, a part of that covenant; it became nothing but a human rite. Now Christ is the one Savior who saves to the uttermost. To add anything to Christ as being necessary to salvation, say circumcision or any human work of any kind, is to deny that Christ is the complete Savior, is to put something human on a par with him, yea to make it the crowning point. That is fatal. A bridge to heaven that is built 99/100 of Christ and even only 1/100 of anything human breaks down at the joint and ceases to be a bridge. Even if Christ be thought of as carrying us 999 miles of the way, and something merely human be required for the last mile, this would leave us hanging in the air with heaven being still far away.

2) **But no little strife and debate having occurred for Paul and Barnabas with them, they arranged for Paul and Barnabas and some others of them to go to the apostles and presbyters in Jerusalem concerning this debate.**

This is Paul's first sharp clash with the Judaizers. and Barnabas is staunchly at his side. We take it that these two men were the most prominent of the teachers in Antioch and hence led the contention against the Judaizers. Again, they had been the missionaries who gathered a number of churches that were mainly Gentile in membership. The attack of the Judaizers was thus in a special way directed against them and this their great work. "No little" is a litotes for "great" strife and debate. The Judaizers made a great disturbance so that many of the members in Antioch who were uncircumcised were thus personally affected by the claims and demands of these men from Judea. They had no official standing, but that did not matter. The issue had to be decided in any case.

The proper way to reach a decision was taken. Antioch might have made the decision independently. That is the procedure followed by many today who are actuated by a sort of morbid individualism which leads one congregation to disregard all others and to act both without them and contrary to them, and the unity of the spirit is disrupted and inward rents and fissures are caused that only hurt the gospel and its work. Antioch even had the Apostle Paul and prophets who were led by the Spirit in its midst, and the first two chapters of Galatians make it clear that Paul was on a perfect par with the apostles of Jerusalem; and yet Antioch did not act independently.

The view that Jerusalem was the head of all the churches and exercised authority over them is not in accord with fact. Neither the apostles in Jerusalem nor the church here occupied a hierarchical position. The entire church was a unit, one spiritual body, in which all alike were brethren who were bound together most intimately. That reality was not a mere theory in the minds of the disciples, it was an actual and a vital bond, one that governed the hearts and the actions of all. Thus the moment a divisive question arose, that question was regarded as one that the entire church must decide.

The issue was, therefore, taken to Jerusalem, the center of the church at that time. The church at Antioch appointed a delegation to take it there. Paul, Barnabas, and others were sent as representatives; we may call them delegates. The subject of ἔταξαν is understood, "they" in the verb signifying the membership of Antioch. Only a grammatical stickler will derive the subject from πρὸς αὐτούς, the Judaizers. But we then rightly ask how they could arrange for and order that delegation sent from Antioch to Jerusalem and even makes the selection of the persons to be sent. In the very next verse we are told that the delegation "was sent forward by the church." This settles also the meaning of "some others of them." These were other members of the church of Antioch and not a number of the Judaizers as some believe. Whether any of these went or not was a matter of indifference and was left to them.

The lengthy addition in the Codex Bezae is a late interpolation which makes the Judaizers the men who direct and arrange everything. Gal. 2:3 shows that Titus accompanied Paul but, it seems, only as Paul's companion and not as one of the delegates. Titus is never mentioned in Acts; how this happens we do not know.

Jerusalem was the center of the church because the Eleven made it their headquarters by working from it as a center and then returning to it. One might think that the question would have been submitted to the apostles alone because they were the immediately called apostles of the Lord, and that thus Paul and the Eleven would have made the authoritative decision. No; just as Barnabas and others are sent along with Paul, so the delegation is sent "to the apostles and elders in

Jerusalem concerning this dispute." The expression "apostles and elders" has but one article which makes it a unit. They are thus the delegates from Jerusalem. None of the other congregations were included; none of them had as yet been vexed with the question under consideration, and none of them was in a position to aid in its solution. Mere numbers do not increase wisdom, and Christian essentials are not decided by numbers and a majority vote. Dr. M. Loy once told a convention that had passed a foolish resolution by a great majority that in the inscrutable providence of God it had been allowed to make an ass of itself.

On elders see 11:30.

3) **They, therefore, having been sent forward by the church, were going through both Phoenicia and Samaria, recounting the conversion of the Gentiles; and they were causing great joy to the brethren.**

On Luke's μὲν οὖν see 1:6. The connective means, "everything being as just described, the delegation was sent forward by the church," the participle implying that an escort accompanied them part of the way, escorts such as this being customary in the case of honored persons when they set out upon a journey. Luke is content with the factual story, but Paul later wrote that he went up to Jerusalem "by revelation" (Gal. 2:1, 2). Going by revelation and being sent as one of a delegation is not a contradiction.

The delegates chose the route overland and thus came through Phoenicia and then Samaria, Jerusalem lying just beyond the latter. The imperfect describes how they passed through these. Congregations had been organized. So they halted again and again and recounted "the conversion of the Gentiles" (their turning to God) in Antioch and on their first missionary journey. Instead of meeting Judaizing objections to the entrance of pagans into the church, the apostles caused only great joy to all the brethren, "all" being significantly added. Judaistic ideas were foreign to all these brethren. We should scarcely call their journey "a triumphal procession" or make the joy "a constant pæan of praise." We think everything was more sober than that.

4) **And having come to Jerusalem, they were received by the church and the apostles and the elders and reported what great things God did in company with them. But there rose up some of the sect of the Pharisees, having believed, declaring, It is necessary to circumcise them and to order them to keep the law of Moses. The apostles and the presbyters, however, were gathered together to see concerning this subject.**

In recording the reception given the delegation from Antioch in Jerusalem the order "by the church," etc., which places the church first, is significant compared with v. 6 where "the church" is omitted so that we might be in doubt regarding its presence if it were not for v. 12, where we see that it was present at this second meeting. At the first reception "the church" is in the foreground. The members as such gave the delegation, and that refers especially to Paul and Barnabas, a most enthusiastic welcome. Luke wants his reader to know that fact. The Judaistic faction was small in numbers; although it was composed of former Jews, the church in Jerusalem was sound in the faith and not fanatic regarding circumcision and the Mosaic regulations. After thus putting "the church" first, in the two remaining groups, which are marked as such by articles, "the apostles" are naturally placed before "the elders."

This must have been a grand gathering. Of the elders who were present we know only James (v. 13). In Gal. 2:9, Paul mentions only two apostles, Peter and

John, as being present, the rest, apparently, being at work elsewhere at this time. It is significant that at this great gathering of welcome Paul and Barnabas simply make a report on "what great things God did in company with them," Luke using the identical clause he used in 13:27, which see. Together they tell the great story of their missionary journey which was undertaken at the instance of the Spirit (13:2) and carried out with such success (including great miracles) in pagan cities. Jerusalem learned the great facts that spoke so forcefully for themselves.

At this meeting Paul and Barnabas say nothing about the Judaizers that had appeared in Antioch and had caused a disturbance there regarding circumcision for Gentile believers. They leave this to the Judaizers themselves. That was a wise procedure. They do not mar the effect of their great narrative by thrusting into it this dispute that had arisen much later, after their missionary work had been completed. By proceeding as they did, Paul and Barnabas really ask on behalf of themselves and on behalf of the church at Antioch which was so deeply involved in their work whether there was anything wrong with "the great things God did in company with them."

5) Some then arose who declared that there was something wrong, something decidedly wrong. Luke does not indicate that these objectors were the same men who had caused the disturbance in Antioch. The view that the Judaizers who had come to Antioch had either themselves ordered some of their number to go up to Jerusalem to present their cause (so the Codex Bezae and those who think it presents the facts) or had induced the congregation at Antioch to send some of their number, fails here where such delegates should appear and speak. Judging from Luke's account, those Judaizers in Antioch had not sent up anyone to present their contention. It was not necessary that

any of them should appear in Jerusalem; in Jerusalem itself men who strongly shared their views would stand up and oppose the delegation of the congregation at Antioch. And such men did stand up and demand not only circumcision for pagan converts (v. 1) but, with complete consistency, the keeping of the Mosaic law in general. In other words, they made the door into the Christian Church not merely faith (see 14:27) but faith plus Judaistic legalism.

In v. 1 Luke writes only "some from Judea" when he describes those who appeared in Antioch; now he characterizes those in Jerusalem as "some of the sect of the Pharisees, having believed," i. e., former Pharisees who had been converted, had been and still were believers, and were thus members of the congregation in Jerusalem. Here we have Luke's definition of the Judaizers, of these disturbers who afterward broke into the Galatian congregations and caused Paul so much trouble, which necessitated his strong Epistle to the Galatians. Some have a wrong conception of them, as though they rejected the entire gospel, the entire Christ, and preached only salvation by the law. But they were believers in Christ and the gospel, members of the church at Jerusalem, but they erred in a most dangerous point, namely in wanting to append to the gospel and Christ the requirement of circumcision (that most especially) and of the other Mosaic regulations. They thought the gospel incomplete without this addition.

Judaizers later charged Paul with emasculating the gospel in order to gain the applause of the Gentiles and win easy victories. Without warrant they claimed Peter as the head of their party. We here learn that they were originally Pharisees, members of that Jewish sect which was most strict in adhering to all the laws of Moses and to the traditions with their 613 additional commandments (Matt. 15:9). From αἵρεσις we have our word "heresy," the original meaning being a set of persons who profess peculiar principles or tenets.

6) The Judaizers feared that Gentile Christianity was like "the boar out of the wood" (Ps. 80:13) who would ravage God's vineyard by breaking down the hedge of the law. From opposing Peter (11:2) and then Paul they went on to become the sect of the Ebionites. It was at a second meeting, one that seems to have been especially called (judging from the passive συνήχθησαν), that the contention of these Judaizers was examined. Luke now properly puts "the apostles and the elders" forward. We see from v. 12 that the congregation, too, was present. In matters of doctrine and practice — this was one of both — all were concerned, but the apostles and the elders naturally took the lead because of their office and their special qualifications. It is necessarily so to this day in spite of the movements that try to put laymen forward unduly and beyond their depth. Some shepherds, too, expect their sheep to lead them; the sheep may enjoy the novelty but are only sheep after all. A fine distinction was made in Jerusalem. That first meeting was called for the purpose of welcoming only, and the Judaizers were not allowed to turn it into anything else; this second meeting had its special purpose, "to see concerning this subject" or λόγος. There was due deliberation.

We may place Gal. 2:1-6, the private conference with the apostles at Jerusalem, before this second meeting. In this letter Paul characterizes the Judaizers as ψευδάδελφοι, pseudo-brethren, not real brethren, who were brought in unawares, without anyone knowing their real convictions, who had no right to membership. This was due to the fact that they falsified the gospel. When R., *W. P.*, says that it is a bit curious that today some scholars claim that for the sake of peace Paul yielded to them and had Titus, his companion, circumcised, he states it rather mildly; in Galatians, Paul claims the exact opposite of what these scholars believe: "to whom I yielded, no not for an hour." Paul was the last man in the world to effect an evil compromise. It seems that he purposely took uncircumcised Titus along as a sample of a Gentile convert and as a direct challenge to the Judaizers, and no apostle even suggested that Paul should have him circumcised if only to placate the Judaizers.

7) **Now much debate having occurred, Peter, having arisen, said to them, etc.** We now see why Luke says nothing about the church in v. 6; the laity did not participate in the debate, the speakers were those immediately concerned, the apostles and the elders officially. We may take it that the Judaizers had their full say, and that their contentions were also answered. All that, however, was only preliminary, and Luke passes it by with a brief genitive absolute.

The decisive address was made by Peter, and hence Luke recounts that with great credit to Peter. Paul and Barnabas had already spoken at length at the first meeting and had recounted their experience which was the very same as Peter's had been. They and Peter were in fullest harmony as direct witnesses of what God had done among the Gentiles. Moreover, Peter had already received full approbation from the congregation in Jerusalem over against the Judaizing legalists (11:18). Thus we see the influence his address now had. Peter did not preside at the meeting; it was James, the chief elder of the congregation in Jerusalem. Peter spoke as no longer being a resident of Jerusalem, which agrees with his leaving as recounted in 12:17. The congregation in Jerusalem was organized like all others and had elders; the apostles did their work in new territory outside of the city.

Men and brethren (see 1:16), **you yourselves know that in olden days God made choice for himself for the Gentiles to hear through my mouth the**

Word of the gospel and to believe. And God, the heart-knower, bore them witness by giving them the Holy Spirit even as also to us. And in no respect did he discriminate between both us and them, by the faith cleansing their hearts. Now, therefore, why are you tempting God to place a yoke upon the neck of the disciples, which neither our fathers nor we were strong enough to bear? But through the grace of the Lord Jesus we believe to be saved after what manner they too.

Peter addresses the entire assembly in the usual fraternal manner but in v. 10 turns to the Judaizers themselves. He appeals to what they on their part know and what happened so long ago. The Greek idiom uses ἀπό (or ἐκ) when reaching back into the past by counting from "the olden days" forward. It was more than ten years ago since the Gentile Cornelius and his house had been brought into the church by faith in the gospel alone.

God did that. The work of Paul and of Barnabas was not an innovation and did not present a new question. Far back in those days God "made choice for himself," elected of his own accord (middle voice), "for the Gentiles to hear (effectively, aorist) through my mouth the Word of the gospel and to believe (effectively, aorist)." At that time God made Peter the medium as he had now made Paul and Barnabas his media. We must review chapter ten in order to see that God was the great agent in bringing Peter to Cornelius by using a vision and an angel. For the first time we meet "the Word of the gospel" whereas hitherto we have had "the Word" or "the Word of God (or of the Lord)."

8) And now Peter brings out the pertinent point in that act of God's. As "the heart-knower" he made no mistake (the same term occurs in 1:24) when "he

bore testimony to them" (to those Gentiles in Caesarea) that they were truly his children by faith alone. He bore this testimony "by giving them the Holy Spirit even as also to us," so that those Gentiles spoke with tongues exactly as the 120 had at the time of Pentecost (see 10:46). The point to be noted is that God gave these Gentiles the same attestation that he had given to the apostles themselves and to the first believers.

9) Peter intensifies this most decisive point: "in no respect did he discriminate (differentiate, judge one way and then another) between both us and them." The Greek always names the first person first, the others last. God made no difference whatever between Jew and Gentile, circumcised and uncircumcised, Levitically clean and unclean. As to this last, the matter of cleanness in God's eyes, "he cleansed their hearts — where alone all true spiritual cleansing occurs — by the faith." Τῇ πίστει with the article is "the faith" in the sense of the Word of the gospel received by faith; and "heart" is to be taken in the Biblical sense, the center of the personality. These unclean Gentiles God cleansed in this true fashion. That is what made Jew and Gentile alike in his sight. Peter's hearers knew the whole story and hence needed to have only its significance for the question in hand pointed out to them.

10) With οὖν and the logical νῦν he makes his deduction and turns to these Judaizers themselves. *Apostrophe ad Pharisaios et severus elenchus.* Bengel. The question is convicting: "Why are you tempting God?" They are not dealing with these Gentiles but with God himself and with his will as he has made it so clearly known. They are tempting or trying God to see whether he will keep still to their contradiction of his will or will resent it and punish them. The infinitive is epexegetical (R., *W. P.*), *Ergaenzung* (B.-D. 392, 1 a), not result (R. 1089): "to place a yoke upon the neck of the disciples," one that is so heavy that neither

our fathers in the old covenant nor we former Jews had strength to bear it (Gal. 5: 1).

Metaphors are often the strongest arguments, for they are really condensed syllogisms. Βαστάσαι, "to bear up with hands or shoulders," fits the figure. The thought is that expressed by Paul in 13:39. No man who lived in the old covenant ever fulfilled the law of Moses and in that sense really bore its yoke. That is why the old covenant had its Day of Atonement and its many arrangements with offerings and sacrifices to remove sins, all these gaining their efficacy through the sacrifice of Christ which they typified and with which they connected the sinner. For that intolerable yoke of the law Christ had substituted his gospel yoke (Matt. 11:29), a wonderful yoke which itself bears every believer. Do these former Pharisees intend again to burden men with the old yoke?

Christ's removal of the yoke of the law made circumcision and kosher eating, etc., no longer obligatory in any sense apart even from the matter of gaining salvation; yet neither were these Jewish practices and modes of living forbidden by Christ. They became adiaphora, matters of liberty and choice, that should not be forced upon others or become a cause of pride and marks of special holiness as compared with Gentile Christians. Peter could continue kosher eating, for instance, but not as though that elevated him above those who did not eat kosher and made him stand higher in God's sight.

11) Over against the Judaistic imposition of a legal yoke ἀλλά, the strong negative "on the contrary," places the declaration: "Through the grace of the Lord Jesus we believe to be saved after what manner they too" (believe to be saved). The phrase with διά is placed forward for the sake of emphasis. The one divine means of salvation is "the grace of the Lord Jesus" and not our observance of the law. Even in the old cove-

nant the saving means was the Old Testament gospel and promise of the Messiah and not the law. "Grace" is the *favor* of the Lord Jesus and the redemption it wrought for the sinner and now applies to him. "Grace" connotes sin, guilt, liability to damnation; "grace" brings remission of sin, guilt, and damnation, and thus salvation. The aorist "to be saved" is effective, "actually and effectively to be saved," rescued spiritually and placed in the condition of safety. In καθ' ὃν τρόπον the antecedent is drawn into the relative clause: "according to that manner according to which" they, too, believe to be saved. There is one and one manner only, the one stated by διά, namely grace.

That address of Peter's was masterly in every way. To appreciate it fully we must visualize the audience and the occasion. It was a perfect answer to any and every Judaistic and legalistic contention. The fact that later Peter himself did not live up to his own words in Antioch and had to be rebuked in public by Paul (Gal. 2:11-21) changes nothing as to the truth and the import of Peter's address here in Jerusalem; it only points a warning for us lesser men.

12) **And all the multitude kept silence and went on hearing Barnabas and Paul recounting what great signs and wonders God did among the Gentiles through them.**

The debate had come to an end. Not a voice from "all the multitude" spoke in contradiction to what Peter had said, and that implies that none of the former Pharisees (v. 5) and no one in the congregation raised the least objection. That silence was eloquent.

Then Barnabas and Paul again spoke, and the imperfect describes how attentively all listened to them. Barnabas spoke first because he was the older man and was better known than Paul in the congregation in Jerusalem. Perhaps he alone spoke for both as we have repeatedly seen Paul speaking for both. They had already made a full report in regard to their success among the Gentiles (v. 4); now they recount "the signs and wonders" (see 2:19; 14:3) God wrought among the Gentiles through them. They thereby clinch the decisive point of Peter's address, namely that God bestowed the same miraculous manifestations on Cornelius and on his house that he had bestowed on the 120 Jewish believers at the time of Pentecost. *God* did those signs and wonders among the Gentiles, for no apostle ever worked a miracle by his own volition. The apostles were only his instruments as the significant διά once more states. Peter's experience was already sufficient, but that experience was multiplied in the case of Barnabas and of Paul. God had thus set his seal of approval on the work of receiving Gentiles into the church by faith alone without circumcision and other Levitical observances.

13) **And after they were silent, James answered, saying, etc.** R., *W. P.*, regards ἐσίγησε in v. 12 and σιγῆσαι in v. 13 as ingressive aorists: "became silent." But no one had been speaking, all had been listening silently. These are mere historical aorists that state only the fact that there was silence. James now speaks. He does so as chairman of the meeting, for he lays a proposition before the assembly which embodies what the results of the discussion ought to be; and that proposition was adopted by all. In our assemblies we require a motion and a second from members on which a vote of yea or nay is taken. Yet even today a good chairman may suggest what the motion should be which someone then formally makes and another seconds. It seems to have been the Jewish custom (see 6:3 for another instance) that the chairman formulated and offered the resolution and himself simply presented it to the assembly for adoption or otherwise. On James see 12:17.

14) Men and brethren, hear me! Symeon did recount how God first looked to it to take out of Gentiles a people for his name. And with this agree the words of the prophets even as it has been written:

> **After these things I will return again**
> **And will build again the Tabernacle of David, the one that has fallen,**
> **And the ruined parts of it I will build up again**
> **And I will upright them again**
> **In order that those remaining of men may seek out the Lord,**
> **And all the Gentiles upon whom has been called my name —**
> **Says the Lord who does these things.**

Known from the eon his work to God!

James belonged to the Hebrews and not to the Hellenists (on the distinction see 6:1). He, no doubt, lived in the Jewish fashion, for in Gal. 2:12 some who came to Antioch from him influenced even Peter to eat only with them and in a marked way to turn from the tables of the Gentiles. This fact made his address the more effective. He first called for attention, probably in order to hush the subdued conversation being carried on in the great assembly. He begins by restating the substance of Peter's address and uses Peter's old Jewish name "Symeon" in its Hebrew form. James, too, stresses the agency of God and refers to Peter's account because that dealt with God's receiving Gentiles into the church. He uses the Greek equivalent of the Hebrew expression ἐπεσκέψατο (see this verb in Luke 1:68, 78; 7:16), which is often employed with reference to gracious visitation, "to look upon someone," "to visit a person." Here the verb has no personal object, and hence we translate, "first looked to it." God gave his personal attention to taking "out of the Gentiles a people for his name."

Bengel notes the *egregium paradoxon* between ἐθνῶν and λαόν which is made the more marked by putting the words in juxtaposition: "pagans" and "sacred people," λαός being constantly used as a designation for Israel. God wanted a *laos* also from the pagan world in addition to the Jews and was now taking it out of that world. The ὄνομα is again God's revelation (see 2:21, 38). For the great saving revelation of himself in Christ Jesus, God took "a people" from the Gentile world. That is what he did for the first time in Caesarea; there he made the beginning.

15) To Peter's report and to all that Barnabas and Paul had added James now appends the Scripture corroboration, the one thing still needed. All the statements (λόγοι) of the prophets "sound together with" (our word symphony) this act of God's, his taking "a people for his name out of the Gentiles." James employs the usual formula for quotation and quotes Amos 9:11, 12. He uses the LXX although it deviates markedly from the Hebrew in one line. The view that James quoted the LXX because he found the main point of the quotation in just this line, is untenable; the Hebrew would be just as fitting. It may well be possible that the whole address of James, in fact, the entire discussion was conducted in Greek and that James used the LXX for this reason. Zahn shows that Greek was regularly spoken in Jerusalem in his *Introduction to the New Testament* I, 43, etc. The supposition that in recording the address of James Luke merely copied his LXX is untenable, for the quotation is not a verbatim reproduction of the LXX and differs from it already in the very first phrase.

The idea that James quotes Amos in preference to Isaiah or some other prophet because Amos speaks of the tent of David, and James was of Davidic descent as "the Lord's brother (Gal. 1:19)," is another of those combinations in which Zahn delights and which he therefore elaborates at great length. This is untenable. The reference to David's Tabernacle is made for far weightier reasons.

16) Amos writes "in that day," i. e., when Israel's punishment will have been inflicted, in the day when the Messianic kingdom will be founded, in the day of the Christian Church. When James spoke, that day had come and hence he quotes interpretatively when he substitutes the phrase "after these things," namely the inflictions of which Amos had spoken. James quoted in order to be understood and not in order to give a mere mechanical reproduction of the prophet's words. Even if he spoke in Aramaic he had to make the Hebrew intelligible. Note that the four main verbs which state what the Lord (Κύριος, v. 18, no article: *Yahweh*) will do are compounds of ἀνά, "again": "I will return again — I will build again — I will upright again"; the LXX, too, has four "again" verbs, but two of them are "raise up again" and two "build up again" to bring about this blessed restoration, for he wants to emphasize the truth that God himself is doing this work that had been begun by Peter, Paul, and Barnabas.

Ἡ σκηνὴ Δαβίδ, "the Tabernacle of David," cannot be "the house of David," David's descendants, either in general or as a royal line. Σκηνή is never employed in that sense. In Jesus, risen and glorified, the throne and the kingdom or rule of David were raised up and established forever. That had been done years ago and was not being done now. "Tabernacle" refers to the Tabernacle of David's time before Solomon was permitted to build the Temple. In that Tabernacle David worshipped with Israel. It thus stood for the church. And it was the church that had fallen because many of its parts were ruined (literally; "the parts that have been turned down"). The church of Israel was, indeed, in a sad state, had been so for years and years. God would restore it.

17) That glorious promise was now being fulfilled. But not in Israel alone, and not by building the church out of Jews only. Amos, like the other prophets, was permitted to see that the great restored Tabernacle of David would include also the Gentiles. The ἄν is rarely used with ὅπως in the New Testament (R. 986); but it does not add "an additional note of uncertainty," for the entire note is one of expectancy, the connective denoting divine purpose, and God's purposes are always realized. The Hebrew reads: "That they may possess the remnant of Edom and of all the heathen," etc.; the LXX translate: "That those remaining of men may seek out [the Lord], and all the Gentiles," etc. It seems as though the translation of the LXX was made from a text that had the Hebrew reading *adam* (men) instead of *'edom* (Edom) and the verb *yidroshu* (seek) instead of *yiroshu* (possess). The question is one that concerns the Hebrew text. James was content with the rendering of the LXX. As far as possessing Edom is concerned, Amos certainly did not have in mind a political possession, for he adds "all the heathen" (*goyim*), and no prophet spoke of a political domination of all the heathen or Gentiles on the part of Israel. This possession would be entirely spiritual. Perhaps that is the reason that James left the LXX as it was.

He was concerned mainly with this word about "all the Gentiles." God's great purpose in restoring David's Tabernacle reached out to "all the Gentiles," including, of course, also Edom, as we have already seen that it included also the Samaritans (8:5, etc.). However the textual question regarding the Hebrew and the LXX is answered, the point of the quotation is not affected as far as the use made of it by James is concerned. The great Messianic restoration was intended most particularly for the Gentiles, their coming into it made David's Tabernacle greater than ever. The limiting relative clause, "upon whom has been called my name," states that this divine purpose will be fulfilled only in the case of the believing Gentiles. The addition ἐπ' αὐτούς is a case of incorporating a redundant antecedent into the relative clause: "upon whom my name has been called, upon them," R. 723. The masculine relative after τὰ ἔθνη is used because persons are referred to.

To call the Lord's name upon the Gentiles is to bring them the revelation of the Lord (see ὄνομα in 2:21, 28; 3:6); note the same expression in James 2:7 (Greek). To have that name called upon one again and again (perfect tense) is to be present where that name and revelation constantly resounds, namely in the worship of God's people. The relative clause thus designates these Gentiles as believing worshippers. "All" considers them as being many. In the A. V. note the marginal note with 9:12, which renders the Hebrew exactly.

The close of the quotation is: "saith the Lord who does these things," λέγει Κύριος ὁ ποιῶν ταῦτα. This statement sets the prophet's seal on his utterance as being the Lord's own word, the word of him who carries out what he says. We cannot omit the article before the participle as a few texts do, because this would result in the impossible sense: "Saith the Lord *by* doing these things," this is contrary also to the Hebrew.

18) A few texts read: λέγει ὁ Κύριος ὁ ποιῶν ταῦτα γνωστὰ ἀπ' αἰῶνος, which is adopted by the R. V. and translated in one way in the text and in another way in the margin. But it is difficult to think that James would have made such an addition to the words of Amos. Far more preferable is the translation of the A. V., which is also well supported textually. The only questions are whether to read the plural "works" or the variant singular "work," to leave the copula ἐστί or to omit it, to

read "God" or "Lord." We take the text to be: "Known from the eon his work to God (or to the Lord)!" a separate exclamatory statement by James himself. After concluding the quotation from Amos, James quite pertinently declares that an eon before the time that God would do a work he already knew what that work would be and thus could foretell it. Of such a kind was this work of having his name called upon the Gentiles. God is doing that work now but knew it an eon ago and foretold it through Amos. An αἰών is an eon or era that is marked in some way, here by the knowledge on the part of God of what would transpire at its end. James adds this statement with which all his hearers must agree in order to bring to their minds the fact that God is now doing a work which he ages ago knew he would do. If it seems strange to some when they now see him doing this work, as he undoubtedly is doing it, let these persons know that God had it in contemplation all along and said so through the statements of his prophets (v. 15), Amos being among them.

19) From the reports of Peter, Paul, and Barnabas and the ancient prophecies concerning their work James draws the conclusion for the question at issue. **Wherefore I for my part judge that we do not annoy those turning from the Gentiles to God but that we write to them to abstain from pollutions of the idols and from fornication and from what is strangled and from blood. For Moses from olden generations has city by city those preaching him by being read in the synagogues Sabbath by Sabbath.**

The formulation ἐγὼ κρίνω, *ego censeo*, "I for my part judge," intends to present to the assembly the question as to whether they on their part judge the same. According to our way of speaking, James is offering a resolution to the assembly for adoption; so in v. 22 we see that adoption promptly followed. The negative part of the resolution was, not to annoy the incoming Gentile believers. They are fitly called "those turning from the Gentiles to God," who thus cease to be Gentiles who are far from God, living in superstition and in idolatry, and become Christians, worshippers of the true God. This turning is conversion.

The negative infinitive is an indirect command: "Do not annoy." It is in indirect discourse after κρίνω (R., *W. P.*). The point lies in the meaning of the infinitive: παρά + ἐν + ὄχλος = to crowd in on someone unnecessarily, here by demanding circumcision and the Levitical requirements. James regards the Judaistic demands made on the Gentile Christians as crowding these Christians in an uncalled for manner, annoying them without warrant (this is the force of παρά, bringing something in on the side). Thus in a distinct though mild way James passes an adverse verdict on all Judaistic legalism and asks the assent of the assembly to this verdict. It is important to note this negative point in the resolution he offers lest we misconceive the sense of the positive part of his resolution. He does not intend to compromise with the Judaizers, to accept at least some of their demands for Gentile Christians and thus in a manner at least to satisfy them.

20) What James proposes that the apostles and the church at Jerusalem shall write to the Gentile Christians is something entirely different. We may translate ἐπιστεῖλαι, "write" or "send a letter or message," ἐπιστολή. The four points thus to be communicated to the Gentile congregations constitute the *fraternal advice* deemed necessary for them in view of their Gentile origin and their position in Gentile and pagan surroundings and as being brethren of Jewish Christians in almost all cities. The idea of James is by no means that of an apostolic decree handed down by apostolic authority which demands legal obedience. In v. 22 the

entire assembly acts. The apostles are not a body which substitutes for Moses and decrees laws similar to those which Moses gave to Israel at God's command. The resolution that James offers is not to be a papal bull. The four points to be sent out are in no sense "a moral catechism," an abbreviation of the decalog or a selection from the decalog. Neither are they a substitute for the so-called Noachian commandments which are reduced from seven to four. Those seven were directed against idolatry, blasphemy, murder, incest, robbery, disobedience to government, eating bloody meat (Gen. 9:4), and were imposed on the proselytes of the gate. There was not the faintest idea of dealing with Gentile Christians as the Jews dealt with proselytes of the gate and of regarding them as second-rate and not as real Christians.

We regard the infinitive with τοῦ exactly as we did the infinitive in v. 19: it is in indirect discourse and replaces an imperative: "Hold yourselves away from." Although ἀλισγήματον (from ἀλισγέω) is found only here, its meaning is assured, "pollution." "Pollutions of idols" is defined in v. 29: pollutions incurred by eating things sacrificed to idols. James is not speaking of idolatry, for no one could be an idolater and a Christian at the same time, and all Gentile Christians had given up idolatry. Yet there was danger for Gentile Christians of pollutions with idols through eating things sacrificed to idols. All manner of idol feasts were celebrated, at which parts of the animals sacrificed to the idol were served as meat to all the guests. Gentile converts would be asked by relatives and friends at least to go along and to enjoy the rich dinner. What harm could there be in that? We know what a grave question this became in Corinth; read I Cor. 8 as the best commentary on this point of the proposal of James. Considered by itself and abstractly, it was not a sin to eat such meat; but it was dangerous to do so for any who had a weak conscience and dangerous for others who had weak consciences to see a Christian at such a feast. Only one safe course remained, namely to stay away. To say this to Gentile Christians was not making a law for them; it was the best and the truest advice to them. Jewish Christians, of course, had neither invitations nor desire to go to such an idol feast.

We need not make the next three genitives depend on "pollutions"; they are connected directly with the infinitive. "From fornication" has caused much discussion since this is forbidden by the Decalog and no limitation is introduced in v. 29. Here again we find our best commentary in I Cor. 6:13b-20, and recall that Paul's letters so frequently warn the Gentile believers against fornication. The point is always that in the Gentile world, even among its noblest men, this sin was not considered a sin but something that was entirely innocent and natural. It was a part of their idol worship. The wisdom of some of the Corinthian Christians argued that fornication was merely an external matter. The old pagan ideas about sexual impurities not being impurities kept clinging to the converts from paganism in some form or other. Hence this warning appears as the second in the list of James. Missionaries still have trouble with their converts on this score. Even in Christian lands moral laxity is justified in peculiar ways as not being immoral at all but only unmoral, merely something natural, "living one's life," etc. The early Gentile converts were in constant danger of being drawn into fornication in one form or the other by their relatives and their friends. Hence Paul's, "Flee fornication!" I Cor. 6:18.

This word of James' is not metaphorical or figurative, nor should it be restricted to incest, forbidden degrees of consanguinity, marriage with a pagan spouse, etc. No restriction is needed because the form of the sin made no difference.

"From a thing strangled and from blood" may be considered together since both alike involve blood. An animal that was not butchered but snared and killed by strangling still had blood in it. To eat such an animal or to eat anything that was prepared with blood, although it was forbidden by Lev. 18:13; Deut. 12:16, 23, was no longer forbidden to Christians since all these Levitical regulations had been abrogated. Why, then, introduce these items? Certainly not in order again to enforce these points of the Levitical law. That would have been Judaistic legalism, and if any part of it was to be imposed, it should not have been one minor point regarding food but circumcision, the *sine qua non* of Judaism. James mentions these two points because the Jewish Christians were especially sensitive regarding them. They, too, knew that these points of the law were abrogated but they still felt a horror of eating blood or any meat that had retained the blood. The Gentile Christians were asked to respect this feeling and thus from motives of brotherly love, and from these alone, to refrain from eating blood and meat that still had its blood.

The principle that underlies these two items is the one Paul so constantly stressed: to use the adiaphora in love, always so as not to offend the brethren, especially the weak. Against presumptuous demands he stood firm as a rock, but otherwise his prime consideration was love. See him voice this principle in I Cor. 8:13, and again in 9:19-23. Many who today deem themselves strong are impotent in this application of love. They scorn the idea that they should consider their brethren, they hurt and stagger the weak without a qualm, and they offend where they are themselves often wrong in fact and where the offense is gratuitous and wholly uncalled for. Go to school to James and take a full course with Paul. One thing that made them so great was this considerate love for the brethren.

The idea that all four points must deal with adiaphora or with universal moral principles, has led to much confusion. As such we regard Harnack's deletion of "the thing strangled" from the text so that he might obtain three commandments of the Decalog, one against idolatry in general, one against all sexual sins, and one against murder ("blood"). Reference is made to the Codex Bezae which omits "the thing strangled" and adds the Golden Rule at the end. Here as elsewhere this lone text and its Latin translation present only what someone thought Luke should have written. "From blood" is often referred to the shedding of human blood, as though Gentile Christians were inclined toward murder! This list is diverse throughout, and no effort will succeed in reducing the four points to the same level.

James was not governed by logical or theoretical considerations but only by the different needs of the Gentile Christians in their peculiar situation at that time. On the one hand they were surrounded by their pagan connections, and on the other they found themselves in the same Christian congregations with Jewish members. Here were idol feasts, where they might both contaminate themselves and greatly hurt others; here was fornication which was nothing to pagans and liable still to seem to be nothing to pagan converts; here was the matter of blood in meat or otherwise which was nothing to them, nothing in fact, and yet still horrible to their Jewish brethren. The one safe course to follow was to avoid these things.

21) "For" adduces a consideration which concerns especially the Jewish Christians and to some degree also former Jewish proselytes of the gate who are now Christians. Ever since synagogues were established in the diaspora, which goes back to the time after the Exile, Moses, meaning his Pentateuch, was preached "city by city" (distributive κατά) by being read "Sab-

bath by Sabbath" (the same κατά) in the synagogues. The hatred of idolatry, the wickedness of fornication, and the prejudice against any food that has blood in it had been most deeply ingrained in Jewish minds and to some extent in the minds of proselytes. Now, indeed, as far as Levitical regulations are concerned, these are abrogated, and James is certainly not trying to revive at least a few of them. They have disappeared forever. But love demands of the Gentile Christians that, apart from any danger to themselves in idol feasts and in fornication, they ought to be considerate of their fellow Christians who had been reared as Jews and who, although they were now freed from the old Jewish legalism, still shrank from the things that were once so strongly forbidden them by the Levitical laws of Moses. Considering this, all Gentile Christians would and should refrain from what might offend. This is not law and legislation but fraternal appeal to Christian love. James stands forth as the full brother of Paul as the latter is revealed in his epistles.

Yet some still think that James offered a compromise, namely that the Gentile Christians should be satisfied to keep at least these few regulations of the Mosaic and the Levitical system. But Christianity never compromises, Christian liberty is to be exercised only in love and in consideration for others, and James moves on this high plane and on it alone. The idea that converted Jews would still attend their synagogues and thus still be bound by the old Mosaic legalism, is contrary to the facts. In Pisidian Antioch and in Iconium the synagogue raged against Christianity. And James speaks of what has been "from olden generations" and not of what Jewish converts may still do.

22) **Then it was resolved by the apostles and the elders together with the entire church that, having elected for themselves men from themselves, they send them to Antioch together with Paul and**

Barnabas, Judas called Barsabbas and Silas, leading men among the brethren, having written by their hand: The apostles and the elders as brethren to the brethren of the Gentiles throughout Antioch and Syria and Cilicia greeting! Since we heard that some who went out from us agitated you with declarations, unsettling your souls, to whom we did not give command, it was resolved by us, after coming to one accord, having elected for ourselves men, to send them to you together with our beloved Barnabas and Paul, men who have delivered up their lives in behalf of the name of our Lord Jesus Christ. We have accordingly commissioned Judas and Silas, they themselves also by word (of mouth) **reporting the same things. For it was resolved by the Holy Spirit and us that no further burden be placed upon you; only abstain from these necessary things: from those sacrificed to idols and from blood and from things strangled and from fornication; from which carefully continuing to guard yourselves, it shall be well with you. Fare well.**

In connections such as this (see also v. 25 and 28) δοκέω with the dative means that the assembly passed a formal resolution (B.-P. 315). This was probably done by a show of hands as in 14:23. In this way "it seemed good" (our versions). The entire church participated in the vote together with the apostles and the elders. The vote was unanimous as v. 25 indicates, ὁμοθυμαδόν. R., *W. P.*, is hard on the Judaizers by declaring that they probably did not vote but still held to their opinions. The vote included everything: assent to the resolution offered by James, sending a commission to Antioch with a letter that embodied that resolution, and the election of Judas and Silas as that commission. Several votes were probably taken although Luke merely states that "it was resolved." The sending of a committee to Antioch was a courteous response to the committee that had been sent from Antioch and at the same time shows the importance of the entire matter. The committee from Jerusalem is to accompany the committee from Antioch, the two are really a joint committee. Even in matters such as this the apostles strongly fostered the unity of the church.

The construction of ἐκλεξαμένους is perfectly regular, it is the accusative subject of πέμψαι and not loose (R., *W. P.*); the participle is a true middle. Concerning Judas we know only what is said here, that he belonged to the leading men in Jerusalem. Because of his added name Barsabbas he is generally regarded to have been a brother of the Joseph Barsabbas mentioned in 1:23. Silas, however, soon became one of the assistants of Paul, whose Hebrew name "Silas" received a companion name of similar sound, the Roman "Silvanus," which Paul used to designate him. Adding or substituting a Greek or a Latin name of a sound similar to the original Hebrew or Aramaic name was a quite common practice. Silvanus was prominent in Jerusalem. He now came into close association with Paul and was thus chosen as the latter's companion on the second missionary journey (v. 40). He must have been a Hellenist and was a Roman citizen (16:37).

23) The nominative participle γράψαντες, having no nominative on which to depend, is a mild anacoluthon and is construed *ad sensum;* apostles, elders, and the whole church wrote "by the hand" of Judas and Silas. Διὰ χειρός means no more than "through"; it is an Aramaic expression. These two received the order to put the adopted resolution into proper written form so that it might be approved by the apostles and the elders.

The resolution was drawn up in the form of a letter; and both its beginning and its ending are worded in the standard style of the day. First was the heading, which was always composed of three elements; the sender's own name (we put the signature at the end), the name of the person to whom the letter is addressed (we put that at the head), then the greeting. Additions may be made to any one of the three elements or to all of them; we have samples in the Epistles. No additions were made in the present letter. "The apostles and the elders" write for themselves and for the entire church but as "brethren." Some texts have "and the brethren," referring to the congregation, but this reading lacks attestation. The apposition "brethren" is highly significant in this communication. The apostles and the elders of Jerusalem speak to the Gentile Christians only as brethren and not as superiors. They call these Christians "the brethren of the Gentiles" and thus acknowledge them as brethren in Christ in the full sense of the word. *Fratres Fratibus Salutem.* Brethren salute brethren. The communication is fraternal and asks to be accepted as such and as such alone.

The letter is, however, sent not only to Antioch but also to all the Gentile brethren "throughout Antioch and Syria and Cilicia." It is a circular letter that is intended to reach all the churches that have been disturbed by the Judaizers. All these brethren were immediately involved. The letter was later carried still farther (16:4) and was used to fortify Gentile Christians everywhere against the appearance of Judaizers. We need not wonder that there were congregations in Syria and in Cilicia; the first dispersion had carried the gospel as far as Antioch, and that means also to other places, and since that time Christians had spread out from these new centers. That Titus had organized them or any of them is a hypothesis. The missionary spirit actuated every believer.

The greeting is only the common secular χαίρειν, an absolute infinitive (R. 944, 1093) with imperative force; the ellipsis of λέγουσιν is not needed to explain the infinitive (B.-D. 389, 480, 5) nor "send" in the A. V.

Only in James 1:1 do we have a Christian letter that has this common brief salutation; the other Epistles use a distinctive Christian formula which is generally expanded. This infinitive is idiomatic and cannot be imitated in translation. The letter was certainly written in Greek. Many copies of it must have been made and spread abroad, one of which Luke certainly obtained.

24) The preamble is elaborate (v. 24-27) and states fully the reason that prompted the letter. First, the Judaizers are completely disowned. The writers say that they had heard about them, that they "went out from us," from the congregation at Jerusalem, and what damage they then did, "agitated you with declarations (λόγοις), unsettling your souls." Since these Judaizers came out from Jerusalem and misrepresented the mother church so badly, it was proper, aside from the request from Antioch, that the mother church should set herself right in the eyes of these Gentile Christians and put an end to the false teaching that had disturbed the daughter-congregations.

While the clause, "to whom we did not give command," is only relative, it is decisive and a complete disavowal. What these Judaizers had done they had done of their own accord. They had no authorization from home. No apostle or elder had given them the least permission to make demands such as they had made. One of the marks of sectarists and fanatics is the fact that they act without a call from either God or man. The devil rides them to spread their divisive and hurtful doctrines. A morbidity to infect others possesses them. Judging from this statement in the letter, we must conclude that the Judaizers who had come to Antioch had carefully refrained from sending a representation to the convention at Jerusalem. The apostles and the elders found out about them and their damaging work only from the delegation that the congregation in Antioch itself had sent. "We heard" is thus the literal fact.

25) And so they passed their resolution (ἔδοξεν ἡμῖν, exactly as in v. 22) to send a special committee of their own to accompany that of Antioch; and this resolution was taken "after coming to one accord," i. e., with full unanimity as to the entire question and as to the mode of procedure. Thus they elected their committee. The Gentile Christians are thus given to understand that a plenary meeting was held, that this meeting acted unanimously, and that it chose this committee. This letter accredited the committee. Its bearers had official standing. This was orderly action and proper authority which was something different from the Judaizers who came unsent, unauthorized, and yet acted as though they spoke the mind of the mother church.

Moreover, this committee is being sent "with our beloved Barnabas and Paul" who are properly mentioned in this order because Barnabas had been a member of the congregation in Jerusalem from early days. This acknowledges the committee from Antioch by naming its two illustrious members. By adding "our beloved" (plural) the letter states in what high esteem these two men were held in Jerusalem, in what accord the mother church was with them, and how fine a thing it was that Antioch had entrusted them with an important mission. All these fine fraternal touches must be appreciated.

Not a word is said about the Judaizers who attempted to voice a contrary opinion. The conclusion is not fair that they were merely brushed aside as defeated disturbers who had lacked the courage to vote against the majority. The opposite is true. After speaking as they did (v. 5) and after hearing Peter, Paul, and Barnabas these men dropped their objections, voted for the proposition, and were satisfied. The mother congregation was unanimous in passing its resolution just as the letter states.

We must not be misled by the rise of Judaistic opinions at a later date. What happened in 11:18, after Peter had been assailed, happened also at this time. The letter would not have been honest in the statement "having come to one accord" if the Judaizers still persisted in their views. The letter would have had to deal with that fact. More than that, the congregation in Jerusalem could not have tolerated in its membership men who persisted in claims which would agitate and unsettle the souls of all Gentile brethren, claims that were subversive of the full powers of the gospel to save. Such members would have to be dealt with and could not be allowed to go on as long as their opinions remained unchanged. No mere majority of the mother church was sending this letter. The unity of the mother church remained intact. That was one great achievement of the meeting which Luke describes. Let our congregations note it and not be satisfied with bare majorities in matters of doctrine and of practice. True unity is too precious and too vital to be sacrificed so easily.

26) The apposition which describes Barnabas and Paul as "men (ἀνθρώποις, *Menschen*) who have delivered up their lives in behalf of the name of our Lord Jesus Christ" is a refined intimation to the effect that the mother church was fully informed in regard to the work Barnabas and Paul had done on their great missionary tour and in regard to the mortal dangers these two had incurred. That made them all the dearer to the mother church. The perfect participle "have delivered up their lives" conveys the idea that this past act is still valid in the present. Ὄνομα is here, too, "the revelation" of Jesus, namely his gospel (see 2:21, 38; 3:6). For the first time in Acts we have the full personal, official, and soteriological designation "our Lord Jesus

Christ," which became standard in the church. Κύριος is the saving Lord, who makes us "his own to live under him in his kingdom and serve him in everlasting righteousness, innocence, and blessedness, even as he is risen from the dead, lives, and reigns to all eternity," a part of Luther's imperishable definition of "our Lord." On "Jesus Christ" see 2:38.

This was not flattery of Barnabas and Paul and not extravagant language to describe what they had done. The words are brief but strike the main point. It was fitting that they themselves were not sent with the letter. Even in such matters it is difficult to excel the apostles and the early church. The church has had much flattery, much insincere praise. That is the sin of hypocrisy. Its praise has often been bestowed where it did not belong and withheld where it did truly belong. To praise in the wrong place and in the wrong way only exposes those who extend and those who accept such praise. When certain persons withhold praise where it is due or perhaps pronounce blame instead of praise, this is one of the unconscious yet most valuable forms of praise which ought to cheer those to whom it is rightfully extended. When Paul was almost stoned to death, the crown was being placed upon his work and upon his head. I Pet. 4:12-14. But when we are buffeted for our faults, let us take it like the malefactor and not be hypocritical martyrs.

27) The letter names the two commissioners to Antioch. What kind of men they are the congregation at Antioch will see for itself, and hence no words of commendation are added. They are commissioned, that is enough to show the confidence the mother church has in them; it was indeed a high honor. In addition to conveying the letter, Judas and Silas are authorized "themselves also by word of mouth, διὰ λόγου, by statement of their own, to repeat the same things." The letter is necessarily brief; Antioch and all the other

congregations will desire to know more. Barnabas and Paul could make an added report in Antioch, but Judas and Silas will be needed for this purpose in the other places, since it cannot be assumed that Barnabas and Paul will have the time for this in Syria and in Cilicia, and even in Antioch it will be most proper that the added information and the answers to questions come from them, at least from them in the first place.

28) And now the resolution adopted at Jerusalem in regard to the question at issue is reported in due form. The resolution is certainly well formulated. But it comes as a surprise to read, "It was resolved by the Holy Spirit and us," since the Holy Spirit has thus far not been mentioned in the entire account. Yet the apostles had the specific promises of Jesus that the Holy Spirit would guide them into all truth, John 16:13. Besides, in regard to this particular question God had made his will too plain for anyone to be in doubt as to what that will was regarding Gentile believers. In the case of Cornelius, Peter had moved only according to the most divine revelations. So it was not presumption but true assurance to write "by the Holy Spirit and us." The principal and the ministerial cause are mentioned side by side (Calov). We are today led by the Spirit in our decisions when we are in accord with his Word; deviation from the Word is forsaking the Spirit and following our own wisdom. The subjective certainty that the Spirit is directing us must always be supported by the objective fact that we are clinging to the Word and not to something we think is the Word.

The good news which the letter communicates is this: "That no further burden be placed upon you," present infinitive, "placed upon you at any time," no further burden beyond the one that necessarily rests on all believers whether they be former Jews or former Gentiles. The idea to be conveyed is that at no time is a peculiar burden to be placed on Gentile believers because they are of Gentile origin. This is exactly what Peter said in v. 10, even the same verb is employed: "to place a yoke upon the neck of the (Gentile) disciples." The letter uses the literal "burden" instead of the figurative "yoke." Yoke and burden are defined by Peter in v. 10 as that which neither the fathers nor the Jewish disciples when they were still Jews could bear: the Mosaic law (see this passage) from which "the grace of the Lord Jesus" made the believers wholly free. Those who assume the easy burden and the light yoke of the Lord Jesus (Matt. 11:29, 30) have no further burden to bear.

At this point we disagree with the translations and with some of the commentators. It is linguistically impossible to construe πλέον . . . πλήν, as is, for instance, done in our versions: "greater than"; πλέον is never so construed. Πλήν never completes a comparison, for it is either a conjunction or a preposition. We, too, never say, "greater except." What has contributed to the grammatical misconstruction is the idea that a compromise was being arranged for the Gentile Christians, namely that they were not to bear the whole law but only a small part of it, not the whole legalistic system of Moses but only certain parts of it. This misconception is augmented when the part which the Gentile Christians were supposed to bear is summed up in three commandments of the Decalog, abstinence from idolatry, from murder, and from fornication. But what about the rest of the Decalog? See the discussion of v. 20. The entire moral law (the ten commandments of the Decalog) were binding upon *all* Christians; but the whole Levitical and ceremonial law, every last part of it, was abrogated for *all* Christians. In this apostolic letter not the part of the latter law is imposed on the Gentile Christians. As far as this Levitical law is concerned, it would have been meaningless to impose this or that point and to pass by the chief point, namely circumcision. So we cannot construe πλέον with πλήν. Place a semicolon after βάρος.

Zahn has the right idea but has difficulty with the infinitive ἀπέχεσθαι because in the ten instances in which the conjunction πλήν occurs it is followed by the imperative; and so he changes the reading to the imperative ἀπέχεσθε: "only . . . abstain," etc. But read R. 943 in regard to the infinitive used as an imperative. A new statement begins with πλήν: "only (or nevertheless) from these necessary things abstain," and then they are named. The infinitive is the more in place since another infinitive precedes so that we may even keep the same construction for both: "It was resolved that no further burden be placed upon you; only (nevertheless) that you abstain from these necessary things," etc. That clears up the grammar; v. 29 should begin with πλήν.

29) But when it is now stated that Gentile Christians should abstain from certain "necessary" things, it would be misleading to reintroduce legal or Levitical, Mosaic necessity. No burden of that kind remains, not even for Jewish Christians. If, for instance, they choose still to eat kosher they may do so as a matter of liberty; the moment they would do it as a matter of law they would be destroying the gospel. We have explained the necessity of the things here mentioned in connection with v. 20; it was a necessity that was due in part to danger for Gentile Christians themselves (idol feasts, fornication) and in part to love for their Jewish fellow Christians (offending them by eating blood or bloody meat). This type of necessity is something that is vastly different from all ancient or modern legalism. It will always rest upon us: the necessity to keep away (ἀπέχεσθαι, hold oneself away from) from everything that might pollute, from anything idolatrous, fornicatious, or otherwise contaminating; the necessity of considering our brethren, their natural

feelings and also their weakness so as never to harm them. This is sound *apostolic advice* that is good for us Gentile Christians to this day. The order of the four items is changed from that found in v. 20, but this seems immaterial.

Because of its preposition and its tense, διατηροῦντες means, "carefully continuing to guard" and defines what is meant by abstaining. If you follow the apostolic advice, "it shall be well with you"; for εὖ πράξετε has the specific meaning of being and not of doing well, and was often used in this sense at the close of a letter. Here, however, ἔρρωσθε, "fare well," is added. It is the Latin *valete*. The form is the perfect passive imperative of ῥώννυμι and literally means: "Be made strong!" or "keep well!"

30) **They, therefore** (see v. 6), **having been dismissed, went down to Antioch and, having gathered the multitude together, delivered the letter. And having read it, they rejoiced over the encouragement.**

Luke is brief. We may take it that the committees were accompanied for a short distance by a goodly number of the members of the congregation in Jerusalem in accord with the custom that was so common at that time. After they arrivevd at Antioch, the πλῆθος was gathered together. Deissmann, *Bible Studies*, 232, offers illustrations from inscriptions of the use of this word for official, political, and religious gatherings; ὄχλος would certainly not be the proper word. Thus in public, at a great gathering of the entire church in Antioch, the letter from Jerusalem was duly delivered.

31) Luke says "they read it" and means that one did the reading for all. The result was joy over the παράκλησις, a word that is not easily translated. It can scarcely mean, "the exhortation," for it applies to the entire letter and not merely to the one hortatory sentence. "The consolation" is little better. Perhaps "the

encouragement" is the best we can do in English, for in the next verse Judas and Silas παρεκάλεσαν (the verb instead of the noun), "encouraged" the brethren. The root idea of the word is "calling one to one's side" for some kind of help and support. We note "the Paraclete," the Holy Spirit as the One called to our side. The effect of the letter was the same in all the other Gentile congregations in which it was read.

32) **Both Judas and Silas themselves also, being prophets, encouraged the brethren by means of many a word and made them firm.**

Our versions punctuate incorrectly. We cannot translate, "being themselves also prophets," because there are no other prophets with whom Judas and Silas are compared. But as the letter brought encouragement, so Judas and Silas themselves also encouraged the brethren. They, no doubt, told the entire story at length; but "being prophets," they did much more. On "prophets" compare 11:27; here the word signifies men who are thoroughly versed in the Word and able authoritatively to set forth the Lord's will from that Word. So they must have done what James began to do when he cited Amos 9 (v. 16-18) and showed "by means of many a word" just what was intended concerning Gentile converts to Christendom; note διὰ λόγου in v. 27. The second verb adds the thought that they thereby confirmed, fixed and settled them in their faith and their conviction regarding what God really willed.

33) **Now, having spent some time, they were dismissed with peace from the brethren to those who commissioned them.**

The two messengers did not return hurriedly, they took their time. "They were dismissed" does not mean that it was finally intimated to them to leave; they certainly would have been welcomed to stay even permanently. "They were dismissed with peace" means that, when they were ready to leave, the congregation itself bade them farewell to depart in peace. As they had been formally received on their arrival, so they did not merely steal away when leaving but were tendered a formal farewell. "From the brethren to those who (had) commissioned them" includes greetings to the apostles, elders, and the congregation in Jerusalem. Why should these two prominent phrases be used if that were not the sense? The brethren in Antioch were no less courteous than those in Jerusalem had been.

34) The Codex Bezae adds: "Silas, however, resolved to remain there (or with them)," and: "And Judas alone went on." Because v. 40 shows that Silas was in Antioch, the writer of this codex imagined that he had never left the place. The idea is in conflict with v. 33, where both Judas and Silas leave. Here, as in so many changes and additions, this codex is unreliable. It is the work of a late scribe who altered the original according to his own ideas. Correct the A. V. by cancelling v. 34.

35) **Paul, however, and Barnabas were tarrying in Antioch, teaching and proclaiming as good news the Word of the Lord in company also with many others.**

We are kept in touch with Paul and with Barnabas, and the imperfect tense intimates that more in regard to them is to follow. While they continued in Antioch they were busy "teaching" the brethren and "proclaiming as good news the Word of the Lord" to pagans in order to bring them to faith. In this they had the company (μετά) of "many others," so rich in teachers and in missionaries was this great congregation. Active, ever active is the word that characterizes Paul — vacations had not yet been invented. Into this time of a few weeks or months, those prior to March in the year 50, the trying incident with regard to Peter must be placed (Gal. 2:11-21). Paul was compelled to correct him publicly, and Barnabas, too, had yielded to

Peter's influence. Luke passes the matter by because it did not influence the course of events; if it had not been for the later attacks of Judaizers on Paul, even he would have left no record of Peter's mistake, but his opponents who were working in Galatia compelled him to write about it in self-defense.

THE SECOND MISSIONARY JOURNEY: PAUL AND SILAS REACH TROAS

36) The second missionary journey starts with a painful incident: Paul and Barnabas part company with each other. **Now after some days Paul said to Barnabas, Having returned now, let us visit the brethren city by city, in which we proclaimed the Word of the Lord, how they fare.**

This occurred "some days" after Judas and Silas had left for Jerusalem; but the number of days were not only a few, for they extend over a number weeks or perhaps months. The proposition is made by Paul. He, too, sees that Antioch is well supplied with teachers and missionary workers, and he had reason to be solicitous about the young congregations that he and Barnabas had founded in heathen territory. So Paul proposes a visit to them, taking them city by city in order to see how they are getting along. Δή = "now," "then." It is a particle that gives precision or emphasis to the words to which it is attached and has no real English equivalent. Πῶς ἔχουσι is an indirect question, literally, "how they have it," "*wie sie sich befinden,*" "how they are getting along." It seems that no news regarding them had come to Antioch.

37) **But Barnabas was wanting to take along with them also John, the one called Mark. Paul, however, was considering it best not to take along with them this one, him who withdrew from them from Pamphilia and did not go with them to the work. And there occurred a clash so that they**

separated from each other, and that Barnabas, taking Mark along, sailed off to Cyprus; but Paul, having chosen for himself Silas, went out after having been given over to the grace of the Lord by the brethren.

The last we heard of Mark was in 13:13, where he left Paul and Barnabas at Pamphilia and returned to Jerusalem. Had he come to Antioch? The same question may be asked with reference to Silas; had he, too, come back to Antioch from Jerusalem? It is generally assumed that both Mark and Silas were again in Antioch. In regard to Silas see the spurious v. 34. It is possible, of course, that both Mark and Silas were in Jerusalem at the time when Paul proposed the journey to Barnabas and that they were summoned from there.

We can understand why Barnabas wanted to take his cousin Mark along just as he had been taken along as an attendant (ὑπηρέτης) in 13:5. Note the imperfect tense to express the desire of Barnabas and in the next verse to indicate the consideration of Paul. R., *W. P.*, interprets these imperfects as durative and as thus marking the tenacity with which each man clung to his idea. But Luke regularly uses imperfect tenses to express the preliminary actions when the final outcome is still in abeyance. Then follows the aorist or several aorists which state what the result was. So here ἐγένετο is followed by ὥστε in v. 39.

38) Paul did not consider it wise to take Mark along, and his reasons are indicated briefly by the two participles. Mark had withdrawn from Paul and Barnabas on the first missionary tour when they reached Pamphilia and had not gone with them to the work. The implication is that the call of the work, the great work to be done, had failed to hold Mark; he let other considerations weigh so heavily that he left Paul and Barnabas at Pamphilia even before the main work was

done and went back to his home in Jerusalem. We have treated the question of this withdrawal in 13:13, which see. Paul faulted Mark for that withdrawal to such an extent that he would not risk a recurrence by again taking Mark along. A man who failed once at a crucial time might well fail again. If we were right in 13:13, in supposing that Mark was afraid to go on because Paul was sick at Perga, Paul was right in refusing to take Mark along. What if Paul again had to battle with sickness? We must endeavor to picture in our minds not only the hardships but also the dangers of these missionary journeys. They certainly required a degree of heroism, and not every man was equal to the task. It would be an injustice to Barnabas to think that he, too, had not blamed Mark for leaving them at Perga. Barnabas had loyally clung to Paul although Mark was his cousin. But now the confidence of Barnabas in Mark was fully restored; it was otherwise in the case of Paul.

39) This is the situation painted by the imperfect tenses which hold the reader in suspense. Now the outcome: neither man yielded to the other. "A clash occurred," παροξυσμός (our word "paroxysm"). We need not overdraw the picture and speak of passionate and bitter words, of hot tempers and anger. Paul and Barnabas were not men of that common, cheap type. This clash was one between incompatible convictions, Barnabas being sure that Mark would prove fit for the task, Paul equally convinced that he would not prove fit. Neither insulted the other nor did anything regrettable. But because they had such opposite convictions in regard to Mark, the two men separated and divided the field, Barnabas going to Cyprus and taking Mark along with him, Paul taking the rest of the field on the mainland. Barnabas and Paul evidently agreed on this division. If they were not to go to the work together, this was a most proper thing to do. They also

agreed that Barnabas was to go to Cyprus. Paul and Barnabas had begun their work at Cyprus because the latter was a Cyprian and knew a good deal about the island. So Cyprus is now allotted to him. We have no reason to assume that the division thus made was not an amicable one. To assume that it was made in heat or passion is quite unwarranted.

Barnabas now passes from sight; the Acts do not mention him again. Paul refers to him in I Cor. 9:6. The great current of gospel history follows Paul, and Luke limits himself to that. However much Barnabas accomplished, his work was like that of most of the Twelve (now Eleven) and of others, it was not a part of the main stream that flowed with such power through Asia Minor and southern Europe and left its mighty mark for the next centuries while the Romans destroyed Jerusalem and the Jews as a nation.

Mark made good with Barnabas in Cyprus. Eventually be became one of Paul's helpers, Col. 4:10; and how dear he became to Paul we see when Paul was facing his end in the Roman prison, II Tim. 4:11. We also see him with Peter, I Pet. 5:13, who calls him his son. He wrote the second Gospel and did it as the mouthpiece of the Apostle Peter. Mark was a man who might be regarded as belonging to the second-class workers in the church but proved to be of great value in supporting two, and that two of the greatest apostles. His early mistake was soon wiped completely from the slate.

40) So Paul took Silas but not in place of Mark but in place of Barnabas. On Silas see v. 22. Due to the acquaintance Paul had had with him in Jerusalem, on the journey to Antioch, and while he had remained in Antioch, Paul found him the man to be put in the place of Barnabas. Silas was even a Roman citizen (16:37), which was an asset not to be despised in an undertaking such as this missionary journey. We meet

him with Peter and Mark (in I Pet. 5:12, 13) as Peter's messenger. It is an interesting pursuit to gather the scattered notices of the New Testament and to reconstruct parts of the biography of these lesser men such as Mark, Silas, Luke, and others. It does not seem, from all accounts, that Silas fully filled the place of Barnabas; Barnabas was the greater man.

Only in regard to Paul does Luke say that on departing for his journey "he was given over to the grace of the Lord by the brethren." This recalls 15:26, and indicates that the brethren in Antioch sided with Paul as far as Mark was concerned and not with Barnabas. This does not imply that they did not wish Barnabas and Mark well and did not commend them to the grace of the Lord. Luke is speaking of a public service at which Paul and Silas were sent on their journey. It seems that Barnabas and Mark had already left Antioch.

41) **And he was going through Syria and Cilicia, making the churches firm.** The singulars used here and in the following narrative indicate the complete leadership of Paul. Barnabas had been more of an equal to Paul, while Mark was no more than an attendant. Silas thus appears as the able assistant of Paul who was less than Barnabas but much more than Mark. This time the searoute was not taken but the route overland. The two travelers circled around the upper part of Syria and then went through the narrow part of Cilicia into the province of Galatia. They thus circled the Gulf of Issus and when doing so passed through the "Syrian Gates," the narrow road that led between steep rocks on the one side and the Gulf on the other. They very likely passed through Tarsus, Paul's old home, and then through the Cilician Gates, the narrow pass over the Taurus range. This route afforded an opportunity to present the apostolic letter to the congregations in this part of Syria and Cilicia

as had been contemplated in the address of the letter itself (v. 23). We have no means of knowing how these congregations were founded. Some think they were Paul's work during the eight years he spent in Tarsus, but this is unlikely. Let us assume that they came into existence as Antioch itself had done, through the disciples that were scattered abroad after Stephen's martyrdom. Details about them and even locations are entirely lacking.

CHAPTER XVI

1) **And he arrived also at Derbe and at Lystra. And lo, a disciple was there, by name Timothy, son of a believing Jewish woman but of a Greek father who was attested by the brethren in Lystra and Iconium. Him Paul wanted to go out with him and, having taken him, he circumcised him because of the Jews who were in those places, for they all knew that his father was a Greek.**

From Cilicia Paul went to the lower corner of Galatia, to Derbe near the border, the last Galatian city he had reached on his first missionary journey. Nothing of importance for Luke's narrative occurred here. But in connection with Lystra, the next city in which he had established a congregation, Luke introduces Timothy, whom Paul made his companion. Καὶ ἰδού is stressed unduly when it is adduced as proof that Paul now met Timothy for the first time, and that he had already become a disciple before Paul met him, and that we are mistaken in concluding from I Cor. 4:17; I Tim. 1:2, 18; II Tim. 1:2, that Paul himself had converted him on his first visit to Lystra. When Paul so repeatedly calls Timothy "my beloved son," this means more than that Timothy was in full accord with him; others who were in equal accord with him are not called "my son." "Lo" is used by Luke when he introduces someone for the first time or when he draws special attention to some person; see the many examples in Luke's Gospel and in Acts (Young's *Concordance*) and note that other writers do the same. Compare the remarks on 15:20.

Because already here Luke states that Timothy came from Lystra, he leaves his name without further designation in 20:4, and the supposition that, like

Gaius, he was from Derbe is untenable. His mother was Eunice and his grandmother Lois (II Tim. 1:5), both were faithful disciples and former Jews; but his father was a Greek and, apparently, had been dead for some time. This had been a mixed marriage, and although both mother and grandmother were Jews, the father had remained pagan, and the son had never been circumcised. Already this marriage shows that the mother and the grandmother were not strong in the Jewish faith; as does also the fact that even after the father's death the son had not been circumcised. Although they had been very indifferent Jews, mother, grandmother, and son were now ardent believers in Christ. One thing the mother had done for her son, she had faithfully taught him the Scriptures (II Tim. 3:14, 15), fully unaware of the fact that she was thereby preparing the boy for his great future work. Paul could not have used him in his work if he had not had this early training in the Old Testament Scriptures.

2) While Lystra and Derbe belonged to the same section, Lystra and Iconium were closer together, and there was regular business and other intercourse between them. That is why Iconium is here named together with Lystra. It implied not a little to have the attestation of the brethren of two such cities, an attestation and testimony as to both character and ability for the work of the church. Here we have the neuter plural in the name Lystra, Luke uses both this plural and the feminine singular.

3) The resumptive demonstrative τοῦτον gathers up all that has been said about Timothy. This was the young man whom Paul desired to take with him as a second assistant in addition to the older Silas, and the aorist implies that this desire was made reality. Much more than Luke could record, of course, entered into this choice of Timothy; Luke states enough to let his reader see that in Timothy Paul found a young man

who was eminently suited to his purpose. In connection with 14:20 R., *W. P.*, regards him as being only fifteen years old and now as being only eighteen although the interval between the two visits of Paul was little more than a year, but this makes Timothy entirely too young. We can only estimate his age, but it was more than that, he was at least twenty-one.

Because Paul wanted to use him in his work he took and circumcised him, not, of course, with his own hand but by the hand of some competent Jewish Christian. Paul did this on account of the Jews in those places, referring not only to Lystra and Iconium but to any others in this territory. He followed the principle laid down in I Cor. 9:19, and did not do this because he was yielding to Judaistic legalism. If Jewish Christians had demanded Timothy's circumcision, Paul would have resisted strongly; he did this very thing in Jerusalem regarding Titus (Gal. 2:3). But if Timothy had not been circumcised he would have been not only useless to Paul in his work but the worst kind of a hindrance, for he would have aroused the prejudices of the Jews whom he might try to approach to such an extent as to prevent even a hearing of the gospel. Timothy would not have dared to speak in any synagogue; even the houses of most Jews would have been closed to him. Timothy would have directed this Jewish prejudice also against Paul and Silas because they had an uncircumcised associate. R., *W. P.*, says rightly: "Timothy was circumcised because of Jewish unbelievers, not because of Jewish believers." All the Jews living in that section also knew that the father of Timothy was a Greek; the question of his circumcision would, therefore, be much discussed by them. The mixed marriage of Timothy's parents had, no doubt, long been an offense to the Jews.

4) **Now, as they were going through the cities, they continued to give to them the resolutions to**

keep, those that had been decided on by the apostles and elders in Jerusalem. The churches, accordingly, were being made firm in the faith and were abounding in number day by day.

The imperfects are descriptive of what continued to happen. Silas is now included, and hence the plurals occur in v. 4. He had been one of the original committee that had been sent to Antioch with the resolutions and was thus better fitted than even Paul for communicating those resolutions also to these predominantly Gentile congregations.

Our versions leave a wrong impression when they translate δόγματα "decrees"; and R., *W. P.*, does not aid us by pointing to Luke 2:1; Acts 17:7; Col. 2:14. To be sure, the word is used with reference to the decrees of rulers and of legal enactments, but that is due to the authors. An emperor declares δοκεῖ μοι, "it seems good to me," and lo, his pleasure is law, a decree; *sic volo, sic jubeo.* But when the apostles, elders, and the church in Jerusalem were assembled in their meeting, it is stated ἔδοξε τοῖς κτλ., and so twice in the letter itself (15:22, 25, 28), when it is used with reference to assemblies, this verb and its datives always means, "it was resolved" and never, "we decree." Δόγματα is the corresponding noun and means "resolutions."

So also τὰ κεκριμένα cannot mean "that have been ordained"; the verb κρίνω does not mean "to ordain," and no assembly ever "ordained" resolutions. This is the very κρίνω which James used in 15:19 when he first offered the resolution to the assembly for vote. Did he "ordain"? He did not. The verb means "to judge," "to decide"; and so here these resolutions were decided on by the assembly in Jerusalem and as such were now offered to the Gentile churches one after another. These were "resolutions" that were "decided on" after full and mature deliberation. They carried weight accordingly. Only the apostles and the elders are here named by Luke, for he has already told us the entire story about these "resolutions" and how they were adopted (15:22). The apostles and the elders are such only because of the church. Preachers often forget that and act as though the church existed because of them, or as though they could disregard it.

5) Οὖν indicates the result, and once more we have the verb "being made firm" in the faith, fixed and solid against attack. "The faith" is objective, firm in *what* the churches believed; Luke has repeatedly used this word in that sense, *quae creditur.* To be made firm in the faith is with strong confidence (subjective) to hold the divine truth and reality given us to hold (objective). The inward first and then the outward: "they were abounding in number day by day," receiving new members in the faith. We take it that these were Gentiles. After the question about the old Levitical regulations had been settled effectively as between Jewish and Gentile Christians, more and more Gentiles flocked to the banner of the cross. That was true success. In order to gain numbers, doctrine and its practice are often sacrificed. The great growth of the apostolic churches was not made at such a sacrifice.

Already at this point the controversy regarding the next three verses is introduced. Where were these "churches," in which "cities" (v. 4)? Derbe and Lystra have already been mentioned. That would leave Iconium (14:1) and Pisidian Antioch (13:14), where Paul and Barnabas had founded churches, and we may include several others in smaller places in this territory on the strength of 13:49 where we are told that the Word of the Lord was carried "through the entire region" of which Antioch was the general center. Since Iconium and Antioch are not especially named in the following, this must be the understanding with reference to the cities and the churches that were visited and informed regarding the apostolic resolutions with the attendant good results.

6) **And they went through the Phrygian and Galatian region, having been prevented by the Holy Spirit from speaking the Word in Asia. And having come down to Mysia, they were trying to go to Bithynia, and the Spirit of Jesus did not let them. And having passed alongside Mysia, they went down to Troas.**

The controversy centers on the question as to what v. 6 really states. The contention ought to cease regarding the participle. No aorist participle expresses subsequent action. Paul and his companions did not go "through the Phrygian and Galatian region" and *then* receive the Spirit's word in regard to Asia. The participle is causal and thus antecedent. They went through the Phrygian and Galatian region *because* they were prevented from speaking the Word in Asia. But why do Ramsay and others think that the participle expresses subsequent action? In order to exclude the so-called north Galatian hypothesis, namely that on this journey Paul founded a number of congregations in northern Galatia (in a line from Synnada to Pessinus, Ancyra, and Tavium), and that his letter to the Galatians was addressed to these northern congregations which were chiefly Celtic. Take a look at the map. We are told that "the Phrygian and Galatian region" means: 1) the part of Phrygia that contained Antioch and Iconium, and 2) the part of Galatia that was Lycaonia and contained Lystra and Derbe (note R. 963). *After* this region had been crossed, we are told, the Spirit made his will known; and then the missionaries did not go to the coast and follow this to Ephesus and north to Troas but went straight across the middle of the province Asia and thus to Troas as some maps draw the journey. But this is not the way in which to refute the northern hypothesis. The participle prevents this.

Luke should have written "the Galatian (Lycaonian) and Phrygian region" and not have reversed the two. Moreover, he should not have led the reader through Derbe and Lystra (v. 1) and the other churches (v. 5) *before* speaking of going through "the Phrygian and Galatian region" in which these very churches were situated. Luke would twice be *reversing* the localities.

What Luke says is this: After visiting Derbe and Lystra (v. 1) and all the other churches founded on the first missionary journey (v. 5), after Paul and his companions were through visiting the churches and were probably at Antioch, the question arose as to what new fields were to be entered; and the natural course seemed to be to turn to the coast of the province of Asia with its great cities such as Ephesus, Smyrna, Sardis, Thyatira, Pergamos, etc., most inviting fields of labor — then the Spirit told them *not* to utter the word in Asia. How the Spirit did that, and to whom he communicated his will, Luke does not state because he is concerned with the fact alone. The supposition that this revelation came to Silas and not to Paul seems unlikely. Our guess is that it came to Paul. What was to be done then? "They went through the Phrygian and Galatian region"; they turned north. Did they preach there, found churches, etc.? Those who advocate the northern hypothesis in regard to the letter to the Galatians say "yes." A whole group of congregations was founded along the line drawn on the maps in a great sweep from Synnada to Pessinus, Ancyra, even Tavium, through the whole of northern Galatia. And this extensive work is read into Luke's simple statement that they διῆλθον, "went through," the Phrygian and Galatian region. Luke does not even say that they preached and writes only χώρα, "region." The theory in regard to these northern cities in Galatia breaks down here at its source. If this theory is correct, why did Luke not insert at least a phrase such as "as far as Tavium"?

Verses 6-8 intend only to show us briefly how the journey from Antioch to Troas was made without a longer stop between these two points, without the founding of a single church in this territory. On leaving Antioch, which was located in the ethnographic section called Phrygia, on the border of the old Pisidia, the missionaries naturally passed through that part of Phrygia. Now a part of Phrygia (an old indefinite ethnographic section) was located in the Roman province Asia, the rest in the Roman province Galatia (in which were Antioch and Iconium). So Luke writes that they went through "the Phrygian and Galatian region," remained in that part of Phrygian territory which was Galatian, did not pass over into that part of Phrygia which was incorporated in the Roman province Asia. Where they turned west we do not know, perhaps it was at Pessinus, but that makes little difference. We have absolutely no intimation that they stopped for work, much less that congregations were founded. Zahn's supposition that they worked but were unsuccessful is untenable.

At this point we see that Ramsay's idea that in Luke's writings χώρα designates an administrative section, a *Regio* in this sense, breaks down. It looks plausible in 13:49, and again in 14:6 (περίχωρον). Ramsay tries to apply his view here and in 18:23; but how does he do this? By having "the Phrygian and Galatian region" mean the Phrygian (with Antioch as its center) and Galatian (embracing Lycaonia with Lystra and Derbe as center). But we have already shown that v. 1-5 place us beyond both of these regions. If two *Regiones*, administrative centers, are referred to, the article τήν should be repeated, and "Galatian" should *precede* "Phrygian." In regard to 18:23 see that passage.

Zahn regards τὴν Φρυγίαν as a noun: they passed through "Phrygia" and also through "Galatian territory" (beyond Phrygia). He does this because Φρυγίαν seems to be a noun in 18:23. But even then, as far as 18:23 is concerned, in 16:6 the adjective is proper. The only difference would be that the missionaries would go farther north before turning toward Troas. But greater difficulty would result in connection with 18:23. On coming from Syrian Antioch, Paul would enter Phrygian territory first and not Galatian as distinct from Phrygian. In both 16:6 and 18:23 all is clear if *one* section is referred to, namely in 16:6 Phrygian Galatia, and in 18:23 Galatian Phrygia, it being immaterial which word comes first. Both are adjectives, both modify χώραν in both passages.

7) So they went down to Mysia and then tried to go into Bithynia. The missionaries could not have come close to Mysia without crossing the province Asia. That is why in v. 6 Luke writes that they were prevented only "from speaking the Word in Asia" and not from crossing the province as such. Now the same is true with regard to Mysia that was said in regard to Phrygia. Both are ethnographic sections that include indefinite stretches of territory, and the maps only estimate their extent, and thus map makers vary greatly. We are unable to plot the route from Pisidian Antioch to Troas on the basis of the meager data which Luke furnishes. How near to Bithynia did their route carry them, and at just what point did the Spirit refuse them permission to enter this northern province with its city Nicea, which later became so well known? Noteworthy is "the Spirit of Jesus" as helping to establish the *filioque* of the Nicene Creed, the confession: "I believe in the Holy Ghost, . . . who proceedeth from the Father *and the Son,* etc." Jesus himself said that he would send the Spirit, John 16:26.

8) Both the fact that the travelers came κατά Mysia and that they went παρά (in the participle) Mysia indicates that they left it to one side and so reached Troas. They probably came through Adramyttium. Troas was not in Mysia or in Asia but was an independent district of its own. The point of these verses is the peculiar way in which Paul and his assistants are made to wander from Pisidian Antioch to Troas and are shunted away from the south and from the north until they drift into this faraway Mediterranean port. No work awaited them anywhere on this long journey, nothing of consequence even here at Troas, but great work waited across the sea in Europe, in southern Macedonia. This is one of the plain cases in which the Spirit closes and opens doors for missionary work. He does so still, and we must dismiss the idea that we may choose the fields *ad libitum.* Louis Harms selected a place in Africa but all in vain; his missionaries had to go elsewhere, where neither Harms nor they had expected to go.

9) **And a vision appeared at night to Paul — a man, a Macedonian, was standing and beseeching him and saying, Having come across to Macedonia, help us! Now when he saw the vision, immediately we sought to go out to Macedonia, concluding that God had called us to proclaim the good news to them.**

Until this time the Holy Spirit had given only negative commands, not to go to the coast cities of the Asian province (v. 6) and not to enter Bithynia (v. 7), and no positive command of any kind. This fact alone refutes the north Galatian hypothesis that, on leaving Pisidian Antioch, Paul had worked and had founded churches in Pessinus, Ancyra, and Tavium and in this section generally. He had no orders to work in even this seaport Troas, for after receiving the vision he promptly left it. If work had been in progress in

Troas, he could not have broken it off so promptly. Now at last comes the positive order to cross into southern Europe and to work there.

Sometimes the Holy Spirit communicated his will directly as in v. 6, 7; how this was done we do not know except that the communication was always understood. At other times, as here, a vision was used, which was granted either in the daytime (10:11) or at night. Paul had a number of such visions (18:9; 23:11; 27:23; II Cor. 12:1, etc.). Διὰ νυκτός means sometime during the night, possibly while Paul slept. It was not a mere dream; for these visions are always plainly supernatural visions and communications. This one was exceedingly simple and also plain in its meaning: "a man, a Macedonian (τις = our indefinite article) was standing" before Paul and beseeching him to come across into Macedonia. The second perfect participle ἑστώς is always used as a present, so we have ἦν with three participles, which are three periphrastic imperfects. The effect is continuation: there he kept standing, beseeching, and saying, "Help us!"

The very fact that he asks Paul to come across into Macedonia makes plain that Paul recognized him as a Macedonian; he also says, "help *us*." He pleads for the entire province. We need not think of peculiar Macedonian dress, accent of speech, and the like. The idea that this was an angel who was asking Paul to come over to help him and his fellow angels fight the spirits of Satan, is a mere fancy. The help desired is plainly spiritual help such as Paul was called to bring by means of the gospel. The Lord was assigning him this Gentile field for his labors. It has been thought that this Macedonian was Luke, the writer of the Acts. This view is based on the assumption that Luke was a Macedonian, a native of Philippi. But it is difficult to imagine how a man of flesh and blood, one of Paul's companions at this time, could possibly appear to Paul in a vision at night. The entire vision is supernatural, sent by God. As God showed Peter all sorts of animals in a vision, so he showed Paul this man in a vision.

10) "Immediately," that means the very next morning, passage was sought on some vessel in order to cross over to Macedonia, the conclusion having been correctly drawn that God had called Paul and his companions to preach the gospel in Macedonia. The vision presented a man pleading for help, and that meant success in the missionary work. This vision has often been regarded as picturing the need of all heathen people, as calling on us to bring them the help of the gospel. That, however, is not strictly correct. To be sure, the whole heathen world is in direct need of the gospel. But we must remember that the Spirit himself prevented Paul from taking the gospel to the coast cities of the province of Asia and to the entire province of Bithynia. Were the heathen of these provinces not in need of the gospel? The better application made of this text is to point out that we would bring the gospel wherever God opens the door for us. The Macedonian man symbolizes, not the whole heathen world, but that specific part of it to which God would at any special time send us. He does not now use visions to direct us, but he does use plain providential indications, and these are the cries to us to come and to help.

This is the first of Luke's famous *"we"* passages found in Acts. Zahn finds an earlier "we" in 11:28, in the reading of the Codex Bezae of that passage: *συνεστραμμένων ἡμῶν*, "we having been drawn closely together," namely in regard to Agabus when he predicted the great drought to the congregation at Antioch. But this codex aims to improve on Luke's text by changing it in scores of places like an editor who revises somebody's manuscript. A number of conclusions are based on this "we" of the Codex Bezae. Since it takes us to Syrian Antioch in the year 40, it is concluded that Luke and Theophilus were natives of Antioch, see the introduction to this volume. But we discount that "we" in 11:28 since it lacks sufficient textual support.

But this "we" that runs through 16:10-17 again through 20:5-21:25, and once more through 27:2-28:16 is a far different matter. It is Luke's quiet and unobtrusive yet distinct testimony that he is the writer of Acts, that he was present with Paul and an eyewitness of the events recorded in these sections. So here in Troas, Luke is with Paul. More than that, he is one of Paul's little party, an assistant such as Silas and Timothy were, for he writes: "Immediately we sought to go out to Macedonia, concluding that God had sent *us* (ἡμᾶς)," etc. Luke acted together with the rest. The aorist "we sought" implies that they at once found what they sought, namely passage on a ship for Macedonia, and so they sailed away as v. 11 states. All four men at once left Troas, there was no reason why even one of them should be left behind. We conclude that no work had been done at Troas on this visit.

But now a series of questions naturally arises. This "we" implies that Luke must have been not only a Christian but one who had also proved himself worthy of being an assistant of Paul's. He suddenly introduces himself as such here at Troas, a place to which the others had come without him, a place to which none of them knew they were going until shortly before they arrived there; for only after they had been forbidden to enter Bithynia did they go to Troas. How, then, does Luke appear here at Troas, appear as an assistant of Paul's. That fact is most remarkable in every way. And let us honestly admit that we do not know the answer. But this ignorance on our part opens the gates to speculation. We have noted Zahn's hypothesis which he bases on the reading of the Codex Bezae in 11:28, and that of a few fathers who think that Luke was a native of Syrian Antioch.

Even when that is granted, we still ask, "How does Luke appear here in Troas just at this time?" It certainly was not due to a previous arrangement, for Paul himself did not know until just a little before this time that he would come to Troas. Luke could not have joined Paul when Paul started from Syrian Antioch or before he got to Pisidian Antioch, for why should Luke then delay the "we" until his mention of Troas? He could not have joined Paul after the latter left Pisidian Antioch, for from that point onward Paul himself was in the dark as to his destination. The hypotheses that ignore these facts are unacceptable for that very reason. And this implies that making Luke a native of Syrian Antioch is not as simple a matter as some have made it. In this and in some other matters we shall have to accustom ourselves to the humble admission that we just do not know and cannot even venture an acceptable guess.

THE SECOND MISSIONARY JOURNEY: PHILIPPI

11) **Having set sail, therefore, from Troas, we made a straight run to Samothrace, and on the next day to Neapolis and then to Philippi, the first city of that part of Macedonia, a colony; and in this city we continued to spend some days.**

Hobart sought to establish the fact that Luke was a physician on the basis of the medical terms occurring in Acts and in the Gospel; when one considers the nautical terms occurring in Acts one might conclude that Luke was a sailor or a sea-captain. Luke, however, never makes his medical profession prominent; and although he was not a sailor, he writes with exactness about harbors and voyages. The term for setting sail is explained in 13:13; to make a straight run is the proper term for sailing straight before a favorable wind without having to tack. It was as though God himself speeded their vessel. So they reached the little island Samothrace at the end of the first day and the harbor Neapolis (New Town) on the mainland the next day. But this harbor was located in the territory of Thrace and not in Macedonia; hence they did not stop here. Their call was directed toward Macedonia. In 20:6 it took Paul five days to get from Neapolis to Troas.

12) So Paul and his company at once went over the well-paved road to Philippi, ten miles distant. As Seleucia was the harbor of Syrian Antioch and Milete that of Ephesus, so Neapolis was the harbor of Philippi. The latter was the old Krenides ("Place of Fountains") which had been made a real city by Philip of Macedon, the father of Alexander the Great. After the battle of Pydna (168 B. C.) the Romans divided Macedonia into four politically separate parts, in the first of which Philippi was located. Amphipolis was the capital of this section. Philippi was located about a mile east of the small river Gangites which flows into the Strymon thirty miles from this point.

In 42 B. C. the battle of Philippi was fought between the Second Triumvirate (Octavius, Antonius, Lepidus) and the republicans of Rome under Brutus and Cassius, which resulted in a defeat for the latter, both of whom were killed. In commemoration of the victory Octavius made Philippi a colony. After the battle of Actium in 31 B. C. Augustus sent more Roman veterans to the colony and raised the standing of Philippi to the highest point by granting it the so-called *jus Italicum,* i. e., putting it on a par with the Roman colonies in Italy. Philippi regarded itself as an entirely Roman city. Its citizens were Roman citizens who enjoyed all the rights of such: freedom from scourging, from arrest except in extreme cases, and the right to appeal to the emperor. The official language was Latin. At the head of the city there were two officials, the *praetores duumviri* or στρατηγοί, who appeared officially with attendant lictors, the *lictores* or ῥαβδοῦχοι, who carried the official bundles of rods or *fasces* with a mace protruding from the center, the symbols of power and of authority. Here, then, was a city that was markedly different from many to which Paul had as yet come.

Since πρώτη is commonly used without the article we may translate, "the first city of that part of Macedonia." And now the controversy begins, for Amphipolis was both the capital and foremost city of that section. Ramsay thinks that this word "first" indicates that Philippi was the native city of Luke, that there was keen rivalry between it and Amphipolis as to which was first, and that Luke naturally favored his own city and loyally wrote "first" in Acts. In other words, Luke was like the ardent advertisers of rival towns are today, each boasting about his own. Considering everything, for instance also the fact that Luke calls only Philippi "a colony" although many other cities mentioned in his narrative were also colonies, a strong case is made for Luke's being a native of Philippi. We know that the very same thing is done with regard to Syrian Antioch. Every mention of it and all that he says about it are stressed to show how intimately Luke knew this Antioch because it was his native town.

These two hypotheses offset each other, and one admires the ingenuity with which they are constructed. Ramsay answers the disputer of his theory by decaring that every mention of Antioch has "the cold and strictly historical tone." But is Luke warm and personal in regard to Philippi? These are hypotheses and not proven facts.

With the support of a few Latins Zahn, following Blass, proposes to read πρώτης instead of πρώτη: "which is a city of the first part of Macedonia." This is an attractive view but lacks sufficient textual support. The best solution still seems to be to construe, "the first (foremost) colony city of that part of Macedonia." This would also agree with ἥτις which is causal: "since this is," etc., and states the reason that Paul chose this city. Luke writes "is" because Philippi still had this distinction at the time he wrote Acts. Paul might have sailed for some other coast city but chose this one for a good reason. The clause is not a mere geographical remark such as that Philippi was the first or nearest city in Macedonia he could reach. Paul and his three companions spent several days here before they started to work. This was necessary. They had to get their bearings. As already stated, this city was materially different from any that Paul had visited before this time. With reference to it alone he uses the word κολωνία. Other cities were colonies because they *had* a Roman colony, Philippi *was* a Roman colony because it was largely inhabited by Romans.

13) **And on the day of the Sabbath we went outside the gate beside a river where we were supposing a prayer-place to be; and having sat down, we began speaking to the women who had come together.**

We take it that this was the first Sabbath after their arrival in Philippi. After inquiring in the city in regard to Jews and a Jewish synagogue, all that the missionaries learned was that the city had very few Jews, and that their only place of worship was located somewhere along the river Gangites, a little over a mile from the walls of the city. The Greek plural is commonly used in the expression "the day of the Sabbath," just as the plural is common also in the names for festivals. So the four walk out along the great Roman road, the Via Egnatia, which they had followed into the city from Neapolis; they follow it on the other side of the city toward the northeast.

"Where we were supposing a prayer-place to be" shows how little information they had. They were not entirely certain that there was a prayer-place along the river nor just where it was if there was one. Some prefer the reading οὗ ἐνομίζετο προσευχὴ εἶναι of the Codex Bezae and take it to mean: *"wo es herkoemmlich war, dass eine Gebetsstaette sei*; but this reading simply means: "where a prayer-place was supposed to be" (passive) and is quite the same as the attested reading ἐνομίζομεν ,"where we supposed" (active).

At least ten men were required to organize a synagogue. No mention is made of Jewish men in Philippi, and it is a question whether any men were connected with the prayer-place beside the Gangites River. None at least were present on this Sabbath. In lieu of a synagogue with its organization, form of service, and proper building, a prayer-place was arranged for an isolated group of Jews, which was called προσευχή, a word that is otherwise used as a designation for prayer to God. A favorite place for such a *proseuche* was beside some river, which was selected, it is supposed, because of the Jewish lustrations although this is not entirely clear. The missionaries found the place. Whether it was a mere enclosure, or some sort of shelter, or just a selected spot, we are unable to say. Only women had gathered there, and we have no idea how they conducted their worship. The four missionaries, no doubt, introduced themselves, and after their status as teachers had been properly established, they sat down and "began speaking to the women who were come together." That this was teaching is understood. Luke says "we began speaking," each of the four in turn, also Luke.

One reason that no men were present may be the fact that, when Claudius expelled the Jews from Rome, the colony city Philippi had followed his example. Only a little group of women — yet Paul did not despise this humble beginning. Let no preacher despise even the smallest audience and imagine that he need not do his best for so few. The very smallness of a group of hearers is sometimes fraught with special blessing for the few who are present. It has often been remarked that the vision showed "*a man*, a Macedonian," and here Paul found a few *women*. Where two or three are gathered in my name, Jesus says, he will be present.

14) **And a woman, by name Lydia, a purple-seller of Thyatira city, one worshipping God, kept hearing; whose heart the Lord opened wide to be heeding the things spoken by Paul.**

A woman was the first Christian convert made in Europe. No wonder her name is cherished by her sisters to this day and by all believers generally. Since Luke introduces personal names by the dative ὀνόματι, we cannot accept the idea that Lydia, Λυδία, is here the appellative "a Lydian," a woman of Lydia, and the supposition that her personal name was either Euodia or Syntyche (Phil. 4:2, 3). We cannot agree with the further surmise that, since racial and place names were often borne by slaves, this was a freed woman, a former slave. But if Luke says only that she was "a Lydian," why did he add "of Thyatira city" when this city is known as the main city and a colony at that in the section of Asia Minor called Lydia, and the main output of the entire section was purple dye and cloth?

Luke combines "a purple-seller of Thyatira" (the plural as a designation for the city as it was for Philippi in v. 11) because in good part the city explains Lydia's business. The purple dye was obtained from a conchylium, the shellfish *Murex trunculus* of Linnæus, and the waters at Thyatira produced the brightest and the most permanent hues. Scarlet fezzes made there are still considered superior. In three inscriptions dating back to the time between Vespasian and Caracalla a corporate guild of dyers is mentioned as having been established in this city. The dye itself was so costly because only a drop of it was secured from a small vessel in the throat of each shellfish. This was the genuine article; a cheaper grade was secured by crushing the fish.

Dyeing was the chief industry of the Lydian land. Lydia herself came from Thyatira and was now located in Philippi. Purple cloth of all kinds would be in high demand in this colony with its many Romans. It formed the trimming of the white Roman toga as well as of the tunic; the rich wore purple (Luke 16:19); prominent ladies loved the royal color; rugs and tapestries contained much rich purple; and besides it was used by officials for state robes and by emperors and their courts. "Royal purple" is still a current phrase.

Lydia dealt in purple goods of all kinds, and it is not necessary to add all kinds of other goods. This sale of purple was a business that required a large capital. Let us take it that Lydia was a widow and was carrying on her dead husband's business by importing from Thyatira and selling in Philippi. She was a business woman, capable, successful, rich. She has "a house" (family), ample accommodations for four men in her beautiful home. In those days, when women were greatly restricted and seldom launched out for themselves to any great extent, all this that is related about Lydia means much.

Paul's first European convert was no ordinary woman. Lydia was a proselyte of the gate; Luke uses the regular term for that idea: σεβομένη τὸν Θεόν (13:43). Since Philippi had no synagogue, it is only fair to conclude that she was drawn to Judaism already in Thyatira. It is not amiss to conclude that she was the leading spirit among the women whom Paul found at the prayer-place. At this time many pagan women of prominence found their way into the synagogues; note a sign of it in 13:50. The worship of the sun god Tyrimnas, to which her native city was devoted, had long lost its hold upon Lydia since she came to know the True God. Her business did not keep her away from the insignificant little prayer-place to reach which she had to travel far on the Sabbath.

We must combine the two duratives "she kept hearing" and "to be heeding," for they imply that Lydia was not converted on that very first Sabbath. From the beginning, however, she heard with a heart that was opened wide (διά in the verb) by the Lord. Little did she dream that Saturday morning what a treasure she was to find in the little retreat by the riverside; but she heard the great Apostle of the Gentiles himself set forth the blessed gospel of Jesus Christ with all fervor and all conviction, and this gospel was corroborated by his three companions. She was finding the pearl of great price.

The Lord opens the heart, but the hand with which he lifts the latch and draws the door is the Word which he makes us hear, and the door opens as we heed, προσέχειν, keep holding our mind to what we hear. No man can open the door of his heart (καρδία is the center of thought and will) himself, nor can he help the Lord to open it by himself lifting the latch and moving the door. The one thing he can do is to bolt the door, i. e., refuse to hear and to heed; and thus he can keep the door closed and bar it even more effectually than it was at first. This prevents conversion.

All the women at the prayer-place heard the missionaries speak, but all did not heed as Lydia did. The grace of hearing, however, none of them thrust away, and they may later have come to faith. The heeding may have followed when they afterward recalled the apostle's words to memory, perhaps discussed them with Lydia, or when they heard the same things preached a second time.

"The grace of hearing no man is able to ward off." Besser. But we must let God work the heeding through the hearing. Then will his blessed purpose be accomplished. Lydia came to faith. Luke says that this was accomplished through "the things spoken by Paul." He thus credits Paul with Lydia's conversion. This was undoubtedly the fact; Paul's companions at most reinforced what he said. In Lydia we have a beautiful example of adult conversion. There is no emotionalism, no ranting of the preacher to work up his hearer, no agitation and shouting by the hearer, but only the silent touch of the Spirit as the ear conveys the blessed truth to the heart, only the true inward assent, the blessed confidence and trust which presently manifest themselves in open confession.

15) **And when she was baptized and her house she besought, saying, If you have judged me to be faithful to the Lord, having come into my house, remain there. And she constrained us.**

Lydia's baptism followed in due order. When, where, and in what manner it was administered Luke does not say. The expression "and her house," meaning her household, leaves undetermined whether she and the rest were baptized at the same time, or she alone at this time and the rest later. The former seems the more probable, since by using a temporal clause Luke connects the baptism with Lydia's invitation to the missionaries to lodge in her house. May we say that at the solemn service in her house, when she and her household were baptized, she then and there insisted that these her teachers make her house their headquarters?

Who made up her "house"? When R., *W. P.*, states that nothing indicates that Lydia's "house" included more than "the women employed by her, who, like her, had heard the preaching of Paul and had believed," and when "possibly" Euodia and Syntyche

(Phil. 4:2, 3) are included in the supposition that Lydia may have employed many slaves and freedwomen in her trade, we fear that these women are assigned to the house in order to evade the statement that there were children. But even then, the more women are introduced, the greater is the likelihood of at least one child being present. Other writers state that οἶκος means servants or workpeople.

Now "her house," as here used, is the regular term for the members of one's immediate family. Thus any children Lydia may have had would be included. The word also includes servants, but *if* there happened to be servants we must not fill every "house" with a number of servants. We think Lydia did have servants; but we also know that Paul would never baptize even as much as one slave simply on the order of that slave's master. If any servants of Lydia's were baptized they of their own volition believed the Word they themselves had heard. "House" does *not* include employees generally, not even when such people believed. They had their own homes. As far as the text is concerned, Luke does not say or imply that the other women who were present at the river came to faith. We think some of them did, but Luke does not say so. It is also unwarranted to make all these women at the river servants or employees of Lydia. It lays them open to the charge that they associated themselves with Lydia only for mercenary reasons. What Paul writes about Euodia and Syntyche in Phil. 4:2, 3 simply states that the two were prominent women who were neither slaves nor mere employees of Lydia but had homes of their own.

One commentator states: "In the household baptisms (Cornelius, Lydia, the jailor, Crispus) one sees 'infants' or not according to his predilections or preferences." But why just "infants"? And why just these four households? Surely, the few baptisms of entire families during the time of the apostles on record were not the only ones that occurred. And the point at issue is in regard to children up to the age of discretion and not only "infants." The whole matter is rather simple. The apostles and their assistants baptized entire households and by baptism received them into the Christian Church. That was the standard apostolic practice. Where is the evidence that οἶκος ever meant less than "household," "family," referred only to the adults to the exclusion of the children? Granted that many servants and slaves were included, the likelihood of there being children is only increased; and who will count all the households thus received by baptism? Mark 10:13-16 settled the question for the apostles.

Equally unsatisfactory is the view that Lydia "submitted to baptism as proof that she was 'faithful to the Lord.' " Is that all her baptism involves? Was it only a submission and a proof that *she* offered? Did the Lord do nothing for her in and through baptism? Was Ananias mistaken when he said to Saul: "Be baptized and wash away — yes, wash away! — thy sins"? Was Lydia baptized "and her house" without the sacrament washing away their sins? Lydia did do something to prove that she was "faithful to the Lord." She besought her teachers to use her home as their lodging place while they remained in Philippi. That sounds as though they had thus far had very poor accommodations in the city. Her invitation was put in such a way that, if it were refused, this would imply that her teachers did not yet esteem her "faithful to the Lord." She uses the condition of reality: "If you have judged me to be faithful to the Lord," i. e., one who truly believes in and trusts the Lord. Paul seems to have declined this invitation at first, and we know that it was his principle to be burdensome to no one.

Luke writes: "And she constrained us," the aorist implying that she succeeded. This is another trait in

Lydia that makes her character lovely in our eyes. Christian hospitality is one of the outstanding virtues of the early church, and Lydia is the first outstanding example of it. In this Lydia from the very beginning gave a distinction to the church at Philippi. For this was the one congregation which later remembered the needs of the apostle and sent him kindly personal gifts, especially when he was in captivity in Rome. How Paul appreciated such remembrances he himself records in Phil. 4:15, etc. What an example for all future time! There are no greetings to Lydia in Paul's letter to the Philippians, in fact, this epistle contains no personal greetings at all. We must offer our own explanation as to the reason for this.

16) **And it came to pass as we were going to the prayer-place that a maid having a divining spirit met us, one such as was bringing her masters much income by divining.**

The accusative with the infinitive is the subject of ἐγένετο. Preaching at the prayer-place evidently continued for many days (v. 18). On one occasion, when Paul and his companions were going out to it, this παιδίσκη — the word commonly used as a designation for slave girl — met them. Luke describes her as "having a spirit," as one possessed. But to πνεῦμα he adds the apposition πύθωνα, which describes the character of this "spirit." This word "Python" originally designated the mythical serpent or dragon that dwelt in the region Pytho at the foot of the Parnassus in Phocis and was said to have guarded the oracle at Delphi until it was slain by the god Apollo. Then the word became the appellation for those who professed to reveal future events such as those associated with the Delphic oracle. It later came to mean merely a ventriloquist. Here the second sense of the word is referred to: the girl had "a spirit, a diviner," i. e., a divining spirit. The supposition that she was afflicted with a peculiar mental derangement that gave certain of her faculties an excessive sensitiveness and keenness is not in accord with Luke's language and describes a pathological condition that is otherwise not known.

This poor girl's terrible affliction was capitalized by "her masters" who had probably purchased her for this very reason. She was bringing (imperfect tense) them "much income" (ἐργασία) by divining (the participle denoting means). The masters charged a price for the information which people desired of the girl. The world has not changed in this respect. Girls are still exploited — just so money can be made through them, no matter what becomes of their souls or their bodies. And divining of all sorts still brings in good money, for men will not believe God but will believe the charlatans who profess to be able to pry into the future. In this case, of course, there was no charlatan but a demon speaking from the girl. Many are ready to believe that this spirit could foretell the future. Let them learn once for all that no devil or demon is able to perform even one genuine miracle, all their "miracles" are "pseudo," lying, spurious, and intended only to deceive, II Thess. 2:9. The spirit in this girl accomplished no more by means of his divining than our fortunetellers do today. Why, this spirit could not and did not know what was awaiting him, namely that in a few days he would be driven out of the girl by the power of Jesus!

17) **She, following after Paul and us, kept yelling, saying, These men are slaves of God, the Highest, such as are proclaiming to you salvation's way. And this she kept doing on many days.**

She met the missionaries, walked past them, then, however, turned around and followed behind them, crying out her information at the top of her voice and continuing this until the very gates of the city were reached. Just imagine the excitement she must have caused. When the Canaanitish woman did a similar thing, the disciples of Jesus could not endure it and asked Jesus to get rid of her, "for she crieth after us."

Two questions may be asked at this point. How did this girl know what she was doing, and why did she have to broadcast it to the world? These are the same two questions that arise with reference to all the demoniacs we read about in the Gospels. The fact that the devils know the Son of God need not be explained. They know him just as they know the other persons of the Godhead. The fact that this girl, apart even from the spirit that possessed her, should know Paul and his companions as preachers of God and of salvation's way is not even surprising. Paul did not in any way keep his work secret. All Philippi was free to know of it. This divining spirit had discovered no secret. He might have learned even more; for we must note that he says nothing about Jesus, or Christ, or God's Son. What he does say is no more than would apply to ordinary Jewish rabbis. It is quite possible that the girl was a Jewess, for she met the missionaries going out to the Jewish prayer-place. "God, the Highest" was a term that was familiar also to pagans; "salvation's way" sounds more Jewish. R., *W. P.*, regards the expression as indefinite: "a way of salvation" and remarks that many such have been offered to men and still are; but the qualitative genitive makes the expression definite: "salvation's way." The spirit is not speaking of *some* way of salvation but of *the one* way proclaimed by these missionaries. In regard to the "somewhat thorny subject" (R. 782) of the article and its absence with nouns and their genitives one must be rather careful.

It is the spirit's crying after the missionaries as such that constitutes the main point. It was intended especially for Paul, he being recognized as the leader;

for the girl did not follow merely "us" but "Paul and us" as Luke carefully writes. Imagine a venerable preacher accompanied by three colleagues going through town with a girl behind them pointing to them and crying, "These are preachers!" Or think of any other four professional men. That would certainly be disconcerting. People would stare, wonder, begin to talk, and ask all sorts of queer questions about such men. That is the wicked spirit's very intention in this case. This explanation suffices, so that we disregard the idea of this spirit's attempted fawning and flattery by his cries, or of expressing fear of stripes and torments and seeking to deprecate his well-known Master's anger.

18) This public demonstration the girl continued for "many days." Paul finally drove out the spirit. Why did he not do so sooner, and why not at once? Miracles are never wrought at the discretion of the human agent. They are in every instance wrought only by the will of the Lord. Paul had no directions from the Lord or his Spirit to act during those "many days," and that is why he did not, in fact, could not act. At last the divine directions came to him, and he promptly drove out the demon.

But Paul, having been deeply distressed and after turning to the spirit, said, I order thee in the name of Jesus Christ to go out of her! And he went out in that very hour.

Neither the first participle nor the second are causal. Not *because* this crying distressed him did Paul drive out the spirit. That is the mistaken idea that suggested the translation "worn out," as though Paul stood it so long, and then his patience was worn out completely. Διαπονηθείς was true already on the first day. The first participle states the inner feeling with which Paul acted, and the second the outward act. And this distress was not due to his own person but to the state of the girl and the effect on his work. We may venture to say that the Lord let it continue as long as he did because he wanted Paul to finish his work in Philippi; for after he drove out the spirit Paul had to leave the city (v. 39, 40).

The spirit is ordered to leave and forthwith leaves. We must construe the dative with the participle: Paul turned to the spirit. The fact that he spoke to the spirit is made plain by what he said. The position of the dative indicates that it is to be construed with the participles, and when it is construed thus, this dative affects also the verb "said" by showing to whom the words were said. "In the name of Jesus Christ" is never to be taken in the sense of "by the authority of," etc., but always: "in connection with the revelation of Jesus Christ." See the explanation in 2:38 ("name" already in 2:21). Follow ὄνομα in all these and in similar connections and clear up this important point. NAME — NAME — NAME goes echoing through the Scriptures.

19) But now the trouble begins. One should suppose that all men would acclaim the deed of the apostle, see in it the hand of "God, the Highest," and a sample of the "salvation" his messengers bring; but worldly eyes took a different view. **But her masters, on seeing that their hope of income was gone out, having laid hold on Paul and Silas, dragged them to the market place to the rulers and, having brought them to the praetors, said, These men are exceedingly stirring up our city, being Jews, and are proclaiming customs which it is not lawful for us to receive or to practice, being Romans. And the multitude rose up together against them. And the praetors, having stripped off their garments, were ordering to beat them with rods. And having put many blows on them, they threw them into prison, having ordered the jailor to keep them safely; who, having received**

such an order, threw them into the inner prison and made their feet fast in the stocks.

This was the reward for the priceless service rendered to the poor victim of the devil.

The fact that the girl was owned by several "masters" is made plain by the plural which cannot here denote a succession of masters. Their hope of income "was gone out." Luke uses the very verb he employed when the spirit "was gone out." The worldly look for monetary gain; the hope for that dims the higher hope, blots it out altogether. Touch the unconverted moneybag and hear what a devilish noice results. A fine example is Demetrius at Ephesus. Just how soon these "masters" discovered their great loss we are unable to say, but it must have been soon, perhaps by the time Paul came back from the prayer-place if that is where he again went this day. These masters were evidently in a rage, judging from the way in which they pounced upon Paul and Silas and dragged them into the *agora* or market place to the rulers. Why Luke and Timothy were not with Paul and Silas is not indicated. The fact that they were absent was providential, for they thereby escaped being compelled to leave the city. The Lord's hand ruled even in apparent disaster. The *agora* was the public square or forum where the people gathered for business and for other purposes. The magisterial offices, courts, etc., were usually located at or near the market place.

We find no difficulty in the two clauses "dragged them to the market place to the rulers," and the next, "having brought them to the praetors." Why should these "rulers" and the "praetors" be the same? It lies on the surface that the two praetors did not attend to petty cases but only to graver matters. These "rulers" were what we should call the police court with its officers, who could be easily reached. This is why Luke says no more about them; they turned the case over to the praetors. We see why, when we note the extravagant charges launched against Paul and Silas. Something that affected the whole city belonged to the two supreme judges.

20) Thus Paul and Silas came before the στρατηγοί, the *duumviri*, mentioned in v. 12, the highest authority in the colonial cities, who tried infractions of the Roman laws. They gloried in the title στρατηγοί which was the proper equivalent of the Latin *praetores*. We are amazed to hear the charge. There is not one word about the girl and her deliverance from the demon and, of course, not a breath about losing the wicked income from her affliction. Instead of this they prefer the inflammatory charge that Paul and Silas were Jews and as such were setting the city by the ears. This was a rank appeal to race prejudice coupled with religious animosity. The single word "Jews" was thrown out like a firebrand. The emperor Claudius had recently expelled all Jews from Rome (18:2), and it was the pride of every colonial city to become more or less a replica of Rome. This would be especially true of a colony that had as many Romans as Philippi had. It had scarcely any Jews in it, not enough even to maintain the smallest kind of a synagogue. And here were two Jews caught in the very act of stirring up the city exceedingly (ἐκ in the verb). No wonder Rome had ousted all Jews.

21) "Jews" — think of it! And now the deadly specification is added: these Jews "are proclaiming customs which it is not lawful for us to receive or to practice, being Romans." "Jews — Romans," take in the full contrast. And do not forget the ungodly pride that is associated with "Romans," men who had conquered and were now ruling the whole world! "Englishmen," "Americans" are superior titles today, but in the whole world of today there is no capital that is at all comparable to Rome in its imperial days, and hence

there is no title of such imperial grandeur as "Romans." It is cunningly mild on the part of these accusers to speak of "customs which it is not lawful for us to receive or practice, being Romans." The very idea of even suggesting that these lords of the world should change their customs and change them for those of Jews — think of it, of Jews! A barb is thrust in: "which it is not lawful." "Not lawful?" —— just negative? why, that would be outright treason!

We must note the shrewdness of this charge. The "customs" are left wholly to the imagination, not one of them is named; all that is said is that they come from "Jews" and are offered to "Romans." The accusers themselves do not know what they mean by these "customs." They know nothing at all about Paul and Silas, have paid no attention to them until this time when the girl is no longer a source of income. They heard only the word "Jews" and may have had only a vague idea as to what a real Jew was. It is safe to say that they had never even heard the word "Christians" (11:26). But their rage and their revenge had to find some outlet. This is a counterpart to the charges which the Sanhedrin launched against Jesus before Pilate. Both were equally based on nothing, both equally hid the real vicious motive, and both even attempted to uphold the interest of Rome. But the Sanhedrists were baser. They had the divine law, these pagans had only idols.

22) The two or three owners of the girl could never have dragged Paul and Silas to the police court with their own hands; but they had men enough with them. And this drew an ὄχλος, a crowd, just as any excitement will. The charge before the praetors repeated only what had been told the rulers or police officers. When it was made again with strident voices, this crowd rose up to support and second the accusers against Paul and Silas. The σύν in the verb refers to the accus-

ers, the crowd was "with" them. They "rose up" means that they became tumultuous with shouts and cries "against them," the two accused "Jews," and κατά ("down") suggests that they shouted: "Down with them! Down with them!" or something of the sort. That is the way of silly crowds. The praetors thus had an ocular demonstration of how the city was being stirred up exceedingly except that not Paul and Silas but these Jew baiters were doing the stirring. The missionaries had worked in great quietness, and their first general advertisement had been the miracle performed on the girl.

The two praetors were simply swept off their feet. They did not have the sense of Pilate. Roman praetors they were but showed not a trace of it before this mob. Roman dignity, Roman justice, Roman law which hears the accused face to face with the accusers, preferably under the open sky — all were lacking in this wild disorder. The praetors order their lictors, the ῥαβδοῦχοι of v. 38 (see v. 12) to strip the accused and to beat them with their official rods. The usual formula was: "Go, lictors, strip off their garments; let them be scourged!" Ῥαβδίζειν = *virgis caedere.* Paul refers to this infliction in II Cor. 11:25, and to two others that are not otherwise recorded. He mentions the shameful treatment which he received here at Philippi in I Thess. 2:2; it was outrageous in the extreme.

The wording: "the praetors, having stripped off their garments" becomes ridiculous when Ramsay lets these praetors strip off their own garments. And not with their own hands did the praetors tear the clothes from the victims; this, as all other actions of violence, was carried out by the hands of the lictors at the command of the praetors. So Pilate, so the Jews crucified Jesus. What one commands or to what one consents he himself thereby does. "To beat them with rods" needs no subject; the lictors did the beating. We must note the imperfect ἐκέλευον. The Jews scourged with forty blows less one, a fixed number; the Romans did not count. So when the lictors went to work they did not know when to stop and after beating a while looked up to the praetors for a signal. These praetors repeatedly ordered them to go on. That is what the imperfect intends to say.

This thing was done right there; the praetors were influenced by the jubilant mob. It thus happened that neither Paul nor Silas could assert their right as Roman citizens whom no Roman court could flog. We may take it that they tried to warn the praetors, but all their efforts were in vain. If any of the lictors heard them they just laughed.

23) All that Luke is able to say is that "they put many blows upon them," for no one kept count. We calmly read these few words as we do those others: "Pilate took and scourged Jesus." But they are filled with excruciating pain and horrible disgrace. Under the many blows the skin would be broken, the blood would ooze out, and inflamed welts would cover the whole back. And all this was wholly illegal according to Roman law, was inflicted on innocent men without process of law to satisfy a few greedy men and a wholly ignorant mob. The gospel and Jesus were not even mentioned during the whole affair. The punishment was intended for Paul and Silas because they were Jews. But this was the calling of the apostles, to suffer innocently for welldoing. If some share of such suffering comes to us, shall we not also take it?

Since they were regarded as two dangerous vagabond Jewish agitators, the praetors intended to look further into their case and remanded them to prison. The Roman prison usually had three distinct parts: the *communiora,* where the prisoners had light and air; the *interiora,* which was shut off by strong iron gates and had bars and locks; and the *tullianum* or dungeon for executions, where prisoners condemned to die were confined. Chrysostom's supposition that in this case the jailor (literally, "the guard of bonds") was the Stephanus mentioned in I Cor. 16:15 is an unreliable guess.

This prison warden received orders not only to lock up Paul and Silas but "to keep them safely," which means that he was held responsible with his own life for their safekeeping as were the guards that kept Peter in 12:4, who lost their lives after his escape. So this warden took no chances and threw them into the dungeon; and even here "he made safe their feet in the wood," i. e., in the stocks, which were both a fetter and an instrument of torture, for the feet were locked wide apart and held in that painful position. Note the middle voice ἠσφαλίσατο, he made them safe on his own account. Bleeding, bruised, sore, without anything to assuage their wounds, Paul and Silas lay in the black dungeon in this painful position. This was the last place in the world to do missionary work but the very place where they were given such work to do by the Lord.

25) **But along midnight Paul and Silas, praying, were singing hymns to God, and the prisoners were attentively listening to them. And suddenly there occurred a great earthquake so that the foundations of the prison were shaken. And forthwith all the doors were opened, and the fetters of all were let go.**

Nihil crus sentit in vervo quum animus in coelo est: "Nothing the limb feels in the stocks when the mind is in heaven." Tertullian. What else could they have done in such pain and wretchedness of body than to pray to God? The present participle and the imperfect verb express simultaneous action: their singing was praying. What hymns they sang we, of course, do not know, but the psalms of David have ever been dear to those who suffer, especially also to those who suffer wrong. We may be sure that their praying hymns were not a weary wail. They were rather a petition for deliverance according to the good and wise counsel of God, a petition for fortitude and strength to bear their cross, and prayers for the furtherance of God's work in the midst of their enemies and for the conversion of many.

Such conduct a Roman prison had never experienced, but, of course, it had never confined such Christians before this. No wonder "the prisoners were attentively listening to them." The jailor had forgotten to fetter their lips, their hearts he could not fetter. "And if among those captives there was a malefactor like the one at the right side of Christ's cross, Paul and Silas sang him into Paradise." Besser. In his city mission work in Berlin, Stoecker employed bands of singing boys, each band under a good leader, and thus sang the gospel into many a cold and arid heart; and this work of the *Kurrendensaenger* may still be going on. Paul was here learning what he afterward put into such comforting language in Romans eight.

26) We know in what way the Twelve and especially Peter were released from prison (5:19; 12:7, etc.), namely through an angel. This time the Lord used an earthquake with results (ὥστε) that were phenomenal and such as the Lord intended to achieve by this means. The Lord is never bound to a single means to achieve his end. *Weg hat er aller Wege, an Mitteln fehlt's ihm nicht.* We see why the Lord used an earthquake in this instance: he intended to release all the prisoners in that prison and not merely Paul and Silas. In Jerusalem and among Jews the Lord used an angel, in Philippi among pagans he used an earthquake. We call the one means supernatural, the other natural, and that may pass as far as the agencies are concerned; but we dare not surrender the conviction that both were

employed by the Lord and in that sense were supernatural.

Now winds, waters, earthquakes, and other disturbances of nature often play curious "pranks" as we call them, but they are in reality not pranks at all. Like the disturbance itself, all that they effect and do is in the hand of divine providence down to the least point. So it was here when the very foundations of the prison were shaken, when all the doors were opened, and all the fetters of the prisoners were let go (ἀνέθη, from ἀνίημι, first aorist passive without augment, note the passive). This does not mean that the doors were thrown ajar; they were opened in the sense that their heavy locks and bars no longer held. So also the fetters and the stocks were made to let go; the bolts in the walls fell out and no longer held the chains; the lock in the stocks was sprung open or burst from the beams. Yet not a single prisoner was hurt. These miraculous features were so plain that all the prisoners could see them.

Just as all the prisoners heard the prayer-hymns which Paul and Silas sang to God, so these prisoners were to see God's miraculous answer to those prayers and praises. They could not but connect the two. As by their singing Paul and Silas were really preaching the Word to these prisoners, so by his deed of power God put his own tangible seal on that word. Strange kind of missionary work! But it is exactly the same as when God supported the apostolic preaching by means of other miracles. In this instance, however, the miracle was new and different.

27) **But the jailor, having been roused out of sleep and having seen that the doors of the prison had been opened, having drawn his short sword, was about to make away with himself, supposing that the prisoners had fled. But Paul called with**

a great voice, saying, Do thyself no harm, for we are all here!

Let us not imagine that this warden had no assistants, that he alone kept the prison and, after locking it up securely, had peacefully gone to bed in his own adjoining house. He had guards, and some of them kept guard all night. They are not important for the story and therefore are ignored. They certainly rushed to the outside when the earthquake began. Note the use of no less than five participles in three tenses in the Greek, and all are placed with exactness. The first two go together: the jailor was aroused from sleep (became ἔξυπνος) and then saw the prison doors, the perfect participle describes these as having been opened and as thus being open. On rushing out the guards had left those through which they fled wide open. This much the jailor saw without lights. Paul and Silas must have gone toward the main entrance which was now wide open; the other prisoners perhaps crowded around or back of them. They were invisible to the jailor who stood outside the building.

Then the jailor drew his short sword, the regular Roman weapon; but this participle has no καί before it because this action is very closely connected with the verb "was about to make away with himself," namely by this means. Finally, the durative participle at the end: "supposing the prisoners to have fled." He saw the gaping door but not a prisoner anywhere. Panic seized him, and the next thought was suicide. The imperfect implies that something intervened. It was Paul's tremendous shout. *When* the jailor got awake (temporal) and *because* he saw (causal), etc., then *by* the act of drawing his sword (means) he was about to kill himself, *since* he was supposing (again causal) the prisoners have fled (perfect, implying that they are far away and still fleeing; it is like the perfect participle used with reference to the doors).

The Roman law dealt severely with jailors who were unable to produce the prisoners who had been put into their custody. If prisoners who were liable to the death penalty were lost, the jailor himself would be promptly executed in their stead. That is why the jailor, despairing of his own life when he thought that all his prisoners had escaped, preferred to kill himself rather than to be ignominiously killed by the praetors. But what a difference between the happy apostles singing amid their suffering, shame, and mortal danger and this pagan Roman who, even before he is certain of his calamity, would resort to suicide! But this was true Roman teaching, for had not Cassius, when he was defeated, covered his face and ordered his freedmen to kill him in his tent here at Philippi? Had not Titinius, his messenger, done the same as being properly "a Roman's part"? Had not Brutus and many others done likewise? This is the pagan wisdom of the world: when everything seems lost, cap it with suicide, a quick death. The worldling's philosophy has not advanced one step since King Saul killed himself. It is the devil's own trick to rush a man into self-destruction; a Judas died by his own hand.

28) We take it that through the open door and in the light which the night afforded Paul saw the action of the jailor and with a great shout stopped him: "Do thyself nothing base!" the peremptory aorist subjunctive in a negative command. The distinction between πράσσειν, "practice," and ποιεῖν, "do," is not always observed although the Greek idiom would prefer the former here. Paul knew the reason and the motive of the jailor and therefore offers the one assurance that would stop him, the statement that all the prisoners were still there. Now you may ask how Paul knew that, and in the following you may ask still more questions that Luke disregards altogether. Just take it for granted that Paul automatically took charge of

matters just as he did later in the desperate situation recorded in 27:21-44. Paul was master here, one who understood exactly what God was doing and never for a moment lost his wits.

We need not wonder that none of the prisoners attempted to flee. The effect of the praying and the singing of Paul and Silas was still in their hearts, and this was combined with the tremendous effect of the earthquake, which to all of them could not but appear as the direct intervention of the God to whom these two had so strangely and so effectively prayed. So they all stood together, and not a man made a wrong move. Let us not forget, however, that the shackles with which they had been bound were removed from their fastenings in the wall but still clung to their wrists or their feet.

29) **And, having asked for lights, he rushed in and, having become trembling, he fell down before Paul and Silas and, having brought them outside, said, Lords, what is necessary for me to do that I be saved?**

Paul's shout checked the jailor's suicidal attempt, and he asked for lights to assure himself that it was true that all of the prisoners were still there. We regard it as scarcely a possibility that the members of the jailor's own family brought those lights, namely torches. We prefer to think of the jailor's assistants who had been on guard and had run out of the building when the earthquake made it rock with an accompanying roar. They ran out but were at hand and obeyed the order to bring lights. There, sure enough, were all the prisoners, not one was gone.

Then the jailor sank to his knees before Paul and Silas, the men whom he had caused extra tortures by locking their feet in the stocks. He was overwhelmed with gratitude to Paul and Silas, to whom he attributed the fact that no prisoner had escaped. He was still shaking because of his terrible experience when he a moment ago was trying to take his life. What a scene for those other prisoners! What thoughts must have raced through their minds? Besser exclaims: "Behold the man from Macedonia! And if he had been the only one in all Macedonia to be brought to salvation, Paul and Silas would gladly have suffered the scourging and the pain of the stocks for this one."

30) After they had lifted him up with gentle yet firm words, he brought them out of the prison. What about the other prisoners? We decline to believe that the jailor himself first bound them securely, and equally that he just left them inside the prison without further attention. Why do some commentators suppose that this jailor was alone? To account for the lights they bring in the family, but to account for the other prisoners the family will not do, so the jailor either attends to them or just leaves them. The jailor's assistants attend to these prisoners.

Where did this jailor take Paul and Silas? Luke writes: προαγαγὼν αὐτοὺς ἔξω, "having led them forward outside" — the prison was left behind. It is Luke's custom to mention only the essential facts, and here the fact is that the great question of the jailor was asked after the jailor had led the prisoners out of the prison.

We do not think that the jailor's question was asked immediately after he and his prisoners were outside of the prison. It must have occurred after the jailor had fully collected himself. Luke does not tell us what led to the question. Zahn thinks that the jailor asked his question just outside of the prison door and that it was not a question but an expression of worry regarding the loss of his position for some negligence with which the praetors might charge him, and that Paul then surprised the poor fellow by giving him an answer when he had expected none. "Saved" is then understood in the sense of saved from losing his position. But this is too unlikely. When was the gospel offered a man who was still upset by panic and worry about his job?

While we do not know just what led to the jailor's question we at once see that beneath the man's rough exterior there beat a poor, wretched human heart. God had reached into his life, this God of Paul and Silas who was greater that Jupiter or any god of Olympus. The man's whole inner nature had been shaken; he had been tossed between life and death. Had he heard Paul and Silas singing in the prison? Did he know their real story? One thing is certain, his word about being saved (ἵνα σωθῶ) is a direct echo of the possessed girl's word about "salvation's way (ὁδὸν σωτηρίας)" in v. 17. Luke is giving us only the final outcome of what happened after the jailor took the missionaries away from the prison.

Κύριοι is only an address of humility. It is an eloquent expression of the jailor's feeling toward Paul and Silas. Undue fear of synergism lays stress on ποιεῖν as though the man intended to say that he would "do" something to merit salvation or to prepare himself for it. The earthquake had removed all high ideas regarding himself from his heart. We have noted this question already in 2:37, and in 9:6. Neither the apostles nor Jesus (in Luke 10:25; 18:18) act as though the question in regard to doing something had anything wrong about it; see the discussion on 2:37. Paul answers this question exactly as it is put by telling the man what he is to "do." The same is true with regard to the clause ἵνα σωθῶ and the verb "to be saved" (see 4:12 regarding "salvation"). Paul answers by using this same great verb, and no one need attempt to show that the sense in which Paul used it was totally different from that implied in the jailor's question.

This man had looked death in the face, and divine "saving" was not a remote subject to him. Whatever imperfect conceptions he may have had, he saw before him two astounding men who were undisturbed by fear amid an earthquake, undismayed by their punishment, who spoke of God in a mighty sense — they had been saved, and the jailor wanted this same salvation. If we knew what preceded his asking this question we should see that the jailor's question came to his lips most naturally. From the answer of Paul and Silas we may conclude that the jailor's family was present. In that question the man laid open his heart.

31) That is why it received an answer that was so crystal clear, an answer that has gone down through the ages, that has answered this same question in unnumbered hearts and satisfied those hearts as nothing else could satisfy them. **And they said, Believe on the Lord Jesus, and thou shalt be saved, thou and thy house. And they spoke to him the Word of the Lord together with all those in his house.**

Here we have the most astounding piece of mission work recorded in Acts: it is done in the small hours of the night for the jailor and his family by the jailor's prisoners! Here we have the gospel in a nutshell, its quintessence expressed in simplest form: faith, Jesus, salvation. Many find a play on words in Paul's answer: as though the missionaries said, look not to us as "lords" but to the One who is truly the "Lord"; but this is imaginary. The common address toward a superior was "lord," and the missionaries did not repudiate the title and its meaning as used by the jailor. When the word was used by believers with reference to Jesus, it meant divine Lord, Lord in the supreme sense, and was thus clear. Luke compresses the answer into a few strong words. As the next verse shows, it was fully expanded so that the gospel was presented to the jailor and to his family in all its saving power.

Πίστευσον is properly the aorist, for the moment one believes, salvation is his. "To believe" always means to put all trust and confidence in the Lord Jesus, in other words, by such trust of the heart to throw the personality entirely into his arms for deliverance from sin, death, and hell. Here ἐπί is used; this trust is to rest on Jesus. This the jailor is to "do." He must do the believing, every individual in his household likewise, for no one can do the believing for others. But faith is not our own production. Even in ordinary life confidence is awakened and produced in us by the one in whom we believe. The same holds true with reference to Jesus who is most worthy of our confidence and trust. To come in contact with him is to be moved to trust him and him alone for salvation. For this reason unbelief is such a crime. It is the refusal to trust him who is supremely worthy of trust.

Jesus has salvation, offers and bestows it. To trust him is to let him give us that salvation. To refuse is to mistrust and distrust him and his salvation, which means to remain unsaved although salvation is actually extended to us. His very name means "Savior." The result of letting Jesus draw us to trust him is to be saved. The future passive "thou shalt be saved" makes Jesus the agent, the one who saves. But this future tense is not to be dated at some distant time, say at the hour of one's death. This future is relative to the preceding aorist in the sense that believing is forthwith followed by being saved. To believe is to accept the divine gift of salvation and at once to have it. This is a logical future: faith — salvation; never in the reverse order. There is no interval of time between them.

"Thou" is expressed already by the verb ending. When the pronoun is added it becomes emphatic: "thou shalt be saved, thou and thy house" (family, household). The jailor's believing will certainly not save his wife, children, etc. As he must believe in his person, so must each member of his house in his or her person. Here again there is family religion as in v. 15,

Lydia "and her house." See v. 15 in regard to the question concerning children.

32) This theme of believing, etc., was fully elaborated by Paul and Silas. The pain and the blows inflicted by the lictors and the torture of the hours in the stocks were practically forgotten by Paul and Silas when it came to preaching the gospel for the saving of souls. Again we meet the individualization: "to him (personally) together with all those in his house (in the same personal way)." The aorists occurring in v. 31, 32 already imply that the speaking was not in vain.

33) **And having taken them aside in that hour of the night, he washed them from the blows, and he was baptized, he and all his, immediately. And having brought them up into the house, he set a table beside them and exulted with his whole house, having believed God.**

Luke writes: *παραλαβὼν αὐτούς*, "having taken them aside in that hour of the night," *παρά*, "aside," where there was water, and there "he washed them from the blows," washed off the dried blood and laved the hot and inflamed welts. Callously this pagan jailor had thrust these men into the prison and added the cruel stocks to their pain; but he now seeks to undo the cruelty inflicted upon the two victims as much as he can. His heart was now completely changed. This was the first work of the man's faith. Pagan cruelty and callousness is changed into Christian mercy and tenderness. Behold what the gospel does! It always does this. And yet many spurn its blessed converting and renewing power.

One of the curiosities of exegesis is the assumption that the jailor took the two men down into the cellar where there was water. Here in the cellar, we are told, the jailor drew a bath, and after the two had bathed in the same cellar, the whole family was baptized. This interpretation is made to depend on the preposition used in the participle: "having taken them *aside*."

If this idea of a cellar is curious, and if the sane view is that the washing took place in the courtyard, one would think that all is then taken care of. Here in the courtyard there would be a well, a cistern in the ground, or a tank above ground, either of the latter two containing rain water from the roof. A basin or a tub would be used for washing the bloody backs of the missionaries, the jailor doing this washing. But immersionists are not satisfied with this explanation. R., *W. P.*, would have us choose between "the pool or tank" mentioned by De Wette and "the rectangular basin (*impluvium*), or even a swimming pool (*kolumbethra*) found within the walls of the prison" mentioned by Kuinol. Please note the names of the authorities used and the main point, somehow to get enough water for an immersion! Now this "tank" is especially interesting! Imagine Paul and Silas in this tank and then the jailor and his family! Now the jailor may have had a tank, but it had a spigot to draw out the water into vessels as it was needed. The water in the tank was kept clean and was not used to wash off blood into it or the filth of bathing bodies. Does this need to be said?

On the question of immersion see 2:41. The jailor and his family were baptized in the ordinary way by an application of water in the name of the Triune God. The quantity of water present is wholly immaterial. Zoeckler offers another curiosity by thinking that the baptismal act was partly *immergendo*, partly *adspergendo*. But why this difference?

Was this baptism performed too hastily? Could instruction and all that was necessary be completed in one night when the family was pagan? We may leave this question with Paul and Silas and the answer they gave. We know that they never baptized before their converts were fully prepared.

34) Why need one think that the jailor lived upstairs above the prison? "Having brought them up into the house" is fully satisfied by his leading Paul and Silas up the few steps from the courtyard to the house and its dining-room. The expression that he placed a table beside them implies that the missionaries had had nothing to eat for some time, apparently since the morning of the previous day. Whether the low table had the food on it when it was brought in we are unable to say. The two dined from couches in the usual way. The jailor did everything in his power for these his great benefactors.

One is struck by the fact that Luke adds a record of the feelings of the jailor and his family. A little while before this black despair had him by the throat with suicide the only escape, now "he exulted," was jubilant, with salvation in his possession. That is what the gospel does; this was a glorious exhibition of its power. Πανοικί (-εί) occurs in the papyri. A little while previously the family was about to be bereaved by a tragic death, now all had life everlasting. R., *W. P.*, thinks the adverb is amphibolous, that it may be construed with either the verb or the participle; but this views the matter only in the abstract. When the jailor exulted, his entire family exulted. The fact that the entire family believed has already been stated. The context leads us to construe the adverb with the verb. The dative after πεπιστευκώς means that the jailor "has believed God," namely what God said. In v. 15 "the Lord" is used in the case of Lydia. Some think that this is due to the fact that she was a Jewess, while the jailor was a pagan. But in v. 31 Paul says: "Believe on the Lord Jesus Christ," and he is speaking to this very pagan. So we conclude that there was no difference between Lydia and the jailor. The identification of the jailor with the Clement mentioned in Phil. 4:3 is only a guess.

35) **Now, day having come, the praetors sent the lictors, saying, Release those men! And the jailor reported the words to Paul: The praetors have sent in order that you be released; now, therefore, having come out, be going in peace. But Paul said to them: Having hided us in public not subjected to trial, men that are Romans, they threw us into prison; and now secretly they are throwing us out? No indeed! But having come themselves, let them lead us out!**

The additions of the Codex Bezae found in this paragraph are no more than a commentator's effort to add to the story here and there. In connection with v. 35 the reader at once wonders how the praetors came to reverse themselves so completely in the morning. The Codex Bezae answers: they came to their offices in the Agora, remembered the earthquake, got frightened because of that, and so sent the lictors to release Paul and Silas. But Luke usually reports just the facts and not the motivation for them when he has no direct knowledge of what this was. He does so here. This right-about-face of the praetors remains unexplained. Whether even Paul and Luke ever found out what brought it about we do not know. They probably guessed as we still do. The supposition that the praetors in some way connected the earthquake with Paul and Silas and the treatment they had received seems unlikely. It is more likely that the praetors discovered the real reason for the false accusations against Paul and Silas and therefore ordered them released.

We also have no difficulty with the order to the jailor, "Release those men!" That command records only the gist of the order and not the whole of it. The lictors were noted in v. 12.

36) The jailor is evidently happy to report this order to his benefactors. Luke mentions only Paul because it was he who refused to be released in this way. The jailor bids the missionaries go in peace. "In peace" is the word of a friend and brother. But where were these two men? Certainly not, as some suppose, in the jailor's house in comfort. Beautiful as that would have been, Paul and Silas would not have risked this for the sake of the jailor himself. If this were found out by the praetors, they would most likely have removed him from his position. They were back in the prison at their own insistence. No one surmised that the praetors would so quickly release them; they, as well as the jailor, expected that the lictors would summon them for trial as soon as possible.

37) Πρὸς αὐτούς is generally taken to mean that the lictors themselves were present, but one cannot be sure; the phrase may well mean that the jailor is to transmit Paul's answer to the lictors. The apostle intends to teach these precipitate praetors a necessary and wholesome lesson, one, too, that is in the interest of the believers in Philippi. These praetors are to understand thoroughly that the men behind the proclamation of the gospel are Roman citizens. And these praetors had flagrantly broken the severe laws which safeguarded the rights of Roman citizens. Paul's answer is according. In unmistakable terms it points out the crime which the praetors had committed and insists on an act of reparation, one which, though it cannot make good the serious wrong done, yet acknowledges that wrong and returns to Paul and Silas the honor they rightly claim. The praetors may congratulate themselves for being let off so easily. This is the purport of Paul's answer to the praetors.

Δέρω means "to skin," "to flay," and thus comes to mean "to beat severely," "to give one a hiding." The praetors had publicly hided Paul and Silas before many witnesses. They had done this to men "not subjected to trial," ἀκατακρίτους, "without having been tried." And these men were "Romans" who were under the aegis of the great Roman law.

The praetors had thrown these Romans into prison. The *Lex Valeria* B. C. 509, and the *Lex Poscia* B. C. 248 made it a crime to inflict blows upon a Roman citizen. Cicero is quoted: "To fetter a Roman citizen was a crime, to scourge him a scandal, to slay him — patricide." Ἀκατάκριτος is found only here and in 22:25, but the meaning "uncondemned" (our versions) cannot be maintained because it would imply that condemned Romans might be beaten, which was not the case. To have condemned them and then to have them beaten would exclude the plea that the thing had been done ignorantly, not knowing that Romans were concerned; the trial would have brought out their Roman citizenship. This word brings out an aggravating circumstance in the crime of the praetors. It signifies "not subjected to trial," B.-P. 45. The praetors had rushed ahead blindly, had not paused even to begin a trial, had merely ordered the beating and the imprisonment. The whole business had been criminally wrong. At the very start of the trial the praetors should have learned that they had Roman citizens before them. These praetors had made themselves liable to severe penalties. We see that Paul fully knows and asserts his rights as a Roman citizen.

Having committed these criminal acts, do these praetors now think they can throw these Roman citizens out secretly and so rid themselves of what they have done? Οὐ γάρ. "Not much!" (R. 1190). As the least reparation he can accept Paul demands that they come in person and lead him and Silas out and thereby acknowledge the wrong and honor the prisoners as Roman citizens. That was in truth little enough. It is plainly implied that Paul and Silas were again in the prison. Paul's claim that he is a Roman is never challenged for the simple reason that to make a false claim to this effect entailed death.

Here we have the first mention of Paul's citizenship, and 22:29 adds that he was born a Roman. His father, then, had this precious right, perhaps also his grandfather. This could not have been due to merely living in Tarsus, an *urbs libera;* the city was not even a Roman colony. Only two possibilities are thus open: the right was purchased (22:28), or it was granted for special service to the state. How the family of Paul obtained it we do not know. The same is true with regard to Silas who was a Roman like Paul. All we know about his being a Roman is what Paul here says.

38) **And the lictors reported these utterances to the praetors; but they became frightened on hearing that they were Romans. And having come, they besought them and, having led them out, began requesting them to go away from the city. And having gone out of the prison, they went in to Lydia; and having seen the brethren, they comforted them and went out.**

Fear came upon the praetors when they heard the report of the lictors and found what crimes they had committed against these Romans. These crimes might easily have cost them their lives. The governor of Macedonia would have given them a summary trial, and an appeal to the emperor would have been hopeless. We may translate the ingressive aorist, "they became terrified."

39) We may be sure that the praetors came in haste and "besought" Paul and Silas with placating words. We see, too, that they did what Paul had demanded and themselves led him and Silas out of the prison. But why did they request that they leave the city? Of course, Luke again states only the fact and omits the reason for it. With the imperfect ἠρώτων he

implies that the praetors kept requesting, but that Paul made no promise — the matter is held in suspense. The reason that the praetors were so concerned to get Paul and Silas out of the city is very apparent. If they remained, the criminal action of these praetors might easily become known among the Roman colonists, and then woe to them! No wonder they so earnestly made this request.

40) After having said that the praetors led Paul and Silas out, Luke repeats, as if to impress it upon his reader, that they "went out of the prison." They literally conferred a favor on the praetors by doing so. Think how they were thrown in, and now how they go out. Luke loves contrasts such as this. The night had brought them no sleep. Without having answered the request of the praetors, the two men went to Lydia, to their lodging place. Here they met τοὺς ἀδελφούς, and for the first time and in this one word we learn that the mission work done in Philippi had been far more successful than Luke has reported. He has sketched only two of the interesting and significant stories connected with this work, that of the first convert, and that of this last event before Paul and Silas left the city. A congregation was left behind when Paul and Silas departed. They comforted all these brethren and, when they were at last ready, they left. But not because of the praetors. They left because the work had been established in Philippi, because it could be left, and because elsewhere work was waiting to be done. Moreover, only Paul and Silas left, Timothy and Luke remained behind. The "we" that began in v. 10 is now dropped: "they went out" of the city, "they," not "we." Timothy and Luke continued to work in Philippi. We again meet the former in 17:14, the latter not until 20:5 ("us").

CHAPTER XVII

THE SECOND MISSIONARY JOURNEY: THESSALONICA AND BEREA

1) Timothy and Luke were left behind in Philippi to continue the work there; Paul and Silas left this city. **Now, having made their way through Amphipolis and Apollonia, they went to Thessalonica where there was a synagogue of the Jews.** They followed the great Roman road, the *Via Egnatia*, for thirty-two miles to Amphipolis, the capital of the first of the four districts into which the Romans had divided the kingdom of Macedonia. The city was thus named from the fact that the river Strymon flowed around nearly all of it. They went on without stopping, another thirty-two miles to Apollonia which was also on the Egnatian Way. Here, too, they did not stop but proceeded about thirty-six miles farther to Thessalonica on the great Roman road, the capital of the second of the four great divisions of Macedonia, which finally became the capital of the entire province. When Cassander rebuilt it he changed its name Therma to Thessalonica in honor of his wife, the sister of Alexander the Great. It shared the commerce of the Aegean Sea with Corinth and with Ephesus. Politically it ranked with Antioch in Syria and Caesarea in Palestine. It is now called Saloniki.

The reason that Paul and Silas made no halt in the two other cities was, in part at least, due to the fact that neither had a synagogue while Thessalonica had one from which work could readily be begun. I Thess. 1:8 shows what a strategic center Thessalonica became, for the gospel sounded forth from it into Macedonia and Achaia. The fact that some cities were passed by when the gospel was brought to a province must not be taken to mean that the gospel was not to be offered to them. This would come later. After it had taken root in the proper centers, the intervening cities and territories would be reached in due time.

2) **And according to the custom for Paul he went in to them and on three Sabbaths reasoned with them from the Scriptures, opening up and submitting on his part that it was necessary for the Christ to suffer and to arise from the dead, and that this One is the Christ, the Jesus whom I on my part am proclaiming to you.**

The phrase in regard to what was customary for Paul helps to indicate why he passed by the two cities and made a halt in Thessalonica: here he could work in his chosen and most rapid way by beginning in the synagogue. Εἰωθός is the neuter of the second perfect participle of ἔθω, the perfect, however, being used with the force of the present: "what is customary." On three consecutive Sabbaths Paul and Silas attended the synagogue and "reasoned with them from the Scriptures." In the case of Jews and proselytes of the gate the prophecies of the Old Testament necessarily formed the basis for a presentation of the gospel of Jesus. The aorist implies that Paul's work was completed in the space of the three Sabbaths. We need not worry about the weekdays, about synagogue services during the week, and the like. Paul's great efforts were made on these three Sabbaths. Then the decision and the division came. The idea that this occurred exceptionally soon is not implied; in Pisidian Antioch the division came already on the second Sabbath.

3) Luke gives us a clear idea as to just how Paul proceeded. After presenting the discourse delivered in Pisidian Antioch in 13:17-41, a brief resume is sufficient at this point. Two present participles which cover the time included in the main verb state Paul's

method: "opening up and submitting on his part" (note the middle voice and also the meaning, M.-M. 490). On the basis of the Scriptures Paul opened up and on his part submitted to his hearers in the synagogue the great facts concerning "the Christ," the promised Messiah, namely that according to God's own Word "it was necessary for the Christ to suffer and to arise from the dead" (see 3:16 on this phrase). What prophecies Paul used we do not know; we naturally think of Isa. 53. The suffering, of course, includes the death, for the resurrection follows; both aorist infinitives state historical facts, and the imperfect ἔδει states the enduring necessity lying in the prophecies and going back to the eternal counsel of God. This was new to the hearers, it had to be opened up to them. The Jews had the prophecies but in spite of them had formed a far different conception of the Christ whom they expected. After opening up the prophecies Paul submitted them to his hearers. Luke says nothing about "heated discussion by the opposing rabbis" on these three Sabbaths. Luke draws a totally different picture in v. 5.

After opening up the Scriptures Paul proceeded to show their fulfillment in Jesus. Here Luke drops into direct discourse: "that this One is the Christ (of the Scripture promises), the Jesus whom I on my part (emphatic ἐγώ) am proclaiming to you." Thus the whole story of Jesus was presented in the light of the Messianic prophecies. We follow the same course to this day even for ourselves who are not of Jewish blood. What makes us so everlastingly sure is this prophecy through the ages with its fulfillment in Jesus. The Old Testament has supreme value in this central part of our faith. To this day the Jews are helpless before their own ancient prophecies with their revelation of the suffering and the risen Savior. Whom did those prophets have in mind if not Jesus? The claim that they had in mind the Jewish nation and not an individual is surmise. If the Jewish nation is the Messiah of the world, who is the Messiah of the Jewish nation? or does it need none? need none when the prophets promised the Messiah to Israel first of all?

4) **And some of them were persuaded and were allotted to Paul and Silas, also of the worshipping Greeks a great multitude, also of women those foremost not a few.**

This success was secured in three weeks, objections to the contrary notwithstanding. Why does Luke specify three Sabbaths if more time than that were necessary to accomplish this? Every reader expects Luke to say what the results were after three Sabbaths. The matter is not changed by inserting a καί before Greeks so that we should have four classes, some Jews, proselytes of the gate, many pagan Greeks, prominent women. This leaves the three Sabbaths as before; but it also leaves τῶν σεβομένων without a noun and makes the prominent women pagans, who, no doubt, were proselytes of the gate. Everywhere women of the upper classes were attracted to Judaism; we have an instance in 13:50. As far as I Thess. 1:9, and 2:16 are concerned, both passages apply to Greek proselytes and do not refer only to converts from paganism. As for the many proselytes of the gate in the Thessalonian synagogue at this time, what of it? Why must the number be reduced?

Only some Jews were converted. We must refer both verbs to all the subjects: Jews, proselytes, including women. All were persuaded and were allotted to Paul and Silas. The translation "consorted with" cannot be accepted (see M.-M. 549). The unexpressed agent in the two passives is the Lord or his grace. The second verb shows that a separation from the synagogue was effected. This implies a good deal, namely that a new organization was brought into being, a Christian congregation. On the two kinds of proselytes see 2:10, and on σεβόμενος, 13:43. Not a few of the proselytes who were converted in Thessalonica were women of the upper classes. All these converts formed a strong church from the very beginning.

5) **But the Jews, roused with jealousy and taking with them of the market-loafers some vicious men and having made a crowd, began to put the city in an uproar. And coming upon the house of Jason, they were seeking to bring them before the people.**

The New Testament is full of the records of the moral obliquity of the Jews who spurned the gospel. They consistently resort to foul, vicious, criminal means in order to crush the heralds of the gospel. Their Judaism never even makes them hesitate. This great historic fact ought to receive more attention. Men who spit upon the gospel are morally vicious and, as soon as the occasion offers, are ready to prove it. Piously they sat in their synagogue in Thessalonica Sabbath after Sabbath and now they plot and execute a regular riot against Paul and Silas — no, not against pagans and idolaters but against two former Jews who were telling them of the Messiah for whom their nation had hoped for so long a time.

Their motive was of the basest kind, jealousy. Paul and Silas had taken so many from their synagogue and had started what to them appeared as an opposition synagogue. The plan was to disrupt it by foul means. So they take along with them "of the market-loafers some vicious men" and put the city into an uproar with a loud and boisterous commotion. These Jews hire the most vicious loafers that loiter around in the market place and with shouts start for the house of Jason where Paul and Silas lodged. A great crowd was attracted by their commotion and ran along with them. The plan was to lay hold of the two and to bring them before the δῆμος, an assembly of the people for public trial. What would happen then one may imagine.

How soon after the third Sabbath this wicked move was made is not indicated; enough time must have elapsed to convince the Jews that the Christian organization promised to become permanent, and that strong measures alone could hope to break it up. After the separation from the synagogue Paul and Silas worked with pagan Greeks who had been made accessible to them through the proselyte Greeks they had gained. This, however, enraged the Jews of the synagogue all the more.

Jason must have been a former Jew. This conclusion is not based on his name, for he bore the name of an ancient king of Thessaly. Many Jews bore foreign names, among the apostles Andrew and Philip had Greek names. Similar-sounding names were often chosen; one who was named Joshua might adopt the name Jason. On coming to Thessalonica, Paul would not lodge with a Gentile in order not to offend the Jews at the very beginning of his labor. The two imperfect tenses leave the outcome in suspense: will these Jews and these thugs lay hold on Paul and on Silas?

6) The imperfect used in this verse is also descriptive. **But not having found them, they were dragging Jason and some brethren to the politarchs, shouting: They that turned the world upside down, these are here also, whom Jason has hospitably received. And these all act contrary to the decree of Caesar, declaring there is a different king, Jesus.**

Paul and Silas were providentially absent as Timothy and Luke had escaped the mob in Philippi (16:19). But Jason was at home and several brethren were with him, and these were made to suffer instead of Paul and Silas by being brought to the politarchs. Thessalonica was a free city and was governed by politarchs ("city-rules"), a senate, and a people's assembly (βουλὴ καὶ δῆμος, *senatus populusque*). This δῆμος is mentioned in

v. 5, and in 19:29-40 we see it in action; but note 19:39 regarding an assembly that is lawfully called.

Πολιτάρχη is not found in Greek literature and was for a long time referred to as one of Luke's errors in historical matters. But now it can be seen in an inscription on an arch which is preserved in the British Museum, in seventeen other inscriptions, fourteen from Macedonia (five of these from Thessalonica); one is from Egypt, and a papyrus letter from Egypt mentions the "politarch Theophilus." M.-M. 525. At the time of Augustus five men composed this board of burgomasters, during the time of Antonius and Marcus Aurelius this number was increased to six. The verb corresponding to the noun has also been found.

The whole mob arrives before the offices of these politarchs, who are forced to investigate as to what is disturbing the peace of the city. They are met with shouting, charges that treason is abroad in the city, and the implication of Jason in particular. Paul and Silas are described as "they that turned the world upside down," τὴν οἰκουμένην (γῆν), "the inhabited earth," meaning the Roman empire as in Luke 2:1. News had evidently come from Philippi regarding the action of the mob there, and it may well have been possible that the Jews had learned about other places where Paul had been. The accusers are, of course, the hostile Jews and not the loafers or the crowd. "These fellows (οὗτοι) are here also" to disturb the city's peace with their treason. The charge is political and hence extremely serious. It is interesting to read in a papyrus letter dated Aug. 4, A. D. 41 that a bad boy used this very verb ἀναστατόω in the sense of "he upsets me."

7) Paul and Silas were, of course, not present to be accused, but poor Jason was: "whom Jason has hospitably received," i. e., and is still harboring. And now the terrible thing that is being done: "These all, Paul, Silas, the brethren captured with Jason, and all others

who follow these leaders, they all act contrary to the decrees of Caesar by declaring there is a different king, namely one called Jesus." One hears the echoes of what the Sanhedrin once charged against Jesus himself. Here Jews again renounce all their Messianic hopes and pose as the most loyal subjects of Caesar.

The emperors never called themselves *rex* because they had kings under them; but in the provinces they were commonly called "king." Here again the Jews lie brazenly, for they know that Jesus is a spiritual and not a political king, and these Jews even shout that Jesus is usurping Caesar's place although Jesus had been crucified about twenty years before this time. They mention the δόγματα (see 16:4) of Caesar to convey the idea that the followers of Jesus are in rebellion against Caesar and against all Roman laws and yield allegiance only to this usurper Jesus.

But they exaggerate unduly. These politarchs had never heard of a Jesus, a pretender to the Roman throne. If the world had been upset, these politarchs had not heard the noise. The only noise they heard was that made by the frenzied shouters before them. These are the points to be noted rather than making an effort to figure out how this charge in regard to Jesus' being a king could have been based on Paul's preaching. We must note how carefully Luke records just what Paul had preached regarding Jesus, namely that he had to suffer (die) and rise from the dead. If we may venture a guess it would be that these Jews of Thessalonica had heard how their Sanhedrin had accused Jesus before Pilate and had succeeded, and so they tried to repeat the accusation before the ignorant politarchs. "Caesar" was a name to conjure with. Had not Pilate bowed before it? would not the politarchs do the same?

8) **And they agitated the crowd and the politarchs, they hearing these things.** The charge had

a disquieting ring. Being thrown into the crowd, who had not heard it before, it excited them. The politarchs were in the same position. But these politarchs were not swept off their feet as the praetors in Philippi had been (16:22). They kept their heads.

9) **And having taken the security from Jason and the rest, they dismissed them.** And that is all that the riotous excitement accomplished. In λαβόντες τὸ ἱκανόν (generic article, R. 763) we have a forensic expression, the equivalent of the Latin *cum satis accepissent* (B.-D. 5, 3, b). The politarchs took money as a security from Jason and the brethren and made certain that Paul and Silas would cease all activity in Thessalonica. Since the politarchs were much in the dark as to what it was all about they intended to take no risks, especially since Caesar was said to be involved and they intended to shield their own positions. What they did was about the least they could do since there was no clearer evidence than that which they had.

10) **But the brethren immediately by night sent forth both Paul and Silas to Berea.** This was the only course open to them in view of the security Jason and others had been compelled to give the politarchs. Somewhere in the city a quiet gathering of the brethren was held at night, and Paul and Silas were spirited away. A small delegation of brethren no doubt accompanied them for a considerable distance as this was so generally done by the Christians. Berea, about fifty miles from Thessalonica, was chosen as the next place for work. This was located in the third district of Macedonia and hence was outside of the jurisdiction of Thessalonica. Paul's moving on to other localities was providential. However much he might have preferred to remain and to work longer, his work was more fruitful when it was transferred to other cities. This is true also regarding his inability to return to Thessalonica. Whether the bond Jason and others had given

to the politarchs was still in force and prevented Paul's return, or whether other causes played in, the result is that we have two letters written to the Thessalonians by him which are priceless to the church of all time.

From these letters we glean that persecution had come upon the Thessalonian brethren after Paul had left them (I Thess. 2:14; 3:3-5; II Thess. 1:6, 7). We again meet Jason in Corinth (Rom. 16:21). Two others, Aristarchus and Secundus of Thessalonica, will go to Jerusalem with Paul (Acts 20:4), and the former will even travel to Rome with the prisoner Paul (27:2). These brief notices speak volumes for what was accomplished in Thessalonica.

Who, on having arrived, kept going away to the synagogues of the Jews. Although it is added relatively, this is an independent statement. Again it is the synagogue which determines the choice of the city for work. The imperfect is iterative so that we need not think that immediately on setting foot in Berea Paul and Silas hurried to the Jewish synagogue. What Luke tells us is that the synagogue was made the scene of their work and continued to be so. Ἀπῄεσαν is the imperfect of ἄπειμι, and this compound is found only here in the New Testament. Because of the ἀπό in the verb it is often supposed that the synagogue was outside of the city, but this is too improbable.

11) **Now these were nobler than those in Thessalonica, such as received the Word with all eagerness, day by day examining the Scriptures whether these things were so. Many of them, therefore, believed, also of the Grecian women, those of good standing, and of men not a few.**

This is one of the most beautiful pages in Paul's missionary labors. In this somewhat secluded town a fair and lovely congregation grows up, a tender violet in a quiet corner, a lovely rose in a fair spot of the garden. Here many of the vicious influences which Paul met so often are absent. Luke compares the Jews of Berea with those of Thessalonica and calls them nobler. The word may mean of noble birth, race, or character, here the latter is evidently intended. The Bereans were better Jews because they had imbibed the true spirit of Israel and the Old Testament. They had allowed the grace of God to mold their hearts through the Old Testament Scriptures. This rendered them incapable of jealousy, lying accusation, and resort to violence, all of which are so directly contrary to God and to his law as recorded in the Word.

As so often, οἵτινες has causal force: "since they were such as," etc. The proof of their nobleness is the fact that they "received the Word with all eagerness," namely the gospel as Paul and Silas preached it to them from the Old Testament. Luke has given us a sample of that preaching in 13:16-41, and a summary in 17:2, 3. The participle describes the manner of this reception. These Bereans were by no means a credulous, uncritical lot, which certainly would have made them far from noble. Their acceptance of the gospel was the result of their "examining day by day the Scripture whether these things were so." Ἀνακρίνω is often used in a forensic sense, especially with regard to the preliminary questioning and examination of a prisoner by the judge. This gives us the sense that applies here. These Jews probed most carefully whether what Paul and Silas taught about Jesus was really in the Old Testament as these preachers claimed. This examination was not superficial, it continued "day by day." The article before the distributive κατά makes the phrase an adverbial substantive. This examination took time because only a few owned copies of the LXX.

The one concern of these Bereans was to find out at firsthand "whether these things were so," the things proclaimed by Paul and Silas. Here there was no initial blind, unreasoned hostility that sought only objections no matter of what kind. Here there was no cold indifference that is careless as to whether "these things" were really true or not and was taken up by other interests. Time, study, search, discussion were fully devoted to the Scriptures and to finding out what they contained in regard to this new teaching.

The attitude of heart thus revealed is the mark of spiritual nobility. The Bereans did not know it, but they have occupied a shining place in the New Testament Scriptures for nearly 2,000 years. This is exactly what Paul and Silas desired: to have them examine, truly examine the Scriptures. That examination, properly made, could result in only one verdict: "These things *are* so!" and that implied faith, intelligent faith, that rested on the one true ground of faith, the Scriptures.

R., *W. P.*, is right when he makes the optative of the indirect question represent the indicative of the corresponding direct question: "Are these things so?" Then, however, εἰ is but the mark of the indirect question and *not* conditional. If, however, εἰ is regarded as the protasis of a condition, this could be only a condition of reality: "if these things *are* (indirect in English: were) so," and not, as R., *W. P.*, thinks, a condition of potentiality: "if these things *might be* so." Of course, ἔχω with an adverb amounts to our "to be": *ob sich diese Dinge so verhalten.*

Here we have an excellent example of the right of private judgment which is part of the royal priesthood of believers. Each man is to have direct access to the Scripture, is to see and to judge for his own person and conscience. Although Paul was an apostle, his preaching had to be tested by the Scriptures. Because he was an apostle he asked for this, demanded it. As an apostle his whole preaching automatically rested on the Scriptures.

But we dare not misunderstand this divine right granted to every man to go to the Scriptures in person. It does not mean that you and I have the right to interpret the Scriptures as we please. Your right and my right is to see and to find the one divine truth which the Spirit placed into the Scriptures. This and this alone is in them. If you claim to find anything else you have not done so at all, you have fooled yourself or have let others fool you. The same is true with regard to every other man. Everyone and all of us together can truly find only this *one* truth and true sense in the Scriptures and will thus be one in faith. And the Scriptures are clear, perfectly adequate to present this one truth to every man. Those who deviate from that one truth, no matter how, can do so only by making the Word mean what it never meant, and *they*, they alone are to blame for such deviation. A great, glorious right indeed, but one that is combined with an equally great and serious responsibility. Do not misconceive the right, but also do not treat the responsibility lightly!

12) Μὲν οὖν as in 1:6. This, then, is the manner in which many of the Jews in Berea "believed." The aorist is simply historical to indicate the fact, or ingressive, "came to believe." The shining way to faith is to receive the preached Word with all eagerness — not with hostility, and to test and to examine every bit of it by the Scriptures and to accept only what agrees with them. Oh, for more Bereans everywhere! Away with preachers and with hearers who treat the Scriptures like an actor's nose of wax that is to be twisted as one may please. To take any man's word for it is Romanism even if it be you and your word, the word of some "great scientist," or of no matter what "high authority" within or without the church. All these are like the Serpent in Eden: they thrust the Word aside, "Yea, hath God said?" and then substitute their own false-

hood for what God did most assuredly say. God said, "In the day that thou eatest thereof thou shalt surely die!" Satan, "Ye shall *not* surely die."

In addition to many Jews also many Grecian women believed, and of the men not a few. The adjective "Grecian" is feminine but refers to "men" as well as to "the women" since women are mentioned first. They were not only more numerous than the men but also more influential. That is brought out by the adjective which is added by a separate article and thus given special stress: τῶν εὐσχημόνων, "of good form," i. e., "of superior social standing." This is the third time that we note that Greek women proselytes of the gate constituted an important element in a Jewish synagogue (13:50; 17:4; and we may note 16:14). Some think that Luke refers to pagan Grecian women and Grecian men or at least to some pagans in addition to proselytes of the gate. But this is untenable. After the Christian congregation had been organized, these Jewish proselytes proved the means for reaching into the pagan world. At the beginning Paul and Silas were fully occupied in the synagogue. "Many," "not a few," Luke writes, thus not all the Jews and the proselytes yet a large number, the nucleus of an excellent congregation.

13) **But when the Jews from Thessalonica realized that the Word of God was proclaimed by Paul also in Berea, they came also there, stirring up and agitating the multitudes. And then immediately the brethren sent away Paul as far as to the sea; and both Silas and Timothy remained there.**

News of the work done by Paul in Berea reached the vicious Jews of Thessalonica, and they at once repeated what the Jews of Pisidian Antioch and of Iconium had done when they hurried to Lystra to stop Paul's work (14:19). They always direct their efforts at Paul, which is plain proof that he towered above his assistants. These are regarded as negligible: he draws the lightning. Silas became involved in difficulty in Philippi only because he happened to be found in Paul's company at the moment (16:19). The same tactics were followed that had been set in motion in Thessalonica. They again probably hired the market loafers and then stirred up and excited the crowds. But again they failed to lay hold on Paul and could find no other victim. One thing must be noted, namely that Luke in no way implicates any of the Berean Jews who had not accepted the gospel; none of them joined in this riot that was instigated by the Thessalonian Jews. When Luke writes that the latter went to this length because "the Word of God was proclaimed by Paul," he speaks from his own point of view, for these Jews never admitted that it was the Word of God.

14) At once and without waiting for night to come the brethren hurried Paul off. They profited by what had happened in Thessalonica. This again was the hand of providence which swiftly moved Paul on to a new field of labor. God merely used the hatred of Paul's enemies to further the divine plans.

And now we come to a debatable point. While ἕως is the assured reading in preference to ὡς, and we must translate "until to the sea," the question arises whether Paul and those with him went by sea or took a route overland. Luke nearly always mentions the harbors even in the case of short voyages, but he mentions none here (Dium, Pydna, or Methone).. Codex Bezae inserts the remark that, because Paul was hindered from preaching in Thessaly, he passed this province by, which makes the impression that this commentating text had in mind a journey by land. The real object, however, is to explain why Paul made a journey as far as Athens. But if Paul went by land, why does Luke mention the sea? It is this mention of the sea that induces us to decide for a journey by sea. The fact that no harbor is indicated we must leave unanswered. The A. V. reads ὡς, "as it were to the sea." Thus Paul and his company would be throwing pursuit of them off the track by a ruse.

Silas had come to Berea with Paul, and so we are not surprised that he was left behind. But Timothy had been left in Philippi with Luke when Paul and Silas moved on from there (16:40). But now Timothy is in Berea and is left with Silas to aid the young church from which Paul is suddenly torn. A glance at Phil. 4:15, 16 reveals that the church at Philippi, where Luke and Timothy had been left, twice sent gifts to Paul while he was in Thessalonica. When he left Philippi he may have been poorly equipped. So the first gift was dispatched a day or two later, Timothy and some companion being the bearers of it. Why Paul was in need in Thessalonica we see from I Thess. 2:9: he worked night and day in order not to be chargeable to his converts. When Timothy returned to Philippi and made this known, a second gift was promptly sent. Phil. 4:15 would indicate that Paul had moved on to Berea and that Timothy found him there. Thus it came about that Timothy and Silas were left at Berea when Paul hurried away.

15) **Now those conducting Paul brought him as far as Athens; and having received command to Silas and Timothy that they come to him as soon as possible, they left.**

Paul did not travel alone even on this journey. Several Bereans conducted him, and that not only to the vessel but all the way to Athens, whose seaport was Pireus. There is silent testimony throughout the story of Acts that the churches solicitously guarded Paul even as here the Bereans send competent men with him who probably had made this journey more than once before this time. Now, why Paul went to Athens and just to Athens, no one can say. Some think that he intended to return to Macedonia as soon as it was safe and base this view on the vision and the call to this province (16:9). But Paul had traveled through all of Macedonia; he was certainly not to confine himself to this one province and must have realized that the work which the Lord intended he should do there in person would come to an end. We thus conclude that Paul intended to begin work in new territory. When the Codex Bezae explains why Paul passed by Thessaly, we see that the explanation is only a comment that is drawn from 16:6, 7. Why had Paul gone through Amphipolis and Appolonia without stopping, and why had he halted nowhere between Pisidian Antioch and Troas, not even stopping in Troas?

After they had arrived in Athens and had enjoyed a brief rest, Paul's conductors return to Berea. But Paul sends instructions with them that Silas and Timothy are to hurry on to Athens. Thus Paul remained alone for a brief period. The aorists imply that Paul's instructions were carried out and that Silas and Timothy did join him "as soon as possible" (ὡς with the superlative) in Athens. The ἵνα clause is simply subfinal and does not state the purpose but the contents of the ἐντολή or command. After Silas and Timothy came to Athens, we know from I Thess. 3:1-6 that in his anxiety regarding Thessalonica Paul sent Timothy back, who also returned to Paul with a most encouraging report. But he joined Paul only after the apostle had gone on from Athens to Corinth (18:5). So Paul sent also Silas back to Macedonia; to what congregation in this territory is not stated. It was probably to Philippi. This mission of Silas' is indicated in Acts 18:5 when Silas and Timothy come to Paul in Corinth. The movements of Paul's assistants are mentioned only incidentally, and Luke makes no attempt to trace them in detail. After 18:5 Silas is not again mentioned, but Timothy is again mentioned in 19:22, and 20:4. We

may add that in 20:4 Sopater of Berea is in the group of men who are with Paul. This is the Sosipater who is with Paul in Corinth, cf., Rom. 16:21, together with Timothy and Jason of Thessalonica. Ἐξῄεσαν is the imperfect of ἔξειμι, "to go forth."

THE SECOND MISSIONARY JOURNEY:
ATHENS

16) Athens, "the eye of Greece, the mother of arts and eloquence," still held this position in the Greek world at the time of Paul's visit to this city. It was filled with great memories of Socrates, Plato, Aristotle, of Sophocles and Euripedes, of Pericles, and of Demosthenes. In its Agora, Socrates had walked with his pupils; here was the Academy of Plato, the Lyceum of Aristotle, the Porch of Zeno, the Garden of Epicurus. The Parthenon, the most beautiful of temples, crowned the Acropolis. Standing on its glorious height, the writer saw pages and pages of the ancient history of Greece and Athens spread out as on a map. The view is unforgettable. At one time Athens dominated all the great cities around the Mediterranean that are located in Asia and in Europe. These political glories had taken wing. It was now only a provincial city in the province of Achaia with Corinth as its capital. This province had been restored to the Senate by Claudius in A. D. 44 and was thus governed by a proconsul.

This was a city that was entirely different from any that Paul had ever visited or was to visit. It is often described as a university town that was similar to those cities of our day that have great universities located in their midst; but this conception is misleading in more ways than one. It was the world center of art, but an art that was devoted chiefly to the idolatries of Greek mythology. Its great attraction today is the ruined Parthenon with the Erechteion on the far left and two amphitheaters far below on the right. Sculpture, Greek architecture, Greek theaters, schools of philosophies, literates of all kinds, all steeped in Greek paganism — this was Athens as Paul saw it in A. D. 52. This is what the pagan Lucian has in mind, "When I first came to Athens I was astonished and delighted to see all the glory of the city." Pagan writers remark regarding the plethora of temples and statues. Petronius satirically remarks that in Athens it was easier to find a god than a man. In his fine description Pausanias states that Athens had more images than all Greece put together. Xenophon calls Athens "one great altar, one great offering to the gods." Livy writes, "In Athens are to be seen images of gods and men of all descriptions and made of all materials." In the Agora every god of the Olympus found a place. Every public building was at the same time a sanctuary that was dedicated to one or to more gods. Besides the ordinary gods there were deifications of Fame, Modesty, Energy, Persuasion, etc.

Two things must be noted with regard to Paul as he appears in Athens. First, his feeling of intense indignation as he surveys the city. The glory he saw was utter shame. He was in no way humbled and abashed by the pride of this pagan flowering; he was only aroused to set the glory of God and of Christ where the glory of idolatry now spread itself. Secondly, Paul was in no way impressed by the philosophic show in this central seat of philosophic cults. The hollowness of it never impressed him more than here among its most ardent votaries. Again his spirit strained at the leash to explode all this supposed wisdom by the divine Wisdom which is Truth. That is why Luke made the record about the work in Athens as it is. The body of it is Paul's great address. The apostle meets the Athenians with a mastery such as they had never seen. All one needs to do is to place side by side the sentences of Paul and the Apology of Plato or any other of Plato's writings. Athens is the measure of Paul.

Now while Paul was expecting them in Athens, his spirit was provoked within him, he beholding the city as being full of idols.

Since it was wholly new to him, Paul inspected this famous city during the first days of his visit while he was awaiting the arrival of Silas and Timothy for whom he had sent (v. 15). Here he beheld a city that was *κατείδωλον*, a word that is found only here but one that is formed with the perfective *κατά*: "excessive as to idols," beyond any other city in this respect. It is, of course, self-evident that Paul was not thinking that the statues were idols instead of only representing imaginary idol beings. All images are idols just because they are representations of such beings. It has been well said that Paul was not impressed by mere art for art's sake, no matter how perfect the art might be. That is the modern canon. But art is never abstract, just as beauty is not. Beauty is a quality in something, and art the means of presenting that beauty. What that something is: falsehood, idolatry, and superstition with a heavy dose of sensualism, when it is presented with beauty and art, is the most vicious prostitution of both. Luke is not given to recording emotions. Hence when he here writes with the imperfect tense that Paul "was provoked," stirred with sharp indignation even in his very spirit because of what he beheld at almost every step, the statement is the greater in force. The worse the prostitution of all this art, the more aroused Paul's inner spirit became. Note that the two present participles in the genitive absolute agree with the durative imperfect tense of the main verb.

17) **Accordingly, he began to reason in the synagogue with the Jews and those worshipping, and**

in the market place every day with those happening to be present.

Luke writes as though Paul had originally intended to wait for Silas and Timothy before he began his work of spreading the gospel in Athens. But, being stirred as he was, he could not delay. Yet he was not radical or rash; he followed his regular course of procedure. He went into the synagogue and reasoned (v. 2) with the Jews and "those worshipping" (see 13:43), the Greek proselytes of the gate. Little attention is often paid to this statement because Luke says no more regarding this work in the synagogue. But Luke says no more about it because he has already said so much in regard to it when sketching this type of work in the other cities and because he intends to tell us something about the work among the pagan Athenians. Paul's success in the synagogue is taken as a matter of course. A congregation was organized in Athens with the converts thus gained. This work in the synagogue was by no means "a slim chance" as it has been called.

Paul also spent a part of every day in the Agora conversing with the pagan Greeks who might happen to be there. This "market place" was by no means devoted only to selling and to buying all sorts of provisions. Nor was it frequented only by busy, bustling crowds that were occupied with nothing else. The Athenian Agora was also the public meeting place for philosophers and their following, for idlers and persons of leisure, a place of conversation, discussion, plus business. Under the great plane trees there stood the statues of some of the most famous men of the city such as Solon, Conon, Demosthenes. The Agora was replete with historical memories. Everywhere the buildings were decorated with sculpture and impressive figures; some of the more prominent were graced with porticos and cloisters and beautified with paintings and ornaments. Here was the famous Painted Porch where philosophers and rhetoricians held forth. Here Zeno, the founder of Stoicism, had become famous. The cultural and the intellectual life of Athens throbbed in the Agora. Here Paul could always find an interested audience and men who were ready for serious discussion.

18) **Moreover, some also of the Epicurean and Stoic philosophers were having discussions with him.**

The imperfect tenses used in v. 16-18 resemble a moving picture and show us what was going on during these days. Yet a progress must be noted: Paul is provoked — he reasons in the synagogue and in the Agora — he has discussions with philosophers — two opinions about Paul are expressed: all this is expressed with imperfects. They lead up to the final outcome which is stated by the two aorists: in v. 19 "they brought" Paul, etc., and in v. 22, Paul "said" in his great address. Unless the tenses are understood and noted, Luke's account is not fully appreciated.

The reasonings in the Agora were carried on with anybody who happened to be present (παρατυγχάνοντες). But it was not long before more important men were attracted, namely professional philosophers of the two great schools that were prominent in Athens, where they had been founded, and also in the entire Roman educational world. These συνέβαλλον (λόγους) αὐτῷ, literally, "kept throwing words or statements together with him," "kept engaging him in discussion," namely day after day. When these professionals engaged Paul in argument, the audience of lesser men increased to a great degree. Paul was creating somewhat of a sensation in Athens. And it is worth noting that he adapted himself to the Athenian ways by first gathering circles of hearers in their Agora and then entering into public discussions with their philosophers.

Luke uses only one article with the two kinds of philosophers, for they constituted one party and Paul alone was on the other side. The discussions were, no doubt, keen although entirely friendly. These philosophers followed this practice almost daily; it was their delight and diversion as well as their profession. They tolerated each other while they fought each other intellectually. They cultivated broad tolerance, and the Jewish fanaticism that always sought Paul's blood was wholly foreign to them. Nothing is said about persecution of Paul in Athens. The story of Socrates who had been tried and condemned to drink the poison hemlock was a matter of the remote past. In his *W. P. R.* groups as follows: "Socrates had turned men's thoughts inward ('know thyself!'), away from the mere study of physics. Plato followed with a profound development of the inner self (metaphysics). Aristotle with his cyclopaedic grasp sought to unify and relate both physics and metaphysics. But Zeno and Epicurus (340-272 B. C.) took a more practical turn in all this intellectual turmoil and raised the issues of everyday life. Zeno (336-260 B. C.) taught at the Stoa (Porch), and so his teaching was called Stoicism." That of Epicurus bore its author's name.

The Epicureans were quite atheistic in their speculation; they thought that the world was formed by a fortuitous concourse of atoms and was not created, not even formed by divine power. While they permitted a certain belief in the gods they treated them as phantoms who were without influence upon the world and upon life; they mocked at the popular mythology but presented nothing better. Thus their view of the soul was materialistic. At death it was dissolved and dissipated in the elements thus ending forever the existence of man. Life, therefore, was not regulated by higher moral or spiritual interests; its highest aim was gratification: gross and sordid, even vicious and criminal if one was inclined that way; or refined and esthetic if one had tastes and aspirations in this direction. Pleasure, ἡδονή, not duty was the substance of this philosophy. The means to attain it was called virtue. This was a doctrine which could not produce anything but selfishness and sensuality when men put it into practice. Note how little advance certain schools of philosophy of today have made beyond this old Epicurus and his following.

The Stoics were pantheists; they condemned the worship of images and the use of temples, and considered them only as ornaments of art. God was merely the Spirit of Reason of the universe; matter was inseparable from this deity, and he was conceived as impressing order and law upon it since he regulated it as an inner principle. The soul was corporeal, at death it was burnt or absorbed into God. The Stoic moral code was higher than that of the Epicureans, their ideal being an austere apathy and unconcern which regarded itself superior to passion as well as to circumstance; pleasure was no good, pain no evil; reason was the guide and decided what was good and what was evil. He who followed reason was perfect and sufficient in himself. When reason saw no more in life, it dictated suicide as the most reasonable thing. Its first two leaders died by their own hand, and the Romans who felt attracted to this sterner philosophy often followed their example. Stoicism was the philosophy of human *pride*. Seneca, Epictetus, and Marcus Aurelius espoused Stoicism. The poets Lucretius and Horace were Epicureans.

Both of these philosophies were diametrically opposed to Christianity with its doctrine of God, the soul, sin, redemption, salvation in Christ, the resurrection of the body, and eternal life.

And some began to say, What would this seed-picker say? and others, He seems to be a proclaimer of foreign divinities; because he was proclaiming as good news Jesus and the resurrection.

Luke does not write "some of them," namely of the philosophers disputing with Paul, but "some" of those who heard the discussions. One group was supercilious and scoffed, the other was more serious and tried to understand. The question: "What would this seedpicker say?" of course, expects no answer. The sense is that what he says amounts to nothing. That is why Paul is called "this seedpicker," σπερμολόγος. The interpretation of this word must be either literal or metaphorical. Since we have no metaphorical equivalent, the literal alternative alone is left. Used originally with regard to a bird "picking up seed" here and there, Athenian slang applied it to a man picking up an idea here and there and passing these on without a real knowledge of their meaning. Tindale's "babbler" was adopted in our versions and is not far from the sense. Moffatt translated by interpreting "fellow with scraps of learning"; Goodspeed's "ragpicker" is incorrect, M.-M. 583. These scoffers saw nothing worth-while in Paul. The question with the optative and ἄν is the apodosis of a condition of potentiality (B.-D. 385, 1; R. 1021), and οὗτος is derogatory (B.-D. 290, 6).

Καταγγελεύς as well as ξένων δαιμονίων are to be understood from the Athenian point of view. The former has finally been found in an inscription in the sense of "announcer" of games, and the latter refers to "divinities" in the pagan sense. They were "foreign" because they were not known in Athens. We might translate "new." R., *W. P.*, thinks that Paul was treading on thin ice when he proclaimed Jesus as God in Athens, for this was contrary to Roman law and introduced a *religio illicita;* but these men did not have in mind the idea of an illegal religion, new divinities rather interested them because they might perhaps offer new ideas. The injection of something that was perhaps criminal on Paul's part is unwarranted.

Luke explains on what this second opinion rested, namely on Paul's preaching as good news — and the Athenians loved news! — "Jesus and the resurrection." Some interpreters ask whether "the resurrection" was understood as a divinity. The imperfect, of course, shows that Luke adds this remark as being his own; but that does not exclude the idea that "the resurrection" was understood as a divinity by these Athenians. The main point is that Luke elucidates the plural "foreign divinities" by "Jesus and the resurrection" and not by a reference to the Trinity. And all know that the Athenians personified and worshipped as divinities all sorts of abstract virtues and truths (see above). We must note, too, that Luke writes only the abstract "the resurrection" and not "his (Jesus') resurrection."

Luke describes this result of Paul's discussions in the Agora to show what a task the apostle was facing, and how hard it was even to make these lovers of philosophy and learning really understand what he meant. It is still so. Science, falsely so-called, often beclouds the intellect to such an extent that spiritual verities are not even intellectually understood, to say nothing of being accepted.

19) **And having taken hold of him, they brought him to the Areopagus, saying: Can we come to know what this new teaching uttered by thee is? for thou art bringing to our ears some things that are foreign. We desire, therefore, to know what these things intend to be. Now all Athenians and the resident foreigners were accustomed to have leisure for nothing other than to be stating something or to be hearing something brand new.**

Ὁ Ἄρειος Πάγος was the Hill of Ares (Mars) and, named from this Hill, the supreme Council of Athens, the Areopagus, which was called the Upper Council to distinguish it from the council of the Five Hundred.

This Upper Council consisted of all who had held the office of Archon, and they were members of it for life. In the days of Chrysostom and of Theophylact it was supposed that Paul had been tried before the Areopagus. Then it was seen that the whole account contains not even a trace of a trial, and so it was thought that Paul was to give an account of his teaching to the high court of Athens on the supposition that this court exercised some sort of oversight over the teachings and the lecturers in Athens. The extreme was reached when a discussion arose regarding the place where Paul spoke, some insisting that it took place on the actual Hill of Mars but only before a dozen or more of philosophers whom some even call "professors"; others that it did not occur on Mars Hill but in the Stoa Basilica where the Council often met.

Now these points are certain. The only motive for requesting Paul to state his teaching was curiosity. The polite request and urging so states, and Luke himself adds that the Athenians always had plenty of time for anything new. The motive was not in the least hostile. We must not be misled by those who had called Paul "this seedpicker," for they were not the ones who now asked him for a full statement of his new doctrine. The address itself undoubtedly fits Paul's audience. The two opening sentences, however, do not fit either Epicurean or Stoic philosophers; what their opinion of the gods was we have seen. Paul addressed a formal or informal meeting of the Council and many Athenians and resident foreigners who flocked in to hear Paul's new teaching. In other words, Paul obtained a grand opportunity to present the gospel teaching concerning God and Jesus to a representative audience of the great and famous city of Athens, and he certainly rose to the occasion.

After going over Mars Hill in 1925 the writer must confess that he found nothing there that might prove helpful in this study. When one faces the Acropolis and the Propyla or entrance to the Parthenon, this rocky ridge lies to the left, and scores of century plants in the intervening space shoot up their tall stalks of bloom, prickly pear also growing in abundance. The hill is rough rock in its natural state. From the Parthenon one looks down upon it. The side that is toward the city is a steep descent, rough and hard to climb. On top we found two holes with conelike stonework in the excavations. The side of the rocky hill away from the city is concave in contour, but all is in its natural rocky state. This slope, like the top, is an utter disappointment as far as even the remotest trace of a place where a court might have assembled is concerned. All the ancient amphitheaters show where the seats were, but on Mars Hill all is natural, apparently untouched rock. In imagination we tried to see Paul and his audience in the concave lower slope, but it was pure imagination. It is inspiring to imagine a Mars Hill with Paul delivering his great address on God before the Athenians on such an eminence, stone seats for the Areopagites, etc., but the Mars Hill of actuality sadly upsets all that.

When we then read the phrases ἐπὶ τὸν Ἄρειον πάγον, in v. 22 ἐν μέσῳ τοῦ Ἀρείου πάγου, and in v. 33 ἐκ μέσου αὐτῶν, the two latter especially compared with ἐν τῷ μέσῳ in 4:7 with regard to the Sanhedrin, we must think of some other place than Mars Hill. Reluctantly we dismiss the Hill and accept "the Areopagus" as being the Council of Archons, and the place of their meeting somewhere along the Agora — the Stoa Basilica will do. Curtiss may have missed it otherwise but not as far as the place is concerned. To speak about the noise of the Agora is inept, for here in the Painted Porch and in the Stoa Basilica and in other places as well all manner of meetings were held, and no noise interfered with them. "They took" Paul and "brought" him. They encouraged this stranger to come and then showed him the way. Politely they ask whether they may know this "new" teaching, and the position of the adjective makes it decidedly emphatic. The second article introduces the ὑπό phrase and also lends it an emphasis (R. 776) and is not superfluous.

20) "New" is explained (γάρ) by ξενίζοντα, "being foreign" (participle), coming to Athens as a stranger guest. That is what attracts these Athenians; that is what is giving Paul this exceptional hearing. These men feel that Paul's teaching is so new, so unlike anything else in Athens that their Areopagites ought also to hear it. Its newness will mightily interest them. They would like to know, too, "what these things intend to be" (the same expression as in 2:12), what their real purpose and aim are.

21) With the parenthetic δέ Luke describes the outstanding characteristic of the Athenians so that we may evaluate this invitation properly. If they had time for nothing else they always had plenty of it for anything "newer," just out and thus newer than what they had heard thus far. They were enamored of "the latest" as we should call it, both they and the resident foreigners who had come there and were living there for a while. They loved both to state and to hear something new. Both Thucidides and Demosthenes rebuke the Athenians for this passion for the new. It tended to make them exceedingly superficial. They might welcome the gospel, the greatest news in the world, but only for an hour; when something newer came along, they would cast the gospel aside as being old. The world still has many religious Athenians. Religion must be progressive, have new doctrines, "advanced ideas," not everlastingly repeat the old "categories or patterns of thought." They are like the vain woman who would never dream of appearing in last year's dress or hat.

22) Paul had learned to take sinners as they are. The gospel had power to transform any of them. The old and ever new gospel was intended for all of them. Two Sanhedrists had been converted (Nicodemus and Joseph of Arimathaea), so here one at least of the Areopagites (v. 34) was converted. **And Paul, having taken his stand in the midst of the Areopagus, said, etc.** The very words show what a dramatic moment this was for Paul. He might have longed to have his helpers with him but he was all alone. All eyes were upon him. In all Greece there was no audience such as this. Without effort on his part it had assembled just for his sake. He was here by invitation, and every ear was keyed to hear anything he might say. He felt the full responsibility resting on him; he knew the Holy Spirit was with him. No wonder Luke records his address.

The outward scene is usually pictured in order to bring out the dramatic side of it: the Acropolis with its wonderful Parthenon towering on the right which contained the golden statue of Minerva, the tutelary divinity of Athens; Mars Hill overlooking the city, the famous Agora beneath the Hill with all the great names of Athenian history attached to its Porches and its halls; the magnificent panorama of land and sea around, scenes of history and of fame that keep our students busy even after 2,000 years. But we shall have to change all this and draw the picture by starting with the men of Paul's audience, Athenians and residents, an assembly that was unique in many ways. It is just as dramatic, but internally and not merely externally. Parthenon, Hill, Agora, city and land; history, poetry, art, philosophy, and all else were there and lent their effect, but Paul faces these Athenian men. Note incidentally that nobody would write, "in the midst of Mars Hill" or any hill; "in the midst" of an assembly — yes. "In the midst of the Areopagus" means in the midst of the body of notables who were called "the Areopagus."

Paul's address is a masterpiece in every way: in its introduction, in its line of thought, in its aptness for the audience, in its climax. It is bold but it does not offend in a bungling manner; it refutes but it does this so as to convince and to win; it states the truth squarely and fully but so as to lift it far above the follies of error; it is reasonable but it is directed at the heart; it seeks to win men but only by glorifying God and the Lord Jesus Christ. It was not quite concluded but it did not fail of divinely given fruit. Just ask yourself, "If you had stood in Paul's place that day, what would you have said?"

The theme is "the Unknown God" (v. 23). This God who is now revealed is the first part (v. 24-29); this God will judge through Jesus Christ, is the second (30, 31); it was probably to be followed by the third: this God delivers from judgment through Jesus Christ. The address is *not* philosophic. It was something brand new to these Athenians but surely refreshing and effective already for that very reason. It elevates both God and his creature, man, in a way which these Athenians had never heard before. Here was the truth — and oh, how insufficient it made their two great philosophies appear! It drove straight at the conscience by its demand for repentance and its announcement of the divine judgment — yes, conscience, the one vulnerable spot in every human being. On the judgment day no man who heard Paul before the Areopagus can excuse himself with the plea that Paul did not tell him what he needed to be told.

Men of Athens, in all things I behold you as unusually devoted to divinities. In fact, in passing through and noting your objects of worship I found even an altar on which had been inscribed, To the Unknown God. Now what without knowing you are

worshipping, this I on my part am proclaiming to you.

Paul's introduction is a gem because it leads so simply and so directly to his theme, which he also states in the clearest and most natural way. He intends to speak only a few minutes and thus keeps the proper proportion for his introduction and approach. Ἄνδρες Ἀθηναῖοι is the form of address used by Demosthenes and by all the orators and is thus exactly suitable for Paul. He is speaking to Athenian citizen. There were three classes of men in Athens: the citizens with the precious right of suffrage in the Assembly and of holding office (the latter being held by almost all in course of time), the residents who had neither right, and the slaves. Luke refers to the residents in v. 21 when he says that they were as avid to hear the latest as the Athenians themselves. Paul does not make the mistake of placing these foreign residents on a par with the citizens. They were not at all on a par with them although some of them were present to hear Paul. To have named them on a par with the citizens would have been resented by the latter. In a synagogue Israelites and proselytes of the gate could be addressed together, but in Athens the Athenians and the mere residents could not be thus joined. While Ἀθηναῖοι is an adjective, it is here used as a noun in apposition with ἄνδρες, an idiom we cannot reproduce as little as we can reproduce ἄνδρες ἀδελφοί.

All uncertainty in regard to Paul's opening statement is unnecessary, including that of Robertson who leaves it to exegesis and to one's personal choice as to how Paul is to be understood. Pausanias and others had told the Athenians just what Paul is telling them, namely that to an unusual degree, above other Grecian cities, they are devoted to the cultus of divinities. That fact was more than obvious. The noun δαιμόνια, which is akin to the adjective, is to be understood in the

Athenian sense of "divinities," all kinds of gods, deified heroes, virtues, etc., and has nothing to do with "demons" in the sense of devils. And δείδω, the verb in the adjective, refers to "fear" in the sense of worship, devotion to the cultus pertaining to these divinities. Their statues, temples, shrines, and altars filled the public places and the city generally; from Zeus and Athene down they all had their devotees, and there were divinities and shrines in every house. Let us remember that the heathen festivals were celebrated in grand style; all these temples had their priests (though not in the sense of a specific class but only as men elected by the Assembly of citizens); public and private functions were accompanied by sacrifices and by rites. This was true of other pagan cities, but Athens stood in the first rank because of the number of its divinities and the multiplicity of its statues and its shrines. This is what Paul refers to when he says: "I behold you as unusually devoted to divinities."

The ὡς belongs to the object: "as devoted," etc. (see examples in R. 481); it is not a conjunction with ὄντα to be supplied: "how or that you are," as B.-D. 416, 1 supposes. The comparative contains no *Vorwurf* (censure) as the A. V.'s "too superstitious" implies. "Superstitious" conveys the wrong idea, and "somewhat" in the R. V. is a mistranslation of the comparative, "very" would be more correct. "Religious" (R. V. margin) also misleads. The Athenians were not "more religious" than pagans generally but had far more divinities to occupy their attention; in v. 18 Paul is regarded as introducing still more divinities, and the Athenians imagined that they had about all of them. What Paul says is that the Athenians were unusually devoted to divinities.

Paul was not addressing only a group of "university professors," a misleading term for philosophers. This idea gives a wrong direction to the address and to the philosophers themselves. Paul had a large audience, and such philosophers as were present, despite their speculations, were agreed with the other citizens in all that pertained to the cultus of the divinities. Some might be called "atheists," but this term was to be taken only in a philosophical sense and did not by any means apply as far as the public and even the private cultus of the divinities was concerned. Let a man assail Athene, the goddess glorified in the Parthenon, and the Assembly would have made short work of him; he would immediately have been brought before one of the panels of Five Hundred (jury and judge in one). Let us remember Athens as it was and get away from every university idea of today.

23) Paul continues by saying that in passing through and inspecting their σεβάσματα or "objects of worship," temples, altars, statues of divinities, he found one βωμόν that especially attracted his attention since it had engraved upon it the words ΑΓΝΩΣΤΩ ΘΕΩ, which is intended to be definite although it is without the article in the Greek: "To the Unknown God." The idea expressed is not "to *some* Unknown God" but to a certain one whom the Athenians did not know as to his actual name, power, work, etc., as they knew their many other divinities. It was wholly immaterial to the apostle as to how and why this altar had been erected in Athens, or what polytheistic conceptions the Athenians might entertain concerning this "God." He intended to regard this altar and its inscription only as a confession on the part of the Athenians that, despite their multitude of divinities, one God existed of whom they themselves said that, while they knew of him, they did not in any way know him.

It is going too far to claim that by this inscription the Athenians intended to set aside all their other gods, or that thereby they virtually set them aside. Paul makes no such deduction for them; he does not try to catch them with a trick of logic, which would have been about the worst thing he could have attempted. He had just said that the Athenians were most notable worshippers of divinities. This altar to the Unknown God was only one among hundreds and not prominent at all and certainly drew no worshippers away from other altars and other gods.

Commentators make much of what is here said by Paul and preserved by Luke. They point us to "the nameless god" mentioned in a vedic hymn; to old Egyptian records that mention "the great god whose name is unknown," "God whose name is hidden," etc.; and to the nine-story teocolli or mound built by the Aztecs and dedicated to the "unknown god, the cause of all causes." Then, as far as Athens is concerned, we hear about Philostratus (A. D. 200-240), about Diogenes Laertius of about the same time, about Pausanias (160-180), who knew of altars to unknown gods; in addition to these pagans we find some of the ancient church fathers who bear similar testimony. In his *Apostelgeschichte* Zahn has an elaborate excursus. Stories as to how such an altar or a number of them came to be erected contribute nothing to Paul's address. We pass all this late material by as being of little interpretative value.

The correct text reads ὃ . . . τοῦτο, "what . . . that," neuter; not masculine: "whom . . . this one." But the unacceptable nature of the latter reading does not lie in the fact that it would introduce the personality of God too soon, for the inscription itself had already introduced that, and Paul continues it in the next statement. Either reading would be proper for Paul's address. The former is better because it says more than the latter. By erecting this strange altar and by the worship connected with it the Athenians were worshipping something about which they knew nothing whatever. They were taking this God for granted but were conceiving him to be one who was similar to their other gods. Paul is here to proclaim the very thing that is far from their knowledge, namely the facts about this God, the facts that will make them realize that all their other gods and divinities are fictions, base delusions, to be forever cast aside. But the thought that the apostle might thus be proclaiming a *religio illicita* contrary to Roman law was wholly foreign to his mind; he was using no turn of language in order shrewdly to evade a legal charge. To think of such an act on his part is to assail his character.

24) **God who made the world and all the things therein, this One, being heaven's and earth's Lord, does not dwell in handmade sanctuaries, nor by men's hands is he served as needing something, he himself giving to all life and breath and all things. And he made out of one man's blood every nation of mankind to settle on the face of the earth, having destined their appointed seasons and the boundaries of their settlement — for them to be seeking God if, indeed, they might touch him and find him, he even being not far from every one of us; for in him we live and move and are, as also some of the poets among you have said, For of him even offspring are we. Being offspring of God, we ought not suppose the divine nature to be like to gold or silver or stone, a thing graven of man's technique and conception.**

Paul is preaching natural theology as he had done in Lystra (14:15, etc.). The Scriptures also contain all of this theology; but in dealing with pagans an appeal to the Scriptures as Scriptures would be useless, hence Paul appeals to the mighty facts themselves as even pagans may see them and realize their direct import. He presents God, the omnipotent Creator, Ruler, and Benefactor, who is absolute and sufficient in himself. He lays special stress on man's relation to God, who as his creature is altogether dependent on him and his gifts, the very offspring of God, who is intended to worship God. All this Paul does in a simple, direct, and grand way by stating the realities as they are and by relying on them as realities that are able of themselves to enlighten and to fill his hearers' hearts with full conviction. Truth needs no argument, it never does, for it is its very nature to convince.

By ὁ Θεός Paul does not have in mind one God among many others such as Zeus, the chief god of Greek paganism, but "God" who alone is God and by his revelation of himself in nature and among men establishes this fact regarding himself. Over against the vain gropings of paganism, including their mythologies and their philosophies, the apostle sets the first chapter of the Bible: "God who made the world (τὸν κόσμον, the ordered universe) and all things therein," great and small, visible and invisible. Nothing came into being of itself or arranged itself, nothing was before God, nothing has its origin apart from him. The philosophies of science to this day disprove themselves whenever they set aside and operate without this elementary reality.

"This One," the emphatic οὗτος, resumes this tremendous reality and then restates it: "being heaven's and earth's Lord," for as the Creator of all he is their one master and ruler who is infinitely greater than any and all things called into being by him. When he is conceived thus as he is in his supreme eminence, the very foundation of idolatry is forever abolished in its emptiness. But Paul does not state this abstractly, he puts it in a concrete way so that the philosopher and the common man alike may get its full force: this Creator-Lord "does not dwell in handmade sanctuaries." How could the Creator and Lord of all be confined in one of the little spots he himself has made? So Solomon once asked regarding the Temple he had built, I Kings 8:27. All these sanctuaries are "handmade," fashioned by human hands. That adjective reveals what they are in comparison with the universe which is made by God who is greater than even this universe.

25) Connected with this first deduction is the second which is involved in it: "nor by men's hands is he served as needing something." The emphasis is on the first phrase, "by men's hands," and then on the final participial phrase, "as needing something." The verb θεραπεύεται is exactly proper to express the thought intended, rendering someone a service that he needs as the sick man must have the service of a physician. The service of worship: adoration, praise, prayer, petition, is a totally different thing. By it we profit and not God, nor does it supply a need in God.

The very reverse is true: "he himself giving to all life and breath and all things"; ζωή, life in its essence and existence, "breath," its continuance in our bodies, "and all things," adding all else to the two supreme gifts of our natural being. Three words, and yet they go to the very heart of our dependence upon God. "He himself giving" is the proper verb even as to the tense. Not only this or that is a gift, but our very existence is such a gift and a gift that flows on and on like a glorious stream. But the moment this mighty reality concerning God is grasped the whole conception of pagan offering and sacrifices as needed by the gods so that they must insist on being supplied, is abolished. So also the multiplicity of gods, one doing this, another that for his votaries; some in one country and nation, some in another. Life and breath have one source; above us is one Creator, Ruler, Preserver, Benefactor.

Paul's presentation must have struck especially the philosophers who had learned in different ways to scorn the gods of Grecian mythology. That really was no great achievement for thinking men. But what had their speculation put in place of the gods? Here at last was the true reason for scorning all pagan gods, not a veiled atheism, a vapid pantheism, or a supercilious skepticism which left the great questions regarding the cosmos, man, the course of men and of nations, etc., unanswered in helpless ignorance but a clear, full, efficient grasp of the truth — the one true and only God before whom all debasements of his being simply fade away.

26) In the same way, by trusting the power of truth to win its way against error, the apostle speaks about anthropology, especially about the intentions of God regarding man. First, the unity of the human race: "And he made out of one man's blood every nation of mankind to settle on the face of the earth." The entire human race in all its different nations sprang from one man. The R. V. follows the texts which drop the word "blood." Zahn marshals the reasons for retaining the word as is done in the other texts, such as the A. V. If ἐξ ἑνός is placed next to πᾶν ἔθνος, the numeral would be neuter: "out of one nation" he made every nation, etc. Standing by itself, ἐξ ἑνός could not be determined as masculine. But if we read ἐξ ἑνὸς αἵματος with πᾶν ἔθνος ἀνθρώπων following, the sense would be, "out of one man's blood every nation of men" and not merely, "out of one blood," etc.

The Athenians were fond of being called αὐτόχθονες, *indigenae*, "indigenous" (see Liddell and Scott on the word). Paul, however, deals with something that is more important than Athenian pride. The different pagan mythologies had their different accounts of man's origin. Over against all of these he places the one true God who created Adam, the one progenitor of the human race. This fact, recorded on the very first page of the Bible, our science has proved over and over again to its own satisfaction, finding also human blood vitally different from all other blood since it permits cross-fertilization in all human races.

Some of the German commentators translate πᾶν ἔθνος ἀνθρώπων "*alles Menschenvolk,*" "all humanity."

They think of ἔθνος as it is used with reference to bees, ants, migrating birds, and the like, as a collective noun; but this does not agree with the very next clause where national diversity is evidently referred to. So we abide by "every nation of men." These God made to settle over all the earth, one here, another there. But not in a haphazard way but as: "having destined their appointed seasons and the boundaries of their settlement," αὐτῶν modifying both "seasons" and "settlement." God allotted to each nation both its period and its geographical location according to the wisdom and beneficence of his providence. Zahn finds much fault with the reading and, as so often, resorts to the Codex Bezae which has: "according to their settlement boundary"; but this reading overlooks the resultant sense, namely that God destined or fixed the seasons according to the boundary of the territory settled — a strange way of doing! Here again this codex, while trying to improve, did the opposite.

God's hand has ever been and still is in history. Nations begin, rise to full development, finally decline. Historians trace out their courses, and thousands of natural causes are found to be at work. But these are but the surface. Underneath, over, within is the unseen Hand that guides and directs according to the supreme Will. We see the pattern from below, as it appears on the wrong side of the cloth; someday we shall see it as God weaves it, the right side, which is beautiful and perfect.

27) Paul is not solving the mysteries of providence. All that he presents in v. 26 with regard to God's doings with the men he made and with the nations he arranged is to bring out the supreme purpose of God regarding men: "for them to be seeking God," etc. Ζητεῖν is the infinitive of purpose, its subject is implied, namely men: "for them to be seeking." The implication is that men had lost God. This was a

thought that was already implied in the reference to idol worship (v. 25), in fact, already in the mention of the altar "to the Unknown God." It is not God's will to remain unknown, he wants men to seek and to find him and to enter into communion with him. All God's dealings with men show that this is his great purpose; God's creation of man and his providence place this beyond doubt. All false ideas about God, in particular agnosticism, atheism, pantheism, skepticism, to say nothing of polytheism and paganism, destroy the right relation of man to God and the attainment of the divine purpose.

The optatives are due to indirect discourse; εἰ is used for ἐάν with original subjunctives. That means that we here have a condition of expectancy. The ἄρα agrees with this and γε emphasizes, expressing, as always, a natural correspondence, namely, in this instance, that what God has done will, indeed, cause men to touch and to find him. So the expectancy is strengthened: "if, indeed, they might touch him and find him." The "haply" of our versions is misleading; it weakens the expectation. We are sorry to note that R., *W. P.*, supports that idea by speaking of a "vague hope" in regard to the condition's being met. Paul expresses a distinct and clear expectation. That is what all ἐάν conditions do; and he even emphasizes it as being proper by ἄρα γε. And καίγε agrees with this, γε strengthening καί; "he even being not far from every one of us." So near is he that one is fully entitled to expect that men will find him. And this is surely the case. The heavens declare the glory of God, everything points to him, the expectation must be that men will find God.

This is, of course, only natural revelation, and it cannot do what lies in the province of Scripture and of supernatural revelation. It cannot save man; but it can and does reveal the existence of God, of his majesty, glory, omnipotence, omniscience, beneficence, righteousness, and justice. So the expectation voiced by Paul is that, to say the least, men may, indeed, touch and find him. Paul is speaking about what God has a right to expect, in fact, the fullest right. The fact that men grossly disappoint him in this expectation is another matter, one that leaves them in the most fearful guilt. On that phase of the subject Paul speaks with equal clearness in Rom. 1:19-23. Here at Athens, however, Paul is trying to open the eyes of pagans to what God has given them: the cosmos to testify of him, their existence in the midst of endless beneficence, their nation in its development in a grand location on the earth with all that thus made Greece and especially Athens great. God had every right to expect that men such as those of Athens would long ago have arrived at a true and an adequate natural conception of their Creator, Ruler, and Benefactor. A silent, shaming question runs through the apostle's words: "Why had the Athenians not done so, they who even regarded themselves as standing so high among the nations?"

28) In order to bring out the idea as to how near God is to man in his natural state, the apostle does not appeal to the abstract omnipresence of God but to this omnipresence in its beneficent effect: "for in him we live and move and are." *To live* is more than *to move,* which even the inanimate creatures may do; *to move* is more than merely *to be,* to exist. Here, then, is an anticlimax. Man should be cognizant of God, for without him he could not live for a moment, could not move hand or foot, could not in any way even exist. This is a cardinal passage on the divine providence of God including the *praeservatio* and the so-called *concursus.* "In him" is more than "through him"; it expresses a wonderful immanence, yet, as the clear enunciation of creation and providence and the abso-

lute self-sufficiency of God show, without even an approach to pantheism.

Gibson has translated the Syriac commentary on Acts written by the Nestorian bishop Ischodad, of Chadeth on the Euphrates, about 850. This bishop quotes a certain Greek poet who wrote in praise of Zeus, and one of the lines reads: "For through thee we live and move and are." From Chrysostom's comment on Titus 1:12, Zahn concludes that this Greek poet was Epimenides, and the title of his composition was, "On Minos and Radamanthys." The Greek original has been lost, and Paul's statement is not metrical in form, nor does he indicate that he is quoting. All that one may say is that Paul may have read Epimenides and have used his statement in a formulation of his own.

He continues, "As also some of the poets among you have said." He refers to several Greek poets, and from one of them he quotes the last half of the hexameter: "Ever and in all ways we all enjoy Jupiter, *for we are also his offspring*." This is taken from Aratus, a countryman of Paul himself, who was born in the Cilician coast town of Soli about 310 B. C., and died about 240. He was a versatile man, a mathematician, astronomer, medic, court poet of the Macedonian king Antigonus Gonatus, editor of Homeric epics for the Syrian king Antiochus I Soter. He lived in Athens for years and was a pupil of Zeno, the founder of Stoicism. In Athens he composed his *Phaenomena*, which promptly became celebrated and was admired in the Greek-speaking world for centuries and was translated into Latin by Cicero and by Caesar Germanicus. Paul had certainly read this composition.

By using the plural "some of the poets among you" he indicates his conversance with others who say about the same thing as Aratus. One of them is the Athenian Stoic Cleanthes who for thirty-two years was leader of the Stoic school. In his famous hymn to Zeus he identifies himself with the whole human race and even with all mortal beings that live and crawl on earth and declares: ἐκ σου γὰρ γένος ἰσμέν, κτλ., "for from him we are offspring." A third poet is probably Timagenes who is named by Chrysostom in this connection, a writer of comedies of whom little is known.

On two other occasions Paul quotes from Greek poets. He quotes Menander in I Cor. 15:33, and a full hexameter from Epimenides of Crete in Titus 1:12. The question is naturally asked as to how far Paul was conversant with Greek literature, in particular with poetry. When Paul quotes verbatim as he did in these three cases he thereby shows a rather thorough acquaintance with Greek literature, he particularly demonstrates that he had studied and retained in memory certain striking passages. Paul was fully equipped to appear before the Athenians. His quiet reference to several of their poets and the exact quotation from one who was famous gently inform his hearers that he is not a stranger to their learning.

The words are quoted as Aratus wrote them; Paul omits neither γὰρ nor καί. We scan : — — | — ∪ ∪ | — ∪ : Τοῦ γὰρ | καὶ γένος | ἐσμέν. Here τοῦ is to be taken in its original sense as a demonstrative pronoun. The quotation from an Athenian poet is in the nature of an *argumentum ad hominem.* Zeus, of course, is not the true God but only the head of the mythological gods; but if the Greek poets themselves declared man to be his γένος (from γίνομαι as having "become" from him), that was an inkling of the real truth that the true God called us into being, preserves, and keeps us as such, in other words, treats us as his "offspring" which we are. The quotation is intended to refer to all that precedes in v. 26-28 and is certainly telling for this particular audience.

29) Paul then draws the simple, self-evident conclusion that God's own offspring certainly ought to know τὸ θεῖον better than to imagine (νομίζειν) that "the divine nature," that which God really is, could possibly be represented and pictured by anything made of gold or silver or stone, however skilfully it may be graven by man's "technique" in these materials and of his "conception" bodied forth in such material. God certainly must be conceived as being infinitely greater than man whom he has made; hence he cannot be like (ὅμοιον) anything that is far beneath man, namely metal and stone although it be worked up ever so artistically by man's art and thought.

Paul acknowledges all the art and the genius manifested in the statues of Athens but points out that, even when these are applied to the highest degree in the finest materials, they do so little justice to God that they do not even do justice to man and the conception he ought to have of his Maker, Ruler, and Benefactor. The idea of the apostle is thus not like that expressed in Isa. 44:9, etc., that the image made by man is itself considered to be a god by its maker. Paul advances beyond that. Such an image, man himself ought to realize, cannot even represent or picture God. Paul intends to say that the Athenians should certainly have touched and found God sufficiently, so that they would know that as the One in whom we live, move, and are, no images of gold, silver, or stone, a thing fashioned by the creature could in the least be like God. And he properly uses τὸ θεῖον, "the divine nature," that which is peculiar to God; for this is what would have to be embodied in an image. On its very face this is an impossibility.

Our versions mistranslate, for τὸ θεῖον is ἡ θειότης, *das Goettliche, das, was Gottes ist,* and not ἡ θεότης, *das Gottsein, das, was Gott ist,* "the Godhead," cf., C.-K. on these words, 490, etc. And what is peculiar to God and places him vastly above all material images is not merely the fact of his being spirit, as has been thought, but his infinite majesty and glory which transcend all human power of conception. These Athenians had been entertaining too low a conception of the divine nature; their city full of statues was a great reflection on their intelligence. No wonder the philosophers rejected the gods that were thus represented. But what had they to put in place of them, gods that had a nature that could be pictured in metal and stone? Nothing! Paul shows them what to put in place of all these gods: the infinite greatness, power, and glory of the one true God who is revealed already in the cosmos of his creation and in man, his offspring. The words of the apostle were few, but in all the philosophies and the poetry of Greece nothing had ever been uttered that even approached the power of these statements of Paul's.

30) After these fundamentals in regard to God and to man have been stated, the apostle advances to the revelation which God made in Christ. He naturally passes over the revelation made in the old covenant (he is speaking to pagans) and shows his hearers what God now offers them. **The times of the ignorance, accordingly, God having overlooked, as regards things now he passes the order along to all men for all everywhere to be repenting inasmuch as he set a day in which he is about to judge the inhabited earth in righteousness in the person of a man whom he ordained, having furnished assurance to all by having raised him up from the dead.** One God, one human race; and now one way of salvation, one judgment: these are the lines of the apostle's address.

Paul did not need to say that the purpose of God that men should seek him had not been met on the part of the Athenians; their polytheistic sanctuaries and statues were evidence enough of their failure in this regard. What did God do? Besser replies: "Had he looked at the Athenians with the fire flames of his holy eyes, there would have been no Athenian this many a day." But God "overlooked the times of the ignorance" by looking at Christ and the plan of salvation for the coming ages. He bore the idolatries of the Gentiles, he ceased not to reveal himself to them in nature and in providence, and because of their guilty ignorance he made them feel his wrath by giving them over to the effects of this ignorance, their depravity. But at last the great day for which God had so long been preparing and waiting in patience and in love had arrived: redemption was complete, the gospel could go forth to all the world.

So Paul says τανῦν, "as regarding things now" (adverbial accusative), since a new era has begun for all mankind through Christ. Now God "is passing the order along to all men for all everywhere to be repenting." He has sent out his heralds to all nations with the call to repent. At this very moment God was giving this order to the Athenians through Paul. Note the universality: "to men" as men — "all everywhere" with not a single exception. It is thus that Paul explains his presence in Athens and his preaching to the Athenians. On μετανοεῖν see 2:38. The present tense is used because of the succession implied in "all everywhere" — ever more men are to repent. They are to turn to the true God from their idols and their ignorance with an inward change of heart. Paul has not yet mentioned Christ; he will do so in a moment. But repentance is in place already on the basis of what Paul has presented thus far.

31) Καθότι is causal, "in consideration of this," "in accord with this reason." And the reason that God now orders all men to repent is the fact that "he did set a day in which he is about to judge the inhabited earth in righteousness." As he appointed certain

times and certain locations to every nation, so he has set a day of final judgment for all men. He is a righteous God, and his judgment will be "in righteousness," in harmony with this principle of his being. It will be a judgment that all men will acknowledge as right; for it will condemn all those who persist in turning away from God and will exonerate all those who allow themselves to be brought to God by his revelation and his grace. As God made all men and intends that they shall seek and find him, so all must appear before his judgment; ἡ οἰκουμένη (γῆ), "the inhabited earth," is here a term for all mankind.

By referring to God's righteous judgment Paul is aiming directly at the consciences of his hearers. His whole presentation has moved in this direction and is now being driven home. For so long a time these Athenians had been blind to God's revelation of himself in nature and in their own being; they were no longer blind since Paul had pointed out God to them in a way that brushed aside all their false representations of the divine nature. Must they now not turn and be drawn to God? How would they meet him at the great day of judgment when righteousness would flood them with its revealing light?

At this point Paul brings in Christ. The great feature about this judgment will be that God will execute it ἐν ἀνδρὶ ᾧ ὥρισεν, "in the person of (ἐν in this sense, R. 587) a man whom he ordained" (the relative is attracted to the case of its antecedent). Paul emphasizes the human nature of Christ as Christ himself does in John 5:27 when he speaks of his executing judgment as "the Son of man." He who died for us and rose again for our justification in his human nature, he shall be the judge at the last day who will pronounce the verdict as to whether a man has accepted or has rejected the redemption bought at such a price. Paul says that *God* will judge in the person of this man, *God* set the day, *God* ordained the man. He is preaching *God* to these pagans in mighty terms. As far as Christ is concerned, they will accept him only as one who was ordained by God.

The thought that all men were to be judged by a man was not new to Paul's hearers; but the mythological form of this idea current among them made this man a nebulous ancient being such as Minos and Radamanthys and thus turned the whole conception into something dim and ineffective. As the apostle had lifted God into a clear vision for his hearers, so he did the same with regard to Christ, the Judge. It was God himself who ordained this man to be the judge, "having furnished assurance to all by having raised him up from the dead." All are to know that God so ordained him, their assurance is God's raising him up. Παρέχω (here the second aorist participle) πίστιν means "to furnish trustworthy assurance or evidence," that assurance being Christ's resurrection. Some refer πίστιν to saving faith and say that the participle extends such faith to all; but this does not agree with the expression itself which means *Buergschaft leisten, Unterpfand gewaehren* (B.-P. 1061). The argument that μετανοεῖν requires that πίστις in the sense of saving faith should follow, does not show that it follows in this expression. Paul had not finished his address, more was to follow.

Paul held his hearers in suspense by not at once naming this man. Who could he be? It was the very question Paul intended to provoke in order the more effectively to present the great truth that God appointed this man Judge because God first of all made him our Savior. The fact that God raised this man from the dead and by that astounding act sealed him as Judge was the first part of Paul's answer to the question as to who this man was. But instead of opening their ears wider to hear more about this man these

Athenians gave way to a scoffing, skeptical spirit. They interrupted Paul, broke off his address, and would hear no more. On ἐκ νεκρῶν see 3:16.

Paul's address in Athens has been called philosophy. Instead of preaching the gospel, Paul is said to have tried something else for the benefit of these educated Athenians. To this is added the statement that Paul failed. This claim is extended, and Paul is thought to have left for Corinth, a thoroughly disappointed and discouraged man. We are told that he never again tried to preach as he had done in Athens. Evidence for these ideas is found in the fact that Luke fails to mention any baptisms that were performed in Athens, any congregation, any appointment of elders. Then I Cor. 2:1-5 is introduced as though Paul returned to Christ crucified and abandoned philosophy when he worked in Corinth. But if Paul's address in Athens was a mistaken resort to philosophy or, softening this, a mistaken mode of trying to reach his hearers, why did Luke report this address in full? Paul succeeded in Athens (v. 34). Luke lays so much stress on this masterly address that he makes it the main part of his report in regard to Athens. The fact that the persons mentioned in v. 34 were baptized goes without saying; Luke does not always mention the baptisms. A congregation was certainly organized, its size is immaterial.

32) **But on hearing the resurrection of the dead some began to mock, others said, We will hear thee concerning this yet again. Thus Paul went out from their midst. Some men, however, closely drawn to him, believed, among whom was also Dionysius, the Areopagite, and a woman by name Damaris, and others with them.**

Already in v. 18 Luke has told us that the resurrection attracted attention. Now the moment Paul mentions it again "some began to mock" with derisive exclamations. We can scarcely imitate ἀνάστασιν νεκρῶν with its absence of articles, *Totenauferstehung,* such a thing as dead men being raised. The very idea was preposterous to these scoffers. It is impossible to determine whether these scoffers were Epicureans or Stoics. We have stated what these philosophers believed regarding the state of the soul after death; the Greeks otherwise believed that the soul lived on. But even the ordinary Greeks had absolutely no conception that the body could or did arise. So they just laughed at Paul. "If the judge before whom thou citest us is one risen from the dead, we little fear him!" Besser.

Others were indeed willing, they said, to hear Paul again about this matter. This is usually taken to be only politeness on the part of those who had invited Paul before this audience. Yet it may well have been real interest so that they did hear Paul again.

33) Thus Paul went out from their midst. The famous address had been held.

34) But now comes the glorious result. Some men were closely drawn to Paul (literally, "glued to him") and could not tear themselves away from him. These constituted the third class among those who had heard Paul. And Luke at once adds that they believed, believed already on the strength of what Paul had said. The aorist is historical. One of these was no less a person than Dionysius, the Areopagite, one of the twelve judges of the Athenian Court. That was, indeed, a signal victory. About 100 to 120 years later, as Eusebius reports (4, 23, 3, also 3, 4, 11), the bishop of Corinth by the same name in a letter to the church at Athens speaks of this Dionysius who was converted by Paul as having been the first bishop of Athens. His very standing as an Areopagite would certainly have made him the man to become chief elder in the infant congregation.

Luke speaks of ἄνδρες "men," and yet adds a woman and even records her name, Damaris. This causes a good deal of discussion. How did it come about that she was present? She was not the wife of Dionysius, which Luke does not state. Some regard her as a ἑταίρα (Liddell and Scott) at the expense of her character, for instance as an educated courtesan. Even her name is altered as though Damaris had been written instead of Damalis (heifer). Abbott-Smith makes the name a derivative from the poetic word for wife δάμαρ, which is better. One thing is certain, her presence helps to answer the view that Paul spoke to only a dozen or a score of philosophers. The very mention of her plus her name proves that she was a woman of consequence who could be present at this meeting to hear Paul and was of great importance in the congregation. There were also others, but all of them were men. But these were the first to believe. Paul remained and continued to work. We need not think that he at once left Athens. This beginning would detain him until he could leave the young flock in security. Because Luke says no more is no reason to think that more converts were not added and that a congregation was properly organized and put on its feet.

NOTE: Manuals on Logic define the *argumentum ad hominem* as an attack on an opponent's character instead of an answer to the subject of discussion. When I speak of Paul's *argumentum ad hominem* on page 733 I do not accept this definition. John 8:48 is not an *argumentum ad hominem* but vicious vilification. He who runs out of argument attacks the person. This is the abandonment of all argument, the open admission of defeat in all argument. The definition of the *argumentum ad hominem* is given by the *Standard Dictionary* under "argumentum": "An argument proving a conclusion from the principles or practices of an opponent himself: often by showing them to be contrary to his argument." *International Cyclopedia:* "An appeal to the known prepossessions or admissions of the person addressed." This *argumentum* is legitimate and sound, and in the sense here defined I use the term throughout.

CHAPTER XVIII

The Second Missionary Journey: Corinth

1) **After these things, having withdrawn from Athens, he went to Corinth.**

The passive of χωρίζειν is used in the middle sense: Paul withdrew from Athens of his own accord; compare 1:4. No persecution drove Paul out of this place. The plural "after these things" refers to all that transpired in Athens. Compare 17:34, where Luke implies that a congregation was organized. The view that Paul took a new and a risky step in Athens by preaching in philosophic form, saw his mistake because of the small result attained, and then left for Corinth cannot be maintained. The proposed premise does not warrant the conclusion. A man who starts in a wrong way does not flee to a new place in order there to start in a right way but remains and starts over again and retrieves his mistake. It is unwarranted to assume anything else in regard to Paul.

It is also unwarranted to think that Paul did not even baptize his converts in Athens but abandoned them. Likewise, that no congregation was organized, and that Paul's effort was abortive. I Cor. 2:1-5 implies the very opposite. Paul continued to preach Christ in all simplicity. He had done so in Athens and continued to do so in the more difficult city of Corinth. As far as the two cities are concerned, the work in Athens was the easier of the two. "After these things" means after the success achieved in Athens, after he had planted a congregation in this city. He withdrew of his own accord because the planting was completed; if more had been needed, Paul would have remained until this, too, had been done, for the matter of leaving lay in his own hands. In other cities he had to leave when he would have remained a while; not so here.

Corinth, once the capital of the Achaean league, was destroyed by Mummius in B. C. 146 and was left in ruins for a century until Julius Caesar rebuilt it in B. C. 46 and made it a *colonia.* In Paul's time it was the capital of the Roman province of Achaia, the chief commercial city of Greece, prosperous and luxuriant, cnly fifty miles from Athens. Back of it towered Acrocorinthus, 1,800 feet high. Situated on the isthmus, it had two harbors, Cenchraea near to it on the Aegean side, and Lechaeum on the opposite side of the isthmus, across which goods were transferred and small ships hauled. A canal now cuts through the isthmus.

It was this situation that made Corinth great, so that it commanded the great trade route between Asia and Rome. This accounts for the mixed population, for ships from all ports docked in its harbors. In Athens, Paul met the Greek mythological gods, to Corinth flocked many men of varied religions, nationalities, languages. It was not accidental that many in the Corinthian congregation spoke with tongues. Corinth had several temples that were devoted to Egyptian deities, which fact is explained by its extensive trade with Alexandria. It was natural for the Alexandrian Apollos to work in Corinth (19:1). Paul wrote his letter to the Romans from Corinth, and the list of Latin names at the end of this letter marks Corinth as being a prominent colony. Although it was a wealthy city, we must not forget that wealth implied many slaves and many poor people below the wealthy stratum. The congregation founded by Paul was drawn chiefly from these two classes of people.

Corinth did not boast of a single outstanding philosopher; its pride was trade and the arts. Corinthian brass was famous, and Corinthian capitals and pillars are still used in architecture. Yet the Greek spirit was strong because Corinth was situated in Greece. We should go wrong in thinking of philosophers, yet speculative ideas were to be found everywhere, just as today many claim γνῶσις (they call it "science") who are anything but scientific or philosophic. The pride of this attitude was characteristic just as it is today.

Corinth was a wicked city even as larger cities of the empire went at this period. The very term "Corinthian" came to mean a profligate. Κορινθιάζομαι, "to Corinthianize," meant to practice whoredom; Κορινθιαστής = a whoremonger; Κορινθία κόρη (girl) = a courtesan. In the old city the worship of Venus boasted of 1,000 female slaves who were free to strangers. Venus worship marked also the restored city although we have no account of the number of the prostitutes connected with the new temple. Money was freely spent in Corinth. Paul's description of pagan vice, Rom. 1:18-32, was written in Corinth. One of the great attractions were the Isthmian games, the custody of which was restored to the new city. Greeks and Romans flocked to the contest, and the mob came in crowds, but the effect was degrading.

2) **And having found a Jew by name Aquila, a Pontic by race, having lately come from Italy, and Priscilla, his wife, because Claudius had ordered all the Jews to withdraw from Rome, he went in to them and, because he was of the same trade, he continued to remain with them and to work, for they were tentmakers by trade.**

Luke records all this because Paul remained in Corinth about eighteen months and his reader should know how he supported himself, and because of the importance of the couple with whom Paul became associated here in Corinth. We shall meet Aquila and his wife in Ephesus and in Rome. "A Pontic by race" means that he was born in the Roman province of Pontus on the borders of the Black Sea. Incidentally, it is worth noting how this man and his wife moved freely from place to place: Pontus, Rome, Corinth, Ephesus, Rome again, etc.

The emperor Claudius reigned 41-54. He was very friendly to the Jews and accorded them various privileges. In 49 Agrippa was still in the company of the emperor, which places the date of the order after that year. Paul came to Corinth in the fall of 51 and left in the spring of 53 (Zahn, *Apostelgeschichte,* 656, in an extended discussion of the dates). About 20,000 Jews lived in Rome. They were first warned against tumultuous actions, finally the decree of expulsion from Rome was issued. The historian Suetonius writes: *Judaeos impulsore Chresto assidue tumultantes Roma expulit.* Although they were not driven out of Italy but only out of Rome, Aquila and Priscilla went as far as Corinth. It is usually thought that "Chrestus" = "Christus," and this view is based on Tacitus who, indeed, writes "Christus" but has *Chrestianos* as a name for Christians. Suetonius, however, speaks of an agitator in Rome, and "Chrestus" is a common name which has nothing to do with "Christ." The assumption must be given up that the clashes referred to by Suetonius occurred between hostile Jews and Christians in Rome concerning Jesus. In 28:17-29 all the leading Jews of Rome readily come to Paul, and after a long day's conference with him many of them were being persuaded by the apostle. This is inconceivable if some years prior to this the lines had been drawn between the Jews and the Christians in Rome so that tumults and the expulsion of the Jews from the city had resulted. See the discussion of 28:17, etc.

After the death of Claudius the Jews returned to Rome. Paul converted more than one half of them as Luke informs us in 28:17-31. To this great body of converted Jews in Rome the Epistle to the Hebrews is addressed after the death of Paul, and everything points to Apollos as the writer of this epistle. See my introduction to Hebrews.

Aquila and Priscilla had established themselves in Corinth in company with many others who were affected by the decree of expulsion. Among the first converts at the time of Pentecost had been Jews from Pontus (2:9), but these had settled in Jerusalem. Aquila and Priscilla had very likely heard about Jesus while they were in Rome. Although Luke does not record their conversion through Paul, it is unwarranted to assume that they had become converts already in Rome. Paul naturally made his abode with a Jew because he always began work in the synagogue. Although they at first associated with one another for business reasons, Paul's employers soon became the most devoted Christians and the closest friends of the apostle.

3) Paul lived and lodged with them during his entire stay in Corinth. Aquila took him into his employ. Both were tentmakers, σκηνοποιοί; they made portable tents out of leather or cloth woven out of goat's hair. There is no reason to think that they manufactured the cloth or prepared the hides. The ancients thought that this Greek word meant shoemakers, or saddlemakers, or leatherworkers in general. Paul earned his own living while he preached the gospel. He did it by his own choice. He discusses the matter at length in I Cor. 9:1-15, and brings out the truth that he, too, had the fullest right to marry a wife and to expect the support of the church. The two imperfect tenses indicate an indefinite stay and occupation.

4) **And he began to discuss in the synagogue every Sabbath and tried to persuade both Jews and Greeks.**

Luke does not need to add that these Greeks were proselytes of the gate; he has done that often enough in previous cases. It is sufficient to know that these Jews and these Greeks were together in the synagogue. We thus have a picture of the first weeks spent in Corinth: Paul working during the week and engaging in discussions in the synagogue on the Sabbath. Every Jewish boy was taught a trade in order to make him independent. Rabbi Juda said, "He that teacheth not his son a trade teacheth him to be a thief." And the Talmud: "What is commanded of a father toward his son? To circumcise him, to teach him the law, to teach him a trade." Nothing is said about success as a result of these discussions. The first imperfect is inchoative: "he began to discuss"; the second is conative: "he tried to persuade" (R. 885). Paul was laying the foundation; he delayed pressing the issue to a final decision.

5) **But when both Silas and Timothy came down from Macedonia, Paul began to hold himself to the Word, continuing to testify earnestly to the Jews that Jesus is the Christ.**

In 17:15 we have discussed the missions on which Timothy and Silas were sent from Athens to Thessalonica and to Philippi. They now returned to Paul in Corinth, probably at the same time, or Timothy came first from Thessalonica with his good news (I Thess. 3:6), and Silas came from Philippi soon after this. In regard to the gifts that Philippi sent to Paul we have remarked already in 17:14. They had already reached him and should not be introduced here in Corinth in order to explain how Paul was able to stop working at his trade for a while. The arrival of his two helpers made Paul press for a decision. "He began to hold himself to the Word" ("spirit" in the A. V. is incorrect), inchoative imperfect of the direct middle (R. 808, also *W. P.*, not passive as our versions translate). He began to devote all his time to the Word, applying himself especially to testifying earnestly to the Jews that Jesus is the Messiah. His earnings during the past few weeks enabled him to do this. The Jews were Paul's special concern; and the issue was whether they would accept Jesus as "the Christ," the Messiah.

6) **But they arraying themselves in opposition and blaspheming, having shaken out his garments, he said to them: Your blood upon your own head! Clean I on my part! From now on I go to the Gentiles! And on departing thence he went to the house of one by name Titus Justus, a worshipper of God, whose house was adjoining the synagogue.**

This was the result attained with regard to the Jews. They ranged themselves in battle array (so literally) and flung railing and blasphemy at Paul and at the idea that Jesus should be the Christ. Paul could follow no other course than to withdraw. The manner in which he does this shows his deep emotion. The act of shaking the garments is symbolic in the same way as shaking off the dust of the feet, with this difference that the one takes place indoors while the other is performed on the street. Both are often misunderstood. Ramsay, for instance, writes, "undoubtedly a very exasperating gesture," others, "a sign of contempt," etc. The act denotes that the dust is left behind and not taken along and thus remains as a witness that the gospel messengers had come and duly delivered their message but had not been received in faith. That dust would testify to the Judge, and none of the guilty would be able to deny its testimony. See 13:51.

This act accompanies Paul's words. These are not a curse or an imprecation but a disclaimer of guilt on Paul's part. Since they reject Jesus as the Christ, damnation must follow. Whose is the fault? It is that of these Jews alone. To speak of blood coming upon one's head is to say that the guilt for shedding someone's blood rests upon the murderer and cries to God for punishment. Here the blood of these Jews who are destroying themselves rests upon their own heads, they are like men committing spiritual suicide. Compare Matt. 23:35, and especially Matt. 27:24, 25. "Clean I on my part!" emphatic ἐγώ, means clean of the blood of these Jews; Paul has left nothing undone to save them. And since because of their violent state he can do no more he repeats what he and Barnabas did in Pisidian Antioch (13:46), he goes to the Gentiles. So the great turning point was reached in Corinth.

7) Forthwith Paul and, of course, Silas and Timothy with him retired from the synagogue and went next door to it to the house of Titus Justus, whom Luke designates as a proselyte of the gate (see 13:43). His house must have been spacious enough to provide ample opportunity for carrying on Paul's work among the Gentiles. The fact that it happened to adjoin the synagogue could not be helped even if this circumstance angred the Jews; σύν — ὅμος, joint, ὅρος, boundary = having joint boundary, adjoining. Titus must have been a Roman citizen, one of the *coloni*, a man of prominence. The Titii were a famous family of potters in Corinth, and the name of this family dates back to 133 B. C., and many of its members were prominent in military and in civil positions. This Titus may have taken the added name Justus on becoming a proselyte of the gate. He should not be confused with the Titus who became one of Paul's assistants. Moreover, his name is frequently spelled Titius.

8) **Crispus, however, the synagogue ruler, believed the Lord with his whole house; and many of the Corinthians, hearing, kept believing and being baptized.**

Titus Justus was a most prominent proselyte of the synagogue, and Crispus was even one of its rulers. When the division came, the synagogue lost both, which was a great victory for Paul. The idea that this synagogue had only one *archisynagogos*, whether he was sole ruler or the head of its group of rulers, must be given up in view of the plural used in 13:15. Crispus was one of several rulers. His entire family went with him. What this implies has been discussed in connection with Lydia in 16:15 and the jailor in 16:33, 34 also in regard to the baptism of children. Paul baptized Crispus with his own hand, I Cor. 1:14. Yet we should be hasty in concluding from the few persons that Paul himself baptized in Corinth that he considered this a minor matter; Matt. 28:19 corrects that opinion.

The "many of the Corinthians" were pagan Greeks who had not been connected with the synagogue. Paul's letters to the Corinthians show that the congregation had comparatively few Jews in its membership. I Cor. 1:12 names a party that called itself after Cephas, and this was probably made up of former Jews. The two imperfects plus the present participle describe a continuous influx of new members, all of whom were converts from heathenism. Most of these, too, must have been whole families, a fact which must not be overlooked when the baptism of children in the apostolic congregations is discussed. The Codex Bezae again rewrites in the way of a commentary, but its comments are not an improvement on Luke's text.

9) All this implied that Paul might consider that the time had come to move on to some new field, for the congregation in Corinth was fully established. Another consideration would influence Paul: the rumblings among the hostile Jews, whose viciousness Paul knew so well from past experience in other fields. He was the focus of this implacable hatred. Since the congregation was well established, Paul might think it wise to move on before the Jews started a move against his person. But the Lord himself detained him in Corinth.

Now the Lord said to Paul at night through a vision: Stop being afraid but go on speaking and be not silent, because I myself am with thee, and no one shall set on thee to ill-treat thee, because I have much people in this city. And he sat a year and six months, teaching among them the Word of God.

The Lord himself spoke to Paul in a vision by night. We must compare 22:18; 16:9; 27:23, and also the other instances when the Lord or his Spirit directed Paul where not to go. They show the immediate divine guidance in the spread of the gospel. It is never our work but always the Lord's even though we are now left to depend only on his providential guidance which opens doors here and closes them elsewhere.

The present imperative in negative commands often means to stop an action already begun (R. 851, etc.). It does so here. Paul had begun to fear lest, by staying too long, he might precipitate an attack upon himself that would do damage to the young and growing congregation. Even after he had left Thessalonica, the congregation in that city had to suffer because of the onset that had been made by the Jews (17:5, etc.). Paul had worried about the Thessalonians and had sent Timothy to find out how matters stood (I Thess. 3:1-6). He learned what they had suffered but also that they had remained firm. Paul was fearing similar trouble in Corinth, which he might obviate by leaving in time. The Lord told him to dismiss all such fears. Nor was he to try to avoid trouble by quietly working on. No, he is to go on speaking (durative, present imperative) and is not to become silent (the aorist subjunctive in a negative command, punctiliar, ingressive, "fall silent"). The idea, of course, is that of relative silence. He is to work quietly so that the vicious Jews would hear little of his work and not be stirred to violence. This was not an order to cast prudence to the winds. This virtue is always in place. It was the preamble to the Lord's assurance that he himself (emphatic ἐγώ) was with Paul to protect him in his work so that no ill would come to the congregation through anything that his free and open work might bring about.

10) "I myself am with thee" vividly recalls Matt. 28:20. Do not ask: "Did Paul not know this promise?" He did, but it meant much to him in his present situation to have it repeated. So we to this day must seek out the Lord's promises in order to assure ourselves of them anew in difficult situations where we need their strengthening power more than at other times.

Paul had been set upon repeatedly. In Philippi Silas had been caught with him, but Paul was the real object of hatred. So the Lord here assures him that in Corinth, despite his boldness of utterance, no one shall set upon him and succeed in ill-treating him (aorist infinitive, effective). We certainly know that this promise was not made on Paul's account as though it was to dispel fears concerning his own person. The Lord states a different reason: the many people he had in this city, "because much people is to me," the common Greek idiom. The Lord speaks by virtue of his omniscience exactly as he does in John 10:16: "Other sheep I have." R., *W. P.*, thinks that the Lord refers to the elect, namely as having been made such by an absolute eternal decree. But God foreordained those whom he foreknew (Rom. 8:29) and excluded no man from his election and eternal salvation by an absolute decree concerning him (I Tim. 2:4; compare v. 6: 13:46)

11) Ἐκάθισε harmonizes with διδάσκων; Paul sat, engaged in teaching. The year and six months comprise his entire stay in the city of Corinth. For immediately after his arrival Paul sat in Corinth and taught. The preceding clause speaks of all the people the Lord had "in this city" and not only in regard to those who were converted after this vision. Hence we cannot

count this year and six months by beginning with the vision, so that his entire stay would approach two years as some reckon; nor can we count the eighteen months from the arrival of Silas and Timothy. The reason for inserting the time of Paul's entire stay at this point is the Lord's order to Paul not to leave immediately after the congregation was fully established. We have no means of estimating how long Paul had been in Corinth when the vision came that told him to remain still longer. Some time after this vision the affair before Gallio occurred; even then Paul remained on (v. 18).

In II Cor. 1:1, Paul speaks of all the saints in Achaia, and in Rom. 16:1 we read of a church in Cenchraea, the seaport of Corinth. How it came about that the gospel was spread so far we see in II Cor. 1:19. While Paul "sat" at work in Corinth itself, Silas (Silvanus) and Timothy were active beyond the confines of the city. It has also been assumed that Paul left the home of Aquila and Priscilla (v. 2) and took up his residence with Titus Justus when the break with the synagogue came (v. 7). But μεταβάς does not imply a change of residence but only a transfer of teaching from the synagogue to this convert's house. Jesus had explicitly said, "Go not from house to house," Luke 10:5-7; Matt. 10:11, "there abide until ye go thence." Paul stopped his work, cf., v. 5, but certainly not for the rest of his long stay in Corinth (I Cor. 9:15). As he earned his own living in Thessalonica (II Thess. 3:8-11), so he did in Corinth in Aquila's shop. When he left Corinth, Aquila and Priscilla went along with him (v. 18), so close was their mutual attachment. It is untenable to assume that Paul left their home a few weeks after coming to Corinth and then lived the following months with a wealthy Gentile Christian. Would Paul treat his dearest friends in this manner (Rom. 16:3, 4)?

12) **Now when Gallio was proconsul of Achaia, with one accord the Jews rose up against Paul and brought him to the tribunal, saying, This fellow overpersuades men to worship God contrary to the law.**

Lucius Junius Gallio bore this name after his adoption by the Roman rhetor Lucius Junius Gallio, a friend of his father's. His original name was Lucius Annaeus Novatus; he was born about 3 B. C., in Corduba, Spain, the son of a lawyer, Lucius Annaeus Seneca. His younger brother, who had the same name as the father, was the Stoic philosopher, poet, educator of Nero, and statesman, generally known as Seneca, who characterized his older brother: *Nemo enim mortalium uni tam dulcis quam hic omnibus* (No one of mortals is so pleasant to one person as he is to all). A third brother was M. Annaeus Mela (or Melas). All three were of a weak physical constitution, and all three were compelled to commit suicide by Nero.

Luke is the only writer who calls Gallio a proconsul although Seneca mentions the fact that he was taken with fever in Achaia. The province of Achaia underwent various shifts in government, being now imperial, then senatorial; but Luke has been amply vindicated when he speaks of it as being senatorial at this time, as being governed by a proconsul. In 1909 a whitish grey limestone inscription from the Hagias Elias quarries near Delphi was found which immortalized a letter from the emperor Claudius to the citizens of Delphi, which contains not only the name of Gallio, "Lucius Junius Gallio, my friend and proconsul of Achaia," but also most valuable dates: the 12th tribunician year of Claudius, for the 26th time acclaimed Imperator. This places us between January 25 and August 1 of the year 52. Zahn corrects Deissmann in regard to the beginning of Gallio's proconsulship. This office was held for only a year and seldom for two. Imperial orders made the time for leaving Rome April 1, and then April 15.

Gallio must have arrived in Corinth before May 1 of the year 52. Deissmann mistakenly assumes his arrival in midsummer and hence dates it about July of the year 51, which would shift all dependent estimates of dates by a year. Many have followed Deissmann, also R. in his books; but the time of year when proconsuls had to leave Rome should clear up this matter.

The absolute date thus secured, May 1, 52 to May 1, 53 for Gallio's proconsulship, affects all dates stated in Acts back to 13:4, and thus shortens by a year the previously accepted calculations for the period covered in 13:1-3. Paul came to Corinth in the fall of 51; the episode before Gallio, who came to Corinth about six months later, must be dated after May, 52. Paul's entire stay covered eighteen months; he thus left Corinth in the spring of 53. This calculation obviates placing any of the journeys into the winter, a point not to be overlooked. The seven lines of the inscription are damaged in some places, but experts are agreed on all omitted letters; the disagreement is due to other points.

The Jews tried the same tactics they had used in Philippi (16:19). The tactics employed by those in Thessalonica were worse (17:5). "They rose up with one accord," formed a crowd (this compound verb occurs only here), seized Paul, and brought him to the βῆμα of the proconsul. This word means step, orator's platform, and then a platform or raised dais for the seat of the judge. Gallio was new in office; the Jews had attempted nothing during the time of office of the previous proconsul but they seem to think that because of their numbers and their vociferation they can move the new governor to punish and to banish Paul. So Paul faces a Roman proconsul for the second time but under totally different circumstances from the first time (13:7).

13) The accusation lodged against Paul is not identical with that made in Philippi (16:20, etc.) or with that made in Thessalonica (17:6, 7). No political

crime is charged against him. The Jewish religion was regarded as a *religio licita,* it could be freely practiced and had the privilege of making converts, although not among Roman citizens. The charge against Paul was not that he practiced a *religio illicita* but that he contravened Roman law by the way in which he practiced the Jewish religion, namely by persuading them to worship God in a way which they as orthodox Jews had to repudiate. They, of course, do not explain that this was done by preaching that Jesus was the Jewish Messiah, a claim which they utterly rejected. Their point is that by deviating from the regular Jewish way of worshipping God, which was sanctioned by Roman law, Paul transgressed that law and its sanction, was acting παρὰ τὸν νόμον.

The charge against Paul is often misunderstood, and it is stated that Gallio's reply did not fit the charge. Then it is assumed that by further questioning Gallio discovered that it was a contention only about Jewish religious questions. But this idea reflects on Luke by assuming that he did not adequately report the charge. Luke reports entirely to the point. Gallio's reply fits the charge as recorded by Luke.

14) **But when Paul was about to open his mouth, Gallio said to the Jews: If it were some injury or criminal wickedness, O Jews, according to reason I would have put up with you; but if they are questions concerning doctrine and names and law peculiar to you, you will see to them yourselves. A judge of these matters I on my part am determined not to be!**

Roman law brought accuser and accused face to face before the judge. After the charge had been made, the accused had the right to offer his defense. It was thus that Paul looked for the signal from Gallio which would permit him to reply to the indictment. Paul was prepared to open his mouth. But Gallio promptly rejected the entire charge. The Jews had no case in court. They were ordered out of court. Their whole effort was a great nuisance to the Roman proconsul who had other things that properly belonged to his jurisdiction to take up his time and his attention.

Note how μέν and δέ (v. 15) balance the two conditional statements. In v. 14 we have a mixed condition: εἰ with the imperfect (protasis, present unreality): "if this were a proper legal case — but it is not"; and the aorist with ἄν (apodosis, past unreality): "I would have entertained it in my court, i. e., when you brought it — but I have not done so." Gallio also indicates what are proper legal cases: a charge involving ἀδίκημα τι, some injury inflicted on the complainant, or ῥᾳδιούργημα πονηρόν (τι understood), some wicked rascality, some slick villany that has been perpetrated in a criminal way. Gallio teaches these Jews a lesson on the functions of a Roman judge. Then "according to reason," i. e., in whatever way reason would apply to the case — and, of course, only in that way — would he have tolerated them. Gallio means that even then it would have been an infliction on him, a case which he would not have enjoyed handling. This Roman proconsul wants these Jews to understand that he knows what sort of people the Jews are. Claudius had to drive them out of Rome (v. 2); Gallio had just come from Rome; and here in Corinth this whole crowd of Jews ("with one accord," v. 12) was invading his court immediately after he had assumed his office and trying to start trouble when everything else was to occupy his attention.

15) The condition of unreality intimates Gallio's conviction that the Jews were bringing no legitimate legal case before him. He follows this with a condition of reality: εἰ with the indicative (protasis), any tense in the apodosis. "If, however, they are — and I am convinced that they are — nothing but disputes concerning doctrine (λόγου) and names and law peculiar to

you (τοῦ καθ' ὑμᾶς, which is stronger than a mere genitive), see to them yourselves." The future is volitive and almost equal to an imperative (R. 874): "you will see to them" — they are your business and not mine. Since he had come from Rome, Gallio knew all about these agitations of the Jews (see v. 12) and indicates this by the three terms he uses, λόγος as a designation for Jewish doctrine, ὀνόματα for the contention about Jewish authorities, and νόμος τοῦ καθ' ὑμᾶς for the Jewish Torah and its contents. These were at the bottom of the tumults that arose in Rome, on account of which the emperor had to expel the Jews. Gallio is determined to have no repetition of this in Corinth. That is why he makes short work of these Jews at the very beginning.

Note that κριτὴς ἐγώ are abutted, which increases the emphasis and is a construction that we cannot duplicate in English: "a judge — I — of these things" — no! With this statement the proconsul throws the case out of court with all the dignity and disdain of a high Roman official. He wants these Jews to understand right here and now that he will have no more of this sort of thing.

Some have misunderstood Gallio's action and his temper on this occasion. They overlook v. 2; they are puzzled as to how Gallio could act with such understanding as v. 15 evidences, and think that Luke omitted some questions which Gallio put to the Jews; then they picture Gallio as the noble Roman who knows where to draw the line between church and state, the Roman who wisely follows Rome's policy of leaving the religions of its subject peoples alone. Gallio is credited with fine statesmanship, noble tolerance, exceptional justice, and great strength of character. But we have a different conception of this scene. Gallio knew what these Jews were after; he used good sense in squelching them forthwith and rather thoroughly; he intended to have no bother and disturbance from that source during his term of office — that is the whole story. A little more must be added.

16) **And he drove them from his tribunal. But having laid hold on Sosthenes, the synagogue ruler, they all began to beat him before the tribunal. And Gallio was concerned about none of these things.**

When Gallio threw the case of these Jews out of court, they should have left the tribunal promptly. Let us remember that the proconsul of a great Roman province was equal to the governor of one of our states, in fact, was like a governor plus the supreme court of his state. Why did Gallio drive those Jews from his tribunal (βῆμα, as in v. 12)? Because they remained after their case had been thrown out. Gallio had to *throw* them out. He ordered his lictors to take their rods and to clear the place. A judge of far lower standing would have done the same.

17) Sosthenes was, no doubt, their spokesman. The idea that this synagogue had but one ἀρχισυνάγωγος is answered by the plural used in 13:15. Nor do we think that Sosthenes was elected in place of Crispus (v. 8). The synagogue always had several rulers, especially one that was as large as this synagogue in Corinth. Sosthenes was the spokesman because of his ability to serve in this capacity, he would have been the spokesman even if Crispus had remained a member of the synagogue.

Now what does it mean that "having laid hold on him, all began to beat him"? Simply this, that he persisted, and that all the lictors began to strike him with their rods, the imperfect implying that they did not need to do this very long.

This obvious sense is questioned because of πάντες, and the question is raised, "Who were they?" Some answer, "The Jews" cf., R., *W. P.* Sosthenes is said to have bungled his job as a spokesman so that the

Jews themselves avenged themselves on him by giving him a beating before the very tribunal. The Codex Bezae is referred to which states that these "all" were a group of Greeks who became incensed at Sosthenes. But these Greeks would have manhandled more than merely one Jew. And what about the statement that "none of these things was a care to Gallio"? Let us at once say that he certainly would have minded it if the Jews had beaten their own spokesman, or if any Greek bystanders had done so.

Some commentators praise Gallio for strength of character in driving the Jews from his tribunal (see v. 16) and then fault him as being a weak character for allowing Sosthenes to be beaten before his tribunal, be it by the Jews or by the Greeks. These views cancel each other, and neither is correct. No proconsul would have tolerated such a thing, nor was such a beating a matter for the police court and not for a proconsul's court. No supreme judge would disregard a lesser crime that is committed in his own court. All is clear when πάντες is referred to the proconsul's own lictors. An obstreperous synagogue ruler would soon have them all around him, striking him, and he would retire with speed. Gallio certainly would not interfere. But "none of these things" refers to far more, namely to the whole affair, of which the hurried departure of Sosthenes was but a small part. The proconsul held himself superior to this whole affair, and so concerned himself no more about the entire matter.

Other suppositions are added. Sosthenes bungled his task because he was already half a Christian, and therefore the Jews beat him, and this helped to make him completely a Christian (R., *W. P.*). This view is based on I Cor. 1:1, where a Sosthenes is mentioned. The fact is overlooked that Paul calls this Sosthenes "a brother" and not "your brother" and in no way connects him with the Corinthians to whom he is writing. The name Sosthenes was one that was frequently found. And I Cor. 1:1 itself answers the assumption that the two were identical.

End of the Second and Beginning of the Third Missionary Journey

18) The second missionary journey did not extend beyond Corinth. Paul left a well-established church in this city. The experience the Jews had with Gallio seems to have satisfied the Jews, for in Paul's letters to Corinth he mentions no persecutions of any kind.

Now Paul, after having remained for many days with the brethren, having taken his leave, started to sail out for Syria, and with him Priscilla and Aquila, having shorn his head at Cenchraea; for he had a vow.

After the action of the proconsul Gallio, Paul had no reason to leave Corinth in a hurry. So he remained for a considerable number of days. We have indicated already in connection with v. 11 that the entire stay in Corinth comprised eighteen months, yet some add also these "days" to the eighteen months. Until the very end of his stay Paul was active in gathering new converts. The dative τοῖς ἀδελφοῖς is to be construed with προσμείνας and not as our versions translate it.

Paul finally bade farewell and set out for Syria. The inchoative imperfect ἐξέπλει, "started out to sail," is in place because the final destination, Syria, was not reached by means of one voyage. We can fix the date rather exactly, due to the inscription discussed in v. 12. It was after March 10, 53. That was the time of the year when shipping was resumed (not already on March 5, as some suppose). We thus see why Paul had to wait until this time. Aquila and Priscilla went with him but only as far as Ephesus. One likes to read between the lines at this point. Did this couple move to Ephesus in order that, after the apostle returned to Ephesus from Syria, he might again live with them and work in their shop? And was it Paul's aim already when he left Corinth to continue his missionary work in Ephesus? These may have been his plans. They would then answer the supposition that, while he was in Corinth, Paul at any time left the home of Aquila and Priscilla in order to live with Titus Justus (see v. 7).

At this point a question is raised. Who had made this vow and what about it? One answer given is, *Paul.* Why? Because the story concerns Paul and not Aquila; because the other participles refer to Paul, hence κειράμενος (aorist middle, causative: "having caused to be shorn") must also refer to him; because the clause with γάρ must modify the main verb and this refers to Paul. Explanations: 1) Paul voluntarily assumed the vow; 2) he had been placed under it since his birth (Gal. 1:15) as a chosen vessel (Acts 9:15). The shearing of the head began the vow; the shearing marked its completion. Paul had to go to Jerusalem to complete it and did go there, this being the reason he could not stay at Ephesus; Paul did not go to Jerusalem on this journey.

The other answer given is, *Aquila.* On the basis of the grammar this must be the answer. If the participle were to refer to Paul, why is it placed so that the nominative "Aquila" comes immediately before the participle, and, most significant of all, why is Aquila named *after* his wife? The latter point cannot be answered by pointing to v. 26; Rom. 16:3; II Tim. 4:19, because every time the wife is mentioned before her husband a reason for doing so exists. In v. 26 it is because Priscilla was more capable of instructing Apollos than her husband. Ever after that Paul ranks her as the first of the two. In character, ability, and devotion she so evidently excelled her husband that her name had to precede his. Here in v. 18 we also have a reason for reversing the names. It cannot be an implied distinction for Priscilla; for what would this be? Only one reason appears, the necessity of getting the nominative "Aquila" next to the nominative participle. That is why Luke did not write σύν with two datives: "with Aquila and Priscilla."

But we confess that no explanation can be given regarding the vow itself and what part shaving the head played in the vow. Num. 16:1, 2 offers no help whatever even when it is thought that Paul was bound by the vow. The supposition that Aquila made the vow when he and his wife left Rome and that cutting his hair marked its completion is only a supposition. So also is the view that vows were assumed before making a dangerous journey, and that Aquila (or Paul) had his hair cut in the seaport Cenchraea immediately before embarking. The objection to this view is the imperfect εἶχε — he had already made the vow. It is also stated that the entire matter is irrelevant when it is referred to Aquila, and that it must refer to Paul because only then would it be of sufficient importance for a record, since it showed that he often voluntarily lived "Jewish" even to the extent of assuming a Jewish vow. But despite all his brevity Luke often adds incidental statements also regarding minor characters. They are not at all intended to bring out some important truth; they do, however, convey to the reader the fact that Luke was informed even in regard to minor details and thus deserves his reader's fullest confidence.

19) **And they arrived at Ephesus, and them he left here. He, however, having gone into the synagogue, reasoned with the Jews. Yet when they requested him to remain a longer time, he did not assent but, after taking leave and saying, I will return again to you, God willing, he put to sea from Ephesus.**

On this occasion Luke departs from his usual custom and does not mention the seaport, namely Panormus. Ephesus, situated on the Cayster River, the capital of the Roman province of Asia, was the most important city in all Asia Minor. The temple of Artemis Diana which had been erected in this city was one of the seven wonders of the ancient world. It was built of the purest marble, was 425 feet long and 220 wide, had 127 columns, each 60 feet high and supporting the roof. It was destroyed by the Goths in 262.

Paul founded the local congregation. Although he had been prevented from going to Ephesus in 16:6, the city was now open to him. Paul spent almost three years of his missionary activity here; Timothy became superintendent of the churches in the entire territory as Paul's representative with headquarters in Ephesus; John spent his last years in this city and wrote his Gospel and his Epistles here. The third Ecumenical Council met here in 431 and defined the doctrine of the church against Nestorius.

The fact that Paul left Aquila and Priscilla here is noted because of what follows in v. 24, etc. Αὐτός is contrasted with κἀκείνους but not as saying that Paul went to the synagogue, and that Aquila and Priscilla did not do so. The contrast lies in the fact that these two were left to stay in Ephesus while Paul remained only long enough to pay one visit to the synagogue. Of course, all three went to the synagogue together. Was it a Sabbath? Quite likely though not certainly. The aorist passive διελέχθη (from the deponent διαλέγομαι) is without passive force, and the aorist states only the fact that Paul discoursed with the Jews and told them about the gospel of Jesus, the Messiah.

20) The impression Paul made was altogether favorable, for he was at once requested to stay in Ephesus for a longer time. But he did not nod his head (so

literally; this word is found only here in the New Testament), did not assent.

21) Luke reports only the facts that Paul bade everybody farewell, promised to return, and then put to sea (see the verb in 13:13) and left Ephesus. The Codex Bezae again inserts a commentary that Paul explained that he had to attend the festival in Jerusalem (the A. V. accepts this reading). We, too, accept it, but not as a part of Luke's text but as comment that offers an apparently correct explanation as to why Paul hurried on from Ephesus. This comment, however, does not answer the question as to why Paul wanted to go to Jerusalem. Those who think that he and not Aquila had made the vow assign as the reason that he intended to complete the vow in Jerusalem according to Num. 16:1-12 by bringing the sacrifices prescribed by the law.

The reason, we think, was far more important and vital. Paul wanted to keep the Gentile churches in contact with the mother congregation at Jerusalem. More than this, he wanted to see the conditions obtaining in Jerusalem; and soon we see him arranging a great collection in all his Gentile congregations for the relief of the brethren at Jerusalem. Since he sailed from Cenchraea about March 10, the festival Paul hoped to attend in Jerusalem was the Passover. Whether he managed to get there in time no one knows. "God willing" (I Cor. 4:19; 16:7; James 4:15) is certainly not a mere phrase in the mouth of the apostle, nor should it ever be in ours whose goings and comings are equally subject to God's will.

22) **And having come down to Caesarea, after having gone up and having greeted the church, he went down to Antioch. And having spent some time, he went out, in succession going through the Galatian and Phrygian region, making firm all the disciples.**

When one starts a voyage one goes up ("is brought up," nautical), and when one ends a voyage one comes down; these are the Greek nautical terms. So our versions very properly translate, "when he had landed." And now we have a controversy as to whether Paul, after landing in Caesarea, went up and greeted the church of Caesarea only or that of Jerusalem also and then went down to Antioch. We submit the following. Κατελθὼν εἰς Καισάρειαν means complete arrival in Caesarea and not merely arrival in the harbor; just as the corresponding expression ἀνήχθη ἀπὸ τῆς Ἐφέσου means departure from Ephesus and not merely from the water of its harbor. Ἀναβάς does not mean walking up from the water's edge to the higher ground of Caesarea (and so greeting the church there) but again corresponds with κατέβη, going down. Participle and main verb are plain when they are understood as referring to going up to Jerusalem and coming down from there to Antioch. When Zahn scores this view as being wrong, he lays stress only on ἀναβάς and contends that the mere participle never means going up to Jerusalem, and that the unmodified ἡ ἐκκλησία is never used with reference to the church at Jerusalem; he does not say a word about κατέβη, and how one could say he "went down" from the coast town of Caesarea to Antioch which is up some distance from the sea; nor does he say one word about the correspondence of "having gone up" with "he came down" although he insists that Paul went to Antioch by land.

Furthermore, why did Paul go to Caesarea at all if he did not intend to go to Jerusalem? There was nothing in the church at Caesarea that attracted him, the attraction was entirely in Jerusalem. He should have taken passage from Ephesus to Seleucia, the harbor of Antioch, and saved the long, hard journey overland from Caesarea to Antioch. Sailing facilities to Seleucia were just as frequent as those to Caesarea. Again, after once getting to Caesarea, it was only a short journey to Jerusalem, and to turn his back on the great church there, with which Paul intended to maintain close connection in the interest of unity, would be an inexplicable act.

But why did Luke not add "to Jerusalem"? Because he did not think that his reader would misunderstand the going up and the coming down. Jerusalem was always up, in leaving it one always came down; and this "up" and this "down" were in large part ethical and not merely physical. For all Jews and all Christians Jerusalem, by virtue of this fact, always had been and still was high up and great. Nothing of sufficient importance for a record transpired on this brief visit; it is unlikely that Paul found even one apostle in Jerusalem. Some make an issue of the fact that in his letter to the Galatians Paul does not mention this visit (his fourth) nor that indicated in 11:30 and 12:25 (his second). There is no issue of any kind, for in Galatians, Paul is writing of those visits to Jerusalem which he made when he conferred with one or another of the apostles.

23) Paul finally returned to Antioch, the congregation from which he had set out on both of his great missionary tours. He had been gone about two years, from the early spring of 51 until April of 53 (for the dating see v. 12, which is exact for this reckoning). He could not immediately tear himself away, so he remained for some time; we think it was several weeks. How much he had to relate, and how much there was to be related to him! The old bonds were strongly reknit. Paul always strengthened the sacred ties. From him many might learn this process and the spirit of unity (not unionism) which completely filled him. The deplorable practice that this or that church does as it pleases without due consideration of the other churches in the fellowship had not yet arisen.

And now *the third missionary journey* begins. It begins as did the second: Paul revisits the congregations founded on his first missionary journey in "the Galatian and Phrygian region." In 16:6 we have discussed this territory. In that passage we must regard the one article in the expression τὴν Φρυγίαν καὶ Γαλατικὴν χώραν as denoting *one region* which was designated as both Phrygian and Galatian, namely Phrygian Galatia, that part of the Roman province Galatia which was at one time included in the ethnographic territory called Phrygian. The effort to find *two* regions in this expression, one Phrygian (or taking this as a noun: Phrygia) and the other Galatian, has brought on the confusion we mention in our comments on chapter 16. This is also the case here where Luke reverses the adjectives. Since it was Phrygian and Galatian at the same time, it may with equal propriety be called Galatian and Phrygian. The noun χώραν may be placed after both adjectives as is done in 16:6, or between them as is done here; it could also be placed immediately after the article. Greek usage allows any one of these three constructions without a change in sense. Instead of noticing this rather obvious fact, some interpreters divide this expression so that *two* territories are found in it, and Φρυγίαν is made a noun, or χώραν is supplied and thus read twice. The grammar is ignored, namely that *one* article (and in both passages we have only one) combines into a unit whatever follows that article.

On this journey Paul traveled alone, and on this third visit he again confirmed the disciples. And the expression "the disciples" refers to the churches or congregations, for every church was composed of disciples. He viewed the progress that had been made, and his one aim was to make them as firm and solid as possible in the faith they had received. His third visit must have been even more delightful to his heart than the first. In view of the letter he was soon to write to these very churches (Galatians) let us note that no defection from the gospel was evident to Paul on this visit.

24) **Now a Jew, Apollos by name, an Alexandrian by race, an eloquent man, arrived in Ephesus, being mighty in the Scriptures.**

Aquila and Priscilla had remained in Ephesus. Paul had gone on and had not as yet returned. During this interval Apollos arrived. He probably came from Alexandria. By saying that he was "a Jew" Luke designates his extraction which was Jewish and not Gentile. He was not Jewish as opposed to Christian. "An Alexandrian by race," τῷ γένει, adds the detail that he was a native-born Alexandrian, had been reared in the great Egyptian city that had been founded by Alexander the Great and named after him. Two of this city's five sections were inhabited by Jews. It had a great university and a library and was the main seat of Jewish-Hellenistic learning. The Jewish-Alexandrine philosophy was developed here; its chief exponent, Philo, was still living. Here the LXX had been translated, a work that was of more influence than any other translation of the Old Testament. The inspired New Testament writers quoted from it. Although they regarded Jerusalem as the great center of their religion, the Alexandrine Jews had their own temple at Leontopolis.

The A. V. version correctly translates λόγιος, "eloquent" as distinguished from the R. V.'s "learned." Apollos was gifted and well-trained dialectically. He had, no doubt, been educated in the famous university of his city. Last and most important of all and added without a connective and by means of a participle, he is described as "being mighty in the Scriptures." The rest of his education had been made subservient to the Scriptures and to the power to use them effectively.

What follows shows that Luke does not have in mind rabbinical ability in the Old Testament, for Apollos used the Bible to preach Jesus Christ as he had learned to know him.

Apollos was not a man who merely echoed the learning of his day, who merely swallowed all that he was taught and let it puff him up with intellectual pride, who disdained everything that did not bear the stamp of the schools. A flood of light falls into the very heart of Apollos when Luke writes, "being mighty in the Scriptures." That is exactly where thousands of highly titled university graduates are pitifully weak. They are perhaps mighty *against* the Scriptures with their learning but not mighty *in* the Scriptures, filled with the spiritual power that has its source *in* the saving truth of Holy Writ.

It was providential that this valuable man came to Ephesus just at this time. The teachers he needed to complete his education had also been providentially brought to Ephesus just at this time. Paul was not there and would not get there for some time. Not even a congregation was found there. Only a humble tentmaker and his equally unpretentious wife were there to take Apollos in hand. But would this eloquent, able university graduate condescend to go to school to a tentmaker, a common artisan, and to his wife who had never attended a university? We shall see. The best university training Apollos ever received was given him in this tentmaker's shop, and the best professor Apollos ever had was this tentmaker's wife, Priscilla. And among the greatest services these two ever rendered the Lord was what they did for Apollos. In the whole story of Acts there is no picture that is more ideal than this of Apollos and Aquila and his wife.

25) **This one had been informed as to the Way of the Lord; and being fervent in the spirit, he spoke and taught accurately the things concerning Jesus al-**

though knowing only the baptism of John. This one also began to speak with boldness in the synagogue, and having heard him, Priscilla and Aquila took him to them and more accurately set forth to him the Way of God.

In the effective Greek fashion οὗτος brings to a focus all that has been said about Apollos and then adds more. By means of the periphrastic past perfect passive "had been informed" we are told that in addition to all his other education Apollos also knew about "the Way of the Lord." Passives of verbs that have two objects still take the one as here (R. 816). Κατηχέω (source of our "catechize," "catechism," "catechetics") is used here as it is in Luke 1:4 and in a few other places in the New Testament without conveying an idea of formal instruction; this idea of formally instructing in the elements of the faith by using also the question method was added later (C.-K. 481).

Not in the Alexandrian schools but from some disciple of the Baptist Apollos had learned something about "the Way of the Lord," i. e., the Christian doctrine. The Hebrew *derek*, "way," one that is laid out and traveled, is used extensively in the Old Testament in a religious and an ethical sense; in Ps. 1:6 it is used in both the good and the evil sense. The Jews later called the entire Christian doctrine and practice *derek hanotsarim*, "the Way of the Christians." So "Way" means doctrine, faith, confession, life, all combined. "Lord" must here mean Jesus, for Apollos taught "the things concerning Jesus." What Apollos thus knew was correct enough as far as it went; the trouble was that it did not go far enough.

Apollos had eagerly accepted this teaching concerning Jesus from the disciples of the Baptist. We shall meet another case of this kind in 19:1, etc., but much less information will be furnished us in regard to that case. It seems that after his death some of the disciples of the Baptist had scattered and had spread some of his teaching here and there without fully knowing about the death and the resurrection of Jesus and what these implied.

And now we learn something about the spirit of Apollos, namely, that he was "fervent in spirit" (dative of relation), ζέω meaning "to boil," "to seethe." What he had discovered did not appeal to him only intellectually, it captivated his very spirit; he glowed with holy enthusiasm and zeal. He spoke and taught all along (imperfect tenses) what he had learned, τὰ περὶ τοῦ Ἰησοῦ, a neat idiom, "the things concerning Jesus" as far as he knew them. He could not keep still about them, he had to impart them also to others; he spoke them to men privately as occasion offered, and he taught them in public, in meetings in the synagogues wherever he happened to be.

This Apollos did ἀκριβῶς, "accurately," the same adverb Luke used in Luke 1:3 in regard to himself. He did not let his zeal carry him away. He became no "enthusiast" in the sense of a fanatic; he avoided the speculations into which the Alexandrian Jews such as Philo might have carried him by mixing error with truth in a philosophic fashion. He kept to exactness. Why some authorities think that Apollos had obtained much from Philo is difficult to understand when Luke excludes this idea with the adverb "accurately." So also "the things concerning Jesus" means the actual facts about Jesus. They included what the Gospels record for us of the Baptist's testimony, which was by no means inconsiderable; they may have included some things from the early work of Jesus himself, which those of the Baptist's disciples who did not attach themselves to Jesus heard toward the end of the Baptist's career and afterward.

Luke marks this limitation in the equipment of Apollos by adding, "knowing only the baptism of

John." By "the baptism of John" the whole teaching and work of the Baptist are referred to. The idea is not that he knew nothing about Christian baptism but that his knowledge did not extend to the completion of the work of Jesus. This, of course, included also the command to baptize all nations and the events that transpired at the time of Pentecost and later. A misleading contrast is introduced by regarding John's baptism as a mere *water baptism* over against the baptism of Jesus, either this itself (Matt. 28:19) or the so-called *Spirit* baptism at the time of Pentecost and what some today call "the baptism of the Spirit," an imaginary sudden seizure by the Spirit without means which produces total sanctification. On this subject compare 1:6. To know only John's baptism was not to know about the crucifixion, the resurrection, the ascension, Pentecost, etc., not to know of the Lord's Supper, the first church at Jerusalem, the mission of the apostles, etc.

Nothing is said about the baptism of Apollos. But we are safe in the conclusion that, if he had been baptized with John's baptism, and if this baptism had not been deemed sufficient, Luke would have touched upon that point, especially in view of what he writes in 19:1, etc. So the facts must be that Apollos had received the baptism of John, and that this was all he needed, exactly as all of the Twelve had received no other baptism than that of John. The case of the persons mentioned in 19:1, etc., is entirely different.

26) This then, a second οὗτος which includes all that had thus far been said of him, was the man who began to speak in the Ephesian synagogue with full freedom, holding nothing back. Aquila and Priscilla must have been surprised when they heard him. But they at once noted his serious limitations. When Luke writes that they "took him to them" (indirect middle voice), we must note all that is involved. Moreover, Luke now places Priscilla's name before her husband's.

In v. 18 the reason for this placement is only grammatical; here it means much more just as it does twice in Paul's letters (Rom. 16:3; II Tim. 4:19, where Paul even uses Prisca instead of the diminutive Priscilla). We conclude that Priscilla was the moving spirit, that she was by nature more gifted and able than her husband, also spiritually fully developed due to her having had Paul in her home for eighteen months while residing in Corinth. Aquila seems to have been a gentle, quiet soul, who was genuine in this unobtrusive way. It seems that the couple was childless.

The beauty of Priscilla's character lies in the fact that she never thrust herself forward, never asserted herself, or made her superiority felt. She was loyally true to Paul's teaching that the husband is the head of the wife. Aquila had found a pearl among women. Priscilla is the direct opposite of Sapphira. The one stimulated her husband to all that was good, the other helped her husband on to his destruction. Priscilla is the example our women need so much today when so many thrust themselves beyond their proper sphere and often do not know where to stop.

It was a delicate undertaking to take Apollos to themselves and to set forth to him more accurately the Way of God. Who were these humble people to teach a university graduate, this orator schooled in the Scriptures? But they managed it perfectly with all tact. The two aorists imply that. Equal credit belongs to Apollos. He accepted the invitation of Priscilla and Aquila. He must have been a man of deep spirituality not to let his superior education, ability, and standing assert themselves and prevent him from going to school to such lowly teachers. He is an example for all the high and mighty men of education today and for the green beginners for whom a little learning is already a dangerous thing. They scorn the old faith, look down even upon godly parents who cling to it and on the church that keeps the sacred fire burning. Apollos shall judge them at that day!

Luke surely wants his reader to understand that Priscilla was the main teacher. The ancients, too, knew about a number of most superior and talented women. Priscilla was not like these. She had no more education than her husband. Her great treasure was the gospel, and her ability was that she could impart it with all lucidity and force. She helped to teach Apollos in all propriety. Since this was private teaching, it in no way conflicted with the apostolic principle that women are to remain silent in the church. Humble people though she and her husband were, they were not abashed before Apollos.

On tries to picture the three sitting together and going into the great gospel story. Apollos must have asked many questions, Paul's name must have been mentioned often. Little had Priscilla and Aquila thought, when they had learned from Paul in Corinth to what use they would have to put their instruction. Apollos eagerly absorbed all they could teach him. Suppose you, wife and husband, had been in their place, how would you have acquitted yourselves? We here see how in the apostolic age so many churches started in places to which no apostle came. The Christians themselves were the missionaries. So well did the apostle ground them in the faith that they themselves were ready always to give an answer to every man that asked them a reason of the hope that was in them, with meekness and fear (I Pet. 3:15).

27) **Now he desiring to go through to Achaia, the brethren having urged him forward, wrote to the disciples duly to receive him: who, having come, contributed much on his part to those who had believed through grace. For strenuously he kept confuting the Jews to a finish in public, showing by the Scriptures Jesus to be the Christ.**

How did Apollos come to think of extending his travels to Achaia, and who were these brethren who urged him forward? Here the Codex Bezae adds to Luke's account. It states that some Corinthians were temporarily in Ephesus and, on hearing Apollos, began to beseech him to go with them to their home city. After he had consented, we are told, "the Ephesians" wrote "to the disciples in Corinth" to receive the man. To be sure, Paul does speak of Apollos' being in Corinth (I Cor. 1:12). So this Codex refers the whole story to Corinth. But had Aquila and Priscilla not recently come from Greece, and had they not told Apollos the whole story about Paul's work there while he lived in their home, and that he had left Silas and Timothy behind? Nor does Apollos deserve special credit for farsightedness in thinking of Achaia and thus farther than Corinth; for we have already seen that Paul extended his work beyond Corinth through Silas and Timothy, and did not Aquila and Priscilla tell Apollos all about that also?

The statement that the transient Corinthians invited Apollos to return with them makes an unpleasant impression. Paul had left Silas and Timothy to continue the work in Corinth, but these Corinthians promptly fell in love with Apollos and induced him to go along with them because they regarded him as a better man than these two assistants of Paul. Yet when Aquila and Priscilla heard Apollos they at once recognized his deficiency. The observation that after having been taught more accurately, Apollos preferred not to continue to speak in the Ephesian synagogue but to go elsewhere, seems far nearer probability than the story which the Codex Bezae inserts. And Luke writes that he went to "Achaia" and not to "Corinth." Apollos was not the type of man who would desire to supplant Paul's assistants in Corinth; he hoped to find work at their side in the spacious province of Achaia.

The fact that he worked also in Corinth, as we gather from Paul's letter, was a later development.

We incidentally read about "the brethren" in Ephesus. So there were a few others besides Aquila and his wife who joined in recommending Apollos to the disciples in Achaia. Just who these brethren were makes little difference. The word of Aquila and Priscilla, who had given Paul a home for so long a time, would go far. This is the first instance of a Christian letter of recommendation. A close study of the apostolic period reveals the frequent use of such letters; Paul, too, wrote some of them. All of them have been lost. In ἀποδέξασθαι the preposition ἀπό adds the idea of "duly" receiving, i. e., as befits the recommendation given.

The Greek relative often has demonstrative force: "he was the one who." Apollos more than lived up to his recommendation. When he reached Achaia, it was his occupation (durative, imperfect) to contribute on his part (note this force of the middle) a great deal to those who had believed (and were thus still believing, perfect participle.) Our versions construe: "had believed through grace." But Luke is scarcely characterizing these believers; he is describing the work of Apollos. His success was not due to his eloquence and his learning but to divine grace, the grace with which he had made contact in the home of Aquila and Priscilla. This is something every preacher ought to put into the notebook of his heart, whether he be a man of learning and eloquence who needs to trust not in himself, or a man of humble gifts who needs to know that grace alone gives true success.

28) Apollos was not equipped to advance the faith of those who believed; his contribution was of a negative kind as Luke also feels constrained to explain (γάρ) lest his reader obtain a wrong impression. He strenuously kept confuting the Jews to a finish (κατά

in the compound verb) in public (the dative of the feminine form of the adjective δημόσιος used as an adverb). And this took place in the Jewish synagogues and not in the Christian congregations. Jewish opponents would not appear in the congregations, nor attempt a controversy there. Nor did this occur in Corinth, for the hostile Jewish synagogue in this place had long before this time been closed to every Christian speaker. It took place, as Luke has said, in Achaia, in new territory, in new synagogues, and the believers who were thus helped were those found in these synagogues.

How Apollos accomplished this complete confuting is stated: "showing by the Scriptures Jesus to be the Christ." This harks back to v. 24, to the learning Apollos had obtained in Alexandria when he studied the Old Testament. He now used all of it in proving most conclusively that Jesus was the Messiah, and in overwhelming all his Jewish opponents. With this brief account Luke concludes his story about Apollos except to say in 19:1 that he was in Corinth where he, no doubt, made his headquarters.

CHAPTER XIX

The Third Missionary Journey: Ephesus

1) Luke takes up the thread broken off at 18:23 and continues with the story of Paul. The accusative Ἀπολλώ is the Attic second declension (R. 260; B.-D. 55, 1g). The account of the twelve men who had not been properly baptized has been criticized as being unlike Luke and far below the high literary level of Acts. This criticism overlooks the fact that the account about Apollos and that about these twelve men must be considered together as dealing with the aftereffects produced by certain disciples of the Baptist. Both accounts are also concerned with Paul. He put his stamp of approval on Apollos. He was with Paul when the latter wrote to the Corinthians from Ephesus (I Cor. 16:12). But Paul corrected the baptism of the twelve men whose case was different from that of Apollos. Not all baptisms were genuine. It is so to this day.

Now it came to pass while Apollos was in Corinth that Paul, having come through the upper parts, came to Ephesus and found some disciples.

Luke uses two of his favorite idioms: ἐγένετο with an accusative with the infinitive as the subject; and ἐν τῷ with the infinitive in the sense of "while." Apollos had left Ephesus before Paul arrived there and had only heard about him from Aquila and Priscilla. "The upper parts" which Paul crossed in order to go directly to Ephesus were "the Galatian and Phrygian region" of 18:23; see the discussion of that passage. Luke's brevity need not imply that the "disciples" were found in Ephesus immediately upon Paul's arrival. When

Paul found them is not stated because it is quite immaterial. Luke is concerned only about what Paul did in their case.

2) **And he said to them, Did you receive the Holy Spirit on coming to believe? They to him, No, we did not even hear whether there is a Holy Spirit. And he said, In what, then, were you baptized? They said, In John's baptism. But Paul said, John baptized with the baptism of repentance, saying to the people to believe in the One coming after him, that is in Jesus. And having heard, they were baptized in the name of the Lord Jesus.**

We do not agree with those who feel that Paul became "suspicious of their looks and conduct." There is no evidence that these disciples were different from others in appearance or in conduct. On meeting these as well as other disciples, Paul and others likewise would naturally try to get acquainted with them and would thus ask about their past life and their connection with the faith. We do the same today. Thus in the most natural way the question was asked: "Did you receive the Holy Ghost on coming to faith?" The participle expresses action that is simultaneous with that of the main verb and is punctiliar to indicate the time when they first came to believe. We have discussed the use of εἰ at the beginning of a direct question in 1:6, and venture the explanation that it is not elliptical but has become a mere interrogatory particle which thus does not call for translation.

Paul's question contained no reference to baptism. The sacrament was only indirectly involved since people who came to faith would naturally also be baptized. What Paul asked these men was whether any charismatic manifestations of the Holy Spirit occurred when they came to faith. In the case of Cornelius and those with him these manifestations came before they were baptized, they usually came afterward, yet not always immediately but sometimes much later as was the case in 8:15, and in most of the later cases they did not occur at all. As proof of this we may point to all the congregations founded by Paul. The question asked by Paul was thus not at all a searching one, as though he were putting these men to a test. Some of the early converts received the temporary grace of charismatic gifts, not, however, the 3,000 who were converted at Pentecost, nor the many thousands that were converted later. Paul thus merely inquired as to what had happened in their case.

3) His innocent question brought out the astonishing fact that these men had never even heard whether or not there was a Holy Ghost. Ἀλλά is here equal to "no" (R. 1186, where it is shown that this conjunction does not always mean "but"). We leave this answer just at it reads. They confess that they had not yet heard of the existence of the Holy Spirit (εἰ ἔστιν). This does not mean that, as in John 7:39, they had, indeed, heard of his existence but not yet of his being given, i. e., of his great coming at the time of Pentecost. Those who hold this view must reckon with Apollos who also had not heard of Pentecost and yet was admittedly not rebaptized.

This is the salient point in this entire account: people who know nothing about the Holy Spirit cannot have received genuine and valid baptism; what they have received in that respect is not a true baptism. That is why Paul at once asks: "In what, then, were you baptized?" This is the static use of εἰς and is equal to ἐν with the idea of sphere (R. 592) so that the sense is: "In connection with what were you baptized?" And "what" (neuter) shows that Paul has in mind "in connection with what name?" When these men were baptized, was the name of the Holy Ghost not used, and had the sacrament not been explained to them sufficiently to make plain the Spirit's connection with it (John 3:3, 5)? It develops that the Spirit's name had not even been mentioned. In regard to εἰς in this paragraph, the R. V. with its "into" is inferior to the A V. with its "unto" and its "in" (v. 5). The R. V. aims to be more literal and exact; unfortunately its translation was made before the new knowledge of the Koine became known. Anyone who still doubts this static use of εἰς should consult the many new grammars and dictionaries and the ostraca and the papyri where copious proof is furnished.

These men give a rather helpless answer. Paul wants to know "in what" they had been baptized, and all they can say is that it it was "in John's baptism." That is the only name they can mention in connection with their baptism. It is quite possible that somebody had baptized them by using only the words: "I baptize you with John's baptism." Disciples and followers of John, who were scattered about even outside of Palestine after John's early death, tried to perpetuate his baptism and his teaching. In every case where people received the baptism of these followers of John it became a casual question as to what such a baptism really amounted to.

4) After receiving only the vague answer, "In John's baptism," Paul explains briefly what John himself did so that these men could compare John himself, his baptism, and his teaching with whatever alleged follower of John they had come into contact with and anything he had done and said. Paul emphasizes two main points in regard to John: 1) he baptized with the baptism of repentance (cognate accusative), the divinely appointed sacrament, genuine, legitimate, proper in every way. The genitive "of repentance" is qualitative. We see what he had in mind in Mark 1:4, 5; Matt. 3:6, especially when we note those to whom John refused baptism, Matt. 3:7-9; Luke 3:7-9. True repentance accompanied John's baptism; the

sacrament itself implied that. It was no *opus operatum*, for it conveyed the forgiveness of sins just as baptism does today. On "repentance" see 2:38. And 2) John's baptism turned every man to faith in the One coming after John, that is, to Jesus. Paul calls him, what John himself had called him, "the One coming," which was the great Messianic name. Repentance had to be linked with faith in him. The fact that this involved the Holy Spirit who alone works repentance and faith need not be stated.

Note that the object is placed before ἵνα in order to give it the greatest emphasis; note also the construction λέγων ἵνα in which this conjunction introduces *what* John demanded (R. 993; B.-D. 392, 1 d). John baptized only repentant and believing confessors just as we do to this day, with this difference, that John demanded faith in the One coming, we faith in the One come. Paul may have spoken at great length, Luke gives his reader the gist of what he said.

5) This was entirely new to these men. They saw from what Paul revealed to them about John's baptism that the baptism they had received was not John's real baptism. Paul discovered it for them when they told him they knew nothing about the Holy Ghost. So they were now baptized. What they had received before was not baptism. But now they were not baptized in the name of the One yet to come. The Lord Jesus had come long ago, and so they were baptized "in the name of the Lord Jesus." This phrase has been explained in 2:38, and always means, "in connection with the revelation of the Lord Jesus"; ὄνομα means "revelation" in all these and similar phrases and never "the authority of."

We still meet analogous cases when people are baptized in non-Trinitarian churches. Theirs is not baptism and for the following valid reason. Baptism was given to the church, and non-Trinitarians are not in any sense the church or a part of it. Denial of the Trinity is denial of the true God, substituting a figment for him, destroying the very substance of baptism, which is to bring a sinner into saving connection, not with an imaginary "God" but with the one true God. We never rebaptize such people, for these people were never baptized. A counterfeit is not real money, never will be. We, therefore, see the great value of this incident reported by Luke.

6) **And when Paul placed his hands on them, the Holy Spirit came upon them, and they began to speak with tongues and to prophesy. Moreover, the men in all were about twelve.**

See 6:6 for the laying on of hands. Here this act must have been accompanied by a prayer for the special manifestation of the Holy Ghost. This is a duplicate to 8:15-17; compare also 9:17. We are able to say why charismatic gifts were bestowed at the time of Pentecost, on the Samaritans, and then on the Gentiles who were with Cornelius. Just why these same gifts were bestowed here is not apparent. But the fact is plain. The two imperfects are inchoative.

It is unwarranted to state that because Luke does not write "with *other* tongues" as he did in 2:4, this was not the same speaking in foreign languages that occurred at the time of Pentecost; that there were two entirely different kinds of speaking with tongues, etc. See 2:4 where the subject is treated at length. Prophesying is added in order to state what was uttered with tongues just as in 2:11, "the great things of God" are mentioned. This word must here be understood in the wider sense as expressing any adequate utterance of divine truth. The Spirit himself spoke through the mouths of these men who were so ignorant but now so richly blessed by him. They now know the Holy Spirit because of their own wonderful experience.

If Luke offers a hint in regard to immersion, R., *W. P.*, ought to point it out instead of claiming that this was "a baptism in water," meaning by immersion. He also advances the old erroneous claim that this baptism did not convey the Holy Spirit nor forgiveness of sins; but Jesus differs with him as to the Spirit in John 3:5, and Peter differs with him as to the remission of sins in Acts 2:38, likewise Ananias in Paul's case in 22:16, and Paul himself in Tit. 3:5. But one should not think that baptism and the charismatic gifts go together. Pentecost excludes such a view, for none of the 3,000 baptized on that day spoke with tongues. The *saving* presence of the Spirit is evident in baptism; his *charismatic* presence is an entirely different thing and is bestowed as the Spirit wills (I Cor. 12:11) for his own special purposes. To conclude that, because the Spirit there came charismatically after the baptism when Paul laid on his hands, therefore the Spirit was not bestowed with saving grace in baptism, and then to stress the idea that this was "a baptism in *water*," is to antagonize John 3:5.

7) "About twelve," like the addition πάντες, "in all," means that not many men were involved and that Luke cared to say no more. Note that πάντες is attributive, is placed after the article, and thus means *im ganzen, zusammen* (B.-D. 275, 7), "the total number of the men" (R. 773.) The incident connected with these men seems to have occurred during the first days that Paul spent in Ephesus and not necessarily before he began his work in the synagogue.

8) The account of what Paul did in Ephesus Luke presents in v. 8-12. **Now having gone into the synagogue, he continued to speak boldly for three months, reasoning and persuading regarding the things concerning the kingdom of God.**

Paul had been most favorably received in the Ephesian synagogue on his first visit and was at that time asked to remain but promised, God willing, to return. So he now again takes up his work. It is exceptional that it was possible for him to continue for as long a period as three months, reasoning, namely on the basis of the Scriptures, and persuading his Jewish hearers "regarding the things concerning the kingdom of God," God's rule of grace in Christ Jesus and all that it included. On this kingdom and on the entire expression see 1:3. We do not regard "persuading" as conative, "trying to persuade" (R., *W. P.*), because both participles must be understood in the same way, and Paul certainly did not merely try to reason. "Trying to persuade" would imply that he failed, but this was by no means the case.

9) Paul took his time. As long as no opposition developed, he had hopes of winning the entire synagogue, and nothing would have delighted him more.

But when some began to harden themselves and began to be disobedient, speaking basely of the Way in the presence of the multitude, having stood away from them, he separated the disciples, day by day reasoning in the school of Tyrannus. Moreover, this went on for two years so that all those inhabiting Asia heard the Word of the Lord, Jews as well as Greeks.

The division finally came, and not through the agency of Paul but through that of the opposing Jews. The two imperfect tenses are inchoative: "they began," etc.; and the first is not passive, "were hardened" (our versions) but the reflexive middle, "began to harden themselves." The point is rather important because the sinner always first hardens himself, and not until that point has been reached does God harden him. In other words, God's hardening is always punitive. His whole effort is directed toward softening the sinner in contrition and faith, but when the sinner resists all these efforts of grace so that the Holy Spirit can no longer work in him by his grace, God abandons him, gives him over to his hardness, and thus hardens him. The outstanding example is Pharaoh who hardened himself five times and was then hardened by God as a punishment. The idea contained in the verb is expressed in the adjective σκληρός (compare it in the compound found in 7:51), "dried out" like a dried branch that no longer bends but is rigid and stiff.

The second imperfect helps to bring out the idea more fully. Paul was busy "persuading," but these Jews "were unpersuaded." The longer Paul applied grace in order to persuade, the worse they became. The verb thus gets to mean both "to be disobedient" and "to be disbelieving," and usually, as here, both ideas flow together. These Jews would not obey the saving call of grace, and that means that they would not believe the saving truth in Jesus. The condition thus described by the two verbs is possible only when grace is applied to the heart; it can never result before grace is applied. It is always abnormal and unreasonable because the sinner ought to yield to grace and to saving truth, i. e., to the power of deliverance, to the *gratia sufficiens.* Because it is so abnormal and unreasonable his self-hardening is extremely guilty, has a guilt that is due wholly to himself (Matt. 23:37). It is a terrible matter for the sinner when saving grace is compelled to withdraw and to abandon him to God's judgment.

The participle states how these Jews manifested their inner hardening and disobedient refusal to believe: they began to speak basely of the Way in the presence of the multitude; compare the expressions found in 13:45; 18:6. "The Way" is here used ethically as it was in 13:10; 16:17. It needs no modifier, it is the Way of salvation κατ' ἐξοχήν. When Luke writes "some" he evidently refers to the leaders of the opposition. They spoke against the Way "in the presence of the multitude," in the synagogue meeting, and sought to turn everybody against the Way that was proclaimed by Paul. To what extent they succeeded is not stated.

The decisive moment had come. Paul "stood away from them," he gave up speaking in the synagogue. It was the only course left to him. It is also impossible to force the gospel upon men who, after they have heard it, reject and revile it. When he withdrew himself he naturally took with him and separated the "disciples" from the synagogue. So Paul had "disciples" in the synagogue at the end of the three months; how many is not stated. Separating them from the synagogue implied the formation of a new congregation. We take it that these "disciples" were in part proselytes of the gate.

The new meeting place was "the school of Tyrannus" where Paul reasoned day by day (distributive κατά). The word σχολή means "leisure" but is here used in the sense of "school." This is the only instance in the New Testament where the word has this meaning. Just what this school was we are unable to say. Some have thought that Tyrannus was a Jew who conducted a school for teaching the law or even maintained a private synagogue. Others think of a regular Greek school for boys and bring descriptions of how each of the boys was conducted to school by his παιδαγωγός, slave mentor, and spent from earliest morning until about eleven o'clock under the teacher. Still others think of a lecture hall for teaching rhetoric and philosophy, or possibly even medicine. This conjecture seems best.

It is a question whether "the school of Tyrannus" was merely the name of the hall which was not in use at the time, or whether Tyrannus was the teacher who was using it at the time it bore this name. The Codex Bezae again amplifies with the comment that Paul used this school from 11 in the morning until 4 in the afternoon, "after business hours" as Ramsay puts it. This intrigues some, and they picture Paul working at his trade from dawn until 11 and then teaching from 11 to 4 — a strenuous life indeed! But it is an impossible supposition to anyone who has visited the Orient. Every place of business closes from noon until 4 o'clock; everybody takes his siesta, does so of necessity, would be compelled to do so especially in a coast town. This is necessary less because of the heat than because of the dangerous actinic power of the vertical rays of the sun during the long summer season. The hours mentioned by the Codex Bezae are the very ones when even such a man as Paul could not have had hearers for most of the year. This Codex must have originated in northern territory.

As in 18:7 Paul used the spacious house of Titus Justus, so he now uses the school of Tyrannus. Both places must have been suitable to his purpose. But no one knows whether Tyrannus was a convert, whether the school building was offered gratis, or whether Paul and the disciples paid rent. One thing is certain, having left the synagogue and the Jewish circle, Paul now extended his work into the great Gentile world.

10) Paul used this hall for two years. In 20:31 Paul himself states that he devoted a τριετία, a period of three years, to his labors in Ephesus. This scarcely implies that he counted after the Jewish fashion and reckoned a part of a year as a year, and two years and three months as three years. The church, too, probably outgrew the old hall and found some more commodious place of meeting. To think of the home of Aquila and Priscilla is untenable. Note the mention of additional time in v. 22. The result of this prolonged labor in Ephesus was that "all who inhabited Asia heard (aorist) the Word of the Lord, both Jews and Greeks." The coast cities and villages of the province of Asia are referred to, the cities mentioned in Rev. 2:1, etc. Jews as well as Greeks had at least heard the

gospel. Paul used Ephesus as a radiating center. While he remained in this metropolis and political center he reached out as far as possible by means of his assistants; how many he employed we cannot estimate. Congregation after congregation was formed. Paul is at the height of his great missionary activity.

11) **Also power works, not those usual, God kept doing through the hands of Paul so that even on the sick there were carried from his skin handkerchiefs and aprons, and the ailments were removed from them, also the wicked spirits went out.**

Luke records only the unusual miracles, δυνάμεις, "power works," that occurred in Ephesus. The feminine participle is added attributively with the article: τὰς τυχούσας; and οὐ is placed before the article and negatives the attribute (not merely the participle, R. 1038, etc.): "not those happening," i. e., ordinarily. This is a litotes for "those exceptional." We take it that Paul did other miracles in the usual way by touching the sufferers with his hands, speaking the word of power with his lips, etc.

12) The remarkable fact was that without his presence or his voice all kinds of sufferers were healed διὰ τῶν χειρῶν, "through his hands," he with his hands giving messengers handkerchiefs and aprons "from his χρώς, body surface, skin." The phrase "through the hands of Paul" states that these handkerchiefs and these aprons were sent by Paul himself; they were not taken surreptitiously, and hence were not used superstitiously. Paul would be the last person to encourage superstition.

Ὥστε with the infinitive expresses actual result. The three infinitives state what actually occurred. The view that people secured the handkerchiefs and the aprons from Priscilla and Aquila before they were washed and without the knowledge of Paul because they imagined that there was some somatic and occult power in them and so applied them to the sick, and that Luke is careful not to say what actually happened — this modernistic view contradicts Luke's plain statement. The three infinitives are even present tenses which denote the frequency with which this occurred. Luke has just said that all dwellers in Asia heard the Word of the Lord. Luke is not speaking of sufferers in Ephesus. These could be brought to Paul personally, or he could go to them. These were sufferers who resided in other cities and villages and were far away from Paul. It was *he* who reached them in the way here indicated.

Read the discussion of 5:15, much of which applies also here. The statement that the Lord "honored superstitious faith" is in an impermissible mixture — superstition and faith are opposites, faith drives out superstition. Many begged Jesus to touch and to heal them. The skin of the hand is not different from the handkerchief or apron touched by that skin of the hand. In every case the *person* through whom the divine power to heal reaches the sufferer is recognized. The difference is only superficial just as Luke says, "Not those happening (ordinarily)" as is the case when the apostle is present in person.

And these unusual miracles, which were wrought at a distance from the apostle, extended also to the demoniacs. Luke writes carefully, "So that also the wicked spirits kept going out." He makes a separate class of these cases and designates them accurately. On demoniacal possession see 5:16, and the writer's discussion in Matt. 4:24; 8:28; Mark 1:23; Luke 4:33. The mention of demoniacs in the present connection means that no case was so serious that this mode of healing was not effective. Paul was only the Lord's instrument; it was the Lord's own power that wrought these "power works," wrought them as freely through Paul's handkerchiefs and aprons as through Paul's hand and spoken word. Paul used aprons in the shop of Aquila in his work as a tentmaker.

No wonder that these "power works" mightily advertised "the Word of the Lord" in Asia. Luke wants us to note this connection. In the following he also indicates to some extent why the Lord wrought these power works in spreading the gospel. Ephesus and Asia were full of superstition, magic, charms, and everything else of that kind. It is reversing things to claim that magical powers were superstitiously attributed also to Paul. The very opposite was the effect: the people turned from all devilish arts, burned their magical books and papers, and accepted the Lord's Word. How could the Lord possibly allow superstitious notions to be associated with his "chosen vessel," the great apostle? As everywhere, these mighty works of the Lord glorified the Lord and sealed his saving Word which is so full of the still higher power that saves men's souls eternally.

13) **Now some of the strolling Jewish exorcists undertook to name over those having the wicked spirits the name of the Lord Jesus, saying, I adjure you by the Jesus whom Paul is preaching!**

We are not surprised to note that there were Jewish exorcists among the charlatans in Ephesus, and that these tried to steal what they thought was the superior method and formula of Paul. They are described as "vagabond" (A. V.), "strolling" (R. V.), "going around" (Greek) like gypsies. They had evidently seen Paul work miracles, not as indicated in v. 11, 12, but in the usual way, by personally applying the name of Jesus. We see that Luke expects his reader to understand that Paul also wrought miracles in this way. These exorcists tried to use the name of Jesus in the same way and upon demoniacs, and Luke adds the very formula they used: "I adjure," etc., ὁρκίζω is construed with two accusatives. They felt that they had to identify Jesus as "the Jesus whom Paul is preaching." They evidently did not know much about this Jesus. Jewish exorcists used the name of Solomon; Josephus, *Ant.* 8, 2, 5 furnishes a description of Solomon's power and relates how an exorcist used Solomon's system before the emperor Vespasian by drawing the demon out of its victim's nose and making the demon upset a cup of water to demonstrate that he had gone out of his victim. These exorcists imagined that Paul somehow had discovered a far more potent name for charming, namely the name "Jesus." So they themselves undertook to use it.

14) **And there were seven sons of a certain Sceva, a Jewish high priest, doing this thing.**

Δέ marks this statement as being parenthetical. Luke specifies that these seven are the exorcists he has in mind. To charge Luke with relating matters in an awkward way is to read him superficially. He wants us to know in a general way that these Jewish exorcists tried to imitate Paul (v. 13). Then he specifically mentions the seven sons of Sceva (v. 14). Then he specifies still further by telling of an actual incident that happened in the case of these seven fellows (v. 15, 16). Where is the awkwardness of this narration? The genitive Σκευᾶ is Doric. No high priest by the name of Sceva appears in any Jewish writing. Luke himself uses the plural "high priests" so as to include the reigning high priest and any who had held the office before him and also those members of the family of the high priest who was functioning in the Sanhedrin. Some think that the heads of the twenty-four courses of ordinary priests were also called "high priests." This title is used in a wider sense when it is here applied to Sceva.

The fact that his seven sons had traveled far from Palestine shows a marked decline of the family. They, no doubt, made much of their parentage and, as all ambitious practitioners of this type are apt to do, most likely sought the patronage of the rich, Gentiles being as welcome to them as Jews. Luke relates their story also because of their prominence as sons of one who could in some way claim to be of high priestly standing. They would naturally be regarded as mighty exorcists. The whole subject of Jewish exorcists which is touched upon by Jesus himself in Matt. 12:27 especially as to what they actually accomplished by their efforts, is still rather obscure. All we can say is that they operated on demoniacs and not on the sick and diseased, and that they help to prove the prevalence of demoniacal possession in their day and thus refute the claim that this affliction was not what the New Testament so plainly indicates that it was.

15) **Answering, the wicked spirit said to them, This Jesus I recognize, and this Paul I am acquainted with. But you, who are you? And springing upon them, the man in whom the wicked spirit was, having overmastered them all, he prevailed against them so that naked and having been wounded they fled out of that house.**

These exorcists must have been thoroughly cured of ever again attempting to use the name of Jesus in connection with a demoniac. Note that Luke distinguishes between the demon in the man and the man himself. The very words uttered could not have been spoken by this man.

The two articles used with "Jesus" and "Paul" are clearly demonstrative: German, *den Jesus, den Paulus,* "the Jesus," "the Paul" of whom you speak. Note the synonyms: "I recognize" (realize whom you mean), which is applicable to one who is no longer on earth; and, "I am acquainted with," which is applicable to Paul who is active in the city. Everything is proper in regard to these two who had been brought to the attention of the demon. "But you, who are you?" with its emphatic ὑμεῖς, asks not merely who they are (sons of Sceva) but who they are as men who name Jesus and Paul to the demon. What possible connection have they with either Jesus or Paul so that any demon should obey them? Do they intend to pose as disciples of this Jesus and companions of this Paul? The demon will show them.

16) In sudden fury the possessed man leaps upon these exorcists, and completely overpowers them with the result that they flee out of that house in consternation. Their clothes have been torn from their bodies, and they themselves have been wounded. And this refers to the entire seven; for ἀμφοτέρων is used in the papyri with reference to more than two (in 23:8 with reference to three). The papyri reveal this broader use of this word at a later time than the composition of the Acts, yet one need not say that in Luke's time it was as yet only colloquial.

The demon filled his victim with supernatural strength. The seven exorcists, no doubt, made the mistake of resisting, which brought on their nakedness and their wounds. Remember how Orientals dressed in those days, and how easy it was to strip them so that they were actually naked. The perfect participle "having been wounded" has its usual present connotation, "being in that condition."

17) **Moreover, this became known to all Jews as well as Greeks inhabiting Ephesus; and fear fell on them all, and the name of the Lord Jesus began to be magnified. Many also of those having believed kept coming, making confession and reporting their practices. Moreover, considerable of those practicing the uncanny arts, having brought together the books, went on burning them up in the presence of all. And they reckoned together the prices of them and found fifty thousand pieces of silver. Thus with**

strength the Word of the Lord continued to grow and prevail.

If the matter had had no results beyond those experienced by the seven exorcists themselves, Luke would probably have passed it by; but great results followed. The entire city heard what had happened. The exorcists were Jews, and so, of course, all the Jews learned the story, but the Greeks also heard about it.

This was not, in our newspaper parlance, a mere "news story" that was soon to be forgotten for another. It gripped the Ephesians very seriously, for they were all given to superstition and magical practices. They all felt directly involved. A glare of light fell on the whole subject, and not because of the dramatic failure of these exorcists, but because the name "Jesus" was involved as having brought on that failure. Here was a new power that operated with stunning effect even against all powers of superstition. In this connection we must not forget the miracles wrought by Paul himself, nor the effort of these exorcists to duplicate them. It was thus that something akin to holy fear fell on all. And Luke at once adds that "the name of the Lord Jesus began to be magnified." The wonder of that name passed from lip to lip. Paul used that name, and the demons were expelled; the exorcists used it, and were themselves crushed. What was back of that name?

18) Luke says no more about this effect on the general population. He turns to the most wholesome effect on the believers themselves and by using the perfect participle describes them as those who have believed and thus continue to do so. Driven by their consciences, they kept coming to the Christian assembly in order to confess and report their practices, namely that they still kept practicing magical arts of all kinds. They saw their delusion in the light of the Savior's name and

that they were still sinning against him and his divine, saving power.

We have the exact counterpart today: Christians who still resort to witchcraft for healing, for warding off evil, for directing their lives in difficulties, and the like. See, for instance, the comprehensive and most excellent work by Wuttke, *Der Deutsche Volksaberglaube.* Every experienced physician and every pastor can tell many a tale. In spite of all enlightenment and education the ilk of those who practice the uncanny arts is still legion. If only the churches themselves could clean house as this was done in Ephesus!

To no small extent the preachers themselves have been guilty in keeping alive superstitious faith in the claims of witchcraft by admitting that its charms are effective. After an extensive study the writer here declares: they never work; they are remnants of paganism; the holy names, symbols, and Scripture words used in them are substitutions for pagan originals, a desecration of the most damnable kind, the devil's delight; they deceive, and this is the real devil's power in them; they are dangerous even when they are tried in fun; they do "work" in countless cases and often produce the saddest physical, mental, and invariably also spiritual damage. Fail not to include spiritualism.

19) With *ἱκανοί* Luke singles out those believers who had *βίβλοι*, little papyrus rolls that were inscribed with magical formulas and symbols. They used them for their own benefit but also for the benefit of others, and often, as at present, had extensive patronage. Now they wanted to get rid of these treasured documents and, therefore, collected them and proceeded to burn them. Note the imperfect found here and in the preceding verse. This confessing and this destroying of magical documents was not done in a day. Another point to be noted is this: all this was done publicly. Note that Luke uses two participles in v. 18 to empha-

size the idea "confessing and reporting"; and in v. 19 the phrase "in the presence of all." This implies that Paul himself directed this entire movement and directed all these believers to proceed in this way. He succeeded in getting some to take the lead, and then all who felt themselves guilty followed. It is of interest to know that Magic Papyri have been discovered in Egypt (Deissmann, *Bible Studies*, 323); pagan writers refer to charms, slips of parchment that contained cabalistic words and sentences which were deposited in little silk bags and worn like amulets. A great trade was carried on in *Ephesia grammata.*

How did they calculate that the price amounted to five myriads of silver, i. e., so many drachmae (at say 17 cents), in all about $8,500? Somebody of a statistical bent of mind must have conceived the idea and then added up the amounts that had been paid for these *bibloi.* That was a lot of money to be consigned to the flames. It was one of the best investments these believers ever made. And no one had the brilliant idea of selling these *bibloi* to the pagans and the Jews and of setting the price aside for *sacred use.* Incidentally, this sum of 50,000 drachmae gives some indication as to the size to which the Ephesian congregation had grown.

20) Two more imperfects show us the continuance of the growth of the Word in the city and in the province, and the second adds the idea of prevailing (the same verb occurs in v. 16) over adverse forces. Οὕτω, "thus," extends back over the entire previous account concerning the work in Ephesus. It is the Word that grew and prevailed in the double sense of extending to more and more converts and of more and more filling their hearts and their lives.

21) Now at last Paul thinks of moving on. **Now when these things were accomplished, Paul purposed in the spirit, on having gone through Macedonia and**

Achaia, to proceed to Jerusalem, saying, After I get there, it is necessary for me to see also Rome.

This plan was duly carried out as Luke records, but the part in regard to seeing Rome was realized in a way that Paul did not expect: he was brought to Rome as a prisoner. Luke presents Paul's final plan of going to Achaia by way of Macedonia (the route overland); Paul had originally planned to go directly to Corinth (sea route), then through Macedonia and back again to Corinth (II Cor. 1:16), and then on to Judea (Jerusalem). During his visit to Macedonia and Achaia Paul wished to inspect the various congregations and also to look after the great collection then in progress for the famine sufferers in Palestine. That is why he here mentions Jerusalem before stating his desire to see Rome. The matter of the great collection is so important that Paul wants it off his hands before turning toward Rome. Regarding the collection and its magnitude compare I Cor. 16:1, etc.; II Cor. 8; Rom. 15:25, etc.

"When these things were accomplished" (literally fulfilled) places us at the end of the two years mentioned in v. 10. Paul's first letter to the Corinthians was written about this time, near Easter 57. Other communications had passed between Paul and the Corinthians during Paul's stay in Ephesus. In I Cor. 5:9 he refers to an earlier letter of which all other trace has been lost. A short time before Paul wrote First Corinthians he sent Timothy to Corinth by the longer and much slower route overland so that the letter arrived before this messenger. Timothy had various things to do in the congregations en route.

Paul's eventual goal is Rome. In Rom. 1:10, 13 he writes to the Romans about his desire to come to them. But Luke carefully states that Paul said only that he must "see" Rome. The commentary on this is Rom. 1:11, 12. The congregation at Rome was not founded by an apostle, and Paul never thought of establishing himself there. It was not for him to build on another man's foundation. His desire to go to Rome was, as far as the Roman Christians were concerned, to impart some spiritual gift to them and to enjoy their mutual faith. Paul was fully aware of the importance of Rome for the church and what might be done in reaching out farther from this center. The consideration that all his plans were made "God willing" Luke does not need again to add (18:21).

22) **Moreover, having commissioned into Macedonia two of those ministering to him, Timothy and Erastus, he himself held out for a time in Asia.**

We know that Timothy proceeded to Corinth through Macedonia. In I Cor. 4:17 Paul informs the Corinthians of his coming, the letter being sent early enough to anticipate his arrival; he again mentions his coming in I Cor. 16:10, 11, and wants him to return to Ephesus immediately after completing the mission indicated in I Cor. 4:17.

Paul says nothing about Erastus in First Corinthians. The Erastus mentioned in Acts is the same person that is mentioned in II Tim. 4:20, but one is uncertain whether he is also the person referred to in Rom. 16:23, who is there called the οἰκονόμος of the city of Corinth, *Rentmeister*, steward or treasurer. Romans was written in Corinth when Paul was there for the second time (20:2, 3). Because he held an important city office, Erastus could scarcely absent himself from the city for a long period of time. One supposition is that he is the Erastus mentioned here, that he was sent to Paul by the Corinthians and because of his financial ability was employed by Paul in the matter of the collection in Macedonia. The trouble with this view is that Luke calls him one of "those ministering" to Paul, one of his steady assistants, that nothing is said about him in First Corinthians, and that he is, nevertheless, mentioned in Romans.

Paul intended to follow the route taken by Timothy and Erastus although we know that he did not expect to start until Timothy had returned from Corinth. Before Paul started for Macedonia he sent Titus directly to Corinth by the sea route so that he might help to settle matters there. Titus was to meet Paul at Troas but was delayed, so that Paul grew anxious and met him in Macedonia and received the best of news from Corinth. Here in Macedonia, Paul wrote Second Corinthians not long before he himself arrived in Corinth.

Luke reports only the fact that, after dispatching Timothy and Erastus to Macedonia, "he himself held out for a time in Asia." First Corinthians, written near Easter, states the reason: a great and effectual door was opened in Ephesus although there were many adversaries (I Cor. 16:10). So Paul planned to stay in Ephesus until Pentecost. We do not know whether he realized his plan. Pentecost came late in May, and May was the month when the great festival of Artemis (Diana) was observed in Ephesus. The tumult staged by Demetrius must have taken place before this festival, and immediately after the tumult Paul departed (20:1). When Luke writes "in Asia" εἰς, is, of course, static; he intends to state that the interests that detained Paul extended beyond Ephesus itself, so that I Cor. 16:10 must not be understood as referring to Ephesus alone.

Summing up all that is involved in these two verses: messengers hurrying to distant parts and to many congregations, Ephesus with its open door, and the province of Asia besides, enemies to add their peculiar zest, one understands II Cor. 11:27: "The care of all the churches." It was enough to break down any man.

23) **Now along that period there occurred no small disturbance about the Way.** It occurred while

Paul was still spending his time in Asia (v. 22) "No small" is a litotes for "great," and "the Way" is the designation frequently found in Acts (see 9:2) for the entire Christian faith and life. This disturbance, which was precipitated by Demetrius, cannot possibly be what Paul refers to in I Cor. 15:32, when he speaks of fighting with wild beasts in Ephesus; for First Corinthians was already in Corinth when Demetrius stirred up the city; Paul also left Ephesus immediately after this episode. The expression used in I Cor. 15:32 is plainly figurative and elaborates the equally figurative term: "I die daily." See the details in the author's commentary on First Corinthians.

24) **For one by name Demetrius, a silversmith, making silver shrines of Artemis, was furnishing for the artisans no small income; whom having collected together, also the workers pertaining to such things, he said: Men, you know that from this income we have our prosperity. Also you behold and hear that this Paul, by persuading, turned away a great multitude not only of Ephesus but of almost all Asia, saying that those formed by hands are not gods. Now not only is there danger for ourselves that this part come into disrepute but also that the temple of the great goddess Artemis be accounted as nothing, and that presently also she be deposed from her majesty — she whom whole Asia and the inhabited earth worships!**

Luke introduces the account of the great disturbance with γάρ. Demetrius has too common a name to make it possible to identify him beyond what Luke here records of him. This applies to III John 12, and to any inscriptions. This Demetrius was no more than a "silversmith, a maker of silver sanctuaries of Artemis." If these artisans had formed a guild, as is generally assumed, he may have been its head. He is described by Luke as furnishing the artisans no small "income," ἐργασίαν. This word has that meaning in 16:16, 19, and scarcely means "business." This reads as though he was a proprietor who himself employed workmen in his profession and also gave out work to others who were not directly in his employ.

25) Note the two terms employed by Luke: "technicians" to designate those who made silver shrines, and "workmen" to characterize those who produced τὰ τοιαῦτα, "the things of a similar kind," which were probably images made of terra cotta. Demetrius arranged to have them meet and then made his inflammatory address. Regarding the temple of Artemis as being the glory of Ephesus see the remarks in 18:19 and consult the Bible Dictionaries for complete descriptions. The fact that only terra cotta images have been found is explained by the value of those made of silver. These were sought for the silver and were melted down. The use to which the little miniatures were put was to serve as offerings in the temple itself and as sacred ornaments in houses; we do not think that they were used as amulets.

Artemis is not Diana (our versions). The latter, the sister of Apollo, is the Roman goddess who was a graceful huntress, while Artemis, specifically "the Artemis of Ephesians," is the goddess whose image was believed to have fallen from heaven here at Ephesus, a female figure with many breasts which symbolized the generative and the nutritive powers of nature. Nor was "Artemis" her original name. She was worshipped in Ephesus and in the entire province of Asia. Elaborate festivities and games were celebrated in her honor which drew crowds from the whole province and beyond. It seems that at this very time, in May, these celebrations were about to take place, and Paul's work threatened materially to reduce the income of Demetrius and of the manufacturers of the shrines of Artemis.

The address of Demetrius is a cunning mixture of self-interest and zeal for the goddess. One suspects that the mercenary motive was the real one, the religious one being added in order to gild the other. All these artistic and other workers certainly knew "that from this income (ἐργασία) we have our prosperity (εὐπορία)."

26) But here is this Paul who is about to destroy this prosperity. Demetrius furnishes an interesting account of what Paul had accomplished. When he says to all these workmen, "you behold and hear," he speaks of what all of them knew about Paul's work. He exaggerates when he says that by his persuading this Paul (derogatory: "this fellow Paul") has turned away a considerable (ἱκανός) multitude not only of Ephesus but of almost all Asia; yet even then, and allowing for the strong language, we see how much Paul had actually accomplished. He certainly had reached out into the province generally.

Demetrius even states to what Paul was persuading so many, namely that manufactured gods are not gods at all; θεοί, without the article, is the predicate. Note the present tense in the phrase οἱ διὰ χειρῶν γινόμενοι, "those coming into being through (human) hands." Demetrius, of course, does not refer to the handmade images as such but to what these images intend to represent. He restates Paul's thought quite correctly. Gods that can be carved and modeled by human hands are *eo ipso* not gods, and this fact is so plain that a mere statement of it already convinces. We think that the two genitives Ἐφέσου and πάσης τῆς Ἀσίας are dependent on ὄχλον, "of Ephesus, of all Asia a multitude," B.-D. 186, 1, and do not agree with R. 494 who states that they are genitives of place: "at Ephesus, at Asia." These genitives are placed forward merely for the sake of emphasis.

Here we have a plain case of knowing the truth and of stating it exactly and yet rejecting it because of a base motive. The sordidness of the motive is not the point although income and prosperity constantly keep men away from the divine truth and its salvation. The devil buys many for a price. Always, however, a secret motive blinds the soul to its own destruction despite the clearness of the truth. We must not suppose that this entire multitude of which Demetrius speaks became Christian. Paul's success was not so inordinate, great as it was. Paul's teaching did, however, cause thousands of pagans to lose faith in the pagan gods, notably in Artemis. Recall 17:18, the skepticism of the philosophic schools, to which we must add a large number who were like Pilate ("What is truth?"), men who saw the emptiness of idolatry although they found no substitute for the gods. Paul's teaching raised the question about the reality of these gods and turned many worshippers away from the shrines and the altars. Men like Demetrius raised an outcry against it. They felt the loss of money.

27) He points out a threefold danger that threatens if this fellow Paul is not stopped in his teaching. Once more we see that the apostle is the center of attention and not his assistants. The lightning always flashes over *his* head. He certainly must have towered high above all his assistants. The first danger is ἡμῖν, "for us ourselves," namely, "that this part come into disrepute," the part involving the manufacture of the shrines. Their sales will decrease heavily. This will be bad enough as Demetrius implies. This lucrative business will most surely decline to an alarming degree. But worse than that, there is danger "also that the temple of the great goddess Artemis be accounted as nothing" (predicative εἰς), and that in consequence few will care to buy miniatures of that temple. Finally, there is danger "that presently also she be deposed from

her majesty — she whom whole Asia and the inhabited earth worships." This will be the crowning calamity if this fellow Paul is not stopped.

We translate τε καί "and . . . also." All the infinitives occurring after κινδυνεύει are future in sense; hence we have μέλλειν with the last, "about to be deposed," followed by the genitive as is the case with verbs that denote separation. One questions whether even in these statements Demetrius is a sincere worshipper of this great goddess. It is, of course, gross exaggeration to claim that the whole *oikoumenē*, "inhabited (earth)," worshipped the Ephesian Artemis, but some allowance must be made for the provincial character of the speaker who imagined that, when the province paid homage to Artemis, the world generally surely did the same.

28) The fire thus kindled burst into a violent conflagration. **Having heard and become full of wrath, they began to shout, saying, Great the Artemis of Ephesians! And the city was filled with confusion; also they began to rush into the theater, having seized Gaius and Aristarchus, Macedonians, travel companions of Paul.**

Luke's description is graphic. They heard, became excited, began to shout. The Codex Bezae adds the comment that they ran into the open street. Luke has not mentioned a building, the meeting may have been held in the Agora. The laudation of their Artemis came naturally to their lips and gave vent to their excitement. The acclamation "great" as well as her designation "the Artemis of Ephesians" merely repeat the cries the votaries shouted at the festivals of the goddess. She is always "the Artemis of Ephesians," for at Ephesus her image had fallen from heaven, and here was located her central sanctuary, so that elsewhere, too, she bore this name.

29) The excitement spread quickly and filled the city with confusion, and everybody poured into the amphitheater that had over 20,000 seats encircling an arena and was the usual place for large public meetings. The move to the theater seems not to have been planned but was begun spontaneously. Public affairs were transacted in these amphitheaters also when tumults ensued.

How the crowd found Gaius and Aristarchus, travel companions of Paul, is not indicated, it was most probably by accident. No special hostility was shown them save that they were forced to go along and thus involuntarily came to witness the entire affair in the theater. These two were evidently recognized as Paul's companions. We see no reason for thinking that the mob wanted these two as victims for "this gladiatorial show," or that they were to be treated to a dose of "popular justice." The mob was leaderless, was one grand confusion. Nobody knew why these two were wanted or what to do with them. The danger, of course, was that at any moment some man might assume the lead and demand some form of violence. No one could foresee how things would end. The whole crowd was irresponsible.

Gaius was a Macedonian and hence was not identical with the Gaius of Derbe (20:4), or with the Gaius of Corinth (I Cor. 1:15; Rom. 16:23). The praenomen Gaius was quite common. The Gaius of III John 1 is certainly another person. Aristarchus was from Thessalonica and is again mentioned in 20:4; 27:2; Col. 4:10; Philemon 24.

30) **And Paul, wanting to go in to the populace, the disciples were not letting him. Moreover, some also of the Asiarchs, being friends to him, by sending to him were beseeching him not to adventure himself into the theater.**

All credit to Paul for both his courage and his readiness to come to the rescue of his assistants. While that mob was carrying on, no man could tell what would happen to Gaius and to Aristarchus, and the worst was no doubt feared. Δῆμος is the term for the people as a political body and is in place here since rushing to the theater appeared to them as an assembling there to settle some matter. The disciples would naturally not think of letting Paul do this. It would have made the situation worse. Paul could not have saved the two, he might even have precipitated a calamity by having himself and these two killed. R. 885 calls this a negative imperfect which denotes resistance to pressure. Instead of implying that the disciples failed, it implies the opposite, that they succeeded, and that is the distinctive thing about this imperfect.

31) In addition there came the message from "some of the Asiarchs," friends of Paul, which earnestly urged him not to risk his life in the theater. Here we have another imperfect which is evidently to be taken in the same sense as the one preceding; it is also action against pressure, and it also implies success. "Not to give himself" is well rendered, "not to adventure himself."

Zahn is evidently mistaken when he thinks that only one Asiarch was appointed for each year. All the evidence is in favor of the view that there were ten for each year. The plural cannot be justified by counting those who had had this honor during preceding years after the analogy of the plural "high priests" although only one was high priest at any time. When Eusebius mentions only one (4, 11) named Philip who refused to release a lion against Polycarp in Smyrna, this has nothing to do with the number of Asiarchs that ruled a province. He was the one who had been elected for Smyrna or resided in that city. Each city elected a representative annually and these elected the ten Asiarchs for the year; one was selected as the president by the proconsul of the province. It was their duty to defray the costs of and to undertake all the arrangements for the national games and the sacred theatrical spectacles. This entailed the expenditure of great sums of money; only the wealthiest could serve, but the honor was eagerly sought. Some authorities add other functions and mix in priests, but this is without warrant.

A remarkable circumstance is the fact that some of these men were friends of Paul and so concerned about him as hastily to send a message on this occasion lest he throw his life away. This is a little chapter on which one might like to have light. Their presence in Ephesus may be explained by the fact that the festivities were to be held at this time (May); otherwise they lived in various cities. To be sure, they wanted to avoid bloodshed in the theater. But they acted from motives of friendship toward Paul. How did it come about that they were Paul's friends, men who were so prominent in the province and friends so loyal? A most remarkable man was this Paul. We are sorry we can say no more about his contact with these Asiarchs. Other provinces, too, had their men: Galatriarchs, Bithyniarchs, Syriarchs.

32) **Some, then, kept shouting one thing, others another; for the assembly was confused, and the majority knew not on what account they had come together.**

Οὖν is resumptive and continues the story from v. 30; ἄλλοι ἄλλο τι is the classical idiom for "some one thing, some another" (R. 747). Luke still speaks of the ἐκκλησία, the word for a proper assembly, but he describes it as being in a condition of confusion. This is the force of the perfect participle συγκεχυμένη. We do not combine this with ἦν to make a periphrastic past perfect passive (R., *W. P.*). This verse has three imperfect tenses, and the perfect participle with ἦν is merely predicative: "was confused" i. e., was in that condition. In fact, the majority (R. 665) knew not (ᾔδεισαν, second past perfect which is always used as an imperfect) why they had come together (the Greek here accommodating the tense just as we do in English) Demetrius had started something that promptly got beyond him. Perhaps he was himself frightened.

33) **Moreover, out of the multitude they brought Alexander, the Jews putting him forward. And Alexander, beckoning with the hand, wanted to make defense to the populace. But having recognized that he was a Jew, there came one shout from all for about two hours crying, Great the Artemis of Ephesians!**

This abortive effort on the part of the Jews is surely most interesting. The view that this Alexander was a converted Jew, and that the Jews forced him forward in order that, as a Christian, he might become the victim of the mob's fury is untenable. They might have forced him forward, but he would never have attempted to speak, and if he spoke he would have accused the Jews who thrust him forward. He certainly was himself a Jew and was willing to speak in defense of the Jews.

In his *Introduction to the New Testament* 2, 16, etc.; 21, etc., Zahn advocated the view that this Alexander is not identical with the one mentioned in I Tim. 1:20, and II Tim. 4:14; but he changed his mind in his *Apostelgeschichte.* The fact that in the latter passage Alexander is called a coppersmith lends color to the view that they were identical. But then he must have been converted to Christianity and must have forsaken the faith according to I Tim. 1:20. As a coppersmith he may well have helped in manufacturing shrines of Artemis; they were made of copper and were then plated with silver and thus were of a cheaper grade than the solid silver shrines. Some Jews made a living by following many trades that were forbidden by their law.

If Alexander was also a metal image worker we can almost know what his address would have presented if he had been allowed to make it. He would have said that he himself helped to make shrines and that thus he and the Jews were not guilty of opposing Artemis, that this was wholly the crime of renegade Jews such as "this fellow Paul" whom Gaius and Aristarchus abetted. But a higher hand controlled this wild hubbub.

The moment Alexander, by the help of the Jews, got to the stage and moved his hand up and down in order to give the usual signal for quiet so that he might speak, pandemonium broke loose. Already the imperfect ἤθελεν indicates that he did not get beyond wanting to speak, and ἀπολογεῖσθαι is the regular verb for making a formal oral defense.

34) The preferred reading is ἐπιγνόντων (with αὐτῶν being understood), a perfectly regular genitive absolute: "they having realized that he was a Jew" ("is" in the Greek is unchanged from the direct discourse) ; the reading ἐπιγνόντες would be a pendent nominative absolute and an unusual construction. Somebody who knew Alexander may have shouted, "A Jew, a Jew!" As though a signal had been given, the thousands that were in the amphitheater raised the original cry, "Great the Artemis of Ephesians!" This absolutely prevented Alexander from speaking. So this Jew also precipitated something that he neither expected nor could control. We need not inject the thought that he was promptly removed from the stage. The great multitude was not in a violent mood, the outlet of its energy remained vocal. Luke writes beautifully, "a voice came as one out of all"; it was an instantaneous, unanimous chorus in which everybody shouted in order to drown out the Jew. That was the first involuntary impulse; but once it was under way.

Alexander was forgotten, and the shouting continued of its own momentum for well on to two hours. Once started, it just could not stop. It exhibited typical mob psychology. There was no leader, no sense, no object and purpose, no consideration even of the foolishness of its own demonstration. This Ephesian clamor seems to hold the world's record for crowd marathon shouting.

35) **And having quieted the multitude, the chancellor says: Ephesian men, Why, who is there of men that does not know the city of the Ephesians as being temple keeper of the great Artemis and of the image fallen from Zeus? These things, then, being undeniable, it is needful that you keep quiet and be doing nothing precipitate. For you brought these men, neither temple robbers, nor blaspheming our goddess. If, therefore, Demetrius and the artisans with him have a legal complaint against anyone, court days are held, and there are proconsuls — let them bring charges against each other. If, however, you are seeking something concerning different matters, it shall be disposed of in a lawful assembly. For also we are in danger of being accused of riot concerning this day, there being no legal cause regarding which we shall be able duly to give a statement concerning this mob.**

The "town clerk" of our versions makes a wrong impression. This γραμματεύς was the chief official of the city; Luther's rendering "chancellor" is still the best. This title is found on Ephesian inscriptions and in the papyri just as Luke has it. It was probably derived from his function of drafting the decrees with the aid of the *strategoi*; but he also had charge of the city funds, was in control of the assembly of the citizens when this was called out to transact city affairs, and communicated with the Roman proconsul who governed the entire province. Free cities such as Ephesus elected their own chancellor and other officers. In different cities the functions of the chancellor varied somewhat. When this city chief appeared on the stage, his very presence affected the howling mob which was already well spent because of its two hours of crying, and he soon had silence and full attention. We do not think that he stood on the stage for some time. His appearance brought prompt silence.

This official's address was decidedly to the point. He was a capable man in his position and showed it. We first note his neat *captatio benevolentiae;* next, the natural deduction as to the impropriety of the mob's procedure; then, the pointing out the proper and legal course that Demetrius or any others were to pursue if they have a case of other business; finally, the implied threat that he and all others present might be called to account for this day's unwarranted and indefensible action. That sobered everybody. If we ask why he did not interfere sooner, the address itself answers that question. What he says about Demetrius and those with him reveals that he did not rush into the meeting uninformed in order to stop the clamor; he waited until he had full and correct information on the entire affair, down to the part Demetrius had played in it. When he had what he needed he interfered. Meanwhile the shouting was doing no special damage.

We cannot duplicate ἄνδρες Ἐφέσιοι ("men, Ephesians") except by making the latter an adjective: "Ephesian men"; and γάρ resembles our "why" at the head of a statement. We may reproduce as follows: "Why, who in the world does not know," etc.? Then follows the complementary participle οὖσαν in indirect discourse (R. 1123) which we may imitate by rendering, does not know "the city of the Ephesians as being temple keeper," etc. This term νεωκόρος (from νεός = νεώς plus κορέω, sanctuary sweeper) is a sort of high title. A coin of A. D. 65 bears this as a title for Ephesus, inscriptions do the same. It was later used also with reference to the imperial cultus in temples that were erected for the emperors. The chancellor's question challenges anybody to name a man in the whole world who does not know that Ephesus is the illustrious warden of "the great Artemis." That was saying a good deal when it was taken literally. In general, of course, Ephesus with its temple of Artemis, one of the seven wonders of the world, was known as the adorer of this goddess.

The addition καὶ τοῦ Διοπετοῦς (Ζεύς, genitive, Διός, plus πίπτω) with ἀγάλματος to be supplied, R. 653, "and of the image fallen down from Zeus," refers to the statue that was so highly revered in Ephesus, a many-breasted female figure whose bottom section was a square pillar carved with ancient symbols of bees, corn and flowers. It was discolored with age, and more like a Hindoo idol than anything else. Perhaps it was dug up at an early age and was a relic of previous idolatry, the image of a goddess whose original name is now no longer known, and was, perhaps, unknown to the Ephesians at the beginning. Having been found thus, it was thought to have fallen from heaven where Zeus was supposed to rule. Being made of ebony, it should have been burned up when, on the night of the birth of Alexander the Great, Herostratus set fire to the temple in order to gain undying fame; the statue escaped destruction because it was at the time not in the temple but was being used in some ceremony.

36) Since the fame of Artemis, her image, and Ephesus as her sanctuary warden were assured in the whole world, what sense was there in all this shouting? "These things, then, being undeniable" answers the speaker's question, answers it for all his hearers. But then they ought to be quiet and not to perpetrate anything rash such as the present proceeding. There is no rhyme or reason in what they are doing. Δέον (neuter participle of δεῖν) ἐστίν is a periphrastic present that is

both classical and vernacular, R. 881; and κατεσταλμένους (we have the aorist active participle in v. 36) with ὑπάρχειν is the perfect passive periphrastic infinitive which is here used as the subject: the needful thing is "for you on your part (ὑμεῖς, emphatic) to have been, and thus still to be, quiet."

37) This is said in view of the fact (γάρ) that they have brought into the theater "these men, neither temple robbers (deeds) nor blaspheming (participle — words) our gods." They have committed no crime against the temple or against the goddess. The chancellor knows about Gaius and Aristarchus and their innocence and fears no contradiction.

38) The two conditions of reality include all other possibilities. The term λόγος may refer to any legal complaint and Demetrius himself and the artisans are named. If they feel that they have been wronged in an illegal way, the chancellor informs them that court days or sessions are regularly conducted, ἀγοραῖοι (ἡμέραι), which were called this because they were held in the Agora under proper judges who conducted trials according to the laws.

He also reminds Demetrius and the artisans that there are such supreme judges as the ἀνθύπατοι; for Asia was a senatorial province which was always under a proconsul. The plural is a general designation for this highest type of judge. The hint is given that, if justice is not secured in the lower courts, the proconsul may hear an appeal. But this mention of proconsuls hints at the seriousness of starting a trial in the courts; the thing may go farther than Demetrius and his men may desire. "Let them bring charges against each other" is neutral in regard to those who may consider themselves wronged.

39) However, it may not be a matter for the law courts but "something concerning different things," referring to such as concern the δῆμος which was com-

posed of the citizen voters in general that could thus legally and properly decide to enact a new law or change one that was already in force. There is slight textual evidence for the reading περαιτέρω, comparative of περαίτερος, "something further beyond." Any matter of this kind "shall be disposed of in the lawful assembly," the ἐκκλησία, the meeting to which, according to law, all the voting citizens are called out (ἐκκαλεῖν). Only the Roman officials could issue this call. One must not lose the force of "lawful." The present assembly was entirely unlawful. Moreover, calling and conducting an "assembly" was always a grave matter and vastly beyond any little grievance a man might have.

40) With γάρ the chancellor states why he is reminding this theaterful of people of these legal ways of proceeding, ways which they should certainly themselves know. He means that the proconsul may look into this day's riot and frankly calls it a στάσις, "riot." Diplomatically he says, "We are in danger of being accused of riot concerning this day." As the city chancellor he himself would, of course, also be involved. He intimates that by taking a hand as he now does and by speaking in a sensible way as he does he is keeping his own skirts clean, but how about Demetrius, his adherents, and all the rest? According to R., *W. P.*, the Romans looked on nothing with so much jealousy as on tumultuous meetings. The chancellor's hearers knew that.

This wild assembly certainly had "no legal cause" whatever; μηδενὸς αἰτίου, neuter, in the genitive absolute denotes cause in the legal sense, one that would be accepted by a judge. Another cause there was, namely the inflammatory harangue of Demetrius; but he would be the last person to desire that the proconsul look into that. "There being no legal cause regarding which we shall be able (i. e., if actually called upon by the proconsul) duly to give a statement concerning this mob (συστροφή)." Ἀποδοῦναι = duly to give, and λόγον is here an acceptable account and explanation. Not one of us, the chancellor says, could offer the least excuse to the proconsul for this day's turmoil. He was certainly right. He began with words that tickled the vanity of this mob, he ended by throwing the fear of proconsular justice into their bones. He certainly cured them of any further demonstration.

41) **And having said these things, he dismissed the assembly.** It was most willing to be dismissed, and the most willing was Demetrius himself who had started things. It began wildly, it ended tamely. That was God's providence. He as yet wanted no martyrs in Ephesus. The chancellor closed this unwarranted "assembly" in proper order and saved at least that much of legality.

Luke's record of this address contains so many specific terms that are used in the same sense in inscriptions, papyri, coins, and other writers, that one is really surprised at Luke's exactness and at the precision with which he introduces term after term. Those who fault him in other places do not praise him here. They are simply silent. But the great fact stands out that Luke is absolutely reliable aside from inspiration. Here is evidence that can be tested from many still available sources; where we have less or no outside sources and can apply no such tests, the record is just as true.

CHAPTER XX

THE THIRD MISSIONARY JOURNEY: FROM EPHESUS TO GREECE AND BACK TO MILETUS

1) The tumult in the theater caused Paul to put into execution the plans that had for some time been maturing in his mind (19:21), the preliminaries of which had already been carried out (19:22), namely the sending ahead of Timothy and of Erastus, the former all the way to Corinth. When Demetrius staged his tumult, Paul was waiting for Timothy's return. If Timothy had not yet returned he must have hastened after Paul and soon joined him.

Now after the uproar ceased, Paul, having summoned the disciples and encouraged them, after taking leave went out in order to go into Macedonia.

The accusative with the infinitive is regarded as a substantive (*τό*) after *μετά*. We know how the tumult came to cease, and therefore this phrase does not state the motive for Paul's departure but only the time of it. We must not think of fear, hurry, flight, or anything of that sort. Paul could have remained in Ephesus but not much longer, for his plans called for his departure in a few days. So he summoned the disciples by sending messengers with word about his leaving. The next day they gathered at their usual meeting place at the appointed time, and Paul addressed encouraging words to them. Then followed the formal farewell (*ἀσπασάμενος*), and Paul left. It is understood that many escorted him for a considerable distance of his journey, for that was a regular custom. It is worth noting, however, that Luke does not write *ἐξελθὼν ἐπορεύθη*, which would imply that Paul now chose this destination in order to have some place to go, but ἐξῆλθε πορεύεσθαι, the infinitive of purpose, "in order to be going," i. e., carrying out a purpose and a plan that had been projected long ago.

2) **And having gone through those parts and having encouraged them with many a word, he came to Greece.**

These few words cover the long journey overland from Ephesus to Corinth. It was interrupted by frequent stops. When Luke writes εἰς τὴν Ἑλλάδα he refers to Greece proper; heretofore he wrote "Achaia," which is the Roman province that included Greece and Thessaly. Before leaving Ephesus, Paul had sent Titus to Corinth as a second messenger who was to go by ship and after completing his mission to return by land and meet Paul in Troas. Although Paul spent much time in the churches that lay between Ephesus and Troas, "encouraging them with many a word," Titus had not appeared when he reached Troas. This worried Paul, for he feared that matters had gone illy in Corinth; so he hurried on into Macedonia, met Titus, received a most encouraging report from him, wrote Second Corinthians (II Cor. 2:13; 7:5; 8:1, etc.), sent it ahead, most likely from Philippi, finished visiting the church in Macedonia, "having encouraged them with many a word" as he had done in the case of the rest, and so reached Greece, and in particular Corinth.

3) **And having spent three months, a plot having been laid against him by the Jews when he was about to set sail for Syria, he became of the opinion to return back through Macedonia.**

We may take it that Paul left Ephesus in May, 57, reached Corinth at the end of that year, and left there so as to arrive in Philippi before Easter of 58. During the three months which he spent chiefly in Corinth he most likely wrote the letter to the Galatians and certainly the letter to the Romans. Then he planned to sail from Cenchraea, the harbor of Corinth, for Syria just as he had done after his first visit in Corinth which continued for eighteen months. But the Jews formed a plot against him and intended to murder him as he was about to set sail. Learning of it in some way, he changed his plans and went by land through Macedonia, thus coming to spend Easter in Philippi.

The Greek reads, "a plot having become for him," αὐτῷ is the indirect object; to this pronoun there is attached μέλλοντι, "for him as about to set sail for Syria." Codex Bezae inserts the remark that the Spirit told Paul to take the route overland, but this is an unnecessary comment, for Paul and his friends knew enough to circumvent the dastardly plot by changing their route as Luke reports they did. On the genitive γνώμης after ἐγένετο see R. 497 and 514: "he became of the opinion"; the infinitive with τοῦ simply modifies the noun as a genitive (R. 1060, 1076) : "he became of the opinion of going back," etc.

4) **Moreover, there were following with him until Asia, Sopater, son of Pyrrhus of Berea; and of Thessalonians, Aristarchus and Secundus; and Gaius, a Derbean, and Timothy; and Asians, Tychicus and Trophimus. These, however, having gone on ahead, were awaiting us at Troas. And we on our part set sail from Philippi after the days of the unleavend bread and came to them to Troas after five days, where we tarried seven days.**

These seven men who accompanied Paul were bearers of the great collection Paul had arranged for in all his Gentile congregations during the two years preceding. A year before this he had written regarding it in I Cor. 16:1, etc.; then again in II Cor. 8 and 9. During the three months spent in Corinth he wrote regarding it in Rom. 15:25, just before he set out to deliver the funds in Jerusalem.

The seven here mentioned began the journey with Paul. The details are uncertain except that we may conclude from 1 Cor. 16:3 that each of the larger congregations elected its bearers of the funds. As the collecting had been done in a systematic way, so the transmission was arranged with an eye to safety, full satisfaction to the givers, and most beneficial effects on both donors and beneficiaries. In 19:21, 22 Paul's plans include the disposal of these funds. He never thought of handling this money himself; he was too wise for that. In fact, 1 Cor. 16:4 reveals that he had not at that time as yet fully decided whether he himself would accompany the bearers of the money or not.

The phrase that the seven were following along "until Asia" which is omitted in some texts because it was probably puzzling, has received various interpretations. One opinion advanced is that Troas is referred to, but then Luke would have written Troas and not Asia, to which Troas did not belong. Moreover, the entire party, including Luke himself, certainly journeyed all the way to Jerusalem. Hence another opinion advanced is that Asia refers, not to the Roman province by that name, but to Asia in general. But this would be the only instance in Acts where the word has such a general meaning.

The best solution seems to be that "until Asia" marks the preliminary objective. The funds that had been gathered in the province of Asia and in the Galatian congregations would certainly not first be carried to Corinth or even to Troas when it was known that Paul would stop at Miletus in the province of Asia. Seven men, plus Luke, which makes eight, started from Europe; these either took charge of the remaining funds that had been gathered in Asia when they stopped at Miletus, or other bearers of those funds joined them there. So these eight followed along until

Asia whence all sailed together for Palestine with all the funds.

One of the company came from Berea, and two came from Thessalonica, Luke from Philippi (v. 6), and thus there were four from the province of Macedonia. Next, one from Derbe, another from Lystra (Timothy, 16:1) are mentioned; these two came from the province of Galatia. Then two, the "Asians," from the province of Asia. This omits the province of Achaia with its various congregations. Why there were no representatives from Achaia, from Corinth in particular, is a problem. We should rather expect at least two from these localities. Some authorities state that Paul was himself entrusted with the funds from Achaia; but we cannot agree with this view, see I Cor. 16:3. We should much rather think of Timothy who was well known to the Corinthians and to the rest in Achaia. Moreover, we do not think that the funds were carried in coin, even in gold coin. That would have been inadvisable because of the distance traveled and because of the route followed. The amount would have been heavy, too bulky, too much exposed to robbery. It was carried in bills of exchange.

Sopater is the Sosipater, a former Jew, mentioned in Rom. 16:21, one of those whom Luke calls "more noble" (17:11). Aristarchus was mentioned in 19:29, but Secundus appears only here; both came from Thessalonica. The Greek reads "Gaius, a Derbean," so that the only mention we have of this Gaius is here (see 19:29); we cannot translate "as Derbean also Timothy." It has already (16:1) been stated that Timothy came from Lystra, hence nothing is added to his name at this point. Trophimus appears again in Jerusalem (21:29), he was an Ephesian and a former Gentile, he is mentioned also in II Tim. 4:20. Tychicus is mentioned often; Paul speaks highly of him in Eph. 6:21 and Col.

4:7, he was probably an Ephesian, II Tim. 4:12; Tit. 3:12.

5, 6) As Luke introduced himself in the "we" section 16:10-17, so he does here. He had apparently been left in Philippi in 16:40 and now appears in this city and joins Paul's company. All we are able to determine is that he had spent the entire interval of about five years in Philippi, working in the congregation and at his profession as a physician.

These seven went directly to Troas and there waited for Luke and Paul. We do not know the reason that Luke and Paul remained behind and took ship "after the days of the unleavened bread." If they wanted to observe these days, i. e., the Jewish Passover week, they could have done so in Troas as well as in Philippi. The view that Paul at times lived "Jewish" without, of course, compelling others to do so, cannot be introduced here, much less the view that he, whether together with Luke or without him, wanted to keep the Jewish festival in the way that was customary to the Jews of the diaspora. The story of Lydia reveals that there were practically no Jews in Philippi. Why should Paul remain here and separate himself from the other seven if participation in such a celebration was his object? Aristarchus was a former Jew, yet he goes on, and the former Gentile Luke alone remains with Paul.

In 16:11 the voyage from Troas to Neapolis, the harbor of Philippi, took only two days, the vessel going in "a straight course" under favorable winds; the return voyage took five days, for apparently the wind which was blowing in the same direction was most unfavorable. Paul had hastened away from Troas on coming from Ephesus (v. 1; II Cor. 2:12, 13). He now makes up for this, and he and his entire party remain there a full week. Luke has thus far said nothing about a congregation in Troas. We shall now hear of one, and II Cor. 2:12 shows why Paul was willing to delay here a week.

7) **Now on the first day of the week, we being gathered together to break bread, Paul kept discoursing with them, being about to leave in the morning, and he was stretching the discourse out until midnight. Moreover, there were lamps sufficient in the upper room where we were gathered together.**

We translate "on the first day of the week," but the phrase is literally "on the first (day) with reference to the Sabbath," i. e., on Sunday. The Jews had no definite names for the days of the week and hence designated them with reference to their Sabbath. The genitive was used in the Greek, and the plural τῶν σαββάτων means "Sabbath" and not "week" (as R., *W. P.*, explains: "Sabbath to Sabbath"). This neuter plural is like the neuter plural that is used in the names of festivals and is thus idiomatic; so also is the cardinal μία instead of the ordinal πρώτη, which is properly explained by R. 671, etc. Luke refers to Sunday exactly as his dative does in Luke 24:1, and Sunday in our sense of the word, so that "until midnight" *follows* the daylight of Sunday. John 20:14 is clear on this point: "It being evening on that day, the first day of the week."

The Jewish day began at sundown, and when Luke writes "Sabbath" and "unleavened" (v. 6) he is using Jewish expressions. But we must note that this company did not assemble after dark, as we do for evening service, but already before dark, hence on Sunday as Jews, too, would say. Moreover, "until midnight" simply follows "on the first day of the week" without saying that it was the midnight of this or of that day. Zahn ingeniously counts back the days Luke mentions and thus finds that the Jewish Easter of this year 58 occurred on a Tuesday, this being the fourteenth of Nisan, but when the astronomers treat the matter they arrive at no unanimity in their calculations as far as dating this Easter according to our calendar is concerned.

It is true that this is the first Christian service, held on a Sunday, that is recorded in Acts; yet little can be proved from it since it was a special service in every way, and Paul and his company left early on Monday morning. It was the last opportunity for him and for them to meet the congregation. We feel that if this had been some other day of the week, such a final service would have been held. If this had been a Sunday morning service, it would be of more help to us in establishing Sunday as the regular day of worship in the apostolic congregation. We, indeed, think that a morning service was held at Troas on this Sunday although no mention of it is made by Luke. We also think that Paul purposely started his journey on Monday. Much more important regarding Sunday as the day of worship is what Paul wrote to the Corinthians several months before this in I Cor. 16:2; for this deals with regular Sunday worship. With this we combine John 20:19, and, as being of great importance, Rev. 1:10. Jewish Christians may for a time have retained the seventh day of the week; but in the Gentile churches, as I Cor. 16:2 certainly shows, the first day was the day of public worship. This day was sacred from the time mentioned in John 20:19, as the day of Christ's resurrection, and at once became more sacred as commemorating also the day of the outpouring of the Holy Spirit. The break with the Jewish Sabbath became decisive the moment the converted Jews withdrew from the synagogue; they no longer wanted to be identified with the hostile Jews, and the keeping of Sunday in place of Saturday thus received a strong impetus from the beginning.

But there is no command anywhere in the New Testament obligating believers to observe Sunday. In the old covenant Saturday was fixed by divine law for the Jews. In the new covenant no day is fixed in any manner by any law. The supposition that Christ or his apostles transferred the legal sanction from Saturday to Sunday is without support. To call our Sunday the Christian "Sabbath" is to apply a wrong and misleading name. Sunday as a day of rest and worship for Christians is just about the opposite of the Jewish Sabbath. The latter was wholly compulsory, the former is altogether voluntary. We keep Sunday because we want and need it for the public worship without which we cannot get along in our Christian life. The Lord wants his Word preached and taught, and that publicly; to do that to the best advantage we must have a set day. The old covenant serves as an example. Thus without any legal constraint whatever, in the most natural and voluntary manner, and in the sensible and wholesome exercise of our New Testament liberty, with the greatest unanimity since the earliest apostolic days, Sunday is our day of public worship. We refuse to attach anything legal to it that may be in conflict with Col. 2:16, or Gal. 5:1. See The Augustana, article 28, §§ 57-60, *C. Tr.* 91, etc.

The perfect participle συνηγμένων has its durative force so that we translate "being gathered together." The purpose of the gathering was "to break bread." This was evidently not merely to dine together but to dine in the Agape which was followed by the Lord's Supper in the usual manner of this time (2:42; I Cor. 10:16) The absence of the article with "bread" is quite immaterial. To imagine that the Agape was celebrated in the early evening, and the Lord's Supper after midnight, because of the expression with the article used in v. 11, is fanciful. After the tables had been cleared away, Paul began to discourse and was stretching his discourse out until midnight, two imperfect tenses, that are descriptive and intimate that something is to follow.

8) Before this follows, we have the parenthetical remark (δέ) about the many lights in the upper room where they were gathered. The remark that it was dark because it was already so far past full moon is inadequate, because lights were needed during any night, moon or no moon. Nor does Luke mention the lamps as a proof that he saw what happened; even if he had not seen it with his own eyes, he could have learned all the facts. Mention of the lamps does not mean that Eutychus had no occasion to go to sleep; or the opposite, that the smoke from the many lamps made the young man drowsy and made him seek the window seat. Luke, of course, proves himself an eyewitness, but he has already stated his presence. The sense of Luke's statement is that the room was brilliantly lighted and not just dimly with a few lamps; hence those near the young man should certainly have seen him nodding, noted his danger, and have aroused him. Luke conveys the idea that in spite of the brilliant light nobody noticed the young man. Some speak of a very large assembly, but "upper room," even when it is crowded, implies only a moderate number of people. The congregation was small, quite so if all present found room for the breaking of bread in this room; ἦμεν with the perfect participle is the periphrastic past perfect.

9) **Now a young man by name Eutychus, sitting at the window, gradually being borne down by sleep while Paul was discoursing, still longer completely borne down by his sleep, fell down from the third story and was taken up dead.**

Eutychus = fortunate, the Latin *Fortunatus;* according to R., *W. P.*, this was common as a name for slaves. His sitting on the window sill was not due to the smoke or the heat from the lamps, for how about the other people? The window sill afforded a seat, somebody took it, and it was this youth. The diminutive θυρίς from θύρα, "little door," is used for our "window." II Cor. 11:33. The present participle καταφερόμενος describes how he was gradually being borne down by sound sleep; then the aorist participle κατενεχθείς states the fact that he was completely borne down or overcome. The significance of the tenses is striking, the more so since the three participles used are without connectives. The genitive absolute, "Paul discoursing still longer," as "still longer" shows, is to be construed with the final participle as showing how the young man became completely unconscious and thus fell out of the window from the third story and was taken up dead.

Luke says "dead" and not "as dead." We have every reason to suppose that as a physician Luke hurried down with the others and examined the youth himself and found that life was extinct. The youth was not hastily and mistakenly pronounced dead. The view that "dead" does not mean that his soul had left the body is untenable, for that is exactly what "dead" means. Equally untenable is the idea that, when death sets in, the soul still hovers near the body. This is the old superstition that is back of so many superstitious practices connected with dying and with funerals. One practice was to move everything in the house and in the barns in order to make the place look strange, so that the soul would not linger to haunt the place. Even the cattle were changed about in the stalls, the beehives moved, etc. Some people still stop all the clocks in the house, turn pictures and mirrors to the wall, or at least throw a sheet over the latter. This explains the Irish wake and its remnant today of sitting up with the dead body. The soul, still present, must be amused, and the greater the hilarity, the better. After the funeral everybody returns to the house for a feast, the soul also returning; in some places a vacant chair was placed at the table, a towel was thrown over its back, and the feast was prolonged. We have remnants of these superstitious practices today although people no longer know just why they do such peculiar things. This is the real basis for the idea that at death the soul hovers near the body for a time. Some commentators have introduced that idea here. Ahaziah fell out of a window without killing himself, II Kings 1:2.

10) Before Paul could run down, the young man had been taken up and, as we may suppose, carried into the house. Were any of his bones broken? Luke is reticent, keeping only to the main facts. **And Paul, having gone down, fell upon him and, after having embraced him, said, Stop making noise! For his soul is in him.**

The commentators are divided in their views. Some think the young man was dead, others that he was not dead. But Luke writes "dead": "was taken up νεκρός," and tells us briefly how this "dead" man was restored to life. Luke even says that Paul proceeded much as Elijah (I Kings 17:21) and Elisha (II Kings 4:34) did in connection with two plain cases of actual death.

Note the clearness of Luke's verb forms, all are aorists. Paul ran down and "fell on" the young man. The verb is finite and not a participle. A participle might express action that is simultaneous with εἶπε, so that Paul spoke *as* he fell on the young man, said that his soul was in him as an explanation as to why he fell on him. But this idea is excluded by the finite verb. This makes fully clear the participle "having embraced" him, for it repeats and amplifies the finite verb "fell on him." The point of Luke's verb forms is that *after* these actions Paul spoke as he did. The young man, taken up dead, has his soul in him, i. e., is alive *after* Paul fell on him and embraced him. Luke says no more — it is enough. Paul brought the dead man's soul back as Elijah and Elisha had done.

Negative commands in the present imperative often mean to stop an action already begun. So here the people had already begun their loud lament for the dead, and Paul tells them to stop it (R. 851, etc.). The verb is the same as that used in Matt. 9:23 with reference to the same noise of lament for the dead; Mark 5:38, 39 has both the noun and the verb. Paul's action is illy explained by saying that, in order not to have the grief over this fatal accident mar his departure, he made use of the charismatic gift bestowed on him and brought the youth back to life. These gifts do not operate at will and for personal reasons. Paul did what Peter had done in the case of Dorcas. Both prayed to know the Lord's will in the case, and not until Paul had embraced the dead man did he know the Lord's will, in other words, not until he spoke as he did.

11) **And having gone up and broken the bread and tasted food and having conversed a long while until dawn, he thus went out. And they brought the lad living and were in not a little comforted.**

Once more we disagree with some commentators, those who think that the Agape and the Lord's Supper were observed after the miracle, after midnight, and base this view on the article in the expression "having broken *the bread.*" We submit, first of all, that in v. 7 Luke states, "we being assembled in order to break bread." This was the purpose of the meeting. The meeting was held early in the evening, at the usual time for the δεῖπνον. Everybody brought food, and it would be strange, indeed, if by his discourse which continued for some five hours Paul had delayed the very purpose for which all had assembled. No, the bread was broken, let us say, about seven o'clock. This action was not hurried. After the meal was over, Paul began his discourse, the length of which Luke accounts for by saying that the apostle was to leave in the morning. We now add that after the miracle Luke speaks only about Paul and not about the company ("we" in v. 7). He breaks the bread — some of that originally brought

— and Luke adds a second participle by way of explanation: he tastes food. Why this singular if all are referred to? And why this second participle if the Lord's Supper is referred to or is included as the chief thing? The answer that Paul acted as the host is not an answer. Why should it be said of any host that he "tasted food"? Luke would be writing rather strangely if he had in mind that *all* waited until so late a time for the Sacrament and that *all* now took food for the first time.

But somebody might object that Paul could not have eaten alone. True. The answer is that Luke has indicated the presence of Paul's assistants only in the lone pronoun ἡμῶν, "we," in v. 7, and has centered attention on Paul in relating the events of this night. So he now says that Paul ate and that Paul went out — his eight helpers are certainly included. They were all to embark with Paul, and so they ate with him. Immediately after midnight, so early? Why stress so? Paul did not hurry. The excitement caused by the miracle did not at once die down. Please allow some of that excitement for Paul himself. He ate in due time and then spent the time until dawn, still quite a space of time (ἐφ' ἱκανόν), in conversation — Luke purposely changes from "to discourse" which he has used in both v. 7 and 9. One may even guess what the conversation was about — the miracle which all had witnessed was in the minds of all.

12) "They brought the lad" is indefinite as to the subject and refers to those present. The view that he had been slowly recovering overlooks the fact that miracles do not operate in that way. When the Lord works a miracle he does so with completeness. The Codex Bezae introduces a curious substitution: "while they were taking farewell, he (Paul) brought the young man in living." This has received an even more curious interpretation: the young man kept hold of Paul's

hand when going downstairs, and he and Paul were the ones most comforted, Paul especially needing this comfort. The story, however, is much simpler. At the end of v. 11 Paul left, and that means that he left the young man and all. The Christians of Troas, of course, also left and thus brought the lad "alive" or "living," the emphasis being on this participle. They had carried him in "dead," now they brought him living and that is what filled them with so much comfort and cheer, literally, "not moderately," a litotes for "exceedingly."

13) **Now we on our part, having gone in advance to the boat, set sail for Assos, intending there to pick up Paul; for so he had arranged, intending himself to go on foot. And when he met us at Assos, having picked him up, we went to Mitylene. And having sailed thence, we arrived on the following day opposite Chios; and on the next day we touched at Samos; and on the coming day we came to Miletus.**

Ramsay's explanation of this coastwise voyage with its regular stops helps to explain also the start. Sometime after midnight the wind sets in from the north and blows regularly until late in the afternoon. So Paul's eight companions went to the boat in advance, i. e., in advance of the start Paul himself made; they had to be aboard by the time the wind rose and the boat weighed anchor. Paul had given directions to them to pick him up (ἀναλαμβάνειν) at Assos, beyond which point the boat did not attempt to go on the first day but lay over for the night. The Assian stone near the city was supposed to have flesh-consuming properties; hence the stone coffins were called *sarcophagi*, "flesh consumers." Paul intended to go afoot, the distance being twenty miles on a good Roman road. Some take πεζεύειν to mean "to go by land" in the sense of to ride (Blass, quoted by M.-M.) ; Zahn cites one lone example, a man riding in a litter, going by the feet of others. The classics use the word with reference to going by land instead of by water, but then it is always afoot and only so by land. We shall have to regard Paul as using his *pedes apostolorum*. The vessel had to pass around Cape Lectum and thus traveled a greater distance. It was beautiful spring weather, Monday, April 25 (Ramsay), which is nearly if not exactly correct (see v. 7 regarding the calendar). Paul, too, had plenty of time.

A number of reasons are presented as to why he chose to walk, and that after being awake the whole night before; we just do not know why he chose to do this.

14) He was duly picked up at Assos, and the boat finished its day's run at Mitylene, a beautiful city on the island of Lesbos. In 1925 the writer passed through these same waters, coming from Constantinople and the Hellespont, past the site of ancient Troy, past Mitylene, landing at devastated Smyrna, passing Chios, Samos, Cos, landing also at Rhodes, passing Paphos at the tip of the island of Cyprus, landing at Lanarka, then arriving at Beiruth. The voyage was filled with memories of Paul. The imperfect συνέβαλλεν is an unexplained tense. Two texts have the aorist συνέβαλεν, the form one expects, but this in no way helps to explain the imperfect that is found in all the other texts. R., *W. P.*, suggests the inchoative sense: "began to meet us," but this is too odd to be satisfactory.

15) The vessel stopped for the night at Mitylene. The next day's run, Tuesday's, took the party opposite the island of Chios. Here they again lay for the night, waiting for the early morning wind. The third day's run took them to the island of Samos. Here the Codex Bezae adds the comment that they "remained" (the night) in Trogyllium. The strait between this small place and the island of Chios is only a mile wide, and

the vessel may, indeed, have anchored at Trogyllium although Luke himself does not say so. Miletus was not far away, yet the vessel did not attempt to reach this harbor where it expected to lie over for several days. Ramsay's explanation is best: the wind died down during the late afternoon and did not rise again until between midnight and dawn. Others attribute the stops during the night to the dark of the moon. Early on Thursday Miletus was reached. It has been thought that Paul and his party chartered the boat, but this is rather improbable.

16) It is based on the following. **For Paul had judged to sail past Ephesus in order that he might not have to spend time in Asia; for he was hastening if it might be possible for him to be at Jerusalem for the day of Pentecost.**

The past perfect κεκρίκει (here without an augment) does not mean that Paul gave the captain of the boat orders where to make a landing, and hence that Paul and his party had chartered the boat. Paul had judged it best when he planned his journey in Troas to sail past Ephesus by embarking in a vessel that would not stop at Ephesus but would dock for some days at Miletus, there discharging its cargo and reloading. Paul's purpose was (ὅπως μή with the subjunctive) not to spend time in Asia. And the reason (γάρ) for this purpose was his desire to get to Jerusalem for Pentecost. He certainly got there even with some days to spare. But he could not have done so if he had taken a boat that stopped at Ephesus. He would have been detained not only in Ephesus but, as Luke says, in Asia, referring to the province with its many important congregations. The clamor for him to stay for a while, to go here and there, would have been too great.

We must not forget that the men who were with him had the funds for the relief work in Jerusalem, and

Paul wanted to be with them when this money was delivered. He had spent a long time in having these funds collected. He had higher purposes than merely relief; his object was the unity of all the churches, a welding together of the Gentile congregations he had founded with the original Jewish congregations in the motherland, especially with Jerusalem. So he felt that he must accompany the committee sent by his Gentile churches. He had left Philippi immediately after the Jewish Easter, had spent a week at Troas, had left there on April 25, and had now arrived at Miletus on April 28. The rest of the journey would be as follows: from Miletus May 1, Rhodes May 2, Patara May 3, Myra May 4, Tyre probably May 7, seven days at Tyre, Ptolemais May 13, Caesarea May 14, giving him time until May 28 to reach Jerusalem. One may freely allow a few more days. These dates are relatively correct for the time between the Jewish Easter and Pentecost even if these festivals did not in the year 58 occur on the dates assigned by Ramsay, for the interval between the two festivals was always fifty days. But a delay at Ephesus would have upset this itinerary as far as spending Pentecost in Jerusalem was concerned. The accusative "for the day of Pentecost" is correct; for Paul did not want to arrive "at Pentecost" (dative) but to be in Jerusalem for the entire day, i. e., arriving a few days in advance.

So "he was hastening," the imperfect tense to indicate hastening all along. "If it might be possible," the condition of potentiality, εἰ with the optative, refers only to unforeseen contingencies on a voyage such as this; Paul himself would have said, "God willing," as he did for instance in 18:21. The effort to put more into this conditional clause, especially the conclusion that Paul did not reach Jerusalem as planned, is without warrant.

17) **Now having sent from Miletus to Ephesus, he summoned the elders of the church. And when they came to him, he said, etc.**

There is no need to inquire as to the messengers nor as to the route they took. Paul had two "Asians" in his party (v. 4); they would be the men to be sent. And they started at once, on the morning the boat docked in Miletus. The distance to Ephesus was about thirty miles. With haste already implied (v. 16), the elders could reach Paul by the end of the next day.

18) We see that they came promptly. After the pathetic leavetaking the elders conducted Paul to the boat (v. 38). The boat would leave before dawn. We thus take it that the address to the elders was made somewhere in Miletus and either in the evening or late in the afternoon. The news that Paul, their beloved apostle, was only thirty miles away and waiting for them must have filled the Ephesian elders with joy and eagerness to reach him. Traveling on such an errand, a distance of thirty miles would offer no difficulty at all even if it was made entirely afoot. In those days men walked. They may have been weary when they arrived, but the sight of their great friend and teacher dispelled all fatigue. So small a group: a few elders, Paul, his eight companions — yet an immortal meeting! The great theater in Miletus where the crowds gathered, which is now in ruins, is forgotten like the nameless crowds that gathered there; but the words this one man Paul spoke to a handful of men somewhere in this harbor city still throb with life and power as when they were uttered that day. Here are immortal truths; here throbs a heart moved with those truths to a tenderness and a love which they alone could beget. Paul's address to the Ephesian elders is a shining page even in the New Testament.

You yourselves know, from the first day that I stepped into Asia, how I was with you the entire

time, serving the Lord with all humble-mindedness and tears and trials that befell me in connection with the plots of the Jews; how nothing of the things profitable did I shrink from proclaiming to you and from teaching you in public and from house to house, testifying both to Jews and Greeks the repentance toward God and faith toward our Lord Jesus Christ.

Paul reviews briefly his life and his work in Ephesus. It was what he had wanted it to be. He is not passing judgment on himself and disregarding the saying that *Eingenlob stinkt,* but appealing to the judgment of the Ephesian elders, men tried and true, who were chosen elders for this very reason: "You yourselves (ὑμεῖς, emphatic) know," etc. Paul's work was entirely open and known, subject to the judgment of friend and of foe alike. Paul knew what these elders thought concerning his work. So begin and carry forward your work, whatever the Lord allots to you, that, when it is finished, you, too, can submit it fearlessly to men tried and true and be assured of what their judgment will be.

To be sure, it is only the judgment of men and not yet that of God. Paul himself points to the difference in I Cor. 4:1-4. He knew that men often bestow both praise and blame in biased fashion, blaming him who does not agree with them, praising him who does, whether they themselves are right or wrong. By what they say of another they thus merely try to justify themselves (Luke 10:29; 16:15). For this reason Paul appeals to the facts regarding himself, facts which stand on their own feet even if men should deny them or pass adverse judgment upon them. And he includes all of them, "from the first day that I stepped into Asia," ἀπό is repeated with the relative: "from the first day on from which," etc. "How I was with you the entire time," extending to three years, indicates a time that was long enough to permit Paul to become thoroughly known.

19) Paul singles out the vital features by mentioning his serving the Lord in ways that were not open to question, secondly (v 20, 21), his teaching the Word in ways that again were not open to question. By δουλεύων he declares that he had ever shown himself a δοῦλος or "slave" of the Lord, one who submitted his own will completely to his divine Lord and took all orders and directions from him alone. Now follow three weighty modifiers that are bound together by one preposition: "with humble-mindedness and tears and trials," etc. These three marked his "slaving for the Lord." Note well, "all, i. e., complete humble-mindedness," the true inner feeling of one who is in truth a slave of the Lord. It always marked Paul's character and was manifested in many different ways that were apparent to men. He had no trace of pride in himself, he laid his very life at his Master's feet The very greatness of this high apostle lay in his lowly-mindedness. He was an example for all lesser men.

One is surprised to hear about "tears," yea, to find "tears" repeated in v 31; compare also II Cor. 2:4; Phil. 3:18. He then mentions trials that came to him from the Jews. At least some of those tears must have been caused by Paul's sad, sad experiences with these men of his own race. We catch only a glimpse of the activity of the Jews in Ephesus in Luke's record (19:33); but it is enough to show us that here, too, they were enemies of Paul. How deeply he felt for his own people, and what price he was ready to pay for their conversion, his own letter, written only a few weeks before in Corinth, Rom. 9:1-3, reveals. Did others also press tears from the eyes of Paul?

Now he was not a feminine type of man in any sense of the word; the more significant are these tears, yea, and noteworthy the fact that he does not shrink from speaking about them. We shall have to make a new mental picture of this man Paul, one that we have perhaps never visioned before. Not for injuries that *he* received did he ever shed tears. These he bore without a quiver of the lip. These tears accompany his working as a slave for the Lord. They were pressed out by a heart that was wrenched with pain when he saw men obdurately rejecting the Lord. That is why these tears probably seem so strange to us — our own callous hearts have not drawn us so completely to the Lord that, as he wept over the obduracy of Jerusalem (Luke 19:41), we, too, might shed tears when we behold similar sights, tears such as those of Paul.

He speaks of trials that were due to plots of the Jews. We know that such plots were made elsewhere; they have run through Luke's record of Paul's life since the apostle's experience at Damascus. It is only natural to find that Ephesus was no exception. Luke perhaps omitted them in his account of the work at Ephesus because they would be mentioned here in his record of Paul's address which Luke himself heard.

20) Ὡς parallels the πῶς occurring in v. 18. First, the Lord in Paul's work; secondly, the Lord's Word, Paul's work of teaching. His one motive and sole purpose was not to conceal or to hold back a single thing of all that was profitable to his hearers. He never tried to save himself or to seek the slightest advantage for himself. It is so easy just to keep still on some points; one may even hide his real motive from himself when doing so and persuade himself that he is following the promptings of wisdom. "I did not shrink," Paul says, and that is the correct word. For we naturally shrink when we anticipate hurt or loss as the result of what we ought to teach and preach.

The infinitive with τοῦ is the ablative after a verb of hindering, denying, etc., and the negative μή is retained although it is not necessary, R. 1094. Note the two infinitives: "from proclaiming and from teaching," both are effective aorists, the one referring to announcements, the other to instructions, both "in public and from house to house," Paul using every opportunity.

21) And now the modal present participle states that all this announcing and this teaching were ever done by way of "testifying both to Jews and Greeks," etc. Paul's own soul and person were put into all his announcing and his teaching. The participle has the effective διά. With his whole soul Paul believed and lived what he propounded to others. It welled up out of his own heart like a living stream. He did not have to put his heart into it; it came out of his heart. This is one secret of Paul's power as missionary, preacher, and teacher. We can tell about it, but that helps very little. The fire of divine truth must catch in the heart, then the flames will glow in testimony and will set other hearts afire. It is like Paul's tears — unknown language to all who do not know it from experience.

Jews and Greeks — Paul made no difference but kept this order (1:8) here as always. The entire gospel is centered in "the repentance toward God and faith toward our Lord Jesus Christ." Let no man violate what Paul here says by persuading himself that this repentance and this faith signify two brief doctrines, all else in the Bible being immaterial, non-fundamental, or whatever word may be chosen. Repentance includes all of the law, and faith all of the gospel, and these two comprise the Scriptures. On repentance see 2:38 where the verb is used. And πιστις is the heart's trust and confidence in "our Lord Jesus Christ," the very name being an epitome of the gospel, see 1:6, 1:21; 2:22, 36. But note that Luke uses only one article with the two nouns: τὴν μετάνοιαν καὶ πίστιν He thereby indicates that repentance and faith constitute a unit idea in Paul's mind. Either noun involves the other; either might be used alone in the present connection. The use of both after one article is more effective, strong, and clear.

22) From the past which has thus been summarized Paul turns to the present and the future. **And now, lo, I on my part, as bound in the spirit, am going to Jerusalem, not knowing the things in it that shall meet me save that the Holy Spirit is testifying to me from city to city, saying that fetters and afflictions are awaiting me. But I deem the life of no account as dear to me in order to finish my course and the ministry which I received from the Lord Jesus, to testify the gospel of the grace of God.**

"And now" marks the turn to the present, and "lo" points to what is indeed remarkable — he who has been so faithful to the Lord and to his Word has fetters and afflictions awaiting him as his reward! As the elders know, he is now on his way to Jerusalem, but he goes as one who "has been and thus is now bound (this is the force of the perfect participle) in the spirit" (locative dative to indicate where the binding holds Paul, namely in his own spirit). An inward constraint urges Paul to go on. The fact that this does not refer merely to the decision of his own will, one that he could alter at any time, should be evident; the passive participle points to a higher agent that holds Paul bound to go to Jerusalem, an agent to whom Paul was wholly submissive in the direction of his life. He confesses that he does not know what things shall meet him in Jerusalem, εἰδώς, the second perfect participle is always used as a present. In τὰ συναντήσοντα we have one of the few future participles which is futuristic and not volitive.

23) Πλήν with a ὅτι clause following is best taken as a preposition, the clause as the object (B.-D. 449, 1), and not as an adverb (R. 646). One thing Paul does know, namely that the Holy Spirit is testifying to him in city after city (κατά is distributive) that fetters

(imprisonment) and afflictions (pressure from all sides) are awaiting him. We must note the implication that, by thus forewarning Paul, the Holy Spirit is really binding him to go to Jerusalem, telling him of the divine will that he endure these things. In his previous record Luke has said nothing about these communications to Paul; he will mention one notable instance a little later, the prophecy of Agabus in Caesarea (21:10-14). For the present Luke lets Paul's own words on this subject suffice. We are to know at least this much, that Paul knew the nature of what he was going to meet.

24) Instead of being deterred, he went bravely on with one mighty purpose dominating him. We see this brave spirit in the words: "But I deem the life of no account as dear to me." The readings vary but not enough to make us doubtful. The middle ποιοῦμαι is used in the sense of "deem," "hold" (Liddell and Scott), much as we, too, use "make" in expressions such as this: "He makes (deems, considers) it an honor or a calamity." Οὐδενὸς λόγου is the genitive of price; and τιμίαν is the necessary limiting predicate adjective (scarcely an apposition, R., *W. P.*). Paul does consider his life of account but not of account as far as it is dear to him himself. He is willing to die at any time for the Lord's name (21:13; Phil. 1:20, 21). The emphasis is on οὐδενὸς λόγου and on τιμίαν ἐμαυτῷ: "Of not one word's value do I consider my life as far as its being dear just to myself is concerned." He would not utter even one word to save his life in order that *he* might have it.

The purpose for which we do a thing is often our reason for doing it; philosophers call this "the final cause." Such is the purpose here, which is expressed by ὡς with the subjunctive. In regard to the reading ὡς, this is almost solidly assured (ὥστε is only a conjecture to match the infinitive); but it is a question whether to read the aorist subjunctive (a possible future indicative) τελειώσω, or the aorist infinitive τελειῶσαι (see R. 987). The former reading would be the last lone example in the New Testament of ὡς as a final particle: "in order that I may finish my course and the ministry," etc.; the latter would be the adverb: "as finishing," etc. Paul is governed by one purpose only, in which his life is not even a pawn; it is the finishing of his apostolic course, meaning the διακονία or ministry which he received from the Lord Jesus. The Lord gave this work of serving to him, and Paul wants to finish it in whatever way the Lord has planned for him. Here is the place to recall that so many of Paul's movements were directly guided by the Lord, for instance, *not* to go to Asia or to Bithynia (16:6, 7), to continue in Corinth (18:9-11), etc.

With an appositional infinitive Paul further describes his office: "to testify the gospel of the grace of God." He is always a master in describing his office. He repeats the testifying which he had mentioned in v. 21 and thereby shows what importance he attached to this significant term. "The gospel" is the good news, and its contents is "the grace of God," the divine favor extended through the atoning merits of Christ to the guilty, damned sinner to free him forever from this guilt and to receive him as God's child. Not a single word used here should be discounted and reduced in substance or in extent. Some call their preaching "gospel" when it does not comply with Paul's description in whole or in part; Paul settles his account with them in Gal. 1:6, 7.

25) The seriousness of what lay before Paul is made fully evident at this point. **And now, lo, I for my part know that not again shall you see my face, you all among whom I went through heralding the kingdom.**

The first words parallel v. 22. Once more we have a surprise — Paul does not expect that these Ephesian elders will ever see his face again! The idea is not that he expects to die in Jerusalem itself — he dos not know where it will be but is convinced that it will be. This conviction runs through Paul's entire address and gives it such an affecting tone. A spiritual father is taking a last leave from his spiritual children.

The emphatic ἐγώ, "I for my part know," helps to indicate that Paul is expressing only his own conviction. Without receiving a warning from the Spirit, he had repeatedly been in mortal danger; now he had had a warning concerning "fetters and afflictions" and thus he thought his course was coming to its end. As a matter of fact, he was imprisoned for four long years. Then he was freed, revisited Corinth, Troas, Miletus (II Tim. 4:13, 20), even Ephesus itself (I Tim. 1:3, compared with 4:13). Nothing is gained by denying that he paid a visit to the latter place, for Paul says, "you all among whom I went through heralding the kingdom," and refers to Ephesus and to many other places he "went through." The Ephesian elders were only representatives of all these places. So these people saw the apostle's face again — he did not die as soon as he had expected.

It is, of course, not necessary to assume that Paul spoke this address by inspiration (rather revelation); for, beyond question, the apostles were not always inspired (did not have a revelation on every point.) Yet this word of Paul's regarding himself is really no proof that on this occasion he spoke without inspiration, it only shows that he had no revelation regarding the time of his death. He differentiates most clearly between what the Holy Spirit actually testified to him (v. 23) and what he himself felt he knew in addition to that testimony. Why should the Spirit not permit him to say that? "Heralding the kingdom" (see 1:3) was Paul's great διακονία, proclaiming the blessed rule "of the grace of God."

26) **For this reason I let testify for myself to you on this day that I am clean from the blood of all. For I did not shrink from proclaiming to you all the counsel of God.**

Διότι, "because," and διό, "therefore," are not always closely differentiated; here the former is used much like the latter. But the middle μαρτύρομαι is most exact; Paul is not testifying (which would be μαρτυρέω) but is letting a great fact that no one can contradict and question testify for him. It is the fact "that I am clean from the blood of all" (compare 18:6) according to Ezek. 3:18-21, which see; ἀπό is ablative in sense and not a Hebraism (R. 576). "Blood" is a pregnant, metonymical term for the guilt involved in bringing about death, here eternal death. On the great judgment day none of the lost from this territory shall be able to point to Paul and say that his is the guilt. Whoever may be guilty, Paul is pure from this terrible stain. The apostle wants this fact to testify to these elders ἐν τῇ σήμερον ἡμέρᾳ, literally, "on the today day," this day of parting, which Paul expects to be final and which these elders will not soon forget.

27) It is one thing to disclaim such bloodguilt; it is quite another to be able to back up that disclaimer as Paul was able to do. "For" proves that the testimony Paul cites is most certainly true. "I did not shrink from proclaiming to you" repeats v. 20 (which see, also as to μή with the infinitive). Here we again have the implication that, if Paul had considered men only or selfish personal advantages, he might, indeed, have kept back this or that part of his teaching, for it often ran counter to Jewish bigotry and heathen prejudice, and it often offended Christian ignorance and narrowness. But Paul ever bore in mind the accounting he would have to render to his Lord at the last day. So he proclaimed "all the counsel of God," the entire will of God, every doctrine and every truth of God, omitting, alter-

ing, toning down nothing. He had no peculiar personal views, he followed no peculiar policy. He especially did not omit what was difficult and hard to set forth, unpalatable and obnoxious to human reason, out of harmony with the spirit of the times. He was neither reactionary nor progressive; for "the whole counsel of God" is changeless. He put justification by faith into the center because God put it there, but he treated a large number of other points as well, each in its place. Now he is ready for his final accounting. Heb. 13:17: "As they that must give account."

Here there is presented the full responsibility of everyone who undertakes to herald the kingdom. No man on earth can lessen it, least of all you yourself. Here let a man examine himself How many preachers have blood on their conscience? Paul purposely used this bloody word Be not ready to absolve yourself too quickly Make sure! Correlate these expressions: "the things profitable" (v 19) — "the repentance toward God and faith toward our Lord Jesus Christ" (v 21) — "the gospel of the grace of God" (v. 24) — "the kingdom" (v 25) — "all the counsel of God" (v. 27) Each casts light on the others.

28) Not until after Paul has dealt fully with himself does he deal with others. Only what he has done does he ask others also to do **Be taking heed to your own selves and to all the flock in which the Holy Spirit set you as overseers, to shepherd the church of God which he purchased for himself through his own blood.**

Προσέχω with and without τὸν νοῦν, "to hold the mind toward something," is our "to take heed", and the present imperative is used to express constant heeding. He who is to take heed of others must first take heed to himself Be clean yourself before you try to cleanse others. Be taught yourself before you try to teach others. Be light yourself before you try to give light to others. Be near to God yourself before you attempt to bring others near. So Paul did, so he bade these elders do, and that pertains to you.

Paul uses the beautiful figure of "the flock" which Jesus himself used in John 10:11, etc.; Luke 12:32. It harks back to the Old Testament. But we must get the full force of the figure as it is contained in the relation of the shepherd to his own flock. We see it in David who fought a lion and a bear at the risk of his own life in order to save only one sheep of the flock. Jesus has intensified and even glorified this figure. He is "the good Shepherd," John 10:11; "the Shepherd and Bishop of your souls," I Pet. 2:25; "the great Shepherd of the sheep," Heb. 13:20. See how he reinstates Peter in John 21:15, etc.

The church is a body, a united flock, and not a large number of individual sheep — a great fact for Christians as well as for pastors. Sheep are not dogs, and we must think of dogs in the Oriental sense, ownerless, scavengers, etc. Sheep as a flock are precious, follow the shepherd, depend on him; it is a crime to be a hireling, to abuse the confidence of the flock; it is the devil's work to scatter the flock. All this and more lies in the word *ποίμνιον*, diminutive from *ποίμνη*, but only in form, not in sense. "All" the flock — Paul binds every sheep upon the hearts of these elders. "All" — not merely the pastor's friends, a faction he has allowed to form that clings to him, the well-to-do, neglecting the poor and the unassuming. The true shepherd knows no dividing line, no factions, loves every sheep, especially the weak and the needy. The lambs as well as the sheep — how often these are neglected! If your heart is not big enough to embrace "all the flock," it is not big enough to shepherd any of the flock.

Paul brings out the sacred obligation and trust connected with the pastorate: "in which the Holy Spirit did set you as overseers." We have nothing to add to what we said in connection with 11:30 in regard to "elders" and their other title "overseers," both of which are used for what we now call "pastors," the former stressing the honor, the latter the type of work. The title "bishops" as distinct from "pastors" is a later use of the term "overseer"; they oversee a diocese of many congregations and their pastors. It is the Holy Spirit who sets or places overseers in the flock. The entire church is under his guidance; and in every true call, ordination, and installation we see the work of the Holy Spirit. It is a vast comfort to every true pastor that the Holy Spirit placed him in the flock he serves. But how about hypocrites in the pastorate, humanly manipulated calls? The devil's work in the church in this and in other directions must be purged out, but its presence here and there in no way alters the Spirit's true work.

In the Greek ποίμνιον and ποιμαίνειν are cognate, the infinitive is the object of "take heed " "To shepherd" is broad and includes the entire work of the pastor: leading, feeding, guarding, etc In John 21:15, 17 Jesus used also βόσκειν, "to pasture" or to feed, which refers especially to teaching, this being the chief feature of the task. Neither Paul nor Jesus know of a flock that leads and manages itself and has a shepherd only to feed it. These inventions plague the church today

There is a difference of opinion regarding the reading, "the church *of God*, which he purchased for himself through his own blood." Some think the reading should be, "the church of *the Lord*." Here are the decisive points. Almost invariably Paul uses the expression "the church of God," in fact, this or an equivalent genitive occurs twenty times and never "the church of the Lord"; "of Christ" is found only two or three times. In other cases the common usage is preferred to an exceptional usage; here the reverse is advocated. We are told that because elsewhere "the church of God" appears, therefore Luke's "the church of the Lord" was changed by scribes also to read "of God." Both readings have good textual support. But if we ask how it came about that there are two readings (plus a few minor variants), the answer is obvious; Luke wrote "of God," and scribes thought they must change this because then it would be stated that God's *blood* bought the church. The issue is not at all in regard to "the church of God" but in regard to the relative clause which has the phrase "through his own blood." Some critics feel that the idea of God's blood should be eliminated from the text.

Some claim that Jesus never called himself God, also that Paul never called Jesus God, hence "God" must be deleted here. Both claims are unwarranted. In regard to Paul see at least Rom. 1:4; 9:5; Col. 2:9; Tit. 2:13; also Col. 1:15-20; Phil. 2:5-11. All Paul's utterances rest on the deity of Jesus, and this is evident in many passages. When those who accept the deity of Jesus shrink from the use of the expression "the blood of God," they are often moved by an unnecessary timidity.

The person of Jesus may be designated by any name, human, divine, merely personal, or official, and then anything may be predicated of him, either of one or of the other nature or of both. This the New Testament does with at times startling effect. The fact that *God* purchased for himself the church through his own *blood* is only of a piece with expressions like: "You killed the Author (Prince) of life" (3:15); "they crucified the Lord of glory" (I Cor. 2:8). Jesus is strikingly named according to his deity, yet being killed, being crucified, having blood is predicated of him. We refuse to divide the Savior by saying in Nestorian fashion that human things can be ascribed to him only as to his human nature, divine things only as to his divine nature. The New Testament calls him by any name regardless of what it predicates of him, just so his person is referred to. And no serious student will adopt Zwingli's evasive expedient that all these glorious Scripture statements are "merely verbal," just words that are not to be taken seriously.

And let us not forget the great reality here expressed so clearly: we are purchased by means of God's blood. Διά expresses means; this blood was the price; as being God's blood its value is infinite and could and did effect the purchase. This is the whole "blood theology" which so many deny. More — here we have the the true value of the church, which every pastor should keep in mind. This church entrusted to his care cost God's blood. Will God be indifferent as to how the church for which he paid such a price is treated? And this passage does not imply a limited atonement, for in II Pet. 2:1 it is said even of those that deny the Lord and go to swift destruction that "the Lord bought them." The church, the sheep, the believers are often mentioned as those who were bought, etc., for the rather obvious reason that among all whom the Lord bought they are the ones, and they alone, who really become his own.

29) Paul's first admonition is general and is based on the mightiest reason. The apostles always used such tremendous reasons as a basis for their admonitions. Now the apostle points to the coming danger. He expected a severe trial for himself; he sees also what is in store for his fellow laborers. **I for my part know that there shall come after my departure grievous wolves to you, not sparing the flock. And from yourselves there shall rise up men uttering perverted things to draw away the disciples after them. Wherefore keep watching, remembering that for a space of three years, night and day, I did not cease with tears to put in mind each one.**

Paul sees the wolves coming. He is neither a pessimist nor an optimist; he has sharp eyes and reads aright the signs of the times. He also knows men. 'Εγὼ οἶδα is used exactly as it was in v. 25. He had no special revelation on this matter regarding Ephesus; yet he did have the warning words of Jesus, Matt. 7:15, about ravening (rending) wolves. Paul uses βαρύς, "heavy," hard to endure, and explains by adding, "not sparing the flock" (John 10:12). A few years later Paul wrote, I Tim. 4:1, etc.

Pointedly he says, "after my departure," ἄφιξις has its later meaning. Zahn marshals his learning against this later meaning and contends that this word means, "after my arrival," i. e., in heaven; but B.-P. contradicts him by a reference to three plain examples. When Paul's apostolic authority is no longer exerted, these wolves in sheep's clothing will invade the church. Of whom was the apostle thinking? First of all, of the Judaizers as his letter which was not long before this time written to the Galatians makes rather certain. But he does not attempt to specify, errorists of other types will also appear. In his later letters he deals with various kinds of them. Not a little debate has centered about these "wolves" mentioned in Matt. 7:15 and here in Paul's address. The point debated is whether errorists are to be included. This has been denied, and we were told that wolves are men who deny Christianity *in toto*. But these men are not really dangerous; even a simple Christian recognizes them for what they are. And what about the sheep's clothing? Now the fact is, every false doctrine rends and tears to the degree that it is false. It is most destructive when it parades as the true teaching of Christ or of his apostles. One fang or false doctrine may cause faith to bleed to death.

30) When Paul speaks of men arising in the church itself who speak twisted, distorted, perverted things, διεστραμμένα (perfect participle from διαστρέφω, "having been and thus still being perverted"), let us not think that these are not wolves. Paul merely drops

the figure. Men that bring in destructive doctrine from other churches are bad enough, but still worse are men that arise in one's own church and teach such doctrines, and the worst are false preachers and pastors. This is not an anticlimax but a climax. The name used for the perverters in v. 30 cannot be milder than that employed with reference to those in v. 29. The wolves spare not the flock, they destroy souls; but these others actually divide the church by drawing poor, deluded disciples after them. They cause great schisms and sects.

What a long procession of these two classes of foes the church has had to suffer during the past ages and especially also in the present age, and the end is not yet! Matt. 24:24, 25. It is a God's wonder that the church exists at all at this date. Paul's two verses are the epitome of one side of her history. But the gospel is still intact, and there is still a host of those that preserve that gospel intact.

31) In the face of the danger thus described, what is the course these Ephesian elders, as well as all shepherds of the church everywhere, must pursue? "Keep watching!" The only deduction they can make (διό) is to keep wide awake, to note and to meet even the first appearance of danger. Paul is, indeed, leaving them, but see what he leaves them: the memory of his example! That memory is still kept alive in the churches to this day. Although he has been dead for a long time, Paul's example still speaks. What he did we can do today. A τριετία is a space of three years, the accusative expresses the extent of time, as do the words "night and day." We are certain that Paul worked in Ephesus for almost three years (19:8, 10, 22; see 19:10). The point is that these elders had had Paul's example before their very eyes for so long a time.

Not once during all this time did Paul slacken his efforts: "night and day I did not cease with tears putting in mind each one." He labored even during the night. The night is put first because watching precedes and not because Paul was still thinking about wolves, for they prowl by day as well as by night. R., *W. P.*, is a little strong when he renders νουθετέω, "to put sense into one." The verb means only "to put in mind." Paul constantly reminded and did that for "each one," thus by individual and personal work, which takes a good deal of time. He kept his eye on every single sheep.

32) The address is perfectly proportioned. The admonition is made brief, it is the more effective for that reason. **And now I commend you to God and to the Word of his grace, the one able to build up and to give the inheritance among all those that have been sanctified.**

This is the final "now," ταννῦν, adverbial accusative: "as to the things now." Paul is parting. Paul is able to do but one more thing, and he now does that: he commends these elders to God, etc. He uses the very word "I commend" which Jesus used when he placed his spirit into his Father's hands. To commend to God is to place into his care and keeping.

By adding, "and to the Word of his grace," etc., (compare "the gospel of the grace of God" in v. 24) Paul states what he expects God to do for these elders. God and the Word of his grace always go together; God lets his grace flow out through that Word. With the attributive participle Paul describes the power of this Word. We construe τῷ δυναμένῳ with τῷ λόγῳ, but there is little difference in force when it is construed with τῷ Θεῷ. The Word (gospel) is the power of God, Rom. 1:16. It is able to do two things: 1) to build us up spiritually in this life, and 2) to give us the inheritance in the life to come.

When we call this building up "edification" we do so only in the New Testament sense of that word. Edification is by no means only the arousing of pleasant religious sensations but an increase, an unfolding of the whole spiritual life, including more and better knowledge, but especially centering the will and the character more deeply in Christ and in his Word. Men who are thus built up are proof against wolves and errors.

The heavenly inheritance is a gift of the Word of grace. In fact, that Word is the divine testament in which we believers are named as the heirs to whom this inheritance is to be conveyed. Only God's sons are his heirs. How could his enemies hope to be such? Luke has used ἅγιοι, "saints," in 9:13 and later; now he uses the substantivized perfect participle in practically the same sense. "The holy ones" are "the ones that have been made and thus now are holy," set apart as belonging to God through Christ by the Holy Spirit's work. Cf. Luther, the explanation of the Third Article of the Creed. Both Greek terms are used in the wider sense; we are holy and hallowed by having all our sins removed in justification and by having in us a new life that ever strives to perform holy works. "Among those sanctified" refers to the saints that are already in heaven. To join them is our hope in Christ.

33) Heavenly-mindedness does away with earthly-mindedness. It is the thought of the heavenly inheritance awaiting us as saints that leads Paul to speak of the manner in which he has lived during these years he has spent in Ephesus. **Silver or gold or robing of no one did I covet. Yourselves realize that for my needs and for those who are with me these hands rendered service. Regarding all things I gave example to you that it is necessary thus by laboring to attend to the weak and to remember the words of the Lord Jesus that he himself said, Blessed it is rather to be giving than to be taking.**

"Robing," garments, was an item in Oriental wealth and is thus listed with silver and gold. The three nouns are genitives after a verb of emotion, R. 508. Even to covet is sin. Paul knew why he placed among the qualifications for the ministry "no lover of money," I Tim. 3:4; Tit. 1:7. Self-seekers disgrace the holy office; clerical speculators disgrace it still more; bidders for "fat" calls and all who commercialize their office are an abomination to the Lord.

34) While Paul himself wrote I Cor. 9:14 and what precedes, it is he who tells us in the following verses why he forewent this right. He speaks to the Ephesian elders only of the fact that he did so and not of his special reason. That someone had slandered him in regard to the great collection, that he had such slander in mind here, and that II Cor. 13:7, etc., is evidence to that effect, is an unwarranted supposition.

"These hands" he must have held out, which were marked with traces of his tentmaking labors in Aquila's shop. He earned his own living and more than that. Some of his money was used for his assistants, "for those who are with me." Why? Because he used them so hard, often sending them on long journeys. While he was residing in Ephesus he covered the entire province of Asia by their aid. Most of his earnings were probably used for this purpose. He invested them in the gospel; ὑπηρετέω = to serve as an underling, Paul served as Aquila's workman, Aquila was his employer. Even today few appreciate what Paul did in this respect.

35) Πάντα is the adverbial accusative and is by the context limited to the subject in hand. The verb ὑποδείκνυμι means "to show somebody a thing by holding it *under* his eyes," thus "to give an example." There is no pronoun "you" in the ὅτι clause, and it is best to take the clause in a general sense, the accusative κοπιῶντας modifying the accusative subject (understood) of the infinitive ἀντιλαμβάνεσθαι, *sich annehmen*: "that it is necessary thus by laboring to attend to the weak," etc.

Who are "the weak," genitive after the verb "to take hold of"? It is best not to take the word in a figurative sense: the spiritually weak who might think that the missionary worked only for money. "The weak" are those who become needy through sickness; the word often means "the sick." Paul does not say outright that he contributed to charity, but he most likely did just as Jesus himself did (John 13:29). Δεῖ may express any kind of necessity, here it expresses a moral necessity.

By thus working to have money to aid the destitute, an obligation resting on all, Paul wants all to be remembering (present infinitive) the words of the Lord Jesus (all of them that bear on this subject, plural), in particular that he said (now quoting one of them): "Blessed it is rather to be giving than to be taking" (two present infinitives to express repeated action). A few *Agrapha* have come down to us, words of Jesus that are not recorded in the four Gospels. This one is so like Jesus and is especially precious. It is a beatitude. The implication is that it is also blessed to take; Paul himself is an excellent example in the way in which he took the gifts sent him by the Philippians (Phil. 4:10-17). But the greater blessedness lies in the right kind of giving. Note the giving that runs through Matt. 25:35-40. God is the most blessed Giver, John 3:16; Acts 14:17. Jesus likewise. His whole ministry was giving, and in death he gave his life for us. The glory of the whole gospel is the fact that it is nothing but GIVING. Paul enjoyed this blessedness to the full, "as poor, yet making many rich," II Cor. 6:10. With a word from Jesus' own lips Paul closed his address.

36) **And having said these things, after bending his knees, he prayed with them all. Moreover, there occurred considerable weeping on the part of all. And having fallen on the neck of Paul, they**

went on kissing him fervently, pained most at the word he had spoken that they were not again to behold his face. And they started to send him forward to the boat.

After having spoken to the elders, Paul now speaks to the Lord. The Greek idiom is "to place the knees," meaning to kneel. The common posture in prayer was to stand and to lift the eyes to heaven; Jesus regularly prayed in this position. Standing in one's presence is to honor that person. Kneeling in prayer expresses deep feeling such as grief, utter helplessness, etc. In Gethsemane Jesus knelt, being sorrowful unto death, but this was exceptional in his case. The attitude should express what is in the heart. Kneeling in the case of too many prayers makes this attitude too common so that it loses its specific significance. Reserve kneeling for confession of sin, for the day of humiliation, the hour of stress, calamity, etc. Paul and his little gathering naturally knelt in this tense, sad hour of parting. It was most affecting and the right way to part.

37) Luke states that they could not restrain their feelings, there was much sobbing. The imperfect κατεφίλουν expresses the lingering of the parting and not only that each man kissed Paul while embracing him, but also that each one could hardly let him go. Here is fully manifested the deep affection Paul inspired. As his enemies hated him with burning intensity, so his friends loved him with glowing fervor.

38) The elders were so overcome because of Paul's word that this was the final parting. "Sorrowing" is too weak a translation; the participle means "pained," "deeply distressed"; and μέλλουσι brings out the thought that now, in a few moments, they would behold him no more, "behold," not merely "see"; their eyes would not again rest upon him. The final imperfect is really dramatic; in the midst of their accompanying Paul to

the boat Luke lets the curtain fall. When Luke wrote his account years afterward he lived this affecting scene over again. He recalled his own wet eyes. Paul is outstanding in the whole scene, his assistants are wholly in the background. It was always thus. Even the rabid Jews always centered only on Paul and disregarded his helpers. He towered above them all. He still towers in the same way. In the New Testament record and in the tradition of the early church only the beloved John is like him in this respect. Because both were so uncompromising in maintaining the doctrines of the gospel they inspired the deepest love in all who knew them best. This presents a tremendous fact on which we cannot ponder enough.

CHAPTER XXI

The Conclusion of the Third Missionary Journey: From Miletus to Jerusalem

Luke made this voyage with Paul and his seven other companions (20:4). These eight carried the great collection which Paul had had his Gentile congregations gather during the past year or more to aid the Jewish brethren in Palestine; that is why his company was so large. Paul himself had no part in carrying the funds. The vessel from Troas was a coaster and was used only as far as Patara.

1) **Now when it came to pass that we set sail** (cf. 13:13) **after having been torn from them, having made a straight run, we came to Cos and on the next day to Rhodes and thence to Patara. And having found a boat crossing over to Phoenicia, having embarked, we set sail. Now having sighted Cyprus and having left it on the left, we continued sailing to Syria and came down to Tyre, for there the boat was to discharge its cargo.** The Greek goes up on the sea and then comes down to land (v. 3); both terms are nautical.

It is a beautiful fancy when Zahn pictures the Ephesian elders and the whole congregation of Miletus (Luke says nothing about such a congregation) standing on the shore waving farewell to Paul and his party who wave in return. Sorry to spoil the picture. Read 20:13 and Ramsay who traveled these waters. At this season the wind regularly springs up from the north before dawn and blows until late afternoon. This explains 20:13-15, each day's run was about so far, and each night they anchored; the daily runs and stops from Miletus to Patara were also due to this fact. First, the straight run to the Island Cos, a distance of forty miles. Here the boat anchored. The next day's run was fifty miles to Rhodes, where the night was spent. Then came the run to Patara, again about forty miles, now toward the east. The probability is that this coaster continued in this fashion and did not venture out into the open sea.

So we must change the picture at Miletus. It was night when the elders escorted Paul to the boat, and when his party tore themselves away. This may have happened shortly before sailing, for the boat would start with the rising of the wind. The straight run of which Luke makes note by using a nautical term shows how favorable the first day's wind was. Cos was an island that was famous for its wines and its fabrics and had attracted many Jews; Κῶ is the second Attic accusative of Κῶς, see Goodwin 196 on νεώς, and B.-D. 44, 1. Rhodes = island of roses (Rhoda in 12: 13 = Rose); it was renowned for its great Colussus, a statue of Apollo that was 105 feet high but is at this time in ruins. The sun was said to shine every day at Rhodes. In 1925 the writer was impressed by the ancient fortifications near the city of Rhodes which date from the time of the crusaders and the Knights of St. John. There were glorious oleanders, flaming hybiscus, gorgeous morning glories, the water was indigo blue. Patara was a notable maritime city on the Lycian coast which once possessed an oracle of Apollo that rivaled that at Delphi.

The Codex Bezae adds that the party went on to Myra (27:5); this is conjecture. If transshipment was made at Myra instead of at Patara, Luke would have written Myra and not omitted it.

2) At Patara the party left the small coaster and took passage on a large merchantman that sailed

across the open sea straight for the Phoenician coast. They had a voyage of about 400 miles before them.

3) All that Luke says in regard to this voyage is that they sighted Cyprus on their left, sailed on to Syria without stopping, meaning to the Phoenician coast, and landed at Tyre, which was famous in the Old Testament, in the New, during the crusades, 1,000 years later. Its very site is now hopelessly altered in literal, frightful fulfillment of Ezek. 26:1-28:19, note especially 26:4, 5, 14, 21. Read Delitzsch, *Commentar ueber den Propheten Ezechiel* (1868), p. 259, etc. Paul sailed close to the tip of Cyprus, where he and Barnabas had achieved a most notable victory at Paphos (13:6, etc.). The writer sailed past the same point, stopped at Lanarka, and then crossed to Syria.

The form of the first aorist active ἀναφάναντες is explained in B.-D. 72; the aorist passive ἀναφανέντες which is found in important texts is incorrect. Ἀναφαίνω γῆν is still the Greek expression for "to sight land" (Smith, *Bible Dictionary,* nautical vocabulary IV, 3009). The imperfect "we went on sailing" means straight on, making no landing in Cyprus. The vessel's cargo was to be discharged in Tyre. This was a fast boat that sailed through without a stop. In R., W. P., ἦν . . . ἀποφορτιζόμενον is explained as a "customary" or "progressive" periphrastic imperfect, see R. 884. R. 1115 is much better. This is not a periphrastic form, the participle is merely predicative and states what kind of a boat this was, "one discharging its cargo there" (in Tyre), just as the participle διαπερῶν in v. 2 describes this boat as one "crossing over" (*es hatte diese Eigenschaft,* B.-D. 339, 2b).

4) **And having discovered the disciples, we remained there seven days, who kept saying to Paul through the Spirit not to be going on to Jerusalem. And when it was that we finished the days, having left, we were starting to journey on, all with wives**

and children bringing us on our way until outside the city. And having bent the knees on the beach, after having prayed, we bade each other farewell, and we went into the boat, but they returned to their homes.

They had to make a search for the disciples in Tyre because the congregation was small. How it came about that there were Christians here is explained by 11:19 and 15:3. Seven days was a long time for Paul to remain in this city; the length of time seems to have been determined by the stay of the vessel at Tyre.

Although they were few in number, the charisma of prophecy was found among these disciples; they knew from one or from the other of their number, to whom the Spirit had granted this special revelation, that imprisonment awaited Paul in Jerusalem. The imperfect *ἔλεγον* states that they kept telling Paul not to go on to Jerusalem, meaning that he was by all means to avoid that city. These disciples understood the Spirit's word as a warning which they should transmit to Paul. Paul did not consider the Spirit's word as a warning, for the Spirit never forbade him to go to Jerusalem; these revelations only forewarned and prepared him to be ready for what awaited him.

5) Luke uses the accusative with the infinitive as the subject of *ἐγένετο*. By writing *ἐξαρτίσαι*, "we finished," Luke conveys the idea that they spent so many days in Tyre, not from choice, but from necessity while waiting for their vessel to proceed. "Having left, we were starting to journey on" (inchoative imperfect), doing the very thing the disciples of Tyre begged us not to do. Although Paul was quite a stranger to them (he had paid this city a fleeting visit in 15:3, and possibly also passed through it in 11:30 and 12:25), and none of the companions of Paul had ever been in Tyre, yet during this one week the bond of attachment became so strong that men, women, and children turned out to a person to bid farewell to Paul

and his company. They realized fully what they had experienced during this week. "To send forward" (as in 20:38) means to go along with one who is departing. "Outside of the city" means to the docks where the boat lay.

On kneeling for prayer see 20:36. A most interesting study are the three pictures of leavetaking presented by Luke: at Miletus (20:36, etc.), here at Tyre, and in the following verses at Caesarea. The intensity of feeling that marks the departure from Miletus is absent in the case of Tyre. These disciples also feel that they will never see Paul again, but he had not been with them for three years but only for seven days. The parting is impressive. They kneel on the beach and separate from each other with earnest prayer. The place was public, but they were not ashamed.

6) There is a tenderness in Luke's three statements: they bade each other farewell, we went into the boat, and they returned home. He witnessed this scene. The article in the phrase "into *the* boat" refers to the boat on which they had come from Miletus, for the sailing of which they had waited a week. Εἰς τὰ ἴδια, literally, "to their own things," is idiomatic for "to their own homes"; the masculine would mean "own people."

7) **Now we, having continued the voyage from Tyre, arrived at Ptolemais and, having greeted the brethren, remained one day with them.**

Ptolemais is the ancient Acco (Judges 1:31), the later Acre (Crusades). Little is said about the stop made here because it was so brief. We see that here, too, a congregation had been founded. On his trips between Antioch and Jerusalem Paul must have passed through Ptolemais as he had through Tyre.

We here take issue with a large number of commentators and with those dictionaries that accept their exegesis. Because of διανύσαντες they say that the voyage ended here at Ptolemais, and that Paul and his party went overland to Caesarea. Zahn mentions cart and horses, and R., *W. P.*, alters the construction. As to the latter point, we cannot accept Robertson's translation, "arrived from Tyre to Ptolemais." If Luke had intended to say that he would have placed *both* phrases *after* the verb. To place "from Tyre" *before* the verb would imply putting an emphasis on this phrase if it were to be construed with this verb. But such an emphasis is entirely out of place. Nor could any reader guess that "from Tyre" is to be construed with the following verb, because the phrase is placed after the participle διανύσαντες exactly as the phrase "at Ptolemais" is placed after κατηντήσαμεν, and neither has an emphasis. The verb διανύω is found only here in the New Testament, and it means not only "to finish" but also "to continue"; see Abbott-Smith, *Lexicon*, for this use in Xenophon and in other writers, in Clement, etc.; see also Liddell and Scott. The New Testament dictionaries which omit this second meaning deal only with the verb as it is found in our passage.

In determining the meaning of a word the context and the author's own thought are usually taken into consideration, and wisely so. Ptolemais is thirty miles south of Tyre, one day's walk on the fine road along the shore, the great highway from Syria to Egypt. Why should Paul remain in Tyre for a period of seven days merely in order to be able to sail these thirty miles and no more? Then spend only one day in Ptolemais? Then spend only a few days in Caesarea? Have some of these commentators forgotten that Paul preferred walking from Troas to Assos while he let his eight companions go by boat (20:13)? Here, then, is another case where correction is needed. Fortunately, it is only in regard to externals, for it matters little whether Paul arrived at Caesarea afloat or afoot.

8) **And having left on the morrow, we came to Caesarea** by boat. This is substantiated by v. 15; for when the party did finally travel by land, namely from Caesarea to Jerusalem, Luke adds ἐπισκευασάμενοι, "having made our preparations," i. e., "having packed up." If the journey overland began at Ptolemais, why is this participle postponed until the mention of the departure from Caesarea?

And having gone to the house of Philip, the evangelist, who was one of the seven, we remained with him.

Philip came to Caesarea in 8:40; but we find no further mention of him until now when he and his daughters are living in Caesarea in a home that is spacious enough to entertain Paul's entire party of nine men. It is most natural to assume that Philip just insisted on lodging all of them himself because he was overjoyed at having all of them with him. Peter began work among the Gentiles in Caesarea (10:1-11, 18) although Luke says nothing about Philip's presence in the city at that time. We also hear nothing about Cornelius at this time; he had probably been transferred to some other garrison. Caesarea was the capital of Judea during the rule of the Romans and was the residence of the procurators. It had a magnificently built harbor, and the whole city had been grandly rebuilt by Herod the Great and named in honor of Caesar. Paul had passed through this city several times.

Philip is called "the evangelist" in order to distinguish him from Philip, the apostle, and is further identified as "of the seven," partitive ἐκ, one of the seven deacons (6:4, etc.), whose office as deacon came to a sudden end during the persecution that scattered the church at Jerusalem after Stephen's martyrdom. On Philip's work as an "evangelist" see 8:5. The participial modifier does not mean that Philip was *the* evangelist of the "seven," i. e., the only one deserving this name. This office was not specific and fixed but fluctuated according to abilities and gifts. What we know about Philip is most attractive; we here catch our final glimpse of him as he served as Paul's host.

9) **To him belonged four daughters, virgins, prophesying.** All we know about them is what Luke relates here. Being "virgins," never having married, they lived with their father; being four in number, they could entertain nine guests without trouble. "Virgins," of course, had nothing to do with "prophesying." In connection with 11:27 we have described the difference between "prophets" and those who were blessed with the charisma of prophesying. That difference is here clearly indicated: Agabus is a "prophet" who was on occasion used by the Spirit for communicating direct revelations and is called "prophet" on that account; Philip's daughters "prophesied," i. e., had the gift of prophecy, the ability to set forth God's will from his Word, the gift for which Paul told all the Corinthians to strive (I Cor. 14:1). Those who exercised this gift were not known by the name "prophet" in the same way that Agabus was; a reading of I Cor. 14 makes that clear.

The distinction here pointed out is often overlooked, especially in the present account. The daughters are considered "prophets" like Agabus; their "prophesying" was noted by Luke because they, too, foretold to Paul what awaited him (20:13; 21:4); it is usually also found remarkable that all four were prophets. The present participle is explained by thinking that one after another of the four stood before Paul and foretold his future. But this is in conflict with all that follows.

Agabus alone foretells. It is plain that the Spirit sent him to Caesarea for this specific purpose. Not until after Agabus had delivered his special message did the dissuading and the weeping set in. The participle is to be construed with ἦν and refers to the past activity of these daughters just as "virgins" refers to their entire past state. These women were like their father, they had the ability to propound the Word; they had what Paul told the Corinthians to value as the very best gift. The present participle states that they exercised this gift diligently.

Luke tersely mentions this fact to their credit and thereby gives credit also to their father. These women are an example to the daughters of all pastors today, and, let us add, to the sons as well. How these ladies exercised their valuable gift is not indicated by Luke; it certainly was not done in conflict with what Paul states in I Cor. 14:34, 35, and in I Tim. 2:11-14. A part of their making known the Word and the will of God included the contents of these very passages regarding the position of women in the church. Let us also recall 2:17 and its exposition.

Zahn supposes that there were two editions of Acts, and that both were issued by Luke himself. He reconstructs the first edition and on the strength of a Provencal thirteenth-century translation assumes that Luke wrote "five" daughters in his first edition. In his commentary he says that Luke made a mistake in his first edition and corrected it in the second after somebody had pointed out the error to him. But see the introduction to this volume regarding this matter of two editions and in regard to Luke's writing "books" that were intended for publication.

10) **While remaining on more days, there came down from Judea a prophet by name Agabus.**

Both ἐπί in the participle and "more days" state that the stay in Philip's home was extended beyond the time at first intended. Paul had time, there were still some days before Pentecost, his date for being in Jerusalem. And we may be sure his hosts and his friends in Caesarea clung to him as long as they possibly could. The participle is the genitive absolute with ἡμῶν understood. "Came down" is correct, Judea being high and rugged, and Caesarea lying on the coast. Agabus appears already in 11:28, yet Luke now introduces him as he introduces an entirely new person, with τίς and the dative "by name." The explanation that Luke kept a diary of this journey and thus merely copied from his diary at this place, reflects on Luke's mentality. The fact that both passages speak about the same Agabus is beyond question. It is also clear that "a prophet" intends to differentiate him from the "prophesying" daughters of Philip. Until we find a better explanation, let us assume that Luke introduces Agabus anew because ten chapters have intervened since he was first mentioned.

11) **And having come to us and having taken the girdle of Paul, after binding his own feet and hands, he said: These things says the Holy Spirit, The man whose is this girdle the Jews will so bind in Jerusalem and will deliver him up into the hands of the Gentiles.**

It must have been at the Spirit's own bidding that Agabus went to Caesarea and then "to us" as Luke writes. We also regard it as providential that Paul's resolution to stay in Caesarea a little longer coincided with the arrival of this message from the Spirit through Agabus.

Note the three aorist participles, the last being added without καί. They are written from the standpoint of the aorist εἶπε, these three actions preceded this last one. Agabus either unfastened the belt from Paul's waist, or, if Paul had laid it aside, took it up. The next action is best conceived as a double action. The prophet tied his own feet together and then wrapped the belt around his wrists. This was symbolic, a sort of picture-prophecy that illustrated to the eye what had already been told Paul about "bonds,"

20:23. We may compare John 21:18; I Kings 22:11; Isa. 20; Jer. 13; Ezek. 4. Agabus was ordered to do this by the Spirit himself as the words which he was ordered to speak show.

Agabus quotes the very words of the Spirit exactly as the ancient prophets did. If this is not verbal Inspiration, pray, what is? The Spirit has no difficulty whatever in communicating his words and his will to a prophet with utmost exactness; nor is there anything in the least "mechanical" about the process, this dreadful feature which modern theologians feel they must eliminate at all hazards even though they destroy Inspiration itself.

The symbolical action accompanies the prediction regarding fetters and thus imprisonment, but the words add a new point, namely that, like Jesus, Paul is to be delivered up to the Gentiles by the Jews. The prophecy, however, stops with that. Paul's fate is not to be that of Stephen and of James, and he was, indeed, set free again (see 20:25). One more point may be noted. The girdle was used to bind up the long, loose outer robe when one walked rapidly or worked; the binding of both feet and hands, then, meant that for a time Paul was not to travel and to work at will as he had done heretofore. Any work that he now did would be done as a prisoner.

12) **Now when we heard these things, both we ourselves and they of that place began beseeching him not to go up to Jerusalem.**

Others were present. The house had many visitors (ἐντόπιοι is found in the classics but only here in the New Testament). Luke really makes a confession when he states that "we ourselves" joined in beseeching Paul not to go to Jerusalem. Had the eight traveling companions said nothing until this time (20:25, 38; 21:4)? It seems so. Their pent up feelings give way at last, and they join with those of Caesarea in trying to prevent Paul from going to the fatal city. Caesarea was the last stopping place, and perhaps the journey to Jerusalem was to be begun the very next day. If Paul was to refrain from going he would have to turn back now.

We need not argue the questions in regard to preventing the fulfillment of a divine prophecy such as this, as to whether it could remain unfulfilled, and as though human effort could have interfered with the fulfillment. Divine determination does not force the fulfillment. We know that the prophecy rests on the event, and not the event on the prophecy. It is thus that the foreknowledge and the prophecy are infallible. The friends of Paul were not actuated by a close reasoning in regard to prophecy but by their abounding affection for the apostle. They dreaded to see him snatched from their midst and thrown into terrible bondage. They act very human in the whole matter by giving way to their natural feeling in these moments when they realize how close the impending calamity looms over their beloved leader.

13) **Then answered Paul: What are you doing, sobbing and crushing my heart? For on my part I am ready not only to be fettered but also to die in Jerusalem in behalf of the name of the Lord Jesus.**

This plain instance reveals how Paul towered above even the best of his assistants. When all had lost their balance under the stress of feeling, Paul kept both his heart and his head. Gently but firmly, with feeling but with that feeling perfectly controlled he rebukes all of these his friends. The question is dramatic and asks them to stop and to consider what they are doing by their sobbing and their crushing of Paul's heart. If they consider his road a hard one, are they not making it much harder for Paul by acting thus? Do they really want to do that?

Συνθρύπτω has been found in but one other place in Greek literature (Liddell and Scott; M.-M. 607); the sense is that of θρύπτω plus σύν "to crush together." No; they should have heartened and encouraged Paul instead of trying to do the opposite. But that is a way which the love of relatives and of friends has; it is generally too mushy and soft.

Paul states the reason (γάρ) for his rebuke and for his implied command that they stop sobbing, etc. Whatever they may think, he for his part (emphatic ἐγώ) is prepared not only for fetters but for death itself. We note the sting in ἐγώ, for it involves the thought that on their part Paul's friends would shrink from martyrdom. Ἔχω with an adverb is always equal to "to be" (it does not mean, "I hold myself," and has no reflexive idea). Paul indicates that the prophecy of Agabus did not involve death. Yet Paul is ready for even the ultimate martyrdom. This was not boasting, for he had already repeatedly faced death. Why, should he, then, now run away, when less than death threatened him? Nor was this bravery, such as that which a soldier manifests in battle. The world admires that, but such bravery disregards only physical death and generally blindly disregards what comes after death. Paul had Christian courage. His motive was spiritual, and he knew what death would bring him (II Tim. 4:8). This is something that is vastly different from mere human bravery.

He states his motive. The highest possible human motive for willingly going into death is stated in Rom. 5:7. The motive with which Paul had so often faced death and would face it again was vastly higher: "to die in behalf of the name of the Lord Jesus." He states it again in II Tim. 4:6 shortly before he was beheaded in Rome. In order to understand this decisive phrase we must know what Paul means by ὄνομα, namely the revelation, the gospel of Jesus (see 2:21, 28; 3:6;

10:43). As his life had been dedicated to this Name and its spread, so he was ever ready to devote also his death to this Name. He finally did that very thing.

14) **Now, he not being persuaded, we became silent after saying, Let the will of the Lord occur!**

Paul remained firm. The present participle states that not only at the end but all along he did not in the least yield to the persuasion of his solicitous friends. Luke, who was present, gives him that testimony. The ingressive aorist ἡσυχάσαμεν (ἡσυχάζω) means: "we became silent," i. e., ceased our efforts to persuade him. This is really another confession on the part of Luke: only Paul's firmness induced Luke and the rest to cease. So far removed were all of them from the noble strength of Paul. Even when they kept still they would rather have persuaded him.

Yet Paul's firmness began to brace them up. That is what one man's correct stand, firmly held, often does. Soon these friends, too, grew firmer. We must note that Luke writes the aorist εἰπόντες and not the durative present λέγοντες (as our versions may lead us to suppose). They said this once, with finality; they did not repeat it or go on saying it. After saying it they were silent — the matter was ended. "The will of the Lord" is his volition, whatever he had decided regarding Paul. They now bowed to that decision. From their anxiety regarding Paul they now turned their thoughts and their wills submissively to the Lord. That was assuming the right attitude. The Lord's will can do nothing but good to those who love him, Rom. 8:28. Some submit reluctantly at first, as Paul's friends did, with a sigh and a tear. From that we must advance to joyful submission, like Paul, with head erect and heart elate. It is sad to see that Calvin reads his idea of the absolute decree of God into "the will of the Lord."

15) **And after these days, having packed up, we went up to Jerusalem. Moreover, there went with**

us also some of the disciples from Caesarea, bringing us to him with whom we were to lodge, Mnason, a Cyprian, an early disciple.

We have indicated in connection with v. 8 that the participle "having packed up" (having made our paraphernalia ready) is inserted to indicate that the journey overland began at Caesarea; see also v. 7. Because Luke says nothing about the time of Paul's arrival in Jerusalem, some assume that he failed to get there by Pentecost as he had planned (20:16); but beginning with his mention of Philippi and Troas, Luke has numbered the days for us until they reached Caesarea. Paul had time to spare even after spending several days in Caesarea. He reached Jerusalem before Pentecost. In 21:27 we read of "the Jews from Asia" who were evidently present for the observation of Pentecost.

16) The partitive genitive is freely used as both the subject and the object; here: "some of the disciples" went with us. Escorts such as this were the regular practice in apostolic times; we have noted that some of the Bereans escorted Paul all the way to Athens. Caesarea was seventy miles from Jerusalem, a journey, even when it was made on asses, that required over two days. Ramsay mentions the use of horses, but a few hours in the saddle on horseback would have worn out Paul's party, to speak of them alone. How many of them could have managed a horse traveling beyond a walk? Asses, yes. The writer rode them in Palestine and in Egypt. His personal opinion is that the entire party used *pedes apostolorum* in the good old fashion to which they were thoroughly accustomed, and led a few asses that carried whatever baggage they had.

How must the idiomatic Greek which incorporates the antecedent in the relative clause and at the same time attracts it to the case of the relative, be resolved? Certainly not by inserting the preposition πρός (B.-D. 294, 5; 378; R. 719) when the relative clause has παρά.

Nor by the simple accusative Μνάσωνα as the object of ἄγοντες: "bringing Mnason" along from Caesarea (R. 719, and *W. P.*). This goes hand in hand with the curious comment of the Codex Bezae that the whole party went to a village and stopped for the night with Mnason who is described as a wealthy landowner. The point of the narrative is never where the travelers stopped for the night (the probability is that they had to lie over for two nights) but where Paul's party lodged in Jerusalem even as Luke has said in v. 15 that "we went up to Jerusalem."

We must resolve the contraction as it itself indicates: ἄγοντες παρὰ Μνάσωνα παρ' ᾧ κτλ., "bringing (us, derived from σὺν ἡμῖν) to Mnason, with whom we should lodge" in Jerusalem during our stay there (R., *W. P.*). The point to be noted is that the friends in Caesarea discussed and decided which would be the best place to lodge the nine men of Paul's party during their stay in Jerusalem. They decided on the home of Mnason, not only because he had ample accommodations, but also because he was "a Cyprian, an early disciple" (datives, appositions to the dative "Mnason"). We do not know just why "a Cyprian" is added although we may think of Paul and Barnabas in Cyprus (Barnabas being a Cyprian).

Since Mnason was one of the early converts, this plainly implies that he must have been well known to the whole church in Jerusalem, and that the friends in Caesarea thought that for this reason he would be the man with whom to lodge Paul. So some went along to bring Paul's party to Mnason. Paul would not have imposed himself upon Mnason, especially not with eight companions even though they brought the great collection from the Gentile congregations with them.

On the subjunctive in relative clauses see R. 955. Such clauses are used for various purposes, and the forms of the verb correspond. Here the relative clause indicates purpose. We know only what Luke here states about Mnason. That he was only too glad to accommodate these guests who were almost formally brought to him by a delegation from Caesarea goes without saying. We may note, too, that the disciples in Caesarea knew him well as Luke plainly implies.

The Fourth Quarter

The Progress of the Gospel with Paul in Custody

Paul is Made a Prisoner

17) The eight brethren mentioned in 20:4 plus Luke are with Paul. They were the delegates who had the great collection Paul had been taking up for the last year and more in all his Gentile congregations for famine sufferers in the churches of Judea. That explains their number. Luke omitted mention of the collection from his record.

Now we having come to Jerusalem, the brethren received us gladly.

The genitive absolute is in place because of v. 16. The seventy miles from Caesarea, we take it, required a little over two days of travel. The news of the arrival of Paul and his party at Mnason's house must have brought many of the brethren in Jerusalem to see these most welcome visitors. Thus the remainder of the day of arrival was spent.

18) **And on the following day Paul went in together with us to James, also all the elders were present.**

It is most natural to assume that this meeting was arranged in advance and that all the elders in Jerusalem assembled at the home of James. In regard to James as the chief elder of the church in Jerusalem see 12:17. No apostles are mentioned, apparently because all were absent from Jerusalem and working in distant places. Luke was present at this meeting as the phrase "together with us" makes certain. But this is the last time he writes "we" until 27:1, when he starts on the voyage to Rome with Paul. But he relates most fully all that intervened, and we must conclude that after Paul's arrest he kept as close to Paul as he could and visited him in his prison in Caesarea as often as he could.

19) **And having saluted them, he recounted one by one each of the things which God did among the Gentiles through his ministry.**

We take it that the collection was duly delivered by Paul's companions after the salutations had been observed. We have previously noted that Paul had entrusted the handling of all funds to them, also that the money must have been in the form of drafts on bankers and could not have been in the form of coins because of the great sum. Then everybody wanted to know all about the apostle's great work, and he told the whole story of what had transpired since his last visit in Jerusalem. We have it in Luke's record. It is not necessary to combine καθ' ἓν ἕκαστον and to complicate the construction by making the phrase a substantive, the object of "recounted"; read καθ' ἓν by itself as an adverbial phrase with distributive κατά, "one by one," and read ἕκαστον as the object: "he recounted each thing." The ὧν contains the genitive antecedent τούτων, which attracts ἅ into its genitive case: "each thing of those which." God is the one who did all these things, and that is the absolute fact; Paul was only his instrument as διά so plainly states. This was not boasting, not self-laudation. Nor was Paul submitting a report to a higher authority. What higher authority had these elders compared with the elders in the churches founded by Paul himself? Paul was informing these elders as he had done in Antioch in 14:27.

20) **And they, having heard it, began to glorify God; also they said to him: Thou beholdest, brother, how many myriads there are among the Jews of those who have believed, and all are zealots for the law; and they had it reported concerning thee that thou teachest all the Jews down among the Gentiles apostasy from Moses, telling them not to circumcise the children, neither to walk in the customs.**

The inchoative imperfect, "they began to glorify," merely implies that they also did something else. When Luke writes that they glorified God he intends to say that they did exactly what Paul himself did, the only right thing to be done. An unwarranted implication is introduced by the remark that these elders in Jerusalem failed to praise Paul. Look at 15:4, 7, 8, 12, 14, 18, and see how throughout the work among the Gentiles all success is attributed to God and to God alone. Here Paul does the very same thing, and these elders respond by recognizing the agency of God and by glorifying God accordingly.

This unwarranted contrast is expanded. It is supposed that Paul was received with coldness although he came with eight men who brought the great collection. If not by the elders, at least by the church in Jerusalem he was regarded with suspicion. We are told that for this reason no meeting of the entire church at Jerusalem was called; and that, after Paul had been imprisoned, no effort was made by the church in his behalf, he was practically abandoned to his fate. In v. 17 "the brethren" are supposed to be only a few special friends of Paul, the rest holding aloof. This picture is incredible on the face of it. It distorts Luke's record by injecting an unwarranted hypothesis. Even the fact that the elders address Paul only as "brother" is given a suspicious turn. Yet "brother" contains the fullest possible acknowledgment by the elders and should be understood only in that sense.

It was a most brotherly act on the part of the elders to inform Paul in regard to the damaging reports that had been spread among the Jewish Christians in Palestine in regard to the character of his work and his teaching. Some are puzzled by the expression "myriads among the Jews of those who have believed" and call this hyperbole. And the 144,000 mentioned in Rev. 7:4-8 are introduced; but this number is purely symbolical like the other numbers mentioned in Revelation. A myriad is the Greek term for 10,000, and it was certainly a fact that tens of thousands of Jews in Palestine had by this time become believers. We saw that at the time of Stephen's death the estimate of 25,000 converts was low, and years had passed since that time.

Now all these Jewish converts were "zealots for the law" (objective genitive). They retained their Jewish way of living, circumcised their children, ate kosher, kept the Sabbath, etc. No one was forbidden to live in this way, and that, undoubtedly, won so many converts in the Jewish land. All the apostles, plus Paul himself, regarded these matters as adiaphora. They became dangerous only when they were regarded as necessary to salvation. The so-called Judaizers regarded them thus; in 15:5 we have considered them when they appeared at the apostolic convention.

21) Κατηχήθησαν does not mean, "they were informed." If they only had been informed, all would have been well. The trouble was that they had no information; they had only false reports. This verb means "to sound," "to echo," with κατά, "to resound," and the passive, "to have this sound get into the ears." These Jewish believers in Palestine suffered because of false rumors regarding Paul The passive purposely hides the agents who sounded forth these rumors. Many leap to the conclusion that the unscrupulous Judaizers are referred to, especially because Paul's letter to the Galatians reveals them as undermining Paul's work in

the Galatian congregations. Their number and their power are then also magnified. Let us keep our balance. We know about these Judaizers; in chapter 15 they received their quietus. We see some of them in Galatia. But all evidence shows that they were never numerous; their power lay, not in their numbers, but in their zeal to spread their error. They were of the fanatic type, a few of them capable of doing much damage. We know of none that were found in Jerusalem at this time and cannot conceive that James and the elders and the apostles who returned from time to time would have tolerated them and their destructive work. It is imagination to locate a party of Judaizers in Jerusalem at this time. Wherever they roamed about they slandered Paul. That was their chief stock in trade.

But these reports, regarding which the elders inform Paul, had also other and probably quite innocent sources. It is more than likely that Jewish converts in the Gentile churches in the provinces dropped many of their former Jewish customs. It made things easier for them in their Gentile surroundings, in labor, trade, travel, etc. The gospel in no way prevented that, it was a natural result. In fact, many Jews of the diaspora failed to live up to the Jewish legal ways, often they could not help it. Many of these Jewish converts came to Palestine; other Christians, too, came and told about them and how they had dropped their Jewish ways. In this way these reports regarding Paul spread in Palestine.

It was impossible to stop and to counteract them, and among Jewish Christians who were still zealous for the law they would find credence. Thus many supposed that Paul actually taught "apostasy from Moses," that all Jews of the diaspora must disavow everything Mosaic, in particular must not circumcise their children nor observe the Jewish customs in their daily walk.

When πάντας is in the attributive position it refers to the total number (R. 773). The infinitives with μή after λέγω replace the imperatives of direct discourse (R. 950, 1046). The concern the elders show when they tell Paul about these reports implies that they themselves had done all they could to brand them as false. Now Paul is himself again in Jerusalem. He will remain only for a little while but long enough to do something that may prove most effective in squelching these reports, something to which all could point to prove what his real position and teaching were. The elders suggest a good plan, one that Paul also cheerfully accepts.

22) **What, then, is to be done? Certainly, they will hear that thou hast come. Do, therefore, this that we tell thee. We have four men who have a vow on them. Having taken these along, let thyself be sanctified with them and pay the expenses for them in order that they may get the head shaved, and all may realize that of the things that have been reported concerning thee there exists not a thing, on the contrary that thou also thyself standest in line, keeping the law.**

By asking, τί οὖν ἐστιν, which is idiomatic for our, "What, then, is to be done?" the elders submit the situation to Paul himself They do not at all dictate but submit to him their solution as to what it is best to do under the circumstances. We also see that Paul accepts their plan. The elders add that certainly (πάντως, "in every way") they will hear that he has come, referring to many Jewish believers in Jerusalem. Paul cannot escape notice; but if he at once acts as proposed, the falseness of the reports about him will at once be apparent to all.

23) The proposal is simple and in harmony with what Paul himself had some time before written to the Corinthians: "Unto the Jews I became as a Jew," etc.,

I Cor. 9:20-23. So to the Jewish Christians he could become as a Jewish Christian in the interest of the gospel. The plan was that Paul join himself to four Jewish Christians who had made a vow in the Jewish manner and were now bringing their vow to an end. The reading ἀφ', "from themselves," is inept, for all such vows were voluntary, none were compulsory; we must read ἐφ', "upon themselves," for the vow rested on them as an obligation to be discharged, not only by keeping it, but also by closing it in the prescribed way.

We may at once dispose of two other points. These four belonged to the church in Jerusalem. "We have (the Greek idiom: there are for us) four men" means that the elders have them in their congregation; that, too, is why they know all about them and the length of time their vow lasts and the fact that they are poor and need somebody to help pay the expense of the sacrifices they must offer. These voluntary vows usually continued from one to three months. That of these men had only a week more to continue. The singular "having a vow" means that all four of them had made the same vow which would continue for the same length of time and end with sacrifices to be offered on the same day. The opinion that four different vows, ending on different days, are referred to has no support in Luke's language.

On the subject of these vows and on the way prescribed for concluding them see Num. 6:1-21. We must note the following points. Taking such vows was an ancient custom which reached back we do not know how far. Numbers 6 merely regulates them. They were entirely voluntary; but, once assumed, they bound the person who could be properly released only in the prescribed manner. These vows were assumed for various reasons: in order to thank God for some special blessing like recovery from sickness, some piece of good fortune, and the like, or in order to obtain some blessing or favor from God. Numbers 6 plainly states what the person vowed: he separated himself, became a nazarite (one separated, *natzir*), 1) by using nothing whatever that was produced by the vine; 2) by letting his hair grow; 3) by remaining away from the dead, even from the closest relative. These three continued for the duration of the vow, the time fixed by the person himself. Such a vow meant that the person would live priestlike, as one who was for the time especially dedicated to God. A breach of the vow by accident or otherwise required that the vow be begun over again. It is reported that Queen Helena made a vow for seven years, but that she was held for twenty-one years. The nature of the vow made it public although the writer is uncertain as to whether it was at once reported to the priests or not. Only in the prescribed way, by offering sacrifices, cutting off the hair and burning it on the altar, etc., could the vow be brought to an end.

How long the vow of the four men had already continued we do not know, and that point is immaterial. Paul is asked to pay the expenses involved in terminating their vow. Incidentally we thus learn about the poverty of the church in Jerusalem, the poverty Paul had come to relieve by his great collection among the Gentile churches. Josephus, *Ant.* 19, 6, 1, reports in regard to Agrippa that he thus helped many nazarites to conclude their vows. To help in such a way was considered not only a good deed, it certainly also showed that the helper honored the Jewish law highly.

24) We now understand what the elders proposed to Paul. He was to take these four men and to have himself sanctified with them by going to the priests in the Temple and informing them that he would be the one to pay their expenses for all the sacrifices that were necessary in order that these four men might have their heads shaved and their hair burned with the sacrifice on the altar in the Temple, thereby being released from

their vow. The passive ἁγνίσθητι, like other passives in the Koine (R. 819), is reflexive and causative: "have thyself sanctified." The verb is used in the technical sense with reference to a ritualistic act (C.-K. 62), the one required in the present instance. The idea expressed is certainly not that Paul is to take a vow or to participate in the vow of these four men. They and not he are to have their hair shaved off and burnt. Paul was only to help these men terminate their vow by furnishing the necessary sacrifices.

Just how a case of this kind was handled by the priests no one is able to say. We can glean only the following: the proceeding lasted a week; the persons who had taken the vow, together with their patron (if they needed one), appeared before the priests. Just what was done with them and with him we do not know, but some ritualistic act was performed. The patron did not merely pay the money for the sacrifices, the priests had to accept and to sanctify him.

We see how this plan of the elders was to operate. There were four men who had taken a vow and not merely one; these were known in the church, known as being under a vow. Paul would go with them, would be seen with them, would be noticed in the Temple courts with them, would be observed when he appeared before the priests. They may have had to go before the priests on several of the seven days. It would quickly become known that Paul was generously participating in the Jewish ritual of concluding a vow for no less than four men. All would realize "that of the things that have been reported concerning thee there is (exists in fact) not a thing." On the contrary (ἀλλά), they would see that Paul was himself standing in line (στοιχεῖς does not mean, "to walk," but, "to stand in line," C.-K. 1025) by keeping the law laid down in Num. 6. All the baseless and perverted reports about Paul would thus be silenced by a *demonstratio ad oculos* that would be far more effective than any verbal preachment. The idea was certainly a good one. The choice of the act, too, was good: the matter of a voluntary vow together with the generosity of helping four men to be absolved from its obligation.

The Koine allows the use of the future indicative after ἵνα, so here ξυρήσονται. We may likewise construe the second verb which is also a future, γνώσονται, with ἵνα or regard it as an independent sentence: "and all shall realize." The ὧν contains the antecedent τούτων: "of these things which," the genitive is due to the antecedent, the subject being ἅ. Κατήχηνται is the perfect passive: "have been (and thus still are) reported." Στοιχέω means to follow a certain mode of life.

25) **But concerning the Gentiles who have believed, we on our part sent the letter after coming to a decision that they keep themselves from that sacrificed to an idol and from blood and from anything strangled and from fornication.**

James was undoubtedly the speaker (v. 18), and he adds this matter regarding the Gentile believers in order to show that what Paul was to do in no way contradicted the decision arrived at in the apostolic convention years before this time (Acts 15:13, etc.). James himself had presided at that convention and himself had formulated the resolution that was unanimously adopted. Paul, too, had been at that convention, for he had been sent as a delegate from Antioch together with Barnabas for the very purpose of having the question regarding the Gentile believers settled.

The emphatic "we" (ἡμεῖς) intends to include Paul. What James says is that the old agreement to which Paul, too, was party stands, namely when we reached our decision and then sent out our letter to all the Gentile congregations, asking them for the sake of unity and harmony to keep themselves clear of four things. See the letter in 15:23-29, and the exposition of the four items in 15:29. James was right: the request that was now being made of Paul conflicted neither in principle nor in fact with the agreement that had once been made and was so acceptable to the Gentile churches everywhere. The fact that the reading ἐπεστείλαμεν is correct over against ἀπεστείλαμεν, "we sent orders," is substantiated by 15:20, where the very same word was used by James, namely ἐπιστεῖλαι.

26) **Then Paul, having taken the men along on the following day after letting himself be sanctified with them, was in the act of going into the Temple, declaring the fulfillment of the days of the sanctification, until the offering was offered in behalf of each one of them.**

Paul proceeded promptly to carry out the plan proposed to him by James and the elders. On the very next day he took the four men along with him and had himself sanctified with them, i. e., accepted by means of the required ritual act as the patron of these men who was to attend to the offerings for them. This was the first necessary act and was attended to the next day after the conference with the elders. Nowhere is it intimated that Paul, too, took a vow although this is sometimes assumed. To help pay the expenses for terminating the vow of other men certainly did not require that the benefactor also take that vow.

After this preliminary matter had been attended to on the first day, the time came for Paul and these men to go to the Temple once more in order to announce to the priests who had the matter of vows in charge that the days required for the sanctification of the patron had expired. All that was left to be done was for the patron to attend to having the offering offered for each one of the men for whom he had assumed this expense. The imperfect εἰσῄει (from εἴσειμι) describes Paul in the act of doing this thing. The announcement, it seems, was required, for the priests handling offerings for vows might be busy with other men who were completing their vows. If they were not, the offerings could be made at once, otherwise a wait ensued perhaps until the next day. It would not do to have too many vowmakers in line. On ἕως οὗ with the indicative see R. 974, etc.

The sentence is perfectly clear when it is read in proper sequence although it is sometimes misunderstood because of failure to follow this sequence and noticing that the taking the men along and being sanctified occurred on the first day, and that the going to the Temple for the announcement of the completion of the sanctification days took place on the last of these days, necessarily on the last. Nor does "each one of them" include Paul. No offering was made for him, nor was his hair to be cut off.

The fact that the number of days consumed was seven we learn from v. 27. But the tense of εἰσῄει is important. This imperfect implies that something intervened, that Paul did not get to make his announcement to the priests and, of course, did not get to have the offerings made for his beneficiaries. As he was passing through the courts of the Temple, the Jews from Asia began their riot.

We pause here in order to answer the charge that, by accepting the proposal of James, Paul became inconsistent, compromised his position, chose expediency instead of principle, became weak in the knees, and what not. We might as well call him a hypocrite. We are also told that his effort proved a total failure. But what was Paul's principle? Read it as recorded in I Cor. 9:19-23. That truly Christian principle Paul was following here when he was becoming a Jewish Christian. In accordance with that principle he had circumcised Timothy (16:3). Only one set of men Paul met with solid opposition, the Judaizers. He gave place to them not even for an hour, nor did he circumcise Titus

(Gal. 2:3-5). When men made observance of Mosaic regulations necessary to salvation, these regulations ceased to be adiaphora; as long as this was not done, they were adiaphora, freely to be used or to be put aside as the interests of the gospel required. In order to silence effectively false reports Paul uses the regulation about vows.

Nor did his effort fail. His very arrest advertised his act and satisfied all Jewish Christians when they learned what he was doing in the Temple on that day.

27) **And when the seven days were being about to be completed, the Jews from Asia, on beholding him in the Temple, began to stir up all the multitude and to lay hands on him, crying: Israelite men, run to help! This fellow is the man who is teaching all everywhere against the people and the law and this place! And still more, he brought also Greeks into the Temple and has made common this holy place! For they had previously seen Trophimus, the Ephesian, in the city with him, whom they were supposing that Paul brought into the Temple.**

The article refers to the customary seven days that were needed for terminating a vow of the type that had been made by these four men. The completion of these days implies more than the mere expiration of the week (see 24:11); it includes the sacrifices and the ritual, this, too, being nearly completed. With the four men for whom he was acting as patron Paul must have been standing in the court of the men at the barrier which fronted on the court of the priests who were attending to the final sacrifices that closed the vow. This occurred on the seventh day.

At that time these Jews from Asia began their uproar. We note the same verb συνχέω, "to pour together," to create confusion, in the description of the Ephesian tumult, and also the noun σύγχυσις (19:29, 32). At least some of these Asian Jews must have come from

Ephesus, for they had recognized the Ephesian Trophimus (v. 29). These were those vicious Jews from whom Paul had separated the believers in Ephesus when he took them from the synagogue and began work in the school of Tyrannus (19:9); during the Ephesian riot in the theater they had put forth Alexander as their spokesman (19:33) They exhibit the same vicious character that all unbelieving Jews display.

Here then, out of a clear sky, with terrific suddenness comes the blow in regard to which the Spirit had forewarned Paul. It comes not from Jewish Christians, not even from Judaizers, not from Palestinians, but from vicious, implacable Jews who came directly from one of Paul's greatest mission centers. Few Jews of Palestine knew Paul by sight, but these Asians did. The riot begins in typical fashion. The Jews were as inflammable as gunpowder, especially in their religious fanaticism and here at the center of their religion, Jerusalem and the Temple. They were noted for that, and we shall see that the Romans had taken measures accordingly. Read the history of the Jews of this period and note the bloody riots that preceded the last days of the Temple. Modern times present many similar bloody riots.

28) So they suddenly seized Paul with loud shouts and denounced him amid a tumult that spread like wildfire. Luke reports some of their wild shouts. They called on all Jews to run to the rescue; βοηθέω means "to run at a cry," thus to hurry and help. They have caught the man who does nothing but teach things that are subversive (κατά, "down on") of the λαός ("the people" in the sense of the one chosen by God), of the Mosaic law (which was sacrosanct to all Jews), and of this place (the Temple and Sanctuary of God). His crime is unmentionable. "All everywhere" is alliterated in the Greek and points out the damage Paul is supposed to be doing.

Worse than this and the climax of his sacrilege, ἔτι, "still more": "he brought (aorist to express the fact) also Greeks (pagans) into the Temple and has made common (perfect to indicate a condition that lasts) this holy place," i. e., has defiled it, than which no greater crime could be imagined by the Jews. In 10:15 we have κοίνου, the same verb that occurs here, and in 10:14 the adjective (which see). On the marble screen, which was three cubits high and separated the court of the Gentiles from the other courts there was to be seen an inscription which forbade Gentiles to enter other courts (Josephus, *Ant.* 15, 11, 5); this inscription was written in Greek and in Roman characters. The Greek inscription has been discovered, for it was built into the walls of a mosque on the Via Dolorosa; it decreed death for the violator.

29) With γάρ Luke explains how these frantic Jews came to charge Paul with bringing Greeks into the Temple. They had previously seen Trophimus, a Gentile Christian from Ephesus, whom they well knew, in the city in company with Paul. Now they saw Paul in the Temple with four men who were strange to them. So they jumped to the conclusion that Paul had brought Trophimus into the forbidden courts. The imperfect implies that for the time being they were thus supposing, and that their mistake became apparent later on. A fine example of what hate does to men's minds. But any pretext was sufficient for these Jews who knew no bounds in their viciousness; and Paul was ever their target.

30) **And the whole city was set in motion, and there occurred a running together of the people. And having laid hold of Paul, they were drawing him outside of the Temple! and immediately the doors were shut.**

"The whole city" is not hyperbole. The writer and a party of others rode around the entire outer walls of the present city on an ass in one hour's time. Although the city might have been larger in Paul's time, we must not think of these ancient cities as being as large as cities are today. Disturbances spread in the most astounding way. So the λαός (the same word that was used in v. 28) ran for the Temple. When Luke writes that they were drawing Paul out of the ἱερόν, we understand this to mean out of the inner courts into the great court of the Gentiles and not also out of this into the street. What follows makes this plain. It took some time considering the confused mob of Jews that must have quickly formed at the balustrade in front of the court of the priests where Paul was first seized. Also the determination as to what to do with him had to be made. The imperfect εἷλκον (from ἕλκω), of course, describes but at the same time indicates that something is to follow.

So the great doors were shut. This refers to the doors that opened into the courts of the men and of the women. On these doors, the one toward the east being the Gate Beautiful, see 3:2. This was done by the Temple police and certainly on an order from their chief *strategos* or commander. We take it that this Levite police force, which was always on hand to keep order especially at the festival seasons, helped to get the crowds out of these most sacred precincts.

31) **And as they were seeking to kill him, information came up to the chiliarch of the cohort that whole Jerusalem was stirred up, who at once, having taken soldiers and centurions, ran down upon them. And they, on seeing the chiliarch and the soldiers, ceased beating Paul.**

Supply αὐτῶν as the subject of the genitive absolute ζητούντων. It was their intention to kill Paul, and the seeking was for the purpose of finding ways and means to this end, the present participle indicating that these were still to be found. The mob surrounding Paul had no leader; in v. 34 different opinions were voiced. This genitive absolute does not imply that the killing was now in progress. Before anything was decided by the mob information came to the chiliarch that whole Jerusalem was seething with commotion. The aorist implies that this interfered with the search for ways of killing Paul.

"Came up" is the proper verb. Northwest of the Temple towered the castle Antonia which had been built by Herod the Great and had been fitted out like a little city. It rested like a citadel on a steep, rocky height of fifty cubits and had towers that were fifty cubits high at all corners, the one toward the Temple, from which the entire Temple area could be overlooked, being seventy cubits high. It was equipped magnificently as a royal palace and in addition served as the garrison for the troops of the Roman procurator. Broad steps led down from this citadel into the court of the Gentiles. The entire arrangement was intended to control every disturbance in the Temple courts below, for here violent turbulence was liable to arise at any time, especially during the Jewish festival periods. Antonia could promptly pour out its full military force right into the midst of a violent mob just as it did on this occasion. Φάσις is the term for information in regard to crime or violence.

A Roman legion consisted of 6,000 men plus a detachment of cavalry and auxiliaries. Each cohort of 1,000 was commanded by a chiliarch or tribune, which was a rank corresponding to that of our colonel. The σπεῖρα or cohort was the sixth part of a legion, 1,000 men, each being under a centurion; as happens also in our armies, the numbers were not always full. Such a *speira* was garrisoned at Antonia at this time. In 23:23 we read about the cavalry that was attached to this force of infantry. The chiliarch's name was Claudius Lysias (23:26), and he was promptly reached on this occasion, which shows that he was on duty in the citadel. The information was alarming: whole Jerusalem in turmoil, and the mobs in the Temple court who could be seen by the lookouts of the castle.

32) Serious business. Orders ring out. The chiliarch takes personal command. With his soldiers and his centurions on the double-quick, down the two flights of steps he comes upon the crowds in the court of the Gentiles. A few minutes sufficed to permit this disciplined force to break through the mob to its center of disturbance. The mob saw him coming with his soldiers, saw that it was the chiliarch himself, and promptly left off beating Paul. We do not think that this beating was administered by the Levite Temple police who carried clubs as weapons. A good blow on the head with only one of these clubs would have rendered Paul unconscious; yet Paul is able to make an address to the mob from the Temple steps. Paul received the buffetings of unarmed men who were impatient to have his mode of death decided. When the castle doors suddenly opened and the Romans rushed out, the whole mob paused.

33) **Then, having come near, the chiliarch laid hold on him and ordered that he be bound with two chains and tried to learn who he was and what he had done. But some kept shouting one thing, some another in the crowd; and not being able to know the certainty because of the uproar, he ordered him to be brought into the castle.**

The moment the chiliarch and his soldiers reached the center of the disturbance where Paul was, "he laid hold on him" (genitive when a part is referred to), but certainly not with his own hands but through his soldiers. The order at once to fetter the apostle with two chains reveals the thought that the chiliarch later expressed in v. 38. The fact must be noted that such chains were at hand. The soldiers had had plenty of experience with riots on the Temple grounds and invariably brought chains along with them in preparation for the prisoners they might take. We do not know how the two chains were applied; one would fetter the hands and one the feet, but not in such a way that Paul could not walk.

When the prisoner was secure, the chiliarch tried to learn by questioning the crowd (R. 884 regards the imperfect as iterative, we prefer to make it conative, R. 885: he tried but failed) who the man was and what he had done. The optative in the first indirect question stands for the indicative of the direct; in the second indirect question the original indicative remains unchanged. The writer or speaker may or may not change to the optative, R. 1043, etc. The chiliarch asked, "Who is this?" then, "What has he done?" The perfect tense (here periphrastic) implies that what has been done stands indefinitely against the man as his crime. This chiliarch questions the crowd on the very spot. It was certainly the proper and wise thing to do.

34) But his effort failed; μὴ δυνάμενος is the nominative. Another reading has a genitive absolute, but the sense is the same. In ἄλλοι ἄλλο τι we have the Greek idiom: "some kept shouting (iterative) something to this effect, others to that effect." Unable to learn anything certain because of the uproar, the chiliarch followed the only course left to him: he ordered his soldiers to bring Paul into the παρεμβολή, really, "camp," *castra,* which in this instance was the castle where the soldiers were in barracks. We must note the present infinitive ἄγεσθαι; the aorist would imply that Paul was brought in forthwith, but the present implies that during the course of the action something else occurred that is to be told.

35) **But when he got to the stairs, it befell that he was borne by the soldiers because of the violence of the multitude, for the crowd of the people was following, shouting, Make away with him!**

The stairs led into the castle. Here the violence of the crowd was so great that the soldiers had to bear Paul up on their hands. They lifted him high in order to get him up at all. On συνέβη (συμβαίνω), "it befell," compare 20:19.

36) Deprived of its victim, the mass of Jews (λαός) raged to get hold of him again as if to tear him to pieces. If the plural masculine κράζοντες is the proper reading, the construction is *ad sensum;* if the singular neuter κρᾶζον is preferred, it is quite ordinary. The cry, αἶρε, recalls the aorist ἆρον, ἆρον uttered against Jesus in John 19:15. The singular calls upon the chiliarch to take Paul away by making an end of him. Some may have shouted the aorist as R., *W. P.*, suggests; the present imperative means that the chiliarch is to busy himself with removing Paul from life.

37) **And, being about to be brought into the castle, Paul says to the chiliarch, Is it permitted to me to say something to thee? And he said: Dost thou know** (how to speak) **in Greek? Art thou not, then, the Egyptian who before these days stirred up and led out into the desert the four thousand men of assassins? And Paul said: I for my part am a Jew, a Tarsian of Cilicia, a citizen of no undistinguished city; and I beg of thee, permit me to speak to the people. And he having permitted it, Paul, standing on the stairs, motioned with the hand to the people. And when a great silence came, he addressed them in the Hebrew language, saying, etc.**

Paul must have been on the upper platform in front of the doors and was now standing on his own feet, and the chiliarch must have been close to him, the crowd now being left behind. Deferentially Paul turns to the chiliarch and asks whether it is permitted that he say something to the chiliarch. On εἰ in a direct question see 1:6; in our opinion it is merely an interrogative particle. When we note what Paul intends to ask we see why he makes this preliminary inquiry. It is well, too, to keep in mind the importance of this military man and the hauteur that so many high officers exhibit to this day. And Paul was a prisoner in chains.

The thing to be noted is Paul's spirit. Manhandled in the worst way, barely saved from a murderous mob, he is so far from being upset that he plans to use this frightful occasion in the interest of the gospel! In order to feel the magnificence of such a spirit imagine yourself in his place at this moment. He naturally addressed the chiliarch in Greek, the current language of the day. Unwittingly he thereby astonished the chiliarch. Ἑλληνιστί is an adverb; to preserve it at least in a phrase we translate, "Dost thou know (how to speak) in Greek?" That was the last thing the chiliarch expected from this prisoner.

38) It upset the conclusion to which he had come. The chiliarch thought that he had in his hands the Egyptian who had recently headed a rebellion and had led 4,000 men into the desert. These were the frightful *sicarii* who were armed with the *sica,* a curved dagger, from which they had received their name. The translation might be "dagger-men"; "assassins" is used because they made a practice of mingling with the crowds on the Temple grounds, especially at the time of the Jewish festivals, when they would carry their daggers under their cloaks and suddenly whip them out to stab to death such persons whom they wanted to make away with. They were also hired to commit murder, and one of their victims was the high priest Jonathan who was killed at the instigation of the present

procurator Felix. See the accounts of Josephus, *Ant.* 20, 8, 5-6; *Wars* 2, 13, 5-6.

This Egyptian was a mountebank, a pretending prophet; Josephus reports the promises he made to his followers. All that the chiliarch mentions about this man is that some days before this he had stirred up a sedition and had led 4,000 of the assassins into the wilderness. Whether this has anything to do with the 30,000 this Egyptian led against the Romans on Mt. Olivet, and whether the figure stated by Josephus is correct, need not concern us; for here, too, as elsewhere Josephus seems to make two stories out of one, the second having only 600 "robbers," 400 of whom were killed by Felix, 200 were captured, the Egyptian himself escaped. Josephus seems to have used Luke's account of the chiliarch's remark and have tried to weave it into his history with the exception of the number 4,000.

Whatever one may decide in regard to the muddled accounts of Josephus, it is clear that the chiliarch knows what he is talking about, for the affair had happened only some days before this. Although he had gone into the wilderness with 4,000 of the cutthroats, the chiliarch thought that this Egyptian had suddenly returned, and that Paul was the man. No wonder he had put double chains on this dangerous fellow. The verb ἀναστατόω, "to upset," to create an uprising, was once thought to occur only in the LXX and in Acts but has been found also in the papyri. But this Egyptian could not speak Greek, and Paul addresses the chiliarch in most excellent Greek. The chiliarch's great credit for capturing the dangerous Egyptian alive thereby disappears on the instant, and one can imagine his surprise and his disappointment.

39) Paul is only too glad to tell who he is. Ἐγώ is emphatic, "I for my part," and marks the contrast with the person the chiliarch had in mind. Ἄνθρωπος is

pleonastic and hence is omitted in the English. Paul is "a Jew" by nationality and not an Egyptian; "a Tarsian (9:11) of Cilicia," who was born in the capital of this Roman province. Significantly he adds, "citizen of no undistinguished city"; note the assonance in πόλεως πολίτης and the litotes "no undistinguished" for "very distinguished." What Paul meant by "citizen" the chiliarch failed to catch as we see in 22:27. Perhaps his general surprise was the cause for this, for Paul was declaring himself a Roman citizen (see 16:37, 38; 22:25, etc.).

Paul's two statements are balanced by μέν and δέ: on the one hand he tells who he is and at once makes the information complete; on the other he now makes the request for which he had asked permission in v. 37. He begs (δέομαι) to be allowed to speak to the people, to the turbulent mob of Jews who were milling around the stairs that was held by the soldiers. Think of the bold, startling idea!

40) The chiliarch gave the permission. That, of course, is all that Luke would say. But, surely, something about this man Paul, something about the way in which he was conducting himself in this ordeal must have registered in the mind of this chiliarch so as to induce him to consent to a petition that was as astonishing as this. The view that he thought that he would thus find out more about the whole affair is superficial; for when Paul spoke in Aramaic ("in the Hebrew language," not "dialect," see 2:8) which the chiliarch did not understand, he did not stop Paul. Perhaps the very boldness of the request, combined with the impression Paul's person was making, gained for Paul what he desired.

Paul occupied many strange pulpits but none stranger than this one: the top platform of the steps leading into the great citadel Antonia; chiliarch, centurions, Roman soldiers protecting the preacher; a vast mob of violent Jews constituting the audience. A little space is cleared at the edge of the platform. The preacher stands there, and, with the chain rattling at his wrist, his hand gives the signal that he desires quiet in order to speak. We often read about this preliminary motion. Do you wonder that "much silence occurred" (Luke's Greek)? Here was a tableau indeed. When did Paul ever have attention such as this?

He now spoke in Aramaic. We need draw no special conclusions from that because it was the natural thing to do when addressing a Jewish audience, and we see the instantaneous effect in 22:2. A Jew addressing Jews would speak Aramaic, however well they both spoke Greek. The fact that many Jews were a little weak in Greek scarcely entered Paul's mind; he likewise had no thought of excluding the chiliarch and the soldiers from his address, for a public speech was public property. In the phrase, "in the Hebrew language," the adjective is employed; in v. 37 "in Greek" has the adverb.

CHAPTER XXII

Paul's Address from the Castle Stairs and Its Outcome

1) *Paul's address* is a recital of facts, a simple, straightforward presentation of the things his Jewish hearers ought to know about him. Then they would not rage as they were now doing, would believe no such wild rumor as that he had brought Gentiles into the courts forbidden to them, but would ponder well the gospel which had made Paul a new man, yea, had turned the persecutor of the Christians into an apostle of their faith.

Men, brethren and fathers, hear now my defense to you! The address begins exactly like that of Stephen in 7:2. While in 21:37 ἄνθρωπος is pleonastic, ἄνδρες in the address is not. It is generally construed with an apposition, here it has a double one, for Paul acknowledges that all Jews are his bloodbrethren, and that any among them who are in authority are honored by him as fathers should be honored. "Brethren and fathers" is thus not to be understood from the Christian and spiritual but from the national standpoint. The address is arresting. These "brethren and fathers" wanted to tear Paul to pieces, were completely disowning him. Yet he calls them by this affectionate title. He rises above their ignorant passion. Calm, self-possessed, master even of this frightful situation, he intends to bring them to their senses.

The pronoun μοῦ, like other enclitic pronominal forms, is entirely unemphatic and yet is quite regularly placed forward. Ἀπολογία is "defense" in the wider sense. Paul intends to present the great facts which ought to convince his hearers that their wild charges and actions are utterly baseless; νῦν is used as an adjective in the attributive position. The request to be heard is like that of Stephen and implies that a detailed account is to follow.

The address may be divided into three distinct parts. Its subject is an explanation as to how Paul, the Jew, became the apostle to the Gentiles. It begins with Paul, the ardent Jew, the persecutor of the Christians (v. 2-5). It proceeds with Paul converted into the witness for the Just One (v. 6-16). It closes with Paul sent away from the Jews to the Gentiles with his testimony (v. 17-21). The address is perfectly adapted to the audience. It presents exactly what these and all other Jews ought to know and to consider in regard to Paul. It touches upon none of the charges made against him in 21:28, 29, yet destroys every basis for them so that no man could even think of making such charges against Paul. In not a single statement does Paul equivocate or manipulate the facts in order to placate or to win approval. Paul excuses nothing, hides nothing, makes no appeal of any kind. He simply tells the great facts of his life and lets them speak for him.

2) **Now on hearing that he was addressing them in the Hebrew language, they were the more quiet.**

Note the tenses: the instant they heard (aorist) that he was addressing them in Aramaic (imperfect) they started to furnish quietness (inchoative imperfect) still more than before. In regard to the language see 21:40. All would have understood Paul if he had spoken Greek; but the fact that he should stand there among the Roman soldiers and use Aramaic instead of Greek surprised this mass of Jews and so pleased them in spite of the speaker that their silence became intent. Luke wants us to catch the contrast: a moment ago the roar of an enraged mob, this moment, after a single sentence from Paul's lips, absolute silence. Visualize the scene; few of a more dramatic nature are found even in the New Testament. What was passing through the mind of the chiliarch as he eyed Paul and glanced at the crowds and yet understood not a word of what the apostle said?

3) **I — I am a man, a Jew, born in Tarsus of Cilicia but reared in this city, educated at the feet of Gamaliel according to the paternal law's exactitude, being a zealot for God even as you yourselves all are today; one who did persecute this Way to death, binding and delivering into prisons both men and women as also the high priest is witness for me and all the eldership, from whom also having received letters to the brethren I was journeying to Damascus to bring also those who were there bound to Jerusalem in order that they might be punished.**

Ἐγώ is emphatic: "I, as far as I am concerned"; and ἀνήρ (not the pleonastic ἄνθρωπος which is often used by Luke as in 16:37, and in 21:39) makes the appositive substantive adjectival as in 10:28; 3:14; Luke 24:17 (B.-D. 242). The three perfect participles refer to states; once born, reared, educated a man remains thus. On Tarsus of Cilicia as Paul's birthplace see 9:11 and 21:39. His place of birth made him a Hellenist, but his rearing and his education, both of which took place in Jerusalem, were those of a Hebrew; on the difference see 6:1. Although born abroad, Paul was reared "in this city," i. e., Jerusalem (26:4). Only the fact is mentioned. At what age he was brought to Jerusalem (the guesses vary between eight and fourteen), and with whom he lived (a much older sister, 23:16?), are left to surmise.

We ought not confuse the second and the third participles; the one means "nourished up" and thus "reared," while the other means "to train a child" and thus "to educate." "At the feet of Gamaliel" is thus to be construed with the latter participle, for it also precedes it for the sake of emphasis: by no less a person than Gamaliel was Paul educated. This famous teacher scarcely trained little boys; Paul means that, when he was of proper age, he became a disciple of Gamaliel. See the remarks on 5:34. We see how old the expression "at the feet" is. The disciples, of course, sat cross-legged on the floor, their *rabban* (a title given only to Gamaliel and to six others; *rabbi* is less, and *rab* still less) sitting the same way on a platform. The Talmud explains: "They are to dust themselves with the dust of his feet."

Paul's having Gamaliel as a teacher already explains the kind of an education he received, but he adds this fact because it is so important for his present hearers: "according to the paternal law's exactitude," πατρῷος, "received from one's father." Paul's Jewish education was limited to the things handed down from the Jewish fathers, and he received it in a form that was most exact and accurate. The genitive alone is enough to make its governing noun definite. No devout Jew in all Israel could have provided a more satisfactory Jewish upbringing and education for his son than that which Paul's father provided for him. Where Paul obtained his knowledge of Greek poetry is another question.

The present participle adds what Paul thus turned out to be: ζηλωτὴς ὑπάρχων τοῦ Θεοῦ, "a zealot for God" (objective genitive), compare 21:20; and dramatically Paul adds: "even as you yourselves all are today," referring to what they had just done to him when they imagined that he had desecrated God's Temple. Paul refers to the same thing mentioned in Rom. 10:2. He is speaking subjectively and now describes the zealot he was.

4) The relative is typically Greek and links the statements together instead of beginning a separate sentence; the verb, however, is the first person. Paul intends to say: this is the man I was, the one "who did persecute this Way to death," just as his hearers had wanted to kill him (21:31). On this and the next verse see 9:1, 2, where "the Way" is also explained. The term is used intensively here, for "those being of the Way" are referred to. "Unto death" means that those who clung to Christianity were to be visited with the extreme penalty. Paul was satisfied with nothing less. This statement, together with 26:10, convinces us that not a few actually suffered death in the persecution under Paul's leadership. The two participles show Paul's means to this terrible end: "binding and delivering into prisons both men and women," sex making no difference.

5) The sentence continues with ὡς: "as also the high priest is witness for me and all the eldership," etc.; μαρτυρεῖ, present tense, "is witness." Paul is speaking about what happened over twenty years before this time. That implies that the present high priest Ananias (23:2) and the present πρεσβυτέριον, i. e., Sanhedrin (naming it according to its dignity, "the eldership") are the witnesses whom Paul can call upon to substantiate what he is saying. The point to be made is this, that Paul's present hearers might doubt that he was at one time such a fierce foe of the very doctrine he was now preaching. Well, here were his witnesses — and not everyone could produce witnesses as high as these, than which Jews could have no higher. Some think that "the high priest" Paul mentions was Caiaphas who held the office at that time and who may well have still been alive. But the unmodified term "the high priest" and the next, "all the eldership," must have suggested to Paul's hearers those men who were now in office. Ananias was, no doubt, one of the

Sanhedrists, he had at least been connected with the Sanhedrin twenty years before this. Many of its members still held their office; besides, the old records of their actions were available. So Paul could call on the entire body for testimony.

In 9:2 only the high priest (Caiaphas) is mentioned in connection with the letters that empowered Paul to persecute the Christians in Damascus. That is due to the fact that he had to sign those letters. Here both he and the Sanhedrin are named as the authority that empowered Paul. In a matter such as this no high priest could act alone. These letters made Paul the agent of the entire Sanhedrin. They were addressed "to the brethren," and "brethren" is used as it was in v. 1. Now follows the imperfect ἐπορευόμην which describes Paul as being in the act of journeying to Damascus and at the same time indicates that something intervened. What happened is told in the following. Note: "from whom I was journeying," all of them were responsible. The future participle ἄξων denotes purpose; these future participles are rare and mark the Koine of the writer as literary language. Paul was to bring any Christians he arrested to Jerusalem as prisoners to be tried and punished by the Sanhedrin. The Koine often ignores the difference between ἐκεῖσε and ἐκεῖ, "thither" and "there"; similarly we say, "Where did he go?" and not always, "whither?" We do not know how the Sanhedrin managed to have its death verdicts carried out.

6) **Now it happened to me, journeying along and drawing near to Damascus, about midday that suddenly out of the heaven there flashed a great light around me. And I fell to the ground, and I heard a voice saying to me, Saul, Saul, why art thou persecuting me? And I on may part answered, Who art thou, Lord? And he said to me, I am Jesus, the Nazarene, whom thou art persecuting. But**

those who were with me beheld the light but did not hear the voice of him who was speaking to me. And I said, What shall I do, Lord? And the Lord said to me, Having arisen, be going into Damascus, and there it shall be told thee concerning the things which have been arranged for thee to do. And when I was not recovering sight due to the glory of that light, being hand-led by those with me, I came into Damascus.

Ἐγένετο is construed with the dative, and its subject is the accusative with the infinitive: "it happened or occurred to me that," etc. The dative "to me" is modified by two descriptive participles: "to me in the act of journeying and drawing near to Damascus." The only point not mentioned in 9:3 is the phrase "about midday," when the sun is at its zenith and shines with the greatest brilliance. Here and in the following we need not repeat the full exegesis already given in 9:3, etc.; we shall touch upon only a few points that have not already been explained.

7) The only variation here is the use of τὸ ἔδαφος, "the bottom" or "ground," and the genitive φωνῆς, which makes us think more of the speaker, while the accusative would refer more to what is said by the speaker.

8) The only addition here is that Jesus calls himself "the Nazarene," a term that is constantly used for identifying Jesus.

9) At this point Paul explains in regard to the Temple police who had been assigned to him to arrest and to bring in the victims. They did not hear τὴν φωνήν, what the speaker said; they did hear τῆς φωνῆς (9:7), that some speaker was speaking to Paul. There is not a contradiction between the accusative used here and the genitive used in 9:7.

10) Here the account is more detailed than in 9:5. Paul asked what he is to do, ποιήσω, the aorist sub-

junctive in a question of deliberation or doubt; he is thereupon told what to do. In 9:5 this is condensed so as to dispense with the question. The conversation was carried on in Aramaic, hence the translation into Greek may show verbal variations. The force of δεῖ in 9:6 is quite the same as that of τέτακται; "it is necessary" for Paul to do what "has been arranged" by the Lord for him to do.

All that this conversation involves regarding Paul's conversion and the view of the critics in regard to it we have treated in chapter nine.

11) Here Paul is briefer and less specific than Luke is in 9:8, 9, but the sense is exactly the same. The imperfect describes how "he was not recovering his sight," and ἀπό states the cause for this lack of recovery. Ἀναβλέπω has its common meaning, "to look up" so as to see and is used freely with reference to those who were blind and then look up again and are able to see. In regard to Paul's condition during the three days of blindness see 9:9.

12) **And one Ananias, a man devout according to the law, attested by all the resident Jews, having come to me and stepped up, said to me, Brother Saul, recover sight! And I in that hour recovered sight to look on him. And he said: The God of our fathers did appoint thee to know his will and to see the Righteous One and to hear a voice out of his mouth, because thou shalt be a witness for him to all men of what things thou hast seen and didst hear. And now, why art thou hesitating? Having arisen, get thyself baptized and get thy sins washed away, calling on his name.**

All that is recorded about the preparation of Ananias for Saul and of the preparation of Saul for Ananias in 9:10-16 Paul omits from his address as not being pertinent to his present purpose. The point of importance for his fanatic Jewish hearers is that this

Ananias, like so many early Jewish believers, was the devoutest kind of a Jew "according to the law," measured by the canon of faithful law observance; εὐλαβής = one who takes hold well in a religious sense, "devout" in religious observance (2:5; 8:2). Lest anyone think that this is merely Paul's opinion, he at once adds: "attested by all the resident Jews," κατοικούντων, attributive present participle. All the Jews in Damascus esteemed Ananias a most faithful Jew; the division between the synagogue and the disciples had not yet occurred.

13) This was the kind of a man, Paul wanted his hearers to note well, who came to him, stepped up (9:17, laid his hands on Paul), and addressed him. What Ananias said is condensed into three Greek words. "Brother Saul" is the same address as that found in 9:17, which see. The aorist imperative, ἀνάβλεψον, "recover thy sight," either summarizes what 9:17 reports in detail, or is the command which Ananias actually uttered but which is omitted in 9:17. How Ananias came to do this, and how it happened that his word proved instantly effective, are here left to the minds of Paul's hearers to think out. The fact that a higher hand was back of it they felt automatically.

"In that very hour" is the Hebrew idiom for "without delay," in 9:18, "immediately." Here the aorist ἀνέβλεψα is construed with εἰς αὐτόν; this construction does not give the verb a meaning that is different from its use without a modifier but is in accord with its Greek meaning, "to recover sight so as to see or look up again with seeing eyes"; Paul saw Ananias with recovered sight. All that underlies this fact Paul again leaves to the minds of his hearers to think upon.

14) Now Paul amplifies Luke's account which merely reports that Paul was baptized then and there, etc. It is important that his hearers know what An-

anias said, not only as leading to the baptism, but also as indicating God's intention regarding Paul's work after that. On the road into Damascus Jesus spoke to Paul from heaven. Already that conveyed volumes to Paul's audience regarding Jesus, for it implied that he had risen from the dead and ascended to heaven. But it is "the God of our fathers," the one true God in whom all Jews and Paul with them believed, of whom Ananias told how "he did appoint thee to know his will," etc., "did put forth into his hand beforehand," exactly as in 3:20. Long in advance of this hour Israel's God had determined to effect three things. The first was that Paul was "to know his will," to come to a full realization (γνῶναι, aorist) of what it contained. "His will," θέλημα, is certainly his volition as it is expressed in the gospel. Actually to realize that will is to believe the gospel and thus to be saved. This had to come first; without it God could not have used Paul in spreading the gospel as an apostle.

Next is "to see the Righteous One and to hear a voice out of his mouth," which qualified Paul for the apostolate. Paul actually *saw* Jesus in glory; see the discussion in 9:5, where I Cor. 9:1; 15:8 are also introduced. We are left under the impression that without a direct vision of the risen Lord, including also "speech (φωνή) out of his mouth" in his glorified state, Paul could not have been an apostle in the full sense of the word, on a par with the Twelve. In his own wonderful way God himself qualified Paul. As for his own will in the matter, 26:19 is amply sufficient. In 7:52, Stephen called Jesus "the Righteous One," in 3:14, Peter called him "the Holy and Righteous One"; here Paul quotes Ananias as using this Messianic title. This title is continually found in the epistles, but it goes back to Isa. 53:11: the Messiah is the very embodiment of righteousness, he is the one who has the divine verdict in his favor in an absolute sense. This title is soteriological: Jesus executed the saving will of God perfectly, Ps. 40:8; John 4:34.

15) Why did God grant all this to Paul? "Because thou shalt be a witness unto him," etc. "To all men" makes clear the full extent of the witness Paul was to bear; his assignment to the Gentiles follows. The expression recalls 21:28, "teaching all everywhere." The ὧν contains the antecedent τούτων, to the case of which ἃ is attracted. Paul was to testify to what he has seen and did hear. The change in tense in this relative clause is marked and thus significant. The perfect "thou hast seen" implies a permanent effect of the seeing, while the aorist "did hear" contents itself with the past fact as such. Paul's having seen Jesus gave him the real qualification for the apostleship; his hearing the voice of Jesus was only an adjunct, B.-D. 342, 3.

16) The question: καὶ νῦν τί μέλλεις; as in the classics (Liddell and Scott), means: "And now why delayest thou?" Ananias is now encouraging Paul on his own account. He tells him what to do. The two aorist imperatives are causative middles: "get thyself baptized and get thyself washed as to thy sins" (B.-D. 317; R. 808). The action expressed by the aorist participle, "calling on his name," is either simultaneous with that of the aorist imperatives or immediately precedes it, the difference being merely formal. "The name" is Jesus in his revelation; and to call on this name involves faith (Rom. 10:13, 14). This is one of the cardinal passages on the saving power of baptism; see the others, 2:38 discussed at length; Luke 3:3; John 3:3, 5; Tit. 3:5; Eph. 5:26. What makes the present passage unmistakably clear is the second imperative. Why was it not enough to say, "Having arisen, let thyself be baptized, calling on his name"? Why was "and

let thyself be washed as to thy sins" inserted if baptism and its water did not do this washing to remove the sins? The answer has yet to be given.

Was Paul to submit to a mere symbolic ceremony? What lay heavy on his conscience was the guilt of his enormous sin of persecuting the Messiah himself (v. 7). With its water that was sanctified by the Word baptism was *to wash away* all this guilt, all these sins. This washing away is the ἄφεσις of 2:38, and Luke 3:3, the "remission," the "removal" of sins. To be sure, this washing away is "picturesque language" (R., *W. P.*); it is figurative, to speak more exactly, and is appropriate in that baptism has water in connection with the Word, Eph. 5:26. But with "picturesque language" R. means that "here baptism pictures the change that had already taken place," i. e., that is all that baptism does. R. does not seem to see that he contradicts Ananias. Whereas Ananias says, "Let thyself *actually* be baptized" (aorist), "let thyself *actually* be washed of thy sins" (again aorist), R. changes the latter and substitutes, "Let *a picture be made of the washing away of thy sins.*" It may be interesting to enact a picture, but that is about all. As βάπτισαι = a real baptism and not the mere picture of one, so ἀπόλουσαι = a real washing and not the mere picture of one.

17) Paul comes to the third part of his address which states how he came to be sent to the Gentiles. **Now it happened to me, on having returned to Jerusalem and while I was engaged in praying in the Temple, that I was in an ecstasy and that I saw him saying to me, Make haste and go out quickly out of Jerusalem because they will not receive thy testimony concerning me!**

Paul passes over the three years that intervened, since they contained nothing pertinent to his present purpose. In 9: 23-30 Luke has reported this visit of

Paul's to Jerusalem. The construction is the same as in v. 6, ἐγένετο with a dative, the subject being an accusative with the infinitive. A genitive absolute is inserted. We do not find an anacoluthon in the participles (R., *W. P.*) ; nor do we believe that the sentence is *sehr ungefuegig* (B.-D. 409,4). It is well arranged, each element falls easily into its place even when translating. While a second dative participle might have been used in place of the genitive absolute, the latter is preferable because it makes the action of praying stand out by itself.

"It happened to me" brings out the idea that Paul had no hand in the matter. The aorist participle states the fact that Paul had returned to Jerusalem, but the present participle in the genitive absolute describes him as being engaged in praying in the Temple. This statement conveyed a great deal to his hearers. Although Paul had been converted to Jesus, the Temple was still the holy place of prayer to him. This prayer must have been offered at the regular hour for Jewish prayer. Paul was in his place with other Jewish worshippers. Desecrate the Temple (21:28) — that was unthinkable to him. Now it was in the sacred Temple itself that Jesus communicated with him and ordered him to go to the Gentiles. Jesus chose that place as being most fitting. Would the Lord of the Temple, he who had revealed himself to Paul in his heavenly glory, desecrate the Temple by a communication he made? On the condition of "ecstasy" see 10:10; we retain this Greek word. This divine communication is not mentioned in 9:30. The two accounts supplement each other. The brethren wanted Paul to leave, the Jews plotted to kill Paul, his hesitation was ended by the vision.

18) Paul "saw him" (the Righteous One, v. 14) when he told Paul what to do. Here Paul again actually saw the glorified Savior; but now not with

blinding effect. The Lord's foreknowledge is here made manifest: the Jews of Jerusalem will not receive Paul's testimony; in accord with that foreknowledge the Lord directs Paul to utter his testimony elsewhere. This is an excellent illustration as to how the divine foreknowledge is used by God. We cannot construe: "receive of thee" (R. V.), because that would require παρά σου; "thy testimony" (A. V.) is correct.

19) **And I on my part said: Lord, they themselves know that for my part I went on imprisoning and hiding in synagogue after synagogue those believing on thee; and when the blood of thy witness Stephen was being shed, I myself also was standing by and agreeing and guarding the robes of those making away with him.**

The point that Paul's hearers are to note in this statement is his desire by all means to remain and to work among the Jews in Jerusalem, in the very place where everybody knew about his fearful persecution of the Christians; he thought that he was best fitted for that. It was the Lord who insisted on his going to the Gentiles. This is the point for Paul's present hearers. As between Paul and the Lord, Paul is not refusing obedience but, like Ananias in 9:13, 14, is telling the Lord his own thoughts.

Both ἐγώ are emphatic; the first conveys the idea that Paul was bold enough to tell the Lord his own thoughts. And they were certainly most reasonable. In fact, that is why Paul now tells them to his present hearers. He was once so violent against the Christians and then became a very apostle of Christianity — surely, that would impress the Jews who knew the facts, make them realize that they, too, should pause, make them ready to follow Paul. We have ἤμην with two present participles, thus periphrastic imperfects; κατά is distributive: "synagogue by synagogue" and not "in every synagogue" (our versions). Paul never reached all of them. Δέρω means to flay, to pull off the skin, to administer a sound hiding. The synagogue courts had power to scourge with rods.

20) Paul purposely goes back to Stephen's death and the position he took at the time of that tragedy, compare the remarks on 7:58 and 8:1. We ought not entertain the idea that Paul considered this dangerous ground; quite the contrary. He considered it most fruitful ground, for it exhibited the blind rage of the Jews which he fully shared at the time and was then converted to fill the very place left vacant by Stephen's bloody death. The tenses are descriptive imperfects and ask Paul's hearers to dwell on these facts so as to gain their full import. Here again ἤμην, now being used with three participles, forms periphrastic imperfects; ἐφεστώς is the second perfect in form but is always used in the sense of the present.

"When the blood of Stephen, thy witness, was being poured out" is Paul's testimony to the martyr in whose frightful death he was implicated. Paul acknowledges his former crime. "Thy witness" (see 1:8) — a man can bear no higher title. "I was agreeing" is explained in 8:1; ἀναιρέω designates murderous taking away and is used again and again to designate the murder of Jesus, "to make away with." Paul officially helped to supervise the making away with Stephen; see 7:58.

21) **And he said to me, Be going because I myself will commission thee far away to Gentiles.**

Ἐγώ is emphatic with authority: *I* am doing this, no matter what thou thinkest. The future tense of the verb denotes more than mere sending, it is the sending on a mission. The accusative μακράν (ὁδόν) is used as an adverb. "To Gentiles" is without the article and refers to people who are Gentiles and not Jews. Paul went out to Gentiles by divine direction alone (9:15). But his great ministry was not to begin even at this time; he had to wait for about thirteen years before he entered upon his first missionary journey.

The Effect of Paul's Address

22) Paul was not allowed to finish; we can only guess as to what he intended to add. **And they continued listening to him up to this statement and lifted up their voice, saying: Make away from the earth with such a fellow! For it ought not to be that he continue to live. And they shouting and jerking off their robes and throwing dust into the air, the chiliarch ordered him to be brought into the castle, directing that he be examined with scourges in order that he might get to know for what cause they were thus crying against him.**

The idea that the reference to the Gentiles acted like a spark in a powder magazine overlooks the fact that at various points the address must have gone against the grain of the mob until the last statement precipitated the outbreak. Paul was not offending his hearers, and yet he was not cringing before them. As always, he was careful in the choice of his language in order to convey exactly what he wanted to convey, but he did convey just what he deemed necessary and committed the result to God's hands. The fact that the mob again lost its head was certainly to be expected. Paul himself certainly did not expect that his story would satisfy these Jews. The wonder of it is that the mob did not become violent just as soon as Paul mentioned the name "Jesus, the Nazarene," in v. 8. The fact that it restrained itself until this time is to be credited to Paul's personality which was expressed so powerfully in his voice and his word.

Paul's object had been attained; when the uproar broke out anew, all who had heard that address and the mighty facts it stated were no longer in the condition indicated in 21:34, some saying one thing, some another, just guessing this and guessing that. They now knew Paul's whole story. Paul had succeeded in putting them under full responsibility. This is always the case with regard to the opposition that meets the gospel and its defenders. We must testify to the facts, as to how we come to believe and to serve the Lord whenever and wherever the opportunity presents itself, "ready always to give an answer to every man that asketh you a reason of the hope that is in you with meekness and fear (reverence)," I Pet. 3:15 The mob began to rage again, but that did not imply that Paul's testimony did not make a deep and lasting impression on some of his hearers in order to bring fruit in due season. Some brands are thus plucked from the burning.

The old shout αἶρε (21:36) is renewed, the singular is addressed to the chiliarch; but Luke now reports more fully: "Make away from the earth with such a fellow (τὸν τοιοῦτον); for it ought not to be that he continue to live (ζῆν, present, durative infinitive)!" Souter prefers the reading that has the neuter participle καθῆκον (sc. ἐστίν), "it is not a fitting thing," but he does so on the basis of the most slender textual evidence; we prefer the reading that has the imperfect καθῆκεν. This tense is the Greek idiom for a propriety, possibility, or obligation that has already existed too long and is still unfulfilled at the present. The Greek thought reaches into the past and from there to the present; the English and the German think only of the present and thus find difficulty in reproducing the Greek. R. 886. So here the thought is: "he should not have been permitted to live this long, should have been removed from the earth long ago."

23) The three present tenses in the genitive absolute describe the actions as continuing; the scene became more and more violent. Κραυγάζω is the proper word to describe the roar of the mob. Some think there

was nothing specific in the casting off of the robes and the throwing of dust into the air. On this supposition ῥιπτέω is translated, "swing their robes to and fro." Throwing off the long, loose outer robes and flinging dust into the air go together and signify that the mob would stone Paul if it only could. On the robes see 7:58; dust is used because stones were not at hand, and, of course, the dust is hurled in the direction of Paul and not just into the air generally.

24) Imagine the chiliarch with this scene before him. Mystified at the beginning (21:34), confused still more by Paul's speech and its explosive result, he saw no other course to be followed than to order that Paul be taken into the castle (see 21:37), there to be examined. Both ἄγεσθαι and ἀνετάζεσθαι (which has at last been found in a papyrus) are present infinitives in indirect discourse for the present infinitives of the direct: "Let him be brought in and put to examination!"

The participle εἰπών (variant εἴπας) is aorist because one command was issued. It is a fine grammatical point as to whether this aorist participle expresses coincident or subsequent action (R. 861); but the real point is that it indicates a separate command and, as a participle, one that is secondary to the bringing in. When the agents are not to be designated, the passive is used (B.-D. 392, 4); so here: "to be brought in," "to be examined." When Pilate examined Jesus, Luke 23:14, ἀνακρίνω is used; we confess that, at least as far as the Scriptures are concerned, this verb is not used with reference to examination by torture as Abbott-Smith, *Lexicon,* claims. We must say the same in regard to ἀνετάζω; it does not include torture. The fact that torture was to be applied to Paul is expressed by the dative plural "with scourges." The truth was to be whipped out of Paul in the fashion that was common in that day. Pilate gave no such order regarding Jesus; this shows that the chiliarch was convinced in his own mind that Paul must be a dangerous criminal and was determined to get a full confession in short order; ἐπιγνῷ is the subjunctive.

25) **Now, when they were stretching him forward for the thongs, Paul said to the centurion standing by, Is it lawful for you to scourge a Roman and one not (yet) subjected to trial? On hearing it the centurion, having gone to the chiliarch, reported, saying: What art thou on the point of doing? For this man is a Roman. And the chiliarch, having come to him, said to him, Tell me, thou, art thou a Roman? And he said, Yes. And the chiliarch answered, For my part I acquired this citizenship with much capital. But Paul said, But I have even been born so.**

We take it that the order to examine Paul with scourges was given by the chiliarch at a moment when no protest could be offered by Paul. Binding Paul with chains was already a serious violation of his Roman rights (v. 29). Now, under command of one of the centurions (there were several, 21:32), the order to apply the lash was promptly being carried out. The mob was left to howl until it was satisfied, the portal was closed, the chiliarch was in his quarters waiting for Paul to be brought to him after his tongue had been loosened by a good dose of the scourges. These were short handles with several thongs affixed to them and a piece of metal or bone fastened at the tip of each thong. Every blow made several stripes, the tips tore ugly gashes in the flesh. Two soldiers, one on each side, struck alternately. The ordeal was always terrible. After being lacerated sufficiently, the victim was to be brought to the chiliarch for questioning, and woe unto him if he did not answer satisfactorily — the scourges would again be applied.

Is προέτειναν an aorist or is it, as Blass surmised, an imperfect? On imperfects in -αν consult B.-D. 80-81;

two texts do have the imperfect ending - ον. The imperfect would be eminently in place here as Zahn also states, "when they began to stretch him forward," Paul spoke and not after they had done so. We thus venture to regard this form as the imperfect.

Another muted point is the dative τοῖς ἱμᾶσιν. Does it mean, "with the thongs," or, "for the thongs"? R. 533, also *W. P.*, leaves the point undecided. The victim designated for scourging was bent forward (πρό in the verb) over a low, heavy pillar, his hands and his feet were tied to rings in the floor, the back was bared and stretched for the lashes. So Jesus was tied down and scourged. This was a different matter from the beating with rods by Roman lictors (16:22, ῥαβδίζειν, compare 16:37). We think that πρό in the verb decides that the sense of the datives is, "for the thongs" of the scourges and not, "with the thongs that bound the victim." Irrespective of the preposition, others decide in the same way.

At this point Paul asked the question about his Roman rights. On εἰ see 1:6; ἄνθρωπον, *Mensch* (not ἀνήρ) is pleonastic. The entire question regarding the rights of a Roman citizen has been treated in 16:37, also the term ἀκατάκριτον. It indicates the aggravating circumstance there as well as here: rushing ahead with the scourging when even the beginning of a trial would have brought to light the prisoner's Roman citizenship. The supreme Roman authorities would deal severely with a judge who did such a thing, for he could not plead ignorance because he had given the prisoner no opportunity to declare his rights. In this instance the chiliarch would be eminently to blame, for no one had as yet even brought a charge against Paul on the basis of which a trial could be held; the chiliarch could point to neither charge nor accusers. The fact to be noted is that by speaking now Paul was not merely saving himself but was saving also the chiliarch.

26) No wonder the centurion hastened to make due report to his superior officer. His exclamatory question reveals how badly he himself is upset: "What art thou on the verge of doing?"

27) So serious was the case that the chiliarch did not think of having Paul brought to him but immediately arose and went to Paul with the demand that Paul tell him whether he was a Roman; *σύ* is emphatic: "Thou, art thou a Roman?" Badly mistaken regarding Paul in the first place (21:38), he now finds himself in an error that is still worse. In 21:39 Paul had called himself "a Tarsian of Cilicia, a citizen of no mean city." That was significant enough although it was not an outright declaration of Roman citizenship. Paul had spoken with great dignity, but that was lost on the chiliarch who had rashly ordered the scourges. The frightened questioner receives a terse, calm, "Yes!" as the only answer. The word is impressive in this dramatic situation; Paul intends it to be so. He was a Roman, and he spoke as one.

Not for one moment is the simple assertion of Roman citizenship questioned by either the praetors in Philippi or here by the chiliarch. We need not ask why. Summary death awaited the man who dared to claim Roman citizenship falsely.

28) Deferentially the chiliarch answers that he on his part bought this citizenship for much capital, *πολλοῦ κεφαλαίου*, genitive of price, which is exactly our word "capital," a great sum of money, the principal as distinguished from the interest. Under the emperors the Roman citizenship was sold in order to fill their exchequer; Dio Cassius (LX, 17) reports that the wife of Claudius thus accumulated money. Perhaps Paul looked rather too poor to have been able to buy the right for himself, and the chiliarch probably thought — again making a bad guess — that he could have secured it in no other way. He naturally thought of himself.

Judging from his name Lysias, he was probably a Greek who took the added name Claudius on becoming a Roman citizen.

With an equally emphatic ἐγώ Paul replies to the implied question: "But I have been born" so. Paul's citizenship was inherited, and in that respect it was superior to that of the chiliarch. We have discussed this point in 16:37. The perfect, "I have been born," denotes also the resultant state and may be translated, "I am born," in our idiom.

Sometimes 16:22 is misunderstood as though Paul there allowed himself to be beaten, and then the question is argued as to why he did not do so here. Again there is a debate regarding the ethics of Paul in making use of his Roman citizenship, in insisting that its rights be respected. The prophecies regarding his bonds are also introduced. But this debate is pointless. Paul had already been bound as had been prophesied. Was the man who deliberately went to Jerusalem against the urgings of his friends (21:4, 12) trying to evade suffering that had been divinely allotted to him? Certainly not. We have seen that, when in Philippi, Paul asserted his own Roman citizenship and that of Silas, this helped the gospel, those praetors learning that the Christians had Roman citizens among them. The same was true in regard to the chiliarch who learned that this Christian apostle was even a born Roman. Did this discovery hurt the gospel cause? The ethics that quietly assume that grace demands of us that we lie down in order that men may trample upon us at will, even in sheer ignorance, is false in its assumption, and no question raised on that assumption calls for a serious reply.

29) **Immediately, therefore, they stood away from him who were about to examine him; moreover, even the chiliarch became afraid, realizing that he was a Roman and that he had bound him.**

The proceedings stopped with suddenness. We have explained in v. 24 what part the scourges were to play in the process of examining Paul. "They that were about to examine him" refers to all the soldiers who had been detailed for the scourging — that was their part; the questioning to learn the cause of the shouting against Paul, as indicated in v. 24, belonged to the chiliarch.

Δέ adds a different point, namely that "even the chiliarch became afraid," ingressive aorist. He had cause for this. In 23:27 we see how he lies in order to cover up his guilt. He realized that he had put a Roman in chains, had committed a crime that might cost him dearly if the procurator learned of it and took a strict view. See 16:37 in regard to the Roman law. The fact that he had acted in ignorance might or might not be accepted as an excuse.

30) **Now on the morrow, wanting to know the certainty why he was accused by the Jews, he loosed him and ordered the high priests and all the Sanhedrin to come together and, having brought Paul down, he set him before them.**

The debate in regard to the time when Paul was unchained leads some commentators to overlook a more important question: Why did the chiliarch himself fail to question Paul regarding "the certainty why he was accused by the Jews"? He did not dare to. Paul was a Roman; no accusers had appeared against him, no crime had been charged. The chiliarch could not even inaugurate a trial by judicial questioning in the case of a Roman without accusers and an alleged crime. In the case of a non-Roman the matter was different. Τό merely makes a substantive of the indirect question which is in apposition to τὸ ἀσφαλές.

We do not entertain the idea that Paul's chains were left upon him until the next day and were taken off just before he was brought before the Sanhedrin.

This chiliarch was frightened when he learned that he had chained Paul. He could plead ignorance for that; but once he knew that Paul was a Roman and then left him chained, he would knowingly have committed a grave crime against Roman law. The remark is pointless, that, having bound him already, it made little difference to leave him bound until the next day; or that he was stubborn and wanted to show his power. The chiliarch was no fool; the chains came off at once.

"On the morrow" places this entire verse into the next day. It does this even when it is construed with the participle, for we cannot refer the action expressed by the two main verbs to the day before, so that wanting to know would occur on the morrow but loosing Paul and ordering a meeting of the Sanhedrin occurred on the original day. This method of solving the difficulty is unsatisfactory. We cannot accept the contention that ἔλυσεν αὐτόν is intended to correspond with ἦν αὐτὸν δεδεκώς, and that both refer to chains. The point overlooked is the order of the actions: loosing — ordering the Sanhedrin to meet — leading Paul down to that meeting. Why this odd order *if* chains are, indeed, referred to? The order should then be: ordering the Sanhedrin — then loosing and leading Paul down. If we drop the idea of chains, all is in line.

Paul was at once freed from his chains but was kept in the castle for the night. The next morning the chiliarch "loosed him," set him free, summoned the Sanhedrin, and with Paul as a free man went down to the Sanhedrin to find out what he could. That implies that he asked Paul to appear before the Sanhedrin, that Paul consented, and that the Sanhedrin was then convened. That implies furthermore that the chiliarch and Paul went down to the Sanhedrin alone and without soldiers. Thus "he made him stand εἰς αὐτούς, into them." This chiliarch had made mistakes enough in regard to Paul, he was going to make no more. As far as the soldiers are concerned, in 23:11 they go down just as the chiliarch here takes Paul down; and that means that, leaving the boisterous meeting, the chiliarch ran up to the soldiers or from below shouted for them to come down and thus brought them down.

The status of Paul was and, in fact, remained peculiar. He was set free but not fully; he was a prisoner, yet not fully. In this sense he is called a δέσμιος in 23:18. He is detained, not because there is anything definite to be charged against him, but because something might be found against him. Regarding chains in 24:27, and again in 26:29, 31 see these passages. Paul is only guarded (φυλάσσεσθαι, 23:35), detained with liberty to meet his friends (τηρεῖσθαι, 24:23) and not chained.

CHAPTER XXIII

Paul Before the Sanhedrin and His Transfer to Caesarea

1) We accept the view that the Sanhedrin met in a lower hall in the fortress Antonia and not in its own hall, the *lischkath haggasith* on the west side of the Temple hill. The soldiers had their παρεμβολή, *castra*, quarters, on the upper floor from which stairs descended to the level of the Temple court; they occupied only this part of the great castle. In 22:30 the chiliarch takes Paul down; the two of them go alone; in 23:10 he orders his troop down to bring Paul back to the quarters of the soldiers. Neither he nor Paul went to another building.

Paul was not turned over to the Sanhedrin for trial; the chiliarch had no authority for such an act. We find no trace of a trial, no accusers, no charge of a crime, no witnesses, etc. The Sanhedrin is present, but not in formal session. The members have come to learn what the chiliarch desires of them in regard to Paul; and his desire is to discover what is really at the bottom of the previous day's uproar and the Jewish demand for Paul's death. By confronting Paul and the Sanhedrin he hopes to find out what is really wrong. This effort proves abortive; it is ill-advised and of a piece with what we have already seen of the chiliarch and his mistakes.

This explains Luke's account. He presents only two incidents from the undirected proceedings, one from the beginning, Paul's clash with the high priest (v. 1-5); one from the conclusion, the clash between the Pharisees and the Sadducees in the Sanhedrin itself (v. 6-10). Whatever else occurred was not worth recording. The chiliarch got nowhere; he should have known that in advance. Having nothing definite to present, all was left to chance from the very beginning.

The language spoken must have been Greek because it was the chiliarch who wanted to know what the trouble was with reference to Paul (22:3). This need cause no surprise, for at the trial of Jesus before Pilate the Sanhedrists had likewise spoken only Greek. We know nothing as to how proceedings began, and as to how Paul was given the floor. The idea that Paul took matters into his own hands cannot be entertained. It is probable that, after entering with Paul at his side, the chiliarch made some preliminary statement. One might suppose that he would have asked the Sanhedrists what they knew about or against this man; but in the case of this erratic chiliarch one cannot be sure. Some think that it was perfectly in order that Paul should speak first; it certainly was not. All we can say is that after some preliminaries Paul was asked to make a statement.

And Paul, having looked earnestly at the Sanhedrin, said: Men and brethren, on my part I have been conducting myself toward God with all good conscience until this day.

The supposition that Paul had weak eyes or some serious ailment of the eyes has been attached to ἀτενίσας and regards the participle as implying that Paul had to strain his eyes in order to see the Sanhedrists. But in 13:9 and in 14:9 this very same participle is used, yet in those places this weakness of the eyes is not stressed by these commentators. Besides, no one thinks of this when this participle is used with reference to other persons. Paul had not seen the Sanhedrin for many years, not since they had appointed him inquisitor-in-chief and head persecutor of the Christians. He would naturally now scrutinize the present personnel with special interest, being confronted by this body as he now was. The assumption that at one time he himself was a member of the Sanhedrin is unfounded. If he had been, that fact would be of such importance as to necessitate repeated mention, especially in Acts and in II Cor. 11:22.

It is notable that Paul addresses the Sanhedrists as "men and brethren" (see 1:16) and does not add "fathers" as he did in 22:1. He speaks to them as being only fellow Jews, fellow nationalists who believe in the same God of Israel. We confess that we see a great deal in this informal address. If these Sanhedrists are important personages, so is Paul. The apostle is conscious of his own high standing. The very character of the man naturally appears great and impressive. There is another thing that seems to be implied in this address, namely that this was not a formal session of the Sanhedrin. It is generally thought to be just that: all are seated in their own hall on the platform reserved for them, the high priest is in his regular place, there are scribes to take down the proceedings, attendant ὑπηρέται to execute orders — the whole court is in official session. This picture is unwarranted. The hall of meeting is in the castle Antonia, the gathering is informal, "men and brethren" is the form of address for a gathering and not for a formal court in session, secretaries and attendants are absent. Luke's entire account reflects this situation.

The meeting was called in order to enlighten the chiliarch in regard to Paul and in regard to anything of a criminal nature chargeable against him as expressed in yesterday's riotous demand for his death; hence the emphatic ἐγώ introducing Paul's declaration of innocence. So also "with all good conscience" is placed emphatically forward. A second emphasis rests on the final phrase "until this day." The verb πολιτεύομαι is commonly used in regard to the conduct of a citizen or of an official, and when it is used in a broader sense it still retains much of this idea. Here the perfect tense with the dative τῷ Θεῷ means: "I have been conducting myself toward God" (dative of relation), the tense already implying what the added phrase "until this day" emphasizes. The force is: "This is the kind of a man now before you." Paul is referring to the charges made yesterday (21:28), especially to the crowning one that he brought some Gentile into the forbidden Temple precincts. Over against these charges he puts the emphatic declaration that his conscience is clear regarding his conduct toward God and all that pertains to God.

The translation of our versions, "I have lived," has led some to think that Paul is speaking of his entire life, as a Jew as well as a Christian, as a bloody persecutor and as a chosen apostle. They then apply the good conscience to this entire career and show that a man may rage against the church with a good conscience as well as work with might and main for its upbuilding. Then the verb is stressed, namely that Paul lived "as God's citizen, as a member of God's commonwealth," although the idea of such a πόλις and such a citizenship is admittedly Greek and Roman and not Jewish although Paul is speaking to Jews. With these ideas another is associated, namely that Paul is summing up his whole address to the rioters of the day before. Underlying it all is the idea that anything Paul may say at any time, and anything anywhere recorded in Scripture, *must* have a most profound meaning. But the Scriptures were written for men generally in order that all might understand.

Paul's simple statement about himself is devoid of profundities. When the Jews crucified Christ, stoned Stephen, sent Paul to his frightful work, "good conscience" was openly, viciously violated. They plotted murder, used a traitor, suborned perjured witnesses, lied, hated, shed innocent blood, committed crime after crime — all with seared consciences. They trampled on the most elementary divine as well as human law. The whole world has ever so testified. Paul had his own awful share in it all. It is unwarranted to let Paul now cover all that with the cloak of a good conscience.

That perfect tense covers the charges preferred in 21:28. Paul's conduct has *not* been hostile to the people (the λαός, Israel), to the law (the νόμος, the divine Torah), nor to this place (God's Temple); in particular, he never dreamed of taking a Gentile such as Trophimus into the forbidden courts. By appealing to his conscience regarding these charges and naming God as its arbiter Paul does what Luther did at Worms: he had examined his conduct before God, he had found his conscience clear but invites any who think his conduct wrong to point out the wrong before God in order that his conscience may condemn him by admitting the guilt. That is the true use of conscience. It is always subject to God and, when it is mistaken, it is always instantly ready to bow to God when the mistake in conduct is pointed out.

We think that Paul speaks only regarding himself. Others have thought that his reference to "all good conscience toward God" intended to strike these Sanhedrists and to intimate to them that they could not say this for themselves. The implication: "Show me before God where my conscience has been and now is wrong!" seems sufficient here.

2) **But the high priest Ananias ordered those standing near him to smite his mouth.**

This is not the Ananias who is called high priest in the Gospels and in Acts 4:7, but the son of Nebedaeus who was nominated by Herod, King of Chalcis, and held this office from 48-59. He was accused of rapine and cruelty by the Samaritans and in 52 had to go to Rome to defend himself. He was killed by the *sicarii.* Josephus, *Ant.* 20, 5, 2; 6, 2; *Wars* 2, 12, 6;

17, 9. His order to strike Paul on the mouth is typical of the violent character of the man. The Sadducees were notorious for their arrogant manners even toward their colleagues (we have a sample in John 11:49). Those standing by were other Sanhedrists. Those who think of a formal session in which all the Sanhedrists were duly seated think "those standing by" were the attendants of the Sanhedrin. But these would be designated as ὑπηρέται and never as "those standing by." Paul was not turned over to the Sanhedrin and its police. The meeting was wholly informal, and many of the members were standing about in the hall.

The ugly act of Ananias' was wholly unprovoked, nasty and mean, and senseless into the bargain. The Sanhedrists were not servants who were to be ordered about. This high priest was in part asserting his authority for the benefit of the chiliarch, a mere subaltern, who had made bold to summon him, the exalted high priest, and the Sanhedrin. The high priest resented Paul's unabashed, manly bearing. This fellow Paul should have cringed and quavered; instead he presumed to speak of his good conscience and blameless conduct even in the very presence of his majesty, the high priest. Did someone strike Paul? We do not think so; some interpreters do. Of course, zealous police attendants would have leaped to execute the mighty one's order, but no such fellows were at hand. The chiliarch should have interfered at this point; a Roman could not be struck. Due to his usual brevity Luke does not report the chiliarch's reaction. If Paul had been struck, the chiliarch would probably have acted, and Luke would have had something to say about this.

3) **Then Paul said to him: Smite thee shall God, thou whitewashed wall! And thou, dost thou**

sit judging me according to the law and acting contrary to law orderest me to be smitten?

Ananias was facing the wrong man. The chiliarch might hesitate, but not so Paul. Instantly he turns to the arrogant fellow, his words charged with outraged anger. For ourselves let us say that Ananias got exactly what he deserved. Paul's ready reply is straight and stunning. The Greek is far more telling than the translation of our versions. The key word is placed forward with the fullest emphasis: "Smite thee shall God, thou whitewashed wall!" literally, "God is about" to do that very thing to thee. The perfect participle has its usual present connotation (like the verb in v. 1): still covered with whitewash. An ugly wall smeared over with whitewash pictures a hypocrite; Jesus used the same word in a similar figure and in the same sense in his denounciation in Matt. 23:27.

As Jesus did when he uttered his invectives, Paul proved the hypocrisy. "Thou" is emphatic; the structure is chiastic and more telling for this reason: the verbs are placed outside, the participles inside, and "to be smitten" is emphatically at the end. The word order of the entire reply is perfect Greek. The contrast between "judging according to the law" and "acting contrary to law" is intense because of the juxtaposition. Here was a fellow who was pretending to be a judge, to obey the supreme obligation of a judge, which is to follow the law and at the very beginning in his judge's seat he violates all law by the lawless order to strike Paul in the face. Surely, that went home. "Thou sittest judging" has been stressed to support the idea of a formal judicial session of the Sanhedrin, but the word need not have that implication. No chiliarch dared to turn a Roman over even to the Sanhedrin for trial. Some were standing, others were sitting, one of these was the high priest. The judgment the chiliarch desired to secure was not a legal verdict, but he hoped to learn something that might serve as a legal charge because it was preferred by responsible accusers. Paul's words imply no more. The very retort Paul made would have been impossible at a formal trial.

4) **But those standing near said, The high priest of God dost thou revile? And Paul said: I knew not, brethren, that he is high priest. For it has been written, Of the ruler of thy people thou shalt not speak basely.**

Here "those standing near" are again mentioned. No mere police attendants would venture to remonstrate with a defendant who was on trial before a supreme court. These were the Sanhedrists who were standing near Paul. They reprove him for the language he used toward the high priest. "Of God" points to the office as having been instituted by God himself. Even then they venture only to ask a question.

5) Paul promptly acknowledges his fault. This consists in the fact that he had spoken ill against the ruler of his people in ignorance. He had inadvertently sinned against an office. He makes this prompt acknowledgment on the basis of Exod. 22:28 (LXX). Even when a ruler does wrong, he must not be cursed because of his office, the LXX has the milder term. Ἐρεῖς is the future tense which is used in commands (from λέγω), here it is construed with the accusative. Paul says in effect that, if he had known that it was the high priest, he would have quietly borne the mean insult and committed the matter to God.

This obvious sense of Paul's reply has not satisfied all of the commentators. Paul's eyesight is introduced as a reason. Some attribute his weakness of the eyes to the blazing light on the road to Damascus as though the Lord had not fully restored Paul's sight! There is also the surmise that Ananias was not wearing his official robes or was not in his official seat. But he wore those robes only when he officiated, and at this meeting there was no official seat, the meeting being informal, being held in a hall in the castle. Again, Paul did not notice who it was that gave the order to smite him on the mouth. Irony is suggested: "I could not think that a man who gave such an order was really a high priest!" The climax is the claim that Luke recorded Paul as lying.

All these views are based on the assumption that Paul knew Ananias, knew that this individual was the high priest, from the seat he occupied, from his dress, from the preliminaries at this meeting, from something else. Yet Paul himself declares that he did not know him, the tense (the past perfect ᾔδειν is invariably used as imperfect) stating that he had not known him all along. The supposition that Ananias was not rightfully high priest at this time, was usurping the office, holding it temporarily, is contrary to the historical facts. So also is the claim that someone else presided. No one presides at an informal meeting, and no one did so here.

The casuistic efforts to clear Paul of all fault are untenable; Paul admits such fault as there was. The action of the Sanhedrists who reprove Paul reveals how men like the Pharisees could remain in office in the Sanhedrin under Sadducaic high priests such as Caiaphas and this wretched Ananias.

6) After having sketched a scene from the beginning of the meeting arranged by the chiliarch, Luke shows how the meeting came to an end. The wording plainly indicates that there was an interval between v. 5 and 6. We accept that fact and therefore do not try to link these two verses together. Some do this even in quite opposite ways. Paul's acknowledgment is said to have satisfied the party of the high priest, and this made Paul try to win also the Pharisees; but again, Paul saw that he had lost out with the high

priest and the Sadducees and so turned to the Pharisees as his only hope. These two views rather cancel each other.

Now Paul, on coming to realize that the one part consisted of Sadducees and the other of Pharisees, went on to shout in the Sanhedrin, Men and brethren, I myself am a Pharisee, a son of Pharisees. Concerning the hope and resurrection of the dead I am called in question. Having said this, there occurred a commotion of the Pharisees and Sadducees, and the crowd was divided. For the Sadducees declare there is no resurrection, nor angel, nor spirit, but the Pharisees confess both.

Since Paul had always known that the Sanhedrin was made up of both Sadducees and Pharisees, Luke's remark that is introduced with γνούς must mean more than that Paul happened to think of these two parties and with quick wit took advantage of that fact and thus caused a division in the Sanhedrin. Something that is not recorded by Luke but is contained in the participle γνούς, etc., had set the two parties against each other. This seems to be substantiated by ἔκραζεν ἐν τῷ συνεδρίῳ; Paul had to shout (descriptive imperfect) at the top of his voice. The Sadducees and the Pharisees were evidently engaged in a loud altercation, and Paul was quite forgotten for the moment.

These points are clear; everything that goes beyond them is guessing, some of it is unsatisfactory, for instance that the altercation took place in regard to the high priest, and that the Pharisees were rather pleased with Paul's sharp retort, or that Paul's address, "men and brethren," was intended to ignore the high priest in a pointed way. Regarding the latter, what about the same address in v. 1; and what about attributing such a low motive to a man like Paul? Luke writes, "in the Sanhedrin," yet some think that Paul was addressing only the Pharisees. The entire Sanhedrin was to know that Paul was a Pharisee. The force of the argument was this: a judicial body that was itself in large part composed of Pharisees could certainly not find fault with a man for being a Pharisee and holding to the main doctrinal contention of Pharisaism. This feature of the argument would, of course, have been just as strong if matters had been reversed, i. e., if Paul had been a Sadducee. In either case the one party would not, the other could not take exception.

"I am a Pharisee, a son of Pharisees," descended from Pharisee ancestry, intends to say, "a genuine Pharisee." In this very Sanhedrin Gamaliel had sat, a Pharisee, one of the great ornaments of Judaism (5:34), under whom Paul himself had received his education (22:3). If Paul had stopped with this, the casuists might arise and charge him with falsehood or at least with equivocation. But he at once adds in what respect he is a genuine Pharisee, namely for holding to the "hope and resurrection of men dead," *Totenauferstehung*. There are no articles in the Greek, hence both terms are used in their broad sense. We may regard the expression as a hendiadys: "hope of resurrection." The fact that this hope involved belief in angels and in spirits, and that Paul, of course, included both in his present confession, we see in a moment. All that we must add here is that any man who has a conviction such as this, especially if he be a Jew, is properly classed with the Pharisees, the outstanding exponents of this conviction. To this day we call those who reject the resurrection "modern Sadducees" although in other respects they may differ entirely from the ancient Sadducees. It is true, today "Pharisee" has come to designate another mark of this ancient sect; it now signifies a formalist or a hypocrite; but this is a late development in the use of the word. There in the Sanhedrin every man understood Paul's declaration exactly as he intended it: he was in no sense a

Sadducee, he was a Pharisee who held to the hope of the resurrection which was defended by all Pharisees against all Sadducees. We are such Pharisees to this day.

More must be added. This hope of the resurrection was the ancient faith of Israel. The claim of the modern Sadducees that the Old Testament was not acquainted with this faith is refuted by Abraham who believed that God could raise his son Isaac from the dead (Heb. 11:9). The Old Testament is rich in similar proof. The Pharisees were genuinely Biblical in regard to this doctrine, and this Jewish sect dates back to the days of the return from the Babylonian exile. Furthermore, the resurrection was the central doctrine of the apostolic gospel (2:32; 3:15; 4:10; 5:28; 13:30, 34; I Cor. 15:4-20). It was so essential because of the resurrection of Jesus as the Christ. Jesus proclaimed his own resurrection (John 2:18-22; Matt. 8:31; 9:31; 10:34), promised to raise up all the dead (John 5:25), especially his believers (John 6:39, 40, 44, 54), rose as promised, and gave his chosen witnesses "many infallible proofs" thereof (Acts 1:3). The folly of the Sadducees in denying the resurrection is exposed in Matt. 22:23, etc. Gamaliel himself threw cold water on the Sanhedrin's readiness to slay the apostles for preaching the resurrection of Jesus (Acts 5:33, etc.). The Christian teaching of the resurrection drew many Pharisees to the faith; we note some of them in 15:5.

Before a body that was composed in part of so many Pharisees Paul says, "*I* am called in question," *I* on the matter of the resurrection, the one great thing which makes me, too, a Pharisee. That was certainly preposterous. We may translate κρίνομαι, "I am being judged," but even then the Sanhedrin is now not in a court session in a trial of Paul. The following verses answer that assumption. Called together to furnish the chiliarch enlightenment in regard to why Paul's death was so violently called for on the previous day, Paul himself tells both the Sanhedrin and the chiliarch what the trouble is regarding him: like the Pharisees, he holds to the hope of the resurrection. Paul was providentially led to make this declaration by something that had once more made evident the opposition that existed between the two sects represented in the Sanhedrin. The charges preferred on the preceding day (21:28) had practically declared that Paul was guilty of teaching a false, a new religion that was subversive of the λαός (Israel), the law (the Old Testament), and the Temple (of what it stood for). Here in the Sanhedrin itself came this opening which enables Paul to declare that the very central part of his teaching constituted what Israel, the Old Testament, and the Temple stood for as every Pharisee knew and maintained, the hope of the blessed resurrection.

Various opinions have been held in regard to Paul's act. Was he really a Pharisee as he declares? See what he says to the Christian Philippians among whom there were scarcely any former Jews, Phil. 3:5. The whole Sanhedrin knew him to be a Christian (24:5). Deception is completely ruled out. Was Paul shrewd and cunning to "divide and conquer"? Did he follow the Jesuitical principle that the end justifies the means? The answer is that the two parties of the Sanhedrin clashed before him in some way that led him to cry out as he did.

7) We see this when Luke states that, after Paul had said this, a *στάσις*, a "commotion" (in 19:40 we translate "riot") occurred "of the Pharisees and Sadducees," two genitives and only one article, which regards both as one body (R. 787). Our versions are inaccurate. This was not a "dissension between" the two but a joint commotion. This riotous proceeding was, of course, due to the division of the parties, but Luke states this separately.

8) Luke explains to his reader (γάρ) that the Sadducees maintain (λέγουσι) that there is no resurrection and, consistent with this, that there is also no angel nor spirit. They held that no spirit exists save God; that the human soul consisted of rarified matter and disappeared with the body (συναφανίσαι); that God is not concerned with our doing or not doing evil, and that each man may do as he pleases; that death ends everything without reward or punishment hereafter. Josephus, *Wars* 2, 8, 14 adds that their treatment even of each other was wild and barbarous; see also *Ant.* 18, 1, 4. A lurid light is thus cast on this ruling faction among the Jews, which embodied the high priesthood itself. While Sadducees and Pharisees combined against Christ and Christianity, they were at sword's point among themselves. This strong opposition broke out at this time. Paul had not caused the clash as already stated. Chrysostom speaks of three points of difference, and it is now recognized that ἀμφότερα is freely used with reference to more than two, in 19:16 with reference to as many as seven.

9) **And there occurred a great clamor. And some of the scribes of the party of the Pharisees, having arisen, began to battle fiercely, saying: Nothing base do we find in this man! But if a spirit did speak to him or an angel — ? And when the commotion became great, the chiliarch, afraid lest Paul be torn in two by them, ordered the military down to snatch him out of their midst and to bring him into the castle.**

This is not a court scene. Nor is it possible that a proper court session should terminate as here described. At the trial of Jesus a horrible scene was enacted (Matt. 26:67) but not until the court session had pronounced its death verdict and had adjourned. Here no court is convened. Most of the Sanhedrists never even sat down. We are able to discover no trace of formality anywhere.

Κραυγή is the word to express a roar of voices as when the spectators at a college football game cheer their side on to victory. This was an exhibition, indeed: the highest dignitaries of Judaism surging in a mass, wildly gesticulating and shouting at each other in the most frantic Oriental fashion. The circumstantial participle ἀναστάντες has nothing to do with getting up from seats; it is exceedingly common as introducing many kinds of action. Here these scribes "started up" to fight the Sadducees with their shouts. All were at it, but Luke has preserved only the shouts of "some of the scribes of the party of the Pharisees." One of the regular names for the Sanhedrin was "the high priests, the elders, and the scribes." These last named were graduates of the rabbinical schools who were learned in the law, "lawyers" in that sense of the word. The most eminent were made members of the Sanhedrin; Gamaliel had been one of these. Most of them were Pharisees. They functioned especially when questions regarding the interpretation of points in the Torah arose. Some of them now went into strenuous action because they felt that they were the ones who were most entitled to speak.

The imperfect is inchoative and, of course, also descriptive: "they began to battle fiercely (διά)." Two of their shouts were: they found nothing bad or base (κακόν) in Paul, and a spirit might have spoken to him. Yet we should be wrong to conclude that these scribes of the Pharisees were greatly concerned about Paul; they were defeating the Sadducees, and in that battle Paul was only a pawn. It would not do to bank too strongly on their verdict that they find nothing wrong with Paul.

Interesting is the aposiopesis, deliberate suppression of a part of a sentence: "But if a spirit did speak to him or angel — ?" i. e., what about it? This was a direct challenge to the Sadducees who believed in neither. This may have been prompted by Paul's recital on the previous day (22:6, etc.). The word "spirit" is more indefinite, "angel" more definite. The Holy Spirit cannot be referred to because the Sadducees were not disbelievers in God; throughout the Gospels no Jew ever took exception to a mention of the Holy Spirit. Some Pharisees became converts, but we know of no Sadducees that were converted.

10) Πολλῆς is predicative and not attributive (our versions). The commotion rose to such a pitch that the chiliarch became frightened lest they tear Paul to pieces: the Sadducees were enraged at Paul, the Pharisees were trying to shield him from attack. The chiliarch promptly called up to the military force on the floor above, where they were in barracks, to snatch Paul out of the seething mass and to be taking him into their *castra* or military quarters. The first infinitive is properly aorist, the second present. Στράτευμα is not "soldiers" but the military, any part of the garrison; and the aorist neuter participle καταβάν = "having come down." It ought to be understood that the chiliarch had no soldiers with him; he and Paul had gone down to the meeting alone. The chiliarch did not rush out to the fortress to get soldiers; all he did was to shout his command at the door of the lower hall to the force on the upper floor. Luke makes this so plain that one wonders why some fail to understand him (see v. 1).

After Paul and the chiliarch had left, the Sanhedrists could fight on as long as they pleased. The pagan chiliarch must have been edified by the exhibition he had witnessed. But the chiliarch had gained nothing by his attempt at a meeting with the Sanhedrin; in fact, he was more in the dark than ever about this Roman who somehow made both the Jewish populace and the Sanhedrin go wild by his presence.

11) Up to this time Paul had had only the divine intimation that he would be bound (a prisoner) and placed into the hands of Gentiles in Jerusalem, and this prophecy had been fulfilled. Now further light falls on his path.

Now on the following night the Lord, having stepped up to him, said: Continue to be of good cheer! For as thou didst testify the things concerning me in Jerusalem, so it is necessary for thee to testify also in Rome.

The present imperative need not imply that Paul was downhearted. It was not because "Paul never needed Jesus more than now" that the Lord appeared to him, ἐπιστάς, came suddenly upon him. This was only the second night of his confinement, and he was the last man to lose courage quickly. The Lord is now adding more light of prophecy and doing so not through others but in his own person. The imperative θάρσει, "continue to be of good cheer (comfort, courage)," looks forward to the long imprisonment ahead of Paul. A spirit, as full of energy as his, might not hold up under such long inactivity as the weary months dragged along, and the clouds did not once lift. The Lord is fortifying him in advance for that. He would very often lean on what the Lord himself now reveals to him.

The commendation of his past testimony in Jerusalem should not be overlooked That address from the castle steps and that declaration before the Sanhedrists have the Lord's full approval. Both were made under trying circumstances, and Paul is to know that he has made no mistakes and is not to tell himself that, perhaps, if he had acted otherwise he would not find himself in confinement for so long a time. This was comfort. But far more. "It is necessary" for the Lord's own plans regarding Paul that his wish and desire to testify also in Rome be fulfilled (see 19:21; and compare Rom. 1:10-15 which was written in Corinth before this journey to Jerusalem). Paul will not go to Rome in the way he had hoped to go; he will be taken there as a prisoner. But he will testify in Rome (effective aorist) — the very thing for which he wanted to get to Rome. The two εἰς are static, R. 593.

Here the great theme of Acts is brought out clearly. The center of the great gospel work is to be transferred *from Jerusalem to Rome.* We are in the year 58, in May, just after Pentecost; in 66 the war would begin that would end in the destruction of Jerusalem and the abolition of the Jews as a nation. The time was getting brief during which Jerusalem would continue to figure as the center of Christendom.

The most important thing is the Lord's statement that Paul is *to testify in Rome* the things he had *testified in Jerusalem.* Not as Paul had testified in Gentile lands to Gentiles, where he had labored so long, but as he had testified in Jerusalem to *Jews.* The point of this statement is the fact that a great work is awaiting Paul in Rome, a work not among the Gentiles in Rome but among *the host of Jews in Rome,* among whom no gospel work had as yet been done. There were eleven large Jewish synagogues in Rome. The Christians in Rome had left these synagogues entirely alone. The Lord is now appointing Paul to convey the gospel to all these Roman Jews. This is precisely what Paul did immediately on reaching Rome. See Luke's account in 28:17, etc. For two years Paul pursued this task among the Jews in Rome. He converted at least four or five of the synagogues in Rome. To this great body of converted Jews in Rome the Epistle to the Hebrews was addressed. See the full details in the Introduction to Hebrews.

12) **But when day came, the Jews, having made a compact, put themselves under a curse, declaring neither to eat nor to drink until they should kill Paul.**

Moreover, they were more than forty who made for themselves this sworn plot, who, having come to the high priests and elders, said: With a curse we did put ourselves under a curse to taste nothing until we shall kill Paul. Now, therefore, do you on your part with the Sanhedrin inform the chiliarch that he should bring him down to you as being about to decide more accurately the matters concerning him; but we on our part, before he gets near, are ready to make away with him.

One is astounded at the open criminality of the Jews. One high priest after another, Sanhedrists, and a large number of others become guilty of it. Read Josephus in regard to this period, he has much more to report. A συστροφή is a compact, and συνωμοσία is a sworn pact, *Verschwoerung.* To place oneself under a curse not to eat or to drink (effective aorist infinitives) is to promise under oath not to do either, and that God's curse may strike those who fail to carry out the promise. This was similar to a vow with a curse for nonfulfillment. "Until they should kill Paul" (R. 974, etc.) marks the limit to which they swore to fast. If they should fail to kill him according to the terms of their oath they would starve to death. It was to be his death by murder or their own death by voluntary starvation. But what is the oath of deliberate murderers worth? This self-anathematization sounds awful, but the rabbis could dissolve the *cherem*, Hebrew for ἀνάθεμα. None of these men starved to death. By their murderous oath they only brought God into their crime, so accursed were they.

13) Forty had entered upon this "swearing together," a number that was large enough to insure success if their cunning scheme to get Paul out of the custody of the soldiers succeeded.

14) But they needed to have the cooperation of "the high priests and the elders." The former were

Ananias and those of high priestly connection in the Sanhedrin, all of them Sadducees, of course; see 4:5, 6 for "the high priests" at the time of Caiaphas. "The elders" might include all the rest of the Sanhedrists; but this cannot be the case here, for the Pharisees mentioned in v. 9 would not dare to learn about the plot. We conclude that at first a few of the leaders were approached by the conspirators who then confided in those whom they could trust to keep secret their scheme. This is stated outright just as though these murderous fellows knew what kind of men their great religious leaders were. The Hebraistic "with an anathema we did anathematize ourselves," the dative for the Hebrew infinitive absolute, means: "we have most solemnly sworn," R. 531. We must notice the difference between ἀνάθεμα and ἀνάθημα, the former denoting something devoted to God for destruction (hence "a curse"), the latter something devoted to God as a gift (hence "a votive offering," Luke 21:5). Verbs of tasting govern the genitive.

15) These Sanhedrists are to induce the entire Sanhedrin to inform the chiliarch "in order that he may bring Paul down to you" (purpose clause), and ὑμᾶς is modified by the following participle: "as about to decide more accurately the matters concerning him," τὰ περὶ αὐτοῦ. The addition of ὡς indicates the ostensible reason; the real reason was far otherwise. It is worth noting that διαγινώσκειν never means, "to make a judicial investigation or to render a judicial decision," C.-K. 251; nor would "more accurate" fit that idea. The Sanhedrin had no power to try Paul. We have shown that in v. 1-10 there is no evidence that a trial was held. Paul was under Roman authority. The chiliarch had called in the Sanhedrin in order to get data in regard to any crime Paul might have committed; it is to this procedure that the verb refers: "to decide for the benefit of the chiliarch more accurately these matters re-

garding Paul." The idea was to let the chiliarch know that the Sanhedrin was now in a better position than it had been on the day before to procure the desired information for him. Of course, it would be necessary for him "to bring down" Paul as the Sanhedrin would have need of him.

What this bringing down implies is indicated by the promise that, before Paul gets near (aorist) to the Sanhedrin, these conspirators are prepared to make away with him, the very verb that was noted as being so significant in 22:20. This time the Sanhedrists would be approaching the chiliarch, and not he them. On his invitation they came to him; now on theirs he would naturally come to them. The first meeting was held in the lower hall of the fortress, on the upper floor of which were the quarters of the soldiers; this proposed meeting was to be held in the hall of the Sanhedrin itself (see v. 1). Paul would have to be conducted across the Temple court, and even if a few soldiers were with him as a guard, forty resolute Jews, armed with daggers, would soon do away with Paul. These forty did not belong to the infamous *sicarii,* assassins, that Jewish scourge which helped to bring on the war, one of whose victims Ananias himself became (see v. 2); but they intended to operate in the same way with daggers concealed under their cloaks, getting close to their intended victim and then suddenly rushing in and murdering him.

What a horrible plot, and these leading Sanhedrists were party to it! Hate blinds utterly. Suppose that Paul had been put to death in this way, was there not a danger that the chiliarch himself might be stabbed in the mêlée?

16) **But the son of Paul's sister having heard of the ambush, after drawing near and going into the castle, made report to Paul. And Paul, having called to himself one of the centurions, said, Take**

this young man away to the chiliarch; for he has something to report to him. Accordingly he, having taken him, brought him to the chiliarch and said, The prisoner Paul, having called me to him, requested that this young man be brought to thee as having something to tell thee.

"The best laid plans of mice and men gang aft aglee," Burns. Providence thwarted the plot of the conspirators in the most simple way. Providence has a way of doing such things.

So Paul has a sister, and she has a son who is already a νεανίας, a young man between twenty and forty. That is all that we actually know. Guesses are, of course, built up about these meager facts: this sister was much older than Paul who had lived at her house in Jerusalem when he studied under Gamaliel, and this nephew was now studying under this same teacher and thus learned of the plot. Others think that the sister lived in Tarsus, but that her son had come to Jerusalem in order to study there. So also we have no intimation as to how the young man heard about the plot. The accusative is used to designate what one hears. Whether he himself was a Christian or not, he certainly was concerned about his uncle's imprisonment and what the Jews were doing about it. The moment he discovers the dastardly plot he goes to warn Paul.

Luke's description is detailed and graphic and delightful to read. Hence he doubles the participles, "coming near and going into the *castra,*" the soldiers' quarters in Antonia. That first participle refers to the outer guard or sentries who had to be approached first. It cannot be construed with the preceding as explaining how he came to hear of the plot: "having come upon them" (R., *W. P.*); for then it ought to precede ἀκούσας, and the preposition used should be ἐπί and not παρά. As a nephew of the prisoner, a harmless young man at that, he had no difficulty in being admitted to see Paul.

17) Paul was in charge of one of the centurions; 21:32 shows that there were several. His request that the young man be taken to the chiliarch naturally met with no difficulty since Paul was a Roman.

18) Luke even records the centurion's report to his superior officer. Ὁ δέσμιος is a noun, "the prisoner." This term refers to anyone who is in confinement. The supposition that the word means "bound to a soldier," whether by one or by two chains, is unwarranted. In 22:29 the chiliarch was frightened to discover that he had put fetters upon a Roman; see 22:30 on this point. Paul was in military custody, and not even a crime had as yet been charged against him. The centurion states the facts of Paul's request in exact military fashion.

19) **And the chiliarch, having taken him by his hand and having withdrawn in private, began to inquire, What is it that thou hast to report to me? And he said: The Jews did agree to make request of thee in order that thou shalt bring down Paul to the Sanhedrin as desiring to inquire something more accurately concerning him. Do not thou, therefore, be persuaded by them; for some of their men, more than forty, are in ambush, such as did put themselves under a curse neither to eat nor to drink until they shall make away with him. And they are ready now, expecting the promise from thee.**

The young man was a bit frightened to appear before the chiliarch himself. In order to reassure him the chiliarch takes hold of his hand in kindly, paternal fashion and withdraws with him in private, κατ' ἰδίαν, a set phrase. When the two are by themselves, he starts to inquire (inchoative) about what the young man has to report. Several questions were probably required, but Luke condenses the whole information. We cannot construe "asked him privately" (R. V.), for the prepositional phrase would then come before the verb and thus be emphatic, which it cannot be; "went aside privately" (A. V.) is correct, the phrase coming after the participle and being unemphatic.

20) In the young man's report the simple plural "the Jews did agree" is not intended to refer to the whole nation; as in v. 12, this is common speech even to this day. Ὅπως is again final (v. 15); the request has this purpose; ἵνα would not do here, for this might refer to what is requested. We have already explained what leading down into the Sanhedrin means (v. 15), and how this was vital for the plot. Here the young man says μέλλων, the singular, as though the plea (ὡς) was that the chiliarch would want to know "something more accurate" about Paul, while in v. 15 the plural predicates this of the Sanhedrists. Both are true, either one or both pleas could be put forward. The masculine μέλλων is not intended to refer to the neuter "Sanhedrin," an anacoluthic substitute for the neuter μέλλον.

21) When the young man tells the chiliarch not to be persuaded by them (the Sanhedrists; aorist subjunctive in negative commands) he innocently voices his own great fear that the chiliarch might yield to the persuasion (aorist to express committing a single act) and is certainly not giving directions to this chief commander. He just begs him not to yield. With γάρ he explains the whole story as we already know it from Luke's account and adds only that the conspirators are now expecting to get the chiliarch's promise regarding the next day.

22) **Accordingly the chiliarch let the young man go, having charged him to divulge to no one**

that thou didst give information on these things to me.

Οὖν refers to all that the young man had told. The infinitive after παραγγείλας is indirect discourse, while the ὅτι clause after ἐκλαλῆσαι is direct discourse; but this is not a mixture of *oratio obliqua et recta* (B.-D. 470, 2; R. 442, 1047) for the obvious reason that each *oratio* has its owns governing verb; in a real mixture both the direct and the indirect *oration* follow one verb of saying. Paul's nephew is not to breathe a word about what he has done. To do so would probably cost him his own life, and the chiliarch may have thought of that; but the chiliarch certainly also wanted completely to veil his own action.

23) **And having called to himself certain two of the centurions, he said: Make ready two hundred soldiers in order that they may march to Caesarea and seventy cavalrymen and two hundred slingers, from the third hour of the night; and to provide beasts in order that, having mounted Paul, they might bring him safely to Felix, the governor — having written a letter having this form.**

The more we read about this chiliarch, the less we think of him. Here he orders out a small army, and that during the night, in order to transfer Paul the distance of seventy miles to Caesarea. With so large a force he could at once have taken Paul away; and for a swift, secret journey by night a small troup of cavalry would have been the proper thing and not a lot of heavy infantry. These remarks are made by a nonmilitary man, but they must stand, nevertheless. The analogy of εἷς τις makes it certain that δύο τινάς (some reverse the words) does not mean "some two," no choice being made (R., *W. P.*), but as R. 742 has it: "certain two" or "two certain ones" who were specially selected, B.-D. 301, 1. These two centurions are to have the troops ready to start the march (aorist) at nine o'clock that night, ἀπό, from that "third hour of the night" on. The night starts at 6 P. M.; the day at 6 A. M., according to Roman reckoning.

It is agreed that the στρατιῶται are hoplites, heavy armed infantry of the line or legionaries, and the ἱππεῖς the regular Roman cavalry. But nobody knows anything certain about the δεξιολάβοι, a word that is not found again except once in the seventh and again in the tenth century. See Meyer's discussion. The word says that they took something in their right hands. Our versions guess "spearmen," taking their cue from the Vulgate "lancers." Our guess is "slingers." It is agreed that they were afoot.

24) Here the *oratio* is mixed. It changes from the direct to the indirect after the one verb εἶπεν. The centurions are to have "beasts" ready in order to place Paul upon them and thus bring him safely through to Felix who is here called "the governor," thus indicating his office by a general term. We think these beasts were asses because anybody can ride them and almost everybody uses them in Palestine, and because we do not think Paul could have managed a horse, and all he had to do was to travel as rapidly as the infantry. Having ourselves ridden asses in the Orient and seen them used there, we venture this opinion. Some think of baggage, Paul's belongings, because of the plural "beasts"; we have our doubts about the baggage. A change of animals was required for Paul.

Felix was powerful and unprincipled. He and his brother Pallas were originally slaves and then became freedmen in the house of a noble Roman lady, Antonia, the mother of Claudius. Pallas became the favorite and the minister of the emperor and in 52 secured the post of procurator of Judea for his brother. Since he was supported by his brother, Felix felt that he could do any wrong he chose. Tacitus writes: "With all cruelty and lust he exercised the power of a king with the spirit of a slave." Suetonius reports that he had three wives in succession: Drusilla, princess of Mauritania; another Drusilla, daughter of Herod Agrippa I and sister of Herod Agrippa II, who left her first husband; the third is unknown. Felix ruled seven or eight years until he was recalled by Nero in 60. He lost his position when Pallas was put to death in 63.

25) The Greek can continue with a nominative participle which is dependent on εἶπε in v. 23. This construction cannot be imitated in English, so our versions begin a new sentence. Roman law required an *elogium*, a written statement, when a subordinate referred a case to his superior, and this the chiliarch was now providing. It really makes no difference whether this document was drawn up in Latin or in Greek; in either case we have the original and not a composition by Luke which contained only the substance. The expression "having this form" (τὸν τύπον τοῦτον), the Latin *exemplum*, means "this wording," *Wortfassung* (Meyer), and not merely this approximate form or content. Rather decisive in regard to this point is the fact that Luke does not attempt to reproduce the document which Festus knew he had to send to the emperor (26:26); that one was sent is certain, but Luke says nothing about it. If Luke knew only the contents of the chiliarch's letter, there is no reason why he should not have been satisfied to relate just that. It would have fully answered his purpose. Because he knew the exact wording he gave it. The letter, too, speaks for its own genuineness, especially the falsification which it contains regarding the time when the chiliarch learned that Paul was a Roman. It is generally conceded that it was an easy matter for Paul or even for Luke himself to hear the letter read and thus to retain it word for word.

26) **Claudius Lysias to the Most Excellent Governor Felix Greeting!** See 15:23 for the ancient

form of letter writing: 1) the writer, 2) the person addressed, 3) the common χαίρειν as a greeting. We now learn the chiliarch's name: his *cognomen* or family name "Lysias" was Greek and a common family name; his *nomen gentile* (indicating the *gens* to which he belonged) was Roman and recalls the emperor Claudius. This circumstance and the fact that he bought his Roman citizenship seem to indicate that he was a freedman like Felix himself. Lysias and his soldiers were not Roman legionaries but auxiliaries. Κράτιστος = "Your Excellency," see Luke 1:4; and "governor" was generally used as a designation for the provincial rulers, in Luke 3:1 for even the emperor.

27) **This man, seized by the Jews and about to be made away with by them, on coming up with the military, I rescued, having learned that he is a Roman. And wanting to know fully the cause on account of which they were accusing him I brought him down into their Sanhedrin; whom I found accused about questions of their law, having no accusation deserving death or bonds. But a plot having been disclosed to me,** (one that) **would be against the man, at once I sent him to thee, having charged also his accusers to make declaration against him before thee.**

It was the business of Lysias to report to the governor all the facts and these in their proper order. He failed on both scores. He says nothing whatever about having put Paul in chains and ordering him to be examined with scourges. We know why. He says that he rescued (second aorist middle of ἐξαιρέω) Paul after having learned that he was a Roman.

The Greek is beyond question. The aorist participle μαθών (from μανθάνω) can express only action that is coincident with or antecedent to that of the main verb, it cannot express subsequent action. Lysias says that he learned that Paul was a Roman and *then* rescued him. Bengel rightly calls this a lie. A few shield the chiliarch by saying that his military brevity makes his report seem inaccurate on this point. The trouble is the great accuracy which makes the deviation from the fact stand out. A relative clause would have told the truth: "whom I found to be a Roman." Lysias makes it appear that he nobly rescued a Roman from fatal attack whereas he really imagined he was capturing an Egyptian rebel and was squelching a riot. He counted on the governor's inability to find out these details and, in case he did find them out, on explaining them so as to escape blame. Among all the Roman officers we meet in the New Testament this chiliarch makes the poorest showing.

28, 29) He reports correctly regarding the Sanhedrin and what he discovered about Paul from it. Paul was in some way being accused "concerning questions of their (religious) law." So Gallio had found and promptly dismissed the entire charge as not belonging before a Roman court (18:14, etc.). Lysias adds that he found no accusation which, if it were established as true, was deserving of the penalty of death or of bonds in the sense of imprisonment. In other words, he writes that, as far as he could discover, Paul should be set free.

30) Why, then, had he not set him free? In order to save Paul from a plot. He turns the entire case over to Felix in order that he may decide whether there is anything worth-while in the Jewish charges. This, too, was not honest, because he knew the question at issue was concerning the resurrection (v. 6) and that on that point the Sadducees opposed Paul just as they opposed all Pharisees. The fact was, the chiliarch wanted to get rid of this case with which he had already burnt his fingers, and with which he had from the beginning really not known what to do. He had to have some

reason for sending Paul to the governor and thus getting rid of him and uses this matter of the plot.

The construction, a genitive absolute followed by a future infinitive, shows the flexibility of the Greek. The future infinitive is rare in the New Testament, and the accusative absolute has virtually disappeared. For this reason Luke did not write μηνυθὲν ἐπιβουλὴν ἔσεσθαι, B.-D. 424. He uses the genitive absolute, "a plot having been disclosed to me," and then adds the future infinitive in indirect discourse, "that it will be against the man," which is both neat and lucid in the Greek.

So Lysias promptly sent Paul to Felix, having charged also the accusers to make declaration (λέγειν) against him before thee (common use of ἐπί, R. 603). A few texts add the perfect passive imperative ἔρρωσο (see the plural in 15:29), a stereotyped form: "Farewell," literally, "become and remain strong." The question of its retention or rejection belongs to the province of the text critics.

31) **The soldiers, therefore, according to what had been ordered for them, having taken up Paul, brought him by night to Antipatris. And on the morrow, having let the cavalry go away with him, returned to the castle.**

The perfect passive participle states that the orders received from the chiliarch were duly executed; all were to march to Antipatris, the seventy cavalrymen alone were to go on from there. Antipatris was forty-two miles from Jerusalem, twenty-six from Caesarea. The question is raised whether, starting at nine o'clock, these soldiers could march forty-two miles before morning. Even if it took them until noon, it was a strenucus tour, indeed. The old Capharsaba was rebuilt by Herod the Great and named Antipatris in honor of his father Antipater; it is now a miserable Mohammedan village.

32) Although Paul rode he must have been exhausted. But the orders were to push right on with only the cavalry. The foolish orders of this chiliarch are quite ridiculous. Riding into Antipatris with 480 armed men, Paul must have been amused, indeed. Think of a lowly apostle with such an army as his escort! The gospel does stir up some strange actions in the world.

33) **Who, having come to Caesarea and having delivered the letter to the governor, presented also Paul to him. And having read it and having inquired from what kind of a province he was and having learned that he was from Cilicia, he said, I will hear thee fully whenever also thy accusers shall be at hand, ordering that he be guarded in the praetorium of Herod.**

It must have been a weary man who tottered into the governor's presence. Παρέστησαν is the first aorist because it is transitive; the second aorist is identical in form but is intransitive.

34) Ποῖος (never used with reference to persons, B.-D. 298, 2) may be general: "from what province," instead of specific: "from what kind of a province," but the thought is the same. The question was important for it referred to jurisdiction. While Cilicia was not an independent Roman province, it was under the propraetor of Syria who ruled it through a legate. Paul had been arrested in Jerusalem and was thus under the jurisdiction of the procurator of Judea; but being a native of Cilicia, his case, if it involved insurrection, might have to be heard before the propraetor of Syria.

35) "I will hear thee fully" (διά in the verb) means as a judge. Felix expects the accusers to whom Lysias refers to put in their appearance. Here we have a case where the aorist participle κελεύσας might be conceived as denoting subsequent action and thus

having a future sense, for the order remanding Paul to the praetorium certainly followed the promise to hear Paul in due time; but the Greek implies no more than that the order was coincident, R. 861.

Herod's praetorium = the palace of Herod the Great in Caesarea, now the official residence of the praetor Felix when he was in this city, his capital. Here he, of course, had his force of soldiers. Paul is merely placed in military custody and not remanded to a prison cell. He was confined to the palace which he could not leave. He wore no manacles or chains. This was due to the fact that he was a Roman. Up to this point no specific charges against him were known; he was held only because it was expected that charges would be preferred during the next few days.

CHAPTER XXIV

PAUL HELD BY FELIX IN CAESAREA

1) **Now after five days there came down the hight priest Ananias in company with certain elders and a spokesman, one Tertullus, who informed the governor against Paul.**

It is natural to count these five days from the time of Paul's arrival at Caesarea; moreover, they have nothing to do with the counting of the twelve days mentioned in v. 10. It took this delegation at least two full days to make the journey from Jerusalem. They must have learned about Paul's transfer the day after it was effected. So they had moved rapidly in order to appear already "after five days." Ananias is the chief accuser perhaps because of 23:3; the μετά phrase places the elders in a secondary position as being "in company with" Ananias. And we translate, "certain elders," πρεσβυτέρων τινῶν, and not "some elders," τινῶν τῶν πρεσβυτέρων. This was not a committee of the Sanhedrin as such that had been duly sent to represent that body; their spokesman does not venture to say that. The opinion that the Sadducees had placated the Pharisees (23:7, etc.) and had gotten together with them in bringing action against Paul is untenable. These few elders in company with Ananias were friends of his, perhaps all were Sadducees as he was. While all were Sanhedrists, their importance extended no farther than this.

Ananias had employed "one Tertullus" (τίς is used by Luke when he introduces new persons) to act as the ῥήτωρ, *orator forensis*, "spokesman," advocate, "prosecuting attorney" (R., *W. P.*), when bringing charges against Paul on behalf of his clients. These lawyers seem to have been as numerous in those days as they are in ours and looked for business over the entire empire. We have not been able to verify the claim that "Tertullus" was a common name among them. The idea that he was employed in this case because these Sanhedrists did not know the mode of legal procedure, is incorrect. For years all the high priests and the Sanhedrin had had all sorts of legal affairs with the Roman procurators and certainly knew all the formalities; it was their business to know them.

The supposition that the proceedings had to be conducted in Latin and that for this reason Tertullus was taken along is also groundless. Paul may have understood enough Latin to follow the address of this rhetor, but he himself certainly replied in Greek, and if he was permitted to use Greek in his defense, the same privilege would be granted his accusers, and all these Sanhedrists knew Greek, all understood Paul's defense. All the proceedings in regard to Jesus before Pilate were conducted in Greek; so also the proceedings before Gallio in Corinth (17:6, etc). The letter of Lysias to Felix was drawn up in Greek. The short address of Tertullus contains so many hapaxlegomena as to make it certain that Luke reports the very original and that this was Greek. Tertullus seems to have been brought along more as an ornament than for any other purpose. Perhaps someone had suggested bringing him and hoped thereby the more to impress the governor. This is the best we are able to say.

"Came down" is the proper word, both physically (Caesarea lying on the seacoast, compare 9:30) and ethically (one always goes up to Jerusalem and down when leaving it). Οἵτινες = "they being such as," and often has causal force; here, "these were the ones who" accused Paul. The aorist ἐνεφάνισαν (the same verb used in 23:15, 22), "they informed the governor against

Paul," is elucidated in the following where we see how they did this. The tense does not imply that they first lodged information and that Paul was then called to appear. Because of the context, "to inform or lodge information" has a legal sense; the information consisted of an accusation presented to a judge.

2) **And he having been called, Tertullus began to accuse him, saying, etc.**

Luke does not need to go into detail and relate that the delegation sent in word of its presence, asked an audience in order to lodge their charges against Paul, and that a time was set for them to appear. Felix sat as the judge. Paul was called; nothing was done until he was present. The Romans always brought accusers and accused face to face before the judge. Paul "was called," he was not brought in. No soldiers stood beside him, and he was not treated as a prisoner, for he was merely held to see whether any charges would be preferred against him. Besides, as a Roman he had to be treated with consideration. "Began to accuse him" means only that the thing was done with due formality.

Blass has stirred up discussion in regard to the brevity of this address which, according to him, is "so bungling that one might come to surmise that Luke intended to persiflage this rhetor as an *infantissimus.*" This induces Blass to adopt the longer version in spite of the weak textual evidence in its favor (v. 6, etc.). Others follow him or at least assume an abbreviation of the entire address. We decline to follow this lead. The preamble is so genuine in every word that it certainly was uttered just as it is recorded. In v. 4 Tertullus himself states to Felix that he will not be tedious but will speak "concisely." Exactly this he does, and most wisely. The indictment ought to be put tersely. The more to the point it is, the more effective will it prove to be. The unsubstantiated insertion only weakens it and is not an indictment. Tertullus knew his business well. Tertullus had a miserably poor case but certainly made the most of it.

Much peace obtaining through thee and reforms occurring for this nation through thy providence both every way and everywhere we accept them, most excellent Felix, with all thankfulness!

This is the so-called *captatio benevolentiae* which is used by ancient and by modern orators in order to gain the favor of the hearer. Some authorities in homiletics have advised its employment even in sermons. It is always dangerous. Unless it is done perfectly it has the opposite effect. It then appears to beg the question by seeking to win by favor and not by the merit of the cause and betrays in advance the weakness of a cause which needs such an appeal. It is vacuous in sermons, for the hearers have come for the very purpose of gratefully receiving the pulpit message. Tertullus chooses his words with utmost care. One sentence is enough, but the flattery is spread on thick.

In order to get the full force of the choice expressions used we must catch what is implied. Thus the first terse genitive absolute, "much peace obtaining through thee," refers to the special honor accruing to a governor when he could be called *Pacator provinciae*. Tertullus is suggesting that Felix deserves this high title. Here read Josephus, *Ant.* 20, 8, 9, etc. Felix did put down some impostors but caused worse conflicts. He used the *sicarii* ("assassins") who became worse than ever (see 21:38), had them murder the successor of Ananias, caused the worst friction in Caesarea, was finally accused by the Jews in Rome, and removed from office by Nero — "much peace" from such a *pacator!*

The same is true regarding the "reforms occurring for this nation (Tertullus was not a Jew) through thy providence both every way and everywhere." They existed only in the insincere imagination of Tertullus. Here again προνοία must not escape attention. It is the Latin *providentia* and appears on many Roman coins where it is combined with the name Caesar: *Providentia Caesaris.* Tertullus suggests that Felix deserves to have his great "providence" immortalized in some such way. In the Scriptures this word is used with reference to man only here; in Rom. 13:14 it is used in a different sense.

Our versions construe the adverbs "both every way and everywhere" with the following verb "we accept"; but this construction is unsatisfactory. Tertullus could not say with great emphasis (because they are placed before the verb these adverbs have fullest emphasis) that the Jews "in every way and everywhere" thankfully accepted this peace and these reforms from Felix; he is lauding Felix and not the Jews. Nor do the adverbs fit this thought. Tertullus should say ἡμεῖς πάντες, "we all" accept. Reforms may "occur in every way and everywhere," but accepting them is not so expressed. The great flattery consists in this that Felix is heaping up "in all kinds of ways and places" his wonderful reforms for these Jews who were in so bad a state until he came with his προνοία or forethought.

3) It, of course, adds to the flattery to tell "His Excellency Felix" (see 23:25) that "we accept with all thankfulness," that these manifold and widespread benefactions are appreciated. But the "we" is only inflectional, is found in the verb ending, and hence is without emphasis and does not mean, "we, the whole nation," (Tertullus was not a Jew) but "we, this delegation," of which Tertullus was a part as spokesman: men such as the high priest himself, such as these great ruling elders, such as Tertullus, their rhetor. Felix certainly wanted to stand well with just these men. He had married the Jewess Drusilla, the daughter of one

Herod and the sister of another, for this very reason. Well, if Felix liked this sort of thing, this sort of thing was what he would like.

4) Now comes the skillful transition. **But in order that I may not further detain thee I entreat thee to hear us briefly in thy clemency.**

It took a skillful rhetor to make this expert turn. Tertullus implies that the *captatio* he has just uttered, brief as it was, which he really ought to have amplified greatly, already cut into the governor's precious time more than it ought. It was a great favor on the part of Felix to listen so long; it would be presumption to ask him to listen to further eulogy. This was actually cream and sugar.

Accusers have a right to be heard when they lodge an indictment. Although these are themselves rulers of the Jews with the high priest himself at their head, Tertullus "entreats the judge," makes the charges as brief as possible, and in this relies on the clemency of Felix, really his well-known clemency. The word is best understood by a comparison with its opposite: a δίκαιος is one who stands on his full rights; an ἐπιεικής is one who makes fair and reasonable concessions, who is mild, clement, moderate. Was Felix surprised to hear what a paragon he was in the eyes of these Jews? Was he made wary by this excessive sweetness on the part of the Jews? Now we perhaps see why they had hired Tertullus: they themselves could never have spoken such honied turns and phrases. Give them credit for procuring this expert!

5) **For having found this man a pest and setting in motion disturbances for all the Jews throughout the inhabited earth, also a ringleader of the sect of the Nazarenes, who also tried to profane the Temple, whom also we seized, from whom thou wilt be able, by thyself examining him, to know fully con-**

cerning all these things of which we on our part are accusing him.

The specifications of Paul's criminality begin with γάρ. Now the participle εὑρόντες, as someone has well said in regard to pronouns that lack antecedents, "has no visible means of support." Neither subject nor predicate follows, nor can they be supplied. B.-D. 467 charges Luke with "careless reproduction" of the address; Moulton cancels this: "Luke cruelly reports the orator *verbatim*" (R. 1135). This is, of course, anacoluthon, which is merely a big word for saying that the usual grammatical order is not followed. B.-D. has suggestions for removing the anacoluthon. Yet this so-called "irregularity" is really quite regular because it is intentional, a deliberate means to an end. Luke does report verbatim and does not give merely "a summary of the charges against Paul" (R., *W. P.*). He does it neither carelessly nor cruelly. Tertullus, pointing contemptuously to "this man," merely throws out his accusations against him. He is an actor and with this anacoluthon simulates his indignant agitation: "Think of it — we having found him a very pest," etc.

"Pest" really says it all, and καί merely specifies Paul's pestiferousness. He is causing commotions for the Jews all over the world, and this he does as the chief leader of the sect of the Nazarenes. This is the only time the Christians are called "Nazarenes," a remark that proves that Luke's record of the address is exact. But the Sadducees, who here appear against Paul, were themselves members and chief leaders of a Jewish sect, see 5:17, where "sect" is explained; the Pharisees were also a "sect." See the στάσις (the very word here used in connection with Paul) between the Sadducees and the Pharisees mentioned in 23:7. Any new "sect" among Jews would naturally cause "commotions" among the members of the other sects.

Were these troubles matters for a Roman procurator? Had Lysias not reported in 23:29 that he found that Paul was accused only of wranglings about the Jewish religious law and therefore of no charge deserving death or bonds? And now this actor-orator foolishly throws in the phrase "throughout the inhabited world" (ἡ οἰκουμένη, sc. γῆ, meaning the Roman Empire). Was Felix the emperor? Could he try a man for commotions that somebody heard about in distant provinces? The A. V. "seditions" and the R. V. "insurrections" are too strong and misleading. A glance at 19:40 and at 23:7, 10 shows that "commotions" or "disturbances" are referred to; and this holds true also in regard to Mark 15:7, and Luke 23:19, 25. Our versions make the reader think of political revolts.

Tertullus made a serious error when he preferred this his strongest accusation; Paul answers him most crushingly.

6) Now comes the charge about profaning the Temple, but it is greatly reduced: "he tried" to do this. After an investigation even these Sadducees had evidently found out that the Asian Jews who had raised this cry and started a riot because of it (21:28) could not substantiate the charge; in v. 19 Paul demands that they should be present if they had anything against him. "He tried" — that is hard to prove. "Whom also we seized" — but did we? The mob on the Temple grounds seized Paul; how can Tertullus extend this little inflectional "we" to include that whole mob?

At this point two texts (E, and 137, and a version) insert: "And would have judged according to our law; but the chiliarch Lysias, having come upon us with great force, led him away out of our hands, ordering his accusers to come unto thee" (see A. V.). See v. 2. There is insufficient textual evidence for the genuineness of this reading; this interpolation is based on the remark of Felix about Lysias, mentioned in v. 22. It weakens the address materially with its implication that Felix had better let the Jews try Paul, and with its alteration of the antecedent of the following relative παρ' οὗ from Paul to Lysias — the latter knew nothing prior to his own arrest of Paul.

8) Tertullus closes by declaring that Felix will be able to verify all that Paul is accused of from Paul himself (παρ' οὗ) by subjecting him to a judicial examination. In other words, the prisoner will not dare to deny the allegations of Tertullus if he is subjected to a proper judicial examination. That certainly concludes the case against him. The point must be noted that ἀνακρίνας refers to the regular judicial examination to which a prisoner might be put (Jesus was so examined, Luke 23:14), but only by the judge himself. Lawyers could not serve in such a function. The proceedings were as follows: a full statement of the charges by the accusers while facing the accused; the right to make a full defense by the accused; the depositions of any witnesses; if necessary, the judges' questioning of the accused.

The spuriousness of the interpolation is at once apparent because it makes Lysias the one to be subjected to a judicial examination "concerning all these things of which we on our part (emphatic) are accusing him" (the verb is construed with two genitives, or ὧν is used for ἅ). Lysias knew nothing about Paul's activity "throughout the inhabited world" and very little of what had happened in Jerusalem; and in no case would he be put under such an examination; he would freely testify without coercion. Παρ' οὗ must apply to Paul as also the correct text shows.

9) **And the Jews also joined in the charge, alleging that these things were so.** Literally, "they with (Tertullus) put upon (Paul) as far as they were concerned (middle voice)"; ἔχειν with an adverb = "to be," *es verhaelt sich also.* It was necessary that they,

the real accusers, acknowledge the indictments made in their name.

10) **And Paul answered, the governor having nodded to him to make his statement.**

This was the regular course of procedure before a Roman tribunal. The judge could also bring out the defendant's side of the case by questioning him; this would be the judicial examination to which Tertullus referred; Pilate did the latter in the case of Jesus; Felix refused to take Tertullus' hint. A nod was enough; λέγειν means "to make a statement," to present his defense and not merely "to speak."

Paul's defense is also brief, yet no one seems to raise objection to that. It does not begin with a *captatio benevolentiae* and contains no flattery. Since Paul intends to refer to Jewish doctrine and practice he fittingly states that he does so the more cheerfully because Felix is fully conversant with these matters. He presents three points in his defense: 1) during the twelve days he has caused no στάσις or commotion anywhere, v. 11-13; 2) he describes the sect to which he confesses he belongs, v. 14-16; 3) he challenges the Asian Jews or any of the Sanhedrists to show that he had done wrong. When we study this defense we admit that we do not see how we could have improved on it in any way.

It was, of course, an easy matter for Paul to answer Tertullus as he did. The one real charge of having caused a commotion was entirely false. As for being the ringleader of a sect and working in the empire generally, what the sect stood for was the all-sufficient answer. Tertullus had nothing on the basis of which he might construct a real accusation before a Roman court; Paul had everything on the basis of which he might present a genuine defense. There is a strong contrast between the two addresses made before Felix. This appears first in the honesty of the two men, secondly, in the appeal to the judge, thirdly, in the presentation of the facts.

Knowing that for many years thou art a judge for this nation, cheerfully do I make defense as to the things concerning myself, thou being able to know fully that there are not more than twelve days for me since I went up in order to worship in Jerusalem. And neither in the Temple found they me reasoning with anyone or causing a press of a crowd, nor in the synagogues, nor along in the city. Nor are they able to prove to thee whereof they are now accusing me.

Felix had been procurator since 52 or 53, and it was now after Pentecost, 58 (see the elaborate discussion in Zahn, *Introduction* III, 469, etc.) ; it seems that he also held an important position under his predecessor Cumanus. Paul does not say that he knows that Felix has been "governor" for many years; he says "judge," and this includes the entire connection Felix has had with "this nation." These past years as judge among Jews have enlightened him as to all things Jewish and certainly also as to the character of their high priests and most of the Sanhedrists. Before a judge who is so well informed and so fully experienced, Paul says, he cheerfully presents his defense regarding the things (adverbial accusative) concerning himself. Felix will understand without a lengthy explanation. This was not flattery such as that used by Tertullus. Any innocent man would regard himself fortunate to have his case tried by a judge of experience in the matters at issue.

11) Without a break Paul passes over into the defense by using a genitive absolute; this is a typical Greek way of moving on to important matters. Paul mentions the number of days he has been in Jerusalem for a double reason: Felix will understand that he came for the Jewish festival of Pentecost a couple of

weeks before this (this lies in the words, "I went up in order to worship in Jerusalem," the future participle denoting purpose, R. 111); secondly, Felix will understand that Paul came in time for the festival and not weeks before it. And all this implies that anything of a public nature which Paul may have done as recently as this will certainly be easy to discover. Paul goes on to deny that he did anything whatsoever of a public nature and challenges any man to prove that he did. The point regarding the number of days spent in Jerusalem is thus most important, and Paul mentions this point first. Some commentators lose the force of this by at once trying to determine how Paul counted the days.

"Not more than twelve days" is a litotes. Paul has in mind eleven days. But Jews and Romans did not begin and end the day in the same way. The Jews start the day at sundown, the Romans at midnight. Paul left at nine in the evening; the Jews might thus add another day, for when they count they regard also a part of a day, however brief, as a day. If this be done, Paul says, they could make the number twelve, but absolutely not more than twelve. The day of Paul's arrival was one day, another was spent in meeting James and the elders (21:17, 18), seven more were needed for the vow, another passed when Paul faced the Sanhedrin (22:30), the final day was the one on which the Jewish plot was reported to Lysias (23:12) — this makes eleven days. But the Jews might count a twelfth because Paul was spirited away after dark (23:23). 'Αφ' ἧς = ἀφ,' ἡμέρας ᾗ, but is used in the sense of "since," R. 717.

Others count differently. Some begin with the departure from Caesarea; they generally count only five days for the vow; they also add in the five days mentioned in 24:1, making them either five since the arrival at Caesarea or five since leaving Jerusalem. Thus they have too many days; hence the number is reduced at either the one end or the other. We object to the interpretation of 21:27; "when the seven days (of the vow) were about being finished." This cannot mean on the fifth of these days but must mean on the seventh when the final sacrifices were about to be brought. The five days mentioned in 24:1 cannot be included because Paul was no longer in Jerusalem.

12) And what about Paul's activity during these days? It is plain that, when he specifies "in the Temple," "in the synagogues," and "throughout (κατά, down through) the city," he is speaking only of the days spent in the city, i. e., since he arrived and before he was taken away — just as we have counted these days. Nowhere did Paul's accusers find him "reasoning with anyone," starting a discussion of any kind. This would not have been wrong; no law, either Jewish or Roman, forbade it. Paul went quietly about his business day after day, did not do even what he might freely have done. And thus he certainly never "caused a press of a crowd." Ἐπίστασις = "collecting a crowd," causing people to halt. "At no time," Paul says, "did I gather a crowd around me." Our versions misunderstand the word as does R., *W. P.*, who translate "onset." What Paul says is that he was so far removed from causing a disturbance that at no time and at no place did he even as much as gather a number of people around him to listen to him.

13) Paul drives this home: "Neither are they able to prove to thee," etc., παραστῆναι, "to place beside," i. e., to place anything beside their bold assertions, anything to substantiate them; and περὶ ὧν = περὶ τούτων περὶ ὧν (or just ὧν, since "accuse" may govern two genitives). If a man keeps making himself a pest by everywhere setting in motion disturbances among the Jews, these Sanhedrists certainly ought to find it the easiest thing in the world to furnish overwhelming proof that Paul had

done this sort of thing in Jerusalem, within the jurisdiction of Felix, during those eleven or twelve days. Paul does not merely demand this proof, he asserts that it cannot be furnished. He meets the charge squarely. "Now" they accuse me, Paul says, now they invent charges, but at the time to which they refer I was doing nothing, and they know it.

14) He advances to *the second point,* the matter of this terrible sect of the Nazarenes. **But this I confess to thee that, according to the Way which they denominate a sect, thus do I serve the God of my fathers, believing all things, those according to the law and those that have been written in the prophets, having hope in God, which also these themselves accept, that there shall be a resurrection of both righteous and unrighteous. Herein do I also myself take pains to have a conscience void of offense toward God and men alway.**

Paul is only too happy to confess his faith before Felix. He does this with reference to the distinction obtaining between Pharisees and Sadducees, the two parties who were so prominent among the Jews and in the Sanhedrin itself (23:8, 6-9), a distinction that was fully known to Felix. As according to Roman law it was no crime to belong to the Sadducees, so it certainly was no crime to be a Pharisee (23:6) in holding to the Biblical teaching which this Jewish party maintained over against the Sadducees.

Λατρεύω is the service all men ought to render to God in distinction from λειτουργέω, the official service rendered by priests; ὁδός is explained in 9:2; the adjective πατρῷος = "of one's father or fathers." Paul confesses that he serves the God of the Israelite fathers according to the Way (doctrine and life combined) which these Sadducaic accusers of his are pleased to call "a sect." Paul does not call it so, nor were the Nazarenes (Christians, v. 5) a αἵρησις like the Sadducees or the

Pharisees. The word means a peculiar tenet which one chooses and holds, and then those who hold such tenets (5:17). But Paul maintained faith in the entire Old Testament in its original teaching as he also makes plain here. In no sense did he hold to some peculiar tenets that differed from the Scriptures.

The same thing applies today. Those who hold to the true and original Scriptural teaching belong to the great body that has held this teaching through the ages; they are the church. Only those are a sect and their teaching a αἵρεσις who advocate some teaching that is contrary to the Scriptures. They usually also sever connections with others, cause a separation, and in this sense, too, form "a sect." This word naturally came to mean "heresy" in the sense of false doctrine.

How little "the Way" was a peculiar tenet Paul brings out in his description of it. Felix knew about this Way and about the Christians; but Paul is missing no opportunities since Felix may have heard only slanders. Tertullus had called Paul "a ringleader of the sect of the Nazarenes." Very well, then Paul ought to know what these Nazarenes stand for. If Tertullus makes him an authority on the Nazarenes, Felix may be assured that Paul knows what he is talking about when he now states what he believes: "believing all things" in both parts of the Old Testament, "those according to the law and those that have been written in the prophets." "The law and the prophets" was a current designation for the Old Testament. Paul mentions "the prophets" most prominently because his accusers were Sadducees, and the Sadducees, while they did not reject the rest of the Scriptures, held mainly to the Pentateuch and thereby made themselves a sect.

15) In v. 14 Paul enunciates his formal principle: all that the Scriptures contain. Now he goes over to the material principle, the one that is so pertinent in

the present case: the resurrection of the dead. He restates what he had shouted into the Sanhedrin in 23:6. Paul holds to the very hope in God which even "these themselves" (the Jews) accept, namely (apposition to "hope"), "that there shall be a resurrection of both righteous and unrighteous." Μέλλειν is followed by the future infinitive and is a periphrastic future. One does not "look for" a hope (R. V.), one "accepts" it.

Paul is turning the tables on his accusers. These Sadducees, of course, do not accept the resurrection, but the Jews as such most emphatically do, and the Pharisees stand in the forefront. In this respect the Pharisees and their great following were not a sect in any sense, but the Sadducees who rejected this hope most decidedly were. Like a boomerang the invidious term "sect," with which Tertullus wanted to discredit Paul and the Nazarenes (v. 5) before Felix, recoils upon the very men he is trying to represent: in regard to this point these Sadducees alone constitute the sect. And the worst of it was that Felix, who knew the Jews, could not but see the point.

Here Paul defines the Old Testament teaching that was held by all the Jews save the Sadducees more closely than Luke does in 23:8, or than it appears in Matt. 22:23, etc., and in John 11:24. A resurrection awaits "both the righteous and the unrighteous," both terms being forensic, those who are declared thus by the eternal Judge. This is, indeed, the teaching of both Testaments, Dan. 12:2; John 5:28, 29. It underlies all the passages that speak of the judgment, such as Matt. 25:31, etc.; Rom. 14:10; II Cor. 5:10; Rev. 20:12; John 12:48; and others. The old Jewish sect which denied that the Old Testament taught the resurrection has many adherents today who generally also assail this teaching as it is found in the New Testament. In

I Cor. 15:1-20 Paul shows how the resurrection is the very foundation of the gospel; those who deny it have no hope, no gospel, no Christ.

16) From the formal and the material principles Paul proceeds to the ethical principle. Because he holds the two former (ἐν τούτῳ) he takes pains to have a conscience void of offense toward God and men alway. Ἀσκῶ means "to practice," to exercise oneself, thus to take pains; ἀπρόσκοπος is passive in force, for one cannot cause God to stumble (this is the active sense) but one can himself stumble by in some way striking against God as well as against men. The word does not contain both ideas. Here Paul repeats what he said in 23:1. Men who like these vicious, lying Sadducees think that their souls die with their bodies (23:8) are capable of any crime in life; Paul, who knows that the unrighteous as well as the righteous shall rise to face God at the last day, would certainly want to keep his conscience "uninjured" (C.-K. 619, *unverletzt*) in every way. He takes pains to do so even now when making his defense. Paul speaks with reference to himself only. Let his accusers and his judge Felix think about themselves.

17) Coming to *the third part* of his defense, Paul challenges his accusers who failed to bring witnesses and who themselves have testified and can testify to nothing.

Now after an interval of several years I came in order to do alms in my nation and offerings in connection with which they found me as having been sanctified in the Temple, not with a crowd, nor with tumult — however, certain Jews from Asia who ought to be present before thee and be accusing if they should have anything against me. Or let these themselves state what wrong they found when I stood before the Sanhedrin other than this one exclamation which I shouted standing among them, Concerning

the resurrection of the dead I, I am being called in question today before you!

This is the only place in Acts where Luke mentions the great collection (see 20:4, etc.), and now he does so only in Paul's address. This had, indeed, brought him to Jerusalem. Δι' ἐτῶν πλειόνων = "at an interval of more (several) years"; Paul had been in Jerusalem in 54 (18:22, see this passage), it was now 58. "In my nation" has static εἰς; Paul had come "to do alms," i. e., to dispense them. These were "offerings"; we may translate, "to do alms, namely (καί) offerings." They were not ordinary alms but gifts that the churches had made to God for their needy Jewish brethren. Because ἐν αἷς follows, some are inclined to think that "offerings" refers to Temple sacrifices, either those made by Paul for the four brethren who had made a vow (21:26), or some that he brought of his own accord. But the latter are included in προσκυνήσων mentioned in v. 11.

18) Our versions misunderstand ἐν αἷς, "whereupon" (A. V.), "amidst which" (R. V.), "in presenting which" (margin). The R. V. plainly thinks of "offerings" that were brought as sacrifices in the Temple. Ἐν is to be taken in its original sense as it is in so many phrases: "in connection with which," i. e., the alms-offerings. Paul is referring to 21:20, etc. Having come to bring alms-offerings, he was advised to help four brethren with their vow; so it was "in connection with these alms" that he happened to be in the Temple, and in helping these brethren he was naturally there "as having been sanctified," which is explained in 21:24, 26. That, Paul tells the governor, is how "they found me in the Temple" as one sanctified in connection with a great alms-offering. It was not necessary to add all the details about helping the four brethren with their vow. But "as one having been sanctified" for ritual purposes of some kind Paul would be present in the Temple "not with a crowd nor with tumult" but as

quietly attending to what his ritual sanctification made incumbent upon him. Felix knew enough about these rituals to understand that fully.

19) "They found me," Paul says, for the moment omitting the subject. Now he adds it: not these Sanhedrists so found him as Tertullus made it appear in v. 5, 6 by falsifying the fact, "but certain Jews from Asia." We should not disconnect this subject from the verb "they found" and say with R., *W. P.*, that "some Jews from Asia" is without a verb in the Greek and then proceed to supply one or perhaps think of an anacoluthon. Paul says: "They found me — but some Jews from Asia," *not* the Sanhedrists, not anybody who saw me in a tumult. This is dramatic speech, hence the subject is placed last with a parenthetical δέ.

In the Greek the relative is often emphatic as it is here in the case of οὕς: "*they* are the ones who," etc. Most assuredly, *they* ought to be present before the governor and be accusing if, indeed, they should have anything against Paul. Why, then, are *they* not present? It is *their* absence that shows what is wrong with these charges of the Sanhedrists. We decline to regard this statement as a mixed conditional sentence as R. 1022 does by making εἰ with the optative a protasis of potentiality and the imperfect ἔδει an apodosis of present unreality. Then in 886 R. makes the imperfect ἔδει the imperfect in an obligation that has not been met. The imperfect could not be both the apodosis of a conditional sentence and also the imperfect of an unfulfilled obligation. Here ἔδει is only the latter. We at once see this when we note that Paul might have stopped with the relative clause: "who ought to be present before thee" (ἐπί as in 23:30, and again in 24:20, 21). The conditional εἰ clause is merely appended: "if they should (might) have anything against me." This is mere potentiality, for what could they honestly have against Paul?

20) But Paul covers every possibility. "Or let these themselves state what wrong they found when I stood before the Sanhedrin," genitive absolute, aorist participle to express the fact of so standing. Note well, in regard to this incident and in regard to this alone could the high priest and his elders testify as eyewitnesses. Then and then alone when the chiliarch had brought him down to face the Sanhedrin (22:30-23:1) had they seen him; for anything that occurred prior to this they would have to produce the proper eyewitnesses. Paul challenges his accusers to state (aorist, make a single deposition) any ἀδίκημα, "wrong sufficient for a judicial charge," on his part that they had witnessed.

The apostle knew his business, and Felix saw that he did. Where were those Asian Jews, the only witnesses who might substantiate the charge that Paul had defiled the Temple by bringing Gentiles into it (v. 6; 21:28)? Their absence spoke for itself. The Sanhedrists would have had them on hand if they had witnessed what they claimed to have seen. The Sanhedrists had witnessed only what Paul did in their meeting in the presence of Lysias. What could they testify?

21) What "other than this one exclamation," etc., ἤ after the interrogative τί (τί ἄλλο): "what other than." The grammars discuss the absence of the article with ταύτης; B.-D. makes this demonstrative predicative and thus removes the difficulty; R. 702 supports the absence of the article by evidence from the inscriptions. Some texts have ἐκέκραξα, a reduplicated aorist, R. 363. Paul says that the only thing to which these Sanhedrists could take objection was his shout in their meeting when he stood among them and because of their wild commotion had to shout in order to make them hear (23:6, ἔκραζε, the same verb): "Concerning the resurrection of the dead (no articles: *Totenauf-*

erstehung) *I, I* am being called in question today before you!" Unless the emphasis on ἐγώ is noted, the point of Paul's shout is lost. How could *he* be even so much as called in question regarding the resurrection when the Sanhedrin itself was full of Pharisees who themselves believed that doctrine? Paul says: "Do these Sanhedrist Sadducees now want to make an ἀδίκημα or crime of that? Well, that is all they have — some crime that would be!"

We do not see how anyone can find an admission of wrong in this statement as though Paul's sensitive conscience made him confess what others would consider venial. He was doing the very opposite. This statement of his regarding the resurrection was all that his accusers had, the last thing in the world which a procurator of the Jews would call a crime unless he wanted to make criminals of nearly all Jews. Without knowing it, Paul was substantiating the statement of the chiliarch's letter that the trouble was "concerning contentions about their (religious) law" (23:29). Paul is delivering the climax of his defense, his strongest point.

But what about his insult to the high priest (23:3)? Why does he say nothing about that? Because the high priest had ordered him to be struck on the mouth, and because this was a crime against a Roman according to Roman law. Ananias had Paul to thank for not bringing that matter to the attention of the Roman judge.

22) **But Felix, knowing rather accurately the things concerning the Way, put them off, stating, When Lysias, the chiliarch, shall come down, I will decide the things concerning you, directing the centurion that he be kept in ward and have indulgence and to hinder none of his own from waiting on him.**

Here the character of Felix begins to reveal itself.

The second perfect participle εἰδώς (always used as a present) is concessive: Felix held Paul "although knowing" the things concerning the Way "rather accurately." The comparative is to be understood in this sense. He was better informed about the entire Christian movement than another man in his place might have been (ὁδός as in v. 14). He sinned against better knowledge when he still detained Paul. That, of course, was a small matter for a man who had done things that were far worse. He, of course, had a plea for putting the case off, but one could not have guessed that plea in advance. He must wait until Lysias could come down to Caesarea. Yet he had all the information that Lysias could present; Lysias, too, as far as we know, never came down, was never asked to do so. The middle aorist ἀνεβάλετο is forensic: "he adjourned them"; and διαγνώσομαι is used as it was in 23:15: "I will decide"; καθ' ὑμᾶς is equal to a genitive but is stronger, the phrase is made a substantive by the article: "your matters." The aorist εἰπών, like the following διαταξάμενος, denotes a single action: he adjourned them "by stating — by directing," etc.

23) Paul was to be detained in light military custody. He could not leave the palace; a centurion had charge of him. Yet he had ἄνεσις, easement, release from the rigors of close imprisonment. In particular (καί) none of his own, relatives or friends, was to be prevented from waiting on him. This verb is significant: any of Paul's friends could act as ὑπηρέται, "underlings," for Paul, i. e., could wait on him as personal servants, do for him what Paul might direct. This sounds fair and gracious, but look at v. 26. That word about the alms-offerings (v. 17) seems to have been caught by Felix; his knowledge of the Way may also have included rather accurate knowledge in regard to Paul's being the great apostle for whose release from

custody the Christian Jews or Gentiles might be willing to pay a goodly sum. He was certainly putting no obstacle in their way.

Philip, the evangelist, lived in Caesarea (21:8), and he surely visited Paul often. The eight who had come to Jerusalem with Paul (20:4), also Paul's nephew (23:16) and other relatives very likely came to visit him. Whether Luke and Aristarchus, who accompanied Paul when he was finally sent to Rome (27:2), remained with him during his entire imprisonment in Caesarea, no one can say. That Paul was chained is unlikely although it is assumed by Zahn; he was a Roman, and Felix was careful. Paul could have all the visitors he desired. These might bring him books, food, etc. He could take exercise in the palace grounds, bathe when he desired, etc. Yet two lonely years lay ahead of him here in Caesarea.

24) Many things occurred during the two years of Paul's imprisonment in Caesarea, but Luke reports only one episode and the attitude of the governor. **Now after some days, Felix, having come with Drusilla, his wife, she being a Jewess, summoned Paul and heard him concerning the faith in Christ Jesus.**

Felix had apparently been absent during the interval of perhaps a few weeks and had now returned. He brought his wife with him, who had not been in Caesarea since Paul's arrival. On the three successive wives of Felix see 23:24. Drusilla was one of the three daughters of Herod Agrippa I (Drusilla, Mariamne, Bernice). Their brother Herod Aprippa II and Bernice are mentioned in 25:13. According to the most probable chronology Drusilla was born in 37; was married to Aziz, King of Emesa, in 52, after he had become a Jew; was induced to leave him through the machinations of Simon, a Cyprian magus, and to marry Felix in 54 or 55. They had a son who, at the age of 20-22, perished with his mother in an eruption of Vesuvius in 79.

It has been remarked that her father killed James, her great-uncle Herod Antipas slew the Baptist, her great-grandfather Herod the Great murdered the babes of Bethlehem in addition to his many other murders. She is said to have been a beautiful woman; although she deserted her first husband, she was otherwise an ardent Jewess. It was at her request, we assume, that Felix summoned Paul in order to have him tell about "the faith in Christ Jesus." Here πίστις is undoubtedly to be taken in the objective sense. In this place Luke writes "Christ Jesus," placing the Messianic title before the personal name "on Jesus Christ," (see 2:38). This expression, of course, did not come from the lips of Felix.

Paul was summoned only for the purpose of an audience with the governor and his wife. Codex B has ἰδίᾳ, "with his own wife." The article alone is sufficient although two texts have αὐτοῦ. On the basis of textual evidence ἰδίᾳ should be eliminated; the surmise of R. 692, that the word hints at Drusilla's character as it was "at present," leaves the textual question unanswered and puts an implication into the word which it does not convey. We have no reason to deny the presence of attendants although Paul may have been accompanied only by a centurion. While curiosity may have prompted Drusilla's request, her religious interest would also move her to wish to see and to hear this man whom so many Jews, including the prominent Sanhedrists, were determined to put to death. Perhaps this casts some light on the fact that Paul was constantly given great consideration. Ramsay thinks that he must have commanded ample financial means to make him a man of standing. True, prisoners who are poor often receive short shrift, but think of Gandhi in the disturbances in India. The treatment Paul received was due to the man himself, his personality, his work and his fame, and the impression he made on friend and on foe alike, and most likely not to his command of funds.

25) **And as he was reasoning about righteousness and self-control and of the judgment about to come, Felix, having become frightened, answered, For the present be going! And when I get occasion I will call thee unto me — at the same time also hoping that money should be given to him by Paul; wherefore also, summoning him rather often, he kept conversing with him.**

Asked to expound the Christian faith, Paul does that very thing and does it most gladly. This occasion is different from any other at which Paul had to speak since his arrest. Here he was at least not defending himself in any way, he was merely satisfying the desire of these high personages. There sat Felix, for the once not as a judge but as a hearer only, with his wife beside him. It was Paul's life calling to preach the gospel, and here he was even asked to preach it. Strange providence, indeed! These two high personages would never of their own accord have gone to a Christian meeting to hear the gospel even when a man like Paul would be the preacher; but here God sends them a preacher, one of the best the world has heard. He turns their own audience chamber into a church. He brings about a situation in which these two sinners give full and close attention to the gospel sermon. Behold, the great hour of grace has struck in the lives of these two! The door of the kingdom was thrown open to them, salvation was reaching out to draw them into its embrace. If they had only known, at least in this their day, the things, that belonged to their peace! Luke 19:42; Heb. 3:7, 8, 15.

The assumption that Paul began his address with a summons to repentance and expected to follow this with a mention of Christ and remission but got no farther than the first part, is unacceptable. The idea that the gospel must always be preached in this order, and that remission cannot be presented until contrition is effected, is contradicted by John 4:7, etc., where Jesus himself preached the gospel first and then followed with the law (v. 16, etc.) and thus converted the Samaritan woman. Either may be preached first. In this instance Luke says in so many words: "And heard him concerning the faith in Christ Jesus." Luke could not have written this if Paul had spoken first regarding the law ("righteousness, self-control, judgment to come") and had then been put off. He presented, first of all, "Christ Jesus," the whole gospel, and after Felix "heard" that, Paul preached the law. It goes without saying that Paul never for a moment thought of merely telling the story of Jesus but aimed at the conversion of his hearers; he preached "the faith," the "Christ," and then the law to bring about contrition.

Luke presents the conclusion of this sermon because of its effect. "Righteousness" is here combined with "self-control and judgment to come" and thus signifies the moral quality when one does what receives the approval of the divine Judge. The term is always forensic; God judges and declares righteous either man's conduct (as here) or his entire status (righteousness in Christ Jesus), C.-K. 315, etc.

The law demands righteousness — could Felix and his wife face God in regard to that demand? Ἐγκρατεία = "self-control," the life that is governed by κράτος, holding all the passions and desires in check; "temperance" is inadequate. This is usually referred to the unlawful marriage of Felix and Drusilla but it extends much farther. Could these two face God with reference to that part of the law? Finally, Paul points to "the judgment about to come," impending (μέλλων) for every man at death and at the last day (II Cor. 5:10, and other passages). Κρίμα is neutral, it may acquit or condemn. Could Paul's hearers face this inescapable judgment? It is this "judgment" that puts teeth into the law of God. The sinner always ignores, hides this coming judgment from his soul; only in this way can he sleep at night, only in this way can he go on in his sins. To have this judgment clearly and effectively presented to him is to strike the one vulnerable place in his soul and conscience.

From Paul we may learn how to preach so as to convert. Only one blow ever goes home through the sinner's armor, and that is the blow of the law with the judgment to come delivered at the conscience with full force. Omit this, and conversion will not result. See how Jesus struck home in John 4:16-18; Peter likewise in Acts 2:36, 37. In this drive at the conscience the sinner must be brought to accuse and to condemn himself just as God will condemn him. The preacher often makes the mistake of doing this accusing and thereby arouses in the people he accuses a false antagonism against himself. Instead of confronting them with God he confronts them with himself and thus ruins his own work. Paul confronted Felix and Drusilla with righteousness, self-control, and the judgment of God and did not inject himself into the picture. He did not preach about unrighteousness and lack of self-control but about the positive side of the law. In all this he was wise. He did not charge these sinners with sins. Sometimes it is in place to say: "Thou art the man!" more often it is in place to let the sinner say this to himself. Paul was the prisoner of Felix, yet he reached this man's conscience without arousing his anger against himself for being presumptuous and rash.

Felix became ἔμφοβος, he got into a condition of fear. Conscience makes cowards of us all. Paul had done his work perfectly. That fear ("trembled," A. V., is incorrect) was produced by confronting Felix with God, his law and his judgment, in a way which gave the man no opportunity to turn upon Paul in rage. The *terrores conscientiae* were beginning to take hold of Felix. Some use the expression that he was "under conviction," and the law intends to convict. The law strikes with great power like a hammer; it pierces the sinner's armor like a sword that reaches the vitals. These effects are the *motus inevitabiles*. When a man is struck in an unprotected spot he inevitably winces even when he does not yield. Luke's account deals only with Felix, hence he says nothing about Drusilla beyond the fact that she was present. We are not at all ready to join in the assumption that she was not "under conviction" and still less ready to say that "like another Herodias her resentment was to be feared." Even the daughter of a Herod had a conscience.

Felix then makes the fatal turn. He hushes the preacher's voice; he thrusts him and his Word away; he deliberately separates himself from the divine power that is taking hold of him in order to save him. Compare *C. Tr.* 835, 12 (point 11); 1077, 40. Call this act and the condition to which it led "wilful resistance" or use some other term, in Felix we have a plain example of breaking the hold of the Word on the heart, cutting the heart off from the power of the Word, the sinner himself by his own guilt preventing his conversion. In this case the thing was done politely: "For the present be going! And when I get (aorist participle) occasion (καιρόν, a convenient season, our versions) I will call thee unto me (middle voice)." In τὸ νῦν ἔχον we have the accusative of time; ἔχω with an adverb = to be, hence the neuter participle: "as the thing now is." The present imperative πορεύου is mild, it is like our, "please, be going," and not at all like the aorist, "Go!" or, "Get out!" But this politeness must not deceive us. In his heart Felix had resolved never to give Paul another opportunity to speak to his conscience in this manner. He saw to it that no convenient season came. By his own determination he cut himself off permanently from the Word. That was fatal. Felix deliberately destroyed himself.

26) The force of the present participle should be noted and the fact that it modifies ἀπεκρίθη. The desire for a bribe was already in the mind of Felix when he became afraid and gave his answer to Paul. There are two thoughts in this participial statement, "at the same time also hoping" for a bribe. His fear was mingled with this greedy hope. Secondly, he now saw more clearly than ever that Paul had committed nothing for which he deserved to be held. While the divine law and its threat of retribution upset Felix for the moment, it failed to check his greed for criminal gain. Although he was frightened he clung to his sin.

Roman law decreed exile and confiscation for a magistrate who accepted bribes, but in the provinces its enforcement was difficult. The way in which Luke states the matter makes us think that Felix had enriched himself with bribes before this. The statement Paul made in v. 17 had very likely helped to raise the cupidity of Felix. A man with a following and a standing like Paul's would have friends who would be ready to pay a good price for his release. And Felix would have willingly released him for such a price. He could easily answer the Jews that he had found no crime in Paul even as they had failed to establish one. At another trial he could have rendered this verdict and have given himself the airs of being a just judge.

These conversations for which he repeatedly summoned Paul had this one purpose in view and no other. Διό makes this certain; "rather often" does the same. "He kept conversing with him" means that he gave

Paul every opportunity to arrange for a bribe; in familiar private conversation this could easily be done, and διό implies that Felix touched on the matter. Yet some have held that Felix gave the apostle opportunity to speak more fully about the faith; but the purpose back of this exegesis seems to be to eliminate the idea that Felix had definitely cut himself off from the Word. This view does not agree with Luke's words. Nor does it gain what is desired; for even if Felix let Paul speak about the faith, he did so only in order to obtain a bribe for Paul's release. This was his answer to what Paul had said about "righteousness," etc. Felix deliberately followed open unrighteousness, and no word about "the judgment to come" could deter him. Luke, however, knows about only one topic of conversation, that directed toward a bribe.

27) **Now two years having been fulfilled, Felix received as a successor Porcius Festus, and wanting to establish favor for the Jews, Felix left Paul behind bound.**

Lysias never came down (v. 22), the trial never advanced. Paul was able to do nothing but to cultivate the great virtue of patience. Since no further trial was held, Paul could not appeal to Caesar as he did when Festus assumed office. Nero had become emperor on October 13, 54. He finally recalled Felix, but even Josephus, *Ant.* 20, 8, 9, assigns no special reason for this act; it was certainly not the disturbance mentioned in 20:7, 8. After the recall Felix was accused by the Jews in regard to the affair mentioned in 20:7, 8 but escaped punishment through the influence of his brother Pallas.

Josephus has little to say about Festus; the *gens* of the Porcii to which he belonged had obtained senatorial rank centuries before this time. He became procurator in 60, put down the *sicarii* (21:38) and other brigands, died in 62, and was succeeded by the evil Albinus.

Felix left Paul bound and thereby desired to deposit a favor for the Jews, i. e., to leave a favor for them (χάριτα, an Ionic and poetical accusative instead of χάριν, R. 265). He evidently desired to placate the Jews, yet after his recall they accused him before Nero. Felix failed in his purpose. One lone variant reads that Paul was left in ward "because of Drusilla." Disappointed in getting no bribe from Paul and hoping to get some consideration from the Jews, he left Paul "bound."

Does this perfect participle with its present connotation, "having been and thus still remaining bound," imply that Paul was kept in chains, one or two chains fettering him to a soldier? In 22:30 this verb does refer back to 22:25 and to the chains there mentioned. But the chiliarch was frightened because he had "bound" Paul with chains. He certainly came into the hands of Felix as a Roman without chains and was left without chains during the two years he remained in the custody of Felix. Would Felix then, on leaving, order that he be chained and so turn him over to Festus? For what reason? Would Felix risk such an act when the prisoner was going into a new governor's custody? We think not. "Bound" means "a prisoner" and no more. Regarding 26:29, 31, and finally 28:20 see these passages.

CHAPTER XXV

Paul Compelled to Appeal to Caesar

1) With the coming of Festus, Paul finally gets action in his long drawn out case. **Festus, therefore, having set foot in his province, after three days went up to Jerusalem from Caesarea.** He came from Rome and landed at Caesarea where the procurators of Judea had their residence. He was new to the land and the people. It was his duty to get his bearings without delay. For this reason he promptly visits Jerusalem, the Jewish capital and famous religious center. "After three days" (Matt. 27:63; Acts 28:17), by common usage, means on the third day, Festus rested in Caesarea only one full day. Judea was not strictly a province (ἐπαρχεία) but a department of the province of Syria which was under a *propraetor* (*legatus Caesaris*). Judea had a procurator (ἐπίτροπος) who, however, was also called ἔπαρχος, which shows that Luke's language is correct.

2) **And the high priests and foremost of the Jews informed him against Paul and began to beseech him, in due form asking favor against him in order that he might summon him to Jerusalem, they fixing an ambush to make away with him along the road.**

The high priest Ananias (23:2; Josephus, *Ant.* 20, 6, 2) was succeeded by Jonathan who was soon killed at the instigation of Felix (*Ant.* 20, 8, 5); he, in turn, was succeeded by Ishmael, the son of Fabi (*Ant.* 20, 8, 8 and 11). Here again the plural "high priests" refers to Ishmael, the high priest proper, and to those Sanhedrists who had special connection with him or his predecessors; 4:6 names those of this ruling party at an earlier day. For "certain elders" which he used in 24:1, Luke now writes "the foremost of the Jews," most of them being the identical elders mentioned in 24:1. They were "the foremost" because they sided with the high priestly party. They naturally waited until a convenient opportunity offered itself during their initial acquaintance with the new governor; then, in order to impress him the more, they, in a body, informed him against Paul (the same verb that was used in 23:15, 22), told the governor what they had against the apostle. Then "they began to beseech him," inchoative imperfect which also implies that the act was in vain, otherwise the aorist would have been used.

3) Yet this beseeching should not be misunderstood. Luke does not write simply, "began beseeching to summon him to Jerusalem." He inserts the participial modifier αἰτούμενοι κτλ., and the middle of this verb is used with reference to asking in the way of business (R. 805). In going over their affairs with the governor these Jewish leaders stated the case of Paul as being one that had been left over from the administration of Felix, and thus, as being involved in this case, they asked in due form this χάρις, favor or kindness, that Festus try the case here in Jerusalem and thus get it off his hands. What reasons they advanced for the transfer we are left to imagine. One such reason may have been that it was much easier to bring Paul to Jerusalem than to have them and their witnesses travel to Caesarea.

We should not miss the force of the verb "beseech." These wily Jews made no demand on the new governor; they let him feel his lofty authority and thus hoped that he would accommodate them in this matter. Nor should we fail to note that Luke is writing from his own standpoint and not from theirs. So he inserts the phrase "against him" (Paul). A trial of Paul here in the midst of his enemies was in their favor, and not in Paul's. Again, Luke adds the purpose (ὅπως) and not the purport of the request — a point that is obscured in our versions; and this purpose extends over the remainder of the sentence: "in order that," etc. Their secret aim was to have Festus summon Paul to Jerusalem; in the meanwhile they would prepare an ambush (23:16) to make away with him (ἀναιρέω, used with reference to the murder of Jesus). As is so often the case in the Greek, the participle states the main feature of the thought, here: "in order that by summoning him to Jerusalem they might fix an ambush," etc.

They reckoned with the ignorance of Festus, who would know nothing about the plot of two years before (23:12-30) to assassinate Paul. So the governor would have Paul conducted by a small escort; and it would be a simple matter to ambush this along the road. In a quick rush of resolute men Paul would be stabbed to death, the attackers would as suddenly disperse, and the Sanhedrists would blame the affair onto the bandits and the *sicarii* (21:38) who were infesting the country. Shrewd indeed! How could Festus fail to fall into the trap? But Luke's imperfect παρεκάλουν already intimates that the beseeching failed.

Here we see the implacable hatred of these Jews. Two years had passed, a third high priest was in office, but their hate is as bloodthirsty as ever. The highest dignitaries of the Jewish Court, the supreme representatives of the Jewish religion, the greatest guardians of righteousness and law, ever stoop to the most vicious crimes. Pagans could have done no worse. But read Josephus in regard to this period of Jewish history. They were heading straight for the great war when this rejected nation was destroyed as a nation. The plot mentioned in 23:12, etc., was hatched by the forty would-be assassins; here it is renewed by the Sanhedrists themselves.

4) It was surely divine providence that prevented Festus from assenting. **Accordingly Festus answered that Paul is in ward in Caesarea, and that he himself is about to be leaving shortly. Therefore, let those empowered among you, says he, having gone down with me, accuse him, if there is anything amiss in the man.**

Thus did the cunning scheme fail a second time. Οὖν merely marks the answer as being due to the request; and ἀπεκρίθη has the accusative with the infinitive in indirect discourse. But why did Festus refuse assent? It was due to his impartiality, we are told, or to the strict order of Roman jurisdiction, or even to his conversance with the previous course of the case. The first two of these are eliminated by v. 9, where the supposed impartiality and the strict Roman order are conspicuous by their absence. The third supposition is ruled out by v. 1; Festus had not had time to investigate a pending case, the very fact on which these wily Jews counted. While we are at it, let us also dismiss the view of a peremptory tone in the refusal. Present imperatives are not peremptory and sharp, and the explanation about returning soon is anything but sharp. Was Felix suspicious? This, too, is not indicated; these Jews were too careful. The providential refusal of Festus was due to his being busy with other matters during these days of his office. He had to get his bearings especially here in Jerusalem during the eight to ten days (v. 6) of his first stay.

Paul was safely in ward in Caesarea (static εἰς; discard the older labored explanation). "Besides" (δέ adds another point) he intended to leave Jerusalem in a few days (ἐν τάχει, "in speed"). These are mere statements of facts as the accusatives and infinitives so plainly show. Festus is neither asserting "his rights" nor offering an excuse. Since Paul is safely in ward in Caesarea, and since the governor will be returning in a few days, this case can wait until that time. Festus had drawn up his program for these days in Jerusalem and declines to send for Paul and to sit on his case and thus disarrange that program. He was acting in an ordinary, sensible way — something the Jews had not counted on. In ignorance of their design the governor frustrated their plot. Moreover, many a plot goes wrong in just such a way. The main person acts only in his own natural way and not as the plotters surmised that he would act.

5) Festus, however, offers to take the Jews back with him when he leaves for Caesarea and then promptly to attend to this case for them. There is nothing of a commanding nature in the imperative; even the subject is left indefinite, Festus does not say, "*You.*" Δυνατοί is taken to mean, "which are of power" (R. V.), "mighty ones" (R., *W. P.*), or "which are able" (A. V.). The last comes nearest to the meaning. Felix means "those empowered among you" (Sanhedrin), the duly empowered representatives of the Sanhedrin. He offers to take them along in his own retinue, which is a favor to them and doubly so when we think of the dangers along the road. The governor was accomodating enough. "Let them accuse him" is, of course, what these men, whoever they would be, would have to do; for Festus has no thought beyond trying the case in the regular Roman fashion. Naturally, too, the conditional clause: "if there is anything amiss (ἄτοπον, out of place) in the man," is one of reality, for only in case Paul had committed some wrong would there be any use in accusing him.

6) What could these Jews do but accede to the governor's suggestion? This plan was an accommodating offer by Festus himself, and the Sanhedrists had no other way than to act pleased and to accept it as a favor. **Now having tarried among them no more than eight or ten days, after having gone down to**

Caesarea, on the morrow, seated on the judgment seat, he ordered Paul to be brought.

The sentence is compact, the three aorist participles present the subsidiary actions in due order as preceding the final act of ordering Paul to be brought. "No more than eight or ten days" means only that long. Luke is not concerned about greater exactness. The Jews accompanied the governor. And on the very next day he obligingly took up the case. At the appointed hour, with the accusers present, Festus sat down on the *βῆμα*, the raised platform bearing the judge's seat (12:21; 18:12).

7) **And he having come, the Jews who had come down from Jerusalem stood around him, bringing many and heavy charges against him, which they could not prove, Paul offering as defense: Neither against the law of the Jews, nor against the Temple, nor against Caesar did I sin in any respect.**

Everything was delayed until Paul was present. The judge occupied his elevated seat, all others stood during the court proceedings here as elsewhere; nor were special places assigned to them so that the accusers freely stood about Paul. The point to be noted is that Roman courts invariably confronted accusers and accused and heard each in the presence of the other. First the accusers were called on to bring and "to show forth," i. e., prove their charges (on the rare *αἰτίωμα* see M.-M.). This time the Jewish delegation had no rhetor to speak for them; was it because Tertullus (24:1, etc.) had proved a disappointment? They "brought down on" Paul "many and heavy charges." Luke does not need to specify them, for they contained nothing new (24:5, 6). Tertullus had been brief and for that very reason more effective. We have seen how he made the best of a poor case. The Jews now try a greater length and try to make their charges sound "heavy," severe, as criminal as possible.

Despite their extended effort "they could not prove them." Note the imperfect ἴσχυον, "they were not (despite all their repetition and heavy words) having strength to shew them forth," actually to show to the judge that they were real charges (note the effective aorist infinitive). It is a repetition of the story told in 24:5, etc. The trouble with hate is its lack of good sense. Here it blinded these Sanhedrists to the complete lack of legal and proper proof for their charges against Paul. What was the sense of pressing a case like this? Moreover, as Sanhedrists and members of the Jewish supreme court they had had long years of training and experience in this very matter of legal proof. In spite of this they foolishly press a hopeless case. This phenomenon occurs regularly: moral obliquity blinds the intellect.

8) The genitive absolute is more than temporal ("while" our versions); it is causal. Paul's defense annihilated this mass of heavy charges. When the Sanhedrists were through, Festus gave Paul the floor (as in 24:10). As Luke does not specify the charges, so he also omits the defense. The charges had everything but proof; the defense, therefore, ended in the decisive statement (recitative ὅτι) of Paul's innocence. Paul sums up his own case: according to all the charges launched by the Jews, and according to the facts presented in Paul's defense, the verdict must be that he sinned "in no respect" (τί, adverbial accusative) either against "the law of the Jews" (the Scripture teaching on the resurrection, 23:6, etc.; 24:14-16, 21), or against the Temple (desecrating it, 21:28) or against Caesar (any Roman law).

Paul had had two years in which to meditate on his case. In his hearing before Felix he had not made a reference to Caesar and Roman law; he does so now. The point is that only infractions against Jewish law and usage had been charged against him, no infractions whatever against Roman law. This point could, of course, be strained; inasmuch as Roman law tolerated the Jewish religion, an act committed against that religion could be viewed as one committed against Roman law. But the Jews had not ventured to present such an argument; the following makes that certain. The reason, then, that Paul mentions Caesar is to bring to the attention of this Roman judge, whom he now sees for the first time, the fact that no infraction of a Roman law has even as much as been charged in this case. The charges deal with Jewish doctrine and practice, and even these charges are baseless. Why, then, does this Roman want to proceed with such a case? "Nor against Caesar" was a telling point, indeed.

9) It is this phrase which gives the trial its decisive turn, and we thus see why Luke preserved this one sentence from Paul's trial. Things are directed into a new channel.

But Festus, wanting to establish favor with the Jews, answering Paul said, Art thou willing, after having gone up to Jerusalem, there to be judged before me concerning these things? But Paul said: Before the judgment seat of Caesar I am standing, where it is necessary for me to be judged. The Jews I wronged in not a thing as thou thyself dost rather well realize. If, therefore, I am a wrongdoer and have perpetrated anything worthy of death I refuse not to die; but if there is nothing of what these are accusing me, no one is able to dispose of me in their favor! I appeal unto Caesar!

We here see how Festus compelled Paul to appeal his case to the emperor himself, namely to Nero, who ruled from 54-68.

The Jews had no case against Paul. Paul's statement in v. 8 should have been made the governor's verdict. But the famous Roman justice was dispensed in this procurator's court as little as it had been in that of his predecessor. By having appeared in force and by making so much sound and fury when presenting their charges against Paul, the Jews succeeded in one thing, not, indeed, in convincing Festus of the truth of their charges, but in making him reluctant to offend them. Just as the outgoing Felix "wanted to establish favor with the Jews" (24:27), so also Festus who had just come in was anxious to do the same. The words employed are the same in each case save that χάριν is used in place of χάριτα. Not justice tipped the balance but the personal interest of the judge. This time Luke writes "answering he said." He adds the participle (a coincident aorist which is used often in the Gospels) to mark the peculiar answer Festus gave, not to both parties, but to Paul. That answer was exactly what the Jews wanted; they at once saw that Festus was yielding to them.

All the evidence was in, no more could be hoped for. The case had been pending for two years. But instead of rendering the one and only verdict demanded by that evidence, i. e., the lack of it, Festus proposes to continue the trial by transferring it to Jerusalem. He is now ready to grant the very thing for which the Jews had besought him in v. 3. He was, of course, ignorant of the Jewish plot that had prompted that request.

How the Jews must have pricked up their ears when they heard the governor's proposal to Paul! Was their plot to be executed after all? But Paul must give his consent. As a Roman citizen before the Roman court in the proper seat of that court (Caesarea) the procurator could not adjourn his case to another place except with Paul's consent; hence the question: "Art thou willing," etc.? Festus says, "There to be judged before me" (ἐπί is used in this sense in 23:30, and several times later.) We think that he meant just what he said, not that he would turn Paul over to the Sanhedrin, but that he himself would be the judge. Grotius translates *me praesente*, "me being present," and has found some followers; but ἐπ' ἐμοῦ does not mean "before me as a spectator" but "as the judge."

10) Paul's answer is a decided refusal. More than that. Paul's mind has been made up for a long time. Despairing of receiving justice, he has evidently resolved at the first fitting opportunity to take his case out of the hands of judges such as these and to appeal to Caesar. That opportunity is now here; he embraces it promptly. Paul's very tone is bold. Already in v. 8 he states what the verdict should be. Now he again minces no words. He tells the governor what the law is, what that governor knows only too well, and what transferring the case to Jerusalem really implies. Festus has mistaken his man. Here is a man who looks him squarely in the eye and is not afraid of his unjust judge. The Lord's promise given in 23:11 certainly had much to do with Paul's present step. He had come to interpret that promise to mean that he was to testify in Rome, not as a free man, but as a prisoner. As far as Jerusalem was concerned, the renewal of the old plot was, of course, unknow to Paul, but the memory of that old plot was enough.

"If Festus was unwilling to give Paul justice in Caesarea where his regular court held forth, what assurance was there that Festus would give it to him at Jerusalem in the atmosphere of intense hostility to Paul?" R., *W. P.* There is a ring in every word Paul utters. "Before the judgment seat (v. 6) of Caesar I am standing," ἑστὼς εἰμι, periphrastic present tense (R.

881). The second perfect form ἑστώς is always used as a present participle. Festus was functioning in Caesarea on Caesar's judgment seat, in administering Caesar's laws. "Where it is necessary that I be judged," where alone my case belongs according to Roman law, I being a Roman citizen. Did Festus have to be reminded of that? That is what the governor should himself have told the Jews in v. 4. If he had intended to do so he had failed to state it properly. Δεῖ, used for all types of necessity, here states that which is laid down in Roman law for Romans. To transfer Paul for a trial in Jerusalem, even one "before me" (Festus), was, to say the least, an irregularity. Paul is *now* standing before the court of Caesar, that court which is being held in its proper place, why is he not judged here and now?

"The Jews I wronged in not a thing, as also thou thyself (καὶ σύ, emphatic) dost rather well realize," both adverb and verb are strong. Κάλλιον is the comparative: "better" than Festus is admitting. No crime against Caesar or his laws had even been alleged; the view that 24:5 implies such a crime misunderstands στάσεις. If the statement about the place where Paul must be tried contained a sting for Festus, this one that "he knew fully" (ἐπιγινώσκεις) and rather well that Paul had wronged the Jews in no way (double accusative, R. 484) stung more deeply. Festus had to take these rebukes in open court. One wonders how the Jews eyed him and took his measure when he heard these plain facts spoken by Paul.

11) Οὖν draws the plain deduction. Paul is either guilty or he is not guilty, and both propositions are stated in straightforward conditions of reality that are balanced by μέν and δέ. It is impossible to reproduce the former in English. Ἀδικῶ is one of few perfective presents (B.-D. 322, even better than R. 881): "if any past crime still stands against me." This is defined and

specified: "and I have perpetrated anything worthy of death," now the perfect. Paul says, "if so," then pass the verdict: "Guilty of death!" And as far as he is concerned, let Festus be assured, he is not refusing to die (object infinitive with τό R. 1059). Παρά in the verb means "from": "to beg off for myself" and thus to escape the penalty due, the dying under the executioner's hands. These Jews had asked for a special favor (χάριν, v. 3) which Festus was now eager to grant, (χάριν, v. 9); if he is found guilty, Paul asks no χάρις of any kind. That was manly language.

"But if there is (exists) nothing of what these are accusing me," then it is certainly the business of Caesar's judgment seat as represented by Festus to declare, "Not guilty!" As in 24:8, ὧν may be τούτων ἅ. Demosthenes used the verb with two genitives: of the person and of the things charged, B.-P. 662, and others. Certainly, "no one is able to dispose of me in their favor." Paul says "no one," but Festus knows that *he* is referred to. "Legally able" is the thought; illegally, of course, anything could be done. The sharp contrast between Paul's not begging off from dying and this making a present of Paul's life to the Jews in answer to their begging, is often not observed. When Festus asked about transferring the trial to Jerusalem, Paul instantly knew that the Jews had asked this as a favor (χάρις, v. 3 and 9), and that is why he uses the verb that is derived from this noun, χαρίσασθαι, "to grant or dispose of me as a favor to them." The expression is purposely indefinite. Was it only that Paul was to be tried in Jerusalem, or was it more, namely to dispose of his life to please the Jews? Paul conveys the truth to Festus that he fully understands what the proposal in regard to Jerusalem involves. And that, too, was plain language.

Now come the two great decisive words to which all else was but preamble: Καίσαρα ἐπικαλοῦμαι, "I appeal to Caesar!" the technical *Caesarem appello.* In the case of any criminal offense a Roman citizen had the right to make this appeal when he felt that the lower court was not giving him justice. The emperor then tried the case himself. This is not exactly like our present practice when appeal is taken to a higher court by one who has lost his case in the lower; the appeal could be made while the trial in the lower court was still in progress. So here no verdict had as yet been pronounced on Paul.

It is reported of Claudius that he assiduously devoted himself to this onerous task; we have no report about Nero, the present emperor. We do not know whether he finally heard Paul's case in person or let it pass through the imperial court; the latter seems to have been the case. It is certain, however, that Paul was acquitted. Even Agrippa could find nothing on the basis of which he might be held (26:32), and Festus did not know what to write to the emperor when he was sending Paul to Rome (25:26). The original provision in Roman law allowed an appeal from a magistrate to the people (Romans). This was called the *provocatio ad populum.* Later the emperor represented the people in these appeals, and so they were made to him.

When Paul says in 28:19 that he was constrained to appeal to Caesar, this certainly does not mean that he appealed reluctantly. It was the proper thing to do; "constrained" points to the open partiality and injustice of Festus. One does not escape reluctantly from the jurisdiction of such a judge but is glad to be able to escape. This appeal was certainly Paul's last legal resort, but this means only that such appeals were intended to be the last resort, and nobody would think of appealing except when this provision in Roman law finally became necessary. Paul's appeal was not the use of a legal technicality, turning from the real merits of justice to a mere form of justice. The Roman law itself with its right of appeal was wholly in support of genuine justice, and Paul so used this right. Therefore Paul should not be faulted on the score of Christian ethics.

12) **Then Festus, having talked with his council, answered: To Caesar thou hast appealed; before Caesar thou shalt go!**

The moment such an appeal was made, the judge had to decide whether there was any reason that the appeal should not be allowed. So Felix withdrew to consult in private with his "council," a number of councillors or legal advisers. Συμβούλιον is rarely used in this sense: M.-M. 597 furnish other examples. The explanation as to why Felix has no council while Festus has one, is not difficult: Festus was new in his office, this was apparently his first case in law, he thus needed counsel. Moreover, the matter was grave even for himself. To have his very first case terminate in an appeal to Caesar was a reflection on his integrity as a judge. No wonder he conferred with his council. We have no means of knowing who sat in this council; the procurator most likely chose his own men. But the view that the decision lay with this council is untenable; the decision lay with the procurator who merely listened to his advisers before deciding.

Paul's appeal had to be allowed. We see that in the announcement that is now made. This was given in a rather sententious form: "To Caesar thou hast appealed; before Caesar thou shalt go!" Paul had made his appeal with so much confidence that we scarcely think that by means of his sententiousness and his tone Festus intended to frighten Paul because of his own action, or that with a sneer he intended to convey the idea that Paul little knew the seriousness of his step. Paul's entire bearing invited no such reaction. Festus is merely imitating a bit of Paul's own tone and bearing. He is merely holding his head high before Paul and these Jews. Paul is taking the case out of his hands in a rather masterful way; Festus must yield to Paul's demand. But we do not think that his sententious dictum and high air deceived anyone and certainly not Paul. The perfect "thou hast appealed" implies that the appeal stands indefinitely; and ἐπί means: "*before* Caesar shalt thou go" and not "*to* Caesar." The future, "thou shalt go," is volitive, peremptory, equal to an imperative (R. 597). Festus *has* to send Paul and pretends that he is forcing Paul to go.

Festus Presents Paul's Case to Agrippa

13) Despite all the high airs Festus tried to give himself in the courtroom, it was he who was put into a quandary by Paul's appeal. Hence this consultation with Agrippa. He had not managed this case well; he betrays that he knows, even as Paul had told him to his face (v. 10), that Paul had committed no wrong against the Jews. One feels that Festus now wishes that he had acquitted Paul and had thus ended this case with credit to himself instead of precipitating this most inconvenient appeal to Caesar. **Now some days having intervened, Agrippa, the king, and Bernice went down to Caesarea saluting Festus.**

This visit was a formal greeting of the new procurator and hence was made so soon after his assumption of office. Agrippa had his capital in Caesarea Philippi (which he renamed Neronias in honor of Nero), north of the Sea of Galilee, and he came down from there to the procurator's capital Caesarea. One ruler honors and welcomes another into office. While each had his own domain, from the Emperor Claudius, Agrippa had received the jurisdiction over the Temple in Jerusalem and the right to name the high priests. This arrangement was still in force under Nero and naturally prompted a formal visit such as this.

The poorly attested future participle ἀσπασόμενοι would denote purpose, "in order to salute," and would remove all difficulty; but the best texts have the aorist ἀσπασάμενοι, which, whether we retain it or not, brings up the question as to whether an aorist participle can ever denote action that is future to that of the main verb. B.-D. 339, 1 evades the difficulty by preferring the future participle. But Luke uses aorist participles in similar connections, and R. 863 defends the use of the aorist here; he states that all of these participles express an action that is simultaneous with that of the main verb and thus denies that they may have a future force; see R. 863 for this case.

Agrippa II, the last king of the Herodian house, was reared in Rome at the court of Claudius and enjoyed this emperor's signal favor. Upon the death of his father Herod Agrippa I in 44 Claudius wanted to make the young prince, who was then seventeen years old, king in his father's place but met with general disapproval. For six additional years he was kept in Rome in order to learn Roman ways, then in 50 was given the Herodian principality of Chalcis in the Lebanons, and gradually a much greater territory in northern and northwestern Palestine. As the ruler of the Temple he had to become conversant with Judaism and to adopt Jewish ways (26:2, 3).

In regard to Bernice, Agrippa's sister, see 24:24. She was the oldest daughter of Herod Agrippa I (Acts 12:1, etc.), had married her uncle Herod, king of Chalcis, and after his death lived in criminal relation with her brother Agrippa II — she was living thus at the time when both came to visit Festus — then persuaded Polemo, king of Cilicia, to marry her in order to hush up the scandal, which he did because of her riches, but she soon left him to continue the incestuous relation with her brother. Eventually, although she was aging and the mother of several children, she became the mistress of Vespasian (Tacitus) and of his son Titus (Suetonius) who finally cast her off. She barely missed becoming empress, and her Jewish religion had long ago been abandoned although at one time she was completing a vow in the Temple (Josephus, *Wars* 2, 15, 1). Her brother died in 101 during the reign of Trajan. In this palace in Caesarea, which had been built by their grandfather Herod the Great, and where their father Agrippa I had lived, these two, Agrippa II and Bernice, had played as children.

14) **And as they were tarrying there more days, Festus put the things concerning Paul up to the king, saying: There is a man left behind by Felix as a prisoner, concerning whom, when I was in Jerusalem, the high priests and the elders of the Jews informed me, duly asking an adverse verdict against him, to whom I answered that it is not the custom for Romans to make disposal of any man by favor before the accused have the accusers face to face and receive room for defense concerning the accusation. They, therefore, having come together here, making no delay, on the next day seated on the judgment seat, I ordered the man to be brought, around whom having taken their stand, the accusers were bringing no charge of what wickednesses I myself was entertaining suspicion but had certain questions concerning their own divinity-devotion against him and concerning one Jesus as being dead, whom Paul was affirming to be living. And I on my part, being at a loss as to the question concerning these things, went on to say whether he was willing to go to Jerusalem and there to be judged concerning these things. But Paul having appealed that he be kept in ward for the decision of the Augustus,**

I ordered that he be kept in ward until I might send him up to Caesar.

Agrippa and Bernice paid more than a formal official visit. They tarried πλείους ἡμέρας, a number of days, the comparative meaning "more" than were necessary for saluting the governor in his new office. And it is this longer stay and the friendly intimacy it brought about that led Festus "to put things concerning Paul up to the king," which act led to all that follows in the next chapter. So Festus tells Paul's story in his own way. This was surely not done to entertain Agrippa as a guest. We here once again see the great importance which men everywhere assigned to Paul — even as a prisoner he towered above all others. Then his was a Jewish case, and the king was the ruler of the Temple. Thus Paul's case naturally came up for discussion.

For some reason the commentators who at other points ask how Luke secured his exact information do not do so when it comes to this conversation. But this is a place where the skeptic may step in and claim that Luke invented this interchange and challenge us to prove that he did not. But Luke was on the ground. Festus and the king did not confer in secret; they were prominent personages and moved about with their attendants. In this address of the governor we find several optatives that are rather exceptional at that. Luke wrote them, and Luke is literary! He wrote them exactly as he wrote other sections that have a LXX and a Hebraistic cast and each time faithfully reported the originals. It is Festus, the educated Roman, who uses these cultivated literary turns of the Greek when speaking to the king, for, of course, they spoke in Greek. All the unusual literary turns of the address are proof that Luke has recorded the very language Festus employed.

So he begins by speaking about a man who was left behind as a prisoner by Felix. It is rather farfetched to put into this participle the idea that Paul was "left behind as junk" and then to score the governor for this estimate of "the greatest of living men and the greatest preacher of all time." A governor does not speak at length to a king in regard to any man whom he considers "junk." He would tell a king the story of only a most important prisoner. "Left behind," of course, means that Festus had received Paul as a legacy. The perfect participle has its present connotation and implies that it seems that even Felix did not know just how to dispose of the man.

15) The importance of Paul is at once made manifest when Festus states how on his first visit to Jerusalem the Jewish rulers themselves, no less than "the high priests and the elders of the Jews," made it their business not only to inform Festus in regard to Paul and their charges against him but asked in due form for "an adverse verdict against him," the middle αἰτούμενοι being used whenever the request is made in a matter of business (R. 805). The Sanhedrists brought up Paul's case as a piece of unfinished business in which they were involved. Καταδίκην plus κατ' αὐτοῦ assume on the part of these Sanhedrists that Paul is guilty, and their request was that Festus should render the adverse verdict against Paul as being due him. Yet Festus fails to mention the fact that the Jews requested the favor of having Paul brought to Jerusalem where this adverse verdict was to be pronounced (v. 3). Agrippa could not guess that.

16) Festus puts on airs when he relates his answer to the Jews. Having been brought up in Rome, Agrippa was well informed in regard to the Roman legal proceeding of confronting the accused (the substantivized present passive participle) and the accusers (noun), especially also in order that the former might

have "room" (τόπος, a proper legal place) for defense (objective genitive) concerning the charge. Festus makes it appear as though he had to inform even Sanhedrists about this ἔθος or "custom" of Roman courts, as though those seasoned veterans in legal matters needed that instruction. We know what he really answered them (v. 4, 5). The point did not concern the confronting of the two but the transferring of the trial from Caesarea, the seat of the procurator's court, to Jerusalem merely in order to please the Jews. Rome was very proud of its court system, which it regarded as being most just to defendant as well as to plaintiff.

Festus uses the very verb χαρίζεσαι (present of customary action) which was employed by Paul in v. 11 (aorist to express the one act in his case). In these connections the term seems to have a legal sense; in 3:14 it is used with reference to Barabbas in a favorable sense, here with reference to Paul in an unfavorable sense. It is difficult to translate the latter without implying something that is not intended; we venture the translation, "to make disposal of any man by favor," the favor in this instance being shown the accusers. The sense is just as indefinite as it was in v. 11 and allows us to think of disposing of a man's life as a grant to his accusers. No; Roman justice certainly intended to exclude this very thing, especially in the case of a Roman, while other Oriental courts were not acquainted with such absolute justice. Behold Festus posing before Agrippa as an incorruptible Roman judge! And yet see how in v. 9, although he knew Paul to be innocent, he failed to pronounce the verdict to that effect and sought to please Paul's accusers; in v. 20 he seeks to cover up this defection from Roman legal justice.

Here we have the first optatives that occur, and they are used after πρὶν ἤ in indirect discourse. The direct would be πρὶν ἢ ἂν (ἐάν) with the subjunctive; and when this is changed into the indirect after a secondary tense of a verb of saying (ἀπεκρίθη) it is either left unchanged (thus in the Koine) or changed to the optative minus ἄν (thus in the classics and in this the only case occurring in the New Testament). R. 970, 1030. The change to the optatives is almost an Atticism and so exceptional in the Koine as to make it rather certain that Luke is reporting Festus' address verbatim. While this point is grammatical it has this added importance.

17) Quite incidentally Festus states that, when he laid down the law to the high priests and the elders, they came together "here," namely in Caesarea. Yet the only law he had laid down was that they must come to Caesarea (v. 4, 5) since nothing else had been broached. He takes full credit for making no delay, for taking the judgment seat on the very next day (βῆμα, v. 6), and for ordering Paul to be brought before him. Why all this minor detail? It permits us to see the character of the man and is further evidence that Luke reported all he said exactly. Another writer would have summarized all of this by a word or two.

18) We now get a fuller account of the points involved in the trial (v. 7, etc.) from the standpoint of the judge who presided, and this is most valuable. The following imperfects (v. 18-20) are beautifully descriptive and unroll the scene like a moving picture. Περὶ οὗ might mean, "concerning whom" (R. V.; never "against whom," A. V.) and thus be construed with the verb: "concerning whom they were bringing no charge."

R. 619 considers the construction with the participle doubtful: "around whom having taken their stand." But in v. 7 we have the same preposition compounded with the same verb: "they stood around him." This convinces us that Festus here relates that in his court the accusers surrounded Paul (see v. 7) with their babel of "many and heavy charges." But to his surprise, as he now tells Agrippa, they were bringing not a single charge of the kind of which he on his part (emphatic ἐγώ) was entertaining suspicion (ὑπονοέω, to have secretly in mind), namely something in the way of actual criminal "wickedness" which would easily be stamped with the verdict guilty. Not a thing of this kind did the Jews have. Πονηρῶν: no charge "of wickednesses" (partitive genitive) is incorporated into the relative clause and also attracts ἅ into the genitive ὧν, R. 718-719.

19) All that the Jews could offer were the ζητήματα reported by Lysias (23:29) "concerning their own δεισιδαιμονία (the adjective occurs in 17:22), divinity-reverence." "Religion" (R. V.) is too broad and does not fit the adjective; "superstition" (A. V.) is unsatisfactory because of its evil connotation. Festus would not call anything Jewish a "superstition" when he is addressing a king who had charge of the Jewish Temple. "Fear or reverence for a deity" is usually regarded as a neutral term, one that may be used in a good or in a bad sense (superstition), the latter use being a later meaning of the word (C.-K. 274, adjective). As far as 17:22 (see this passage) and the present use are concerned, we are unable to find an evil sense in it.

Καί adds by bringing a specification: "and in particular" this question "about one (named) Jesus as being dead, whom Paul was affirming to be living." The participle is predicative and not attributive: "one dead, Jesus"; and the perfect tense = "having died and thus being dead"; it describes a state. It was the same issue in regard to the resurrection that had been raised two years before (23:6-9; 24:15, 21) when the Sadducees were on the side of the opposition. Since the Sadducees failed to raise this issue before Felix (24:1-9) but left that to Paul, we conclude that the same thing happened again before Festus; among the "many and grave" charges mentioned in v. 7 Paul's faith in the resurrection was omitted although the charges came from the Sadducees. Paul himself, therefore, mentioned this point in his defense. It was crushing as far as his accusers were concerned, for the whole host of good Jewish Pharisees believed in the resurrection, and what Sadducee would dare to charge before a pagan procurator that that was a mortal crime? But that was what Paul's Sadducaic accusers were doing with him.

This point of Jewish doctrine, the resurrection of the dead, centered in Jesus. He died, and the accusers of Paul vehemently asserted, not only that he did not arise, but that resurrection as such was an absolute impossibility; while Paul affirmed both, in particular that Jesus was living, ζῆν, risen and living forever. Festus states the whole matter correctly. He must have been astonished to hear Paul's affirmation in his court — the first time, we take it, that he had ever heard it. Agrippa was better informed regarding Jesus and the Christians. The tone in which Festus speaks is one of entire aloofness; one Jesus — dead — Paul asserting that he is alive — terrible agitation among the high priests and elders in consequence.

By this very tone Festus condemns himself. What business had he as a high Roman judge to sit in court on a case relating to such questions of reverence for divinity that were complicated by assertions and denials of the resurrection? Gallio, cf. 18:14-16, was a different judge — he drove the Jews out of his court. Festus let them stand around Paul and keep up their contentions as though they were legitimate legal charges.

20) Now the confession is made outright: "And I on my part, being at a loss as to the question (the accusative as at times in the classics, R. 472) concern-

ing these things," etc. "Being at a loss" — why? We know why. It was because this judge wanted to curry favor with the accusers (v. 9). No, he does not say that! As a true judge he should not have been at a loss for one moment any more than Gallio had been.

So Festus says that he went on to say to Paul "whether he was willing to go to Jerusalem and there to be judged concerning these things." He does not say "to be judged before me" as he did in v. 9; let us hope that he had this in mind, yet who can be sure? But it is plain that the preamble does not fit the conclusion. How can this judge propose to transfer this case to Jerusalem merely because he knows nothing about a purely religious question? Would he know any more about it in Jerusalem? And if he ever learned more on that question whether one who had died was really still living or not, what did that matter in a Roman court? Here there is another classical optative in indirect discourse which replaces the indicative of the direct although at the speaker's option (R. 1031). This is another indication that Luke reports verbatim.

21) Another participle introduces Paul's appeal to Caesar but hides the fact that the action of Festus himself had forced Paul to resort to this appeal. Festus says that Paul appealed "for him to be kept in ward for the decision (the verb is used in 24:22) of the Augustus," and then that he ordered "him to be kept in ward," etc., the aorist passive infinitive being constative, the present passive infinitive durative. Just why this being kept in ward is stressed by this repetition is not apparent since Paul would naturally be in ward until arrangements could be made to send him to Rome. While ἀναπέμψω can be either the aorist subjunctive or the future indicative in the present construction, we are satisfied to regard it as the former.

"Caesar," originally a family name, became a title that was applied to the emperors. Σεβαστός, the verbal adjective "reverenced or worshipped," was assumed by Octavius in B. C. 27 as the *agnomen* that summed up all his various offices in preference to *Rex* that was so offensive to the Romans as to have led to the death of Julius Caesar. It then became a title, the equivalent of the Latin Augustus, and was more imposing than "Caesar." The Greek Σεβαστός was in keeping with the emperor deification and worship, being derived from the verb σεβάζομαι (σέβομαι), "to worship." See R., *W. P.* Translate, "the Augustus" (A. V. without "the") and not, "the emperor" (R. V.).

22) **And Agrippa to Festus, I was also myself wishing to hear the man. Tomorrow, he says, thou shalt hear him.**

In the Greek the verb of saying need not be written: "to Festus" is enough. The imperfect ἐβουλόμην is used for the sake of courtesy, as much as to say, "I was just wishing while you were speaking to get to hear the man," *den Menschen*, not *den Mann*. As is done in the English, the statement is put into the past although the reference is to the present. The form is a compliment to the interesting story told by Festus. The aorist ἀκοῦσαι is ingressive: "get to hear." The present indicative would be too blunt: βούλομαι, "I wish to hear." See R. 885, 919, *W. P.* Festus promptly accedes to the wish; he will arrange for Agrippa to hear Paul on the very next day. It is difficult to say whether from the beginning Festus planned to induce Agrippa to make this request so as to be able to stage the hearing that followed; or whether Agrippa's wish alone brought about the hearing. Divine providence prepared this new great opportunity for Paul to testify. Agrippa's desire to hear *den Menschen* was most probably real. Paul's fame and the

Christian movement especially among the Jews were surely known to the king and would arouse his interest. Beyond this the king's desire did not go.

23) **Accordingly, on the morrow, Agrippa and Bernice having come with much pomp, and they having gone into the audience hall with both chiliarchs and men of prominence, and Festus having given the order, there was brought in Paul.**

This translation follows the Greek very closely in order to show just what Luke conveys. There are three genitive absolutes to express the subordinate actions, and all the high personages figure only in these actions, then follow the main action and the chief person, just two words and subject and predicate reversed, this emphasizing both: "brought in was Paul." This sentence is a masterpiece in its description of the scene. It depicts how the stage is gradually set, one brilliant and impressive entrance is made after another, the king and his sister with their retinue come in great pomp, then others (the subject is indefinite), visitors perhaps are also present to congratulate Festus on his accession to the procuratorship, Festus, too, of course, has not only his five chiliarchs in gala uniform (five cohorts were stationed in Caesarea) but also the men of highest prominence in the city — all these are presented in their most pompous array and display. What an assemblage! The great stage is set. Festus gives the order. Then follow two simple words without a modifier, which are in striking contrast with the long preamble of genitive absolutes: ἤχθη ὁ Παῦλος, "there was brought in Paul." For him, for this humble apostle of Jesus Christ, for this lone, poor prisoner, this magnificent assembly of royalty, of rule, of military rank, of highest civil prominence has been arranged. Thus do imperial and royal courts assemble in all their splendor, and when the grand climax arrives, the portals swing open, and the emperor or the king enters.

Yes, all eyes were riveted on Paul. All had come in grand attire in order to hear this man. Festus had set this stage for Paul. Such is the esteem which this apostle commanded. When Ramsay thinks that Paul was treated thus because he had much money at his command, he is mistaken; for no millionaire prisoner was such a stage ever set. What were Paul's feelings when he was ushered into this ἀκροατήριον, the great audience hall in the palace of Herod the Great that had been built for just such assemblages as this? If he had had advance notice regarding this audience, he surely did not expect such a magnificent gathering. We shall see that he measured up fully to the occasion the Lord's providence here provided for him.

The greatest man present was Paul. The sacred pages record the other names only because they tell about Paul. He wore no insignia of rank but only his ordinary tunic and robe, he was the one man in common dress in glaring contrast with all the rest. Regarding Agrippa and Bernice, Luke even mentions "much pomp," φαντασία, display, which we take as a reference to their dress as well as to their retinue. Luke writes no articles with "chiliarchs" and "men, etc.," and thus stresses what they were: chiliarchs came, men of prominence came, etc. Κατ' ἐξοχήν appears only here in the New Testament and in inscriptions of the first century, yet it has become a standard phrase which we still use in its original Greek just as we employ the French *par excellence.* The article makes the phrase an adjective (do not supply οὖσιν with τοῖς), and ἐξοχή = a projection, an eminence. These κατά phrases are stronger than mere genitives would be.

In the nature of the case Paul "was brought." It would not surprise us if the very centurion who had him in charge conducted him into the hall and to the place assigned to him before this audience. In view of 26:29 we shall already here say that it is inconceivable to us that Paul was brought in wearing a chain or chains which either fastened his wrist to a soldier or fettered his wrists or ankles. It is inconceivable that to this audience this Roman procurator should present a Roman citizen and one who had never been charged with violence, who had been pronounced not guilty of death or bonds (23:29; 25:25; 26:31), who had as a Roman appealed to the emperor — in chains. When chains were used, Luke uses the proper word, as in 21:33 and in 28:20. Were Luke and perhaps another friend or two of Paul's (27:2) with him on this occasion as his attendants? We wish we might be positive; as it is, all we can say is that this is not unlikely. Festus would never think of displaying anything but fairness, yea, open generosity before this assembly.

24) **And Festus says: King Agrippa and all men present with us, you behold this one about whom all the multitude of the Jews petitioned me both in Jerusalem and here, shouting that he must not live any longer. But I on my part understood that he had committed nothing worthy of death. Moreover, he himself having appealed to the Augustus, I gave judgment to send him, concerning whom I have no certain thing to write to my lord. Wherefore I brought him before you and especially before thee, King Agrippa, in order that, examination having taken place, I may get what I shall write. For it seems unreasonable to me that, sending a prisoner, I signify not also the complaints against him.**

It behooves Festus to open the proceedings, which he does with this address. He had, no doubt, thought it out carefully. It fully reveals the character of the man. Although it is intended to be impressive and to justify the gathering of this assembly, it is weak in its supposed strong point. Agrippa is to make due ἀνάκρισις, "judical examination," of Paul in order to aid Festus in formulating proper "complaints" against Paul. We have such a preliminary examination in John 18:33-38, but nothing even faintly like it here in the case of Paul. Agrippa was not competent to examine; all he could do and did do was to let Paul speak for himself.

One is surprised at the openness with which Festus confesses the false and helpless position into which he alone had maneuvered himself in this case. That audience could not have thought highly of him on the basis of his own address. On the other hand, what he feels obliged to say about Paul, about the clamor of the Jews for his death when he, the governor, found no basis for that clamor, and the appeal to the Augustus, which he, the governor, had to allow, made Paul stand out before this audience. Here there was a rather helpless and inefficient governor and a most unusual, interesting, and effective prisoner.

The address is simple and direct. The king is named first as the person who is being honored by Festus through this occasion. Τοῦτον, used with reference to Paul, is not derogatory as this demonstrative often is. The hyperbole, "all the multitude of the Jews," unconsciously expresses the governor's estimate of Paul and is thus not mere exaggeration. Moreover, Festus thought that the Jews generally were opposed to Paul, and that the Sanhedrists represented their view. The second aorist ἐνέτυχον, like the noun ἔντευξις, is here used in the technical sense, "petitioned me," plural since the subject is collective. Festus combines the original petition which was presented in Jerusalem (v. 3) and what followed "here" in Caesarea (v. 7) into one, for the shouting was done "here." The infinitive δεῖν expresses the demand of the Jews that Paul must no longer go on living (ζῆν, present, durative). All eyes must have turned toward Paul. So this was the one for whose death "the multitude of the Jews" clamored! A Latin and a Syriac version, especially the latter, expand the address considerably.

25) The pride of the Roman judge now asserts itself in the emphatic ἐγώ and in the statement that Festus was not swept away by this petition and this clamor of the Jews but as a judge of great insight "grasped" that Paul had committed (perfect infinitive which is retained from the direct form of the thought) nothing worthy of death. Festus is honest regarding this vital point — credit to him for that. But why had he as a just Roman judge then not acquitted this innocent man? Why is it that Paul had to appeal to the Augustus (v. 21), and that Festus "gave judgment" ("determined" in our versions is incorrect — it was a judicial act) to send him (present tense, the sending had not yet occurred)? What was amiss we know from v. 9; Festus passes over it in silence. In private, alone with Agrippa (v. 20, 21), he told at least what he had done although he hid the real motive.

This he presents to the assembly: the Jewish clamor for Paul's death — his own conviction of Paul's innocence — the appeal of Paul to Caesar which was duly allowed.

26) Now comes the difficulty. When a Roman who had appealed his case was sent to the emperor, *literae dimissoriae* had to accompany the prisoner, which presented the αἰτίαι or "complaints" lodged against him (v. 27). Festus confesses that he has "no certain thing" to write to Caesar. To obtain what he lacks, he says, he has brought Paul before this company, in particular before Agrippa, ἐπί is again to be understood (23:30 and repeatedly) in this sense. Festus expects the king to conduct an ἀνάκρισις, to develop "what I shall write." Τί is the interrogative in

an indirect question and not the indefinite τί, "somewhat" (our versions); and γράψω may be either the subjunctive, "may write," or the future indicative, "shall write," for in the direct question either may be used (R. 875).

We note how Festus makes the difficulty appear, and what his difficulty really was. Agrippa had been assigned a task he could not accomplish; in 26:31, 32 we see that Festus was eventually left just where he had put himself in the first place by seeking to acquire the favor of the Jews (v. 9). Festus makes it appear that without further ado Paul appealed to Caesar when he (Festus) regarded him as innocent of a capital crime. He makes it appear that he was about to acquit Paul when Paul impeded all further action by voicing his appeal (see 26:32). Even then the fault remains that Festus "gave judgment to send him" (v. 25), accepted and allowed the appeal. He should have denied this appeal, promptly answered it by complete acquittal, and thus removed all grounds for appeal. But no, angered by Paul's manly language and prompt appeal to Caesar, he had accepted that appeal in a foolish, sententious manner. So he had cast his own fat into the fire.

The truth was even worse. Festus knew in detail what the Jewish accusations really were, that they were not crimes but matters of faith (v. 18, 19), things that did not belong before a Roman court. When this had been made clear at the trial, and when Festus then sought to gain Jewish favor and proposed to send Paul to Jerusalem for further trial (v. 9), Paul appealed to Caesar. Add these real facts, and the full difficulty of Festus becomes clear. He dared not write the true facts to the emperor, that he had driven Paul to appeal, and that in a temper he had accepted that appeal. He dared not confess his own injustice. Now he was helpless, without imagination enough to lie his way out of the tangle in some at least plausible manner. Those Jewish "complaints" were unfit to send to Nero; his own conviction of Paul's innocence he dared not write, for Nero would at once demand to know why justice had not been done by Festus in accord with that conviction, why this procurator troubled him with an appeal that the prisoner should never have needed to make.

Festus calls Nero "my lord." Octavius and Tiberius had refused the title Κύριος as being too much like *rex* and like the master of slaves. The other emperors accepted it, Nero among them; Antonius Pius even put it on his coins. This title Κύριος played a great role in these times. Read Deissmann, *Light from the Ancient East,* 353-361. *Kyrios,* "Son of God," and the adjective "divine" were applied to the emperors when deifying them just as Κύριος was applied to pagan gods. Many Christians became martyrs for refusing to utter this deifying title in worship of the emperor. "In the case of Polycarp, at Smyrna in the year 155 it was a question of the 'lord'-formula. What is the harm of saying 'lord Caesar'? the Irenarch Herod and his father Nicetes asked the saint seductively." Polycarp refused and died. Another, Speratus of Scili in Numidia, replied: "I know of no imperium of this world, . . . I know my lord, the King of kings, and Emperor of all nations."

27) "Unreasonable" indeed, or, as we may translate, "contrary to reason," it would be to send a prisoner to Caesar and not to signify the "complaints" or charges on the basis of which he is sent. That sums up the difficulty of Festus who had no adequate presentation of the case which he could forward without confessing his own guilt, and then he would have no case to present. The accusative πέμποντα is the subject of the infinitive σημᾶναι with με understood.

CHAPTER XXVI

PAUL'S ADDRESS BEFORE AGRIPPA

1) Festus spoke about an ἀνάκρισις, a judicial examination of one accused (25:26). How he thought Agrippa should conduct such a probe we, of course, do not know, nor what new material he hoped to gain from such an examination for his report to Caesar. Paul had always been free and open. Pilate gave Jesus a judicial examination, cf., John 18:33-38; Agrippa attempts no such questioning. He knew the whole case only at second hand, had not himself heard the accusers nor any witnesses, was in no position to do at this date and before this magnificent audience what belonged in the courtroom in the presence of the accusers and what Festus should have done so thoroughly as to require no re-doing.

We must note that all the present proceedings with regard to Paul are exceptional in the highest degree. Paul is now *not* on trial. All proceedings relative to a trial were automatically stopped the moment Paul's appeal to the emperor was accepted by Festus; any further trial must be held in the emperor's court. The appeal, once accepted, could not be withdrawn. That would, indeed, seem to have been one way out of the governor's trouble, namely to exchange a retraction of the appeal for acquittal and safe release. Aside from a legal possibility of this kind, the procurator's Roman pride closed that avenue, for it would have been an open confession of fault on his part, and thus in v. 32 we see that such a course is not contemplated. After Festus drove Paul to appeal so that he had to accept that appeal, he had to go through with the appeal.

What, then, could Agrippa do when Festus turned Paul over to him for an ἀνάκρισις before this grand assembly in the display hall of the palace (see 25:23)? He did about the only thing he could do. **Now Agrippa said to Paul, It is permitted to thee to speak in thy own behalf.**

The king asks Paul to present his own case, and the durative infinitive bids him do so at length. This permission did not exclude questioning, and questioning might have followed if Paul had created a suspicion that he was hiding something. Paul, however, had nothing to hide and presented his case so that no room was left for even a single question. Thus no judicial examination could even be started unless we call Paul's address itself such an examination.

Then Paul by stretching forth his hand began to make his defense.

Paul would have been within his legal rights if he had refused to present his case. This was not a court, not a trial; Agrippa had no jurisdiction over him; his appeal placed him into the emperor's court alone. Paul is aware of all this, fully aware of it. Yet he makes his defense at the request of Agrippa; but its climax shows that he has a far higher object than merely proving his own innocence of any crime. That had to be included as being basic for his real object, the presentation of the gospel to Agrippa and to all his hearers.

Paul converted this great hall into a church and acted as the preacher. He made this entire assembly, which had come here in pomp and display in order to enjoy a novel spectacle, something of which it had not at all thought, namely hearers of the gospel of Jesus Christ. God had created this golden opportunity for his chosen apostle "to bear Jesus' name before the Gentiles and kings" (9:15), and he embraced this opportunity to the full. The fact of his being a prisoner made the opportunity only more dramatic and impressed his testimony more deeply. The Lord does this sort of thing with sinners, even with the mightiest. When they least expect it, he confronts them with the gospel in order to save them. Here the Lord employs a pagan to provide a church, to bring all these sinners together, to fetch a preacher, to introduce him most effectively, and then himself to sit down to listen with the rest. Alas, neither Festus nor Agrippa spoke as Cornelius had spoken to Peter here in Caesarea: "Now, therefore, are we all here present before God to hear all things that are commanded thee of God" (9:33).

The imperfect is inchoative, "began to make his defense." To stretch out the hand is not the same as motioning with the hand (12:17; 13:16). The latter is done in order to obtain silence, the former is a natural oratorical raising of the hand in a gesture toward the king whom Paul addresses. This shows perfect ease and mastery, dignified and appropriate bearing. With a respectful inclination of the head and a sweep of the hand this master-speaker acknowledges and accepts the king's permission and does, indeed, speak, but also in that king's behalf. A number of interpreters say that Paul's hand was chained to a soldier who stood guard beside him; we regard that view untenable (see 25:23, last paragraph). It seems that the fright of the chiliarch mentioned in 22:29, which was caused by having bound Paul with chains (22:25) and the present status of the apostle, this gala assembly, and other decisive considerations are overlooked.

Paul's address is simple, lucid, straight to the point. Dramatically it rises to its climax (v. 21-23). The best way to feel its power and to understand how it gripped the pagan Festus and made him exclaim aloud (v. 24) although Agrippa alone was addressed, is to read Paul's words aloud while imagining oneself to be in his place before that audience. The theme of the address is stated in its opening phrase: Περὶ πάντων ὧν ἐγκαλοῦμαι ὑπὸ Ἰουδαίων, "*Concerning all things of which I am being accused by Jews.*" After the introduction (v. 2, 3) there follow five sections of biographical material in elaboration of the reason that Paul is being accused for believing in the crucified Christ, the Light unto the people (Israel) and to the Gentiles. The story begins with

1) *The ardent young Pharisee* who believes in Israel's great hope of the resurrection and is now accused by Jews for that very hope (v. 4-8). It proceeds by presenting this Pharisee as

2) *The violent persecutor* of all the saints who believed in the name of Jesus (v. 9-11), who then, in the full swing of his persecution, is made

3) *A minister and witness* of the glorified Jesus, who is sent, under his protection, especially to the Gentiles (v. 12-18) and for this reason

4) *Almost killed* by Jews when he is caught in the Temple (v. 19-21) and yet is

5) *A constant witness to this day* of the old prophecies that have now been fulfilled in the suffering and the risen Christ (v. 22, 23).

The address is most compact. From start to finish it presents just what drives Jews (note: not *the* Jews) to accuse and to seek to kill Paul. It omits every side issue and all points that are immaterial to the main issue. Failure to understand this has produced the discussion in regard to agreement with Luke's narration in 9:1, etc., and Paul's other address in 22:1, etc. The biographical data are made to focus in *the hope of the resurrection* which was held by Israel, which hope was realized in Jesus who is *the Christ.*

Paul took the cue from Festus instantly: "especially before thee, king Agrippa," and addressed Agrippa alone. But Paul did not thereby ignore Festus as though he were through with him or disregarded the rest of the audience. The reverse is true. By addressing the king alone every ear was made the keener to catch what the king was supposed to be especially able to understand. This gained for Paul even more than many a speaker tries to secure by centering his attention on one auditor alone. The fact that Paul gripped every person present is clearly evidenced by the circumstance that it was Festus who cried out at last (v. 24) although Paul was not addressing him. Being the procurator, he could interrupt Paul, others in the assembly had to restrain themselves. But into the ears of every Gentile present sank most deeply every significant statement Paul made about Jesus and the Gentiles (v. 17, 18, 20, 23). And every Jew present was struck by what Paul said about the hope of the promise made to the fathers by God about the twelve tribes serving God night and day in that hope (v. 6, 7), about the prophets and Moses (v. 22), and about this Jesus of Nazareth realizing the ancient hope by his resurrection to glory as "the Christ" (v. 23). Today we must struggle to feel the tremendous impact upon all that was made by almost every statement of this living address. It presented the full sweep of the gospel in the life of its greatest witness who glowed with its power as few have ever glowed.

Add the living voice, the ring of profoundest conviction, the truth instinctively felt as truth. Where had these personages ever heard such a voice and such truth before? Paul was witnessing in supreme fashion (v. 22, 23) on repentance, forgiveness, the inheritance of heaven, the works meet for repentance (v. 18, 20), for Jew and Gentile alike in the risen Christ. It was personal, straight to the soul, the more effective for being only biographical. Then came the dramatic end: the cry of Festus and Paul's telling answer, the question to Agrippa, his answer, and Paul's reply. Paul was reaching home. Who had anticipated anything like this from one who was nothing but a Jewish prisoner? Dignitaries in ranks, a procurator, a king — and a prisoner! And this prisoner dominated them all.

When one now enters upon the details of the address, their variety and the discussion of them must not dim the power that floods through them and reveals the Lord's chosen witness at the height of his work. What he said at his two trials in Rome where he was acquitted in the one and sent to the axman's block in the other, is not reported to us. Did he face Nero himself? To what height did his testimony then rise? The record left us does not extend that far.

2) **Concerning all things of which I am being accused by Jews, King Agrippa, I consider myself happy as being about to make defense before thee today, especially thou being an expert regarding all both the customs and questions among Jews. Wherefore I beg, patiently to hear me.**

In the very first phrase Paul strikes squarely the subject about which Festus was in difficulty; Paul will speak about all the Jewish accusations and evade none. On ὧν see 24:8, 13. Note the absence of the article: "by Jews"; this absence is repeated. Jews they were, these Sadducees, not "*the* Jews," not even representative Jews. When comparing Paul's opening words with those of Tertullus in 24:2-4, we at once see the great difference. The latter are open and insincere flattery, the former register a pertinent and a valuable fact. Agrippa had had the control of the Temple plus the appointment of the high priests by gift from Caesar, was himself a Jew as far as religion was concerned, and thus knew both the customs and the questions of the Jews. Paul says he is glad to present his case before a man possessed of this information. He certainly was. It was far different from dealing with a pagan like Felix to whom all these Jewish matters were new, strange, perhaps incomprehensible.

A few verbs have the perfect in the present sense. Such a verb is ἥγημαι, "I consider." When it is used, as here, with the reflexive pronoun "myself," the force of the middle voice in the verb itself is probably largely lost, R. 690. As in 23:30, ἐπί is again to be taken in the sense of "before."

3) We construe μάλιστα with ὄντα. Most interesting is γνώστην ὄντα σε, which B.-D. 137, 3 calls "a constructionless accusative," which is a meaningless term, and R. 1130, with similar hesitancy, calls it "a possible accusative absolute," although it is practically the only one occurring in the New Testament. Some texts insert ἐπιστάμενος, "knowing thee as being an expert," which, however, fails to explain the other texts. Why hesitate in regard to this lone appearance of an accusative absolute: "thou being an expert," γνώστην with the objective genitive, "one who knows all the Jewish customs and questions"? Κατά is stronger than a mere genitive would be: "among (throughout) Jews" — again no article. Agrippa knew all the Jewish customs or practices, likewise all the questions which divided the Jews into parties such as the Pharisees, Sadducees, Herodians. Paul implies that the more a man knows about these matters, the more easily he will see how innocent Paul is of any crime or fault regarding Jews.

Paul intends to present his entire case and thus begs Agrippa to hear him (aorist to indicate complete hearing) patiently. Paul begins with perfect calmness and dignity. We have already stated why he addressed the king alone. One sentence suffices for the introduction. It stated very much the right thing in the right way both for the king and for the audience.

4, 5) First *the ardent young Pharisee.* With the neat transitional μὲν οὖν Paul presents this period of his life. **Now my manner of life from youth up, as spent from the beginning in my nation and in Jerusalem, know all Jews having knowledge of me from**

the first, if they be willing to testify, that according to the strictest sect of our worship I lived a Pharisee. And now on hope of the promise made to our fathers I stand as being judged — unto which our twelve tribes, with intentness serving God night and day, hope to attain — concerning which hope I am being accused by Jews, O king! Why is it judged incredible with you if God raises the dead? Paul's life in its earlier period was like an open book to all Jews who knew him at the time, and we know that these were many, including the whole Sanhedrin of those years.

In only two other places do we find the word βίωσις, "manner of life," *Lebensweise;* and ἐκ designates the starting point. "In my nation" is general; "also in Jerusalem" specifies the Jewish capital in particular. It was necessary to specify Jerusalem, for here Paul was educated (22:3), and here he rose to his height as a Pharisee. We must construe together: "all Jews formerly knowing me from the first," and thus need no article, "all *the* Jews"; and ἴσασι is the literary Attic form for the vernacular οἴδασι. The condition of expectancy: "if they be willing to testify," assumes such willingness, and the ὅτι clause states what their testimony would be: "that according to the strictest sect of our worship I lived a Pharisee," the predicative "Pharisee" being placed last for the sake of emphasis. On "sect" see 5:17.

Θρησκεία is the *cultus exterior,* and a θρῆσκος is one who is diligent in all cultus acts. This word is eminently in place because Pharisees were most scrupulous in regard to outward religious observances (Matt. 23:14, etc.). In v. 7 Paul uses λατρεύω, to serve God with sacrifice, a service that was obligatory for all. Paul rightly calls the Pharisees "the strictest sect" (one of the three superlatives in the New Testament that end in -τατος) ; they were, indeed, most exacting in their formalism. Paul includes this as well as their work-righteousness and spurious holiness when he here says that he lived as a Pharisee.

6) Here, however, the point to be noted is that the Pharisees ever held fast to and defended most strenuously the hope of the promise of the resurrection against the small though powerful sect of the Sadducees (23:8). In regard to this doctrine Paul was as much as ever a strenuous Pharisee. He is becoming dramatic. Every Jew who knew him in his early years will testify that he was a genuine Pharisee. "And now" he is being judged on the ground (ἐπί) of his hoping for the fulfillment of the promise made to the fathers by God! What a contradictory situation! Paul as yet purposely withholds the substance of this hope and promise, namely the resurrection of the dead. It is assumed that Agrippa the Jew at once understands. Others will understand in a moment. "On hope" = for hoping, for having such a hope; and "of the promise" is the objective genitive, hope of the promise being hope in its fulfillment.

"God" himself, the God in whom Agrippa believes, the great God of Israel to whom all Jews bow in distinction from all pagans, made this glorious promise, made it "to the fathers," whom all Jews are proud to acknowledge as their fathers. The Scriptures are not mentioned but only the great fact which they report, this glorious, this supreme promise. When Paul lived as a Pharisee here in Jerusalem, no Jew ever dreamed of bringing him to judgment before a court, Jewish or pagan, for hoping in this promise; but now — here he stands, accused and being judged, and before a pagan judge (Festus) to whom this hope and this promise mean nothing!

7) Two relative clauses follow; but in order to get their force we must remember that in the Greek relatives such as these have demonstrative force. Thus,

"unto which" = "unto which very promise (i. e., its fulfillment) the twelve tribes, with intentness serving God night and day, hope to arrive." This accusation against Paul is one that charges criminality against the δωδεκάφυλον of Israel itself. This substantivized adjective = *das Zwoelfstaemmegeschlecht,* the twelve-tribe-body.

It is unwarranted to say that Paul "had no knowledge of the 'lost ten tribes'." He certainly knew the history of the ten tribes which constituted the northern kingdom called Israel. Their deportation left some few behind, who, mixed with Gentiles, became the Samaritans, the enemies of the Jews. Some eventually returned from exile but were amalgamated with the Jews (Judah and Benjamin). Many remained in the foreign land and became mixed with the Jews of the Babylonian captivity in the so-called Dispersion. But the bulk of the ten tribes was really "lost." They were idolatrous in their own northern kingdom and were absorbed in foreign paganism so that all trace of them disappeared. Smith, *Bible Dictionary* I, 387, and other accounts. Paul uses δωδεκάφυλον with reference to the Jews in general who are found in the world as still representing the original twelve tribes. James 1:1 addresses "the twelve tribes" and has in mind all Jews who had been converted to Christianity in the Diaspora. Thus they were still more reduced in number and yet were the representatives of the original twelve tribes.

The neuter present participle λατρεῦον modifies δωδεκάφυλον and is modal: this body of the twelve tribes hopes to attain the promise, i. e., its fulfillment, "by serving with intentness night and day," by rendering that service to God which is obligatory upon all. Ἐκτενείᾳ is a stretched-out, straining effort like that of a runner making for his goal. "Night and day" (the same order of words found in 20:31) is the usual form for our "day and night." The verb "hopes" is vital in the statement by resuming the noun "hope"; *on hope* Paul is being judged, and the twelve-tribe-body *ever hopes* with the same hope.

Clinching this contrast and bringing out the monstrosity involved, Paul repeats the noun hope and again uses a relative with demonstrative force: "concerning which hope," i. e., "concerning *this very hope* I am being accused by Jews, O king!" The thing is almost incredible although, alas, true. Think of it. "Jews" are accusing one of their own race for holding to the hope that has ever lifted their nation above paganism! Again "Jews," minus the article, and here especially we feel that Paul has in mind "people who call themselves Jews but are not real Jews at all" — Jews, renegades to the great hope of Judaism. The simple Greek vocative is best rendered "O king."

8) From the address, "king," Paul turns to the assembly in general with a dramatic rhetorical question. Whereas he has thus far spoken of "hope" and "the promise made by God" he now mentions the substance of that promise and that hope. "Why is it judged incredible with you if God raises the dead?" In spite of the marked singular vocative "king" and the equally marked plural "with you," it has been supposed that the king is included in this plural "you." No; Agrippa was not a Sadducee, especially not with reference to this doctrine. This does not imply that he was a Pharisee. He was a Jew like the mass of the people were, an adherent of no particular party and thus, like this mass, a believer in the resurrection, the hope of all Israel, excluding only the small sect of the Sadducees. Paul's entire address to the king, notably also its climax (v. 27-29), is not an effort to convince a Sadducee of the resurrection but a joyful testimony to a Jewish believer in the resurrection of Paul's own faith in that hope as realized especially in Jesus, the

risen Christ. Thus understood, all is clear and convincing, otherwise all would be out of line.

We have shown why Paul makes his address to Agrippa, but the whole audience is before him. It is largely pagan, and therefore this Jewish hope in the resurrection was "incredible." Like Jesus (Matt. 22:23-33), Paul would have met a Sadducee with the Scriptures. These pagans he meets with the one word "God," the God who *is* God. With one crushing blow he strikes their incredulity and ignorance. The question comes like a flash. Its answer is as plain as day. It is not only credible that God should raise the dead, it is wholly incredible that he should not — if, indeed, he is God and not merely one of the pagan gods. Paul wisely uses a question and thereby throws the burden of answering wholly upon his hearers. That question undoubtedly struck home. It was simplicity itself and could not easily be thrown off. It staggered the pagan mind with a thought it had never seriously entertained. Agrippa was a Jew and as such believed in the resurrection, and before these pagans Paul was bringing out this faith as one that was shared by the Jewish king. This question was thus an impenetrable shield that was suddenly raised by Paul in order to cover also the king before these pagans. Incredible — no, this king is believing nothing incredible by holding to Israel's supreme hope!

The condition, εἰ with the indicative, is one of reality: "if God raises the dead," and assumes that he indeed does. This εἰ is not ὅτι, nor is it to be taken in the sense of ὅτι (declarative), R. 1024. While either could be used, the one is different from the other; we make the same difference in thought between an assumption and a mere fact as such. The present tense "raises the dead" makes the condition general, he raises them at any time as his will may determine. Paul includes every resurrection, those reported in the Old Testament, those in the New — had he not himself brought Eutychus back to life (20:10, etc.)?—in particular the resurrection of Jesus to glory and the resurrection at the end of the world. The absence of the article with νεκρούς draws attention to the quality of the noun: "dead," such as are dead.

In this first part of the address Paul shows that the basic issue in his accusations is the great hope of Israel in God's promise of the resurrection. All these accusations fall in a heap the moment this issue becomes clear.

9) In the second part of the address Paul presents his career as *the violent persecutor* of all that was marked by the name of Jesus of Nazareth. Although he was a Pharisee and believed in the resurrection he acted just like those who are now thirsting for his blood. Note that μὲν οὖν marks the second part as it does the first (v. 4), both are only transitional, "now," not "verily" (our versions).

Now I myself (emphatic ἐγώ) **thought for myself that I had to commit many hostile things against the name of Jesus, the Nazarene; which also I did in Jerusalem. And I myself both shut up many of the saints in prisons, having received the authority from the high priests, and when they were being made away with, I gave my vote. And throughout all the synagogues, by often punishing them, I was forcing them to blaspheme; and being exceedingly enraged against them, I was pursuing them to even the outside cities.** This account of Paul's evil activities is fuller than the statements found in 9:1 and 22:4, 5.

Paul takes the entire blame for this mad persecution of the Christians upon himself: "I myself thought for myself," etc., (personal construction of this verb). Δεῖν, expressing any type of necessity, here denotes that of personal conviction; it is the infinitive in indirect discourse. At this point Paul introduces "the name of Jesus" and calls him "the Nazarene" just as Peter did in 2:22; see also 3:6; 4:10. Agrippa at once understands, the rest of the audience also. At once also that name reveals as in a flash what Paul aimed at when he spoke of the promise, the hope, and God raising the dead, namely this that God raised up Jesus as the Messiah. Not until he reaches the end (v. 23) is this stated outright; here, in the second section of the address, it is Paul's opposition to this Jesus that is sketched.

On the lips of Paul, even in a connection such as this, "the name" means "the revelation" (see 2:21, and all the other passages that have this significant ὄνομα). Paul says that his overpowering conviction was that this NAME and all it embraced and conveyed must be abolished root and branch: "it was necessary to commit many hostile things against the name," etc.

10) This very thing, too, he did (the relative with the same force it has in v. 7) first in Jerusalem and then also in the outside cities (v. 11). With the emphatic ἐγώ he again assumes the full responsibility. It was *he* who, having received "the (i. e., necessary) authority from the high priests," locked up many of the saints in prisons. By calling them "saints" Paul confesses his great guilt; Luke uses this term in 9:13 and elsewhere. Now follows the worst part: "they being made away with," the present participle being iterative to indicate the frequent trials, "I cast my vote," i. e., affirmatively, an idiomatic expression in the Greek (see the similar terms in 1:26; 19:19). Ἀναιρέω, "to make away with," is the significant verb which is used so often with reference to Jesus beginning with 2:23, then also with reference to the attempts against Paul himself. Paul voted for the death of many Christians.

Stephen's martyrdom was followed by others. We see no way of mitigating this fact although attempts to do so have been made. See the remarks on 9:1. How the Sanhedrin managed the executions and obtained the procurator's assent we are unable to say.

Is κατήνεγκα ψῆφον to be understood literally? The ancient Greeks voted with pebbles, white ones for acquittal, black ones for conviction. The writer has seen this method of voting employed even at the present time: a box attached to a long handle, had a drawer containing white and black marbles, each voter picked out one and dropped it through a hole in the top of the box, the marbles used for voting falling into an upper drawer. The verb "to blackball" is derived from this way of voting.

The main point, however, concerns the question as to how Paul came to have a vote in these trials, and whether he voted by actually casting a pebble or not. Was he himself a Sánhedrist? And since this body was composed of married men, was he at that time married and later became a widower? We can be certain of the main fact expressed in these questions, namely that Paul never belonged to the Sanhedrin as one of its members. The record shows so many contacts of Paul with the Sanhedrin that, if he had been one of the members, that fact would undoubtedly have been stated. It would have been too pertinent to have been passed over in silence in 7:58-8:3; 9:1, etc.; 22:3-5, and elsewhere. This lone remark about Paul's voting is too slender a support to suffice as a basis for so great a fact. With that falls the thought of his marriage.

The one thing we do not know is the capacity in which Paul voted. One way out of the difficulty is to regard this voting as figurative, as consenting heartily to the death of these saints; but we see no reason for this peculiar figure and prefer to predicate a real vote.

Was Paul, perhaps, empowered to vote as the accredited agent of the Sanhedrin, the agent who had apprehended these as being the most guilty persons?

11) As the next greatest crime Paul mentions the fact that throughout all the synagogues of Jerusalem he often forced the saints to blaspheme, and when they fled, he pursued them even to outside cities. The point to be decided is whether the imperfect ἠνάγκαζον is conative (R., *W. P.*): "tried to force," i. e., without succeeding, or whether the tense is iterative: forced again and again. The fact that Paul has already said that he brought many to death is adduced in support of the former idea, those who remained firm were executed; those who yielded, blasphemed. Other considerations point in the same direction. We have two parallel imperfects; ἠνάγκαζον and ἐδίωκον, and it is natural to understand them in the same way. But the latter cannot be conative: "tried to pursue," for Paul did this very thing. Now it is possible to regard one imperfect as conative and the other as iterative, but such a construction would be very odd. The adverb: "by *often* punishing them I was forcing," etc., certainly agrees only with the iterative sense. Finally, we have iteration in the preceding: "when they were being made away with," and it is most natural to continue this in connection with the next-mentioned atrocities.

As much as we should like to believe that no saint of that time denied the faith, we fear that a good many did. Paul uses the infinitive "to blaspheme" (also iterative present tense), namely to revile Jesus as not being the Christ. This verb is spoken from Paul's present standpoint. He now sees that he forced these poor Christians to utter what was really blasphemy. The fact that Paul went to outside cities before he attempted his journey to Damascus is stated only here; but it is natural to think that he would not at once leap from Jerusalem to Damascus. It is easy to see Paul's reason for so fully stating his rage against the Name of Jesus: Agrippa is to understand that Paul was even more bloodthirsty against this Name than his accusers now are. They are persecuting him and him alone; Paul was wiping out all the Christians near and far away. But let us not lose the connection: the promise of God, the hope of the fathers and of the twelve tribes centers and culminates in Jesus, in his glorious resurrection. This is the inner connection, and Paul now continues with this.

12) In his third part Paul states how this Jesus met and checked him in the midst of his bloody career, yea, turned him into *a minister and witness* of this Jesus. Even now Paul does not mention Christ's resurrection — he does not need to do so. That and the glorious enthronement stand out by themselves. Agrippa is to tell himself a few things as Paul proceeds. Before him stands the fiercest enemy Jesus had ever had, this enemy converted into the most fervent apostle — a miraculous transformation that is unaccountable save for what Paul now tells.

In connection with which things, while journeying to Damascus with authority and commission of the high priests, at midday along the road I saw, O king, a light that shone from heaven beyond the brilliance of the sun around me and those journeying with me. And, we all having fallen to the ground, I heard a voice saying to me in the Hebrew language, Saul, Saul, why art thou persecuting me? Hard for thee to be kicking against goads! And I said, Who art thou, Lord? And the Lord said, I, I am Jesus, whom thou art persecuting!

Ἐν οἷς is neither "whereupon" (our versions) nor "on this errand" (R. V. margin) but "in connection with which matters," the relative is again used as in v. 7 and 10: "in connection with the very things just stated," especially Paul's ravaging the outside cities.

We need not repeat what has been said in 9:2-5, and 22:5, etc. The double: "authority and commission" emphasizes this point; the expedition was to execute a task that had been officially "turned over" to Paul.

13) The fact that the light appeared "at midday" is told also in 22:6. When the Syrian sun which is always intense was at its zenith and its maximum intensity, this miraculous light which was beyond the sun's brilliance suddenly flooded Paul and his companions. Note the dramatic vocative, "O king!" at this point. It happened years ago but is as vivid to Paul as it was at the time when the miracle occurred.

14) The fact that "all" fell prostrate when the superearthly light enveloped them is reported only here. As regards ἀκούω with the accusative (here; 9:4; 22:9) and again with the genitive (9:7; 22:7), the explanation that at times no difference is intended, is questionable. The genitive connotes the person speaking, the accusative the thing spoken. Examine these five passages from this angle. Paul is speaking in the presence of Romans and of Greeks and thus mentions that what he heard spoken (accusative φωνὴν λέγουσαν) was by way of the Hebrew (meaning Aramaic) language (not "dialect," see 2:6), which explains "Saul, Saul" as the name applied to him who now went by the name of Paul. The words: "Hard for thee to be kicking against goads!" belong only in Paul's present narration; copyists interpolated them in 9:5 (A. V.). The statement is proverbial and has been traced in Greek poetry and Greek prose through five centuries B. C. and four A. D. A goad, a sharp stick, was used to prod oxen to a more rapid pace; feeling its prod, they might kick back and thereby only wound themselves more severely, and σκληρόν is to be understood in this sense. This saying is not found in Jewish literature.

Since Jesus spoke to Paul in Aramaic, the question arises whether Paul gave only the sense of the Aramaic, or whether Jesus spoke these very words in Aramaic. The former seems to be correct. But this does not imply that in some other Scripture passages which have the word κέντρον or "sting" we may find the original Aramaic expression employed here by Jesus. We cannot substitute the sting of a scorpion for the goads prodding oxen (I Cor. 15:55, 56; Hos. 13:14; Rev. 9:10). A sting that kills and against which no one kicks his heel is far from a goad that pricks and, when kicked against, hurts only the more.

Figurative language often becomes lucid when its connection with the literal is noted. That is the case here. "Why persecutest thou me?" and the repetition, "whom thou persecutest," were the goads of the law that were driven into the conscience of Saul. See 9:5: the force of the question aimed at contrition. Paul might in anger kick against these goads. They would strike more deeply, affect him the more painfully. The statement was thus a call to contrition by yielding to the blows of the law. We find no thought here which intimates that the Lord's will is irresistible. We likewise decline to extend the reference to the entire future life of Paul, especially to its providential leadings. This word refers only to the sharp, penetrating question of Jesus, this stab of the law into Saul's tough conscience.

15) Paul's question and the Lord's answer are reported exactly as they are recorded in 9:5.

16) Then, instead of narrating the rest in historical form as Luke does in 9:16, etc., Paul adds only a summary of all that the Lord communicated to him regarding the apostleship to which he had been chosen. For this is the point Paul intends to impress: he, the worst persecutor, is made a minister and witness by the Lord's own gracious act. To tell all about Ana-

nias whom the Lord used as his instrument in dealing with Paul would only complicate the narrative and blur the chief point Paul is impressing by bringing in unessential details. So also in retelling what the Lord communicated to him Paul uses language that is largely his own, a wording that conveys fully and precisely to this audience what the Lord said and had in mind.

But arise and stand upon thy feet. For this did I appear to thee to appoint thee for myself as a helper and a witness both of the things thou didst see and of the things I will let thee see, delivering thee from the people and from the Gentiles to whom I myself am commissioning thee, to open their eyes in order to turn them from darkness to light and from the authority of Satan to God in order that they receive remission of sins and a lot among those that have been sanctified by faith in me.

Ἀλλά breaks off and turns to something else, see 9:5. The command to arise is intensified by the order to stand on the feet. That is all that Paul could do; he was blind and could not walk without being led. All this Paul omits in order to center attention completely upon what the Lord communicated to him through Ananias.

This communication is introduced by γάρ, which is merely explanatory in many instances. Here it explains that Paul is to get up on his feet and to move on in order to receive these communications which are at once stated. "I appeared unto thee" states directly that Paul saw Jesus in the superearthly light. To Agrippa and to all who knew how Jesus had been crucified this simple statement conveyed volumes, following, as it did, v. 6-8 regarding Israel's hope of the promise of the resurrection. As the risen, ascended, glorified Christ he appeared to this persecutor Paul. That shattered every denial of his resurrection, no matter by whom it was made, every denial of his Messiahship, no matter by whom it was made.

The middle infinitive denotes purpose: "to appoint thee for myself as a helper and a witness," etc. On the verb see 3:20, where it is used with reference to Jesus as being one appointed. The predicate nouns make clear what Paul was to be. A ὑπηρέτης is an "underling"; the Levite Temple police were called "underlings," and when Mark accompanied Paul and Barnabas on their first missionary tour he was their "helper" or "attendant," their ὑπηρέτης. Thus Paul was to be subject to the Lord's orders and do what the Lord told him.

At the same time he was to be the Lord's "witness," one who is qualified to testify in regard to what he has seen with his own eyes. This refers specifically to Christ as risen and glorified and puts Paul on a par with the other apostles as the chosen witnesses (1:8). Both terms describe Paul's apostleship. The Lord's personal appearance was only mediate, namely as qualifying Paul for his office, for the testimony he was to bear to Jews and especially to Gentiles. Here we have the explanation of all the work Paul had done, for which certain Jews hated him so intensely.

Of what Paul was to be a witness is stated by two relative clauses, each with ὧν (τούτων ἅ). They puzzle the grammarians, namely με in the first, and ὧν in the second with the future passive ὀφθήσομαι. It is rather certain that both ὧν, being connected as they are with "both — and," are to be construed alike. So we decline to construe τούτων δι' ἅ (Winer) in the second instance. The addition of "me" in the first clause does not have adequate textual support. Read: "a witness of what things thou didst see" (like the A. V., and the R. V. margin); not: "wherein thou didst see me" (like the R. V.). On the second clause see R. 819, etc. The proposal to make both ὧν attractions from οἷς ("wherein," R. V.) is untenable. R. 806 (bottom) notes that Blass considers that the passive, rather than the middle, has a permissive sense. We submit the question whether this passive is not permissive: "a witness of what things I shall let thee see." We note that Zahn at least has *sehen lassen wird* (permissive). While B.-P. 918 suspects that the reading is not in order, he translates: *Zeuge fuer das, als was du mich gesehen hast, und fuer das, als was ich dir* (*noch*) *erscheinen werde,* both ἅ are regarded as being predicative. The sense is fortunately plain. Paul is to testify in regard to this sight of the risen and the glorified Jesus and of other appearances the Lord may yet grant him. The two relatives, however, stress the features or particulars of these appearances as the object of Paul's testimony.

17) The fact that ἐξαιρούμενος means "delivering thee" and thus modifies the subject of ὀφθήσομαι and does not refer back to ὤφθην is evident. The New Testament uses this word only in the former sense. Luke, for instance, does so in 7:10; 12:11; 23:27, Paul in Gal. 1:4; also the LXX, and Isa. 48:10 is scarcely an exception. To introduce the classics and the papyri as evidence for the second meaning without presenting the evidence for the other is unfair. The thought is that Jesus promises "to take out" Paul, out of the dangers that threaten him in his witness-bearing. The idea that the Lord is choosing Paul out of the midst of Jews and out of the midst of Gentiles is unwarranted as far as Gentiles are concerned. Since mortal danger threatened Paul first from the Jews (9:23, etc., 29), these are named first.

Now Paul mentions his commission: "to whom I myself am commissioning thee" or "do commission thee." It need not surprise us that the Jews are included in this statement, for even when Paul labored among the Gentiles he always began his work with the

Jews. Agrippa and all those present are to know that Paul went out to bear his testimony under a specific order from no less a master than the risen Christ himself, and that the protection of this glorious Master accompanied him in all his work.

18) The three infinitives with τοῦ denote purpose, and the second depends on the first, the third on the second, connectives being out of place. Paul uses his own language in describing the purpose that Jesus wanted him to carry out. The aorists are effective. The Jews certainly needed to have their eyes opened as well as the Gentiles. By opening their eyes he was to turn them from darkness to light, from falsehood to truth, and thus from the authority of Satan (whose domain is darkness and evil) to God (who is light and dwells in light). And by this turning to God (conversion) both Jews and Gentiles were to receive remission of sins (ἄφεσις, explained in 2:38) and thus "a lot among those that have been sanctified by faith in me" (Jesus). Κλῆρος is "lot," a portion or part allotted, and not "inheritance" (our versions), which would be κληρονομία. An inheritance awaits its possessor, a lot is at once his. Those who believe immediately find their place among the ἡγιασμένοι (explained in 20:32). Emphatically at the end comes πίστει, to which τῇ, also with emphasis, adds εἰς ἐμέ: "by faith, that (faith) which is in me" (directed toward me). Faith is the subjective means of sanctification. And this stress on faith shows that sanctification is here to be understood in the wider sense as separation unto God and Christ by all that cuts us loose from Satan (justification and remission and holy living).

Here Paul is doing his apostolic witnessing, preaching the gospel to king and procurator and all these grandees and their attendants. Although they scarcely realize it, Paul is making this hall a church, is reaching out to their souls, is opening their eyes, etc., is trying to make the blessed lot theirs. That is the wonderful thing about this meeting. If Festus wanted a "judicial examination" of Paul (25:26), Agrippa needed no probing questions to bring out everything. Paul was only too glad to tell it all himself because Jesus had made him a great witness.

19) In this fourth part of the address Paul explains that he was *almost killed* for having thus borne witness to the Lord. This is the real cause of the rage of the Jews against him. **As a result, King Agrippa, I was not disobedient to the heavenly vision but proceeded to proclaim first to those both in Damascus and Jerusalem and as far as the country district of Judea and (finally) to the Gentiles to repent and to turn to God, doing works worthy of repentance. On account of these things Jews, having seized me in the Temple, were trying to murder me.**

With ὅθεν, "whence," Paul states the result of all that precedes. The renewed address, "King Agrippa," marks the importance of what Paul now states. The negative statement: "I was not disobedient," is a litotes, "I was obedient"; yet by putting it negatively Paul intends to suggest that he might after all have proved disobedient. For all that the Lord did and said implies a sudden and amazing reversal for Paul: from deadly persecution of Jesus to ardent testimony for Jesus. The aorist is best taken as stating only the fact. "The heavenly vision" intends to include the entire revelation of Jesus, that given directly to Paul on the road outside of Damascus plus that which came to him through Ananias.

This passage is often interpreted in a rather narrow manner. It refers not only to the obedience of conversion but equally and even especially to that of testifying as an apostle. Paul might have hesitated in regard to the latter, might have wished only to repent of his persecutions and to live quietly as a repentant disciple.

But he obeyed in all respects. As far as Paul's conversion is concerned, this statement of his shows that grace does not work irresistibly (Matt. 23:37). Faith is often called obedience to Christ, unbelief disobedience. But there is a difference between them. The obedience of faith, the yielding of the will in conversion, is wholly the result of the gracious operation of God; while the disobedience of unbelief, the wilful, obdurate rejection of Christ, is wholly the work of man himself. When Paul declares that he was not disobedient he takes no credit for himself. The credit belongs *in toto* to the heavenly vision vouchsafed to him. He does imply, however, that disobedience on his part would have been a damnable act. To yield to grace is normal, for it is accomplished by *gratia sufficiens*; to spurn this grace is abnormal, a monstrous act that is criminal in the highest degree.

20) The imperfect ἀπήγγελλον intends to describe all of Paul's proclaiming of the gospel, which also was not as yet finished. He mentions briefly all the places where he preached. But the wording has puzzled many and has thus produced various interpretations. Some find four places that are coordinated, others three, whereas the two τοῖς present only two, the same two that were mentioned in v. 17: the λαός (Jews) and the Gentiles. For many the chief difficulty lies in the accusative πᾶσαν τὴν χώραν, which is apparently out of line with the three datives. This disturbed even the ancient text critics who felt that they must insert εἰς before this accusative, and later commentators have followed them. They, of course, use εἰς because of the accusative; they really would like to have ἐν with the dative or a simple dative.

The adverb "first" refers not to Damascus alone but to everything that is mentioned up to the Gentiles. For Damascus and Jerusalem are here a unit, they are written after one preposition and joined by "both and."

And the accusative of extent is attached, not as a co-ordinate place, but in the sense of "as far as" (R. 469). This is very necessary, indeed. A dative would be misleading, for it would state that Paul worked in the country of Judea as he did in the two cities named. This was not the case as we see from Gal. 1:18-24; Acts 9:26-30; 22:17-21. He was in Jerusalem for only two weeks, the people of Judea did not know him. This accusative states that Paul's proclaiming Christ in Damascus and in Jerusalem got to be known all over Judea as something that was almost incredible. The second τοῖς then states the second field of Paul's operations, the Gentiles, to whom he finally went. Thus Paul traces his past movements in a most exact manner.

But the chief point is what he kept proclaiming to Jews and then to Gentiles. He told them to repent (see 2:38), to turn to God (v. 18), and to show it by doing works worthy of repentance, ἄξια, of such weight as to show that they belonged to repentance. That is what Paul had done, and nothing but that. What was wrong about that? Could anyone possibly say that Jews should *not* repent, *not* turn to God, *not* do corresponding works? And what Jew could say that the Gentiles should *not* do the same? Why, in the very address Paul was now making and in these very statements he was uttering he was continuing the same work, calling on his present audience which was made up of Jew and Gentile to repent, turn, do those works.

21) But "on account of these things," Paul tells Agrippa, "Jews," (no article), when they found an opportunity, seized him in the Temple and were trying to beat him to death with their hands (21:27, etc.). Yes, "Jews" — the last people on earth who should have wanted such blessed work stopped! Here Agrippa has the true facts of Paul's case, what was really behind all this business of trials, accusations, etc.

22) Now the fifth part of the address: Paul *a constant witness to this day.* As in v. 4 and again in v. 9, so here, too, οὖν marks a new turn of thought, one that accords with what precedes. **Having, therefore, obtained help from God, to this day I stand testifying to both small and great, declaring nothing beyond what the prophets did utter as about to occur, also Moses, on whether the Christ is subject to suffering, and whether he as the first of the resurrection of the dead will announce light to the people and to the Gentiles.**

It was due to the help of God alone that those Jews did not accomplish what they tried, to murder Paul. Ἐπικουρία is the help afforded by an ally who hastens to support. Since these foes were thirsting for Paul's blood, he would have perished if he had been left alone. The article before the added phrase lends this emphasis: it was the special help, "that from God" the Almighty himself, who rules in the midst of his enemies. The second aorist participle τυχών with a neuter object means: "having obtained."

Paul does not complain about the treatment he received from the Jews, his own nationalists. Two years of Roman imprisonment have not embittered him against those who occasioned it by their murderous attack upon him in the Temple. Not one harsh or hateful word appears in his address. What he sees is this wonderful help of God which came to his rescue at that critical moment and by rescuing him then enabled him to stand as a constant confessor to this very day.

A note of victory is sounded in ἕστηκα, "I stand." The perfect of this verb is always used in the present sense. Nothing has been able to move or to overthrow Paul in his testifying. His word recalls Luther's famous utterance at Worms: "Here I stand," etc., and he, too, said something about God helping him.

"To this day" is pertinent because of the illustrious audience brought to Paul for his testimony. We prefer the reading μαρτυρόμενος, "testifying to both small and great" (i. e., low and high, among the latter even a governor and a king) to μαρτυρούμενος, "attested by both small and great." The double indirect object has singulars and is individualizing. As a matter of fact, "small and great" did not always "attest" Paul, and therefore this reading is not acceptable. All the apostles were witnesses (1:8), and v. 16 shows how Jesus qualified Paul especially and appointed him as such a witness. "Testifying" was his one office and business. And he testified the same thing to all; whether a man was small in importance or great changed nothing of that testimony.

The important point in what Paul says about his unchanging testimony is the fact that he declares not a single thing beyond what the prophets have long ago spoken, at the head of them Moses himself, regarding what was to occur. Ἐκτὸς ὧν = τούτων ἅ, and μελλόντων thus also becomes genitive. Note the emphasis on Moses because he is named at the end. "The things about to occur" are the Messianic things. Moses and the prophets said they would come. Some of them had come: redemption, the outpouring of the Spirit, the establishment of the new covenant, and a new covenant people; others, such as the final judgment, were yet to come. Now Paul spoke of these things in absolute accord with Moses and the prophets whenever he spoke either of those features already come or of the others that were yet to come. One of the tremendous features of his testimony, especially to the Jews, was this very point of actual and literal fulfillment of the Messianic prophecies.

Where was the crime in clinging so closely to Moses and the prophets? What Jew would dare to condemn Paul for that? And what Roman court could find a crime in that? The condemnation would fall back on Moses and the prophets themselves. By accusing Paul, these Jews were outlawing their own prophets, their own Old Testament mediator. Paul is driving straight at Agrippa as a Jew. He is surrounding him so with these prophets and Moses that, unless he wants to repudiate them, by believing their Messianic utterances, he must accept also their fulfillment in Jesus. Here is a sample of the effective way in which Paul operated upon Jews with Moses and the prophets.

23) Paul is, however, never content with general terms and statements. In v. 17, 18 he specifies in detail; at the end of v. 20 he again does so. So he here mentions the two points that are absolutely vital in telling just what Moses and the prophets foretold and what has now actually been fulfilled. His wording is such as to include both the prophecies involved and their fulfillment as accomplished. This explains the two εἰ of indirect questions in part. We give up the idea that εἰ = ὅτι (R. 1024) or that these clauses are protases, which either include the apodosis or need none. We question whether εἰ is ever equal to ὅτι, and that idea is advanced here because Paul might have said "that" but said something else instead.

Paul states the two questions on which all his discussions with Jews regarding the prophets and Moses and the fulfillment of their utterances turned. Both εἰ clauses are appositions to μελλόντων γίνεσθαι, this genitive being attracted from its accusative as modifying ὧν, an original ἅ. Both clauses are original accusatives that have been attracted to genitives. Construe: "what things the prophets and Moses uttered as about to occur, as to whether," etc. The R. V. and its two marginal efforts are unsatisfactory because the case of these clauses is not noted, their case as appositions.

As Moses and the prophets spoke, so Paul testifies. And first of all "on whether the Christ is subject to suffering." All of them plus Paul do most emphatically so affirm. The question is put in a general form by being stated in regard to "the Christ." In support of his affirmation Paul had all the prophecies, but he had them as now literally fulfilled in Jesus, "the Christ." The Jews would have no Messiah who could (and did) suffer and die. The very thought was an offense to them. But the prophecies and their fulfillment were solidly against them. They would have only a Christ who would be an earthly conquering and triumphant hero. M.-M. 473, and others, make παθητός the only verbal in τος that has a weakened sense, "capable of suffering," *patibilis* (a sort of active) ; C.-K. 841, however, writes "seems" and leaves the meaning doubtful. Regard this verbal as a plain passive: "subject to suffering." Jesus was not merely capable of suffering, he was subjected to suffering just as the prophecies declared.

Dramatically and without a connective the second clause is added: "on whether he as the first of the resurrection of the dead will announce light," etc. Like παθητός, πρῶτος is placed emphatically forward. And we must read as a unit: πρῶτος ἐξ ἀναστάσεως νεκρῶν (ἐξ does not mean "by," R. V.; the A. V. is much truer), *als Erster aus Totenauferweckung* = "first risen from the dead." The Greek omits the articles, and thus each term has its full qualitative force. This "first" conveys a great power. As the first he would have to break the power of death and the tomb in order to arise. Thus he could, indeed, announce "light" to the people (λαός, Jews) and to the Gentiles. Death and the tomb are dark, "light" is their opposite. And this light is the hope (v. 6, 7) of our own blessed resurrection through him who is "first." Col. 1:18. The Christ was to rise by his own power, corruption was not even to touch

him (2:27, 31). He was not to enter this life again and, like Lazarus, to die a second time but to rise glorified, to live in glory forever. This the Sadducees would deny emphatically. Not so the Pharisees and the people generally. Their great difficulty was the lowly, crucified Jesus, the fact that he should be this "first," and that these prophecies should thus center in him and in this resurrection glory.

Here μέλλει with the present infinitive is a circumscribed future with prophetic force. Once more (v. 17, 20) we have side by side "the people" (Jews) and "the Gentiles." This kind of a Christ could be what he was for no single nation such as the Jews. His light (v. 18) with all its spiritual and eternal blessings was too great, too universal for that. But with the term "Gentiles" Paul again touched all the Romans and the non-Jews present. This light of the suffering, risen, and glorified Christ was for all of them.

24) Not until one puts himself fully into the situation can he catch just what the interruption by Festus means. **But he offering these things in defense, Festus, with the voice elevated, says, Thou ravest, Paul! Much learning is turning thee to raving!**

The procurator can contain himself no longer. The intensity of feeling produced by Paul's presentation charged Festus like an electric current which finally leaped out in a flash. Involuntarily the man explodes. This effect, so dramatically revealed, lets us feel how the rest of this audience must likewise have been stirred in varying degrees. While the governor Festus speaks, those of less authority refrain from speaking. Agrippa among them. Festus had turned Paul over to Agrippa (25:26), and Paul had throughout addressed Agrippa as the one to whom he had been referred. This makes the interruption by Festus the more astonishing.

He at first listened with the hope of hearing something that might serve him in writing to the emperor (25:27). That hope vanished promptly. Paul spoke again about the matters Festus had mentioned to Agrippa in 25:19 and with such power as to make the governor react. This Roman pagan had evidently never read the Greek Old Testament, and all the things said about Jesus, the Nazarene, dead, risen to glory, appearing to Paul in divine light, and commissioning him to proclaim light, repentance, etc., were utterly beyond him, a new world that startled and crashed into all his old pagan conceptions.

"With the voice loud (elevated, note the predicative position of the adjective)" betrays the tension of Festus. His shout, "Thou ravest, Paul!" is neither anger nor resentment; it is self-defense, a thrust to remove all that Paul was saying. In this respect it was like that word of the fools at Pentecost, who called the apostles and believers drunk (2:13). If Paul is just raving, if his mind is unbalanced, that excuses Festus — he may brush aside all that Paul says. It is a helpless, pitiful, foolish self-defense, the only thing this Roman can think of in order to thrust Paul's words aside.

Moreover, Festus' word is not sincere. If he really thought Paul unbalanced mentally he would not shout at him, he would smile in pity and try to catch Agrippa's eye with a significant look, gesture, or whisper. If Paul were crazy, the case would automatically end despite Paul's appeal to Caesar. No governor would send a lunatic to the emperor's court.

It is significant that Festus does not stop with the shout, "Thou ravest, Paul!" He adds the explanation that much learning is turning Paul to raving. By τὰ πολλὰ γράμματα he cannot refer to books, for Paul had no library while he was in prison. Festus is not mitigating his charge of raving, he is trying to substantiate it.

And by doing so he shows that his shout is not caused by anger. But this supposed cause of raving is the insipid notion that, when a man devotes himself too much, in the opinion of men, to one subject, he is off balance, and that, when he speaks with all his heart and soul on that subject, he shows that he is deranged. The explanation is like the charge: a helpless attempt to remove all that is said so effectively. In his *W. P.* R. makes the present tenses inchoative as though Paul was starting to go mad, beginning to turn to raving. But this idea of "going mad right before them all" as though Festus was frightened about that, does not lie in the tenses.

25) **But Paul says, I am not raving, Most Excellent Festus. On the contrary, I am speaking forth utterances of truth and sanity. For the king knows concerning these things, to whom also I speak, using entire freedom; for I am persuaded that not a single one of these things is hidden from him, for this thing has not been done in a corner.**

Without speaking in a loud voice, with perfect composure and telling clarity, Paul promptly answers the governor's excited allegations. The manner in which Paul replies shows the wildness of those allegations. "As long as Paul was exceedingly mad (v. 11) and raved he passed for a bright fellow; but when he knew that he had been raving and became a Christian, they thought him mad." Lindhammer.

With all due respect but with directness Paul denies that he is raving. On κράτιστε, "Your Excellency," compare 23:26, and Luke 1:4. The dignified way in which Paul accords this title to Festus could not fail to have its effect. To the governor's shouted, "Paul!" he calmly replies, "Your Excellency Festus." The negation is fortified by its corresponding affirmation. Just the opposite is the fact: Paul is speaking forth utterances that are marked by truth and sanity (qualifying genitives which are far stronger than adjectives). Luke alone uses ἀποφθέγγεσθαι (2:4), a choice verb which was used by the LXX with reference to prophesying, and by later Greek writers with reference to oracles. It fits well into Paul's dignified statement. Ἀλήθεια = reality, "truth" in this sense; it is objective. Σωφροσύνη = "sanity" or saneness, the direct opposite of μανία, "insane or raving"; this term is subjective. The two terms are straight to the point.

26) Festus tried to substantiate his judgment of Paul by a common notion; Paul substantiates his denial by appealing to Agrippa himself as a witness: "For the king knows concerning these things," but the Greek reverses subject and predicate and thus places emphasis on both. The implication is that Festus, who hears of these things for the first time, is not, because of their strangeness, justified in thinking them the ravings of an unbalanced mind. The addition, "to whom also I speak, using entire freedom" (παρρησιαζόμενος), has a causal note, for it states why Paul spoke as he did: he was addressing the king, a person who was fully informed on the subject. To him, Paul says, he could speak without hesitation or reserve, for he would understand. Although he had been reared and educated at Rome, Agrippa adhered to Judaism. He had been made guardian of the Temple with power to appoint the high priests and thus was obliged even officially to know all about Jewish affairs, the Jewish Scriptures, etc.

Yet Paul is careful when he refers to this knowledge of the king. With a second and then with a third γάρ he explains. It is his subjective assurance that the king knows. The emphasis rests on λανθάνειν and on οὐδέν: "there has escaped him of these things, I am assured, not a single thing." The subject of λανθάνειν is τὶ followed by οὐδέν, and αὐτόν is the object. R. 1094.

The Greek doubles the negatives and thereby makes them stronger in a way that seems odd to the English ear: "I am *not* persuaded that *not* a thing escapes him." Paul felt certain that none of the things he had referred to in his address had been lost on Agrippa. It would have been foolish to have introduced other things.

Paul even adds the reason for this assurance: "this thing has not been done in a corner." Subject and predicate are again reversed with a strong emphasis on "this thing." Paul says, "these things," the plural spreading out the details, and then, "this thing," the singular regarding everything as a great unit. All that was said about Jesus was transacted in the very capital of the nation, and the Sanhedrin and the procurator Pilate were involved, and Jesus was a national figure, whose fame filled even the surrounding lands. "Not in a corner" is not only a powerful litotes for, "on what for Judaism at least was the world stage," but it at the same time informs this ignorant governor that what Paul has been talking about is not some notion that was developed in his own deranged mind, nor an obscure little affair that nobody knows anything about, but a thing that is so great and vital, so public and far-reaching, that Agrippa has been obliged to give it his full royal attention.

Festus resembles Lysias in making a move, now one, now another, and each time realizing just too late that it was the wrong move. We must not overlook the fact that even in this august presence (see 25:23) Paul just naturally gravitates to the position of master of the situation. He is a prisoner before a king and a procurator in all their pomp of power, yet it is he who takes things into his hands. He makes no false moves; he keeps true to his mission, his great purpose; he scores at every turn.

27) Paul had accomplished a great deal when he had stirred Festus into excited exclamation. Now Paul does more, he questions Agrippa, the king himself. The king was to give Paul an ἀνάκρισις, a probing examination such as a judge gave a prisoner in ancient days (prosecutors do it now), and Paul had given complete information to the king so that he found no room for a question. And now Paul has put himself into a position where he can question the king who was to question him. The tables have somehow turned. Paul's question is, however, pastoral, personal, spiritual as alone befits Paul and his mission. In the most natural way he turns from the procurator with whom he has finished to the king and asks: **Dost thou, King Agrippa, believe the prophets?** Perhaps startled a bit, the king hesitates, and Paul gives the answer for him: **I know that thou dost believe.** Πιστεύεις with the dative asks whether the king believes that what the prophets say is true, is fact and not fancies or lies. Paul is not asking too much, he is inquiring only as to Agrippa's *assent.* When he makes answer for the king, the answer is the only creditable one Agrippa could give as an honest Jew. How could he reply that he does *not* believe the prophets?

But we must catch the full implications. Agrippa does not adopt Paul's answer, neither does he repudiate it. Paul had brought out the truth that the prophets and Moses, too, had declared that these things should occur: the Christ suffering and dying and then as the First-risen bringing light and salvation to Jews and to Gentiles (v. 23). Any Jew who believed the prophets would thus after what Paul had said have to face the further question as to whether he believed these supreme utterances of the prophets. Then the next question would confront him, whether these prophecies were fulfilled in Jesus, the Nazarene. A straight *yes* to Paul's question, Agrippa saw, led straight into these admissions. Yet a *no* would repudiate his Judaism — and he was the Temple guardian and the appointer of high priests! Agrippa shrank from both. He is one of the many who, when they are brought face to face with the truth by the great alternatives of the Word, dodge the issue. Felix did the same before this same apostle. A *tertium* is always possible: the unmanly, cowardly act of evasion.

28) **But Agrippa to Paul: In short order thou art persuading me to become a Christian! Paul, however, I would wish to God that both in short order and in great measure not only thou but all those hearing me today become such as also I myself am, except these bonds!**

The omission of the verbs of saying in these two verses makes the narrative more dramatic even as what they narrate is the dramatic climax of Paul's address. The history of the exegesis of these two verses is too long and too varied to be surveyed here. Ἐν ὀλίγῳ cannot mean "almost" (A. V.), and the revival hymn, "Almost persuaded," loses its Scriptural basis. Agrippa's word is not a scoff, nor is it "spoken ironically and in contempt." To find a twinkle of humor in it, to which Paul replies with a similar humorous touch, is too frivolous to need refutation. Confronted by a *yes* or *no* alternative, Agrippa evades both and in the presence of this high company assumes a superior tone. In the discussion of the linguistic difficulties the real point of Agrippa's remark is lost. From the simple question of believing the prophets Agrippa at once leaps to the question of becoming a Christian. Paul's question asks in regard to the *first* step toward Christianity, Agrippa answers in regard to the *final* goal. He saw it all and lets Paul know this.

He used even the word "Christian" (see 11:26) which originated in Syrian Antioch and thus became known to him since he ruled a part of Syria. The word itself, as well as the whole reply, betray the intimate knowledge Agrippa had of the things to which Paul had referred even as Paul also was sure he had this knowledge. Of the two preferred readings γενέσθαι and ποιῆσαι we select the former. Zahn calls it "incomparably better attested," we think well attested is sufficient. In his answer Paul, too, uses this infinitive. It agrees with the active πείθεις far better than ποιῆσαι does, which would fit only the passive πείθῃ which is found in one text. But this point is of minor importance and scarcely involves the sense as such.

The real question concerns ἐν ὀλίγῳ in Agrippa's answer, and then the combination of this phrase with ἐν μεγάλῳ in Paul's rejoinder. Many authorities think that this combination rules out the idea of time in ἐν ὀλίγῳ because it is certainly ruled out in ἐν μεγάλῳ. But this view overlooks two points. The phrases are combined by καί — καί, "both — and," which the R. V. translates "whether — or," but the text should then have ἤ. Combined thus, Paul's phrases present no alternative but the contrary, the second presents an addition. If Paul had intended to use alternatives he would have paired ἐν ὀλίγῳ with ἐν πολλῷ, and the R. V. translates as though he had done so: "with little or with much," i. e., Paul would like to see Agrippa become a Christian whether it took little or much to make him one. Or Paul would have paired ἐν ὀλίγῳ with ἐν μακρῷ; "whether with little or with long time." Paul did neither, nor did he use ἤ, "or," and have alternatives. He said ἐν μεγάλῳ, which is diverse and which the correlatives καί — καί add: "both in short order (time) and in great degree (measure)." Compare Zahn.

Agrippa charges Paul with persuading him to Christianity "in short order," i. e., by means of his believing the prophets. Ἐν ὀλίγῳ has the emphasis. The sense is: "Thou art rushing me off my feet!" There is no inchoative or conative idea in πείθεις (R. 880). Agrippa imagines that he sees through Paul's scheme and with an air of lofty superiority that is intended to impress the company lets Paul know that he sees through his plan of operation. Here we see the man's evasion. He turns from the prophets and their plain, compelling utterances about the Christ by looking only at Paul and Paul's purpose. He gets rid of the great fact that it ought to be only a short cut from the prophets and the prophecies to faith in Christ for any true and sincere Jew who believes these holy prophets of God. No; whatever Agrippa thinks of these prophets, letting them point him so directly to Jesus as the Christ is out of the question for him, a Herod, a king, although a Jew in profession.

29) Paul's reply meets the king squarely. Since Agrippa centers on Paul instead of on the prophets presented to him by Paul, the apostle bares his whole heart to the king, yea, to all here present: "I would wish (or pray) to God that both in short order and in great degree not only thou but all those hearing me today become such as also I myself am, etc.!" Here is not a man who is by a quick turn trying to coerce the king into becoming a Christian; here is a man whose whole soul is wrapped up in God, whose one fervent prayer could ever be only this, to see all men, just as he himself is, completely won for God, for the prophets of God, and for the Christ of God revealed by God through these prophets — yea, see them thus "both in short order," the time cannot be too short, "and in great degree or measure," with no halfway measures about it. Nor does Paul hesitate to make himself the pattern for Agrippa and for all those hearing him today. His strong ἐγώ is full of holy pride. It confesses joyfully what Paul is as a Christian. He knows in

whom he believes. Would to God that all this company, with the king making the beginning, might do the same! I Cor. 7:7.

Paul repeats the king's "in short order" and completes it with "in great measure." Instead of yielding and saying that he has no such hurry in mind he does the opposite and adds even great measure. It does Paul an injustice to let him say that a longer time would also be satisfactory. Aside from the fact that he says the opposite, delays in following the prophets often prove fatal. The optative with ἄν is a protasis of potentiality and in exclamations is always without an apodosis. The aorist γενέσθαι is in place, for full actuality is referred to. The margin "in all respects," desired by the American Committee of the R. V., reveals that these translators did not understand Paul's telling phrases.

On the basis of the final phrase "except these bonds" the commentators feel that Paul stood before this illustrious company in chains; the author followed this lead in his *St. Paul*, 222, etc. In 25:23 we have given the reasons why we consider this idea a mistake. We here note the plural παρεκτὸς τῶν δεσμῶν τούτων, which should make one pause. Would Paul appear before this audience manacled with more than one chain? No one calls this a plural of the category. Where chains are referred to we have the word for them as in Luke 8:29 and in Acts 22:25 and 28:20. This plural δεσμά (at times the masculine) occurs frequently, and we submit that in no instance does it signify "chains." Begin with v. 31, which is rather plain, also 16:26, and then look through the epistles. We rest on this survey.

Δέσμιος, too, means only "prisoner." "Bonds" (neuter plural) = bondage, imprisonment, all that confines a man as a δέσμιος. Even in 28:16 we feel certain that no chains were used; 28:20 is different. Roman law forbade the use of chains on Roman citizens when they became prisoners. We thus do not think that Paul made a dramatic gesture when he uttered this final phrase and held up his arm with the clanking chain or both arms with two chains — and they have been described as being long enough for that purpose.

30) **And the king rose up and the governor and Bernice and those sitting with them. And having withdrawn, they continued to speak to each other, saying, Nothing worthy of death or of bonds is this man doing. But Agrippa said to Festus, This man might have been released if he had not appealed to Caesar.**

The king ended the audience by rising to leave. It had been arranged at his request (25:22), and thus he was privileged to prolong or to shorten it, the governor politely deferring to him. Agrippa had felt Paul's touch upon his heart, and from this strange and unexpected power he withdrew. It was his hour of grace, and when he withdrew he left salvation behind him. How many are like him along the road the gospel has traveled! The others also arose according to rank. That is why Bernice is mentioned after the governor. It was done in state and with due precedence. Some are ready to say that. as far as a saving effect was concerned, Paul's efforts had been in vain. We hesitate in regard to that. The gospel has its own way of not returning void. It was lost upon the main personages, but was it lost on all who heard Paul that day?

31) They withdrew and discussed the case. While the imperfect is descriptive it is more; it holds the reader in suspense for the final aorist in v. 32. The verdict of all the dignitaries that are privileged to speak is unanimous: Paul is guilty of nothing that deserves either death or bonds, and here δεσμά certainly means only imprisonment and not "chains." It is the same verdict that Festus himself had publicly pro-

nounced at the opening of the audience in 25:25; it was the more readily reiterated now.

32) This leads to the final word, which was spoken directly to Festus by Agrippa, that Paul might have been released if he had not appealed to Caesar. That is all that Agrippa, to whom Paul's case had been especially presented, could say. Small comfort for Festus this "might have been." It was he who has mismanaged the case and maneuvered himself into this awkward position of having to send to Caesar a prisoner who had been pronounced innocent by himself and by all others who had heard him. What the helpless and inefficient fellow finally wrote to Caesar no one knows; it was certainly nothing incriminating. When the court of Caesar tried Paul's case, he was promptly acquitted.

The condition is that of past unreality, the apodosis without ἄν as so often with certain verbs, R. 1014. Ordinarily aorists are used in order to place the unreality in the past. Here this is achieved by the past in the protasis and by the imperfect plus a perfect infinitive in the apodosis. The sentence is conditional and nothing more, past unreality even in the apodosis (R. 887 regards it as present). We dissent from R. 886 in having the imperfect ἐδύνατο function also as the tense used in an unfulfilled possibility. In our opinion it cannot serve in such a double capacity. See another case of this in 24:19.

What prevented Paul's release under the present circumstances was not only the fact that he had appealed but that he had appealed effectively, Festus having formally accepted the appeal (25:12) in open court before the Sanhedrists who had appeared as accusers. Agrippa puts it mildly, in reality it was Festus who had tied his own hands.

CHAPTER XXVII

From Caesarea to Malta

1) Luke's account of the voyage to Rome is considered a masterpiece, the best record of an extended ancient voyage, which throws more light on seafaring matters of that time than any other description. He is a landman and writes as such but is well-informed and most accurate. Consult Ramsay, *St. Paul the Traveller and the Roman Citizen*, 314, etc.

Now when it was determined for us to sail away for Italy, they proceeded to deliver Paul and certain other prisoners to a centurion by name Julius, of the Augustan cohort. And having embarked in an Adramyttian ship about to sail to the places along Asia, we put to sea, Aristarchus, a Macedonian of Thessalonica, being with us.

No further efforts were made in Paul's case; it was decided to ship him to Italy. The imperfect παρεδίδουν describes the transfer into the centurion's custody; it presents the course of the action (B.-D. 327) instead of merely the fact (aorist). The other prisoners were not other Romans who had made an appeal to Caesar but men condemned to death, who were to be sent to Rome for the gladiatorial shows, to die in these for the amusement of the Roman populace. Rome drew extensively on the provinces for such victims. We imagine that they were used chiefly to face wild animals and not as gladiators in matched battles with each other. These prisoners may have been pagan criminals; ἑτέρους, which is not always used as being distinct from ἄλλους, may or may not designate men who were distinct from Paul. The fact that they were distinct and in a class by themselves seems assured.

While he was in custody in Caesarea, Paul was in charge of a centurion (24:23) who was responsible for his safekeeping; so when he was now sent to Rome he was again placed in charge of such an officer. Luke gives us his name "Julius," which, like Cornelius and Claudius, is the name of the gens, a name that was borne by three emperors and by the dictator Julius Caesar. "An Augustan cohort" is not identical with the Italian cohort mentioned in 10:1. Ramsay, *St. Paul the Traveller,* etc., 348, follows the historian Mommsen: "Augustus had reduced to a regular system the maintenance of communications between the center of control in Rome and the armies stationed in the great frontier provinces. Legionary centurions, called commonly *frumentarii,* went to and fro between the armies; and were employed for numerous purposes that demanded communication between the emperor and his armies and provinces. They acted not only for commissariat purposes (whence the name), but as couriers, and for police purposes, and for conducting prisoners; and in time they became detested as agents and spies of Government. They all belonged to legions stationed in the provinces and were considered to be on detached duty when they went to Rome; and hence in Rome they were 'soldiers from abroad,' *peregrini.*"

What Ramsay further adds from Mommsen is without substantiation: "While in Rome they resided in a camp on the Caelian Hill, called *castra peregrinorum*; in this camp there were always a number of them present, changing from day to day, as some came and others went away. This camp was under the *princeps peregrinorum,* and it is clear that the *stratopedrach* in Acts 28:16 (A. V. 'captain of the guard') is the Greek name for that officer." Zahn, *Introduction, I,* 552, etc., states that the existence of this *princeps castrorum peregrinorum,* of his troops, and his barracks prior to the military reorganization made by the emperor Severus, has yet to be shown. Julius delivered Paul to the *praefectus praetorio,* the emperor's judicial deputy who administered criminal justice. It was this General of the Praetorian Guard who ordered Paul kept in the mild custody indicated in 28:16. All this is of great importance for understanding Phil. 1:13 (A. V. margin) and explains how Paul was able to come in contact with many of the Praetorian Guard.

2) The home port of the vessel boarded for the transport was Adramyttium at the head of the bay in Mysia, opposite the island of Lesbos. The vessel was only a coasting vessel which intended to stop only in different ports along the coast of Asia Minor and was similar to the vessel which Paul's party took for Patara at Troas (20:13-21:1). Luke accompanies Paul on this voyage. Here for the last time the "we" appears in the narrative and informs the reader of Luke's presence. Paul's second companion is Aristarchus, who is identified as the man mentioned in 20:4 by the addition, "a Macedonian of Thessalonica." He was one of the party commissioned to bring the great collection to Jerusalem. We first met him in 19:29 in Ephesus, and Col. 4:10 and Philemon 24 show that he remained with Paul during his confinement in Rome.

It is debated as to how Luke and Aristarchus managed to make this voyage to Rome with Paul. Ramsay thinks that they went as Paul's slaves, the apostle being able to take them along as such. Would Paul have stooped to such a pretense? R., *W. P.,* thinks that Luke managed to go along as Paul's physician — but what about Aristarchus? We do not need such explanations. We note how Felix treated Paul in 24:23, 24, how Festus arranged a grand audience for

Paul in 25:22-26:32, how Julius treated Paul in 27:3. Is not this enough to show Paul's importance and standing in the eyes of the Roman authorities? Why, then, hesitate in regard to this privilege of taking his two companions on the voyage to Rome? Because in the subsequent narrative Luke does not mention Aristarchus by name, some conclude that Aristarchus went only as far as Myra where Paul was transferred to another vessel. But Luke does not mention even himself by name; he had no occasion to do so. The "we" that runs through the narrative beginning with v. 3 includes all that were in the vessel and alternates with "they." Read on and note the varying subjects. Luke as well as Aristarchus recede into the background. Paul is the man that stands out. On the nautical use of ἀνήχθημεν and its counterpart κατήχθημεν (v. 3) see 13:13. The former occurs repeatedly in these last two chapters, the latter again in 28:12.

3) **And on the next day we were brought down to Sidon. And Julius, using Paul in humane manner, permitted that, having gone to his friends, he obtain attention.**

On the first run "we were brought down" (from the high sea to the harbor) to Sidon, sixty-seven miles away. "We touched" in our versions is not quite correct, for the verb may imply a permanent stop. Here, of course, it indicates only a temporary one.

Χράομαι governs the dative, τυγχάνω the genitive. When Luke inserts the participial modifier that Julius used Paul in a humane way, *in menschenfreundlicher Weise*, we see how greatly he, Paul, and Aristarchus appreciated this act. It was exceptional in every way to permit *a prisoner* and his two friends to land in a port, to go to his other friends there, and to trust that he would return when the vessel would sail on. One of the notable things in the records of the Gospels and the Acts is the fact that all the centurions whom we meet were fine men; the chiliarch Lysias — but he was a chiliarch — stands beneath them all. It was this centurion's humaneness that prompted his act. One almost suspects that he had known Paul for some time. How could he otherwise have trusted Paul so much? We do not believe that he sent Paul ashore chained to a soldier or under any kind of military guard. A man who had to be chained and guarded would not have been sent ashore at all. We feel certain that after the fright of Lysias (22:29; 22:25) Paul was not chained again until in 28:10. Paul was not under criminal charges. He certainly could have escaped here at Sidon. But what would such conduct have availed him? Paul was not that kind of man!

These friends in Sidon were Christians, and we now hear about them for the first time. But we decline to accept the idea that they had been notified concerning Paul's arrival, had even again and again gone to the docks expecting the vessel, were there to receive him as their guest on his arrival. Paul, Luke, and Aristarchus knew that they were to sail only when the order for Paul's embarking was issued. Not until then, most likely not until after they had put out to sea, did they know the route and the places at which they would touch. The "attention" Paul obtained was hospitality. Luke and Aristarchus and friends in Caesarea had surely provided all that was needed as baggage for the journey. Medical attention cannot be thought of in Sidon; Luke, the physician, was on board ship for the entire voyage, which in itself was invigorating. The stop at Sidon lasted a day or more and was probably made for the purpose of taking freight aboard.

Ramsay and others explain why a coast vessel was taken to Myra, which passed to the east of Cyprus. No large vessel for a direct voyage from Caesarea to

Rome via Alexandria was available. The winds from the west necessitated the slow voyage along the coast to Myra. The latter was a prominent port where a larger vessel for Rome might be found. It was probably left to the centurion to determine how he would proceed from Myra, whether, as he did, across the open sea with the risks involved at this season of the year or whether, continuing up the coast to Troas, across to Neapolis, and then by land to Dyrrachium, and thence to Brundisium and Rome. On this subject, as on various points involved in Luke's account of the actual voyage, nautical authorities acquainted with ancient sailing possibilities and practices alone are able to speak with full assurance.

4) **And having put to sea from thence, we sailed under the lee of Cyprus because the winds were contrary. And having sailed across the open sea down along Cilicia and Pamphilia, we came down to Myra of Lycia.**

Ships had no difficulty in sailing from Myra to the Syrian harbors because they could use the winds which blew with great steadiness from the west or the northwest. Paul and his party that had the great collection had come this way, from Patara to Tyre (21:1-3). This route left Cyprus on the left and passed the tip of the island at Paphos. But these very winds prevented sailing in the opposite direction, from Syrian ports to the Lycian coast; so they hugged the lee of Cyprus on their left and were sheltered from the contrary western winds by the island.

5) Then they followed the coast of Cilicia and Pamphilia by availing themselves of temporary local land breezes and the steady westward current that runs along the coast. This was often accomplished with slow progress and necessitated anchoring along the winding coast when the winds from the west were too contrary. Luke does not say how long it took

to reach Myra. A few authorities insert "through fifteen days." Someone apparently made this estimate. While it is not from Luke's pen it may be a correct comment.

6) **And the centurion having there found an Alexandrian ship sailing for Italy, he embarked us in it.**

No stop had been made since leaving Sidon. Myra lay inland about two and one half miles; its port, Andriace, had an excellent harbor and did a large shipping business, Alexandrian grain ships for Rome making this port. We hear about no Christians at Myra. Here transshipment was made by the centurion into an Alexandrian freighter bound for Italy. This was a large vessel; we find that it carried 276 souls (v. 37), it was a grain ship with accomodations also for passengers. The presence of this Alexandrian vessel in Myra is explained by commentators (landmen) as being due to the same contrary winds, the ship being driven off its course. Ramsay assures us that the contrary is true, that these winds had given the ship a direct run from Alexandria to Myra at this season of the year (autumn), and that only exceptionally could a run have been made directly from Alexandria to Crete. The vessel was ready to sail, and the transshipment was made without delay.

7) **Now sailing slowly in many days and having come with difficulty down along Cnidus, the wind not letting us forward, we sailed under the lee of Crete down along Salmone; and with difficulty coasting along it, we came to a place called Fair Havens, near to which was the city of Lasea.**

The city of Cnidus lies at the angle of the coast where, in turning almost northward, the coast no longer protects against winds from the north. That is why the vessel turned southward toward Crete. The distance from Myra to Cnidus, thirteen miles, was made slowly. They again passed Rhodes (21:1) but had to anchor and wait for opportunity to proceed so often that days were consumed thereby.

The genitive absolute is to be construed with the statement in regard to sailing under the lee of Crete. Προσεάω is one of those words that are found nowhere else in the Greek (M.-M. 547) although its sense is plain: πρός + ἐάω, "to let toward"; Ramsay: "as the wind did not permit our straight course onwards." They made for the southern coast of the island of Crete and passed its eastern promontory, Cape Salmone. To pass to the north of Crete was too hazardous because they would be exposed to north winds along a coast that afforded only a few harbors for shelter.

8) As it was was, they coasted along the southern side of Crete with difficulty; παραλέγομαι, to coast along, M.-M., 487. When Luke writes, "a certain place called Fair Havens," he means that it was not a significant place. This place was not well known. Luke mentions the city near it; but neither harbor nor city are otherwise mentioned in Greek literature. The former, however, has been identified as a small bay two leagues east of Cape Matala, at which point most of the protection from the contrary winds ends.

9) **Now considerable time having elapsed, and the voyage being already dangerous because also the Fast had already gone by, Paul went on to advise them by saying: Men, I take the view that the voyage will be with injury and much loss not only of the cargo and the ship but also of our lives. But the centurion was persuaded more by the sailing master and the captain than by the things being stated by Paul.**

The "considerable time" that had elapsed refers, not to a long stay in Fair Havens, but to the total time consumed since leaving Caesarea. If the stay in Fair Havens were referred to, Luke would have spoken of "days" and not of "time." The stay in Fair Havens before the decision was made as to going on must have been very brief.

The second genitive absolute explains that the time had already come when any voyage was considered dangerous, so also this one. "Dangerous" is specific, for it refers to the period between the middle of September and the first part of November; after November 11 all navigation ceased until March 10 (see 18:18). "The Fast" was well along in this period which was considered dangerous for sea voyages. If the year was 59, it would be October 5; if the year 60, near that date.

What causes comment is the fact that Luke here mentions a Jewish festival, "the Fast," a name for the Day of Atonement as a designation of time for Theophilus, both he and Luke being Gentile Christians. But this is not so strange. Paul and Aristarchus had most likely kept the Fast by fasting that day, and thus the day was noted by Luke in his diary (if he kept one) and in his memory. We can thus also approximate the date when the voyage from Caesarea began, it was after the middle of August. The Feast of Tabernacles, which came five days after the Fast, need not be taken into account so that a date after the Fast and before Tabernacles must be assumed. Tabernacles could not be celebrated on a vessel, and it was a festival that was far less likely than the great Fast to be observed by Jewish Christians.

The imperfect παρῄνει plus ἐπείθετο, which are descriptive, prepare for the aorist ἔθεντο βουλήν; we are told what was transpiring up to the moment when the decision was made. Luke fails to record how Paul came to make his statement so that we are left to our imagination. Did Paul introduce the subject by stating his own view, the others then getting together for a decision? Or was a council held to which Paul, although a prisoner, was invited? In either case we see how Paul gravitated to the front. He was that kind of man. In this case he also had his past experience as a seafarer who had been shipwrecked three times and had been adrift on wreckage in the sea (II Cor. 11:25) for a day and night to draw on.

10) With θεωρῶ Paul states his view: "I take the view." He is not offering a prophecy. What he says is that a continuation of the voyage so late in the season is sure to end in disaster. We have ὅτι followed by the accusative with the infinitive, which is called a mixture of two constructions (B.-D. 397, 6; R. 1047) although it is used in the classics and in the papyri. Paul sees injury and loss ahead, both of cargo and of vessel as well as of the lives of those in the ship. Μέλλειν ἔσεσθαι is a circumscribed future which is found three times in the New Testament, R. 887. According to Paul's view the proper course to follow was to remain in Fair Havens. He probably said so outright but in a deferential and a fitting manner.

11) The centurion carefully weighed Paul's words yet felt that what the sailing master and the captain said had greater weight and so sided with them. The κυβερνήτης is the chief pilot or "sailing master," and ναύκληρος, "the captain," (examples from the papyri in M.-M.). Correct the terms found in our versions. The view is mistaken that the centurion had the final decision in the matter, that he presided at a council, that he was merely taking the advice of the others, and that he had charge of the delivery of the cargo of grain. He was only a centurion, he had charge only of the prisoners and their delivery, he was sent

from Caesarea, and no one knew that he would be able to secure passage on a grain ship. He did *not* have the decisive word, nor was the decision made by him. This was a government vessel, the government was its owner. The sailing master is named before the captain, his word certainly counted as much as that of the latter. All that Luke says about the centurion is that he eventually agreed with these two.

12) **Now since the harbor was not well situated for wintering, the majority resolved to put to sea from there if somehow, after having arrived at Phoenix, they might winter (there), a harbor looking down the southwest wind and down the northwest wind.**

The compound ἀνεύθετος, which is found only here in the Greek, means "not well placed." It was "commodious" (A. V.) enough but did not provide sufficient protection against winter storms. Οἱ πλείους = "the majority." Now we see why the centurion is mentioned. If Paul had succeeded in persuading him, it would have been a case of two against two. Now it was three against one. The supposition that other persons besides these four had a part in the matter is excluded. These three resolved for the reason assigned, if possible, to reach the better harbor of Phoenix, to put to sea from Fair Havens. Ἔθεντο βουλήν does not mean "advised" (our versions). "To take or to give counsel" (R., *W. P.*) is also incorrect. They had no one from whom to take it, no one to whom to give it. Βουλή is a resolution, and ἔθεντο means, "they set it for themselves," thus, "they resolved." And the aorist states the final outcome of the two preceding imperfects, Paul's advising and the centurion's refusal to be persuaded by that advice. Ἀναχθῆναι is used at it was in 13:13; 27:2; etc.

Εἴπως with the optative is *not* a condition of potentiality (Robertson's fourth class condition, *W. P.*), because it occurs in indirect discourse. "Here after primary tenses we should have ἐάν and the subjunctive, or εἰ with the future indicative" (R. 1030), for this is a condition of expectancy (Robertson's third class) or of reality (Robertson's first). The change to the optative in the indirect discourse is optional with the writer. "The indicative or the subjunctive could have been retained," R. 1044. Nor do we think that this clause expresses purpose. Conditional clauses are distinct from purpose clauses. They said (direct discourse) : "If we may somehow be able to winter," etc. They expected to but took some risk. Φοῖνιξ = Phoenix (named from "palm") = Penice (two syllables, A. V.), a harbor on the southern coast of Crete opposite the little isle Cauda (v. 16).

What does βλέποντα κατὰ λίβα καὶ κατὰ χῶρον mean? The point is a quite minor one. The vessel never reached this harbor. It makes little difference to us which way it faced, and whether the coast is now altered or not. To say that Luke never saw it is beside the mark, for this sailing master and this captain knew it so well that they left the one harbor for the other. The debate is keen, and not only on the part of the commentators, but even on the part of officers of the navy who have surveyed this coast and others who have examined it with charts, pictures, and debate resulting.

Λίψ is the wind that blows from the southwest, χῶρος the one from the northwest; there is no debate regarding this. There appear, however, to be two harbors in question, one that is now called Lutro, which one enters from the east; the other which by some is called Phineka, which one enters from the west (Zahn, a bight named "Plaka B." on the latest maps). We see the clash in our versions: "lieth toward the south *west* and north *west*," A. V.; "looking north-*east* and south-*east*," R. V., the one version looking κατά, "against" the wind, the other looking κατά, "down" the wind and thus translating the supposed sense of the Greek words. For ourselves we can say only this: "A harbor *into* which the so prevalent western winds could blow would be far worse than Fair Havens, into which these winds do not blow. How could a northwest wind reach a harbor on the south of Crete?" And now let us leave this question. See Smith, *Bible Dictionary*, III, 2481, for one view, and Zahn for the other.

13) **Now, when the south wind started to blow gently, supposing to have achieved their purpose, having weighed anchor, they began coasting along Crete rather closely.**

After they had decided to get to Phoenix, some forty miles for Fair Havens, the first opportunity that offered itself was when a gentle south wind started to blow; the gentleness lies in ὑπό in the participle, and its aorist is ingressive. The sailing master, the captain, and the centurion at once supposed that they had achieved the purpose they had set, namely reaching Phoenix; κρατέω is followed by the genitive. Since this wind was blowing, they thought they were as good as there. So they quickly weighed anchor, αἴρω, "to draw up," "to lift," in the nautical sense. Then they started to coast along the shore of Crete (inchoative imperfect, the verb being the same as the participle used in v. 8) "rather closely," well inshore, ἆσσον, comparative of ἄγχι. The tense, of course, implies that something unexpected intervened. But the venture itself seemed to have everything in its favor: only forty miles to go, and ugly westerly winds changed into a gentle southern breeze which could be used to good advantage in slipping along the coast.

14) **Not long after, however, there beat down from it a typhonic wind, the one called Euraquilo. And the ship having been seized and not able to face the wind, having given way, we were driven on.**

The description is terse and graphic. The gentle south wind was deceptive. "Not much after" is a litotes for "quite soon." The totally unexpected happened. "Down from it" (feminine, Crete), from the Cretan mountains, 7,000 feet high, a typhonic wind, for which the sailors had the name Euraquilo, struck the vessel. The adjective is derived from Τυφῶν, "the malignant demon *par excellence* of magic" (M.-M. 646), from which we still have "typhoon." When Luke adds the name of this hurricane he conveys the idea that this type of wind was well known. We see what made sailing so dangerous at this season of the year, and what Paul meant by his warning in regard to going on. The resolve to winter in Phoenix was really a compromise. It had been proposed to go only to this point. But even while traversing this short distance the vessel was promptly caught in the gale. The name εὐρακύλων (εὖρος, east wind and the Latin *aquilo,* northeast) is unimportant as far as its hybrid etymology is concerned; this name was given the wind because of its terrible character. The variant εὐροκλύδων, textually weakly supported and probably a corruption = northeast wind causing great waves. The aorist ἔβαλε reports wherein the preceding imperfect ended.

15) The vessel being thus suddenly seized (aorist) and not being able to face the wind (to look it in the eye, nautical for beating up against it; δυναμένου present tense to denote the condition), "having given way, we were being borne on," the aorist participle to indicate the act of giving the vessel over to the typhoon, and the imperfect verb, the continued result, and aorists to tell what the outcome was. Here Luke's "we"

includes the entire group on the ship. They were helplessly swept onward in the grip of the hurricane. They simply ran with the wind and did not in any way beat up against it as they could and would have done in an ordinary gale.

16) **And having run under the lee of a small island called Cauda, we succeeded with difficulty to secure the boat; which having hoisted, they started using frappings, undergirding the ship; and fearing lest they fall off into the Syrtis, having lowered the tackle, they were thus borne along.**

Note well how Luke writes: in v. 14, 15, he tells how the typhoon struck until ἐφερόμεθα, "we were borne on"; then v. 16, 17, how they got into the lee of the island, did what they could, and thus still ἐφέροντο, "they were borne on." These two imperfects are mates: borne on and still borne on. Cauda or Clauda, called Gaudo by the Greeks today, Gozzo by the Italians, twenty-three miles from Crete, is a little triangular isle, one side facing east, the second southwest, the third north. They managed "to run under the lee" of this isle; note in v. 4, "to sail under the lee." This lee was the southwest angle of the isle which shielded the vessel somewhat from the northwest hurricane.

With difficulty they managed to secure the ship's boat here. When they left Fair Havens, this only boat which they possessed was towed. Then the sudden typhoon swept down on them and afforded no opportunity to take the boat in. It had been promptly swamped and was thus now hauled in with considerable difficulty. Luke writes ἰσχύσαμεν, "we succeeded," as though he had been one of those who helped to secure the boat. Some imagine that, when the typhoon struck, the boat had been put out (even loaded down) in order to act as a drag. But if this had been done, Luke would have mentioned the fact.

He writes instead as though the boat had been towed as a matter of course. The boat was too valuable to be cut adrift; in case of the ship's foundering it afforded some means of escape. It was probably of a considerable size.

17) The first task was to hoist the boat. This done, they began to use frappings to undergird the ship. Βοηθείαις is to be construed with ἐχρῶντο, which always has the dative, and the present participle describes how the frappings were used. Luke now uses the third person, for this task the sailors alone could perform, and the imperfect pictures the work as consuming some time. These βοηθεῖαι were ὑποζώματα, strong cables that were passed under the ship transversely around its waist in order to support the timbers lest they spring their joints and let in the water and cause the ship to founder. The Athenian triremes used such frappings. Some speak of passing these cables around the ship horizontally, from stem to stern, an idea that is unacceptable, not only because the thing could not be done, but because, if done, would be quite useless. The planking of the hull was horizontal, and a transverse cable alone would help to secure it against springing joints. Ancient ships generally foundered because of the spreading of the planks of the hull; frappings were thus carried as regular equipment. The straining of the heavy mast in a violent storm often forced timbers to spread. Even in the case of modern vessels severe storms force open the steel plates and cause foundering despite powerful pumps.

The next step was to escape a different danger, that of being driven into the Syrtis. There were two, one a smaller (now the Gulf of Cabes), and the other the larger one here referred to (now the Gulf of Sidra). These were sandbanks which shifted because of wind and waves. This Syrtis lying between Carthage and Cyrene was so dreaded by all ancient sailors that "Syrtis" became a common expression with the poets. These northeast hurricanes were known to blow for days as we see that this one did. When they were first caught on the coast of Crete, nothing availed but to run before the wind; but to continue thus involved being driven into these sand bars with a fatal ending. The ship's course had to be changed at all hazard.

When this is understood, we shall reject the explanation of the German commentators who think that χαλάσαντες τὸ σκεῦος means lowering the gear into the water in order to slow down the scudding vessel. Some think of stones or weights that were dragged by ropes; Zahn names rudder, sails, ropes, anchors, but does not mention further details except to state that the sails were furled, and the anchors were thrown out. But this would not have changed the ship's course, it would only have delayed the calamity of the Syrtis. And the ship's course *was* changed; see the maps. It was driven westward and a little northward so that it eventually (the hurricane lasted fourteen days) reached Malta. The indispensable book for a proper understanding of the entire voyage and most of its details is that by J. Smith, *The Voyage and Shipwreck of St. Paul,* 4th ed., 1880.

What was lowered in the lee of Cauda was the mainsail; the yardarm and this sail were brought down. The ship was laid to, pointed into the wind as closely as possible, having only a small topsail to help to hold it there; she was laid on her starboard tack, the right side slanting acutely to the wind, so that the gale sent her westward and a little northward. The resultant drift 8° north of west, according to the strength of the gale, would be between ¾ and 2 miles per hour. Taking the mean rate of 1½ miles per hour, 36 per day, would bring the ship the 480 miles to Malta in about 13 days, exactly as Luke has described its course. These calculations of Smith are certainly most satisfactory. "Thus they were borne on" in the new course.

18) **And we being exceedingly tempest-tossed, they started jettisoning, and on the third day with their own hands they hurled out the furniture of the ship. And neither sun nor stars appearing for a number of days, and no small tempest continuing to hold on, as for anything further, there began to be taken away all around every hope of our being saved.**

The hurricane did not abate in the least as the genitive absolute (causal) states. Thus jettisoning started the next day in order to lighten the ship (A. V.), literally: "they began to make an outthrow," imperfect, inchoative. Luke fails to state what was heaved overboard. Those who think of the grain are mistaken (v. 38); it was probably some of the heavy supercargo, pieces of freight that were, perhaps, lashed to the deck or easily reached through the hatches. The tense implies that not all of it was jettisoned.

19) But on the third day with their own hands they heaved overhoard τὴν σκευήν of the ship, its furniture (R. V. margin) and not the tackling (our versions). The latter would be τὰ σκεύη or τὰ ὅπλα. Because of αὐτόχειρες the A. V. translates, "we with our own hands," which Ramsay thinks more graphic. Everybody lent a hand, even Luke. But the text has the third person, and now the aorist to indicate a complete job. Beds, tables, chairs, chests were thrown overboard. Desperation was growing. But they did not cast overboard the tackling, the spars, broken masts or the anchors. We note four anchors in v. 29

and 40, and the hoisting of the mainsail in v. 40, which means that the mast held, and that the spars were in place. Moreover, the ship was held to its course and not abandoned to drift helplessly.

20) Neither sun nor stars appearing for days (πλείονας, "more," i. e., a number of them), it was impossible to make a reckoning and to establish the position of the ship. "No small tempest continuing to hold on," literally, "to lie on," means that the severity of the gale had not abated. Luke does not name the number of days; he had lost count. In this desperate condition, "as for anything further," λοιπόν, "furthermore," Deissmann, *Light, etc.*, 176, (16), 188 (5 and 20), "there began to be taken away all around (περιῃρεῖτο, imperfect of περιαιρέω) all hope of our being saved" (ἡμᾶς, not, "as far as we were concerned," R., *W. P.*, for it is the subject of the infinitive). We need not ask whether Paul, too, was losing hope, for Luke uses the inchoative imperfect which even in the case of the others does not imply complete loss of hope.

21) **And there having been much going without food, then, having taken his stand in their midst, Paul said: It was necessary, O men, for you by obeying me not to put to sea from Crete and to escape this injury and loss. And as to you, I exhort you to be of good cheer, for there shall be not a single loss** (by sea) **of life from among you, only of the ship. For there stood beside me this night of the God, whose I am, whom also I serve, an angel, saying, Fear not, Paul! It is necessary for thee to stand before Caesar. And lo, God has graciously granted thee all those sailing with thee. Therefore be of good cheer, men, for I believe God that it shall be thus according to what manner he has spoken to me. However, it is necessary for us to fall onto some island.**

Since the conditions during these days were as described, even the preparation of food had scarcely been attempted to say nothing about eating sufficiently. Ἀσιτία is "foodlessness," and there had been much of this, namely men going without food, perhaps eating a bite only at great intervals, giving way to despair, and being weak and exhausted. This completes Luke's picture of the desperate condition of vessel, crew, and passengers.

We have already seen so much of Paul's strong character and of the leadership and the mastery with which he was endowed, that all this does not need again to be introduced. Of course, he had lost none of this during these desperate days. Now, however, it is not this strength of soul that makes him "take a stand in the midst of them," but the divine message God sent him by an angel during the night. He is not attempting to put new heart and courage into all these despairing men merely by his own personal power but chiefly by this divine revelation which he has received, which, indeed, concerns all on board the ship. He had made no special move until this time; the one he now makes is undertaken by God's own direction. Luke records Paul's words in full.

The imperfect ἔδει expresses a past necessity or obligation that was not met. This idiom is difficult to the English and the German ear, starting, as it does, in the past and reaching to the present. R. 886 and 919-920 describe it well although we doubt the statement on p. 920 that this imperfect is practically an apodosis of a second-class conditional sentence (present unreality) without ἄν; we think only of one function, not of this second one of a conditional thought. Back there in Fair Havens they should have obeyed Paul when he urged them not to put to sea, but they failed to do so.

Δεῖ always takes the accusative with the infinitive,

and here the infinitive ἀνάγεσθαι, "to be putting to sea" (nautical, see 13:13), has its implied accusative subject ὑμᾶς modified by the participle πειθαρχήσαντάς μοι. The thing they ought to have done as being right and necessary was: "by obeying me not to go on putting to sea from Crete." Κερδῆσαι adds what the result of not putting to sea would have been: "and escape (aorist, the one act of escaping) this injury and loss." The verb means "to gain" but is used idiomatically with terms such as injury and loss; the gain lies in escaping the loss. Our versions draw the negative μή also to this second infinitive: "not to gain this injury," etc., which is incorrect (B.-P. 672, and others).

22) This reminder of the past great mistake was not intended in the sense of, "I told you so," as is the manner of petty natures. Paul reminds the authorities of the ship in regard to what they now see, that they should have obeyed him, in order that they may not again disbelieve and disobey. One serious mistake was enough. So now (ταvῦν, "as to present affairs," complement of μέν in v. 21) he exhorts them to be of good cheer and to drop their hopeless despair. But this is not a rallying of the last bit of desperate courage, at least to die fighting. Paul has more, far more: God's own positive assurance that not a single loss (ἀποβολή, nautical: "loss by sea," by being thrown overboard, Smith, *Bible Dictionary,* the nautical vocabulary, IV, 3009) of life among all of them shall occur although the vessel itself shall be lost. Paul thus states in brief what God had communicated to him. Looking at that communication, we see that it promised nothing cheering in regard to the ship, and the outcome, too, shows that Paul understood correctly that the ship would not be saved.

23) And now, in explanation (γάρ) of this so positive assurance and prophecy, Paul tells all his ship-

mates what God himself promised him by one of his angels in a vision during the past night. As soon as possible Paul announced the news in the morning. The genitive "of God" with its two modifiers is placed forward for the sake of emphasis. All these men were pagans although there may have been a Jew or two among them. That makes clear the reason for this emphasis. And Paul's tone and bearing must be added, his joy in confessing the one true God before these pagans, "whose I am," who is my God, to whom alone I belong with heart and soul, who holds me in his hand as his very own; "whom also I serve," λατρεύω (in the service due him from everyone, not λειτουργέω, official service as an apostle), serve faithfully as his true worshipper. What were pagan gods in comparison with this "God"? Let all these men understand well this great confession of God on Paul's part. Whether these pagans understood ἄγγελος as "angel," in the way Paul meant the word, or only as "messenger," in the general sense, made little difference, for only a spirit from God and from heaven could stand beside Paul during the night and speak the message which Paul now repeats.

24) In prohibitions the present imperative often means to stop an action already begun (R. 851, etc.), yet here the sense is scarcely, "Stop being afraid!" but, as in various other instances, "Remain unafraid!" for the angel's message was, indeed, a blessed one. It was brief and consisted of two decisive statements. The first is that Paul must, indeed, appear before Caesar. The necessity implied in δεῖ is here that of God's will which was plainly intimated to Paul already in 23:11, so that before Festus he had also appealed to Caesar (25:11, 12). With regard to God it had been settled, and he would bring it to pass that the apostle should stand before Caesar. We hesitate to stress the angel's statement to mean that Nero himself

was to hear Paul's case and not merely Nero's imperial judge in Rome.

More than this, and no small addition, as "lo" makes clear. God has graciously granted Paul the lives of all his shipmates. May we not assume that Paul had earnestly prayed for them, and that this was God's answer? The angel does not say so as he does in Luke 1:13, and Acts 10:4, hence we cannot be certain. But this is beyond question: it was for Paul's sake that God spared the lives of all these men. They had him, under God, not themselves to thank for the extension of their day of grace. God has often done similar things for the sake of his children. "Graciously granted" to Paul, with its perfect tense implying that this was now their condition, is a word to cause us to pause although so many pass over it lightly. All might have perished in the waves, and God might have saved Paul alone, or Paul and Luke and Aristarchus. Surely, it was not the keeping of all alive that is so important in this divine grant. They now hear that they belong to Paul by the gift of the Almighty who will save them from this tempest when their hope was almost gone. And Paul belongs to God as one who truly serves him. Is God not telling them that through Paul's mediation they, too, like him, are to be this true God's own in order to serve him? They were to see and to hear much more about God, and we may, indeed, conclude that many of these men "sailing with Paul" came also to be saved in the higher sense.

25) Calamity, the imminence of frightful death, is one of God's means for opening men's ears to his Word and to the thought of eternity. Paul's words found willing hearers. No one scoffed at the vision of the angel and the message. Again, and for the mighty reason assigned, Paul bids them take heart by assuring them that he trusts what God has said (πιστεύω with

the dative of the person). In καθ' ὃν τρόπον the antecedent is drawn into the relative clause. The Greek is more cumbersome; we say, "just as." Paul confesses his confidence in God and in the message. He does it in order to awaken a like confidence in all his shipmates. One man's faith and confident confession are to aid other men in joining him. The strong faith is to support the weak, hesitant, timid. This was more than a star of hope in the black night of death; this was God himself, his angel, his great message, a burst of sunlight. "I believe God." This word is placed on each man's lips in order to confess it with Paul.

26) From the angel's words Paul makes the deduction that "we must fall onto some island," δεῖ to indicate the necessity lying in the situation. On ἐκπεσεῖν εἰς note v. 17, in v. 29 this verb is used with κατά; our versions translate interpretatively, "be cast upon." Paul's judgment was correct. It was so in v. 10, where he spoke without revelation or inspiration. Where he speaks of the loss of lives in addition to the other loss, he was right; for the fact that no lives were lost was due wholly to God's intervention and gracious gift. We take it that Paul spoke on the morning before the fourteenth night (v. 27).

27) **But when the fourteenth night came, we being borne on through in the Adria, along the middle of the night the sailors began to suspect that some land was drawing near to them. And on sounding they found twenty fathoms; and on standing through a little and having sounded again, they found fifteen fathoms. And fearing lest, perhaps, they fall along rough places, having thrown out four anchors from the stern, they kept praying for day to come.**

In regard to the time, the fourteenth night as compared with the distance covered from Crete to Malta, see v. 17. This protracted tempest which continued unabated after fourteen days and nights shows the danger of navigation at this season (September 15-November 11), and why all navigation ceased from November 11 to March 10. We see no reason for "to and fro" as a translation of διά in διαφερομένων; "through" is sufficient, for they held their course in the same direction as before.

"The Adria" (not "the Adriatic" in our sense) is the sea between Malta, Italy, Greece, and Crete; later "the Adria" was extended to the coast of Cyrene. About midnight the sailors on duty began to suspect that some land was approaching. It is an interesting textual question whether to accept the reading προσάγειν, or with one codex and a Latin version or two the reading προσαχεῖν, *resonare sibi*, the Doric for προσηχεῖν. The former is, indeed, used intransitively in the sense of "to approach," and the commentators explain that the verb is subjective, the sailors thinking of the land as coming toward them. But, in reality, during the thick, starless night (v. 20) they detected the nearness of land by the first sound of the breakers and the surf beating on the coast. This new sound was at first faint because of the storm, hence ὑπενόουν, "began to suspect some land sounding toward them." One also sees how this more unusual infinitive by a slight alteration became, "was approaching," when landmen copied the text. See M.-M. 546 for Moulton's opinion that "resounding toward them" was a technical nautical term.

28) The sailors promptly cast the sounding lead and found the depth to be twenty fathoms, the ὀργυιά or "stretch" being the distance between the tips of the middle fingers with the arms outstretched. "And when they had gone a little further" (A. V.). like, "after a little space" (R. V.), is interpretative for "having stood on through a little," διά being used to indicate the

interval. Then the sounding showed only fifteen fathoms, which indicated that they were rapidly approaching land. The noise they had begun to hear was certainly the roar of the breakers.

29) They now feared that "they might fall out down on rough places," the verb ἐκπίπτω being used as it was in v. 17 and 26. Those breakers sounded ominous in the dead of night as though the coast were full of rocks and reefs toward which the ship was rapidly drifting. Forthwith they threw out four anchors from the stern, all the anchors they had in the stern, in order to prevent the ship, if possible, from going straight onto the rocks. We see no reason for calling this anchoring from the stern "unusual" under the circumstances. This was not an anchoring in a calm bay or in waters where a position could be chosen but in a storm. The effect of the anchoring from the stern seems to be ill understood. The ship was not driving head on, i. e., running before the wind. This would have carried it southwest into the great Syrtis. Under the lee of Cauda the prow had been pointed north or north by east. The impact of the wind on the starboard side drove the vessel west by north. Thus it was now in danger of being hurled port or larboard side onto the rocks. The moment the stern anchors held, the ship swung to the left as on a pivot, its prow pointing down wind, southwest, more or less directly toward the shore. With the casting of the anchors the rudder was released, and the topsail was quickly taken in.

All this was done in the dark while the booming shore was wholly invisible, and only its general direction was being indicated by the sound. To say that anchoring from the prow would have caused the ship to swing about and to snap the anchor cables is unwarranted. The stern would have swung about and not the prow, nor would there have been more danger of snapping than by causing the prow to swing around by anchoring at the stern. It is not easy to show just why the stern was chosen. The assumption that it had already been determined to beach the ship, and that the calculation had already been made that in doing this with the prow down wind the ship might be controlled enough to choose a favorable spot ashore, overlooks the total darkness. All that can safely be said is that, if the anchors would not hold, it was thought best to head inshore at some kind of an angle. But the anchors held, and all now prayed for day to come so that they might be able at least to see.

30) **But the sailors seeking to flee out of the ship and having lowered the boat into the sea on pretext as though intending to lay out anchors from the prow, Paul said to the centurion and the soldiers, Unless these remain in the ship, you yourselves cannot be saved. Then the soldiers cut away the ropes of the boat and let her fall off.**

This scheme of the sailors was cunning, indeed. Once in the boat under the cover of the dark night, who could tell but what they were swept away from the ship by accident? They thought that they had more chance of getting ashore alive by means of the boat than by risking their lives in the ship, whose stern anchors might not hold the ship until daylight. Those who think that the sailing master and the captain (v. 11) were not party to the scheme forget that these officers of the vessel alone could order more anchors lowered.

The scheme progressed as far as lowering the boat into the sea (aorist to express the fact). One of the main officers gave the order and added the second regarding the additional anchors. It is Luke who calls this "a pretext." With ὡς and the participle (genitive, continuing the genitive absolute, R. 966) he states what was used as the pretext, namely "intending (μελλόντων) to lay out anchors from the prow." Ἐκτείνω ἄγκυραν is used in this sense, Smith, *Bible Dictionary*, vocabulary IV, 3009. This was really an excellent plan. By means of the boat the anchors of the prow would be carried as far back as possible on each side of the ship so that, if the four stern anchors began to slip, these others would grip, and all of the anchors together would hold.

31) It was the keen eye of Paul that detected the treachery. His speaking to the centurion and the soldiers and not to the ship's officers shows plainly that the latter were party to the scheme, in fact, were the very men who were trying to effect it. One word from Paul is enough: "Unless these remain in the ship, you yourselves (ὑμεῖς, emphatic) cannot be saved." Paul says nothing about himself and all the other passengers. It was enough that the centurion and his soldiers (who heard Paul) should lose their lives. But had Paul, by God's own revelation, not declared that not a single life would be lost? He had, indeed; nor was even one man lost. But God uses natural means, was even now using Paul, the centurion and his soldiers, and these wicked sailors. After the desertion of the latter no man would have been left to manage the ship (as in v. 39-41). It is idle to ask the hypothetical question as to what really would have happened *if* the scheme of the sailors had succeeded. Nearly all of such "if" questions are useless. When God foretells the future, he does so by foreseeing every detail and every means with the same certainty as though they had already occurred. Thus Paul's frustration of the wicked scheme of the sailors was known to God when he gave him the prophecy.

32) Upon the centurion's orders the ropes that held the boat were promptly slashed through by the soldiers and the boat let go (ἐάω, nautical, see Smith above).

33) **Until day was about to come, Paul was beseeching them all to partake of food, saying: For the fourteenth day today you are continuously waiting foodless, having taken nothing to yourselves. Wherefore I beseech you to partake of food, for this is in the interest of your own safety, for of not one of you a hair from the head shall perish. And on having said this and having taken bread, he gave thanks to God in the presence of them all and, having broken it, he began to eat. And having become of good cheer, all also themselves took food. Now we were in the ship to the total number of souls two hundred seventy-six.**

What a scene! It is still pitch-dark night, the storm is still howling as it had done during thirteen other nights, the surf is roaring on the uncertain coast, dim lanterns afford the only light, a vessel full of despairing people is expecting to be drowned in the wild sea! It is Paul who once more steps to the front. He connects the prophecy with the present situation: all lives will be saved, but the vessel will be lost. What could and should now be done? Here was a true leader in an emergency. He made all these people eat in order to hearten and to strengthen them for what lay ahead.

We may take it that little food had been served during these two weeks. Few had cared to eat beyond snatching a bite now and then, many of those who were not sailors had been seasick and had given up entirely. It was no small task to rally all of them. How Paul had borne up during the long ordeal we do not know but he had by God's help and had courage enough for all of them. And had not God himself "graciously granted" all those sailing with him to Paul as a special gift to him (v. 24)? Had God not thus placed them in his charge? Just as it had been the case with regard to the sailors, whom God would use and who must not abandon the ship, so now it was the case with regard to the food which was to hearten and to strengthen all of them: this was another means in God's hands, and Paul was God's agent. God achieves so many of his ends by blessing the proper, sensible means.

Luke has preserved Paul's urgent words. The accusative "for the fourteenth day today" states the extent of the time of their having continued foodless. As is done so often in the Greek, the participle expresses the main idea, and the verb the adverbial thought: προσδοκῶντες διατελεῖτε, *ihr wartet ununterbrochen* (B.-D. 414), "you wait continuously" (Abbott-Smith, *Manual Greek Lexicon,* 112), and "foodless" is not to be taken absolutely, but as "having taken to yourselves nothing" in the way of a real meal. Since they were expecting death at any moment, who wanted to eat, how many could eat?

34) Paul rouses them out of this despair. He urges them to partake of food, for this is in the interest (πρός, "towards") of their own safety or deliverance. It is safety that lies ahead, not death; and the possessive adjective ὑμετέρας is stronger than the pronoun ὑμῶν, "your own safety." "For of not one of you shall a hair from the head perish" intensifies the assurance of coming safety and is based on the prophecy mentioned in v. 24. The sense is that, without the least bodily injury, every person on the ship shall be saved. The word is the same as that used in Luke 18:21. A variant reading has, "shall fall from the head," in agreement with 1 Sam. 14:45; II Sam. 14:11; I Kings 1:52; compare Matt. 10:30; Luke 12:7. Paul's faith dismisses all doubts and questions; he voices it in the strongest language in order to hearten all the others.

35) To his words he adds his example, for acts always speak more effectively than words. He took

bread, gave thanks to God before them all, broke it, and began to eat. This action said more than Paul's words; it showed all of them how to eat, namely with thanksgiving to God. It must not escape the reader that "he gave thanks" is a main verb which raises this act above those expressed by the participles. "In the presence of them all," perhaps all pagans, is important. Of course, this was grace before meat, but it was the confession of the true God before pagans, it was preaching this God to all of them as the fount of every blessing, as their one Deliverer in their frightful danger. So simple and yet so significant an act! No, Paul did not just break and eat; praying before eating was no formality with him, one that might be omitted at a time such as this. Prayer and thanksgiving were more essential in this hour than in more normal ones.

It is strange to find Blass and some others introducing the Lord's Supper or at least the Agape because Paul took the bread, gave thanks, and broke it. Bread was always taken, broken, and eaten, and all Jews were taught to eat with thanksgiving. Our method of biting into sliced bread was never used, nor was bread sliced in those days. Paul did not ask all to give thanks with him; he did not regard all these men as a Christian or a Jewish family for the reason that they were nothing of the kind. Luke and Aristarchus regarded Paul's thanksgiving as intended also for them; the rest listened, and even that was good for them. They saw a man of God acting like one even under dire circumstances.

36) Cheered and heartened, at least to some degree, they all also themselves took food. So much Paul had gained.

Because v. 21-26, and again, resting on them, v. 33-35, introduce the supernatural element, critics eliminate them. This critical canon, applied to Acts generally, would leave it a senseless wreck. As regards this one chapter Ramsay writes to the point: "In the voyage Luke pictures Paul on a higher plane than common men, advising more skillfully than the skilled mariners, maintaining hope and courage when all were in despair, and breathing his hope and courage into others, playing the part of a true Roman in a Roman ship (let us rather say of a true Christian in a heathen ship), looked up to even by the centurion, and in his single self the savior of the lives of all. But the interpolation-theory would cut out the center of the picture." Yes, it would do worse.

37) Δέ is parenthetical because of the nature of the statement. On the size of ancient vessels see Smith, *Bible Dictionary* IV, 3004. Josephus was wrecked in the same part of the Levant in a vessel which carried 600 souls. The average ship was between 500 and 1,000 tons, carrying one man for every 1½ tons. We need not trouble about the variant reading "about seventy-six" in place of "two hundred seventy-six." But πᾶσαι is attributive and thus means "the total number." It is Paul who towers above them all.

38) **And having been satisfied with food, they proceeded to lighten the ship by throwing out the wheat into the sea.**

This was done before daylight. Everybody had eaten well. New life and vigor promptly showed themselves. After verbs of tasting we have the genitive. It was a real task to bring up the wheat from the holds and to heave it overboard, but the work was done with zest. The verb κουφίζω is nautical (Smith, cited above), and the tense indicates the action as being in progress. The lighter the vessel, the higher she would ride, and the farther up on the shore would she be thrown. That ship and cargo were doomed had been plain for some time.

39) **But when it became day, they recognized not the land; but they were aware of a sort of bay**

having a beach, into which they resolved, if they could, to drive the ship. And having cast loose the anchors, they let them go into the sea; at the same time having loosed the yokes of the paddle-rudders and having hoisted the foresail to the blow, they held for the beach. But lighting upon a place between the seas, they grounded the vessel; and the prow having become fixed, remained immovable, but the stern began to break by the violence.

The climax is reached, and Luke is both detailed and most accurate. Any careful reader sees this, but those who have investigated the actual locality where Paul's ship was wrecked are astonished at Luke's wonderful account. It is well to note how he records only the vital points, each just briefly but so as to furnish a perfect picture. One must carefully follow the imperfects from v. 38 on to v. 41; they are like a moving picture. It is difficult to reproduce them in English but they are beautiful in the Greek. Only in v. 41 the aorist stands out, ἐπέκειλαν; they "beached" the vessel. With one heave it grounded.

Day finally arrived, the shore began to become visible through the spray, but though the sailors strained their eyes, they "were not recognizing" (imperfect) the land. But "they were noting" (again imperfect) a sort of (τινά) bay or inlet (not "creek," A. V.) with a beach. The ship had been driven just past Koura Point on the northwest slope of Malta, this Point forming the east boundary of what has since been called St. Paul's Bay. Today the water is twenty fathoms deep at this place, and in a storm breakers beat upon this point. The west side of this bay shows a decreasing depth. After passing the Point breakers would sound also from the opposite direction but in time to allow casting anchor. The English government survey states that anchors will hold here. On this western side of the bay there lies the island Salmonetta, so that from the vessel it would look like part of the mainland. But this west coast is made up entirely of high rocks, against which it was hopeless to beach the ship. That is why the sailors were so happy when they saw an indentation with a beach, one place where, by driving the ship ashore, they might hope to save at least their lives. So "they were resolved (imperfect), if they could (protasis, condition of potentiality), to drive the ship" into this inlet (we prefer the reading ἐξῶσαι, from ἐξωθέω. There was no hope of saving the ship, ἐκσῶσαι, a variant reading). The translation of the A. V. is far better than that of the R. V., for βουλεύω does not mean, "to take counsel whether," etc., but, "to resolve that," etc. (B.-P. 228; also others.)

40) The things that were thus done are grouped: an aorist participle with an imperfect verb, then, connected by ἅμα ("at the same time"), two aorist participles and another imperfect verb. After casting loose the four anchors at the stern they let go of them for good (εἴων, from ἐάω, is nautical; probably also περιελόντες, from περιαιρέω). The ship was thus adrift, was head on with the wind. At the same moment the two paddle-rudders were again fixed for use. Ancient vessels had no hinged rudder but had two long oar-like rudders, one on each side of the stern. The two were often operated together by being joined by cross-bars, ζεῦγλαι, the same as ζευκτήριαι, "yokes" (cf. Liddell and Scott on these words and on πηδάλιον). While the anchors at the stern held the ship, the rudders were drawn up and fastened so as to be out of the way. Now the fastenings of the yokes were loosed (ἀνέντες, second aorist participle), and the rudders slipped into the water and once more controlled the ship. At that moment, too, the foresail was hoisted to the blow of the wind. While ἀρτέμων is very rare, all nautical authorities are agreed that it means top foresail, which could be hoisted from the deck.

Thus "were they holding for the beach," the foresail and the rudders controlling the vessel so as to head in the direction desired. Τῇ πνεούσῃ is the present feminine participle converted into a noun: "to the blow," B.-P. 1090. This was not a "breeze," αὔρᾳ, Abbott-Smith and R., *W. P.*, but a howling gale. Equally unacceptable is the supposition of Breusing and the German commentators that the rudders were released in order *not* to be used; for without them the ship could not have been pointed toward that inlet beach. That certainly was a swift run for the shore!

41) But instead of reaching this goal they fell in with (περιπίπτω, "encountered," M.-M. 507) "a place dividing the sea," a sand bar that either projected from the beach or lay in front of it, the sea washing up from both sides (διθάλασσον).

James Smith thinks this sand bar was the submerged isthmus between the isle Salmonetta and the coast, and his word carries great weight. Nevertheless, we question this view, for Luke makes it very plain that, while running for the inlet beach, they unexpectedly struck this sand bar "between seas." It seems to be this adjective which our versions translate, "where two seas met" (following Luther's *der auf beiden Seiten Meer hatte*), that favors this view of the submerged isthmus, for any isthmus has sea on both sides. But the word means, "between seas," between deeper places on its two sides, thus "through the sea" and across the course of the ship which was making for the main shore and the inlet beach. This is the view of the German naval men reflected in B.-P. 304 who translates τόπος διθάλασσος *Aussengrund.* So we do not say with Ramsay that the ship could not have struck a more fortunate place. It was not fortunate, it was unavoidable. "They grounded the vessel" on this bar and were still some distance from the beach. This is the only place where Luke changes from πλοῖον to ναῦς in referring to the same vessel.

With μέν and δέ balancing the statements the effect is described and imperfects are again employed. The prow, fixed fast in the sand bar, continued to remain immovable, but the stern began to be broken by the violence, certainly not of the shock, but of the pounding waves. The imperfects leave us with this situation while the next incident is told.

42) **Now the resolution of the soldiers was to kill the prisoners so that not one, by swimming out, escape. But the centurion, being resolved to save Paul, hindered them from the project and ordered those able to swim, by going overboard, to get out as the first to the land, and the rest, some on boards, some on whatever things from the ship. And so it came to pass that all came safe through to the land.**

The soldiers were accountable for the prisoners with their own lives (see 12:18, 19). It was in order to protect their own lives for their accounting to the emperor for their prisoners that they resolved to kill all of them so that not one, by escaping, might cause them to be held accountable with their own lives. To say that they "owed this to their honor" is unwarranted. Here again βουλή is not "counsel" but an actual resolution; see the verb in v. 39, "to resolve." The soldiers did not merely advise this but agreed on it and told the centurion about their resolution. The texts vary between the subjunctive διαφύγῃ and the optative διαφύγοι, either being correct (R. 987).

43, 44) But the centurion vetoed the project (τοῦ βουλήματος, more than "purpose"), not because he was "more humane," but for a different reason. He was personally more in danger of forfeiting his own life than his soldiers in case one of his prisoners should manage to escape. Under other circumstances he himself would have ordered the prisoners killed. His soldiers counted on that. It is generally assumed that his "being resolved to save Paul" implies the alternative of killing all the prisoners, Paul included, or of killing none. But he certainly could have ordered all killed except Paul. And this the more readily because all the other prisoners had been condemned to death and were being sent to their death in Rome (see v. 1), while no sentence whatever had been passed on Paul. This centurion was grateful to Paul as the man who had practically saved his life by his courageous actions. But more is implied. This centurion was impressed by Paul's prophecy that God had "graciously granted" to Paul (v. 24) all his shipmates, including himself (the centurion). That word of prophecy gripped the centurion and made him veto the entire proposition of the soldiers; for Paul's sake he spared all the prisoners. Verbs of hindering take the genitive.

So he gave the command that all the prisoners and the soldiers who could swim should, by dropping overboard (ἀπό in the participle), get to the land as the first ones (πρώτους), so that they might help also any of the rest in getting to land. The sailors, of course, were able to swim and take care of themselves. The passengers, including Luke and Aristarchus, used boards (planks) or anything else that served to keep them afloat. The gale drove the waves ashore so that all of these had only to keep afloat in order to be thrown toward land. The aorist ἐκέλευσε implies that the order was promptly carried out.

"And thus it came to pass" (this ἐγένετο which is often used by Luke after the fashion of the LXX) marks something weighty and notable. The entire 276 "came through safe to land" (were brought safely through, passive). The angel's word was fulfilled (v. 24), and that in spite of everything that worked to the contrary even to the very last.

CHAPTER XXVIII

From Malta to Rome

1) The terrible experience on the sea was over at last. Exhausted, dripping, yet glad to be alive, sailors, soldiers, prisoners, passengers dragged themselves onto the beach. **And having gotten through safe, then we knew that the island was called Melite. And the barbarians went on showing us unusual kindness, for, kindling a fire, they took us all to themselves because of the present rain and because of the cold.**

Not until this time did they know where they had been wrecked. Καλεῖται, "is called," is retained in the indirect discourse. Μελίτη is correct, not Μελιτήνη, a clerical error. This is our present Malta with its great harbor Valetta. The author visited this harbor and had rough seas on leaving and only sailed past St Paul's Bay. Just how the sailors realized that they had been wrecked on Malta is not indicated. The fact that the inhabitants told them seems to be ruled out because they are not mentioned until the next sentence. Although Malta has been made important and populous by the British, even in ancient times it had trade, and its great harbor Valetta was known and often visited by sailors since it lay on the route of vessels bound for Rome.

2) "The barbarians" means neither savages nor barbarous people. In the language of the day mankind was made up of three groups of people: Jews, Greeks, and barbarians. All who did not speak Greek but native languages were termed "barbarians" in the sense of foreign people. These Maltese were a colony

of Phoenicians who thus spoke Punic. Yet we should not think that none of them were at least to some degree conversant with the Greek. As far as the Punic itself was concerned, its relation to Hebrew is close enough so that Paul who was master of Hebrew (as distinct from Aramaic) could understand and could make himself understood even without relying on such knowledge of the Greek as the natives may have had.

To the credit of these people Luke reports their unusual humanitarian kindness, *Menschenfreundlichkeit,* literally, "not the kindness that happens" right along. Παρεῖχον = "they went on furnishing" this exceptional kindness. To have 276 shipwrecked people suddenly thrust upon them during the wintry season with a storm still raging, in rain and cold, was no small visitation. Without hesitation "they took them to themselves." "Us all," Luke writes, stressing the great crowd. They took charge of the whole sorry lot and, in order to do what was most necessary first, kindled a great fire (πυρά is found only here and in the next verse in the New Testament) to help dry and warm them. The protracted gale must have brought much rain during the past fourteen days. It is not mentioned until now because it, together with the cold, was the reason for the kindling of the fire. The second perfect participle ἐφεστῶτα, which is always used in the present sense, "standing upon them" = the "present" rain. We may think of some kind of shelter under which the fire was made. Luke restricts himself to this evidence of humaneness because of what follows and leaves it to his reader to think of further kindness, for the shipload of 276 persons remained among the natives for about three months and needed practically everything that was necessary for their sustenance.

3) **Now Paul having packed together some pile of brushwood and having placed it on the fire, a viper, on coming out from the heat, fastened to his**

hand. And when the barbarians saw the beast hanging from his hand they went on to say to each other, Surely, this man is a murderer whom, though brought to safety out of the sea, justice did not let live! Now he, having shaken the beast off into the fire, suffered no harm. But they were expecting him presently to swell or to fall down suddenly dead; but expecting (this) **for a long while and beholding nothing amiss occurring to him, having changed their minds, they went on to say that he was a god.**

It is worth noting that Paul is among those who gather fuel for the fire. It was a sensible procedure to keep bestirring oneself in such a wet and cold condition, but it also reveals the spirit of the man. See him with a big lot of brushwood (the plural φρύγανα) in his arms, placing it upon the fire! Just such traits help to reveal his greatness. Somehow there was a viper among the wood that was burning, whether among the brush Paul had brought or in some other. Torpid from the cold, on getting warm it became active and struck its poisonous fangs into Paul's hand. The claim is made that Malta has no woods and has no vipers or poisonous snakes but only a small non-poisonous constrictor, that clings and bites. Hence Luke's story is not true. Until recent years wood was found at St. Paul's Bay; in 1853 Lewing believed he saw a viper near this very bay. But the population is now 1,200 to the square mile, which means that woods and poisonous snakes may have disappeared.

4) The viper hung from Paul's hand; all of the natives saw it hanging there. It had struck its fangs into the hand. It did not merely coil around the hand so that some might *think* the fangs were inserted, while in reality they were not. Take the miracle out of this record and a pointless story is left. But these natives

saw what they saw, and not only they, for Luke mentions them only because of what they said. The imperfect ἔλεγον (again in v. 6) describes instead of merely stating the fact. And these natives knew the full effect of a viper's strike, knew it from sad experiences in their own midst. On vipers compare Matt. 3:7; Luke 3:7; Matt. 12:34; 23:33.

Here we have a case of the natural sense of justice even among heathen men, conscience is still working in them. They are sure that crime is overtaken by retribution, and that this retribution often comes in a strikingly visible manner. These natives spoke in Punic, which Paul understood. But they probably did not speak at this moment but afterward; at this time they most likely just whispered to each other and eyed each other significantly. Πάντως, "looking at this in every way" = "certainly." They were sure that Paul (*dieser Mensch*) was a murderer and mentioned this crime as being most worthy of the doom of death. Although he had been brought to safety out of the sea (concessive participle), justice did not let him live, the aorist speaking of Paul as already being virtually dead.

Perhaps we may capitalize "Justice" as being personified, but it was scarcely a pagan deity that was worshiped on the island; it is enough to think of "justice" in the abstract sense. The idea is that justice always claims its victim; one may escape it now and again, in the end escape is hopeless. Justice works in its own strange and mysterious ways; one can never tell just when and how it reaches its victim. We should not call this superstition. Superstition is mentioned later and in a different way. To this day men know the workings of justice, in fact, cannot escape thinking of them.

5) Ὁ μὲν οὖν is balanced by the following οἱ δέ, and οὖν returns to Paul after telling about the natives. Paul

just flipped the viper into the fire and suffered no ill consequences whatever, the aorist expressing the permanent fact.

6) What the natives expected was that he would presently swell as a result of the poison, or that he would suddenly fall down dead. Μέλλειν is to be construed with both infinitives and expresses what was impending: "him about to be swelling or falling suddenly." They kept looking for either result to occur at any moment. In their experience this had always come about without much delay. The imperfect "were expecting" conveys the idea that in this case the expected did not eventuate.

For a long while they kept on expecting and yet observing "not a thing amiss happening to him." This was a marvel in their eyes. It was, as we know, a manner of fulfillment of the promise of Jesus stated in Mark 16:18, and in Luke 10:19. The miracle was wrought by the Lord in the interest of the gospel. Paul would remain in Malta only three months. Although 276 were cast on the island, the Lord at once directed the fullest attention to this one man Paul. In his own miraculous way even on this mere island the Lord opened the door for the apostle. It is for this reason that Luke makes a record of the miracle.

After waiting until their own expectation was completely dead, the natives finally turned their thoughts completely around. Μεταβαλόμενοι is the second aorist participle, and properly so, since the change of mind was one act. Since deadly serpent poison had no effect whatever on Paul, these pagan natives knew only one alternative, they declared "him to be a god," i. e., some one of their gods appearing in human form. This was a strange repetition of Acts 14:11, 12. And here is where we find the superstition above referred to.

Now what did Paul do to correct these natives? How did he succeed, and what happened? Has not

Luke written enough about Paul so that we may answer these questions ourselves? Although he was a prisoner, Paul did much for the gospel in Malta. Luke gives us just a glimpse. Paul reached even the headman on the island and many others besides, for the door had been opened to him at once.

7) **Now in the neighborhood of that place estates belonged to the Protos of the island by name Publius, who, having received us, lodged us in friendly-minded manner for three days.**

Ἐν τοῖς περὶ τὸν τόπον ἐκεῖνον, "in those (parts) around that place," i. e., in the neighborhood of the locality where the natives had first tried to help the shipwrecked crowd. The χωρία· (plural) were estates, perhaps an extensive villa with other buildings. They belonged to the Πρῶτος of the island, and this was his official title as the governor under the prætor of Sicily, to whose jurisdiction Malta belonged somewhat as Judea belonged to Syria. The reality of this title is established by a Phœnician-Greek inscription bearing the Greek title Πρῶτος Μελιταίων. This Prōtos was the Sicilian prætor's representative or legate, one of the permanent residents who had been appointed to this office. "Publius" was his *praenomen,* and its use by Luke in place of the *cognomen* may indicate the intimate relation with the man into which Paul and his companions came.

As is so often the case, here, too, the relative has demonstrative force: "it was he who," no less a person than he. We understand ἡμᾶς to include the entire 276. That is why his "estates" are mentioned. He found room to lodge and to feed the entire number; and he did this "in friendly-minded manner," in the same spirit which the natives had manifested (v. 2), and for three days, i. e., until other provisions were arranged for the prolonged, enforced stay. The wreck occurred in the early morning, and the three days must have begun with that day. Luke wants us to understand that this was a noble act on the part of Publius although as the governor of the island he, no doubt, felt it incumbent upon himself to take care of the personnel of a government grain ship and of the soldiers of the emperor.

8) **Now it was that the father of Publius was lying afflicted with fever attacks and dysentery, to whom Paul entering in and, on having prayed, healed him by laying on his hands.**

This case was serious, for the man was lying completely prostrated, afflicted (M.-M.) with fevers (plural, fever attacks that recurred) and dysentery (our very word which is derived from the Greek itself). The claim that this ailment is unknown on Malta is unwarranted, for it occurs everywhere. When feverish conditions develop, the patient may easily lose his life.

Here we have an instance in which the first participle is used with almost the force of a finite verb, for "to whom" applies only to Paul's going in and not to the act of healing, which has its own pronoun. Paul evidently asked to see the sick man and so went in to him. Many interpreters pass lightly by Paul's praying as if this conveyed nothing special regarding Paul and the miracle, as if it was similar to a pastor's prayer for the sick. But Paul prayed exactly as Peter did in 9:40 (see that passage) in order to learn the Lord's will concerning this desperately sick man. The apostles never healed at will; they performed miracles only on the Lord's or the Spirit's intimation. So here Paul prayed not for the sick man but for himself: did the Lord intend to heal this man through Paul or did he not? And the Lord directed Paul to heal. Forthwith the miracle was wrought. The laying on of hands (see 6:6) accompanied this act as in so many instances recorded regarding Jesus. The Lord was furthering Paul's work in Malta.

9) **And when this was done, also the rest, those in the island having diseases, proceeded to come and to be cured; who also honored us with many honors, and they added for us on putting to sea the things for our needs.**

In view of the rest of Acts it is impossible to believe that on Malta only miracles were wrought and that no gospel was preached in connection with them. What happened as a result of the shipwreck was that the gospel with its great seal of miracles was spread through the island. Paul could, of course, not go about, being a prisoner; so the miracle caused the people voluntarily to come to the place where he was. The two imperfects describe what occurred continually. We have no report on the part of Luke and no other record of a church in Malta except the tradition that Publius became the first bishop. The gospel never returns void. Malta could be no exception. Neither here nor anywhere else does Luke even intimate that he himself also wrought miracles. To say that "he no doubt had his share in the cures" by working miracles or by using his medical skill, is without warrant.

10) The benefactions that came to them through Paul (Luke and Aristarchus helping him with the preaching and the teaching) evoked the strongest gratitude. "They honored us with many honors." Luke uses the personal pronoun freely in this last "we" section, beginning with 27:1, sometimes with reference to Paul, himself, and Aristarchus alone (some think the latter went only as far as Myra, 27:5), again with reference to all the voyagers. Here the context suggests that "us" is to be taken in the narrow sense. What the "honors" were is not specified. But when they put to sea again, the grateful people supplied them with all that they needed for the further voyage. We take ἐπέθεντο to mean, "they added"; the A. V. is better than the R. V. on this point. We find it misleading

when R., *W. P.*, intimates that "honors" has the sense of payment for professional services, honorarium. When did an apostle ever regard his healings as "professional services" or accept an honorarium?

11) **Now after three months we put to sea in a ship that had wintered in the island, an Alexandrian one, with the sign Dioscuri. And having been brought down to Syracuse, we remained there for three days; whence, on having gone around, we arrived at Rhegium, and after one day a south wind having come on, we came on the second day to Puteoli, where, on finding brethren, we were urged to remain with them for seven days. And thus we came to Rome.**

The regular shipping season opened on March the tenth (see 18:18). Some think that the start from Malta was made a little earlier, but Luke is not concerned about fixing the exact day. The Alexandrian ship had wintered in the grand harbor of Valetta, which is now heavily fortified by Britain and enclosed by heights, all save the entrance. This Alexandrian ship was quite likely also a government grain vessel. Whether the entire 276 took passage on this ship or only the centurion with his soldiers and his prisoners is left undetermined.

This is the only vessel whose name Luke records: "Dioscuri," Διός (genitive of Ζεύς) plus κόροι = "boys of Zeus" (the Attic used the dual form, the Koine the plural), meaning the twins, Castor and Pollux, born to Leda. These two were the tutelary gods of sailors, and their images were either painted or carved on both sides of the prow; παρασήμῳ (either a noun or an adjective) is like the appositional name in the dative because of the construction after ἐν although the vessel's name might have been given in the nominative. Ramsay thinks that Luke has given this vessel's name because on previous voyages he saw the names of the ships for the first time when he embarked in them, but in this case he heard the name long before embarkation. On the verb "put to sea" and its opposite see 13:13.

12) The run of eighty miles to Syracuse on the east of Sicily was accomplished without incident. In regard to the history that makes this harbor interesting see Conybeare and Howson, *Life and Epistles of the Apostle Paul,* and other writers. This reference applies also to the other localities and to their histories. Why the vessel remained for three days, whether Paul went ashore, and what the tradition is worth that he founded the church in Syracuse, are questions on which Luke does not offer a hint.

13) Two uncials read περιελόντες (αἱρέω), which is thought to mean, "having cast off"; but even if we supply the noun "anchors," as we have it in 27:40, this reading is unsatisfactory. Περιελθόντες, "having gone around," is correct and means, "by tacking" we arrived at Rhegium, on the toe-tip of Italy, the city whose tutelary gods were the same Dioscuri, Castor and Pollux. Only by tacking were these seventy miles negotiated.

Here, however, after a wait of one day, the south wind began to blow, the very wind that was needed to get safely through the Straits of Messina. The very next day they were ably aided by this most favorable wind in making the 182 miles to Puteoli, the magnificent harbor of Naples, Puteoli lying on its northern side eight miles from Naples. Paul thus saw three famous volcanoes, Aetna on the island of Sicily, and after passing the straits, Stramboli rising like a cone out of the Mediterranean, and Vesuvius near Naples. They still stand out in the writer's memory, for he saw them on his voyage from Naples to Malta. At Paul's time, however, Vesuvius was inactive, and its westward slopes were covered with vines; at that time no one dreamed that in but a few years (A. D. 79) a ruin similar to that which came upon Sodom and Gomorrah would descend upon the fair cities about its base. During this awful eruption Drusilla, the wife of Felix, and their son were destroyed.

Puteoli was one of the great harbors for ships coming from Alexandria. Luke's exactness has been remarked, for the old sailing vessels would require just about twenty-four to twenty-six hours with a good south wind in making a straight run. The Greek uses the plural adjective: we "as second-day people," instead of the adverb, "on the second day."

14) It is not a surprise that Paul found "brethren" at Puteoli. A strong colony of Jews lived here; the distance to Rome was not great. Christianity naturally spread in various directions from Rome. "We were urged to remain with them for seven days" is concise for the urging to stay as long as possible; the time was extended seven days by permission of the centurion. The idea does not commend itself that the centurion left Paul in charge of a few soldiers in Puteoli for a week while he and the other soldiers took the other prisoners on to Rome; for on his arrival in Rome he had to turn over all his prisoners with all documents relative to them plus his own complete report. One does not see how he could have left Paul behind. Yet Luke's aorist "we were urged" implies that this urging brought about the stay of a week; and we must note that "we" includes the entire party, the centurion as well as Paul, Luke, and Aristarchus. Let us take it as a signal favor to Paul that the centurion delayed so long in Puteoli. He regarded Paul as the one who had saved his life and surely was attracted to the apostle for other personal reasons. Luke leaves this to his reader's inference in an account which, in these last two chapters, quietly but plainly reveals the full power of the apostle's wonderful personality.

"Thus," after this gracious delay of a whole week in Puteoli, "we came to Rome." The emphasis is on the adverb "thus" and not on the phrase. It conveys the idea that, although months had been required for the voyage from Caesarea to Rome, the centurion did not now hurry Paul onward. Because the arrival in Rome is again mentioned in v. 16, some let the two statements say different things — an unnecessary effort. In v. 16 the clause is of minor import and merely resumes v. 14. The idea that in v. 14 "to Rome" means "Rome" in a wide sense, including the entire territory of the city, the whole *ager Romanus,* "the state Rome," while in v. 16 "to Rome" means "the walls of Rome," is supposition. No reader would discover that the same phrase had such diverse meanings. Moreover, Luke has done this before, taking us to the goal and then adding something that transpired on the way.

Paul is reaching his great goal Rome. This getting to Rome is also the climax of Acts. Luke has every reason to emphasize this fact by a repetition. In regard to the journey overland to Rome with all the old historical ornamentation read Conybeare and Howson (above), chapter XXIV.

15) **And from thence the brethren, having heard the things concerning us, came for meeting with us as far as Appii Forum and Three Taverns; whom having seen, Paul, giving thanks to God, took courage.**

It was a distance of 125 miles from Puteoli to Rome. The brethren who came to Appii Forum went some forty miles, about one-half of the distance; those who stopped at Three Taverns went thirty miles, one-fourth of the distance. We need not wonder how word got to Rome during the week of Paul's stay in Puteoli. This city was on one of the great Roman roads that had heavy traffic of all kinds: "We are on the most crowded approach to the metropolis of the world, in the midst of prætors and proconsuls, embassies, legions, and turms of horse, 'to their provinces hasting or on return,' which Milton, in his description of the city enriched with the spoils of nations, has called us to 'behold' in various habits on the Appian Road." It was a very simple matter to send word to Rome.

This action on the part of the Christians in Rome, delegations coming out thirty and forty miles to meet Paul, is exceedingly significant. They had heard τὰ περὶ ἡμῖν, "all about us," and that brought them to meet and to greet the great apostle. The fact that he was a prisoner for the sake of the gospel increased their estimation of him. We know, of course, how brethren loved to go great distances with Paul when he bade them good-by — some Bereans went all the way to Athens. But here they come out to meet him and to bring him in, and two delegations at that, the one either starting sooner than the other or traveling at a faster pace and thus meeting Paul the sooner. We take it that both delegations were numerous as, indeed, the church in Rome was not small.

Three years before this time Paul had sent his great epistle to Rome by the hands of Phœbe. A number of brethren who had known Paul were now in Rome. They were most likely also a part of these delegations that came out to meet him. Paul was the first apostle to reach Rome. The church in Rome had been founded long before this time. Christians who found each other in the capital had just gotten together and established a congregation in this great center. Peter got to Rome after Paul had been there. No event as great as this coming of Paul's to Rome had transpired in the history of the church. No wonder that we hear about these delegations. Ἄχρις marks the points to which they came.

The Forum of Appius was named after the Censor Appius Claudius who built this part of "the queen of roads" in 312 B. C. Paul most probably reached the Appian Way at Capua. Appii Forum was a rough place; R., *W. P.*, reports that it was the haunt of thieves, thugs, and swindlers. If Paul was happily surprised at meeting a delegation from Rome so far from the city, what were his feelings when he met another ten miles farther on at Three Taverns? This was only a village on the Appian Way. The centurion's party traveled afoot, and it must have taken some five days in getting to Rome. Paul did not travel that distance in chains. See the discussion in 25:23, and again in 26:29. Add all that we have seen of the fine treatment accorded to Paul by this centurion. The fact that Paul was a Roman would keep him free from chains although there is much to be added. After 22:25 we do not read about a chain until in 28:20, which see.

Luke writes that when Paul saw these delegations "thanking God, he took courage." Paul's heart was too devoted to the gospel to lead us to think that Luke implies that he thought only of himself. Since he had landed in Puteoli and found brethren there he had no special cause for discouragement. He certainly had not forgotten the Lord's promise that, as he had testified at Jerusalem, so also he would have to testify in Rome (23:11). He now thanked God and took courage because in these delegations from Rome he saw how the Lord was beginning to prepare the way for him that, although a prisoner, he might, nevertheless, do his part in bearing witness in Rome. In a few days the Lord's guidance in this matter was fully revealed: Paul was able to testify daily for two years.

16) **And when we came into Rome, it was permitted to Paul to stay by himself with the soldier guarding him.**

All that Luke says is that the authorities at Rome treated Paul with great consideration. Since all the other prisoners had already been sentenced to death they were confined in the *castra*, παρεμβολή, i. e., barracks of soldiers, but Paul was granted permission to live by himself, in his own rented house, with only a soldier to guard him until his case could be disposed of. This statement confines itself to the main fact, the mild form of the *custodia militaris*. The soldier guard was changed at regular intervals so that during the space of two years Paul became acquainted with many of these men. Phil. 1:13 shows that the impression made upon these men was far-reaching. While Paul was confined to his dwelling, many kept coming to him daily, which enabled him to keep on testifying, and each soldier guard heard everything that was said during his hours on duty, to say nothing about the conversations which Paul had with such individual guards.

What has caused the main discussion in regard to this passage is the poorly attested reading which inserts: "The centurion delivered the prisoners to the στρατοπεδάρχης." This seems to be a comment which the A. V. regards as a part of the text. Now it is undoubtedly correct that the centurion completed his commission by turning over his prisoners to the imperial officer and not to the emperor Nero in person, who certainly would not himself attend to such minor matters. The centurion would hand over the documents regarding the prisoners which had been entrusted to him by Festus in Caesarea. At the same time he would make a complete report on his voyage, including all that we know about Paul's actions. We lack all knowledge as to what Festus finally put into his report to the emperor's court, but he could not have reported anything resembling a serious charge. Paul, moreover, was a Roman. Add the centurion's favorable account, and we see why Paul was treated so mildly until his case could be considered.

But who was this officer to whom the centurion reported and who gave Paul this permission? We have already answered this question in connection with 27:1. It was the *praefectus praetorio* (or *praetorii*), in the Greek the στρατοπεδάρχης (or -ος). Under Tiberius and during the first years of the reign of Claudius and again during the last years of Nero's rule there were two such commanders of the Prætorian Guards, but during the years 51-62, which period includes the time of Paul's arrival at Rome, there was only one, Sex. Afranius Burrus, an excellent man, who was very influential in young Nero's court. From what is known it does not seem likely that Nero himself handled the cases of appeal, but that Burrus was delegated to do this (Zahn, *Apostelgeschichte* 851, etc.). Claudius attended to these duties in person. These findings rest on such evidence as there is; even the variant reading has the singular. The barracks of the Prætorians were located at the *Porta Viminalis* in the northeast part of the city. Paul was brought in through the *Porta Capena* and thus passed through the busy part of Rome. From the time of Tiberius until that of Vespasian the Prætorian Guards consisted of nine cohorts of 1,000 men each (Zahn, *Introduction* I, 554).

We assume that Luke and Aristarchus lived in the same house with Paul. It seems to have been spacious enough to receive many visitors. We can only surmise who paid the rent. We note the gifts received from the Philippians through Epaphroditus (Phil. 2:25; 4:10-14). Many Christians from the Orient visited Paul, brethren who had stood near to the apostle and loved him. Here he wrote his letters to the Ephesians, Colossians, Philippians, etc. He was a busy man during these years, and his work began at once.

PAUL IN ROME

17) Luke might have added v. 30, 31 or their substance and thus brought his record to a close. The reader notes that the intervening section, v. 17-28, does no more than to state how Paul established contact with the many Jews at Rome. Yet v. 17-28 is a vital part of Acts. It states far more than that Paul finally arrived in Rome where he then spent two whole years. Acts describes how the gospel moved from Jerusalem to Rome. This was not accomplished by the mere fact that *Paul* reached Rome. The main point is that this apostle performed a most important work among *the Jews* in Rome, the capital of the world. See the exposition of Acts 23:11. Paul had attempted to do work among the Jews in Jerusalem, but without success (Acts 9:26-30). The Lord appointed him to do the great work among the Jews in Rome. In a few years Jerusalem would be destroyed, not one stone would be left upon another; but here in Rome, in the very capital of the destroyers of Jerusalem, a multitude of converted Jews, whole synagogues, were to continue. Thus from Jerusalem the church moved to Rome in the person of these converted Jews — *by the work of Paul.*

The importance of this section at the close of Acts is thus evident.

And it came to pass that after three days he called together to himself those that were foremost of the Jews. Now, they having come together, he proceeded to say to them: I, men and brethren, though having done nothing adverse to the people or to the customs, those pertaining to the fathers, was delivered a prisoner from Jerusalem into the hands of the Romans, who, having judicially examined me, were resolving to release me for the reason that no cause for death existed in my case.

But the Jews objecting, I was forced to appeal to Caesar, not (however) as having anything whereof to accuse my nation. For this cause, therefore, I called you her to see and to speak with you, for on account of the hope of Israel I bear on me this chain.

The immediate task was to find a proper house and to rent it, to get the necessary furniture, etc. That took three days. We should not think that Paul thereupon first formed contact with the Jews and did not form contact with the Christians until later. The contact with all the foremost Christians had already been made when these went to meet Paul at Appii Forum and at Three Taverns and traveled with him the last two days of his journey. That was loving contact, indeed. So now the apostle thinks about the Jews. The middle implies that he called them together to or for himself, and call together is correct, for we have a record of no less than eleven synagogues in Rome, and there may have been even more. "Those being foremost of the Jews" (the participle is placed correctly, R. 777) are their leading men, a few from each synagogue. Christian friends at Rome very likely helped Paul to draw up a list and then went to these Jews with the apostle's invitation, he being a prisoner. So they came together, and with ἔλεγε, the imperfect, Luke describes how Paul proceeded to address them. Introductions were, of course, in order as the men arrived singly or in groups, and Paul's statement to them was made after all were assembled.

This statement is a brief account of Paul's present status, firsthand information from Paul himself in regard to his being brought to Rome as a prisoner. It is made solely for the purpose of giving information. On the address "men and brethren" see 1:16; the apostles always used it when addressing Jews. Ἐγώ is emphatic and forward because these Jews needed to be informed in regard to Paul: "I, as far as I am concerned."

"As having done nothing adverse or hostile to the people (λαός meaning the Jewish people) or to the customs pertaining to the fathers (meaning the religious practices derived from the fathers of ancient Israel)," I was delivered as a prisoner. It is an understatement because, when Paul was arrested, he was engaged in one of these very customs (21:23, etc.). Understatements such as this — we find them frequently — are most wise. When a man claims too much, especially in his own case, he is doubted in regard to all that he may say; but when he claims less than he might he is the more readily believed. This is something that many forget. These Jews soon learned the full details in regard to what Paul was doing in the Temple when the Asiatic Jews caused the awful riot on the basis of their utterly baseless surmise.

Paul says that he was delivered as a prisoner "from Jerusalem" (not "in") into the hands of the Romans and thereby refers to his transfer to Caesarea under Felix. "Romans" is the right word, for he was a prisoner of the Roman authorities.

18) We have more than the ordinary relative οἵ, for οἵτινες = "who were such as." Paul summarizes the judicial examinations to which he was subjected (note ἀνάκρισις, the noun, the examination Festus asked Agrippa to make, 25:26). The imperfect ἐβούλοντο, "they were resolving" (A. V. is again better than the R. V.), conveys the idea that this resolution was not carried out. Διά with the substantivized infinitive states the reason why the Romans wanted to release Paul: "because that no cause for death (no crime of that nature) existed in my case (ἐν ἐμοί, see R. 587, paragraph 6)." Paul says only, "no capital crime," but the willingness "to release" him implies that also

no lesser crime could be charged against him, one deserving "bonds," imprisonment (23:29; 26:31).

19) But "the Jews" objected, which refers to those in authority, Sanhedrists, the present participle denoting continued objection. Then in order to end the matter (that expressed in the imperfect ἐβούλοντο and in the present participle, the two actions that were hanging fire) Paul made his appeal to Cæsar. But he at once adds that this was not done "as having something for which to accuse his nation." These Jews in Rome might leap to the conclusion that Paul had this intention. Charges against procurators and against officials were often lodged with the emperor. And Paul certainly could have lodged charges against the Sanhedrists. He does not by any means exonerate them, he says only that he made his appeal to Cæsar without such an intent.

20) Οὖν refers to the result. So Paul is now here in Rome on this appeal of his. And for this reason he invited all the Jewish leaders in Rome in order to see them himself and to talk to them himself so that they might get everything at firsthand and not in some garbled manner in a roundabout way. But all this is not done because of Paul's personal interest. Why should he trouble all these leading Jews in Rome with that? With γάρ Paul introduces the real reason that he tells them about himself; it is "on account of the hope of Israel that I bear this chain." We have Paul's own commentary regarding this "hope" in 23:6; 24:15; 26:6, 7. It is the promise of Moses and the prophets (26:22), the resurrection of the Messiah which was fulfilled in Jesus, against which the Sadducees of the Sanhedrin raged, which the Pharisees, however, also firmly held (23:6-9). It was because of this very heart of the gospel that Paul was a prisoner. Because the gospel with its crown of hope was so bound up with Paul's arrest and appeal to Cæsar he wanted no mis-

understanding regarding it among the Jewish leaders in Rome lest the gospel cause receive damage through false reports. Note that περίκειμαι is used as the passive of περιτίθημι (R. 815), the accusative of the thing is retained from the active of the latter verb (R. 816) ; all of which the English cannot duplicate or imitate: "I have lying around (my wrist) this chain."

See v. 15 in regard to Paul's having been chained previous to this time. When Burrus (v. 16) placed him into this mildest form of military custody by permitting him to live in his own house with only a single soldier to guard him, this Præfect, the emperor's direct representative, ordered that Paul be fastened to the soldier guard with a chain. It was done as a simple precaution, to obviate the necessity of increasing the guard. Also, and this is often overlooked by those who have Paul in "chains" (nearly always plural) since in his fright Lysias removed the two with which he had fettered Paul (21:33; 22:29), the order of Burrus was something entirely different from chaining as carried out by other magistrates, all of whom dared place no fetters on a Roman. Roman law forbade that. The confusion on this point needs clearing up, and the assumption that, because Paul was chained to a soldier in Rome, he had been in chains since Lysias transferred him to Felix, is without warrant.

21) **And they said to him: We for our part neither received writings concerning thee from the Jews, nor did one of the brethren, on getting here, report or tell anything wicked concerning thee. But we deem it proper to hear from thee what thou thinkest, for as concerning this sect, it is known to us that it is spoken against everywhere.**

The emphatic ἡμεῖς, "we for our part," matches Paul's emphatic ἐγώ. We need not discuss the question as to whether the Sanhedrists had been able to send letters or documents to the Jews at Rome prior to the time of Paul's arrival, when we consider the difficulties Paul had encountered on his voyage. The fact is, the Sanhedrists did not pursue the matter any farther. As a body they themselves were divided in regard to Paul (23:6-9) and thus could take no united action; moreover, they had already failed twice, in the case of both Felix and Festus. All the leading Jews thus state that they are without official information about Paul and his difficulty with the Jewish authorities at Jerusalem.

But they are also without private information. No Jewish brother, "on getting here," (παραγενόμενος) has made a private report in any synagogue or has talked in private Jewish circles concerning anything wicked in regard to Paul. Πονηρόν is more than "harm" (our versions), it denotes something vicious or wicked, actively so. We take it that this statement covers the whole period of Paul's imprisonment in Caesarea (two years), for the participle refers to actual arrivals in Rome of individual Jews from Jerusalem, and there had been not a few such arrivals. Some of the many Jews residing in Rome had certainly gone to the great festivals and returned, and others had come to Rome from abroad. The statement is thus rather important. After the riot precipitated by the Asiatic Jews (21:27, etc.), and after Paul was rushed to Caesarea, the Sanhedrists who were opposed to Paul had not advertised their opposition in Jerusalem. Their two attempts against Paul in Caesarea before Felix and before Festus had not become known. The Jews in Rome had heard nothing.

22) But these admissions pertained only to what Paul had just told them in regard to his arrest and his appeal to Cæsar. These prominent Jews in Rome had a general knowledge in regard to Paul, had probably heard much about him and his work. We note how, on Paul's invitation, they had at once come to him. So

they say that they deem it worth-while (ἀξιοῦμεν) to hear from him himself what he holds in his mind, what his ideas and convictions are. Not, however, as though they as yet knew nothing on that score; what makes it seem proper for them to hear Paul is the fact that "this sect" (see 24:5) is spoken against everywhere. They mean "everywhere" among Jews; they are not thinking of Gentiles as some suppose.

We are warranted in concluding that no apostle and, in fact, no outstanding exponent of Christianity (such as Apollos, for instance) had as yet appeared in Rome. Paul is the first to appear, and his great reputation has preceded him. We conclude furthermore that no special mission work had as yet been attempted in the synagogues of Rome. All these prominent Jews deem it worth-while to come and to hear Paul expound his teaching to them. We know that in all the cities in whose synagogues Paul had preached sometimes a decisive schism had been very soon effected, and the unbelieving Jews turned to vicious and implacable hostility. Nothing similar to this is evident in Rome on Paul's arrival. All these leading Jews are ready to hear the apostle.

We finally conclude that the Christian congregation at Rome had quietly organized itself through the believers' just getting together of themselves without a clash with the synagogues. No conflict had taken place, no Jewish persecution had flared up. These leading Jews looked only askance at the Christians, knew only that the Jews in all other cities spoke against the Christians. This is a situation that is entirely new in the story of Acts and is most interesting on that account. It promises at least something. Paul finds a great work to do. Although he is the special apostle to the Gentiles, this work inviting him is to be done among Jews. In other places the work always began with the Jews before a Christian congregation could be formed. Here in Rome matters are reversed: a strong Christian congregation already exists, yet the Jewish work is not done. We must, however, not expect too much; these leading Jews look at "this sect" as one that is everywhere spoken against. Paul must know that this fact counts heavily with them. His work will be uphill.

23) **And having appointed a day for him, there came to his lodging even more, to whom he proceeded to expound, earnestly testifying regarding the kingdom of God, persuading them concerning Jesus from both the law of Moses and the prophets from morning until evening. And some were being persuaded by the things said, but some were unbelieving.**

It surely says much concerning Paul that these leading Jews, after hearing Paul's story about his imprisonment, appointed a day when they would hear him at length on the great subject of the gospel of Christ. Although the church had existed in Rome for so many years, these Jews had not as yet been fully confronted with the gospel. Paul has been there only three days, and the beginning of this great and most necessary work has already been made. Let us not charge the Christians at Rome with negligence. Think of the difficulty of the task, the power and the ability required to do it in the proper way. God has his man for it, he had brought him in his own good time, it is now that he sends the hour of grace to the Jews in Rome. Πλείονες means that even more came on the appointed day than had come in answer to Paul's first invitation.

Textual evidence is divided between the aorist ἦλθον and the imperfect ἧκον, the former stating only the fact, "they came," the latter being descriptive. We must note that all of the main verbs that follow in the narrative (not, of course, in the quotation from Isaiah and in Paul's final word) are imperfects, all of them being descriptive of the actions, all of them unrolling the scene like a moving picture. If the first main verb were an aorist, this would constitute an exception. Moreover, ἦλθον would be the common verb, ἧκον one that is more unusual which was likely exchanged for the other by some scribe. We see the reason that a special day was appointed. The Jews probably came in the afternoon in answer to that first invitation. Paul wanted an entire day, "from morning (early) until evening." While the foremost Jews had come on that first day, their number probably did not include all the men of importance. Rabbis of learning and importance who had been absent from the first meeting were also desired even by Paul himslf. On the day appointed they were all on hand — a most notable gathering, indeed!

Paul's rented house was certainly filled to capacity. He was face to face with the entire Jewish leadership of the capital of the world. God wanted a man like Paul for this. One wonders about the Roman soldier to whom the apostle was chained, the one pagan witness to this great conference. It was also his hour of grace. What did he report about it to the other soldiers and to his superior officer after he was relieved and returned to the Prætorian barracks?

Luke records only the subject and the general line of thought of that day's discussion. Paul "proceeded to expound" (imperfect). The two present participles are just as descriptive as the imperfect. Both participles expand the imperfect tense of the main verb. The three form a close unit. Paul's work during that whole day was a setting forth (ἐκτίθημι), but with most earnest personal testifying (διά in the participle for earnestness) and with loving persuasion. That was Paul's way of dealing with all Jews, but Luke records it here because of the great occasion. His was apostolic testimony (26:16). When we copy Paul's method of expounding, testifying, persuading, we can testify only in a limited way, on the basis of Christian experience and not on the basis of direct vision of Jesus and a direct revelation to us. All that we can do with the apostolic testimony is what alone Paul could do with Moses and the prophets, namely expound it.

On the kingdom see 1:3. Paul testified about the whole rule of God's grace, that rule which culminates in glory, in which he made Jesus both Prince and Savior (5:31), both Lord and Christ (3:36). It was the entire plan of salvation. The Jews had it in "the law of Moses and in the prophets." This expression refers to the entire Old Testament which is so commonly called "Moses and the prophets." It is here that Paul's persuading of the Jews concerning Jesus comes in. He attempted to move them to accept what Moses and the prophets had foretold and what had been fulfilled so completely in Jesus, in his sacrificial death, in his glorious resurrection, and in his eternal exaltation. The appeal was most effective in the case of Jews who lived in their glorious Scriptures.

24) Here Luke might have used aorists when reporting the final outcome, namely, that some were actually persuaded, some not. But he continues with descriptive imperfects because the outcome of this day's work was not complete at the end of this day. Paul scored a great success, but what he had said this day continued to work for a much longer time. It was not a matter of the Jewish leaders alone but of all Judaism in Rome. What Luke presents is the fact that the things Paul was saying (note that this is a present participle and not an aorist) were making some nod their heads in assent while others were shaking their heads in incredulity. And he leaves it at that. Paul had started on his great success, and it was only a question as to how far it would extend. And Luke writes οἱ μέν — οἱ δέ, "some — some," and not, "a few — but

most." He certainly does not overstate. Paul won perhaps half of these Jewish leaders on that first day, probably more than half. Imagine what that means to the Jews in Rome; a stream of them would pour into the Christian Church. Here we see what the Lord had in mind when he told Paul: "Thou must bear witness also at Rome" (23:11).

25) "From early until evening" sounds as though there was no interruption for eating food; all were so taken up with what Paul was presenting. **And being disagreed with each other, they were withdrawing after Paul spoke one word: Well did the Holy Spirit make utterance through Isaiah, the prophet, to your fathers, saying:**

> **Go to this people and say:**
> **By hearing you shall hear and in no wise understand;**
> **And seeing you shall see and shall in no wise perceive.**
> **For this people's heart did become thickened,**
> **And with their ears they heard heavily,**
> **And their eyes they closed**
> **Lest, perhaps, they perceive with their eyes**
> **And with their ears hear**
> **And with their heart understand**
> **And turn again,**
> **And I heal them.**

Be it therefore known to you that to the Gentiles this saving thing of God was commissioned; they on their part, too, will hear.

Ὄντες only describes and does not state a cause. They did not leave *because* they were disagreed, as though they would otherwise not have left. They were leaving *while* they were disagreed with each other. Since this is evident already in v. 24, its being stated here means that there had been discussion not only with Paul but also with each other, some seconding Paul's exposition, others bringing objections. Since the situation was thus, "they were loosing themselves," i. e., were leaving. The imperfect tense is not inchoative, "were starting to leave," but merely descriptive. Since it is the last imperfect used in this scene, the force of this final verb and tense is both important and unmistakable. One might expect an aorist: "they left," and the last imperfect used in this scene, the force of this final verb and tense is both important and unmistakable. One might expect an aorist: "they left," and think that that was the end of the matter; but no, it was by no means the end, this imperfect (an open tense) states that leaving was not the end but only a move that was followed by much more. What did follow? The spurious v. 29 answers by adding that after Paul's final statement "the Jews went away (ἀπῆλθον, note this aorist) while having much dispute among themselves." But this really says nothing beyond what is already fully implied in the participial clause in regard to being disagreed. But the aorist used in this v. 29 is misleading, for it conveys the idea that this leaving with dispute ended the matter. It did nothing of the kind. Luke has his own statement as to how this thing proceeded and ended; he has it in v. 30, 31, which see.

Luke's account is misunderstood when it is supposed that, while the Jews were leaving, Paul detained them for an additional moment until he uttered this final word; or that this final word brought about the leaving. Ὄντες is to be construed with the imperfect ἀπελύοντο plus the aorist εἰπόντος. It was evening, time to be going. Paul closed what he had to say on this day with the final statement which Luke has preserved. Then the leaving of the Jews in disharmony with themselves took place. There is no thought that Paul tried to have the last word. There was much animated talk among the Jews as they left, and we have seen what the open imperfect conveys in regard to the future.

In order to get the force of Paul's citation from Isaiah (6:9, 10) we must not forget that Paul's whole exposition was a persuading from the law of Moses and the prophets. Passage after passage had been used, and it is thus that Paul adds one more as the last one. Its intent is like that of the rest, to persuade. But it would persuade by means of the warning example of the unbelieving fathers. Paul does *not* say that Isaiah prophesied concerning his present Jewish hearers. God sent Isaiah with a dire message to the Jews of the prophet's day ("to your fathers"). Paul intends to say to his present Jewish hearers: "It will pay you to think twice about what God had Isaiah tell those fathers of yours!" Why? History at times repeats itself. Paul means: "Let no Jew today repeat the mistake of those fathers so that Isaiah's words would apply also to him!" For this is true as we see from Matt. 13:14, 15, and again from John 12:40, 41, where Jesus used this same word of Isaiah's: it includes all those who in later years did and still now do what those obdurate Jewish fathers did in Isaiah's day. All later obdurates place themselves into the same class with those fathers and thus bring on a new fulfillment of the prophet's words. When Zahn thinks that Paul avoids identifying himself with Isaiah so as not to leave the impression that the prophet had Paul in mind in his effort to convert the Jews, his view is unacceptable. Paul uses Isaiah's word as history, mighty grave history. There stands the mistake of the wicked fathers. Let no man repeat it!

Paul quotes just "one utterance"; he might have used more, but this one was enough. He names "the Holy Spirit" as though the Jews knew this Third Person of the Godhead fully. They did. The Old Testament revealed the Trinity. In the days of the Baptist we find no Jew objecting to the Three Persons. The Jews had not yet become Unitarian.

Here we again have the entire doctrine of Verbal Inspiration in most simple language. "The Holy Spirit made utterance through Isaiah, the prophet, by saying." The thing is *a fact, just a fact.* "Theory"? no theory nor hypothesis appear. The Holy Spirit is the speaker. He "made utterance, saying." He used Isaiah, the prophet, as his medium, for διά states the medium. At times we read, "through the mouth of the prophet," which makes *Verbal* Inspiration still clearer. The Spirit spoke what he wanted to say by using the prophet as his mouthpiece, the entire prophet with mind, heart, will, and tongue, in a way so dynamic (favorite term), so removed from anything mechanical (favorite term in objections), so little like one uses an automaton (another objection), that human language has never more clearly expressed this simple fact. If you ask *how* the Spirit did or could do this, we refer you to Isaiah himself or to some other man whom the Spirit inspired verbally; but we doubt that he could tell you just how the Spirit did what beyond the least question he did.

26) Luke quotes the Spirit's preamble (this is omitted as not being necessary in Matt. 13:14, 15): "Go to this people and state" (εἰπέ or εἰπόν, the imperative being written either way, B.-D. 81, 1). Note that Isaiah is told verbally just what to state and, of course, stated that and only that. By hearing they are to hear and not to undersand (συνῆτε from συνίημι, second aorist subjunctive); and by seeing (participle) they are to see and not perceive (βλέπειν, looking at something, and ἰδεῖν, actually seeing what something means; the difference in meaning is due to the tenses). The negation οὐ μή is the strongest negation the Greek has and is used with subjunctives as here and with future indicatives.

The subjunctives are here used in main clauses and are simply volitive futures, aorists that convey finality.

Through Isaiah the Spirit is pronouncing judgment upon the Jews of that day. So long had they refused to understand, refused to perceive. Their day of grace was at an end, judgment alone was left them. And the form of the judgment matches the form of the obdurate sin. The Word they heard and would not understand they are now not to understand; the miracles and the grace they saw and would not perceive as such they are now not to perceive. The Word that was sent to them as a savor of life unto life is now sent to them as a savor of death unto death. This is the subsequent (not the antecedent) will of God, namely the will which takes into account man's actions and attitude and is based on these. It is the judicial will and it pronounces judgment. It is the Spirit's act of hardening the sinners. This is always judicial, always subsequent. The outstanding example is Pharaoh. Five times he hardened his heart, and not until then did God harden his heart for him. This is terrible, indeed, to hear the divine verdict that we shall not understand or perceive but be forever excluded from the saving grace of the Word. Paul quotes the prophet's word that was addressed to the fathers in order to make these Jews in Rome aware of their own danger.

27) The A. V., like the Vulgate and Luther, translates the Hebrew of Isaiah as though it had the vowel pointing of imperatives, whereas the LXX, the Syriac, and the Arabic versions render it as though it had the vowel pointing of indicatives. Matthew 13:14, 15 and Luke follow the latter, which, therefore, must be correct as far as the original Hebrew and its proper vowel pointing are concerned. The Spirit states the reason for his verdict (γάρ). Those fathers had exhausted their day of grace. The aorists state the awful facts as facts. "This people's heart did thicken," i. e., perma-

nently so. Because it was encased in a thick, gross mass of fat, no effort of the Spirit reached it so as to move it in any way. It would be futile for the Spirit to try to penetrate that thick wall. He has no power of grace that is able to pierce through it. Judgment alone is left. The aorist states that the case is settled.

First the heart, and in the Scriptures this is always the center of the personality, the seat of mind, emotions, and especially also of will. Then come the ears and the eyes, the two great avenues to the heart. The Spirit uses the ears, for he operates through the Word. "With their ears they did hear heavily," i. e., so that the Word never got to the heart. The Spirit uses the eyes so that men may see his works of grace and salvation. "Their eyes they did close." The aorists state final, permanent acts. The Spirit finally had to give up all efforts of grace. Both channels were completely blocked.

And all this the Jews of Isaiah's time did with the deliberate, malignant purpose: "lest, perhaps, they perceive with their eyes and with their ears hear (note the chiasm) and with their heart understand." Eyes, ears, heart are now in reverse order. At this point the Hebrew mentions the three but only the heart and the eyes in the preceding. Those versions that add a clause in regard to ears do so interpretatively, which we may let pass, since ears are mentioned in the purpose clause. This clause makes manifest the damnableness of all fixed obduracy. The obdurate are determined not to see, hear, perceive. Jesus said regarding obdurate Jerusalem: "I would, but you would not — henceforth your house is left unto you desolate (judgment)," Matt. 23:37.

The negative purpose clause continues: "lest, perhaps, they turn again (under the Spirit's grace), and I heal them." The two belong together: we turn when the Lord heals. The turning is that of conversion, this verb is often used in this sense (9:35; 11:21; etc.), active with reference to our turning, passive with reference to God's turning us. Soteriological healing is referred to, and the final verb is a future indicative after three subjunctives; in the Koine this occurs repeatedly (R. 988) so as to need no comment. Men are determined *not* to turn from damnation, *not* to be healed by the Spirit. They love darkness rather than light (John 3:19), they treat salvation as a plague What is left but judgment and doom?

28) Paul's own final statement that these Roman Jews must know that God's salvation was commissioned to the Gentiles, and that these will, indeed, hear it (i. e., receptively, with faith), is nothing but a restatement of what this same prophet Isaiah declares in 65:1, etc.; compare Rom. 10:20, 21. The second aorist passive ἀπεστάλη is historical, for the commissioning had already been made through the prophets. And the sense is plain: because those fathers absolutely refused God's salvation, God extended it to the Gentiles, and they will, indeed, accept it. They were now doing so. Paul is asking these Jews whether they, too, would exclude themselves as those fathers of old had done. When even the Gentiles hear, will they fail to hear? Paul's tone is authoritative throughout. "Well did the Spirit speak, etc. (v. 25) — be it known to you," etc. Facts need not apologize for being what they are. Truth has its crown of authority and must be enthroned in our hearts while wearing that crown. Paul uses the neuter adjective as a noun: "this saving thing of God," which is more concrete than the abstract noun "this salvation."

29) See under v. 25.

30) After having written all the narrative imperfects, beginning in v. 23, Luke now writes the aorist although he follows it with a final imperfect. The outcome of this most important meeting with the Jews of

Rome was not the fact that they went away (aorist ἀπῆλθον of the spurious v. 29) but this that Paul remained for two years in Rome, etc.

Now he remained for a whole space of two years in his own rented place and kept receiving all those coming in to him, preaching the kingdom of God and teaching the things concerning the Lord Jesus Christ with all freedom of utterance, unhindered.

As far as this great conference with the leading Jews of Rome was concerned, the end did not come on that day. It took two whole years before Paul's case was decided by the imperial court. It was decided in his favor. It would have been strange, indeed, if, after all other Roman judges had found nothing against Paul (23:29; 24:26, etc.; 25:18, 25; 26:30, etc), the emperor's court should have condemned him. More inexplicable still would be Luke's failure to note with at least a final sentence or two that at the end of the two years Paul was condemned to death if such had been the case. In Phil. 1:23, etc.; 2:24; Philemon 22 (written in Rome near the end of the two years) Paul confidently expected to be freed. Besides, we have the uncontradicted tradition that after his acquittal Paul undertook a final missionary journey which carried him to Spain; he also revisited some of the fields of his first labor immediately after his release and prior to his journey to Spain. Read also the remarks at the close of our introduction to Acts.

Because he lived in his own hired place it was possible for him to receive all the visitors who desired to come to him, and the imperfect records that he continued such receptions. We do not need the ill-attested addition "both Jews and Greeks." As far as the Jewish leaders were concerned, Luke's manner of using the tenses of the verb implies that they were among those who came again and did this repeatedly. That is enough, for men who had definitely turned to unbelief would never come again. Μίσθωμα is the price paid and only here seems to be used passively to designate that for which the price was paid. Although he was confined to his dwelling and under a soldier guard (v. 16), Paul's great testimony in Rome went on (23:11). The Lord employed this novel way of filling Rome with direct apostolic testimony.

31) Luke concludes his great account with the rhythmic participial modifiers: "preaching the kingdom of God (see v. 23, and 1:3) and teaching the things concerning the Lord Jesus Christ (in 1:21, "the Lord Jesus") with all freedom of utterance, unhindered." This ending deserves more notice than it usually receives. It reveals the fact that Luke's chief interest in Acts is this apostolic promulgation of the gospel and far less the person involved. To show how the apostolic testimony resounded in Rome in so strange a way especially among the Jews, is Luke's goal. He has reached that goal and so lays down his pen.

We note the two significant verbs "preaching" (heralding) and "teaching"; both form a unit of work and are vital. Although he was a prisoner, Paul was in no way restricted; he had full παρρησία, freedom to say all and everything. Luke even adds the adverb "unhindered." Burrus, the commander of the Praetorian Guards, placed no restrictions upon Paul. That was, indeed, remarkable, but it was the Lord's doing. He had brought his great witness to Rome and he enabled that witness to testify freely, fully, to the glory of his Name.

We feel safe in saying that in all of Paul's career he scored no greater success in a single day's work than on the day which Luke describes in v. 23, etc. He converted half of the rabbis and leaders of the eleven synagogues in the capital of the world! Οἱ μέν — οἱ δέ (v. 24) = 50 — 50 according to our way of speaking. This

Jewish work of Paul's went on for two entire years. Converting the rabbis and the leaders could mean only one thing, namely that these rabbis took the gospel of Paul into their synagogues with the result that whole synagogues were converted, and the members who refused conversion withdrew to other synagogues.

The assumption that all these converted rabbis and these Jews left their synagogues and joined the original mixed congregation in Rome, is unwarranted. Four, five, perhaps even more of the eleven synagogues became Christian churches. To this great body of converted Jews in Rome the Epistle to the Hebrews was addressed by Apollos after Paul's death. See my introduction to Hebrews. See also the introduction to First Peter in regard to Peter's work in Rome and his death in the year 64. New light is shed on the whole work done in Rome when we finally combine all the data that are available in the New Testament.

Among these data we must include Rom. 16 with all its salutations. The question is solved in regard to the composition of the original congregation in Rome, whether it was mostly Jewish (Zahn and others) or Gentile. In Rom. 16 Paul greeted *all the members* of the congregation. He lists *all* the prominent persons and tells us which are Jewish, which Gentile, and which of the Jewish members were personally known to him, also which had been converted even before he himself was converted. See my exposition of Rom. 16 for full details.

It is most remarkable that Paul should invite all the πρῶτοι of the Jews in Rome to his house, and that *these leaders should come!* Weigh this fact. The old congregation in Rome had left the Roman Jews severely alone. That is why the Lord spoke the order and the promise stated in 23:11. The converted Jews in the old congregation, who had come to faith in Jerusalem at the time of Pentecost and after, had had a terrible experience with the Sanhedrin and the Jews of Jerusalem during the days following Stephen's martyrdom and thus, when the congregation in Rome was formed and progressed, let the Jews in Rome alone. Moreover, the Jews living in Rome had often been turbulent so that Claudius, their friend, had been compelled to expel them from Rome (18:2). All this should be exceedingly plain.

The Lord more than fulfilled the desire of Paul to go to Rome. He gave him the greatest work among Jews to be done in Rome. What Paul did among pagan Romans we can only surmise from what Luke states in v. 30, 31. Paul's wonderful success with the Jews in Rome is more than enough to make us praise the Lord's Name.

Soli Deo Gloria